THE POWER OF FINE LITERATURE
THE MASTERY OF LANGUAGE ARTS

PRENTICE HALL LITERATURE

Begin each selection with the Guide for Reading.

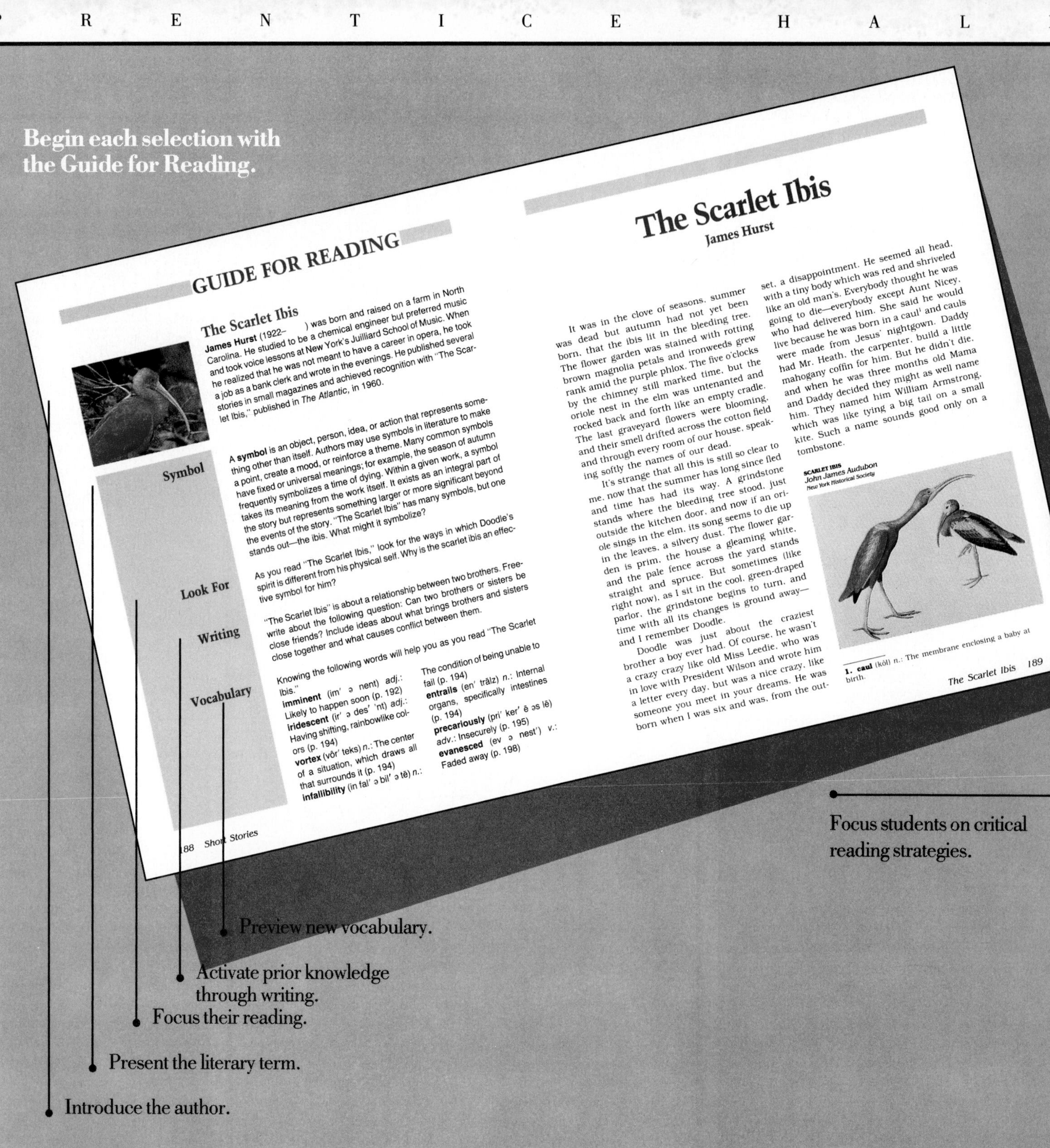

GUIDE FOR READING

The Scarlet Ibis

James Hurst (1922–) was born and raised on a farm in North Carolina. He studied to be a chemical engineer but preferred music and took voice lessons at New York's Juilliard School of Music. When he realized that he was not meant to have a career in opera, he took a job as a bank clerk and wrote in the evenings. He published several stories in small magazines and achieved recognition with "The Scarlet Ibis," published in *The Atlantic*, in 1960.

Symbol

A **symbol** is an object, person, idea, or action that represents something other than itself. Authors may use symbols in literature to make a point, create a mood, or reinforce a theme. Many common symbols have fixed or universal meanings; for example, the season of autumn frequently symbolizes a time of dying. Within a given work, a symbol takes its meaning from the work itself. It exists as an integral part of the story but represents something larger or more significant beyond the events of the story. "The Scarlet Ibis" has many symbols, but one stands out—the ibis. What might it symbolize?

Look For

As you read "The Scarlet Ibis," look for the ways in which Doodle's spirit is different from his physical self. Why is the scarlet ibis an effective symbol for him?

Writing

"The Scarlet Ibis" is about a relationship between two brothers. Freewrite about the following question: Can two brothers or sisters be close friends? Include ideas about what brings brothers and sisters close together and what causes conflict between them.

Vocabulary

Knowing the following words will help you as you read "The Scarlet Ibis."

imminent (im' ə nent) *adj.*: Likely to happen soon (p. 192)
iridescent (ir' ə des' 'nt) *adj.*: Having shifting, rainbowlike colors (p. 194)
vortex (vôr' teks) *n.*: The center of a situation, which draws all that surrounds it (p. 194)
infallibility (in fal' ə bil' ə tē) *n.*: The condition of being unable to fail (p. 194)
entrails (en' trālz) *n.*: Internal organs, specifically intestines (p. 194)
precariously (pri ker' ē əs lē) *adv.*: Insecurely (p. 195)
evanesced (ev ə nest') *v.*: Faded away (p. 198)

188 Short Stories

The Scarlet Ibis

James Hurst

It was in the clove of seasons, summer was dead but autumn had not yet been born, that the ibis lit in the bleeding tree. The flower garden was stained with rotting brown magnolia petals and ironweeds grew rank amid the purple phlox. The five o'clocks by the chimney still marked time, but the oriole nest in the elm was untenanted and rocked back and forth like an empty cradle. The last graveyard flowers were blooming, and their smell drifted across the cotton field and through every room of our house, speaking softly the names of our dead.

It's strange that all this is still so clear to me, now that the summer has long since fled and time has had its way. A grindstone stands where the bleeding tree stood, just outside the kitchen door, and now if an oriole sings in the elm, its song seems to die up in the leaves, a silvery dust. The flower garden is prim, the house a gleaming white, and the pale fence across the yard stands straight and spruce. But sometimes (like right now), as I sit in the cool, green-draped parlor, the grindstone begins to turn, and time with all its changes is ground away—and I remember Doodle.

Doodle was just about the craziest brother a boy ever had. Of course, he wasn't a crazy crazy like old Miss Leedie, who was in love with President Wilson and wrote him a letter every day, but was a nice crazy, like someone you meet in your dreams. He was born when I was six and was, from the outset, a disappointment. He seemed all head, with a tiny body which was red and shriveled like an old man's. Everybody thought he was going to die—everybody except Aunt Nicey, who had delivered him. She said he would live because he was born in a caul[1] and cauls were made from Jesus' nightgown. Daddy had Mr. Heath, the carpenter, build a little mahogany coffin for him. But he didn't die, and when he was three months old Mama and Daddy decided they might as well name him. They named him William Armstrong, which was like tying a big tail on a small kite. Such a name sounds good only on a tombstone.

SCARLET IBIS
John James Audubon
New York Historical Society

1. **caul** (kôl) *n.*: The membrane enclosing a baby at birth.

The Scarlet Ibis 189

Focus students on critical reading strategies.

Preview new vocabulary.

Activate prior knowledge through writing.

Focus their reading.

Present the literary term.

Introduce the author.

The Power of Fine Literature, The Mastery of Critical Reading.

Integrate the power of fine literature with critical reading to stimulate an active response.

Begin each unit with Reading Actively.

READING ACTIVELY

Nonfiction

Some people seem to gain more from their reading of nonfiction than others. Why? Most likely, they gain more because they read with an active mind. To read nonfiction successfully, you must interact with the information the author presents. Ask questions about this information and make predictions about where the information is leading. Pause to answer your predictions and to check your predictions. At appropriate points, stop to summarize the information you have received so far.

Use the following strategies to help you read actively.

Question Ask questions about the information the author presents. What does the author reveal about the topic? Determine whether the author's conclusions seem based on the information given. In addition, question the author's purpose for writing.

Predict Think about what you already know about the topic. Make predictions about the conclusions you think the author will reach based on this information. As you read, you will find out whether your predictions are accurate.

Clarify As you read, try to find the answers to your questions and check the accuracy of your predictions. In this way, you will monitor, or guide, your own reading and so gain the fullest understanding of the information presented.

Summarize Every now and then, pause to summarize, or review, the information the author has presented so far. What important points has the author made? How has the author supported this information?

Pull It Together Determine the main idea of the entire selection. What did you find out about the topic? How do you feel about the topic?

On the facing page is a model showing how an active reader might read an essay.

310 *Nonfiction*

MODEL

from **In Search of Our Mothers' Gardens**

Alice Walker

Questions: What is the meaning of the title? What is the author's purpose for writing this essay?

My mother made all the clothes we wore, even my brothers' overalls. She made all the towels and sheets we used. She spent the summers canning vegetables and fruits. She spent the winter evenings making quilts enough to cover all our beds.

During the "working" day, she labored beside—not behind—my father in the fields. Her day began before sunup, and did not end until late at night. There was never a moment for her to sit down, undisturbed, to unravel her own private thoughts; never a time free from interruption—by work or the noisy inquiries of her many children. And yet, it is to my mother—and all our mothers who were not famous—that I went in search of the secret of what has fed that muzzled[1] and often mutilated,[2] but vibrant,[3] creative spirit that the black woman has inherited, and that pops out in wild and unlikely places to this day.

Clarification: The author's purpose is to uncover the secret of the black woman's creative spirit.

from *In Search of Our Mother's Gardens* 311

Direct students to a model showing examples of active reading.

Up to 100 Grammar in Action lessons in each ATE . . . the teachable moment for skills mastery.

5 Discussion What sides of the narrator's character are revealed in this paragraph?

6 Reading Strategy Ask students to summarize Doodle's progress and to predict what further progress he might make.

7 Discussion Is Doodle a good name for William Armstrong? Why?

8 Discussion What character traits does the narrator's behavior reveal?

9 Discussion What kind of unspoken pact develops between the brothers?

tains billowed out in the afternoon sea breeze, rustling like palmetto fronds.[2]

5 It was bad enough having an invalid brother, but having one who possibly was not all there was unbearable, so I began to make plans to kill him by smothering him with a pillow. However, one afternoon as I watched him, my head poked between the irons posts of the foot of the bed, he looked straight at me and grinned. I skipped through the rooms, down the echoing halls, shouting, "Mama, he smiled. He's all there! He's all there!" and he was.

6 When he was two, if you laid him on his stomach, he began to try to move himself, straining terribly. The doctor said that with his weak heart this strain would probably kill him, but it didn't. Trembling, he'd push himself up, turning first red, then a soft purple, and finally collapse back onto the bed like an old worn-out doll. I can still see Mama watching him, her hand pressed tight across her mouth, her eyes wide and unblinking. But he learned to crawl (it was his third winter), and we brought him out of the front bedroom, putting him on the rug before the fireplace. For the first time he became one of us.

As long as he lay all the time in bed, we called him William Armstrong, even though it was formal and sounded as if we were referring to one of our ancestors, but with his creeping around on the deerskin rug and beginning to talk, something had to be done about his name. It was I who renamed him. 7 When he crawled, he crawled backwards, as if he were in reverse and couldn't change gears. If you called him, he'd turn around as if he were going in the other direction, then he'd back right up to you to be picked up. Crawling backward made him look like a doodle-bug, so I began to call him Doodle, and in time even Mama and Daddy thought it was a better name than William Armstrong. Only Aunt Nicey disagreed. She said caul babies should be treated with special respect since they might turn out to be saints. Renaming my brother was perhaps the kindest thing I ever did for him, because nobody expects much from someone called Doodle.

Although Doodle learned to crawl, he showed no signs of walking, but he wasn't idle. He talked so much that we all quit listening to what he said. It was about this time that Daddy built him a go-cart and I had to pull him around. At first I just paraded him up and down the piazza, but then he started crying to be taken out into the yard and it ended up by my having to lug him wherever I went. If I so much as picked up my cap, he'd start crying to go with me and Mama would call from wherever she was, "Take Doodle with you."

8 He was a burden in many ways. The doctor had said that he mustn't get too excited, too hot, too cold, or too tired and that he must always be treated gently. A long list of don'ts went with him, all of which I ignored once we got out of the house. To discourage his coming with me, I'd run with him across the ends of the cotton rows and careen him around corners on two wheels. Sometimes I accidentally turned him over, but he never told Mama. His skin was very sensitive, and he had to wear a big straw hat whenever he went out. When the going got rough and he had to cling to the sides of the go-cart, 9 the hat slipped all the way down over his ears. He was a sight. Finally, I could see I was licked. Doodle was my brother and he was going to cling to me forever, no matter what I did, so I dragged him across the burning cotton field to share with him the only beauty I knew, Old Woman Swamp. I pulled the go-cart through the saw-tooth fern, down into the green dimness where the pal-

2. palmetto fronds: Palm leaves.

Grammar in Action

When a writer uses **concrete details,** readers can see, hear, smell, taste, and feel what the writer is describing. For instance, if a writer merely says "dog," the reader will only have a vague or general idea of the type of animal the writer has in mind. If a writer specifies "German shepherd," however, readers will have a much more specific picture.

Notice how James Hurst uses concrete, specific details to enliven the following description:

> . . . I dragged him across the *burning cotton field* to share with him the only beauty I knew, Old Woman Swamp. I pulled the go-cart through the *saw-tooth fern,* down into the *green dimness* where the *palmetto fronds* whispered by the stream, lifted him out and set him down in the *soft rubber grass* beside a *tall pine.* His eyes were round with wonder as he gazed about him, and his little hands began to stroke the *rubber grass.* Then he began to cry.

Without the concrete details, this passage would be much less effective:

Enrich your skills teaching with Grammar in Action lessons.

The Power of Fine Literature, The Mastery of Grammar and Usage Skills.

Use fine literature as a springboard to teach grammar and usage skills.

BOYS IN A PUNT
N. C. Wyeth
Courtesy of Dr. and Mrs. William A. Morton, Jr.

Humanities Note

Fine art, *Boys in a Punt*, by N.C. Wyeth. Newel Convers Wyeth (1882–1945), who was born in Needham, Massachusetts, lived during the time that is now known as the Golden Age of American Illustration—the time from the mid-1870's to approximately the 1920's. The age was so named because of the number of creative and well-known illustrators whose work was published during that period, including Winslow Homer, Howard Pyle, and N.C. Wyeth.

By the time he was a teenager, Wyeth knew he wanted to be an artist and enrolled in the Howard Pyle School of Illustration in Philadelphia, where he was taught by Howard Pyle.

While in school, Wyeth frequently took trips to Pyle's home at Chadds Ford, Pennsylvania, to roam the hills and woods of the Brandywine Valley. He later permanently moved to this area to raise his own family. Much of Wyeth's finest work, including *Boys in a Punt* was inspired by the rural life around him.

You might use the following questions for discussion.

1. The tone of a painting is the painter's attitude toward the subject. It may be established through the colors the artist chose or the composition. What is the tone of this painting? How does the tone of the painting complement the tone of the story?
2. Do you think Wyeth's illustration is appropriate for this story? Explain.

I pulled him across the field into a pretty swamp. It was dark and wet. I set him on the ground. He was startled and cried.

The many concrete details that Hurst includes enable readers to experience the swamp along with the two boys.

Student Activity 1. Identify the vague, general terms in the shorter passage above. Then locate the concrete details in Hurst's passage that bring the description to life.

Student Activity 2. Rewrite the vague shorter passage so that it is more concrete. However, make your description of Old Woman Swamp different from Hurst's.

191

Reinforce learning with blackline masters in the Teaching Portfolio.

Guide learning with on-the-spot practice.

A writing program within a literature program.

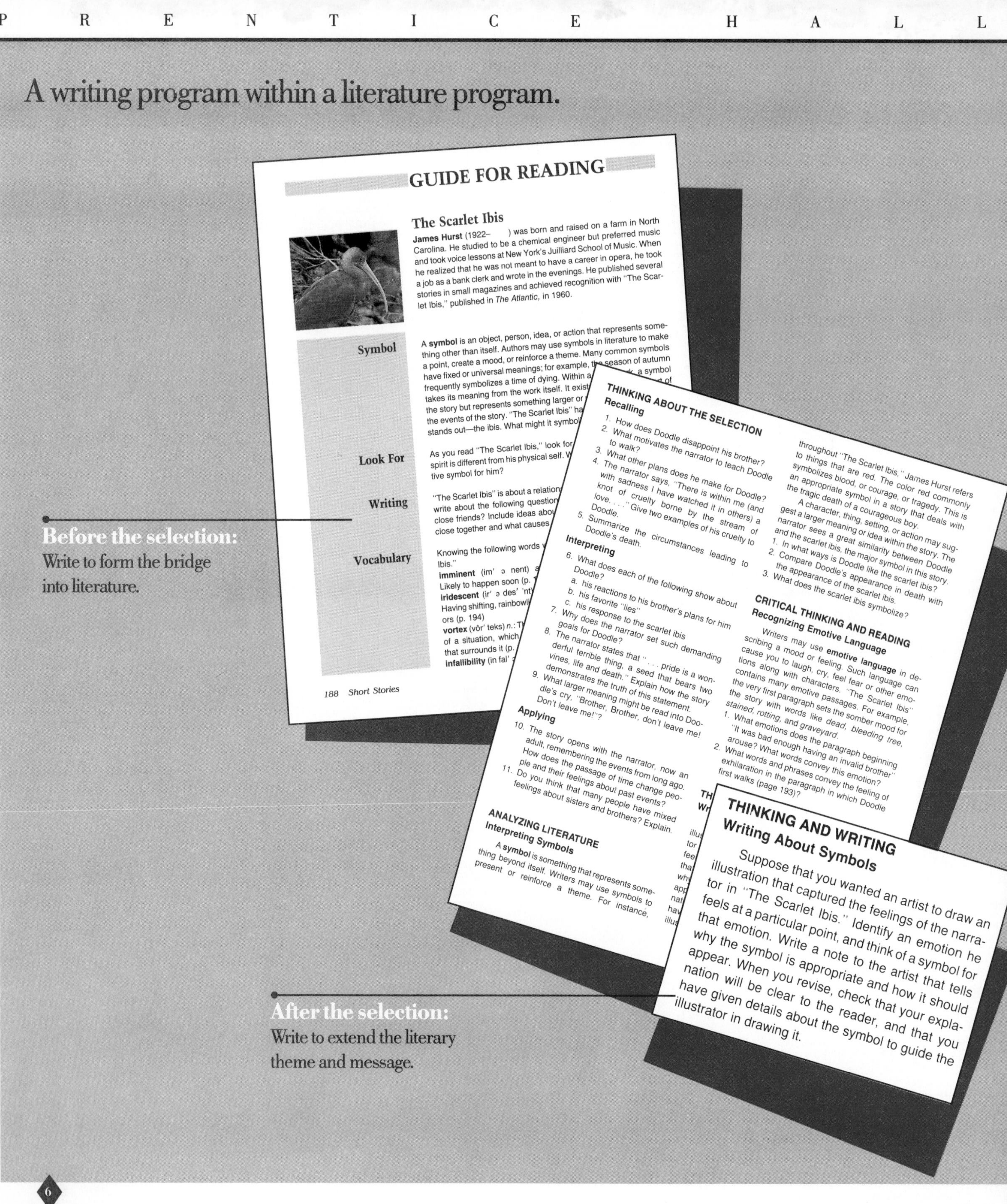

GUIDE FOR READING

The Scarlet Ibis

James Hurst (1922–) was born and raised on a farm in North Carolina. He studied to be a chemical engineer but preferred music and took voice lessons at New York's Juilliard School of Music. When he realized that he was not meant to have a career in opera, he took a job as a bank clerk and wrote in the evenings. He published several stories in small magazines and achieved recognition with "The Scarlet Ibis," published in *The Atlantic*, in 1960.

Symbol

A **symbol** is an object, person, idea, or action that represents something other than itself. Authors may use symbols in literature to make a point, create a mood, or reinforce a theme. Many common symbols have fixed or universal meanings; for example, the season of autumn frequently symbolizes a time of dying. Within a … a symbol takes its meaning from the work itself. It exist… the story but represents something larger or … the events of the story. "The Scarlet Ibis" ha… stands out—the ibis. What might it symbol…

Look For

As you read "The Scarlet Ibis," look for … spirit is different from his physical self. W… tive symbol for him?

Writing

"The Scarlet Ibis" is about a relation… write about the following question… close friends? Include ideas abo… close together and what causes…

Vocabulary

Knowing the following words … Ibis."

imminent (im′ ə nent) a… Likely to happen soon (p. …

iridescent (ir′ ə des′ 'nt)… Having shifting, rainbowl… ors (p. 194)

vortex (vôr′ teks) *n.*: T… of a situation, which… that surrounds it (p. …

infallibility (in fal′ …

188 Short Stories

THINKING ABOUT THE SELECTION

Recalling

1. How does Doodle disappoint his brother?
2. What motivates the narrator to teach Doodle to walk?
3. What other plans does he make for Doodle?
4. The narrator says, "There is within me (and with sadness I have watched it in others) a knot of cruelty borne by the stream of love. . . ." Give two examples of his cruelty to Doodle.
5. Summarize the circumstances leading to Doodle's death.

Interpreting

6. What does each of the following show about Doodle?
   a. his reactions to his brother's plans for him
   b. his favorite "lies"
   c. his response to the scarlet ibis
7. Why does the narrator set such demanding goals for Doodle?
8. The narrator states that ". . . pride is a wonderful terrible thing, a seed that bears two vines, life and death." Explain how the story demonstrates the truth of this statement.
9. What larger meaning might be read into Doodle's cry, "Brother, Brother, don't leave me! Don't leave me!"?

Applying

10. The story opens with the narrator, now an adult, remembering the events from long ago. How does the passage of time change people and their feelings about past events?
11. Do you think that many people have mixed feelings about sisters and brothers? Explain.

ANALYZING LITERATURE

Interpreting Symbols

A **symbol** is something that represents something beyond itself. Writers may use symbols to present or reinforce a theme. For instance, throughout "The Scarlet Ibis," James Hurst refers to things that are red. The color red commonly symbolizes blood, or courage, or tragedy. This is an appropriate symbol in a story that deals with the tragic death of a courageous boy.

A character, thing, setting, or action may suggest a larger meaning or idea within the story. The narrator sees a great similarity between Doodle and the scarlet ibis, the major symbol in this story.

1. In what ways is Doodle like the scarlet ibis?
2. Compare Doodle's appearance in death with the appearance of the scarlet ibis.
3. What does the scarlet ibis symbolize?

CRITICAL THINKING AND READING

Recognizing Emotive Language

Writers may use **emotive language** in describing a mood or feeling. Such language can cause you to laugh, cry, feel fear or other emotions along with characters. "The Scarlet Ibis" contains many emotive passages. For example, the very first paragraph sets the somber mood for the story with words like *dead, bleeding tree, stained, rotting,* and *graveyard.*

1. What emotions does the paragraph beginning "It was bad enough having an invalid brother" arouse? What words convey this emotion?
2. What words and phrases convey the feeling of exhilaration in the paragraph in which Doodle first walks (page 193)?

THINKING AND WRITING

Writing About Symbols

Suppose that you wanted an artist to draw an illustration that captured the feelings of the narrator in "The Scarlet Ibis." Identify an emotion he feels at a particular point, and think of a symbol for that emotion. Write a note to the artist that tells why the symbol is appropriate and how it should appear. When you revise, check that your explanation will be clear to the reader, and that you have given details about the symbol to guide the illustrator in drawing it.

Before the selection:
Write to form the bridge into literature.

After the selection:
Write to extend the literary theme and message.

The Power of Fine Literature, The Mastery of Writing.

Choose from 5 writing activities for each selection.

Extend the power and breadth of your writing program with these additional activities:

- Fine Art Writing activities
- Selection Test essay questions
- Unit Test essay questions
- You the Writer Writing assignment
- You the Critic Writing assignment
- Writing Across the Curriculum activities
- Student writing models

Plus – Writing About Literature Handbook

A writing course right in the student book

COMPOSITION

Thinking and Writing

Discuss the assignment with the students. Make sure they understand that the illustration should reveal emotion rather than story action.

Prewriting: Provide classroom time for students to identify the different feelings expressed by the narrator throughout the story. Have them write a list of the character's emotions. Have them suggest symbols that might represent each of the emotions on their list. Finally, have them discuss the purpose of an illustration—to enhance the text which it accompanies.

Writing: Allow time for students to write their first draft in class.

Revising: Provide time for students to revise their writing. Direct them to make sure that their explanation is clear and that they have included details about the symbol. Have them proofread their note and prepare a final draft. Finally, have students read each other's notes and select the ones they would give to artists.

Guidelines for Evaluating Thinking and Writing

Keep the following questions in mind when evaluating students' papers.

1. Does the note describe a symbol that might be illustrated?
2. Does the note explain in what ways the symbol is appropriate to the emotions of the narrator during a particular part of the story?
3. Is the appearance of the symbol suggested with details?
4. Are the sentences grammatically correct? Are they punctuated correctly? Are the words spelled correctly?

ALTERNATE COMPOSITION ASSIGNMENTS

Three writing assignments follow: Less Challenging, More Challenging, and The Student as Critic.

Less Challenging

Imagine that you are directing a television play of "The Scarlet Ibis." What stage settings will you need to convey the atmosphere and action of the story? Write a report to your set designer listing the scenery you will need and describing the atmosphere each set should have. First make a list of settings that are important to the story. Freewrite about the atmosphere each setting should convey. Then write a first draft of your report. Revise the report, checking that your list is complete and is clearly stated. Finally, proofread your report and prepare a final draft.

More Challenging

Imagine that you are one of the parents in the story. What do you say to your son when you learn about Doodle's death? Are you angry that the older boy encouraged Doodle to exercise? Do you appreciate his guilt and shame? What thoughts do you have about the dead ibis? Keeping in character, freewrite to explore your feelings about the event. Then write a diary entry that conveys your feelings. Revise your entry, making sure that you have discussed the ibis and that you ... proofread ... draft.

The Student as Critic

The following excerpt is the first sentence from "The Summer of Two Figs," another story by James Hurst.

> How like life that summer was—born of fulsome promise to fade into falling leaves unfulfilled, like the seven yards of white silk crepe which was bought to make Mama a party dress, but was requisitioned for a shroud.

Think about the meaning of this quotation. How does it apply to "The Scarlet Ibis"? Then write a short composition comparing the excerpt with the first paragraph of "The Scarlet Ibis." In your composition, discuss one of the following: (1) the author's use of symbols to create a mood; (2) the author's choice of words according to their sound as well as their meaning. First identify the similarities between the two passages. Make a list of details from each passage that support your ideas. Organize your ideas around a thesis statement. Then write a first draft of your composi-

Three additional writing activities in the Teaching Portfolio meet the needs of all ability levels:

- Less Challenging
- More Challenging
- The Student as Critic

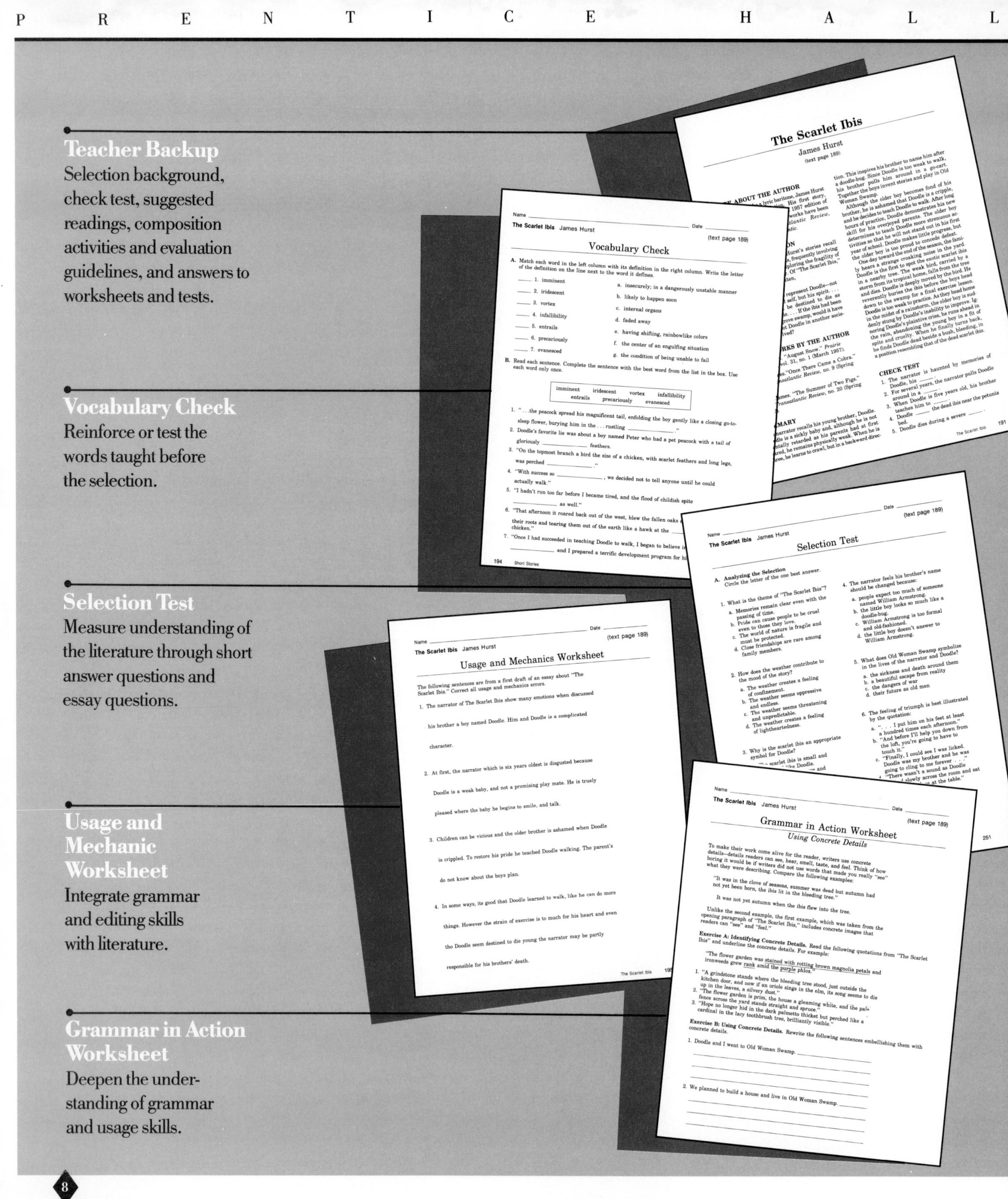
Teacher Backup
Selection background, check test, suggested readings, composition activities and evaluation guidelines, and answers to worksheets and tests.
Vocabulary Check
Reinforce or test the words taught before the selection.
Selection Test
Measure understanding of the literature through short answer questions and essay questions.
Usage and Mechanic Worksheet
Integrate grammar and editing skills with literature.
Grammar in Action Worksheet
Deepen the understanding of grammar and usage skills.
The Scarlet Ibis
James Hurst
Vocabulary Check
Selection Test
Usage and Mechanics Worksheet
Grammar in Action Worksheet
Using Concrete Details

The Teaching Portfolio – Redefining the Concept of Support for all the Language Arts.

Everything you need to teach a selection is in one place.

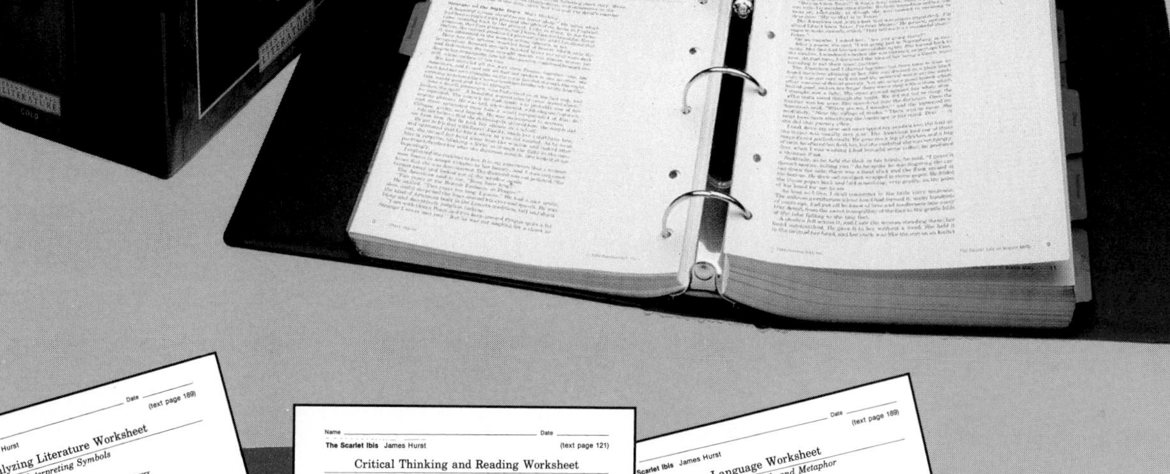

Name ______ Date ______

The Scarlet Ibis James Hurst (text page 189)

Analyzing Literature Worksheet

Interpreting Symbols

These are two broad categories of symbols used in literature. One category includes objects that suggest a consistent meaning in whatever context they are used. As discussed in the Guide for Reading, such symbols include the season of autumn as a time of transition and perhaps death. The other category of symbols includes objects that assume significance in a given work. For example, James Hurst uses the scarlet ibis as a symbol of Doodle's exoticism and transience.

On the lines below each question, write an answer that demonstrates the symbolic significance you have drawn from "The Scarlet Ibis."

1. Throughout the story, the author provides the names of specific plants and birds. What characteristics do these names have in common? How does the emphasis on the natural world support the theme of the story?
2. What colors other than red are emphasized in the story? What significance are these colors given?
3. Find evidence in the story that describes the weather, the time of day, and the time of year during which Doodle's death occurs. What symbolic significance is implied by these facts?

196 Short Stories

Name ______ Date ______

The Scarlet Ibis James Hurst (text page 121)

Critical Thinking and Reading Worksheet

Making Inferences About Characters

A reader makes inferences based on the thoughts, feelings, and actions of a story's characters. Following is a series of facts from "The Good Deed." On the lines below each fact, identify a major inference you can draw from the fact.

1. Mr. Pan risked his life and spent much money to bring his mother to New York.
2. Old Mrs. Pan sits far from the window.
3. Although they were already in love, Mr. and Mrs. Pan allowed their marriage to be arranged by their elders.
4. The old woman crosses the street with her grandson.
5. Mr. Pan arranges for Lili to make another visit to his mother.
6. Young Mr. Lim suggests that Lili meet him on Sunday.

127

Date ______

Scarlet Ibis James Hurst (text page 189)

Language Worksheet

Identifying Simile and Metaphor

Simile and metaphor are forms of descriptive language with which a writer may draw a comparison between two seemingly dissimilar things. A *metaphor* states that one object *is* another object, whereas a *simile* states that one object is similar to or resembles another object. For example, the narrator of "The Scarlet Ibis" uses a metaphor when he explains that "pride is a seed that bears two vines." On the other hand, the statement "Hope . . . perched like a cardinal in the lacy toothbrush tree" contains a simile.

Decide whether the following sentences contain similes or metaphors. For each sentence, write "simile" or "metaphor" on the line at the right.

1. The oriole nest rocked back and forth like an empty cradle. 1. ______
2. The last graveyard flowers were speaking softly the names of our dead. 2. ______
3. The sick-sweet smell of bay flowers hung everywhere like a mournful song. 3. ______
4. He collapsed onto the grass like a half-empty flour sack. 4. ______
5. When the sun burned orange in the top of the pines, we'd drop our jewels into the stream. 5. ______
6. I pulled the go-cart down into the green dimness where the palmetto fronds whispered by the stream. 6. ______
7. The rain fell straight down like ropes hanging from the sky. 7. ______
8. The grindstone begins to turn, and time with all its changes is ground away. 8. ______

The Scarlet Ibis 197

Analyzing Literature Worksheet
Extends understanding of the literary element.

Critical Thinking and Reading Worksheet
Promotes reading and reasoning.

Language Worksheet
Beyond vocabulary to word origins, synonyms, dialects – and more.

Fine Art Transparencies

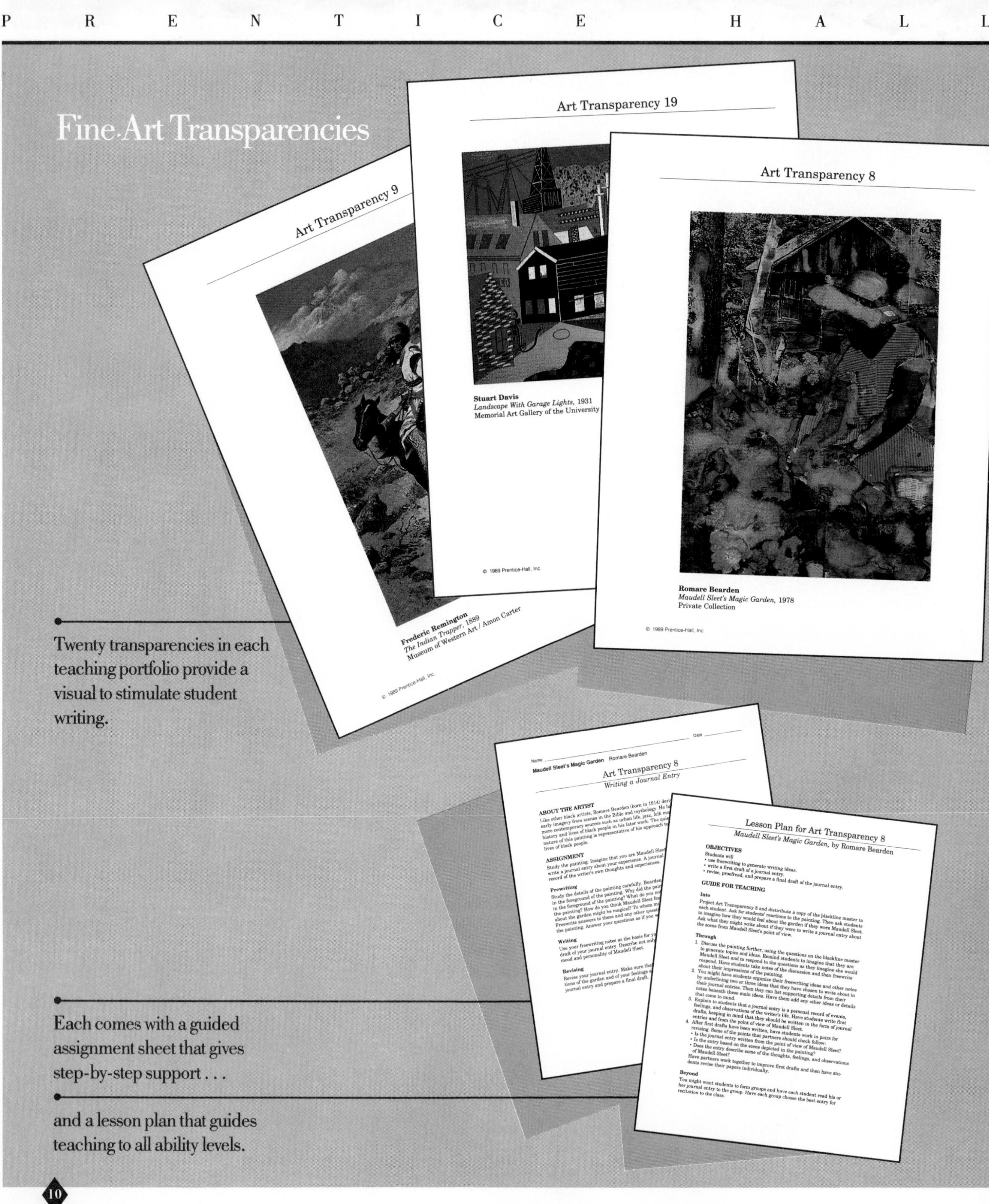

Twenty transparencies in each teaching portfolio provide a visual to stimulate student writing.

Each comes with a guided assignment sheet that gives step-by-step support . . .

and a lesson plan that guides teaching to all ability levels.

Capture the Power of Integrating Fine Literature and the Humanities.

A fine arts program and classic cinema connected with literature.

The Library of Video Classics

- Four feature length films per grade level, including the novel and the play.
- Viewing guides link the film with the literature to stimulate new ideas.

Each Viewing Guide provides:

- Previewing and After Viewing Questions – enhance critical thinking skills.
- Speaking and Listening activities – promote oral language skills through the impact of film.
- Writing activities – creative topics enhance students responsiveness.
- Ability level notes – ideas to challenge each student.

Direct students to new discoveries with the dynamic combination of literature and cinema.

Study Guides

What if your favorite novel or play is not in Prentice Hall Literature? We still provide you with teaching support. Complete teaching guides for 40 novels and plays give you fresh insights to make the classic even more interesting and relevant. Each guide contains:

- Author Background
- Synopses of Plot, Setting, Theme and More
- Chapter-by-Chapter Teaching Plans
- Writing Assignments
- Guidelines for Dealing With Provocative Themes
- Blackline Master Handouts and Test

Tailor the Literature Program to Your Own Classes.

Library of Great Works

Now, the time-honored longer works of American, British, and world cultures available with Prentice Hall Literature

- Classic, unabridged editions
- Hardbound versions insure lasting value
- A Novel Study Guide for expert teaching support to bring the work to life

Great Works

Adventures of Huckleberry Finn
Brothers Karamazov
Candide
Death of a Salesman
Don Quixote
Great Gatsby
Hamlet
Importance of Being Earnest
Lord of the Flies
Nineteen Eighty Four
Our Town
Pride and Prejudice
Red Badge of Courage
Scarlet Letter
Siddartha
Tartuffe
Things Fall Apart
Wuthering Heights

Computer Test Bank

Customize your literature testing program with instant tests on each selection

For each selection choose from:

- Selection test
- Essay questions with evaluation guidelines
- Answer key

For each unit, choose from:

- Short answer test
- Essay tests

Powerful word processor for your made to order options.

- Write an unlimited number of new questions
- Delete questions

User friendly format for quick answers.

- Menus
- 800 customer service number

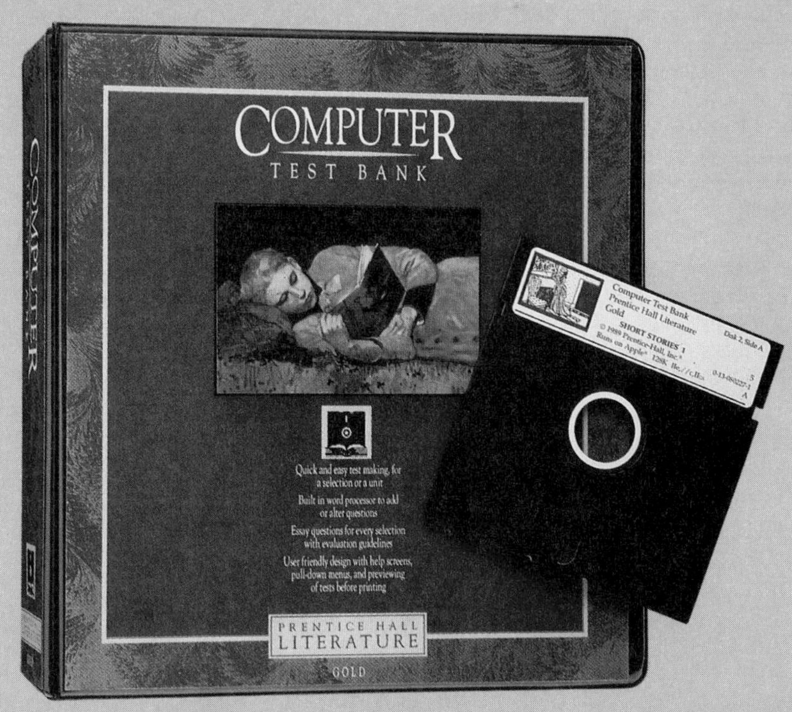

Master Teacher Board

Roger Babusci
(Pennsylvania Teacher of the Year, 1983)
Schenley High School
Pittsburgh, Pennsylvania

Loutish Burns
(Houston Teacher of the Year, 1981)
Louie Welch Middle School
Houston, Texas

Guy Doud
(National Teacher of the Year, 1986)
Brainerd Senior High School
Brainerd, Minnesota

Terri Fields
(Arizona Teacher of the Year, 1986)
Sunnyslope High School
Phoenix, Arizona

Kermeen Fristrom
(1985 Distinguished Service Award of Merit, California)
San Diego City Schools
San Diego, California

LeRoy Hay
(National Teacher of the Year, 1983)
Manchester High School
Manchester, Connecticut

Beth Johnson
(Florida Teacher of the Year, 1982)
Kathleen Senior High School
Lakeland, Florida

Evaline Kruse
(California Teacher of the Year, 1985)
Audubon Junior High School
Los Angeles, California

Jane McKee
(West Virginia Teacher of the Year, 1986)
Man High School
Man, West Virginia

Robert Seney
(Texas Curriculum Association's Exemplary Showcase Award for Literature)
Albright Middle School
Houston, Texas

Pat Weaver
(1985 National Outstanding Dissertation for Curriculum)
Arlington Independent School District
Arlington, Texas

Consultants

Joan Baron
University of Connecticut
Storrs, Connecticut

Charles Cooper
University of California
San Diego, California

Nancy Nelson Spivey
Carnegie Mellon University
Pittsburgh, Pennsylvania

Contributing Writers

Sumner Braunstein
Former Teacher and Curriculum Planner
Campus High School
The City College, New York

Nancy Coolidge
Former English Teacher
Escondido High School
Escondido, California

Frances Earle
Former English Teacher
Miralest High School
Palos Verdes, California

Sharon Glick
Formerly affiliated with Detroit Public Schools
Detroit, Michigan

Annotated Teacher's Edition

PRENTICE HALL LITERATURE

SILVER

SECOND EDITION

PRENTICE HALL
Englewood Cliffs, New Jersey
Needham, Massachusetts

ISBN 0-13-713074-0

10 9 8 7 6 5 4 3 2 1

Cover and Title Page: *The Inspiration of Christopher Columbus*, 1856, José Maria Obregón, Museo Nacional de Arte, Mexico City

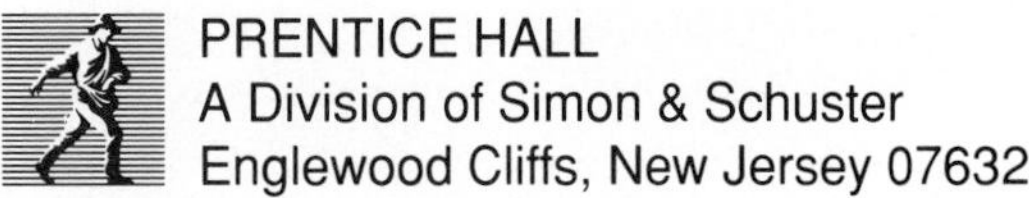

PRENTICE HALL
A Division of Simon & Schuster
Englewood Cliffs, New Jersey 07632

CONTENTS

The Prentice Hall Literature Program
OVERVIEW

THE STUDENT BOOK

The Prentice Hall Literature Program is a complete literature program, offering high-quality, appealing, traditional and contemporary literary selections, with study aids that will guide students into, through, and beyond the literature.

Organization

The selections are organized by genre to encourage comprehensive study of the types of literature. The following list shows the units and the sections within each unit into which the selections are organized:

The Short Story: Plot, Character, Setting, Theme
Drama: One-act Plays, a Full-length Play
Nonfiction: Biographies and Personal Accounts, Essays for Enjoyment, Essays in the Content Areas
Poetry: Narrative Poetry, Figurative Language and Imagery, Lyric Poetry, Facets of Nature, Perceptions, Choices
American Myths, Legends, and Folktales
The Novel: A Complete Novel

The number and variety of selections offer choice and flexibility in meeting curriculum requirements as well as student needs and interests.

Unique Features

Because the Prentice Hall Literature Program puts emphasis on the reading and appreciation of literature, it offers several unique features to help students become active readers.

Reading Actively Each unit begins with a feature called Reading Actively, which includes a set of strategies for effectively reading the literature in the unit. The strategies involve the reader in the text before reading and while reading. Such involvement and reaction are necessary if students are to understand and appreciate the material. The active reading strategies include the following:

For prose: questioning, predicting, summarizing, clarifying
For drama: visualizing, questioning, predicting, clarifying, summarizing
For poetry: questioning, clarifying, listening, paraphrasing, summarizing

In the short story, nonfiction, and poetry units, this feature is followed by a Model for Reading Actively. This Model is annotated to demonstrate and explain to students how a good reader might use the active reading strategies to understand a selection. Students are encouraged to use these strategies as they read other selections in the unit. This feature provides a method of scaffolding—giving students help and support while they acquire the skills to become successful readers of literature. To give students further practice with this process, there is an additional selection in the Teaching Portfolio which students can annotate themselves.

Guide for Reading All other selections begin with a Guide for Reading. This page, which precedes the selection, contains useful prereading information. The Guide for Reading prepares students for successful reading in five ways:

- A biography of the author provides insight into how the author came to write the selection.
- A literary focus section introduces the literary concept that is taught with the selection.
- The Look For provides a specific goal—thematic, stylistic, or meaning-oriented—to guide the students' reading of the selection.
- A motivational writing activity puts students in an appropriate frame of mind.
- A vocabulary list presents, in glossary format, words from the selection that might present difficulty in reading.

This Guide for Reading provides the necessary background to encourage comprehension, motivates students to read, and gives them technical support to read successfully.

Putting It Together The short story, nonfiction, and poetry units also end with a feature called Putting It Together. This feature serves as a summary for reading and analyzing the particular types of literature and comprehending the literary elements and devices that are in them. For examples, the Putting It Together for short stories reviews plot, character, theme, and setting, and analyzes the application of these elements in a particular story. In the Teaching Portfolio, there is an additional selection that the students can annotate themselves.

Each selection is self-contained and complete so that you can use the selections in any order.

After Reading

Features at the end of the selection are designed to foster comprehension and encourage constructive response, either personal or literary. They also encourage the growth of skills needed by students to become independent readers. These features comprise five areas:

Thinking About the Selection: These study questions are built upon three levels of comprehension: the literal, the interpretive, and the applied. The questions are grouped by three levels of increasing complexity: recalling (literal), interpreting (inference, analysis), and applying (generalization, extension, judgment). The different levels may be used as appropriate for different ability levels, or may be used to take all students through different levels of thinking.

Analyzing Literature: This section develops and reinforces the literary concept or skill introduced on the Guide for Reading page and applies it to the selection. It helps students to understand literary concepts and appreciate writers' techniques, thereby enabling them to respond appropriately to literature.

Critical Thinking and Reading: This section introduces students to those critical thinking and critical reading skills that are necessary for understanding literature. It gives them an opportunity to apply these skills to the literary selections.

Understanding Language: Knowledge and appreciation of language are developed in this section, which contains activities on language prompted by the selection. The activities may be geared toward helping students appreciate writers' use of language, master skills needed to increase their vocabulary, or prepare for SATs.

Thinking and Writing: This is a composition assignment arising from the selection. This assignment, which may be creative or analytical, is process-oriented, suggesting steps for prewriting, drafting, and revising.

End of Unit

Focus on Reading At the end of each unit is a two-page lesson focusing on one reading skill appropriate to the type of literature students have read. For example, at the end of the short story unit, students take an in-depth look at relationships and see how patterns of relationships affect the stories they have read. At the end of the poetry unit, students review and practice making inferences about poetry. Each lesson is structured so that it provides an explanation of the skill, examples, and activities.

You the Writer, You the Critic At the end of each unit, there are six additional writing activities. Three of them, under You the Writer, are creative; three of them, under You the Critic, are analytical. Each activity is developed through the steps of the writing process.

End of Book

Three handbooks are provided at the end of *Prentice Hall Literature*: Handbook of Writing About Literature, Handbook of Critical Thinking and Reading Terms, and Handbook of Literary Terms and Techniques.

Handbook of Writing About Literature The Handbook of Writing About Literature is divided into five sections. The first section introduces the process of writing. The second requires students to analyze and interpret literature and teaches them how to write about the specific elements of literary works. The third requires students to interpret and synthesize while teaching how to write about the work as a whole. The fourth provides instruction in evaluating literary works. The fifth guides the students in the creation of their own literary works.

This Handbook may be used for direct instruction or as support for the individual writing assignments in *Prentice Hall Literature*.

Handbook of Critical Thinking and Reading Terms The Handbook of Critical Thinking and Reading Terms provides an alphabetical arrangement of the terms taught in the Critical Thinking and Reading activities at the end of selections. Some entries expand upon the original definition and provide one or more examples. Other entries provide additional terms and definitions. This Handbook can be used to preteach terminology or to review information. It can also be used as an easy reference guide for students as they work on individual Critical Thinking and Reading assignments.

Handbook of Literary Terms and Techniques The Handbook of Literary Terms and Techniques provides an alphabetical guide to the literary terms introduced on the Guide for Reading page and taught in the Analyzing Literature activities at the end of selections. Each entry provides a full definition of the term or technique with one or more examples. The handbook can be used for preteaching, for review, or as a support for students as they work on individual Analyzing Literature activities.

TEACHING SUPPORT

THE ANNOTATED TEACHER'S EDITION

The Annotated Teacher's Edition of *Prentice Hall Literature* is designed to be used both for planning and for actual in-class teaching. It offers planning aids and specific teaching suggestions for all selections. This planning and teaching material appears in the side columns next to the reduced student pages of each selection. These annotations, which correspond to the student material on that page, help you give your students positive and relevant experiences with literature by asking the right questions at the right time and by pointing out what is significant.

Preparing the Lesson: Focus

The annotations on the opening pages of the selection help you plan your presentation of the material. Each selection begins with notes that suggest ways to introduce or enhance the prereading instruction or activities presented in the students' Guide for Reading. These notes help you present the material or adapt it for **less advanced** or **more advanced** students. In addition, an occasional **spelling tip** gives a hint for remembering the spelling of a troublesome word. Objectives for each selection are keyed to the end-of-selection material. This pages also includes a complete list of support material for this selection in the Teaching Portfolio and other program components. In the column next to the first page of the selection, you will find a **motivation/ prior knowledge** suggestion and a **purpose-setting question** to prepare the students to read the selection. Frequently, **thematic ideas** are given. These suggest other selections in this book that treat themes similar to those under discussion. You may want to use these selections together to integrate and reinforce universal concepts and themes. **ESL strategies** suggest ways to make selections accessible to ESL students. All of these annotations help you effectively prepare your lesson.

Teaching the Lesson: Presentation

You may use the notes throughout the pages of the selection to direct your discussion in class. As you and your students read the selection, you will find additional notes that enable you to customize the lesson for your class. They let you increase your students' involvement in the work and enrich their reading of it, while enabling them to deal with the particular genres. The following kinds of notes may direct your class discussions:

Master Teacher Notes These classroom tips from master teachers give an approach, a strategy, or a very special bit of information that enlivens the selection or increases appreciation.

Humanities Notes For each piece of fine art in the student book, there is a humanities note giving information on the work of art and the artist. These notes generally point out features of the piece of art that relate it to the work of literature with which it is presented. Additionally, the humanities note concludes with questions that you may use if you wish to discuss the art as part of your discussion of the work.

Enrichment Enrichment notes provide additional information on points of interest that arise in selection. You may use this information to enrich your students' knowledge of the background of a selection and appreciation of it.

Reading Strategies Strategies to promote student comprehension of the literary text reinforce the emphasis on enabling students to read literature.

Clarification Words, phrases, or ideas that might be obstacles to student understanding are clarified to ensure comprehension.

Discussion Throughout the selection, you will find additional questions and points for discussion. These help you proceed through the selection with students, eliciting their understanding and appreciation of significant passages.

Literary Focus To promote understanding of the writer's techniques, literary focus annotations direct attention to those aspects of the selection that reflect the literary concept presented with it.

Critical Thinking and Reading These notes reinforce the critical thinking and reading skills developed throughout the program.

Reader's Response These notes ask a question designed to prompt the students' personal response to the selection.

Grammar in Action Grammar in Action notes integrate language arts skills. These notes demonstrate the writer's use of particular grammatical or style points. They present a direct link between grammar and writing.

Occasional **commentary** and **primary source** notes add background or insight to the selection.

There are probably more notes than you need for presenting any given selection. We emphasize the importance of selecting those annotations that are best suited to your classes and course of instruction.

Closure and Extension

Answers are provided for all questions in each feature following the selections. Where questions are open-ended, we present a suggested response or suggest points that students should note in their answers.

The annotations after the selection also include the following:

Challenge These questions take students beyond those given with the instruction.

Publishing Student Writing For many selections, additional notes suggest ways of publishing the writing students have done in the Thinking and Writing feature.

Writing Across the Curriculum Where appropriate, you will see suggestions for additional assignments or suggestions for relating the Thinking and Writing assignment to students' work in another discipline.

In addition, you will find teaching suggestions for the special features in the student book—Reading Actively, Putting It Together, Focus on Reading, and You the Writer, You the Critic.

THE TEACHING PORTFOLIO

The Teaching Portfolio provides support for teaching and testing all of the selections and skills in *Prentice Hall Literature*.

Fine-Art Transparencies

Twenty fine-art transparencies with blackline masters are provided in the Teaching Portfolio. These can be used to introduce selections and motivate students to read, or they may be used as additional writing assignments in response to art. The fine art is keyed into the selections through Master Teacher Notes in the Annotated Teacher's Edition. In the Portfolio, each transparency is accompanied by a writing assignment for students and a lesson plan for teaching that assignment.

Beginning of Unit

Each unit begins with a list of objectives and a skills chart listing literary elements and skills covered in the unit. The chart also identifies all the blackline masters in the Teaching Portfolio that correlate to each selection.

The Selections

Full teaching support is provided for each selection. This support material is organized by selection for your convenience. The support for each selection consists of the following: Teacher Backup, Grammar in Action Worksheet, Usage and Mechanics Worksheet, Vocabulary Check, Analyzing Literature Worksheet*, Critical Thinking and Reading Worksheet*, Language Worksheet* (there are always two of the starred three), and a Selection Test.

Teacher Backup Teacher Backup material is provided for each selection. This material consists of more information about the author, a critical quotation about the author, a summary of the selection, and a list of other works by the author. In addition, there is a Check Test that you can use to check if students have read the selection. Help in teaching and evaluating the writing assignment in the student text is provided as well as three alternative composition assignments for the students. One of these is less challenging than the assignment in the student text, one is more challenging, and one requires the student to write in response to literary criticism. Finally, answers to all worksheets and tests are provided.

Grammar in Action Worksheets These worksheets provide additional instruction and practice on the topic presented with a selection in the Annotated Teacher's Edition.

Usage and Mechanics The Usage and Mechanics Worksheet provides sentences dealing with the selection that contain errors in usage and mechanics. They provide additional practice with the skill presented in the Grammar in Action Worksheet. Such common problems as run-on sentences, sentence fragments, and subject–verb agreement are incorporated into these sentences as well as errors in spelling and punctuation. We suggest you have your students correct these sentences orally so that they can discuss each problem.

Vocabulary Check The Vocabulary Check tests mastery of the vocabulary words listed on the Guide for Reading page before each selection. This blackline master can be used as a test or as an in-class or at-home assignment.

Worksheets The Analyzing Literature Worksheet, Critical Thinking and Reading Worksheet, and Language Worksheet support and expand upon the skills taught at the end of the selection in the student book.

Selections Test A Selection Test is provided for each selection. This test requires students to demonstrate comprehension and interpretation of the selection and to apply the skills taught at the end of the selection. The test includes an essay question and a reader's response question.

Annotated Models For each selection that is annotated as a model in the student book (at the beginning of the short story, nonfiction, and poetry units), a selection is provided in the Teaching Portfolio for students to annotate themselves.

End of Unit

Each unit ends with two unit tests: a short-answer test and an essay test, with guidelines for evaluating student responses to the essay test questions. In addition, a list of suggested projects, a bibliography, and list of audio-visual aids are included.

End of Portfolio

At the end of the Teaching Portfolio are models of strong and weak student writing and a guide to evaluating student writing.

STUDY GUIDES

Study Guides for major novels and plays are available with *Prentice Hall Literature*. These guides will help you teach many of the works of your choice as part of your total literature program. Each guide contains an overview of the novel or play, chapter-by-chapter lessons, assignments leading to essays and imaginative writing, guidelines for dealing with provocative themes, a bibliography, and blackline masters of skills and a test for the work.

COMPUTER TEST BANK

The computer test bank provides the selection test and unit tests from the Teaching Portfolio on a computer disk. The program allows you to modify the selection tests by deleting items from the short-answer selection tests supplied, choosing a different essay question, and writing your own test questions. You can save your test for future use.

LIBRARY OF VIDEO CLASSICS

The Library of Video Classics provides videotapes of films made of major works in this level. Each tape is accompanied by a Viewing Guide, which gives background on the film or director; a planning overview for the film; and previewing and after-viewing questions and activities.

Composition Strand in Prentice Hall Literature

The following chart shows all composition activities and their location in the program. The activities are organized to take students into, through, and beyond the literature.

Feature	In the Student Materials	In the Teacher Materials	Benefit
Into the Literature			
"Writing" activity *before* each selection	"Guide for Reading" page before each selection in student text	"Guide for Reading" teaching note in margin of Annotated Teacher's Edition	Writing before reading is an ideal technique for getting students into literature
Through the Literature			
"Thinking and Writing" composition activity after each selection	End of each selection in student text	In Teaching Portfolio: teaching notes for activity labeled with writing process steps; evaluation checklist for grading writing In ATE: suggestions for publishing student writing	The writing activity that follows each selection provides an immediate opportunity to respond to the literary experience. The activity is in writing process format.
Three additional composition activities for *each* selection: Less Challenging, More Challenging, The Student as Critic		Additional activities are in the Teaching Portfolio. These can be used as assignments, or as essay questions for tests.	Three additional activities for *each* selection let you meet the needs for lower ability levels, or provide enrichment.
"Handbook of Writing About Literature," made up of two-page writing lessons	Handbook section of at least 50 pages at the end of each student text	Notes and support for using the handbook in the Teaching Portfolio	Guided lessons lead students step-by step through case studies and activities.
"Unit Test" essay questions that address several selections in a unit		Tests in Teaching Portfolio comes with evaluation checklists	Sharpen critical thinking and writing with thoughtful topics that compare and contrast thematic ideas, literary elements, and unit content.
Beyond the Literature			
"You the Writer" creative writing activity with each unit	End of each unit in student text	Guidelines for evaluating student writing are in Annotated Teacher's Edition	Students try their hand at expressive writing aided by imaginative prompts and step-by-step encouragement.
"You the Critic" literary criticism activity with each unit	End of each unit in student text	Teaching notes and guidelines for evaluating student writing in Annotated Teacher's Edition	Challenge analytical skills as your students respond to literary criticism.
"Writing Across the Curriculum" suggestions		Suggestions in Annotated Teacher's Edition	Broaden writing opportunities to other subjects. Notes suggest assignments and interactions with other departments.
"Fine Art Writing Activity" (from full color art transparency)	Handout sheet	Twenty fine art color transparencies with accompanying blackline masters in Teaching Portfolio	Use the dynamic combination of literature and writing for a humanities-based writing activity.
"Student Writing Models"		In the Teaching Portfolio: examples of strong and weak student compositions	Use the powerful motivator of peer learning to prompt better writing responses.

Skills Chart for Selections in Each Unit

The following chart shows the literary elements and integrated language arts skills covered with each selection. An asterisk (*) indicates that a worksheet appears in the Teaching Portfolio.

SHORT STORIES

Selection	Analyzing Literature	Critical Thinking and Reading	Understanding Language/ Speaking and Listening	Thinking and Writing	Grammar in Action
Reading Activity					
"The Story-Teller," Saki, p. 3	Understanding the title	Comparing and contrasting stories*	Using a glossary*	Creating a story	Using vivid adjectives and adverbs* Appreciating unusual word choice*
Plot					
"Rain, Rain, Go Away," Isaac Asimov, p. 13	Understanding plot*	Understanding the sequence of events*	Using negative prefixes	Writing a short story	Understanding dialogue*
"Christmas Day in the Morning," Pearl S. Buck, p. 21	Understanding flashback*	Understanding time order	Using context clues*	Writing an extended definition	Understanding compound–complex sentences*
"The Adventure of the Speckled Band," Sir Arthur Conan Doyle, p. 27	Examining conflict	Understanding logical reasoning*	Choosing the meaning that fits the context*	Understanding your thinking	Using *who* and *whom** Understanding adjective clauses* Understanding compound sentences* Understanding passive voice*
"The Captain and His Horse," Beryl Markham, p. 47	Investigating suspense*	Making predictions*	Interpreting metaphors	Writing about suspense	Using demonstrative pronouns*
"A Retrieved Reformation," O. Henry, p. 61	Understanding the surprise ending*	Recognizing allusions	Finding meanings to fit the context*	Writing about a surprise ending	Using dashes* Understanding pronouns and antecedents*
"The Rule of Names," Ursula K. Le Guin, p. 69	Investigating fantasy	Separating realistic and fantastic details*	Identifying synonyms*	Writing a fantasy	Using semicolons* Varying sentence patterns and length* Appreciating degrees of comparison*

SHORT STORIES (continued)

Selection	Analyzing Literature	Critical Thinking and Reading	Understanding Language/ Speaking and Listening	Thinking and Writing	Grammar in Action
"Charles," Shirley Jackson, p. 79	Investigating point of view*	Making inferences about the plot	Using the suffix *-ly* to form adverbs*	Writing from another point of view	Understanding dialogue*
Character					
"The House Guest," Paul Darcy Boles, p. 85	Understanding character traits*	Comparing and contrasting characters*	Showing contrast	Writing as a character	Using transitions*
"Gentleman of Río en Medio," Juan A. A. Sedillo, p. 93	Identifying major and minor characters	Comparing and contrasting attitudes*	Understanding words from Spanish*	Comparing and contrasting cultures	
"Raymond's Run," Toni Cade Bambara, p. 97	Recognizing round and flat characters*	Identifying reasons	Understanding idioms*	Writing an extension of the story	Understanding parallelism* Using consistent verb tense*
"The Day the Sun Came Out," Dorothy M. Johnson, p. 107	Understanding characterization*	Making inferences about characters	Appreciating dialect*	Comparing and contrasting characters	
"The Day I Got Lost," Isaac Bashevis Singer, p. 113	Understanding narrator*	Understanding caricature	Reporting on caricature in advertising Understanding synonyms and antonyms*	Writing a story	Using appropriate verb tense*
Setting					
"The Land and the Water," Shirley Ann Grau, p. 119	Understanding setting*	Making inferences about setting	Choosing meanings to fit the context*	Describing a setting	Using semicolons* Understanding sentence fragments*
"Grass Fire," Loula Grace Erdman, p. 129	Understanding descriptive details*	Analyzing the effect of setting on plot	Understanding similes*	Using descriptive details	Using adjectives*
"Crime on Mars," Arthur C. Clarke, p. 137	Understanding time as part of setting	Identifying scientific details*	Recognizing new words*	Continuing a science-fiction story	Using adverbs*
"The Tell-Tale Heart," Edgar Allan Poe, p. 145	Describing atmosphere or mood	Choosing words to create atmosphere*	Choosing the meaning that fits the context*	Writing to create atmosphere	Understanding connotations*

SHORT STORIES (continued)

Selection	Analyzing Literature	Critical Thinking and Reading	Understanding Language/ Speaking and Listening	Thinking and Writing	Grammar in Action
"The Drummer Boy of Shiloh," Ray Bradbury, p. 151	Recognizing historical details*	Identifying appropriate historical details	Preparing a program of Civil War songs Understanding synonyms*	Writing about a historical setting	Understanding dialogue* Using active voice*
Theme					
"The Ninny," Anton Chekhov, p. 159	Understanding theme	Making inferences based on dialogue*	Finding the meaning from the context*	Writing an extension of the story	
"The Six Rows of Pompons," Toshio Mori, p. 163	Understanding key statements*	Comparing and contrasting attitudes*	Understanding meaning from context	Writing an essay about theme	
"Thank You, M'am," Langston Hughes, p. 169	Using character to understand theme	Identifying generalizations*	Presenting readers' theater Understanding compound words*	Writing about a character	Understanding verb predicates*
"The Gift-Giving," Joan Aiken, p. 175	Understanding significant actions	Summarizing*	Understanding homonyms*	Writing about theme	Using commas* Using varied sentence structure* Using semicolons*
"The Man Without a Country," Edward Everett Haie, p. 185	Recognizing symbols	Paraphrasing*	Choosing the meaning that fits the context*	Writing about theme	Using colons* Understanding action verbs* Using sentence variety*
"Flowers for Algernon," Daniel Keyes, p. 201	Understanding point of view and theme*	Comparing and contrasting views	Understanding synonyms and antonyms*	Writing about theme	Understanding 1st-person narration* Understanding adverb clauses* Understanding 2nd-person point of view* Understanding participles and participial phrases*
Putting It Together					
"The Medicine Bag," Virginia Driving Hawk Sneve, p. 225	Reviewing the short story*	Evaluating a story*	Appreciating another language	Continuing a story	Using descriptive words* Using transitions*

SKILLS CHART: DRAMA

Selection	Analyzing Literature	Critical Thinking and Reading	Understanding Language/ Speaking and Listening	Thinking and Writing	Grammar in Action
The Ugly Duckling, A. A. Milne, p. 245	Understanding the one-act play	Recognizing parody*	Completing analogies*	Writing to cast the characters	Understanding sentence fragments* Using dashes*
Back There, Rod Serling, p. 263	Appreciating staging*	Recognizing the playwright's purpose	Identifying word roots*	Writing about staging the play	Understanding participial phrases*
Let Me Hear You Whisper, Paul Zindel, p. 277	Understanding conflict in drama*	Understanding controversy*	Appreciating specialized vocabulary	Writing a response to critical comment	Understanding compound sentences* Understanding sentence fragments*
The Diary of Anne Frank, Act I, Frances Goodrich and Albert Hackett, p. 303	Appreciating the use of flashback	Predicting outcomes*	Recognizing words from German*	Writing about the effect of flashback	Understanding simple sentences* Connecting ideas of equal weight* Understanding infinitive verbs* Understanding imperative sentences*
The Diary of Anne Frank, Act II, p. 345	Understanding characters and theme*	Finding support for opinions*		Writing a letter to the editor	Using contractions* Understanding ellipses*

SKILLS CHART: NONFICTION

Selection	Analyzing Literature	Critical Thinking and Reading	Understanding Language/ Speaking and Listening	Thinking and Writing	Grammar in Action
Reading Actively					
From *One Writer's Beginnings,* Eudora Welty, p. 377	Understanding the informal essay	Comparing and contrasting opinions*	Tracing word histories*	Writing about beginnings	Understanding complex sentences*

NONFICTION (continued)

Selection	Analyzing Literature	Critical Thinking and Reading	Understanding Language/ Speaking and Listening	Thinking and Writing	Grammar in Action
Biographies and Personal Accounts					
"Harriet Tubman: Guide to Freedom," Ann Petry, p. 383	Understanding biography	Recognizing subjective details*	Using Latin roots	Writing a biography	Understanding subject-verb agreement* Understanding subordinate clauses*
"Roberto Clemente: A Bittersweet Memoir," Jerry Izenberg, p. 393	Understanding the memoir*	Identifying primary sources	Doing an interview Using prefixes and suffices to determine meaning	Writing a memoir	Using dashes*
From *I Know Why the Caged Bird Sings,* Maya Angelou, p. 403	Understanding autobiography	Inferring the author's purpose*	Choosing the meaning that fits the context*	Writing an autobiographical sketch	Using vivid adjectives*
"Cub Pilot on the Mississippi," Mark Twain, p. 411	Understanding conflicts*	Separating fact from opinion	Using contrast clues*	Writing about conflict	Appreciating dialect* Using precise, carefully selected verbs*
From *Of Men and Mountains,* William O. Douglas, p. 421	Understanding narrator in autobiography*	Recognizing the effect of point of view*	Appreciating words from Greek myths	Writing from another point of view	Using semicolons* Understanding repetition*
Essays for Enjoyment					
"Sancho," James Frank Dobie, p. 431	Understanding a narrative essay	Putting events in chronological order*	Understanding words from Spanish	Writing a letter	Understanding prepositional phrases*
"Debbie," James Herriot, p. 439	Understanding characters in an essay	Comparing and contrasting characters*	Understanding technical words*	Comparing and contrasting cats	Understanding quotation marks*
"My Wild Irish Mother," Jean Kerr, p. 445	Understanding the humorous essay	Identifying exaggeration*	Finding homophones*	Writing a humorous essay	Using sophisticated sentences*
"Forest Fire," Anais Nin, p. 453	Understanding descriptive essays*	Separating fact and opinion	Identifying word origins*	Writing a descriptive essay	
"The Indian All Around Us," Bernard DeVoto, p. 457	Understanding an expository essay*	Identifying main idea*	Investigating word origins	Writing an expository essay	Using commas*

NONFICTION (continued)

Selection	Analyzing Literature	Critical Thinking and Reading	Understanding Language/ Speaking and Listening	Thinking and Writing	Grammar in Action
"The Trouble with Television," Robert MacNeil, p. 463	Understanding the persuasive essay*	Recognizing connotative language	Using combining forms Choosing the meaning that fits the context*	Writing a persuasive essay	Using topic sentences*
Essays in the Content Areas					
"Shooting Stars," Hal Borland, p. 469	Understanding observation*	Recognizing observation and inference*	Appreciating words from myths	Observing	
"The Sounds of Richard Rodgers," Ellen Goodman, p. 473	Setting a purpose for reading	Recognizing subjective details*	Appreciating music terms*	Writing about an artistic person	
"Dial Versus Digital," Isaac Asimov, p. 477	Varying your rate of reading	Finding main ideas*	Using the prefix *counter**	Writing about technology	
"Hokusai: The Old Man Mad About Drawing," Stephen Longstreet, p. 481	Taking notes*	Finding implied main ideas	Appreciating art terms*	Writing about art	
"Talking About Writing," Ursula K. Le Guin, p. 485	Understanding outlining*	Sequencing events	Using dictionary terms*	Writing advice about performing a skill	
Putting It Together					
"A to Z in Foods as Metaphors," Mimi Sheraton, p. 491	Understanding an essay's purpose*	Interpreting metaphorical language*	Identifying mixed metaphors	Writing about language arts	Understanding parenthetical expressions*

SKILLS CHART: POETRY

Selection	Analyzing Literature	Critical Thinking and Reading	Understanding Language/ Speaking and Listening	Thinking and Writing	Grammar in Action
Reading Actively					
"Mushrooms," Sylvia Plath, p. 503	Understanding personification*	Reading lines	Finding synonyms*	Using personification	Understanding capitalization*

POETRY (continued)

Selection	Analyzing Literature	Critical Thinking and Reading	Understanding Language/ Speaking and Listening	Thinking and Writing	Grammar in Action
Narrative Poetry					
"Paul Revere's Ride," Henry Wadsworth Longfellow, p. 509	Understanding a narrative poem	Sequencing events*	Understanding choral reading Using a thesaurus*	Summarizing the events in the poem	
"William Stafford," Anonymous, p. 517	Understanding features of a ballad	Reading inverted sentences*	Selecting a voice for a dramatic reading Understanding multiple meanings of words*	Evaluating the ballad	
"Columbus," Joaquin Miller, p. 521	Understanding rhythm and refrain	Making inferences about theme*	Appreciating old-fashioned words*	Writing a poem about a historical figure	
"Barbara Frietchie," John Greenleaf Whittier, p. 525	Creating characters*	Making inferences about characters	Choosing a meaning to fit context*	Writing a definition of a hero	Understanding verb tenses*
Figurative Language and Imagery					
"Lyric 17," Jose Garcia Villa, p. 532 "O Captain! My Captain!": Walt Whitman, p. 534 "Jetliner," Naoshi Koriyama, p. 536	Understanding similes Understanding similes, metaphors, and personification* Understanding metaphors Understanding personification		Appreciating diction	Writing similes Writing about figurative language	
"By Morning," May Swenson, p. 540 "Reflections Dental," Phyllis McGinley, p. 542 "Ring Out, Wild Bells," Alfred, Lord Tennyson, p. 544	Recognizing and interpreting imagery Understanding humorous images			Using images to compose a poem Writing a patterned poem	
"The Secret Heart," Robert P. Tristram Coffin, p. 548	Interpreting symbols carefully*		Understanding synonyms and antonyms*	Paraphrasing a poem	

POETRY (continued)

Selection	Analyzing Literature	Critical Thinking and Reading	Understanding Language/ Speaking and Listening	Thinking and Writing	Grammar in Action
"Advice to a Girl," Sara Teasdale, p. 550					
"Taught Me Purple," Evelyn Tooley Hunt, p. 551				Writing about symbolism	
Lyric Poetry					
"Four Little Foxes," Lew Sarett, p. 556	Understanding lyric poetry		Recognizing sensory language		
"Harlem Night Song," Langston Hughes, p. 558		Making inferences about mood*			
"Blue-Butterfly Day," Robert Frost, p. 559				Writing a lyric poem	
"For My Sister Molly Who in the Fifties," Alice Walker, p. 560			Appreciating vivid language*		
"Silver," Walter de la Mare, p. 564	Understanding alliteration*				
"Forgotten Language," Shel Silverstein, p. 565	Understanding parallel structure		Understanding poetic language*		
"Blow, Blow, Thou Winter Wind," William Shakespeare, p. 566					
"Hog Calling," Morris Bishop, p. 569	Understanding limericks*			Writing a limerick	
"I Raised a Great Hullabaloo," Anonymous, p. 569			Using rhythmic language*		
Facets of Nature					
Two Haiku, Basho and Moritake, p. 573	Understanding haiku		Choosing words*	Writing a haiku	
"January," John Updike, p. 576	Recognizing sensory language*		Writing sensory language*	Using sensory language	

POETRY (continued)

Selection	Analyzing Literature	Critical Thinking and Reading	Understanding Language/ Speaking and Listening	Thinking and Writing	Grammar in Action
"Winter Moon," Langston Hughes, p. 578				Writing a poem	
"Song of the Sky Loom," Tewa Indian, p. 579		Paraphrasing a poem			
"New World," N. Scott Momaday, p. 580			Giving a choral reading		Understanding verb tense*
Perceptions					
"The City Is So Big," Richard Garcia, p. 586	Understanding free verse*				
"Concrete Mixers," Patricia Hubbell, p. 587		Reading free verse*			
"Southbound on the Freeway," May Swenson, p. 588				Writing free verse	
"400-Meter Free Style," Maxine Kumin, p. 591	Understanding concrete poetry*		Choosing the meaning that fits the context*	Writing a concrete poem	
Choices					
"Identity," Julio Noboa Polanco, p. 598	Hearing the speaker's voice*		Finding synonyms*		
"The Road Not Taken," Robert Frost, p. 600		Interpreting differences in metaphors			
"The Choice," Dorothy Parker, p. 604	Understanding tone				
"Journey to the Interior," Adrien Stoutenburg, p. 606	Understanding speaker and tone*		Appreciating concrete words*		
"Staying Alive," David Wagoner, p. 609	Understanding figurative language*		Finding figurative language*	Writing an interpretation of a poem	

POETRY (continued)

Selection	Analyzing Literature	Critical Thinking and Reading	Understanding Language/ Speaking and Listening	Thinking and Writing	Grammar in Action
Putting It Together					
"The Story-Teller," Mark Van Doren, p. 615	Understanding rhyme*	Defining poetry*	Finding antonyms	Retelling a story	

SKILLS CHART: AMERICAN MYTHS, LEGENDS, AND FOLK TALES

Selection	Analyzing Literature	Critical Thinking and Reading	Understanding Language/ Speaking and Listening	Thinking and Writing	Grammar in Action
"The Origin of Fire," Ella E. Clark, p. 627	Understanding a myth*	Understanding cause and effect	Appreciating homographs*	Writing a myth	
"They Have Yarns," Carl Sandburg, p. 631	Understanding a yarn*		Appreciating compound words*	Writing a yarn	
"The Girl Who Hunted Rabbits," Zuñi Indian Legend, p. 635	Understanding a legend	Making inferences from a legend*	Choosing meaning to fit context	Retelling a legend	Understanding conjunctions* Understanding prepositional phrases
"Paul Bunyan of the North Woods," Carl Sandburg, p. 643	Understanding a folktale	Making generalizations about a folktale*	Appreciating homophones	Writing a response to critical comment	
"Pecos Bill: The Cyclone," Harold W. Felton, p. 647	Understanding conflict in a folktale*	Identifying reasons*	Appreciating words from Spanish	Writing a description of a conflict	Using precise words*
"Hammerman," Adrien Stoutenberg, p. 655	Understanding the folk hero	Making inferences about characters*	Dramatizing a folktale Choosing effective synonyms*	Writing another adventure	
"John Henry," Traditional, p. 663	Understanding the oral tradition*		Sharing other ballads about folk heroes Determining word meaning from Latin roots*	Comparing and contrasting selections	
"The Foggy Stew," Harold W. Felton, p. 669	Understanding exaggerations	Interpreting the storyteller's purpose*	Understanding comparison of adjectives*	Writing with exaggeration in a folktale	

AMERICAN MYTHS, LEGENDS, AND FOLK TALES (continued)

Selection	Analyzing Literature	Critical Thinking and Reading	Understanding Language/ Speaking and Listening	Thinking and Writing	Grammar in Action
"Johnny Appleseed," Rosemary Carr Benét, p. 675	Understanding characterization*	Making inferences about characters*	Completing word analogies*	Comparing and contrasting	
"Davy Crockett's Dream," Davy Crockett, p. 679 "Tussle with a Bear," Davy Crockett, p. 681	Understanding a yarn*	Recognizing exaggeration	Appreciating dialect*	Creating a yarn	

SKILLS CHART: THE NOVEL
THE PEARL, John Steinbeck

Selection	Analyzing Literature	Critical Thinking and Reading	Understanding Language/ Speaking and Listening	Thinking and Writing	Grammar in Action
The Pearl, Chapters 1–3, John Steinbeck, p. 695	Understanding characters*		Appreciating words from Spanish*	Writing from Juana's point of view	Using dashes* Understanding intensive and reflexive pronouns*
The Pearl, Chapters 4–6, p. 717	Understanding plot and theme	Recognizing cause and effect*	Appreciating vivid verbs*	Responding to literary criticism*	Understanding gerunds* Understanding participles* Using specific verbs*

PRENTICE HALL LITERATURE

COPPER

BRONZE

SILVER

GOLD

PLATINUM

THE AMERICAN EXPERIENCE

THE ENGLISH TRADITION

WORLD MASTERPIECES

i

Master Teacher Board

Roger Babusci
(Pennsylvania Teacher of the Year, 1983)
Schenley High School
Pittsburgh, Pennsylvania

Loutish Burns
(Teacher of the Year, 1981)
Louie Welch Middle School
Houston, Texas

Guy Doud
(National Teacher of the Year, 1986)
Brainerd Senior High School
Brainerd, Minnesota

Terri Fields
(Arizona Teacher of the Year, 1986)
Sunnyslope High School
Phoenix, Arizona

Kermeen Fristrom
(1985 Distinguished Service Award)
San Diego City Schools
San Diego, California

LeRoy Hay
(National Teacher of the Year, 1983)
Manchester High School
Manchester, Connecticut

Beth Johnson
(Florida Teacher of the Year, 1982)
Kathleen Senior High School
Lakeland, Florida

Evaline Kruse
(California Teacher of the Year, 1985)
Audubon Junior High School
Los Angeles, California

Jane McKee
(West Virginia Teacher of the Year, 1986)
Man High School
Man, West Virginia

Robert Seney
(Texas Curriculum Association's Exemplary Showcase Award for Literature)
Albright Middle School
Houston, Texas

Pat Weaver
(1985 National Outstanding Dissertation for Curriculum)
Arlington Independent School District
Arlington, Texas

Consultants

Joan Baron
University of Connecticut
Storrs, Connecticut

Charles Cooper
University of California
San Diego, California

Nancy Spivey
Carnegie-Mellon Institute
Pittsburgh, Pennsylvania

Contributing Writers

Kathleen Janson
former English teacher
Bay Ridge High School
Brooklyn, New York

Cathleen G. Welsh
Reading Specialist and English teacher
William Penn High School
Wilmington, Delaware

ii

PRENTICE HALL
LITERATURE

SILVER

SECOND EDITION

PRENTICE HALL
Englewood Cliffs, New Jersey
Needham, Massachusetts

Humanities Note

Fine Art, *The Inspiration of Christopher Columbus,* by José Maria Obrégon, 1856. Obrégon (1832–1902) was a Mexican artist who was trained in the European academic style by a French artist, Pelegrin Clavé, an immigrant to Mexico. Clavé's late classical manner was a strong influence on Obrégon, who painted historical subjects and Biblical themes. But Obrégon's best-known works were paintings depicting the history of Mexico; he thereby contributed to the nationalistic sentiment that characterized much Mexican art.

In fact the 1850s, during the rule of Maximilian, was a period in Mexican art in which scenes of American history were very popular. This painting of Christopher Columbus was typical of the Europeanized style and subject matter of painting in the Mexican academy. Many of the paintings by Obrégon and his colleagues showed Europeans arriving in Mexico (or North America), thus stressing the European origins of many Mexicans. Obrégon's most noted works, however, were pictures of events from the ancient history of pre-Spanish Mexico.

In this rather romanticized view, Columbus is seen staring out to sea, charts and compass in hand. Bathed in the golden light of the setting sun, he looks out at the world he will explore.

ISBN 0-13-691742-9

10 9 8 7 6 5 4 3 2 1

Art credits begin on page 858.

COVER AND TITLE PAGE: *The Inspiration of Christopher Columbus* (detail), 1856, José María Obregón, Museo Nacional de Arte, Mexico City

PRENTICE HALL
A Division of Simon & Schuster
Englewood Cliffs, New Jersey 07632

STAFF CREDITS FOR PRENTICE HALL LITERATURE

Editorial: Eileen Thompson, Ellen Bowler, Philip Fried, Daniel Jackson, Doug McCollum, Jane Standen, Richard Hickox, Carol Schneider, Kelly Ackley

Design: Sue Walrath, Nancy Sharkey, Leslie Osher

Photo Research: Libby Forsyth

Production: Penny Hull, Suse Cioffi, Joan McCulley, Marlys Lehmann, Lisa Meyerhoff, Cleasta Wilburn

Editorial Systems: Andrew Grey Bommarito, Ralph O'Brien

Marketing: Carol Newman, Mollie Ledwith, Tom Maksym

Manufacturing: Laura Sanderson, Denise Herckenrath

Permissions: Doris Robinson

ACKNOWLEDGMENTS

Grateful acknowledgment is made to the following for permission to reprint copyrighted material:

American Way
"Dial Versus Digital" by Isaac Asimov. Reprinted by permission of *American Way,* inflight magazine of American Airlines, copyright 1985 by American Airlines.

Atheneum Publishers, an imprint of Macmillan Publishing Company
"Concrete Mixers" from *8 A.M. Shadows by* Patricia Hubbell, Copyright © 1965 Patricia Hubbell. Reprinted with the permission of Atheneum Publishers, an imprint of Macmillan Publishing Company.

Robert Bly
"Driving to Town Late To Mail a Letter" from *Silence In the Snowy Fields,* Wesleyan University Press, 1962. Copyright © 1962 by Robert Bly, reprinted with his permission.

(contiued on page 855)

CONTENTS

SHORT STORIES

v

DRAMA

NONFICTION

vi

POETRY

vii

viii

AMERICAN MYTHS, LEGENDS, AND FOLKTALES

THE NOVEL

ix

PRENTICE HALL
LITERATURE
SILVER

CHILDREN AND PIGEONS IN THE PARK, CENTRAL PARK, 1907
Millard Sheets
Photograph Courtesy of Kennedy Galleries, New York

SHORT STORIES

A short story is one of the most popular forms of literature. Even though it is fiction, a product of the author's imagination, you may become interested in reading it because it deals with people, places, actions, and events that seem familiar. At other times it may stir your imagination because it deals with the fantastic—or unusual. Whatever your reason for enjoying a particular short story, you will find that because it is short, you can usually read it in one sitting.

A short story is made up of elements: plot, character, setting, point of view, and theme. The plot is the sequence of events in the story. The characters are the people, and sometimes the animals, that play a role in the story. The setting is where and when the events take place. Often the plot, characters, and setting work together to reveal a theme, or insight into life.

Adventure stories, mysteries, science-fiction, animal tales—these are just a few of the varied types of short stories that authors write. In this unit you will encounter many of these types, and you will learn strategies to help you understand and appreciate short stories more thoroughly.

Humanities Note

Fine art, *Children and Pigeons in the Park*, by Millard Sheets. Millard Sheets, an American painter, designer, illustrator, and graphic artist, was born in 1907 in California. He studied art in Los Angeles at the Chouinard Art Institute and at the University of Southern California. His travels throughout the world broadened his artistic perceptions. Millard Sheets has made diverse contributions to the art world. He has taught, designed murals, illustrated for *Life* magazine, created architectural designs, designed sets in Hollywood, and won many awards for his outstanding watercolor paintings.

Children and Pigeons in the Park is a watercolor. The style can be called Impressionistic and the subject lighthearted. The activity suggests stories in progress. Quick lively brush strokes give a bright spontaneity to the scene. The fresh and diverse color lends to it an appropriate sun-dappled appearance. This painting has the same familiar appeal today as it did when it was painted.

Focus

Reading Actively Research has shown that effective reading requires an active process on the part of the reader. The strategies listed on this page enable students to become thoughtful, active readers of fiction.

To introduce the process outlined on this page, ask students to discuss the ways they normally read a story. What strategies have they found that work for them? Have they encountered any difficulties? Then discuss the strategies listed here. Explain that these strategies will help students become more effective readers. The model on the following pages contains annotations with the types of questions, predictions, clarifications, and summaries that an active reader might make while reading. It also shows the way an active reader might pull together these details after reading. Have students pay attention to these annotations as they read. Also ask them to create their own questions, predictions, summaries, and clarifications, and finally to react to the story.

For further practice with the process, use the selection in the Teaching Porfolio, "The Baroque Marble," pp. 8–15, which students can annotate themselves. Encourage students to continue to use these strategies when reading other stories.

READING ACTIVELY

The Short Story

Good readers become actively involved. They read not only with their eyes but, more important, with a questioning mind. This means that they interact with the story, considering the events, the characters, where the story takes place, and the story's meaning.

Question

As you read, ask questions and then read to find the answers to these questions. What questions does the title bring to mind? Ask how a situation came about. Question why a character acts a certain way or makes a particular remark. Wonder about how the setting affects the characters and the events. Then read to find the answers to your questions.

Predict

Make predictions about what will happen. Base these predictions on clues in the story, on your own experience, and on your knowledge of how a story works. For example, when reading an action-filled adventure story, you may predict "I'm sure he will get off that runaway train before it goes over the cliff." Of course, some predictions will turn out to be true, while others, as in life, will not.

Clarify

Take time to clarify points. Stop to find the answers to your own questions. Check your predictions to see if they turned out to be true. Then discard predictions that turned out to be inaccurate and make new predictions based on your latest information.

Summarize

Occasionally, stop to summarize. At appropriate points in the story, review the main events. Identify what seems to be important, and consider the significance of this information.

Pull It Together

Think about the story after you are done reading. Pull together all the details and consider the effect of the story as a whole. What does the story mean to you? How do you feel about it?

Using these strategies will help you become a more effective reader. You will be better able to recall details, interpret meaning, and apply this meaning to your life.

On the following pages is a model of how an active reader might read a story.

Objectives

1. To learn how to read a short story actively
2. To understand the various possible meanings of a story's title
3. To compare and contrast two stories
4. To write a short, imaginative story

Support Material

Teaching Portfolio
Teacher Backup, pp. 5–7
Grammar in Action Worksheets, *Appreciating Unusual Word Choice*, pp. 16–17; *Using Vivid Adjectives and Adverbs*, pp. 18–19
Usage and Mechanics Worksheet, p. 20
Critical Thinking and Reading Worksheet, *Comparing and Contrasting Stories*, p. 21
Language Worksheet, *Using a Glossary*, p. 22
Selection Test, pp. 23–24

MODEL

The Story-Teller

Saki

Question: Who is the storyteller? Will this story be about this character?

It was a hot afternoon, and the railway carriage was correspondingly sultry, and the next stop was at Templecombe, nearly an hour ahead. The occupants of the carriage were a small girl, and a smaller girl, and a small boy. An aunt belonging to the children occupied one corner seat, and the further corner seat on the opposite side was occupied by a bachelor who was a stranger to their party, but the small girls and the small boy emphatically occupied the compartment. Both the aunt and the children were conversational in a limited, persistent way, reminding one of the attentions of a housefly that refused to be discouraged. Most of the aunt's remarks seemed to begin with "Don't," and nearly all of the children's remarks began with "Why?" The bachelor said nothing out loud.

Question: Why does the author compare the group to a housefly? What does this comparison indicate about the group?

"Don't, Cyril, don't," exclaimed the aunt, as the small boy began smacking the cushions of the seat, producing a cloud of dust at each blow.

"Come and look out of the window," she added.

The child moved reluctantly to the window. "Why are those sheep being driven out of that field?" he asked.

"I expect they are being driven to another field where there is more grass," said the aunt weakly.

"But there is lots of grass in that field," protested the boy; "there's nothing else but grass there. Aunt, there's lots of grass in that field."

"Perhaps the grass in the other field is better," suggested the aunt fatuously.[1]

"Why is it better?" came the swift, inevitable question.

"Oh, look at those cows!" exclaimed the aunt. Nearly every field along the line had contained cows or bullocks, but she spoke as though she were drawing attention to a rarity.

---

1. fatuously (fach′ oo wəs′ lē) *adv.*: In a foolish way.

Presentation

Motivation/Prior Knowledge You might ask your students what are some of the characteristics a story must have to hold people's attention. What characteristics must a storyteller have? Tell your students that as they read this story, they should see if both the story and storyteller fit their description of what makes a good tale and teller.

Thematic Idea Another selection that deals with the theme of unconventional behavior getting a positive response is "Cub Pilot on the Mississippi (page 411).

Purpose-Setting Question The model question asked with the title sets a purpose for reading.

Master Teacher Note What does interacting with a story mean? It means students should ask themselves questions about the material and then read to answer the questions.

It means students should predict what will happen based on what they already know. As they read they should check to find out if their predictions are correct.

It means students should summarize to check their comprehension. If they do not understand a passage, they should reread it.

It means they should take time to clarify when something in the story is not clear.

Finally, it means pulling together all the details in the story and thinking about its meaning.

As students first work with these strategies, you may have to help them formulate good questions and make valid predictions.

Reading Strategy Remind students that the questions, predictions, clarifications, and summaries shown with "The Story-Teller" are samples. Not everyone would ask the same questions and make the same predictions.

Master Teacher Note A short story writer must get the reader involved in the story very quickly from the beginning. Saki does this by using strong descriptive words and phrases. Point out some of these words and have your students locate others. Ask your students what general impression they have formed about the people in the story up to this point.

After reading the whole story, have your students make three columns on their paper: children, aunt, bachelor. Then have them write the descriptive words used by Saki to portray each of these characters.

"Why is the grass in the other field better?" persisted Cyril.

Prediction: The bachelor will not put up with this behavior for long.

The frown on the bachelor's face was deepening to a scowl. He was a hard, unsympathetic man, the aunt decided in her mind. She was utterly unable to come to any satisfactory decision about the grass in the other field.

Clarification: This group is really annoying. So this is what the author was suggesting by comparing them to a fly.

The smaller girl created a diversion by beginning to recite "On the Road to Mandalay."[2] She only knew the first line, but she put her limited knowledge to the fullest possible use. She repeated the line over and over again in a dreamy but resolute and very audible voice; it seemed to the bachelor as though someone had had a bet with her that she could not repeat the line aloud two thousand times without stopping. Whoever it was who had made the wager was likely to lose his bet.

Question: Is the aunt the storyteller that the title refers to?

"Come over here and listen to a story," said the aunt, when the bachelor had looked twice at her and once at the communication cord.[3]

2. **"On the Road to Mandalay":** Poem by Rudyard Kipling. Its first line is "By the old Moulmain Pagoda, lookin' eastward to the sea . . ."
3. **communication cord:** Signal switch pulled to call the conductor.

Grammar in Action

Skillful writers use **vivid adjectives** and **adverbs** to communicate their intended meaning. Vivid, specific words convey the author's vision of events to the reader.

In the following passages notice Saki's vivid adjectives and adverbs:

> The children moved *listlessly* toward the aunt's end of the carriage. Evidently her reputation as a story-teller did not rank high in their estimation.

> In a *low, confidential* voice, interrupted at *frequent* intervals by *loud, petulant* questions from her listeners, she began an *unenterprising* and *deplorably uninteresting* story . . .

Notice the words that describe the actions of the children: they move *listlessly*, interrupt *frequently* with *loud* and *petulant* questions. Notice the description of the aunt's storytelling: she speaks in a *low, confidential* voice and begins an *unenterprising* and

The children moved listlessly toward the aunt's end of the carriage. Evidently her reputation as a story-teller did not rank high in their estimation.

Prediction: The aunt's story will not prove a success.

In a low, confidential voice, interrupted at frequent intervals by loud, petulant[4] questions from her listeners, she began an unenterprising and deplorably uninteresting story about a little girl who was good, and made friends with everyone on account of her goodness, and was finally saved from a mad bull by a number of rescuers who admired her moral character.

"Wouldn't they have saved her if she hadn't been good?" demanded the bigger of the small girls. It was exactly the question that the bachelor had wanted to ask.

"Well, yes," admitted the aunt lamely, "but I don't think they would have run quite so fast to her help if they had not liked her so much."

"It's the stupidest story I've ever heard," said the bigger of the small girls, with immense conviction.

"I didn't listen after the first bit, it was so stupid," said Cyril.

The smaller girl made no actual comment on the story, but she had long ago recommenced a murmured repetition of her favorite line.

Clarification: The aunt's story is a failure. It does not keep the children interested or quiet.

"You don't seem to be a success as a story-teller," said the bachelor suddenly from his corner.

The aunt bristled in instant defense at this unexpected attack.

"It's a very difficult thing to tell stories that children can both understand and appreciate," she said stiffly.

Prediction: The bachelor will tell a story the children will like.

"I don't agree with you," said the bachelor.

"Perhaps *you* would like to tell them a story," was the aunt's retort.

"Tell us a story," demanded the bigger of the small girls.

"Once upon a time," began the bachelor, "there was a little girl called Bertha, who was extraordinarily good."

Clarification: So there are two storytellers—the aunt and the bachelor.

The children's momentarily aroused interest began at once to flicker; all stories seemed dreadfully alike, no matter who told them.

"She did all that she was told, she was always truthful, she kept her clothes clean, ate milk puddings as though they

4. **petulant** (pech' oo lənt) *adj.*: Impatient.

deplorably uninteresting story. Saki's vivid adjectives and adverbs create these effective images of both the children and their aunt.

Student Activity. Using your memory, a dictionary, or a book of synonyms, find other vivid words that could express how the children moved and interrupted, how the aunt spoke, and what kind of a story she began.

Enrichment Point out to your **more advanced** students how the storyteller pulls the children into what has started out as a story "dreadfully" like all the others by flattering them and through the use of the oxymoron "horribly good." Explain that an oxymoron is a figure of speech in which opposite or contradictory ideas or terms are combined. Ask your students if they could think of their own oxymorons. Some other examples are "thunderous silence" and "sweet sorrow."

were jam tarts, learned her lessons perfectly, and was polite in her manners."

"Was she pretty?" asked the bigger of the small girls.

"Not as pretty as any of you," said the bachelor, "but she was horribly good."

There was a wave of reaction in favor of the story; the word horrible in connection with goodness was a novelty that commended itself. It seemed to introduce a ring of truth that was absent from the aunt's tales of infant life.

"She was so good," continued the bachelor, "that she won several medals for goodness, which she always wore, pinned on to her dress. There was a medal for obedience, another medal for punctuality, and a third for good behavior. They were large metal medals and they clinked against one another as she walked. No other child in town where she lived had as many as three medals, so everybody knew that she must be an extra good child."

"Horribly good," quoted Cyril.

"Everybody talked about her goodness, and the Prince of the country got to hear about it, and he said that as she was so very good she might be allowed once a week to walk in his park, which was just outside the town. It was a beautiful park, and no children were ever allowed in it, so it was a great honor for Bertha to be allowed to go there."

"Were there any sheep in the park?" demanded Cyril.

"No," said the bachelor, "there were no sheep."

"Why weren't there any sheep?" came the inevitable question arising out of that answer.

The aunt permitted herself a smile, which might almost have been described as a grin.

Clarification: The bachelor is a good storyteller. The children *do* like his story.

"There were no sheep in the park," said the bachelor, "because the Prince's mother had once had a dream that her son would either be killed by a sheep or else by a clock falling on him. For that reason the Prince never kept a sheep in his park or a clock in his palace."

The aunt suppressed a gasp of admiration.

"Was the Prince killed by a sheep or by a clock?" asked Cyril.

"He is still alive, so we can't tell whether the dream will come true," said the bachelor unconcernedly; "anyway, there were no sheep in the park, but there were lots of little pigs running all over the place."

Grammar in Action

Word choice is important in speaking and writing. Carefully chosen, accurate words that are specific and clear-cut are qualities of good writing. Skillful writers are also sensitive to the different shades of meanings for words that have similar definitions. It is wise to use synonyms for variety in writing, but be aware of the connotations, or, suggestive meanings of the words you choose. Examples of words that have similar meanings but different connotations are *fib/lie, mad/angry,* and *happy/jubilant.* When using a thesaurus to substitute synonyms, be sure that the word you choose has appropriate connotations.

Writers who want to describe a unique image or express an uncommon idea sometimes use **unusual word choice.** Using adjectives that are not commonly associated with a particular subject can startle the reader into a clear understanding of the writer's meaning. For example, when the bachelor in Saki's story uses unusual word choice, the narrator explains how the bachelor's word choice affected his listeners. In describing Bertha, the bachelor says "she was *horribly* good." In response to the bachelor's word choice, the narrator explains:

"What color were they?"

"Black with white faces, white with black spots, black all over, gray with white patches, and some were white all over."

The story-teller paused to let a full idea of the park's treasures sink into the children's imaginations; then he resumed:

"Bertha was rather sorry to find that there were no flowers in the park. She had promised her aunts, with tears in her eyes, that she would not pick any of the kind Prince's flowers, and she had meant to keep her promise, so of course it made her feel silly to find that there were no flowers to pick."

"Why weren't there any flowers?"

"Because the pigs had eaten them all," said the bachelor promptly. "The gardeners had told the Prince that you

There was a wave or reaction in favor of the story; the word horrible in connection with goodness was a novelty that commended itself. It seemed to introduce a ring of truth that was absent from the aunt's tales of infant life.

Saki's use of unusual word choice is an example of how effective carefully chosen words can be.

Student Activity. Using Saki's phrase "horribly good" as a model, write five more phrases that are composed of uncommonly associated words. Try to pair words that are almost opposites in meaning, such as "loud silence."

Enrichment Have students note the entry of the wolf—a symbol for evil. Why does a wolf become symbolic for evil in stories? What other story immediately comes to mind when you think of a wolf? Bring in a copy of the original "Little Red Riding Hood" story by the Grimm brothers and a copy of a modern version. Read both versions to your students and have them contrast the endings. Then have your students contrast those two endings to the ending of this story.

More About the Author Saki took his pen name from the cupbearer in Omar Khayyam's *Rubaiyat.* He specialized in short pieces with unexpected endings, though his stories frequently satirized the genteel class. Besides his many stories, he wrote novels and dramas. What other authors also specialized in stories with unexpected endings?

couldn't have pigs and flowers, so he decided to have pigs and no flowers."

There was a murmur of approval at the excellence of the Prince's decision; so many people would have decided the other way.

"There were lots of other delightful things in the park. There were ponds with gold and blue and green fish in them, and trees with beautiful parrots that said clever things at a moment's notice, and hummingbirds that hummed all the popular tunes of the day. Bertha walked up and down and enjoyed herself immensely, and thought to herself: 'If I were not so extraordinarily good, I should not have been allowed to come into this beautiful park and enjoy all that there is to be seen in it,' and her three medals clinked against one another as she walked and helped to remind her how very good she really was. Just then an enormous wolf came prowling into the park to see if it could catch a fat little pig for its supper."

Prediction: This story is quite different from the aunt's. Perhaps the good little girl will not be saved this time.

"What color was it?" asked the children, amid an immediate quickening of interest.

"Mud color all over, with a black tongue and pale gray eyes that gleamed with unspeakable ferocity. The first thing that it saw in the park was Bertha; her pinafore[5] was so spotlessly white and clean that it could be seen from a great distance. Bertha saw the wolf and saw that it was stealing toward her, and she began to wish that she had never been allowed to come into the park. She ran as hard as she could, and the wolf came after her with huge leaps and bounds. She managed to reach a shrubbery of myrtle bushes, and she hid herself in one of the thickest of the bushes. The wolf came sniffing among the branches, its black tongue lolling out of its mouth and its pale gray eyes glaring with rage. Bertha was terribly frightened, and thought to herself: 'If I had not been so extraordinarily good, I should have been safe in the town at this moment.' However, the scent of the myrtle was so strong that the wolf could not sniff out where Bertha was hiding, and the bushes were so thick that he might have hunted about in them for a long time without catching sight of her, so he thought he might as well go off and catch a little pig instead. Bertha was trembling very much at having the wolf

Question: Will Bertha escape?

5. pinafore (pin′ ə fôr′) *n.*: A sleeveless, apronlike garment worn by little girls over a dress.

prowling and sniffing so near her, and as she trembled the medal for obedience clinked against the medals for good conduct and punctuality. The wolf was just moving away when he heard the sound of the medals clinking and stopped to listen; they clinked again in a bush quite near him. He dashed into the bush, his pale gray eyes gleaming with ferocity and triumph, and dragged Bertha out and devoured her to the last morsel. All that was left of her were her shoes, bits of clothing, and the three medals for goodness."

Clarification: So Bertha does meet with a bad end after all.

"Were any of the little pigs killed?"

"No, they all escaped."

"The story began badly," said the smaller of the small girls, "but it had a beautiful ending."

"It is the most beautiful story that I ever heard," said the bigger of the small girls, with immense decision.

"It is the *only* beautiful story I have ever heard," said Cyril.

Question: Why do the children like this story so much?

A dissentient[6] opinion came from the aunt.

"A most improper story to tell to young children! You have undermined the effect of years of careful teaching."

"At any rate," said the bachelor, collecting his belongings preparatory to leaving the carriage, "I kept them quiet for ten minutes, which was more than you were able to do."

"Unhappy woman!" he observed to himself as he walked down the platform of Templecombe station; "for the next six months or so those children will assail her in public with demands for an improper story!"

Putting It Together: The bachelor's story is much better than the aunt's. Perhaps children prefer stories that stir their imagination to ones that teach a lesson.

6. dissentient (di sen' shənt) *adj.*: Differing from the majority.

Saki (1870–1916) is the pen name of H. H. Munro, one of England's finest short-story writers. Born in Burma, after his mother's death he was sent to England, where he was brought up by his grandmother and two strict aunts. In 1893 he moved back to Burma, where he received a posting in the military police. However, ill health forced him to leave this posting and return to England. Here he began his career as a writer. Did you notice how Saki poked fun at aunts in "The Story-Teller"?

Reader's Response What is your reaction to the ending of the bachelor's story? Do you agree with the smaller girl that it had a "beautiful ending"? Explain.

Closure and Extention

ANSWERS TO THINKING ABOUT THE SELECTION

Recalling

1. The children are noisy and restless.
2. The aunt hopes to quiet the children by telling a story. The children are unexcited because her reputation as a storyteller does not rank high in their estimation.
3. The aunt at first grins when she suspects that the bachelor will have no more success than she did. When he succeeds in holding the children's attention, she admires his abilities as a storyteller, but she thoroughly disapproves of his story's moral, which she considers "improper" and "subversive." Unlike the aunt, the bachelor succeeds in entertaining the children and making them behave.

Interpreting

4. The aunt's answers are either logically practical or evasive. The bachelor's answers are imaginative and fanciful, but never evasive.
5. The aunt's story is "unenterprising" and told mainly to establish a moral.
6. The children consider the aunt's notion of goodness to be horribly uninteresting. The bachelor's "horribly good" heroine, therefore, more closely approximates the children's notion of reality. The children like the bachelor's inventive responses to their questions, the imaginative details of his story, the unexpected conclusion to his plot, and the lack of a proper moral.

(Questions begin on p. 10.)

Applying

7. Answers will differ. Moral lessons are usually intended to increase the moral awareness of the reader and to bring about a suitable improvement in behavior. These stories may be effective, depending on the way in which they are told.

ANSWERS TO ANALYZING LITERATURE

1. The first storyteller is the aunt. She is described as "belonging to the children," suggesting that they control her behavior rather than vice versa. When she is not exclaiming at the children, she speaks "weakly," "fatuously," and "in a low, conversational voice" that is entirely unsuited for effective storytelling. Moreover, she believes the goal of storytelling is primarily to correct behavior, not to entertain.
2. The second storyteller is the bachelor. As the aunt notes, he is hard and unsympathetic, but toward her and not the children despite the nuisance they create. His story is as much an act of revenge against her ineffectual attempt to subdue the children. By attending to the children's needs as an audience, the bachelor succeeds in entertaining the children while delivering a sharp moral lesson to the aunt.
3. The third storyteller is Saki.
4. Saki's tale suggests that a story must be imaginative and entertaining and include surprising twists while adhering to the audience's expectations of reality. A moral, if it exists at all, should never be the storyteller's primary purpose.

(Answers begin on p. 9.)

ANSWERS TO CRITICAL THINKING AND READING

1. Both girls are little and good, but the girl in the bachelor's story is horrible because of her goodness.
2. Both girls are threatened by dangerous animals, but unlike the aunt's heroine the girl in the bachelor's story is not saved because of her goodness, but devoured.
3. The aunt's story is part of Saki's narration and contains little descriptive detail. The bachelor's story is quoted directly and contains much descriptive detail that the children find fascinating.
4. The aunt's lesson is that goodness acts as a shield against physical harm. The bachelor's lesson is the opposite. A dangerous animal does not care whether its prey is good or bad. In fact, goodness may put the victim at a disadvantage.
5. Unlike the aunt's unenterprising and deplorably uninteresting story, the bachelor's is imaginative and entertaining. Moreover, the bachelor's characterization of the "horribly good" girl, his plot, and his moral have "a ring of truth" that is absent from the aunt's story.
6. Answers will differ. Most students will probably prefer the bachelor's story because it is more entertaining.

Challenge The use of irony is a technique writers employ when they wish to heighten the contrast between the expected and the actual outcome of events in life. What is the irony in this story?

THINKING AND WRITING

For help with this assignment, students can refer to Lesson 17, "Writing a Short Story," in the Handbook of Writing About Literature.

Publishing Student Writing If you know any teachers in the local elementary school, ask them if they would like copies of some of the better stories to read their children.

THINKING ABOUT THE SELECTION

Recalling

1. Describe the children's behavior at the beginning of the trip.
2. Why does the aunt decide to tell the children a story? Why are the children unexcited by this prospect?
3. How does the aunt react to the bachelor's story? What was he able to accomplish with his story that the aunt had not been able to do?

Interpreting

4. Why are the children never satisfied by the aunt's answers to their questions? How are the bachelor's answers different?
5. What makes the aunt's story "deplorably uninteresting"?
6. How does the word *horribly* inject "a ring of truth" into the bachelor's story? What other details of the bachelor's story do the children particularly like?

Applying

7. Why do people tell stories to children that teach moral lessons? Are these stories effective? Explain your answer.

ANALYZING LITERATURE

Understanding the Title

The author of a story usually chooses the title very carefully. It may call attention to a character or suggest something about the plot. It may even hint at the theme, or central idea, that the story expresses. The title of this story calls attention to the storytellers in it.

1. Describe the first storyteller. Include in your description as many key features of this character's personality as you can.
2. Describe the second storyteller. Indicate as many key features as you can.
3. There is also a third storyteller—one who does not appear as a character. Who is this storyteller?
4. What does the third storyteller's tale suggest about the art of telling stories?

CRITICAL THINKING AND READING

Comparing and Contrasting Stories

When you compare two things you show how they are alike. When you contrast, you show how they are different. Think about the story the aunt tells and the story the bachelor tells.

1. Compare and contrast the girl in each story.
2. Compare and contrast what happens in each story.
3. Compare and contrast the use of descriptive detail.
4. Compare and contrast the moral, or lesson.
5. Why do the children enjoy the bachelor's story so much more than the aunt's?
6. Which story did you enjoy more? Explain your answer.

THINKING AND WRITING

Creating a Story

Imagine you, like the bachelor in this story, have to entertain a group of unruly children. Create a story that would stir their imagination and keep them involved. First decide on your main character. Will this character be horribly good, or impossibly perfect, or wonderfully bratty? Next decide what happens to this character. Write the first draft of this story. Revise it, making sure it holds enough details to keep your audience interested. Prepare a final draft and share it with your classmates.

Plot

JAMES FOLLY GENERAL STORE AND POST OFFICE
Winfield Scott Clime
Three Lions

Humanities Note

Fine art, *James Folly General Store and Post Office,* Winfield Scott Clime. Winfield Scott Clime (1881–1958), an American painter and watercolorist, was born in Philadelphia. He studied art at the Corcoran Art School in Washington, D.C. and at the Art Students League of New York. His paintings are represented in the collections of several American museums.

James Folly General Store and Post Office is American genre painting at its finest. Painted with humor and skillful realism, it shows a small town scene of early twentieth-century America. This painting is a charming reminder of the General Store that has all but disappeared.

Focus

More About the Author Isaac Asimov derived his interest in writing science fiction from reading the many magazines stocked in his father's candy store in Brooklyn. He nurtured that interest and began to write at eighteen while majoring in biochemistry at Columbia College and earning his Ph.D. Ask students to discuss the relationship between science and science fiction. In what ways does having a science background help a science-fiction writer?

Literary Focus Suggest that there may be many conflicts in a plot. Can, for example, curiosity cause conflict? What types of conflicts can develop between people? With other forces? How can one person have a conflict within him or her?

Look For Ask your students to list, as they read, the several incidents of the story. Tell them to be able to explain how each incident leads to the next. Is the resolution temporary or permanent?

Writing/Prior Knowledge Have students discuss how different people might feel about rain. How might a baseball player feel? A farmer? A police officer? A meteorologist? Do you think people's feelings about the rain depend on their occupations? Then have students complete the freewriting assignment.

Vocabulary Have your **less advanced** students read the words aloud so you can be sure they can pronounce them.

GUIDE FOR READING

Rain, Rain, Go Away

Isaac Asimov (1920–   ), born in the Soviet Union, came to the United States when he was three. Asimov once remarked, "I imagine there must be such a thing as a born writer; at least, I can't remember when I wasn't on fire to write." Asimov has the ability to combine science with fiction to create astounding science-fiction and fantasy stories. He has won a Locus Award, a National Science Fiction Writers Award, a Nebula Award, and a Hugo Award. In "Rain, Rain, Go Away," Asimov gives a new twist to an old song.

Plot

Plot is the series of related actions or events in a short story. This sequence of events centers on a **conflict,** which is a struggle between opposing forces, or on a problem that must be solved. The plot includes exposition, in which the situtation is revealed. The events build toward a **climax,** the point of highest interest. They continue toward a **resolution,** in which the story comes to a close.

Look For

As you read "Rain, Rain, Go Away," look for clues that indicate what makes the Sakkaros special. How does one action or event lead to another as the plot develops? How does each event make you curious about what will happen next? What is the climax?

Writing

Why do you think children sing the song "Rain, Rain, Go Away"? Freewrite about rain and its effect on you. Are you usually pleased when it rains? Does your feeling about rain depend on what you want to do when it rains? Do you always feel the same about rain?

Vocabulary

Knowing the following words will help you as you read "Rain, Rain, Go Away."

forestall (fôr stôl′) *v.*: Prevent (p. 13)
meticulous (mə tik′yoo ləs) *adj.*: Extremely careful about details (p. 15)
affectation (af′ek tā′shən) *n.*: Artificial behavior intended to impress others (p. 15)
semblance (sem′bləns) *n.*: Outward appearance (p. 16)
centrifugal (sen trif′yə gəl) *adj.*: Tending to move away from the center (p. 16)
celestial (səl es′chəl) *adj.*: Of the sky (p. 18)

Objectives

1. To understand the elements of a short story's plot
2. To understand sequence of events
3. To create words with negative prefixes
4. To write a short story

Support Material

Teaching Portfolio
Teacher Backup, pp. 25–27
Grammar in Action Worksheet, *Understanding Dialogue,* pp. 28–29
Usage and Mechanics Worksheet, p. 30
Vocabulary Check, p. 31
Analyzing Literature Worksheet, *Understanding Plot,* p. 32
Critical Thinking and Reading Worksheet, *Understanding Sequence of Events,* p. 33
Selection Test, pp. 34–35

Rain, Rain, Go Away

Isaac Asimov

"There she is again," said Lillian Wright as she adjusted the venetian blinds carefully. "There she is, George."

"There who is?" asked her husband, trying to get satisfactory contrast on the TV so that he might settle down to the ball game.

1 "Mrs. Sakkaro," she said, and then, to forestall her husband's inevitable "Who's that?" added hastily, "The new neighbors, for goodness sake."

"Oh."

"Sunbathing. Always sunbathing. I wonder where her boy is. He's usually out on a nice day like this, standing in that tremendous yard of theirs and throwing the ball against the house. Did you ever see him, George?"

"I've heard him. It's a version of the Chinese water torture.[1] Bang on the wall, biff on the ground, smack in the hand. Bang, biff, smack, bang, biff—"

"He's a *nice* boy, quiet and well-behaved. I wish Tommie would make friends with him. He's the right age, too, just about ten, I should say."

"I didn't know Tommie was backward about making friends."

"Well, it's hard with the Sakkaros. They keep so to themselves. I don't even know what Mr. Sakkaro does."

"Why should you? It's not really anyone's business what he does."

"It's odd that I never see him go to work."

"No one ever sees me go to work."

"You stay home and write. What does *he* do?"

"I dare say Mrs. Sakkaro knows what Mr. Sakkaro does and is all upset because she doesn't know what *I* do."

"Oh, George." Lillian retreated from the window and glanced with distaste at the television. (Schoendienst was at bat.) "I think we should make an effort; the neighborhood should."

"What kind of an effort?" George was comfortable on the couch now.

"To get to know them."

"Well, didn't you, when she first moved in? You said you called."

"I said hello but, well, she'd just moved in and the house was still upset, so that's all it could be, just hello. It's been two months now and it's still nothing more than hello, sometimes.—She's so odd."

"Is she?"

"She's always looking at the sky; I've seen her do it a hundred times and she's
never been out when it's the least bit cloudy. 2
Once, when the boy was out playing, she called to him to come in, shouting that it was going to rain. I happened to hear her

---

1. Chinese water torture: A form of torture in which the slow, steady drip of water on the victim's head can drive him or her mad.

Presentation

Motivation/Prior Knowledge To heighten the suspense of this story, it is best to have students read it with very little introduction. Ask them to imagine that new neighbors have just moved in next door. What would be some things they would want to know about these new neighbors?

Thematic Idea Other selections that deal with the theme of fantasy are "The Rule of Names" (page 69) and "The Gift Giving" (page 175).

Purpose-Setting Question Does Mrs. Sakkaro seem like a real person, someone you might know?

1 **Discussion** What does the name "Sakkaro" sound like? Point out that Karo is a brand name for a corn syrup. You might also point out that the name sounds like the first syllable in "saccharin." Why do you think the author chose this name for this family?

2 **Discussion** Why does Mrs. Wright think Mrs. Sakkaro is odd?

3 **Discussion** What type of climate is Arizona known for?

4 **Discussion** Why do you think Mrs. Sakkaro is so preoccupied with the weather?

5 **Critical Thinking and Reading** Explain that sometimes an author gives clues about events that will happen later in the plot. This technique is called foreshadowing. Ask the students what they think the author is hinting at. What other references to water or rain have there been since the beginning of the story?

and I thought, Oh no, wouldn't you know and me with a wash on the line, so I hurried out and, you know, it was broad sunlight. Oh, there were some clouds, but nothing, really."

"Did it rain, eventually?"

"Of course not. I just had to run out in the yard for nothing."

George was lost amid a couple of base hits and a most embarrassing bobble that meant a run. When the excitement was over and the pitcher was trying to regain his composure, George called out after Lillian, who was vanishing into the
3 kitchen, "Well, since they're from Arizona, I dare say they don't know rainclouds from any other kind."

Lillian came back into the living room. "From where?"

"From Arizona, according to Tommie."

"How did Tommie know?"

"He talked to their boy, in between ball chucks, I guess, and he told Tommie they came from Arizona and then the boy was called in. At least, Tommie says it might have been Arizona, or maybe Alabama or some place like that. You know Tommie and his nontotal recall. But if they're that nervous about the weather, I guess it's Arizona and they don't know what to make of a good rainy climate like ours."

"But why didn't you ever tell me?"

"Because Tommie only told me this morning and because I thought he must have told you already and, to tell the absolute truth, because I thought you could just manage to drag out a normal existence even if you never found out. Wow—"

The ball went sailing into the right field stands and that was that for the pitcher.

Lillian went back to the venetian blinds and said, "I'll simply just have to make her acquaintance. She looks *very* nice.—Oh, look at that, George."

George was looking at nothing but the TV.

Lillian said, "I know she's staring at that cloud. And now she'll be going in. 4,5
Honestly."

George was out two days later on a reference search in the library and came home with a load of books. Lillian greeted him jubilantly.

She said, "Now, you're not doing anything tomorrow."

"That sounds like a statement, not a question."

"It *is* a statement. We're going out with the Sakkaros to Murphy's Park."

"With—"

"With the next-door neighbors, George. *How* can you never remember the name?"

"I'm gifted. How did it happen?"

Grammar in Action

Dialogue is conversation between characters. By beginning a new paragraph for each speaker, the writer makes it easy for the reader to follow a conversation. When a writer wants the reader to move through dialogue in a rapid, realistic manner, he or she will omit the introductory, concluding, and interrupting expressions and begin new paragraphs.

In the following excerpt, notice the lack of explanatory expressions. However, the reader knows the change in speaker because each time Lillian and George speak, there is a new paragraph:

> She said, "Now, you're not doing anything tomorrow."
> "That sounds like a statement, not a question."
> "It is a statement. We're going out with the Sakkaros to Murphy's Park."
> "With—"
> "With the next-door neighbors, George. *How* can you never remember the name?"
> "I'm gifted. How did it happen?"
> "I just went up to their house this morning and rang the bell."

"I just went up to their house this morning and rang the bell."

"That easy?"

"It wasn't easy. It was hard. I stood there, jittering, with my finger on the doorbell, till I thought that ringing the bell would be easier than having the door open and being caught standing there like a fool."

"And she didn't kick you out?"

"No. She was sweet as she could be. Invited me in, knew who I was, said she was so glad I had come to visit. *You* know."

"And you suggested we go to Murphy's Park."

"Yes. I thought if I suggested something that would let the children have fun, it would be easier for her to go along with it. She wouldn't want to spoil a chance for her boy."

"A mother's psychology."

"But you should see her home."

"Ah. You had a reason for all this. It comes out. You wanted the Cook's tour.[2] But, please, spare me the color-scheme details. I'm not interested in the bedspreads, and the size of the closets is a topic with which I can dispense."

It was the secret of their happy marriage that Lillian paid no attention to George. She went into the color-scheme details, was most meticulous about the bedspreads, and gave him an inch-by-inch description of closet-size.

"And *clean?* I have never seen any place so spotless."

"If you get to know her, then, she'll be setting you impossible standards and you'll have to drop her in self-defense."

"Her kitchen," said Lillian, ignoring him, "was so spanking clean you just couldn't believe she ever used it. I asked for a drink of water and she held the glass underneath the tap and poured slowly so that not one drop fell in the sink itself. It 6
wasn't affectation. She did it so casually that I just knew she always did it that way. And when she gave me the glass she held it with a clean napkin. Just hospital-sanitary."

"She must be a lot of trouble to herself. Did she agree to come with us right off?"

"Well—not right off. She called to her husband about what the weather forecast was, and he said that the newspapers all said it would be fair tomorrow but that he was waiting for the latest report on the radio."

"*All* the newspapers said so, eh?"

"Of course, they all just print the official weather forecast, so they would all agree. 7
But I think they do subscribe to all the newspapers. At least I've watched the bundle the newsboy leaves—"

"There isn't much you miss, is there?"

"Anyway," said Lillian severely, "she called up the weather bureau and had them tell her the latest and she called it out to her husband and they said they'd go, except they said they'd phone us if there were any unexpected changes in the weather."

"All right. Then we'll go." 8

The Sakkaros were young and pleasant, dark and handsome. In fact, as they came down the long walk from their home to where the Wright automobile was parked, George leaned toward his wife and breathed into her ear, "So *he's* the reason."

"I wish he were," said Lillian. "Is that a handbag he's carrying?"

---

2. Cook's tour: A brief, well-organized tour named after a British travel agent.

6 **Discussion** Why do you think the kitchen looks like it was never used? Do you think it was never used? Why do you think Mrs. Sakkaro was so careful getting the glass of water?

7 **Discussion** Does Mr. Sakkaro appear to be as interested in the weather as his wife? How can you tell?

8 **Reading Strategy** Have students summarize the events that have occurred so far in the story and predict what will happen at Murphy's Park.

"That easy?"

"It wasn't easy. It was hard. I stood there, jittering, with my finger on the doorbell, till I thought that ringing the bell would be easier than having the door open and being caught standing there like a fool."

"And she didn't kick you out?"

Asimov places the only explanatory phrase at the beginning of the dialogue, but he skillfully leads the reader through the conversation in a rapid and realistic manner. Beginning a new paragraph each time the speaker changes makes it easy to follow the conversation.

Student Activity. Make up your own dialogue between two people but do not use any explanatory phrases. Each person should speak at least five times. You might make up an imaginary conversation between a boy asking a girl out to a movie or between you and one of your parents on the day you show them your report card.

9 Discussion Why would the boy bring an aneroid barometer?

10 Discussion What does a "student of human nature" do?

"Pocket-radio. To listen to weather forecasts, I bet."

9 The Sakkaro boy came running after them, waving something which turned out to be an aneroid barometer,[3] and all three got into the back seat. Conversation was turned on and lasted, with neat give-and-take on impersonal subjects, to Murphy's Park.

The Sakkaro boy was so polite and reasonable that even Tommie Wright, wedged between his parents in the front seat, was subdued by example into a semblance of civilization. Lillian couldn't recall when she had spent so serenely pleasant a drive.

She was not the least disturbed by the fact that, barely to be heard under the flow of the conversation, Mr. Sakkaro's small radio was on, and she never actually saw him put it occasionally to his ear.

It was a beautiful day at Murphy's Park; hot and dry without being too hot; and with a cheerfully bright sun in a blue, blue sky. Even Mr. Sakkaro, though he inspected every quarter of the heavens with a careful eye and then stared piercingly at the barometer, seemed to have no fault to find.

Lillian ushered the two boys to the amusement section and bought enough tickets to allow one ride for each on every variety of centrifugal thrill that the park offered.

"Please," she had said to a protesting Mrs. Sakkaro, "let this be my treat. I'll let you have your turn next time."

When she returned, George was alone. "Where—" she began.

"Just down there at the refreshment stand. I told them I'd wait here for you and we would join them." He sounded gloomy.

3. aneroid (an′ ər oid) **barometer:** An instrument that registers air pressure changes on a dial and is used to predict weather changes. A "falling barometer" indicates an increase in air pressure and the likelihood of rain.

"Anything wrong?"

"No, not really, except that I think he must be independently wealthy."

"What?"

"I don't know what he does for a living. I hinted—"

"Now who's curious?"

"I was doing it for you. He said he's just a student of human nature." 10

"How philosophical. That would explain all those newspapers."

"Yes, but with a handsome, wealthy man next door, it looks as though I'll have impossible standards set for me, too."

"Don't be silly."

"And he doesn't come from Arizona."

"He doesn't?"

"I said I heard he was from Arizona. He looked so surprised, it was obvious he didn't. Then he laughed and asked if he had an Arizona accent."

Lillian said thoughtfully, "He has some kind of accent, you know. There are lots of Spanish-ancestry people in the Southwest so he could still be from Arizona. Sakkaro could be a Spanish name."

"Sounds Japanese to me.—Come on, they're waving. Oh, look what they've bought."

The Sakkaros were each holding three sticks of cotton candy, huge swirls of pink foam consisting of threads of sugar dried out of frothy syrup that had been whipped about in a warm vessel. It melted sweetly in the mouth and left one feeling sticky. 11

The Sakkaros held one out to each Wright, and out of politeness the Wrights accepted.

They went down the midway, tried their hand at darts, at the kind of poker game where balls were rolled into holes, at knocking wooden cylinders off pedestals. They took pictures of themselves and recorded their voices and tested the strength of their handgrips.

Eventually they collected the youngsters, who had been reduced to a satisfactorily breathless state of roiled-up[4] insides, and the Sakkaros ushered theirs off instantly to the refreshment stand. Tommie hinted the extent of his pleasure at the possible purchase of a hot-dog and George tossed him a quarter. He ran off, too.

"Frankly," said George, "I prefer to stay here. If I see them biting away at another cotton candy stick I'll turn green and sicken on the spot. If they haven't had a dozen apiece, I'll eat a dozen myself." 12

"I know, and they're buying a handful for the child now."

---

4. roiled-up *adj.*: Stirred up, agitated, unsettled.

11 **Discussion** Have you ever eaten two sticks of cotton candy at one sitting? Do you think you could? Did the Wrights really want their stick?

12 **Discussion** How does Mr. Wright feel about the Sakkaros' consumption of cotton candy?

13 **Discussion** How do the Wrights feel about the Sakkaros' reaction to the offer of a hamburger and an orange drink? Point out that they think it was odd, but not abnormal.

14 **Discussion** How does Mrs. Wright react to Mrs. Sakkaro's insistence that George drive faster?

15 **Discussion** How do you think Helen was going to finish the sentence?

16 **Discussion** Which character from "The Wizard of Oz" reminds you of this description? Discuss the scene where the Wicked Witch of the West shriveled up and died.

17 **Discussion** Is the story's conclusion expected or unexpected? Why?

Enrichment Have students imagine that the Sakkaros were able to reach their home safely before it began to rain. Ask students if they think the Wrights would have still wanted to be friends with their mysterious neighbors. Would the Sakkaros ever reveal their secret to the Wrights and explain their true origin? Have your **more advanced** students write a new ending for Asimov's story in which they tell what happens after the Sakkaros reach home safely. Have the students make sure that their new endings deal with both the Sakkaros and the Wrights.

Enrichment Ask students if the ending was predictable and satisfying? Could the story have been eerier and more mysterious if the Sakkaros' meltability had been brought out in other ways—perhaps by a series of events rather than one? Have the students write another version of the story, preferably as a television script. Ask if any student has seen a "Twilight Zone" program. How would this story fit into the show's format?

"I offered to stand Sakkaro a hamburger and he just looked grim and shook his head. Not that a hamburger's much, but after enough cotton candy, it ought to be a feast."

"I know. I offered her an orange drink
13 and the way she jumped when she said no, you'd think I'd thrown it in her face.—Still, I suppose they've never been to a place like this before and they'll need time to adjust to the novelty. They'll fill up on cotton candy and then never eat it again for ten years."

"Well, maybe." They strolled toward the Sakkaros. "You know, Lil, it's clouding up."

Mr. Sakkaro had the radio to his ear and was looking anxiously toward the west.

"Uh-oh," said George, "he's seen it. One gets you fifty, he'll want to go home."

All three Sakkaros were upon him, polite but insistent. They were sorry, they had had a wonderful time, a marvelous time, the Wrights would have to be their guests as soon as it could be managed, but now, really, they had to go home. It looked stormy. Mrs. Sakkaro wailed that all the forecasts had been for fair weather.

George tried to console them. "It's hard to predict a local thunderstorm, but even if it were to come, and it mightn't, it wouldn't last more than half an hour on the outside."

At which comment, the Sakkaro youngster seemed on the verge of tears, and Mrs. Sakkaro's hand, holding a handkerchief, trembled visibly.

"Let's go home," said George in resignation.

The drive back seemed to stretch interminably. There was no conversation to speak of. Mr. Sakkaro's radio was quite loud now as he switched from station to station, catching a weather report every time. They were mentioning "local thundershowers" now.

The Sakkaro youngster piped up that the barometer was falling, and Mrs. Sakkaro, chin in the palm of her hand, stared dolefully at the sky and asked if George could not drive faster, please.

"It does look rather threatening, doesn't it?" said Lillian in a polite attempt
to share their guests' attitude. But then 14
George heard her mutter, "Honestly!" under her breath.

A wind had sprung up, driving the dust of the weeks-dry road before it, when they entered the street on which they lived, and the leaves rustled ominously. Lightning flickered.

George said, "You'll be indoors in two minutes, friends. We'll make it."

He pulled up at the gate that opened onto the Sakkaro's spacious front yard and got out of the car to open the back door. He thought he felt a drop. They were *just* in time.

The Sakkaros tumbled out, faces drawn with tension, muttering thanks, and started off toward their long front walk at a dead run.

"Honestly," began Lillian, "you would
think they were—" 15

The heavens opened and the rain came down in giant drops as though some celestial dam had suddenly burst. The top of their car was pounded with a hundred drum sticks, and halfway to their front door the Sakkaros stopped and looked despairingly upward.

Their faces blurred as the rain hit; blurred and shrank and ran together. All
three shriveled, collapsing within their 16
clothes, which sank down into three sticky-wet heaps.

And while the Wrights sat there, transfixed with horror, Lillian found herself unable to stop the completion of her remark: 17
"—made of sugar and afraid they would melt."

Reader's Response Mr. Sakkaro calls himself a "student of human nature." What does "Rain, Rain, Go Away" tell you about human nature?

Closure and Extension

ANSWERS TO THINKING ABOUT THE SELECTION

Recalling

1. Mrs. Wright notes the Sakkaros' seemingly excessive fear of rain and the overly cautious manner in which Mrs. Sakkaro handles a glass of water.
2. According to Mrs. Wright, ". . . if I

THINKING ABOUT THE SELECTION

Recalling

1. Name two events involving the Sakkaros that make the Wrights curious about them, even before the outing to Murphy's Park.
2. Why does Mrs. Wright suggest Murphy's Park for an outing with the Sakkaros?
3. How do the Sakkaros show their nervousness about the weather on their trip?
4. Why do the Sakkaros insist on going home?

Interpreting

5. Why does Mrs. Sakkaro fill the glass of water for Mrs. Wright so carefully?
6. What is unusual about what the Sakkaros eat at the park? Why do they refuse other food?
7. What does Mr. Sakkaro probably mean when he says he is a student of human nature?
8. Where do you think the Sakkaros are from? Find evidence to support your answer.
9. How is Mrs. Wright's statement at the end of the story truer than even she expects?

Applying

10. Mrs. Wright's last sentence describes people who are behaving almost too carefully. A similar common saying is, "He looks as if he is walking on eggs." What other expressions describe especially careful behavior?

ANALYZING LITERATURE

Understanding Plot

Plot is a sequence of events or related actions. Usually, a **conflict** or a problem, such as Mrs. Wright's desire to know about the Sakkaros, is presented. Next, the action builds up to the high point, or **climax,** of the story. Finally, the action moves to a **resolution,** or final outcome.

1. Name two events that move the plot toward the climax of the story.
2. What is the climax of the story?
3. How is the conflict resolved?

CRITICAL THINKING AND READING

Understanding the Sequence of Events

Authors carefully plan the **sequence,** or order, of events in stories. Often they arrange events in **chronological order,** which shows how one event follows another in time. For example, Lillian first invites the Sakkaros to Murphy's Park; then the families go there.

On a piece of paper, write the numbers of the following events in chronological order:

1. The Wrights discuss their new neighbors.
2. The adults play games on the midway.
3. The Wrights and the Sakkaros go to the park.
4. The Sakkaros move to the neighborhood.
5. The Sakkaros race for their front door.

UNDERSTANDING LANGUAGE

Using Negative Prefixes

A **prefix** is a letter or group of letters added at the beginning of words to form a new word or to change the meaning of the original word. A **negative prefix** reverses the meaning of the original word. For example, *un-* added to *happy* creates the negative word *unhappy.*

Add one of the following negative prefixes to each word below: *mis-*, *non-*, *dis-*, *in-*, *il-*, *im-*.

1. agreeable	2. possible	3. active
4. logical	5. spell	6. sense

THINKING AND WRITING

Writing a Short Story

Sometimes a story starts by an author wondering "What if?" Use your imagination to complete the statement: What if the people next door really were __________. Then imagine an outing with your neighbors. Write the first draft of a short story telling about the consequences of their true identity. Include dialogue between the characters. When you revise, be sure to start a new paragraph when you change speakers.

suggested something that would let the children have fun, it would be easier for her to go along with it. She wouldn't want to spoil a chance for her boy."

3. Mr. Sakkaro brings a pocket radio for monitoring weather forecasts. The son carries a barometer. The family warily inspects the sky for signs of clouds.
4. They fear that it is about to rain.

Interpreting

5. Mrs. Sakkaro is afraid of spilling water on herself, knowing how destructive water can be to her.
6. The Sakkaros eat only cotton candy, that is, sugar. Normal food and drink, which contain water, would dissolve them.
7. Answers will differ. Suggested response: Mr. Sakkaro probably means that he himself is not human and must, therefore, observe human nature in order to act as if he were a human being.
8. Answers will differ. Suggested response: The Sakkaros are definitely not from Arizona. They are probably alien creatures who have come to Earth to study human nature. Their financial independence, strange diet, and unearthly physical composition suggest extraterrestrial origins.
9. The Sakkaros are indeed composed entirely of sugar and do melt.

(Answers begin on p. 18)

Applying

10. Answers will differ. Suggested response: Another expression is "handle with kid gloves."

ANSWERS TO ANALYZING LITERATURE

1. The two most crucial events are the outing in the park and the hurried drive home as the rainstorm approaches.
2. The climax occurs when the rain begins.
3. The Sakkaros dissolve and the Wrights finally understand the motivation underlying their neighbors' strange behavior.

ANSWERS TO CRITICAL THINKING AND READING

4, 1, 3, 2, 5

ANSWERS TO UNDERSTANDING LANGUAGE

1. disagreeable
2. impossible
3. inactive
4. illogical
5. misspell
6. nonsense, nonactive

Challenge Explain that Asimov's story is a fantasy—that is, it deals with events that could not possibly happen in real life. Even though the story is fantastic, Asimov gives his characters logical motivation for their actions. Have students choose specific actions in the story and tell the motivation for each.

THINKING AND WRITING

For help with this assignment, students can refer to Lesson 17, Writing a Short Story, in the Handbook of Writing About Literature.

Publishing Student Writing You might want to publish a "What if" class magazine. Type some of the better stories and duplicate enough copies for your students.

Focus

More About the Author Pearl S. Buck was not highly regarded by critics. She was faulted, before winning the Pulitzer Prize, for having written too few books and, after winning, for writing too many. Despite lack of strong critical support, Ms. Buck, along with Mark Twain, is today the most frequently translated author in Europe and the Orient. Ask students to discuss the relationship between popular success and literary merit. In what ways can popular success be a drawback for a serious writer?

Literary Focus If students have read "Rain, Rain, Go Away," ask them to explain how Asimov used chronology to organize his story. How might he have used flashback if he had used a narrator, such as Mrs. Wright, who, in her old age, wanted to tell about a good deed that turned out bad? How might such an arrangement have led to a tale with an obvious moral?

Look For Point out to students that being aware of a writer's techniques increases a reader's enjoyment of a story. Explain that writers use flashback because they want to make a comparison between the present and the past, usually to show how the past has influenced the present.

Writing/Prior Knowledge Explain to your students that their paragraphs will be better if they begin by explaining briefly at what point in time the movie or television narrative began and how far back in time the flashback extended. Remind students that they are to focus on the connection between these two points in time.

Spelling Tip Point out the different spellings of the s sound in these two words. In *placidly*, the s sound is spelled *c*, and in *acquiescent*, the s sound is spelled *sc*.

GUIDE FOR READING

Christmas Day in the Morning

Pearl S. Buck (1892–1973) grew up in China where her parents were missionaries. After teaching in China and the United States, she became a full-time writer of nonfiction and fiction. Her most famous novel, *The Good Earth,* earned her a Pulitzer Prize, and in 1938 she won the Nobel Prize for Literature. Buck was active throughout her life in child welfare work. Her caring about people is clearly seen in "Christmas Day in the Morning," where Buck shows that the greatest gift we have to give one another is love.

Flashback

A **flashback** is a scene inserted into a story showing events that occurred in the past. Usually the events in a story are arranged **chronologically;** that is, the order in which the events occurred in time is the order in which they appear in the story. Sometimes, however, an author might want to show something that happened at an earlier time than the events of the story. To do so, the author uses a flashback. In "Christmas Day in the Morning," the author uses a flashback to show why Robert, now an aging grandfather, has had special feelings about Christmas since he was fifteen.

Look For

As you read "Christmas Day in the Morning," look for the flashback. Why do you think the author includes this flashback in the story? How does it help explain Robert's actions?

Writing

Think of a movie or television program you have seen recently that contained a flashback. Explain why you think the flashback was included. Would the story have been as effective if the author had told it in strict time order?

Vocabulary

Knowing the following words will help you as you read "Christmas Day in the Morning."

placidly (plas′id lē) *adv.*: Calmly; quietly (p. 22)

acquiescent (ak′wē es′ənt) *adj.*: Agreeing without protest (p. 22)

Objectives

1. To understand the use of flashback in a short story
2. To understand time order in a story containing a flashback
3. To use context clues to determine the meanings of words
4. To write an extended definition

Support Material

Teaching Portfolio

Teacher Backup, pp. 37–39
Grammar in Action Worksheet, *Understanding Compound-Complex Sentences*, pp. 40–41
Usage and Mechanics Worksheet, p. 42
Vocabulary Check, p. 43
Analyzing Literature Worksheet, *Understanding a Flashback*, p. 44
Language Worksheet, *Using Context Clues*, p. 45
Selection Test, pp. 46–47

Christmas Day in the Morning

Pearl S. Buck

He woke suddenly and completely. It was four o'clock, the hour at which his father had always called him to get up and help with the milking. Strange how the habits of his youth clung to him still! Fifty years ago, and his father had been dead for thirty years, and yet he waked at four o'clock in the morning. He had trained himself to turn over and go to sleep, but this morning, because it was Christmas, he did not try to sleep.

Yet what was the magic of Christmas now? His childhood and youth were long past, and his own children had grown up and gone. Some of them lived only a few miles away but they had their own families, and though they would come in as usual toward the end of the day, they had explained with infinite gentleness that they wanted their children to build Christmas
1 memories about *their* houses, not his. He was left alone with his wife.

Yesterday she had said, "It isn't worthwhile, perhaps—"

And he had said, "Oh, yes, Alice, even if there are only the two of us, let's have a Christmas of our own."

Then she had said, "Let's not trim the tree until tomorrow, Robert—just so it's ready when the children come. I'm tired."

He had agreed, and the tree was still out in the back entry.

Why did he feel so awake tonight? For it was still night, a clear and starry night. No moon, of course, but the stars were extraordinary! Now that he thought of it, the stars seemed always large and clear before the dawn of Christmas Day. There was one star now that was certainly larger and brighter 2
than any of the others. He could even imagine it moving, as it had seemed to him to move one night long ago.

He slipped back in time, as he did so easily nowadays. He was fifteen years old 3
and still on his father's farm. He loved his father. He had not known it until one day a few days before Christmas, when he had overheard what his father was saying to his mother.

"Mary, I hate to call Rob in the mornings. He's growing so fast and he needs his sleep. If you could see how he sleeps when I go in to wake him up! I wish I could manage alone."

"Well, you can't, Adam." His mother's voice was brisk. "Besides, he isn't a child anymore. It's time he took his turn."

"Yes," his father said slowly. "But I sure do hate to wake him."

When he heard these words, something in him woke: his father loved him! He had never thought of it before, taking for granted the tie of their blood. Neither his father nor 4,5
his mother talked about loving their

Presentation

Motivation/Prior Knowledge Discuss with students the spirit of love that Christmas symbolizes for Christians—the birth of a child, the joy and love of that birth, and the giving of gifts to celebrate the love. Ask what the most precious gift is that could be given to them. Steer the discussion away from material gifts. Ask students what gifts were precious to them.

Purpose-Setting Question What role does love play in this story?

Thematic Idea Other selections that deal with the theme of a gift of oneself are the excerpt from "I Know Why the Caged Bird Sings" (page 403), in which Mrs. Flowers gives Marguerite personal attention, and "The Gift Giving" (page 175), in which Sammle and Mark give Grandmother a gift of love.

1 **Discussion** Do you agree with his children? How does the grandfather in the story feel about spending Christmas alone with his wife? How does his wife feel?

2 **Discussion** What star is Robert referring to?

3 **Literary Focus** Discuss how the author is inserting a flashback to tell what happened to Robert when he was fifteen. Discuss other stories where the authors used flashbacks.

4 **Discussion** In what ways did the simple fact of knowing that his father loved him make a difference in Robert's life? Could he have gone on without knowing this?

5 **Master Teacher Note** Discuss the idea that it is difficult for some parents to tell children that they love them. Why might this be? Is it easier to show love than to tell it? Is it more meaningful?

6 **Discussion** Have you ever done a chore around the house as a gift for one of your parents? Why did you choose this way of giving a gift? How did it make you feel?

children—they had no time for such things. There was always so much to do on a farm.

Now that he knew his father loved him, there would be no more loitering in the mornings and having to be called again. He got up after that, stumbling blind with sleep, and pulled on his clothes, his eyes tight shut, but he got up.

And then on the night before Christmas, that year when he was fifteen, he lay for a few minutes thinking about the next day. They were poor, and most of the excitement was in the turkey they had raised themselves and in the mince pies his mother made. His sisters sewed presents and his mother and father always bought something he needed, not only a warm jacket, maybe, but something more, such as a book. And he saved and bought them each something, too.

He wished, that Christmas he was fifteen, he had a better present for his father. As usual he had gone to the ten-cent store and bought a tie. It had seemed nice enough until he lay thinking the night before Christmas, and then he wished that he had heard his father and mother talking in time for him to save for something better.

He lay on his side, his head supported by his elbow, and looked out of his attic window. The stars were bright, much brighter than he ever remembered seeing them, and one star in particular was so bright that he wondered if it were really the Star of Bethlehem.

"Dad," he had once asked when he was a little boy, "what is a stable?"

"It's just a barn," his father had replied, "like ours."

Then Jesus had been born in a barn, and to a barn the shepherds and the Wise Men had come, bringing their Christmas gifts!

The thought struck him like a silver dagger. Why should he not give his father a special gift too, out there in the barn? He could get up early, earlier than four o'clock, and he could creep into the barn and get all the milking done. He'd do it alone, milk and clean up, and then when his father went in to start the milking, he'd see it all done. And he would know who had done it.

He laughed to himself as he gazed at the stars. It was what he would do, and he mustn't sleep too sound.

He must have waked twenty times, scratching a match each time to look at his old watch—midnight, and half past one, and then two o'clock.

At a quarter to three he got up and put on his clothes. He crept downstairs, careful of the creaky boards, and let himself out. The big star hung lower over the barn roof, a reddish gold. The cows looked at him, sleepy and surprised. It was early for them too.

"So, boss," he whispered. They accepted him placidly and he fetched some hay for each cow and then got the milking pail and the big milk cans.

He had never milked all alone before, but it seemed almost easy. He kept thinking about his father's surprise. His father would come in and call him, saying that he would get things started while Rob was getting dressed. He'd go to the barn, open the door, and then he'd go to get the two big empty milk cans. But they wouldn't be waiting or empty; they'd be standing in the milkhouse, filled.

"What the—" he could hear his father exclaiming.

He smiled and milked steadily, two strong streams rushing into the pail, frothing and fragrant. The cows were still surprised but acquiescent. For once they were behaving well, as though they knew it was Christmas.

The task went more easily than he had ever known it to before. Milking for once was 6
not a chore. It was something else, a gift to

Grammar in Action

Compound-complex sentences indicate a mature style of writing. A compound-complex sentence consists of two or more independent clauses and one or more subordinate clauses.

Reread these sentences from "Christmas Day in the Morning":

It had seemed nice enough until he lay thinking the night before Christmas, and then he wished that he had heard his father and mother talking in time for him to save for something better.

The stars were bright, much brighter than he ever remembered seeing them, and one star in particular was so bright that he wondered if it were really the Star of Bethlehem.

He'd do it alone, milk and clean up, and then when his father went in to start the milking, he'd see it all done.

Each of these sentences is compound: each has two independent clauses joined with a comma and the conjunction *and*. Notice that

ALBERT'S SON
Andrew Wyeth
Nasjonalgalleriet, Oslo

his father who loved him. He finished, the two milk cans were full, and he covered them and closed the milkhouse door carefully, making sure of the latch. He put the stool in its place by the door and hung up the clean milk pail. Then he went out of the barn and barred the door behind him.

Back in his room he had only a minute to pull off his clothes in the darkness and jump into bed, for he heard his father up. He put the covers over his head to silence his quick breathing. The door opened.

"Rob!" his father called. "We have to get up, son, even if it is Christmas."

"Aw-right," he said sleepily.

"I'll go on out," his father said. "I'll get things started."

The door closed and he lay still, laughing to himself. In just a few minutes his father would know. His dancing heart was ready to jump from his body. 7

The minutes were endless—ten, fifteen, he did not know how many—and he heard his father's footsteps again. The door opened and he lay still.

"Rob!"

"Yes, Dad—"

"You son of a—" His father was laughing, a queer sobbing sort of a laugh. "Thought you'd fool me, did you?" His father was standing beside his bed, feeling for him, pulling away the cover.

"It's for Christmas, Dad!"

He found his father and clutched him in a great hug. He felt his father's arms go

7 **Discussion** How does Robert feel about his gift?

Humanities Note

Fine art, *Albert's Son,* 1959, by Andrew Wyeth. Andrew Wyeth (1917–), an American, is best known for his realistic and thoughtful pictures of people and places in rural Pennsylvania and Maine. All his figures are portraits of real people, especially his family and neighbors.

Tell students that this is a tempera painting. The word "tempera" refers to a technique in which egg yolk is added to paint. Tempera dries quickly, so the brushstrokes do not blend easily. In a tempera painting, most shapes are sharp and clear. Tones are bright and details are exact and strong. Elicit from your students how Wyeth's skill in using a tempera brush has brought forth the remarkable precision of the hairs—countless of them, each finely drawn—on the boy's head and of the hay in the loft.

You might ask students the following questions.

1. What feeling do you see in the boy's face?
2. How has Wyeth created this feeling?
3. Is the painting an appropriate illustration for this story? Why?

there is a complete sentence on each side of the conjunction. The comma and conjunction could be replaced by a period and a capital letter.

Each of these sentences is also complex: each contains at least one subordinate clause beginning with a relative pronoun (*that*) or a subordinating conjunction (*until, when*).

Student Activity 1. Copy the example sentences. Underline the independent clauses, put parentheses around the subordinate clauses, and circle the comma and conjunction.

Student Activity 2. Write three compound-complex sentences of your own. You might try to follow the pattern of the example sentences.

8 **Discussion** How did Robert's father feel about receiving the gift? Ask students to explain the change that occurred in the relationship between the father and son that Christmas Day.

9 **Literary Focus** As the flashback scene ends, ask why the author used this technique. Discuss how the author used flashback to create the meaning on this Christmas day. Be sure the students are aware of how the chronological sequence of events differs from the order of events when the flashback device is used.

10 **Discussion** Is the true joy of life the ability to love? Are there people who are genuinely unable to love anyone?

11 **Enrichment** Have students make a list of the things they could do to show their love to someone. What could others do to show love to them?

Reader's Response What is the best gift you've ever given or received? Why?

Teaching to the Ability Levels Many writers over the centuries have offered their definitions and descriptions of love. Have your **more advanced** students use *Bartlett's Familiar Quotations* or another quotation book to locate definitions or descriptions of love with which they strongly agree or disagree. Then have them write a paragraph in which they present a quotation and explain why they agree or disagree with it.

around him. It was dark and they could not see each other's faces.

"Son, I thank you. Nobody ever did a nicer thing—"

"Oh, Dad, I want you to know—I do want to be good!" The words broke from him of their own will. He did not know what to say. His heart was bursting with love.

"Well, I reckon I can go back to bed and sleep," his father said after a moment. "No, hark—the little ones are waked up. Come to think of it, son, I've never seen you children when you first saw the Christmas tree. I was always in the barn. Come on!"

He got up and pulled on his clothes again and they went down to the Christmas tree, and soon the sun was creeping up to where the star had been. Oh, what a Christmas, and how his heart had nearly burst again with shyness and pride as his father told his mother and made the younger children listen about how he, Rob, had got up all by himself.

8, 9 "The best Christmas gift I ever had, and I'll remember it, son, every year on Christmas morning, so long as I live."

They had both remembered it, and now that his father was dead he remembered it alone: that blessed Christmas dawn when, alone with the cows in the barn, he had made his first gift of true love.

Outside the window now the great star slowly sank. He got up out of bed and put on his slippers and bathrobe and went softly upstairs to the attic and found the box of Christmas-tree decorations. He took them downstairs into the living room. Then he brought in the tree. It was a little one—they had not had a big tree since the children went away—but he set it in the holder and put it in the middle of the long table under the window. Then carefully he began to trim it.

It was done very soon, the time passing as quickly as it had that morning long ago in the barn. He went to his library and fetched the little box that contained his special gift to his wife, a star of diamonds, not large but dainty in design. He had written the card for it the day before. He tied the gift on the tree and then stood back. It was pretty, very pretty, and she would be surprised.

But he was not satisfied. He wanted to tell her—to tell her how much he loved her. It had been a long time since he had really told her, although he loved her in a very special way, much more than he ever had when they were young.

He had been fortunate that she had loved him—and how fortunate that he had been able to love! Ah, that was the true joy of life, the ability to love! For he was quite sure that some people were genuinely unable to love anyone. But love was alive in him, it still was. 10

It occurred to him suddenly that it was alive because long ago it had been born in him when he knew his father loved him. That was it: love alone could waken love. 11

And he could give the gift again and again. This morning, this blessed Christmas morning, he would give it to his beloved wife. He could write it down in a letter for her to read and keep forever. He went to his desk and began his love letter to his wife: *My dearest love . . .*

When it was finished he sealed it and tied it on the tree where she would see it the first thing when she came into the room. She would read it, surprised and then moved, and realize how very much he loved her.

He put out the light and went tiptoeing up the stairs. The star in the sky was gone, and the first rays of the sun were gleaming in the sky. Such a happy, happy Christmas!

Closure and Extension

ANSWERS TO THINKING ABOUT THE SELECTION
Recalling

1. He spends it alone with his wife. His children and grandchildren usually arrive later in the day.
2. Rob was awakened to help his father milk the cows.

THINKING ABOUT THE SELECTION

Recalling

1. How does Robert spend Christmas now?
2. Why did young Rob's father wake him every morning at 4:00 A.M.?
3. How did Rob learn that he loved his father?
4. What gift did young Rob plan to give his father? Why does he alter his plan?
5. How did Rob's father show his gratitude for Rob's gift?

Interpreting

6. Why is the gift young Rob gives his father special? How does giving it make Rob feel?
7. Explain the significance of the two gifts the adult Robert gives his wife.
8. When Robert first awakens at the beginning of the story, he wonders where the magic of Christmas is now. How do his feelings change by the end of the story? What has brought about the change?

Applying

9. Do you agree with Robert that people who can love are fortunate? Explain your answer.
10. This story tells of one gift of love. What other gifts of love are there?

ANALYZING LITERATURE

Understanding a Flashback

A **flashback** presents events of the past in the midst of a story in the present. Pearl Buck uses a flashback to relate a Christmas in Robert's youth to a Christmas today. As a reader, you need to be able to tell when a flashback begins and when it ends.

1. When does the flashback begin in "Christmas Day in the Morning"?
2. How does the reader know when it is over?
3. What is the effect of the flashback?
4. How does the flashback prove Robert's statement: "Love alone could waken love"?

CRITICAL THINKING AND READING

Understanding Time Order

When an author uses flashbacks, events in the plot are not all in time or chronological order. To understand the story, you must mentally put the events in chronological order as you read.

Tell whether each event happens in the past as part of the flashback or in the present.

1. Robert overhears his father talking about him.
2. Robert writes a love letter to his wife.
3. Rob gets up at quarter to three to milk cows.

UNDERSTANDING LANGUAGE

Using Context Clues

One way to find the meaning of unfamiliar words is to use the context. The **context** of a word is the words and phrases that surround it. Often, the context gives clues to the meaning. Notice the context clue for *auburn:* "Her auburn hair gleamed like copper." The word *copper* indicates that auburn hair is the color of copper.

Use the context to determine the meanings of the following italicized words.

1. ". . . there would be no more *loitering* in the mornings and having to be called again."
2. "The cows were still surprised but *acquiescent.* For once they were behaving well, as though they knew it was Christmas."

THINKING AND WRITING

Writing an Extended Definition

An **extended definition** includes examples of what you are defining and points out important aspects that cannot be explained in a brief definition. Brainstorm about what the word *love* means to you. Make a list of examples of kinds of love with which you are familiar. Then, write an extended definition of the word *love.* Use specific examples from your list to illustrate your definition. Check carefully to see that you have covered as many types of love as you can.

3. When Rob overhears his father say that he regrets having to wake his son each morning, the boy realizes that his father loves him. This realization makes Rob aware of his own love for his father.
4. Rob had planned to give his father an inexpensive tie. Knowing that his father truly loves him, he decides to give his father a special gift instead. He will get up extra early and milk the cows himself.
5. His father hugs and thanks Rob and tells the rest of the family that Rob's gift was the best he had ever received.

Interpreting

6. Unlike an impersonal tie, Rob's gift is special because it is a true expression of love from one individual to another. Giving this gift makes Rob feel "the true joy of life, the ability to love."
7. Robert's gifts to his wife signify his unspoken love for her.
8. Robert's gloomy thoughts change to happiness in the knowledge of his love for his wife. Remembering his father's love for him and how he was able to return it to his father brings about the change.

Applying

9. Students' answers may differ depending on their own experiences of sharing love.
10. Answers will differ. Students should note that any gift of love requires giving of oneself from the heart rather than the pocketbook.

(Answers begin on p. 24.)

ANSWERS TO ANALYZING LITERATURE

1. It begins in the eighth paragraph: "He slipped back in time . . ."
2. There is an obvious shift from the past back to the present: ". . . and now that his father was dead he remembered it alone."
3. The flashback shows what the main character is thinking and establishes the motivation for his actions in the present.
4. The flashback serves as a vivid example of how the father's love wakened love in the boy. Furthermore, it shows how past love can stir a person to love in the present.

ANSWERS TO CRITICAL THINKING AND READING

1. past
2. present
3. present

Challenge Have your students create time lines to illustrate the difference between strict chronological order in Asimov's "Rain, Rain, Go Away" and the disjointed time order caused by the flashback technique in Buck's story.

ANSWERS TO UNDERSTANDING LANGUAGE

1. *Loitering* means "wasting time by lagging behind." The clue is *having to be called again.*
2. *Acquiescent* means "yielding quietly without protest." The clue is *behaving well, as though they knew it was Christmas.*

THINKING AND WRITING

Publishing Student Writing Have some students read aloud their extended definitions of love to the rest of the class. How many different types of love were considered?

Focus

More About the Author Sir Arthur Conan Doyle refused to believe his Sherlock Holmes stories were as important as his many other works. The public loudly disagreed. In fact, Doyle wrote a story in 1893 in which Holmes was killed. But public demand forced Doyle to bring Holmes back to life in another story. Ask students what may motivate a practicing physician to want to write stories.

Literary Focus Ask students to recall the conflicts in Ms. Buck's and Dr. Asimov's stories. Ask if they would expect a conflict in a mystery or detective story to be different. How would it differ?

Look For Explain to your students that part of Holmes's conflict with Dr. Roylott involves red herrings, or false clues. Have them look for the red herrings that Doyle has put in the story to lead readers to expect they have solved the murder of Julia before Holmes does.

Writing/Prior Knowledge Some students might wish to write about the rewards gained by current fictional detectives in books or a film. How do their rewards differ from Holmes's?

Vocabulary It would be helpful for students to also know the following words: *agitation* (p. 28), *perpetrated* (p. 30), *avert* (p. 30), *fortnight* (p. 31), *impending* (p. 32), *averse* (p. 34), *insolence* (p. 36), and *cunning* (p. 37).

Spelling Tip Point out that the vocabulary words in the Guide for Reading are all multisyllabic. Emphasize that careful pronunciation of the syllables will help in spelling these words.

GUIDE FOR READING

The Adventure of the Speckled Band

Arthur Conan Doyle (1859–1950) was born in Edinburgh, Scotland. He began to study medicine and took up writing mystery stories in his early twenties. According to one of his professors, Doyle was often more accurate in guessing the occupation of patients than in diagnosing their illnesses. By 1886 Doyle had published his first Sherlock Holmes mystery, "A Study in Scarlet." In "The Adventure of the Speckled Band," you will see that Holmes, like Doyle himself, displays extraordinary powers of observation.

Conflict

A **conflict** is a struggle between opposing forces or characters. Often a conflict occurs between two characters or between a character and the forces of nature. Conflict adds interest to a story, since it makes us wonder who will win.

Look For

In "The Adventure of the Speckled Band" Sherlock Holmes stands in the way of Dr. Roylott's achieving his goal. Look for the way the conflict is developed. Are the characters evenly matched? Why does one character finally win over the other?

Writing

When Holmes's client offers to pay him, Holmes responds, "As to my reward, my profession is its own reward." Do you think you would enjoy being a detective as much as Holmes does? Freewrite, exploring your thoughts about being a detective.

Vocabulary

Knowing the following words will help you as you read "The Adventure of the Speckled Band."

defray (di frā') *v.*: Pay the money for the cost of (p. 29)
manifold (man'ə fōld') *adj.*: Many and varied (p. 29)
dissolute (dis'ə lo͞ot') *adj.*: Unrestrained (p. 30)
morose (mə rōs') *adj.*: Ill-tempered; gloomy; sullen (p. 30)
convulsed (kən vuls'd') *v.*: Suffered a violent, involuntary spasm (p. 32)
imperturbably (im'pər tʉr'bə blē) *adv.*: Unexcitedly; calmly (p. 35)
reverie (rev'ər ē) *n.*: Daydreaming (p. 40)
tangible (tan'jə b'l) *adj.*: Having form and substance; that can be touched or felt by touch (p. 40)

Objectives

1. To examine conflict in a short story
2. To understand logical reasoning
3. To write about deductive reasoning

Support Material

Teaching Portfolio
Teacher Backup, pp. 49–52
Grammar in Action Worksheets, *Using Who and Whom*, pp. 53–54; *Understanding Adjective Clauses*, pp. 55–56; *Understanding Compound Sentences*, pp. 57–58; *Understanding Passive Voice*, pp. 59–60
Usage and Mechanics Worksheet, p. 61
Vocabulary Check, p. 62
Critical Thinking and Reading Worksheet, *Understanding Logical Reasoning*, p. 63
Language Worksheet, *Choosing the Meaning That Fits the Context*, p. 64
Selection Test, pp. 65–66
Library of Video Classics: *The Speckled Band*

The Adventure of the Speckled Band

Sir Arthur Conan Doyle

On glancing over my notes of the seventy odd cases in which I have during the last eight years studied the methods of my friend Sherlock Holmes, I find many tragic, some
1 comic, a large number merely strange, but none commonplace; for, working as he did rather for the love of his art than for the acquirement of wealth, he refused to associate himself with any investigation which did not tend towards the unusual, and even the fantastic. Of all these varied cases, however, I cannot recall any which presented more singular features than that which was associated with the well-known Surrey family of the Roylotts of Stoke Moran. The events in
2,3 question occurred in the early days of my association with Holmes when we were sharing rooms as bachelors in Baker Street. It is possible that I might have placed them upon record before but a promise of secrecy was made at the time, from which I have only been freed during the last month by the untimely death of the lady to whom the pledge was given. It is perhaps as well that the facts should now come to light, for I have reasons to know that there are widespread rumors as to the death of Dr. Grimesby Roylott which tend to make the matter even more terrible than the truth.

It was early in April in the year 1883 that I woke one morning to find Sherlock Holmes standing, fully dressed, by the side of my bed. He was a late riser, as a rule, and as the clock on the mantelpiece showed me that it was only a quarter past seven, I blinked up at him in some surprise, and perhaps just a little resentment, for I was myself regular in my habits.

"Very sorry to wake you up, Watson," said he, "but it's the common lot this morning. Mrs. Hudson has been awakened, she retorted upon me, and I on you."

"What is it, then—a fire?"

"No; a client. It seems that a young lady has arrived in a considerable state of excitement who insists upon seeing me. She is waiting now in the sitting room. Now, when young ladies wander about the metropolis at this hour of the morning, and get sleepy people up out of their beds, I presume that it is something very pressing which they have to communicate. Should it prove to be an interesting case, you would, I am sure, wish to follow it from the outset. I thought, at any 4
rate, that I should call you and give you the chance."

"My dear fellow, I would not miss it for anything."

I had no keener pleasure than in following Holmes in his professional investiga- 5, 6
tions, and in admiring the rapid deductions, as swift as intuitions, and yet always found-

Presentation

Motivation/Prior Knowledge Tell students that this story is about the famous detective, Sherlock Holmes, and his assistant, Dr. Watson. The often heard phrase, "Elementary, my dear Watson" is associated with the stories by Sir Arthur Conan Doyle. Ask students what they think a mystery about a speckled band might be.

Purpose-Setting Question How is the conflict resolved between Sherlock Holmes and Dr. Roylott?

1 **Teaching to Ability Levels** Have your more advanced students note the length of the first sentence and all of the sentences in the first paragraph. Have them take the first sentence apart grammatically—phrases, clauses, and punctuation marks. Note that the story's complexity is reflected in the sentence structure.

2 **Discussion** Who is the narrator?

3 **Literary Focus** Discuss first-person point of view. Explain that it is the position from which the story is told. In the first-person point of view, the narrator is a character in the story who uses the pronoun "I" while narrating.

4 **Discussion** How does Sherlock Holmes treat Dr. Watson?

5 **Discussion** What does Dr. Watson think of Holmes? What qualities of an investigator does Watson attribute to Holmes?

6 **Master Teacher Note** Explain the differences between inductive and deductive reasoning. Present two reasoning exercises—inductive from the specific to the general; deductive from the general to the specific. Have students identify each. Explain that Holmes is known for his ability to solve baffling crimes through clever observation and deduction.

7 **Discussion** What does this tell you about Sherlock Holmes?

ed on a logical basis, with which he unraveled the problems which were submitted to him. I rapidly threw on my clothes and was ready in a few minutes to accompany my friend down to the sitting room. A lady dressed in black and heavily veiled, who had been sitting in the window, rose as we entered.

"Good morning, madam," said Holmes cheerily. "My name is Sherlock Holmes. This is my intimate friend and associate, Dr. Watson, before whom you can speak as freely as before myself. Ha! I am glad to see that Mrs. Hudson has had the good sense to light the fire. Pray draw up to it, and I shall order you a cup of hot coffee, for I observe that you are shivering."

"It is not cold which makes me shiver," said the woman in a low voice, changing her seat as requested.

"What, then?"

"It is fear, Mr. Holmes. It is terror." She raised her veil as she spoke, and we could see that she was indeed in a pitiable state of agitation, her face all drawn and gray, with restless, frightened eyes, like those of some hunted animal. Her features and figure were those of a woman of thirty, but her hair was shot with premature gray, and her expression was weary and haggard. Sherlock Holmes ran her over with one of his quick, all-comprehensive glances.

"You must not fear," said he soothingly, bending forward and patting her forearm. "We shall soon set matters right, I have no doubt. You have come in by train this morning, I see."

"You know me, then?"

"No, but I observe the second half of a return ticket in the palm of your left glove. 7
You must have started early, and yet you had a good drive in a dogcart[1] along heavy roads, before you reached the station."

1. **dogcart:** Small horse-drawn carriage with seats arranged back-to-back.

Grammar in Action

Who and **whom** are personal pronouns that indicate case; *who* is nominative, and *whom* is objective. The nominative case, *who,* is used as a subject. Often, *who* is the subject of a question, such as "Who is Sherlock Holmes?" *Who* can also begin a subordinate clause in a complex sentence. For example, *who* is the subject of a subordinate clause when Helen Stoner says that she is living with her stepfather, "who is the last survivor of the oldest Saxon families . . ."

The objective case, *whom,* is used as the direct object of a verb, and the object of a preposition. In the following sentence from the story, *whom* is the direct object of a verb:

> "I have heard of you, Mr. Holmes, I have heard of you from Mrs. Farintosh, whom you helped in the hour of her sore need."

Doyle uses *whom* as the object of a preposition as Helen Stoner says,

> ". . . that even he to whom of all others I have a right to look for help and advice looks upon all that I tell him about it as fancy."

The lady gave a violent start and stared in bewilderment at my companion.

"There is no mystery, my dear madam," said he, smiling. "The left arm of your jacket is spattered with mud in no less than seven places. The marks are perfectly fresh. There is no vehicle save a dogcart which throws up mud in that way, and then only when you sit on the left-hand side of the driver."

"Whatever your reasons may be, you are perfectly correct," said she. "I started from home before six, reached Leatherhead at twenty past, and came in by the first train to Waterloo. Sir, I can stand this strain no longer; I shall go mad if it continues. I have no one to turn to—none, save only one, who cares for me, and he, poor fellow, can be of little aid. I have heard of you, Mr. Holmes, I have heard of you from Mrs. Farintosh, whom you helped in the hour of her sore need. It was from her that I had your address. Oh, sir, do you not think that you could help me, too, and at least throw a little light through the dense darkness which surrounds me? At present it is out of my power to reward you for your service, but in a month or six weeks I shall be married, with the control of my own income, and then at least you shall not find me ungrateful."

Holmes turned to his desk and, unlocking it, drew out a small case book, which he consulted.

"Farintosh," said he. "Ah yes, I recall the case; it was concerned with an opal tiara. I think it was before your time, Watson. I can only say, madam, that I shall be happy to devote the same care to your case as I did to that of your friend. As to reward, my profession is its own reward; but you are at liberty to defray whatever expenses I may be put to, at the time which suits you best. 8 And now I beg that you will lay before us everything that may help us in forming an opinion upon the matter."

"Alas!" replied our visitor, "the very horror of my situation lies in the fact that my fears are so vague, and my suspicions depend so entirely upon small points, which might seem trivial to another, that even he to whom of all others I have a right to look for help and advice looks upon all that I tell him about it as fancy. He does not say so, but I can read it from his soothing answers and averted eyes. But I have heard, Mr. Holmes, that you can see deeply into the manifold wickedness of the human heart. You may advise me how to walk amid the dangers which encompass me."

"I am all attention, madam."

"My name is Helen Stoner, and I am living with my stepfather, who is the last 9 survivor of one of the oldest Saxon families

8 Discussion How does Holmes feel about his job? Does his attitude sound practical? How do you suppose he can support himself with this type of attitude about payment for his services?

9 Enrichment Tell students that this story is set in London and the English countryside in the 1880s. Set the period for this story by bringing in pictures of Victorian London, especially those showing horsedrawn carriages and steam-driven trains. To help students visualize the manor house at Stoke Moran, show them pictures of typical English great houses.

Whenever *whom* follows a preposition, it is the object of the preposition.

Student Activity 1. Identify the case and purpose of the pronouns *who* and *whom* in the following sentences from the story:

> "This is my intimate friend and associate, Dr. Watson, before whom you can speak as freely as before myself."
>
> "I have no one to turn to—none, save only one, who cares for me, and he, poor fellow, can be of little aid."

Student Activity 2. Write a paragraph in which you summarize the important details in the story at this point, correctly using the pronouns *who* and *whom*.

10 **Clarification** An income of £250 was worth, at the time, about $1250. The total income, once amounting to about $5000, had fallen to about $3750.

11 **Discussion** What do you learn about Helen's stepfather?

in England; the Roylotts of Stoke Moran, on the western border of Surrey.''

Holmes nodded his head. ''The name is familiar to me,'' said he.

''The family was at one time among the richest in England, and the estates extended over the borders into Berkshire in the north, and Hampshire in the west. In the last century, however, four successive heirs were of a dissolute and wasteful disposition, and the family ruin was eventually completed by a gambler in the days of the Regency. Nothing was left save a few acres of ground, and the two-hundred-year-old house, which is itself crushed under a heavy mortgage. The last squire dragged out his existence there, living the horrible life of an aristocratic pauper; but his only son, my stepfather, seeing that he must adapt himself to the new conditions, obtained an advance from a relative, which enabled him to take a medical degree and went out to Calcutta, where, by his professional skill and his force of character, he established a large practice. In a fit of anger, however, caused by some robberies which had been perpetrated in the house, he beat his native butler to death and narrowly escaped a capital sentence. As it was, he suffered a long term of imprisonment and afterwards returned to England a morose and disappointed man.

''When Dr. Roylott was in India he married my mother, Mrs. Stoner, the young widow of Major-General Stoner, of the Bengal Artillery. My sister Julia and I were twins, and we were only two years old at the time of my mother's remarriage. She had a
10 considerable sum of money—not less than £1000 a year[2]—and this she bequeathed to Dr. Roylott entirely while we resided with him, with a provision that a certain annual sum should be allowed to each of us in the event of our marriage. Shortly after our return to England my mother died—she was killed eight years ago in a railway accident near Crewe. Dr. Roylott then abandoned his attempts to establish himself in practice in London and took us to live with him in the old ancestral house at Stoke Moran. The money which my mother had left was enough for all our wants, and there seemed to be no obstacle to our happiness.

''But a terrible change came over our stepfather about this time. Instead of making friends and exchanging visits with our neighbors, who had at first been overjoyed to see a Roylott of Stoke Moran back in the old family seat, he shut himself up in his house and seldom came out save to indulge in ferocious quarrels with whoever might cross his path. Violence of temper approaching to mania has been hereditary in the men of the family, and in my stepfather's case it had, I believe, been intensified by his long residence in the tropics. A series of disgraceful brawls took place, two of which ended in the police court, until at last he became the
terror of the village, and the folks would fly 11
at his approach, for he is a man of immense strength, and absolutely uncontrollable in his anger.

''Last week he hurled the local blacksmith over a parapet into a stream, and it was only by paying over all the money which I could gather together that I was able to avert another public exposure. He had no friends at all save the wandering gypsies, and he would give these vagabonds leave to encamp upon the few acres of bramble-covered land which represent the family estate, and would accept in return the hospitality of their tents, wandering away with them sometimes for weeks on end. He has a passion also for Indian animals, which are sent over to him by a correspondent, and he

---

2. £1000: One thousand pounds. £ is the symbol for pound or pounds, the British unit of money.

Grammar in Action

Adjective clauses enable a writer to include information that is important but not important enough to stand as a separate sentence. Adjective clauses are easy to recognize because they begin with one of five words called relative pronouns: *that, which, who, whom,* and *whose.* Adjective clauses are subordinate clauses: although they contain a subject and a verb, they cannot stand alone as a sentence. They are attached to and modify a word in an independent clause.

Adjective clauses can help a writer vary sentence length. Instead of writing two short shoppy sentences, a writer can combine them, making one into an adjective clause.

The following sentences or excerpts by Sir Arthur Conan Doyle contain adjective clauses:

> Nothing was left save a few acres of ground, and the two-hundred-year-old house, which is itself crushed under a heavy mortgage.

> In a fit of anger, however, caused by some robberies which had been perpetrated in the house . . .

has at this moment a cheetah and a baboon, which wander freely over his grounds and are feared by the villagers almost as much as is their master.

"You can imagine from what I say that my poor sister Julia and I had no great pleasure in our lives. No servant would stay with us, and for a long time we did all the work of the house. She was but thirty at the time of her death, and yet her hair had already begun to whiten, even as mine has."

"Your sister is dead, then?"

"She died just two years ago, and it is of her death that I wish to speak to you. You can understand that, living the life which I have described, we were little likely to see anyone of our own age and position. We had, however, an aunt, my mother's maiden sister, Miss Honoria Westphail, who lives near Harrow, and we were occasionally allowed to pay short visits at this lady's house. Julia went there at Christmas two years ago, and met there a major in the Marines, to whom she became engaged. My stepfather learned of the engagement when my sister returned and offered no objection to the marriage; but within a fortnight of the day which had been
12 fixed for the wedding, the terrible event occurred which has deprived me of my only companion."

Sherlock Holmes had been leaning back in his chair with his eyes closed and his head sunk in a cushion, but he half opened his lids now and glanced across at his visitor.

"Pray be precise as to details," said he.

"It is easy for me to be so, for every event of that dreadful time is seared into my memory. The manor house is, as I have already said, very old, and only one wing is now inhabited. The bedrooms in this wing are on the ground floor, the sitting rooms being in the central block of the buildings. Of these bedrooms the first is Dr. Roylott's, the second my sister's, and the third my own. There is no communication between them, but they all open out into the same corridor. Do I make myself plain?"

"Perfectly so."

"The windows of the three rooms open out upon the lawn. That fatal night Dr. Roylott had gone to his room early, though we knew that he had not retired to rest, for my sister was troubled by the smell of the strong Indian cigars which it was his custom to smoke. She left her room, therefore, and came into mine, where she sat for some time, chatting about her approaching wedding. At eleven o'clock she rose to leave me, but she paused at the door and looked back.

" 'Tell me, Helen,' said she, 'have you ever heard anyone whistle in the dead of the night?'

" 'Never,' said I.

" 'I suppose that you could not possibly whistle, yourself, in your sleep?'

" 'Certainly not. But why?'

" 'Because during the last few nights I have always, about three in the morning, heard a low, clear whistle. I am a light sleeper, and it has awakened me. I cannot tell where it came from—perhaps from the next room, perhaps from the lawn. I thought that I would just ask you whether you had heard it.'

" 'No, I have not. It must be the gypsies in the plantation.'

" 'Very likely. And yet if it were on the lawn, I wonder that you did not hear it also.'

" 'Ah, but I sleep more heavily than you.'

" 'Well, it is of no great consequence, at any rate.' She smiled back at me, closed my door, and a few moments later I heard her key turn in the lock."

"Indeed," said Holmes. "Was it your custom always to lock yourselves in at night?"

"Always."

12 **Discussion** If Helen's sister Julia had married, what would she have received?

The money which my mother had left was enough for all our wants . . .

Instead of making friends and exchanging visits with our neighbors, who had at first been overjoyed to see a Roylott of Stoke Moran back in the old family seat, he shut himself up in his old house and seldom came out . . .

. . . and he would give these vagabonds leave to encamp upon the few acres of bramble-covered land which represent the family estate . . .

Student Activity 1. Write out the adjective clauses in the example sentences and excerpts.

Student Activity 2. Write five of your own sentences with adjective clauses. Try to use a different relative pronoun in each.

"And why?"

"I think that I mentioned to you that the doctor kept a cheetah and a baboon. We had no feeling of security unless our doors were locked."

"Quite so. Pray proceed with your statement."

"I could not sleep that night. A vague feeling of impending misfortune impressed me. My sister and I, you will recollect, were twins, and you know how subtle are the links which bind two souls which are so closely allied. It was a wild night. The wind was howling outside, and the rain was beating and splashing against the windows. Suddenly, amid all the hubbub of the gale, there burst forth the wild scream of a terrified woman. I knew that it was my sister's voice. I sprang from my bed, wrapped a shawl round me, and rushed into the corridor. As I opened my door I seemed to hear a low whistle, such as my sister described, and a few moments later a clanging sound, as if a mass of metal had fallen. As I ran down the passage, my sister's door was unlocked, and revolved slowly upon its hinges. I stared at it horror-stricken, not knowing what was about to issue from it. By the light of the corridor lamp I saw my sister appear at the opening, her face blanched with terror, her hands groping for help, her whole figure swaying to and fro like that of a drunkard. I ran to her and threw my arms round her, but at that moment her knees seemed to give way and she fell to the ground. She writhed as one who is in terrible pain, and her limbs were dreadfully convulsed. At first I thought that she had not recognized me, but as I bent over her she suddenly shrieked out in a voice which I shall never forget, 'Oh, Helen! It was the band! The speckled band!' There was something else which she would fain have said, and she stabbed with her finger into the air in the direction of the doctor's room, but a fresh convulsion seized her and choked her words. I rushed out, calling loudly for my stepfather, and I met him hastening from his room in his dressing gown. When he reached my sister's side she was unconscious, and though he poured brandy down her throat and sent for medical aid from the village, all efforts were in vain, for she slowly sank and died without having recovered her consciousness. Such was the dreadful end of my beloved sister."

"One moment," said Holmes; "are you sure about this whistle and metallic sound? Could you swear to it?"

"That was what the county coroner asked me at the inquiry. It is my strong impression that I heard it, and yet, among the crash of the gale and the creaking of an old house, I may possibly have been deceived."

"Was your sister dressed?"

"No, she was in her nightdress. In her right hand was found the charred stump of a match, and in her left a matchbox."

"Showing that she had struck a light and looked about her when the alarm took place. That is important. And what conclusions did the coroner come to?"

"He investigated the case with great care, for Dr. Roylott's conduct had long been notorious in the county, but he was unable to find any satisfactory cause of death. My evidence showed that the door had been fastened upon the inner side, and the windows were blocked by old-fashioned shutters with broad iron bars, which were secured every night. The walls were carefully sounded, and were shown to be quite solid all round, and the flooring was also thoroughly examined, with the same result. The chimney is wide, but is barred up by four large staples. It is certain, therefore, that my sister was quite alone when she met her

Grammar in Action

Writers join closely related ideas of equal importance in **compound sentences.** By joining several ideas in one sentence, the writer shows the logical relationship between the ideas and eliminates choppy sentences.

A compound sentence consists of two or more independent clauses joined with a comma and one of the coordinating conjunctions: *and, but, for, nor, or, so, yet.* The following sentences from "The Adventure of the Speckled Band" are compound:

The wind was howling outside, and the rain was beating and splashing against the windows.

I ran to her and threw my arms around her, but at that moment her knees seemed to give way and she fell to the ground.

She writhed as one who is in terrible pain, and her limbs were dreadfully convulsed.

At first I thought that she had not recognized me, but as I bent over her she suddenly shrieked out in a voice which I shall never forget . . .

end. Besides, there were no marks of any violence upon her."

"How about poison?"

"The doctors examined her for it, but without success."

"What do you think that this unfortunate lady died of, then?"

"It is my belief that she died of pure fear and nervous shock, though what it was that frightened her I cannot imagine."

"Were there gypsies in the plantation at the time?"

"Yes, there are nearly always some there."

"Ah, and what did you gather from this allusion to a band—a speckled band?"

"Sometimes I have thought that it was merely the wild talk of delirium, sometimes that it may have referred to some band of people, perhaps to these very gypsies in the plantation. I do not know whether the spotted handkerchiefs which so many of them wear over their heads might have suggested the strange adjective which she used."

Holmes shook his head like a man who is far from being satisfied.

"These are very deep waters," said he; "pray go on with your narrative."

"Two years have passed since then, and my life has been until lately lonelier than ever. A month ago, however, a dear friend, whom I have known for many years, has done me the honor to ask my hand in marriage. His name is Armitage—Percy Armitage—the second son of Mr. Armitage, of Crane Water, near Reading. My stepfather has offered no opposition to the match, and we are to be married in the course of the spring. Two days ago some repairs were started in the west wing of the building, and my bedroom wall has been pierced, so that I have had to move into the chamber in which my sister died, and to sleep in the very bed in which she slept. Imagine, then, my thrill of terror when last night, as I lay awake, thinking over her terrible fate, I suddenly heard in the silence of the night the low whistle which had been the herald of her own death. I sprang up and lit the lamp, but nothing was to be seen in the room. I was too shaken to go to bed again, however, so I dressed, and as soon as it was daylight I slipped down, got a dogcart at the Crown Inn, which is opposite, and drove to Leatherhead, from whence I have come on this morning with the one object of seeing you and asking your advice."

"You have done wisely," said my friend. "But have you told me all?"

"Yes, all."

"Miss Roylott, you have not. You are screening your stepfather."

"Why, what do you mean?"

For answer Holmes pushed back the frill of black lace which fringed the hand that lay upon our visitor's knee. Five little livid spots, the marks of four fingers and a thumb, were printed upon the white wrist.

"You have been cruelly used," said Holmes.

The lady colored deeply and covered over her injured wrist. "He is a hard man," she said, "and perhaps he hardly knows his own strength."

There was a long silence, during which Holmes leaned his chin upon his hands and stared into the crackling fire.

"This is a very deep business," he said at last. "There are a thousand details which I should desire to know before I decide upon our course of action. Yet we have not a moment to lose. If we were to come to Stoke Moran today, would it be possible for us to look over these rooms without the knowledge of your stepfather?"

"As it happens, he spoke of coming into town today upon some most important business. It is probable that he will be away all

I rushed out, calling loudly for my stepfather, and I met him hastening from his room in his dressing gown.

Student Activity 1. Reread the example sentences substituting a period for the comma and the coordinating conjunction. What difference do you notice?

Student Activity 2. Write five sets of two simple but related sentences. Exchange papers with a partner, and write the shorter sentences as one compound sentence. Be sure to use a comma before the coordinating conjunction that joins the two sentences.

13 **Reading Strategy** Have students summarize the events that have occurred so far in the story. Ask them if they have any ideas as to the cause of Julia's death.

day, and that there would be nothing to disturb you. We have a housekeeper now, but I could easily get her out of the way."

"Excellent. You are not averse to this trip, Watson?"

"By no means."

"Then we shall both come. What are you going to do yourself?"

"I have one or two things which I would wish to do now that I am in town. But I shall return by the twelve o'clock train, so as to be there in time for your coming."

"And you may expect us early in the afternoon. I have myself some small business matters to attend to. Will you not wait and breakfast?"

"No, I must go. My heart is lightened already since I have confided my trouble to you. I shall look forward to seeing you again this afternoon." She dropped her thick
13 black veil over her face and glided from the room.

"And what do you think of it all, Watson?" asked Sherlock Holmes, leaning back in his chair.

"It seems to me to be a most dark and sinister business."

"Dark enough and sinister enough."

"Yet if the lady is correct in saying that the flooring and walls are sound, and that the door, window, and chimney are impassable, then her sister must have been undoubtedly alone when she met her mysterious end."

"What becomes, then, of these nocturnal whistles, and what of the very peculiar words of the dying woman?"

"I cannot think."

"When you combine the ideas of whistles at night, the presence of a band of gypsies who are on intimate terms with this old doctor, the fact that we have every reason to believe that the doctor has an interest in preventing his stepdaughter's marriage, the dying allusion to a band, and, finally, the fact that Miss Helen Stoner heard a metallic clang, which might have been caused by one of those metal bars that secured the shutters, falling back into its place, I think that there is good ground to think that the mystery may be cleared along those lines."

"But what, then, did the gypsies do?"

"I cannot imagine."

"I see many objections to any such theory."

"And so do I. It is precisely for that reason that we are going to Stoke Moran this day. I want to see whether the objections are fatal, or if they may be explained away. But what in the name of the devil!"

The ejaculation had been drawn from my companion by the fact that our door had been suddenly dashed open, and that a huge man had framed himself in the aperture. His costume was a peculiar mixture of the professional and of the agricultural, having a black top hat, a long frock coat, and a pair of high gaiters,[3] with a hunting crop swinging in his hand. So tall was he that his hat actually brushed the crossbar of the doorway, and his breadth seemed to span it across from side to side. A large face, seared with a thousand wrinkles, burned yellow with the sun, and marked with every evil passion, was turned from one to the other of us, while his deep-set, bile-shot eyes, and his high, thin, fleshless nose, gave him somewhat the resemblance to a fierce old bird of prey.

"Which of you is Holmes?" asked this apparition.

"My name, sir; but you have the advantage of me," said my companion quietly.

---

3. gaiters (gāt′ ərz) *n.*: A high overshoe with a cloth upper.

"I am Dr. Grimesby Roylott, of Stoke Moran."

"Indeed, Doctor," said Holmes blandly. "Pray take a seat."

"I will do nothing of the kind. My stepdaughter has been here. I have traced her. What has she been saying to you?"

"It is a little cold for the time of the year," said Holmes.

"What has she been saying to you?" screamed the old man furiously.

"But I have heard that the crocuses promise well," continued my companion imperturbably.

"Ha! You put me off, do you?" said our new visitor, taking a step forward and shaking his hunting crop. "I know you, you scoundrel! I have heard of you before. You are Holmes, the meddler."

My friend smiled.

"Holmes, the busybody!"

His smile broadened.

"Holmes, the Scotland Yard Jack-in-office!"

Holmes chuckled heartily. "Your conversation is most entertaining," said he. "When you go out close the door, for there is a decided draft."

"I will go when I have said my say. Don't you dare to meddle with my affairs. I know that Miss Stoner has been here. I traced her! I am a dangerous man to fall foul of! See here." He stepped swiftly forward, seized the poker, and bent it into a curve with his huge brown hands.

"See that you keep yourself out of my grip," he snarled, and hurling the twisted poker into the fireplace he strode out of the room.

"He seems a very amiable person," said Holmes, laughing. "I am not quite so bulky, but if he had remained I might have shown him that my grip was not much more feeble than his own." As he spoke he picked up the steel poker and, with a sudden effort, straightened it out again. 14

14 **Discussion** How does Holmes's physical strength compare to Dr. Roylott's? How does his physical appearance compare to the doctor's?

15 Discussion How does Holmes feel about Dr. Roylott thinking he is a member of Scotland Yard?

16 Clarification A trap was a one-horse, two-wheeled carriage on springs.

15 "Fancy his having the insolence to confound me with[4] the official detective force! This incident gives zest to our investigation, however, and I only trust that our little friend will not suffer from her imprudence in allowing this brute to trace her. And now, Watson, we shall order breakfast, and afterwards I shall walk down to Doctors' Commons, where I hope to get some data which may help us in this matter."

It was nearly one o'clock when Sherlock Holmes returned from his excursion. He held in his hand a sheet of blue paper, scrawled over with notes and figures.

"I have seen the will of the deceased wife," said he. "To determine its exact meaning I have been obliged to work out the present prices of the investments with which it is concerned. The total income, which at the time of the wife's death was little short of £1100, is now, through the fall in agricultural prices, not more than £750. Each daughter can claim an income of £250, in case of marriage. It is evident, therefore, that if both girls had married, this beauty would have had a mere pittance,[5] while even one of them would cripple him to a very serious extent. My morning's work has not been wasted, since it has proved that he has the very strongest motives for standing in the way of anything of the sort. And now, Watson, this is too serious for dawdling, especially as the old man is aware that we are interesting ourselves in his affairs; so if you are ready, we shall call a cab and drive to Waterloo. I should be very much obliged if you would slip your revolver into your pocket. An Eley's No. 2 is an excellent argument with gentlemen who can twist steel pokers into knots. That and a toothbrush are, I think, all that we need."

At Waterloo we were fortunate in catching a train for Leatherhead, where we hired 16
a trap at the station inn and drove for four or five miles through the lovely Surrey lanes. It was a perfect day, with a bright sun and a few fleecy clouds in the heavens. The trees and wayside hedges were just throwing out their first green shoots, and the air was full of the pleasant smell of the moist earth. To me at least there was a strange contrast between the sweet promise of the spring and this sinister quest upon which we were engaged. My companion sat in the front of the trap, his arms folded, his hat pulled down over his eyes, and his chin sunk upon his breast, buried in the deepest thought. Suddenly, however, he started, tapped me on the shoulder, and pointed over the meadows.

"Look there!" said he.

A heavily timbered park stretched up in a gentle slope, thickening into a grove at the highest point. From amid the branches there jutted out the gray gables and high rooftop of a very old mansion.

"Stoke Moran?" said he.

"Yes, sir, that be the house of Dr. Grimesby Roylott," remarked the driver.

"There is some building going on there," said Holmes; "that is where we are going."

"There's the village," said the driver, pointing to a cluster of roofs some distance to the left; "but if you want to get to the house, you'll find it shorter to get over this stile, and so by the footpath over the fields. There it is, where the lady is walking."

"And the lady, I fancy, is Miss Stoner," observed Holmes, shading his eyes. "Yes, I think we had better do as you suggest."

We got off, paid our fare, and the trap rattled back on its way to Leatherhead.

"I thought it as well," said Holmes as we

4. confound . . . with: Mistake me for.
5. pittance (pit′ 'ns) *n.*: A small or barely sufficient allowance of money.

climbed the stile, "that this fellow should think we had come here as architects, or on some definite business. It may stop his gossip. Good afternoon, Miss Stoner. You see that we have been as good as our word."

Our client of the morning had hurried forward to meet us with a face which spoke her joy. "I have been waiting so eagerly for you," she cried, shaking hands with us warmly. "All has turned out splendidly. Dr. Roylott has gone to town, and it is unlikely that he will be back before evening."

"We have had the pleasure of making the doctor's acquaintance," said Holmes, and in a few words he sketched out what had occurred. Miss Stoner turned white to the lips as she listened.

"Good heavens!" she cried, "he has followed me, then."

"So it appears."

"He is so cunning that I never know when I am safe from him. What will he say when he returns?"

"He must guard himself, for he may find that there is someone more cunning than himself upon his track. You must lock yourself up from him tonight. If he is violent, we shall take you away to your aunt's at Harrow. Now, we must make the best use of our time, so kindly take us at once to the rooms which we are to examine."

The building was of gray, lichen-blotched[6] stone, with a high central portion and two curving wings, like the claws of a crab, thrown out on each side. In one of these wings the windows were broken and blocked with wooden boards, while the roof was partly caved in, a picture of ruin. The central portion was in little better repair, but the right-hand block was comparatively modern, and the blinds in the windows, with the blue smoke curling up from the chimneys, showed that this was where the family resided. Some scaffolding had been erected against the end wall, and the stonework had been broken into, but there were no signs of any workmen at the moment of our visit. Holmes walked slowly up and down the ill-trimmed lawn and examined with deep attention the outsides of the windows.

"This, I take it, belongs to the room in which you used to sleep, the center one to your sister's, and the one next to the main building to Dr. Roylott's chamber?"

"Exactly so. But I am now sleeping in the middle one."

"Pending the alterations, as I understand. By the way, there does not seem to be any very pressing need for repairs at that end wall."

"There were none. I believe that it was an excuse to move me from my room."

"Ah! that is suggestive. Now, on the other side of this narrow wing runs the corridor from which these three rooms open. There are windows in it, of course?"

"Yes, but very small ones. Too narrow for anyone to pass through."

"As you both locked your doors at night, your rooms were unapproachable from that side. Now, would you have the kindness to go into your room and bar your shutters?"

Miss Stoner did so, and Holmes, after a careful examination through the open window, endeavored in every way to force the shutter open, but without success. There was no slit through which a knife could be passed to raise the bar. Then with his lens he tested the hinges, but they were of solid iron, built firmly into the massive masonry. "Hum!" said he, scratching his chin in some perplexity, "My theory certainly presents some difficulties. No one could pass through these shutters if they were bolted. Well, we

6. lichen-blotched (lī′ kən blächt) *adj.*: Covered with patches of fungus.

17 Discussion Note Holmes's careful screening of the room. Ask students if they can think of some conclusions about Miss Stoner's death.

shall see if the inside throws any light upon the matter."

A small side door led into the whitewashed corridor from which the three bedrooms opened. Holmes refused to examine the third chamber, so we passed at once to the second, that in which Miss Stoner was now sleeping, and in which her sister had met with her fate. It was a homely little room, with a low ceiling and a gaping fireplace, after the fashion of old country houses. A brown chest of drawers stood in one corner, a narrow white-counterpaned bed in another, and a dressing table on the left-hand side of the window. These articles, with two small wickerwork chairs, made up all the furniture in the room save for a square of Wilton carpet in the center. The boards round and the paneling of the walls were of brown, worm-eaten oak, so old and discolored that it may have dated from the original building of the house. Holmes drew one of the chairs into a corner and sat silent, while his eyes traveled round and round and up and down, taking in every detail of the apartment.

"Where does that bell communicate with?" he asked at last, pointing to a thick bell-rope which hung down beside the bed, the tassel actually lying upon the pillow.

"It goes to the housekeeper's room."

"It looks newer than the other things?"

17 "Yes, it was only put there a couple of years ago."

"Your sister asked for it, I suppose?"

"No, I never heard of her using it. We used always to get what we wanted for ourselves."

"Indeed, it seemed unnecessary to put so nice a bell-pull there. You will excuse me for a few minutes while I satisfy myself as to this floor." He threw himself down upon his face with his lens in his hand and crawled swiftly backward and forward, examining minutely the cracks between the boards. Then he did the same with the woodwork with which the chamber was paneled. Finally he walked over to the bed and spent some time in staring at it and in running his eye up and down the wall. Finally he took the bell-rope in his hand and gave it a brisk tug.

"Why, it's a dummy," said he.

"Won't it ring?"

"No, it is not even attached to a wire. This is very interesting. You can see now

that it is fastened to a hook just above where the little opening for the ventilator is."

"How very absurd! I never noticed that before!"

"Very strange!" muttered Holmes, pulling at the rope. "There are one or two very singular points about this room. For example, what a fool a builder must be to open a ventilator into another room, when, with the same trouble, he might have communicated with the outside air!"

"That is also quite modern," said the lady.

"Done about the same time as the bell-rope?" remarked Holmes.

"Yes, there were several little changes carried out about that time."

"They seem to have been of a most interesting character—dummy bell-ropes, and ventilators which do not ventilate. With your permission, Miss Stoner, we shall now carry our researches into the inner apartment."

Dr. Grimesby Roylott's chamber was larger than that of his stepdaughter, but was as plainly furnished. A camp bed, a small wooden shelf full of books, mostly of a technical character, an armchair beside the bed, a plain wooden chair against the wall, a round table, and a large iron safe were the principal things which met the eye. Holmes walked slowly round and examined each and all of them with the keenest interest.

"What's in here?" he asked, tapping the safe.

"My stepfather's business papers."

"Oh! you have seen inside, then?"

"Only once, some years ago. I remember that it was full of papers."

"There isn't a cat in it, for example?"

"No. What a strange idea!"

"Well, look at this!" He took up a small saucer of milk which stood on the top of it.

"No; we don't keep a cat. But there is a cheetah and a baboon."

"Ah, yes, of course! Well, a cheetah is just a big cat, and yet a saucer of milk does not go very far in satisfying its wants, I daresay. There is one point which I should wish to determine." He squatted down in front of the wooden chair and examined the seat of it with the greatest attention.

"Thank you. That is quite settled," said he, rising and putting his lens in his pocket. "Hello! Here is something interesting!"

The object which had caught his eye was a small dog lash hung on one corner of the bed. The lash, however, was curled upon itself and tied so as to make a loop of whipcord.

"What do you make of that, Watson?"

"It's a common enough lash. But I don't know why it should be tied."

"That is not quite so common, is it? Ah, me! it's a wicked world, and when a clever man turns his brains to crime it is the worst of all. I think that I have seen enough now, Miss Stoner, and with your permission we shall walk out upon the lawn."

I had never seen my friend's face so grim or his brow so dark as it was when we turned from the scene of this investigation. We had walked several times up and down the lawn, neither Miss Stoner nor myself liking to break in upon his thoughts before he roused himself from his reverie.

"It is very essential, Miss Stoner," said he, "that you should absolutely follow my advice in every respect."

"I shall most certainly do so."

"The matter is too serious for any hesitation. Your life may depend upon your compliance."[7]

"I assure you that I am in your hands."

"In the first place, both my friend and I must spend the night in your room."

Both Miss Stoner and I gazed at him in astonishment.

"Yes, it must be so. Let me explain. I believe that that is the village inn over there?"

"Yes, that is the Crown."

"Very good. Your windows would be visible from there?"

"Certainly."

"You must confine yourself to your room, on pretense of a headache, when your stepfather comes back. Then when you hear him retire for the night, you must open the shutters of your window, undo the hasp,[8] put your lamp there as a signal to us, and then withdraw quietly with everything which you are likely to want into the room which you used to occupy. I have no doubt that, in spite of the repairs, you could manage there for one night."

"Oh, yes, easily."

"The rest you will leave in our hands."

"But what will you do?"

"We shall spend the night in your room, and we shall investigate the cause of this noise which has disturbed you."

"I believe, Mr. Holmes, that you have already made up your mind," said Miss Stoner, laying her hand upon my companion's sleeve.

"Perhaps I have."

"Then, for pity's sake, tell me what was the cause of my sister's death."

"I should prefer to have clearer proofs before I speak."

"You can at least tell me whether my own thought is correct, and if she died from some sudden fright."

"No, I do not think so. I think that there was probably some more tangible cause. And now, Miss Stoner, we must leave you, for if Dr. Roylott returned and saw us our journey would be in vain. Goodbye, and be brave, for if you will do what I have told you, you may rest assured that we shall soon drive away the dangers that threaten you."

Sherlock Holmes and I had no difficulty in engaging a bedroom and sitting room at the Crown Inn. They were on the upper floor, and from our window we could command a view of the avenue gate, and of the inhabited wing of Stoke Moran Manor House. At dusk we saw Dr. Grimesby Roylott drive past, his huge form looming up beside

7. **compliance** (kəm plī′ əns) *n.*: Agreeing to a request.

8. **hasp** *n.*: Hinged metal fastening of a window.

Grammar in Action

Action verbs can be either active or passive. When a verb is active, the subject of the verb performs the action. By contrast, in the **passive voice,** the subject of a verb receives the action. In general, passive voice is to be avoided because it is not specific and weakens your writing by making it less interesting. However, passive voice is useful when you don't know who performed the action. For example, Doyle uses the passive voice as Watson narrates: "The trap drove on, and a few minutes later we saw a sudden light spring up among the trees as the lamp *was lit* in one of the sitting rooms." In addition, passive voice can be used when you know who performed the action but don't wish to specify the individual.

Passive voice is recognizable because a passive verb has two parts: a form of the verb "to be" and a past participle. Remarking on Miss Stoner's sister's bed, Sherlock Holmes says, "It *was clamped* to the floor." Here is the conjugation of passive forms of the verb *lamp* with the pronoun *it:*

Tense	**Passive Form**
Present	it is clamped

the little figure of the lad who drove him. The boy had some slight difficulty in undoing the heavy iron gates, and we heard the hoarse roar of the doctor's voice and saw the fury with which he shook his clinched fists at him. The trap drove on, and a few minutes later we saw a sudden light spring up among the trees as the lamp was lit in one of the sitting rooms.

"Do you know, Watson," said Holmes as we sat together in the gathering darkness, "I have really some scruples as to taking you tonight. There is a distinct element of danger."

"Can I be of assistance?"

"Your presence might be invaluable."

"Then I shall certainly come."

"It is very kind of you."

"You speak of danger. You have evidently seen more in these rooms than was visible to me."

"No, but I fancy that I may have deduced a little more. I imagine that you saw all that I did."

"I saw nothing remarkable save the bell-rope, and what purpose that could answer I confess is more than I can imagine."

"You saw the ventilator, too?"

"Yes, but I do not think that it is such a very unusual thing to have a small opening between two rooms. It was so small that a rat could hardly pass through."

"I knew that we should find a ventilator before ever we came to Stoke Moran."

"My dear Holmes!"

"Oh, yes, I did. You remember in her statement she said that her sister could smell Dr. Roylott's cigar. Now, of course that suggested at once that there must be a communication between the two rooms. It could only be a small one, or it would have been remarked upon at the coroner's inquiry. I deduced a ventilator."

"But what harm can there be in that?"

"Well, there is at least a curious coincidence of dates. A ventilator is made, a cord is hung, and a lady who sleeps in the bed dies. Does not that strike you?"

"I cannot as yet see any connection."

"Did you observe anything very peculiar about that bed?"

"No."

"It was clamped to the floor. Did you ever see a bed fastened like that before?"

"I cannot say that I have."

"The lady could not move her bed. It must always be in the same relative position to the ventilator and to the rope—or so we may call it, since it was clearly never meant for a bell-pull."

"Holmes," I cried, "I seem to see dimly 18
what you are hinting at. We are only just in
time to prevent some subtle and horrible 19
crime."

"Subtle enough and horrible enough.
When a doctor does go wrong he is the first
of criminals. He has nerve and he has
knowledge. Palmer and Pritchard were 20
among the heads of their profession. This
man strikes even deeper, but I think, Watson, that we shall be able to strike deeper still. But we shall have horrors enough before the night is over; for goodness' sake let us have a quiet pipe and turn our minds for a few hours to something more cheerful."

About nine o'clock the light among the trees was extinguished, and all was dark in the direction of the Manor House. Two hours passed slowly away, and then, suddenly, just at the stroke of eleven, a single bright light shone out right in front of us.

"That is our signal," said Holmes, springing to his feet; "it comes from the middle window."

As we passed out he exchanged a few words with the landlord, explaining that we were going on a late visit to an acquaint-

18 **Discussion** By now Watson has an idea of the cause of death. Ask students again if they have any ideas.

19 **Literary Focus** Point out how the author is building toward the climax and resolution. Little by little clues are being given to the reader.

20 **Clarification** William Palmer was executed in 1856 for the murder of a friend by poison. Edward Pritchard, a Glasgow practitioner, was hung in 1865 for poisoning his wife and mother-in-law.

Past	it was clamped
Future	it will be clamped
Present Perfect	it has been clamped
Past Perfect	it had been clamped
Future Perfect	it will have been clamped

Student Activity 1. Locate three more examples of passive voice on pages 41–42. Why is the use of passive voice appropriate in the examples you found?

Student Activity 2. Compose five sentences in which you use the passive voice, and briefly explain why passive voice is appropriate in each sentence.

ance, and that it was possible that we might spend the night there. A moment later we were out on the dark road, a chill wind blowing in our faces, and one yellow light twinkling in front of us through the gloom to guide us on our somber errand.

There was little difficulty in entering the grounds; for unrepaired breaches gaped in the old park wall. Making our way among the trees, we reached the lawn, crossed it, and were about to enter through the window when out from a clump of laurel bushes there darted what seemed to be a hideous and distorted child, who threw itself upon the grass with writhing limbs and then ran swiftly across the lawn into the darkness.

"My God!" I whispered; "did you see it?"

Holmes was for the moment as startled as I. His hand closed like a vise upon my wrist in his agitation. Then he broke into a low laugh and put his lips to my ear.

"It is a nice household," he murmured. "That is the baboon."

I had forgotten the strange pets which the doctor affected. There was a cheetah, too; perhaps we might find it upon our shoulders at any moment. I confess that I felt easier in my mind when, after following Holmes's example and slipping off my shoes, I found myself inside the bedroom. My companion noiselessly closed the shutters, moved the lamp onto the table, and cast his eyes round the room. All was as we had seen it in the daytime. Then creeping up to me and making a trumpet of his hand, he whispered into my ear again so gently that it was all that I could do to distinguish the words:

"The least sound would be fatal to our plans."

I nodded to show that I had heard.

"We must sit without light. He would see it through the ventilator."

I nodded again.

"Do not go asleep; your very life may depend upon it. Have your pistol ready in case we should need it. I will sit on the side of the bed, and you in that chair."

I took out my revolver and laid it on the corner of the table.

Holmes had brought up a long thin cane, and this he placed upon the bed beside him. By it he laid the box of matches and the stump of a candle. Then he turned down the lamp, and we were left in darkness.

How shall I ever forget that dreadful vigil? I could not hear a sound, not even the drawing of a breath, and yet I knew that my companion sat open-eyed, within a few feet of me, in the same state of nervous tension in which I was myself. The shutters cut off the least ray of light, and we waited in absolute darkness. From outside came the occasional cry of a night bird, and once at our very window a long-drawn catlike whine, which told us that the cheetah was indeed at liberty. Far away we could hear the deep tones of the parish clock, which boomed out every quarter of an hour. How long they seemed, those quarters! Twelve struck, and one and two and three, and still we sat waiting silently for whatever might befall.

Suddenly there was the momentary gleam of a light up in the direction of the ventilator, which vanished immediately, but was succeeded by a strong smell of burning oil and heated metal. Someone in the next room had lit a dark lantern.[9] I heard a gentle sound of movement, and then all was silent once more, though the smell grew stronger. For half an hour I sat with straining ears.

---

9. dark lantern: A lantern with a shutter that can hide the light.

Then suddenly another sound became audible—a very gentle, soothing sound, like that of a small jet of steam escaping continually from a kettle. The instant that we heard it, Holmes sprang from the bed, struck a match, and lashed furiously with his cane at the bell-pull.

"You see it, Watson?" he yelled. "You see it?"

But I saw nothing. At the moment when Holmes struck the light I heard a low, clear whistle, but the sudden glare flashing into my weary eyes made it impossible for me to tell what it was at which my friend lashed so savagely. I could, however, see that his face was deadly pale and filled with horror and loathing.

He had ceased to strike and was gazing up at the ventilator when suddenly there broke from the silence of the night the most horrible cry to which I have ever listened. It swelled up louder and louder, a hoarse yell of pain and fear and anger all mingled in the one dreadful shriek. They say that away down in the village, and even in the distant parsonage, that cry raised the sleepers from their beds. It struck cold to our hearts, and I stood gazing at Holmes, and he at me, until the last echoes of it had died away into the silence from which it rose.

"What can it mean?" I gasped.

"It means that it is all over," Holmes answered. "And perhaps, after all, it is for the best. Take your pistol, and we will enter Dr. Roylott's room."

With a grave face he lit the lamp and led the way down the corridor. Twice he struck at the chamber door without any reply from within. Then he turned the handle and entered, I at his heels, with the cocked pistol in my hand.

It was a singular sight which met our eyes. On the table stood a dark lantern with the shutter half open, throwing a brilliant beam of light upon the iron safe, the door of which was ajar. Beside this table, on the wooden chair, sat Dr. Grimesby Roylott, clad in a long gray dressing gown, his bare ankles protruding beneath, and his feet thrust into red heelless Turkish slippers. Across his lap lay the short stock with the long lash which we had noticed during the day. His chin was cocked upward and his eyes were fixed in a dreadful, rigid stare at the corner of the ceiling. Round his brow he had a peculiar yellow band, with brownish speckles, which seemed to be bound tightly round his head. As we entered he made neither sound nor motion.

"The band! the speckled band!" whispered Holmes.

I took a step forward. In an instant his strange headgear began to move, and there reared itself from among his hair the squat diamond-shaped head and puffed neck of a loathsome serpent.

"It is a swamp adder!" cried Holmes; 21
"the deadliest snake in India. He has died 22
within ten seconds of being bitten. Violence does, in truth, recoil upon the violent, and the schemer falls into the pit which he digs for another. Let us thrust this creature back into its den, and we can then remove Miss Stoner to some place of shelter and let the county police know what has happened."

As he spoke he drew the dog whip swiftly from the dead man's lap, and throwing the noose round the reptile's neck he drew it from its horrid perch and, carrying it at arm's length, threw it into the iron safe, which he closed upon it.

Such are the true facts of the death of Dr. Grimesby Roylott, of Stoke Moran. It is not necessary that I should prolong a narrative which has already run to too great a

21 **Teaching to Ability Levels** You might have your **more advanced** students research poisonous snakes. Is there a real snake that fits the description of the one in this story? If so, what is the identity of the snake?

22 **Clarification** There are certain statements made about the snake in the story that are not true of any snake. You might wish to point these out to your class.

1. No snake bite would kill "within ten seconds."
2. Snakes are deaf. It could not hear the doctor's whistle.
3. No snakes drink milk by choice unless water is not available.

length by telling how we broke the sad news to the terrified girl, how we conveyed her by the morning train to the care of her good aunt at Harrow, of how the slow process of official inquiry came to the conclusion that the doctor met his fate while indiscreetly playing with a dangerous pet. The little which I had yet to learn of the case was told me by Sherlock Holmes as we traveled back next day.

"I had," said he, "come to an entirely erroneous conclusion which shows, my dear Watson, how dangerous it always is to reason from insufficient data. The presence of the gypsies, and the use of the word *band*, which was used by the poor girl, no doubt to explain the appearance which she had caught a hurried glimpse of by the light of her match, were sufficient to put me upon an entirely wrong scent. I can only claim the merit that I instantly reconsidered my position when, however, it became clear to me that whatever danger threatened an occupant of the room could not come either from the window or the door. My attention was speedily drawn, as I have already remarked to you, to this ventilator, and to the bell-rope which hung down to the bed. The discovery that this was a dummy, and that the bed was clamped to the floor, instantly gave rise to the suspicion that the rope was there as a bridge for something passing through the hole and coming to the bed. The idea of a snake instantly occurred to me, and when I coupled it with my knowledge that the doctor was furnished with a supply of creatures from India, I felt that I was probably on the right track. The idea of using a form of poison which could not possibly be discovered by any chemical test was just such a one as would occur to a clever and ruthless man who had had an Eastern training. The rapidity with which such a poison would take effect would also, from his point of view, be an advantage. It would be a sharp-eyed coroner, indeed, who could distinguish the two little dark punctures which would show where the poison fangs had done their work. Then I thought of the whistle. Of course he must recall the snake before the morning light revealed it to the victim. He had trained it, probably by the use of the milk which we saw, to return to him when summoned. He would put it through this ventilator at the hour that he thought best, with the certainty that it would crawl down the rope and land on the bed. It might or might not bite the occupant, perhaps she might escape every night for a week, but sooner or later she must fall a victim.

"I had come to these conclusions before ever I had entered his room. An inspection of his chair showed me that he had been in the habit of standing on it, which of course would be necessary in order that he should reach the ventilator. The sight of the safe, the saucer of milk, and the loop of whipcord were enough to finally dispel any doubts which may have remained. The metallic clang heard by Miss Stoner was obviously caused by her stepfather hastily closing the door of his safe upon its terrible occupant. Having once made up my mind, you know the steps which I took in order to put the matter to the proof. I heard the creature hiss as I have no doubt that you did also, and I instantly lit the light and attacked it."

"With the result of driving it through the ventilator."

"And also with the result of causing it to turn upon its master at the other side. Some of the blows of my cane came home and roused its snakish temper, so that it flew upon the first person it saw. In this way I am no doubt indirectly responsible for Dr.
Grimesby Roylott's death, and I cannot say 23
that it is likely to weigh very heavily upon my conscience."

23 **Discussion** How surprised were you by the ending? Had you any ideas as to the cause of Miss Stoner's death?

Enrichment Encourage your students to read other stories by Sir Arthur Conan Doyle. Discuss the observation powers of Sherlock Holmes. How is he different from private investigators on television or in the movies?

Reader's Response Holmes believes it is dangerous to reason from insufficient data. Support his belief with an example from your own experience.

Closure and Extension

ANSWERS TO THINKING ABOUT THE SELECTION

Recalling

1. Fearing for her life, she has come to ask Holmes, as she says, to "advise me how to walk amid the dangers which encompass me."
2. From the return ticket in her hand, Holmes notes that Helen has come to London by train. From the mud on her left sleeve, he deduces that she traveled to the train station in a dogcart. From the fingerprint bruises on her wrist, he deduces that she has been "cruelly used" by her stepfather.
3. Soon after his wife's death, Dr. Roylott abandons plans for resuming his practice in London and moves with his stepdaughters to his ancestral home at Stoke Moran.

   Helen's mother bequeathed her annual income of £1000 entirely to her husband for as long as her daughters resided with him. Upon marrying, each daughter was to be provided with "a certain annual sum."
4. Helen reports having heard a low whistle followed a few moments later by a clanging sound. Her sister's last words were: "Oh Helen! It was the band! The speckled band!"
5. Having followed Helen, Dr. Roylott warns Holmes not to meddle in his private affairs and threatens Holmes with violence if he does. Holmes remains unperturbed and says the visit adds zest to the investigation.
6. They spend the night in Helen's room in total darkness, quietly waiting for Dr. Roylott to make his move against Helen, whom Holmes has safely sent to her old room.
7. The speckled band is a swamp adder, a poisonous snake resembling a yellow band with brownish speckles.

Interpreting

8. Holmes had thought that Julia's last words referred to the band of gypsies encamped on Dr. Roylott's estate and to the spotted handkerchiefs that they customerily wore on their heads. Holmes's interpretation is an example of reasoning from insufficient data because he makes his conjecture prematurely, before reviewing all the evidence.
9. Like Julia, Helen is planning to marry. Helen now sleeps in the bed that Julia occupied on the night of her death. Furthermore, Helen has heard the low whistle that Julia had heard.
10. These items provide the avenue for the snake to travel from Dr. Roylott's room to his victim's bed. The snake traveled through the ventilator, down the rope, and onto the bed anchored beneath it.
11. Holmes shows a keen interest in

THINKING ABOUT THE SELECTION

Recalling

1. Why has Helen Stoner come to see Holmes?
2. What does Holmes learn about Helen by observing her?
3. What does Dr. Roylott do shortly after his wife's death? What are the terms of her will?
4. What two sounds did Helen hear after she was awakened by her sister's scream? What are her sister's last words?
5. Why does Dr. Roylott pay a visit to Holmes? How does Holmes react to Roylott's visit?
6. How do Holmes and Watson spend the night at Stoke Moran?
7. What is the speckled band?

Interpreting

8. What had Holmes thought was the significance of Julia's last words? How is this an example of reasoning from insufficient data?
9. Name three ways that Helen's situation now is similar to Julia's just before Julia's death.
10. Explain the significance of the dummy bell rope, the ventilator leading to Dr. Roylott's room, and the bed anchored to the floor in Julia's room.
11. Explain the significance of each of the four clues Holmes finds in Roylott's room.
12. What is Roylott's motive for the crimes?
13. How does Roylott's plan backfire?

Applying

14. Sherlock Holmes uses his powers of observation well. Name three ways to improve your own powers of observation.

ANALYZING LITERATURE

Examining Conflict

Conflict is a struggle between opposing forces or characters. One type of conflict involves a struggle of one character with another. Often the characters are fairly evenly matched.

1. How does Roylott prove his physical strength? How does Holmes prove to be his match?
2. In what way does Holmes's nerve, or courage, help him win the conflict?
3. How does his superior intellect help him win?
4. What does Holmes say that indicates he recognizes nerve and intellect in Dr. Roylott?

CRITICAL THINKING AND READING

Understanding Logical Reasoning

A detective reasons in a logical way to solve a crime. Holmes uses a process of elimination. First he gathers all the information he can about Julia's death. Then he tests each piece of information to see if it leads to the truth. If not, Holmes eliminates it from his thinking. For example, when Holmes realizes that gypsies could not have gotten into Julia's room, he stops thinking they might be responsible for her death. In this way, he can focus his skills on fewer and fewer facts or clues, fitting them together in a sequence of events that will lead to the solution.

1. What early clues suggest that Dr. Roylott has something to hide from the authorities?
2. How did you know Dr. Roylott would make an attempt on Helen's life that very night?

THINKING AND WRITING

Understanding Your Thinking

Holmes uses deductive reasoning to solve problems. For example, after observing Helen, he concludes that she drove in a dogcart along heavy roads before reaching the train station. He bases his conclusion on evidence: Her jacket is splattered with fresh mud and the only vehicle that throws up mud that way is a dogcart.

Write the first draft of a composition explaining how you have solved a problem through deductive reasoning, such as solving a television mystery. Revise to make sure your reasoning is clear. Prepare a final draft.

(Answers begin on p. 44.)

Dr. Roylott's large iron safe, a saucer of milk atop the safe, the seat of the wooden chair, and a small dog lash tied into a loop.

The safe is where Dr. Roylott keeps the snake. He uses the saucer of milk to lure the snake back when he whistles. He stands on the chair to coax the snake through the ventilator. He uses the dog lash as a noose to restrain the snake while handling it.

12. Dr. Roylott's motive is greed. By murdering his stepdaughters, he hopes to maintain control over their mother's bequest to them.
13. Instead of Helen, Dr. Roylott becomes the snake's victim when Holmes lashes at it with a cane and chases it back through the ventilator toward Dr. Roylott.

Applying

14. Answers will differ. They might suggest describing what you see to someone else who hasn't seen it, taking notes on what you see, and asking yourself questions about what you see.

ANSWERS TO ANALYZING LITERATURE

1. Dr. Roylott bends Holmes's fireplace poker "into a curve with his huge brown hands." Holmes proves himself Roylott's equal by bending it back to normal.
2. Holmes had deduced that Dr. Roylott will use a snake to try to murder Helen. Nevertheless, he is willing to wait in the dark room for Dr. Roylott to make his move. Holmes displays additional nerve when he lashes out at the snake with his cane.
3. His superior intellect allows him to deduce the facts surrounding the first murder, note the similarities between that murder and Helen's present predicament, and predict Dr. Roylott's next move.
4. He says, "When a doctor does go wrong, he is the first of criminals. He has nerve and he has knowledge."

ANSWERS TO CRITICAL THINKING AND READING

1. Dr. Roylott's murdering of his butler and subsequent imprisonment are bits of personal history he might want to hide from the authorities in England. However, the unexplained death of his wife in a train accident, his hasty departure from London, and his subsequent antisocial behavior suggest that he might have killed his wife to control her money.
2. Julia had heard a low whistle on several nights just before her death, and now Helen has heard that whistle, too. After Holmes deduces exactly how Julia was murdered, he realizes that Dr. Roylott has been trying to murder Helen ever since she moved into Julia's room and will try again that night.

Challenge Point out that even simple, commonplace mysteries depend on deductive reasoning in order to be solved. Ask students if they have ever lost or misplaced something only to find it later. How did they go about finding it? Did they follow a Holmesian process of elimination, or did they proceed haphazardly?

THINKING AND WRITING

For help with this assignment, students can refer to Lesson 20, Writing a Personal Essay, in the Handbook of Writing About Literature.

Publishing Student Writing Have students read aloud their compositions on deductive reasoning. Do the compositions clearly explain the problems that were subsequently solved?

Focus

More About The Author Beryl Markham's father was a scholar, horse breeder, adventurer, and farmer. With his four-year-old daughter, he left England to live in Africa "because it was new and you could feel the future of it under your feet." His daughter inherited from him his fierce independence and love of adventure. Once students have read the story, ask them whether they can see the influence of Markham's father in the story.

Literary Focus Ask students to think of suspenseful stories, novels, movies, or television shows they have enjoyed. Ask them to try to remember if the plots offered hints about events to come. How do such hints add to the suspense of a plot?

Look For Tell students they are about to read an action-packed suspense story. Suggest that, as they read, they identify the words the author chooses to create suspense.

Writing/Prior Knowledge Suggest that, for the freewriting activity, students may use examples of loyalty from fiction, biography, news stories, film, and television as well as from their own experience.

Vocabulary Some students may be unfamiliar with the following words: benevolent (p. 47), frugality (p. 48), lavished (p. 48), futile (p. 48), counterpane (p. 51), flanking (p. 51), stealth (p. 51), tawny (p. 52).

Spelling Tip The word *derisively* follows the general rule for adding the suffix *ly* to change an adjective to an adverb. The spelling of *euphemistically* is irregular in that *al* is added to the adjective *euphemistic* before the suffix.

GUIDE FOR READING

The Captain and His Horse

Beryl Markham (1902–1986) was born in Leicester, England, and raised in Kenya, where she spent her days hunting with the Murani natives and helping her father breed horses. She was the first woman in Africa to obtain a race horse trainer's license. She also had a passion for flying and obtained her pilot's license; in 1936 she made a historic solo flight across the Atlantic. "The Captain and His Horse," her first short story, is based on a true incident which took place in Njoro during World War I.

Suspense and Foreshadowing

Suspense is the quality of a story that makes the reader curious and excited about what will happen next. A suspenseful plot keeps the reader interested in how the plot unravels and what the outcome will be. Beryl Markham creates suspense in the story by maintaining a sense of anticipation while the narrator and the Baron hunt kongoni.

Suspenseful plots often contain **foreshadowing,** clues that hint at later events in the story. In describing the Baron, the narrator calls him a soldier, preparing the reader for what happens to the Baron at the end of the story.

Look For

As you read "The Captain and His Horse," notice the language that creates suspense. Look for details that characterize the suspenseful mood as the characters confront danger. Try to make predictions about what will happen next.

Writing

The characters in "The Captain and His Horse" show loyalty. Freewrite about what loyalty means to you. Include examples of incidents in which you or someone you know has shown loyalty.

Vocabulary

Knowing the following words will help you as you read "The Captain and His Horse."

static (stat′ ik) *adj.*: Not changing or progressing (p. 47)
euphemistically (yo͞o′ fə mis′ ti kə lē) *adv.*: As a less direct term that substitutes for an offensive word or phrase (p. 47)
nebulous (neb′ yə ləs) *adj.*: Vague; unclear (p. 47)
indiscretion (in′ dis kresh′ ən) *n.*: Lack of judgment. (p.49)
plebeian (plē bē′ ən) *adj.*: Common; ordinary (p. 50)
derisively (di rī′ siv lē) *adv.*: As if to ridicule (p. 50)
wistful (wist′ fəl) *adj.*: Expressing vague yearnings (p. 50)
atones (ə tōnz′) *v.*: Makes amends for wrongdoing (p. 55)

Objectives

1 To investigate suspense in a short story
2 To make predictions about the events in a short story
3 To interpret metaphors
4 To write about suspense

Support Material

Teaching Portfolio
Teacher Backup, pp. 67–70
Grammar in Action Worksheet, *Using Demonstrative Pronouns*, pp. 71–72
Usage and Mechanics Worksheet, p. 73
Vocabulary Check, p. 74
Analyzing Literature Worksheet, *Understanding Suspense and Foreshadowing*, p. 75
Critical Thinking and Reading Worksheet, *Making Predictions*, p. 76
Selection Test, pp. 77–78

The Captain and His Horse

Beryl Markham

The world is full of perfectly well-meaning people who are sentimental about the horse. They believe that God in His wisdom charged the horse tribe with two duties; the first being to serve man generally, and the second being to eat lump sugar from the palms of kindly strangers. For centuries the horse has fulfilled these obligations with little complaint, and as a result his reputation has become static, like that of a benevolent mountain, or of an ancient book whose sterling[1] qualities most people accept without either reservation or investigation. The horse is "kind," the horse is
1 "noble." His virtues are so emphasized that his character is lost.

The personalities of many horses have remained in my mind from early East African days. Horses peopled my life then and, in a measure, they still people my memory. Names like these—Cambrian, the Baron, Wee MacGregor—are to me bright threads
2 in a tapestry of remembrance hardly tarnished after all these years.

3 Now there is war, and it is hard to say a thing or think a thing into which that small but most tyrannical of words does not insert
4 itself. I suppose it is because of this that the name of the Baron comes most often to me—because of this and, of course, because, among other things, the Baron was himself a warrior. There was a war, too, 5
when I was a girl of thirteen living on what was euphemistically called a Kenya farm, but which was in fact a handful of cedar huts crouching on alien earth and embraced 6
by wilderness. That was the old war, the nearly forgotten war, but it had the elements of all wars: it bred sorrow and darkness, it bred hope, and it threw strong lights on the souls of men, so that you could see, sometimes, courage that you never knew was there.

Like all wars—like this one—it produced strange things. It brought people together who had never before had a common 7
cause or a common word. One day it brought to my father's farm at Njoro[2] a small company of sick and tired men—mounted on horses that were tired, too—who had the scars of bullets in their flesh.

It goes without saying that the men were cast of heroic stuff. I remember them. A man who has fought for six months in blinding desert heat and stinging desert cold and lives only to fight again has no respect for the word "heroic." It is a dead word, a verbal 8
medal[3] too nebulous to conceal even the smallest wound. Still, you can utter it—you can write it for what it is worth.

1. **sterling** (stʉr′ liŋ) *adj.*: Of high quality; excellent.

2. **Njoro** (ny ōr′ ō) *n.*: Place in Kenya, Africa.

3. **verbal medal:** A word that acts as an award for distinguished action.

Presentation

Motivation/Prior Knowledge Ask students to relate stories from personal experience, books, movies, or television in which a person's life was in danger. What effect did the experience have on the person? Did the person change or gain any insights about life?

Purpose-Setting Question What does the main character learn in this story?

Thematic Idea Other stories containing foreshadowing are "Rain, Rain, Go Away," on page 13, and "A Retrieved Reformation," on page 61.

1 **Discussion** Ask students what the narrator means. Can they think of any people in history of whom we could say the same thing?

2 **Reading Strategy** Ask students to think about why a tapestry is a good representation of the past. What do the "bright threads" of the tapestry stand for?

3 **Clarification** The narrator is referring to World War II.

4 **Reading Strategy** Ask students to explain why the narrator is reminded of the Baron.

5 **Clarification** Tell students that the narrator is referring to World War I. During the War, German troops from German East Africa invaded Kenya, which was controlled by Great Britain.

6 **Discussion** Ask students what the narrator means by "alien earth."

7 **Discussion** Ask students how war might bring such people together.

8 **Discussion** Ask students why some soldiers have no respect for the word "heroic."

9 **Clarification** Explain to students that in this context, the word *husbands* means saves or uses carefully.

10 **Clarification** Explain that a mud-and-daub house is made of dried mud covered with a material such as plaster.

11 **Discussion** Ask students why does the narrator call Africa a "gentle land." Would you describe the part of the world in which you live as gentle? How would you describe it?

Master Teacher Note You might arrange for the class to view Public Broadcasting System's (PBS) documentary, *World Without Walls: Beryl Markham's African Memoir*. Your local public library or public broadcasting station may provide information on how to obtain the video.

But these men came on horses. Each man rode a horse, each was carried to the restful safety of our farm not by an animal, but by his companion, by his battle friend.

"Who are they?" I asked my father.

He is a tall man, my father, a lean man,
9 and he husbands his words. It is a kind of frugality, a hatred of waste, I think. Through all his garnered[4] store of years, he has regarded wasted emotion as if it were strength lavished on futile things. "Save strength for work," he used to say, "and tears for sorrow, and space it all with laughter."

We stood that morning on the little porch
10 of our mud-and-daub house, and I asked my father who these men were with torn clothes and bearded faces and harsh guns in such a gentle land. It is true that leopards came at night and that there were lions to be met with on the plains and in the valleys not
far away. But we had learned to live with 11
these and other beasts—or at least they had learned to live with us—and it seems to me now that it was a land gentle beyond all others.

"They are soldiers of the British army," my father said, "and they are called Wilson's Scouts. It is very simple. They have never seen you before, but they have been fighting for your right to grow up, and now they have come here to rest. Be kind to

4. **garnered** (gär′ nərd) *adj.*: Collected.

them—and above all, see to it that their horses want nothing. In their way, they are soldiers, too."

"I see," I said. But I was a child and I saw very little. In the days that followed, the tired men grew strong again and most of their wounds healed, and they would talk in the
12 evening as they sat around our broad table.
The men would sit under hurricane lamps
13 whose flames danced when a joke was
made, or grew steady again when there was silence. Sometimes the flames would falter, and I could stand in the room for long minutes nursing a failing lamp and hearing what there was to hear.

I heard of a German, General von 14
Lettow-Vorbeck, who, with his Prussian-officered troops based in German East Africa, was striking north to take our country. It seemed that these troops were well-enough trained, that they responded to orders without question, like marionettes responding to strings. But they were lost men; they were fighting British settlers, they were trying to throw Englishmen out of their homes—an
undertaking in which I sensed, even then, 15
the elements of flamboyant ambition, and not a small measure of indiscretion.

They were well-enough trained, these Germans, but, among other things, they had Wilson's Scouts to consider; hard-riding volunteer colonials whose minds were unhampered with military knowledge, but whose hearts were bitter and strong—and free. No, it seemed
to me, as I listened to them, that 16
the enemy they fought was close to his grave. And as things
developed, he was, when I met 17
the Baron, already anticipating its depth.

There was a captain in our small group of cavalrymen, and he would sometimes talk about the Baron—short snatches of talk of the kind that indicated that everybody everywhere must, of course, have heard of him. The captain would say things like this. He would say, "It looked difficult to me. There was a *donga*[5] six feet across and

---

5. *donga* (dăŋ′ gə) *n.*: In South Africa, a channel of water in a large, treeless, grassy area.

12 **Clarification** Tell students that a hurricane lamp is a lantern with a glass cylinder to keep the flame from being blown out.

13 **Discussion** Ask students how they account for the motion or stillness of the flames.

14 **Enrichment** Explain that until World War II, Prussia was the largest and most powerful state in the German Empire, and its armies were among the best drilled and disciplined in the world. Prussian desire for more land was one of the causes of World War I. Now, much of the land once called Prussia lies in East Germany, Poland, and Russia.

15 **Discussion** Explain the difference between the German soldiers and Wilson's Scouts. Ask students who they think would make better soldiers?

16 **Reading Strategy** Ask students to explain in their own words why the narrator thought the Germans would lose the war.

17 **Reading Strategy** Have students specify to what words in the previous sentence do "he" and "its" refer.

18 Clarification Tell students that the expression, "caught one in the shoulder" means that the Baron was shot in the shoulder.

19 Clarification Explain that in this context, the word *jealous* means proud.

20 Discussion Why does the narrator say that the Baron might have been named derisively? Can you think of similar kinds of names for a very small dog, a huge tiger, or a tiny goldfish?

21 Reading Strategy Ask students how this description provides a contrast between the narrator and the Baron. Suggest that students watch for other contrasts between the two as they read.

22 Discussion What might the narrator mean by "big thoughts," and "broad purposes"? What big thoughts might be in the minds of teenagers today?

23 Critical Thinking and Reading Ask students how a horse might prove himself a soldier? What might the narrator mean by "something more"? What can you predict on the basis of this sentence?

24 Enrichment Tell students that Machakos is a city in Kenya that lies southeast of Nairobi, Kenya's capital.

deep with wait-a-bit thorns, and three of the enemy on the other side, but the Baron wasn't worried and so I couldn't be. We cleaned them out after a little skirmish 18 —though the Baron caught one in the shoulder. He holds it still.'' And the other men would shake their heads and drink their drinks, which I knew was just a quiet way of paying tribute to the Baron.

He was the pride of the regiment, of course, but when I first saw him in the stable my father had given him near our thoroughbreds, I was disappointed. I couldn't have helped that; I was used to sensitive, symmetrical, highly strung hors- 19 es, clean-bred and jealous of their breeding.

But the Baron was not like this. He was crude to look at. Surrounded by the aristocrats of his species, the Baron seemed a 20 common animal, plebeian. It was almost as if he had been named derisively. At our first meeting he stood motionless and thoughtful —a dark brown gelding[6] with a boxlike head. There was thick hair around his pasterns and fetlock joints, and he wore his rough coat indifferently, the way a man without vanity, used to war, will wear his tattered tunic.

It is a strange thing to say of a horse, but when I went into the Baron's stable I felt at once both at ease and a little inferior. I think it was his eyes more than anything—they were dark, larger than the eyes of most 21 horses, and they showed no white. It wasn't a matter of their being kind eyes—they were eyes that had seen many things, understanding most of them and fearing none. They held no fire, but they were alive with a glow of wisdom, neither quiet nor fiercely burning. You could see in his eyes that his soul had struck a balance.

He turned to me, not wanting to smell my hair or to beg for food, but only to present himself. His breathing was smooth and unhurried, his manner that of an old friend, and I stroked his thick hard neck that was like a stallion's, because I could think of nothing else to do. And then I left quietly, though there was no need for silence, and walked through one of our pastures and beyond the farm into the edge of the Mau forest, where, if you were a child, it was easier to think.

I thought for a long time, concluding nothing, answering nothing, because there was nothing I could answer.

22 The war, the wounded men, the big thoughts, the broad purposes—all were still questions to me, beyond my answering. Yet I could not help but think that the dark brown gelding standing there in his stable was superior, at least to me, because he made it evident that he had no questions and needed no answers. He was, in his way, as my father had said, a soldier, too.

23 It is easy enough to say such a thing, but as one day nudged another through that particular little corridor of time the Baron proved himself a soldier—and it seems to me now, something more.

I don't think I ever learned the full name of the young captain who owned him, but that was not my fault. There was little formality about Wilson's Scouts. The men at our farm were part of a regiment, but more than that they were a brotherhood. They called their captain ''Captain Dennis'' or just Dennis. Wilson himself, the settler of 24 Machakos who had first brought them together was simply ''F.O.B.'' because those were his initials.

Captain Dennis took the Baron out of his stable one morning, and two of the other men got their horses, and when they were all saddled and bridled—while I leaned against the stable door watching the Baron with what must have been wistful eyes—Captain Dennis led the big gelding over to

6. **gelding** (gel′ diŋ) *n.*: A castrated male horse.

Grammar in Action

Sometimes demonstrative words—words that specify—are used as pronouns. *This, that, these,* and *those* can be used as **demonstrative pronouns.** A demonstrative pronoun may refer to a whole thought rather than to just one or more nouns. As with any pronoun, the writer must be careful that the antecedent (the word or words to which the pronoun refers), is clear to the reader. The antecedent usually precedes the pronoun; however, the pronoun should be close enough to its antecedent so that the reference is clear.

The demonstrative pronoun *this* appears at the end of the following passage from "The Captain and His Horse." As you read over the passage, note to what the word *this* refers.

> The days were clear and many-colored. You could sit in your saddle and look at the huge mountains and at the river valleys, green, and aimless as fallen threads on a counterpane—and you could not count the colors or know them, because some were nameless. Some colors you never saw again, because each day the light was different, and often the colors you saw yesterday never came back. But none of *this* meant much to me that morning.

To what does *this* refer?

me and handed me the reins. The captain was a lanky man with fierce gray eyes and a
25 warm smile that laughed at their fierceness —and I think at me as well.

He said, "You've been watching the Baron like that for weeks and I can't stand
26 it. We're going to shoot kongonis[7] with revolvers from horseback, and you're coming along."

I had a currycomb[8] in my hand and I turned without saying anything and hung the comb on its peg in the stable. When I came out again my father was standing next to the captain with a revolver in his hand. It
27 was a big revolver, and when my father gave it to me he said:

"It's a little heavy, Beryl, but then you never had much fun with toys. What the captain can't teach you, the Baron will. It doesn't matter if you don't hit a kongoni, but don't come back without having learned something—even if it's the knowledge that you can't shoot from horseback."

The captain smiled, and so did my father. Then he kissed me and I mounted the Baron and we rode away from the farm—the captain, two cavalrymen, and myself—through some low hills and down into the Rongai Valley, where the kongonis were.

To say that it was a clear day is to say almost nothing of that country. Most of its days were clear as the voices of the birds that unfailingly coaxed each dawn away from the night. The days were clear and many-colored. You could sit in your saddle and look at the huge mountains and at the river valleys, green, and aimless as fallen
28 threads on a counterpane—and you could not count the colors or know them, because some were nameless. Some colors you never saw again, because each day the light was different, and often the colors you saw yesterday never came back.

But none of this meant much to me that morning. The revolver slung at my waist in a rawhide holster, the broad, straight backs of the cavalrymen riding ahead, the confident pace of the Baron—all these made me feel very proud, but conscious of my youth, smaller, even, than I was.

We hit the bowl of the valley, and in a little while the captain raised his hand, and we looked east into the sun and saw a herd of game about a mile away, feeding in the yellow grass. I had hunted enough on foot to know the tricks: move upwind toward your 29
quarry;[9] keep the light behind you if you can; fan out; be quiet; if there is cover, use it. The captain nodded to me and I waved a hand to show that I would be all right by myself, and then we began to circle, each drifting away from the others, but still joined in the flanking maneuver.

The grass in the Rongai Valley is waist-high and it does not take much of a rise in the plain to hide a man and his horse. In a moment the Baron and I were hidden, and so were the men hidden from us, but the herd of game was just there toward the sun, gathered in a broad clearing—perhaps five thousand head of kongonis, zebras, wildebeests, and oryxes[10] grazing together.

I rode loose-reined, giving the brown gelding his head, watching his small alert ears, his great bowed neck, feeling the strength of his forthright stride—and I felt that he was hunting with me. He moved with stealth, in easy silence, and I dropped my hand to the revolver, self-consciously, and realized that it was really I who was 30
hunting with him.

He was not an excitable horse, yet he

---

7. kongonis (kôŋ′ gə nēz) *n.*: Large African antelopes.
8. currycomb (kʉr′ ē kōm′) *n.*: A circular comb used to groom a horse's coat.

9. quarry (kwôr′ ē) *n.*: An animal being hunted.
10. wildebeests (wil′ də bēsts′) **and oryxes** (or′ iks əs) *n.*: Large African antelopes.

25 **Reading Strategy** The narrator uses a physical description to characterize Captain Dennis. What can students tell about his personality from the description?

26 **Clarification** Explain that kongoni are large, African antelopes armed with curved, spear-sharp horns that may exceed five feet in length.

27 **Discussion** Do you find it unusual that a father would give a young girl a revolver and allow her to hunt? How do you account for his actions?

28 **Enrichment** Markham's description brings to mind the series paintings by Claude Monet (*Rouen Cathedral, Water Lilies, Haystacks*), in which the same scene is depicted in different lights. Showing students reproductions of these paintings will make the description more concrete.

29 **Literary Focus** What parts of this paragraph heighten the suspense of the story?

30 **Discussion** What does the narrator mean?

Student Activity 1. Rewrite the sentence "But none of this meant much to me that morning" substituting a specific phrase for the demonstrative pronoun *this*. How does the use of the pronoun enhance the reading of the passage?

Student Activity 2. Write as Beryl Markham does about a beautiful place you have seen. You might describe a natural scene such as a view from a mountaintop or a quiet place in the woods, or you might choose the interior of a beautiful building you have visited. Use demonstrative pronouns in your description, but be careful not to overuse them, and make sure they are placed correctly.

31 **Discussion** What does this passage tell you about the character of the narrator at the time of the story?

32 **Literary Focus** Ask students how the author creates suspense in these two paragraphs.

33 **Critical Thinking and Reading** Ask students to predict whether the narrator will kill the kongoni. Ask them on what do they base their predictions.

34 **Literary Focus** Ask students how the author builds suspense in this paragraph.

35 **Literary Focus** Ask students to specify what tense the author has been using. Why do they think she shifts to the present? Ask students to watch for the point at which the author switches back to the past.

36 **Discussion** What is the narrator's state of mind? Have you ever been so excited that you have forgotten everything around you?

37 **Clarification** Explain that the men are angry because the narrator has frightened away the herd of animals they were hunting.

seemed to become even more calm as the distance between the game and ourselves narrowed, while I grew more tense. I sat more rigidly upon the back of the Baron than anyone should ever sit upon the back of any horse, but I had the vanity of youth; I was not to be outdone—not even by soldiers.

By the time the identity of the game had become clear—the horns of oryxes reflecting sunlight like drawn rapiers,[11] the ungainly bulk of wildebeests, zebras flaunting their elaborate camouflage, eland[12] and kongonis in the hundreds—by the time the outlines of their bodies had become distinct to my eyes, I was so on fire with anticipation
31 that I had forgotten my companions.

The Baron and I took advantage of what cover there was and crept up on the outer fringe of the herd until we could smell the dust they stirred to motion with their hooves. Then the Baron stopped and I leaned forward in the saddle. I was breathing unevenly, but the Baron scarcely
32 breathed at all.

Not a hundred yards away, a kongoni stood in long grass, half buried in it. The sun was on him, playing over his sleek fawn coat, and he looked like a beast carved from teakwood and polished by age. He was motionless, he was still, he was alert. High in the shoulders, the line that ran sloping to his hips was scarcely curved, and it forewarned us of his strength and his speed.

33 It didn't occur to me that I might have been wiser in choosing a smaller animal. One half as big would have been faster than most horses, with perhaps more endurance, but this one was a challenge I could not resist. In a quick instant of apprehension I
34 peered in all directions, but there was no one near. There were only the Baron, the kongoni, and myself, none of us moving, none of us breathing. Not even the grass moved, and if there were birds they were motionless too.

Leaning low over the Baron's crest, I begin to whisper, smothering my excitement in broken phrases. I ease the reins forward, giving him full head, pressing my hands upon his neck, talking to him, telling 35
him things he already knows: "He's big! He's the biggest of all. He's out of the herd, he's alone, he's ours! Careful, careful!"

The Baron is careful. He sees what I see, he knows more than I know. He tilts his ears, his nostrils distend[13] ever so slightly, the muscles of his shoulders tighten under his skin like leather straps. The tension is so great that it communicates itself to the kongoni. His head comes up and he trembles, he smells the air, he is about to plunge.

"Now!"

The word bursts from my lips because I can no longer contain it; it shatters the stillness. Frightened birds dart into the air, the kongoni leaps high and whirls, but we are off—we are onto him, we are in full gallop, and as the tawny rump of our prey fades into the tawny dust that springs from 36
his heels, I am no longer a girl riding a horse; I am part of the dust, part of the wind in my face, part of the roar of the Baron's hooves, part of his courage, and part of the fear in the kongoni's heart. I am part of everything and it seems that nothing in the world can ever change it.

We run, we race. The kongoni streaks for the open plain. Somewhere to the left there is the drumming of a thousand hooves and the voices of men—angry men with a right to be angry. I have committed the unpardon- 37
able; I have bolted their game, but I can't help it.

11. rapiers (rā′ pē ərz) *n.*: Slender, two-edged swords.
12. eland (ē′ lənd) *n.*: Oxlike African antelopes with spirally twisted horns.

13. distend (di stend′) *v.*: Stretch; expand.

We're on our own now—the Baron and I—and no sense of guilt can stop us.

We gain, we lose, we hold it even. I grope for the revolver at my thigh and pull it from its sheath. I have used one before, but not like this. Always before it has been heavy in my hand, but now it is weightless; now it fits my hand. Now, I think, I cannot miss.

Rocks, anthills, leleshwa bush, thorn trees—all rush past my eyes, but I do not see them; they are swift streaks of color, unreal and evanescent.[14] And time does not move. Time is a marble moment. Only the Baron moves, his long muscles responding to his will, surging in steady, driving rhythm.

Closer, closer. Without guidance the Baron veers to the left, avoiding the dust that envelops the racing kongoni, exposing him to my aim—and I do aim. I raise the gun to shoulder height, my arm sways, I lower it. No. Too far, I can't get a bead. Faster! It's no good just shooting. I've got to hit his heart. Faster! I do not speak the word; I only frame it on my lips, because the Baron knows. His head drops ever so slightly and he stretches his neck a bit more. Faster? There, you have it—this is faster!

And it is. I raise my arm again and fire twice and the kongoni stumbles. I think he stumbles. He seems to sway, but I am not sure. Perhaps it is imagination, perhaps it is hope. At least he swerves. He swerves to the right, but the Baron outgenerals him; the Baron is on his right flank before I can shift my weight in the saddle.

Then something happens. I want to shoot again, but I can't—there's nothing to shoot at. He's gone—our kongoni's gone.
38 He's disappeared as if his particular god had that moment given him wings. The Baron slows, my hand drops to my side and I mumble my frustration, staring ahead.

It's a *donga*, of course—a pit in the plain, deeper than most, crowded with high grass, its sides steep as walls. Our prize has plunged into it, been swallowed in it, and there is nothing to do except to follow.

That's my impulse, but not the Baron's. He looks from side to side, sudden suspicion in his manner, tension in his body. He slows 39
his pace to scarcely more than a canter[15] and will not be urged. At the rim of the *donga* he almost stops. It is steep, but in the high grass that clothes it I can see the wake of the kongoni, and I am impatient.

"There! Get onto him!"

For the first time I slap the Baron with the flat of my hand, coaxing him forward. He hesitates, and there is so little time to waste. 40
Why is he failing me? Why stop now? I am disappointed, angry. I can't return empty-handed. I won't.

"Now then!"

My heels rap sharply against his ribs, my hand is firmer on the reins, my revolver is ready—and the Baron is a soldier. He no longer questions me; surefooted and strong, 41
half walking, half sliding, he plunges over the rim of the *donga* at such an angle that I brace myself in my stirrups and shut my eyes against the plumes of dust we raise. When it is gone, we are on level ground again, deep in grass still studded with morning dew—and the path of the kongoni is clear before us, easy to see, easy to follow.

We have lost time, but this is no place for speed. Our prey is hiding, must be hiding. Now, once more, we stalk; now we hunt. Careful. Quiet. Look sharply, watch every moving thing; gun ready, hands ready.

I'm ready, but not the Baron. His manner has changed. He is not with me. I can feel it. He responds, but he does not anticipate my will. Something concerns him, and

14. evanescent (ev′ ə nes′ ənt) *adj.*: Tending to fade from sight.

15. canter (kant′ ər) *n.*: A smooth, moderate gallop.

38 Reading Strategy Ask students how the tone of the story changes in this passage. How does the author achieve this change in tone?

39 Critical Thinking and Reading Ask students how the Baron's behavior has changed. Why might he be hesitating? What do students predict will happen next?

40 Discussion How would you describe the narrator's actions? Is she being brave or foolish? What would you advise her to do now?

41 Discussion What does the narrator mean by, "the Baron is a soldier"? What are the qualities of a good soldier?

42 Critical Thinking and Reading Ask students what the narrator is catching from the Baron? What does their nervousness foreshadow?

43 Literary Focus Ask students how the author builds suspense in this paragraph. What question do students ask themselves at this point in the story?

44 Reading Strategy Ask students whether this interruption in the action increases or decreases the suspense.

42 I'm getting nervous too—I'm catching it from him. It won't do. It's silly.

I look around. On three sides we are surrounded by steep banks easier to get down than up—and just ahead there's nothing but bush and high grass that you can't see into. Even so there's a way out—straight ahead through the bush. That's where the kongoni went—it's where we'll go.

"Come on!"

43 I jab the Baron's ribs once more and he takes a step forward—a single step—and freezes. He does not tremble. With his ears and his eyes and by the sheer power of his will, he forces me into silence, into rigidity, into consciousness of danger.

I feel and see it at the same moment. Wreathed in leaves of shining grass, framed in the soft green garland of the foliage, there is an immense black head into which are sunk two slowly burning eyes. Upon the head, extending from it like lances[16] fixed for battle, are the two horns of a buffalo. I am young, but I am still a child of Africa—and I know that these, without any question, are Africa's most dreaded weapon.

Nor is our challenger alone. I see that not one but a dozen buffalo heads are emerging from the bush, across our path like links in an indestructible chain—and behind us the walls of the *donga* are remote and steep and friendless. Instinctively I raise my revolver, but as I raise it I realize that it won't help. I know that even a rifle wouldn't help. I feel my meager store of courage dwindle, my youthful bravado[17] becomes a whisper less audible than my pounding heart. I do not move, I cannot. Still grasping the reins, but unaware of them, the fingers of my left hand grope for the Baron's mane and cling there. I do not utter them, but the words are in my heart. I am afraid. I can do nothing. I depend on you!

Now, as I remember that moment and write it down, I am three times older than I was that day in the *donga*, and I can humor my ego, upon occasion, by saying to myself 4
that I am three times wiser. But even then I knew what African buffaloes were. I knew that it was less dangerous to come upon a family of lions in the open plain than to

16. lances (lans′ əz) *n.*: Long wooden weapons with sharp metal spearheads.

17. bravado (brə vä′ dō) *n.*: Pretended courage; false confidence.

come upon a herd of buffaloes, or to come upon a single buffalo; everyone knew it—everyone except amateur hunters who liked to roll the word "lion" on their lips. Few lions will attack men unless they are goaded into it; most buffaloes will. A lion's charge is swift and often fatal, but if it is not, he bears no grudge. He will not stalk you, but a buffalo will. A buffalo is capable of mean cunning that will match the mean cunning of the men who hunt him, and every time he
45 kills a man he atones for the death at men's hands of many of his species. He will gore you, and when you are down, he will kneel upon you and grind you into the earth.

I remember that as I sat on the Baron's back the things I had heard about buffaloes swept swiftly into my mind. I remember fingering the big revolver, suddenly becoming heavy in my hand, while the buffaloes moved closer in strategic[18] order.

18. **strategic** (strə tē′ jik) *adj.*: Having to do with advantageous results.

45 **Clarification** The African buffalo weighs about 1800 pounds and carries five-foot curved horns. It is reputed to be Africa's most dangerous animal. Although it is normally peaceful unless provoked, a buffalo may stalk and charge a human, even without provocation.

46 **Literary Focus** Although the narrator's situation seems hopeless, we know that she will escape, simply because she lives to tell the story. What, then, is the source of suspense? What questions does the author leave unanswered?

47 **Critical Thinking and Reading** The author gives readers a clue as to what will happen next by reminding us of the Baron. How do students predict the narrator will escape?

48 **Discussion** Do you believe that animals can reason? Can you think of any stories from your own experience or from fiction in which an animal acted intelligently?

49 **Discussion** What thoughts might go through your mind if you were in a similarly dangerous situation.

They stood in an almost mathematical semicircle across the only avenue of escape from the *donga.* They did not gather together for the charge, they did not hurry. They did not have to. They saw to it that every loophole was blocked with their horns, and it seemed that even the spaces between their bodies were barred to us by the spears of light that bristled from their bright, black hides. Their eyes were round and small and they burned with a carnelian[19] fire. They moved upon us with slow leisurely steps, and the intensity of their fury was hypnotic. I could not move.

I would not think, because to think was to realize that behind us there was only a wall of earth impossible to climb in time.

As the nearest bull raised his head, preliminary to the final charge, I raised my revolver and with strange detachment, watched my own hand tremble. It wasn't any good. Thinking of my father, fear changed to guilt and then back to fear again, and then to resignation. All right—come
46 on, then. Let's get it over. It's happened to lots of others and now it's going to happen to me. But I had forgotten my companion. All this time the Baron had not moved. Yet
47 neither had he trembled, nor made a sound.

You can find many easy explanations for the things that animals do. You can say that they act out of fear, out of panic, that they cannot think or reason. But I know that this
48 is wrong; I know now that the Baron reasoned, though what he did at the precise instant of our greatest danger seemed born more of terror than of sense.

He whirled, striking a flame of dust from his heels; he reared high into the air until all his weight lay upon his great haunches, until his muscles were tightened like springs. Then he sprang toward the farthest, steepest wall—while behind us came the drumming, swelling thunder of the herd.

For perhaps a hundred yards the *donga* was broad and flat, and then it ended. I remember that the wall of earth loomed so closely in front of my eyes that they were blinded by it. I saw nothing, but just behind us I could hear the low, the almost soothing undertones of destruction. There was a confident, an all-but-casual quality in the sound; not hurried, hardly in crescendo,[20] not even terrifying, just steady—and inescapable.

Another minute, I thought—a whole
minute at least. It's a lot of time, it's sixty 49
seconds. You can do a lot of living in sixty seconds.

And then the Baron turned. I do not know how he turned—I do not know how, running at such speed, he could have turned so swiftly and so cleanly—and I do not know how it was that I stayed in the saddle. I do know that when, at a distance of less than a hundred feet, we faced the onrushing buffaloes once more, they had been beaten, outgeneraled, frustrated, they had lost their battle. An instant ago they had presented an impassable barrier, but now their ranks were spread; now their line was staggered and there were spaces between their beautiful, embracing horns that not one but two horses might have galloped through.

The Baron chose the widest breach and sprinted. He moved toward the open end of the *donga* in great exultant[21] leaps, springing like a reedbuck,[22] laughing in his heart. And when the *donga* was far behind us and the sun was hot on our backs and sweat

19. carnelian (kär nēl′ yən) *adj.*: Having the color of red quartz.

20. crescendo (kri shen′ dō) *adj.*: In music, a gradual increase in loudness and intensity.

21. exultant (eg zult′ ′nt) *adj.*: Triumphant.

22. reedbuck (rēd′ buk′) *n.*: A small African antelope with widely spread hooves and ringed horns.

50 stood on the Baron's flanks, we came slowly up the wagon track that led to the farm.

I remember that my father and Captain Dennis were talking near the doorway of our house when I rode by, and it may have been that they were smiling; I am not sure. But at least I said nothing and they said nothing, 51 and in a few days all the soldiers left, and it

50 **Literary Focus** Now that the narrator is safe, how does the author continue to keep the reader in suspense? What does the reader still want to know about the final outcome?

51 **Discussion** Why do you think the narrator's father says nothing? Do you think he is satisfied that she has learned something? What might he suspect she has learned?

52 Clarification Tell students that World War I ended in 1918.

53 Critical Thinking and Reading Ask students what emotion the Colonel's facial expressions reveal. Do they predict that Captain Dennis survived, or not?

54 Clarification Tell students that the letters CO stand for commissioned officer.

55 Clarification Explain that Kilimanjaro is a mountain in Kenya. Kibo, one of its two peaks, is the highest point in Africa. Kibo peak is always covered with snow and ice about 200 feet deep.

56 Discussion Why did Captain Dennis disobey orders? Do you think he did the right thing? Do you agree that he was a fool?

57 Reading Strategy Ask students to identify the narrator's father's tone? Do they think he believes what he is saying?

58 Literary Focus Ask students what effect does this long silence has on the reader.

59 Discussion How were Captain Dennis, the Baron, and the colonel different from the Prussian soldiers mentioned earlier?

60 Discussion What is the reason for the colonel's anger?

Reader's Response Most of the action of this story takes place when the narrator is thirteen years old, but her experiences and ideas are probably very different from yours. Does this affect your enjoyment of the story? In what ways are you able to relate to the character in spite of the differences?

Cooperative Learning Viewed in one way, "The Captain and His Horse" is a growing-up story. A group of students may want to compile a list of titles, authors,

was not until five years had passed that I heard the Baron's name again.

My father spoke it first. We sat at our table one night, and with us sat the colonel of the East African Mounted Rifles. He was not an imposing man; he was red-faced and he looked a little like the colonels in the cartoons you used to see, though of course he was out of uniform.

52 The war was over and the men had returned to their farms—or some men had. Only a handful of Wilson's Scouts survived, and the colonel and my father talked about that, and then my father asked about Captain Dennis, and the colonel's face got red-
53 der. At least he made a grimace with his lips that could only have meant displeasure.

"Dennis," he said, "ah, yes. We had a lot of confidence in him, but he proved a fool. Went dotty[23] over some horse."

My father and I looked at each other. "The Baron," my father said.

The colonel nodded. "That was it. The Baron—big brute with a head like a cartridge case. I remember him."

"What happened?" said my father.

The colonel coughed. He flipped a large hand over on the table and shrugged. "One
54 of those things. CO sent Dennis through von Lettow's lines one night to pick up a spot of
55 news. It was south of Kilimanjaro. Not nice country, but he got through on that clumsy half-breed of his—or almost got through, that is."

"They got him, did they?" said my father.

"Got him in the face with grenade shrapnel,"[24] said the colonel. "Not fatal though. With a little sense he would have made it. He clung to that horse and the horse brought him almost all the way back. Then Dennis went off his chump.[25] Disobeyed orders. Had to be rescued. Blasted fool."

My father nodded but said nothing.

"Blasted fool," repeated the colonel. "He was within a mile of our lines with all the information we wanted—then he quit."

"It seems hard to believe," I said. 56

"Not at all," said the colonel, looking at me with stern eyes. "It was that horse. The brute suddenly went under. Dennis found he'd been shot in the lung. The Baron went down and Dennis wouldn't leave him—sat there the whole night with his face half shot away, trying first aid, holding the brute's head in his lap." The colonel looked at my father with sudden anger. "He'd disobeyed orders. You see that, don't you?"

My father let a smile, half gay, half sad, twist his lips. "Oh clearly! Orders are orders. No room for sentiment in war. You 57
had Captain Dennis court-martialed,[26] of course?"

A hurricane lamp makes almost no sound, but for a long time after my father's question there was no sound but the sound of our hurricane lamp. It gave a voice to
silence—the colonel's silence. He looked at 58
both of us. He looked at the table. Then he stared at the wrinkled palms of his clumsy hands until we thought he would never utter another word, but he did.

He stood up. "It took a little time," he said, "but finally Dennis recovered—the Baron died with his head toward our guns. In the end I had them both decorated for bravery beyond the call of duty—the captain and his horse. You see," the colonel 59
added angrily, "I'm afraid I'm a blasted fool 60
myself."

---

23. dotty (dät′ ē) *adj.*: Crazy.
24. shrapnel (shrap′ nəl) *n.*: Fragments of an exploded bomb.

25. chump (chump) *n.*: British slang expression meaning insane or crazy.
26. court-martialed (kôrt′ mär′ shəld) *v.*: Tried or convicted in military court for breaking military law.

and brief summaries of other stories they have read in which a character has an experience that results in learning and growth. Post the suggested reading list in the classroom for other students who would like to read more stories with this theme.

Another group may want to compile a similar suggested reading list of stories in which an animal saves a person's life.

Closure and Extension

ANSWERS TO THINKING ABOUT THE SELECTION

Recalling

1. War brings people together who otherwise would have nothing in common.
2. The Baron has the upper hand. Students might support this answer by saying that the Baron became more calm as Beryl grew more tense; or by citing the passages, ". . . it was really I who was hunting with him," and "The Baron is careful. He sees what I see, he knows more than I know."
3. She loses her courage, becomes terrified, feels totally dependent upon the Baron, loses the ability to think, and gives up hope.

THINKING ABOUT THE SELECTION

Recalling

1. According to the narrator, what strange things does the war produce?
2. Who has the upper hand, the narrator or the Baron, in the hunt for kongoni? Explain.
3. What happens to the narrator as she and the Baron are challenged by the buffalo?

Interpreting

4. The narrator calls the word *heroic* "a verbal medal." What does she mean?
5. Why does the narrator trust the Baron?
6. Interpret what the narrator's father means by saying "No room for sentiment in war" when he was discussing Captain Dennis's loyalty to the wounded Baron.
7. What do the narrator and Captain Dennis have in common?
8. The narrator's father tells her not to come back without learning something. Explain what she learns.

Applying

9. Early in the story, the father says, "Save strength for work and tears for sorrow, and space it all with laughter." Interpret what his words mean and explain whether or not you consider them a useful philosophy.
10. Put yourself in Captain Dennis's shoes. When the Baron went down, would you have left him or stayed with him? Explain. If you were the colonel, would you have had Captain Dennis court-marshalled or decorated? Explain.

ANALYZING LITERATURE

Investigating Suspense

When you read this story, did you find yourself sitting on the edge of your seat? Were you excited to find out what would happen next? **Suspense** is the quality of a story that keeps you wondering about the outcome. Sometimes a writer **foreshadows** the outcome by hinting at upcoming events.

1. When does the suspense in this story reach its greatest intensity?
2. Find the hint that foreshadows Captain Dennis's disobedience.
3. List two other examples of foreshadowing.
4. Why do you think people enjoy reading suspenseful stories?

CRITICAL THINKING AND READING

Making Predictions

As you read, you make **predictions,** intelligent guesses, about what will happen next based on evidence. For example, you can predict the approaching danger as you notice the Baron becoming nervous.

1. What helped you predict that the narrator had had an extraordinary experience with the Baron?
2. What did you predict when the Baron refused to move toward the kongoni?

UNDERSTANDING LANGUAGE

Interpreting Metaphors

A **metaphor** is an implied comparison between unlike things. For example, by calling the Baron a soldier, the narrator describes him as having the qualities of a human soldier.

Find and explain the metaphor in the following sentence: "I feel my meager store of courage dwindle, my youthful bravado becomes a whisper less audible than my pounding heart."

THINKING AND WRITING

Writing About Suspense

The writer Max Lerner has said: "The turning point in the process of growing up is when you discover the core strength within you . . ." Discuss this quotation with your classmates. Was there ever a time when you discovered the strength within yourself? Write a composition about an incident that marks your passage from childhood. Revise your composition, making sure you have explained how the incident made you aware that you were growing up. Finally, proofread your paper.

ANSWERS TO ANALYZING LITERATURE

1. Suspense is most intense as the narrator and the Baron are charged by the buffalo.
2. The colonel says that Captain Dennis "proved a fool. Went dotty over some horse."
3. Answers may differ. Students might cite the passage in which Captain Dennis describes how the Baron had once before gotten out of a difficult situation in a donga, or the passage in which the narrator's father tells her, "It doesn't matter if you don't hit a kongoni, but don't come back without having learned something."
4. Students might answer that, because suspense stories are so engrossing, they offer an escape from everyday life; or that they allow us to feel the excitement of danger and adventure absent from most of our lives.

ANSWERS TO CRITICAL THINKING AND READING

1. The narrator says, "the Baron proved himself a soldier—and it seems to me now, something more."
2. Students may answer that they thought the Baron sensed danger.

ANSWERS TO UNDERSTANDING LANGUAGE

The narrator compares her "youthful bravado" to a whispering voice, suggesting that her foolish boastfulness has been silenced.

THINKING AND WRITING

For help with this assignment, students can refer to Lesson 20, "Writing a Personal Essay," in the Handbook of Writing About Literature.

Interpreting

4. She means that the soldiers have earned the right to be called heroic by their courageous actions.
5. She trusts the Baron because she feels he is braver, wiser, and more experienced than she is.
6. He means that, in war, giving in to one's feelings rather than simply following orders may be dangerous. However, he is being facetious; his facial expression reveals that he suspects the colonel of acting on his feelings.
7. They are both courageous and daring, and they share feelings of love and respect for the Baron, who saved both their lives.
8. The narrator learns to think before she acts, to respect the wisdom and experience of others, and to stay calm in the face of danger. In other words, she learns to act as an adult rather than as a child.

Applying

9. The narrator's father is advising her not to overreact to trivial situations, but to expend physical and emotional energy only on important things and to keep sight of the humor in life.
10. Answers will differ.

Writing Across the Curriculum
Many animals native to Africa are unknown in this part of the world. Have students research animals of Africa. You might want to inform the social studies and biology departments of this assignment.

Focus

More About the Author O. Henry's early interest in writing was a result of his education by Evelina, his maiden sister and surrogate mother, after his mother's death. She would begin stories and have her brother add incidents to continue and conclude them. This interest also resulted in his stealing money from the First National Bank in order to continue publishing *Rolling Stone,* a humor magazine he began in 1891. Ask students in what ways might prison life lead to contemplation and writing.

Literary Focus Ask students whether Asimov's "Rain, Rain, Go Away" had a surprise ending. How did Asimov prepare readers for that surprise? Do all surprise endings have to be happy?

Look For Point out that some clues may be red herrings. Remind students, for example, of the gypsies and exotic animals on the Roylott estate in "The Adventure of the Speckled Band."

Writing/Prior Knowledge Remind students that thinking about a story's title is an important part of reading actively. You might have students review the questions for reading actively (page 2) that accompany Saki's "The Story-Teller."

Vocabulary The following words may give your **less advanced** students some difficulty: *compulsory* (p. 55), *chronicled* (p. 55), *genially* (p. 56), *clemency* (p. 56), *sauntered* (p. 59), and *implements* (p. 60).

GUIDE FOR READING

A Retrieved Reformation

O. Henry (1862–1910) was born William Sidney Porter in North Carolina. In his youth he worked as a reporter, a bank teller, and a draftsman. He lived in Austin, Texas, in the country of Honduras, in Pittsburgh, and in New York City. He even spent three years in an Ohio penitentiary. It was there that he wrote his first short stories. It was also there that he learned about a bank robber and a safecracker who became models for Jimmy Valentine, the hero of "A Retrieved Reformation."

The Surprise Ending

Sometimes writers surprise you at the ending of a story. A **surprise ending** is an unexpected twist at the end of a story that you did not predict. Even though an ending is a surprise, it must be believable. Writers make surprise endings believable by giving you a few hints about the ending without giving it away. O. Henry is known for startling his readers with surprise endings.

Look For

As you read "A Retrieved Reformation," look for the clues that point to the surprise ending.

Writing

Look up the words *retrieve* and *reformation* in a dictionary and write their definitions. Then write a paragraph predicting what this story is about by considering its title "A Retrieved Reformation."

Vocabulary

Knowing the following words will help you as you read "A Retrieved Reformation."

assiduously (ə sij′o͞o əs lē) *adv.*: Carefully and busily (p. 61)
eminent (em′ə nənt) *adj.*: Well-known; of high achievement (p. 62)
retribution (re′ trə byo͞o′ shən) *n.*: A punishment deserved for a wrong done (p. 62)
specious (spē′shəs) *adj.*: Seeming to be true without really being so (p. 63)
guile (gīl) *n.*: Craftiness (p. 63)
alterative (ôl′ tə rāt′ iv) *adj.*: Causing a change (p. 63)
unobtrusively (un əb tro͞o′siv lē) *adv.*: Without calling attention to oneself (p. 64)

Objectives

1 To understand the surprise ending of a short story
2 To recognize allusions
3 To use context to find the meanings of words
4 To write about a surprise ending of a short story

Support Material

Teaching Portfolio
Teacher Backup, pp. 79–81
Grammar in Action Worksheets, *Using Dashes,* pp. 82–83; *Understanding Pronoun/Antecedent/Agreement,* pp. 84–85
Usage and Mechanics Worksheet, p. 86
Vocabulary Check, p. 87
Analyzing Literature Worksheet, *Understanding the Surprise Ending,* p. 88
Language Worksheet, *Finding Meanings to Fit the Context,* p. 89
Selection Test, pp. 90–91

A Retrieved Reformation

O. Henry

A guard came to the prison shoe-shop, where Jimmy Valentine was assiduously stitching uppers, and escorted him to the front office. There the warden handed Jimmy his pardon, which had been signed that morning by the governor. Jimmy took it in a tired kind of way. He had served nearly ten months of a four-year sentence. He had expected to stay only about three months, at the longest. When a man with
1 as many friends on the outside as Jimmy
Valentine had is received in the "stir" it is hardly worthwhile to cut his hair.

"Now, Valentine," said the warden, "you'll go out in the morning. Brace up, and make a man of yourself. You're not a bad fellow at heart. Stop cracking safes, and live straight."

"Me?" said Jimmy, in surprise. "Why, I never cracked a safe in my life."

"Oh, no," laughed the warden. "Of course not. Let's see, now. How was it you happened to get sent up on that Springfield
2 job? Was it because you wouldn't prove an
alibi for fear of compromising somebody in extremely high-toned society? Or was it simply a case of a mean old jury that had it in for you? It's always one or the other with you innocent victims."

"Me?" said Jimmy, still blankly virtuous. "Why, warden, I never was in Springfield in my life!"

"Take him back, Cronin," smiled the warden, "and fix him up with outgoing clothes. Unlock him at seven in the morning, and let him come to the bullpen.[1] Better think over my advice, Valentine."

At a quarter past seven on the next morning Jimmy stood in the warden's outer office. He had on a suit of the villainously fitting, ready-made clothes and a pair of the stiff, squeaky shoes that the state furnishes to its discharged compulsory guests.

The clerk handed him a railroad ticket and the five-dollar bill with which the law expected him to rehabilitate himself into
good citizenship and prosperity. The war- 3
den gave him a cigar, and shook hands. Valentine, 9762, was chronicled on the books "Pardoned by Governor," and Mr. James Valentine walked out into the sunshine.

Disregarding the song of the birds, the waving green trees, and the smell of the flowers, Jimmy headed straight for a restaurant. There he tasted the first sweet joys of liberty in the shape of a chicken dinner. From there he proceeded leisurely to the depot and boarded his train. Three hours set him down in a little town near the state line. He went to the café of one Mike Dolan and shook hands with Mike, who was alone behind the bar.

"Sorry we couldn't make it sooner, Jimmy, me boy," said Mike. "But we had

1. **bullpen** *n.*: A barred room in a jail, where prisoners are kept temporarily.

Presentation

Motivation/Prior Knowledge Tell students that O. Henry's stories are known for their surprise endings. In this story, the main character is a bank robber. Ask them to try to predict the "twist" at the end of this story.

Thematic Idea Another selection that deals with the theme of the need for acceptance is "The Man Without a Country" (page 185).

Purpose-Setting Question What role does love play in this story?

1 **Discussion** How would having "friends on the outside" help Jimmy shorten his prison stay?

2 **Discussion** According to the warden, what type of friends does Jimmy have?

3 **Literary Focus** Discuss how O. Henry uses irony in his stories. Calling a prisoner a "compulsory guest" is one example. Have students read the next paragraph to find another example of irony.

4 **Discussion** What is Mike Dolan really asking Jimmy?

5 **Literary Focus** Point out that "a scant eight hundred dollars" is ironic again since this story was written in the early 1900s and eight hundred dollars would hardly have been considered "scant."

that protest from Springfield to buck against, and the governor nearly balked. Feeling all right?"

"Fine," said Jimmy. "Got my key?"

He got his key and went upstairs, unlocking the door of a room at the rear. Everything was just as he had left it. There on the floor was still Ben Price's collar-button that had been torn from that eminent detective's shirt-band when they had overpowered Jimmy to arrest him.

Pulling out from the wall a folding-bed, Jimmy slid back a panel in the wall and dragged out a dust-covered suitcase. He opened this and gazed fondly at the finest set of burglar's tools in the East. It was a complete set, made of specially tempered steel, the latest designs in drills, punches, braces and bits, jimmies, clamps, and augers,[2] with two or three novelties invented by Jimmy himself, in which he took pride. Over nine hundred dollars they had cost him to have made at—, a place where they make such things for the profession.

In half an hour Jimmy went downstairs and through the café. He was now dressed in tasteful and well-fitting clothes, and carried his dusted and cleaned suitcase in his hand.

4 "Got anything on?" asked Mike Dolan, genially.

"Me?" said Jimmy, in a puzzled tone. "I don't understand. I'm representing the New York Amalgamated Short Snap Biscuit Cracker and Frazzled Wheat Company."

This statement delighted Mike to such an extent that Jimmy had to take a seltzer-and-milk on the spot. He never touched "hard" drinks.

A week after the release of Valentine, 9762, there was a neat job of safe-burglary done in Richmond, Indiana, with no clue to the author. A scant eight hundred dollars was all that was secured. Two weeks after 5 that a patented, improved, burglar-proof safe in Logansport was opened like a cheese to the tune of fifteen hundred dollars, currency; securities and silver untouched. That began to interest the rogue-catchers.[3] Then an old-fashioned bank-safe in Jefferson City became active and threw out of its crater an eruption of bank-notes amounting to five thousand dollars. The losses were now high enough to bring the matter up into Ben Price's class of work. By comparing notes, a remarkable similarity in the methods of the burglaries was noticed. Ben Price investigated the scenes of the robberies, and was heard to remark:

"That's Dandy Jim Valentine's autograph. He's resumed business. Look at that combination knob—jerked out as easy as pulling up a radish in wet weather. He's got the only clamps that can do it. And look how clean those tumblers were punched out! Jimmy never has to drill but one hole. Yes, I guess I want Mr. Valentine. He'll do his bit next time without any short-time or clemency foolishness."

Ben Price knew Jimmy's habits. He had learned them while working up the Springfield case. Long jumps, quick getaways, no confederates,[4] and a taste for good society—these ways had helped Mr. Valentine to become noted as a successful dodger of retribution. It was given out that Ben Price had taken up the trail of the elusive cracksman, and other people with burglar-proof safes felt more at ease.

One afternoon, Jimmy Valentine and his suitcase climbed out of the mail hack[5] in

2. drills . . . augers (ô′ gərz): Tools used in metalwork.

3. rogue-catchers *n.*: The police.

4. confederates (kən fed′ər its) *n.*: Accomplices; partners in crime.

5. mail hack: A horse and carriage used to deliver mail to surrounding towns.

Grammar in Action

Dashes are helpful tools for skillful writers. They are used to set off information that is loosely related to the rest of the sentence—not essential, but desired by the writer to make the meaning clearer. Explanations, examples, and interrupting comments can be added to sentences with dashes. Note O. Henry's use of dashes:

Ben Price had learned Jimmy's habits. He had learned them while working up the Springfield case. Long jumps, quick getaways, no confederates, and a taste for good society—these ways had helped Mr. Valentine to become noted as a successful dodger of retribution.

Mr. Ralph Spencer, the phoenix that arose from Jimmy Valentine's ashes—ashes left by the flame of a sudden and alternative attack of love—remained in Elmore, and prospered.

In the first example, the explanation of Jimmy's ways comes at the

Elmore, a little town five miles off the railroad down in the blackjack country of Arkansas. Jimmy, looking like an athletic young senior just home from college, went down the board sidewalk toward the hotel.

A young lady crossed the street, passed him at the corner and entered a door over which was the sign "The Elmore Bank." Jimmy Valentine looked into her eyes, forgot what he was, and became another man. She lowered her eyes and colored slightly. Young men of Jimmy's style and looks were scarce in Elmore.

Jimmy collared a boy that was loafing
6 on the steps of the bank as if he were one of the stockholders, and began to ask him questions about the town, feeding him dimes at intervals. By and by the young lady came out, looking royally unconscious of the young man with the suitcase, and went her way.

"Isn't that young lady Miss Polly Simpson?" asked Jimmy, with specious guile.

"Naw," said the boy. "She's Annabel Adams. Her pa owns this bank. What'd you come to Elmore for? Is that a gold watch chain? I'm going to get a bulldog. Got any more dimes?"

Jimmy went to the Planters' Hotel, registered as Ralph D. Spencer, and engaged a room. He leaned on the desk and declared his platform[6] to the clerk. He said he had come to Elmore to look for a location to go into business. How was the shoe business,
7 now, in the town? He had thought of the shoe business. Was there an opening?

The clerk was impressed by the clothes and manner of Jimmy. He, himself, was something of a pattern of fashion to the thinly gilded[7] youth of Elmore, but he now perceived his shortcomings. While trying to figure out Jimmy's manner of tying his four-in-hand,[8] he cordially gave information.

Yes, there ought to be a good opening in the shoe line. There wasn't an exclusive shoe store in the place. The dry-goods and general stores handled them. Business in all lines was fairly good. Hoped Mr. Spencer would decide to locate in Elmore. He would find it a pleasant town to live in, and the people very sociable.

Mr. Spencer thought he would stop over in the town a few days and look over the situation. No, the clerk needn't call the boy. He would carry up his suitcase, himself; it was rather heavy.

Mr. Ralph Spencer, the phoenix[9] that arose from Jimmy Valentine's ashes—ashes left by the flame of a sudden and 8
alterative attack of love—remained in Elmore, and prospered. He opened a shoe store and secured a good run of trade.

Socially he was also a success, and made many friends. And he accomplished the wish of his heart. He met Miss Annabel Adams, and became more and more captivated by her charms.

At the end of a year the situation of Mr. Ralph Spencer was this: he had won the respect of the community, his shoe store was flourishing, and he and Annabel were engaged to be married in two weeks. Mr. Adams, the typical, plodding, country banker, approved of Spencer. Annabel's pride in him almost equalled her affection. He was as much at home in the family of Mr. 9
Adams and that of Annabel's married sister as if he were already a member.

6. **platform** *n.*: Here, statement of intention.
7. **thinly gilded** *adj.*: Coated with a thin layer of gold: here, appearing well-dressed.
8. **four-in-hand** *n.*: A necktie.
9. **phoenix** (fē′niks), *n.*: In Egyptian mythology, a beautiful bird that lived for about 600 years and then burst into flames; a new bird arose from its ashes.

6 **Discussion** What happens to Jimmy Valentine when he sees the young lady?

7 **Discussion** Where did Jimmy learn about the shoe business?

8 **Discussion** Do you think love has the power to reform people? Do you believe this new character?

9 **Reading Strategy** Have your students summarize the events that have occurred so far in the story and predict what will happen to Ralph Spencer.

end of the sentence; therefore, only one dash is used to separate it from the rest of the sentence. In the second example, the explanation of the ashes is in the middle of the sentence; a dash is needed before and after the nonessential material.

If you are typing or using a word processor, use two hyphens to indicate a dash. When you are writing by hand, make the dash a little longer than a hyphen.

Student Activity 1. Find four other places where O. Henry uses dashes. Discuss the effective use of the dashes. Do you think other punctuation marks would have been better? Do dashes seem to emphasize meaning differently than commas do? If so, how?

Student Activity 2. Write a paragraph describing Jimmy Valentine. Use dashes to set off information that is loosely related to the rest of the sentence.

10 Discussion How do you think Ben Price found Jimmy after more than a year had gone by?

11 Discussion What do you think Ben is planning to do?

12 Discussion Why did Jimmy bring his tools into the bank? Do you think he is planning to rob a bank again?

One day Jimmy sat down in his room and wrote this letter, which he mailed to the safe address of one of his old friends in St. Louis:

> Dear Old Pal:
>
> I want you to be at Sullivan's place, in Little Rock, next Wednesday night, at nine o'clock. I want you to wind up some little matters for me. And, also, I want to make you a present of my kit of tools. I know you'll be glad to get them—you couldn't duplicate the lot for a thousand dollars. Say, Billy, I've quit the old business—a year ago. I've got a nice store. I'm making an honest living, and I'm going to marry the finest girl on earth two weeks from now. It's the only life, Billy—the straight one. I wouldn't touch a dollar of another man's money now for a million. After I get married I'm going to sell out and go West, where there won't be so much danger of having old scores brought up against me. I tell you, Billy, she's an angel. She believes in me; and I wouldn't do another crooked thing for the whole world. Be sure to be at Sully's, for I must see you. I'll bring along the tools with me.
>
> Your old friend,
>
> Jimmy.

On the Monday night after Jimmy wrote
10 this letter, Ben Price jogged unobtrusively into Elmore in a livery buggy.[10] He lounged about town in his quiet way until he found out what he wanted to know. From the drugstore across the street from Spencer's shoe store he got a good look at Ralph D. Spencer.

"Going to marry the banker's daughter are you, Jimmy?" said Ben to himself, softly. "Well, I don't know!"

The next morning Jimmy took breakfast at the Adamses. He was going to Little Rock that day to order his wedding suit and buy
something nice for Annabel. That would be 11
the first time he had left town since he came to Elmore. It had been more than a year now since those last professional "jobs," and he thought he could safely venture out.

After breakfast quite a family party went downtown together—Mr. Adams, Annabel, Jimmy, and Annabel's married sister with her two little girls, aged five and nine. They came by the hotel where Jimmy still boarded, and he ran up to his room and brought along his suitcase. Then they went on to the bank. There stood Jimmy's horse and buggy and Dolph Gibson, who was going to drive him over to the railroad station.

All went inside the high, carved oak railings into the banking-room—Jimmy included, for Mr. Adam's future son-in-law was welcome anywhere. The clerks were
pleased to be greeted by the good-looking, 12
agreeable young man who was going to marry Miss Annabel. Jimmy set his suitcase down. Annabel, whose heart was bubbling with happiness and lively youth, put on Jimmy's hat, and picked up the suitcase. "Wouldn't I make a nice drummer?[11] said Annabel. "My! Ralph, how heavy it is! Feels like it was full of gold bricks."

"Lot of nickel-plated shoehorns in there," said Jimmy, coolly, "that I'm going to return. Thought I'd save express charges by taking them up. I'm getting awfully economical."

---

10. livery buggy: A horse and carriage for hire.

11. drummer *n.*: A traveling salesman.

Grammar In Action

To maintain clarity in your writing, make sure **pronouns** and **antecedents agree.** An antecedent is the noun for which a pronoun stands. Personal pronouns, those that refer to the person speaking, the person spoken to, or the person, place, or thing spoken about, must agree with antecedents in person and number. Person indicates whether a pronoun refers to an individual in the first person, second person, or third person. Number indicates whether a pronoun is singular or plural.

A common agreement error occurs when a pronoun does not have the same person as its antecedent. In the following sentence, a second person pronoun, you, refers to a third person antecedent; "*Jimmy* has decided to take the straight road, the only road *you* can take if you're honest." The sentence should read, "*Jimmy* has decided to take the straight road, the only road *he* can take if he's honest."

Singular antecedents must have singular pronouns, and plural antecedents must have plural pronouns. Notice how O. Henry's pronouns and antecedents agree in number.

The Elmore Bank had just put in a new safe and vault. Mr. Adams was very proud of it, and insisted on an inspection by everyone. The vault was a small one, but it had a new, patented door. It fastened with three solid steel bolts thrown simultaneously with a single handle, and had a time lock. Mr. Adams beamingly explained its workings to Mr. Spencer, who showed a courteous but not too intelligent interest. The two children, May and Agatha, were delighted by the shining metal and funny clock and knobs.

While they were thus engaged Ben Price sauntered in and leaned on his elbow, looking casually inside between the railings. He 13

13 **Reading Strategy** What do you think will happen next?

"After breakfast quite a family party went downtown together—Mr. Adams, Annabel, Jimmy, and Annabel's married sister with *her* two little girls, aged five and nine. *They* came by the hotel where Jimmy still boarded, and *he* ran up to *his* room and brought along *his* suitcase."

In your writing, make sure pronouns agree with antecedents in person and number. In addition, be sure to place pronouns close to antecedents to avoid vague pronoun references.

Student Activity 1. Each of the following pronouns appears in Jimmy's letter on page 64: *them, I, some, another, she.* Identify the antecedent of each pronoun.

Student Activity 2. Locate five more pronouns on pages 64–65, identify their antecedents, and explain how they agree in person and number.

14 **Discussion** What has Jimmy decided to do? Why did he ask for Annabel's rose?

15 **Discussion** Do you think Annabel will still want to marry Jimmy now that she is bound to find out about his past?

16 **Discussion** Are you surprised by Ben's actions? Why did he let Jimmy go free? Is the end of the story satisfying? Point out to students that unless a surprise ending is believable, readers will consider it disappointing and a "cop-out."

Enrichment Suggest to the students that they create their own story, about a "bad" person who goes "good." Allow time for classroom discussion and brainstorming. Perhaps this could even be a group-effort story.

Master Teacher Note Although Ben Price permits Valentine to keep his new identity, Ralph still needs to explain to his fiancée and to her father why he happened to have his burglar tools with him. Will Ralph be able to maintain his reputation as a successful shoe merchant, or will his real identity have to be revealed? Have your students write a final scene to "A Retrieved Reformation" in which Ralph explains why he was able to free little Agatha from the bank vault.

Reader's Response From the surprise ending, we can infer that Ben Price thinks Jimmy has changed his ways. Do you think Jimmy is a reformed citizen? Explain.

told the teller that he didn't want anything; he was just waiting for a man he knew.

Suddenly there was a scream or two from the women, and a commotion. Unperceived by the elders, May, the nine-year-old girl, in a spirit of play, had shut Agatha in the vault. She had then shot the bolts and turned the knob of the combination as she had seen Mr. Adams do.

The old banker sprang to the handle and tugged at it for a moment. "The door can't be opened," he groaned. "The clock hasn't been wound nor the combination set."

Agatha's mother screamed again, hysterically.

"Hush!" said Mr. Adams, raising his trembling hand. "All be quiet for a moment. Agatha!" he called as loudly as he could. "Listen to me." During the following silence they could just hear the faint sound of the child wildly shrieking in the dark vault in a panic of terror.

"My precious darling!" wailed the mother. "She will die of fright! Open the door! Oh, break it open! Can't you men do something?"

"There isn't a man nearer than Little Rock who can open that door," said Mr. Adams, in a shaky voice. "My God! Spencer, what shall we do? That child—she can't stand it long in there. There isn't enough air, and, besides, she'll go into convulsions from fright."

Agatha's mother, frantic now, beat the door of the vault with her hands. Somebody wildly suggested dynamite. Annabel turned to Jimmy, her large eyes full of anguish, but not yet despairing. To a woman nothing seems quite impossible to the powers of the man she worships.

"Can't you do something, Ralph—*try*, won't you?"

He looked at her with a queer, soft
14 smile on his lips and in his keen eyes.

"Annabel," he said, "give me that rose you are wearing, will you?"

Hardly believing that she heard him aright, she unpinned the bud from the bosom of her dress, and placed it in his hand. Jimmy stuffed it into his vest pocket, threw off his coat and pulled up his shirt sleeves. With that act Ralph D. Spencer passed away and Jimmy Valentine took his place.

"Get away from the door, all of you," he commanded, shortly.

He set his suitcase on the table, and opened it out flat. From that time on he seemed to be unconscious of the presence of anyone else. He laid out the shining, queer implements swiftly and orderly, whistling softly to himself as he always did when at work. In a deep silence and immovable, the others watched him as if under a spell.

In a minute Jimmy's pet drill was biting smoothly into the steel door. In ten minutes—breaking his own burglarious record—he threw back the bolts and opened the door.

Agatha, almost collapsed, but safe, was gathered into her mother's arms.

Jimmy Valentine put on his coat, and walked outside the railings toward the front door. As he went he thought he heard a
far-away voice that he once knew call 15
"Ralph!" But he never hesitated.

At the door a big man stood somewhat in his way.

"Hello, Ben!" said Jimmy, still with his strange smile. "Got around at last, have you? Well, let's go. I don't know that it makes much difference, now."

And then Ben Price acted rather strangely.

"Guess you're mistaken, Mr. Spencer," he said. "Don't believe I recognize you. Your
buggy's waiting for you, ain't it?" 16
And Ben Price turned and strolled down the street.

Closure and Extension

ANSWERS TO THINKING ABOUT THE SELECTION

Recalling

1. Valentine was convicted for "cracking safes." The governor grants Valentine clemency because he has "many friends on the outside."
2. He resumes his life of crime as a safecracker.
3. From the pattern of robberies, Ben deduces that the perpetrator must be Valentine and sets out to bring him to justice.
4. Valentine becomes another man when he looks into the banker's daughter's eyes. The change is caused by a "sudden and alterative attack of love."
5. When his fiancée's niece is accidentally locked in a vault, Valentine risks his new way of life to free her.

THINKING ABOUT THE SELECTION

Recalling

1. Why is Valentine in prison? Why is he pardoned?
2. Out of prison, how does Valentine support himself?
3. Why does Ben start looking for Jimmy again?
4. At what point in the story does Valentine become another man? What causes this change?
5. Why does Valentine use his old talents once again?

Interpreting

6. Find three details in the story that support the idea that Valentine really has changed.
7. Why does Ben pretend not to know Jimmy?
8. Explain the meaning of the story's title.

Applying

9. People speak of turning points in their lives, when they seem to change greatly. Can people really change? Support your answer.

ANALYZING LITERATURE

Understanding the Surprise Ending

A **surprise ending** depends on an unexpected resolution of the main conflict. To make the surprise ending believable, authors include hints in the story that point toward the ending.

1. How did you think this story would end? Which clues led you to expect this ending?
2. How did the story really end? What clues did the author plant leading to this ending?

CRITICAL THINKING AND READING

Recognizing Allusions

An **allusion** is a reference in a work of literature to a person, place, or thing in another work, such as literature, art, music, history, painting, mythology. For example, O. Henry writes, "Mr. Ralph Spencer, the phoenix that arose from Jimmy Valentine's ashes—ashes left by the flame of a sudden and alterative attack of love —remained in Elmore, and prospered." The phoenix is a mythical bird that lived in the Arabian wilderness. Every 500 or 600 years it would burn itself up and rise from its ashes anew.

1. In what way is Valentine like a phoenix?
2. How does this allusion help you predict that Valentine is now truly Ralph Spencer?

UNDERSTANDING LANGUAGE

Finding Meanings to Fit the Context

One unabridged dictionary lists thirty-four meanings for the word *serve*. In the following sentence you can tell the appropriate meaning of *served* from its context: "He had *served* nearly ten months of a four-year sentence." Here *serve* means "spent."

Use the context to choose the correct definitions for the following italicized words.

1. "After breakfast quite a family *party* went downtown together. . . ."
   a. social gathering
   b. group of people
   c. defendant in a suit
2. "Or was it simply a *case* of a mean old jury that had it in for you?"
   a. problem
   b. instance
   c. legal claim

THINKING AND WRITING

Writing About A Surprise Ending

Stephen Leacock, a writer and critic, once wrote about O. Henry: "No one better than he can hold the reader in suspense. Nay, more than that, the reader scarcely knows that he is 'suspended,' until at the very close of the story, O. Henry, so to speak, turns on the lights, and the whole tale is revealed as an entirety." Discuss Leacock's statement with your classmates. Then write a paper using examples from the story to agree or disagree with this opinion. Revise your paper to make sure you have organized your support in a logical order. Proofread for correct sentence structure, spelling, and punctuation.

(Answers begin on p. 66.)

ANSWERS TO ANALYZING LITERATURE

1. Answers will differ, depending on how much students read into the story's title. However, the presence of Ben Price, the "eminent detective," and his seemingly chance arrival in Elmore should lead most students to expect that he will arrest Valentine.
2. The story ends surprisingly. Ben Price does not arrest Valentine. The clues to this ending lie mainly in O. Henry's sympathetic characterization of Valentine. Another clue is that Ben does not arrest Valentine immediately. Instead, Price hesitates and observes Valentine in his new identity.

ANSWERS TO CRITICAL THINKING AND READING

1. Honest Ralph Spencer rises phoenixlike from the ashes of dishonest Jimmy Valentine.
2. The allusion implies a permanent, irreversible transformation as well as rebirth and renewal.

ANSWERS TO UNDERSTANDING LANGUAGE

1. b
2. b

Challenge Ask students if they know of any allusions to mythology in the names of spacecraft. Examples include Mercury and Apollo.

Publishing Student Writing Have several students read aloud their paragraphs in class. Discuss whether the paragraphs adequately refer to Leacock's quotation, clearly state the writer's agreement or disagreement, and include sufficient and logical support.

Interpreting

6. Valentine abandons his plans to rob the bank in Elmore. He remains in town and opens a successful shoe store. He writes a letter to an old friend in which he admits to a change and arranges to give away his burglary tools. For the sake of love, he is willing to risk exposure to save his fiancée's niece.
7. Ben Price has observed that Valentine has changed his life. When he witnesses Valentine's rescue of the little girl, he becomes convinced of the change and is willing to allow the reformed criminal to continue leading an honest life as Ralph D. Spencer.
8. In saving the girl, Valentine throws away his new identity as a reformed man. Ben Price retrieves that reformed identity by conspiring to keep Valentine's true identity a secret.

Applying

9. Answers will differ. Students should realize, however, that change, whether in the form of growth or decay, is everywhere in nature and human society.

Focus

More About the Author The *K* in Le Guin's name stands for Kroeber, the surname of her father, a pioneering anthropologist. Her mother, Theodora, was a writer, and her home, as a result of prominent parents, was a gathering place for scientists. Ask students how they think such an environment could influence the future of a young writer.

Literary Focus Have the class recall some fairy tales or Disney movies. What was fantastic in the stories of Hansel and Gretel or Snow White, for example? Could a witch really live in a gingerbread house? Has there ever really been a talking mirror?

Look For Point out that while events in fantasies cannot happen in real life, writers are careful not to stretch details beyond the point of believability.

Writing/Prior Knowledge Some students may not like such stories and can just as easily write their reasons for disliking them. Some students may wish to write about talking animals, such as Garfield, and tell why they are either amusing or tiresome.

Vocabulary Have your **less advanced** students use each word in a sentence orally before reading the story.

GUIDE FOR READING

The Rule of Names

Ursula K. Le Guin (1929–) was born in California and earned her undergraduate and graduate degrees from eastern universities. Her first published writings appeared when she was thirty-two years old. Since then she has received a Science Fiction Writers Award for best short story, a Nebula Award, and a Hugo Award. Le Guin writes mainly science fiction and fantasy. "The Rule of Names," while a complete story on its own, sets the scene for three of Le Guin's later novels.

Fantasy

Fantasy is a type of fiction that is based on the impossible. The plot of a fantasy may take place in an imaginary place, such as a make-believe country, and have imaginary characters, often with supernatural powers, such as wizards. While fantasy is similar to science fiction, it does not need to be based on scientific reality. Instead, it may use magic or other unnatural powers in the plot.

Look For

As you read "The Rule of Names," look for the events that could not possibly happen in real life. Which characters have supernatural powers? How does the author make these characters appear real?

Writing

Why do we like to imagine creatures like dragons and wizards that cannot possibly exist? Freewrite about your answer.

Vocabulary

Knowing the following words will help you as you read "The Rule of Names."

walleyed (wôl′ īd′) *adj.*: Having eyes that turn outward (p. 69)
damask (dam′əsk) *n.*: A fine fabric of silk or linen with a woven design; tablecloth and napkins made of damask (p. 69)
incantation (in′ kan tā′ shən) *n.*: Magic words used to cast a spell (p. 71)
taciturn (tas′ə turn′) *adj.*: Not likely to talk (p. 73)
stolid (stäl′id) *adj.*: Showing little or no emotion (p. 73)
crockery (kräk′ər ē) *n.*: Earthenware dishes, pots, and so on (p. 75)
cataract (kat′ə rakt′) *n.*: Large waterfall (p. 75)
taunted (tônt′əd) *v.*: Jeered at; mocked (p. 76)

Objectives

1 To investigate fantasy in a short story
2 To distinguish between realistic and fantastic details
3 To identify synonyms
4 To write a short fantasy

Support Material

Teaching Portfolio
Teacher Backup, pp. 93–95
Grammar in Action Worksheets, *Using Semicolons*, pp. 96–97; *Varying Sentence Patterns and Sentence Lengths*, pp. 98–99; *Appreciating Degrees of Comparison*, pp. 100–101
Usage and Mechanics Worksheet, p. 102
Vocabulary Check, p. 103
Critical Thinking and Reading Worksheet, *Separating Realistic and Fantastic Details*, p. 104
Language Worksheet, *Identifying Synonyms*, p. 105
Selection Test, pp. 106–107
Art Transparency 1, *St. George and the Dragon*

The Rule of Names

Ursula K. Le Guin

Mr. Underhill came out from under his hill, smiling and breathing hard. Each breath shot out of his nostrils as a double puff of steam, snow-white in the morning sunshine. Mr. Underhill looked up at the bright December sky and smiled wider than ever, showing snow-white teeth. Then he went down to the village.

"Morning, Mr. Underhill," said the villagers as he passed them in the narrow street between houses with conical, overhanging roofs like the fat red caps of toadstools. "Morning, morning!" he replied to each. (It was of course bad luck to wish anyone a *good* morning; a simple statement of the time of day was quite enough, in a place so permeated with Influences as Sattins Island, where a careless adjective might change the weather for a week.) All of them spoke to him, some with affection, some with affectionate disdain. He was all the
1 little island had in the way of a wizard, and so deserved respect—but how could you respect a little fat man of fifty who waddled along with his toes turned in, breathing steam and smiling? He was no great shakes as a workman either. His fireworks were fairly elaborate but his elixirs[1] were weak. Warts he charmed off frequently reappeared after three days; tomatoes he enchanted grew no bigger than cantaloupes; and those rare times when a strange ship stopped at Sattins Harbor, Mr. Underhill always stayed under his hill—for fear, he explained, of the evil eye. He was, in other words, a wizard the way walleyed Gan was a carpenter: by default. The villagers made do with badly-hung doors and inefficient spells, for this generation, and relieved their annoyance by treating Mr. Underhill quite familiarly, as a mere fellow-villager. They even asked him to dinner. Once he asked some of them to dinner, and served a splendid repast, with silver, crystal, damask, roast goose, sparkling Andrades '639, and plum pudding with hard sauce; but he was so nervous all through the meal that it took the joy out of it, and besides, everybody was hungry again half an hour afterward. He did not like anyone to visit his cave, not even the anteroom, beyond which in fact nobody had ever got. When he saw people approaching the hill he always came trotting out to meet them. "Let's sit out here under the pine trees!" he would say, smiling and waving towards the fir grove, or if it was raining, "Let's go have a drink at the inn, eh?" though everybody knew he drank nothing stronger than well-water.

Some of the village children, teased by that locked cave, poked and pried and made raids while Mr. Underhill was away; but the small door that led into the inner chamber was spell-shut, and it seemed for once to be an effective spell. Once a couple of boys,

1. elixirs (i lik′ sərz) *n.*: Magic potions.

Presentation

Motivation/Prior Knowledge Discuss with your students the characteristics of fantasy: the magic of wizards and magicians, the presence of unusual creatures like fire-breathing dragons, and the superstitious beliefs of the characters. Tell students that they are about to enter the magical world of fantasy. As they read this story, ask them to pick out three examples of the elements of fantasy in the plot.

Master Teacher Note The dragon has figured as a mythical beast in the folklore of many European and Asian cultures. Show students Art Transparency 1, *St. George and the Dragon* by Raphael in the Teaching Portfolio. St. George, the patron saint of England, is rescuing a princess from a dragon by slaying the beast with a lance. Have students look at the dragon. How does it compare with their ideas about the appearance and behavior of dragons? Tell them that "The Rule of Names" also features a dragon. Have them notice as they read how the dragon in this story is similar to and different from other dragons.

Purpose-Setting Question Why is the rule of names important?

1 **Reading Strategy** After reading the second paragraph, have students summarize what they have to know about Mr. Underhill. Does he appear to be a skilled, respected wizard? Does he appear to be contented and happy with his life? What does the phrase "affectionate disdain" mean?

Thematic Idea Other selections that deal with the theme of fantasy are "Rain, Rain, Go Away" (page 13) and "The Gift Giving" (page 175).

2 Language Note the use of alliteration. Explain that alliteration is the repetition of an initial sound in two or more words of a phrase or sentence. Have students try writing a sentence describing a person who is angry. Make sure each sentence contains at least two words that start with the same sound.

3 Discussion Does Mr. Underhill seem like the type of wizard who would produce such sounds? Why?

4 Discussion Why do you think the island has these two rules?

thinking the wizard was over on the West Shore curing Mrs. Ruuna's sick donkey, brought a crowbar and a hatchet up there, but at the first whack of the hatchet on the door there came a roar of wrath from inside, and a cloud of purple steam. Mr. Underhill had got home early. The boys fled. He did not come out, and the boys came to no harm, though they said you couldn't believe
2 what a huge hooting howling hissing hor-
3 rible bellow that little fat man could
make unless you'd heard it.

His business in town this day was three dozen fresh eggs and a pound of liver; also a stop at Seacaptain Fogeno's cottage to renew the seeing-charm on the old man's eyes (quite useless when applied to a case of detached retina,[2] but Mr. Underhill kept trying), and finally a chat with old Goody[3] Guld, the concertina-maker's[4] widow. Mr. Underhill's friends were mostly old people. He was timid with the strong young men of the village, and the girls were shy of him. "He makes me nervous, he smiles so much," they all said, pouting, twisting silky ringlets round a finger. "Nervous" was a newfangled word, and their mothers all replied grimly, "Nervous my foot, silliness is the word for it. Mr. Underhill is a very respectable wizard!"

After leaving Goody Guld, Mr. Underhill passed by the school, which was being held this day out on the common. Since no one on Sattins Island was literate, there were no books to learn to read from and no desks to carve initials on and no blackboards to erase, and in fact no schoolhouse. On rainy days the children met in the loft of the Communal Barn, and got hay in their pants; on sunny days the schoolteacher, Palani, took them anywhere she felt like. Today, surrounded by thirty interested children under twelve and forty uninterested sheep under five, she was teaching an important item on the curriculum: the Rules of Names. Mr. Underhill, smiling shyly, paused to listen and watch. Palani, a plump, pretty girl of twenty, made a charming picture there in the wintry sunlight, sheep and children around her, a leafless oak above her, and behind her the dunes and sea and clear, pale sky. She spoke earnestly, her face flushed pink by wind and words. "Now you know the Rules of Names already, children. There are two, and they're the same on every island in the world. What's one of them?"

"It ain't polite to ask anybody what his name is," shouted a fat, quick boy, interrupted by a little girl shrieking, "You can't 4
never tell your own name to nobody my ma says!"

"Yes, Suba. Yes, Popi dear, don't screech. That's right. You never ask anybody his name. You never tell your own. Now think about that a minute and then tell me why we call our wizard Mr. Underhill." She smiled across the curly heads and the woolly backs at Mr. Underhill, who beamed, and nervously clutched his sack of eggs.

"'Cause he lives under a hill!" said half the children.

"But is it his truename?"

"No!" said the fat boy, echoed by little Popi shrieking, "No!"

"How do you know it's not?"

"'Cause he came here all alone and so there wasn't anybody knew his truename so they couldn't tell us, and *he* couldn't—"

"Very good, Suba. Popi, don't shout. That's right. Even a wizard can't tell his truename. When you children are through school and go through the Passage, you'll leave your childnames behind and keep only

---

2. detached retina: A serious visual disorder due to damaged nerve tissue at the back of the eyeball.
3. Goody *n.*:Short form of *goodwife*, a term formerly used for married women of low social standing.
4. concertina (kän′ sər tē′ nə) **maker's** *adj.*: Belonging to the person who makes a musical instrument like a small accordion.

Grammar In Action

Semicolons are most frequently used to join independent clauses that may or may not be connected by the coordinating conjunctions *and, but,* and *or.* In the following sentence from "The Rule of Names," LeGuin uses semicolons to join two independent clauses and a third independent clause beginning with the conjunction and:

"Warts he charmed off frequently reappeared after three days; tomatoes he enchanted grew no bigger than cantaloupes; and those rare times when a strange ship stopped at Sattins Harbor, Mr. Underhill always stayed under his hill . . ."

Semicolons also join independent clauses that are connected by a conjunctive adverb such as *however, for example,* or *thus.* Sometimes semicolons are used to separate independent clauses that are exceptionally long or contain commas as in the following sentence from the story:

"Once he asked some of them to dinner, and served a splendid repast, with silver, crystal, damask, roast goose, sparkling Andrades 639, and plum pudding with hard

Cover of A WIZARD OF EARTH-SEA
Yvonne Gilbert

your truenames, which you must never ask for and never give away. Why is that the rule?"

The children were silent. The sheep bleated gently. Mr. Underhill answered the question: "Because the name is the thing,"
5 he said in his shy, soft, husky voice, "and the truename is the true thing. To speak
6 the name is to control the thing. Am I right, Schoolmistress?"

She smiled and curtseyed, evidently a little embarrassed by his participation. And he trotted off towards his hill, clutching his eggs to his bosom. Somehow the minute spent watching Palani and the children had made him very hungry. He locked his inner door behind him with a hasty incantation, but there must have been a leak or two in the spell, for soon the bare anteroom of the cave was rich with the smell of frying eggs and sizzling liver.

The wind that day was light and fresh out of the west, and on it at noon a little boat came skimming the bright waves into Sattins Harbor. Even as it rounded the point a sharp-eyed boy spotted it, and knowing, like

5 Discussion Why are those rules so important? Why is it important to control something?

6 Enrichment Have your students rename some common objects in the room. Have them use nonsense words to label a chair, table, desk, blackboard, etc. Ask students if their perception of an object's true identity changes with the nonsense renaming. Do words create reality? If we know the right words, can we change or create reality?

Humanities Note

Illustration, cover for *A Wizard of Earth-Sea,* Yvonne Gilbert. British illustrator Yvonne Gilbert is an accomplished artist who has been commissioned to illustrate many book covers. She created this painting for Ursula K. Le-Guin's *A Wizard of Earth-Sea.* The whimsical coloring is suitable to the fantastic nature of the story. Gilbert's use of light and dark serves to draw the eye of the viewer to the figure in the right foreground; though small in scale, this figure becomes the center of interest for the illustration. The unique point of view from above adds interest and drama to the scene.

You might want to ask the following questions to discuss the art:

1. Can you describe what is taking place in this scene?
2. Does the sea serpent seem fearsome to you?

> sauce; but he was so nervous all through the meal that it took the joy out of it, and besides, everybody was hungry again half an hour afterward."

In all cases, semicolons are used to combine related ideas.

Student Activity 1. Identify two other examples of LeGuin's use of semicolons in "The Rule of Names." Explain why semicolons are appropriate in the sentences you found.

Student Activity 2. Compose three sentences in which you correctly use semicolons.

7 **Discussion** Why isn't Mr. Underhill interested in the foreign boat?

8 **Discussion** Why might it be bad to have two wizards in one village?

every child on the island, every sail and spar of the forty boats of the fishing fleet, he ran down the street calling out, "A foreign boat, a foreign boat!" Very seldom was the lonely isle visited by a boat from some equally lonely isle of the East Reach, or an adventurous trader from the Archipelago.[5] By the time the boat was at the pier half the village was there to greet it, and fishermen were following it homewards, and cowherds and clam-diggers and herb-hunters were puffing up and down all the rocky hills, heading towards the harbor.

7 But Mr. Underhill's door stayed shut.

There was only one man aboard the boat. Old Seacaptain Fogeno, when they told him that, drew down a bristle of white brows over his unseeing eyes. "There's only one kind of man," he said, "that sails the Outer Reach alone. A wizard, or a warlock, or a Mage . . ."

So the villagers were breathless hoping to see for once in their lives a Mage, one of the mighty White Magicians of the rich, towered, crowded inner islands of the Archipelago. They were disappointed, for the voyager was quite young, a handsome black-bearded fellow who hailed them cheerfully from his boat, and leaped ashore like any sailor glad to have made port. He introduced himself at once as a sea-peddlar. But when they told Seacaptain Fogeno that he carried an oaken walking-stick around with him, the old man nodded. "Two
8 wizards in one town," he said. "Bad!" And his mouth snapped shut like an old carp's.

As the stranger could not give them his name, they gave him one right away: Blackbeard. And they gave him plenty of attention. He had a small mixed cargo of cloth and sandals and piswi feathers for trimming cloaks and cheap incense and levity stones and fine herbs and great glass beads from Venway—the usual peddlar's lot. Everyone on Sattins Island came to look, to chat with the voyager, and perhaps to buy something—"Just to remember him by!" cackled Goody Guld, who like all the women and girls of the village was smitten with Blackbeard's bold good looks. All the boys hung round him too, to hear him tell of his voyages to far, strange islands of the Reach or describe the great rich islands of the Archipelago, the Inner Lanes, the roadsteads white with ships, and the golden roofs of Havnor. The men willingly listened to his tales; but some of them wondered why a trader should sail alone, and kept their eyes thoughtfully upon his oaken staff.

But all this time Mr. Underhill stayed under his hill.

"This is the first island I've ever seen that had no wizard," said Blackbeard one evening to Goody Guld, who had invited him and her nephew and Palani in for a cup of rushwash tea. "What do you do when you get a toothache, or the cow goes dry?"

"Why, we've got Mr. Underhill!" said the old woman.

"For what that's worth," muttered her nephew Birt, and then blushed purple and spilled his tea. Birt was a fisherman, a large, brave, wordless young man. He loved the schoolmistress, but the nearest he had come to telling her of his love was to give baskets of fresh mackerel to her father's cook.

"Oh, you do have a wizard?" Blackbeard asked. "Is he invisible?"

"No, he's just very shy," said Palani. "You've only been here a week, you know, and we see so few strangers here. . . ." She also blushed a little, but did not spill her tea.

Blackbeard smiled at her. "He's a good Sattinsman, then, eh?"

---

5. archipelago (ar′kə pel′ ə gō′) *n.*: A chain of many islands.

Grammar in Action

Good writers **vary their sentence patterns and sentence lengths** in order to make their writing more interesting. Sentences of the same pattern and length are often tedious and dull; readers find it difficult to concentrate on the passage. On the other hand, sentences with different patterns and lengths help readers stay involved with the passage and communicate the writer's message more successfully.

Read the following passage from "The Rule of Names" and notice the length of sentences and the various ways in which sentences are started by the writer:

> As the stranger could not give them his name, they gave him one right away: Blackbeard. And they gave him plenty of attention. He had a small mixed cargo of cloth and sandals and piswi feathers for trimming cloaks and cheap incense and levity stones and fine herbs and great glass beads from Venway—the usual peddlar's lot. Everyone on Sattins Island came to look, to chat with the voyager, and perhaps to buy something—"Just to remember him by!" cackled Goody

"No," said Goody Guld, "no more than you are. Another cup, nevvy?[6] Keep it in the cup this time. No, my dear, he came in a little bit of a boat, four years ago was it? Just a day after the end of the shad run, I recall, for they was taking up the nets over in East Creek, and Pondi Cowherd broke his leg that very morning—five years ago it must be. No, four. No, five it is, 'twas the year the garlic didn't sprout. So he sails in on a bit of a sloop loaded full up with great chests and boxes and says to Seacaptain Fogeno, who wasn't blind then, though old enough goodness knows to be blind twice over, 'I hear tell,' he says, 'you've got no wizard nor warlock at all, might you be wanting one?' 'Indeed, if the magic's white!' says the Captain, and before you could say cuttlefish Mr. Underhill had settled down in the cave under the hill and was charming the mange off Goody Beltow's cat. Though the fur grew in grey, and 'twas an orange cat. Queer-looking thing it was after that. It died last winter in the cold spell. Goody Beltow took on so at that cat's death, poor thing, worse than when her man was drowned on the Long Banks, the year of the long herring-runs, when nevvy Birt here was but a babe in petticoats." Here Birt spilled his tea again, and Blackbeard grinned, but Goody Guld proceeded undismayed, and talked on till nightfall.

Next day Blackbeard was down at the pier, seeing after the sprung board in his boat which he seemed to take a long time fixing, and as usual drawing the taciturn Sattinsmen into talk. "Now which of these is your wizard's craft?" he asked. "Or has he got one of those the Mages fold up into a walnut shell when they're not using it?"

"Nay," said a stolid fisherman. "She's oop in his cave, under hill."

"He carried the boat he came in up to his cave?"

"Aye. Clear oop. I helped. Heavier as lead she was. Full oop with great boxes, and they full oop with books o' spells, he says. Heavier as lead she was." And the stolid fisherman turned his back, sighing stolidly. Goody Guld's nephew, mending a net nearby, looked up from his work and asked with equal stolidity, "Would ye like to meet Mr. Underhill, maybe?"

Blackbeard returned Birt's look. Clever black eyes met candid blue ones for a long moment; then Blackbeard smiled and said, "Yes. Will you take me up to the hill, Birt?"

"Aye, when I'm done with this," said the fisherman. And when the net was mended, he and the Archipelagan set off up the village street towards the high green hill above it. But as they crossed the common Blackbeard said, "Hold on a while, friend Birt. I have a tale to tell you, before we meet your wizard."

"Tell away," says Birt, sitting down in the shade of a live-oak.

"It's a story that started a hundred years ago, and isn't finished yet—though it 9
soon will be, very soon. . . . In the very heart of the Archipelago, where the islands crowd thick as flies on honey, there's a little isle called Pendor. The sealords of Pendor were mighty men, in the old days of war before the League. Loot and ransom and tribute came pouring into Pendor, and they gathered a great treasure there, long ago. Then from somewhere away out in the West Reach, where dragons breed on the lava isles, came one day a very mighty dragon. Not one of those overgrown lizards most of you Outer Reach folk call dragons, but a big, 10
black, winged, wise, cunning monster, full 11
of strength and subtlety, and like all dragons loving gold and precious stones above all things. He killed the Sealord and his

6. **nevvy** *n.*: *Nephew* in dialect form.

9 Literary Focus Discuss the story within a story. Explain that flashback is a technique in which the writer presents scenes that shift back to an earlier time period. If students have read "Christmas Day in the Morning," ask them to tell about the flashback scene in that story. What other stories have they read that have a flashback?

10 Discussion Have students look at the picture of the dragon on the following pages and give their opinions about its appearance. Is it suitable? Why or why not? Would they change anything?

11 Master Teacher Note Elicit from your students other stories or tales in which a monster or dragon hurts or controls the people. For example, the Grimm brothers wrote several fairy tales involving dragons.

Guld, who like all the women and girls of the village was smitten with Blackbeard's bold good looks. All the boys hung round him too, to hear him tell of his voyages to far, strange islands of the Reach or describe the great rich islands of the Archipelago, the Inner Lanes, the roadsteads with white ships, and the golden roofs of Havnor. The men willingly listened to his tales; but some of them wondered why a trader should sail alone, and kept their eyes thoughtfully upon his oaken staff.

A few of the sentences in the passage above are short; the rest are long and complex. How does each sentence begin?

Student Activity. Write your own paragraph modeling it after the example. Begin it with the same sentence (you may change some of the words if you wish), and follow it with sentences that are similar in structure to those in the passage.

12 **Discussion** Why do you think Blackbeard is on Sattins Island? Who is the wizard Blackbeard is referring to?

13 **Discussion** Why does knowing the wizard's name make Blackbeard mightier?

14 **Discussion** On page 73, the Captain said the people on the island wanted a wizard that performed white magic. Here, Blackbeard learned the name through black magic. What is the difference between these two types of magic?

soldiers, and the people of Pendor fled in their ships by night. They all fled away and left the dragon coiled up in Pendor Towers. And there he stayed for a hundred years, dragging his scaly belly over the emeralds and sapphires and coins of gold, coming forth only once in a year or two when he must eat. He'd raid nearby islands for his food. You know what dragons eat?''

Birt nodded and said in a whisper, ''Maidens.''

''Right,'' said Blackbeard. ''Well, that couldn't be endured forever, nor the thought of him sitting on all that treasure. So after the League grew strong, and the Archipelago wasn't so busy with wars and piracy, it was decided to attack Pendor, drive out the dragon, and get the gold and jewels for the treasury of the League. They're forever wanting money, the League is. So a huge fleet gathered from fifty islands, and seven Mages stood in the prows of the seven strongest ships, and they sailed towards Pendor. . . . They got there. They landed. Nothing stirred. The houses all stood empty, the dishes on the tables full of a hundred years' dust. The bones of the old Sealord and his men lay about in the castle courts and on the stairs. And the Tower rooms reeked of dragon. But there was no dragon. And no treasure, not a diamond the size of a poppy-seed, not a single silver bead . . . Knowing that he couldn't stand up to seven Mages, the dragon had skipped out. They tracked him, and found he'd flown to a deserted island up north called Udrath; they followed his trail there, and what did they find? Bones again. His bones—the dragon's. But no treasure. A wizard, some unknown wizard from somewhere, must have met him single-handed, and defeated him—and then made off with the treasure, right under the League's nose!''

The fisherman listened, attentive and expressionless.

''Now that must have been a powerful 12
wizard and a clever one, first to kill a dragon, and second to get off without leaving a trace. The lords and Mages of the Archipelago couldn't track him at all, neither where he'd come from nor where he'd made off to. They were about to give up. That was last spring; I'd been off on a three-year voyage up in the North Reach, and got back about that time. And they asked me to help them find the unknown wizard. That was clever of them. Because I'm not only a wizard myself, as I think some of the oafs here have guessed, but I am also a descendant of the Lords of Pendor. That treasure is mine. It's mine, and knows that it's mine. Those fools of the League couldn't find it, because it's not theirs. It belongs to the House of Pendor, and the great emerald, the star of the hoard, Inalkil the Greenstone, knows its master. Behold!'' Blackbeard raised his oaken staff and cried aloud, ''Inalkil!'' The tip of the staff began to glow green, a fiery green radiance, a dazzling haze the color of April grass, and at the same moment the staff tipped in the wizard's hand, leaning, slanting till it pointed straight at the side of the hill above them.

''It wasn't so bright a glow, far away in Havnor,'' Blackbeard murmured, ''but the staff pointed true. Inalkil answered when I called. The jewel knows its master. And I know the thief, and I shall conquer him. He's a mighty wizard, who could overcome a
dragon. But I am mightier. Do you want to 13
know why, oaf? Because I know his name!''

As Blackbeard's tone got more arrogant, Birt had looked duller and duller, blanker and blanker; but at this he gave a twitch, shut his mouth, and stared at the Archipelagan. ''How did you . . . learn it?'' he asked very slowly.

Blackbeard grinned, and did not answer. 14

''Black magic?''

''How else?''

Grammar in Action

Adjectives and adverbs can be used to compare two or more nouns or actions that share common characteristics. The different forms that the adjectives and adverbs take are called degrees of comparison. The three degrees are the **positive,** the **comparative,** and the **superlative.**

The positive degree is used when no comparison is made. For example:

> Blackbeard's tone was *arrogant.*

In the following example the comparative degree is used because two things are being compared:

> As Blackbeard's tone got *more arrogant,* Birt had looked *duller and duller, blanker and blanker;* . . .

The superlative degree is used when three or more things are compared:

> Blackbeard's tone was the *most arrogant* tone Birt had ever heard.

Most single syllable words form their comparative and superlative degrees by adding *-er,* and *-est: dull, duller, dullest.* Longer words

Birt looked pale, and said nothing.

"I am the Sealord of Pendor, oaf, and I will have the gold my fathers won, and the jewels my mothers wore, and the Greenstone! For they are mine.—Now, you can tell your village boobies the whole story after I have defeated this wizard and gone. Wait here. Or you can come and watch, if you're not afraid. You'll never get the chance again to see a great wizard in all his power." Blackbeard turned, and without a backward glance strode off up the hill towards the entrance to the cave.

Very slowly, Birt followed. A good distance from the cave he stopped, sat down under a hawthorn tree, and watched. The Archipelagan had stopped; a stiff, dark figure alone on the green swell of the hill before the gaping cave-mouth, he stood perfectly still. All at once he swung his staff up over his head, and the emerald radiance shone about him as he shouted, "Thief, thief of the Hoard of Pendor, come forth!"

There was a crash, as of dropped crockery, from inside the cave, and a lot of dust came spewing out. Scared, Birt ducked. When he looked again he saw Blackbeard still standing motionless, and at the mouth of the cave, dusty and dishevelled, stood Mr. Underhill. He looked small and pitiful, with his toes turned in as usual, and his little bowlegs in black tights, and no staff—he never had had one, Birt suddenly thought. Mr. Underhill spoke. "Who are you?" he said in his husky little voice.

"I am the Sealord of Pendor, thief, come to claim my treasure!"

At that, Mr. Underhill slowly turned pink, as he always did when people were
15 rude to him. But he then turned something else. He turned yellow. His hair bristled out, he gave a coughing roar—and was a yellow
16 lion leaping down the hill at Blackbeard, white fangs gleaming.

But Blackbeard no longer stood there. A gigantic tiger, color of night and lightning, bounded to meet the lion. . . .

THE SEA SERPENT
Arthur Rackham
Arthur Rackham's Book of Pictures

The lion was gone. Below the cave all of a sudden stood a high grove of trees, black in the winter sunshine. The tiger, checking himself in mid-leap just before he entered the shadow of the trees, caught fire in the air, became a tongue of flame lashing out at the dry black branches. . . .

But where the trees had stood a sudden cataract leaped from the hillside, an arch of silvery crashing water, thundering down upon the fire. But the fire was gone. . . .

15 Reading Strategy Encourage students to read this part slowly and visualize these transformations. Have them retell the changes each wizard underwent.

16 Humanities Note Ask students what kind of music should be played for this battle between the formidable wizard adversaries. To capture the magical aspects of their duel, play "Scene III" of Wagner's opera *Das Rheingold* (Deutsche Grammophon, 2740145). Here crashes of lightning and thunder cause clouds to vanish and an arched rainbow bridge to appear.

Humanities Note

Fine Art, *The Sea Serpent,* Arthur Rackham. The notable English illustrator Arthur Rackham (1867–1936) studied drawing at the Lambeth Academy in London. His inventive style won him many commissions throughout his career. The genius of this prolific artist is now fully recognized and his work has been elevated to the status of fine art.

The illustration *The Sea Serpent* is one of twenty-five plates from a collection of Rackham's works, "A Book of Pictures," published in 1913. This delightful composition is done in the "art nouveau" style. The fanciful creature, speeding through the waves with a tiny girl clinging to his back is executed with the graceful flow of line characteristic of Rackham's work. Tiny details, such as the shells and limpets clinging to the serpent and the strand of seaweed flying from the child's foot are what made the work of Charles Rackham so appealing.

You might ask the following questions to discuss the art:

1. Has Rackham shown the serpent as a creature to be feared? Explain.
2. How does the artist's conception of a sea serpent compare with yours?

often form their comparative and superlative forms by using the words *more* and *most: arrogant, more arrogant, most arrogant.*

Student Activity. The following sentences contain adjectives in the positive degree. Rewrite each of them first in the comparative and then in the superlative degree. You will probably have to change the wording slightly or add more words.

1. The principal's tone was demanding.
2. When the test results were announced, the students were hopeful.
3. The guest was rude to his host.
4. The science test was difficult.
5. The English test was simple.
6. The movie star was handsome.

17 Discussion What happened at the climax of the story when Birt's eyes were closed?

18 Discussion How did Mr. Underhill look when he came out of his cave? Ask students how they felt about the ending of the story. Were they surprised, shocked, enchanted?

Enrichment Encourage classroom artists to make drawings of scenes from this story.

Literary Focus Have students go back to the first paragraph and note the use of foreshadowing. Remind students that sometimes an author gives you hints at later events in the plot. What hints are given in the first paragraph about the dragon and Mr. Underhill?

Master Teacher Note Have your **more advanced** students compare "The Rule of Names" to Asimov's "Rain, Rain, Go Away" (page 13). In which ways can both be considered fantasies? Which one contains more realistic details? How do both involve the consequences of making false assumptions about people's appearances? Have students list as many similarities and differences between the two stories as they can discover. This can be done individually or as a group assignment.

Reader's Response Do you agree that "to speak the name is to control the thing"? In your opinion, how important are names?

For just a moment before the fisherman's staring eyes two hills rose—the green one he knew, and a new one, a bare, brown hillock ready to drink up the rushing waterfall. That passed so quickly it made Birt blink, and after blinking he blinked again, and moaned, for what he saw now was a great deal worse. Where the cataract had been there hovered a dragon. Black wings darkened all the hill, steel claws reached groping, and from the dark, scaly, gaping lips fire and steam shot out.

Beneath the monstrous creature stood Blackbeard, laughing.

"Take any shape you please, little Mr. Underhill!" he taunted. "I can match you. But the game grows tiresome. I want to look upon my treasure, upon Inalkil. Now, big dragon, little wizard, take your true shape. I command you by the power of your true name—Yevaud!"

Birt could not move at all, not even to blink. He cowered, staring whether he would or not. He saw the black dragon hang there in the air above Blackbeard. He saw the fire lick like many tongues from the scaly mouth, the steam jet from the red nostrils. He saw Blackbeard's face grow white, white as chalk, and the beard-fringed lips trembling.

"Your name is Yevaud!"

"Yes," said a great, husky, hissing voice. "My truename is Yevaud, and my true shape is this shape."

"But the dragon was killed—they found dragon-bones on Udrath Island—"

"That was another dragon," said the dragon, and then stooped like a hawk, tal-
17 ons outstretched. And Birt shut his eyes.

When he opened them the sky was clear, the hillside empty, except for a reddish-blackish trampled spot, and a few talon-marks in the grass.

Birt the fisherman got to his feet and ran. He ran across the common, scattering sheep to right and left, and straight down the village street to Palani's father's house. Palani was out in the garden weeding the nasturtiums. "Come with me!" Birt gasped. She stared. He grabbed her wrist and dragged her with him. She screeched a little, but did not resist. He ran with her straight to the pier, pushed her into his fishing-sloop the *Queenie*, untied the painter,[7] took up the oars and set off rowing like a demon. The last that Sattins Island saw of him and Palani was the *Queenie*'s sail vanishing in the direction of the nearest island westward.

The villagers thought they would never stop talking about it, how Goody Guld's nephew Birt had lost his mind and sailed off with the schoolmistress on the very same day that the peddlar Blackbeard disappeared without a trace, leaving all his feathers and beads behind. But they did stop talking about it, three days later. They had other things to talk about, when Mr. Underhill finally came out of his cave.

Mr. Underhill had decided that since his truename was no longer a secret, he might
as well drop his disguise. Walking was a lot 18
harder than flying, and besides, it was a long, long time since he had had a real meal.

7. **painter** *n.*: Here, a rope tied to a boat.

Closure and Extension

ANSWERS TO THINKING ABOUT THE SELECTION
Recalling

1. Mr. Underhill is a wizard and cares for the villagers much as a doctor would.
2. His elixirs are weak. His charms for warts wear off quickly. His enchanted tomatoes grow no bigger than cantaloupes.
3. Never ask anyone his name, and never tell your own, because to speak the name is to control the thing.
4. He has come to retrieve a treasure that he claims belonged to his ancestors. He has been guided to the island by his magic staff,

THINKING ABOUT THE SELECTION

Recalling

1. What is Mr. Underhill's role in the village?
2. Give two examples that indicate how well Mr. Underhill performs his job.
3. What are the two Rules of Names?
4. Why does Blackbeard come to Sattins Island? How is he guided there?
5. What shapes does Mr. Underhill take during the battle? What is his true shape?
6. What happens to Blackbeard at the end of the story?

Interpreting

7. Why does Blackbeard feel that knowing Mr. Underhill's true name would enable him to defeat Underhill?
8. What "other things" do the villagers have to talk about at the end of the story?
9. What clues does the author provide throughout the story to Mr. Underhill's true identity?

Applying

10. Explain why names used for people or things do or do not affect the way you feel about them.

ANALYZING LITERATURE

Investigating Fantasy

The elements of **fantasy** include imaginary places, strange characters, and the use of magic and supernatural powers in plots.

1. What powers do the villagers know Mr. Underhill to have?
2. What are his true powers?
3. What powers does Blackbeard have?
4. Why does he lose the battle to Mr. Underhill?

CRITICAL THINKING AND READING

Separating Realistic and Fantastic Details

Although the details in a work of fiction may all be products of the author's imagination, some might possibly happen in life. These are realistic details. Others are simply fantastic; those could not possibly happen in real life. Label the following details from "The Rule of Names" as either realistic or fantastic.

1. "A careless adjective might change the weather for a week."
2. "He loved the schoolmistress, but the nearest he had come to telling her of his love was to give baskets of fresh mackerel to her father's cook."
3. "A stiff dark figure alone on the green swell of the hill before the gaping cave-mouth, he stood perfectly still."
4. "Where the cataract had been there hovered a dragon."

UNDERSTANDING LANGUAGE

Identifying Synonyms

Synonyms are words that mean almost the same thing. *Happy* and *joyful* are synonyms, for example.

Identify the synonym for each italicized word in these sentences:

1. The wizard asked some of the villagers to *dinner* where he served a splendid repast of roast goose.
2. The staff was *leaning,* slanting so that it pointed at the side of the hill.

THINKING AND WRITING

Writing a Fantasy

Think of an event that could not possibly happen in real life. Use it as the plot of a short fantasy. Write your fantasy, including characters and details that will make your story interesting as well as fantastic. When you have written your first draft, revise it to make sure that your ideas are presented clearly and that what you have written is fantasy. Finally, share your fantasy with your classmates.

(Answers begin on page 76.)

which glows and points the way toward one of the jewels when he calls out its name.

5. He takes the shape of a yellow lion, a high grove of trees, a cataract of silvery crashing water, and a blackwinged dragon. The last is his true shape.
6. He disappears or is perhaps killed by the dragon, for nothing remains at the battle site except "a reddish-blackish trampled spot, and a few talonmarks in the grass."

Interpreting

7. As Mr. Underhill explained to the schoolchildren, to speak a name is to control the thing it signifies.
8. They have Mr. Underhill's true shape to talk about and the dragon's appetite for maidens.
9. Clues include the double puff of steam emerging from his nostrils; his horrible roar of wrath and the cloud of purple steam when the boys try to break into his cave; the fact that he lives in a cave; the hoard of heavy and mysterious boxes that he keeps hidden in his inner chamber; the nervous feeling that maidens have whenever he smiles at them.

Applying

10. Answers will differ. Most people are affected by the sounds of names, and names in fiction are often chosen for the effect they will have on a reader's impressions of the characters. You might point out that some fictional names have come to designate particular traits—for example, Scrooge, Romeo, and Pollyanna.

ANSWERS TO ANALYZING LITERATURE

1. They know he has powers over human and animal health and over the growth of crops.
2. His true powers are formidable and destructive, as his changes in shape demonstrate.
3. As a wizard, he has powers comparable to Mr. Underhill's.
4. As a wizard, Blackbeard can match Mr. Underhill's powers. However, Blackbeard's true shape, a Sealord of Pendor, is no match for Mr. Underhill's dragon.

ANSWERS TO CRITICAL THINKING AND READING

1. fantastic
2. realistic
3. realistic
4. fantastic

ANSWERS TO UNDERSTANDING LANGUAGE

1. repast
2. slanting

Challenge Choose and describe three examples of the elements of fantasy in the plot of "The Rule of Names."

THINKING AND WRITING

For help with this assignment, students can refer to Lesson 17, Writing a Short Story, in the Handbook of Writing About Literature.

Publishing Student Writing Have some students draw pictures showing scenes from their fantasies. Make a bulletin board display of these stories and accompanying artwork.

Focus

More About the Author Shirley Jackson first knew fame when, in 1948, the *New Yorker* printed her short story, "The Lottery." Now widely anthologized, the piece brought the magazine its greatest reader response: 450 letters from twenty-five states, two territories, and six foreign countries. Point out that the character Laurie in this story was modeled directly from Jackson's real son. Discuss the importance of a writer's experience in creating fiction and ways of enlarging and making an actual happening into a made-up story.

Literary Focus Have your students glance back at the short stories they have read thus far to decide which one is told in a first-person point of view. Point out that only "The Adventure of the Speckled Band" has a first-person narrator—Watson.

Look For Have students find lines or sentences as they read that show evidence that a mother, rather than a father, is telling the story. For starters, ask if a father would pay as much attention to the boy's clothing as the mother does in the first paragraph.

Writing/Prior Knowledge Before students write, you might have them discuss characteristics that make a person unforgettable. Then have them complete the writing assignment. For extra credit, you might ask students to use their writing as the basis for a formal composition.

Vocabulary Have your less advanced students read the words aloud so you can be sure they can pronounce them.

Spelling Tip Point out that four of these words are adverbs ending in *-ly*. In each of these cases, there is no change in the spelling of the adjective to which the *-ly* is added when forming the adverb.

GUIDE FOR READING

Charles

Shirley Jackson (1919–1965) was born in San Francisco and was graduated from Syracuse University. Jackson was married and had four children. As a writer, she produced mainly two types of stories—spine-tingling tales of supernatural events and hilarious stories about family life. She once said that she wrote because "It's the only chance I get to sit down" and because it gave her an excuse not to clean her closets. The main character in "Charles" is patterned after Jackson's own son Laurie.

Point of View

In writing a short story, the author chooses the character through whose eyes he or she wants you to see the story. **Point of view** is the way an author chooses to see and tell a story. One point of view an author may use is first-person narrative. In a **first-person narrative,** a character tells the story, referring to himself or herself as "I," and presenting only what he or she knows about events.

"Charles" is a first-person narrative, told by Laurie's mother. You learn at the same time as she does about the events in Laurie's kindergarten class.

Look For

As you read "Charles," look for all the details the mother learns about Charles. Think about why the author may have decided to tell her story using first-person narrative point of view.

Writing

"Charles" tells the story of an unforgettable boy. Think about people you know who are unforgettable. What is it that makes them unforgettable? Write about some of the things that make a person unforgettable to you.

Vocabulary

Knowing the following words can help you as you read "Charles."

renounced (ri nounst) *v.*: Gave up (p. 79)
swaggering (swag′ər iŋ) *v.*: Strutting; walking with a bold step (p. 79)
insolently (in′sə lənt lē) *adv.*: Boldly disrespectful in speech or behavior (p. 79)
simultaneously (sī′məl tā′nē əs lē) *adv.*: At the same time (p. 80)
elaborately (i lab′ər it lē) *adv.*: Painstakingly (p. 80)
incredulously (in krej′o͞o ləs lē) *adv.*: With doubt or disbelief (p. 81)
haggard (hag′ərd) *adj.*: Having a tired look (p. 81)

Objectives

1 To understand first-person point of view in a short story
2 To make inferences about the plot
3 To extend the story by writing from a different point of view

Support Material

Teaching Portfolio

Teacher Backup, pp. 109–111
Grammar in Action Worksheet, *Using Dialogue,* pp. 112–113
Usage and Mechanics Worksheet, p. 114
Vocabulary Check, p. 115
Analyzing Literature Worksheet, *Investigating Point of View,* p. 116
Language Worksheet, *Using the suffix -ly to Form Adverbs,* p. 117
Selection Test, pp. 118–119

Charles

Shirley Jackson

The day my son Laurie started kindergarten he renounced corduroy overalls with bibs and began wearing blue jeans with a belt; I watched him go off the first morning
1 with the older girl next door, seeing clearly that an era of my life was ended, my sweet-voiced nursery-school tot replaced by a long-trousered, swaggering character who forgot to stop at the corner and wave good-bye to me.

He came home the same way, the front door slamming open, his cap on the floor, and the voice suddenly become raucous[1] shouting, "Isn't anybody *here?*"

At lunch he spoke insolently to his father, spilled his baby sister's milk, and remarked that his teacher said we were not to take the name of the Lord in vain.

"How *was* school today?" I asked, elaborately casual.

"All right," he said.

"Did you learn anything?" his father asked.

Laurie regarded his father coldly. "I didn't learn nothing," he said.

"Anything," I said. "Didn't learn anything."

"The teacher spanked a boy, though," Laurie said, addressing his bread and butter. "For being fresh," he added, with his mouth full.

"What did he do?" I asked. "Who was it?"

Laurie thought. "It was Charles," he said. "He was fresh. The teacher spanked him and made him stand in a corner. He was awfully fresh."

"What did he do?" I asked again, but Laurie slid off his chair, took a cookie, and left, while his father was still saying, "See here, young man."

The next day Laurie remarked at lunch, as soon as he sat down, "Well, Charles was bad again today." He grinned enormously and said, "Today Charles hit the teacher."

"Good heavens," I said, mindful of the Lord's name, "I suppose he got spanked again?"

"He sure did," Laurie said. "Look up," he said to his father.

"What?" his father said, looking up. 2

"Look down," Laurie said. "Look at my thumb. Gee, you're dumb." He began to laugh insanely.

"Why did Charles hit the teacher?" I asked quickly.

"Because she tried to make him color with red crayons," Laurie said. "Charles wanted to color with green crayons so he hit the teacher and she spanked him and said nobody play with Charles but everybody did."

The third day—it was Wednesday of the first week—Charles bounced a see-saw on to the head of a little girl and made her bleed, and the teacher made him stay inside all during recess. Thursday Charles had to stand in a corner during story-time because he kept pounding his feet on the

---

1. **raucous** (rô′ kəs) *adj.*: Boisterous; disorderly.

Presentation

Motivation Prior Knowledge Ask students if they can remember any impish, naughty children who always seemed to get into trouble when they were in kindergarten. What were some of the things the children did in school? Ask occasionally what tone one of the experiences suggests. Is it funny? Sad? Ironic? Sentimental? Ask your students if Charles is like the children they remember.

Thematic Idea Other selections that deal with humorous characters are "The Day I Got Lost" (page 113) and "My Wild Irish Mother" (page 445).

Purpose-Setting Question Why is Laurie so interested in Charles's behavior?

1 **Discussion** Who is telling the story? What has happened to Laurie since he started kindergarten?

2 **Discussion** How is Laurie behaving toward his father?

3 Discussion Why do you think Laurie stayed after school with Charles?

4 Discussion How do you think Charles's teacher will handle him? Will she punish him? Suspend him? Would the school suspend a kindergartener? How would you deal with Charles if you were his teacher?

5 Discussion How is Charles affecting Laurie's family?

floor. Friday Charles was deprived of blackboard privileges because he threw chalk.

On Saturday I remarked to my husband, "Do you think kindergarten is too unsettling for Laurie? All this toughness, and bad grammar, and this Charles boy sounds like such a bad influence."

"It'll be all right," my husband said reassuringly. "Bound to be people like Charles in the world. Might as well meet them now as later."

On Monday Laurie came home late, full of news. "Charles," he shouted as he came up the hill; I was waiting anxiously on the front steps. "Charles," Laurie yelled all the way up the hill, "Charles was bad again."

"Come right in," I said, as soon as he came close enough. "Lunch is waiting."

"You know what Charles did?" he demanded, following me through the door. "Charles yelled so in school they sent a boy
3 in from first grade to tell the teacher she had to make Charles keep quiet, and so Charles had to stay after school. And so all the children stayed to watch him."

"What did he do?" I asked.

"He just sat there," Laurie said, climbing into his chair at the table. "Hi, Pop, y'old dust mop."

"Charles had to stay after school today," I told my husband. "Everyone stayed with him."

"What does this Charles look like?" my husband asked Laurie. "What's his other name?"

"He's bigger than me," Laurie said. "And he doesn't have any rubbers and he doesn't ever wear a jacket."

Monday night was the first Parent-Teachers meeting, and only the fact that the baby had a cold kept me from going; I wanted passionately to meet Charles's mother. On Tuesday Laurie remarked suddenly, "Our teacher had a friend come to see her in school today."

"Charles's mother?" my husband and I asked simultaneously.

"Naaah," Laurie said scornfully. "It was a man who came and made us do exercises, we had to touch our toes. Look." He climbed down from his chair and squatted down and touched his toes. "Like this," he said. He got solemnly back into his chair and said, picking up his fork, "Charles didn't even *do* exercises."

"That's fine," I said heartily. "Didn't Charles want to do exercises?"

"Naaah," Laurie said. "Charles was so fresh to the teacher's friend he wasn't *let* do exercises."

"Fresh again?" I said.

"He kicked the teacher's friend," Laurie said. "The teacher's friend told Charles to touch his toes like I just did and Charles kicked him."

"What are they going to do about
Charles, do you suppose?" Laurie's father 4
asked him.

Laurie shrugged elaborately. "Throw him out of school, I guess," he said.

Wednesday and Thursday were routine; Charles yelled during story hour and hit a boy in the stomach and made him cry. On Friday Charles stayed after school again and so did all the other children.

With the third week of kindergarten Charles was an institution in our family; the baby was being a Charles when she cried all afternoon; Laurie did a Charles when he filled his wagon full of mud and
pulled it through the kitchen; even my 5
husband, when he caught his elbow in the telephone cord and pulled the telephone and a bowl of flowers off the table, said, after the first minute, "Looks like Charles."

During the third and fourth weeks it looked like a reformation in Charles; Laurie reported grimly at lunch on Thursday of the third week, "Charles was so good today the teacher gave him an apple."

Grammar in Action

Grammatical rules for **dialogue** require exact positioning of other punctuation marks with quotation marks. Quotation marks separate dialogue from the narration of the story. Commas are most commonly used to separate the spoken words from the explanatory phrase; however, when the spoken words are in question form, a question mark must be used.

Notice the punctuation that Shirley Jackson uses in the following excerpt:

"Charles's mother?" my husband and I asked simultaneously.

"Naaah," Laurie said scornfully. "It was a man who came and made us do exercises, we had to touch our toes. Look." He climbed down from his chair and squatted down and touched his toes. "Like this," he said. "He got solemnly back into his chair and said, picking up his fork, "Charles didn't even *do* the exercises."

"That's fine," I said heartily. "Didn't Charles want to do exercises?"

"What?" I said, and my husband added warily, "You mean Charles?"

"Charles," Laurie said. "He gave the crayons around and he picked up the books afterward and the teacher said he was her helper."

"What happened?" I asked incredulously.

"He was her helper, that's all," Laurie said, and shrugged.

"Can this be true, about Charles?" I asked my husband that night. "Can something like this happen?"

"Wait and see," my husband said cynically.[2] "When you've got a Charles to deal with, this may mean he's only plotting." He seemed to be wrong. For over a week Charles was the teacher's helper; each day he handed things out and he picked things up; no one had to stay after school.

"The PTA meeting's next week again," I told my husband one evening. "I'm going to find Charles's mother there."

"Ask her what happened to Charles," my husband said. "I'd like to know."

"I'd like to know myself," I said.

On Friday of that week things were back to normal. "You know what Charles did today?" Laurie demanded at the lunch table, in a voice slightly awed. "He told a little girl to say a word and she said it and the teacher washed her mouth out with soap and Charles laughed."

"What word?" his father asked unwisely, and Laurie said, "I'll have to whisper it to you, it's so bad." He got down off his chair and went around to his father. His father bent his head down and Laurie whispered joyfully. His father's eyes widened.

"Did Charles tell the little girl to say *that?*" he asked respectfully.

"She said it *twice,*" Laurie said. "Charles told her to say it *twice.*"

"What happened to Charles?" my husband asked.

"Nothing," Laurie said. "He was passing out the crayons."

Monday morning Charles abandoned the little girl and said the evil word himself three or four times, getting his mouth washed out with soap each time. He also threw chalk.

My husband came to the door with me that evening as I set out for the PTA meeting. "Invite her over for a cup of tea after the meeting," he said. "I want to get a look at her."

"If only she's there," I said prayerfully.

"She'll be there," my husband said. "I don't see how they could hold a PTA meeting without Charles's mother."

At the meeting I sat restlessly, scanning each comfortable matronly face, trying to determine which one hid the secret of Charles. None of them looked to me haggard enough. No one stood up in the meeting and apologized for the way her son had been acting. No one mentioned Charles.

After the meeting I identified and sought out Laurie's kindergarten teacher. She had a plate with a cup of tea and a piece of chocolate cake; I had a plate with a cup of tea and a piece of marshmallow cake. We maneuvered[3] up to one another cautiously, and smiled.

"I've been so anxious to meet you," I said. "I'm Laurie's mother."

"We're all so interested in Laurie," she said.

"Well, he certainly likes kindergarten," I said. "He talks about it all the time."

"We had a little trouble adjusting, the

---

2. cynically (sin′ i k′l ē) *adv.*: With disbelief as to the sincerity of people's intentions or actions.

3. maneuvered (mə no͞o′ vərd) *v.*: Moved in a planned way.

In the first paragraph, the quoted material is a question; therefore, a question mark to end the quotation is placed inside the last quotation mark. There is a period at the end of the entire statement.

In the second paragraph, Laurie's first statement is an interjection. It is followed by a comma and then the quotation mark. A period follows the explanatory phrase. Notice that when Laurie begins speaking again, a new set of quotation marks is needed, and the dialogue continues in the same paragraph.

Notice the repetition of this pattern in the third paragraph.

Student Activity. Write your own dialogue in which you use commas, periods, and question marks with quotation marks. Make up a dialogue similar to Laurie's in which you relate a school experience. You might begin with: "Guess what! You'll never believe what ______ did in school today!" I exclaimed as I roared through the door.

first week or so," she said primly, "but now he's a fine little helper. With occasional lapses, of course."

"Laurie usually adjusts very quickly," I said. "I suppose this time it's Charles's influence."

"Charles?"

"Yes," I said, laughing, "you must have your hands full in that kindergarten, with Charles."

"Charles?" she said. "We don't have any Charles in the kindergarten." 6

THINKING ABOUT THE SELECTION

Recalling

1. Give three examples of Charles's poor behavior in school.
2. Give three examples of Laurie's poor behavior at home.
3. How does Charles's teacher deal with him?
4. What does Laurie's mother learn when she goes to the PTA meeting?

Interpreting

5. Why did Laurie act the way he did in school?
6. What clues to Laurie's behavior in school can you find in his behavior at home?
7. Why do you think Laurie invented Charles?

Applying

8. Imagine you were Laurie's parent. What would you do about Laurie's behavior?

ANALYZING LITERATURE

Investigating Point of View

"Charles" is a **first-person narrative.** A character, Laurie's mother, tells the story. As the narrator, she uses language such as "my son" and "I said." The plot reveals information only as Laurie's mother learns it. The story's ending is as much of a surprise to her as it is to you.

1. Before the PTA meeting, how does Laurie's mother learn about incidents in school?
2. Why is a first-person point of view effective for developing the plot of "Charles"?

CRITICAL THINKING AND READING

Making Inferences About the Plot

An **inference** is a conclusion based on evidence. Sometimes an author does not state directly everything that is happening. The reader must make inferences based on clues given. For example, the author does not tell you directly that Laurie's behavior at home changes after he starts kindergarten, but you infer it.

Find and list four clues from which you can make the inference that Charles is Laurie.

THINKING AND WRITING

Writing from Another Point of View

Make a list of several questions you might want to ask the parents of Laurie if you were his kindergarten teacher. Use the questions to write a new scene at the PTA meeting between Laurie's mother and his teacher. Instead of writing the episode from the point of view of Laurie's mother, write your episode from the point of view of Laurie's teacher. The pronouns "I" and "me" will refer to the teacher in your scene. Remember that she knows only about what has happened at school.

Revise your story to make sure you have maintained a consistent point of view. Finally, proofread your story and share it with your classmates.

6 **Discussion** Were you surprised by the ending? When did you first suspect that Charles and Laurie were the same person?

Reader's Response Why do you think children Laurie's age have active imaginations? Were you especially imaginative when you were five? Explain.

Closure and Extension

ANSWERS TO THINKING ABOUT THE SELECTION

Recalling

1. Examples of Charles's poor behavior include being "awfully fresh," hitting the teacher, bouncing the seesaw on the head of a classmate, throwing chalk, yelling in class, kicking the gym instructor, hitting a classmate in the stomach, and using profanity.
2. Examples of Laurie's poor behavior at home include slamming the door, speaking insolently to his father, and filling his wagon with mud and pulling it through the kitchen.
3. She spanks him, makes him stand in the corner, deprives him of blackboard privileges, makes him stay after school, and washes his mouth out with soap.
4. She learns that there is no boy named Charles in the class.

Interpreting

5. Answers will differ. Laurie was probably testing the limits of his teacher's endurance.
6. Laurie's behavior at home is essentially the same as Charles's behavior in school.
7. Answers will differ. Laurie probably invented Charles because he has mixed feelings about his behavior. He knows his parents would disapprove if they knew the truth. Nevertheless, he is pleased that Charles is able to draw so much attention to himself.

Applying

8. Answers will differ. Some may opt for Laurie's teacher's methods. Others may suggest confronting Laurie and admonishing him.

ANSWERS TO ANALYZING LITERATURE

1. She gets her information only from Laurie.
2. It gives the plot the illusion of truth, as if the events described actually happened to the "I" of the story. As a result, the fictional story seems to be nonfiction.

ANSWERS TO CRITICAL THINKING AND READING

When his mother first learns of Charles and asks what he did that was fresh, Laurie is reluctant to answer, as if he has something to hide. When his father asks about Charles's appearance and last name, Laurie is evasive and responds vaguely. When Charles's behavior temporarily improves, so do Laurie's table manners. We never actually "see" Charles. The only evidence that he exists is hearsay.

THINKING AND WRITING

Publishing Student Writing As students read aloud their new scene, have the rest of the class keep the following questions in mind.

1. Does the scene shift the first-person point of view from Laurie's mother to the teacher?
2. Is the new point of view consistent with the teacher's limited knowledge of Laurie?

Character

WOMAN WITH PARASOL
Claude Monet
Scala/Art Resource

Humanities Note

Fine art, *Woman with Parasol,* 1875, by Claude Monet. Claude Monet (1840-1926) was one of the most prominent of the French Impressionist painters. Impressionism was a movement in painting characterized by the breaking down of form and light into flecks of color. Monet is often considered the purest of the Impressionist painters. The title of one of his paintings, *Impression: Sunrise,* inspired the name of the entire movement, Impressionism. Monet's belief in painting out of doors, directly onto the canvas, did much to redefine the fixed concepts of painting at the end of the nineteenth century.

In *Woman with Parasol,* the models were Monet's wife and their son Jean. The painting is not a portrait so much as a study of the effects of strong sunlight on figures and landscape. The features and outlines of the figures are blurred by the intensity of the light. Yet a portrayal of character comes through. The variety of colors used in the grassy bank is apparent upon close examination but is blended by the eye into a more homogeneous hue when viewed from a distance. The artist painted with frantic speed to try to record the light before it changed. The resulting directness and spontaneity truly capture the essence of a bright and breezy summer scene.

Master Teacher Note To introduce the element of character in stories, show Art Transparency 2, *Farewell to Lincoln Square* by Raphael Soyer, from the Teaching Portfolio. Have students look at the people in this painting. Ask by what means the artist made each person individual. What might be the character of the girl in the center of the painting, as revealed by her functional clothing, downcast expression, and dispirited posture? How do the expressions of the other characters reveal what they are thinking or feeling? What is the effect of the artist's use of color on the mood of the painting? You might then ask how writers, without visual means, create characters in stories.

Focus

More About the Author Many of Paul Boles's plays were written for radio, a genre he much admired. Have students discuss some of the problems producers of radio plays have to contend with: conveying setting; choosing sound effects; and suggesting costumes. What advantage do television plays have over those on radio? What qualities are important for actors in each medium—voice, age, and appearance?

Literary Focus Have students work in small groups to develop characters who demonstrate certain traits, such as courage, snobbery, shyness, or generosity. Each group should select one trait and construct a short skit in which a principal character's words and actions clearly reveal that trait. The rest of the class can then try to identify the trait.

Look For Point out to your **less advanced** students that the narrator will be Mitch and that he will describe Bridgie's character in great detail. Explain that Mitch will not describe himself as vividly. Direct students to focus on Mitch's actions and reactions to Bridgie in order to discover his character traits.

Writing/Prior Knowledge Remind students to use examples of their character's words and actions to support the trait that they assign to the person.

Vocabulary Most students will have no difficulty with these words. You might have them use each word in a sentence orally before reading the story.

GUIDE FOR READING

The House Guest

Paul Darcy Boles (1916–1984) was born in Ashley-Hudson, Indiana, and was the author of novels, short stories, plays, and criticism. Some of his short stories were first published in magazines. Among these stories was "The House Guest," which first appeared in *Seventeen* in 1975. During that year, the problems of unrest and conflict in Northern Ireland were frequently reported in the news. The house guest in this story is a young girl from Northern Ireland.

Character Traits

Character traits are the qualities that make up a character's personality. For example, a character may be honest, generous, stubborn, or scheming. You can discover these character traits through a character's actions and words and through the writer's description of the character. Some characters may show only one major character trait, while others, like real people, show a number of different traits.

Looking For

As you read "The House Guest," pay attention to the characters of Bridgie and Mitch. Look for the ways in which their character traits are revealed. What are they like? Do you think you would enjoy knowing them?

Writing

"The House Guest" tells of a young Irish girl who comes to live with an American family for a few weeks and touches their lives. Think of someone you have met who stands out in your mind. List that person's character traits in order of importance—from what is most outstanding about the person to what is least memorable. Then describe the person's full character.

Vocabulary

Knowing the meaning of the following words will help you as you read "The House Guest."

intern (in'tərn) *n.*: A doctor serving a training period in a hospital after completing medical school (p. 85)

mammoth (mam'əth) *adj.*: Huge (p. 87)

crooning (kro͞on'iŋ) *adj.*: Singing or humming in a low, gentle way (p. 90)

mutual (myo͞o' cho͞o əl) *adj.*: Having the same relationship toward each other (p. 90)

Objectives

1 To understand how character traits are revealed in a short story
2 To compare and contrast characters
3 To combine sentences by using contrasting words as connectives
4 To write a letter

Support Material

Teaching Portfolio

Teacher Backup, pp. 121–123
Grammar in Action Worksheet, *Using Transitions*, pp. 124–125
Usage and Mechanics Worksheet, p. 126
Vocabulary Check, p. 127
Analyzing Literature Worksheet, *Understanding Character Traits*, p. 128
Critical Thinking and Reading Worksheet, *Comparing and Contrasting Characters*, p. 129
Selection Test, pp. 130–131
Art Transparency 3, *Seated Girl with Dog*, by Milton Avery

The House Guest

Paul Darcy Boles

I'm writing this at the downstairs desk where I do homework or just fool around. It's the same desk Bridgie used to come up to and stand behind sometimes. After a second or so I would feel her standing there. Then I would turn around, making it slow because she's a kid you don't want to scare. She has big dark blue eyes, red hair about the color of the sun before it's really up. She doesn't have much of a chin; her cheekbones are high and like smooth little rocks under the clear skin. She's no beauty. I mean, she's just what she is.

When I turned around and she was there as I'd thought, I would say, "Can I help you, Bridgie?" She would shake her head; she'd just wanted to see if *I* was all right. And when she'd made sure I was, she would just turn around and walk off. My mother and father told me she did the same thing with them: stood and looked
1 at them for a couple of seconds, then walked off . . . satisfied they were still themselves and handy.

She was only with us for six short weeks. It was one of these red-tape deals through the United States government: you
2 signed up to keep a kid from Northern Ireland in your home as a guest. The idea was to show the kids what America was like, as if anybody could do that even in six years. Anyhow, I was all for it; my brother is an intern and he's working in Rome for a year, and I never had a sister.

The night Bridgie first came, after my parents brought her from the city to our town, she didn't talk much at all. I don't mean she ducked her head or looked awk- 3
ward or fiddled with her feet or hid behind the furniture. It was just that she clammed up.

She had a small green bag with some extra clothes in it and an old doll that had been whacked around quite a bit. That was the whole works, except for the clothes she wore. Next day my mother took her to a couple of shops in town and bought her some new stuff. She still wasn't talking a lot, only pleases and thank-yous, and when my mother took the new clothes out of the boxes to hang them up, Bridgie touched them, very politely, as if they belonged to somebody else and she shouldn't make any fuss. She was nine years old.

At first it kept on being kind of eggshelly
around her. You see, we weren't supposed to 4
ask her anything heavy about how things were in the place she'd come from. She'd been born in Belfast, grew up there. She had four brothers and two sisters. She was next
to the oldest. Her mother had died a year 5
and a half before and her father took care of the family the best he could.

We got all that from the bunch of statis-

Presentation

Motivation/Prior Knowledge Ask your students if they have ever known a foreigner visiting the United States. What did these people notice about the people and places they visited?

Purpose-Setting Question Would you like to know this guest?

Master Teacher Note Many stories have been written about dogs. Show Art Transparency 3, *Seated Girl with Dog* by Milton Avery in the Teaching Portfolio. Ask students how they think the girl feels about the dog, and why. What are other examples of stories involving people and dogs?

1 **Discussion** What does this tell you about Bridgie?

2 **Clarification** Discuss with students the strife in Northern Ireland between the Catholics and Protestants. In 1920 the British Parliament divided Ireland into two separate countries. The southern countries, inhabited by Catholics, became an independent nation: the Irish Republic. The northern county of Ulster, largely Protestant, remained part of Great Britain. Protestant Irish in Northern Ireland did not want to become part of the Irish Republic. But many Catholics in Northern Ireland wanted a United Ireland. Catholic discontent led to violence on both sides in 1969.

3 **Enrichment** To appreciate the fear in a traumatized child, you might read excerpts from *Children in Conflict: Growing Up in Northern Ireland* by Morris Fraser.

4 **Discussion** What does "being kind of eggshelly" mean?

5 **Enrichment** Bring in photographs of the violence in Northern Ireland that can occur almost every day. How might such civil strife affect the way a child grows up?

6 **Discussion** What is a "noble idea"? Do you think this was a wise plan?

7 **Discussion** What do these two paragraphs tell you about Bridgie's life in Northern Ireland?

8 **Discussion** Note that she refers to herself as a kid then when at the time of this story she is only nine years old. What does that tell you about "kids" in Northern Ireland? Do you think there might be places in the United States where children grow up much faster than if they lived elsewhere?

9 **Discussion** What is meant by "big, iron reasons"?

tics that came before we even saw her. The people running this show wanted the kids to "fit easily into the American environment" without being pestered. I guess that was a
6 noble idea, but it left an awful lot you couldn't say or ask.

You can hear a good deal of traffic from our dining room, not anything thunderous, but backfires and people pretending they're A.J. Foyt[1] when they zoom down the street. And a couple of times at dinner when this happened, you could see Bridgie stiffen up. She'd get quiet as a rabbit, and it wasn't even that so much as it was the way she looked out of the corners of her eyes. As if
7 she were searching for a neat, dark place to hide in.

It didn't wreck her appetite, though. I don't mean she was a born pig, I just mean she always ate fast and never left anything on the plate. Oh, sure, my mother is a decent cook, but this was a different thing. I noticed she never asked for second helpings, either, but she'd take them when they were handed to her, even if she looked kind of amazed about getting them.

It was not until the third day she was with us that she really started to open up a little. We were all sitting around yakking after the evening's parade of news on TV. There had been a clip of a building, or what was left of it, that had been bombed in Dublin. The commentator had said, in that level voice they use for good news, terrible news and in between, that the trouble was moving out of Belfast, that it wasn't "contained" anymore. Bridgie had been sitting straight as six o'clock, hands in her lap, and suddenly she said, "My da was in Dublin the once."

There was a good-sized stop in the talk; then my mother asked, "Did he go on a holiday?"

She gave her head a small shake. She wore her hair in two braids wound tight around her head like pale silk ropes. "Nah, ma'am. He went there in a van to help his mate he worked with down at the docks. His mate was movin' to Dublin. When my da come back he brought us a dog."

"What kind?" I asked. "What'd he look like?"

Her eyes went a pretty fair distance
away, "Ah, I was a kid then. I hardly remem- 8
ber ut." She looked around blinking, her eyes that same way, as if she were looking into the fireplace where the fire was jumping around in some pine logs and trying to see backward. Then she said, "But soft he was, with fine ears that stuck up when he was happy." She turned back from the fire and her shoulders went up in little wings, shrugging. "He come up missin' inside the week though. My ma never took to him, him makin' messes and all. But he couldn't o' helped it, so young."

That night after Bridgie had been tucked in bed by my mother in the room next to my parents', I asked my mother whether we could adopt Bridgie or something. My mother said that wasn't possible, she'd already asked about it. Bridgie's family needed her
too much, for one thing. There were a lot of 9
those big, iron reasons. After my mother explained them we just sat there thinking about her. I kept wishing it was the kind of world where I happened to be President, or anyhow head of the State Department or something, and could cut through some rules.

The next day was Saturday. My mother took Bridgie into the city for lunch and a flick and some sight-seeing. The flick was something made for kids, very ha-ha, and my mother said that all through it Bridgie sat without moving and not laughing either,

1. **A. J. Foyt:** A race-car driver.

Grammar in Action

Writers use **transitions** to make clear the relationship between ideas. Transitions link ideas and guide the reader through a passage. Transition words and phrases can show chronological order, order of importance, comparison and contrast, and other relationships between ideas.

On these pages the writer uses a number of transition words to move the action through several days:

It was not *until the third day* . . .

. . . *then* my mother asked . . .

That night after Bridgie had been tucked in bed . . .

After my mother explained . . .

The next day was Saturday . . .

After that . . .

Finally they got to the crafts part of the store . . .

. . . so *a few nights after that* I talked her into going ice skating with me down at the lake.

with the buttered-popcorn-and-soft-drink bunch hollering around them.

She liked the Carl Akeley elephants and the stuffed-looking Eskimo families in the Field Museum, but the thing she liked best was a bunch of puppies in a pet-shop window. She had to be just about dragged away. "But we can't get her a dog; it would be too cruel when she had to give it up," my mother said. "She couldn't take it back to Ireland . . ."

After that my mother took her to one of the mammoth toy stores. She walked her through the doll section, but Bridgie wasn't hot about dolls. "I've got the one already," she said. "Ut's good enough."

THE CLOTH DOLL
Robert Duncan

Humanities Note

Fine Art, *The Cloth Doll,* Robert Duncan. *The Cloth Doll* by American artist Robert Duncan is a touching portrait of girlhood. The child, in a somewhat vulnerable, contemplative pose, is surrounded by traditionally feminine objects—a broom, a wide gardening hat, and a shelf of jars. The doll in her lap may symbolize a child she may one day bear.

The placement of the girl, facing left, serves to draw the viewers attention to her. The eye is led from the upper left to the top of the head by the corner of the shelf. The mass of the figure and blank wall is counter-balanced by the chair and broom on the right. The importance of the sundry objects in the painting is diminished by their totality being cropped from the picture plane. This device further serves to focus our attention on the girl. You might want to ask students the following questions about the art:

1. Based on her pose and what we can see of her expression, what might the girl be thinking and feeling?
2. Does this girl remind you of Bridgie?

The use of these transitions helps to connect the events logically through time. Skillful writers use transitions throughout their writing; however, they do not need to include transitions in all of their paragraphs.

Student Activity 1. Read through the rest of the story and write down all of the transition words and phrases that you can find.

Student Activity 2. Write a paragraph in which you describe a series of related events. Use transition words to show the logical connection between the events. You might describe how your baseball team scored four runs in the bottom of the ninth inning to win the game. Or you might describe the events on the night of October 31 (Halloween). Make up your own series of events to describe. Be sure that they follow one after the other.

10 **Discussion** Why is this family doing so much for Bridgie? Is it just because they feel sorry for her? Is it because they feel it is their "duty"?

11 **Discussion** What do you think she is making?

12 **Discussion** Contrast Mitch's ability to walk around his neighborhood and Bridgie's inability to do so in Northern Ireland. Explain that districts, or neighborhoods, in Northern Ireland are often armed camps separating the warring factions from one another.

Finally they got to the crafts part of the store, and there Bridgie finally found something she was really warm for. It was a big leatherworking set with a lot of colored chunks of leather in red, blue, green and yellow, and the knives and tooling instruments and all the rest. It was about the most advanced leatherworking set I'd ever seen, and I asked Bridgie if she'd like me to help her get started with it.

"Nah," she said, "I'm quick at the readin' and I can soak in the directions. Don't put yourself out for me, Mitch."

I wanted to put myself out for her all right, though, so a few nights after that I talked her into going ice skating with me down at the town lake. She didn't exactly skate when we got there, but I pushed her around on the skates I rented for her. After a while it started to snow, and going home I carried Bridgie on my back and she carried my skates. I pranced like a horse in the snow and once I heard her laugh.

But on the porch back home when I was brushing snow off her shoulders she said, "I shouldn't 'a gone. I've missed out a whole night o' my leatherin'."

"That's supposed to be fun too," I said. "Like skating. How're you coming with it?"

"I'm learnin'," she said. "It went slow at the first. Them directions was set down by a blitherin' lump. But now I'm swarmin' around it." Then she said, fast, "Please, Mitch, I'd like a place to work outside the fine room where I do my sleepin'."

I'd happened to look in that room and see her working, chewing her tongue and frowning and fierce. She'd been so into it she hadn't even seen me. Now she said, "It's not the need o' elbow room, there's plenty o' that. It's I'm afraid o' carvin' up the pretty floor. There's the workshop out in your garage, the one next to where ya keep the ottomobiles. It's even got the heater, if ya could spare the oil for that."

I swept out the workroom and got the heater jets open and working the next morning 10 before I went to school. It was a place I'd spent a whole lot of my own time in as a young child, working like a fiend on model airplanes and boats. When I got home that afternoon I found she'd spent most of the day out there; I walked out of the back door and went to the workroom window, but she wasn't inside. Then she came around the corner of the garage from the lane in back of it. Her hair was mussed and she looked as though she'd been doing a hundred-yard dash. "Ah, I had to take me a walk," she said. "Ut gets scrooged up, laborin' so over the bench the many hours."

I started into the workroom to turn off the lights, but she ran ahead of me. "Here, I'll do ut." She flipped them off. I could see she didn't want me to see what she was making. She shut the door. On the way back to the house she said, looking at the ground, "Ya won't peach[2] on me? Ya won't tell? Sometimes I just like swingin' around the 11 neighborhood. I won't get lost and shame ya."

We were almost at the back porch steps. She said, "It's fine, walkin' where ya please. Not havin' to stay in the District."

"District?" I said.

"Ah, that's the boundaries. You don't go past 'em unless you're a fool bent on destruction. The District is where you and your people stay inside of."

I'd never even started to think how it would be living inside a few blocks and not 12 stepping over a line. I did then.

She was out in the workroom the next day after breakfast; my mother told me she came in for lunch and then swept right out again. She did the same thing after dinner

2. peach *v.*: To inform against someone.

till I went out and called her in because it was her bedtime. My mother said she was a little worried about all this hangup with leathercraft, but my father said, "Maybe privacy is the rarest thing we can give her," and my mother gave in to that. I didn't tell them about the walks around the neighborhood; Bridgie could take care of Bridgie, all right.

A couple of days before it was time for her to go back—something we weren't mentioning, any of us—my mother and father sailed off in the evening to visit some town friends. Then about nine-thirty my mother called to tell me they were going to stay longer than they'd planned, and to be sure to get Bridgie in from the workroom by around ten. After that, though, the phone rang again; it was some mad, dashing girl I'd been interested in for what seemed a hundred years. It wasn't till we'd finally said good night that I sat up and noticed it was ten-thirty.

I bolted[3] out in the night, down the back porch steps and yelled for Bridgie. There wasn't any answer; the whole night seemed quiet as a piece of white steel. I crunched

3. **bolted** *v.*: Dashed out suddenly.

STREET VISTA IN WINTER
Charles Burchfield
Kalamazoo Institute of Arts

Humanities Note

Fine Art, *Street Vista in Winter,* Charles Burchfield. The American painter Charles Burchfield (1893–1967) studied at the Cleveland Institute of Art. Teachers there were profoundly impressed by his work and encouraged him to develop his intense, personal style of painting. He is remembered today for his emotional, inventive landscape studies and dramatic, evocative portrayals of buildings.

Street Vista in Winter is another of the many midwestern street views painted by Charles Burchfield. There is no life on this street except the bleak glare of the winter sun. The blank faces of the houses lurk behind the inky trunks of the bare trees. Over all is an aura of expectancy. As with all of Burchfield's work, *Street Vista in Winter* does more than merely record a snowy winter street. You might ask students what the painting suggests to them. For example, does it suggest loneliness and isolation? You might also ask students if they have seen similar scenes where they live or where they have visited.

13 Discussion What is so touching about what she is saying to the dog? What does this tell you about Bridgie and her sense of values? What does this tell you about her ability to care and to love?

14 Discussion Note the mention of government control. Is this something we think of often?

15 Discussion How do you think Bridgie reacted to the bombing?

Reader's Response Would you like to spend a summer or some period of time living with a family in a foreign country? Why or why not? If you were to live in another country temporarily, where would you like to live and why?

Master Teacher Note Ask why the United States has always been a haven for people in need. Have students relate any knowledge of exchange students or refugees living with United States families. Discuss the humanitarian effort in giving homes and new lives to refugees from Vietnam and Cambodia.

through the snow that had fallen the day before and looked in at the workroom window. The bench light was off.

A second later, I saw her footprints, leading back to the lane.

Halfway down the lane, though, the footprints started to get mixed up with tire tracks and were harder to make out. But that was all right because by then I could see Bridgie herself. She was easy to spot, down at the end of the lane where the boulevard started and not far from the streetlight, kneeling down beside a ribby old black and tan dog. The dog looked as though it might have had Airedale in it, along with four or five other breeds; on its hind legs it would have been about as tall as Bridgie was.

She didn't turn around, maybe didn't hear me, when I came up closer. She was fitting a new collar around the dog's neck. It was acting pretty patient; she talked to it in a kind of low crooning-scolding way. "Hold your head up," she was saying. "You'll be proud and solid as the Rock of Cashel now,
13 and don't be tryin' to scrape ut off or lose ut. Ut's your ticket to some fine homes. They'll feed ya up. They'll think ya been a pet, they'll b'lieve you're valuable . . ."

About that time, she saw me. She gave the green leather collar another pat, just the same, before she stood up. It was tooled with a lot of careful flowers, and I recognized one of the brass buckles from the giant leatherworking set.

"Well, you've caught me out," she said. "That was the last of the leather, so ut's just as well. I fitted out an even dozen creatures. It was hard findin' 'em all, some I had to folla for blocks. But none had the collars before, and now they have. It makes their chances o' havin' a home much grander. You're not angered?"

I didn't say anything. I just stuck a hand down to her and she took it. We went back along the lane. She said, "The collar's a kind o' door key. Ya'd be faster to take in a dog with a collar, wouldn't ya, now?" I still didn't say anything and she looked up at me. "There's no hard feelin's, for the immense cost o' the leatherin' outfit?"

I said, "It's okay, Bridgie."

Then I lifted her up (for nine she doesn't weigh a lot) and carried her home.

Before she went up to bed she said, "You're glad o' me? You'll ask me back some day when ut's allowed by our mutual gov- 14
ernments?"

"Sure," I said. I kissed her on the forehead. She grinned quickly and broadly, and said, "Yah! Mush!" then backed away and skipped off and upstairs.

I'm writing this at the desk Bridgie used to come up to and stand behind while she looked at me to make sure I was still here. I'm still here. Tonight on the news there
were some cut-ins from Belfast: bombings 15
and shootings. A while ago I heard a dog outside in the dark howling a little, then going away. I don't know if it had a collar on or not. I turned around when I heard it, but Bridgie wasn't there, of course. She's back home in her District, but maybe that's not exactly true either . . . because I think Bridgie's District is the world.

THINKING ABOUT THE SELECTION

Recalling

1. Why is Bridgie staying with Mitch's family?
2. Which gift does she like the most?
3. Why does Bridgie go for walks alone?

Interpreting

4. Why do you think Bridgie stiffens when she hears cars backfire?
5. Bridgie eats fast and never leaves anything. What does this indicate about her life in Belfast? Find another detail that supports this idea.
6. Find three details that indicate she remembers well the dog she had at home but is covering up her feelings.
7. What does Bridgie mean when she says, "The collar's a kind o' door key." Draw a comparison between Bridgie and dogs she collars.
8. Explain Mitch's statement that "Bridgie's District is the world."

Applying

9. Mitch says, "I'd never even started to think how it would be living inside a few blocks and not stepping over a line. I did then." Discuss what such a life must be like.

ANALYZING LITERATURE

Understanding Character Traits

Character traits are the qualities of a character's personality. They are revealed through a character's actions and words. For example, in "The House Guest," Mitch says about Bridgie, "I noticed she never asked for second helpings, either, but she'd take them when they were handed to her, even if she looked kind of amazed about getting them." This passage shows that Mitch is being perceptive, or observant.

What traits about the character indicated are shown by the following lines from the story?

1. Bridgie: "The night Bridgie first came . . . she didn't talk much at all . . . It was just that she clammed up."
2. Mitch: "I wanted to put myself out for her all right, though, so a few nights after that I talked her into going ice skating with me. . . . "

CRITICAL THINKING AND READING

Comparing and Contrasting Characters

A **comparison** shows the similarities between two or more characters. A **contrast** shows the differences between them.

1. Mitch can walk where he pleases, have second helpings, and live in a peaceful area. How is Bridgie's home life different from Mitch's?
2. Bridgie shows kindness to dogs. How does Mitch similarly show kindness to Bridgie?

UNDERSTANDING LANGUAGE

Showing Contrast

Certain words and phrases such as *although, but, different, however, whereas, on the other hand, unlike, while,* and *yet* indicate contrast.

Combine the pairs of sentences into one sentence by using a word or phrase that shows a contrast. Use a comma or semicolon, if needed.

1. In Ireland, Bridgie's family is confined to their district. In the U.S., Mitch's family is free to travel wherever they wish.
2. Mother worries Bridgie is spending too much time at her leatherworking. Father feels privacy may be the best thing they can give Bridgie.

THINKING AND WRITING

Writing as a Character

Imagine that you are Bridgie back in Northern Ireland. Write a letter to Mitch telling him about how your stay with his family affected you. Give specific examples of the experiences that meant the most to you.

Closure and Extension

ANSWERS TO THINKING ABOUT THE SELECTION

Recalling

1. Bridgie is visiting Mitch's family as part of a United States government program designed to bring children from Northern Ireland to America.
2. Bridgie's favorite gift is an advanced leatherworking set.
3. Bridgie goes for walks to look for stray dogs. She then gives each one a leather collar.

Interpreting

4. Bridgie stiffens because the noise reminds her of all the violence and gunshots in Northern Ireland.
5. It indicates that there was never enough food. Another indication was that she never asked for second helpings, but always ate them when they were handed to her.
6. She remembers that the dog was soft with fine ears that stuck up when he was happy. He'd disappear for several days at a time. He'd make messes in the house. She covers up her feelings by saying she hardly remembers the dog because she was so young.
7. Bridgie feels that people will be more willing to take in and feed a lost dog than a homeless one. Bridgie relates to the dogs because she feels alone, too.
8. Suggested Response: Bridgie is so good and caring that everyone in the world would want to know her.

Applying

9. Answers will differ. Some students might say they would be very scared of the bombings and violence. Others might find living in such a limited area confining.

ANSWERS TO ANALYZING LITERATURE

1. Answers will differ. It could show that Bridgie is shy and quiet, or that she is nervous or scared.
2. Mitch is friendly and caring.

ANSWERS TO CRITICAL THINKING AND READING

1. Bridgie never seemed to have enough food at home. Belfast was under constant attack. She was also limited in where she could walk, restricted by boundaries.
2. Mitch, at first, asks his mother if they could adopt Bridgie. He takes her ice skating and offers to help her with her leatherworking set.

ANSWERS TO UNDERSTANDING LANGUAGE

1. In Ireland, Bridgie's family is confined to their district, whereas in the United States, Mitch's family is free to travel wherever they wish.
2. Mother is worried that Bridgie is spending too much time at her leatherworking, although Father feels that privacy may be the best thing they can give Bridgie.

Writing Across the Curriculum

The civil strife that has affected Northern Ireland for decades has its roots deep in political and religious history. Have your students use periodicals and historical reference books to research the causes of Northern Ireland's troubles. Which factions are fighting? What are their goals? What historical arguments does each side use to justify its goals? You might want to inform the history department of this research assignment. They might provide guidance for students on conducting research.

GUIDE FOR READING

Gentleman of Río en Medio

Juan A. A. Sedillo (1902–1982) was born in New Mexico and lived in the Southwest. He was a lawyer and public servant, as well as a writer. "Gentleman of Río en Medio" is based on an actual legal case that arose over a conflict about the ownership of some property. In this story, Sedillo makes use of his legal background and his understanding of people.

Major and Minor Characters

A story usually has both major and minor characters. A **major character** is the most important person in the story. You learn the most about this character when you read the story. A **minor character** is a person of less importance in the story, but who is necessary for the story to develop. You learn only a little about each minor character in the story.

Look For

As you read "Gentleman of Río en Medio," look for what you learn about Don Anselmo. Why is he so important to the story? Who are the less important characters?

Writing

Don Anselmo is called "the *gentleman* of Río en Medio." What makes someone a gentleman? Freewrite, exploring your thoughts on this matter.

Vocabulary

Knowing the following words will help you as you read "Gentleman of Río en Medio."

negotiation (ni gō′shē ā′ shən) *n.*: Bargaining or discussing to reach an agreement (p. 93)

gnarled (närld) *adj.*: Knotty and twisted (p. 93)

innumerable (i no͞o′mər ə bəl) *adj.*: Too many to be counted (p. 93)

broached (brōcht) *v.*: Started a discussion about a topic (p. 94)

Focus

More About the Author Juan A. A. Sedillo is from New Mexico. The magazine *New Mexico* each month carries evidence that many people within the United States do not recognize New Mexico as part of the nation. They reprint letters and notices by people labeling the state as part of Mexico. Have students locate New Mexico on a map and name its capital. Have them find out how and why the United States acquired the land. The information will provide background for the cultural differences described in the story.

Literary Focus This story is primarily a two-character piece, with a major and a minor character. Who are the major and minor characters in other stories students have read? How can students tell?

Look For Ask the class to think also about reasons for the minor characters to be in the plot. What minor conflict are these characters engaged in? How does this plot resolve the major plot and lead to the final line of the story?

Writing/Prior Knowledge When students have finished freewriting, ask them to use their writing to form a single sentence definition: A gentleman is a person who . . .

Vocabulary Have your **less advanced** students read the words aloud so you can be sure they can pronounce them.

Spelling Tip Point out the silent *g* at the beginning of *gnarled* and the double *n* in *innumerable.*

Objectives

1. To understand the differences between major and minor characters in a short story
2. To compare and contrast cultural celebrations

Support Material

Teaching Portfolio

Teacher Backup, pp. 133–135

Usage and Mechanics Worksheet, p. 136

Vocabulary Check, p. 137

Critical Thinking and Reading Worksheet, *Comparing and Contrasting Attitudes,* p. 138

Language Worksheet, *Understanding Words From Spanish,* p. 139

Selection Test, pp. 140–141

Gentleman of Río en Medio

Juan A. A. Sedillo

It took months of negotiation to come to an understanding with the old man. He was in no hurry. What he had the most of was time. He lived up in Río en Medio,[1] where his people had been for hundreds of years. He tilled the same land they had tilled. His house was small and wretched, but quaint. The little creek ran through his land. His orchard was gnarled and beautiful.

The day of the sale he came into the office. His coat was old, green and faded. I thought of Senator Catron,[2] who had been such a power with these people up there in
1 the mountains. Perhaps it was one of his old Prince Alberts.[3] He also wore gloves. They were old and torn and his finger tips showed through them. He carried a cane, but it was only the skeleton of a worn-out umbrella. Behind him walked one of his innumerable kin—a dark young man with eyes like a gazelle.

The old man bowed to all of us in the room. Then he removed his hat and gloves, slowly and carefully. Chaplin[4] once did that in a picture, in a bank—he was the janitor. Then he handed his things to the boy, who stood obediently behind the old man's chair.

THE SACRISTAN OF TRAMPAS (detail)
Paul Burlin
Museum of New Mexico

There was a great deal of conversation, about rain and about his family. He was very proud of his large family. Finally we got down to business. Yes, he would sell, as he
had agreed, for twelve hundred dollars, in 2, 3
cash. We would buy, and the money was ready. "Don[5] Anselmo," I said to him in Spanish, "We have made a discovery. You remember that we sent that surveyor, that

---

1. Río en Medio (rē' ō en mā' dē ō)
2. Senator Catron (ka'trən): Thomas Benton Catron, senator from New Mexico, 1912–1917.
3. Prince Alberts: Long, double-breasted coats.
4. Chaplin: Charlie Chaplin (1889–1977), actor and producer of silent films in the United States.

5. don: A Spanish title of respect, similar to *Sir* in English.

Presentation

Motivation/Prior Knowledge Explain to students that this is not an action story but rather one that develops a character. Discuss the term "gentleman." Have students describe gentlemen whom they know.

Purpose-Setting Question What role does honor play in this story?

1 **Discussion** Why is formal dress important to this man even though his clothing is torn and faded?

2 **Discussion** Who is the narrator?

3 **Literary Focus** Note that this story is a first-person narrative. Here a character tells the story, referring to himself as "I", and presenting only what he knows. Everything we learn about the gentleman comes through another person's observations and dealings with the man. Ask why the author may have decided to tell his story using the first-person point of view.

Humanities Note

Fine art, *The Sacristan of Trampas,* by Paul Burlin (1886–1969). Burlin, an American, studied at the National Academy of Design in New York City and in England and Paris. He was an early Sante Fe School painter, painting Indian portraits and landscapes. He applied personal approaches to color and distortion that were not approved of or understood by his colleagues in Sante Fe.

Before you discuss the painting, explain the meaning of its title. A sacristan is an official in charge of the room in a church where sacred vessels are kept.

Ask the following questions.

1. Does the person in this painting remind you of Don Anselmo? If so, in what ways?
2. Is this work an appropriate choice to accompany this story? Why?

Thematic Idea Another selection that deals with the theme of the importance of personal dignity is "The Ninny" (page 159).

4 Discussion What does this tell you about Don Anselmo?

5 Master Teacher Note Ask why Don Anselmo insists on honoring the terms of the original contract, even though they were based on faulty information and are to his disadvantage. Discuss the importance of honor and of keeping one's word at all costs. You might tell students about the character of Brutus in *Julius Caesar*. Brutus, a man of true honor, says in Act I, Scene 2, "I love the name of honor more than I fear death." Indeed, Brutus kills himself when his honor is stained.

6 Reading Strategy Have students summarize the story up to this point and predict what will happen at the meeting.

engineer, up there to survey your land so as to make the deed. Well, he finds that you own more than eight acres. He tells us that your land extends across the river and that you own almost twice as much as you thought." He didn't know that. "And now, Don Anselmo," I added, "These Americans are *buena gente*,[6] they are good people, and they are willing to pay you for the additional land as well, at the same rate per acre, so that instead of twelve hundred dollars you will get almost twice as much, and the money is here for you."

The old man hung his head for a moment in thought. Then he stood up and stared at me. "Friend," he said, "I do not like to have you speak to me in that manner." I kept still and let him have his say. 4 "I know these Americans are good people, and that is why I have agreed to sell to them. But I do not care to be insulted. I have agreed to sell my house and land for twelve hundred dollars and that is the price."

I argued with him but it was useless. 5 Finally he signed the deed and took the money but refused to take more than the amount agreed upon. Then he shook hands all around, put on his ragged gloves, took his stick and walked out with the boy behind him.

A month later my friends had moved into Río en Medio. They had replastered the old adobe house, pruned the trees, patched the fence, and moved in for the summer. One day they came back to the office to complain. The children of the village were overrunning their property. They came every day and played under the trees, built little play fences around them, and took blossoms. When they were spoken to they only laughed and talked back good-naturedly in Spanish.

I sent a messenger up to the mountains for Don Anselmo. It took a week to arrange another meeting. 6 When he arrived he repeated his previous preliminary performance. He wore the same faded cutaway,[7] carried the same stick and was accompanied by the boy again. He shook hands all around, sat down with the boy behind his chair, and talked about the weather. Finally I broached the subject. "Don Anselmo, about the ranch you sold to these people. They are good people and want to be your friends and neighbors always. When you sold to them you signed a document, a deed, and in that deed you agreed to several things. One thing was that they were to have the complete possession of the property. Now, Don Anselmo, it seems that every day the children of the village overrun the orchard and spend most of their time there. We would like to know if you, as the most respected man in the village, could not stop them from doing so in order that these people may enjoy their new home more in peace."

Don Anselmo stood up. "We have all learned to love these Americans," he said, "Because they are good people and good neighbors. I sold them my property because I knew they were good people, but I did not sell them the trees in the orchard."

This was bad. "Don Anselmo," I pleaded, "When one signs a deed and sells real property one sells also everything that grows on the land, and those trees, every one of them, are on the land and inside the boundaries of what you sold."

"Yes, I admit that," he said. "You know," he added, "I am the oldest man in the village. Almost everyone there is my relative and all the children of Río en Medio

6. ***buena gente*** (bwā′ nä hen′ tā)

7. **cutaway** (kut′ ə wā′) *n.*: A coat worn by men for formal daytime occasions.

Closure and Extension

ANSWERS TO THINKING ABOUT THE SELECTION

Recalling

1. It took months because Don Anselmo was in no hurry to sell his house and land. His people had lived in Río en Medio for hundreds of years.
2. They offered additional money because they discovered that he owned twice as much land as they originally thought. He reacts to the offer by refusing the additional money.
3. They complain that the children of the village overrun the orchard and spend most of their time there. Don Anselmo tells the Americans that the trees in the orchard belong to the children of the village.
4. The Americans buy the trees from the children.
5. He was formally dressed, with a

are my *sobrinos* and *nietos*,[8] my descendants. Every time a child has been born in Río en Medio since I took possession of that house from my mother I have planted a tree for that child. The trees in that orchard are not mine, *Señor*, they belong to the children of the village. Every person in Río en Medio born since the railroad came to Santa Fé owns a tree in that orchard. I did not sell the trees because I could not. They are not mine."

There was nothing we could do. Legally we owned the trees but the old man had been so generous, refusing what amounted 7
to a fortune for him. It took most of the following winter to buy the trees, individually, from the descendants of Don Anselmo in the valley of Río en Medio.

---

8. *sobrinos* (sō brē′ nōs) and ***nietos*** (nyā′ tōs): Spanish for "nieces and nephews" and "grandchildren."

THINKING ABOUT THE SELECTION

Recalling

1. Why does it take months to reach the first agreement with Don Anselmo?
2. Why do the Americans offer additional money for the property? How does Don Anselmo react to the offer?
3. What complaint do the Americans have after they have bought the property? What is Don Anselmo's response to their complaint?
4. How do the Americans solve their problem?
5. Describe how Don Anselmo acts when he comes into the office to finalize the sale. What does his behavior suggest about him?

Interpreting

6. What does Don Anselmo's refusal of more money for the land suggest about him? Find one other detail that supports this impression.
7. What does the Americans' solution to the problem suggest about them? Find one other detail that supports this impression.
8. What makes Don Anselmo the "Gentleman of Río en Medio"?

Applying

9. Put yourself in the Americans' place. Explain how you would have solved their problem.

ANALYZING LITERATURE

Identifying Major and Minor Characters

In a work of literature, the **major** character is the person the story is about—the one about whom you learn the most and who plays the largest role in the tale. The **minor** characters play less essential roles.

1. What role does Don Anselmo play in this story?
2. What do you learn about him as the story progresses?
3. What role do the Americans play in the story?
4. What role does the narrator play?

THINKING AND WRITING

Comparing and Contrasting Cultures

Imagine that you have just received a letter from a pen pal in Mexico. Your pen pal has described his or her birthday celebration and has asked you how you celebrate your birthday. Write a letter to your pen pal explaining how you celebrate birthdays. Include not only what you do but your attitude about birthdays. After you have drafted your letter, revise it to make sure that your explanation is clear. Proofread your letter and prepare a final draft.

(Answers begin on p. 94.)

7 **Discussion** How was this a situation in which everyone won? Do these situations happen frequently? Can you recall a time when a problem was solved in such a way that everyone won?

Reader's Response Do you consider Don Anselmo an honorable character? Why or why not?

Enrichment Which is more important to Don Anselmo, observing the language of the contract, which he knows is binding, or letting the children play under the trees he planted for them? Elicit how the trees are a moral commitment he has made to posterity. Guide the discussion to have the class understand situations in which moral and legal values may impose different claims.

Challenge The dispute between Don Anselmo and the new American owners of his land is settled in a friendly way. Ask students what might have happened if the new owners had resorted to the law instead.

THINKING AND WRITING

Publishing Student Writing Make a birthday bulletin board. Ask students if they can bring in photos of their birthday celebrations. Hang these on the bulletin board next to their letters.

Writing Across the Curriculum The practice of planting trees to mark a special occasion is an ancient and widespread custom. Trees might be planted, as in the story, to celebrate the birth of a child; or to memorialize a death; or to mark the site of a historical event. Ask students what trees in your neighborhood or city have been planted for a special reason. Have them interview public officials and neighbors. You might want to inform the history department of this assignment.

faded coat, torn gloves, and the skeleton of an umbrella for a cane. When he entered the room he bowed to everyone. It suggests that he is poor, yet proud.

Interpreting

6. It suggests that he is a man of his word. He makes sure the Americans understand that he does not own the trees in the orchard. They belong to the children in the village.
7. The Americans make an effort to understand and tolerate the customs of Don Anselmo. They also show a willingness to compromise. They buy back the trees from the children.
8. He is a gentleman because he is courteous and has a strong sense of honor.

Applying

9. Answers will differ. Suggested response: I would have done as the Americans did. I would have brought back the trees from the children.

ANSWERS TO ANALYZING LITERATURE

1. He is the major character.
2. He is a gentleman—courteous and honest.
3. They are minor characters.
4. He is one of the Americans, a minor character.

Focus

More About the Author "Raymond's Run" appeared in a 1971 anthology edited by Toni Cade Bambara called *Tales and Stories for Black Folks.* In the preface she urged her readers to take the contents "seriously as valuable lessons in human behavior and examples of living history." Students should note the critic's quote carefully. What "new awareness" allows black women to "create their own choices about the kinds of women they will be"? How does the quote apply to women of all colors?

Literary Focus Have students consider other stories for examples of round and flat characters. Which of the two main characters is more fully developed? Which reveals only admirable character traits? Point out that often round characters exhibit at least two traits at odds with each other with a resulting inner conflict. Direct students to look for evidence of this struggle within Squeaky and for the way she resolves the conflict.

Look For Bambara gives many clues that foreshadow Squeaky's change. Point out that readers will find most of these clues in the girl's thoughts and conversations. Students might also jot down examples, as they read, of idiomatic language that helps to make Squeaky's character realistic.

Writing/Prior Knowledge Remind students to include in their freewriting the names of both the show and characters, as well as the channel on which it appeared.

Vocabulary Have your **less advanced** students use each word in a sentence orally before reading the story.

GUIDE FOR READING

Raymond's Run

Toni Cade Bambara (1939–) was born in New York City and educated in the United States and Europe. She has studied mime and dance and has taught students of all ages, from preschoolers to college students. A critic has said that Bambara writes of "black women at the edge of a new awareness, who create their own choices about the kinds of women they will be." In "Raymond's Run," Squeaky reaches that point and makes a clear choice about the kind of person she intends to be.

Round and Flat Characters

Characters are sometimes described as being round or flat. **Round** characters are like real people. They are complex, revealing several sides to their personality and growing and changing as the story progresses. **Flat** characters are one-dimensional, often revealing a single personal quality and staying the same throughout the story.

Look For

As you read "Raymond's Run," look for the descriptive details that make Squeaky come alive for you. Does she seem like a real person, someone you might know? What sides do you see to her personality? How does she change as the story progresses?

Writing

Think of a television show or movie that you like. List all the characters. Which ones seem round or fully developed? Select one of the round characters and freewrite, exploring all the aspects of his or her personality.

Vocabulary

Knowing the meaning of the following words will help you as you read "Raymond's Run."

prodigy (präd′ə jē) *n.*: A child of extraordinary genius (p. 99)
glockenspiels (gläk′ən spēlz′) *n.*: Musical instruments, like xylophones, that are carried upright and often used in marching bands (p. 100)
periscope (per′ə skōp) *n.*: An instrument containing mirrors and lenses to see objects not in a direct line from the viewer; often used in submarines to see objects above the water (p. 101)

Objectives

1 To understand the differences between round and flat characters
2 To identify the reasons that motivate a character
3 To understand the meanings of idioms
4 To write an extension of the story

Support Material

Teaching Portfolio

Teacher Backup, pp. 143–146
Grammar in Action Worksheets, *Understanding Parallelism,* pp. 147–148; *Using Consistent Verb Tense,* pp. 149–150
Usage and Mechanics Worksheet, p. 151
Vocabulary Check, p. 152
Analyzing Literature Worksheet, *Recognizing Flat and Round Characters,* p. 153
Language Worksheet, *Understanding Idioms,* p. 154
Selection Test, pp. 155–156

Raymond's Run

Toni Cade Bambara

I don't have much work to do around the house like some girls. My mother does that. And I don't have to earn my pocket money by hustling; George runs errands for the big boys and sells Christmas cards. And anything else that's got to get done, my father does. All I have to do in life is mind my brother Raymond, which is enough.

1 Sometimes I slip and say my little brother Raymond. But as any fool can see he's much bigger and he's older too. But a lot of people call him my little brother cause he needs looking after cause he's not quite right. And a lot of smart mouths got lots to say about that too, especially when George was minding him. But now, if anybody has anything to say to Raymond, anything to say about his big head, they have to come by me. And I don't play the dozens[1] or believe in standing around with somebody in my face doing a lot of talking. I much rather just knock you down and take my chances even if I am a little girl with skinny arms and a squeaky voice, which is how I got the name Squeaky. And if things get too rough, I run. And as anybody can tell you, I'm the fastest thing on two feet.

There is no track meet that I don't win the first place medal. I use to win the twenty-yard dash when I was a little kid in kindergarten. Nowadays it's the fifty-yard dash. And tomorrow I'm subject to run the quarter-meter relay all by myself and come in first, second, and third. The big kids call me Mercury[2] cause I'm the swiftest thing in the neighborhood. Everybody knows that—except two people who know better, my father and me.

1. the dozens: A game in which the players insult one another; the first to show anger loses.

2. Mercury *n.*: In Roman mythology, the messenger of the gods, known for great speed.

Presentation

Motivation/Prior Knowledge This is a story told humorously by a very strong character. Have students note the humorous phrases she uses. Most students will have no difficulty recognizing the humor in this story.

Thematic Idea Another selection that deals with an older sister helping a younger sibling is "For My Sister Molly Who in the Fifties," by Alice Walker, on page 560.

Purpose-Setting Question What role does humor play in this story?

1 **Discussion** What have you learned about the main character from the first two paragraphs? How do you feel about her?

2 **Critical Reading** Have students compare and contrast the different approach to excellence each girl takes.

3 **Master Teacher Note** Squeaky's directness makes her angry with girls who are not direct, but evasive—Cynthia, for example. Ask your students which character traits they find least tolerable. For those who have read J.D. Salinger's *The Catcher in the Rye,* have them explain why the book's hero, Holden Caulfield, was also angry with the world's phonies. Have students contrast how he and Squeaky dealt with this anger. Bring out how Holden would pump gas, pretending he was mute, to escape communicating with people. Squeaky would fight them.

He can beat me to Amsterdam Avenue with me having a two fire-hydrant headstart and him running with his hands in his pockets and whistling. But that's private information. Cause can you imagine some thirty-five-year-old man stuffing himself into PAL[3] shorts to race little kids? So as far as everyone's concerned, I'm the fastest and that goes for Gretchen, too, who has put out the tale that she is going to win the first place medal this year. Ridiculous. In the second place, she's got short legs. In the third place, she's got freckles. In the first place, no one can beat me and that's all there is to it.

I'm standing on the corner admiring the weather and about to take a stroll down Broadway so I can practice my breathing exercises, and I've got Raymond walking on the inside close to the buildings cause he's subject to fits of fantasy and starts thinking he's a circus performer and that the curb is a tight-rope strung high in the air. And sometimes after a rain, he likes to step down off his tightrope right into the gutter and slosh around getting his shoes and cuffs wet. Or sometimes if you don't watch him, he'll dash across traffic to the island in the middle of Broadway and give the pigeons a fit. Then I have to go behind him apologizing to all the old people sitting around trying to get some sun and getting all upset with the pigeons fluttering around them, scattering their newspapers and upsetting the wax-paper lunches in their laps. So I keep Raymond on the inside of me, and he plays like he's driving a stagecoach, which is O.K. by me so long as he doesn't run me over or interrupt my breathing exercises, which I have to do on account of I'm serious about my running and don't care who knows it.

3. **PAL** *adj.*: Police Athletic League.

Now some people like to act like things come easy to them, won't let on that they practice. Not me. I'll high prance down 34th Street like a rodeo pony to keep my knees strong even if it does get my mother uptight so that she walks ahead like she's not with me, don't know me, is all by herself on a shopping trip, and I am somebody else's crazy child.

Now you take Cynthia Procter for instance. She's just the opposite. If there's a test tomorrow, she'll say something like, "Oh I guess I'll play handball this afternoon and watch television tonight," just to let you know she ain't thinking about the test. Or like last week when she won the spelling bee for the millionth time, "A good thing you got 'receive,' Squeaky, cause I would have got it wrong. I completely forgot about the spelling bee." And she'll clutch the lace on her blouse like it was a narrow escape. Oh, brother. 2,

But of course when I pass her house on my early morning trots around the block, she is practicing the scales on the piano over and over and over and over. Then in music class, she always lets herself get bumped around so she falls accidently on purpose onto the piano stool and is so surprised to find herself sitting there, and so decides just for fun to try out the ole keys and

Grammar in Action

When ideas within a sentence are of equal weight or importance, effective writers put them in the same grammatical form. This technique, called **parallelism,** gives rhythm and balance to writing.

Look at the following sentence from "Raymond's Run." Read the sentence aloud. Notice how smoothly it flows from your tongue. This smoothness is a result of parallel structure.

> Then I have to go behind him apologizing to all the old people sitting around trying to get some sun and getting upset with the pigeons fluttering around them, scattering their newspapers and upsetting the wax-paper lunches in their laps.

The old people are doing two things. They are "sitting around trying to get some sun" and they are "getting upset with the pigeons." Notice that both these activities are given equal weight since they are placed in the same grammatical form. Both begin with a participle, an *-ing* form of the verb used as an adjective. Notice how much less effective the following passage is:

what do you know—Chopin's[4] waltzes just spring out of her fingertips and she's the most surprised thing in the world. A regular prodigy. I could kill people like that.

I stay up all night studying the words for the spelling bee. And you can see me anytime of day practicing running. I never walk if I can trot and shame on Raymond if he can't keep up. But of course he does, cause if he hangs back someone's liable to walk up to him and get smart, or take his allowance from him, or ask him where he got that great big pumpkin head. People are so stupid sometimes.

4 So I'm strolling down Broadway breathing out and breathing in on counts of seven, which is my lucky number, and here comes Gretchen and her sidekicks—Mary Louise who used to be a friend of mine when she first moved to Harlem from Baltimore and got beat up by everybody till I took up for her on account of her mother and my mother used to sing in the same choir when they were young girls, but people ain't grateful, so now she hangs out with the new girl Gretchen and talks about me like a dog; and Rosie who is as fat as I am skinny and has a big mouth where Raymond is concerned and is too stupid to know that there is not a big deal of difference between herself and Raymond and that she can't afford to throw stones. So they are steady coming up Broadway and I see right away that it's going to be one of those Dodge City[5] scenes cause the street ain't that big and they're close to the buildings just as we are. First I think I'll step into the candy store and look over the new comics and let them pass. But that's chicken and I've got a reputation to consider. So then I think I'll just walk straight on through them or over them if necessary. But as they get to me, they slow down. I'm ready to fight, cause like I said I don't feature a whole lot of chit-chat, I much prefer to just knock you down right from the jump and save everybody a lotta precious time.

"You signing up for the May Day races?" smiles Mary Louise, only it's not a smile at all.

A dumb question like that doesn't deserve an answer. Besides, there's just me and Gretchen standing there really, so no use wasting my breath talking to shadows.

"I don't think you're going to win this time," says Rosie, trying to signify with her hands on her hips all salty, completely forgetting that I have whupped her many times for less salt than that.

"I always win cause I'm the best," I say straight at Gretchen who is, as far as I'm concerned, the only one talking in this ventriloquist-dummy routine.

Gretchen smiles but it's not a smile and I'm thinking that girls never really smile at each other because they don't know how and don't want to know how and there's probably no one to teach us how cause grown-up girls don't know either. Then they all look at Raymond who has just brought his mule team to a standstill. And they're about to see what trouble they can get into through him.

"What grade you in now, Raymond?"

"You got anything to say to my brother, you say it to me, Mary Louise Williams of Raggedy Town, Baltimore."

"What are you, his mother?" sasses Rosie.

"That's right, Fatso. And the next word out of anybody and I'll be *their* mother too." So they just stand there and Gretchen shifts from one leg to the other and so do they. Then Gretchen puts her hands on her hips

4. **Chopin** (shō′ păn): Frédéric François Chopin (1810–1849), Polish composer and pianist.
5. **Dodge City:** The location of the television program "Gunsmoke," which often presented a gunfight between the sheriff and an outlaw.

4 **Literary Focus** Point out the length of the first sentence in this paragraph. Explain that this story is told from a first-person point of view where the narrator is a character in the story. All events are described from Squeaky's viewpoint, which may or may not be slanted. Here we are inside Squeaky's mind.

Then I have to go behind him apologizing to all the old people sitting around trying to get some sun. These people got upset with the pigeons. . . .

Student Activity 1. Read the sample sentence again. Which three groups of words describe what the pigeons were doing? What grammatical form begins each of these groups of words? Do you think the use of parallelism makes this part of the sentence more or less effective? Explain.

Student Activity 2. Using the second part of Toni Cade Bambara's sentence as a pattern, complete each of the following sentences.

1. They were getting upset with the dogs. . . .
2. They were getting annoyed by the children. . . .
3. They were getting bothered by the mosquitoes. . . .
4. They were getting angry at the peddlers. . . .

5 Discussion How does Squeaky see herself? Is she honest about herself and her abilities?

and is about to say something with her freckle-face self but doesn't. Then she walks around me looking me up and down but keeps walking up Broadway, and her sidekicks follow her. So me and Raymond smile at each other and he says, "Gidyap" to his team and I continue with my breathing exercises, strolling down Broadway toward the ice man on 145th with not a care in the world cause I am Miss Quicksilver herself.

I take my time getting to the park on May Day because the track meet is the last thing on the program. The biggest thing on the program is the May Pole dancing, which I can do without, thank you, even if my mother thinks it's a shame I don't take part and act like a girl for a change. You'd think my mother'd be grateful not to have to make me a white organdy dress with a big satin sash and buy me new white baby-doll shoes that can't be taken out of the box till the big day. You'd think she'd be glad her daughter ain't out there prancing around a May Pole getting the new clothes all dirty and sweaty and trying to act like a fairy or a flower or whatever you're supposed to be when you should be trying to be yourself, whatever that is, which is, as far as I am concerned, a poor
5 black girl who really can't afford to buy shoes and a new dress you only wear once a lifetime cause it won't fit next year.

I was once a strawberry in a Hansel and Gretel pageant when I was in nursery school and didn't have no better sense than to dance on tiptoe with my arms in a circle over my head doing umbrella steps and being a perfect fool just so my mother and father could come dressed up and clap. You'd think they'd know better than to encourage that kind of nonsense. I am not a strawberry. I do not dance on my toes. I run. That is what I am all about. So I always come late to the May Day program, just in time to get my number pinned on and lay in the grass till they announce the fifty-yard dash.

I put Raymond in the little swings, which is a tight squeeze this year and will be impossible next year. Then I look around for Mr. Pearson, who pins the numbers on. I'm really looking for Gretchen if you want to know the truth, but she's not around. The park is jam-packed. Parents in hats and corsages and breast-pocket handkerchiefs peeking up. Kids in white dresses and light-blue suits. The parkees unfolding chairs and chasing the rowdy kids from Lenox as if they had no right to be there. The big guys with their caps on backwards, leaning against the fence swirling the basketballs on the tips of their fingers, waiting for all these crazy people to clear out the park so they can play. Most of the kids in my class are carrying bass drums and glockenspiels and flutes. You'd think they'd put in a few bongos or something for real like that.

Then here comes Mr. Pearson with his clipboard and his cards and pencils and whistles and safety pins and fifty million other things he's always dropping all over the place with his clumsy self. He sticks out in a crowd cause he's on stilts. We used to call him Jack and the Beanstalk to get him mad. But I'm the only one that can outrun him and get away, and I'm too grown for that silliness now.

"Well, Squeaky," he says checking my name off the list and handing me number seven and two pins. And I'm thinking he's got no right to call me Squeaky, if I can't call him Beanstalk.

"Hazel Elizabeth Deborah Parker," I correct him and tell him to write it down on his board.

"Well, Hazel Elizabeth Deborah Parker, going to give someone else a break this year?" I squint at him real hard to see if he is

Grammar In Action

Consistent verb tense is an important quality of good writing. Just as clauses within a sentence should be parallel in structure, the verb tense in which a writer chooses to tell a story should be consistently past or present. For example, a writer who is describing events that already happened using past tense should maintain past tense throughout the story.

Occasionally, writers shift tenses when necessary. For example, in "Raymond's Run," Toni Cade Bambara writes predominantly in the present tense. She shifts to past tense when she depicts Squeaky reflecting on incidents that happened outside the boundaries of her story. For most of the story, however, Squeaky uses present tense to narrate events that happened in the past. Through present tense narration, Squeaky paints a picture of the May Day program so that we can see the events as they happen, through the eyes of Squeaky's memory. Relating past events in present tense as Bambara does makes the story more immediate to the reader.

Notice how Bambara shifts to past tense in the paragraph which begins "I was once a strawberry". Squeaky's attention drifts temporarily away from the action of the May Day races as she remembers an early childhood scene. Then toward the end

seriously thinking I should lose the race on purpose just to give someone else a break.

"Only six girls running this time," he continues, shaking his head sadly like it's my fault all of New York didn't turn out in sneakers. "That new girl should give you a run for your money." He looks around the park for Gretchen like a periscope in a submarine movie. "Wouldn't it be a nice gesture if you were . . . to ahhh . . ."

I give him such a look he couldn't finish putting that idea into words. Grownups got a lot of nerve sometimes. I pin number seven to myself and stomp away—I'm so burnt. And I go straight for the track and stretch out on the grass while the band winds up with "Oh the Monkey Wrapped His Tail Around the Flag Pole," which my teacher calls by some other name. The man on the loudspeaker is calling everyone over to the track and I'm on my back looking at the sky trying to pretend I'm in the country, but I can't, because even grass in the city feels hard as sidewalk and there's just no pretending you are anywhere but in a "concrete jungle" as my grandfather says.

The twenty-yard dash takes all of the two minutes cause most of the little kids don't know no better than to run off the track or run the wrong way or run smack into the fence and fall down and cry. One little kid, though, has got the good sense to run straight for the white ribbon up ahead, so he wins. Then the second-graders line up for the thirty-yard dash and I don't even bother to turn my head to watch cause Raphael Perez always wins. He wins before he even begins by psyching the runners,

of the paragraph Squeaky shifts back to present tense and announces:

> "I am not a strawberry. I do not dance on my toes. I run. That is what I am all about. So I always come late to the May Day program, just in time to get my number pinned on and lay in the grass till they announce the fifty-yard dash."

Bambara carefully maintains present tense throughout the story, except for occasional, intentional shifts to past tense.

Student Activity 1. As you read the rest of the story, record examples of shifts in verb tenses. Explain why it is necessary for Bambara to shift tenses.

Student Activity 2. Imitate Bambara's writing style by writing an original paragraph about an experience in your past which you narrate in the present tense.

telling them they're going to trip on their shoelaces and fall on their faces or lose their shorts or something, which he doesn't really have to do since he is very fast, almost as fast as I am. After that is the forty-yard dash, which I use to run when I was in first grade. Raymond is hollering from the swings cause he knows I'm about to do my thing cause the man on the loudspeaker has just announced the fifty-yard dash, although he might just as well be giving a recipe for angel food cake cause you can hardly make out what he's saying for the static. I get up and slip off my sweat pants and then I see Gretchen standing at the starting line kicking her legs out like a pro. Then as I get into place I see that ole Raymond is in line on the other side of the fence, bending down with his fingers on the ground just like he knew what he was doing. I was going to yell at him but then I didn't. It burns up your energy to holler.

Every time, just before I take off in a race, I always feel like I'm in a dream, the kind of dream you have when you're sick with fever and feel all hot and weightless. I dream I'm flying over a sandy beach in the early morning sun, kissing the leaves of the trees as I fly by. And there's always the smell of apples, just like in the country when I was little and use to think I was a choo-choo train, running through the fields of corn and chugging up the hill to the orchard. And all the time I'm dreaming this, I get lighter and lighter until I'm flying over the beach again, getting blown through the sky like a feather that weighs nothing at all. But once I spread my fingers in the dirt and crouch over for the Get on Your Mark, the dream goes and I am solid again and am telling myself, Squeaky you must win, you must win, you are the fastest thing in the world, you can even beat your father up Amsterdam if you really try. And then I feel my weight coming back just behind my knees then down to my feet then into the earth and the pistol shot explodes in my blood and I am off and weightless again, flying past the other runners, my arms pumping up and down and the whole world is quiet except for the crunch as I zoom over the gravel in the track. I glance to my left and there is no one. To the right a blurred Gretchen, who's got her chin jutting out as if it would win the race all by itself. And on the other side of the fence is Raymond with his arms down to his side and the palms tucked up behind him, running in his very own style and the first time I ever saw that and I almost stop to watch my brother Raymond on his first run. But the white ribbon is bouncing toward me and I tear past it racing into the distance till my feet with a mind of their own start digging up footfuls of dirt and brake me short. Then all the kids standing on the side pile on me, banging me on the back and slapping my head with their May Day programs, for I have won again and everybody on 151st Street can walk tall for another year.

"In first place . . ." the man on the loudspeaker is clear as a bell now. But then he pauses and the loudspeaker starts to whine. Then static. And I lean down to catch my breath and here comes Gretchen walking back for she's overshot the finish line too, huffing and puffing with her hands on her hips taking it slow, breathing in steady time like a real pro and I sort of like her a little for the first time. "In first place . . ." and then three or four voices get all mixed up on the loudspeaker and I dig my sneaker into the grass and stare at Gretchen who's staring back, we both wondering just who did win. I can hear old Beanstalk arguing with the man on the loudspeaker and then a few others running their mouths about what the stop watches say.

Then I hear Raymond yanking at the fence to call me and I wave to shush him, but he keeps rattling the fence like a gorilla in a cage like in them gorilla movies, but then like a dancer or something he starts climbing up nice and easy but very fast. And it occurs to me, watching how smoothly he climbs hand over hand and remembering how he looked running with his arms down to his side and with the wind pulling his mouth back and his teeth showing and all, it occurred to me that Raymond would make a very fine runner. Doesn't he always keep up with me on my trots? And he surely knows how to breathe in counts of seven cause he's always doing it at the dinner table, which drives my brother George up the wall. And I'm smiling to beat the band cause if I've lost this race, or if me and Gretchen tied, or even if I've won, I can always retire as a runner and begin a whole new career as a coach with Raymond as my champion. After all, with a little more study I can beat Cynthia and her phony self at the spelling bee. And if I bugged my mother, I could get piano lessons and become a star. And I have a big rep as the baddest thing around. And I've got a roomful of ribbons and medals and awards. But what has Raymond got to call his own? 6

So I stand there with my new plan, laughing out loud by this time as Raymond

6 **Discussion** Squeaky has come to an important realization here. Up until this point, she has shown great love and affection for her brother. Ask students to give examples from the story. But now, she is about to give him a greater gift, something of his own. What does this tell us about her character?

7 **Discussion** Discuss what kind of growth this smile of respect shows. Ask the students how this scene represents an important aspect of growing up. Have students recount any instances in which they came to recognize an opponent's true worth. Why was doing so a way of maturing?

Enrichment Discuss with students their feelings about competition and their competitors. Is athletic competition a good preparation for dealing with life? Explain.

Reader's Response In your eyes, what is Squeaky's most outstanding quality? In what way or ways do you find her most admirable?

jumps down from the fence and runs over with his teeth showing and his arms down to the side, which no one before him has quite mastered as a running style. And by the time he comes over I'm jumping up and down so glad to see him—my brother Raymond, a great runner in the family tradition. But of course everyone thinks I'm jumping up and down because the men on the loudspeaker have finally gotten themselves together and compared notes and are announcing "In first place—Miss Hazel Elizabeth Deborah Parker." (Dig that.) "In second place—Miss Gretchen P. Lewis." And I look over at Gretchen wondering what the P stands for. And I smile. Cause she's good, no doubt about it. Maybe she'd 7 like to help me coach Raymond; she obviously is serious about running, as any fool can see. And she nods to congratulate me and then she smiles. And I smile. We stand there with this big smile of respect between us. It's about as real a smile as girls can do for each other, considering we don't practice real smiling every day you know, cause maybe we too busy being flowers or fairies or strawberries instead of something honest and worthy of respect . . . you know . . . like being people.

THINKING ABOUT THE SELECTION

Recalling

1. How did Squeaky gain her name? Why is she also called Mercury? Why does she refer to herself as "Miss Quicksilver"?
2. What would Squeaky's mother like her to do in the May Day program? Why doesn't Squeaky do this?
3. What does Mr. Pearson want her to do during the race? How does she react even before he can finish putting this idea into words?
4. How does Squeaky feel before each race? How does she "psych herself up" or encourage herself to win?
5. What does Squeaky realize about herself at the end of the race? What does she realize about Raymond?

Interpreting

6. Squeaky's main responsibility is taking care of Raymond. How does she feel about this responsibility? Find evidence to support your answer.
7. How does Squeaky act toward people who talk smart to her? What does this behavior suggest about her?
8. When Squeaky runs into Gretchen, Mary Louise, and Rosie, she thinks, "Besides, there's just me and Gretchen standing there really. . . ." What does this thought indicate about her feelings toward the other girls? Why does she feel this way about them?
9. Early in the story, how did Squeaky feel about girls smiling at each other? Why do she and Gretchen smile at each other at the end of the race? What does this change suggest that Squeaky has learned?
10. Why is this story called "Raymond's Run" instead of "Squeaky's Run"?

Applying

11. What makes you respect other people?
12. Squeaky suggests that it is difficult for girls in

Closure and Extension

ANSWERS TO THINKING ABOUT THE SELECTION

Recalling

1. She got her name because she has a squeaky voice. She is sometimes called Mercury because she runs very fast. She refers to herself as "Miss Quicksilver" because she runs so fast.
2. Her mother wants her to participate in the May Pole dance. Squeaky doesn't want her mother to buy her a white organdy dress and white baby-doll shoes that she would only wear once. She feels her mother can't afford this expense.
3. Mr. Pearson asks Squeaky to let someone else win the race. Squeaky gives him "such a look that he couldn't finish putting that idea into words."
4. Before each race Squeaky feels as if she is in a dream. She dreams she is flying over a sandy beach in the early morning sun. Then she tells herself that she must win, that she is the fastest thing in the world, and that she could even beat her father if she really tried.
5. At the end of the race she decides to coach Raymond in running because Raymond has nothing to call his own. She realizes that while she has always loved her brother she is now going to give him a greater gift, something of his own. She realizes that Raymond would make a fine runner.

Interpreting

6. Squeaky loves her brother and doesn't mind taking care of him. When taking Raymond outdoors, she makes sure he walks on the inside close to the buildings so he won't step off the curb and run into traffic.
7. Squeaky would "knock you down" if you talk smart to her. It suggests that she is aggressive, direct, and immature.
8. It indicates that she doesn't feel Mary Louise and Rosie are important enough even to acknowledge. She feels this way because Mary Louise used to be her friend when Mary Louise first moved to Harlem. Squeaky had befriended her, but she wasn't grateful and

our society to be "something honest and worthy of respect." Explain why you agree or disagree with her opinion.

ANALYZING LITERATURE
Recognizing Round and Flat Characters

Writers often people their stories with both round and flat characters. The **round** characters grow and change as the story progresses. The **flat** characters generally reveal only one side of their personality and may serve to highlight the positive qualities of the round characters.

1. Describe how Squeaky grows and changes as the story progresses.
2. In what way does Cynthia Procter serve as a foil to Squeaky? That is, how does she serve to point up Squeaky's positive characteristics?
3. In what way do Mary Louise and Rosie serve as a foil to Squeaky? In what way do they also serve as a foil to Gretchen?

CRITICAL THINKING AND READING
Identifying Reasons

A **reason** is the information that explains or justifies a condition, an action, or a decision. A reason may be a fact, an opinion, a situation, or an occurrence. In "Raymond's Run," for example, the reason for Squeaky's nickname is that she has a squeaky voice.

Give the reasons for the following situations in "Raymond's Run."

1. Squeaky changes her view of Gretchen.
2. At the end, Squeaky feels that winning the race does not matter.

UNDERSTANDING LANGUAGE
Understanding Idioms

An **idiom** is an expression that has a meaning all its own. This meaning is different from the literal meaning of the words. For example, *to catch one's eye* is an idiom that means "to get one's attention." To take this meaning literally can mean making a serious mistake.

The meaning of idioms is generally understood. Sometimes you can understand that words are being used as idioms from the context, or surrounding words and ideas. Often an idiom can give the flavor of a character, or a clearer idea of what the character is like.

What is the meaning of each *italicized* idiom?

1. "Rosie is too stupid to know that there is not a big deal of difference between herself and Raymond and that she can't afford *to throw stones.*"
2. "Grown-ups got a lot of nerve sometimes. I pin number seven to myself and stomp away, I'm so *burnt.*"

THINKING AND WRITING
Writing an Extension of the Story

Imagine Squeaky in a different situation—for example, during Raymond's first race after she has coached him. Write about the race from Squeaky's point of view, speaking as "I." First make an outline of what you will write. Think about what advice Squeaky will give Raymond: how she will feel and think before, during, and after the race; and how the race will end. Then write this part of the story. Revise your story, making sure you have told it consistently from Squeaky's point of view. Proofread your story and share it with your classmates.

(Answers begin p. 104.)

now hangs out with Gretchen. Squeaky doesn't like Rosie because she talks against Raymond.

9. She feels that girls never really smile at each other because they don't know how and there is no one to teach them. At the end of the race, they smile because they respect each other. It suggests that Squeaky has matured and now accepts Gretchen as a worthy competitor.
10. It's called "Raymond's Run" because Raymond runs the race on the other side of the fence. Seeing him run "in his very own style," Squeaky resolves to forego running to coach him.

Applying

11. Answers will differ. Some students might say that the people they respect are honorable, honest, friendly, sincere, and good friends.
12. Answers will differ. Students that agree might say that girls are catty and competitive. Those that disagree could argue that girls like Squeaky are honest and worthy of respect.

ANSWERS TO ANALYZING LITERATURE

1. At first Squeaky is defensive and immature in her relationships with the other girls. If anyone says something she disagrees with, instead of talking about it, Squeaky responds by starting a fight. By the end of the story, she realizes her opponent's worth, and wants to work with her in coaching Raymond.
2. Cynthia is not honest about the efforts she exerts in order to excel. Squeaky prides herself on her honesty and lets everyone see how much she practices for the race.
3. Mary Louise used to be Squeaky's friend until Mary Louise became friends with Gretchen. Squeaky used to protect her from bullies. Now she talks against Squeaky. Rosie is fat and talks against Raymond. The two girls serve as a foil to Gretchen because Gretchen is the only one of the three that has any positive qualities. She grows and matures, accepting Squeaky at the end of the story.

ANSWERS TO CRITICAL THINKING AND READING

1. Squeaky sees that Gretchen is a serious runner. Gretchen acknowledges Squeaky's win by nodding her congratulations.
2. Squeaky realizes that she can give more than just love to Raymond. She can help him to win races of his own.

ANSWERS TO UNDERSTANDING LANGUAGE

1. criticize
2. angry

Challenge Squeaky uses many idioms and slang expressions that are typical of New York City neighborhoods. Ask your students what idioms and slang expressions are common in your area. Have them make a list of at least five.

THINKING AND WRITING

For help with this assignment, students can refer to Lesson 17, "Writing a Short Story," in the Handbook of Writing About Literature.

Publishing Student Writing Have some of the better essays read aloud in class.

Focus

More About the Author Dorothy Johnson made her home in Missoula, Montana. In her writing about the West, she takes a realistic look both at the white settlers and the Indians they displaced and frequently battled. She lived in New York City for several years, writing western stories, working as a magazine editor, and missing the mountains. When she returned to Montana she said, "We have all this wonderful space with practically nobody in it." Through her stories, she has gained a reputation for historical accuracy, brevity of style, and themes dealing with courage and strength of ordinary people. How do you think Montana has affected her stories dealing with the West?

Literary Focus After students have read the definitions, have them refer to other stories they have read for specific examples. Elicit examples of characters' speech and actions that indirectly characterize them.

Look For Tell the class that this story concerns a pioneer family moving west. Ask students to look for details that indicate the financial condition of the group, the character of the father, and possible reasons for Mary's wishing to join the group. Ask them to be able to give reasons why one of the group is more rounded than the others.

Writing/Prior Knowledge Suggest to students that their heroes can come from literature, film, real life, or even from their ideas of what a hero should be.

Vocabulary It would be helpful for students to know the following words also: **venison** (p. 107), **tarp** (p. 107), **gaunt** (p. 108), and **rummaged** (p. 109).

GUIDE FOR READING

The Day the Sun Came Out

Dorothy M. Johnson (1905–1984) lived most of her life in Montana, where she was born. Many of her stories have western or Indian themes. In fact, Johnson was an honorary member of the Blackfoot tribe; her Indian name is Kills-Both-Places. Two of Johnson's books were adapted in the popular movies "The Man Who Shot Liberty Valance," and "A Man Called Horse." "The Day the Sun Came Out" is one of her many stories about courage and strength in ordinary people.

Direct and Indirect Characterization

Characterization is the way a writer presents a character in a story. A writer may use direct or indirect characterization. In **direct characterization,** the writer tells you what a character is like. For example, the writer might state that Joe is a stubborn man.

In **indirect characterization,** the writer reveals a character through what he or she looks like, says, and does, and lets you draw conclusions about what the character is like. For example, the writer might describe an incident in which Joe acts stubbornly.

Look For

As you read "The Day the Sun Came Out," look for the methods the author uses to create the characters. What do you learn in particular about Mary? How do you learn this? See if you agree that she is heroic.

Writing

Think about someone you consider a hero. Freewrite about the reasons why you consider this person a hero.

Vocabulary

Knowing the meaning of the following words will help you as you read "The Day the Sun Came Out."

teamsters (tēm′stərz) *n.*: People who drive teams of horses to haul a load (p. 107)

homesteaders (hōm′ sted′ ərz) *n.*: Settlers who received land from the United States government in exchange for living on it and farming it for a period of time (p. 107)

savoring (sā′vər iŋ) *v.*: Enjoying; appreciating (p. 110)

Objectives

1 To understand the difference between direct and indirect characterization in a short story
2 To make inferences about characters
3 To appreciate dialect
4 To compare and contrast characters from two short stories

Support Material

Teaching Portfolio

Teacher Backup, pp. 157–159
Usage and Mechanics Worksheet, p. 160
Vocabulary Check, p. 161
Analyzing Literature Worksheet, *Understanding Characterization,* p. 162
Language Worksheet, *Appreciating Dialect,* p. 163
Selection Test, pp. 164–165

The Day the Sun Came Out

Dorothy M. Johnson

We left the home place behind, mile by slow mile, heading for the mountains, across the prairie where the wind blew forever.

1 At first there were four of us with the one-horse wagon and its skimpy load. Pa and I walked, because I was a big boy of eleven. My two little sisters romped and trotted until they got tired and had to be boosted up into the wagon bed.

2 That was no covered Conestoga, like Pa's folks came West in, but just an old farm wagon, drawn by one weary horse, creaking and rumbling westward to the mountains, toward the little woods town where Pa thought he had an old uncle who owned a little two-bit sawmill.

3 Two weeks we had been moving when we picked up Mary, who had run away from somewhere that she wouldn't tell. Pa didn't want her along, but she stood up to him with no fear in her voice.

"I'd rather go with a family and look after kids," she said, "but I ain't going back. If you won't take me, I'll travel with any wagon that will."

Pa scowled at her, and her wide blue eyes stared back.

"How old are you?" he demanded.

"Eighteen," she said. "There's teamsters come this way sometimes. I'd rather go with you folks. But I won't go back."

"We're prid'near out of grub," my father told her. "We're clean out of money. I got all I can handle without taking anybody else." He turned away as if he hated the sight of her. "You'll have to walk," he said.

So she went along with us and looked after the little girls, but Pa wouldn't talk to her.

On the prairie, the wind blew. But in the mountains, there was rain. When we stopped at little timber claims along the way, the homesteaders said it had rained all summer. Crops among the blackened stumps were rotted and spoiled. There was no cheer anywhere, and little hospitality. The people we talked to were past worrying. They were scared and desperate. 4

So was Pa. He traveled twice as far each day as the wagon, ranging through the woods with his rifle, but he never saw game. He had been depending on venison, but we never got any except as a grudging gift from the homesteaders.

He brought in a porcupine once, and that was fat meat and good. Mary roasted it in chunks over the fire, half crying with the smoke. Pa and I rigged up the tarp sheet for

Presentation

Motivation/Prior Knowledge Ask students to think about the title of this story. What does it suggest this story might be about?

Motivation for Reading Ask students to think about the title of this story. What does it suggest this story might be about?

Thematic Idea Another selection that deals with the theme of courage is "Grass Fire" (page 129).

Purpose-Setting Question What role does courage play in this story?

1 **Discussion** Who is the narrator of the story? Is he still eleven years old?

2 **Discussion** After reading the first three paragraphs, what do you think is the mood of the story? What descriptive words has the author used to convey this feeling? Have some students substitute words and phrases that would change the mood of the first three paragraphs to one of eager anticipation about a new home.

3 **Discussion** What is your first impression of Mary? You might also discuss the choice of the name Mary for this character. Ask students why they think the author chose this name. Students should be aware that authors carefully select the names of their characters. The name Mary is plain, simple, and has religious connotations. It might suggest love, sacrifice, and suffering.

4 **Discussion** What is the mood of this paragraph? What does it say about the homesteaders?

5 Literary Focus Bring out that, to the boy, this is the first time that his father has recognized Mary's presence. Note that this story is told from the first-person point-of-view. With a first-person narrator, the reader only knows what the narrator has observed or felt. Therefore, it may not be the first time that the father has recognized Mary's presence but only the first time that the boy is aware of his doing so.

6 Discussion What is the mood of the father? What must have happened in his life to make him feel this way? If he really feels this way, why is he bothering to go into town, which is probably four days away, to get food?

7 Discussion Why can't big boys cry?

a shelter to keep the rain from putting the fire clean out.

The porcupine was long gone, except for some of the tried-out[1] fat that Mary had saved, when we came to an old, empty cabin. Pa said we'd have to stop. The horse was wore out, couldn't pull anymore up those grades on the deep-rutted roads in the mountains.

At the cabin, at least there was shelter. We had a few potatoes left and some cornmeal. There was a creek that probably had fish in it, if a person could catch them. Pa tried it for half a day before he gave up. To this day I don't care for fishing. I remember my father's sunken eyes in his gaunt, grim face.

He took Mary and me outside the cabin to talk. Rain dripped on us from branches overhead.

"I think I know where we are," he said. "I calculate to get to old John's and back in about four days. There'll be grub in the town, and they'll let me have some whether old John's still there or not."

5 He looked at me. "You do like she tells you," he warned. It was the first time he had admitted Mary was on earth since we picked her up two weeks before.

"You're my pardner," he said to me, "but it might be she's got more brains. You mind what she says."

6 He burst out with bitterness, "There ain't anything good left in the world, or people to care if you live or die. But I'll get grub in the town and come back with it."

He took a deep breath and added, "If you get too all-fired hungry, butcher the horse. It'll be better than starvin'."

He kissed the little girls good-by and plodded off through the woods with one blanket and the rifle.

The cabin was moldy and had no floor. We kept a fire going under a hole in the roof, so it was full of blinding smoke, but we had to keep the fire so as to dry out the wood.

The third night, we lost the horse. A bear scared him. We heard the racket, and Mary and I ran out, but we couldn't see anything in the pitch-dark.

In gray daylight I went looking for him, and I must have walked fifteen miles. It seemed like I had to have that horse at the cabin when Pa came or he'd whip me. I got plumb lost two or three times and thought maybe I was going to die there alone and nobody would ever know it, but I found the way back to the clearing.

That was the fourth day, and Pa didn't come. That was the day we ate up the last of the grub.

The fifth day, Mary went looking for the horse. My sisters whimpered, huddled in a quilt by the fire, because they were scared and hungry.

I never did get dried out, always having to bring in more damp wood and going out to yell to see if Mary would hear me and not get lost. But I couldn't cry like the little girls did, because I was a big boy, eleven years old. 7

It was near dark when there was an answer to my yelling, and Mary came into the clearing.

Mary didn't have the horse—we never saw hide nor hair of that old horse again—but she was carrying something big and white that looked like a pumpkin with no color to it.

She didn't say anything, just looked around and saw Pa wasn't there yet, at the end of the fifth day.

---

1. tried-out fat: Fat or lard that has been boiled or melted.

"What's that thing?" my sister Elizabeth demanded.

"Mushroom," Mary answered. "I bet it hefts ten pounds."

"What are you going to do with it now?" I sneered. "Play football here?"

"Eat it—maybe," she said, putting it in a corner. Her wet hair hung over her shoulders. She huddled by the fire.

My sister Sarah began to whimper again. "I'm hungry!" she kept saying.

"Mushrooms ain't good eating," I said. "They can kill you."

"Maybe," Mary answered. "Maybe they can. I don't set up to know all about everything, like some people."

"What's that mark on your shoulder?" I asked her. "You tore your dress on the brush."

"What do you think it is?" she said, her head bowed in the smoke.

"Looks like scars," I guessed.

"'Tis scars. They whipped me, them I used to live with. Now mind your own business. I want to think."

Elizabeth whimpered, "Why don't Pa come back?"

"He's coming," Mary promised. "Can't come in the dark. Your pa'll take care of you soon's he can."

She got up and rummaged around in the grub box.

"Nothing there but empty dishes," I growled. "If there was anything, we'd know it."

Mary stood up. She was holding the can with the porcupine grease.

"I'm going to have something to eat,"
8 she said coolly. "You kids can't have any yet.
And I don't want any squalling,[2] mind."

2. **squalling** (skwôl′liŋ) *n.*: Crying or screaming.

It was a cruel thing, what she did then.
She sliced that big, solid mushroom and 9
heated grease in a pan.

The smell of it brought the little girls out of their quilt, but she told them to go back in so fierce a voice that they obeyed. They cried to break your heart.

I didn't cry. I watched, hating her.

I endured the smell of the mushroom frying as long as I could. Then I said, "Give me some."

"Tomorrow," Mary answered. "Tomor-
row, maybe. But not tonight." She turned to 10
me with a sharp command: "Don't bother
me! Just leave me be."

She knelt there by the fire and finished frying the slice of mushroom.

If I'd had Pa's rifle, I'd have been willing 11
to kill her right then and there.

She didn't eat right away. She looked at the brown, fried slice for a while and said, "By tomorrow morning, I guess you can tell whether you want any."

The little girls stared at her as she ate. Sarah was chewing an old leather glove.

When Mary crawled into the quilts with
them, they moved away as far as they could 12
get.

I was so scared that my stomach heaved, empty as it was.

Mary didn't stay in the quilts long. She took a drink out of the water bucket and sat down by the fire and looked through the smoke at me.

She said in a low voice, "I don't know how it will be if it's poison. Just do the best you can with the girls. Because your pa will come back, you know. . . . You better go to bed. I'm going to sit up."

And so would you sit up. If it might be
your last night on earth and the pain of 13
death might seize you at any moment, you

8 **Reading Strategy** Have the students summarize the story up to this point and have them predict what will happen when Mary eats the mushroom.

9 **Discussion** Why was it a cruel thing that she did? Does the boy know why she is doing this?

10 **Master Teacher Note** Have the class create a portrait of this remarkable woman. Frame questions to draw out her strength and devotion to the children. Why does she test the mushroom on herself? Discuss other remarkable heroes in fiction. What made them heroes?

11 **Discussion** Why was the boy so angry with Mary?

12 **Discussion** Why did the girls move away from Mary?

13 **Discussion** How has the boy's attitude toward Mary changed here?

Humanities Note

Lithograph, *A Log Cabin in a Clearing on the American Frontier,* 1826. The scene is a cabin that might well have served the family in this story. Have the students concentrate on the woman standing in the doorway. Using her as a focus, have the class compare and contrast her with Mary. Based on her age and appearance, could this be the woman in the story? Have the students support their opinions by referring to specific aspects of the story.

1. What message is given by the stumps on the left? Why has this land been cleared, perhaps recently?
2. Are there any other signs that a family of pioneer times occupied this cabin and land?
3. Is this work of art appropriate to illustrate this story? As you answer, think of the characters, the feeling, and the details in both the art and the story.

14 **Discussion** Even in their distressful situation, Mary looks at the world as if it were beautiful. Why?

15 **Enrichment** Note the change in mood from here to the end of the story. This would be a good place to discuss word connotations and the vivid word choices that authors make in order to convey mood and feeling. Have your students make a list of the dreary words used in the beginning of the story and contrast them with the hopeful, more cheerful words used in these paragraphs.

16 **Discussion** What are the characteristics of a wonderful person? What characteristics does Mary have? Ask the students to go back through the story to find words and phrases that were used to describe Mary.

A LOG CABIN IN A CLEARING ON THE AMERICAN FRONTIER, 1826
The Granger Collection

would sit up by the smoky fire, wide-awake, remembering whatever you had to remember, savoring life.

We sat in silence after the girls had gone to sleep. Once I asked, "How long does it take?"

"I never heard," she answered. "Don't think about it."

I slept after a while, with my chin on my chest. Maybe Peter dozed that way at Gethsemane as the Lord knelt praying.

Mary's moving around brought me wide-awake. The black of night was fading.

"I guess it's all right." Mary said. "I'd be able to tell by now, wouldn't I?"

I answered gruffly, "I don't know."

Mary stood in the doorway for a while,
14 looking out at the dripping world as if she
found it beautiful. Then she fried slices of
the mushroom while the little girls danced
15 with anxiety.

We feasted, we three, my sisters and I, until Mary ruled, "That'll hold you," and would not cook any more. She didn't touch any of the mushroom herself.

That was a strange day in the moldy cabin. Mary laughed and was gay; she told stories, and we played "Who's Got the Thimble?" with a pine cone.

In the afternoon we heard a shout, and my sisters screamed and I ran ahead of them across the clearing.

The rain had stopped. My father came plunging out of the woods leading a pack horse—and well I remember the treasures of food in that pack.

He glanced at us anxiously as he tore at the ropes that bound the pack.

"Where's the other one?" he demanded.

Mary came out of the cabin then, walking sedately. As she came toward us, the sun began to shine.

My stepmother was a wonderful woman. 16

Reader's Response Why do you think Mary didn't explain why she ate the mushroom before allowing the children to have any? Should she have taken a different approach? Explain.

Master Teacher Note What does the verb tense in the last sentence suggest? Why might the narrator have written this story? You might ask the students to think of someone whom they love who is no longer alive. Have them write a tribute to that person in the form of a story of a memorable experience that they had with that person.

THINKING ABOUT THE SELECTION

Recalling

1. Describe how the family travels.
2. Why doesn't Pa want Mary to join them?
3. Why does Pa leave his family and Mary alone?
4. Why does Mary go looking for the horse?
5. How do the children feel about Mary as she eats the mushroom?

Interpreting

6. Find two details indicating that Pa has come to respect Mary by the time he leaves.
7. Why won't Mary let the children eat the mushroom until the next day?
8. The Bible says Peter dozed while Jesus waited for the soldiers to take him. Why does the boy in this story compare himself to Peter?
9. Explain the significance of the last line: "My stepmother was a wonderful woman."
10. Why does this story have the title it does?

Applying

11. Would you have told the children why they couldn't have the mushroom? Explain.
12. Explain why you think Mary is heroic or not.

ANALYZING LITERATURE

Understanding Characterization

In **direct characterization,** writers state directly what a character is like. For example, Johnson has the boy say, "I was so scared that my stomach heaved, empty as it was." When the writer uses **indirect characterization,** she shows the character's personality through the character's words and actions. For example, Mary says, "If you won't take me, I'll travel with any wagon who will." This suggests Mary is determined. Tell whether the writer is using direct or indirect characterization in the following:

1. "Pa didn't want her along, but she stood up to him with no fear in her voice."
2. "I don't know how it will be if it's poison. Just do the best you can with the girls."

CRITICAL THINKING AND READING

Making Inferences About Characters

Inferences are conclusions draw from evidence. When writers use indirect characterization, you must make inferences about the character's feelings and personality.

1. When Mary crawls into the quilts after eating the mushroom, the two girls move as far away from her as they can. What are they feeling?
2. When Mary looks at the dripping world the morning after she ate the mushroom, she finds it beautiful. What was she feeling the night before? What is she feeling now?
3. When Pa returns he looks anxiously for Mary. How do you think he is feeling about Mary?

UNDERSTANDING LANGUAGE

Appreciating Dialect

Dialect is a way of speaking found in a particular region or group. It usually differs from the standard language in grammar, vocabulary, or pronunciation. Writers use dialect to place characters in a certain time and to give them local color.

Pa says, "If you get too all-fired hungry, butcher the horse." Such dialect was used by Americans in the 1800's.

Rewrite these sentences in standard English:

1. '"We're prid'near out of food. We're clean out of money.'"
2. "And I don't want any squalling, mind."

THINKING AND WRITING

Comparing and Contrasting Characters

Mary displays great courage. Select a courageous character from another story. First list the ways in which Mary and this character are alike. Then list the ways in which they are different. Write the first draft of a composition comparing and contrasting the two characters. Revise, making sure your details are in a logical order. Finally, proofread your paper.

Closure and Extension

ANSWERS TO THINKING ABOUT THE SELECTION

Recalling

1. There were originally four people traveling with a one-horse wagon and its skimpy load.
2. Pa didn't want Mary because there was little food and no money left.
3. Pa left to get more food.
4. Mary went looking for the horse because the boy was afraid his father would whip him for losing the horse.
5. They thought she was doing a cruel thing and were angry with her.

Interpreting

6. He tells the boy to do as Mary tells him. He says that Mary might have "more brains" than the boy.
7. Mary wants to make sure that the mushroom isn't poisonous.
8. There was nothing the boy could do to help Mary. He just had to wait to see what would happen to her.
9. Pa married Mary, and she became the boy's stepmother. The boy is telling the story after his stepmother had died.
10. Mary was a wonderful person. When she came into the family, everything became better.

Applying

11. Answers will differ. Some students might say they would because the children were mature enough to understand what she was doing. Other students might say they would not because it would scare the youngsters.
12. Answers will differ. Most students will probably say yes because she risked her life by eating the mushroom.

ANSWERS TO ANALYZING LITERATURE

1. direct characterization
2. indirect characterization

ANSWERS TO CRITICAL THINKING AND READING

1. They are angry with her for not sharing the mushroom with them.
2. She was scared that she might die. She feels relieved that she wasn't poisoned and looks at the world differently than before.
3. He realized that he missed Mary when he was away and that he really cares for her.

ANSWERS TO UNDERSTANDING LANGUAGE

1. "Our food supply is nearly gone. We don't have any money."
2. "And I don't want any fighting."

Challenge The external conflict in "The Day The Sun Came Out" centers on a family's struggle to survive hunger in a hostile environment. Ask students to imagine some of the other threats from nature that the pioneer family might have encountered, such as severe weather or dangerous animals.

THINKING AND WRITING

For help with this assignment, students can refer to Lesson 16, "Writing a Comparative Evaluation," in the Handbook of Writing About Literature.

Publishing Student Writing Send some of the better essays to the school newspaper for publication. The paper might devote a page to courageous people in literature.

Focus

More About the Author Almost all of Isaac Singer's work appeared first in the *Jewish Daily Forward,* a Yiddish newspaper in New York City. Point out that Singer lectures in perfect, though highly accented, English. Why might he choose to write in Yiddish despite the fact that he has lived most of his life in New York?

Literary Focus Remind the class that a first-person narrator does not necessarily indicate the author is speaking of his or her own life. It means you are getting one character's viewpoint, which may or may not be slanted.

Look For Ask your students to prepare to discuss the way Professor Shlemiel sees himself. Is he ashamed or embarrassed by his problem? How many things that he does have been done by the students? Do they suspect the author himself might be guilty of some?

Writing/Prior Knowledge Some students may find it easier to write about themselves by exaggerating their own occasional moments of forgetfulness.

Vocabulary Most students will have no difficulty with these words. You might have them use each word in a sentence orally before reading the story.

GUIDE FOR READING

The Day I Got Lost

Isaac Bashevis Singer (1904–) was born in Poland, where he received a traditional Jewish education. In 1935 he settled in New York City, where he became a U.S. citizen. Singer writes in Yiddish, a language of some East European Jews and their descendants. In 1978 he was awarded the Nobel Prize for literature. Many of his stories involve people with exaggerated traits. In "The Day I Got Lost," the professor typifies a shlemiel, a Yiddish word for a bungler or unlucky person.

Narrator

A **narrator** is the person who tells a story. In this story, the narrator speaks in the first person as "I." He tells the story as he experiences it, presenting only his own thoughts, feelings, observations, and interpretations of events.

In "The Day I Got Lost" the way the narrator tells the story adds to its humor. Professor Shlemiel tells his story matter-of-factly; he does not realize how utterly ridiculous it is.

Look For

As you read "The Day I Got Lost," look for the differences between the way Professor Shlemiel sees the situation he is in and the way you see it. How does this difference make his story even funnier?

Writing

Freewrite for five minutes about a day in the life of any forgetful person. Think about all the funny things that could happen and exaggerate them. Make your tone light, not serious.

Vocabulary

Knowing the following words will help you as you read "The Day I Got Lost."

eternal (i tur′ n'l) *adj.*: Everlasting (p. 114)
destined (des′ tind) *v.*: Determined by fate (p. 114)
forsaken (fər sā′ kən) *adj.*: Abandoned; desolate (p. 115)
pandemonium (pan′ də mō′ nē əm) *n.*: A scene of wild disorder (p. 115)

Objectives

1 To understand the character of the narrator in a short story
2 To understand how caricature can create a humorous effect
3 To report on the use of caricature in advertisements
4 To write a humorous sequel to the story

Support Material

Teaching Portfolio
Teacher Backup, pp. 167–169
Grammar in Action Worksheet, *Understanding Verb Tense,* pp. 170–171
Usage and Mechanics Worksheet, p. 172
Vocabulary Check, p. 173
Analyzing Literature Worksheet, *Understanding the Narrator,* p. 174
Language Worksheet, *Understanding Synonyms and Antonyms,* p. 175
Selection Test, pp. 176–177

The Day I Got Lost

Isaac Bashevis Singer

It is easy to recognize me. See a man in the street wearing a too long coat, too large shoes, a crumpled hat with a wide brim, spectacles with one lens missing, and carrying an umbrella though the sun is shining, and that man will be me, Professor Shlemiel.[1] There are other unmistakable clues to
2 my identity. My pockets are always bulging with newspapers, magazines, and just papers. I carry an overstuffed briefcase, and I'm forever making mistakes. I've been living in New York City for over forty years, yet whenever I want to go uptown, I find myself walking downtown, and when I want to go east, I go west. I'm always late and I never recognize anybody.

I'm always misplacing things. A hundred times a day I ask myself, Where is my
3 pen? Where is my money? Where is my handkerchief? Where is my address book? I am what is known as an absentminded professor.

For many years I have been teaching philosophy in the same university, and I still have difficulty in locating my classrooms. Elevators play strange tricks on me. I want to go to the top floor and I land in the basement. Hardly a day passes when an elevator door doesn't close on me. Elevator doors are my worst enemies.

In addition to my constant blundering
4 and losing things, I'm forgetful. I enter a coffee shop, hang up my coat, and leave without it. By the time I remember to go back for it, I've forgotten where I've been. I lose hats, books, umbrellas, rubbers, and above all manuscripts. Sometimes I even forget my own address. One evening I took a taxi because I was in a hurry to get home. The taxi driver said, "Where to?" And I could not remember where I lived.

"Home!" I said.

"Where is home?" he asked in astonishment.

"I don't remember," I replied.

"What is your name?"

"Professor Shlemiel."

"Professor," the driver said, "I'll get you

1. **Shlemiel** (shlə mēl'): Version of the slang word schlemiel, an ineffectual, bungling person.

Presentation

Motivation/Prior Knowledge Ask your students if they have ever been lost. How did they feel? How did they get "found"?

Purpose-Setting Question Have you ever known a shlemiel like the Professor?

1 **Literary Focus** What is a caricature? Bring out that in a caricature, a person's personality is ludicrously exaggerated. In what ways is Professor Shlemiel a caricature? What other caricatures do you know? Discuss some comic caricatures like Archie and Veronica. How are they caricatures of teenagers? What about Popeye? How is he a caricature of a sailor?

2 **Discussion** What does the Yiddish word *shlemiel* mean? What is the author's purpose in so naming the Professor? Do you know any other characters in either films or television who share his personality traits? What about in real life?

3 **Discussion** Have any of these things ever happened to you? Point out that from the beginning of the story, the reader should feel some affinity to this professor since we all do some of the things he does.

4 **Master Teacher Note** Ask your students why some people have such terrible memories. Is it because they have too much to do? Or because they are thinking of other things? What are the consequences for them and others of this forgetfulness? Have students relate incidents they know of. The bungling Inspector Clouseau of *The Pink Panther* series might be a familiar figure to many students. Ask how indulgent are the victims of his memory lapses?

5 Reading Strategy Have students predict what the Professor will do next.

6 Discussion What would you have done in this predicament?

to a telephone booth. Look in the telephone book and you'll find your address."

He drove me to the nearest drugstore with a telephone booth in it, but he refused to wait. I was about to enter the store when I realized I had left my briefcase behind. I ran after the taxi, shouting, "My briefcase, my briefcase!" But the taxi was already out of earshot.

In the drugstore, I found a telephone book, but when I looked under S, I saw to my horror that though there were a number of Shlemiels listed, I was not among them. At that moment I recalled that several months before, Mrs. Shlemiel had decided that we should have an unlisted telephone number. The reason was that my students thought nothing of calling me in the middle of the night and waking me up. It also happened quite frequently that someone wanted to call another Shlemiel and got me by mistake. That was all very well—but how was I going to get home?

I usually had some letters addressed to me in my breast pocket. But just that day I had decided to clean out my pockets. It was my birthday and my wife had invited friends in for the evening. She had baked a huge cake and decorated it with birthday candles. I could see my friends sitting in our living room, waiting to wish me a happy birthday.
5 And here I stood in some drugstore, for the life of me not able to remember where I lived.

Then I recalled the telephone number of a friend of mine, Dr. Motherhead, and I decided to call him for help. I dialed and a young girl's voice answered.

"Is Dr. Motherhead at home?"

"No," she replied.

"Is his wife at home?"

"They're both out," the girl said.

"Perhaps you can tell me where they can be reached?" I said.

"I'm only the babysitter, but I think they went to a party at Professor Shlemiel's. Would you like to leave a message?" she said. "Who shall I say called, please?"

"Professor Shlemiel," I said.

"They left for your house about an hour ago," the girl said.

"Can you tell me where they went?" I asked.

"I've just told you," she said. "They went to your house."

"But where do I live?"

"You must be kidding!" the girl said, and hung up.

I tried to call a number of friends (those whose telephone numbers I happened to think of), but wherever I called, I got the same reply: "They've gone to a party at Professor Shlemiel's."

As I stood in the street wondering what
to do, it began to rain. "Where's my umbrel- 6
la?" I said to myself. And I knew the answer at once. I'd left it—somewhere. I got under a nearby canopy. It was now raining cats and dogs. It lightninged and thundered. All day it had been sunny and warm, but now that I was lost and my umbrella was lost, it had to storm. And it looked as if it would go on for the rest of the night.

To distract myself, I began to ponder the ancient philosophical problem. A mother chicken lays an egg, I thought to myself, and when it hatches, there is a chicken. That's how it has always been. Every chicken comes from an egg and every egg comes from a chicken. But was there a chicken first? Or an egg first? No philosopher has ever been able to solve this eternal question. Just the same, there must be an answer. Perhaps I, Shlemiel, am destined to stumble on it.

It continued to pour buckets. My feet were getting wet and I was chilled. I began to sneeze and I wanted to wipe my nose, but my handkerchief, too, was gone.

At that moment I saw a big black dog. He was standing in the rain getting soaked and

Grammar in Action

In composing a story, the writer selects the time in which it will be told: the present, the past, or the future. The writer then uses the appropriate **verb tense** consistently in the story. Notice the verbs in the following passages from "The Day I Got Lost":

In the drugstore, I found a telephone book, but when I looked under S, I saw to my horror that though there were a number of Shlemiels listed, I was not among them.

I usually had some letters addressed to me in my breast pocket. But just that day I had decided to clean out my pockets. It was my birthday and my wife had invited friends in for the evening.

Then I recalled the number of a friend of mine . . .

The verbs are in the past tense or the past perfect tense: *was, had, had decided, was, had invited, recalled.* The two past perfect

looking at me with sad eyes. I knew immediately what the trouble was. The dog was lost. He, too, had forgotten his address. I felt a great love for that innocent animal. I called to him and he came running to me. I talked to him as if he were human. "Fellow, we're
7 in the same boat," I said. "I'm a man shlemiel and you're a dog shlemiel. Perhaps it's also your birthday, and there's a party for you, too. And here you stand shivering and forsaken in the rain, while your loving master is searching for you everywhere. You're probably just as hungry as I am."

I patted the dog on his wet head and he wagged his tail. "Whatever happens to me will happen to you," I said. "I'll keep you with me until we both find our homes. If we don't find your master, you'll stay with me. Give me your paw," I said. The dog lifted his right paw. There was no question that he understood.

A taxi drove by and splattered us both. Suddenly it stopped and I heard someone shouting, "Shlemiel! Shlemiel!" I looked up and saw the taxi door open, and the head of a friend of mine appeared. "Shlemiel," he called. "What are you doing here? Who are you waiting for?"

"Where are you going?" I asked.

"To your house, of course. I'm sorry I'm late, but I was detained. Anyhow, better late than never. But why aren't you at home? And whose dog is that?"

"Only God could have sent you!" I exclaimed. "What a night! I've forgotten my address, I've left my briefcase in a taxi, I've lost my umbrella, and I don't know where my rubbers are."

"Shlemiel," my friend said, "if there was ever an absentminded professor, you're it!"

When I rang the bell of my apartment, my wife opened the door. "Shlemiel!" she shrieked. "Everybody is waiting for you. Where have you been? Where is your briefcase? Your umbrella? Your rubbers? And who is this dog?"

Our friends surrounded me. "Where have you been?" they cried. "We were so worried. We thought surely something had happened to you!"

"Who is this dog?" my wife kept repeating.

"I don't know," I said finally. "I found him in the street. Let's just call him Bow Wow for the time being."

"Bow Wow, indeed!" my wife scolded. "You know our cat hates dogs. And what about the parakeets? He'll scare them to death."

"He's a quiet dog," I said. "He'll make friends with the cat. I'm sure he loves parakeets. I could not leave him shivering in the rain. He's a good soul."

The moment I said this the dog let out a bloodcurdling howl. The cat ran into the room. When she saw the dog, she arched her back and spat at him, ready to scratch out his eyes. The parakeets in their cage began flapping their wings and screeching. Everybody started talking at once. There was pandemonium.

Would you like to know how it all ended? 8

Bow Wow still lives with us. He and the cat are great friends. The parakeets have learned to ride on his back as if he were a horse. As for my wife, she loves Bow Wow even more than I do. Whenever I take the dog out, she says, "Now, don't forget your address, both of you."

I never did find my briefcase, or my umbrella, or my rubbers. Like many philosophers before me, I've given up trying to solve the riddle of which came first, the chicken or the egg. Instead, I've started writing a book
called *The Memoirs of Shlemiel.* If I don't 9
forget the manuscript in a taxi, or a restaurant, or on a bench in the park, you may read them someday. In the meantime, here is a sample chapter.

7 Discussion Note the use of the word *shlemiel* not as the professor's name. Why does he call the dog "a dog shlemiel"?

8 Reading Strategy Have your students predict the end of the story.

9 Discussion Do you think he'll ever finish his book? Why? Would you read his memoirs? Why?

Enrichment For students who enjoyed reading this story, suggest they read some short stories by another famous Yiddish writer, Sholom Aleichem. He wrote humorous stories about Jewish life in Russia and Jewish immigration to the United States.

Master Teacher Note Explain that Singer's brand of exaggeration differs from Twain's. Twain exaggerates individual details by stretching them out of proportion to reality. Singer exaggerates by piling one realistic detail on top of another until the sum defies belief. In a sense, Singer's technique is deadpan. Can students think of any stand-up comics who use this kind of delivery?

Reader's Response Choose an aspect of your personality or the personality of a friend and describe how it could be exaggerated for a humorous effect in a caricature.

verbs (*had decided, had invited*) indicate an action that was completed earlier. (Past perfect verbs are formed by using *had* with the past form of the verb.)

Student Activity 1. Find ten more verbs in the story that are in the past tense, and three verbs in the past perfect tense.

Student Activity 2. Write a paragraph in which you tell about something that happened to you in the past few days. Underline all of the verbs you use. Check over your writing or have a partner check it to make sure that you used the past tense throughout.

Closure and Extension

ANSWERS TO THINKING ABOUT THE SELECTION

Recalling

1. His most outstanding trait is his forgetfulness.
2. First he looks up his address in a telephone book. Then he tries to telephone a friend.
3. Everybody is at Shlemiel's house for his birthday party.
4. He met a friend who was taking a taxi to his birthday party.
5. He feels sorry for the dog who was wet and hungry.

Interpreting

6. They were both wet from the rain and hungry. The dog appeared lost, as was Professor Shlemiel.
7. He is constantly losing or misplacing things. He can't remember addresses and phone numbers. He gets splattered by cars and almost misses his own birthday party.
8. The end of Professor Shlemiel's day was ridiculous because he brought a dog home who he claimed was very quiet. But the dog ran after the cat and scared the parakeet and everyone at his party started talking at once. There was pandemonium.

Applying

9. Answers will differ. Examples include any of the super heroes, such as Superman.

ANSWERS TO ANALYZING LITERATURE

1. He tells you what he looks like, that he is always late, and that he never recognizes anybody. He also says he always misplaces things and is absentminded.
2. His wife and friends view him as absentminded and careless. His wife says, "Now, don't forget your address, both of you." His friends query, "Where have you been? . . . We were so worried. We thought surely something had happened to you!"
3. Answers will differ. Students may say the story wouldn't be as funny if Mrs. Shlemiel told it. It's funnier because Professor Shlemiel sees these traits in himself. If Mrs. Shlemiel told the story, it could be interpreted as a wife's opinion of her husband.

ANSWERS TO CRITICAL THINKING AND READING

1. He loses his rubbers and umbrella and then it starts to rain. Elevator doors close on him. He gets splashed by a taxi in the rain.
2. He is an absentminded professor in that he always misplaces things. He misplaces his pen, his money, his handkerchief, or his address book. He loses hats, books, and manuscripts. He even forgets his own address and phone number.
3. Answers will differ. Most students will probably say no. The idea that he is so absent-minded should be the main focus of the story. If Professor Shlemiel were more well-rounded, he wouldn't be as funny.

Challenge Tell the class that the word *pandemonium* translates literally as a place of all demons. When they create pandemonium, therefore, what are they?

THINKING AND WRITING

For help with this assignment, students can refer to Lesson 17, "Writing a Short Story," in the Handbook of Writing About Literature.

THINKING ABOUT THE SELECTION

Recalling

1. What is Shlemiel's most outstanding trait?
2. In what two ways does Professor Shlemiel try to find out his own address?
3. Why can't he get in touch with anybody?
4. How does Professor Shlemiel get home?
5. Why does he bring the dog home with him?

Interpreting

6. In what ways are Shlemiel and the dog alike?
7. In what ways is the professor a true shlemiel, or bungler?
8. Explain what is ridiculous about the outcome of Professor Shlemiel's day.

Applying

9. Describe a character from books, movies, or television whose traits are exaggerated to be funny. An example is the classic comic strip character Popeye the Sailor Man, whose strength is exaggerated to create humor.

ANALYZING LITERATURE

Understanding Narrator

The **narrator,** or person who tells the story, is Professor Shlemiel, who speaks in the first person as "I." You experience the story through his eyes, knowing only his thoughts and feelings; you do not learn the views of anyone else, such as his wife or his friend in the taxi. However, as an active reader, you read between the lines, and see humor where Schlemiel does not.

The serious way in which Professor Shlemiel tells his ridiculous story adds to its humor.

1. What does Shlemiel tell you about himself?
2. How do you think Professor Schlemiel's wife views him? How do you think his friends view him? Find evidence to support your answer.
3. How do you think this story would have been different if Mrs. Schlemiel had told it?

CRITICAL THINKING AND READING

Understanding Caricature

Caricature is the distortion or exaggeration of the peculiarities in a character's personality. Often a writer will use caricature to create a humorous effect. The exaggerated traits can be amusing or ridiculous in themselves, or they can cause preposterous situations.

1. A schlemiel is a bungler. How is Schlemiel a perfect example of this type of person?
2. In what way is he a perfect example of an absent-minded professor?
3. The author reveals only one side of the Professor's personality and blows this side out of proportion. Would this story have been as amusing if the author had presented the Professor as a well-rounded individual? Explain.

SPEAKING AND LISTENING

Reporting on Caricature in Advertising

Advertisements, and television commercials often show people selling products who are caricatures of some sort: the harried housewife, the helpful salesperson. Caricatures appeal to people because they are easily understood.

Collect several advertisements that show people selling a product. Give an oral report describing the caricature of people portrayed.

THINKING AND WRITING

Writing a Story

Write a story telling of another day in the life of Shlemiel. First freewrite for three minutes about what an absent-minded professor might do. Imagine as many ridiculous incidents as you can. Using this freewriting, write in the first person. Make your tone serious as you describe the humorous events. Revise, making sure you have used exaggeration. Proofread your story and share it with your classmates.

Setting

LAVENDER AND OLD LACE
Charles Burchfield
From the collection of the New Britain Museum of American Art

Publishing Student Writing Have some of the better essays read aloud in class.

Humanities Note

Fine art, *Lavender and Old Lace,* by Charles Burchfield. The American artist Charles Burchfield (1893-1967) was schooled in painting at the Cleveland Institute of Art. His teacher there, Henry Keller, encouraged Burchfield to develop an individualistic style of painting. To finance his painting career, Charles Burchfield worked at many things, including designing wallpaper, illustrating, and teaching art classes. He eventually gained fame for his intense and imaginative paintings of nature and his moody, psychological studies of buildings.

The painting *Lavender and Old Lace* is a watercolor painted between 1939 and 1947. This brooding study of a Victorian house is filled with gloom and mystery. Burchfield has made the building come alive as if its awareness grew on the emotions of those that dwelled there. The melancholy air is nurtured by the overshadowing tree and the gingerbread trim, which hangs from the house like a malevolent growth. Burchfield referred to this painting as "an elegy." He used the twilight time of evening and the crowding vegetation to instill a sense of mystery into this painting. Burchfield's ability to give life to inanimate objects and plant forms is apparent in this work.

Master Teacher Note To Introduce the element of setting, have students look at Art Transparency 4, *Diner* by Richard Estes, in the Teaching Portfolio. Explain that a writer uses words to create a seting that expresses time, place, and mood. Ask students what they think is the time and place of the painting. What details of the diner's style and appearance give them this impression? Does the use of lighting, shadow, and color produce any particular mood? What might take place in this diner?

Focus

More About the Author Though Shirley Ann Grau has written some travel essays, she is essentially a regionalist, preferring to write mainly about New Orleans and the coast, terrain, and bayous of Louisiana. At the same time she is often able, as she is in this story, to make her setting so universal that the story could occur in New England, California, or almost anywhere there is a coast bounding a treacherous piece of water. How might her writings reflect her love of solitude and dislike of travel?

Literary Focus After students have read the definition of setting, have them consider the settings of some of the stories they have read. Why, for example, are specific settings needed in some stories and not in others?

Look For How much control can people exercise over the water?

Writing/Prior Knowledge You might collect and present several pictures of the sea in various moods and weathers. Before asking students to write, divide the class into groups and allow time for the groups to discuss what they see in the pictures. Each group should be able to see several pictures before writing begins.

Vocabulary You might have students use each word in a sentence orally before reading the story.

GUIDE FOR READING

The Land and the Water

Shirley Ann Grau (1929–) has lived in New Orleans most of her life. She attended Tulane University and raised four children while writing novels, short stories, and journal articles. *Black Prince and Other Stories* is a collection of stories Grau has written especially for teen-agers. "The Land and the Water," like many of her other short stories, is set in Louisiana. This story is an example of the importance of nature and its forces in stories Grau creates.

Setting

The **setting** of a story is the time and place of the action. In a short story the setting is usually presented through detailed descriptions. In some stories the setting plays a very important role. It affects what happens to the characters and what they learn about life.

Look For

"The Land and the Water" takes place by the ocean. As you read, look for ways the ocean affects the plot and the characters. What role does weather play in the story? What feeling does it create?

Writing

Think of times you have seen an ocean or pictures of an ocean. How does weather or the season affect the ocean? List words and phrases that describe the ocean in all its different moods.

Vocabulary

Knowing the following words will help you as you read "The Land and the Water."

stifled (stī′ f'ld) *adj.*: Muffled; suppressed (p. 119)
luminous (lo͞o′ mə nəs) *adj.*: Glowing in the dark (p. 122)
scuttling (skut′ 'liŋ) *v.*: Running or moving quickly (p. 122)
lee (lē) *n.*: Sheltered place; the side away from the wind (p. 122)
spume (spyo͞om) *n.*: Foam; froth (p. 122)
swamped (swämp'd) *v.*: Sank by filling with water (p. 123)
tousled-looking (tou′ z'ld lo͝o′kiŋ) *adj.*: Rumpled or mussed (p. 123)
impenetrable (im pen′ i trə b'l) *adj.*: Not able to be passed through (p. 126)

Objectives

1 To understand the setting of a short story
2 To make inferences about a story's setting
3 To choose a definition that fits the context of a word
4 To write a description of a setting

Support Material

Teaching Portfolio
Teacher Backup, pp. 179–181
Grammar in Action Worksheets, *Using Semicolons,* pp. 182–183, *Understanding Sentence Fragments,* pp. 184–185
Usage and Mechanics Worksheet, p. 186
Vocabulary Check, p. 187
Analyzing Literature Worksheet, *Understanding Setting,* p. 188
Language Worksheet, *Choosing Meaning to Fit the Context,* p. 189
Selection Test, pp. 190–191

The Land and the Water

Shirley Ann Grau

From the open Atlantic beyond Tim-
1 balier Head a few scattered foghorns grunted, muffled and faint. That bank[1] had been hanging offshore for days. We'd been watching the big draggers[2] chug up to it, get dimmer and dimmer, and finally disappear in its grayness, leaving only the stifled sounds of their horns behind. It had been there so long we got used to it, and came to think of it as always being there, like another piece of land, maybe.

The particular day I'm thinking about started out clear and hot with a tiny breeze—a perfect day for a Snipe or a Sailfish.[3] There were a few of them moving on the big bay, not many. And they stayed close to
2 shore, for the barometer was drifting slowly down in its tube and the wind was shifting slowly backward around the compass.[4]

Larger sailboats never came into the bay—it was too shallow for them—and these small ones, motorless, moving with the smallest stir of air, could sail for home, if the fog came in, by following the shore—or if there was really no wind at all, they could be paddled in and beached. Then their crews could walk to the nearest phone and call to be picked up. You had to do it that way, because the fog always came in so quick. As it did that morning.

My sister and I were working by our dock, scraping and painting the little dinghy.[5] Because the spring tides washed over this stretch, there were no trees, no bushes even, just snail grass and beach lettuce and pink flowering sea lavender, things that liked salt. All morning it had been bright and blue and shining. Then all at once it turned gray and wet, like an unfalling rain, moveless and still. We went right on sanding and from being sweaty hot we turned sweaty cold, the fog chilling and dripping off our faces.

"It isn't worth the money," my sister said. She is ten and that is her favorite sentence. This time it wasn't even true. She was the one who'd talked my father into giving us the job.

I wouldn't give her the satisfaction of an
answer, though I didn't like the wet any 3
more than she did. It was sure to make my hair roll up in tight little curls all over my

1. **bank** *n.*: Mass of fog.
2. **draggers** *n.*: Fishing boats that use large nets to catch fish.
3. **Snipe . . . Sailfish:** names of sailboats.
4. **barometer . . . compass:** The decrease in barometric pressure and change in wind direction indicate that a storm is approaching.

5. **dinghy** (din' gē) *n.*: Small rowboat.

Presentation

Motivation/Prior Knowledge On the board, paraphrase Louise Gossett's quote about Shirley Grau: "People are not free agents protected by their environment but, rather, stoics reconciled to the violence of nature that assails them." Ask students to explain the meaning of the quote. They will probably need help with the vocabulary. Ask them to decide, after finishing the story, whether or not the story illustrates the critic's quote.

Thematic Idea Another selection that deals with the effect of a natural disaster is "Grass Fire" (page 129).

Purpose-Setting Question What role does nature play in this story?

1 **Clarification** Timbalier Head is south of New Orleans, Louisiana. It is on the Gulf of Mexico.

2 **Discussion** What does a falling barometer mean?

3 **Discussion** Who is the narrator of the story? What is her relationship to the ten-year-old girl?

Humanities Note

Perkins Cove, by Jane Betts. Those students who have enjoyed summer visits to the Maine coast will recognize the fishing village shown here. Point out the tidy design of the houses near the dock. A customer is seen stopping at the small snack bar. A gangway goes from the land's edge to a floating dock, and to complete this ordered hamlet, there is a mountain in the background. The portrait of a rational way of life is meant to be deceiving. Those who know the Maine coast know how menacing the water can become and how dangerous it is to go out on it once the fog comes in. Tragedy has come to many fishermen. Parts of boats have been found floating miles from shore or washed up on the beach.

1. Why was this picture of a peaceful scene chosen to accompany a story of a drowning?
2. Do you agree with using this painting to accompany the story? Why or why not?
3. Would you have chosen another one instead? Explain.

4 **Discussion** What does the phrase "The land and the water all looked the same . . ." mean?

PERKINS COVE
Jane Betts
Collection of Wendy Betts

head and I would have to wash it again and sleep on the hard metal curlers to get it back in shape.

Finally my sister said, "Let's go get something to drink."

When we turned around to go back up to the house, we found that it had disappeared. It was only a couple of hundred yards away, right behind us and up a little grade, a long slope of beach plum and poison ivy, salt burned and scrubby. You couldn't see a
4 thing now, except gray. The land and the water all looked the same; the fog was that thick.

There wasn't anything to drink. Just a lot of empty bottles waiting in cases on the back porch. "Well," my sister said, "let's go tell her."

She meant my mother of course, and we didn't have to look for her very hard. The house wasn't big, and being a summer house, it had very thin walls: we could hear her playing cards with my father in the living room.

They were sitting by the front window. On a clear day there was really something to see out there: the sweep of the bay and the pattern of the inlets and, beyond it all, the dark blue of the Atlantic. Today there was nothing, not even a bird, if you didn't count the occasional yelp of a seagull off high overhead somewhere.

"There's nothing to drink," my sister said. "Not a single thing."

"Tomorrow's grocery day," my mother said. "Go make a lemonade."

Grammar in Action

Semicolons are used to join independent clauses in certain instances. If the meaning of the two clauses is closely related, and a coordinating conjunction is either unnecessary or unwanted because it would change the meaning, writers use semicolons.

In the following example from "The Land and the Water," a period would be too much of a break, and a comma with a conjunction wouldn't sound right. Therefore, the writer chooses a semicolon; it is the correct punctuation mark for this instance.

The land and the water all looked the same; the fog was just that thick.

If two independent clauses are joined with either a conjunctive adverb (*also, besides, furthermore, consequently, however, indeed, instead, moreover, nevertheless, otherwise, therefore, thus*) or a transitional expression (*as a result, at this time, for instance, in fact, on the other hand, that is*), a semicolon goes before the conjunctive adverb or the transitional expression, and a comma follows it.

A semicolon is also used to separate independent clauses if there are two or more commas within any of the independent

5 "Look," my father said, "why not go back to work on the dinghy? You'll get your money faster."

So we went, only stopping first to get our oilskin hats. And pretty soon, fog was dripping from the brims like a kind of very gentle rain.

6 But we didn't go back to work on the dinghy. For a while we sat on the edge of the dock and looked at the minnow-flecked water, and then we got out the crab nets and went over to the tumbled heap of rocks to see if we could catch anything. We spent a couple of hours out there, skinning our knees against the rough barnacled[6] surfaces. Once a seagull swooped down so low he practically touched the tops of our hats. Almost but not quite. I don't think we even saw a crab, though we dragged our nets around in the water just for the fun of it. Finally we dug a dozen or so clams, ate them, and tried to skip the shells along the water. That was how the afternoon passed, with one thing or the other, and us not hurrying, not having anything we'd rather be doing.

We didn't have a watch with us, but it must have been late afternoon when they all came down from the house. We heard them before we saw them, heard the brush of their feet on the grass path.

It was my mother and my father and Robert, my biggest brother, the one who is eighteen. My father had the round black compass and a coil of new line. Robert had a couple of gas lanterns and a big battery one. My mother had the life jackets and a little wicker basket and a thermos bottle. They all went out along the narrow rickety dock and began to load the gear into my father's *Sea Skiff*. It wasn't a big boat and my father had to take a couple of minutes to pack it, stowing the basket way up forward under the cowling[7] and wedging the thermos bottle on top of that. Robert, who'd left his lanterns on the ground to help him, came back to fetch them.

"I thought you were at the McKays," I said. "How'd you get over here?"

"Dad called me." He lifted one eyebrow. "Remember about something called the telephone?" And he picked up his gear and walked away.

"Well," my sister said.

They cast off, the big outboard sputtered gently, throttled way down. They would have to move very slowly in the fog. As they swung away, Robert at the tiller, we saw my father set out his compass and take a bearing off it.

My mother watched them out of sight, which didn't take more than a half minute. Then she stood watching the fog for a while and, I guess, following the sound of the steady put-put. It seemed to me, listening to it move off and blend with the sounds of the bay—the sounds of a lot of water, of tiny waves and fish feeding—that I could pick out two or three other motors.

Finally my mother got tired of standing on the end of the dock and she turned around and walked up to us. I expected her to pass right by and go on up to the house. But she didn't. We could hear her stop and stand looking at us. My sister and I just scraped a little harder, pretending we hadn't noticed.

"I guess you're wondering what that was all about?" she said finally.

"I don't care," my sister said. She was lying. She was just as curious as I was.

6. barnacled (bär′ nə k′ld) *adj.*: Covered with small shellfish that attach themselves to rocks, ships, wood, and whales.

7. cowling *n.*: A removable metal covering for an engine.

5 **Literary Focus** How has the author established the setting and the tempo of life of summer vacationers in a seaside resort? In reviewing the story with the class, explain how the reference to getting pocket money for painting the dinghy is a note of normalcy, not preparing the reader for future developments.

6 **Discussion** In your own words, describe how the sisters spent the afternoon.

clauses or when another comma might result in confusion. Look at the following example:

> The story was touching, sensitive, and humorous; but the movie version was soapy and slapstick.

Student Activity. Write three sentences in which you demonstrate each of the uses of the semicolon. Be sure that each of the independent clauses is closely related in meaning.

7 **Discussion** What is the girl's reaction to the people in the sailboat? Contrast her mother's reaction to hers.

8 **Language** Note the use of descriptive language here. What is the fog compared to? Explain that a simile is a comparison of two unlike things using *like* or *as*. You might have your **more advanced** students write their own similes about fog.

My mother didn't seem to have heard her. "It's Linda Holloway and Stan Mitchell and Butch Rodgers."

We knew them. They were sailing people, a little older than I, a little younger than my brother Robert. They lived in three houses lined up one by the other on the north shore of Marshall's Inlet. They were all right kids, nothing special either way, sort of a gang, living as close as they did. This year they had turned up with a new sailboat, a twelve-foot fiberglass job that somebody had designed and built for Stan Mitchell as a birthday present.

"What about them?" my sister asked, forgetting that she wasn't interested.

"They haven't come home."

"Oh," I said.

"They were sailing," my mother said. "The Brewers think they saw them off their place just before the fog. They were sort of far out."

"You mean Dad's gone to look for them?"

She nodded.

"Is that all?" my sister said. "Just somebody going to have to sit in their boat and wait until the fog lifts."

My mother looked at us. Her curly red
7 hair was dripping with the damp of the fog and her face was smeared with dust. "The Lord save me from children," she said quietly. "The glass is twenty-nine eighty and it's still going down fast."

We went back up to the house with her, to help fix supper—a quiet nervous kind of supper. The thick luminous fish-colored fog turned into deep solid night fog. Just after supper, while we were drying the dishes, the wind sprang up. It shook the whole line of windows in the kitchen and knocked over every single pot of geraniums on the back porch.

"Well," my mother said, "it's square into the east now."

A low barometer and a wind that had gone backwards into the east—there wasn't one of us didn't know what that meant. And it wasn't more than half an hour before there was a grumble of approaching thunder and the fog began to 8
swirl around the windows, streaming like torn cotton as the wind increased.

"Dad'll come back now, huh?" my sister asked.

"Yes," my mother said. "All the boats'll have to come back now."

We settled down to television, half watching it and half listening to the storm outside. In a little while, an hour or so, my mother said, "Turn off that thing."

"What?"

"Turn it off, quick." She hurried on the porch, saying over her shoulder: "I hear something."

The boards of the wide platform were wet and slippery under our feet, and the eaves of the house poured water in steady small streams that the wind grabbed and tore away. Between the crashes of thunder, we heard it too. There was a boat coming into our cove. By the sound of it, it would be my father and Robert.

"Is that the motor?" my mother asked.

"Sure," I said. It had a little tick and it was higher pitched than any of the others. You couldn't miss it.

Without another word to us she went scuttling across the porch and down the stairs toward the cove. We followed and stood close by, off the path and a little to one side. It was tide marsh there, and salt mud oozed over the tops of our sneakers. The cove itself was sheltered—it was in the lee of Cedar Tree Neck—but even so it was pretty choppy. Whitecaps were beginning to run high and broken, wind against tide, and the spume from them stung as it hit your face and your eyes. You could hear the real stuff blowing overhead, with the

CLOUDS AND WATER, 1930
Arthur Dove
Metropolitan Museum of Art, The Alfred Stieglitz Collection, 1949 © 1979 by the Metropolitan Museum of Art

peculiar sound wind has when it gets past half a gale.

My father's boat was sidling up to the dock now, pitching and rolling in the broken water. Its motor sputtered into reverse and then the hull rubbed gently against the pilings. They had had a bad time. In the quick lightning flashes you could see every scupper[8] pouring water. You could see the slow weary way they made the lines fast.

"There wasn't anything else to do," my father was saying as they came up the path, beating their arms for warmth, "with it blowing straight out the east, we had to come in."

Robert stopped a moment to pull off his oilskins. Under them his shirt was as drenched as if he hadn't had any protection at all.

"We came the long way around," my father said, "hugging the lee as much as we could."

"We almost swamped," Robert said.

Then we were at the house and they went off to dry their clothes, and that was that. They told us later that everybody had come in, except only for the big Coast Guard launch. And with only one boat it was no wonder they didn't find them. 9

The next morning was bright and clear and a lot cooler. The big stretch of bay was still shaken and tousled-looking, spotted with whitecaps. Soon as it was light, my father went to the front porch and looked

8. scupper *n.*: An opening in a ship's side that allows water to run off the deck.

Humanities Note

Fine art, *Clouds and Water,* 1930, by Arthur Dove. Dove was a man who loved the water. Born in 1880, in 1920 he began living on a houseboat on the Harlem River, which runs east of Manhattan in New York City. In 1923, he and another artist bought a yawl on which they lived, cruising the waters of Long Island Sound for seven years. The environment of the rivers, bay, and sound in and around New York City gave Dove the inspiration and the subjects to paint.

1. Ask students to describe both the colors and shapes of this painting. Of what are they suggestive?
2. Guide students into an awareness of the twisting, dark lines that define the clouds, hills, and water. In what ways do these lines speak of the gathering, and virtual imminence, of a giant storm?
3. Is Dove saying that these tiny sailboats will be engulfed and overwhelmed by the storm? Or will they survive it?
4. Is this work of art appropriate to illustrate this story? Explain your answer.

9 **Reading Strategy** Have students summarize the story up to this point and predict what happened to the three people in the sailboat.

Humanities Note

Fine art, *Softly,* by Vivian Caldwell. The waves here are gentle. There is a slight foam as they very softly break. Indeed, there is nothing threatening about this water. It is pleasant to look at. Its peacefulness makes one want to jump in. The bluish green at the top of the water and the yellowish green of its body help to achieve this tranquil aspect.

1. Why has this painting been used to illustrate a work in which boys are drowned? Perhaps to suggest how deceptive calm water is or that water cannot be trusted.
2. Does this oil painting properly illustrate the story? Why or why not?

and looked with his glasses. He checked the anemometer[9] dial, and shook his head. "It's still too rough for us." In a bit the Coast Guard boats—two of them—appeared, and a helicopter began its chopping noisy circling.

It was marketing day too, so my mother, my sister, and I went off, as we always did. We stopped at the laundromat and the hardware, and then my mother had to get some pine trees for the slope behind the house. It was maybe four o'clock before we got home.

The wind had dropped, the bay was almost quiet again. Robert and my father were gone, and so was the boat. "I thought they'd go out again," my mother said. She got a cup of coffee and the three of us sat watching the fleet of boats work their way back and forth across the bay, searching.

Just before dark—just when the sky was beginning to take its twilight color—my father and Robert appeared. They were burned lobster red with great white circles around their eyes where their glasses had been.

"Did you find anything?" my sister asked.

My father looked at my mother.

9. **anemometer** (an′ ə mäm′ ə tər) **dial:** The dial on an instrument that determines wind speed and sometimes direction.

SOFTLY
Vivian Caldwell
Private Collection

Grammar in Action

Accomplished writers sometimes break grammatical rules. However, when they break a rule, they usually do so for a specific purpose. Students learn that sentences must have a subject and a verb. If one or both is missing, the result is a **sentence fragment.** Sentence fragments are generally considered unacceptable. However, notice how skillfully fragments have been used in the following paragraph:

But not to sleep. We played cards for an hour or so, until we couldn't stand that any more. Then we did a couple of crossword puzzles together. Finally we just sat in our beds, in the chilly night, and listened. There were the usual sounds from outside the open window, sounds of the land and the water. Deer moving about in the brush on their way to eat the wild watercress and wild lettuce that grew around the spring. The deep pumping sounds of an owl's wings in the air. Little splashes from the bay—the fishes and the muskrats and the otters.

"You might as well tell them," she said. "They'll know anyway."

"Well," my father said, "they found the boat."

"That's what they were expecting to find, wasn't it?" my mother asked quietly.

He nodded. "It's kind of hard to say what happened. But it looks like they got blown on East Shoal with the tide going down and the chop tearing the keel out."[10]

"Oh," my mother said.

"Oh," my sister said.

"They found the boat around noon."

My mother said: "Have they found them?"

"Not that I heard."

"You think," my mother said, "they could have got to shore way out on Gull Point or some place like that?"

"No place is more than a four-hour walk," my father said. "They'd have turned up by now."

And it was later still, after dark, ten o'clock or so, that Mr. Robinson, who lived next door, stopped by the porch on his way home. "Found one," he said wearily. "The Mitchell boy."

"Oh," my mother said, "oh, oh."

"Where?" my father asked.

"Just off the shoal,[11] they said, curled up in the eel grass."

"My God," my mother said softly.

Mr. Robinson moved off without so much as a good-by. And after a while my sister and I went to bed.

But not to sleep. We played cards for an hour or so, until we couldn't stand that any more. Then we did a couple of crossword puzzles together. Finally we just sat in our beds, in the chilly night, and listened. There were the usual sounds from outside the open windows, sounds of the land and the water. Deer moving about in the brush on their way to eat the wild watercress and wild lettuce that grew around the spring. The deep pumping sounds of an owl's wings in the air. Little splashes from the bay—the fishes and the muskrats and the otters.

"I didn't know there'd be so many things moving at night," my sister said.

"You just weren't ever awake."

"What do you reckon it's like," she said, "being on the bottom in the eel grass?"

"Shut up," I told her.

"Well," she said, "I just asked. Because I was wondering."

"Don't."

Her talking had started a funny shaking quivering feeling from my navel right straight back to my backbone. The tips of my fingers hurt too, the way they always did.

"I thought the dogs would howl," she said.

"They can't smell anything from the water," I told her. "Now quit."

She fell asleep then and maybe I did too, because the night seemed awful short. Or maybe the summer dawns really come that quick. Not dawn, no. The quiet deep dark that means dawn is just about to come. The birds started whistling and the gulls started shrieking. I got up and looked out at the dripping beach plum bushes and the twisted, salt-burned jack pines, then I slipped out the window. I'd done it before. You lifted the screen, and lowered yourself down. It wasn't anything of a drop—all you had to watch was the patch of poison ivy. I circled around the house and took the old deer trail down to the bay. It was chilly, and I began to wish I had brought my robe or a coat. With just cotton pajamas my teeth would begin chattering very soon.

I don't know what I expected to see. And

10. the chop tearing the keel out: The choppy waves tearing out the beam supporting the boat frame.

11. shoal (shōl) *n.*: Sand bar.

Student Activity 1. Find the four sentence fragments in the example paragraph. Explain why you think each is effective in this passage.

Student Activity 2. Write your own paragraph in which you describe a similar situation: you and a sister or brother or friend cannot for some reason fall asleep right away. Model your paragraph after the example—and this time you get to use sentence fragments, provided that you use them effectively.

10 Discussion What do you think the girl is referring to?

11 Discussion This is a story of initiation. Into what?

Reader's Response Have you ever had an experience similar to the narrator's in which you were "spooked" by something that probably wasn't real? Explain the circumstances of your experience and describe your reaction at the time. If you have not had such an experience, what do you think caused the narrator's fear at the end of the story?

I didn't see anything at all. Just some morning fog in the hollows and around the spring. And the dock, with my father's boat bobbing in the run of the tide.

The day was getting close now. The sky overhead turned a sort of luminous dark blue. As it did, the water darkened to a lead-colored gray. It looked heavy and oily and impenetrable. I tried to imagine what would be under it. I always thought I knew. There would be horsehoe crabs and hermit crabs and blue crabs, and scallops squirting their way along, and there'd be all the different kinds of fish, and the eels. I kept telling myself that that was all.

But this time I couldn't seem to keep my thoughts straight. I kept wondering what it must be like to be dead and cold and down in the sand and mud with the eel grass brushing you and the crabs bumping you and the fish—I had felt their little sucking mouths sometimes when I swam.

The water was thick and heavy and the color of a mirror in a dark room. Minnows broke the surface right under the wharf. I jumped. I couldn't help it.

10 And I got to thinking that something might come out of the water. It didn't have a name or a shape. But it was there.

I stood where I was for a while, trying to fight down the idea. When I found I couldn't do that, I decided to walk slowly back to the house. At least I thought I was going to walk, but the way the boards of the wharf shook under my feet I know that I must have been running. On the path up to the house my bare feet hit some of the sharp cut-off stubs of the rosa rugosa bushes, but I didn't stop. I went crashing into the kitchen because that was the closest door.

The room was thick with the odor of frying bacon, the softness of steam: my mother had gotten up early. She turned around when I came in, not seeming surprised—as if it was the most usual thing in the world for me to be wandering around before daylight in my pajamas.

"Go take those things off, honey," she said. "You're drenched."

"Yes ma'am," I told her.

I stripped off the clothes and saw that they really were soaking. I knew it was just the dew and the fog. But I couldn't help thinking it was something else. Something that had reached for me, and missed. Something that was wet, that had come from the water, something that had splashed me as it went past. 11

THINKING ABOUT THE SELECTION

Recalling

1. What are the two girls doing at the beginning of the story?
2. Why do the girls' father and brother go out in the boat?
3. Why do they return when they do?
4. What happens to the three lost people?

Interpreting

5. How does the girl react to the boy's death? Why does she slip out of her house just before dawn?
6. What comparison is the author suggesting when the girl's clothing gets wet at the end of the story? What is the "something else" the girl feels has reached for her and missed?

Closure and Extension

ANSWERS TO THINKING ABOUT THE SELECTION
Recalling

1. They were scraping and painting their little dinghy.
2. They went out searching for three people in a sailboat.
3. They returned because it started to thunder, the wind increased, and the fog got thicker.
4. They were killed in the storm.

Interpreting

5. She is very upset with the news and can't sleep. She leaves her house to go down to the dock in search of something she cannot define.
6. The author suggests that the something that reached for her was her own death. She has become aware of her own mortality.
7. She learns to question her own mortality. She has also learned that although the surface of nature can look calm and peaceful, it can change all too quickly, without much warning and without reason.
8. The land in the title might refer to the people living on it and life in general. The water might represent death. The title stands for life and death.

7. What does the girl learn about life?
8. What do you think the land represents to the girl? What do you think the water represents? Why is this story called "The Land and the Water"?

Applying

9. The author Joseph Conrad has written, ". . . for all the celebration it has been the object of . . . , the sea has never been friendly to man." Explain the meaning of these words. How do they relate to this story?

ANALYZING LITERATURE

Understanding Setting

Setting is the time and place of a story. Sometimes the setting is so important it affects what the characters do and what they feel. In "The Land and the Water," for example, the ocean almost becomes a character in the story.

1. At what time of year does "The Land and the Water" take place? How do you know this?
2. Describe the weather during the course of this story.
3. In what way does the setting affect what the characters do and what they feel?
4. In what way can the setting be thought of as almost a character in this story?

CRITICAL THINKING AND READING

Making Inferences About Setting

An **inference** is a judgment or conclusion based on evidence. Not all information about the setting of a story is stated directly by the author. You must also make inferences about the setting from the clues given by the author just as you do about the other elements of a story.

1. What evidence helped you make the inference that this is not the family's first summer here?
2. What clues indicate that the land and sea are unaffected by what has happened?

UNDERSTANDING LANGUAGE

Choosing Meaning To Fit the Context

When you look up an unfamiliar word in a dictionary, you may find more than one definition. Then you must decide which definition fits the context in which the word appears. Try substituting each definition for the word in the sentence and see which one makes the most sense.

For example, in the sentence "The Grand Canyon is a *singular* tourist attraction," *singular* can mean "one of a kind," "odd; peculiar" or "extraordinary." By replacing the word with each definition, you can see that in this sentence *singular* means "one of a kind."

From a dictionary choose the best definition for each of the following italicized words.

1. "That *bank* had been hanging offshore for days."
2. The motor "had a little tick and it was higher *pitched* than any of the others."
3. "And I didn't see anything at all. Just some morning fog in the hollows and around the *spring*."

THINKING AND WRITING

Describing a Setting

Choose one of the pieces of art used to illustrate "The Land and the Water." List descriptive details about it. Include details about the way the picture makes you feel—or your mood. Use your list to write a description of the art. Use vivid, specific words so that a friend who has not seen the picture will be able to envision it. When you finish read over your paper to be sure your friend will be able to visualize the illustration you described.

Applying

9. The sea is unpredictable and has caused many accidents and deaths. In this story, it caused the deaths of three young people.

ANSWERS TO ANALYZING LITERATURE

1. It takes place during the summer. The author describes the day as "clear and hot with a tiny breeze." Also there were many sailboats out in the bay.
2. The story starts out on a beautiful, clear day. It suddenly becomes very foggy, with a falling barometer and shifting wind. The weather worsens and it begins to thunder and the fog thickens. The wind starts blowing at gale force. The next day is "bright and clear and a lot cooler."
3. When the weather gets stormy, the story becomes grim. The characters worry about the people out at sea and the girl contemplates "what it must be like to be dead."
4. The setting is almost a character because it affects everyone's thoughts and actions. People react to the storm as they might to another character in the story.

ANSWERS TO CRITICAL THINKING AND READING

1. The family knew the area well and reacted quickly when told of the three young people lost at sea.
2. The sea went back to normal height and the storm subsided.

(Answers begin on p. 126.)

ANSWERS TO UNDERSTANDING LANGUAGE

1. a long mound or heap, as of clouds
2. that quality of a sound determined by the frequency of vibration of the sound waves reaching the ear: the greater the frequency, the higher the pitch
3. a flow of water from the ground, often a source of a stream, pond, etc.

Challenge The narrator in "The Land and the Water" is deeply moved when she learns that Stan Mitchell has drowned. Considering her feelings about the ocean at the end of the story, as well as what she has learned about life, ask students what they think she would have to say to the dead boy's parents.

THINKING AND WRITING

For help with this assignment, students can refer to Lesson 7, Writing About Setting, in the Handbook of Writing About Literature.

Writing Across the Curriculum Artists have long found the ocean an interesting and challenging subject to paint. In the library, have students look through art books to find paintings by artists who specialize in seascapes. Students might specifically look for works by Winslow Homer or J.M. W. Turner. Have students choose one painting that especially appeals to them and write what precisely they like about it—its mood, its colors, or the ideas it suggests about life. You might want to inform the art department of this writing assignment. Art teachers might provide guidance for students.

Focus

More About the Author Loula Grace Erdman was educated at Central Missouri and Columbia Universities before beginning to teach in Amarillo, Texas. Late in life she achieved great popularity for her novels, short stories, and children's literature. Many of Erdman's stories have been anthologized and nearly all of her books are available in braille. Ask your students what they can infer from knowing that Erdman's works have been widely translated. Discuss what might make a written work popular.

Literary Focus Bring in some pictures of nature working havoc—storms at sea, floods, forest fires, and electrical storms, for example. Then, after students have read the explanation of descriptive details, divide the class into groups and have them note the descriptive details and make comparisons. What do waves look as if they'd like to do? What does lightning resemble? What does a raging river remind them of?

Look For Help students appreciate what the prairie was like before people turned the vast grassland into cultivated fields. Explain that some of the people lived in sod houses. Discuss why they could not build with wood and why the prairie environment afforded little or no water to use in fighting fires.

Writing This exercise can be used as a quick grammar review with your **less advanced** students. When the freewriting ends, ask how many students used *fire* as a noun, as a verb, as an adjective, or in a meaning different from that of a blaze.

Vocabulary It would help your students to know the following words also: *cunning* (p. 129), *diabolical* (p. 129), *semblance* (p. 130), *anticipate* (p. 131), *archvillain* (p.132), and *plunged* (p. 133).

GUIDE FOR READING

Grass Fire

Loula Grace Erdman (1884–1976) was born in Missouri and later moved to Texas. There she became a school teacher and a professor and novelist-in-residence at West Texas State University. Erdman's novels have been translated into many languages, including German, Italian, Arabic, and Indonesian. She once wrote, "I tend to write about people I could ask in for a cup of coffee or a spot of tea." Her characters, ordinary people who can show extraordinary courage, may help to explain the popularity of her works.

Descriptive Details

A writer can make a story come alive by using vivid descriptive details to describe a character's appearance, the setting, or the actions of characters in a story. In "Grass Fire" the author uses descriptive details to tell of the struggle to stop a grass fire on the prairie. She describes in detail each implement used to fight the fire so that you can see them clearly in your mind.

Look For

As you read "Grass Fire," look for the descriptive details that make you feel you are caught in the fire yourself. What impression do you get of the fire? How do the descriptive details make you feel?

Writing

Fire! The word immediately brings us to attention. Freewrite about the effect of the word *fire*.

Vocabulary

Knowing the following words will help you as you read "Grass Fire."

nesters (nest′ ərz) *n.*: Homesteaders on the prairies in the mid-1800's (p. 129)
dugout (dug′ out′) *n.*: A shelter built into a hillside (p. 130)
carcass (kär′ kəs) *n.*: The dead body of an animal (p. 131)
acrid (ak′ rid) *adj.*: Sharp, bitter; stinging to the taste or smell (p. 132)
distended (dis tend′ id) *adj.*: Stretched out; swollen (p. 133)
horde (hôrd) *n.*: A large moving crowd or throng (p. 133)
divested (də vest′ id) *adj.*: stripped; (p. 133)
cower (kou′ ər) *v.*: To crouch or huddle from fear (p. 134)

Objectives

1 To understand how an author uses descriptive details in a short story
2 To analyze the effect a story's setting has on plot
3 To understand the meaning of similes
4 To write a vivid description of a picture

Support Material

Teaching Portfolio
Teacher Backup, pp. 193–195
Grammar in Action Worksheet, *Understanding Adjectives*, pp. 196–197
Usage and Mechanics Worksheet, p. 198
Vocabulary Check, p. 199
Analyzing Literature Worksheet, *Understanding Descriptive Details*, p. 200
Language Worksheet, *Understanding Similes*, p. 201
Selection Test, pp. 202–203
Art Transparency 5, *Fire Fight Fire*

Grass Fire

from *The Edge of Time*

Loula Grace Erdman

They said, "It's a big one—look at the smoke—"

As a single unit the men moved to their horses, the party forgotten. Where there had been only a light a few moments ago, now there were little red tongues of flame, licking scallops[1] against the sky. Like imps dancing they formed a solid line against the horizon.

"It's headed north," someone said. "And with the wind the way it is—"

North. Away from the river. And, Bethany thought—knew Wade was thinking, too—toward their place. North. For Wade and her, that was the direction in which fear lay.

They set about fighting the fire, ranchers, cowboys and nesters alike, moving together in an undivided attack, held by a common purpose. In their approach there was no talk of me and mine. They saw the fire against the horizon and they moved toward it, determined to use every cunning as if they were fighting an enemy half-human, half-demon. For the fire, indeed, had about it a human-like cunning, a diabolical cruelty.

"You stay here," Wade said to Bethany. "Later you can help bring us something to eat, and some water."

He didn't say, "You couldn't get home now if you wanted to. Not without riding miles out of your way, you couldn't—"

They stayed at the Newsome place, waiting. The men fought, and they used whatever weapons they could lay their hands upon.

They took the plow and put it to a new use. They plowed strips of prairie sod, not for seeding, but to prevent the growth of the 1
seeds of fire. Fireguards, they called these plowed strips. But the red monster hurdled them as if they were not there. Sometimes the wind picked up cow chips, tossing them lightly across the barrier, starting a new fire 2
in fresh fuel. Even the cow chips, which had served them well, seemed to turn against them—friends until now, they had joined the enemy.

The men made backfires[2] between the main blaze and the territory they wished to protect, placing them with cunning, watching them with a care a doctor shows a patient to whom he has given a problematical medicine in a last desperate effort to save him. There was no water here, the

1. licking scallops: Making a pattern of curves against the sky.

2. backfire *n.*: A fire started to stop or check advancing prairie fire or forest fire.

Presentation

Motivation/Prior Knowledge Discuss with your students the terror of fire. Ask if they have ever seen a fast moving grass fire or if they have ever been witness to any kind of life-threatening fire. How is it that fires like this break out and spread so quickly? How do firefighters hope to stop such fires?

Thematic Idea Another selection that deals with the theme of courage is "The Day the Sun Came Out" (page 107), and with the theme of the effect of a natural disaster is "The Land and the Water" (page 119).

Master Teacher Note Life on the frontier—its hardships and joys—has been immortalized in art and literature. Place Art Transparency 5, "Fire Fight Fire" by Currier & Ives in the Teaching Portfolio on the overhead projector. Discuss with students other kinds of natural disasters that affected the lives of the pioneers. In "Grass Fire," a prairie fire threatens the settlers.

Purpose-Setting Question Why is Lizzie both ordinary and extraordinary?

1 **Discussion** How does a fireguard work?

2 **Discussion** Explain that personification is a figure of speech that gives an inanimate object human characteristics. Who is the fire compared to? Who are cow chips compared to?

Humanities Note

Fine art, *Herd of Buffalo Fleeing from Prairie Fire,* 1888, by Meyer Straus. Straus (1831–1905) was born in Bavaria but lived most of his life in the United States. Before discussing this painting, give some background information on the American buffalo. Great herds once roamed over North America between the Appalachian Mountains on the east and the Rockies on the west. The Indians depended upon their flesh for food and their hides for clothing. In 1850, about 20 million of these animals still thundered over the western plains. In the late 1800's, white American hunters slaughtered millions of buffalo. This killing deprived the Indians of their main source of food and almost wiped out the buffalo. By 1889, only 551 buffalo could be found alive in the United States.

1. Why is the herd of buffalo running?
2. What does the wagon wheel in the lower portion of the picture tell you about human habitation in the area?
3. Is this work of art appropriate to illustrate this story? Why or why not?

3 **Enrichment** Have students note the description "took command." In situations like this, is there usually someone who emerges as the strong, courageous leader? Do situations like this bring out these characteristics?

HERD OF BUFFALO FLEEING FROM PRAIRIE FIRE
M. Straus
Amon Carter Museum

natural enemy of fire, so they must make a semblance of that enemy.

3 It was Lizzie Dillon who took command of the women. She, who had weathered everything, felt no great fear of a grass fire.

"They'll stop it," she said calmly. "They always do. Sometimes it takes longer'n others, but they do it—"

She could be calm, Bethany thought rebelliously. About her place there were no row crops drying, no curtains at dugout windows. No maiden blush rose was taking root beside her door. For Lizzie Dillon, there was nothing to lose. If her burrow was destroyed, she and her mate and her young would move to another.

It was as simple as that.

"Come morning," Lizzie went on. "I reckon we'd best take them a bite to eat—we can load it in my wagon—"

"I'll go with you," Bethany said. "I'll ride Star—"

Morning came, eerie and unreal. The sun rose red in the east, in the west was that other grim redness.

"It ain't quite so big," Lizzie said. "They're a-whippin it; I knowed they would. We'll take the stuff to eat now, and the water."

They packed the food left from the party into pans and boxes. Among them, they got a small barrel on the wagon, filled it with

Grammar in Action

Adjectives enliven our language. They enable writers to describe precisely. **Adjectives** modify nouns or pronouns. They sharpen the meaning of the noun they modify by adding information that answers one of these questions: *What kind? Which one? How many? How much?*

Reread the following sentences from "Grass Fire" and notice the adjectives that enhance or add to the meaning of the sentences.

The trail over which they passed, Lizzie driving the *rickety* wagon and Bethany riding Star, ran through the grass already blackened by fire. It looked like *soft, dark* cloth, *thick* and *heavy.* When the *horses'* feet touched it, a *black* dust arose. The smell was *acrid, choking,* like the smell of fire itself.

She had turned to speak to Bethany, and what she saw when she looked around brought a *strange* expression to her face. . . . Her face was *quiet* and *intent* as she waited for her judgment to tell her what she wanted to know.

water. Mrs. Newsome's face showed gray and old in the light of dawn. Bethany knew that she herself should be tired, but she was beyond fatigue, beyond feeling of any kind.

Mrs. Dillon awakened the children and got them into the wagon.

"Shouldn't some of us go with you?" Milly asked uncertainly.

"You best stay here and take care of the baby," Lizzie Dillon said kindly. "And you ought to lay down and rest, Mrs. Newsome. You're plum wore out from the party. Git up, Bess. Git up, Kate—"

Lizzie Dillon drove on. The woman did not look back; she drove with sureness and confidence. Bethany followed her, never questioning her decisions. The children sat quiet in the wagon as if they too were sure of her rightness. Afterwards Bethany remembered that not once during all that trip did the children make any trouble, grow rest-
4 less, ask for some of the food or water which was in the wagon with them. They had been trained in a sort of quiet acceptance of what came. They had been schooled to follow without question the ways of their elders in times of emergency.

They came upon the firefighters by midmorning. The men had just killed an old bull and split him wide open, so that his carcass formed a large flat surface. They had tied ropes to his legs, and two men rode to a side, with the other ends of the ropes tied to their saddle horns.

Four cowboys whom Bethany remembered only vaguely were making ready to drag this strange piece of fire-fighting equipment across the grass, where it was burning farther up the line.

"Wouldn't you like some water?" Bethany asked. "And—and something to eat?"

She felt a little embarrassed to be offering them the dainty remnants of the Newsome party supper. Working men needed real food, not party stuff.

They swung down off their horses, which stood with eyes turned questioningly toward their masters, as if they would know the reason for this strange burden they carried. Live cows they knew—plunging and kicking. They could brace their weights with them, even almost anticipate their movements. But this dead thing—

"Yes, ma'am," they said. "We could use some water and some grub, all right."

Bethany looked at the dead bull, tied fast between the horses.

"Seems sort of a shame," she said. "Killing cattle, I mean—"

"Well, Ma'am," one of them said softly, "maybe so. But I reckon this one would be right proud to know he helped stop a fire."

They would drag this carcass across the burning grass, putting out the flames with it. Maybe it was like that everywhere, Bethany was thinking. A few have to suffer so 5
that things will be easier for others.

"How are they a-comin'?" Lizzie asked. "They are a-stoppin' it, ain't they?"

"I can't say, Ma'am," he told her. "Sometimes we think so, and then the wind changes and blows it back into new places—like as not where none of us are working."

He bent over to beat out a small spark with his slicker. The gesture was automatic. The spark had landed on the trail, was out almost before it struck. But all the same, you put out a fire, however small, when and where you saw it. The monster they were fighting now had probably been a spark no larger than this one at one time.

"Seems like the wind blows from all directions at once when we get to fighting a fire," he said. He got back on his horse. "Guess we'd better be getting along. Thanks

4 **Discussion** Why did the children respond so well in an emergency? Is this always the case? Can anyone think of another instance in which schoolchildren had to act responsibly in dangerous situations?

5 **Master Teacher Note** Discuss the idea that some suffer so that things will be easier for others. Can students give you any examples from their own life experiences? Have them think about what they have learned in their history classes about pioneers in any field, about their hardships and about their failures. Do students think their failures might be the seeds of ideas for the next generation?

Lizzie slapped the lines over the *horses'* backs. They started off at a *smart* trot, tossing their heads in *nervous* excitement.

Student Activity 1. Look over the sample sentences and determine which of the four questions each adjective answers.

Student Activity 2. Find five more adjectives on these pages. Tell which noun each describes, and which of the four questions it answers.

Student Activity 3. Write five sentences without adjectives. Pass your paper to other students in the class and ask them to add adjectives to describe the nouns in your sentences. Try to change the meaning of the sentence by using different adjectives a second time.

6 Reading Strategy Have your students predict what she saw. What do you think will happen next?

7 Discussion What did this tell her about the fire?

for the grub and water."

"We'll drive on up the trail," Lizzie told him. "No fire up thataway, is there?"

"Haven't heard of one."

"Tell the others where we're headed, and that we got stuff to eat."

"That's right kind of you, Ma'am," he said. "Most of them are back a ways where the fire is worst, but I'll tell them. Maybe they can sort of spell each other off and come for some."

"Tell them I'm workin' on toward home," she said. "I'll git them kids out of the wagon and then bring back some fresh grub and water."

"That's fine," the boy said. "Looks like we may be at this for quite a spell yet. So long—"

He rode off.

"If you see my husband," Bethany called after him, "will you tell him I've gone home?"

Home! It seemed like weeks, like years, since she had seen the little dugout. She felt she could not wait to be back there again. And if she went, as she knew now she must, Wade should have word so that he would not go back to Newsomes' looking for her, once the fire was over.

"I'm Mrs. Cameron," she added.

"Yes, Ma'am, I know," the boy called back to her. "I danced with you last night."

Last night! That was an eon ago. She rode off, trying to remember what had happened in that long-gone time.

The trail over which they passed, Lizzie driving the rickety wagon and Bethany riding Star, ran through the grass already blackened by fire. It looked like soft, dark cloth, thick and heavy. When the horses' feet touched it, a black dust arose. The smell was acrid, choking, like the smell of fire itself. Off to their right they could see flames against the sky; the fire, then, was on two sides of them—to the right and behind them. Where it would go next, or whether it would spread at all, was a matter that rested not only with the zeal of the fighters, but on that archvillain, the wind. At any time a new fire could break out, seemingly without cause, sometimes in places widely separated. What was it Tobe Dillon had said one time? "Sometimes I think fire jest breaks out by itself, here—"

Ahead of them now an expanse of unburned grass fanned out. Seeing it, Lizzie said, "Looks like we ain't a-goin' to have a chance to git rid of this grub."

She had turned to speak to Bethany, and what she saw when she looked around brought a strange expression to her face. 6
She stopped the wagon, stood up. She put her forefinger in her mouth, then held it up to the air. Her face was quiet and intent as 7
she waited for her judgment to tell her what she wanted to know. Finally she turned to Bethany.

"Miz Cameron," she said, "the wind is a-changin'. We'd best git down the trail as fast as we can. It don't look so good—back of us—"

Bethany looked around. The thing she saw made panic well up in her.

On three sides of them was fire—behind, to the left, and to the right. More than that—the wind was behind them, pushing the fire forward as a child would roll a hoop. Only the way ahead was clear. And, even as they faced front again, it seemed that the bright edge of fire was spreading closer to the trail.

"I think you'd best tie your horse to the endgate and git in the wagon with the kids," Lizzie said quietly.

There was something about her voice that made Bethany obey instantly, without question. She tied Star's reins to the back of the wagon; she got in the wagon and sat down with the Dillon children. They received her with unblinking regard, as they would have received any other fresh discomfort. One of the older girls reached over to pick up the baby. She held it close to her, dropped her face against its head.

Lizzie slapped the lines over the horses' backs. They started off at a smart trot, tossing their heads in nervous excitement. Star, following behind, also seemed uneasy. Bethany hoped she had tied him securely. It would be too bad if he broke loose in his nervousness and fright. Turning to check the knot, she saw what was probably the strangest sight she had ever beheld.

The wild things were coming—running
swiftly, with terror-distended nostrils. Side
by side they ran, the coyote, the antelope,
the lobo,[3] the deer. Cattle came too, and the
birds, and the jack rabbits, their great ears
erect. Hunted and hunter were as one,
8 joined in a great exodus[4] of fear and horror,
fleeing the thing that was more fearful than
fear itself. Desire to kill was lost in desire to
live. The strange horde passed the wagon as
if they knew that man, their enemy, was
fleeing as they fled.

And now the fright of the horses almost matched that of their wild brothers. Only Lizzie's expert handling of the lines kept them steady at all. The wagon rattled perilously. *What if it falls to pieces entirely,* Bethany thought. *We'll be left in the path of the fire!* Why hadn't she stayed on Star? She heard Lizzie's voice calling to her. The woman did not turn, but kept her eyes on the fear-maddened horses.

"Now listen, Miz Cameron, and you kids—you do what I tell you to—"

Lizzie had long since lost the last of her
hairpins. Her black hair was hanging loose,
whipping back from her face like some
strange banner which they must all follow.
And, as if she knew they felt this, she gave
her directions, quick and tense, like a general who sees one chance to win a battle, 9
and that only if his men obey him without
question.

The boys were to peel off their shirts, she said, and Bethany was to take them and wetten them with what was left of the water they had fetched for the men. One of the shirts Bethany must put on her head, protecting her face with it as much as possible. The other she was to hand Lizzie, who would do the same. The kids were to get under the quilt.

"—and Eli, you shuck out of them britches of yores—"

Eli, already divested of his shirt, hung back.

"Eli—" His mother's voice was terrible. Eli, hearing it, forgot false modesty. He pulled off his pants, and then plunged under the quilt.

"Now you git them britches real wet, too," she told Bethany, "and when a spark blows in on the wagon, you beat it out with them. See—?"

"Yes," Bethany said, dipping Eli's pants into the keg of water.

"And if the wind lands a burning chip in the wagon, you jest shovel it out with one of them plates Miz Newsome put the grub on."

"Yes," Bethany said again, locating a plate from the box of food. Part of the cake was still on it, that fancy party cake which looked all the more foolish now in the face of the red terror that menaced them.

Bethany looked around. The red wall was closing in. By now it was a sound and a smell and a red light. She realized what had happened—a new fire had broken out so swiftly and unexpectedly that there were no

---

3. lobo (lō' bō) *n.*: Gray wolf.
4. exodus (ek' sə dəs) *n.*: Departure.

8 **Enrichment** We tend to forget about the effects of fire on the creatures of the prairie. Have students note the sentence "Desire to kill was lost in desire to live." Can students support this with examples from other stories they have read or from real life situations?

9 **Discussion** Note the comparison of Lizzie to a general. What does this suggest?

10 Discussion What does this tell you about Lizzie?

11 Discussion How did Bethany feel toward Lizzie? Was this feeling deserved?

12 Discussion How does Lizzie feel at the end of the story? How do you think you would feel in her place?

Reader's Response What do you think enables people to persevere in the face of certain defeat or failure?

Thematic Idea Have your students compare Lizzie to Mary from the story "The Day the Sun Came Out," page 107. How are they similar? Do you know any people like this? Do you think you could be like this if the situation warranted it? How do people get this way?

Enrichment Imagine you are a reporter for the *Prairie Gazette.* You have heard of Lizzie Dillon's heroic act during the recent prairie fire. Think about how you might write about Lizzie in a news article. Jot down responses to the six basic questions of journalism. *Who* is Lizzie Dillon? *What* did she do? *When* did she do it? *Where* did the events occur? *Why* did Lizzie act as she did? *How* did she accomplish what she did? Use your responses to write a news article entitled "Prairie Woman Saves Family and Friend from Flames."

fighters near it. If they came out of this, it would be because Lizzie Dillon brought them out.

"And now," Lizzie said, knowing that her commands were understood and heeded, "now—we'll jest make a run fur it."

She stood up in the wagon and struck the horses. "Git up," she said, although it did not seem possible that they were capable of any greater speed.

The road was a narrowing wedge whose outlines were sketched in fire. The fire did not seem so much to come toward them as they seemed themselves to drive into the face of it. Even through the wet shirt, Bethany could feel the heat. The smoke stung her nostrils; water streamed from her eyes. A flying disc of fire shot into the wagon—a burning cow chip which hit the quilt under which the children were cowering. Bethany scooped it up on Mrs. Newsome's plate, threw it over the side of the wagon. She beat out the smoking place on the quilt with Eli's wet pants.

By now, the team was frantic. They sped across the prairie, down the trail. Lizzie
10 Dillon still stood up in the wagon, leaning forward slightly, as if she would push them along with her own stout heart. The air was full of chips, flaming like meteors. The wagon swayed from side to side. Once Star stumbled. Maybe he had stepped in a prairie dog hole, broken his leg. If he had, Bethany knew what she must do—at once, and with no holding back. She must untie him, leave him there to perish in the fire.

He righted himself, came on after the wagon, as if he knew that in that action lay safety, lay life itself.

"Good old Star," she whispered, feeling her cheeks wet, knowing it was not moisture from the Dillon boy's shirt.

Could they make it?

Lizzie had said they would. She was matching her instinct, her wisdom, against the cunning of the fire. More than that
—she was matching the courage of a moth- 11
er who was taking her children to safety. They had a chance.

The path was very narrow now. The path was not there at all. There was only a line—a thin line—a line through which no human being could pass, and live.

Bethany shut her eyes. Her lips moved stiffly; she knew she was praying, but did not know what words she said. The texture of them was there, though, the need, the appeal.

To perish by fire! To die in a blaze, there in the wagon with Lizzie and the children, with little Eli and the girl who held the baby against her breast. A wave of love for the doomed children passed over her; she wished that she, too, might reach under the quilt and hold one of them close to comfort it in this last hour.

To die by fire. Never to see Wade again. Never.

She felt the slowing pace of the horses. All was over. Lizzie, too, had given up. Lizzie knew it was no use. Bethany reached out blindly for one of the children.

"Well, Miz Cameron," she heard Lizzie say shakily, "we're through—"

Bethany opened her eyes. The prairie stretched out ahead of them, free of fire. Behind them, a red wall had closed in.

"Looks like it's already burned off here," Lizzie said, surveying the burnt grass ahead of them. "Must have happened last night."

They were on burnt grass. They were
safe. 12

"You kids can come out now if you are a mind to," Lizzie said. "Eli, we'll turn our backs whilst you put on yore britches. And don't you fret about 'em being wet—"

THINKING ABOUT THE SELECTION

Recalling

1. Why does the fact that the fire is heading north frighten Bethany?
2. Find three methods the men use to fight the fire.
3. Describe how the wild animals behave during the fire.
4. Why did Bethany, Lizzie, and the children have to race to escape the fire?
5. How do Lizzie and Bethany know that they have escaped the grass fire?

Interpreting

6. What kind of person is Lizzie Dillon? Why is she able to command the women?
7. At one point Bethany thinks, "A few have to suffer so that things will be easier for others." What does this statement indicate about prairie life?
8. How can you tell from the story that grass fires are common occurrences on the prairie? What makes them so dangerous on the prairie?

Applying

9. "Grass Fire" portrays one of the terrible dangers of prairie life in the 1800's. What other dangers did the settlers face? What might have been some benefits of life on the prairie?

ANALYZING LITERATURE

Understanding Descriptive Details

Descriptive details create a picture of an event, character, or place. Erdman uses descriptive details, for example, to help you to picture Lizzie: "Lizzie Dillon still stood up in the wagon, leaning forward slightly, as if she would push them along with her own stout heart."

1. Find three details that show how frightened the prairie animals are by the approaching fire.
2. Give three examples of details describing the last frantic race to escape the fire.

CRITICAL THINKING AND READING

Analyzing the Effect of Setting on Plot

"Grass Fire" could take place only on a prairie. The setting, therefore, causes the plot to develop as it does.

1. Why do grass fires spread so rapidly on a prairie?
2. Why is it difficult to extinguish a grass fire on the prairie?

UNDERSTANDING LANGUAGE

Understanding Similes

A **simile** is a figure of speech that compares two unlike things. A simile uses the words *like* or *as* in the comparison. Read the following simile: "More than that—the wind was behind them, pushing the fire forward as a child would roll a hoop." Here the word *as* is used to compare the way the wind pushes the fire to the way a child rolls a hoop.

1. Identify the simile in this sentence: "The air was full of chips, flaming like meteors." What is the effect of this simile?
2. Write a simile comparing each of the following people or things with something else: Lizzie; the wagon on which Lizzie, Bethany, and the children rode; the men who fought the fire.

THINKING AND WRITING

Using Descriptive Details

Look at the picture that illustrates "Grass Fire." List details about the picture that you could use to help a friend who had not seen it envision the scene. Write a description for your friend using the details you have listed. If possible, include a simile. Revise your writing to be sure your description is clear and vivid. Proofread your writing and share it with your classmates.

Closure and Extension

ANSWERS TO THINKING ABOUT THE SELECTION

Recalling

1. Her home is located there.
2. They built fireguards by plowing strips of prairie sod. They made backfires between the main blaze and the territory they wished to protect. They killed an old bull and dragged his carcass across the burning grass.
3. They ran swiftly past the wagon, ignoring the people in it.
4. The fire was on three sides of them —behind, left, and right.
5. They saw the prairie stretched ahead of them, free of fire.

Interpreting

6. Lizzie is courageous and determined. She is a strong leader, with the ability to take charge of a situation and to do what is needed.
7. It shows that life was very hard for everyone. However, some people's hardships helped make life easier for others.
8. Everyone knew what to do when the fire was spotted. The men went to fight the fire and the women to bring them food and water. The fires are dangerous because there is no water on the prairie.

Applying

9. Answers will differ. Some dangers might include lack of water and food, attacks by wild animals, and snowstorms. Benefits may include room to build homes and farms, rich farm land, and the idea of being the first to do something.

ANSWERS TO ANALYZING LITERATURE

1. They were running swiftly with terror-distended nostrils. The jack rabbits ran with their ears erect. They ignored the wagon of people.
2. Answers will differ. Lizzie's black hair was hanging loose, whipping back from her face. Bethany protected her face from the smoke and heat with a wet shirt. The smoke stung Bethany's nostrils and water streamed from her eyes.

ANSWERS TO CRITICAL THINKING AND READING

1. The land is flat, and when the grass is dry, fire can spread very quickly.
2. There is a lack of water.

ANSWERS TO UNDERSTANDING SIMILES

1. The simile is "flaming like meteors." It makes the reader see the air more vividly.
2. Answers will differ.

Challenge How are the children in this story both ordinary and extraordinary?

THINKING AND WRITING

Publishing Student Writing If possible, get a picture of a prairie grass fire and hang it on a bulletin board. Hang some of the better descriptions around it.

Writing Across the Curriculum Forest fires destroy thousands of acres every year in the United States. Have your students go to the library to learn about the causes of forest fires and how they are brought under control. Then have them write a short informative report summarizing their findings. You might want to inform the history department of this writing assignment. History teachers might provide guidance for students on conducting their research.

Focus

More About the Author Arthur C. Clarke is also active in promoting space travel and communication and in underwater exploration and photography. For a year he had the only television set in Sri Lanka and a special dish antenna, a loan from India and the United States as a reward for originating the concept of satellite communication. Have your students discuss the advantages and disadvantages for a writer, such as Clarke, who lives apart from the Western world. What recent problems in Sri Lanka may have upset the author's routine?

Literary Focus Point out that most science fiction is set in the future, but that some is also set in the present or past. Explain that some fiction, such as *1984,* is set so little ahead of publication that that time is already past. What might be the purpose of such settings?

Look For Suggest that your students note the name of the city where the crime occurred as an important clue to what will happen. It might help for them to look up *prime meridian* and *date line* in a dictionary.

Writing/Prior Knowledge To motivate students, suggest they think about the confusion possible to people phoning Hawaii or a friend in Spain while going by the time on their home clock. What sort of reception, if any, might they get?

Vocabulary Have your less advanced students read the words aloud so you can be sure they can pronounce them.

Spelling Tip Point out the exceptional spelling, *cean,* of the ending sound in *crustacean.*

GUIDE FOR READING

Crime on Mars

Arthur C. Clarke (1917–) grew up in England. Now he lives in Sri Lanka, a small island country off the coast of India. Because he lives in a remote area, Clarke keeps up with world events by subscribing to twenty scientific journals, by listening to the news on his shortwave radio, and by using a modem with his computer. Author of countless science-fiction novels and short stories, Clarke also wrote the screenplay of *2001: A Space Odyssey*. "Crime on Mars" is not only a science-fiction story but also a mystery story.

Time as an Element of Setting

Setting includes the time as well as the location of a story. In some stories the time period is important, and it is therefore reflected in the characters' dress, customs, actions, and beliefs. The time of a story can be any time in the past, present, or future. Science-fiction stories, like "Crime on Mars," are usually set in the future.

Look For

This story has also been published under another title, "The Trouble with Time." As you read, look for reasons why this title is also appropriate.

Writing

Time sometimes causes trouble right here on earth. Having time zones that differ from one section of the country to another and changing from daylight savings time to another time can cause confusion. Freewrite about how traveling from one time zone to another or turning the clocks forward or backward can cause trouble.

Vocabulary

Knowing the following words can help you as you read "Crime on Mars."

enigma (ə nig′ mə) *n.*: An unexplainable matter or event (p. 138)
sects (sekts) *n.*: Small groups of people with the same leaders and beliefs (p. 138)
crustaceans (krus tā′ shəns) *n.*: Shellfish, such as lobsters, crabs, or shrimp (p. 138)
aboriginal (ab′ə rij′ə n′l) *adj.*: First; native (p. 138)
reconnoitering (rē′ kə noit′ ər iŋ) *v.*: Making an exploratory examination to get information about a place (p. 139)
artifacts (är′ tə fakts′) *n.*: Any objects made by human work, left behind by a civilization (p. 139)
discreet surveillance (dis krēt′ sər vā′ ləns): careful, unobserved watch kept over a person, especially one who is a suspect or a prisoner (p. 142)

Objectives

1 To understand that time is an important aspect of setting
2 To identify scientific details in a science-fiction setting
3 To recognize that new words are added to the English language
4 To write an extension of the short story

Support Material

Teaching Portfolio
Teacher Backup, pp. 205–208
Grammar in Action Worksheets, *Understanding Adverbs,* pp. 209–210
Usage and Mechanics Worksheet, p. 211
Vocabulary Check, p. 212
Critical Thinking and Reading Worksheet, *Identifying Scientific Details,* p. 213
Language Worksheet, *Recognizing New Words,* p. 214
Selection Test, pp. 215–216

Crime on Mars

Arthur C. Clarke

"We don't have much crime on Mars," said Detective Inspector Rawlings, a little
1 sadly. "In fact, that's the chief reason I'm going back to the Yard.[1] If I stayed here much longer, I'd get completely out of practice."

We were sitting in the main observation lounge of the Phobos Spaceport, looking out
2 across the jagged, sun-drenched crags of the tiny moon. The ferry rocket that had brought us up from Mars had left ten minutes ago, and was now beginning the long fall back to the ocher-tinted[2] globe hanging there against the stars. In half an hour we would be boarding the liner for Earth—a world upon which most of the passengers had never set foot, but which they still called "home."

"At the same time," continued the Inspector, "now and then there's a case that makes life interesting. You're an art dealer, Mr. Maccar; I'm sure you heard about that spot of bother at Meridian City a couple of months ago."

"I don't think so," replied the plump, olive-skinned little man I'd taken for just another returning tourist. Presumably the
3 Inspector had already checked through the passenger list; I wondered how much he knew about me, and tried to reassure myself that my conscience was—well—reasonably clear. After all, everybody took *something* out through Martian Customs—

"It's been rather well hushed up," said the Inspector, "but you can't keep these things quiet for long. Anyway, a jewel thief from Earth tried to steal Meridian Museum's greatest treasure—the Siren Goddess."

"But that's absurd!" I objected. "It's priceless, of course—but it's only a lump of sandstone. You couldn't sell it to anyone—
you might just as well steal the Mona Lisa."[3] 4

The Inspector grinned, rather mirthlessly. "*That's* happened once," he said. "Maybe the motive was the same. There are collectors who would give a fortune for such an object, even if they could only look at it themselves. Don't you agree, Mr. Maccar?"

"That's perfectly true. In my business, you meet all sorts of crazy people."

"Well, this chappie—name's Danny Weaver—had been well paid by one of them. And if it hadn't been for a piece of fantastically bad luck, he might have brought it off."

The Spaceport P.A. system apologized for a further slight delay owing to final fuel checks, and asked a number of passengers to report to Information. While we were waiting for the announcement to finish, I

---

1. Yard: Scotland Yard, headquarters of the London police force.
2. ocher (ō′ kər)**-tinted** *adj.*: Yellow-colored.

3. Mona Lisa: Priceless portrait by Leonardo da Vinci (1452-1519), an Italian painter.

Presentation

Motivation/Prior Knowledge Tell your class they are going ahead in time to Mars, which is now colonized by Earthlings. How do they imagine the colonists are able to breathe, to eat and drink, or to navigate? What new inventions and skills will be needed before such colonization can actually occur? What sorts of aboriginal Martians might have to be controlled? Next, have students consider the title. Does it suggest a "civilized" planet?

Purpose-Setting Question What sorts of crimes do you expect to happen on Mars?

1 **Discussion** What does this first sentence tell you about the story?

2 **Literary Focus** Point out to students that this story is told in the first-person point of view. What does this mean? What does this tell you about the events that are described?

3 **Discussion** How does this scene compare to present times in an airport? Discuss how the inspector has information about passengers; there is a customs through which travelers must pass, and some travelers try to smuggle things through customs.

4 **Discussion** Why wouldn't you be able to sell the Mona Lisa to anyone?

recalled what little I knew about the Siren Goddess. Though I'd never seen the original, like most other departing tourists I had a replica[4] in my baggage. It bore the certificate of the Mars Bureau of Antiquities, guaranteeing that "this full-scale reproduction is an exact copy of the so-called Siren Goddess, discovered in the Mare Sirenium by the Third Expedition, A.D. 2012 (A.M. 23)."

It's quite a tiny thing to have caused so much controversy. Only eight or nine inches high—you wouldn't look at it twice if you saw it in a museum on Earth. The head of a young woman, with slightly oriental features, elongated earlobes, hair curled in tight ringlets close to the scalp, lips half parted in an expression of pleasure or surprise—that's all. But it's an enigma so baffling that it's inspired a hundred religious sects, and driven quite a few archaeologists[5] round the bend. For a perfectly human head has no right whatsoever to be found on Mars, whose only intelligent inhabitants were crustaceans—"educated lobsters," as the newspapers are fond of calling them. The aboriginal Martians never came near to achieving space flight, and in any event their civilization died before men existed on Earth. No wonder the Goddess is

4. **replica** (rep′ li kə) *n.*: A copy of a work of art.

5. **archaeologists** (är′ kē äl′ ə jistz) *n.*: Scientists who study the life and culture of ancient peoples.

Grammar in Action

Adverbs make sentence meaning more specific. They answer one of these questions: *Where? When? In what manner? To what extent?* Notice the adverbs (in italics) and the questions they answer in the following sentences from "Crime on Mars":

Where?: He stayed *there* until about midnight, just in case there were any enthusiastic researchers still in the building.

When?: Danny was counting on this, when he checked into the hotel in Meridian West, *late* Friday afternoon.

In what manner?: "Danny's plan was *beautifully* simple," continued the Inspector.

To what extent?: Beyond those electronic shields is the *utterly* hostile emptiness of the Martian Outback, where a man will die in seconds without protection.

In addition to making meaning precise, adverbs enable writers to expand sentences and to vary sentence patterns.

the solar system's number-one mystery; I don't suppose we'll find the answer in my lifetime—if we ever do.

"Danny's plan was beautifully simple," continued the Inspector. "You know how absolutely dead a Martian city gets on Sunday, when everything closes down and the colonists stay home to watch the TV from Earth. Danny was counting on this, when he checked into the hotel in Meridian West, late Friday afternoon. He'd have Saturday for reconnoitering the Museum, an undisturbed Sunday for the job itself, and on Monday morning he'd be just another tourist leaving town. . . .

"Early Saturday he strolled through the little park and crossed over into Meridian East, where the Museum stands. In case you don't know, the city gets its name because it's exactly on longitude one hundred and eighty degrees; there's a big stone slab in the park with the prime meridian engraved on it, so that visitors can get themselves photographed standing in two hemispheres at once. Amazing what simple things amuse some people.

"Danny spent the day going over the Museum, exactly like any other tourist determined to get his money's worth. But at closing time he didn't leave; he'd holed up in one of the galleries not open to the public, where the Museum had been arranging a Late Canal Period reconstruction but had run out of money before the job could be finished. He stayed there until about midnight, just in case there were any enthusiastic researchers still in the building. Then he emerged and got to work."

"Just a minute," I interrupted. "What about the night watchman?"

The Inspector laughed.

"My dear chap! They don't have such luxuries on Mars. There weren't even any alarms, for who would bother to steal lumps of stone? True, the Goddess was sealed up neatly in a strong glass-and-metal cabinet, just in case some souvenir hunter took a fancy to her. But even if she were stolen, there was nowhere the thief could hide, and of course all outgoing traffic would be searched as soon as the statue was missed."

That was true enough. I'd been thinking in terms of Earth, forgetting that every city on Mars is a closed little world of its own 7
beneath the force-field that protects it from the freezing near-vacuum. Beyond those electronic shields is the utterly hostile emptiness of the Martian Outback, where a man will die in seconds without protection. That makes law enforcement very easy; no wonder there's so little crime on Mars. . . .

"Danny had a beautiful set of tools, as specialized as a watchmaker's. The main item was a microsaw no bigger than a soldering iron; it had a wafer-thin blade, driven at a million cycles a second by an ultrasonic power pack. It would go through glass or 8
metal like butter—and left a cut only about as thick as a hair. Which was very important for Danny, since he had to leave no traces of his handiwork.

"I suppose you've guessed how he intended to operate. He was going to cut through the base of the cabinet, and substitute one of those souvenir replicas for the real Goddess. It might be a couple of years before some inquisitive expert discovered the awful truth; long before then the original would have traveled back to Earth, perfectly disguised as a copy of itself, with a genuine certificate of authenticity. Pretty neat, eh?

"It must have been a weird business, working in that darkened gallery with all those million-year-old carvings and unexplainable artifacts around him. A museum on Earth is bad enough at night, but at least it's—well—*human*. And Gallery Three,

5 **Discussion** What do you think everyone watches on television on Sundays?

6 **Discussion** What is the importance of the prime meridian? Why would visitors want a picture of themselves in two hemispheres?

7 **Enrichment** Artistic students might like to draw their conceptions of these Martian cities.

8 **Thematic Idea** In which other short story did the main character have a beautiful set of tools used to cut through metal? How are Danny and Jimmy Valentine from "A Retrieved Reformation" (page 61) alike? How are they different?

Student Activity 1. Find ten other examples of adverbs on these pages.

Student Activity 2. Make up ten sentences in which you use adverbs. You might use as examples the model sentences given here or the other sentences on these pages in which you found adverbs.

9 **Reading Strategy** Have students summarize the story up to this point and tell why they think the museum opened up for the day.

which houses the Goddess, is particularly unsettling. It's full of bas-reliefs[6] showing quite incredible animals fighting each other; they look rather like giant beetles, and most paleontologists[7] flatly deny that they could ever have existed. But imaginary or not, they belonged to this world, and they didn't disturb Danny as much as the Goddess, staring at him across the ages and defying him to explain her presence here. She gave him the creeps. How do I know? He told me.

"Danny set to work on that cabinet as carefully as any diamond cutter preparing to cleave a gem. It took most of the night to slice out the trap door, and it was nearly dawn when he relaxed and put down the saw. There was still a lot of work to do, but the hardest part was over. Putting the replica into the case, checking its appearance against the photos he'd thoughtfully brought with him, and covering up his traces might take most of Sunday but that didn't worry him in the least. He had another twenty-four hours, and would positively welcome Monday's first visitors so that he could mingle with them and make his inconspicuous exit.

"It was a perfectly horrible shock to his 9
nervous system, therefore, when the main

6. **bas-reliefs** (bä′ rə lēfs′) *n.*: Sculpture in which figures are carved on a flat surface, such as a wall, so that they stand out from the background.
7. **paleontologists** (pā′ lē än täl′ ə jists) *n.*: Scientists who investigate prehistoric forms of life by studying plant and animal fossils.

10 Discussion What is Meridian City's chief claim to fame?

11 Discussion Who is the watchman? Why is it ironic that Danny became the watchman?

12 Discussion Why is Mr. Maccar "green about the gills"?

13 Discussion Why is the trip going to be so interesting?

Reader's Response Imagine living in a self-contained city on Mars. What would you like and dislike about living there?

Enrichment As Clarke describes it, the environment of Mars is a hostile setting, especially the Martian Outback. Have your students write a paragraph describing the Martian Outback. What do you imagine makes this setting so hostile? What are the Martian terrain, weather, atmosphere, and wildlife like? You might help your **less advanced** students by giving them the first sentence of their paragraphs: "In the Martian Outback, a person will die in seconds without protection." Then have them explain why this statement is true.

doors were noisily unbarred at eight-thirty and the museum staff—all six of them—started to open up for the day. Danny bolted for the emergency exit, leaving everything behind—tools, Goddesses, the lot. He had another big surprise when he found himself in the street; it should have been completely deserted at this time of day, with everyone at home reading the Sunday papers. But here were the citizens of Meridian East, as large as life, heading for plant or office on what was obviously a normal working day.

"By the time poor Danny got back to his hotel, we were waiting for him. We couldn't claim much credit for deducing that only a
10 visitor from Earth—and a very recent one at that—could have overlooked Meridian City's chief claim to fame. And I presume you know what *that* is."

"Frankly, I don't," I answered. "You can't see much of Mars in six weeks, and I never went east of the Syrtis Major."

"Well, it's absurdly simple, but we shouldn't be too hard on Danny; even the locals occasionally fall into the same trap. It's something that doesn't bother us on Earth, where we've been able to dump the problem in the Pacific Ocean. But Mars, of course, is all dry land; and that means that *somebody* has to live with the International Date Line. . . .[8]

"Danny, you see, had worked from Meridian West. It was Sunday over there all right—and it was still Sunday when we picked him up back at the hotel. But over in Meridian East, half a mile away, it was only Saturday. That little trip across the park had made all the difference; I told you it was rotten luck."

There was a long moment of silent sympathy; then I asked, "What did he get?"

"Three years," said Inspector Rawlings.

"That doesn't seem very much."

"Mars years; that makes it almost six of ours. And a whacking fine which, by an odd coincidence, came to just the refund value of his return ticket to Earth. He isn't in jail, of course; Mars can't afford that kind of nonproductive luxury. Danny has to work for a living, under discreet surveillance. I told you that the Meridian Museum couldn't afford a night watchman. Well, it has one now. Guess who."

"All passengers prepare to board in ten minutes! Please collect your hand baggage!" ordered the loud-speakers.

As we started to move toward the air lock,[9] I couldn't help asking one more question.

"What about the people who put Danny up to it? There must have been a lot of money behind him. Did you get them?"

"Not yet; they'd covered their tracks pretty thoroughly, and I believe Danny was telling the truth when he said he couldn't give us any leads. Still, it's not my case; as I told you, I'm going back to my old job at the Yard. But a policeman always keeps his eyes open—like an art dealer, eh, Mr. Maccar? Why, you look a bit green about the gills. Have one of my space-sickness tablets."

"No, thank you," answered Mr. Maccar, "I'm quite all right."

His tone was distinctly unfriendly; the social temperature seemed to have dropped below zero in the last few minutes. I looked at Mr. Maccar, and I looked at the Inspector. And suddenly I realized that we were going to have a very interesting trip.

---

8. International Date Line: Imaginary line drawn north and south that marks the beginning of different time zones. When it is Sunday on one side of the line, it is Saturday on the other.

9. air lock: An airtight compartment between two places that have different air pressures.

Closure and Extension

ANSWERS TO THINKING ABOUT THE SELECTION

Recalling

1. He discusses the case of a jewel thief from Earth trying to steal the Siren Goddess from the Meridian Museum.
2. He considers the crime absurd because no one could sell the statue since it is so well-known. The Inspector feels that the thief might just want to look at the statue, not sell it.
3. The Siren Goddess is eight or nine inches high. It has the head of a young woman, with slightly oriental features, elongated earlobes, hair curled in tight ringlets close to the scalp and lips half parted in an expression of pleasure or surprise. It's an enigma because no intelligent human-looking inhabitants were ever on Mars before the Earthlings arrived.
4. Danny's plan was to check into a hotel in Meridian West on late Friday afternoon. He'd use Saturday to reconnoiter the Museum. On Sunday, when everyone was watching television, he'd steal the statue and on Monday morning he'd leave town.
5. When Danny went to the Museum a half mile across the park, he crossed the prime meridian. It became Saturday and the Museum was open. The police know that

THINKING ABOUT THE SELECTION

Recalling

1. About what crime does the Inspector tell the narrator and Mr. Maccar?
2. Why does the narrator consider such a crime absurd? What is the Inspector's explanation for the motive?
3. Describe the Goddess. Why is it an enigma?
4. How did Danny plan to steal the Goddess?
5. What goes wrong with Danny's plan? Why are the police able to find him so easily?

Interpreting

6. Which detail at the beginning of the story indicates that the Inspector has checked through the passenger list?
7. For what two reasons does the Inspector tell this story?
8. What does the narrator mean when he says, "And suddenly I realized that we were going to have a very interesting trip"?

Applying

9. Compare and contrast the life of the settlers on Mars as shown in this story with the life of settlers of the American frontier.

ANALYZING LITERATURE

Understanding Time as Part of Setting

The setting of a short story includes both its location and the time in which it takes place. Both are very important in "Crime on Mars."

1. Why is there so little crime on Mars?
2. Why is the city named Meridian City?
3. How does time foil Danny's plot?

CRITICAL THINKING AND READING

Identifying Scientific Details

"Crime on Mars" is a science-fiction story set in a spaceport. The spaceport is on one of the moons of the planet Mars. In a science-fiction story, many of the details are based on scientific information. Upon this scientific base, however, the author's imagination creates imaginary characters and situations. Some details in science fiction have a scientific base and some are imaginary.

Label each of the following details as based on science or purely imaginary.

1. "The ferry rocket that had brought us up from Mars had left ten minutes ago, and was now beginning the long fall back to the ocher-tinted globe hanging there against the stars."
2. "For a perfectly human head has no right whatsoever to be found on Mars, whose only intelligent inhabitants were crustaceans —'educated lobsters,' as the newspapers are fond of calling them."
3. "Beyond those electronic shields is the utterly hostile emptiness of the Martian Outback, where a man will die in seconds without protection."

UNDERSTANDING LANGUAGE

Recognizing New Words

Languages grow to accommodate changes in the world. New words are added to the English language as the need for them arises. The areas of science and technology, in particular, have produced words that would not have appeared in any dictionary twenty-five years ago.

Look up the following words in a recent dictionary. Write the meaning of each.

1. camcorder 2. modem 3. condominium

THINKING AND WRITING

Continuing a Science-Fiction Story

Imagine that you are the person telling the story "Crime on Mars." Continue the story by writing a newspaper account of what happened between the Inspector and Mr. Maccar during their trip from Mars and after they landed on earth. Make sure your account contains enough details to be clear and interesting. Proofread your account and share it with your classmates.

(Answers begin on p. 142.)

2. The city got its name because it's exactly on longitude one hundred and eighty degrees.
3. Danny worked from Meridian West where it was Sunday at the hotel. But the Museum was across the park in Meridian East.

ANSWERS TO CRITICAL THINKING AND READING

1. science 2. imaginary 3. science

ANSWERS TO UNDERSTANDING LANGUAGE

1. a combination of a camera and a recorder
2. a device that converts data to a form that can be transmitted, as by telephone, to data-processing equipment, where a similar device reconverts it
3. an arrangement under which a tenant in an apartment building or in a complex of multiple-unit dwellings holds full title to his or her unit and joint ownership in the common grounds

Challenge Ask students if they know of any puzzling archaeological finds of today. Two examples are Stonehenge and the Easter Island statues.

THINKING AND WRITING

Publishing Student Writing Make a class newspaper of the trip. Type some of the better accounts and make enough copies for each student in your class.

Writing Across the Curriculum Mars has been a goal of explorers ever since the beginning of the space age. Have students prepare a report entitled "Exploring Mars: Past, Present, and Future." What Earth probes have visited Mars? What did they discover? What plans do the United States and the Soviet Union have for further exploration of Mars? Have students use recent periodicals to answer these questions. You might want to inform the science department of this assignment.

only a recent visitor from Earth could have overlooked that fact.

Interpreting

6. The Inspector knew that Mr. Maccar was an art dealer.
7. One reason was to entertain the people while they waited for their flight back to Earth. But the main reason was to implicate Mr. Maccar as the person who put Danny up to stealing the statue.
8. He realized that the Inspector knew that Mr. Maccar was the person who put Danny up to the robbery.

Applying

9. Answers will differ. Some points might be that both people were pioneers in a new area and had to live under trying conditions. However, American frontier settlers had much more room to expand, while those on Mars had to live in a closed little world.

ANSWERS TO ANALYZING LITERATURE

1. There is so little crime on Mars because there was nowhere the thief could hide and all outgoing traffic would be searched. Every city was a closed little world beneath the forcefield that protects it from the freezing near-vacuum. Beyond these shields is the Martian Outback, where people would die without protection.

GUIDE FOR READING

The Tell-Tale Heart

Edgar Allan Poe (1809–1849) was born in Boston. He wrote many short stories, poems, and essays before he died at the age of 40. During his life Poe endured personal tragedies including the death of his mother, a difficult stay in a foster home, a college career shortened by debts and misconduct, the death of his wife at a young age, and years of poverty. These tragedies influenced Poe's writing so that his short stories were filled with horror. "The Tell-Tale Heart" is one of the best examples of Poe's tales of terror.

Atmosphere and Mood

The **atmosphere** or **mood** of a story is the overall emotional feeling that the details the author uses create. Sometimes you may be able to describe the atmosphere in a single word—sad, frightening, or mysterious, for example. Authors create atmosphere by their descriptions of settings, characters, and events. They choose their words carefully so that you will be affected by their writing in the way they want you to be.

Look For

As you read "The Tell-Tale Heart," look for the descriptive details that help create the atmosphere of the story. How do these details make you feel? What emotions do they stir up in you?

Writing

Make notes about words or descriptions you might include in a story to create an atmosphere or mood of horror. You will probably want to include descriptions of the weather, the time, and the place where your story takes place.

Vocabulary

Knowing the following words will help you as you read "The Tell-Tale Heart."

acute (ə kyo͞ot′) *adj.*: Sensitive (p. 145)
dissimulation (di sim′ yə lā′ shən) *n.*: The hiding of one's feelings or purposes (p. 145)
profound (prə found′) *adj.*: Seeing beyond what is obvious (p. 145)
sagacity (sə gas′ ə tē) *n.*: High intelligence and sound judgment (p. 146)
crevice (krev′ is) *n.*: A narrow opening (p. 147)
suavity (swä′ və tē) *n.*: Graceful politeness (p. 148)
gesticulations (jes tik′ yə lā′ shəns) *n.*: Energetic hand or arm gestures (p. 148)
derision (di rizh′ ən) *n.*: Contempt; ridicule (p. 148)

Focus

More About the Author In his short life, Edgar Allan Poe invented the detective story. His poetry—coolly received in this country, as was the rest of his output—inspired a school of poetry in France. He was so ignored by his generation that when, twenty-six years after his death, a stone was finally erected over his grave, the only American writer to attend the ceremony was Walt Whitman. Point out that, though Poe is an American author, most of his stories are not set in American locales. Ask why a writer of horror stories might choose to set a tale, for example, in an Italian wine cellar or an island in a swampy pond.

Literary Focus Have your students recall the short stories by Doyle and Le Guin. Which setting in "The Adventure of the Speckled Band" created the best atmosphere for terror? What in Mr. Underhill's island lent credibility to the eventual transformation of the two wizards? How would it be possible for a writer to create suspenseful terror in an old man's bedroom? in a person's mind?

Look For Ask students to consider as they read which element of the story is the most eerie. Is it the narrator, the room, the suspenceful plot, or something else? Suggest that the descriptive details will help them decide what contributes to the eeriness.

Writing/Prior Knowledge Before your students begin writing, mention that a nineteenth-century writer once began his tale with "It was a dark and stormy night." Ask why people today make fun of that first sentence. Why is it a poor opening? How might it have been improved?

Vocabulary Have your students use each word in a sentence orally before reading the story.

Objectives

1 To describe the atmosphere or mood of a short story
2 To choose words that create a specific atmosphere
3 To write a scene that creates a Poelike mood of horror

Support Material

Teaching Portfolio
Teacher Backup, pp. 217–219
Grammar in Action Worksheet, *Appreciating Connotations*, pp. 220–221
Usage and Mechanics Worksheet, p. 222
Vocabulary Check, p. 223
Critical Thinking and Reading Worksheet, *Choosing Words to Create Atmosphere*, p. 224
Language Worksheet, *Choosing the Meaning that Fits the Context*, p. 225
Selection Test, pp. 226–227

The Tell-Tale Heart

Edgar Allan Poe

True!—nervous—very, very dreadfully
1 nervous I had been and am; but why *will*
you say that I am mad? The disease had
sharpened my senses—not destroyed—
not dulled them. Above all was the sense
of hearing acute. I heard all things in the
heaven and in the earth. I heard many
2 things in hell. How, then, am I mad? Hearken![1] and observe how healthily—how
calmly I can tell you the whole story.

It is impossible to say how first the idea entered my brain; but once conceived, it haunted me day and night. Object there was none. Passion there was none. I loved the old man. He had never wronged me. He had never given me insult. For his gold I had no desire. I think it was his eye! yes, it was this! One of his eyes resembled that of a vulture—a pale blue eye, with a film over it. Whenever it fell upon me, my blood ran cold; and so by degrees—very gradually—I made up my mind to take the life of the old man, and thus rid myself of the eye forever.

Now this is the point. You fancy me mad. Madmen know nothing. But you should have seen *me*. You should have seen how wisely I proceeded—with what caution—with what foresight—with what dissimulation I went to work! I was never kinder to the old man than during the whole week before I killed him. And every night, about midnight, I turned the latch of his door and opened it—oh, so gently! And then, when I had made an opening sufficient for my head, I put in a dark lantern, all closed, closed, so that no light shone out, and then I thrust in my head. Oh, you would have laughed to see how cunningly I thrust it in! I moved it slowly—very, very slowly, so that I might not disturb the old man's sleep. It took me an hour to place my whole head within the opening so far that I could see him as he lay upon his bed. Ha!—would a madman have been so wise as this? And then, when my head was well in the room, I undid the lantern cautiously—oh, so cautiously—cautiously (for the hinges creaked)—I undid it just so much that a
single thin ray fell upon the vulture eye. And 3
this I did for seven long nights—every night just at midnight—but I found the eye always closed; and so it was impossible to do the work; for it was not the old man who vexed me, but his evil eye. And every morning, when the day broke, I went boldly into the chamber, and spoke courageously to him, calling him by name in a hearty tone, and inquiring how he had passed the night. So you see he would have been a very profound old man, indeed, to suspect that every night, just at twelve, I looked in upon him while he slept.

Upon the eighth night I was more than usually cautious in opening the door. A watch's minute hand moves more quickly

1. **Hearken** (här′ kən) *v.*: Listen.

Presentation

Motivation/Prior Knowledge Discuss the idea of terror. Ask your students if they have ever been terrified or filled with horror. Discuss horror movies or stories they have read. Tell your class that Poe was a master of suspense and horror stories and that this is one of his most famous.

Purpose-Setting Question How might a disturbed person behave if forced to live in close contact with a man or woman whose appearance is in some way abhorrent?

1 **Discussion** What does the first sentence stress? How does it immediately suggest terror?

2 **Literary Focus** Who is telling the story? Discuss first-person point of view. Here the narrator is a character in the story. The "I" narrator tells us only his thoughts. He cannot enter the minds of the other characters.

3 **Discussion** What does the term "vulture eye" suggest? How does this add to the mood of the story? Bring out that it suggests a beast of prey, hunching over, waiting for its victim.

4 **Thematic Idea** What other short story had a character not move a muscle for a period of time? Compare and contrast Gordon from "Accounts Settled," page 47, to the narrator of this story.

than did mine. Never, before that night, had I *felt* the extent of my own powers—of my sagacity. I could scarcely contain my feelings of triumph. To think that there I was, opening the door, little by little, and he not even to dream of my secret deeds or thoughts. I fairly chuckled at the idea; and perhaps he heard me; for he moved on the bed suddenly, as if startled. Now you may think that I drew back—but no. His room was as black as pitch with the thick darkness (for the shutters were close fastened, through fear of robbers), and so I knew that he could not see the opening of the door, and I kept pushing it on steadily, steadily.

I had my head in, and was about to open the lantern, when my thumb slipped upon the tin fastening, and the old man sprang up in the bed, crying out—"Who's there?"

I kept quite still and said nothing. For a 4
whole hour I did not move a muscle, and in
the meantime I did not hear him lie down. He was still sitting up in the bed, listening; —just as I have done, night after night, hearkening to the deathwatches[2] in the wall.

Presently I heard a slight groan, and I knew it was the groan of mortal terror. It was not a groan of pain or of grief—oh, no!—it was the low stifled sound that arises from the bottom of the soul when overcharged with awe. I knew the sound well. Many a night, just at midnight, when all the world slept, it has welled up from my own bosom, deepening, with its dreadful echo, the terrors that distracted me. I say I knew it well. I knew what the old man felt, and pitied him, although I chuckled at heart. I knew that he had been lying

2. deathwatches (deth' woch' əz) *n.*: Wood-boring beetles that make a tapping noise in the wood they invade. They are thought to predict death.

Grammar in Action

The **connotation** of a word is the feelings and associations it arouses. Through their choice of words, writers suggest meaning, mood, and atmosphere. Careful readers can pick up on this word connotation and can more accurately feel the writer's intended meaning. Since the purpose of writing is to convey a message or feeling to a reader, skillful writers are aware of word connotation and select words which bring the intended meaning to mind. For example, a writer describing a garden party on a summer day would probably choose bright, cheerful words such as *golden, glowing,* and *glittering* to describe the scene. On the other hand, a writer describing an eerie, deserted mansion would probably use words like *dreary, bleak,* and *ghostly.*

Edgar Allan Poe is a master at choosing words with connotations that fit his desired mood. Read the following paragraph from "The Tell-Tale Heart" and think about which words connote the evil, dark atmosphere and mood that he wants to create.

> Presently I heard a slight groan, and I knew it was the groan of mortal terror. It was not a groan of pain or of grief—oh,

awake ever since the first slight noise, when he had turned in the bed. His fears had been ever since growing upon him. He had been trying to fancy them causeless, but could not. He had been saying to himself—"It is nothing but the wind in the chimney—it is only a mouse crossing the floor," or "it is merely a cricket which has made a single chirp." Yes, he has been trying to comfort himself with these suppositions: but he had found all in vain. *All in vain;* because Death, in approaching him,
5 had stalked with his black shadow before
him, and enveloped the victim. And it was the mournful influence of the unperceived shadow that caused him to feel—although he neither saw nor heard—to *feel* the presence of my head within the room.

When I had waited a long time, very patiently, without hearing him lie down, I resolved to open a little—a very, very little crevice in the lantern. So I opened it—you cannot imagine how stealthily, stealthily—until, at length, a single dim ray, like the thread of the spider, shot from out the crevice and fell upon the vulture eye.

It was open—wide, wide open—and I grew furious as I gazed upon it. I saw it with perfect distinctness—all a dull blue, with a hideous veil over it that chilled the very marrow in my bones; but I could see nothing else of the old man's face or person for I had directed the ray as if by instinct, precisely upon the spot.

And now—have I not told you that what you mistake for madness is but over-acuteness of the senses?—now, I say, there came to my ears a low, dull, quick sound, such as a watch makes when enveloped in
6 cotton. I knew *that* sound well, too. It was
the beating of the old man's heart. It increased my fury, as the beating of a drum stimulates the soldier into courage.

But even yet I refrained and kept still. I scarcely breathed. I held the lantern motionless. I tried how steadily I could maintain the ray upon the eye. Meantime the hellish tattoo of the heart increased. It grew quicker and quicker, and louder and louder every instant. The old man's terror *must* have been extreme! It grew louder, I say, louder every moment!—do you mark me well? I have told you that I am nervous: so I am. And now at the dead hour of the night, amid the dreadful silence of that old house, so strange a noise as this excited me to uncontrollable terror. Yet, for some minutes
longer I refrained and stood still. But the 7
beating grew louder, louder! I thought the heart must burst. And now a new anxiety seized me—the sound would be heard by a neighbor! The old man's hour had come! With a loud yell, I threw open the lantern and leaped into the room. He shrieked once—once only. In an instant I dragged him to the floor, and pulled the heavy bed over him. I then smiled gaily, to find the deed so far done. But, for many minutes, the heart beat on with a muffled sound. This, however, did not vex me; it would not be heard through the wall. At length it ceased. The old man was dead. I removed the bed and examined the corpse. Yes, he was stone, stone dead. I placed my hand upon the heart and held it there many minutes. There was no pulsa-
tion. He was stone dead. His eye would 8
trouble me no more.

If still you think me mad, you will think so no longer when I describe the wise precautions I took for the concealment of the body. The night waned, and I worked hastily, but in silence. First of all I dismembered 9
the corpse. I cut off the head and the arms and the legs.

I then took up three planks from the flooring of the chamber, and deposited all

5 **Literary Focus** Discuss personification. In personification, something abstract is given human attributes. What is death personified as? How does this add to the mood of the story?

6 **Discussion** How does the narrator react to the sight of the old man's eye and the beating of his heart?

7 **Master Teacher Note** Poe's horror tales have often been adapted to film. One element of his style lends itself to movie editing techniques. He stretches or contracts time for psychological emphasis. Filmmakers do the same with images. Have your students find passages where time is suspensefully slowed or where lengthy but dull real-time events are encapsulated in a few words.

8 **Reading Strategy** Have students summarize the story up to this point and have them predict what will happen next. Will the narrator get away with his crime? Will the police catch him?

9 **Enrichment** Ask your **more advanced** students why they think some writers and artists gravitate to the macabre. What artistic fulfillments are possible through it? Elicit names of artists who deal with the macabre. You might also show paintings in Paul Haesart's book *James Ensor* (N.Y.: Harry N. Abrams, 1959) Ask your students which of the paintings they identify with Poe's stories.

no!—it was the low stifled sound that arises from the bottom of the soul when overcharged with awe. I knew the sound well. Many a night, just at midnight, when all the world slept, it has welled up from my own bosom, deepening, with its dreadful echo, the terrors that distracted me. . . . *All in vain;* because Death, in approaching him, had stalked with his black shadow before him, and enveloped the victim. And it was the mournful influence of the unperceived shadow that caused him to feel—although he neither saw nor heard—to *feel* the presence of my head within the room.

Student Activity 1. Which words in the example passage suggest the evil, perverse atmosphere that Poe wants to create?

Student Activity 2. With the class, brainstorm for a mood or feeling that you wish to convey to a reader. Then write a paragraph that suggests this mood or feeling. Without coming right out and telling the reader what the mood or feeling is, choose words and actions that suggest your intent.

10 **Discussion** How does the narrator at first react to the police?

11 **Discussion** What do you think is making the noise? Is it a real noise or just in the narrator's mind?

12 **Master Teacher Note** Poe's horror tales are exciting because they emphasize sensual experience. In describing sights and sounds he pulls our imaginations along, forcing us to "feel" the emotional events unfolding. Have your students point out passages where seeing and hearing are key elements in the ongoing narrative.

13 **Discussion** Why did he reveal the parts of the body to the officers?

Reader's Response Although the narrator's anxiety is brought on by the crime he knows he has committed, such anxiety plagues everyone at one time or another. Describe an experience you've had in which the normal circumstances of your surroundings (lights, sounds, temperature) seemed exaggerated and bothered you intensely. What was the real cause of your anxiety?

Enrichment Encourage your artistic students to draw or paint the scene with the old man in bed and the light shining on his eye. Ask them what colors they would use.

Enrichment Have your students imagine that they are one of the police officers in "The Tell-Tale Heart." You have just witnessed the narrator's nervous behavior and heard his startling admission of guilt. As the arresting officer you must write an official account of the circumstances leading to his arrest. How would you explain the narrator's strange behavior? What besides his confession proves his guilt? Write an official report.

between the scantlings.[3] I then replaced the boards so cleverly, so cunningly, that no human eye—not even *his*—could have detected anything wrong. There was nothing to wash out—no stain of any kind—no blood-spot whatever. I had been too wary for that. A tub had caught all—ha! ha!

When I had made an end of these labors, it was four o'clock—still dark as midnight. As the bell sounded the hour, there came a knocking at the street door. I went down to open it with a light heart—for what had I *now* to fear? There entered three men, who introduced themselves, with perfect suavity, as officers of the police. A shriek had been heard by a neighbor during the night; suspicion of foul play had been aroused; information had been lodged at the police office, and they (the officers) had been deputed to search the premises.

10 I smiled—for *what* had I to fear? I bade the gentlemen welcome. The shriek, I said, was my own in a dream. The old man, I mentioned, was absent in the country. I took my visitors all over the house. I bade them search—search *well*. I led them, at length, to *his* chamber. I showed them his treasures, secure, undisturbed. In the enthusiasm of my confidence, I brought chairs into the room, and desired them *here* to rest from their fatigues, while I myself, in the wild audacity of my perfect triumph, placed my own seat upon the very spot beneath which reposed the corpse of the victim.

The officers were satisfied. My *manner* had convinced them. I was singularly at ease. They sat, and while I answered cheerily, they chatted of familiar things. But, ere long, I felt myself getting pale and
11 wished them gone. My head ached, and I fancied a ringing in my ears: but still they sat and still chatted. The ringing became more distinct:—it continued and became more distinct: I talked more freely to get rid of the feeling: but it continued and gained definitiveness—until, at length, I found that the noise was *not* within my ears.

No doubt I now grew *very* pale—but I talked more fluently, and with a heightened voice. Yet the sound increased—and what
could I do? It was *a low, dull, quick sound* 1
—much such a sound as a watch makes when enveloped in cotton. I gasped for breath—and yet the officers heard it not. I talked more quickly—more vehemently; but the noise steadily increased. I arose and argued about trifles, in a high key and with violent gesticulations; but the noise steadily increased. Why *would* they not be gone? I paced the floor to and fro with heavy strides, as if excited to fury by the observations of the men—but the noise steadily increased. Oh! what *could* I do? I foamed—I raved—I swore! I swung the chair upon which I had been sitting, and grated it upon the boards, but the noise arose over all, and continually increased. It grew louder—louder—*louder!* And still the men chatted pleasantly, and smiled. Was it possible they heard not?—no, no! They heard!—they suspected!—they *knew!*—they were making a mockery of my horror!—this I thought, and this I think. But anything was better than this agony! Anything was more tolerable than this derision! I could bear those hypocritical smiles no longer! I felt that I must scream or die!—and now again! hark! louder! louder! louder! *louder!*—

"Villains!" I shrieked, "dissemble[4] no
more! I admit the deed!—tear up the 1
planks!—here, here!—it is the beating of his hideous heart!"

---

3. scantling (skant′ lin) *n.*: A small beam or timber.

4. dissemble (di sem′ b'l) *v.*: To conceal under a false appearance; to conceal the truth of one's true feelings or motives.

THINKING ABOUT THE SELECTION

Recalling

1. Why does the narrator decide to kill the old man?
2. How long does it take him to accomplish his plan?
3. Why do the police arrive, even though the narrator planned the murder so carefully?

Interpreting

4. How does the narrator reveal his cunning throughout the course of the crime? How does he reveal his powers of concentration?
5. When the police arrive, why does the narrator place his chair over the spot where the old man lies buried?
6. Do you think the police suspect the truth from the beginning? Explain your answer.
7. Do you think anyone but the narrator hears the beating of the old man's heart? Explain your answer. Why does he hear it so loudly?
8. What finally drives the narrator to confess?
9. At the beginning of the story, the narrator says that he is not mad. Explain why you agree or disagree with him.
10. To whom may he be recounting his tale?

Applying

11. Why do people like to read tales of terror?

ANALYZING LITERATURE

Describing Atmosphere or Mood

Atmosphere or **mood** is the overall feeling created in a story. Poe builds the atmosphere by the use of words, details, and pictures that allow you to feel what the characters feel. In the scene where the old man awakes, for instance, Poe includes these details and pictures: ". . . he moved on the bed suddenly, as if startled," "His room was as black as pitch," and "I kept pushing it in, steadily, steadily." These details help you to feel the atmosphere of terror.

1. Look at the paragraph that begins "Presently I heard a slight groan" (page 146). List three details that help you to feel what the old man feels at this time.
2. Look at the paragraph that begins "I then took up three planks from the flooring" (page 147). List three details that create the mood of the narrator at this time.
3. Look at the paragraph that begins "No doubt I now grew *very* pale" (page 148). List three details that create the narrator's mood at this point.

CRITICAL THINKING AND READING

Choosing Words to Create Atmosphere

To create a particular atmosphere, you must choose words carefully. For example, notice the word *vulture* in the following sentence by Poe: "One of his eyes resembled that of a *vulture*." To create a different atmosphere an author might say: "His eyes resembled those of a *puppy*."

For each of the following words, a comparison is given that creates a mood. Create a different mood by writing another sentence comparing the item to something different.

1. *moon:* The golden globe of the moon lit up the road as though it were a street light.
2. *store:* The tiny store displays so many jewels that it resembles a huge jewelry box.
3. *cat:* The eyes of the cat gleamed like stars.

THINKING AND WRITING

Writing to Create Atmosphere

Imagine that Edgar Allan Poe were writing a story using the descriptions you wrote before you read this story. Write one scene as he might have written it. When you have finished, check your scene to make sure that you have used words and phrases that create a mood of horror.

Closure and Extension

ANSWERS TO THINKING ABOUT THE SELECTION

Recalling

1. He decided to kill the old man because one of the old man's eyes resembled that of a vulture and made his blood run cold.
2. It took him eight nights to kill the old man.
3. The police came to the house because a neighbor had heard a shriek.

Interpreting

4. He quietly entered the old man's room for seven nights before he found the old man's eye open on the eighth night. On the eighth night he waited for one hour without moving until he made his move to kill the old man.
5. He placed his seat over the corpse because he was so sure he committed the perfect crime and would not be found out.
6. Answers will differ. If students say yes, they should bring out that the police sat down and talked to the narrator long after he explained the reason for the shriek. If they say no, they could point out that the police never directly questioned the narrator about the old man. He confessed without them ever accusing him.
7. No, the narrator is mad. The heart really isn't beating; he just imagines it. He hears it so loudly because the police are in the room and he suspects that they know of his crime.
8. He finally confesses because he thought the police suspected and were making a mockery of his horror. He was in agony and anything was better than the agony.
9. Answers will differ. However, most students will probably disagree with him. The whole idea of killing the old man because his eye resembled a vulture and then cutting him up and burying him in the house are not the thoughts of a sane person.
10. Answers will differ. He might be telling the story to his doctor or psychiatrist.

Applying

11. Answers will differ. Students might say that they like being scared. It's a form of escapism, where their everyday cares and worries are left behind.

ANSWERS TO ANALYZING LITERATURE

1. The three details might be "the groan of mortal terror"; "it was the low stifled sound that arises from the bottom of the soul when overcharged with awe"; and "it has welled up from my own bosom, deepening, with its dreadful echo the terrors that distracted me."
2. The three details might be "so cleverly, so cunningly"; "I had been too wary for that"; and "ha! ha!"
3. The three details might be "I gasped for breath"; "I foamed—I raved—I swore!"; and "I swung the chair upon which I had been sitting."

ANSWERS TO CRITICAL THINKING AND READING

1. through 3. Answers will differ.

THINKING AND WRITING

Publishing Student Writing Have the better scenes read aloud in class. Have students note what words and phrases were used to create the mood of horror.

Focus

More About the Author Ray Bradbury has been a full-time author since 1943. He has published both long and short fiction, children's books, plays, and film scripts, including the one for *Moby Dick*. The movie *Fahrenheit 451* was based on his novel of the same name. Point out to your students that Bradbury was not born until fifty-five years after the Civil War, the setting of "The Drummer Boy of Shiloh." How do students suppose Bradbury was able to re-create a period of which he had no firsthand experience?

Literary Focus After your students have read the explanation of historical setting, discuss what they know about the Civil War period. How was warfare then different from the way it is today? Consider such details as uniforms, weapons and methods of fighting.

Look For To demonstrate how they should look for details, have the class read silently the first three paragraphs, telling them to note details of setting. Then have them close their books and recall the exact month, the name of the creek, any buildings that were mentioned, the time of day, and the kind of orchard. Considering this is a story about the Civil War, what is ironic about this setting?

Writing/Prior Knowledge Remind your students that they should consider soldiers in a variety of battle situations, such as a parachutist about to jump, a hospital orderly awaiting casualties, a sailor on a submarine, or a youth among veteran Marines.

Vocabulary It would be helpful for students to know the following words also: *miraculously* (p. 151), *lunar* (p. 151), *legitimately* (p. 153), and *hindside* (p. 154).

GUIDE FOR READING

The Drummer Boy of Shiloh

Ray Bradbury (1920–   ) was born in Waukegan, Illinois, and began his working life as a newsboy. Bradbury writes chiefly science-fiction and fantasy stories, such as his famous book *The Martian Chronicles*. The feelings and people that Bradbury writes about, however, could exist in any time or place. He writes stories of people—real, honest people—such as the Civil War drummer boy and the general in the "The Drummer Boy of Shiloh." This story is not science fiction, however; it is an example of historical fiction.

Historical Setting

Stories may be set in a real place in a past time. If these stories are accurate in the way the places, times, and historical events are described, the stories are said to have a **historical setting.** Though the setting and some characters and events may be realistic, most of the characters and events are fictional. "The Drummer Boy of Shiloh," for example, has as its setting the battlefield at Shiloh, Tennessee, on the night before a famous Civil War battle. Although drummer boys and generals really were there, the ones you will meet in the story are creations of the author's imagination.

Look For

As you read "The Drummer Boy of Shiloh," look for details about when and where the story takes place. Does the historical setting change the way you view the story?

Writing

How do you think young soldiers feel the night before a major battle? Freewrite about how they might feel and what they might think about.

Vocabulary

Knowing the following words will help you as you read "The Drummer Boy of Shiloh."

askew (ə skyo͞o′) *adv.*: Crookedly (p. 151)
benediction (ben′ ə dik′ shən) *n.*: A blessing (p. 151)
riveted (riv′ it əd) *adj.*: Fastened or made firm (p. 153)
compounded (käm pound′ əd) *adj.*: Mixed or combined (p. 153)
remote (ri mōt′) *adj.*: Distant (p. 153)
resolute (rez′ ə lo͞ot′) *adj.*: Showing a firm purpose; determined (p. 154)
tremor (trem′ ər) *n.*: Shaking or vibration (p. 155)
muted (myo͞ot′ əd) *adj.*: Muffled; subdued (p. 155)

Objectives

1. To recognize the details that establish a historical setting
2. To recognize details inappropriate to particular historical settings
3. To prepare a program of Civil War songs
4. To write about a historical setting

Support Material

Teaching Portfolio

Teacher Backup, pp. 229–231
Grammar in Action Worksheets, *Understanding Dialogue,* pp. 232–233, *Understanding Active Voice,* pp. 234–235
Usage and Mechanics Worksheet, p. 236
Vocabulary Check, p. 237
Analyzing Literature Worksheet, *Recognizing Historical Details,* p. 238
Language Worksheet, *Understanding Synonyms,* p. 239
Selection Test, pp. 240–241

The Drummer Boy of Shiloh

Ray Bradbury

1 In the April night, more than once, blossoms fell from the orchard trees and lit with rustling taps on the drumskin. At midnight a peach stone left miraculously on a branch through winter, flicked by a bird, fell swift and unseen, struck once, like panic, which jerked the boy upright. In silence he listened to his own heart ruffle away, away—at last gone from his ears and back in his chest again.

2 After that, he turned the drum on its side, where its great lunar face peered at him whenever he opened his eyes.

His face, alert or at rest, was solemn. It was indeed a solemn time and a solemn night for a boy just turned fourteen in the peach field near the Owl Creek not far from the church at Shiloh.[1]

". . . thirty-one, thirty-two, thirty-three . . . "

Unable to see, he stopped counting.

Beyond the thirty-three familiar shadows, forty thousand men, exhausted by nervous expectation, unable to sleep for romantic dreams of battles yet unfought, lay crazily askew in their uniforms. A mile yet farther on, another army was strewn helter-skelter, turning slow, basting themselves[2] with the thought of what they would do when the time came: 3 a leap, a yell, a blind plunge their strategy, raw youth their protection and benediction.

Now and again the boy heard a vast wind come up, that gently stirred the air. But he knew what it was—the army here, the army there, whispering to itself in the dark. 4 Some men talking to others, others murmuring to themselves, and all so quiet it was like a natural element arisen from South or North with the motion of the earth toward dawn.

5 What the men whispered the boy could only guess, and he guessed that it was: "Me, I'm the one, I'm the one of all the rest who won't die. I'll live through it. I'll go home. The band will play. And I'll be there to hear it."

Yes, thought the boy, that's all very well for them, they can give as good as they get!

6 For with the careless bones of the young men harvested by night and bindled[3] around campfires were the similarly strewn steel bones of their rifles, with bayonets fixed like eternal lightning lost in the orchard grass.

1. Shiloh (shī′ lō): The site of a Civil War battle in 1862; now a national military park in southwest Tennessee.

2. basting themselves: Here, letting their thoughts pour over them as they turn in their sleep.

3. bindled (bin′ d′ld) *adj.*: Bedded.

Presentation

Motivation/Prior Knowledge Have your students discuss their ideas of fear. What are some common fears people have? What is the difference between irrational and rational fears? What are some ways people overcome their fears? Ask them to consider as they read whether Joby's fear is rational or irrational.

Thematic Idea Another selection that deals with the theme of a teenager's response to war is *The Diary of Anne Frank* (page 303).

Purpose-Setting Question What role does fear play in this story?

1 **Discussion** What sounds do you hear in the first paragraph? From the boy's reaction to the falling pit, what do you know about his thoughts?

2 **Language** Note the use of figurative language in the second paragraph. Metaphors are used by writers to compare unlike objects in order to produce a startlingly real image in the mind of the reader. What is being compared in this paragraph? Have the students note the many other uses of metaphors in this story.

3 **Discussion** What does Bradbury mean by "raw youth their protection and benediction"?

4 **Language** Have your students say the word "murmur" aloud several times. How does it sound? The reproduction of the sound in the word itself is called onomatopoeia. Writers frequently use this device to heighten the sense of reality in a scene.

5 **Discussion** What is it about human nature that produces this thought instead of the negative one of imminent death?

6 **Discussion** Have your students reread this sentence and fix the image in their minds. What is being compared?

Humanities Note

Fine art, *Drummer Boy,* by Julian Scott. Scott (1846–1901), is an American painter who was born in Vermont. After serving in the army during the Civil War, he decided to study fine art. He attended the school of the National Academy and studied with the painter Leutze until 1868.

Ask the class if this is the face of an innocent boy untouched by war or do we see in it the experience of having known and survived battle. Have your students explain their perceptions based on their findings in the canvas and reactions to the portrait. Have students study the face.

1. What character do you see in it?
2. Is this the face of an automaton, drumming out marching and fighting music in a mechanical way, doing what he has been told to do? Or, is there a sense of independence in the face: a young man, strong of spirit, aware of the importance of his drum in rallying the spirit of his fellow Union soldiers?
3. How else do you perceive this young man-boy?

DRUMMER BOY
Julian Scott
N. S. Mayer

Grammar in Action

Writers punctuate **dialogue** to separate it from the rest of the story. Direct speech by characters is set off in quotation marks. Explanatory words or phrases, such as *he said* or *whispered the boy,* are separated from the speaker's words with a comma.

Sometimes the explanatory phrase appears before the quotation. Look at how Bradbury punctuates this situation:

> Then, after a moment, he said, "So there you are, that's it. Will you do that, boy? Do you know now you're general of the army when the general's left behind?"

Bradbury places a comma after the explanatory phrase and capitalizes the opening word in the quotation.

Often the explanatory phrase is at the end of the quotation:

> "Fool question," said the general.

When the phrase appears at the end, the comma is placed inside the quotation mark, and the first letter of the explanatory phrase is a small letter.

Me, thought the boy, I got only a drum, two sticks to beat it, and no shield.

7 There wasn't a man-boy on this ground tonight who did not have a shield he cast, riveted or carved himself on his way to his first attack, compounded of remote but nonetheless firm and fiery family devotion, flag-blown patriotism and cocksure immortality strengthened by the touchstone of very real gunpowder, ramrod, Minié ball[4] and flint. But without these last, the boy felt his family move yet farther off away in the dark, as if one of those great prairie-burning
8 trains had chanted them away never to return—leaving him with this drum which was worse than a toy in the game to be played tomorrow or some day much too soon.

The boy turned on his side. A moth brushed his face, but it was a peach blossom. A peach blossom flicked him, but it was a moth. Nothing stayed put. Nothing had a name. Nothing was as it once was.

If he lay very still, when the dawn came up and the soldiers put on their bravery with
9 their caps, perhaps they might go away, the war with them, and not notice him lying small here, no more than a toy himself.

"Well, now," said a voice.

The boy shut up his eyes, to hide inside himself, but it was too late. Someone, walking by in the night, stood over him.

"Well," said the voice quietly, "here's a soldier crying *before* the fight. Good. Get it over. Won't be time once it all starts."

And the voice was about to move on when the boy, startled, touched the drum at his elbow. The man above, hearing this, stopped. The boy could feel his eyes, sense
10 him slowly bending near. A hand must have come down out of the night, for there was a little *rat-tat* as the fingernails brushed and the man's breath fanned his face.

"Why, it's the drummer boy, isn't it?"

The boy nodded, not knowing if his nod was seen. "Sir, is that *you?*" he said.

"I assume it is." The man's knees cracked as he bent still closer.

He smelled as all fathers should smell, of salt sweat, ginger tobacco, horse and boot leather, and the earth he walked upon. He had many eyes. No, not eyes—brass but- 11
tons that watched the boy.

He could only be, and was, the general.

"What's your name, boy?" he asked.

"Joby," whispered the boy, starting to sit up.

"All right, Joby, don't stir." A hand pressed his chest gently, and the boy relaxed. "How long you been with us, Joby?"

"Three weeks, sir."

"Run off from home or joined legitimately, boy?"

Silence.

"Fool question," said the general. "Do you shave yet, boy? Even more of a fool. There's your cheek, fell right off the tree overhead. And the others here not much 12
older. Raw, raw, the lot of you. You ready for tomorrow or the next day, Joby?"

"I think so, sir."

"You want to cry some more, go on ahead. I did the same last night."

"*You*, sir?"

"It's the truth. Thinking of everything ahead. Both sides figuring the other side will just give up, and soon, and the war done in weeks, and us all home. Well, that's not how it's going to be. And maybe that's why I cried."

"Yes, sir," said Joby.

The general must have taken out a cigar now, for the dark was suddenly filled with the smell of tobacco unlit as yet, but chewed as the man thought what next to say.

4. **Minié** (min′ ē), ball: A cone-shaped rifle bullet that expands when fired.

7 **Discussion** Why does Bradbury use the term "man-boy" here?

8 **Discussion** How does the boy feel about his family?

9 **Discussion** Do you think that thoughts of cowardice would be normal for a boy of fourteen under these circumstances? Explain.

10 **Language** Which word in this sentence is another example of onomatopoeia?

11 **Language** In this metaphor, to what does the author compare brass buttons?

12 **Discussion** What does comparing the boy's cheeks to peach blossoms suggest?

Master Teacher Note Ask some students to interview soldiers who fought in wars. Have them ask about their thoughts on the subjects of survival, the night before an assault, and how well prepared they felt. What sounds did they hear? Did they have trust and faith in their commanding officers? If possible, have some war veterans come to class to be interviewed.

Frequently, the explanatory phrase comes in the middle of a sentence in the quotation:

> "Well," said the voice quietly, "here's a soldier crying *before* the fight. Good. Get it over. Won't be time once it all starts."

In this situation, a comma is placed inside the quotation mark before the explanatory phrase and another is placed immediately after the phrase and before the continuing quotation. Because the explanatory phrase interrupts a single sentence, the first word of the second part of the quotation is not capitalized.

Student Activity. Create a dialogue between two people. Place the explanatory phrases at the beginning, in the middle, and at the end of quotations. Include some lines of dialogue with no explanatory phrase.

13 **Master Teacher Note** Have your students reread the general's monologue. What is he saying about the upcoming battle? What do you think about what he is saying? Do you agree? Why or why not? This paragraph could produce a lively discussion about war. Ask why war touches even the strongest. Do you believe any soldier—firm-jawed, iron-willed—does not suffer the general's apprehension of the slaughter to come?

14 **Discussion** Why does the author suggest that the sun might not show its face here?

15 **Discussion** Why does the general compare the soldiers to wild horses?

16 **Discussion** Why does the general compare the army of soldiers to waves rolling in on a beach?

17 **Enrichment** Is this good advice for fighting men? Tell your **more advanced** students that this speech is based on Henry's advice to his troops in Shakespeare's *Henry V*, Act III, Scene 1: "Then imitate the action of the tiger,/Stiffen the sinews, summon up the blood. . . /Now set the teeth and stretch the nostril wide." Ask your students why Bradbury made use of Henry's speech.

13 "It's going to be a crazy time," said the general. "Counting both sides, there's a hundred thousand men, give or take a few thousand out there tonight, not one as can spit a sparrow off a tree, or knows a horse clod from a Minié ball. Stand up, bare the breast, ask to be a target, thank them and sit down, that's us, that's them. We should turn tail and train four months, they should do the same. But here we are, taken with spring fever and thinking it blood lust, taking our sulfur with cannons instead of with molasses, as it should be, going to be a hero, going to live forever. And I can see all of them over there nodding agreement, save the other way around. It's wrong, boy, it's wrong as a head put on hindside front and a man marching backward through life. More innocents will get shot out of pure enthusiasm than ever got shot before. Owl Creek was full of boys splashing around in the noonday sun just a few hours ago. I fear it will be full of boys again, just floating, at sundown tomorrow, not caring where the tide takes them."

The general stopped and made a little pile of winter leaves and twigs in the darkness, as if he might at any moment strike 14 fire to them to see his way through the coming days when the sun might not show its face because of what was happening here and just beyond.

The boy watched the hand stirring the leaves and opened his lips to say something, but did not say it. The general heard the boy's breath and spoke himself.

15 "Why am I telling you this? That's what you wanted to ask, eh? Well, when you got a bunch of wild horses on a loose rein somewhere, somehow you got to bring order, rein them in. These lads, fresh out of the milkshed, don't know what I know, and I can't tell them: men actually die, in war. So each is his own army. I got to make *one* army of them. And for that, boy, I need you."

"Me!" The boy's lips barely twitched.

"Now, boy," said the general quietly, "you are the heart of the army. Think of that. You're the heart of the army. Listen, now."

And, lying there, Joby listened. And the general spoke on.

If he, Joby, beat slow tomorrow, the heart would beat slow in the men. They would lag by the wayside. They would drowse in the fields on their muskets. They would sleep forever, after that, in those same fields—their hearts slowed by a drummer boy and stopped by enemy lead.

But if he beat a sure, steady, ever faster rhythm, then, then their knees would come up in a long line down over that hill, one knee after the other, like a wave on the ocean shore! Had he seen the ocean ever? Seen the waves rolling in like a well-ordered cavalry charge to the sand? Well, that was it, that's what he wanted, that's what was needed! Joby was his right hand and his left. He gave the orders, but Joby set the pace! 16

So bring the right knee up and the right foot out and the left knee up and the left foot out. One following the other in good time, in brisk time. Move the blood up the body and make the head proud and the spine stiff and the jaw resolute. Focus the eye and set the teeth, flare the nostrils and tighten the hands, put steel armor all over the men, for blood moving fast in them does indeed make men feel as if they'd put on steel. He must keep at it, at it! Long and steady, steady and long! Then, even though shot or torn, those wounds got in hot blood—in blood he'd helped stir—would feel less pain. If their blood was cold, it would be more than slaughter, it would be murderous nightmare and pain best not told and no one to guess. 17

The general spoke and stopped, letting his breath slack off. Then, after a moment,

Grammar in Action

The voice of a verb shows whether or not the subject is performing the action. In **active voice,** the subject performs the action of the verb. In "The Drummer Boy of Shiloh," the general uses active voice when he says ". . . men actually die, in war." The subject, men, perform the action of the verb "to die." In the passive voice, the sentence would read, ". . . men are actually killed, in war;" the subject receives rather than performs the action.

Active voice clearly expresses action while specifying who or what performs the action. Therefore, active voice strengthens your writing. Consider the active voice in the following paragraph:

"The *general stopped* and *made* a little pile of winter leaves and twigs in the darkness, as if *he might* at any moment *strike fire* to them to see his way through the coming days when the *sun might* not *show* its face because of what was happening here and just beyond."

How do the active verbs give the reader a specific impression of what is happening in the paragraph?

THE BATTLE OF SHILOH, TENNESSEE (6–7 APRIL 1862), 1886
Kurz and Allison
The Granger Collection

he said, "So there you are, that's it. Will you do that, boy? Do you know now you're general of the army when the general's left behind?"

The boy nodded mutely.

"You'll run them through for me then, boy?"

"Yes, sir."

"Good. And, maybe, many nights from tonight, many years from now, when you're as old or far much older than me, when they ask you what you did in this awful time, you will tell them—one part humble and one part proud—'I was the drummer boy at the battle of Owl Creek,' or the Tennessee River, or maybe they'll just name it after the church there. 'I was the drummer boy at Shiloh.' Good grief, that has a beat and sound to it fitting for Mr. Longfellow. 'I was the drummer boy at Shiloh.' Who will ever hear those words and not know you, boy, or what you thought this night, or what you'll think tomorrow or the next day when we must get up on our legs and *move!*"

The general stood up. "Well, then. Bless you, boy. Good night."

"Good night, sir." And tobacco, brass, boot polish, salt sweat and leather, the man moved away through the grass.

Joby lay for a moment, staring but unable to see where the man had gone. He swallowed. He wiped his eyes. He cleared his throat. He settled himself. Then, at last, very slowly and firmly, he turned the drum so that it faced up toward the sky.

He lay next to it, his arm around it, feeling the tremor, the touch, the muted thunder as, all the rest of the April night in the year 1862, near the Tennessee River, not far from the Owl Creek, very close to the church named Shiloh, the peach blossoms 18
fell on the drum.

18 **Discussion** What kind of feeling do you have as you think about the peach blossoms falling on the drum during the night?

Reader's Response The general calls Joby "the heart of the army." How would you feel about having the responsibility Joby has?

Humanities Note

Fine art, *The Battle of Shiloh, Tennessee* (6–7 April 1862), 1886. This is a lithograph produced by the Kurz and Allison Company. Artists, hired by magazines, newspapers, and printing companies were sent to the front to record, with drawings and watercolors, battles, skirmishes, and scenes of camp life. Ask the class how this lithograph relates to the fears of the young drummer boy. Question the class as to their understanding of the battle. Bring out that the infantry ranged along the river, facing one another and the opposing artillery batteries are in the upper left and right of the print.

1. What is the purpose of the Union cavalry being grouped on the hill? What are these horse soldiers waiting for?
2. Does this seem to be a bona fide battle scene? Or is it a romanticized product of the artist's imagination of what war is like? Have your students justify their viewpoints.
3. Is this work of art appropriate to illustrate this story? As you answer, think about the characters, the feeling, the details in both the art and the story.

Enrichment Your more advanced students could be encouraged to read *The Red Badge of Courage* by Stephen Crane and report to the class the feelings that the main character had about going to battle.

Student Activity 1. Locate three more examples of active voice in "The Drummer Boy of Shiloh." Identify the active verbs and explain how active voice enhances the story.

Student Activity 2. Use active voice in a short paragraph on each of the following topics:

a. a summary of "The Drummer Boy of Shiloh"
b. a character sketch of the general
c. a character sketch of the drummer boy

Closure and Extension

ANSWERS TO THINKING ABOUT THE SELECTION

Recalling

1. The boy just turned fourteen.
2. He is thinking about the battle to be fought tomorrow morning.
3. The general cried thinking of everything ahead.
4. He needs Joby to lead the men into battle with a steady, fast beat of his drum.

Interpreting

5. Answers will differ. Joby might have run away from home because of an argument with his parents or because he didn't like school.
6. Answers will differ. The general might have stopped because he heard Joby crying.
7. Joby is the "heart of the army" because he sets the beat that the army moves by.
8. He means that Joby will be leading the men into battle, as a general would.
9. He felt calmer and stopped crying. The general had instilled a sense of duty and responsibility in the drummer boy.

Applying

10. The drummer boy never lost his fear, he was just able to master it. He was right to feel fear about tomorrow's battle, but after his talk with the general, he was able to face his fear.

ANSWERS TO ANALYZING LITERATURE

1. The five details might be "Owl Creek was full of boys . . ."; "I was the drummer boy at the battle of Owl Creek, or the Tennessee River, or maybe they'll just name it after the church there"; "I was the drummer boy at Shiloh"; ". . . near the Tennessee River . . ."; and ". . . not far from the Owl Creek, very close to the church named Shiloh."
2. The five details might be "In the April night . . ."; "At midnight . . ."; ". . . at sundown tomorrow, not caring where the tide takes them"; ". . . pile of winter leaves and twigs in the darkness . . ."; and ". . . all the rest of the April night in the year 1862."

ANSWERS TO CRITICAL THINKING AND READING

1. Jeep
2. General Custer
3. Douglas MacArthur

Challenge The calm and beauty of the peach orchard offers a sharp contrast to Joby's fears about the next day's battle. What do you think Bradbury was suggesting by creating this contrast?

THINKING AND WRITING

For help with this assignment, students can refer to Lesson 7, "Writing About Setting," in the Handbook of Writing About Literature.

Writing Across the Curriculum Though the general in Bradbury's story is not identified, the historical details provide clues that Bradbury probably had General W. T. Sherman in mind. Have students find a history book that describes the Battle of Shiloh. What similarities support the notion that Bradbury's fictional general was modeled after Sherman? What might disprove the theory? Have

THINKING ABOUT THE SELECTION

Recalling

1. How old is the drummer boy?
2. What is the boy thinking about as he lies in the orchard?
3. Why has the general cried the night before?
4. Why does the general say he needs Joby?

Interpreting

5. Why do you think Joby joined the army?
6. Why do you think the general stops to talk to the boy?
7. In what way is Joby "the heart of the army"?
8. What does the general mean when he says, "Do you know now you're general of the army when the general's left behind?"
9. How do you think the boy felt after his talk with the general?

Applying

10. Mark Twain once said, "Courage is resistance to fear, mastery of fear—not absence of fear." How does this quotation apply to "The Drummer Boy of Shiloh"?

ANALYZING LITERATURE

Recognizing Historical Details

To create a historical setting, an author includes details that help you recognize and visualize the setting of the story accurately. When Bradbury says "in the peach field near the Owl Creek not far from the church at Shiloh," he introduces a setting where a historical event occurred. As the story continues, he includes other details that are historically accurate.

1. List at least five details in the story that place the setting geographically.
2. List at least five details in the story that place the setting in time.

CRITICAL THINKING AND READING

Identifying Appropriate Historical Details

Authors must be careful to include only details that describe a place and time accurately if they want their historical settings to be true.

Name the item in each of the following groups that does not belong in the same historical setting with the others.

1. battlefield at Shiloh; drummer boy; Jeep; general
2. Cape Canaveral; rocket; television crew; General Custer
3. George Washington; Benjamin Franklin; Douglas MacArthur; Patrick Henry

SPEAKING AND LISTENING

Preparing a Program of Civil War Songs

Look in the card catalog of the public or school library to find song books or records with Civil War songs. List the call numbers and other important information for each book and record. Then, locate the song books and records. Working with some of your classmates, arrange and present a program of Civil War music for your class.

THINKING AND WRITING

Writing About a Historical Setting

Suppose you were preparing a time capsule for someone to open one hundred years from now. List and write about the items you would include in it to give people of the future a clear picture of the place and time you live in today. Explain why you would include each item. Make sure your spelling, grammar, and punctuation are correct.

Theme

ROOMS BY THE SEA
Edward Hopper
Yale University Art Gallery

Humanities Note

Fine art, *Rooms by the Sea,* 1951, by Edward Hopper. The American artist Edward Hopper (1882-1967) was born in Nyack, New York. At the age of seventeen he enrolled in the art class of New York artist Robert Henri. He gained technical training from this class but was not influenced by Henri's style. Later, he went to Paris to continue his studies. While there, he kept to himself, avoiding fellow Ameri cans. Such reserved behavior was a lifelong characteristic. Strongly individualistic, Hopper quietly pursued his own style of art and painted the lonely rooms, houses, and urban scenes for which he is best remembered.

In this painting, *Rooms by the Sea,* the sunlight cuts into an open doorway, creating a sharp diagonal shape on the wall and floor. This diagonal of light is repeated in another room glimpsed on the left. The simple, spare colors and clean bareness of the canvas create an almost abstract geometrical effect. The rooms seem still, lonely, and isolated. The sea, right outside of the door, seems an almost surreal presence. To Edward Hopper, this painting was simply a study of sunlight. He felt that any psychological interpretations were left to the viewer.

Master Teacher Note Use the overhead projector to show Fine Art Transparency 20, *The Trapper,* by Rockwell Kent, in the Teaching Portfolio. Ask students what themes the art calls to mind.

your students write a short paper either proving or disproving that Bradbury's general was Sherman. You might inform the history department of this assignment.

Focus

More About the Author Anton Chekhov was the son of an emancipated serf. Although he graduated from medical school, he did not pursue his medical practice because he discovered that he preferred to write. Most of his stories concern the troubles, shortcomings, and tragedies of common people. Ask students to discuss the relationship between Chekhov's background and the kind of people he wrote about. Why was he more interested in common people than in aristocrats? Whom was he more likely to portray sympathetically? Why?

Literary Focus Every story has a theme. There is a relationship between strong theme and good writing. Identify the theme in some other stories that you have read lately. Note if there is a relationship between the clarity of the theme and how much you liked the story.

Look For Chekhov advised writers, "Take two or three persons, describe their mutual relations, and leave it at that." How does "The Ninny" fit that description? Keep this question in mind as you read the story.

Writing/Prior Knowledge Have students discuss what it means to be "an artist of life." This is how Tolstoy described Chekhov. Then have students complete the freewriting assignment.

Vocabulary Most students will have no difficulty with these words. You might have them use each word in a sentence orally before reading the story.

Spelling Tip In order to help students spell *perspiration* correctly, remind them that the first three letters are *per,* not *pre.*

GUIDE FOR READING

The Ninny

Anton Pavlovich Chekhov (1860–1904), a twentieth-century master storyteller and playwright, was born in southern Russia. He studied medicine in Moscow, supporting his family by writing comic stories. After Chekhov published his first book in 1886, he concentrated on writing. He also wrote plays, among them the classics *The Three Sisters* and *The Cherry Orchard.* That Chekhov sought to "paint life in its true aspects, and to show how far this life falls short of the ideal life" can be seen in "The Ninny."

Theme

Theme is the central idea of a story, or the general idea about life that is revealed through a story. Sometimes the theme of a story is stated directly. Sometimes you must draw a conclusion about it—by considering all of the story's elements. In "The Ninny" the theme is stated directly in the conclusion that the employer draws about certain people.

Look For

As you read "The Ninny," look for what it reveals about life. How does Chekhov show that this life "falls short of the ideal life"?

Writing

What makes people stand up for themselves? Freewrite, exploring your thoughts on this question.

Vocabulary

Knowing the meaning of the following words will help you as you read "The Ninny."

perspiration (pur′ spə rā′ shən) *n.*: Sweat (p. 159)

nitwit (nit′ wit′) *n.*: Stupid or silly person (p. 160)

ninny (nin′ ē) *n.*: Fool (p. 160)

Objectives

1 To identify and understand the theme of a short story
2 To make inferences based on a story's dialogue
3 To choose the meaning that fits a word's context
4 To write an extension of the story

Support Material

Teaching Portfolio

Teacher Backup, pp. 243–245
Usage and Mechanics Worksheet, p. 246
Vocabulary Check, p. 247
Critical Thinking and Reading Worksheet, *Making Inferences Based on Dialogue,* p. 248
Language Worksheet, *Finding the Meaning from Context,* p. 249
Selection Test, pp. 250–251

The Ninny

Anton Chekhov

Translated by Robert Payne

Just a few days ago I invited Yulia Vassilyevna, the governess of my children, to
1 come to my study. I wanted to settle my account with her.

"Sit down, Yulia Vassilyevna," I said to her. "Let's get our accounts settled. I'm sure
2 you need some money, but you keep standing on ceremony and never ask for it. Let me see. We agreed to give you thirty rubles[1] a month, didn't we?"

"Forty."

"No, thirty. I made a note of it. I always pay the governess thirty. Now, let me see. You have been with us for two months?"

"Two months and five days."

"Two months exactly. I made a note of it. So you have sixty rubles coming to you. Subtract nine Sundays. You know you don't tutor Kolya on Sundays, you just go out for a walk. And then the three holidays . . ."

Yulia Vassilyevna blushed and picked at
3 the trimmings of her dress, but said not a word.

"Three holidays. So we take off twelve rubles. Kolya was sick for four days—those days you didn't look after him. You looked after Vanya, only Vanya. Then there were the three days you had toothache, when my wife gave you permission to stay away from the children after dinner. Twelve and seven makes nineteen. Subtract. . . . That leaves . . . hm . . . forty-one rubles. Correct?"

Yulia Vassilyevna's left eye reddened and filled with tears. Her chin trembled. She 4
began to cough nervously, blew her nose, and said nothing.

"Then around New Year's Day you broke a cup and saucer. Subtract two rubles. The cup cost more than that—it was an heirloom, but we won't bother about that. We're the ones who pay. Another matter. Due to 5
your carelessness Kolya climbed a tree and tore his coat. Subtract ten. Also, due to your carelessness the chambermaid ran off with Vanya's boots. You ought to have kept your eyes open. You get a good salary. So we dock off five more. . . . On the tenth of January you took ten rubles from me."

"I didn't," Yulia Vassilyevna whispered.

"But I made a note of it."

"Well, yes—perhaps . . ."

"From forty-one we take twenty-seven. That leaves fourteen."

Her eyes filled with tears, and her thin, pretty little nose was shining with perspira- 6
tion. Poor little child!

"I only took money once," she said in a trembling voice. "I took three rubles from your wife . . . never anything more."

1. **rubles** (ro͞o′ b'lz) *n.*: Units of money used in Russia, now the Soviet Union.

Presentation

Motivation/Prior Knowledge Have students imagine that they live in late nineteenth-century Russia. These were the final years of czarist rule, and there was much social unrest. Living conditions among the middle class were very poor, and jobs were scarce. In this context, have students imagine that they are working in a fine home doing a job they enjoy—taking care of young children. If their employer reduced their wages, rationalizing his actions with untruths, would they protest? Would they try to point out his errors and remind him of their original agreement?

Thematic Idea Another selection that deals with the theme of the importance of personal dignity is "Gentleman of Rio en Medio" (page 93).

Purpose-Setting Question Is Yulia Vassilyevna a "ninny"?

1 **Discussion** Who is in control of this situation? How can you tell?

2 **Critical Thinking and Reading** Why would someone have to "ask" for their agreed-upon salary? What does this indicate about the relationship between Yulia Vassilyevna and her employer?

3 **Critical Thinking and Reading** What is Yulia's state of mind?

4 **Discussion** Since Yulia is becoming upset at this injustice why does she say nothing?

5 **Discussion** Are any of these charges legitimate reasons for Yulia's employer to reduce her wages? Why or why not?

6 **Critical Thinking and Reading** What impression do you get of Yulia's employer? Would you want to work for him? What does he think of Yulia?

7 **Discussion** Is this a surprising turn of events? Why has Yulia's employer done this? Does Yulia deserve such treatment? Why or why not?

8 **Critical Thinking and Reading** Do you think Yulia could have received payment in her other jobs if she had spoken up? Why or why not?

9 **Discussion** Yulia's employer does not understand why she didn't protest. Why doesn't he understand? Why is he so insensitive?

10 **Critical Thinking and Reading** Why does Yulia smile bitterly? Why does she offer no explanations? Do you think Yulia is a "ninny"? Explain your answer.

11 **Discussion** Why is it so easy for Yulia's employer to be strong? Why is it not easy for Yulia? What social factors might account for their behavior?

Reader's Response Do you agree with the narrator that it is easy to be strong in this world? Explain.

"Did you now? You see, I never made a note of it. Take three from fourteen. That leaves eleven. Here's your money, my dear. Three, three, three . . . one and one. Take it, my dear."

I gave her the eleven rubles. With trembling fingers she took them and slipped them into her pocket.

"*Merci,*"[2] she whispered.

I jumped up, and began pacing up and down the room. I was in a furious temper.

"Why did you say *'merci'*?" I asked.

7 "For the money."

"Don't you realize I've been cheating you? I steal your money, and all you can say is *'merci'!*"

"In my other places they gave me nothing."

"They gave you nothing! Well, no wonder! I was playing a trick on you—a dirty 8
trick. . . . I'll give you your eighty rubles, they are all here in an envelope made out for you. Is it possible for anyone to be such a nitwit? Why didn't you protest? Why did you keep your mouth shut? Is it possible that
there is anyone in this world who is so 9
spineless? Why are you such a ninny?"

She gave me a bitter little smile. On her
face I read the words: "Yes, it is possible." 10

I apologized for having played this cruel trick on her, and to her great surprise gave her the eighty rubles. And then she said "*merci*" again several times, always timidly, and went out. I gazed after her, thinking
how very easy it is in this world to be strong. 11

---

2. *Merci* (mer sē′): French for "Thank you."

Closure and Extension

ANSWERS TO THINKING ABOUT THE SELECTION

Recalling

1. She should be paid forty rubles a month.
2. One of the children was sick for four days. Yulia had had a toothache. Yulia broke a cup and saucer. One of the children tore his coat and another lost his boots. The employer claimed that Yulia borrowed money.
3. Yulia is visibly upset but remains quiet.
4. Eleven rubles are left.
5. He pays her eighty rubles.

Interpreting

6. She is afraid she'll lose her job.
7. Her subservience annoys him, and he is trying to teach her a lesson. But he is also insensitive to her helplessness and her dependent social status.

Applying

8. Answers will differ. Suggested response: In today's society, a per-

THINKING ABOUT THE SELECTION

Recalling

1. According to the governess, how much should she be paid per month?
2. Name three reasons why the employer subtracts money from the governess's salary.
3. How does the governess behave as the employer goes over their accounts?
4. What amount is left after the accounting?
5. How much money does the employer actually pay the governess?

Interpreting

6. Why does the governess not protest her employer's actions?
7. Why does the employer trick the governess?

Applying

8. How would you help a friend like the governess stand up for himself or herself if, for example, this person were not rewarded as had been promised for doing extra work?

ANALYZING LITERATURE

Understanding Theme

Theme is the general idea or insight about life that is revealed through a story. Theme may be directly stated, or it may be revealed through dialogue and events. In "The Ninny," the theme is stated directly by a character.

1. What is the theme of this story?
2. State the theme in your own words.
3. Do you agree with this theme? Give reasons for your answers.

CRITICAL THINKING AND READING

Making Inferences Based on Dialogue

An **inference** is a conclusion that can be drawn from information you are given. In a story you can make inferences about a character based on what he or she says—or does not say. For example, if a character chatters endlessly, you might infer that this character is nervous or self-centered. If another character observes people quietly and says little; you might infer that this character is serious and thoughtful.

1. In this story, the governess whispers or speaks hesitantly "in a trembling voice"—or says nothing at all. On the basis of this, what do you infer about her character?
2. What can you infer about the employer from his "furious" speech at the end of the story?
3. What do you infer about him from his trick?

UNDERSTANDING LANGUAGE

Finding the Meaning from the Context

One way to figure out the meaning of a word is by looking at its **context**—the words and sentences that surround it. Suppose you did not know the meaning of *nervously*. In the story, the governess's eye reddens, she begins to cry, her chin trembles, and she coughs *nervously*. Clearly she is upset and anxious. You might conclude, from the context, that *nervously* means "uneasily," "restlessly," or "fearfully."

Choose the best definition for the following italicized words, based on context.

1. Mr. Breen stormed and shouted, his face red, his hair flying, his manner *berserk*.
   a. surprised b. hurt c. frenzied
2. Cheryl, smiling and nodding pleasantly, *acquiesced to* any plan, rather than refuse.
   a. rejected b. agreed to c. opposed

THINKING AND WRITING

Writing an Extension of the Story

How do you think the governess will act the next time she is paid by the employer? Freewrite for three minutes about this scene as you imagine it. Then turn your freewriting into a draft of this scene. Include description and dialogue. When you revise your draft, be sure that the characters' actions are shown clearly. Proofread your story and share it with your classmates.

son in Yulia's position could approach her employer as an equal and discuss her situation intelligently. You could advise your friend to approach his or her employer for a frank discussion or to write a letter to the employer outlining problems and solutions. Another advantage that your friend would have over Yulia is that there are government agencies, such as the National Labor Relations Board, that protect employees who are being cheated by their employers.

ANSWERS TO ANALYZING LITERATURE

1. The theme is "how very easy it is in this world to be strong."
2. Answers will differ. Students should respond that, for someone in the employer's position, it is easy to be forceful and assertive. However, for someone in Yulia's position, it is far from easy because of her low social status.
3. Answers will differ. Students should see, however, that the employer's statement is based entirely on his point of view. Students may agree that it is easy for people to be strong if they just believe in themselves and stand up for the truth. Students may disagree that it is easy to be strong if they think that strength depends on a person's position in life. Or they may say that strength means different things to different people, and perhaps Yulia, too, was strong in her own way.

(Answers begin on p. 160.)

ANSWERS TO CRITICAL THINKING AND READING

1. Yulia is fearful and shy.
2. The employer is self-confident, superior, and condescending.
3. Answers will differ. Suggested response: The employer is angry at Yulia's shyness and wants to teach her a lesson. Students may also say that he is insensitive and condescending and that he cannot put himself in Yulia's place to understand why she acts the way she does.

ANSWERS TO UNDERSTANDING LANGUAGE

1. c. frenzied
2. b. agreed

Challenge Analyze Yulia's strength in the story. How is her behavior a form of strength? How is it different from her employer's definition of what it means to be strong?

THINKING AND WRITING

For help with this assignment, students can refer to Lesson 17, "Writing a Short Story," in the Handbook of Writing About Literature.

Publishing Student Writing After students have written their descriptions and dialogue, have the students break into small groups. Have pairs of students read other students' dialogues aloud. This will be the best test of whether the dialogue is realistic and effective. Post the best dialogue in the classroom.

Writing Across the Curriculum You might want to have students research and report on nineteenth-century Russian society. If you do, perhaps inform the social studies department of this assignment. Social studies teachers might provide guidance for students in conducting their research.

Focus

More About the Author Toshio Mori's first collection of stories included twenty-two about the Japanese communities in Oakland and San Leandro, California. The stories received mixed reviews because of their unconventional style of language. One critic noted about Mori, "His is the language of a writer dependent on the dictionary rather than on an extensive knowledge of connotations, and for this very reason often wonderfully fresh and spontaneous." Ask students to comment on this review. What advantages and disadvantages are there in being "dependent on the dictionary"? Why might a writer be unfamiliar with the connotations of the English language? Why might this unfamiliarity result in good, clear writing?

Literary Focus Even in everyday conversation, note key statements in people's speech that alert you to the main point they are making.

Look For Your less advanced students may find key statements difficult to identify. It may be helpful to preview the Analyzing Literature questions on page 167 as guides for reading.

Writing/Prior Knowledge Have students discuss the meaning of this quotation: "Responsibility's like a string we can only see the middle of. Both ends are out of sight." Then have them complete the freewriting assignment.

Vocabulary Most students will have no difficulty with these words. You might have them use each word in a sentence orally before reading the story.

Spelling Tip You might point out that *lagged* is an example of a word whose final consonant is doubled when an inflectional ending beginning with a vowel is added.

GUIDE FOR READING

The Six Rows of Pompons

Toshio Mori (1910–1980) wrote short stories and novels about the Japanese-Americans of northern California. Mori was born in Oakland, California; his parents were Japanese immigrants. Mori's collection of stories, *Yokohama, California,* was published in 1949. The stories—including "The Six Rows of Pompons"—take place in the years before World War II. This story shows the qualities that the author William Saroyan has identified in Mori's writing: "understanding sympathy, generosity and kindliness."

Key Statements

Theme is the central idea of a story, or the general idea about life that is revealed through a story. Sometimes the theme is implied, or suggested. A **key statement** in the story is a sentence that may point to the implied theme or help you see what the theme is. A key statement may be made directly by a character.

Look For

As you read "The Six Rows of Pompons," look for key statements by the characters that suggest the theme of the story.

Writing

In "The Six Rows of Pompons" a young boy learns responsibility. Imagine someone has been given a serious responsibility for the first time. Freewrite about how this person would feel.

Vocabulary

Knowing the following words will help you as you read "The Six Rows of Pompons."

rampage (ram′ pāj) *n.*: An outbreak of violent behavior (p. 163)

enthusiasm (in thōō zē az′m) *n.*: Intense or eager interest (p. 165)

lagged (lagd) *v.*: Fell behind (p. 165)

anxious (aŋk′ shəs) *adj.*: Eagerly wishing (p. 165)

Objectives

1. To understand the relationship between key statements and the implied theme
2. To compare and contrast the attitudes of two characters
3. To understand the meaning of words from context
4. To write an essay about theme

Support Material

Teaching Portfolio

Teacher Backup, pp. 253–255

Usage and Mechanics Worksheet, p. 256

Vocabulary Check, p. 257

Analyzing Literature Worksheet, *Understanding Key Statements,* p. 258

Critical Thinking and Reading Worksheet, *Comparing and Contrasting Attitudes,* p. 259

Selection Test, pp. 260–261

The Six Rows of Pompons

Toshio Mori

When little Nephew Tatsuo[1] came to live with us he liked to do everything the adults were doing on the nursery, and although his little mind did not know it, everything he did was the opposite of adult conduct, unknowingly destructive and disturbing. So Uncle Hiroshi[2] after witnessing several weeks of rampage said, "This has got to stop, this sawing the side of a barn and nailing the doors to see if it would open.
1 But we must not whip him. We must not crush his curiosity by any means."

And when Nephew Tatsuo, who was seven and in high second grade, got used to the place and began coming out into the fields and pestering us with difficult questions as "What are the plants here for? What is water? Why are the bugs made for? What are the birds and why do the birds sing?" and so on, I said to Uncle Hiroshi, "We must do something about this. We cannot answer questions all the time and we cannot be correct all the time and so we will do harm. But something must be done about this beyond a doubt."

"Let us take him in our hands," Uncle Hiroshi said.

So Uncle Hiroshi took little Nephew Tatsuo aside, and brought him out in the fields and showed him the many rows of pompons[3] growing. "Do you know what these are?" Uncle Hiroshi said. "These things here?"

"Yes. Very valuable," Nephew Tatsuo said. "Plants."

"Do you know when these plants grow 2
up and flower, we eat?" Uncle Hiroshi said.

Nephew Tatsuo nodded. "Yes," he said, "I knew that."

"All right. Uncle Hiroshi will give you six rows of pompons," Uncle Hiroshi said. "You own these six rows. You take care of them. Make them grow and flower like your uncle's."

"Gee!" Nephew Tatsuo said.

"Do you want to do it?" Uncle Hiroshi said.

"Sure!" he said.

"Then jump right in and start working," Uncle Hiroshi said. "But first, let me tell you something. You cannot quit once you start. You must not let it die, you must make it grow and flower like your uncles'."

"All right," little Nephew Tatsuo said, "I 3
will."

"Every day you must tend to your plants. Even after the school opens, rain or shine," Uncle Hiroshi said.

"All right," Nephew Tatsuo said. "You'll see!"

1. **Tatsuo** (tät so͞o' ō).
2. **Hiroshi** (hēr ō' shē).
3. **pompons** (päm' pänz') *n.*: Flowers that have small, rounded heads, such as chrysanthemums.

Presentation

Motivation/Prior Knowledge Have students imagine that they have been given the task of watching over a seven-year-old child for a few days. Each day they must think of a productive activity to keep the child occupied. What kinds of activities can they think of? Are there activities that are both enjoyable and constructive?

Master Teacher Note The men in this story run a flower nursery. This is not an unusual occupation for Japanese people, whose tradition of flower arranging dates from the 500's. You may want to bring in some photos of typical Japanese floral arrangements, which contain leaves and stems as decorative elements as well as flowers. A Japanese floral arrangement is made to look as natural as if the flowers were growing outdoors.

Thematic Idea Another selection that deals with the theme of lessons in living is "Thank You, M'am" (page 169).

Purpose-Setting Question What role does responsibility play in this story?

1 **Discussion** How sensitive is Uncle Hiroshi to Nephew Tatsuo? How can you tell that he's good with children?

2 **Discussion** What does Uncle Hiroshi mean when he says that when the plants flower, we eat? What business is the family in?

3 **Discussion** What conditions does Uncle Hiroshi set for giving Tatsuo his own rows of pompons?

4 **Critical Thinking and Reading** Do you think Tatsuo would have noticed the bugs before receiving his own rows to work on? Why does he notice them now?

5 **Discussion** How does Uncle Hiroshi help Tatsuo? Does he do the work for Tatsuo or let Tatsuo do it himself? Why?

So the old folks once more began to work peacefully, undisturbed, and Nephew Tatsuo began to work on his plot. However, every now and then Nephew Tatsuo would run to Uncle Hiroshi with much excitement.

"Uncle Hiroshi, come!" he said. "There's bugs on my plants! Big bugs, green bugs with black dots and some brown bugs. What shall I do?"

"They're bad bugs," Uncle Hiroshi said. "Spray them." 4

"I have no spray," Nephew Tatsuo said excitedly.

"All right. I will spray them for you today," Uncle Hiroshi said. "Tomorrow I will get you a small hand spray. Then you must spray your own plants."

Several tall grasses shot above the pompons and Uncle Hiroshi noticed this. Also, he saw the beds beginning to fill with young weeds.

"Those grasses attract the bugs," he said. "Take them away. Keep the place clean."

It took Nephew Tatsuo days to pick the weeds out of the six beds. And since the weeds were not picked cleanly, several weeks later it looked as if it was not touched at all. Uncle Hiroshi came around sometimes to feel the moisture in the soil. "Tatsuo," he said, "your plants need water. Give it plenty, it is summer. Soon it will be too late." 5

Nephew Tatsuo began watering his plants with the three-quarter hose.

"Don't hold the hose long in one place and short in another," Uncle Hiroshi said. "Keep it even and wash the leaves often."

In October Uncle Hiroshi's plants stood tall and straight and the buds began to appear. Nephew Tatsuo kept at it through summer and autumn, although at times he looked wearied and indifferent. And each time Nephew Tatsuo's enthusiasm lagged Uncle Hiroshi took him over to the six rows of pompons and appeared greatly surprised.

"Gosh," he said, "your plants are coming up! It is growing rapidly; pretty soon the flowers will come."

"Do you think so?" Nephew Tatsuo said.

6 "Sure, can't you see it coming?" Uncle Hiroshi said. "You will have lots of flowers. When you have enough to make a bunch I will sell it for you at the flower market."

"Really?" Nephew Tatsuo said. "In the flower market?"

Uncle Hiroshi laughed. "Sure," he said. "That's where the plant business goes on, isn't it?"

One day Nephew Tatsuo wanted an awful lot to have us play catch with him with a tennis ball. It was at the time when the nursery was the busiest and even Sundays were all work.

"Nephew Tatsuo, don't you realize we are all men with responsibilities?" Uncle Hiroshi said. "Uncle Hiroshi has lots of
7 work to do today. Now is the busiest time. You also have lots of work to do in your beds. And this should be your busiest time. Do you know whether your pompons are dry or wet?"

"No, Uncle Hiroshi," he said. "I don't quite remember."

"Then attend to it. Attend to it," Uncle Hiroshi said.

Nephew Tatsuo ran to the six rows of pompons to see if it was dry or wet. He came running back. "Uncle Hiroshi, it is still wet," he said.

"All right," Uncle Hiroshi said, "but did you see those holes in the ground with the piled-up mounds of earth?"

"Yes. They're gopher holes," Nephew Tatsuo said.

"Right," Uncle Hiroshi said. "Did you catch the gopher?"

"No," said Nephew Tatsuo.

"Then attend to it, attend to it right away," Uncle Hiroshi said.

One day in late October Uncle Hiroshi's pompons began to bloom. He began to cut and bunch and take them early in the morning to the flower market in Oakland.[4] And by this time Nephew Tatsuo was anxious to see his pompons bloom. He was anxious to see how it feels to cut the flowers of his plants. And by this time Nephew Tatsuo's six beds of pompons looked like a patch of tall weeds left uncut through the summer. Very few pompon buds stood out above the tangle.

Few plants survived out of the six rows. In some parts of the beds where the pompons had plenty of water and freedom, the stems grew strong and tall and the buds were big and round. Then there were parts
where the plants looked shriveled and the 8
leaves were wilted and brown. The majority of the plants were dead before the cool weather arrived. Some died by dryness, some by gophers or moles, and some were dwarfed by the great big grasses which covered the pompons altogether.

When Uncle Hiroshi's pompons began to flower everywhere the older folks became worried.

"We must do something with Tatsuo's six beds. It is worthless and his bugs are coming over to our beds," Tatsuo's father
said. "Let's cut it down and burn them 9
today."

"No," said Uncle Hiroshi. "That will be a very bad thing to do. It will kill Nephew Tatsuo. Let the plants stay."

So the six beds of Nephew Tatsuo remained intact, the grasses, the gophers, the bugs, the buds and the plants and all. Soon

4. **Oakland** (ōk′ lənd): A port city in western California, on San Francisco Bay.

6 **Critical Thinking and Reading** What is Uncle Hiroshi's technique for encouraging Tatsuo?

7 **Literary Focus** What is the key statement here? Explain your answer.

8 **Discussion** Why didn't Tatsuo's rows flourish like his uncle's? Was it his fault? What might Tatsuo have learned from this?

9 **Discussion** Why does Tatsuo's father want to burn Tatsuo's flower beds? Why does Uncle Hiroshi disagree?

10 **Critical Thinking and Reading** What is Uncle Hiroshi trying to teach Tatsuo by selling his pompons?

11 **Discussion** How does Tatsuo react when his pompons are sold?

12 **Discussion** Why does Uncle Hiroshi feel that Tatsuo should spend the money he earned?

13 **Discussion** What has Uncle Hiroshi learned about Tatsuo? What kind of person might Tatsuo grow up to be?

14 **Critical Thinking and Reading** What does Uncle Hiroshi mean by this? How does he expect Tatsuo to change?

15 **Critical Thinking and Reading** What is Tatsuo's "unfinished work"? What are the men talking about?

Reader's Response What has helped you to learn responsibility? What do you take pride in the way Tatsuo takes pride in his pompons?

after, the buds began to flower and Nephew Tatsuo began to run around calling Uncle Hiroshi. He said the flowers are coming. Big ones, good ones. He wanted to know when can he cut them.

"Today," Uncle Hiroshi said. "Cut it
10 today and I will sell it for you at the market
tomorrow."

Next day at the flower market Uncle Hiroshi sold the bunch of Nephew Tatsuo's pompons for twenty-five cents. When he came home Nephew Tatsuo ran to the car.

"Did you sell it, Uncle Hiroshi?" Nephew Tatsuo said.

"Sure. Why would it not sell?" Uncle Hiroshi said. "They are healthy, carefully cultured pompons."

Nephew Tatsuo ran around excitedly.
First, he went to his father. "Papa!" he said,
11 "someone bought my pompons!" Then he
ran over to my side and said, "The bunch
was sold! Uncle Hiroshi sold my pompons!"

At noontime, after the lunch was over, Uncle Hiroshi handed over the quarter to Nephew Tatsuo.

"What shall I do with this money?" asked Nephew Tatsuo, addressing all of us, with shining eyes.

"Put it in your toy bank," said Tatsuo's father.

"No," said Uncle Hiroshi. "Let him do what he wants. Let him spend and have a taste of his money."

"Do you want to spend your quarter,
12 Nephew Tatsuo?" I said.

"Yes," he said.

"Then do anything you wish with it," Uncle Hiroshi said. "Buy anything you want. Go and have a good time. It is your money."

On the following Sunday we did not see Nephew Tatsuo all day. When he came back late in the afternoon Uncle Hiroshi said, "Nephew Tatsuo, what did you do today?"

"I went to a show, then I bought an ice cream cone and then on my way home I watched the baseball game at the school, and then I bought a popcorn from the candy man. I have five cents left," Nephew Tatsuo said.

"Good," Uncle Hiroshi said. "That shows a good spirit."

Uncle Hiroshi, Tatsuo's father, and I sat in the shade. It was still hot in the late afternoon that day. We sat and watched Nephew Tatsuo riding around and around the yard on his red tricycle, making a furious dust.

"Next year he will forget what he is doing this year and will become a wild animal and go on a rampage again," the father of Tatsuo said.

"Next year is not yet here," said Uncle Hiroshi.

"Do you think he will be interested to raise pompons again?" the father said.

"He enjoys praise," replied Uncle Hiroshi, "and he takes pride in good work well 13
done. We will see."

"He is beyond a doubt the worst gardener in the country," I said. "Probably he is the worst in the world."

"Probably," said Uncle Hiroshi.

"Tomorrow he will forget how he enjoyed spending his year's income," the father of Tatsuo said.

"Let him forget," Uncle Hiroshi said.
"One year is nothing. We will keep this six 14
rows of pompon business up till he comes to
his senses."

We sat that night the whole family of us, Uncle Hiroshi, Nephew Tatsuo's father, I, Nephew Tatsuo, and the rest, at the table and ate, and talked about the year and the
prospect of the flower business, about Uncle
Hiroshi's pompon crop, and about Nephew
Tatsuo's work and, also, his unfinished 15
work in this world.

Closure and Extension

ANSWERS TO THINKING ABOUT THE SELECTION

Recalling

1. Uncle Hiroshi tells Tatsuo that he must care for his plants every day, rain or shine.

THINKING ABOUT THE SELECTION

Recalling

1. What instructions does Uncle Hiroshi give Tatsuo about growing pompons?
2. What problems does Tatsuo have with his pompons?
3. Why does Tatsuo's father suggest cutting Tatsuo's flowers down and burning them?
4. What does Hiroshi encourage Tatsuo to do with the money he got for his flowers?

Interpreting

5. Why do the older folks dislike Tatsuo's questions? How is Hiroshi different from them?
6. Why does Hiroshi give Tatsuo the pompons?
7. Why does Hiroshi ask Tatsuo, "Don't you realize we are all men with responsibilities"?
8. Compare and contrast Tatsuo at the beginning and the end of the story. Will he remember the lesson next spring? Explain.

Applying

9. How can someone be taught responsibility?

ANALYZING LITERATURE

Understanding Key Statements

Key statements are those that help you understand the theme of a story, especially a story whose theme is implied, or suggested. In "The Six Rows of Pompons," for example, Uncle Hiroshi says, "You cannot quit once you start." This key statement says that staying with a project to the end is part of being responsible. It points to the implied theme that responsibility can be taught lovingly through experience rather than through punishment.

Explain how the following key statements lead you to understand the implied theme.

1. "That will be a very bad thing to do. It will kill Nephew Tatsuo."
2. "One year is nothing. We will keep this six rows of pompons business up till he comes to his senses."

CRITICAL THINKING AND READING

Comparing and Contrasting Attitudes

When you look at similarities, you **compare.** When you look at differences, you **contrast.** Comparing and contrasting characters' attitudes can help you understand the implied theme. Tatsuo's father and Uncle Hiroshi both want to teach Tatsuo responsibility, but their attitudes differ on how to teach it.

Contrast their attitudes on the following, and explain what this suggests about theme.

1. Bugs from Tatsuo's bed start going over to the other beds.
2. Tatsuo earns money for his flowers.

UNDERSTANDING LANGUAGE

Understanding Meaning from Context

Many words have more than one meaning. You can tell from the **context,** or surrounding words and ideas, which meaning is correct.

Using the context in the sentences, choose the correct meaning of the italicized words.

1. "Some died by dryness, some by gophers or *moles* . . ."
   a. a dark-colored spot on the human skin
   b. a small, insect-eating mammal
2. "Let him spend and have a *taste* of his money."
   a. sense stimulated by the taste buds
   b. a slight experience of something

THINKING AND WRITING

Writing an Essay About Theme

Imagine that you are Tatsuo recalling this experience when you are thirteen. First freewrite for three minutes about your pompon-growing experience. Then use these ideas to draft a letter to Uncle Hiroshi describing what the experience taught you about responsibility. Proofread your letter and prepare a final draft.

(Answers begin on p. 166.)

2. Tatsuo's pompons have bugs, weeds, and gophers.
3. Tatsuo's father suggests this because the bugs from Tatsuo's beds are attacking the men's flowers.
4. Hiroshi encourages Tatsuo to spend his money.

Interpreting

5. Tatsuo's questions are bothersome to people who are trying to work, and many of the questions are unanswerable. Tatsuo is a child.
6. Hiroshi gives Tatsuo the pompons to keep him busy in a productive way and to teach him a sense of responsibility.
7. Hiroshi wants Tatsuo to identify with the men and take his responsibilities seriously.
8. At the beginning of the story, Tatsuo doesn't know what it means to work hard. He pesters the adults with childish questions. At the end, he has learned the value of hard work, has taken pride in his work, and has learned a sense of responsibility. However, even at the end, he is still a child at heart, riding his tricycle around in a circle. Answers to the second part of this question will differ. Students will either say that he won't remember because he's too young or that he will remember because the experience had a great impact on him.

Applying

9. Answers will differ. Suggested Responses: Give them a job to do themselves that they can take pride in, trust them with an important task, let them take the consequences of their own actions.

ANSWERS TO ANALYZING LITERATURE

1. This key statement says that the pompons are very important to Tatsuo. It points to the implied theme that once you give someone a job to do, you must respect his hard work.
2. This key statement says that just one year of tending pompons is unimportant, but the lesson should be continued until Tatsuo becomes more mature. It points to the implied theme that having responsibility for something is a maturing experience.

ANSWERS TO CRITICAL THINKING AND READING

1. Tatsuo's father wants to cut down Tatsuo's beds and burn the flowers to get rid of the bugs. Uncle Hiroshi, on the other hand, feels such an action would destroy any sense of responsibility that Tatsuo may have been developing.
2. Tatsuo's father wants him to save the money he has earned. Hiroshi disagrees, feeling it is important that the boy enjoy an immediate reward for his work.

ANSWERS TO UNDERSTANDING LANGUAGE

1. b. a small, insect-eating mammal
2. b. a slight experience of something

Challenge Explain how responsibility can influence a child's character. Describe examples of how a child's energy can be channeled into productive and beneficial outlets. For example, discuss the benefits to a child of owning a pet.

THINKING AND WRITING

For help with this assignment, students can refer to Lesson 11, Writing About Theme, in the Handbook of Writing about Literature.

GUIDE FOR READING

Thank You, M'am

Langston Hughes (1902–1967) was born in Joplin, Missouri. He attended Columbia University for a year and held a number of odd jobs before the publication of his first collection of poetry in 1926. Hughes published many volumes of poetry and fiction, as well as essays, histories, and dramas. He was awarded numerous prizes and grants and is often called the "Poet Laureate of Harlem," which is a section of New York City in northern Manhattan. "Thank You, M'am" is one of Hughes's many stories about city life for blacks.

Key to Theme: Character

The way that a character in a story changes and grows often can be a key to theme. Sometimes a character may grow through being helped by others. In "Thank You, M'am," Mrs. Jones helps Roger by treating him with respect and understanding. By thinking about what Mrs. Jones says to Roger, you can understand the implied theme of the story.

Look For

As you read "Thank You, M'am," look for the reasons the characters may have for behaving as they do. How does understanding the reasons behind their actions help you infer the theme?

Writing

In "Thank You, M'am," Mrs. Luella Bates Washington Jones changes a young boy's life. Freewrite about what makes a person memorable.

Vocabulary

Knowing the following words will help you as you read "Thank You, M'am."

willow-wild (wil' ō wild') *adj.*: Slender and pliant, like a reed blowing in the wind (p. 169)

kitchenette-furnished (kich ə net' fur' nisht) *n.*: Having a small, compact kitchen (p. 171)

presentable (pri zen' tə b'l) *adj.*: Suitable to be seen by others (p. 171)

Focus

More About the Author When Langston Hughes began to be published, he was criticized for his extensive use of black colloquialisms. Hughes responded that although his characters were not people "whose shoes were always shined," they were good people, too. Now that his works have been translated into German, French, Spanish, Russian, Yiddish, and Czech, do you think the criticism was valid? Ask students to discuss how people of such diverse backgrounds can appreciate black American colloquial dialogue. Why does it speak to all people?

Literary Focus Character and theme are often inextricably bound. The way the characters act and react exemplify the theme of a story. Suggest that students ask themselves, "What is this story about?" and the characters will tell them.

Look For Ask the class to consider the implications of three sentences when they have finished the story: "There's nobody home at my house"; "I have done things, too, which I would not tell you, son—neither tell God, if He didn't already know"; "When I get through with you, sir, you are going to remember Mrs. Luella Bates Washington Jones."

Writing The theme of one person changing another person's life for the better is a popular one. Have students think of songs, movies, or television programs in which one person changes another's life. Then have them complete the freewriting assignment.

Vocabulary Most students will have no difficulty with these words. You might have them use each word in a sentence orally before reading the story.

Objectives

1. To understand an implied theme through a story's characters
2. To identify generalizations about the characters
3. To give a dramatic reading of a selection
4. To write a letter from the point of view of a story's character

Support Material

Teaching Portfolio

Teacher Backup, pp. 263–265
Grammar in Action Worksheet, *Understanding Compound Predicates,* pp. 266–267
Usage and Mechanics Worksheet, p. 268
Vocabulary Check, p. 269
Critical Thinking and Reading Worksheet, *Identifying Generalizations,* p. 270
Language Worksheet, *Understanding Compound Words,* p. 271
Selection Test, pp. 262–273

Thank You, M'am

Langston Hughes

She was a large woman with a large purse that had everything in it but hammer and nails. It had a long strap and she carried it slung across her shoulder. It was about eleven o'clock at night, and she was walking alone, when a boy ran up behind her and tried to snatch her purse. The strap broke with the single tug the boy gave it from behind. But the boy's weight, and the weight of the purse combined caused him to lose his balance so, instead of taking off full
1 blast as he had hoped, the boy fell on his back on the sidewalk, and his legs flew up. The large woman simply turned around and kicked him right square in his blue-jeaned sitter. Then she reached down, picked the boy up by his shirt front, and shook him until his teeth rattled.

After that the woman said, "Pick up my pocketbook, boy, and give it here."

She still held him. But she bent down enough to permit him to stoop and pick up her purse. Then she said, "Now ain't you
2 ashamed of yourself?"

Firmly gripped by his shirt front, the boy said, "Yes'm."

The woman said, "What did you want to do it for?"

The boy said, "I didn't aim to."

She said, "You a lie!"

By that time two or three people passed, stopped, turned to look, and some stood watching.

"If I turn you loose, will you run?" asked the woman.

"Yes'm," said the boy.

"Then I won't turn you loose," said the woman. She did not release him.

"I'm very sorry, lady, I'm sorry," whispered the boy.

"Um-hum! And your face is dirty. I got a great mind to wash your face for you. Ain't you got nobody home to tell you to wash your face?"

"No'm," said the boy.

"Then it will get washed this evening," said the large woman starting up the street, dragging the frightened boy behind her.

He looked as if he were fourteen or fifteen, frail and willow-wild, in tennis shoes and blue jeans.

The woman said, "You ought to be my son. I would teach you right from wrong.
Least I can do right now is to wash your face. 3
Are you hungry?"

"No'm," said the being-dragged boy. "I just want you to turn me loose."

"Was I bothering *you* when I turned that corner?" asked the woman.

"No'm."

Presentation

Motivation/Prior Knowledge Have students imagine that they have been surprised by someone's act of kindness and concern for them. Perhaps it came at a particularly significant point in their lives and made a profound difference in the way they view the world. Would they always remember this person? Would they try to perform an act of kindness toward someone else? Have students explore how a brief encounter with someone can change a life.

Master Teacher Note Point out to students that purse snatching is a major urban crime problem. Hughes set many of his stories in Harlem which, because of its socio-economic problems, is plagued with various types of street crime. Harlem was once the black jazz capital of the world, however, and many people are striving to restore Harlem's dignity through urban renewal programs. Bring in photographs of Harlem jazz clubs of the '20's and contrast them with photographs of Harlem tenements and urban renewal projects today.

Thematic Idea Another selection that deals with the theme of lessons in living is "Six Rows of Pompons" (page 163).

Purpose-Setting Question What role does compassion play in this story?

1 **Discussion** How experienced at purse snatching do you think this boy is? How can you tell?

2 **Literary Focus** How does Hughes use colloquial language to provide information on the characters and setting of the story?

3 **Critical Thinking and Reading** Does the woman regard the boy as a criminal? How does she treat him? Why is she getting involved with him?

Humanities Note

Fine Art, *Mother Courage,* Charles White. The African-American painter, graphic artist, and educator Charles White was born in poverty in Chicago, Illinois. From age seven, he drew and painted constantly. Through the support of his mother and the numerous awards his talent earned him, White received his education at the Chicago Art Institute, the Art Students League of New York, and the Taeler de la Grafica in Mexico. His powerful, articulate style extols the dignity, history, and strength of African-American people.

Mother Courage, a linoleum cut print, was done in 1968 as a magazine illustration. The graceful solidity of this solitary figure illustrates Charles White's skill as a draughtsman. He brings us face to face with his subject, a strong black woman, aptly named "Mother Courage." White's works are exhibited in major collections nationwide.

You might want to ask students the following questions about the art:

1. Why do you think White entitled this piece Mother Courage?
2. What are other possible titles for this piece?

4 **Critical Thinking and Reading** What do you think Mrs. Jones is going to do to the boy? How do you think the boy is feeling?

MOTHER COURAGE, 1974
Charles White
National Academy of Design

"But you put yourself in contact with *me,*" said the woman. "If you think that that
4 contact is not going to last awhile, you got another thought coming. When I get through with you, sir, you are going to remember Mrs. Luella Bates Washington Jones."

Sweat popped out on the boy's face and he began to struggle. Mrs. Jones stopped, jerked him around in front of her, put a half

Grammar In Action

A good way to combine sentences when writing is to use **compound predicate.** A compound predicate is two or more verbs that have the same subject and are joined by a conjunction such as *and, but,* and *or.* Writers who wish to vary their sentence structure and combine related phrases use compound verbs. The result is a sequence of actions performed by one subject in one sentence.

Using compound predicates allows a writer to illustrate a series of actions more effectively. One simple sentence after another can interrupt the flow of actions, whereas compound predicates capture the actions to give the reader a sense of timing. Notice how Langston Hughes uses compound predicates in the following two sentences.

> Mrs. Jones stopped, jerked him around in front of her, put a half nelson about his neck, and continued to drag him up the street. When she got to her door, she dragged the boy inside, down a hall, and into a large kitchenette-furnished room at the rear of the house.

Consider how drawn out the first series of events would read if Hughes had separated each action:

nelson[1] about his neck, and continued to drag him up the street. When she got to her door, she dragged the boy inside, down a hall, and into a large kitchenette-furnished room at the rear of the house. She switched on the light and left the door open. The boy could hear other roomers laughing and talking in the large house. Some of their doors were open, too, so he knew he and the woman were not alone. The woman still had him by the neck in the middle of her room.

She said, "What is your name?"

"Roger," answered the boy.

"Then, Roger, you go to that sink and wash your face," said the woman, whereup-
5 on she turned him loose—at last. Roger looked at the door—looked at the woman —looked at the door—*and went to the sink.*

"Let the water run until it gets warm," she said. "Here's a clean towel."

"You gonna take me to jail?" asked the boy, bending over the sink.

"Not with that face, I would not take you nowhere," said the woman. "Here I am trying to get home to cook me a bite to eat and you snatch my pocketbook! Maybe you ain't been to your supper either, late as it be. Have you?"

6 "There's nobody home at my house," said the boy.

"Then we'll eat," said the woman. "I believe you're hungry—or been hungry —to try to snatch my pocketbook."

"I wanted a pair of blue suede shoes," said the boy.

"Well, you didn't have to snatch *my*
7 pocketbook to get some suede shoes," said Mrs. Luella Bates Washington Jones. "You could of asked me."

"M'am?"

The water dripping from his face, the boy looked at her. There was a long pause. A very long pause. After he had dried his face and not knowing what else to do dried it again, the boy turned around, wondering what next. The door was open. He could make a dash for it down the hall. He could run, run, run, run, *run!*

The woman was sitting on the day bed. After awhile she said, "I were young once and I wanted things I could not get."

There was another long pause. The boy's mouth opened. Then he frowned, but not knowing he frowned.

The woman said, "Um-hum! You thought I was going to say *but,* didn't you? You thought I was going to say, *but I didn't snatch people's pocketbooks.* Well, I wasn't 8
going to say that." Pause. Silence. "I have done things, too, which I would not tell you, son—neither tell God, if He didn't already know. So you set down while I fix us something to eat. You might run that comb through your hair so you will look presentable."

In another corner of the room behind a screen was a gas plate and an icebox. Mrs. Jones got up and went behind the screen. The woman did not watch the boy to see if he was going to run now, nor did she watch her purse which she left behind her on the day bed. But the boy took care to sit on the far side of the room where he thought she could easily see him out of the corner of her eye, if she wanted to. He did not trust the woman *not* to trust him. And he did not want to be mistrusted now.

"Do you need somebody to go to the store," asked the boy, "maybe to get some 9
milk or something?"

"Don't believe I do," said the woman, "unless you just want sweet milk yourself. I was going to make cocoa out of this canned milk I got here."

---

1. **half nelson:** A wrestling hold using one arm.

5 **Discussion** Why does Roger cooperate when he could run?

6 **Discussion** What does this suggest about Roger's home life?

7 **Critical Thinking and Reading** What kind of person is Mrs. Jones?

8 **Discussion** Do you think Mrs. Jones's past makes her more sympathetic to Roger? Why or why not?

9 **Critical Thinking and Reading** Why does Roger make this offer? Do you think it's genuine?

> After Mrs. Jones stopped, she jerked him around in front of her. Then she put a half nelson about his neck. Next, she continued to drag him up the street.

Although each sentence in the paragraph above is grammatically correct, the paragraph does not read as smoothly as Hughes' version nor is it as interesting.

Study another sentence in which Hughes uses a compound predicate.

> Roger looked at the door—looked at the woman—looked at the door—and went to the sink.

In the sentence above Hughes uses dashes rather than commas to set the actions apart from each other while combining them.

Student Activity 1. Write a series of simple sentences which illustrate a series of actions. Exchange papers with classmates and rewrite the sentences using compound predicates.

Student Activity 2. Using sentences with compound predicates, describe an exciting event you have witnessed or seen on television or at the movies.

10 **Literary Focus** Discuss Mrs. Jones's character. What qualities does she have? Why does she show Roger kindness instead of calling the police? What can you infer about her past from the way she treats Roger?

11 **Discussion** What effect do you think this gift has on Roger? Do you think he has learned a lesson from Mrs. Jones?

12 **Critical Thinking and Reading** What else do you think Roger wanted to say to Mrs. Jones? Are you surprised that Roger never saw her again? Do you think Roger will ever forget her?

Humanities Note

Fine Arts *The Sunny Side of the Street,* Philip Evergood. The American artist, Philip Evergood (1901–1973), was a social-realist painter. He obtained his education at many fine art schools in Europe, England, and New York City. His striking, bright canvasses are powerful comments on American life and social tragedy.

The Sunny Side of the Street was painted in 1950. The crowded exuberance of this street scene is typical of Evergood and exemplifies his devotion to painting his personal response to life experience. His technique of laying one flat color field next to another is an expressive device used to evoke an emotional response in the viewer. The odd perspective and proportion of the painting were used for the same result.

The paintings of Philip Evergood are lively and rich with the symbols of American life. The poor and underprivileged people of America were his favorite subject.

You might want to ask the following questions about the art:

1. What associations do you make with this scene?
2. What is your emotional response to this scene?

SUNNY SIDE OF THE STREET
Philip Evergood

"That will be fine," said the boy.

10 She heated some lima beans and ham she had in the icebox, made the cocoa, and set the table. The woman did not ask the boy anything about where he lived, or his folks, or anything else that would embarrass him. Instead, as they ate, she told him about her job in a hotel beauty shop that stayed open late, what the work was like, and how all kinds of women came in and out, blondes, redheads, and brunettes. Then she cut him a half of her ten-cent cake.

"Eat some more, son," she said.

11 When they were finished eating she got up and said, "Now, here, take this ten dollars and buy yourself some blue suede shoes. And next time, do not make the mistake of latching onto *my* pocketbook *nor nobody else's*—because shoes come by devilish like that will burn your feet. I got to get my rest now. But I wish you would behave yourself, son, from here on in."

She led him down the hall to the front door and opened it. "Goodnight! Behave yourself, boy!" she said, looking out into the street.

The boy wanted to say something else other than, "Thank you, m'am," to Mrs. Luella Bates Washington Jones, but he couldn't do so as he turned at the barren 1 stoop and looked back at the large woman in the door. He barely managed to say, "Thank you," before she shut the door. And he never saw her again.

Reader's Response Mrs. Jones trusts Roger even though he has proven himself untrustworthy. In other words, she gives him a chance to prove that he can be trusted. Describe a situation in which you were given a chance to prove yourself when the odds were against you.

THINKING ABOUT THE SELECTION

Recalling

1. What does Mrs. Jones do when Roger tries to steal her purse?
2. What does she say she would teach Roger if he were her son?
3. What reason does Roger give for trying to steal her purse? How does Mrs. Jones respond to this reason?
4. Why does Mrs. Jones give Roger ten dollars?

Interpreting

5. Why doesn't Roger run away from Mrs. Jones's apartment at the first opportunity?
6. What does the following tell about Roger: "He did not trust the woman *not* to trust him. And he did not want to be mistrusted now."
7. Early in the story, Mrs. Jones says, "When I get through with you, sir, you are going to remember Mrs. Luella Bates Washington Jones." How do her words turn out to be true?
8. At the end of the story, why does Roger want to say more than just "Thank you, m'am"?

Applying

9. Can you change people's behavior through kindness and understanding? Explain.

ANALYZING LITERATURE

Using Character to Understand Theme

The way that a character changes is often a clue to the theme of a story. In this story, Mrs. Jones's treatment of Roger brings about a change in him that points to the theme.

1. How does Mrs. Jones show that she respects Roger? In what ways does she treat him with understanding and kindness?
2. Explain how you think Mrs. Jones's treatment makes Roger feel about himself.
3. How does Roger change?
4. What do you think is the theme of this story?

CRITICAL THINKING AND READING

Identifying Generalizations

A **generalization** is a conclusion you draw from similarities among a large number of cases. A **hasty generalization** is a conclusion that is based on too few cases. For example, if the pizza is good the first time you eat at a new pizza parlor, you might conclude that the pizza there is *always* good. This would be a hasty generalization, because the number of cases is too small.

1. What generalization had Roger made about older women walking alone at night?
2. What did Roger learn about applying this generalization to this particular case?

SPEAKING AND LISTENING

Presenting Readers' Theater

In Readers' Theater, two or more speakers give a dramatic reading of a literature selection. The words and the way they are spoken are more important than the gestures used.

With classmates, prepare and present a Readers' Theater version of "Thank You, M'am." Decide how the characters will speak or present themselves. Then write a script and practice reading, putting emphasis on oral interpretation of the characters and their actions. Finally, present your Readers' Theater to your classmates.

THINKING AND WRITING

Writing About a Character

Imagine that you are Roger twenty years after the story. You decide to write a letter to Mrs. Jones describing why the event in the story was so important to you. In your letter, include a statement about how the event helped shape your future decisions and actions. Revise your letter, making sure that your reasoning is clear. Proofread your letter and prepare a final draft.

Closure and Extension

ANSWERS TO THINKING ABOUT THE SELECTION

Recalling

1. Mrs. Jones kicks him and then picks him up and drags him to her house.
2. She says she would teach him right from wrong.
3. Roger tried to steal her purse to buy blue suede shoes. Mrs. Jones responds that Roger could simply have asked her for the money.
4. Mrs. Jones gives Roger the money so he won't steal anymore and because she says that shoes bought with stolen money would "burn" his feet.

Interpreting

5. Answers will differ. Suggested Response: Roger is curious and has nowhere to go anyway.
6. Answers will differ. Suggested Response: He knew the woman had reason to mistrust him, but he wanted her to trust him now that she was being so kind to him.
7. Answers will differ. Suggested Response: Mrs. Jones's words are even truer than she expected because she makes Roger's dream come true.
8. Answers will differ. Suggested Response: Roger wants to say more because he is moved and grateful for her kindness and generosity.

Applying

9. Answers will differ. Suggested Response: Kindness and understanding can change a person's behavior, especially if the person is unaccustomed to being treated well. Being treated with dignity can give a person a feeling of self-worth so that he or she wants to improve.

ANSWERS TO ANALYZING LITERATURE

1. Mrs. Jones shares her dinner with Roger, doesn't ask him any personal questions that might embarrass him, and gives him ten dollars for the shoes he wants.
2. Answers will differ. Suggested Response: Roger probably felt ashamed of himself for trying to steal Mrs. Jones's purse. He probably also felt that he was a human being deserving of kindness and respect.
3. Answers will differ. Suggested Response: Roger relaxes, becomes more trusting, and grateful for human kindness.
4. Answers will differ. Students should see that experiencing a little kindness and generosity of spirit can make a big difference in someone's life.

ANSWERS TO CRITICAL THINKING AND READING

1. Roger probably thought that all older women walking alone at night were vulnerable and helpless.
2. Roger learned that some older people are strong and fearless despite the fact that they're old.

Challenge Discuss how the story makes a universal statement about people through only two characters. Describe both Mrs. Jones's background and Roger's home life, as they are suggested in the story. How do these characters represent larger segments of society?

THINKING AND WRITING

For help with this assignment, students can refer to Lesson 9, "Writing About Character," in the Handbook of Writing About Literature.

Focus

More About the Author Joan Aiken is the daughter of American poet Conrad Aiken. Her work includes long and short fiction, poems, plays, children's books, and horror stories. But she is so well known as a children's writer that when her collection of adult horror stories was published, it was reviewed in the children's book review section of some major newspapers. Ask students to discuss how this mistake could have occurred. Why do horror stories appeal to both children and adults? What do children's and adult's horror stories have in common?

Literary Focus After students have read the story, have them identify the significant actions. In literature as in life, the significant actions are often not obvious as they are happening. They can only be recognized later, when the "big picture" has been revealed.

Look For Your less advanced students may find significant action a difficult concept to grasp. It may be helpful to preview the Analyzing Literature questions on page 183 so that these questions can guide their reading.

Writing/Prior Knowledge Have students discuss the meaning of this quotation. "The manner of giving is worth more than the gift." Then have them complete the freewriting assignment.

Vocabulary These words also may give students some difficulty: *patchwork* (p. 175); *brow-medal, carbine* (p. 176); *ceremonial* (p. 177); *brooch, blotched* (p. 178); *luminous, translucent* (p. 179); *bales,* (p. 181); *precipitately, dejected,* and *scandalized* (p. 182).

Spelling Tip Point out that *crevasse* is not a homophone for *crevice.* Knowing the differences in pronunciation and meaning may help students with spelling.

GUIDE FOR READING

The Gift-Giving

Joan Aiken (1924–   ), born in the English village of Rye, Sussex, is known for her tales of fantasy and suspense. As a child, she often made up stories to amuse herself and her brother on long walks. But she reached a much larger audience at age seventeen, when her fantasy story "But Today Is Tuesday" was read on a children's radio program. Joan Aiken believes stories should never pretend that life is not tough, but virtue should triumph in the end.

Significant Actions

A **significant action** is one that stands out from the other actions and events in a story as being particularly important. A significant action may not be extraordinary in itself, but it can point to the story's theme, or central idea. Recognizing significant actions can lead you to the theme of the story.

Look For

As you read "The Gift-Giving," look for actions that seem important. What do they suggest about the story's theme?

Writing

Think about what you would choose as a gift for a friend. Freewrite for five minutes about this meaningful gift.

Vocabulary

Knowing the following words will help you as you read "The Gift-Giving."

hummock (hum′ ək) *n.*: A mound or small hill (p. 176)
ingots (iŋ′ gətz) *n.*: Metal cast into bars for storage or transportation (p. 177)
crevasse (kri vas′) *n.*: A deep, narrow opening from a split or a crack, as in a cliff (p. 178)
gentians (jen′ chənz) *n.*: Herbs with blue flowers (p. 178)
expound (ik spound′) *v.*: To explain in careful detail (p. 178)
wizened (wiz′ ənd) *adj.*: Shrunken, and wrinkled with age (p. 179)
keystone (kē′ stōn) *n.*: A wedge-shaped piece at the top of an arch that locks into place other pieces (p. 180)
muslin (muz′ lin) *n.*: Plain-woven, cotton fabric (p. 182)

Objectives

1. To understand the relationship between significant actions and the implied theme of a short story
2. To summarize a short story
3. To write an essay comparing and contrasting the themes of two short stories

Support Material

Teaching Portfolio

Teacher Backup, pp. 275–278
Grammar in Action Worksheets, *Understanding Verb Tense,* pp. 279–280, *Varying Sentence Structure,* pp. 281–282, *Using Semcolons,* pp. 283–284
Usage and Mechanics Worksheet, p. 285
Vocabulary Check, p. 286
Critical Thinking and Reading Worksheet, *Summarizing,* p. 287
Language Worksheet, *Understanding Homonyms,* p. 288
Selection Test, pp. 289–290
Art Transparency 6, *The Banjo Lesson*

The Gift-Giving

Joan Aiken

1 The weeks leading up to Christmas were always full of excitement, and tremendous anxiety too, as the family waited in suspense for the Uncles, who had set off in the spring of the year, to return from their summer's traveling and trading: Uncle Emer, Uncle Acraud, Uncle Gonfil, and Uncle Mark. They always started off together, down the steep mountainside, but then, at the bottom, they took different routes along the deep narrow valley, Uncle Mark and Uncle Acraud riding eastward, toward the great plains, while Uncle Emer and Uncle Gonfil turned west, toward the towns and rivers and the western sea.

Then, before they were clear of the mountains, they would separate once more, Uncle Acraud turning south, Uncle Emer taking his course northward, so that, the children occasionally thought, their family was scattered over the whole world, netted out like a spider's web.

Spring and summer would go by in the usual occupations, digging and sowing the steep hillside garden beds, fishing, hunting for hares, picking wild strawberries, making hay. Then, toward St. Drimma's Day,[1] when the winds began to blow and the snow crept down, lower and lower, from the high peaks, Grandmother would begin to grow restless.

Silent and calm all summer long she sat in her rocking chair on the wide wooden porch, wrapped in a patchwork comforter, with her blind eyes turned eastward toward the lands where Mark, her dearest and firstborn, had gone. But when the winds of Michaelmas[2] began to blow, and the wolves grew bolder, and the children dragged in sacks of logs day after day, and the cattle were brought down to the stable under the house, then Grandmother grew agitated indeed. 2

When Sammle, the eldest granddaughter, brought her hot milk, she would grip the girl's slender brown wrist and demand: "Tell me, child, how many days now to St. Froida's Day?" (which was the first of December).

"Eighteen, Grandmother," Sammle would answer, stooping to kiss the wrinkled cheek.

"So many, still? So many till we may hope to see them?"

"Don't worry, Granny, the Uncles are *certain* to return safely. Perhaps they will be early this year. Perhaps we may see them before the feast of St. Melin" (which was December the fourteenth).

And then, sure enough, sometime during the middle weeks of December, their 3

1. St. Drimma's Day: Throughout this story, Aiken interweaves imaginary and real holidays.

2. Michaelmas: The old English name for the feast day of Saint Michael and All Angels, September 29.

Presentation

Motivation/Prior Knowledge Have students imagine that one of their family traditions has been disrupted by the loss of a family member. How might a new tradition both rejuvenate the family and commemorate the missing family member?

Master Teacher Note In some families, the love of a musical instrument is passed down from generation to generation. Show Art Transparency 6, *The Banjo Lesson* by Henry Ossawa Tanner in the Teaching Portfolio. What feeling seems to be part of the lesson? What do the two people in the painting show? What role does music play in the painting? In "The Gift-Giving" on page 225, pipe playing during gift giving is a special tradition.

Purpose-Setting Question What role does ceremony play in this story?

Thematic Idea Other selections that deal with the theme of fantasy are "The Rule of Names" (page 69) and "Rain, Rain, Go Away" (page 13).

1 **Enrichment** The custom of gift giving at Christmas time probably began in ancient Rome and northern Europe. By 1100, Saint Nicholas had become a popular symbol of gift giving in many European countries. Today, Saint Nicholas still brings presents in some countries, including Austria, Belgium, and Germany. Santa Claus brings gifts in the United States, Canada, and Australia. Other countries have their own traditions and versions of Santa Claus.

2 **Discussion** Why did Grandmother become agitated at the end of September?

3 **Critical Thinking and Reading** Who do the Uncles remind you of as they come home laden with gifts in the middle of December?

4 Discussion Why is the whole village in a festive mood? How important are the Uncles?

great carts would come jingling and trampling along the winding valleys. Young Mark (son of Uncle Emer), from his watchpoint up a tall pine over a high cliff, would catch the flash of a baggage-mule's brass browmedal, or the sun glancing on the barrel of a carbine, and would come joyfully dashing back to report. "Granny! Granny! The Uncles are almost here!"

Then the whole household, the whole village, would be filled with as much turmoil as that of a kingdom of ants when the spade breaks open their hummock. Wives would build the fires higher, and fetch out the best linen, wine, dried meat, pickled eggs; set dough to rising, mix cakes of honey and

Grammar in Action

One use of the **comma** is to separate items in a series. Sentences containing series of words, phrases, or clauses must be punctuated with commas. Commas signal the reader to pause slightly, echoing the way people pause as they speak. Without commas, items in a series would run together and confuse the reader.

There are two cases in which commas are not necessary to separate items in a series. One case is when each item is joined to the next by a conjunction. For example: "We were met at the bottom by the children and the servants and half the village." Another exception concerns words that are considered to be one item. Paired words such as *cup and saucer, salt and pepper,* and *macaroni and cheese* do not have commas between the items in the pair.

Several sentences in "The Gift–Giving" contain series of words, phrases, and clauses. In the following sentence, commas separate a series of words as well as a series of verb phrases:

> "Wives would build the fires higher, and fetch out the best *linen, wine, dried meat, pickled eggs; set dough to rising, mix cakes of honey and oats, bring up stone jars of preserved strawberries from the cellars . . .*"

oats, bring up stone jars of preserved strawberries from the cellars; and the children, with the servants and half the village, would go racing down the perilous zigzag track to meet the cavalcade at the bottom.

The track was far too steep for the heavy carts, which would be dismissed and the carters paid off to go about their business. Then with laughter and shouting, amid a million questions from the children, the loads would be divided and carried up the mountainside on muleback, or on human shoulders. Sometimes the Uncles came home at night, through falling snow, by the
5 smoky light of torches; but the children and the household always knew of their arrival beforehand, and were always there to meet them.

"Did you bring Granny's Chinese shawl, Uncle Mark? Uncle Emer, have
6 you the enameled box for her snuff that Aunt Grippa begged you to get? Uncle Acraud, did you find the glass candlesticks? Uncle Gonfil, did you bring the books?"

"Yes, yes, keep calm, don't deafen us! Poor tired travelers that we are, leave us in peace to climb this devilish hill! Everything is there, set your minds at rest—the shawl, the box, the books—besides a few other odds and ends, pins and needles and fruit and a bottle or two of wine, and a few trifles for the village. Now, just give us a few minutes to get our breath, will you, kindly—" as the children danced round them, helping each other with the smaller bundles, never ceasing to pour out questions: "Did you see the Grand Cham? The Akond of Swat? The Fon of Bikom?
The Seljuk of Rum? Did you go to Cathay? 7
To Muskovy? To Dalai?[3] Did you travel by ship, by camel, by llama, by elephant?"

And, at the top of the hill, Grandmother would be waiting for them, out on her roofed porch, no matter how wild the weather or how late the time, seated in majesty with her furs and patchwork quilt around her, while the Aunts ran to and fro with hot stones to place under her feet. And the Uncles always embraced her first, very fondly and respectfully, before turning to hug their wives and sisters-in-law.

Then the goods they had brought would be distributed through the village—the scissors, tools, medicines, plants, bales of cloth, ingots of metal, cordials, firearms, and musical instruments; after that there would be a great feast.

Not until Christmas morning did Grandmother and the children receive the special gifts that had been brought for them by the Uncles; and this giving always took the same ceremonial form.

Uncle Mark stood behind Grandmother's chair, playing on a small pipe that he
had acquired somewhere during his travels; 8
it was made from hard black polished wood, with silver stops, and it had a mouthpiece made of amber. Uncle Mark invariably[4] played the same tune on it at these times, very softly. It was a tune that he had heard for the first time, he said, when he was

---

3. Grand Cham . . . Dalai: Throughout this story, Aiken interweaves imaginary and real place names.
4. invariably (in ver′ ē ə blē) *adv.*: Without change.

5 **Critical Thinking and Reading** Do you detect a magical quality about the Uncles and their travels? How does Aiken use language to evoke this magical atmosphere?

6 **Discussion** The Uncles return bearing gifts for the whole family and even for the village. What legendary character do they remind you of?

7 **Discussion** Why does Aiken use both imaginary and real place names? Why do the children ask such exotic questions?

8 **Critical Thinking and Reading** Why were the gifts not given to the family until Christmas morning? How important is tradition in this family?

Student Activity 1. Identity two more examples of items in a series that are separated by commas from pages 176–177. Explain why the commas are necessary. What would be confusing to the reader if there were no commas?

Student Activity 2. Describe a habitual or ritual activity that is a part of your life. Include sentences that contain series of items correctly punctuated with commas.

9 **Discussion** Can this phenomenon be explained in any rational or medical terms? Why is Christmas a magical time for this family? Why is Christmas a magical time for many families?

10 **Discussion** Why was Grandmother so happy in the months following Christmas?

much younger, once when he had narrowly escaped falling into a crevasse on the hillside, and a voice had spoken to him, as it seemed, out of the mountain itself, bidding him watch where he set his feet and have a care, for the family depended on him. It was a gentle, thoughtful tune, which reminded Sandri, the middle granddaughter, of springtime sounds, warm wind, water from melted snow dripping off the gabled roofs, birds trying out their mating calls.

While Uncle Mark played on his pipe, Uncle Emer would hand each gift to Grandmother. And she—here was the strange thing—she, who was stone-blind all the year long, could not see her own hand in front of her face, she would take the object in her fingers and instantly identify it. "A mother-of-pearl comb, with silver studs, for Tassy . . . it comes from Babylon. A silk shawl, blue and rose, from Hind, for Argilla. A wooden game, with ivory pegs, for young Emer, from Damascus. A gold brooch, from
9 Hangku, for Grippa. A book of rhymes, from Paris, for Sammle, bound in a scarlet leather cover."

By stroking each gift with her old, blotched, clawlike fingers, frail as quills, Grandmother, who lived all the year round in darkness, could discover not only what the thing was and where it came from, but also the color of it, and that in the most precise and particular manner, correct to a shade. "It is a jacket of stitched and pleated cotton, printed over with leaves and flowers; it comes from the island of Haranati, in the eastern ocean; the colors are leaf-brown and gold and a dark, dark blue, darker than mountain gentians—" for Grandmother had not always been blind; when she was a young girl she had been able to see as well as anybody else.

"And this is for you, Mother, from your son Mark," Uncle Emer would say, handing her a tissue-wrapped bundle, and she would exclaim, "Ah, how beautiful! A coat of tribute silk, of the very palest green, so that the color shows only in the folds, like shadows on snow; the buttons and the button-toggles are of worked silk, lavender-gray, like pearl, and the stiff collar is embroidered with white roses."

"Put it on, Mother!" her sons and daughters-in-law would urge her, and the children, dancing 'round her chair, clutching their own treasures, would chorus, "Yes, put it on, put it on! Ah, you look like a queen, Granny, in that beautiful coat! The highest queen in the world! The queen of the mountain!"

Those months after Christmas were Grandmother's happiest time. Secure, 10
thankful, with her sons safe at home, she would sit in the warm fireside corner of the big wooden family room. The wind might shriek, the snow gather higher and higher out of doors, but that did not concern her, for her family, and all the village, were well supplied with flour, oil, firewood, meat, herbs, and roots. The children had their books and toys, they learned lessons with the old priest, or made looms and spinning wheels, carved stools and chairs and chests with the tools their uncles had brought them. The Uncles rested and told tales of their travels; Uncle Mark played his pipe for hours together, Uncle Acraud drew pictures in charcoal of the places he had seen, and Granny, laying her hand on the paper covered with lines, would expound while Uncle Mark played: "A huge range of mountains, like wrinkled brown lines across the horizon; a wide plain of sand, silvery blond in color, with patches of pale, pale blue; I think it is not water but air the color of water. Here are strange lines across the sand where men once plowed it, long, long ago; and a great

Grammar in Action

Vary your writing by beginning sentences with different structures. Notice how effective Joan Aiken is at beginning her sentences in a variety of ways:

> While Uncle Mark played on his pipe, Uncle Emer would hand each gift to Grandmother.

> And she—here was the strange thing—she, who was stone-blind all the year long, could not see her own hand in front of her face, she would take the object in her fingers and instantly identify it.

> By stroking each gift with her old, blotched, clawlike fingers, frail as quills, Grandmother, who lived all the year round in darkness, could discover not only what the thing was and where it came from, but also the color of it, and that in the most precise and particular manner, correct to a shade.

patch of crystal green, with what seems like a road crossing it. Now here is a smaller region of plum-pink, bordered by an area of rusty red. I think these are the colors of the earth in these territories; it is very high up, dry from height, and the soil glittering with little particles of metal."

"You have described it better than I could myself!" Uncle Acraud would exclaim, while the children, breathless with wonder and curiosity, sat cross-legged 'round her chair. And she would answer, "Yes, but I cannot see it at all, Acraud, unless your
11 eyes have seen it first, and I cannot see it without Mark's music to help me."

"How does Grandmother *do* it?" the children would demand of their mothers, and Argilla, or Grippa, or Tassy would answer, "Nobody knows. It is Grandmother's gift. She alone can do it."

The people of the village might come in, whenever they chose, and on many evenings
12 thirty or forty would be there, silently listening, and when Grandmother retired to bed, which she did early for the seeing made her weary, the audience would turn to one another with deep sighs, and murmur, "The world is indeed a wide place."

But with the first signs of spring the Uncles would become restless again, and begin looking over their equipment, discussing maps and routes, mending saddlebags and boots, gazing up at the high peaks for signs that the snow was in retreat.

Then Granny would grow very silent. She never asked them to stay longer, she never disputed their going, but her face seemed to shrivel, she grew smaller, wizened and huddled inside her quilted patchwork.

And on St. Petrag's Day, when the Uncles set off, when the farewells were said and they clattered off down the mountain through the melting snow and the trees with pink luminous buds, Grandmother would fall into a silence that lasted, sometimes, for as much as five or six weeks; all day she would sit with her face turned to the east, wordless, motionless, and would drink her milk and go to her bed-place at night still silent and dejected; it took the warm sun and sweet wild hyacinths of May to raise her spirits.

Then, by degrees, she would grow animated, and begin to say, "Only six months, now, till they come back."

But young Mark observed to his cousin Sammle, "It takes longer, every year, for Grandmother to grow accustomed."

And Sammle said, shivering though it was warm May weather, "Perhaps one year, when they come back, she will not be here. She is becoming so tiny and thin; you can see right through her hands, as if they were leaves." And Sammle held up her own thin brown young hand against the sunlight to see the blood glow under the translucent skin.

"I don't know how they would bear it," said Mark thoughtfully, "if when they came back we had to tell them that she had died."

But that was not what happened.

One December the Uncles arrived much later than usual. They did not climb the mountain until St. Misham's Day, and when they reached the house it was in silence. 13
There was none of the usual joyful commotion.

Grandmother knew instantly that there was something wrong. "Where is my son Mark?" she demanded. "Why do I not hear him among you?" And Uncle Acraud had to tell her: "Mother, he is dead. Your son Mark will not come home, ever again."

"How do you *know?* How can you be *sure?* You were not there when he died?"

"I waited and waited at our meeting place, and a messenger came to tell me. His

11 **Discussion** How close is Grandmother's relationship with her sons? How is she sometimes able to "see"?

12 **Discussion** What is Grandmother's gift? Did anyone outside the family recognize her gift? Could anyone explain it?

13 **Reading Strategy** Predict what bad news the Uncles have. Why is there no joyful commotion in the house?

"And this is for you, Mother, from your son, Mark," Uncle Emer would say, handing her a tissue-wrapped bundle, . . .

The first example begins with an adverb clause; the second has both a clause set off with dashes and an adjective clause modifying the subject at the beginning; the third starts with a participial phrase followed by a prepositional phrase; and the last one begins with a direct quotation. All are effective ways to vary sentence beginnings and produce interesting writing.

Student Activity 1. Find four other sentences in this story that you think begin in an effective manner. Discuss with the class why the sentences you have chosen are effective ways to start a sentence.

Student Activity 2. Write four of your own sentences modeling them after Aiken's.

14 **Critical Thinking and Reading** What does her son's ring tell Grandmother? What is the significance of her having to handle the ring before she can accept Uncle Mark's death?

15 **Discussion** What effect does Uncle Mark's death have on Grandmother?

16 **Critical Thinking and Reading** What is Sammle's plan? What does she hope to achieve?

caravan had been attacked by wild tribesmen, riding north from the Lark Mountains. Mark was killed, and all his people. Only this one man escaped and came to bring me the story."

14 "But how can you be *sure?* How do you know he told the *truth?*"

"He brought Mark's ring."

Emer put it into her hand. As she turned it about in her thin fingers, a long moan went through her.

"Yes, he is dead. My son Mark is dead."

"The man gave me this little box," Acraud said, "which Mark was bringing for you."

Emer put it into her hand, opening the box for her. Inside lay an ivory fan. On it, when it was spread out, you could see a bird, with eyes made of sapphires, flying across a valley, but Grandmother held it listlessly, as if her hands were numb.

15 "What is it?" she said. "I do not know what it is. Help me to bed, Argilla. I do not know what it is. I do not wish to know. My son Mark is dead."

Her grief infected the whole village. It was as if the keystone of an arch had been knocked out; there was nothing to hold the people together.

That year spring came early, and the three remaining Uncles, melancholy and restless, were glad to leave on their travels. Grandmother hardly noticed their going.

16 Sammle said to Mark: "You are clever with your hands. Could you not make a pipe—like the one my father had?"

"I?" he said. "Make a pipe? Like Uncle Mark's pipe? Why? What would be the point of doing so?"

"Perhaps you might learn to play on it. As he did."

"I? Play on a pipe?"

"I think you could," she said. "I have heard you whistle tunes of your own."

"But where would I find the right kind of wood?"

"There is a chest, in which Uncle Gonfil once brought books and music from Leiden. I think it is the same kind of wood. I think you could make a pipe from it."

"But how can I remember the shape?"

"I will make a drawing," Sammle said, and she drew with a stick of charcoal on the whitewashed wall of the cowshed. As soon as Mark looked at her drawing he began to contradict.

"No! I remember now. It was not like that. The stops came here—and the mouthpiece was like this."

Now the other children flocked 'round to help and advise.

"The stops were farther apart," said Creusie. "And there were more of them and they were bigger."

"The pipe was longer than that," said

Grammar in Action

Semicolons are internal punctuation marks that provide clarity and help the writer express a close connection between ideas. Semicolons indicate a pause in reading; however, the pause should be a little greater than that of a comma, but not as strong as that of a period. Notice the use of semicolons in the following:

But it took him several weeks of difficult carving; the black wood of the chest proved hard as iron.

And when the pipe was made, and the stops fitted, it would not play; try as he would, not a note could he fetch out of it.

Mark was dogged, though, once he had set himself to a task; he took another piece of the black chest and began again.

Only Sammle stayed to help him now; the other children had lost hope, or interest, and had gone back to their summer occupations.

Sandri. "I have held it. It was as long as my arm."

"How will you ever make the stops?" said young Emer.

"You can have my silver bracelets that Father gave me," said Sammle.

"I'll ask Finn the smith to help me," said Mark.

Once Mark had got the notion of making a pipe into his head, he was eager to begin. But it took him several weeks of difficult carving; the black wood of the chest proved hard as iron. And when the pipe was made, and the stops fitted, it would not play; try as he would, not a note could he fetch out of it.

Mark was dogged, though, once he had
set himself to a task; he took another piece
of the black chest and began again. Only
17 Sammle stayed to help him now; the other
children had lost hope, or interest, and
gone back to their summer occupations.

The second pipe was much better than the first. By September, Mark was able to play a few notes on it; by October he was playing simple tunes made up out of his head.

"But," he said, "if I am to play so that Grandmother can see with her fingers—if I am to do *that*—I must remember your father's special tune. Can *you* remember it, Sammle?"

She thought and thought. "Sometimes," she said, "it seems as if it is just beyond the edge of my hearing—as if somebody were playing it, far, far away, in the woods. Oh, if only I could stretch my hearing a little farther!"

"Oh, Sammle! Try!"

For days and days she sat silent or wandered in the woods, frowning, knotting her forehead, willing her ears to hear the tune again; and the women of the household said, "That girl is not doing her fair share of the task."

They scolded her and set her to spin, weave, milk the goats, throw grain to the hens. But all the while she continued silent,
listening, listening, to a sound she could
not hear. At night, in her dreams, she
sometimes thought she could hear the
tune, and she would wake with tears on 18
her cheeks, wordlessly calling her father
to come back and play his music to her,
so that she could remember it.

In September the autumn winds blew cold and fierce; by October snow was piled around the walls and up to the windowsills. On St. Felin's Day the three Uncles returned, but sadly and silently, without the former festivities; although, as usual, they brought many bales and boxes of gifts and merchandise. The children went down, as usual, to help carry the bundles up the mountain. The joy had gone out of this tradition, though, and they toiled silently up the track with their loads.

17 **Discussion** How important was this project to Mark and Sammle? How can you tell?

18 **Critical Thinking and Reading** What can you infer about the tune from the fact that Sammle cannot recall it?

In each of the examples, the writer has chosen to use semicolons to connect two independent clauses. In so doing, she has connected the two parts more closely related than if she had used a period and a capital letter.

Student Activity 1. Find four more examples of the use of the semicolon. Substitute a period for the semicolon. Is there a difference in shade of meaning or feeling of the passage when you completely separate the independent clauses?

Student Activity 2. Choose one of the sample sentences shown. Using this sentence as a pattern, write your own sentence about one of the characters and events in "The Gift-Giving."

19 **Discussion** Why do you think the echo reminded Sammle of the tune?

20 **Discussion** What do the children hope to accomplish with the tune?

21 **Critical Thinking and Reading** What had gone out of the gift ceremony? Why was it no longer special?

22 **Discussion** How do the Aunts and Uncles react to Mark's playing? How does Grandmother react?

23 **Critical Thinking and Reading** Why can Grandmother "see" again? What does the tune mean to her? How have the children accomplished their goal?

Reader's Response Part of the joy of holidays is the ceremonious gatherings of people, families, and friends. What occasions do you find enjoyable because they bring people together?

It was a wild, windy evening; the sun set in fire, the wind moaned among the fir trees, and gusts of sleet every now and then dashed in their faces.

"Take care, children!" called Uncle Emer as they skirted along the side of a deep gully, and his words were caught by an echo and flung back and forth between the rocky walls: "Take care—care—
19 care—care— care . . ."

"Oh!" cried Sammle, stopping precipitately and clutching the bag that she was carrying. "I have it! I can remember it! *Now* I know how it went!"

And, as they stumbled on up the snowy hillside, she hummed the melody to her cousin Mark, who was just ahead of her.

"Yes, that is it, yes!" he said. "Or, no, wait a minute, that is not *quite* right—but it is close, it is very nearly the way it went. Only the notes were a little faster, and there were more of them—they went up, not down—before the ending tied them in a knot—"

"No, no, they went down at the end, I am almost sure—"

Arguing, interrupting each other, disputing, agreeing, they dropped their bundles in the family room and ran away to the cowhouse where Mark kept his pipe hidden.

For three days they discussed and argued and tried a hundred different versions; they were so occupied that they hardly took the trouble to eat. But at last, by Christmas morning, they had reached agreement.

"I *think* it is right," said Sammle. "And if it is not, I do not believe there is anything more that we can do about it."

"Perhaps it will not work in any case," said Mark sadly. He was tired out with
20 arguing and practicing.

Sammle was equally tired, but she said, "Oh, it *must* work. Oh, let it work! Please let it work! For otherwise I don't think I can bear the sadness. Go now, Mark, quietly and quickly, go and stand behind Granny's chair."

The family had gathered, according to Christmas habit, around Grandmother's rocking chair, but the faces of the Uncles were glum and reluctant, their wives dejected and hopeless. Only the children showed eagerness, as the cloth-wrapped bundles were brought and laid at Grandmother's feet.

She herself looked wholly dispirited and cast down. When Uncle Emer handed her a slender, soft package, she received it apathetically,[5] almost with dislike, as if she 21
would prefer not to be bothered by this tiresome gift ceremony.

Then Mark, who had slipped through the crowd without being noticed, began to play on his pipe just behind Grandmother's chair.

The Uncles looked angry and scandalized; Aunt Tassy cried out in horror: "Oh,
Mark, wicked boy, how *dare* you?" but 22
Grandmother lifted her head, more alertly than she had done for months past, and began to listen.

Mark played on. His mouth was quivering so badly that it was hard to grip the amber mouthpiece, but he played with all the breath that was in him. Meanwhile, Sammle, kneeling by her grandmother, held, with her own warm young hands, the old, brittle ones against the fabric of the gift. And, as she did so, she began to feel what Grandmother felt.

Grandmother said softly and distinctly: "It is a muslin shawl, embroidered in gold
thread, from Lebanon. It is colored a soft 23
brick red, with pale roses of sunset pink, and thorns of silver-green. It is for Sammle . . ."

---

5. apathetically (ap′ ə thet′ ik lē), *adv.*: Indifferently.

THINKING ABOUT THE SELECTION

Recalling

1. Describe the gift-giving ceremony that enables Grandmother to see.
2. When does Grandmother lose this ability?
3. What do Sammle and Mark do that enables Grandmother to see again?

Interpreting

4. Grandmother is the central figure that holds the family together. Why is it important for her to resume this role?
5. At the end of the story, "Sammle, kneeling by her grandmother, held, with her own warm young hands, the old brittle ones against the fabric of the gift. And, as she did so, she began to feel what Grandmother felt." What does this suggest about Sammle?
6. Describe what each of the following characters sees in "The Gift-Giving": Grandmother, the Uncles, Sammle.
7. What are two possible meanings of the title "The Gift-Giving"?

Applying

8. Some families pass down traditions that enrich the family, such as a special ceremony or an annual family reunion. What are some other traditions that are passed down in families?

ANALYZING LITERATURE

Understanding Significant Actions

A **significant action** is any action or event in a story that gives you a clue to the theme. A significant action stands out from the others as more important.

1. What ceremony seems significant in "The Gift-Giving"?
2. What are the parts of this ceremony?
3. How often does the ceremony occur?
4. What do you think is the theme of "The Gift-Giving"?

CRITICAL THINKING AND READING

Summarizing

A **summary** is a brief report covering the main points of a story. When you summarize, you must distinguish between the major and minor details. For example, that the Uncles returned home once a year near Christmas is a major detail; that they carried their bundles on mules or on their backs is a minor detail. All of the major details should be in a summary.

1. Which of the following details would you include in a summary of "The Gift-Giving"?
   a. The uncles bring gifts for the family.
   b. During the gift-giving ceremony, Grandmother, who is blind, magically can see.
   c. Uncle Mark first hears the pipe tune when he escapes falling into a crevasse.
   d. Uncle Mark dies.
   e. Uncle Acraud brings Uncle Mark's ring to prove that he had died.
   f. Grandmother loses her ability to see.
   g. Sammle and Mark make a new pipe and song for Grandmother, enabling her to see again.
2. Using the details you selected, write a summary of "The Gift-Giving."

THINKING AND WRITING

Writing About Theme

Select another story that you have read. State the themes of "The Gift-Giving" and the story you chose. List the similarities and differences between them. Then use these ideas to write an essay comparing and contrasting the themes of the two stories. Revise your essay. Proofread it, checking carefully for correct spelling and punctuation.

Closure and Extension

ANSWERS TO THINKING ABOUT THE SELECTION

Recalling

1. Grandmother's son Mark stands behind her chair and plays a special tune on his pipe while each gift is handed to Grandmother to describe.
2. Grandmother loses this ability when Mark is killed.
3. Sammle and Mark make a new pipe and Mark learns to play the tune.

Interpreting

4. It is important so the family can be happy again and enjoy the gift-giving ceremony on Christmas morning.
5. It suggests that Sammle has inherited her grandmother's gift of "seeing" with her fingers.
6. Grandmother "sees" the gifts through the eyes of her sons. The Uncles see their mother as the central figure in the family. Sammle sees the gift-giving ceremony as a life-giving tradition in the family.
7. Two possible meanings of the title are the giving of gifts by the Uncles to the family and the village and the giving of the gift of sight to Grandmother once a year.

Applying

8. Answers will differ.

ANSWERS TO ANALYZING LITERATURE

1. The gift-giving ceremony seems significant because it revitalizes Grandmother and the entire family.
2. The Uncles return with gifts, Grandmother sits in a place of honor, her son Mark plays his pipe behind her, and Grandmother describes each gift in detail and tells for whom it is intended.
3. This ceremony occurs once a year.
4. Answers will differ. Suggested Response: Family traditions enrich family members and are passed down from one generation to the next.

ANSWERS TO CRITICAL THINKING AND READING

1. a. The Uncles bring gifts for the family.
   b. During the gift-giving ceremony, Grandmother, who is blind, magically can see.
   d. Uncle Mark dies.
   f. Grandmother loses her ability to see.
   g. Sammle and Mark make a new pipe and song for Grandmother, enabling her to see again.
2. Answers will differ, but students' summaries should include all the main points listed in item 1.

Challenge How will the family tradition continue after Grandmother dies? What would have happened if Mark and Sammle had not made a new pipe and re-created the magic tune?

THINKING AND WRITING

For help with this assignment, students can refer to Lesson 11, "Writing About Theme," in the Handbook of Writing About Literature.

Focus

More About the Author Edward Everett Hale was the grandnephew of the Revolutionary War hero Nathan Hale whose last words, "I only regret that I have but one life to give for my country," have become famous. Nathan Hale was hanged as a spy by the British in New York City in 1776 when he was only twenty-one years old. Ask students to discuss if having a famous ancestor could influence a writer. Would Edward Hale have been more likely than another writer to write from a historical or military perspective, for example?

Literary Focus Many objects that you see everyday are symbolic. Some of these are so common that you don't even realize that what you're looking at is a symbol. For example, a swirling, striped pole is the symbol for a barber shop.

Look For Your less advanced students may find it useful to write down each symbolic object, action, or idea in the story and, next to each, what it stands for.

Writing/Prior Knowledge Have students discuss the meaning of this quotation. "There's no place like home." Then have them complete the freewriting assignment. For extra credit, you might ask them to use their freewriting as the basis for a formal composition.

Vocabulary These words may also give students some difficulty: *catastrophe, court-martials* (p. 186); *frenzy, plantation, adjourned, etiquette* (p. 187); *insignia, minstrel* (p. 189); *beggarly, farce* (p. 190); *rammer, cockpit* (p. 191); *dispatches* (p. 192); *midshipman, schooner* (p. 193); *volubly, liberality* (p. 194); *accumulated* (p. 197); *manifold,* and *transgressions* (p. 198).

GUIDE FOR READING

The Man Without a Country

Edward Everett Hale (1822–1909), the grandnephew of American Revolutionary War hero Nathan Hale, began writing stories when he was a boy. He later published his own small newspaper. After graduating from Harvard University, Hale became a Unitarian minister and a journalist, but continued writing short stories, essays, and novels. His well-known story "The Man Without a Country" seemed so realistic that many people who read it in *The Atlantic Monthly* in 1863 believed it was true.

Symbols

A **symbol** is an object, an action, or an idea that stands for something other than itself. For example, a lion is an animal that lives in Africa and Asia, but it is also a symbol of courage and strength. In a story, a writer may use symbols that are familiar to most readers or symbols that occur only in that story. Recognizing and understanding symbols can help you understand a story's theme, or central idea.

Look For

As you read "The Man Without a Country," look for objects, actions, or ideas that stand for something other than themselves. How do they point to the theme?

Writing

In "The Man Without a Country" Philip Nolan claims he never wants to hear of home again. There have been many sayings about the idea of home, such as "Home is where the heart is." Freewrite for three minutes about what *home* means to you. Write down any thoughts, feelings, words, or images that you associate with *home.*

Vocabulary

Knowing the following words will help you as you read "The Man Without a Country."

obscure (äb skyoor') *adj.*: Hidden; not obvious (p. 185)
availed (ə vāld') *v.*: Made use of (p. 185)
stilted (stil' təd) *adj.*: Unnatural; very formal (p. 185)
swagger (swag' ər) *n.*: Arrogance or boastfulness (p. 187)
intercourse (int' ər kôrs) *n.*: Communication between people (p. 188)
blunders (blun' dərz) *n.*: Foolish or stupid mistakes (p. 191)

Objectives

1 To recognize symbols in a short story
2 To paraphrase the theme of a short story
3 To write about the theme of a short story

Support Material

Teaching Portfolio
Teacher Backup, pp. 291–293
Grammar In Action Worksheets, *Using Colons,* pp. 294–295; *Understanding Action Verbs,* pp. 296–297; *Using Sentence Variety,* pp. 298–299
Usage and Mechanics Worksheet, p. 300
Vocabulary Check, p. 301
Critical Thinking and Reading Worksheet, *Paraphrasing,* p. 302
Language Worksheet, *Choosing the Meaning that Fits the Context,* p. 303
Selection Test, p. 304–305

1 The Man Without a Country

Edward Everett Hale

2 I suppose that very few casual readers of the *New York Herald* of August 13, 1863, observed, in an obscure corner, among the "Deaths," the announcement:

NOLAN. Died, on board U.S. Corvette *Levant*, Lat. 2° 11′ S., Long. 131° W., on the 11th of May, PHILIP NOLAN.

Hundreds of readers would have paused at the announcement had it read thus: "Died, May 11, THE MAN WITHOUT A COUNTRY." For it was as "The Man Without a Country" that poor Philip Nolan had generally been known by the officers who had him in charge during some fifty years, as, indeed, by all the men who sailed under them.

There can now be no possible harm in telling this poor creature's story. Reason enough there has been till now for very strict secrecy, the secrecy of honor itself, among the gentlemen of the Navy who have had Nolan in charge. And certainly it speaks well for the profession and the personal honor of its members that to the press this man's story has been wholly unknown —and, I think, to the country at large also. This I do know, that no naval officer has mentioned Nolan in his report of a cruise.

But there is no need for secrecy any longer. Now the poor creature is dead, it seems to me worthwhile to tell a little of his story, by way of showing young Americans 3
of today what it is to be "A Man Without a Country."

Philip Nolan was as fine a young officer as there was in the "Legion of the West," as the Western division of our army was then called. When Aaron Burr[1] made his first dashing expedition down to New Orleans in 1805, he met this gay, dashing, bright young fellow. Burr marked[2] him, talked to him, 4
walked with him, took him a day or two's voyage in his flatboat,[3] and, in short, fascinated him. For the next year, barrack life was very tame to poor Nolan. He occasionally availed himself of the permission the great man had given him to write to him. Long, stilted letters the poor boy wrote and rewrote and copied. But never a line did he have in reply. The other boys in the garrison[4] sneered at him, because he lost the fun which they found in shooting or rowing while he was working away on these grand letters to his grand friend. But before long the young fellow had his revenge. For this

1. Aaron Burr: American political leader (1756–1836). Burr was U.S. Vice-President from 1801 to 1805. He was believed to have plotted to build an empire in the Southwest.
2. marked *v.*: Here, paid attention to.
3. flatboat *n.*: Boat with a flat bottom.
4. garrison (gar′ ə s′n) *n.*: Military post or station.

Presentation

Motivation/Prior Knowledge Have students imagine that they have been banished from the United States. They can never see their homes, friends, or family again. Furthermore, they are forbidden to hear or discuss any news of home. How would they feel? Can they imagine any crime that would deserve this harsh punishment? What attitude would they adopt in order to survive?

Master Teacher Note Explore with students the meaning of patriotism and love of country. Motivate this discussion by reading Robert Browning's "Home Thoughts from Abroad," an expatriate's thoughts about his beloved homeland. Read aloud some lines from the song "America the Beautiful." Play recordings of "Freedom" and "The Only Home I Know Of" (RCA Red Seal ARL1-101a) from the musical *Shenandoah*. Examine with students what inspired each of these works.

Purpose-Setting Question What role does love of homeland play in this story?

1 **Enrichment** This story was written during the Civil War to inspire patriotism and love of country. As you read the story, note the references to a united country.

2 **Critical Thinking and Reading** Although this is a fictional story, note the techniques the author uses to make it seem like fact.

3 **Discussion** Why is the narrator telling the story of Philip Nolan?

4 **Clarification** Aaron Burr traveled through the American West recruiting men for what many believed was his plan to invade Mexico. It was also suspected that Burr was scheming to detach part of the Southwest from the United States. He was tried for treason in 1807 but was acquitted.

Thematic Idea Another selection that deals with the theme of the need for acceptance is "A Retrieved Reformation" (page 61).

Humanities Note

Fine art, *Officer of the Watch on the Horseblock,* 1851, *From Heck's Iconographic Encyclopedia.* Before photographs, etchings ings were used to represent people, places, and things realistically. This nine-teenth-century engraving shows a typical naval scene. Before the advent of elaborate navigational and tracking equipment, men had to take turns on a ship watching for changes in weather conditions, other ships, and enemy attacks.

1. How is this engraving like a photo?
2. What do you learn about life aboard a nineteenth-century ship from this picture?

5 **Discussion** Why did Burr pursue Nolan?

6 **Critical Thinking and Reading** What had Burr accomplished with Nolan? Why was Nolan loyal to Burr?

OFFICER OF THE WATCH ON THE HORSEBLOCK
Heck's Iconographic Encyclopedia, 1851
The New York Public Library

time His Excellency, the Honorable Aaron Burr, appeared again under a very different aspect. There were rumors that he had an army behind him and an empire before him. At that time the youngsters all envied him. Burr had not been talking twenty minutes with the commander before he asked him to send for Lieutenant Nolan. Then, after a little talk, he asked Nolan if he could show him something of the great river and the plans for the new post. He asked Nolan to
5 take him out in his skiff to show him a
canebrake[5] or a cottonwood tree, as he said —really to win him over; and by the time the sail was over, Nolan was enlisted body and soul. From that time, though he did not yet know it, he lived as a man without a country.

What Burr meant to do I know no more than you. It is none of our business just now. Only, when the grand catastrophe came —Burr's great treason trial at Richmond —some of the lesser fry at Fort Adams[6] got up a string of court-martials on the officers there. One and another of the colonels and majors were tried, and, to fill out the list, little Nolan, against whom there was evidence enough that he was sick of the service, had been willing to be false to it, and
would have obeyed any order to march any- 6
where had the order been signed "By command of His Exc. A. Burr." The courts dragged on. The big flies[7] escaped—rightly, for all I know. Nolan was proved guilty enough, yet you and I would never have heard of him but that, when the president

5. **canebrake** (kān′ brāk′) *n.*: A dense area of cane plants.

6. **Fort Adams:** The fort at which Nolan was stationed.

7. **big flies:** Burr and the other important men who may have been involved in his scheme.

Grammar in Action

The **colon** is used to direct attention to the information following it. One of the most important uses of the colon is to introduce a list of miscellaneous items that follow an independent clause. (Never use a colon to introduce a list that does not follow an independent clause.) As an introductory device, the colon preceeds quotations. When you want to quote something you heard someone say or something you read, use a colon to introduce the quote. Note how the colon is used to introduce what Nolan said in "The Man Without a Country."

". . . when the president of the court asked him at the close whether he wished to say anything to show that he had always been faithful to the United States, he cried out, in a fit of frenzy:

"'Damn the United States! I wish I may never hear of the United States again!"

An especially important function of the colon is to signal important ideas or information. You may have seen the colon on medication labels or labels on toxic products such as cleaners. For instance, "Warning: If taken internally, consult a physician immediately."

of the court asked him at the close whether he wished to say anything to show that he had always been faithful to the United States, he cried out, in a fit of frenzy:

"Damn the United States! I wish I may
7 never hear of the United States again!"

I suppose he did not know how the words shocked old Colonel Morgan, who was holding the court. Half the officers who sat in it had served through the Revolution, and their lives had been risked for the very idea which he cursed in his madness. He, on his part, had grown up in the West of those days. He had been educated on a plantation where the finest company was a Spanish
8 officer or a French merchant from Orleans. His education had been perfected in commercial expeditions to Vera Cruz, and I think he told me his father once hired an Englishman to be a private tutor for a winter on the plantation. He had spent half his youth with an older brother, hunting horses in Texas; and to him "United States" was scarcely a reality. I do not excuse Nolan; I only explain to the reader why he cursed his country and wished he might never hear her name again.

From that moment, September 23, 1807, till the day he died, May 11, 1863, he never heard her name again. For that half-century and more he was a man without a country.

Old Morgan, as I said, was terribly shocked. If Nolan had compared George Washington to Benedict Arnold, or had cried, "God save King George," Morgan would not have felt worse. He called the court into his private room, and returned in fifteen minutes, with a face like a sheet, to say: "Prisoner, hear the sentence of the Court! The Court decides, subject to the
9 approval of the President, that you never hear the name of the United States again."

Nolan laughed. But nobody else laughed. Old Morgan was too solemn, and the whole room was hushed dead as night for a minute. Even Nolan lost his swagger in a moment. Then Morgan added: "Mr. Marshal, take the prisoner to Orleans in an armed boat, and deliver him to the naval commander there."

The marshal gave his orders and the prisoner was taken out of court.

"Mr. Marshal," continued old Morgan, "see that no one mentions the United States to the prisoner. Mr. Marshal, make my repects to Lieutenant Mitchell at Orleans, and request him to order that no one shall mention the United States to the prisoner while he is on board ship. You will receive your written orders from the officer on duty here this evening. The court is adjourned."

Before the *Nautilus*[8] got round from New Orleans to the Northern Atlantic coast with the prisoner on board, the sentence had been approved, and he was a man without
a country. 10

The plan then adopted was substantially the same which was necessarily followed ever after. The Secretary of the Navy was requested to put Nolan on board a government vessel bound on a long cruise, and to direct that he should be only so far confined there as to make it certain that he never saw or heard of the country. We had few long cruises then, and I do not know certainly what his first cruise was. But the commander to whom he was entrusted regulated the etiquette and the precautions of the affair, and according to his scheme they were carried out till Nolan died.

When I was second officer of the *Intrepid,* some thirty years after, I saw the original paper of instructions. I have been sorry ever since that I did not copy the whole of it. It ran, however, much in this way:

---

8. *Nautilus:* The naval ship to which Nolan was assigned.

7 **Discussion** Do you think Nolan meant that? Why did he say it?

8 **Critical Thinking and Reading** What is the difference between the way Colonel Morgan and the other officers perceived the United States and the way Nolan perceived it? Could Nolan's background have led to his involvement with Burr? Explain your answer.

9 **Discussion** How serious does Nolan's sentence sound? What are its ramifications?

10 **Critical Thinking and Reading** What does it mean to be without a country? What are the disadvantages?

Student Activity 1. Locate three other sentences in which the colon is used. How is it used in each sentence?

Student Activity 2. Compose three sentences in which you use the colon to signal items in a list, quotations, and important information you wish to emphasize.

11 Discussion Explain the relevance of the following saying, "Be careful of what you wish for because you may get it." How does this apply to Nolan?

12 Discussion Why didn't the men like to eat with Nolan? Identify other problems Nolan might have had with his shipmates by being the man without a country.

Washington (with a date, which must have been late in 1807).

Sir:

You will receive from Lieutenant Neale the person of Philip Nolan, late a lieutenant in the United States Army.

11 This person on his trial by court-martial expressed, with an oath, the wish that he might "never hear of the United States again."

The court sentenced him to have his wish fulfilled.

For the present, the execution of the order is entrusted by the President to this department.

You will take the prisoner on board your ship, and keep him there with such precautions as shall prevent his escape.

You will provide him with such quarters, rations, and clothing as would be proper for an officer of his late rank, if he were a passenger on your vessel on the business of his government.

The gentlemen on board will make any arrangements agreeable to themselves regarding his society. He is to be exposed to no indignity of any kind, nor is he ever unnecessarily to be reminded that he is a prisoner.

But under no circumstances is he ever to hear of his country or to see any information regarding it; and you will especially caution all the officers under your command to take care that this rule, in which his punishment is involved, shall not be broken.

It is the intention of the government that he shall never again see the country which he has disowned. Before the end of your cruise you will receive orders which will give effect to this intention.

Respectfully yours,

W. Southard,
for the Secretary of the Navy.

The rule adopted on board the ships on which I have met "the man without a country" was, I think, transmitted from the beginning. No mess[9] liked to have him permanently, because his presence cut off all talk of home or of the prospect of return, of politics or letters, of peace or of war—cut off 1
more than half the talk men liked to have at sea. But it was always thought too hard that he should never meet the rest of us, except to touch hats, and we finally sank into one system. He was not permitted to talk with the men, unless an officer was by. With officers he had unrestrained intercourse, as far as they and he chose. But he grew shy, though he had favorites: I was one. Then the captain always asked him to dinner on Monday. Every mess in succession took up the invitation in its turn. According to the size of the ship, you had him at your mess more or less often at dinner. His breakfast he ate in his own stateroom. Whatever else he ate or drank, he ate or drank alone. Sometimes, when the marines or sailors had any special jollification,[10] they were permitted to invite "Plain Buttons," as they called him. Then Nolan was sent with some officer, and the men were forbidden to speak of home while he was there. I believe the theory was that the sight of his punishment did them good. They called him "Plain But-

9. mess *n.*: Here, a group of people who routinely have their meals together.

10. jollification (jäl′ ə fi kā′ shən) *n.*: Merry-making.

13 tons,'' because, while he always chose to wear a regulation army uniform, he was not permitted to wear the army button, for the reason that it bore either the initials or the insignia of the country he had disowned.

I remember, soon after I joined the Navy, I was on shore with some of the older officers from our ship and some of the gentlemen fell to talking about Nolan. Someone told of the system which was adopted from the first about his books and other reading. As he was almost never permitted to go on shore, even though the vessel lay in port for months, his time at the best hung heavy. Everybody was permitted to lend him books, if they were not published in America and made no allusion to it. These were common enough in the old days. He had almost all the foreign papers that came into the ship, sooner or later; only somebody must go over them first, and cut out any advertisement or stray paragraph that referred to America. This was a little cruel sometimes, when the back of what was cut out might be innocent. Right in the midst of one of Napoleon's battles poor Nolan would find a great hole, because on the back of the page of that paper there had been an advertisement of a packet[11] for New York, or a scrap from the President's message. This was the first time I ever heard of this plan. I remember it, because poor Phillips, who was of the party, told a story of something which happened at the Cape of Good Hope on Nolan's first voyage. They had touched at the Cape, paid their respects to the English Admiral and the fleet, and then Phillips had borrowed a lot of English books from an officer. Among them was *The Lay of the Last Minstrel*,[12] which they had all of them heard of, but which most of them had never seen. I think it could not have been published long. Well, nobody thought there could be any risk of anything national in that. So Nolan was permitted to join the circle one afternoon when a lot of them sat on deck reading aloud. In his turn, Nolan took the book and read to the others; and he read very well. Nobody in the circle knew a line of the poem, only it was all magic and chivalry, and was ten thousand years ago. Poor Nolan read steadily through the fifth canto,[13] stopped a minute and drank something, and then began, without a thought of what was coming:

> Breathes there the man, with soul so
> dead
> Who never to himself hath said,—

It seems impossible to us that anybody ever heard this for the first time; but all these fellows did then, and poor Nolan himself went on, still unconsciously or mechanically:

> This is my own, my native land! 14

Then they all saw that something was to pay; but he expected to get through, I suppose, turned a little pale, but plunged on:

> Whose heart hath ne'er within him
> burned,
> As home his footsteps he hath
> turned
> From wandering on a foreign
> strand?—
> If such there breathe, go, mark him
> well,—

11. packet *n.*: A boat that carries passengers, freight, and mail along a regular route.

12. *The Lay of the Last Minstrel:* Narrative poem by Sir Walter Scott, Scottish poet and novelist (1771–1832).

13. canto (kan′ tō) *n.*: A main division of certain long poems.

13 Critical Thinking and Reading What effect do you think Nolan's nickname had on him?

14 Discussion Why is this line so significant to Nolan?

15 Discussion Why was reading the poem so devastating for Nolan?

16 Critical Thinking and Reading How do you think Nolan felt every time he got close to his home shore?

By this time the men were all beside themselves, wishing there was any way to make him turn over two pages; but he had not quite presence of mind for that; he gagged a little, colored crimson, and staggered on:

For him no minstrel raptures swell;
High though his titles, proud his
  name,
Boundless his wealth as wish can
  claim,
Despite these titles, power, and
  pelf,[14]
The wretch, concentered all in
  self,—

and here the poor fellow choked, could not go on, but started up, swung the book into
15 the sea, vanished into his stateroom, "And by Jove," said Phillips, "we did not see him for two months again. And I had to make up some beggarly story to that English surgeon why I did not return his Walter Scott to him."

That story shows about the time when Nolan's braggadocio[15] must have broken down. At first, they said, he took a very high tone, considered his imprisonment a mere farce, affected to enjoy the voyage, and all that; but Phillips said that after he came out of his stateroom he never was the same man again. He never read aloud again, unless it was the Bible or Shakespeare, or something else he was sure of. But it was not that merely. He never entered in with the other young men exactly as a companion again. He was always shy afterwards, when I knew him—very seldom spoke unless he was spoken to, except to a very few friends. Generally he had the nervous, tired look of a heart-wounded man.

When Captain Shaw was coming home, rather to the surprise of everybody they made one of the Windward Islands, and lay off and on for nearly a week. The boys said the officers were sick of salt-junk,[16] and meant to have turtle-soup before they came home. But after several days the *Warren* came to the same rendezvous;[17] they exchanged signals; she told them she was outward bound, perhaps to the Mediterranean, and took poor Nolan and his traps[18] on the boat to try his second cruise. He looked very blank when he was told to get ready to join her. He had known enough of the signs of the sky to know that till that moment he was going "home." But this was a distinct evidence of something he had not thought of, perhaps—that there was no going home
for him, even to a prison. And this was the 16
first of some twenty such transfers, which brought him sooner or later into half our best vessels, but which kept him all his life at least some hundred miles from the country he had hoped he might never hear of again.

It may have been on that second cruise —it was once when he was up the Mediterranean—that Mrs. Graff, the celebrated Southern beauty of those days, danced with him. The ship had been lying a long time in the Bay of Naples, and the officers were very intimate in the English fleet, and there had been great festivities, and our men thought they must give a great ball on board the ship. They wanted to use Nolan's stateroom for something, and they hated to do it without asking him to the ball; so the captain said they might ask

14. pelf *n.*: Ill-gotten wealth.
15. braggadocio (brag′ ə dō′ shē ō) *n.*: Here, pretense of bravery; Nolan acts as if he does not mind his imprisonment.
16. salt-junk *n.*: Hard salted meat.
17. rendezvous (rän′ dā vo͞o) *n.*: Meeting place.
18. traps *n.*: Here, bags or luggage.

Grammar in Action

Action verbs show the action in sentences. An action verb is **intransitive** if the receiver of the action is not named in the sentence. Since there is no person or object receiving the action of the verb, the emphasis is placed on the subject. For example,

he gagged   he staggered

Writers use intransitive action verbs to heighten the action of their subject. Notice how vividly Nolan's actions are described:

. . . but he had not quite presence of mind for that; he *gagged* a little, *colored* crimson, and *staggered* on: . . .

. . . and here the poor fellow *choked,* could not go on, but *started* up, swung the book into the sea, *vanished* into his stateroom . . .

The verbs show what Nolan is doing; they place the emphasis of the sentence on the subject.

him, if they would be responsible that he did not talk with the wrong people, "who would give him intelligence."[19] So the dance went on. For ladies they had the family of the American consul, one or two travelers who had adventured so far, and a nice bevy of English girls and matrons.

Well, different officers relieved each other in standing and talking with Nolan in a friendly way, so as to be sure that nobody else spoke to him. The dancing went on with spirit, and after a while even the fellows who took this honorary guard of Nolan ceased to fear any trouble.

As the dancing went on, Nolan and our fellows all got at ease—so much so, that it seemed quite natural for him to bow to that
7 splendid Mrs. Graff, and say, "I hope you have not forgotten me, Miss Rutledge. Shall I have the honor of dancing?"

He did it so quickly, that Fellows, who was with him, could not hinder him. She laughed and said, "I am not Miss Rutledge any longer, Mr. Nolan; but I will dance all the same." She nodded to Fellows, as if to say he must leave Mr. Nolan to her, and led him off to the place where the dance was forming.

Nolan thought he had got his chance. He had known her at Philadelphia, and at other places had met her. He began with her travels, and Europe, and then he said boldly—a little pale, she said, as she told me the story years after—"And what do you hear from home, Mrs. Graff?"

And that splendid creature looked through him. How she must have looked through him!

"Home! Mr. Nolan! I thought you were the man who never wanted to hear of home again!"—and she walked directly up the deck to her husband, and left poor Nolan alone. He did not dance again.

A happier story than either of these I have told is of the war.[20] That came along soon after. I have heard this affair told in three or four ways—and, indeed, it may have happened more than once. In one of the great frigate[21] duels with the English, in which the navy was really baptized, it happened that a round-shot[22] from the enemy entered one of our ports[23] square, and took right down the officer of the gun himself, and almost every man of the gun's crew. Now you may say what you choose about courage, but that is not a nice thing to see. But, as the men who were not killed picked themselves up, and as they and the surgeon's people were carrying off the bodies, there appeared Nolan in his shirt sleeves, with the rammer in his hand, and, just as if he had been the officer, told them off with authority—who should go to the cockpit with the wounded men, who should stay with him—perfectly cheery, and with that
way which makes men feel sure all is right 18
and is going to be right. And he finished loading the gun with his own hands, aimed it, and bade the men fire. And there he stayed, captain of that gun, keeping those fellows in spirits, till the enemy struck[24]—sitting on the carriage while the gun was cooling, though he was exposed all the time—showing them easier ways to handle heavy shot—making the raw hands laugh at their own blunders—and when the gun cooled again, getting it loaded and fired

19. intelligence *n.*: Here, news about his country.

20. the war: The War of 1812 between the United States and Great Britain.
21. frigate (frĭg′ it) *n.*: A fast-sailing warship equipped with guns.
22. round-shot: A cannonball.
23. ports *n.*: Here, portholes or openings for cannonballs.
24. struck, (struk) *v.*: Lowered their flag to admit defeat.

17 Reading Strategy Predict what Nolan will ask Mrs. Graff and what her response will be.

18 Discussion How did Nolan act in the War of 1812? What did he do to save his ship? Why did he do it?

Student Activity. Write several sentences in which you use vivid action verbs to describe what someone is doing. You might describe an embarrassed classmate who has forgotten his lines in a play, or describe a child learning how to ride a bicycle. A thesaurus may be helpful for finding vivid words.

Humanities Note

Fine art, *U.S.S. Constitution and H.M.S. Guerriere (Aug. 19, 1812)* by Thomas Birch. Thomas Birch (1779–1851) emigrated to the United States from England in 1793. A boat trip down the Delaware River sparked Birch's interest in the sea and ships.

During the War of 1812, Thomas Birch painted a series of historical views of American naval victories. The painting *U.S.S. Constitution and H.M.S. Guerriere (Aug. 19, 1812)* is from this series. The painting is a glorified impression of the encounter of the two ships.

1. Evaluate Nolan's act of bravery in view of how a typical sea battle looked.
2. Study the painting and identify the features that made these ships so vulnerable.
3. Which side is winning? How can you tell?

19 **Discussion** Do you think Nolan has a reason to hope that he'll be pardoned now? Is this why he acted courageously?

20 **Reading Strategy** Summarize the story to this point and predict what will happen to Nolan.

USS CONSTITUTION AND HMS GUERRIERE (Aug. 19, 1812)
Thomas Birch
U.S. Naval Academy Museum

twice as often as any other gun on the ship. The captain walked forward by way of encouraging the men, and Nolan touched his hat and said, "I am showing them how we do this in the artillery, sir."

19 And this is the part of the story where all the legends agree; the commodore said, "I see you do, and I thank you, sir; and I shall never forget this day, sir, and you never shall, sir."

And after the whole thing was over, and the commodore had the Englishman's sword[25] in the midst of the state and ceremony of the quarter-deck, he said, "Where is Mr. Nolan? Ask Mr. Nolan to come here."

And when Nolan came, he said, "Mr. Nolan, we are all very grateful to you today; you are one of us today; you will be named in the dispatches." 20

25. **the Englishman's sword:** A defeated commander would turn over his sword to the victor.

Grammar in Action

Sentence variety within a paragraph produces a more interesting passage, and reflects a careful molding of the sentences by the writer to form exact meaning and emphasis. The overuse of short, simple sentences as well as the overuse of complex, convoluted sentences can create either monotonous or confusing paragraphs. Sentence variety is essential to good writing.

Notice the sentence variety Hale uses in the following passage:

All that was nearly fifty years ago. If Nolan was thirty then, he must have been near eighty when he died. He looked sixty when he was forty. But he never seemed to me to change a hair afterwards. As I imagine his life, from what I have seen and heard of it, he must have been in every sea, and yet almost never on land. Till he grew very old, he went aloft a great deal. He always kept up his exercise, and I never heard that he was ill. If any other man was ill, he was the kindest nurse in the world; and he knew more than half the surgeons do. Then if anybody was sick or died, or if the captain wanted him to, on any other occasion, he was always ready to read prayers. I have said that he read beautifully.

And then the old man took off his own sword of ceremony, gave it to Nolan, and made him put it on. The man told me this who saw it. Nolan cried like a baby, and well he might. He had not worn a sword since that infernal day at Fort Adams. But always afterwards on occasions of ceremony, he wore that quaint old French sword of the commodore's.

The captain did mention him in the dispatches. It was always said he asked that
1 Nolan might be pardoned. He wrote a
special letter to the Secretary of War, but nothing ever came of it.

All that was nearly fifty years ago. If Nolan was thirty then, he must have been near eighty when he died. He looked sixty when he was forty. But he never seemed to me to change a hair afterwards. As I imagine his life, from what I have seen and heard of it, he must have been in every sea, and yet
2 almost never on land. Till he grew very old,
he went aloft a great deal. He always kept up his exercise, and I never heard that he was ill. If any other man was ill, he was the kindest nurse in the world; and he knew more than half the surgeons do. Then if anybody was sick or died, or if the captain wanted him to, on any other occasion, he was always ready to read prayers. I have said that he read beautifully.

My own acquaintance with Philip Nolan began six or eight years after the English war, on my first voyage after I was appointed
a midshipman. From the time I joined, I
3 thought Nolan was a sort of lay chaplain—a
chaplain with a blue coat. I never asked about him. Everything in the ship was strange to me. I knew it was green to ask questions, and I suppose I thought there was a "Plain Buttons" on every ship. We had him to dine in our mess once a week, and the caution was given that on that day nothing was to be said about home. But if they had told us not to say anything about the planet Mars or the Book of Deuteronomy,[26] I should not have asked why; there were a great many things which seemed to me to have as little reason. I first came to understand anything about "The Man Without a Country" one day when we overhauled a dirty little schooner which had slaves[27] on board. An officer named Vaughan was sent to take charge of her, and after a few minutes, he sent back his boat to ask that someone might be sent to him who could speak Portuguese. None of the officers did; and just as the captain was sending forward to ask if any of the people could,
Nolan stepped out and said he should be
glad to interpret, if the captain wished, as 24
he understood the language. The captain
thanked him, fitted out another boat with him, and in this boat it was my luck to go.

When we got there, it was such a scene as you seldom see, and never want to. Nastiness beyond account, and chaos run loose in the midst of the nastiness. There were not a great many of the Negroes; but by way of making what there were understand that they were free, Vaughan had had their handcuffs and anklecuffs knocked off. The Negroes were, most of them, out of the hold and swarming all round the dirty deck, with a central throng surrounding Vaughan and addressing him in every dialect.

As we came on deck, Vaughan looked down from a hogshead,[28] which he had mounted in desperation, and said, "Is there anybody who can make these people understand something?"

---

26. Book of Deuteronomy (do͞ot′ ər än′ ə mē): The fifth book of the Bible.

27. slaves: In 1808 it became illegal to bring slaves into the United States. In 1842 the U.S. and Great Britain agreed to use ships to patrol the African coast, to prevent slaves being taken.

28. hogshead (hôgz′ hed′) *n.*: A large barrel or cask.

21 **Discussion** Is it surprising that Nolan isn't pardoned? Do you think he should be?

22 **Critical Thinking and Reading** Why did Nolan always go aloft, or up to the crow's nest? What was he hoping to see?

23 **Discussion** Why would the narrator of this story have thought at first that Nolan was a chaplain? What kind of man had Nolan become?

24 **Critical Thinking and Reading** Why do you think Aaron Burr had been interested in Nolan? Does he seem like a typical seaman? Explain your answer.

Hale uses both simple and complex sentences in order to produce a smooth, readable style of writing.

Student Activity. Write a paragraph in which you describe someone as Hale did in the example. Strive to vary your sentences by using both simple sentences and complex ones.

25 Discussion Why is this speech so difficult for Nolan? What statement is the author making about slavery? As this story was written during the Civil War, which side would you say the author was on?

26 Critical Thinking and Reading Contrast the Nolan at the beginning of the story with the Nolan who makes this speech. What makes this speech so unexpected and meaningful?

Nolan said he could speak Portuguese, and one or two fine-looking Kroomen who had worked for the Portuguese on the coast were dragged out.

"Tell them they are free," said Vaughan.

Nolan explained it in such Portuguese as the Kroomen could understand, and they in turn to such of the Negroes as could understand them. Then there was a yell of delight, clenching of fists, and leaping and dancing by way of celebration.

"Tell them," said Vaughan, well pleased, "that I will take them all to Cape Palmas."

This did not answer so well. Cape Palmas was practically as far from the homes of most of them as New Orleans or Rio de Janeiro was; that is, they would be eternally separated from home there. And their interpreters, as we could understand, instantly said, *"Ah, non Palmas,"* and began to protest volubly. Vaughan was rather disappointed at this result of his liberality, and asked Nolan eagerly what they said. The drops stood on poor Nolan's white forehead, as he hushed the men down, and said, "He says, 'Not Palmas.' He says, 'Take us home; take us to our own country; take us to our own house; take us to our own children and our own women.' He says he has an old father and mother who will die if they do not see him. And this one says he left his people all sick, and paddled
25 down to Fernando to beg the white doctor to come and help them, and that these devils caught him in the bay just in sight of home, and that he has never seen anybody from home since then. And this one says," choked out Nolan, "that he has not heard a word from his home in six months."

Vaughan always said he grew gray himself while Nolan struggled through this interpretation. I, who did not understand anything of the passion involved in it, saw that the very elements were melting with fervent heat and that something was to pay somewhere. Even the Negroes themselves stopped howling, as they saw Nolan's agony and Vaughan's almost equal agony of sympathy. As quick as he could get words, Vaughan said, "Tell them yes, yes, yes; tell them they shall go to the Mountains of the Moon, if they will. If I sail the schooner through the Great White Desert, they shall go home!"

And after some fashion Nolan said so. And then they all fell to kissing him again.

But he could not stand it long; and getting Vaughan to say he might go back, he beckoned me down into our boat. As we started back he said to me, "Youngster, let that show you what it is to be without a family, without a home, and without a country. And if you are ever tempted to say a word or to do a thing that shall put a bar between you and your family, your home, and your country, pray God in His mercy to take you that instant home to His own heaven. Think of your home, boy; write and send, and talk about it. Let it be nearer and nearer to your thought the farther you have to travel from it, and rush back to it when you are free, as that poor slave is doing now.
And for your country, boy" and the words 2
rattled in his throat, "and for that flag," and he pointed to the ship, "never dream a dream but of serving her as she bids you, though the service carry you through a thousand hells. No matter what happens to you, no matter who flatters you or who abuses you, never look at another flag, never let a night pass but you pray God to bless that flag. Remember, boy, that behind all these men you have to do with, behind officers, and government, and people even, there is the Country herself, your Country, and that you belong to her as you belong to your own mother. Stand by her, boy, as you would stand by your mother!"

I was frightened to death by his calm, hard passion; but I blundered out that I

would, by all that was holy, and that I had never thought of doing anything else. He hardly seemed to hear me; but he did, almost in a whisper, say, "Oh, if anybody had
7 said so to me when I was of your age!"

I think it was this half-confidence of his, which I never abused, that afterward made us great friends. He was very kind to me. Often he sat up, or even got up, at night, to walk the deck with me, when it was my watch. He explained to me a great deal of my mathematics, and I owe to him my taste for mathematics. He lent me books and helped me about my reading. He never referred so directly to his story again; but from one and another officer I have learned, in thirty years, what I am telling.

After that cruise I never saw Nolan again. The other men tell me that in those fifteen years he aged very fast, but he was still the same gentle, uncomplaining, silent sufferer that he ever was, bearing as best he could his self-appointed punishment. And now it seems the dear old fellow is dead. He has found a home at last, and a country. 28

Since writing this, and while considering whether or not I would print it, as a warning to the young Nolans of today of what it is to throw away a country, I have received from Danforth, who is on board the *Levant,* a letter which gives an account of Nolan's last hours. It removes all my doubts about telling this story.

Here is the letter:

Dear Fred,

I try to find heart and life to tell you that it is all over with dear old

WARRANT OFFICERS' MESS
from Heck's Iconographic Encyclopedia, 1851
New York Public Library

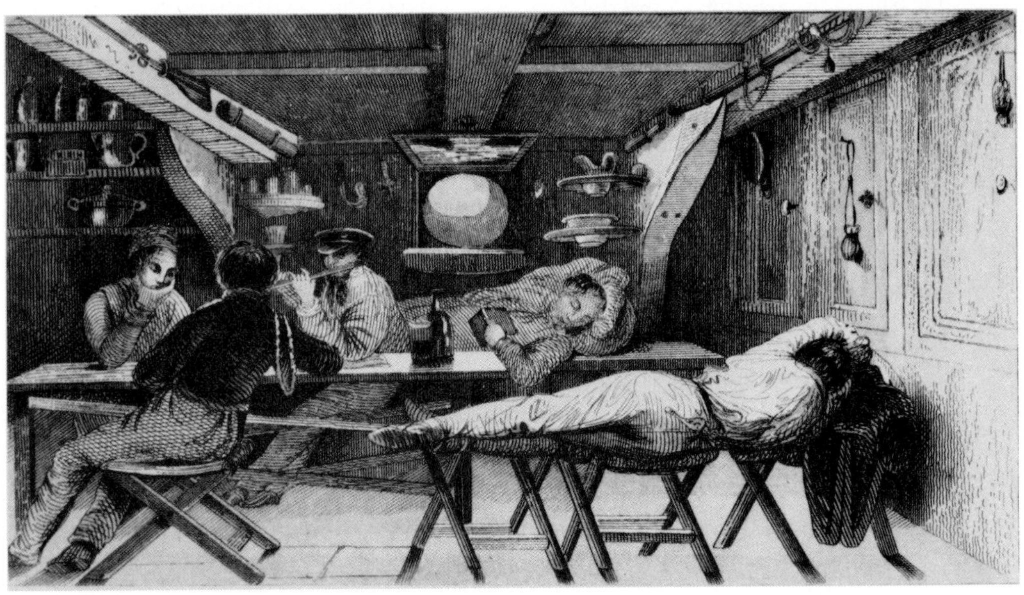

27 Critical Thinking and Reading Might Nolan's life have been different if someone had taught him what it means to belong to a country? How did Nolan learn this lesson?

28 Discussion What does the author mean by this?

Humanities Note

This nineteenth-century engraving shows an officers' mess. The artist strove to depict the scene as realistically and in as much detail as possible.

1. Judging from the engraving, what was life like aboard these ships? What is the dominant feeling of the men?
2. What must Nolan's life have been like if this shows a typical moment of rest for the seamen?
3. Identify the details that make the engraving realistic and photographic?

29 **Literary Focus** What symbols decorate Nolan's room? What do they stand for? How meaningful have they become for Nolan? Why?

30 **Critical Thinking and Reading** According to Nolan, what had Burr's plan been?

Nolan. I have been with him on this voyage more than I ever was, and I can understand wholly now the way in which you used to speak of the dear old fellow. I could see that he was not strong, but I had no idea the end was so near. The doctor has been watching him very carefully, and yesterday morning came to me and told me that Nolan was not so well, and had not left his stateroom —a thing I never remember before. He had let the doctor come and see him as he lay there—the first time the doctor had been in the stateroom —and he said he should like to see me. Do you remember the mysteries we boys used to invent about his room in the old *Intrepid* days? Well, I went in, and there, to be sure, the poor fellow lay in his berth, smiling pleasantly as he gave me his hand, but looking very frail. I could not help a glance round, which showed me what a little shrine he had made of the box he was lying in. The Stars and Stripes were draped up above and around a picture of Washington and he had painted a majestic eagle,
29 with lightning blazing from his beak and his foot just clasping the whole globe, which his wings overshadowed. The dear old boy saw my glance, and said, with a sad smile, "Here, you see I have a country!" And then he pointed to the foot of his bed, where I had not seen before a great map of the United States, as he had drawn it from memory, and which he had there to look upon as he lay. Quaint, queer old names were on it, in large letters: "Indiana Territory," "Mississippi Territory," and "Louisiana Territory," as I suppose our fathers learned such things: but the old fellow had patched in Texas, too: he had carried his western boundary all the way to the Pacific, but on that shore he had defined nothing.

"O Captain," he said, "I know I am dying. I cannot get home. Surely you will tell me something now? —Stop! stop! Do not speak till I say what I am sure you know, that there is not in this ship, that there is not in America a more loyal man than I. There cannot be a man who loves the old flag as I do, or prays for it as I do, or hopes for it as I do. There are thirty-four stars in it now, Danforth, though I do not know what their names are. There has never been one taken away. I know by that that there has never been any successful Burr. O Danforth, Danforth," he
sighed out, "how like a wretched 30
night's dream a boy's idea of personal fame or of separate sovereignty seems, when one looks back on it after such a life as mine! But tell me—tell me something—tell me everything, Danforth, before I die!"

I swear to you that I felt like a monster that I had not told him everything before. "Mr. Nolan," said I, "I will tell you everything you ask about. Only, where shall I begin?"

Oh, the blessed smile that crept over his white face! He pressed my hand and said, "Bless you! Tell me their names," and he pointed to the stars on the flag. "The last I know is Ohio. My father lived in Kentucky. But I have guessed Michigan and Indiana and Mississippi—that was where Fort Adams was—they make twenty. But where are your other fourteen? You have not cut up any of the old ones, I hope?"

Well, that was not a bad text, and I told him the names in as good order as I could, and he bade me take down his beautiful map and draw them in as I best could with my pencil. He was wild with delight about Texas, told me how his cousin died there; he had marked a gold cross near where he supposed his grave was; and he had guessed at Texas. Then he was delighted as he saw California and Oregon;—that, he said, he had suspected partly, because he had never been permitted to land on that shore, though the ships were there so much. Then he asked whether Burr ever tried again—and he ground his
31 teeth with the only passion he
showed. But in a moment that was over. He asked about the old war—told me the story of his serving the gun the day we took the *Java*. Then he settled down more quietly, and very happily, to hear me tell in an hour the history of fifty years.

How I wished it had been somebody who knew something! But I did as well as I could. I told him of the English war. I told him about Fulton[29] and the steamboat beginning. I told him about old Scott,[30] and Jackson;[31] told him all I could think of about the Mississippi, and New Orleans, and Texas, and his own old Kentucky.

I tell you, it was a hard thing to condense the history of half a century into that talk with a sick man. And I do not now know what I told him—of emigration, and the means of it—of steamboats, and railroads, and telegraphs—of inventions, and books, and literature—of the colleges, and West Point, and the Naval School—but with the queerest interruptions that ever you heard. You
see it was Robinson Crusoe asking 32
all the accumulated questions of fifty-six years!

I remember he asked, all of a sudden, who was President now; and when I told him, he asked if Old Abe was General Benjamin Lincoln's son. He said he met old General Lincoln, when he was quite a boy himself, at some Indian treaty. I said no, that Old Abe was a Kentuckian like himself, but I could not tell him of what family; he had worked up from the ranks. "Good for him!" cried Nolan; "I am glad of that." Then I got talking about my visit to Washington. I told him about the Smithsonian, and the Capitol. I told him everything I could think of that would
show the grandeur of his country 33
and its prosperity.

And he drank it in and enjoyed it as I cannot tell you. He grew more and more silent, yet I never thought he was tired or faint. I gave him a glass of water, but he just wet his lips, and told me not to go away. Then he asked me to bring the Presbyterian Book of Public Prayer which lay there, and said, with a smile, that it would open at the right place—and so it did. There was his double red mark down the page; and I knelt

29. Fulton: Robert Fulton (1765–1815), who invented the steamboat.
30. Scott: General Winfield Scott (1786–1866), who served in the War of 1812 and the Mexican War.
31. Jackson: Andrew Jackson (1767–1845), seventh President of the United States (1829–1837) and a general in the War of 1812.

31 Critical Thinking and Reading What does Nolan think of Burr now?

32 Clarification Robinson Crusoe was a character created by Daniel Defoe in 1719. Crusoe was marooned on a desert island, removed from news of the world, for twenty-eight years.

33 Critical Thinking and Reading Describe how Nolan must have felt while hearing about the "grandeur of his country."

34 Critical Thinking and Reading How have these prayers acted as Nolan's penance for his crime? Do you think his punishment was appropriate or overly harsh? Explain your answer.

35 Discussion Discuss the meaning of the Biblical quotation. Why was it appropriate for Nolan?

36 Critical Thinking and Reading Why does Nolan want a tombstone even though he will be buried at sea? Based on the epitaph he wrote for himself, how did Nolan judge himself? Did he think he had been too severely punished for his crime?

Reader's Response In your opinion, was Nolan's punishment fair? Explain.

down and read, and he repeated with me:

For ourselves and our country, O gracious God, we thank Thee, that, notwithstanding our manifold transgressions of Thy holy laws, Thou hast continued to us Thy marvelous kindness . . .

and so to the end of that thanksgiving. Then he turned to the end of the same book, and I read the words more familiar to me:

Most heartily we beseech Thee with Thy favor to behold and bless Thy servant, the President of the United States, and all others in authority.

"Danforth," said he, "I have re-
34 peated those prayers night and
morning—it is now fifty-five years."
And then he said he would go to sleep. He bent me down over him and kissed me; and he said, "Look in my Bible, Captain, when I am gone." And I went away.

But I had no thought it was the end. I thought he was tired and would sleep. I knew he was happy, and I wanted him to be alone.

But in an hour, when the doctor went in gently, he found Nolan had breathed his life away with a smile.

We looked in his Bible, and there was a slip of paper at the place where he had marked the text:

They desire a country, even a
heavenly: where God is not
ashamed to be called their God: for 35
He hath prepared for them a city.[32]

On this slip of paper he had written:

Bury me in the sea; it has been my home, and I love it. But will not someone set up a stone for my memory at Fort Adams or at Orleans, that my disgrace may not be more than I ought to bear? Say on it:

In Memory of 36
PHILIP NOLAN,
Lieutenant in the Army of the United States.
He loved his country as no other man has loved her; but no man deserved less at her hands.

---

32. They desire . . . a city: A passage from Hebrews 11:16.

Closure and Extension

ANSWERS TO THINKING ABOUT THE SELECTION

Recalling

1. The narrator is a man who served with Nolan on a ship. He tells the story to show young Americans what it means to be without a country.
2. Nolan is tried for his participation in subversive activities with Aaron Burr.
3. Nolan says, "Damn the United States! I wish I may never hear of the United States again!" The judge is shocked and grants Nolan his wish as a punishment.
4. Nolan's sentence is to "never hear the name of the United States again." The sentence will be carried out by assigning Nolan to different ships for the rest of his life. The men on each ship are instructed not to mention home to Nolan, and his reading material is censored.
5. Books must be checked for references to the United States, and

THINKING ABOUT THE SELECTION

Recalling

1. Who is the narrator of this story? What is the narrator's purpose in telling the story?
2. Why is Nolan brought to trial?
3. What rash words does Nolan utter when the judge asks him if he wishes to say anything? What effect do these words have on the judge?
4. What is Nolan's sentence? Explain the plan to carry out the sentence.
5. What precautions have to be taken with Nolan before giving him books? What precautions have to be taken before giving him periodicals?
6. How does Nolan create a country for himself in his stateroom?
7. What is Nolan's last wish?

Interpreting

8. How is it that Aaron Burr is able to win over the young Nolan so easily?
9. Why does the poem *The Lay of the Last Minstrel* have such an effect on Nolan? Why does Nolan cry when he receives the sword of the commodore?
10. After interpreting for the slaves to be sent home, why does Nolan advise the narrator to love and serve his country?
11. How has Nolan changed during the course of the story?

Applying

12. What epitaph would you write for Nolan?
13. Do you think Nolan's punishment fit his crime? Explain your answer.

ANALYZING LITERATURE

Recognizing Symbols

A **symbol** can be a word, an object, or an action in a story that represents, or stands for, something else. For example, a snake is a reptile, but it can also symbolize evil.

The writer usually emphasizes or repeats a symbol, or places it in a particular place in the story. The symbol's meaning depends on the context of the story. A story may have more than one symbol.

1. What do Nolan's plain buttons symbolize?
2. What symbol of honor does the commodore of Philip Nolan's ship give him for bravery in the battle with a British frigate?
3. What do the Stars and Stripes draped in Philip Nolan's stateroom symbolize?
4. What do these symbols suggest about the importance of one's country?

CRITICAL THINKING AND READING

Paraphrasing

Paraphrasing is restating in your own words something you read or hear; you do not repeat the words *exactly*.

Paraphrasing may help you understand better what you read or hear. To paraphrase the theme, or central idea, of a story, read and consider what the story is about. Then state its main points in your own words.

1. Paraphrase the story's theme: "And for your country . . . never dream a dream but of serving her as she bids you, though the service carry you through a thousand hells."
2. Paraphrase Nolan's epitaph: "He loved his country as no other man has loved her; but no man deserved less at her hands."

THINKING AND WRITING

Writing About Theme

Suppose Fred read the obituary in *The New York Herald* and wanted to set the record straight about Philip Nolan's true feelings about his country. List examples from the story of how Nolan felt about the U.S. Then, as Fred, write a letter to the editor describing Nolan's feelings and giving the examples. Revise your letter, making sure you have stated your points clearly. Revise your essay and prepare a final draft.

(Answers begin on p. 198.)

references to the country must be cut out of periodicals.

6. Nolan places symbols of the United States all over his room and a map which he filled in himself.
7. Nolan's last wish is that he be buried at sea but that a tombstone be erected for him on land.

Interpreting

8. Burr impresses Nolan and courts him. Burr singles him out to show him different sights so that ordinary barracks life seems boring to Nolan by comparison.
9. The poem affects Nolan because it is about the feeling most people get about seeing their native land after traveling and about the wretchedness of those who don't experience this feeling. Nolan cries because he had not worn a sword since his trial, and he is very moved by the commodore's gesture of giving over his sword of honor.
10. Nolan gives this advice because he has learned a hard lesson himself about not loving his country and the consequences of this.
11. Nolan has changed from a brash, swaggering young officer to a humble, uncomplaining servant of his fellow men.

Applying

12. Answers will differ. Students should see that, in the final analysis, Nolan did serve his country well.
13. Answers will differ. Students will either say that Nolan's punishment fit his crime because he got what he asked for, or they will say that his punishment was in excess of his crime since he spoke in haste and proved his bravery and loyalty to his country over the years.

ANSWERS TO ANALYZING LITERATURE

1. Nolan's plain buttons symbolize that he belongs to no country and so can wear no country's insignia.
2. The commodore gives Nolan his sword.
3. The Stars and Stripes symbolize the United States.
4. The symbols suggest that your country is part of your identity and is worthy of respect.

ANSWERS TO CRITICAL THINKING AND READING

1. Answers will differ. Suggested Response: Always serve your country even if it's difficult.
2. Answers will differ. Suggested response: Nolan loved his country but did not deserve any of the benefits of belonging to a country.

Challenge How might Nolan have avoided his punishment? How could he have behaved before Colonel Morgan? Why did Nolan laugh at his sentence? Even after he was sentenced, how might Nolan have saved himself and regained his country?

THINKING AND WRITING

For help with this assignment, students can refer to Lesson 11, "Writing About Theme," in the Handbook of Writing About Literature.

Writing Across the Curriculum You might want to have students research and report on Aaron Burr or the War of 1812. If you do, perhaps inform the social studies department of this assignment. Social studies teachers might provide guidance for students in conducting their research.

GUIDE FOR READING

Flowers for Algernon

Daniel Keyes (1927–), raised in Brooklyn, New York, is an English professor. He has worked at many jobs, including that of photographer, merchant seaman, and editor. His many works of fiction include the novels *The Touch* (1968) and *The Fifth Sally* (1980). Keyes's best-known story, "Flowers for Algernon," won the Hugo Award of the Science Fiction Writers of America in 1959. It was later adapted for the movie *Charly* and the Broadway musical *Charlie and Algernon.*

Point of View and Theme

Theme is the central insight into life communicated by the events in the story. Sometimes we see the events unfold from one character's point of view. It is as though we stand in this character's shoes and see with this character's eyes. In a story that unfolds this way, we come to understand the theme gradually, as we see what this character sees and sometimes even more than what he or she sees.

Look For

As you read "Flowers for Algernon," look for the way in which the theme emerges from the story. How does Charlie's view of the world change as the story progresses? What do you see in the characters and events Charlie encounters that he does not?

Writing

Charlie takes part in an experiment to make him smart. What makes a person smart? Freewrite about the meaning of the word *intelligence.*

Vocabulary

Knowing the following words will help you as you read "Flowers for Algernon."

tangible (tan′ jə bəl) *adj.*: Observable; understandable (p. 213)
specter (spek′ tər) *n.*: A disturbing thought (p. 213)
refute (ri fyo͞ot′) *v.*: Disprove (p. 214)
vacuous (vak′ yo͞o wəs) *adj.*: Empty; shallow (p. 215)
obscure (äb skyo͝or′) *v.*: Hide (p. 217)
convolutions (kän′ və lū′ shəns) *n.*: Uneven ridges on the brain's surface (p. 218)
fissures (fish′ ərs) *n.*: Narrow openings (p. 218)
introspective (in′ trə spek′ tiv) *adj.*: Looking into one's own thoughts and feelings (p. 218)

Focus

More About the Author Daniel Keyes was a teacher of high school English for many years before he became a university professor of English. "Flowers for Algernon" reflects his first-hand knowledge of teaching and learning. Ask students to discuss the relationship between teaching literature and writing it. Would a deep appreciation for literature motivate someone to become a writer?

Literary Focus Although the narrator of "Flowers for Algernon" is the main character, you see events from other characters' points of view as well as Charlie's. In fact, because of Charlie's limitations, the reader understands the events better than does the main character.

Look For Your less advanced students may find it helpful to pinpoint Charlie's levels of progress and decline. Using the progress reports in the story, have students note when Charlie begins to understand events around him, when he surpasses those around him, and when he begins to lose his intelligence.

Writing/Prior Knowledge Have students discuss the different nuances attached to such words as *shrewd, quick,* and *wise.* Then have them complete the freewriting assignment.

Vocabulary These words also may give students some difficulty: *plateau* (p. 209); *conscious, unconscious, psychology* (p. 210); *coattails* (p. 212); *specialization* (p. 213); *calculus, variations, psychoexperimentalist, invariably* (p. 214); *infuriated* (p. 215); *sensational, applicability* (p. 217); *regressed, impaired, glandular, progressive, amnesia, deterioration, syndromes,* and *proportional* (p. 218).

Objectives

1 To use point of view to understand theme
2 To compare and contrast views
3 To write about theme

Support Material

Teaching Portfolio
Teacher Backup, pp. 307–309
Grammar in Action Worksheets, pp. *Understanding First-Person Narration,* pp. 310–311; *Understanding Adverb Clauses,* pp. 312–313; *Understanding First, Second, and Third-Person Voice;* pp. 314–315, *Using Participles and Participial Phrases,* pp. 316–317
Usage and Mechanics Worksheet, p. 318
Vocabulary Check, p. 319
Analyzing Literature Worksheet, *Understanding Point of View and Theme,* p. 320
Language Worksheet, *Understanding Synonyms and Antonyms,* p. 321
Selection Test, pp. 322–323

Flowers for Algernon

Daniel Keyes

progris riport 1—martch 5 1965

Dr. Strauss says I shud rite down what I think and evrey thing that happins to me from now on. I dont know why but he says
1 its importint so they will see if they will use me. I hope they use me. Miss Kinnian says maybe they can make me smart. I want to be smart. My name is Charlie Gordon. I am 37 years old and 2 weeks ago was my brithday. I have nuthing more to rite now so I will close for today.

progris riport 2—martch 6

I had a test today. I think I faled it. and I think that maybe now they wont use me. What happind is a nice young man was in the room and he had some white cards with ink spillled all over them. He sed Charlie what do you see on this card. I was very skared even tho I had my rabits foot in my pockit because when I was a kid I always faled tests in school and I spillled ink to.

I told him I saw a inkblot. He said yes and it made me feel good. I thot that was all but when I got up to go he stopped me. He said now sit down Charlie we are not thru yet. Then I dont remember so good but he wantid me to say what was in the ink. I dint
2 see nuthing in the ink but he said there was picturs there other pepul saw some picturs. I coudnt see any picturs. I reely tryed to see. I held the card close up and then far away. Then I said if I had my glases I coud see better I usally only ware my glases in the movies or TV but I said they are in the closit in the hall. I got them. Then I said let me see that card agen I bet Ill find it now.

I tryed hard but I still coudnt find the picturs I only saw the ink. I told him maybe I need new glases. He rote somthing down on a paper and I got skared of faling the test. I told him it was a very nice inkblot with littel points all around the eges. He looked very sad so that wasnt it. I said please let me try agen. Ill get it in a few minits becaus Im not so fast somtimes. Im a slow reeder too in Miss Kinnians class for slow 3
adults but I'm trying very hard.

He gave me a chance with another card that had 2 kinds of ink spilled on it red and blue.

He was very nice and talked slow like Miss Kinnian does and he explaned it to me that it was a *raw shok.*[1] He said pepul see things in the ink. I said show me where. He said think. I told him I think a inkblot but that wasnt rite eather. He said what does it remind you—pretend somthing. I closd my eyes for a long time to pretend. I told him I pretned a fowntan pen with ink leeking all over a table cloth. Then he got up and went out.

I dont think I passd the *raw shok* test.

Edited for this edition.

1. raw shok: A misspelling of Rorschach (rôr′ shäk) test, a psychological test involving inkblots that the subject describes.

Presentation

Motivation/Prior Knowledge Have students imagine that they have the opportunity to participate in an experiment to develop a very special talent. The only drawback is that they will probably have the special ability for a limited period of time. Then they will go back to the way they were. Would they want to participate in such an experiment? Would it be too painful to go back to normal? Would having the ability even for a short time make the experience worthwhile?

Thematic Idea Another selection that deals with technology is *Let Me Hear You Whisper* (page 277), and with the theme of need for acceptance is *The Diary of Anne Frank* (page 303).

Purpose-Setting Question How do Charlie's perceptions change in this story?

1 **Critical Thinking and Reading** What impression do you immediately form of Charlie Gordon? If he had not stated his age, how old would you have thought he was?

2 **Discussion** What is Charlie supposed to do in this test? How is he misinterpreting it? Is this a test that can be passed or failed?

3 **Discussion** How can you tell that Charlie tries very hard to understand things?

4 Reading Strategy What do you think Charlie is referring to here? Predict what will happen to Charlie.

5 Discussion What are the doctors asking Charlie to do now?

6 Discussion Are mice that smart? What do you suspect about Algernon?

progris report 3—martch 7

Dr Strauss and Dr Nemur say it dont matter about the inkblots. I told them I dint spill the ink on the cards and I coudnt see anything in the ink. They said that maybe they will still use me. I said Miss Kinnian never gave me tests like that one only spelling and reading. They said Miss Kinnian told that I was her bestist pupil in the adult nite scool becaus I tryed the hardist and I reely wantid to lern. They said how come you went to the adult nite scool all by your-
4 self Charlie. How did you find it. I said I askd pepul and sumbody told me where I shud go to lern to read and spell good. They said why did you want to. I told them becaus all my life I wantid to be smart and not dumb. But its very hard to be smart. They said you know it will probly be tempirery. I said yes. Miss Kinnian told me. I dont care if it herts.

Later I had more crazy tests today. The nice lady who gave it me told me the name and I asked her how do you spellit so I can rite it in my progris riport. THEMATIC APPERCEPTION TEST.[2] I dont know the frist 2 words but I know what *test* means. You got to pass it or you get bad marks. This test lookd easy becaus I coud see the picturs. Only this time she dint want me to tell her the picturs. That mixd me up. I said the man yesterday said I shoud tell him what I saw in the ink she said that dont make no difrence. She said make up storys about the pepul in the picturs.

I told her how can you tell storys about pepul you never met. I said why shud I make up lies. I never tell lies any more becaus I always get caut.

She told me this test and the other one the raw-shok was for getting personalty. I laffed so hard. I said how can you get that thing from inkblots and fotos. She got sore and put her picturs away. I dont care. It was sily. I gess I faled that test too.

Later some men in white coats took me to a difernt part of the hospitil and gave me a game to play. It was like a race with a white mouse. They called the mouse Algernon. Algernon was in a box with a lot of twists and turns like all kinds of walls and they gave me a pencil and a paper with lines and lots of boxes. On one side it said START and on the other end it said FINISH. They said it was *amazed*[3] and that Algernon and me had the same *amazed* to do. I dint see how we
could have the same *amazed* if Algernon 5
had a box and I had a paper but I dint say nothing. Anyway there wasnt time because the race started.

One of the men had a watch he was trying to hide so I woudnt see it so I tryed not to look and that made me nervus.

Anyway that test made me feel worser than all the others because they did it over 10 times with difernt *amazeds* and Algernon won every time. I dint know that mice 6
were so smart. Maybe thats because Algernon is a white mouse. Maybe white mice are smarter than other mice.

progris riport 4—Mar 8

Their going to use me! Im so exited I can hardly write. Dr Nemur and Dr Strauss had a argament about it first. Dr Nemur was in the office when Dr Strauss brot me in. Dr Nemur was worryed about using me but Dr Strauss told him Miss Kinnian rekem-

---

2. THEMATIC (*th*ē mat′ ik) **APPERCEPTION** (ap′ ər sep′ shən) **TEST:** A personality test in which the subject makes up stories about a series of pictures.

3. amazed: A maze, or confusing series of paths. Often, the intelligence of animals is assessed by how fast they go through a maze.

mended me the best from all the pepul who she was teaching. I like Miss Kinnian becaus shes a very smart teacher. And she said Charlie your going to have a second chance. If you volenteer for this experament you mite get smart. They dont know if it will be perminint but theirs a chance. Thats why I said ok even when I was scared because she said it was an operashun. She said dont be scared Charlie you done so much with so little I think you deserv it most of all.

So I got scaird when Dr Nemur and Dr Strauss argud about it. Dr Strauss said I had
something that was very good. He said I
had a good *motor-vation.*[4] I never even
knew I had that. I felt proud when he said 8
that not every body with an *eye-q*[5] of 68
had that thing. I dont know what it is or
where I got it but he said Algernon had it
too. Algernons *motor-vation* is the cheese
they put in his box. But it cant be that 9
because I didnt eat any cheese this week.

4. motor-vation: Motivation, or desire to work hard and achieve a goal.
5. eye-q: I.Q., intelligence quotient, a way of measuring human intelligence.

7 Critical Thinking and Reading How does Miss Kinnian feel about Charlie? Why did she recommend him for this experiment?

8 Enrichment Intelligence quotient, or IQ, is based on a comparison of a person's score on an intelligence test with the scores of others on the same test. Average adult IQ ranges from 90 to 110.

9 Critical Thinking and Reading What is Charlie's motivation?

10 **Critical Thinking and Reading** Why are the doctors arguing? Why does Dr. Nemur think Charlie will be a good subject for the experiment? What is their goal?

11 **Discussion** Is it possible to make a conscious effort to think? How is Charlie's way of thinking different from the average person's?

Then he told Dr Nemur something I dint understand so while they were talking I wrote down some of the words.

He said Dr Nemur I know Charlie is not what you had in mind as the first of your new brede of intelek** (coudnt get the word) superman. But most people of his low ment** are host** and uncoop** they are usualy dull apath** and hard to reach. He has a good natcher hes intristed and eager to please.

10 Dr Nemur said remember he will be the first human beeng ever to have his intelijence trippled by surgicle meens.

Dr Strauss said exakly. Look at how well hes lerned to read and write for his low mentel age its as grate an acheve** as you and I lerning einstines therey of **vity without help. That shows the intenss motorvation. Its comparat** a tremen** achev** I say we use Charlie.

I dint get all the words and they were talking to fast but it sounded like Dr Strauss was on my side and like the other one wasnt.

Then Dr Nemur nodded he said all right maybe your right. We will use Charlie. When he said that I got so exited I jumped up and shook his hand for being so good to me. I told him thank you doc you wont be sorry for giving me a second chance. And I mean it like I told him. After the operashun Im gonna try to be smart. Im gonna try awful hard.

progris ript 5—Mar 10

Im skared. Lots of people who work here and the nurses and the people who gave me the tests came to bring me candy and wish me luck. I hope I have luck. I got my rabits foot and my lucky penny and my horse shoe. Only a black cat crossed me when I was comming to the hospitil. Dr Strauss says dont be supersitis Charlie this is sience. Anyway Im keeping my rabits foot with me.

I asked Dr Strauss if Ill beat Algernon in the race after the operashun and he said maybe. If the operashun works Ill show that mouse I can be as smart as he is. Maybe smarter. Then Ill be abel to read better and spell the words good and know lots of things and be like other people. I want to be smart like other people. If it works perminint they will make everybody smart all over the wurld.

They dint give me anything to eat this morning. I dont know what that eating has to do with getting smart. Im very hungry and Dr Nemur took away my box of candy. That Dr Nemur is a grouch. Dr Strauss says I can have it back after the operashun. You cant eat befor a operashun . . .

Progress Report 6—Mar 15

The operashun dint hurt. He did it while I was sleeping. They took off the bandijis from my eyes and my head today so I can make a PROGRESS REPORT. Dr Nemur who looked at some of my other ones says I spell PROGRESS wrong and he told me how to spell it and REPORT too. I got to try and remember that.

I have a very bad memary for spelling. Dr Strauss says its ok to tell about all the things that happin to me but he says I shoud tell more about what I feel and what I think. When I told him I dont know how to think he said try. All the time when the bandijis were on my eyes I tryed to think. Nothing happened. I dont know what to think about. Maybe if I ask him he will tell me how I can think now that Im suppose 1
to get smart. What do smart people think about. Fancy things I suppose. I wish I knew some fancy things alredy.

Progress Report 7—mar 19

Nothing is happining. I had lots of tests and different kinds of races with Algernon. I

Grammar in Action

In **first-person narration,** the story is told from the narrator's point of view ("I"). As a character in the story, the narrator relates the events of the story from his or her unique perspective. We learn about the events of the story as well as other characters in the story through the narrator's impressions. Therefore, in some cases, the truth or accuracy of the information may be questionable. When reading a story written in the first-person point of view, it is always a good idea to think about the reliability of the narrator.

In first person narration, we are likely to learn the most about the narrator and his or her innermost thoughts and feelings, as is certainly the case with Charlie Gordon in "Flowers for Algernon." Charlie Gordon's narration reveals essential information about his character, as well as the other characters. His unique spelling and punctuation alert the reader to his mental handicap, while his observations indicate the keenly perceptive quality of his character. Consider the following excerpt:

> "Sometimes somebody will say hey look at Joe or Frank or George he really pulled a Charlie Gordon. I don't know why they say that but they always laff."

With its lack of punctuation and misspelling, this passage and hate that mouse. He always beats me. Dr Strauss said I got to play those games. And he said some time I got to take those tests over again. Thse inkblots are stupid. And those pictures are stupid too. I like to draw a picture of a man and a woman but I wont make up lies about people.

12 I got a headache from trying to think so much. I thot Dr Strauss was my frend but he dont help me. He dont tell me what to think or when Ill get smart. Miss Kinnian dint come to see me. I think writing these progress reports are stupid too.

Progress Report 8—Mar 23

Im going back to work at the factory. They said it was better I shud go back to work but I cant tell anyone what the operashun was for and I have to come to the hospitil for an hour evry night after work. They are gonna pay me mony every month for lerning to be smart.

Im glad Im going back to work because I miss my job and all my frends and all the fun we have there.

Dr Strauss says I shud keep writing things down but I dont have to do it every day just when I think of something or something speshul happins. He says dont get discoridged because it takes time and it happins slow. He says it took a long time with Algernon before he got 3 times smarter then he was before. Thats why Algernon beats me all the time because he had that operashun too. That makes me feel better. I coud probly do that *amazed* faster than a reglar mouse. Maybe some day Ill beat Algernon. Boy that would be something. So far Algernon looks like he mite be smart perminent.

Mar 25 (I dont have to write PROGRESS REPORT on top any more just when I hand it in once a week for Dr Nemur to read. I just have to put the date on. That saves time)

We had a lot of fun at the factery today. Joe Carp said hey look where Charlie had his operashun what did they do Charlie put some brains in. I was going to tell him but I remembered Dr Strauss said no. Then Frank Reilly said what did you do Charlie forget your key and open your door the hard way. That made me laff. Their really my friends and they like me. 13

Sometimes somebody will say hey look at Joe or Frank or George he really pulled a Charlie Gordon. I dont know why they say that but they always laff. This morning Amos Borg who is the 4 man at Donnegans used my name when he shouted at Ernie the office boy. Ernie lost a packige. He said Ernie what are you trying to be a Charlie Gordon. I dont understand why he said that. I never lost any packiges.

Mar 28 Dr Straus came to my room tonight to see why I dint come in like I was suppose to. I told him I dont like to race with Algernon any more. He said I dont have to for a while but I shud come in. He had a present for me only it wasnt a present but just for lend. I thot it was a little television but it wasnt. He said I got to turn it on when I go to sleep. I said your kidding why shud I turn it on when Im going to sleep. Who ever herd of a thing like that. But he said if I want to get smart I got to do what he says. I told him I dint think I was going to get smart and he put his hand on my sholder and said Charlie you dont know it yet but your getting smarter all the time. You wont notice for a while. I think he was just being nice to make me feel good because I dont look any smarter.

Oh yes I almost forgot. I asked him when I can go back to the class at Miss Kinnians school. He said I wont go their. He said that soon Miss Kinnian will come to the hospitil

12 **Discussion** Do you see any evidence of a change in Charlie yet?

13 **Discussion** Are Joe Carp and Frank Reilly really Charlie's friends? Why does Charlie think they are?

others like it tells us that Charlie has a low level of intelligence, but at the same time, we learn that he is observant and sensitive. Narration from another character's point of view might not have revealed Charlie's awareness that he is being ridiculed.

Student Activity 1. Choose another passage from the story in which first-person narration reveals important information to the reader.

Student Activity 2. Using first-person narration, write a few short paragraphs about an event that would not have the same meaning if it were narrated by someone other than you.

14 Discussion Notice how Charlie spells "don't" two different ways here. What do you think is happening to him?

15 Literary Focus Although Charlie is narrating this story from his point of view, what do you know about Joe Carp and Frank Reilly that Charlie doesn't know? Do you think it's better that Charlie doesn't know?

to start and teach me speshul. I was mad at her for not comming to see me when I got the operashun but I like her so maybe we will be frends again.

Mar 29 That crazy TV kept me up all night. How can I sleep with something yelling crazy things all night in my ears. And the nutty pictures. Wow. I dont know what it says when Im up so how am I going to know when Im sleeping.

Dr Strauss says its ok. He says my brains are lerning when I sleep and that will help me when Miss Kinnian starts my lessons in the hospitl only I found out it isnt a hospitil its a labatory. I think its all crazy. If you can get smart when your sleeping why do people go to school. That thing I dont think will work. I use to watch the late show and the late late show on TV all the time and it never made me smart. Maybe you have to sleep while you watch it.

PROGRESS REPORT 9—April 3

14 Dr Strauss showed me how to keep the TV turned low so now I can sleep. I don't hear a thing. And I still dont understand what it says. A few times I play it over in the morning to find out what I lerned when I was sleeping and I dont think so. Miss Kinnian says Maybe its another langwidge or something. But most times it sounds american. It talks so fast faster then even Miss Gold who was my teacher in 6 grade and I remember she talked so fast I coudnt understand her.

I told Dr Strauss what good is it to get smart in my sleep. I want to be smart when Im awake. He says its the same thing and I have two minds. Theres the *subconscious* and the *conscious* (thats how you spell it). And one dont tell the other one what its doing. They dont even talk to each other. Thats why I dream. And boy have I been having crazy dreams. Wow. Ever since that night TV. The late late late late late show.

I forgot to ask him if it was only me or if everybody had those two minds.

(I just looked up the word in the dictionary Dr Strauss gave me. The word is *subconscious. adj. Of the nature of mental operations yet not present in consciousness; as, subconscious conflict of desires.)* There's more but I still dont know what it means. This isnt a very good dictionary for dumb people like me.

Anyway the headache is from the party. My frends from the factery Joe Carp and Frank Reilly invited me to go with them to Muggsys Saloon for some drinks. I dont like to drink but they said we will have lots of fun. I had a good time.

Joe Carp said I shoud show the girls how I mop out the toilet in the factory and he got me a mop. I showed them and everyone laffed when I told that Mr Donnegan said I was the best janiter he ever had because I like my job and do it good and never come late or miss a day except for my operashun.

I said Miss Kinnian always said Charlie be proud of your job because you do it good.

Everybody laffed and we had a good time and they gave me lots of drinks and Joe said Charlie is a card when hes potted. I dont know what that means but everybody likes me and we have fun. I cant wait to be smart like my best frends Joe Carp and Frank Reilly. 1

I dont remember how the party was over but I think I went out to buy a newspaper and coffe for Joe and Frank and when I came back there was no one their. I looked for them all over till late. Then I dont remember so good but I think I got sleepy or sick. A nice cop brot me back home. Thats what my landlady Mrs Flynn says.

But I got a headache and a big lump on my head and black and blue all over. I think maybe I fell. Anyway I got a bad headache and Im sick and hurt all over. I dont think Ill drink anymore.

April 6 I beat Algernon! I dint even know I beat him until Burt the tester told me. Then the second time I lost because I got
16 so exited I fell off the chair before I finished. But after that I beat him 8 more times. I must be getting smart to beat a smart mouse like Algernon. But I dont *feel* smarter.

I wanted to race Algernon some more but Burt said thats enough for one day. They let me hold him for a minit. Hes not so bad. Hes soft like a ball of cotton. He blinks and when he opens his eyes their black and pink on the eges.

I said can I feed him because I felt bad to beat him and I wanted to be nice and make frends. Burt said no Algernon is a very specshul mouse with an operashun like mine, and he was the first of all the animals to stay smart so long. He told me Algernon is so smart that every day he has to solve a test to get his food. Its a thing like a lock on a door that changes every time Algernon goes in to eat so he has to lern something new to get his food. That made me sad because if he coudnt lern he woud be hungry.

I dont think its right to make you pass a test to eat. How woud Dr Nemur like it to have to pass a test every time he wants to
7 eat. I think Ill be frends with Algernon.

April 9 Tonight after work Miss Kinnian was at the laboratory. She looked like she was glad to see me but scared. I told her dont worry Miss Kinnian Im not smart yet and she laffed. She said I have confidence in you Charlie the way you struggled so hard to read and right better than all the others. At werst you will have it for a littel wile and
your doing something for sience. 18

We are reading a very hard book. I never read such a hard book before. Its called *Robinson Crusoe*[6] about a man who gets merooned on a dessert Iland. Hes smart and figers out all kinds of things so he can have a house and food and hes a good swimmer. Only I feel sorry because hes all alone and has no frends. But I think their must be somebody else on the iland because theres a
picture with his funny umbrella looking at 19
footprints. I hope he gets a frend and not be lonly.

April 10 Miss Kinnian teaches me to spell better. She says look at a word and close your eyes and say it over and over until you remember. I have lots of truble with *through* that you say *threw* and *enough* and *tough* that you dont say *enew* and *tew*. You got to say *enuff* and *tuff*. Thats how I use to write it before I started to get smart. Im confused but Miss Kinnian says theres no reason in spelling.

Apr 14 Finished Robinson Crusoe. I want to find out more about what happens to him but Miss Kinnian says thats all there is. *Why*

Apr 15 Miss Kinnian says Im lerning fast. She read some of the Progress Reports and she looked at me kind of funny. She says Im a fine person and Ill show them all. I asked her why. She said never mind but I
shoudnt feel bad if I find out that everybody 20
isnt nice like I think. She said for a person who god gave so little to you done more then

6. *Robinson Crusoe* (kroo͞′ sō): Novel written in 1719 by Daniel Defoe, a British author.

16 Discussion Does it appear that the operation was successful?

17 Discussion Why does Charlie decide to be friends with Algernon? What do they have in common?

18 Critical Thinking and Reading What is Charlie doing for science?

19 Discussion How significant is the conclusion that Charlie draws from looking at the picture of Robinson Crusoe? Compare this conclusion with some of Charlie's earlier conclusions? How are they different?

20 Discussion Why is Miss Kinnian worried about Charlie?

21 Discussion What do you notice about Charlie's writing after he learns about the comma?

a lot of people with brains they never even used. I said all my frends are smart people but there good. They like me and they never did anything that wasnt nice. Then she got something in her eye and she had to run out to the ladys room.

21 *Apr 16* Today, I lerned, the *comma*, this is a comma (,) a period, with a tail, Miss Kinnian, says its importent, because, it makes writing, better, she said, sombeody, coud lose, a lot of money, if a comma, isnt, in the, right place, I dont have, any money, and I dont see, how a comma, keeps you, from losing it,

But she says, everybody, uses commas, so Ill use, them too,

Apr 17 I used the comma wrong. Its punctuation. Miss Kinnian told me to look up long words in the dictionary to lern to spell them. I said whats the difference if you can read it anyway. She said its part of your education so now on Ill look up all the words Im not sure how to spell. It takes a long time to write that way but I think Im remember-

22 ing. I only have to look up once and after that I get it right. Anyway thats how come I got the word *punctuation* right. (Its that way in the dictionary). Miss Kinnian says a period is punctuation too, and there are lots of other marks to lern. I told her I thot all the periods had to have tails but she said no.

You got to mix them up, she showed? me'' how. to mix! them(up,. and now; I can! mix up all kinds'' of punctuation, in! my writing? There, are lots! of rules? to lern; but Im gettin'g them in my head.

One thing I? like about, Dear Miss Kinnian: (thats the way it goes in a business letter if I ever go into business) is she, always gives me' a reason'' when—I ask. She's a gen'ius! I wish! I cou'd be smart'' like, her;

(Punctuation, is; fun!)

April 18 What a dope I am! I didn't even understand what she was talking about. I read the grammar book last night
23 and it explanes the whole thing. Then I saw it was the same way as Miss Kinnian was trying to tell me, but I didn't get it. I got up in the middle of the night, and the whole thing straightened out in my mind.

Miss Kinnian said that the TV working in my sleep helped out. She said I reached a plateau. Thats like the flat top of a hill.

After I figgered out how punctuation worked, I read over all my old Progress Reports from the beginning. Boy, did I have crazy spelling and punctuation! I told Miss Kinnian I ought to go over the pages and fix all the mistakes but she said, "No, Charlie, Dr. Nemur wants them just as they are. That's why he let you keep them after they were photostated, to see your own progress. You're coming along fast, Charlie."

That made me feel good. After the lesson I went down and played with Algernon. We don't race any more.

April 20 I feel sick inside. Not sick like for a doctor, but inside my chest it feels empty like getting punched and a heartburn at the same time.

I wasn't going to write about it, but I guess I got to, because its important. Today was the first time I ever stayed home from work.

Last night Joe Carp and Frank Reilly invited me to a party. There were lots of girls and some men from the factory. I remembered how sick I got last time I drank too much, so I told Joe I didn't want anything to drink. He gave me a plain coke instead. It tasted funny, but I thought it was just a bad taste in my mouth.

We had a lot of fun for a while. Joe said I should dance with Ellen and she would teach me the steps. I fell a few times and I couldn't understand why because no one else was dancing besides Ellen and me. And all the time I was tripping because somebody's foot was always sticking out.

Then when I got up I saw the look on Joe's face and it gave me a funny feeling in my stomack. "He's a scream," one of the girls said. Everybody was laughing.

Frank said, "I ain't laughed so much since we sent him off for the newspaper that night at Muggsy's and ditched him."

"Look at him. His face is red."

"He's blushing. Charlie is blushing."

"Hey, Ellen, what'd you do to Charlie? I never saw him act like that before."

I didn't know what to do or where to turn. Everyone was looking at me and laughing and I felt naked. I wanted to hide myself. I ran out into the street and I threw up. Then I walked home. It's a funny thing I
never knew that Joe and Frank and the 24
others liked to have me around all the time to make fun of me.

Now I know what it means when they say "to pull a Charlie Gordon."

I'm ashamed.

22 **Discussion** What are some of the signs that Charlie is getting smarter?

23 **Critical Thinking and Reading** How can you tell that Charlie is not learning in traditional ways?

24 **Discussion** What does Charlie realize here? Why is he ashamed?

25 **Critical Thinking and Reading** What insights does Charlie's analysis give you on the physically or mentally handicapped?

26 **Discussion** Has Charlie's point of view matured yet? How can you tell?

27 **Clarification** An IQ of 200 would be very high. It would indicate that a person was very intelligent.

PROGRESS REPORT 11

April 21 Still didn't go into the factory. I told Mrs. Flynn my landlady to call and tell Mr. Donnegan I was sick. Mrs. Flynn looks at me very funny lately like she's scared of me.

I think it's a good thing about finding out how everybody laughs at me. I thought about it a lot. It's because I'm so dumb and I don't even know when I'm doing something dumb. People think it's funny when a dumb
25 person can't do things the same way they can.

Anyway, now I know I'm getting smarter every day. I know punctuation and I can spell good. I like to look up all the hard words in the dictionary and I remember them. I'm reading a lot now, and Miss Kinnian says I read very fast. Sometimes I even understand what I'm reading about, and it stays in my mind. There are times when I can close my eyes and think of a page and it all comes back like a picture.

Besides history, geography and arithmetic, Miss Kinnian said I should start to learn a few foreign languages. Dr. Strauss gave me some more tapes to play while I sleep. I still don't understand how that conscious and unconscious mind works, but Dr. Strauss says not to worry yet. He asked me to promise that when I start learning college subjects next week I wouldn't read any books on psychology—that is, until he gives me permission.

I feel a lot better today, but I guess I'm still a little angry that all the time people were laughing and making fun of me because I wasn't so smart. When I become intelligent like Dr. Strauss says, with three
26 times my I.Q. of 68, then maybe I'll be like everyone else and people will like me and be friendly.

I'm not sure what an *I.Q.* is. Dr. Nemur said it was something that measured how intelligent you were—like a scale in the drugstore weighs pounds. But Dr. Strauss had a big arguement with him and said an I.Q. didn't weigh intelligence at all. He said an I.Q. showed how much intelligence you could get, like the numbers on the outside of a measuring cup. You still had to fill the cup up with stuff.

Then when I asked Burt, who gives me my intelligence tests and works with Algernon, he said that both of them were wrong (only I had to promise not to tell them he said so). Burt says that the I.Q. measures a lot of different things including some of the things you learned already, and it really isn't any good at all.

So I still don't know what I.Q. is except
that mine is going to be over 200 soon. I 2
didn't want to say anything, but I don't see how if they don't know *what* it is, or *where* it is—I don't see how they know *how much* of it you've got.

Dr. Nemur says I have to take a *Rorshach Test* tomorrow. I wonder what *that* is.

April 22 I found out what a *Rorshach* is. It's the test I took before the operation —the one with the inkblots on the pieces of cardboard. The man who gave me the test was the same one.

I was scared to death of those inkblots. I knew he was going to ask me to find the pictures and I knew I wouldn't be able to. I was thinking to myself, if only there was some way of knowing what kind of pictures were hidden there. Maybe there weren't any pictures at all. Maybe it was just a trick to see if I was dumb enough too look for something that wasn't there. Just thinking about that made me sore at him.

"All right, Charlie," he said, "you've seen these cards before, remember?"

"Of course I remember."

The way I said it, he knew I was angry,

Grammar in Action

When writers want to express one idea in relation to another within one sentence, they frequently use **adverb clauses.** An adverb clause begins with a subordinating conjunction (words like *after, although, as, because, since,* and others) and contains a subject and a verb. It expresses an idea that is less important than the idea expressed in the main clause. Adverb clauses cannot stand alone as a sentence.

The following sentences contain adverb clauses:

People think it's funny *when a dumb person can't do things the same way they can.*

Dr. Strauss gave me some more tapes to play *while I sleep.*

When I become intelligent like Dr. Strauss says, with three times my I.Q. of 68, then maybe I'll be like everyone else and people will like me and be friendly.

While he was making his notes, I peeked out of the corner of my eye to read it.

and he looked surprised. "Yes, of course. Now I want you to look at this one. What might this be? What do you see on this card? People see all sorts of things in these inkblots. Tell me what it might be for you—what it makes you think of."

I was shocked. That wasn't what I had expected him to say at all. "You mean there are no pictures hidden in those inkblots?"

He frowned and took off his glasses. "What?"

"Pictures. Hidden in the inkblots. Last time you told me that everyone could see them and you wanted me to find them too."

28 He explained to me that the last time he had used almost the exact same words he was using now. I didn't believe it, and I still have the suspicion that he misled me at the time just for the fun of it. Unless—I don't know any more—could I have been *that* feeble-minded?

We went through the cards slowly. One of them looked like a pair of bats tugging at some thing. Another one looked like two men fencing with swords. I imagined all sorts of things. I guess I got carried away. But I didn't trust him any more, and I kept turning them around and even looking on the back to see if there was anything there I was supposed to catch. While he was making his notes, I peeked out of the corner of my eye to read it. But it was all in code that looked like this:

WF + A DdF-Ad orig. WF-A
SF + obj

The test still doesn't make sense to me. It seems to me that anyone could make up lies about things that they didn't really see. How could he know I wasn't making a fool of him by mentioning things that I didn't really imagine? Maybe I'll understand it when Dr. Strauss lets me read up on psychology.

April 25 I figured out a new way to line up the machines in the factory, and Mr. Donnegan says it will save him ten thousand dollars a year in labor and increased production. He gave me a $25 bonus.

I wanted to take Joe Carp and Frank Reilly out to lunch to celebrate, but Joe said he had to buy some things for his wife, and Frank said he was meeting his cousin for lunch. I guess it'll take a little time for them to get used to the changes in me. Everybody seems to be frightened of me. When I 29
went over to Amos Borg and tapped him on the shoulder, he jumped up in the air.

People don't talk to me much any more or kid around the way they used to. It makes the job kind of lonely.

April 27 I got up the nerve today to ask Miss Kinnian to have dinner with me tomorrow night to celebrate my bonus.

At first she wasn't sure it was right, but I asked Dr. Strauss and he said it was okay. Dr. Strauss and Dr. Nemur don't seem to be getting along so well. They're arguing all the time. This evening when I came in to ask Dr. Strauss about having dinner with Miss Kinnian, I heard them shouting. Dr. Nemur was saying that it was *his* experiment and *his* research, and Dr. Strauss was shouting back that he contributed just as much, because he found me through Miss Kinnian and he performed the operation. Dr. Strauss said that someday thousands of neurosurgeons[7] might be using his technique all over the world.

Dr. Nemur wanted to publish the results of the experiment at the end of this month. Dr. Strauss wanted to wait a while longer to be sure. Dr. Strauss said that Dr. Nemur

---

7. neurosurgeons (noor' ō sʉr' jənz) *n.*: Doctors who operate on the nervous system, including the brain and spine.

28 **Discussion** How is Charlie's current performance on the Rorschach test different from his first?

29 **Discussion** As Charlie becomes more intelligent, how do his co-workers respond to him?

Notice the punctuation of adverb clauses in the examples. If the adverb clause is at the end of the sentence, usually there is no comma before it. If the adverb clause is at the beginning of the sentence, it must be followed by a comma.

Student Activity 1. Look at each of the sample sentences. What two ideas are expressed in each sentence? Which idea is more important?

Student Activity 2. Write four of your own sentences in which you include an adverb clause. Two of the sentences should have the adverb clause before the main clause, and two should have the adverb clause after the main clause.

30 Discussion What makes Charlie's speculation about the doctors so amazing?

31 Critical Thinking and Reading What is it that Charlie doesn't want to think of?

was more interested in the Chair[8] of Psychology at Princeton than he was in the experiment. Dr. Nemur said that Dr. Strauss was nothing but an opportunist who was trying to ride to glory on *his* coattails.

When I left afterwards, I found myself
trembling. I don't know why for sure, but it
was as if I'd seen both men clearly for the
first time. I remember hearing Burt say that
Dr. Nemur had a shrew of a wife who was
30 pushing him all the time to get things published so that he could become famous.
Burt said that the dream of her life was to
have a big shot husband.

Was Dr. Strauss really trying to ride on his coattails?

April 28 I don't understand why I never noticed how beautiful Miss Kinnian really is. She has brown eyes and feathery brown hair that comes to the top of her neck. She's only thirty-four! I think from the beginning I had the feeling that she was an unreachable genius—and very, very old. Now, every time I see her she grows younger and more lovely.

We had dinner and a long talk. When she said that I was coming along so fast that soon I'd be leaving her behind, I laughed.

"It's true, Charlie. You're already a better reader than I am. You can read a whole page at a glance while I can take in only a few lines at a time. And you remember every single thing you read. I'm lucky if I can recall the main thoughts and the general meaning."

"I don't feel intelligent. There are so many things I don't understand."

She took out a cigarette and I lit it for her.

"You've got to be a *little* patient. You're accomplishing in days and weeks what it takes normal people to do in half a lifetime. That's what makes it so amazing. You're like a giant sponge now, soaking things in. Facts, figures, general knowledge. And soon you'll begin to connect them, too. You'll see how the different branches of learning are related. There are many levels, Charlie, like steps on a giant ladder that take you up higher and higher to see more and more of the world around you.

"I can see only a little bit of that, Charlie, and I won't go much higher than I am now, but you'll keep climbing up and up, and see more and more, and each step will open new worlds that you never even knew existed." She frowned. "I hope . . . I just hope to God—"

"What?"

"Never mind, Charles. I just hope I wasn't wrong to advise you to go into this in the first place."

I laughed. "How could that be? It worked, didn't it? Even Algernon is still smart."

We sat there silently for a while and I knew what she was thinking about as she watched me toying with the chain of my rabbit's foot and my keys. I didn't want to think of that possibility any more than elderly people want to think of death. I *knew* that this was only the beginning. I knew what she meant about levels because I'd seen some of them already. The thought of leaving her behind made me sad.

I'm in love with Miss Kinnian.

PROGRESS REPORT 12

April 30 I've quit my job with Donnegan's Plastic Box Company. Mr. Donnegan insisted that it would be better for all concerned if I left. What did I do to make them hate me so?

The first I knew of it was when Mr. Donnegan showed me the petition. Eight hundred and forty names, everyone con-

8. chair: Professorship.

Grammar in Action

Although stories are usually narrated from one point of view consistently, other points of view also provide important insight or commentary. For example, "Flowers for Algernon" is told from the first-person point of view, but in dialogue, **second-person** is also used. Although works of literature are rarely told from the second-person point of view, dialogue frequently uses second-person.

The sentence "I don't understand why I never noticed how beautiful Miss Kinnian really is" is an example of information we can only learn through first-person narration. However, second-person voice ("you") also provides important information from other characters' perspectives. The following excerpt illustrates the second-person point of view:

> "'You've got to be a little patient. You're accomplishing in days and weeks what it takes normal people to do in half a lifetime. That's what makes it so amazing. You're like a giant sponge now, soaking things in."
>
> It is unlikely that Charlie would have made such an observation.

nected with the factory, except Fanny Girden. Scanning the list quickly, I saw at once that hers was the only missing name. All the rest demanded that I be fired.

Joe Carp and Frank Reilly wouldn't talk to me about it. No one else would either, except Fanny. She was one of the few people I'd known who set her mind to something and believed it no matter what the rest of the world proved, said or did—and Fanny did not believe that I should have been fired. She had been against the petition on principle and despite the pressure and threats she'd held out.

"Which don't mean to say," she remarked, "that I don't think there's something mighty strange about you, Charlie. Them changes. I don't know. You used to be a good, dependable, ordinary man—not too bright maybe, but honest. Who knows what
32 you done to yourself to get so smart all of a sudden. Like everybody around here's been saying, Charlie, it's not right."

"But how can you say that, Fanny? What's wrong with a man becoming intelligent and wanting to acquire knowledge and understanding of the world around him?"

She stared down at her work, and I turned to leave. Without looking at me, she said: "It was evil when Eve listened to the snake and ate from the tree of knowledge. It was evil when she saw that she was naked. If not for that none of us would ever have to grow old and sick, and die."

Once again now I have the feeling of shame burning inside me. This intelligence has driven a wedge between me and all the people I once knew and loved. Before, they laughed at me and despised me for my ignorance and dullness; now, they hate me for my knowledge and understanding. What do they want of me?

They've driven me out of the factory. Now I'm more alone than ever before . . .

May 15 Dr. Strauss is very angry at me for not having written any progress reports in two weeks. He's justified because the lab is now paying me a regular salary. I told him I was too busy thinking and reading. When I pointed out that writing was such a slow process that it made me impatient with my poor handwriting, he suggested that I learn 33
to type. It's much easier to write now because I can type nearly seventy-five words a minute. Dr. Strauss continually reminds me of the need to speak and write simply so that people will be able to understand me.

I'll try to review all the things that happened to me during the last two weeks. Algernon and I were presented to the American Psychological Association sitting in convention with the World Psychological Association last Tuesday. We created quite a sensation. Dr. Nemur and Dr. Strauss were proud of us.

I suspect that Dr. Nemur, who is sixty—ten years older than Dr. Strauss—finds it necessary to see tangible results of his work. Undoubtedly the result of pressure by Mrs. Nemur.

Contrary to my earlier impressions of him, I realize that Dr. Nemur is not at all a genius. He has a very good mind, but it struggles under the specter of self-doubt. He wants people to take him for a genius. Therefore, it is important for him to feel that his work is accepted by the world. I believe 34
that Dr. Nemur was afraid of further delay because he worried that someone else might make a discovery along these lines and take the credit from him.

Dr. Strauss on the other hand might be called a genius, although I feel that his areas of knowledge are too limited. He was educated in the tradition of narrow specialization; the broader aspects of background were neglected far more than necessary—even for a neurosurgeon.

32 **Discussion** Why have the people at the factory turned against Charlie?

33 **Discussion** Why hasn't Charlie written any progress reports in two weeks? What is Dr. Strauss's solution?

34 **Critical Thinking and Reading** What do you notice about Charlie's perception of the doctors?

Student Activity 1. After each sentence, tell whether the sentence is in the first or second-person voice:

1. I'm in love with Miss Kinnian.
2. I realize that Dr. Nemur is not at all a genius.
3. You remember everything you read.
4. But how can you say that, Fanny?
5. I've quit my job with Donnegan's plastic box company.

Student Activity 2. Compose a dialogue between Charlie and one of the other characters in the story in which you use first and second-person point of view.

35 **Discussion** Why is this humorous? Is knowing Latin, Greek, and Hebrew a small accomplishment?

36 **Critical Thinking and Reading** What do you think the look on Dr. Strauss's face means?

37 **Critical Thinking and Reading** How is Charlie handling his new intelligence? Is it making him happy? Why or why not?

I was shocked to learn that the only ancient languages he could read were Latin,
35 Greek and Hebrew, and that he knows almost nothing of mathematics beyond the elementary levels of the calculus of variations. When he admitted this to me, I found myself almost annoyed. It was as if he'd hidden this part of himself in order to deceive me, pretending—as do many people I've discovered—to be what he is not. No one I've ever known is what he appears to be on the surface.

Dr. Nemur appears to be uncomfortable around me. Sometimes when I try to talk to him, he just looks at me strangely and turns away. I was angry at first when Dr. Strauss told me I was giving Dr. Nemur an inferiority complex. I thought he was mocking me and I'm oversensitive at being made fun of.

How was I to know that a highly respected psychoexperimentalist like Nemur was unacquainted with Hindustani[9] and Chinese? It's absurd when you consider the work that is being done in India and China today in the very field of his study.

I asked Dr. Strauss how Nemur could refute Rahajamati's attack on his method and results if Nemur couldn't even read them in the first place. That strange look on Dr. Strauss' face can mean only one of two things. Either he doesn't want to tell Nemur
36 what they're saying in India, or else—and this worries me—Dr. Strauss doesn't know either. I must be careful to speak and write clearly and simply so that people won't laugh.

May 18 I am very disturbed. I saw Miss Kinnian last night for the first time in over a week. I tried to avoid all discussions of intellectual concepts and to keep the conversation on a simple, everyday level, but she just stared at me blankly and asked me what I meant about the mathematical variance equivalent in Dorbermann's *Fifth Concerto.*

When I tried to explain she stopped me and laughed. I guess I got angry, but I suspect I'm approaching her on the wrong level. No matter what I try to discuss with her, I am unable to communicate. I must review Vrostadt's equations on *Levels of Semantic
Progression.* I find that I don't communicate 37
with people much any more. Thank God for books and music and things I can think about. I am alone in my apartment at Mrs. Flynn's boarding house most of the time and seldom speak to anyone.

May 20 I would not have noticed the new dishwasher, a boy of about sixteen, at the corner diner where I take my evening meals if not for the incident of the broken dishes.

They crashed to the floor, shattering and sending bits of white china under the tables. The boy stood there, dazed and frightened, holding the empty tray in his hand. The whistles and catcalls from the customers (the cries of "hey, there go the profits!" . . . "*Mazeltov!*" . . . and "well, *he* didn't work here very long . . ." which invariably seems to follow the breaking of glass or dishware in a public restaurant) all seemed to confuse him.

When the owner came to see what the excitement was about, the boy cowered as if he expected to be struck and threw up his arms as if to ward off the blow.

"All right! All right, you dope," shouted the owner, "don't just stand there! Get the broom and sweep that mess up. A broom . . . a broom, you idiot! It's in the kitchen. Sweep up all the pieces."

The boy saw that he was not going to be

9. Hindustani (hin′ do͞o stan′ ē) *n.*: A language of northern India.

Grammar in Action

Skillful writers use participles in order to enhance the meaning of sentences. **Participles** are verb forms used as adjectives to describe a noun or pronoun. Present participles end in *-ing;* past participles usually end in *-ed* (irregular verbs form their past participle in various ways: *-t, -en* among others).

Participles along with their own modifiers and complements are called **participial phrases** and can also be used to describe nouns and pronouns in sentences.

Note the use of participles and participial phrases in the following sentences from "Flowers for Algernon":

They crashed to the floor, *shattering and sending bits of white china under the tables.* The boy stood there, *dazed* and *frightened, holding the empty tray in his hand.*

His *frightened* expression disappeared and he smiled and hummed as he came back with the broom to sweep the floor.

As his vacant eyes moved across the crowd of *amused* onlookers, he slowly mirrored their smiles . . .

punished. His frightened expression disappeared and he smiled and hummed as he came back with the broom to sweep the floor. A few of the rowdier customers kept up the remarks, amusing themselves at his expense.

"Here, sonny, over here there's a nice piece behind you . . ."

"C'mon, do it again . . ."

"He's not so dumb. It's easier to break 'em than to wash 'em . . ."

As his vacant eyes moved across the crowd of amused onlookers, he slowly mirrored their smiles and finally broke into an uncertain grin at the joke which he obviously did not understand.

I felt sick inside as I looked at his dull, vacuous smile, the wide, bright eyes of a child, uncertain but eager to please. They were laughing at him because he was mentally retarded.

And I had been laughing at him too.

38 Suddenly, I was furious at myself and all those who were smirking at him. I jumped up and shouted, "Shut up! Leave him alone! It's not his fault he can't understand! He can't help what he is! But . . . he's still a human being!"

The room grew silent. I cursed myself for losing control and creating a scene. I tried not to look at the boy as I paid my check and walked out without touching my food. I felt ashamed for both of us.

39 How strange it is that people of honest feelings and sensibility, who would not take advantage of a man born without arms or legs or eyes—how such people think nothing of abusing a man born with low intelligence. It infuriated me to think that not too long ago I, like this boy, had foolishly played the clown.

And I had almost forgotten.

I'd hidden the picture of the old Charlie Gordon from myself because now that I was intelligent it was something that had to be pushed out of my mind. But today in looking at that boy, for the first time I saw what I had been. *I was just like him!*

Only a short time ago, I learned that people laughed at me. Now I can see that unknowingly I joined with them in laughing at myself. That hurts most of all.

I have often reread my progress reports and seen the illiteracy, the childish naïveté,[10] the mind of low intelligence peering from a dark room, through the keyhole, at the dazzling light outside. I see that even in my dullness I knew that I was inferior, and that other people had something I lacked— 40 something denied me. In my mental blindness, I thought that it was somehow connected with the ability to read and write, and I was sure that if I could get those skills I would automatically have intelligence too.

Even a feeble-minded man wants to be like other men.

A child may not know how to feed itself, or what to eat, yet it knows of hunger.

This then is what I was like. I never knew. Even with my gift of intellectual awareness, I never really knew.

This day was good for me. Seeing the past more clearly, I have decided to use my knowledge and skills to work in the field of increasing human intelligence levels. Who is better equipped for this work? Who else 41 has lived in both worlds? These are my people. Let me use my gift to do something for them.

Tomorrow, I will discuss with Dr. Strauss the manner in which I can work in this area. I may be able to help him work out the problems of widespread use of the technique which was used on me. I have several good ideas of my own.

---

10. naïveté (nä ēv′ tā) *n.*: Simplicity.

38 Discussion Why does Charlie react this way?

39 Discussion Do you think this is true? Why might people be less sensitive to the mentally handicapped than to the physically handicapped?

40 Reading Strategy Summarize Charlie's evaluation of his mental condition as it was before the operation.

41 Discussion What does Charlie decide to work on? What can you tell about him from his decision?

Seeing the past more clearly, I have decided to use my knowledge and skills to work in the field of increasing human intelligence levels.

The participles and participial phrases describe the nouns and pronouns in the above sentences and make them more vivid. Like adjectives, participles act to intensify meaning.

Student Activity 1. Write four sentences about Charlie. Use a participle in each sentence.

Student Activity 2. Write four of your own sentences based on "Flowers for Algernon." Begin each sentence with a participial phrase.

42 **Critical Thinking and Reading** Why is Algernon's behavior a bad sign for Charlie?

43 **Literary Focus** How has Charlie's point of view changed in the course of the story?

44 **Reading Strategy** Summarize Charlie's progress from when the bandages were removed to this point.

There is so much that might be done with this technique. If I could be made into a genius, what about thousands of others like myself? What fantastic levels might be achieved by using this technique on normal people? On *geniuses?*

There are so many doors to open. I am impatient to begin.

PROGRESS REPORT 13

42 *May 23* It happened today. Algernon bit me. I visited the lab to see him as I do occasionally, and when I took him out of his cage, he snapped at my hand. I put him back and watched him for a while. He was unusually disturbed and vicious.

May 24 Burt, who is in charge of the experimental animals, tells me that Algernon is changing. He is less cooperative; he refuses to run the maze any more; general motivation has decreased. And he hasn't been eating. Everyone is upset about what this may mean.

May 25 They've been feeding Algernon, who now refuses to work the shifting-lock problem. Everyone identifies me with Algernon. In a way we're both the first of our kind. They're all pretending that Algernon's behavior is not necessarily significant for me. But it's hard to hide the fact that some of the other animals who were used in this experiment are showing strange behavior.

Dr. Strauss and Dr. Nemur have asked me not to come to the lab any more. I know what they're thinking but I can't accept it. I am going ahead with my plans to carry their
43 research forward. With all due respect to both of these fine scientists, I am well aware of their limitations. If there is an answer, I'll have to find it out for myself. Suddenly, time has become very important to me.

May 29 I have been given a lab of my own and permission to go ahead with the research. I'm on to something. Working day and night. I've had a cot moved into the lab. Most of my writing time is spent on the notes which I keep in a separate folder, but from time to time I feel it necessary to put down my moods and my thoughts out of sheer habit.

I find the *calculus of intelligence* to be a fascinating study. Here is the place for the application of all the knowledge I have acquired. In a sense it's the problem I've been concerned with all my life.

May 31 Dr. Strauss thinks I'm working too hard. Dr. Nemur says I'm trying to cram a lifetime of research and thought into a few weeks. I know I should rest, but I'm driven on by something inside that won't let me stop. I've got to find the reason for the sharp regression in Algernon. I've got to know *if* and *when* it will happen to me.

June 4

LETTER TO DR. STRAUSS *(copy)*

Dear Dr. Strauss:

Under separate cover I am sending you a copy of my report entitled, "The Algernon-Gordon Effect: A Study of Structure and Function of Increased Intelligence," which I would like to have you read and have published. 44

As you see, my experiments are completed. I have included in my report all of my formulae, as well as mathematical analysis in the appendix. Of course, these should be verified.

Because of its importance to both you and Dr. Nemur (and need I say to

myself, too?) I have checked and rechecked my results a dozen times in the hope of finding an error. I am sorry to say the results must stand. Yet for the sake of science, I am grateful for the little bit that I here add to the knowledge of the function of the human mind and of the laws governing the artificial increase of human intelligence.

I recall your once saying to me that an experimental *failure* or the
5 *disproving* of a theory was as important to the advancement of learning as a success would be. I know now that this is true. I am sorry, however, that my own contribution to the field must rest upon the ashes of the work of two men I regard so highly.

Yours truly,

Charles Gordon

encl.: rept.

June 5 I must not become emotional. The facts and the results of my experiments are clear, and the more sensational aspects of my own rapid climb cannot obscure the fact that the tripling of intelligence by the surgical technique developed by Drs. Strauss and Nemur must be viewed as having little or no practical applicability (at the

45 **Critical Thinking and Reading** What had Dr. Strauss meant by this? Is this how science works? Explain your answer.

46 **Reading Strategy** Paraphrase Charlie's experimental conclusion.

47 **Discussion** What are the signs that the experiment was not a success after all?

48 **Critical Thinking and Reading** How does Charlie's behavior parallel Algernon's?

49 **Discussion** Is Charlie worse off now than he was before the operation? Why?

present time) to the increase of human intelligence.

As I review the records and data on Algernon, I see that although he is still in his physical infancy, he has regressed mentally. Motor activity[11] is impaired; there is a general reduction of glandular activity; there is an accelerated loss of coordination.

There are also strong indications of progressive amnesia.

As will be seen by my report, these and other physical and mental deterioration syndromes can be predicted with statistically significant results by the application of my formula.

The surgical stimulus to which we were both subjected has resulted in an intensification and acceleration of all mental processes. The unforeseen development, which I have taken the liberty of calling the "Algernon-Gordon Effect," is the logical extension of the entire intelligence speedup. The hypothesis here proven may be described simply in the following terms: Artificially increased intelligence deteriorates at a
46 rate of time directly proportional to the quantity of the increase.

I feel that this, in itself, is an important discovery.

As long as I am able to write, I will continue to record my thoughts in these progress reports. It is one of my few pleasures. However, by all indications, my own mental deterioration will be very rapid.

I have already begun to notice signs of emotional instability and forgetfulness, the first symptoms of the burnout.

47 *June 10* Deterioration progressing. I have become absent-minded. Algernon died two days ago. Dissection shows my predictions were right. His brain had decreased in weight and there was a general smoothing out of cerebral convolutions as well as a deepening and broadening of brain fissures.

I guess the same thing is or will soon be happening to me. Now that it's definite, I don't want it to happen.

I put Algernon's body in a cheese box and buried him in the back yard. I cried.

June 15 Dr. Strauss came to see me again. I wouldn't open the door and I told him to go away. I want to be left to myself. I have become touchy and irritable. I feel the darkness closing in. I keep telling myself how important this introspective journal will be. 48

It's a strange sensation to pick up a book that you've read and enjoyed just a few months ago and discover that you don't remember it. I remembered how great I thought John Milton[12] was, but when I picked up *Paradise Lost* I couldn't understand it at all. I got so angry I threw the book across the room.

I've got to try to hold on to some of it. Some of the things I've learned. Oh, God, please don't take it all away.

June 19 Sometimes, at night, I go out for a walk. Last night I couldn't remember where I lived. A policeman took me home. I have the strange feeling that this has all happened to me before—a long time ago. I keep telling myself I'm the only person in the world who can describe what's happening to me.

June 21 Why can't I remember? I've got to fight. I lie in bed for days and I don't know who or where I am. Then it all comes 49

11. motor activity: Movement, physical coordination.

12. John Milton: British poet (1608–1674).

13. fugues (fyo͞ogz) **of amnesia** (am nē′ zhə): Periods of loss of memory.

back to me in a flash. Fugues of amnesia.[13] Symptoms of senility—second childhood. I can watch them coming on. It's so cruelly logical. I learned so much and so fast. Now my mind is deteriorating rapidly. I won't let it happen. I'll fight it. I can't help thinking of the boy in the restaurant, the blank expression, the silly smile, the people laughing at him. No—please—not that again . . .

June 22 I'm forgetting things that I learned recently. It seems to be following the classic pattern—the last things learned are the first things forgotten. Or is that the pattern? I'd better look it up again . . .

I reread my paper on the "Algernon-
Gordon Effect" and I get the strange feeling
50 that it was written by someone else. There
are parts I don't even understand.

Motor activity impaired. I keep tripping over things, and it becomes increasingly difficult to type.

June 23 I've given up using the typewriter completely. My coordination is bad. I feel that I'm moving slower and slower. Had a terrible shock today. I picked up a copy of an article I used in my research, Krueger's "Uber psychische Ganzheit," to see if it would help me understand what I had done. First I thought there was something wrong with my eyes. Then I realized I could no longer read German. I tested myself in other languages. All gone.

June 30 A week since I dared to write again. It's slipping away like sand through my fingers. Most of the books I have are too hard for me now. I get angry with them because I know that I read and understood them just a few weeks ago.

I keep telling myself I must keep writing these reports so that somebody will know what is happening to me. But it gets harder to form the words and remember spellings. I have to look up even simple words in the dictionary now and it makes me impatient with myself.

Dr. Strauss comes around almost every day, but I told him I wouldn't see or speak to anybody. He feels guilty. They all do. But I don't blame anyone. I knew what might happen. But how it hurts.

July 7 I don't know where the week
went. Todays Sunday I know because I can
see through my window people going to
church. I think I stayed in bed all week but I
remember Mrs. Flynn bringing food to me
a few times. I keep saying over and over Ive 51
got to do something but then I forget or
maybe its just easier not to do what I say Im
going to do.

I think of my mother and father a lot these days. I found a picture of them with me taken at a beach. My father has a big ball under his arm and my mother is holding me by the hand. I dont remember them the way they are in the picture. All I remember is my father arguing with mom about money.

He never shaved much and he used to scratch my face when he hugged me. He said he was going to take me to see cows on a farm once but he never did. He never kept his promises . . .

July 10 My landlady Mrs Flynn is very worried about me. She said she doesnt like loafers. If Im sick its one thing, but if Im a loafer thats another thing and she wont have it. I told her I think Im sick.

I try to read a little bit every day, mostly stories, but sometimes I have to read the same thing over and over again because I dont know what it means. And its hard to write. I know I should look up all the words in the dictionary but its so hard and Im so tired all the time.

50 Discussion Why is Charlie's deterioration so rapid? Do you think it would have been better for him never to have been intelligent than to go through the agony of losing all his new skills?

51 Critical Thinking and Reading What does Charlie's writing indicate about his condition?

52 Discussion Why does Charlie put flowers on Algernon's grave? Why is "Flowers for Algernon" a good title for this story?

53 Discussion What new problem is Charlie going to have with people now?

54 Critical Thinking and Reading How do you think Miss Kinnian feels about the results of the experiment? How can you tell?

55 Discussion Why does Mr. Donnegan give Charlie his old job back?

56 Literary Focus Identify the latest change in Charlie's point of view.

Then I got the idea that I would only use the easy words instead of the long hard ones. That saves time. I put flowers on Algernons grave about once a week. Mrs.
52 Flynn thinks Im crazy to put flowers on a mouses grave but I told her that Algernon was special.

July 14 Its sunday again. I dont have anything to do to keep me busy now because my television set is broke and I dont have any money to get it fixed. (I think I lost this months check from the lab. I dont remember)

I get awful headaches and asperin doesnt help me much. Mrs. Flynn knows Im really sick and she feels very sorry for me. Shes a wonderful woman whenever someone is sick.

July 22 Mrs. Flynn called a strange doctor to see me. She was afraid I was going to die. I told the doctor I wasnt too sick and that I only forget sometimes. He asked me did I have any friends or relatives and I said no I dont have any. I told him I had a friend called Algernon once but he was a mouse and we used to run races together. He looked at me kind of funny like he thought I was crazy.

He smiled when I told him I used to be a genius. He talked to me like I was a baby and
53 he winked at Mrs Flynn. I got mad and chased him out because he was making fun of me the way they all used to.

July 24 I have no more money and Mrs Flynn says I got to go to work somewhere and pay the rent because I havent paid for over two months. I dont know any work but the job I used to have at Donnegans Plastic Box Company. I dont want to go back there because they all knew me when I was smart and maybe they'll laugh at me. But I dont know what else to do to get money.

July 25 I was looking at some of my old progress reports and its very funny but I cant read what I wrote. I can make out some of the words but they dont make sense.

Miss Kinnian came to the door but I said go away I dont want to see you. She cried and I cried too but I wouldnt let her in because I didnt want her to laugh at me. I told her I didn't like her any more. I told her I didn't 5
want to be smart any more. Thats not true. I still love her and I still want to be smart but I had to say that so shed go away. She gave Mrs. Flynn money to pay the rent. I dont want that. I got to get a job.

Please . . . please let me not forget how to read and write . . .

July 27 Mr. Donnegan was very nice when I came back and asked him for my old job of janitor. First he was very suspicious but I told him what happened to me then he 5
looked very sad and put his hand on my shoulder and said Charlie Gordon you got guts.

Everybody looked at me when I came downstairs and started working in the toilet sweeping it out like I used to. I told myself Charlie if they make fun of you dont get sore because you remember their not so smart as you once thot they were. And besides they were once your friends and if they laughed 5
at you that doesnt mean anything because they liked you too.

One of the new men who came to work there after I went away made a nasty crack he said hey Charlie I hear your a very smart fella a real quiz kid. Say something intelligent. I felt bad but Joe Carp came over and grabbed him by the shirt and said leave him alone or Ill break your neck. I didnt expect

Joe to take my part so I guess hes really my friend.

Later Frank Reilly came over and said Charlie if anybody bothers you or trys to take advantage you call me or Joe and we
7 will set em straight. I said thanks Frank and I got choked up so I had to turn around and go into the supply room so he wouldnt see me cry. Its good to have friends.

July 28 I did a dumb thing today I forgot I wasnt in Miss Kinnians class at the adult center any more like I use to be. I went in and sat down in my old seat in the back of the room and she looked at me funny and she said Charles. I dint remember she ever called me that before only Charlie so I said hello Miss Kinnian Im ready for my lesin today only I lost my reader that we was

57 **Discussion** Why do Joe and Frank want to defend Charlie now? Could Charlie have been right about their friendship after all?

58 **Critical Thinking and Reading** How has Charlie made a complete cycle? How has his experience changed him?

59 **Discussion** What does Charlie think caused him to become dumb again? What is his plan for the future? Why is Charlie such a poignant character?

60 **Critical Thinking and Reading** Why is Charlie so concerned with marking Algernon's grave?

Reader's Response Explain what Charlie means by saying "Its easy to make frends if you let pepul laff at you."

using. She startid to cry and run out of the room and everybody looked at me and I saw they wasnt the same pepul who use to be in my class.

Then all of a suddin I rememberd some things about the operashun and me getting smart and I said holy smoke I reely pulled a Charlie Gordon that time. I went away before she come back to the room.

Thats why Im going away from New York
58 for good. I dont want to do nothing like that agen. I dont want Miss Kinnian to feel sorry for me. Evry body feels sorry at the factery and I dont want that eather so Im going someplace where nobody knows that Charlie Gordon was once a genus and now he cant even reed a book or rite good.

Im taking a cuple of books along and even if I cant reed them Ill practise hard and maybe I wont forget every thing I lerned. If I try reel hard maybe Ill be a littel bit smarter then I was before the operashun. I got my rabits foot and my luky penny and maybe they will help me.

If you ever reed this Miss Kinnian dont be sorry for me Im glad I got a second chanse to be smart becaus I lerned a lot of things that I never even new were in this world and Im grateful that I saw it all for a littel bit. I dont know why Im dumb agen or what I did wrong maybe its becaus I dint try hard enuff. But if I try and practis very hard maybe Ill get a littl smarter and know what all the words are. I remember a littel bit how nice I had a feeling with the blue book that has the torn cover when I red it. Thats why Im gonna keep trying to get smart so I can have that feeling agen. Its a good feeling to
know things and be smart. I wish I had it 59
rite now if I did I woud sit down and reed all the time. Anyway I bet Im the first dumb person in the world who ever found out somthing importent for sience. I remember I did somthing but I dont remember what. So I gess its like I did it for all the dumb pepul like me.

Goodbye Miss Kinnian and Dr Strauss and evreybody. And P.S. please tell Dr Nemur not to be such a grouch when pepul laff at him and he woud have more frends. Its easy to make frends if you let pepul laff at you. Im going to have lots of frends where I go.

P.P.S. Please if you get a chanse put some
flowrs on Algernons grave in the bak 60
yard . . .

Closure and Extension

ANSWERS TO THINKING ABOUT THE SELECTION

Recalling

1. Charlie is keeping a journal at his doctor's suggestion so that his progress can be monitored.
2. Miss Kinnian believes Charlie should take part in the experiment because he has a good attitude and is highly motivated to learn. She fears that his new intelligence will not be permanent.
3. He thinks he failed because he didn't see anything and the man testing him left the room without speaking. He comes to learn that the inkblots are supposed to remind you of familiar shapes and that it is not a pass-fail type of test.
4. Dr. Strauss says that Charlie has a good nature, is interested, and is eager to please. Also, Charlie has already learned a lot considering his low IQ. Dr. Nemur apparently wanted to begin with a subject whose IQ was higher than Charlie's.
5. The people are afraid of Charlie and are uncomfortable around him. He leaves because his co-workers have signed a petition asking for his resignation.
6. Charlie feels that his paper was written by someone else.
7. Charlie leaves because he doesn't want people to feel sorry for him because of his loss of intelligence.

Interpreting

8. Charlie slowly becomes smarter and smarter, then becomes irritable, and then deteriorates just like Algernon.
9. His accuracy of spelling and punctuation is an indication of his progress and regression. Both get

THINKING ABOUT THE SELECTION

Recalling

1. Why is Charlie keeping a journal?
2. Why does Miss Kinnian believe Charlie should take part in this experiment? Why does she also fear for him?
3. Why does Charlie believe he failed the Rorschach test? What does he come to learn about the Rorschach test?
4. Why does Dr. Strauss think that Charlie is a fit subject for the experiment? Why does Dr. Nemur disagree?
5. How do Charlie's coworkers treat him after he becomes smart? Why does he leave his job?
6. In his June 22 report, what feeling about his scientific paper does Charlie reveal?
7. Why does Charlie decide to leave New York?

Interpreting

8. Explain how Charlie's development parallels Algernon's.
9. How do the spelling and punctuation in Charlie's reports contribute to your view of his progress? How do the books he reads contribute?
10. How is Charlie at the end of the story different from Charlie at the beginning?
11. Do you think "Flowers for Algernon" is a good title for this story? Explain your answer.

Applying

12. As Charlie grows smarter, he asks questions. Explain why the ability to ask questions is an important part of intelligence.

ANALYZING LITERATURE

Understanding Point of View and Theme

When a story is told by a character in it, you see events through this character's eyes. What this character learns helps reveal the theme.

1. What kind of person is Charlie?
2. At the beginning of the story, Charlie views Miss Kinnian, Dr. Strauss, and Dr. Nemur as almost perfect human beings. How does he view them as he grows smarter? How does he view them at the end of the story?
3. Find three examples in the story of how Charlie's views of friendship change.
4. What is the theme of this story?

CRITICAL THINKING AND READING

Comparing and Contrasting Views

When you examine the similarities between two subjects, you **compare** them. When you examine the differences, you **contrast** them.

In "Flowers for Algernon," Charlie's perceptions change as he moves from unintelligence to genius and back again. The views of the people around him also change.

1. Contrast Charlie's reaction to the first party (page 206) with the second (page 209).
2. Compare Charlie's general attitude at the end when he visits the classroom by mistake (page 221) with his attitude at the beginning.
3. Contrast Miss Kinnian's attitude toward Charlie before his operation with that on April 28 (page 212).

THINKING AND WRITING

Writing About Theme

Assume that at the time of the June 10 progress report, Charlie learns another retarded person has the opportunity to undergo the same operation. Freewrite for three minutes as Charlie about his feelings about the operation. Then write a letter in which Charlie gives the person advice on whether to have the operation. Revise your letter, making sure you have presented your case clearly. Proofread, checking for spelling, grammar, and punctuation.

(Answers begin on p. 222.)

gradually better until Charlie is expressing himself perfectly and on a high level. The books he reads also parallel his development since he begins with *Robinson Crusoe* and peaks by reading scientific reports in German.

10. The Charlie at the end is different from the Charlie at the beginning in that he believes he can one day be intelligent again if he only tries hard enough.
11. Answers will differ. Suggested response: It is a good title because it means both that the subjects of the experiments should be remembered and honored and that Charlie deserves praise for participating in the experiment.

Applying

12. Answers will differ. Suggested response: The ability to ask questions is an important part of intelligence because the intelligent mind is an inquiring mind. Intelligent people seek knowledge and, therefore, ask questions.

ANSWERS TO ANALYZING LITERATURE

1. Answers will differ. Suggested response: Charlie is a sweet, innocent person who is shy about his disability but eager to learn and to please. Even after he becomes intelligent, he wants to use his intelligence to help others like himself.
2. As he grows smarter, he first recognizes their limitations and then believes that they are not at all knowledgeable. At the end, he views them as his friends.
3. Three examples are that he can no longer communicate with Miss Kinnian because she doesn't understand him, that he no longer trusts people, such as the technician who gave him the Rorschach test, and that he recognizes that his doctors had their own reasons for performing the experiment that had nothing to do with being good to him.
4. Answers will differ. Suggested response: Being intelligent does not mean being happy. In fact, it's better to be who you really are than to try to be someone you're not.

ANSWERS TO CRITICAL THINKING AND READING

1. Charlie believes the first party was fun. He doesn't see that his co-workers are laughing at, not with, him. At the second party, however, Charlie is embarrassed because he realizes that his co-workers are making fun of him and mocking his disability.
2. Charlie's attitude at the end is similar to his general attitude at the beginning. He is humble, self-deprecating, and innocently friendly.
3. Miss Kinnian first treats Charlie like a student and a child. On April 28, she is in awe of his accomplishments and talks to him as an equal.

Challenge Why doesn't Charlie notice Miss Kinnian until after the operation? He considered her a friend before, but on April 28, he states in his journal, "I'm in love with Miss Kinnian." What does this say about Charlie's emotional progress? Is it logical for him to fall in love with his teacher? If he had remained intelligent, would he still have been in love with her?

THINKING AND WRITING

For help with this assignment, students can refer to Lesson 11, "Writing About Theme," in the Handbook of Writing About Literature.

Putting It Together Students have already studied each of the literary elements summarized on this age in the short story unit. The purpose of Putting It Together is to emphasize the interrelationship of these elements. By reading actively, students can study these elements, understand their effect on each other, and their contribution to the overall effect of the story.

The plot affects the other elements of a short story. The events of the story affect the actions and emotions of characters, as well as the time and place of the action. The theme is usually revealed through the outcome of the climax as well as the actions of the characters.

Remind students that the Putting It Together process is part of reading actively. As they are reading the selection, they should not only consider the elements that make up the story, but should also question, predict, clarify, and summarize. This interaction will increase their understanding and enjoyment of the story, and help them to be better readers.

For further practice with these elements, use the selection in the Teaching Portfolio, "The Hummingbird That Lived Through Winter," pp. 264–265, with which students can record their own annotations.

PUTTING IT TOGETHER

The Short Story

A short story is a brief work of fiction made up of elements known as plot, characters, setting, and theme. All these elements should combine to create a single effect. You will gain the most enjoyment by reading actively. Like a detective, an active reader looks for clues to elements of a story and discovers how they work together.

Plot

The plot is the sequence of events. While reading a story, make sure you follow the sequence of events. Do you know the order in which events occur? Do you understand how they are related to each other? Can you identify the conflict, or central problem? How does the author create suspense and keep you interested in the events? Can you identify the climax and resolution of the conflict? Do you understand how the actions affect the characters?

Characters

The characters are the people, and sometimes the animals, who take part in the story's events. Who is the main character? Who are the minor characters? What are the character traits and motivations of the different characters? Does the author use both direct and indirect characterization? Which of the characters seem most lifelike? How are the characters influenced by the setting?

Setting

The setting is the place and time of the events. As you read, visualize the setting. Where does the story take place? How much detail does the author give you about the setting? Do events occur in the present, the past, or the future? Do events occur over a long or short period of time? What kind of atmosphere or mood does the author create? How does this mood affect the whole story?

Theme

The theme is a general idea about life that a story communicates. Ask yourself whether the story you are reading has a theme. Not all stories do. Does the main character change in a significant way that reveals the theme? Does the main character learn something about life? Is the theme stated directly or implied?

The comments in the margin of the story that follows review for you the elements of the short story. They also show questions an active reader might ask about these elements while reading.

Objectives

1 To understand how different elements work together in a short story
2 To review a short story
3 To evaluate a story
4 To appreciate words from other languages
5 To continue a story

Support Material

Teaching Portfolio

Teacher Backup, pp. 325–327
Putting It Together, "The Story of Keesh," pp. 328–333
Grammar in Action Worksheets, *Using Descriptive Words,* pp. 334–335; *Using Compound Sentences,* pp. 336–337
Usage and Mechanics Worksheet, p. 338
Analyzing Literature Worksheet, *Reviewing the Short Story,* p. 339
Critical Thinking and Reading Worksheet, *Evaluating a Short Story,* p. 340
Selection Test, pp. 341–342

MODEL

The Medicine Bag

Virginia Driving Hawk Sneve

Theme: The title may provide an important clue to the theme. What is a medicine bag?

My kid sister Cheryl and I always bragged about our Sioux[1] grandpa, Joe Iron Shell. Our friends, who had always lived in the city and only knew about Indians from movies and TV, were impressed by our stories. Maybe we exaggerated and made Grandpa and the reservation sound glamorous, but when we'd return home to Iowa after our yearly summer visit to Grandpa, we always had some exciting tale to tell.

We always had some authentic Sioux article to show our listeners. One year Cheryl had new moccasins[2] that Grandpa had made. On another visit he gave me a small, round, flat, rawhide drum that was decorated with a painting of a warrior riding a horse. He taught me a real Sioux chant to sing while I beat the drum with a leather-covered stick that had a feather on the end. Man, that really made an impression.

Character: The main character seems to be a teen-age boy who enjoys impressing his friends with his Sioux heritage. What does his desire to impress his friends indicate about him?

We never showed our friends Grandpa's picture. Not that we were ashamed of him, but because we knew that the glamorous tales we told didn't go with the real thing. Our friends would have laughed at the picture because Grandpa wasn't tall and stately like TV Indians. His hair wasn't in braids but hung in stringy, gray strands on his neck, and he was old. He was our great-grandfather, and he didn't live in a tepee,[3] but all by himself in a part log, part tar-paper shack on the Rosebud Reservation[4] in South Dakota. So when Grandpa came to visit us, I was so ashamed and embarrassed I could've died.

Plot: The boy is experiencing an internal conflict. He loves his grandfather but is also embarrassed by him. How will he work out his problem?

There are a lot of yippy poodles and other fancy little dogs in our neighborhood, but they usually barked singly

---

1. Sioux (so͞o) *n.*: Native-American tribes of the northern plains of the United States and nearby southern Canada.
2. moccasins (mäk′ ə s′nz) *n.*: Heelless slippers of soft flexible leather, originally worn by native Americans.
3. tepee (tē′ pē) *n.*: A cone-shaped tent of animal skins, used by the Plains Indians.
4. Rosebud Reservation: A small Indian reservation in south-central South Dakota.

Presentation

Motivation/Prior Knowledge Have students discuss traditions that are passed along from one generation to the next, from father to son, mother to daughter, family to family, and generation to generation. What kinds of things can be passed along? Why are these traditions important?

Master Teacher Note Students might appreciate the story more if they had an idea of what life on an Indian reservation was like. You could show students pictures of some reservations. You could probably obtain pictures of Indian reservations from reference books in your school or local library.

Thematic Idea Another selection that deals with the theme of passing traditions along to the next generation is "The Gift Giving," on page 175.

Purpose-Setting Question How does Martin's attitude toward his grandfather and his Sioux heritage change during the story?

Master Teacher Note Have students read each annotation carefully and try to answer the questions. Also, they will probably have some questions of their own. Encourage students to ask these questions as a basis for class discussion. You might also consider having the class read the selection out loud. An oral recitation will enable students to discuss the story and the annotations as a group.

at the mailman from the safety of their own yards. Now it sounded as if a whole pack of mutts were barking together in one place.

I got up and walked to the curb to see what the commotion was. About a block away I saw a crowd of little kids yelling, with the dogs yipping and growling around someone who was walking down the middle of the street.

Plot: Notice how this internal conflict is shown by his feeling hot and cold at the same time. Will he go to his grandfather's assistance?

I watched the group as it slowly came closer and saw that in the center of the strange procession was a man wearing a tall black hat. He'd pause now and then to peer at something in his hand and then at the houses on either side of the street. I felt cold and hot at the same time as I recognized the man. "Oh, no!" I whispered. "It's Grandpa!"

Setting: The confusion in this scene reflects the confusion in the boy's mind. Which sensory details are especially vivid?

I stood on the curb, unable to move even though I wanted to run and hide. Then I got mad when I saw how the yippy dogs were growling and nipping at the old man's baggy pant legs and how wearily he poked them away with his cane. "Stupid mutts," I said as I ran to rescue Grandpa.

When I kicked and hollered at the dogs to get away, they put their tails between their legs and scattered. The kids ran to the curb where they watched me and the old man.

"Grandpa," I said and felt pretty dumb when my voice cracked. I reached for his beat-up old tin suitcase, which was tied shut with a rope. But he set it down right in the street and shook my hand.

"*Hau, Takoza,* Grandchild," he greeted me formally in Sioux.

All I could do was stand there with the whole neighborhood watching and shake the hand of the leather-brown old man. I saw how his gray hair straggled from under his big black hat, which had a drooping feather in its crown. His rumpled black suit hung like a sack over his stooped frame. As he shook my hand, his coat fell open to expose a bright red satin shirt with a beaded bolo tie[5] under the collar. His get-up wasn't out of place on the reservation, but it sure was here, and I wanted to sink right through the pavement.

"Hi," I muttered with my head down. I tried to pull my hand away when I felt his bony hand trembling, and looked up to see fatigue in his face. I felt like crying. I couldn't think of

5. bolo (bō′ lō) **tie,** *n.*: A man's string tie, held together with a decorated sliding device.

Grammar in Action

Writers carefully select vivid, interesting **descriptive words** to enliven their writing and to create the desired image in the mind of the reader. They choose specific and precise words to communicate to the reader.

Carefully reread this description of Grandfather and note the vividness of the picture you receive from the writer. Vivid words are underlined.

All I could do was stand there with the whole neighborhood watching and shake the hand of the *leather-brown* old man. I saw how his gray hair *straggled* from under his big black hat, which had a *drooping feather,* in its crown. His *rumpled* black suit hung *like a sack* over his *stooped* frame. As he shook my hand, his coat fell open to expose a bright *red satin* shirt with a *beaded* bolo tie under the collar. His get-up wasn't out of place on the reservation, but it sure was here, and I wanted to sink right through the pavement.

Student Activity 1. Find ten other vivid words in "The Medicine Bag." Discuss with your classmates your reasons for selecting each word.

anything to say so I picked up Grandpa's suitcase, took his arm, and guided him up the driveway to our house.

Mom was standing on the steps. I don't know how long she'd been watching, but her hand was over her mouth and she looked as if she couldn't believe what she saw. Then she ran to us.

"Grandpa," she gasped. "How in the world did you get here?"

She checked her move to embrace Grandpa and I remembered that such a display of affection is unseemly to the Sioux and would embarrass him.

"*Hau,* Marie," he said as he shook Mom's hand. She smiled and took his other arm.

As we supported him up the steps, the door banged open and Cheryl came bursting out of the house. She was all smiles and was so obviously glad to see Grandpa that I was ashamed of how I felt.

Character: Cheryl's reaction to Grandpa is very different from the boy's. How does this contrast make the boy feel?

"Grandpa!" she yelled happily. "You came to see us!"

Grandpa smiled, and Mom and I let go of him as he stretched out his arms to my ten-year-old sister, who was still young enough to be hugged.

"*Wicincala,* little girl," he greeted her and then collapsed.

He had fainted. Mom and I carried him into her sewing room, where we had a spare bed.

After we had Grandpa on the bed, Mom stood there helplessly patting his shoulder.

"Shouldn't we call the doctor, Mom?" I suggested, since she didn't seem to know what to do.

"Yes," she agreed with a sigh. "You make Grandpa comfortable, Martin."

I reluctantly moved to the bed. I knew Grandpa wouldn't want to have Mom undress him, but I didn't want to, either. He was so skinny and frail that his coat slipped off easily. When I loosened his tie and opened his shirt collar, I felt a small leather pouch that hung from a thong[6] around his neck. I left it alone and moved to remove his boots. The scuffed old cowboy boots were tight, and he moaned as I put pressure on his legs to jerk them off.

Plot: Grandpa appears to be ill. Will his illness play a role in the plot?

I put the boots on the floor and saw why they fit so tight.

6. thong, *n.*: A narrow strip of leather.

Enrichment The Sioux Indians at one time lived throughout the northern plains of North America. Among the many divisions are the Santee Sioux, the Yankton Sioux, and the Teton Sioux.

Originally, the Sioux, as well as other Plains Indian groups, lived in villages along rivers and streams, where they farmed and hunted small game. However, the introduction of the horse by the Spanish in the 1600's changed their lives greatly. Daily life became centered on the great buffalo herds and the tribes became mobile.

The Teton Sioux, the group that Grandpa is part of, agreed to settle on a reservation in 1868. They rebelled in 1876, and groups led by Crazy Horse and Sitting Bull were responsible for killing General Custer and all of his command at Little Big Horn in Montana. But the superiority of the U.S. Army, in men and weapons, forced the Teton Sioux to eventually surrender in the autumn of 1876.

Student Activity 2. Write a description of someone who looks a little odd or out of place. Enhance it with vivid and precise words. Have a partner go over the first draft and circle words that could be improved.

Each one was stuffed with money. I looked at the bills that lined the boots and started to ask about them, but Grandpa's eyes were closed again.

Mom came back with a basin of water. "The doctor thinks Grandpa is suffering from heat exhaustion," she explained as she bathed Grandpa's face. Mom gave a big sigh, *"Oh, hinh,* Martin. How do you suppose he got here?"

We found out after the doctor's visit. Grandpa was angrily sitting up in bed while Mom tried to feed him some soup.

"Tonight you let Marie feed you, Grandpa," spoke my dad, who had gotten home from work just as the doctor was leaving. "You're not really sick," he said as he gently pushed Grandpa back against the pillows. "The doctor said you just got too tired and hot after your long trip."

Grandpa relaxed, and between sips of soup, he told us of his journey. Soon after our visit to him, Grandpa decided that he would like to see where his only living descendants lived and what our home was like. Besides, he admitted sheepishly, he was lonesome after we left.

Theme: The characters in this story come from two different cultures. Will the importance of heritage be an aspect of theme?

I knew that everybody felt as guilty as I did—especially Mom. Mom was all Grandpa had left. So even after she married my dad, who's a white man and teaches in the college in our city, and after Cheryl and I were born, Mom made sure that every summer we spent a week with Grandpa.

I never thought that Grandpa would be lonely after our visits, and none of us noticed how old and weak he had become. But Grandpa knew, and so he came to us. He had ridden on buses for two and a half days. When he arrived in the city, tired and stiff from sitting for so long, he set out, walking, to find us.

He had stopped to rest on the steps of some building downtown, and a policeman found him. The cop, according to Grandpa, was a good man who took him to the bus stop and waited until the bus came and told the driver to let Grandpa out at Bell View Drive. After Grandpa got off the bus, he started walking again. But he couldn't see the house numbers on the other side when he walked on the sidewalk, so he walked in the middle of the street. That's when all the little kids and dogs followed him.

Character: Here the boy feels proud of his grandfather. What qualities does he admire?

I knew everybody felt as bad as I did. Yet I was so proud of this eighty-six-year-old man, who had never been away from the reservation, having the courage to travel so far alone.

Grammar in Action

Transitions are words or phrases used to link sentences and paragraphs to create coherence. Coherence involves ideas that follow each other logically and meaningfully. Transitions make connections between sentences and paragraphs read smoothly.

Transitions can show location (*beneath, over*) and time (*today, when*). They can be used to compare (*like, as*), or to contrast (*yet, but, however*). Transitions also serve to show emphasis (*again, indeed*), to conclude or summarize (*finally, thus*), to add information (*also, in addition*), and to clarify (*that is, in other words*). *Many transitions in "The Medicine Bag" serve to clarify or to show time. For example, the transition finally* indicates an action that occurs last;

> "Finally, one day after school, my friends came home with me because nothing I said stopped them."

It is usually a good idea to begin paragraphs with a transition the way the author does with the word *finally*.

Sometimes conjunctions serve as transitions; "But after they left," Mom said, "No more visitors for a while, Martin." Starting a sentence with a conjunction is a valid way to connect related sentences, but be careful not to rely too heavily on conjunctions

"You found the money in my boots?" he asked Mom.

"Martin did," she answered, and roused herself to scold. "Grandpa, you shouldn't have carried so much money. What if someone had stolen it from you?"

Grandpa laughed. "I would've known if anyone tried to take the boots off my feet. The money is what I've saved for a long time—a hundred dollars—for my funeral. But you take it now to buy groceries so that I won't be a burden to you while I am here."

"That won't be necessary, Grandpa," Dad said. "We are honored to have you with us, and you will never be a burden. I am only sorry that we never thought to bring you home with us this summer and spare you the discomfort of a long trip."

Grandpa was pleased. "Thank you," he answered. "But do not feel bad that you didn't bring me with you, for I would not have come then. It was not time." He said this in such a way that no one could argue with him. To Grandpa and the Sioux, he once told me, a thing would be done when it was the right time to do it, and that's the way it was.

Theme: The last sentence here seems significant. What does it mean?

"Also," Grandpa went on, looking at me, "I have come because it is soon time for Martin to have the medicine bag."

We all knew what that meant. Grandpa thought he was going to die, and he had to follow the tradition of his family to pass the medicine bag, along with its history, to the oldest male child.

Theme: Here is the medicine bag mentioned in the title. What does the medicine bag mean to Grandpa? What will it mean to Martin?

Enrichment In addition to their belief in the Great Spirit Wakantanka, members of the Sioux tribe also believe in guardian spirits that help individuals through the difficulties in life. The vision quest is a ceremony that helps a person find a guardian spirit. The medicine bag is a representation of the guardian spirit and is believed to have special powers.

as transitions. Overusing conjunctions as transitions weakens your writing.

Student Activity 1. Identify five more examples of transitions in "The Medicine Bag" and explain how each is used.

Student Activity 2. Write a brief review of one of your favorite stories in this unit. Strive for coherence by using transitions.

Discussion One of the primary reasons that Virginia Driving Hawk Sneve chooses to write about Native Americans is her "hope to correct the many misconceptions . . . too long perpetrated by non-Indian authors who have written about us." You might discuss some of the misconceptions about Indians as they are portrayed on television and in movies. How do the images students have of Indians contrast with the appearance and behavior of Grandpa? What misconceptions does Martin believe his friends have about his grandfather?

"Even though the boy," he said still looking at me, "bears a white man's name, the medicine bag will be his."

Plot: Martin again feels inner turmoil. How will he resolve his problem?

I didn't know what to say. I had the same hot and cold feeling that I had when I first saw Grandpa in the street. The medicine bag was the dirty leather pouch I had found around his neck. "I could never wear such a thing," I almost said aloud. I thought of having my friends see it in gym class or at the swimming pool and could imagine the smart things they would say. But I just swallowed hard and took a step toward the bed. I knew I would have to take it.

But Grandpa was tired. "Not now, Martin," he said, waving his hand in dismissal. "It is not time. Now I will sleep."

So that's how Grandpa came to be with us for two months. My friends kept asking to come see the old man, but I put them off. I told myself that I didn't want them laughing at Grandpa. But even as I made excuses, I knew it wasn't Grandpa that I was afraid they'd laugh at.

Nothing bothered Cheryl about bringing her friends to see Grandpa. Every day after school started, there'd be a crew of giggling little girls or round-eyed little boys crowded around the old man on the patio, where he'd gotten in the habit of sitting every afternoon.

Grandpa would smile in his gentle way and patiently answer their questions, or he'd tell them stories of brave warriors, ghosts, animals; and the kids listened in awed silence. Those little guys thought Grandpa was great.

Finally, one day after school, my friends came home with me because nothing I said stopped them. "We're going to see the great Indian of Bell View Drive," said Hank, who was supposed to be my best friend. "My brother has seen him three times so he oughta be well enough to see us."

Character: Grandpa understands his grandson very well. What else will Martin learn about him?

When we got to my house, Grandpa was sitting on the patio. He had on his red shirt, but today he also wore a fringed leather vest that was decorated with beads. Instead of his usual cowboy boots, he had solidly beaded moccasins on his feet that stuck out of his black trousers. Of course, he had his old black hat on—he was seldom without it. But it had been brushed, and the feather in the beaded headband was proudly erect, its tip a brighter white. His hair lay in silver strands over the red shirt collar.

I stared just as my friends did, and I heard one of them murmur, "Wow!"

Grandpa looked up, and, when his eyes met mine, they twinkled as if he were laughing inside. He nodded to me, and my face got all hot. I could tell that he had known all along I was afraid he'd embarrass me in front of my friends.

"*Hau, hoksilas,* boys," he greeted and held out his hand.

My buddies passed in a single file and shook his hand as I introduced them. They were so polite I almost laughed. "How, there, Grandpa," and even a "How-do-you-do, sir."

"You look fine, Grandpa," I said as the guys sat on the lawn chairs or on the patio floor.

"*Hanh,* yes," he agreed. "When I woke up this morning, it seemed the right time to dress in the good clothes. I knew that my grandson would be bringing his friends."

"You guys want some lemonade or something?" I offered. No one answered. They were listening to Grandpa as he started telling how he'd killed the deer from which his vest was made.

Grandpa did most of the talking while my friends were there. I was so proud of him and amazed at how respectfully quiet my buddies were. Mom had to chase them home at supper time. As they left, they shook Grandpa's hand again and said to me,

"Martin, he's really great!"

"Yeah, man! Don't blame you for keeping him to yourself."

"Can we come back?"

But after they left, Mom said, "No more visitors for a while, Martin. Grandpa won't admit it, but his strength hasn't returned. He likes having company, but it tires him."

That evening Grandpa called me to his room before he went to sleep. "Tomorrow," he said, "when you come home, it will be time to give you the medicine bag."

I felt a hard squeeze from where my heart is supposed to be and was scared, but I answered, "OK, Grandpa."

All night I had weird dreams about thunder and lightning on a high hill. From a distance I heard the slow beat of a drum. When I woke up in the morning, I felt as if I hadn't slept at all. At school it seemed as if the day would never end and, when it finally did, I ran home.

Plot: The writer vividly portrays the turmoil going on in Martin's mind. Will Martin learn anything from Grandpa the next day that helps him?

Grandpa was in his room, sitting on the bed. The shades were down, and the place was dim and cool. I sat on the floor in front of Grandpa, but he didn't even look at me. After what seemed a long time he spoke.

"I sent your mother and sister away. What you will hear today is only for a man's ears. What you will receive is only for a man's hands." He fell silent, and I felt shivers down my back.

"My father in his early manhood," Grandpa began, "made a vision quest[7] to find a spirit guide for his life. You cannot understand how it was in that time, when the great Teton Sioux were first made to stay on the reservation. There was a strong need for guidance from *Wakantanka*,[8] the Great Spirit. But too many of the young men were filled with despair and hatred. They thought it was hopeless to search for a vision when the glorious life was gone and only the hated confines of a reservation lay ahead. But my father held to the old ways.

"He carefully prepared for his quest with a purifying sweat bath, and then he went alone to a high butte top[9] to fast and pray. After three days he received his sacred dream—in which he found, after long searching, the white man's iron. He did not understand his vision of finding something belonging to the white people, for in that time they were the enemy. When he came down from the butte to cleanse himself at the stream below, he found the remains of a campfire and the broken shell of an iron kettle. This was a sign that reinforced his dream. He took a piece of the iron for his medicine bag, which he had made of elk skin years before, to prepare for his quest.

Theme: This anecdote helps clarify the theme. What does the iron shell represent? How did his vision help him reconcile, or make peace between, the Indian world and the white world?

"He returned to his village, where he told his dream to the wise old men of the tribe. They gave him the name *Iron Shell*, but neither did they understand the meaning of the dream. The first Iron Shell kept the piece of iron with him at all times and believed it gave him protection from the evils of those unhappy days.

---

7. vision quest: A search for a revelation that would aid understanding.

8. Wakantanka (wä' kən tank' ə) *n.*: The Sioux religion's most important spirit—the creator of the world.

9. butte (byo͞ot) **top,** *n.*: The top of a steep hill standing alone in a plain.

"Then a terrible thing happened to Iron Shell. He and several other young men were taken from their homes by the soldiers and sent far away to a white man's boarding school. He was angry and lonesome for his parents and the young girl he had wed before he was taken away. At first Iron Shell resisted the teacher's attempts to change him, and he did not try to learn. One day it was his turn to work in the school's blacksmith shop. As he walked into the place, he knew that his medicine had brought him there to learn and work with the white man's iron.

"Iron Shell became a blacksmith and worked at the trade when he returned to the reservation. All of his life he treasured the medicine bag. When he was old, and I was a man, he gave it to me, for no one made the vision quest any more."

Grandpa quit talking, and I stared in disbelief as he covered his face with his hands. His shoulders were shaking with quiet sobs, and I looked away until he began to speak again.

"I kept the bag until my son, your mother's father, was a man and had to leave us to fight in the war across the ocean. I gave him the bag, for I believed it would protect him in battle, but he did not take it with him. He was afraid that he would lose it. He died in a faraway place."

Again Grandpa was still, and I felt his grief around me.

"My son," he went on after clearing his throat, "had only a daughter, and it is not proper for her to know of these things."

Discussion The author has also stated that she wished "to present an accurate portrayal of American Indian life as I have known it [and] to interpret Indian history from the viewpoint of the American Indian." What aspects of the story about the medicine bag are uniquely from an Indian perspective? How does learning about the Indians from this perspective change your ideas about them?

More About the Author Virginia Driving Hawk Sneve has spent most of her life in her native state, South Dakota. She was born in Rosebud, the location of the Sioux Indian reservation and her writing has been primarily concerned with portraying Indians and their heritage from a Native American point of view. This writing has included fiction, as well as historical articles.

Reader's Response Do you agree with Grandpa that "a thing [will] be done when it [is] the right time to do it? Explain.

He unbuttoned his shirt, pulled out the leather pouch, and lifted it over his head. He held it in his hand, turning it over and over as if memorizing how it looked.

Theme: The medicine bag serves as a symbol? What does it symbolize?

"In the bag," he said as he opened it and removed two objects, "is the broken shell of the iron kettle, a pebble from the butte, and a piece of the sacred sage."[10] He held the pouch upside down and dust drifted down.

"After the bag is yours you must put a piece of prairie sage within and never open it again until you pass it on to your son." He replaced the pebble and the piece of iron, and tied the bag.

I stood up, somehow knowing I should. Grandpa slowly rose from the bed and stood upright in front of me holding the bag before my face. I closed my eyes and waited for him to slip it over my head. But he spoke.

"No, you need not wear it." He placed the soft leather bag in my right hand and closed my other hand over it. "It would not be right to wear it in this time and place where no one will understand. Put it safely away until you are again on the reservation. Wear it then, when you replace the sacred sage."

Grandpa turned and sat again on the bed. Wearily he leaned his head against the pillow. "Go," he said. "I will sleep now."

Putting It Together: Martin comes to accept both sides of his heritage when he learns from his grandfather the true meaning of the medicine bag.

"Thank you, Grandpa," I said softly and left with the bag in my hands.

That night Mom and Dad took Grandpa to the hospital. Two weeks later I stood alone on the lonely prairie of the reservation and put the sacred sage in my medicine bag.

---

10. sage (sāj) *n.*: Plant belonging to the mint family.

Virginia Driving Hawk Sneve (1933–) grew up on the Sioux Reservation in South Dakota. This writer and teacher has won many awards for her fiction, including the Council on Interracial Books Award and the Western Writers of America award. In books such as *Jimmy Yellow Hawk, High Elk's Treasure,* and *When the Thunder Spoke,* she draws on her intimate knowledge of Sioux life. Her Sioux heritage also plays an important role in "The Medicine Bag."

Closure and Extension

ANSWERS TO THINKING ABOUT THE SELECTION

Recalling

1. Martin is embarrassed because he had always bragged about his grandfather and he thinks that when his friends see him they will be disappointed by his actual appearance.
2. The three reasons Grandpa gives for his visit are that he wants to see where his only relatives live, that he is lonely, and that it is time to give Martin the medicine bag.
3. The purpose of the vision quest is to find a spirit guide for the life of a Sioux Indian. He received the name Iron Shell because he found the white man's iron in his vision and then afterwards found an old kettle, which was a confirmation. When he told the elders of the tribe about his experience, they gave him the name.
4. Martin takes the medicine bag and follows Grandpa's instructions by standing alone on the prairie of the reservation and putting the sacred sage into the medicine bag.

Interpreting

5. The Grandpa that Martin at first brags about is portrayed as the type of Indian seen in movies, glamorous and exaggerated. In real life, Grandpa was not tall and stately; he was old and had stringy gray hair.
6. The Sioux heritage that he brags about is the cultural heritage that includes crafts and songs. The heritage that he learns about from Grandpa is the spiritual heritage.
7. The night after he gives Martin the medicine bag and explains its meaning, Grandpa must go to the hospital. He passed the bag along because he knew that he would die soon.
8. Suggested response: Martin comes to stand alone on the prairie because he has come to accept the spiritual heritage of the Sioux that was passed on to him by Grandpa.

Applying

9. Answers will differ. Suggested response: It is important for people to maintain their cultural heritage because this heritage is the basis for their world view and beliefs. Without this, people would have difficulty dealing with the troubles and unexplainable aspects of their lives.

THINKING ABOUT THE SELECTION

Recalling

1. Why is Martin embarrassed when Grandpa comes to visit? How is Cheryl's reaction to Grandpa's visit different from Martin's?
2. What three reasons does Grandpa give for his visit?
3. What is the purpose of a vision quest? How did Grandfather's father receive the name Iron Shell?
4. What does Martin do at the end of the story?

Interpreting

5. Compare and contrast the real Grandpa with the Grandpa Martin at first brags to his friends about.
6. How is the Sioux heritage Martin at first brags about different from the Sioux heritage he learns about from Grandpa?
7. What happens to Grandpa at the end of the story?
8. Explain how Martin comes to stand alone on the lonely prairie?

Applying

9. Why is it important for people to maintain their cultural heritage?

ANALYZING LITERATURE

Reviewing the Short Story

The elements of plot, character, setting, and theme all work together to create a total effect. Think of all of these elements and apply them to "The Medicine Bag."

1. Give a brief summary of the story, focusing on the conflict and the resolution.
2. Compare and contrast Martin and his grandfather.
3. Explain how time and place are important in this story.
4. How would you express the theme?

CRITICAL THINKING AND READING

Evaluating a Story

To evaluate a story means to judge how successfully it works. Using your knowledge of literary elements and how they work in short stories, you can comment on what you think works best in any story.

Prepare an answer to one of the following questions. Present your answer in a brief oral report to your classmates.

1. Do you think the characters in "The Medicine Bag" were well drawn?
2. Do you think the conflict was presented successfully?
3. What does the story say about the importance of a cultural heritage?

UNDERSTANDING LANGUAGE

Appreciating Another Language

A writer will sometimes use words from another language to help draw the characters more vividly. For example, in "The Medicine Bag" the author peppers Grandpa's speech with Sioux words.

1. What words does Grandpa use to greet Martin?
2. What word does he use to greet Cheryl?
3. What word does he use for the Great Spirit?

THINKING AND WRITING

Continuing a Story

Imagine you are Martin thirty years in the future. You now have a son of your own and want to pass on the medicine bag. Write a continuation of this story telling what you would say to your son. Revise your story, making sure you have clearly expressed the importance of the medicine bag to you. Finally, proofread your story and share it with your classmates.

(Answers begin on p. 234.)

They also lose a part of their personal identity.

ANSWERS TO ANALYZING LITERATURE

1. Suggested response: The story begins with Grandpa's visit to Martin's family. The conflict develops within Martin between his love for Grandpa and the ways of the Sioux, and his fears and embarrassment about how his friends will react to the reality of Grandpa and his different way of life. The conflict is heightened when he learns that Grandpa has come to give him his medicine bag. The story progresses as first his sister's, and then his own friends meet and are extremely impressed with Grandpa. The story reaches the climax when Grandpa explains the history and meaning of the medicine bag and gives it to Martin. Martin comes to fully accept his Indian heritage. The resolution of the story is his grandfather's inevitable illness and his own journey to the reservation to fulfill Grandpa's instructions concerning the bag.
2. Martin is a young man, raised in the city by his Indian mother and white father. Grandfather is an old, full-blooded Sioux Indian who has lived his entire life on a rural reservation. While Grandpa is completely immersed in the culture of the Sioux Indians, Martin at first only enjoys the glorified aspects of his grandfather and his Sioux heritage.
3. The time and place are important to this story because the setting in a city in contemporary times contrasts even more sharply Martin's upbringing and beliefs with those of his grandfather.
4. Suggested response: The theme is the importance of maintaining the traditional cultural beliefs of one's heritage despite an ever-changing world.

ANSWERS TO CRITICAL THINKING AND READING

1. Answers will differ. Students should support their answers with details from the story and from their knowledge of the literary element of character.
2. Answers will differ. Students should present their argument by using examples from the story and the definition of conflict to support their ideas.
3. Answers will differ. Students should use examples from the story to support their ideas and generally should follow the idea expressed in the theme.

Challenge Have **more advanced** students list the main points of each oral report and, using these notes for support, decide whether or not the story was well written.

ANSWERS TO UNDERSTANDING LANGUAGE

1. "Hau, Takoza"
2. "Wicincala"
3. "Wakantanka"

THINKING AND WRITING

For help with this assignment, students can refer to Lesson 17, "Writing a Short Story," in the Handbook of Writing About Literature.

Writing Across the Curriculum You might want to have students research and report on different aspects of the history of Native Americans. If you do, perhaps inform the social studies department. Social studies teachers might provide ideas and guidance for students in researching.

FOCUS ON READING

Write the following three sentences on the chalkboard:

Tim threw the ball before the batter expected.

Tim threw the ball because the batter was not paying attention.

Tim expected the batter to miss, but instead she hit a homerun.

Ask students to identify the sentence that shows time order, the one that shows cause and effect, and the one that shows comparison and contrast.

ANSWERS TO THE ACTIVITY

Signal Words: At first, when, now, first, next, then, finally
Time Order:
Charlie thinks he failed the inkblot test.
Algernon keeps beating him in the mazes.
Miss Kinnian tells him they will use him.
Charlie is ecstatic.
They do use him in the operation.
His intelligence is tripled.
He finds that his old spelling and punctuation were all wrong.
He realizes that Joe and Frank had been making fun of him.
He sees what Dr. Nemur and Dr. Strauss were really like.
He perceives that Miss Kinnian is beautiful.

FOCUS ON READING

Understanding Relationships

One way to increase your understanding of what you read it is to understand the relationships that exist in the plot, setting, and characters. **Time order, cause and effect,** and **comparison and contrast** are the most important relationships you will need to know.

Time Order

Time order refers to the sequence of events. In most stories events are arranged chronologically, that is, in the order in which they occurred. Writers often use signal words to help you see the sequence of events. Be aware of the following time-order signal words:

first	then	before	later	during	when	previously
at last	next	after	earlier	finally	now	preceding

Activity

Read the following paragraph and jot down the time-order signal words. Then list the events in chronological order.

> At first Charlie thought they wouldn't use him, for he was sure he had failed the inkblot test. And what is more, Algernon kept beating him in the mazes. Consequently, when Miss Kinnian told him he had been chosen for the operation, he had been ecstatic because he wanted to be smart. Now that his intelligence had tripled, he was amazed by how different things were from the way he once saw them. First he found out that his old spelling and punctuation were all wrong. Next he realized that Joe and Frank had been making fun of him. Then he saw what Dr. Nemur and Dr. Strauss were really like. Finally he perceived that Miss Kinnian was beautiful.

Cause and Effect

Cause-and-effect relationships help you understand why something occurs and how it is connected to other events. A **cause** is a reason for something happening. An **effect** is the result of some action or cause. Watch for the following signal words.

as	so	therefore	accordingly	consequently	so that
for	thus	as a result	in order that	because	since

Read these sentences:

At first Charlie thought they wouldn't use him, for he was sure he had failed the inkblot test.
Charlie thought they wouldn't use him because Algernon kept beating him in the mazes.
Because he was now smart, he perceived that Miss Kinnian was beautiful.

Note that the first two sentences have the same effect but two different causes. Often there are several reasons for something happening. In the first two sentences, the cause falls at the end of the sentence. In the third, it falls at the beginning.

Activity

Look again at the activity paragraph on page 236. Find at least five cause-and-effect relationships in the paragraph and write them in complete sentences, using one of the signal words.

Comparison and Contrast

Comparing involves finding ways that things are similar, while **contrasting** involves noting ways that they are different. Words such as *both, similar,* and *just as much* indicate a comparison relationship. The following words are used to show contrasting relationships:

but	although	in contrast	in spite of	on the contrary	whereas
yet	however	nevertheless	instead	on the other hand	while

Activity

Write a well-developed paragraph comparing and contrasting Charlie as he appeared at the beginning of the story and at the end. Brainstorm to determine how the two Charlies are alike and how they are different. Jot down words that would describe the first Charlie and ones that would characterize the last Charlie. Write your paragraph, including signal words to indicate the relationships. Use the information in this paragraph to write a second paragraph in which you determine whether Charlie was better off before the operation or after. Give reasons to support your decision.

ANSWERS TO THE ACTIVITY

Cause and Effect:
Suggested Responses:

Charlie thought they wouldn't use him, for he was sure he had failed the inkblot test.
Charlie thought they wouldn't use him because Algernon kept beating him in the mazes.
Charlie thought they wouldn't use him; consequently, when Miss Kinnian told him he had been chosen for the operation, he was ecstatic.
Now he saw things differently as a result of the operation.
As a result of his tripled intelligence, he saw that Miss Kinnian was beautiful.

Guidelines for Evaluating

Comparison and Contrast

1. Does the paragraph compare and contrast Charlie at the beginning of the story and at the end?
2. Does it use adequate evidence from the short story to support the comparison and contrast?
3. Is the paragraph well organized?
4. Is it free from grammar, punctuation, and mechanics problems?

The writing assignments on page 238 have students write creatively, while those on page 239 have them think about the short stories and write critically.

The writing assignments on page 238 have students write creatively, while those on page 239 have them think about the short stories and write critically.

YOU THE WRITER
Guidelines for Evaluating Assignment 1

1. Has the student maintained a consistent point of view?
2. Has the student used a first-person narrator?
3. Has the student revealed only information the narrator would know?
4. Is the episode free from grammar, usage, and mechanics errors?

Guidelines for Evaluating Assignment 2

1. Does the description of the setting create a unified effect?
2. Does it include specific details of time and place?
3. Is the description well organized?
4. Is the description free from grammar, usage, and mechanics errors?

Guidelines for Evaluating Assignment 3

1. Does the short mystery explain how the "perfect crime" might be committed?
2. Does it provide the clue needed to solve the crime?
3. Is the solution logical?
4. Is the mystery free from grammar, usage, and mechanics errors?

YOU THE WRITER

Assignment

1. Select a character other than the narrator in one of the short stories and retell part of the story from his or her point of view. Use first-person narration.

Prewriting. Select one episode, or event, from the story. List the main action in that part of the story. Include the thoughts of the character you chose. Do not list other characters' thoughts.

Writing. Write the first draft of your episode. Remember to use first-person point of view.

Revising. Ask another student to read your episode. Can the person tell from which character's point of view you wrote? If not, you need to rewrite that section of your story. Reveal only what one character knows.

Assignment

2. The setting can contribute to the mood of a short story. Choose a particular mood you want to convey—tension? hostility? joy? peacefulness? Then describe a story setting that reflects that mood. Use specific details of time and place. Do not describe a character. Write only a physical description of time and place.

Prewriting. Record your mood in the middle of the page. Jot down details of a setting that creates this mood. Cluster these details.

Writing. Write the first draft of your description of a setting. Make sure the details you include help create the mood.

Revising. Review your first draft. Check to see that your description is unified; that is, that all the details help create a single impression, or mood.

Assignment

3. Mysteries are popular because they challenge the reader to solve the crime before the detective does. Try writing a short mystery. Think about how your "perfect crime" might be committed and what clues a detective would need in order to solve it.

Prewriting. Brainstorm to form a list of "perfect crimes." Choose one and list some clues a detective would need.

Writing. Write the first draft of your story. Be sure you clearly explain the problem that is to be solved.

Revising. Revise your story to make sure you have included enough background to the crime and all the necessary clues. Make sure that the solution is logical.

YOU THE CRITIC

Assignment

1. Choose a short story in which the main character faces a challenge. Write an essay describing the challenge, how the character deals with it, and the outcome.

Prewriting. Prepare an outline, with an emphasis on challenge. Use the outline to organize your thoughts.

Writing. Begin your essay with an extended definition of the word *challenge*. End this introductory paragraph with your premise. Use your outline to explain the challenge, fill in details of the character's actions, and flesh out how the challenge was met and its outcome.

Revising. Read over your essay. Check to see that you have presented your points clearly and arranged them in logical order.

Assignment

2. A symbol is an object, an action, or an idea that stands for something other than itself. Choose one of the short stories and write an essay exploring how symbolism is used.

Prewriting. Freewrite about the story you chose. Let your mind roam freely, jotting down thoughts about anything that might be a symbol.

Writing. Write the first draft of an essay. Be sure your essay deals with the symbols in a logical order. Try organizing your ideas according to an order-of-importance pattern.

Revising. Revise your first draft. Check to see that you have stated clearly what the symbols are and what they represent.

Assignment

3. Some of the short stories you read focus on a young person's viewpoint. Choose two young people from either two different stories or the same one. Compare these two characters, explaining how they are alike and what they learn about life.

Prewriting. Make two lists, one for each character. List the qualities and characteristics each person has.

Writing. Begin your essay by telling how the two characters are alike. Include at least three details from your lists. Use key words such as *similar, both,* and *comparison* to tell how the two characters relate. Then tell what they learn about life. Again, include details from your lists. Conclude with a sentence that summarizes the comparison of the two characters.

Revising. Revise your writing. Check to see that you used several key words to signal the comparisons.

YOU THE CRITIC

Guidelines for Evaluating Assignment 1

1. Does the essay describe a challenge that a main character faces, how the character deals with it, and the outcome?
2. Does the essay begin with an extended definition?
3. Does the introductory paragraph end with a premise?
4. Is the essay free from grammar, usage, and mechanics errors?

Guidelines for Evaluating Assignment 2

1. Does the essay deal with the symbols by using order of importance?
2. Does the essay state clearly what the symbols are and what they stand for?
3. Has the student adequately supported his or her point?
4. Is the essay free from grammar, usage, and mechanics errors?

Guidelines for Evaluating Assignment 3

1. Are there at least three details showing how the two characters are alike?
2. Does the comparison tell what the characters learn about life?
3. Are there key words to signal the comparisons?
4. Is the comparison free from grammar, usage, and mechanics errors?

FIRST ROW ORCHESTRA, 1951
Edward Hopper
Hirshhorn Museum and Sculpture Garden, Smithsonian Institution

DRAMA

What do you think of when you hear the word *drama?* Do you think of the theater with actors, a stage, costumes, sets, and a live audience? Do you think of the movies with action presented on a large screen? Do you think of the pleasure of sitting home and watching a drama unfold on television? Or do you think of hearing a play over the radio? The live theater, the movies, television, and radio—all are means by which drama comes to us.

A play is written to be performed. Therefore, when you read a play, you must visualize how it would appear and sound to an audience. By using your imagination, you can build a theater in your mind. Because a play is written to be performed, it uses certain conventions you do not encounter in short stories. It contains stage directions that tell the actors how to speak and how to move upon the stage. Most of the story is presented through dialogue, the words the characters speak. In addition it is divided into short units of action called "scenes" and larger ones called "acts."

In this unit you will encounter three short plays: a twist on a fairy tale, a romance, and a play with a social comment. In addition you will read one full-length play based on the diary of a young girl.

Humanities Note

Fine art, *First Row Orchestra,* 1951, by Edward Hopper. Edward Hopper (1882-1967) was an American painter of sunlight on houses, lonely streets, and scenes that most Americans take for granted. His education in art consisted of a painting class in New York City and a trip to Paris to learn and paint. He was an introspective and dedicated artist who pursued his own realistic style. His paintings transform the ordinary into something unforgettable.

First Row Orchestra, a look at the front row of a theater before the curtain goes up, is typical of Hopper's detached way of observing people. He politely records their pre-show settlings without attempting to interpret their personalities. The architectural features of the theater are painted with a minimum of detail, anything that can not be seen in a quick glance has been eliminated. It is a pure uncomplicated depiction, from an interesting point of view, of an audience preparing to experience drama on stage.

Reading Actively The drama presented in this unit runs from light comedy to tragedy. Students are introduced to the drama unit with the humorous play *The Ugly Duckling.* Even in this short play, students should get a sense of how the actors would move and speak on stage. You might point out to students that some critics believe that a written script is not a play until it has been performed before an audience. Drama is the most dynamic literary form.

Enrichment Help students distinguish between comedy and tragedy. What makes them different, and how do the actors achieve their different effects? Elicit from students that comedy often involves some exaggerated belief, occurrence, or behavior. Although comedy does present characters in social situations, it does not for the most part raise the serious moral or philosophical questions found in tragedy. Tragedy, on the other hand, maintains a serious mood despite some lighter moments. Tragedy asks important questions about the meaning of life, death, morality, and human relationships. Aristotle defined the emotional impact of tragedy as "the arousal of pity and fear." Ask students what other emotions are aroused by a play such as *The Diary of Anne Frank.*

READING ACTIVELY

Drama

The word *drama* brings to mind the world of the theater. It is an exciting world—a curtain rising on a stage with sets, lights, and actors in costume. But drama includes more than the theater. Because drama is a story told in dialogue by performers before an audience, the definition includes television plays, radio plays, and even movies. In all these kinds of drama, actors make a world come alive before an audience.

Plays are meant to be performed, but it is possible just to read a play. When you read a play, you can make it come alive by staging it in your imagination. The play that you are reading is a script. It contains not only the words that the actors speak but also the stage directions the playwright provides to indicate how to put on the play. Stage directions tell what the stage should look like, what the characters wear, how they speak their lines, and where they move.

Stage directions use a particular vocabulary. *Right, left, up, down,* and *center* refer to areas of the stage as the actors see it. To help you visualize what is meant when a stage direction tells an actor to move down left, for example, picture the stage like this:

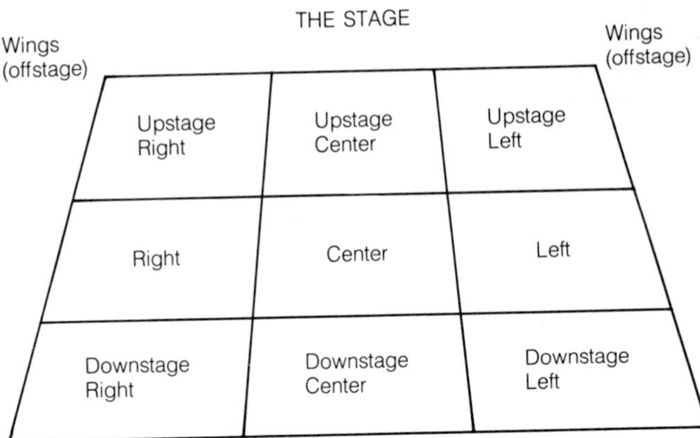

When you are reading drama, right and left are the opposite of what you know. Remember that these are directions for actors, not viewers. Whether as reader, viewer, or actor, though, you too can enjoy the world of drama.

Becoming an active reader of drama will increase your understanding and enjoyment of plays. Reading actively includes seeing the play in your mind while you continually question the meaning of what the characters are saying and doing.

Use the following strategies to help you read drama actively. These strategies will help you to enjoy and appreciate the plays in this unit.

Visualize

Use the directions and information supplied by the playwright to picture the stage and the characters in action. Create the scene in your mind. Hear the characters' voices. See their gestures. Doing so will give meaning to their words.

Question

Question the meaning of each character's words and actions. What motives and traits do the words and actions reveal? What situation does each character face?

Predict

Once you recognize the conflict and understand the characters' motives, predict what you think will happen. How will the conflict be resolved? What will become of each character?

Clarify

If a character's words or actions are not clear to you, stop and try to make sense of them. You may need to look for clues in earlier words or actions. As you read, look also for answers to your questions, and check your predictions.

Summarize

Pause occasionally to review what has happened. What do you know about the story being told through the characters' actions and words?

Pull It Together

Pull together all the elements of the play. What does the play mean? Is there a message, or is the play purely entertainment? What does the play say to you about life?

Reading Strategies A feature that makes plays different from other forms of literature is the stage directions. If students are unfamiliar with reading drama, they may initially find these insertions intrusive. On the contrary, stage directions are integral to the successful rendition of the play. Be sure students understand what the stage directions mean and their purpose. To read the play actively, students must not overlook the stage directions, which will help them to visualize the action and characters.

More About the Author Ask students to recall details from Milne's Winnie the Pooh stories. Then have students look up the meaning of the word *whimsical* and ask them to explain why the Pooh stories were whimsical. Tell students that some critics did not find Milne's whimsical outlook amusing. Ask students to suggest reasons why critics might have disapproved of a whimsical play for adults.

Literary Focus Discuss the similarities between one-act plays and short stories. Then have students consider some of the important differences. They might contrast the short story writer's use of description to create setting with the playwright's reliance on a physical set. Have students think of short stories that could or could not easily be dramatized.

Look For Point out to students that unexpected twists, disguises, and mistaken identities are traditional features of comic plays like *The Ugly Duckling.*

Writing/Prior Knowledge Have your students discuss the various ideas they wrote about beauty. Have students suggest ways in which the ideas could be illustrated, either visually or dramatically.

Vocabulary Have your more advanced students write single sentences in which they use each word with either an antonym or a group of words suggesting the opposite meaning. Examples: His thinking was shallow, rather than profound. Instead of paying homage to their leader, the mob shouted abuses.

Spelling Tip Words ending in *-or,* like *predecessor,* almost always refer to rank or position. Some examples are *ambassador, editor, juror, counselor, exterior, junior.*

GUIDE FOR READING

The Ugly Duckling

Alan Alexander Milne (1882–1956) was a British writer best remembered for his children's books featuring Winnie the Pooh and Christopher Robin, which he wrote for his son. Most of Milne's writing, however, was done for an adult audience. From 1906 to 1914, he was an assistant editor and contributor to the British humor magazine *Punch.* In addition to writing many mystery stories, Milne wrote nearly thirty plays. In *The Ugly Duckling* Milne presents a love story with a humorous twist.

The One-Act Play

A one-act play is similar in some ways to a short story. Like a short story, it presents only a few characters and its plot develops quickly. It usually takes place on a single set. Often it has a single theme, or general idea about life, which is presented through dialogue.

Look For

As you read *The Ugly Duckling,* look for the ways in which it is similar to a short story. What is the plot? Who are the main characters? Where does it take place? What does it reveal about life? Also look for the ways in which the characters and situations are not quite what you expected.

Writing

You have probably heard the expression "Beauty is in the eye of the beholder," which means that each person sees beauty somewhat differently. Freewrite for five minutes about what beauty means to you.

Vocabulary

Knowing the following words will help you as you read *The Ugly Duckling.*

profound (prə found′) *adj.*: Deep (p. 246)
posterity (päs ter′ ə tē) *n.*: Future generations (p. 246)
predecessor (pred′ ə ses′ ər) *n.*: One who comes before another in time (p. 246)
homage (häm′ ij) *n.*: Public expression of honor (p. 247)
nonchalantly (nän′ shə länt′ lē) *adv.*: In a casual way (p. 248)
cryptic (krip′ tik) *adj.*: Having hidden meaning (p. 248)
ruse (ro͞oz) *n.*: A trick or plan for fooling someone (p. 251)

Objectives

1 To recognize characters, plot, settings, and theme in the one-act play
2 To recognize parody in the play
3 To write a persuasive letter to cast the characters of the play

Support Material

Teaching Portfolio
Teacher Backup, pp. 363–366
Grammar in Action Worksheets, *Understanding Sentence Fragments,* pp. 367–368, *Using Dashes,* pp. 369–370,
Usage and Mechanics Worksheet, p. 371
Vocabulary Check, p. 372
Critical Thinking and Reading Worksheet, *Recognizing Parody,* p. 373
Language Worksheet, *Completing Analogies,* p. 374
Selection Test, pp. 375–376

The Ugly Duckling

A. A. Milne

CHARACTERS

The King	**The Chancellor**[1]	**Prince Simon**
The Queen	**Dulcibella**	**Carlo**
The Princess Camilla		

[*The* SCENE *is the Throne Room of the Palace; a room of many doors, or, if preferred, curtain-openings: simply furnished with three thrones for Their Majesties and Her Royal Highness the* PRINCESS CAMILLA*—in other words, with three handsome chairs. At each side is a long seat: reserved, as it might be, for His Majesty's Council (if any), but useful, as to-day, for other purposes. The* KING *is asleep on his throne with a handkerchief over his face. He is a king of any country from any story-book, in whatever costume you please. But he should be wearing his crown.*]

A VOICE. [*Announcing*] His Excellency the
1 Chancellor! [*The* CHANCELLOR, *an elderly man in hornrimmed spectacles, enters, bowing. The* KING *wakes up with a start and removes the handkerchief from his face.*]

KING. [*With simple dignity*] I was thinking.

CHANCELLOR. [*Bowing*] Never, Your Majesty, was greater need for thought than now.

1. **chancellor** (chan′ sə lər) *n.*: An official secretary.

KING. That's what I was thinking. [*He struggles into a more dignified position.*] Well, what is it? More trouble?

CHANCELLOR. What we might call the old trouble, Your Majesty.

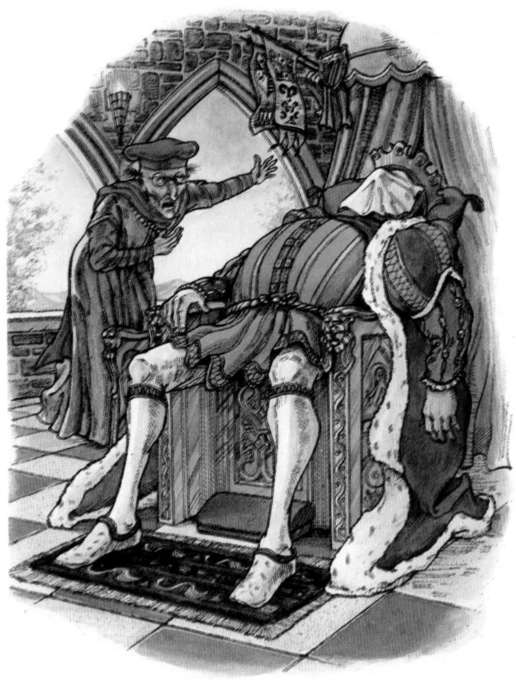

Presentation

Motivation/Prior Knowledge Have a student retell the fairy tale "The Ugly Duckling," by Hans Christian Andersen. Ask students what they might expect if this theme were used in a play about a fairytale kingdom where the princess is not as pretty as a princess is supposed to be.

Literary Focus With more advanced students, you might want to discuss farce before you proceed with the play. Students also need to know that humorous plays deal with exaggeration because that intensifies the humor. The actions of the King and Queen in this play are especially exaggerated. The actions of the Prince and Princess are not because, by not exaggerating their behavior, the reader tends to be more sympathetic to the young lovers.

Purpose-Setting Question What are the ways in which this is not a typical fairy-tale kingdom? In what ways is it?

1 **Enrichment** Horn-rimmed spectacles are a fairly recent invention. They do not belong in a fairy-tale kingdom. What effect does this anachronism have on the play? Does it help make it more humorous? Have students discuss other anachronisms they have read in stories or plays.

2 Master Teacher Note A good reader can make this dialogue very amusing. Ask several students to read aloud this section of the play and have the class listen for differences in interpretations. This could lead to a discussion of individual interpretation in drama and how, each time a play is staged, it is different from other stagings because of the way in which the actors and directors interpret the characters.

3 Master Teacher Note The artist who didn't make the Princess appear beautiful in her portrait suffered a dire fate. People who have their portraits painted usually want to look attractive. Bring in some reproductions of famous portraits or have students recall some that they have viewed. Examples to bring to class might be the "Helga" portraits by Andrew Wyeth. Ask the class if the subjects in the portraits are attractive. Do the students think they looked that way in real life or was their appearance altered by the artist? It is characteristic of Wyeth, for example, to paint a portrait which is not a portrait; it is an expression of affection and a vivid memory. Ask the students, if their portraits were being painted, whether they would prefer reality or a flattering illusion.

4 Discussion Discuss the idea of beauty from within. Is beauty only skin deep?

5 Enrichment The Chancellor notes that Her Royal Highness has great beauty of character. Have students consider whether such ploys to make people feel better are socially useful. Has anyone in the class used similar "compliments"? How did the people receiving them react?

KING. It's what I was saying last night to the Queen. "Uneasy lies the head that wears a crown," was how I put it.[2]

CHANCELLOR. A profound and original thought, which may well go down to posterity.

KING. You mean it may go down well with posterity. I hope so. Remind me to tell you some time of another little thing I said to Her Majesty: something about a fierce light beating on a throne.[3] Posterity would like that, too. Well, what is it?

CHANCELLOR. It is in the matter of Her Royal Highness' wedding.

KING. Oh . . . yes.

CHANCELLOR. As Your Majesty is aware, the young Prince Simon arrives today to seek Her Royal Highness' hand in marriage. He has been traveling in distant lands and, as I understand, has not—er—has not—

KING. You mean he hasn't heard anything.

CHANCELLOR. It is a little difficult to put this tactfully, Your Majesty.

KING. Do your best, and I will tell you afterwards how you got on.

2 **CHANCELLOR.** Let me put it this way. The Prince Simon will naturally assume that Her Royal Highness has the customary—so customary as to be, in my own poor opinion, slightly monotonous—has what one might call the inevitable[4]—so inevitable as to be, in my opinion again, almost mechanical—will assume, that she has the, as *I* think of it, faultily faultless, icily regular, splendidly—

KING. What you are trying to say in the fewest words possible is that my daughter is not beautiful.

CHANCELLOR. Her beauty is certainly elusive,[5] Your Majesty.

KING. It is. It has eluded you, it has eluded me, it has eluded everybody who has seen her. It even eluded the Court Painter. His last words were, "Well, I did my best." His successor[6] is now painting the view across the water-meadows from the West Turret. He says that his doctor has advised him to keep to landscape.

CHANCELLOR. It is unfortunate, Your Majesty, but there it is. One just cannot understand how it can have occurred.

KING. You don't think she takes after *me*, at all? You don't detect a likeness?

CHANCELLOR. Most certainly not, Your Majesty.

KING. Good. . . . Your predecessor did.

CHANCELLOR. I have often wondered what happened to my predecessor.

KING. Well, now you know. [*There is a short silence.*]

CHANCELLOR. Looking at the bright side, although Her Royal Highness is not, strictly speaking, beautiful—

KING. Not, truthfully speaking, beautiful—

CHANCELLOR. Yet she has great beauty of character.

KING. My dear Chancellor, we are not consid-

---

2. This quotation is actually from the play *King Henry IV* by William Shakespeare.
3. This reference was actually made by Alfred, Lord Tennyson, in the "Dedication" to his epic poem *Idylls of the King*.
4. inevitable (in ev′ ə tə b′l) *adj.*: Unavoidable.
5. elusive (i lo͞o′ siv) *adj.*: Hard to grasp mentally.
6. successor (sək ses′ ər) *n.*: A person that follows or comes after another.

ering Her Royal Highness' character, but her chances of getting married. You observe that there is a distinction.

CHANCELLOR. Yes, Your Majesty.

KING. Look at it from the suitor's[7] point of view. If a girl is beautiful, it is easy to assume that she has, tucked away inside her, an equally beautiful character. But it is impossible to assume that an unattractive girl, however elevated in character, has, tucked away inside her, an equally beautiful face. That is, so to speak, not where you want it—tucked away.

CHANCELLOR. Quite so, Your Majesty.

KING. This doesn't, of course, alter the fact that the Princess Camilla is quite the nicest person in the Kingdom.

CHANCELLOR. [*Enthusiastically*] She is indeed, Your Majesty. [*Hurriedly*] With the exception,[8] I need hardly say, of Your Majesty—and Her Majesty.

KING. Your exceptions are tolerated[9] for their loyalty and condemned[10] for their extreme fatuity.[11]

CHANCELLOR. Thank you, Your Majesty.

KING. As an adjective for your King, the word "nice" is ill-chosen. As an adjective for Her Majesty, it is—ill-chosen. [*At which moment* HER MAJESTY *comes in. The* KING *rises. The* CHANCELLOR *puts himself at right angles.*]

QUEEN. [*Briskly*] Ah. Talking about Camilla? [*She sits down.*]

KING. [*Returning to his throne*] As always, my dear, you are right.

QUEEN. [*To* CHANCELLOR] This fellow, Simon —What's he like?

CHANCELLOR. Nobody has seen him, Your Majesty.

QUEEN. How old is he?

CHANCELLOR. Five-and-twenty, I understand.

QUEEN. In twenty-five years he must have been seen by somebody.

KING. [*To the* CHANCELLOR] Just a fleeting glimpse.

CHANCELLOR. I meant, Your Majesty, that no detailed report of him has reached this country, save that he has the usual personal advantages and qualities expected of a Prince, and has been traveling in distant and dangerous lands.

QUEEN. Ah! Nothing gone wrong with his eyes? Sunstroke or anything?

CHANCELLOR. Not that I am aware of, Your Majesty. At the same time, as I was venturing[12] to say to His Majesty, Her Royal Highness' character and disposition are so outstandingly—

QUEEN. Stuff and nonsense. You remember what happened when we had the Tournament of Love last year.

CHANCELLOR. I was not myself present, Your Majesty. I had not then the honor of—I was abroad, and never heard the full story.

QUEEN. No; it was the other fool. They all rode up to Camilla to pay their homage—it was the first time they had seen her. The heralds blew their trumpets, and announced that

---

7. suitor (soot′ ər) *n.*: A man courting or wooing a woman.
8. exception (ik sep′ shən) *n.*: Exclusion.
9. tolerated (täl′ ə rāt′ ′d) *v.*: Allowed; permitted.
10. condemned (kən dem″d) *v.*: Disapproved of.
11. fatuity (fə too′ ə tē) *n.*: Stupidity.

12. venturing (ven′ chər iŋ) *v.*: Expressing at the risk of criticism, objection, or denial.

247

6 **Discussion** How does this stage direction create humor?

7 **Discussion** Discuss the outcome of the Tournament of Love. How would students expect a typical fairy-tale tournament to end?

she would marry whichever Prince was left master of the field when all but one had been unhorsed. The trumpets were blown again, they charged enthusiastically into

6 the fight, and—[*The* KING *looks nonchalantly at the ceiling and whistles a few bars.*]—don't do that.

KING. I'm sorry, my dear.

7 **QUEEN.** [*To* CHANCELLOR] And what happened? They all simultaneously fell off their horses and assumed a posture of defeat.

KING. One of them was not quite so quick as the others. I was very quick. I proclaimed him the victor.

QUEEN. At the Feast of Betrothal held that night—

KING. We were all very quick.

QUEEN. The Chancellor announced that by the laws of the country the successful suitor had to pass a further test. He had to give the correct answer to a riddle.

CHANCELLOR. Such undoubtedly is the fact, Your Majesty.

KING. There are times for announcing facts, and times for looking at things in a broad-minded way. Please remember that, Chancellor.

CHANCELLOR. Yes, Your Majesty.

QUEEN. I invented the riddle myself. Quite an easy one. What is it which has four legs and barks like a dog? The answer is, "A dog."

KING. [*To* CHANCELLOR] You see that?

CHANCELLOR. Yes, Your Majesty.

KING. It isn't difficult.

QUEEN. He, however, seemed to find it so. He said an eagle. Then he said a serpent; a very high mountain with slippery sides; two peacocks; a moonlight night; the day after to-morrow—

KING. Nobody could accuse him of not trying.

QUEEN. *I* did.

KING. I *should* have said that nobody could fail to recognize in his attitude an appearance of doggedness.[13]

QUEEN. Finally he said "Death." I nudged the King—

KING. Accepting the word "nudge" for the moment, I rubbed my ankle with one hand, clapped him on the shoulder with the other, and congratulated him on the correct answer. He disappeared under the table, and, personally, I never saw him again.

QUEEN. His body was found in the moat next morning.

CHANCELLOR. But what was he doing in the moat, Your Majesty?

KING. Bobbing about. Try not to ask needless questions.

CHANCELLOR. It all seems so strange.

QUEEN. What does?

CHANCELLOR. That Her Royal Highness, alone of all the Princesses one has ever heard of, should lack that invariable[14] attribute of Royalty, supreme beauty.

QUEEN. [*To the* KING] That was your Great-Aunt Malkin. She came to the christening. You know what she said.

KING. It was cryptic. Great-Aunt Malkin's besetting weakness. She came to *my* christening—she was one hundred and one then, and that was fifty-one years ago. [*To*

---

13. **doggedness** (dôg' id nis) *n.*: Stubbornness.
14. **invariable** (in ver' ē ə b'l) *adj.*: Not changing; constant.

Grammar in Action

A **sentence fragment** is only part of a sentence. It lacks a subject or a predicate or both, and it does not express a complete thought. For example,

Went to the christening. (lacks subject)
She the one! (lacks predicate)
On the way home. (lacks subject and predicate)

Good writers avoid sentence fragments in most formal writing situations. However, when writing dialogue, they may include fragments to capture the way people actually speak.

Notice the fragments in the following examples:

QUEEN. His body was found in the moat next morning.
CHANCELLOR. But what was he doing in the moat, Your Majesty?
KING. *Bobbing about.* Try not to ask needless questions.

KING. It was cryptic. *Great-Aunt Malkin's besetting weakness.* She came to *my* christening—she was one hundred and one *the* CHANCELLOR] How old would that make her?

CHANCELLOR. One hundred and fifty-two, Your Majesty.

KING. [*After thought*] About that, yes. She promised me that when I grew up I should have all the happiness which my wife deserved. It struck me at the time—well, when I say "at the time," I was only a week old—but it did strike me as soon as anything could strike me—I mean of that nature—well, work it out for yourself, Chancellor. It opens up a most interesting field of speculation. Though naturally I have not liked to go into it at all deeply with Her Majesty.

QUEEN. I never heard anything less cryptic. She was wishing you extreme happiness.

KING. I don't think she was *wishing* me anything. However.

CHANCELLOR. [*To the* QUEEN] But what, Your Majesty, did she wish Her Royal Highness?

QUEEN. Her other godmother—on my side—had promised her the dazzling beauty for which all the women in my family are famous—[*She pauses, and the* KING *snaps his fingers surreptitiously in the direction of the* CHANCELLOR.]

CHANCELLOR. [*Hurriedly*] Indeed, yes, Your Majesty. [*The* KING relaxes.]

QUEEN. And Great-Aunt Malkin said—[*To the* KING]—what were the words?

KING.
I give you with this kiss
A wedding-day surprise.
Where ignorance is bliss
'Tis folly to be wise.

I thought the last two lines rather neat. But what it *meant*—

then, and that was fifty-one years ago. [To the Chancellor] How old would that make her?
CHANCELLOR. *One hundred and fifty-two, Your Majesty.*
KING. [*After thought*] *About that, yes.*

In the give-and-take of conversation, people often answer questions with fragments and respond to the answers with fragments. Why do you think this is so?

Student Activity 1. Rewrite the examples, turning each sentence fragment into a complete sentence. How does this change affect the way the dialogue sounds?

Student Activity 2. Write a conversation in which the King, the Queen, and the Chancellor speculate on the meaning of Great-Aunt Malkin's riddle. Use fragments where appropriate to capture the natural flow of speech.

8 **Discussion** How is this drawbridge different from other fairy-tale drawbridges? This is another uncommon characteristic of this kingdom.

QUEEN. We can all see what it meant. She was given beauty—and where is it? Great-Aunt Malkin took it away from her. The wedding-day surprise is that there will never be a wedding day.

KING. Young men being what they are, my dear, it would be much more surprising if there *were* a wedding day. So how— [*The* PRINCESS *comes in. She is young, happy, healthy, but not beautiful. Or let us say that by some trick of make-up or arrangement of hair she seems plain to us: unlike the* PRINCESS *of the story books.*]

PRINCESS. [*To the* KING] Hallo, darling! [*Seeing the others*] Oh, I say! Affairs of state? Sorry.

KING. [*Holding out his hand*] Don't go, Camilla. [*She takes his hand.*]

CHANCELLOR. Shall I withdraw, Your Majesty?

QUEEN. You are aware, Camilla, that Prince Simon arrives today?

PRINCESS. He has arrived. They're just letting down the drawbridge.

KING. [*Jumping up*] Arrived! I must—

PRINCESS. Darling, you know what the drawbridge is like. It takes at *least* half an hour to let it down.

8 **KING.** [*Sitting down*] It wants oil. [*To the* CHANCELLOR] Have *you* been grudging it oil?

PRINCESS. It wants a new drawbridge, darling.

CHANCELLOR. Have I Your Majesty's permission—

KING. Yes, yes. [*The* CHANCELLOR *bows and goes out.*]

QUEEN. You've told him, of course? It's the only chance.

KING. Er—no. I was just going to, when—

QUEEN. Then I'd better. [*She goes to the door.*] You can explain to the girl; I'll have her sent to you. You've told Camilla?

KING. Er—no. I was just going to, when—

QUEEN. Then you'd better tell her now.

KING. My dear, are you sure—

QUEEN. It's the only chance left. [*Dramatically to heaven*] My daughter! [*She goes out. There is a little silence when she is gone.*]

KING. Camilla, I want to talk seriously to you about marriage.

PRINCESS. Yes, father.

KING. It is time that you learnt some of the facts of life.

PRINCESS. Yes, father.

9 **KING.** Now the great fact about marriage is that once you're married you live happy ever after. All our history books affirm this.

PRINCESS. And your own experience too, darling.

10 **KING.** [*With dignity*] Let us confine ourselves to history for the moment.

PRINCESS. Yes, father.

KING. Of course, there *may* be an exception here and there, which, as it were, proves the rule; just as—oh, well, never mind.

11 **PRINCESS.** [*Smiling*] Go on, darling. You were going to say that an exception here and there proves the rule that all princesses are beautiful.

KING. Well—leave that for the moment. The point is that it doesn't matter *how* you marry, or *who* you marry, as long as you *get* married. Because you'll be happy ever after in any case. Do you follow me so far?

PRINCESS. Yes, father.

KING. Well, your mother and I have a little plan— 12

PRINCESS. Was that it, going out of the door just now?

KING. Er—yes. It concerns your waiting-maid.

PRINCESS. Darling, I have several.

KING. Only one that leaps to the eye, so to speak. The one with the—well, with everything.

PRINCESS. Dulcibella?

KING. That's the one. It is our little plan that at the first meeting she should pass herself off as the Princess—a harmless ruse, of which you will find frequent record in the history books—and allure[15] Prince Simon to his—that is to say, bring him up to the—In other words, the wedding will take place immediately afterwards, and as quietly as possible—well, naturally in view of the fact that your Aunt Malkin is one hundred and fifty-two; and since you will be wearing the family bridal veil—which is no doubt how the custom arose—the surprise after the ceremony will be his. Are you following me at all? Your attention seems to be wandering.

PRINCESS. I was wondering why you needed to tell me.

KING. Just a precautionary measure, in case you happened to meet the Prince or his attendant before the ceremony; in which

---

15. allure (ə loor′) *v.*: Tempt; attract.

9 **Discussion** This is the way life is supposed to be in a fairy tale. Have any students read a fairy tale where this did not take place? Is this always true in reality?

10 **Discussion** How does the King really feel about his wife?

11 **Discussion** Does Princess Camilla understand the situation?

12 **Reading Strategy** Have students summarize the play up to this point and predict what the King plans to do.

13 Enrichment Are ruses like this common in literature? Ask students if they know of other stories or plays where appearances were altered in order to attain a certain outcome. In the Roman myth "Baucis and Philemon," for example, the gods Jupiter and Apollo came to earth disguised as mortals looking for adventures.

14 Master Teacher Note The following scene between the King and Dulcibella is particularly funny. She simply cannot act like a princess, but the King so much wants this ruse to work that he tries to coach her. This can be extremely funny when read aloud and acted out. Choose a particularly outgoing student to read Dulcibella's part.

case, of course, you would pass yourself off as the maid—

13 **PRINCESS.** A harmless ruse, of which, also, you will find frequent record in the history books.

KING. Exactly. But the occasion need not arise.

A VOICE. [*Announcing*] The woman Dulcibella!

KING. Ah! [*To the* PRINCESS] Now, Camilla, if you will just retire to your own apartments, I will come to you there when we are ready for the actual ceremony. [*He leads her out as he is talking; and as he returns calls out.*] Come in, my dear! [DULCIBELLA *comes in. She is beautiful, but dumb.*] Now don't be frightened, there is nothing to be frightened about. Has Her Majesty told you what you have to do?

DULCIBELLA. Y-yes, Your Majesty.

14 **KING.** Well now, let's see how well you can do it. You are sitting here, we will say. [*He leads her to a seat.*] Now imagine that I am Prince Simon. [*He curls his moustache and puts his stomach in. She giggles.*] You are the beautiful Princess Camilla whom he has never seen. [*She giggles again.*] This is a serious moment in your life, and you will find that a giggle will not be helpful. [*He goes to the door.*] I am announced: "His Royal Highness Prince Simon!" That's me being announced. Remember what I said about giggling. You should have a far-away look upon the face. [*She does her best.*] Farther away than that. [*She tries again.*] No, that's too far. You are sitting there, thinking beautiful thoughts—in maiden meditation,[16] fancy-free,[17] as I remember saying to Her Majesty once . . . speaking of somebody else . . . fancy-free, but with the mouth definitely shut—that's better. I advance and fall upon one knee. [*He does so.*] You extend your hand graciously—*graciously;* you're not trying to push him in the face—that's better, and I raise it to my lips—so—and I kiss it—[*He kisses it warmly.*]—no, perhaps not so ardently[18] as that, more like this [*He kisses it again.*], and I say, "Your Royal Highness, this is the most—er—Your Royal Highness, I shall ever be—no—Your Royal Highness, it is the proudest—" Well, the point is that *he* will say it, and it will be something complimentary, and then he will take your hand in both of his, and press it to his heart. [*He does so.*] And then—what do *you* say?

DULCIBELLA. Coo!

KING. No, *not* Coo.

DULCIBELLA. Never had anyone do *that* to me before.

KING. That also strikes the wrong note. What you want to say is, "Oh, Prince Simon!" . . . Say it.

DULCIBELLA. [*Loudly*] Oh, Prince Simon!

KING. No, no. You don't need to shout until he has said "What?" two or three times. Always consider the possibility that he *isn't* deaf. Softly, and giving the words a dying fall, letting them play around his head like a flight of doves.

DULCIBELLA. [*Still a little overloud*] O-o-o-h, Prinsimon!

KING. Keep the idea in your mind of a flight of *doves* rather than a flight of panic-stricken elephants, and you will be all right. Now I'm going to get up and you must, as it

16. meditation (med' ə tā' shən) *n.*: Deep thought.
17. fancy-free: Carefree.

18. ardently (är' d'nt lē) *adv.*: Passionately; with intense feeling.

were, *waft*[19] me into a seat by your side. [*She starts wafting.*] *Not* rescuing a drowning man, that's another idea altogether, useful at times, but at the moment inappropriate. Wafting. Prince Simon will put the necessary muscles into play—all you require to do is to indicate by a gracious movement of the hand the seat you require him to take. Now! [*He gets up, a little stiffly, and sits next to her.*] That was better. Well, here we are. Now, I think you give me a look: something, let us say, half-way between a worshipful attitude and wild abandonment,[20] with an undertone of regal dignity, touched, as it were, with good comradeship. Now try that. [*She gives him a vacant look of bewilderment.*] Frankly, that didn't quite get it. There was just a little something missing. An absence, as it were, of all the qualities I asked for, and in their place an odd resemblance to an unsatisfied fish. Let us try to get at it another way. Dulcibella, have you a young man of your own?

DULCIBELLA. [*Eagerly, seizing his hand*] Oo, yes, he's ever so smart, he's an archer,[21] well not as you might say a real archer, he works in the armory,[22] but old Bottlenose, *you* know who I mean, the Captain of the Guard, says the very next man they ever has to shoot, my Eg shall take his place, knowing Father and how it is with Eg and me, and me being maid to Her Royal Highness and can't marry me till he's a real soldier, but ever so loving, and funny like, the things he says, I said to him once, "Eg," I said—

KING. [*Getting up*] I rather fancy, Dulcibella, that if you think of Eg all the time, *say* as little as possible, and, when thinking of Eg, see that the mouth is not more than partially open, you will do very well. I will show you where you are to sit and wait for His Royal Highness. [*He leads her out. On the way he is saying*] Now remember—*waft*—*waft*—not *hoick*.[23] [PRINCE SIMON *wanders in from the back unannounced. He is a very ordinary-looking young man in rather dusty clothes. He gives a deep sigh of relief as he sinks into the* KING'S *throne. . . .* CAMILLA, *a new and strangely beautiful* CAMILLA, *comes in.*] 15

PRINCESS. [*Surprised*] Well!

PRINCE. Oh, hallo!

PRINCESS. Ought you?

PRINCE. [*Getting up*] Do sit down, won't you?

PRINCESS. Who are you, and how did you get here?

PRINCE. Well, that's rather a long story. Couldn't we sit down? You could sit here if you liked, but it isn't very comfortable.

PRINCESS. That is the King's Throne.

PRINCE. Oh, is that what it is?

PRINCESS. Thrones are not meant to be comfortable.

PRINCE. Well, I don't know if they're meant to be, but they certainly aren't.

PRINCESS. Why were you sitting on the King's Throne, and who are you?

PRINCE. My name is Carlo.

PRINCESS. Mine is Dulcibella.

PRINCE. Good. And now couldn't we sit down?

---

19. waft (waft) *v.*: Signal to; wave.

20. abandonment (ə ban′ dən mənt) *n.*: Unrestrained freedom of actions or emotions; surrender to one's impulses.

21. archer (är′ chər) *n.*: A person who shoots with bow and arrow.

22. armory (är′ mər ē) *n.*: A storehouse for weapons; arsenal.

23. hoick (hoik) *interj.*: A hunter's call to the hounds.

15 Reading Strategy Ask students if their predictions about the King's plan were correct. Summarize what has happened so far in the play. What do you think will happen when the Prince meets Camilla?

PRINCESS. [*Sitting down on the long seat to the left of the throne, and, as it were, wafting him to a place next to her*] You may sit here, if you like. Why are you so tired? [*He sits down.*]

PRINCE. I've been taking very strenuous exercise.

PRINCESS. Is that part of the long story?

PRINCE. It is.

PRINCESS. [*Settling herself*] I love stories.

PRINCE. This isn't a story really. You see, I'm attendant on Prince Simon who is visiting here.

PRINCESS. Oh? I'm attendant on Her Royal Highness.

PRINCE. Then you know what he's here for.

PRINCESS. Yes.

PRINCE. She's very beautiful, I hear.

PRINCESS. Did you hear that? Where have you been lately?

PRINCE. Traveling in distant lands—with Prince Simon.

PRINCESS. Ah! All the same, I don't understand. Is Prince Simon in the Palace now? The drawbridge *can't* be down yet!

PRINCE. I don't suppose it is. *And* what a noise it makes coming down!

PRINCESS. Isn't it terrible?

PRINCE. I couldn't stand it any more. I just had to get away. That's why I'm here.

PRINCESS. But how?

PRINCE. Well, there's only one way, isn't there? That beech tree, and then a swing and a grab for the battlements, and don't ask me to remember it all—[*He shudders.*]

PRINCESS. You mean you came across the moat by that beech tree?

PRINCE. Yes. I got so tired of hanging about.

PRINCESS. But it's terribly dangerous!

PRINCE. That's why I'm so exhausted. Nervous shock. [*He lies back and breathes loudly.*]

PRINCESS. Of course, it's different for *me*.

PRINCE. [*Sitting up*] Say that again. I must have got it wrong.

PRINCESS. It's different for me, because I'm used to it. Besides, I'm so much lighter.

PRINCE. You don't mean that *you*—

PRINCESS. Oh yes, often.

PRINCE. And I thought I was a brave man! At least, I didn't until five minutes ago, and now I don't again.

PRINCESS. Oh, but you are! And I think it's wonderful to do it straight off the first time.

PRINCE. Well, *you* did.

PRINCESS. Oh no, not the first time. When I was a child.

PRINCE. You mean that you crashed?

PRINCESS. Well, you only fall into the moat.

PRINCE. Only! Can you *swim?*

PRINCESS. Of course.

PRINCE. So you swam to the castle walls, and yelled for help, and they fished you out and walloped you. And next day you tried again. Well, if *that* isn't pluck[24]—

PRINCESS. Of course I didn't. I swam back, and did it at once; I mean I tried again at once. It wasn't until the third time that I

---

24. pluck (pluk) *n.*: Courage.

Grammar in Action

Dashes are useful punctuation marks in writing conversation. They indicate a sudden change in thought, a dramatic interrupting idea, or a break in conversation. Notice the dramatic effect they create in *The Ugly Duckling*.

> **PRINCE.** You don't mean that *you*—
> **PRINCESS.** Oh yes, often.

> **PRINCESS.** There's a way of getting over from this side, too; a tree grows out from the wall and you jump into another tree—I don't think it's quite so easy.

> **PRINCE.** Perhaps it might be as well if you taught me how to swim first. I've often heard about swimming but never—
> **PRINCESS.** You can't swim?

> **PRINCESS.** . . . Nobody knows this—except you.

In conversation, there is usually a lot of give and take. One speaker interrupts another. One speaker breaks off a thought in the middle. Another speaker begins a sentence one way, then changes his or actually did it. You see, I was afraid I might lose my nerve.

PRINCE. Afraid she might lose her nerve!

PRINCESS. There's a way of getting over from this side, too; a tree grows out from the wall and you jump into another tree—I don't think it's quite so easy.

PRINCE. Not quite so easy. Good. You must show me.

PRINCESS. Oh, I will.

PRINCE. Perhaps it might be as well if you taught me how to swim first. I've often heard about swimming but never—

PRINCESS. You can't swim?

PRINCE. No. Don't look so surprised. There 16 are a lot of other things which I can't do. I'll tell you about them as soon as you have a couple of years to spare.

PRINCESS. You can't swim and yet you crossed by the beech-tree! And you're *ever* so much heavier than I am! Now who's brave?

PRINCE. [*Getting up*] You keep talking about how light you are. I must see if there's anything to it. Stand up! [*She stands obediently and he picks her up.*] You're right, Dulcibella. I could hold you here forever. [*Looking at her*] You're very lovely. Do you know how lovely you are?

PRINCESS. Yes. [*She laughs suddenly and happily.*]

PRINCE. Why do you laugh?

PRINCESS. Aren't you tired of holding me?

PRINCE. Frankly, yes. I exaggerated when I said I could hold you forever. When you've been hanging by the arms for ten minutes over a very deep moat, wondering if it's too late to learn how to swim—[*He puts her down.*]—what I meant was that I should *like* to hold you forever. Why did you laugh?

PRINCESS. Oh, well, it was a little private joke of mine.

PRINCE. If it comes to that, I've got a private joke too. Let's exchange them.

PRINCESS. Mine's very private. One other woman in the whole world knows, and that's all.

PRINCE. Mine's just as private. One other man knows, and that's all.

PRINCESS. What fun. I love secrets. . . . Well, here's mine. When I was born, one of my godmothers promised that I should be very beautiful.

PRINCE. How right she was.

PRINCESS. But the other one said this:

> I give you with this kiss
> A wedding-day surprise.
> Where ignorance is bliss
> 'Tis folly to be wise.

And nobody knew what it meant. And I grew up very plain. And then, when I was about ten, I met my godmother in the forest one day. It was my tenth birthday. Nobody knows this—except you.

PRINCE. Except us.

PRINCESS. Except us. And she told me what her gift meant. It meant that I *was* beautiful—but everybody else was to go on being ignorant, and thinking me plain, until my wedding-day. Because, she said, she didn't want me to grow up spoiled and willful and 17 vain, as I should have done if everybody had always been saying how beautiful I was; and the best thing in the world, she said, was to be quite sure of yourself, but not to expect admiration from other people. So ever since then my mirror has told me

16 **Discussion** Note that the Prince admits he can't swim. He also acknowledges not being able to do many other things. How is he different from other fairy-tale princes?

17 **Discussion** What does the Princess say will happen on her wedding day?

her mind entirely and starts a new line of thought. Did you notice how the use of dashes helps the writer capture the give-and-take of normal conversation in the examples?

Student Activity. What do you think will happen when the Prince and the Princess discover each other's true identity? Write a conversation between these two characters dramatizing this event. Use dashes to indicate sudden changes in thought, dramatic interrupting ideas, and breaks in conversation.

I'm beautiful, and everybody else thinks me ugly, and I get a lot of fun out of it.

PRINCE. Well, seeing that Dulcibella is the result, I can only say that your godmother was very, very wise.

PRINCESS. And now tell me *your* secret.

PRINCE. It isn't such a pretty one. You see, Prince Simon was going to woo Princess Camilla, and he'd heard that she was beautiful and haughty and imperious—all *you* would have been if your godmother hadn't been so wise. And being a very ordinary-looking fellow himself, he was afraid she wouldn't think much of him, so he suggested to one of his attendants, a man called Carlo, of extremely attractive appearance, that *he* should pretend to be the Prince, and win the Princess's hand; and then at the last moment they would change places—

PRINCESS. How would they do that?

PRINCE. The Prince was going to have been married in full armor—with his visor[25] down.

PRINCESS. [*Laughing happily*] Oh, what fun!

PRINCE. Neat, isn't it?

PRINCESS. [*Laughing*] Oh, very . . . very . . . very.

PRINCE. Neat, but not so terribly *funny.* Why do you keep laughing?

PRINCESS. Well, that's another secret.

PRINCE. If it comes to that, *I've* got another one up my sleeve. Shall we exchange again?

PRINCESS. All right. You go first this time.

PRINCE. Very well. . . . I am not Carlo.

---

25. visor (vī′ zər) *n.*: In ancient armor, a movable part of the helmet that could be lowered to cover the upper part of the face, with slits for seeing.

[*Standing up and speaking dramatically*] I am Simon!—*ow!* [*He sits down and rubs his leg violently.*]

PRINCESS. [*Alarmed*] What is it?

PRINCE. Cramp. [*In a mild voice, still rubbing*] I was saying that I was Prince Simon.

PRINCESS. Shall I rub it for you? [*She rubs.*]

PRINCE. [*Still hopefully*] I am Simon.

PRINCESS. Is that better?

PRINCE. [*Despairingly*] I am Simon.

PRINCESS. I know.

PRINCE. How did you know?

PRINCESS. Well, you told me.

PRINCE. But oughtn't you to swoon[26] or something?

PRINCESS. Why? History records many similar ruses.

PRINCE. [*Amazed*] Is that so? I've never read history. I thought I was being profoundly original.

PRINCESS. Oh, no! Now I'll tell you *my* secret. For reasons very much like your own the Princess Camilla, who is held to be extremely plain, feared to meet Prince Simon. Is the drawbridge down yet?

PRINCE. Do your people give a faint, surprised cheer every time it gets down?

PRINCESS. Naturally.

PRINCE. Then it came down about three minutes ago.

PRINCESS. Ah! Then at this very moment your man Carlo is declaring his passionate love for my maid, Dulcibella. That, I think, is funny. [*So does the* PRINCE. *He laughs heartily.*] Dulcibella, by the way, is in love with a man she calls Eg, so I hope Carlo isn't getting carried away.

PRINCE. Carlo is married to a girl he calls "the little woman," so Eg has nothing to fear.

PRINCESS. By the way, I don't know if you heard, but I said, or as good as said, that I am the Princess Camilla.

PRINCE. I wasn't surprised. History, of which I read a great deal, records many similar ruses.

PRINCESS. [*Laughing*] Simon!

PRINCE. [*Laughing*] Camilla! [*He stands up.*] May I try holding you again? [*She nods. He takes her in his arms and kisses her.*] Sweetheart!

PRINCESS. You see, when you lifted me up before, you said, "You're very lovely," and my godmother said that the first person to whom I would seem lovely was the man I should marry; so I knew then that you were Simon and I should marry you.

PRINCE. I knew directly I saw you that I should marry you, even if you were Dulcibella. By the way, which of you *am* I marrying?

PRINCESS. When she lifts her veil, it will be Camilla. [*Voices are heard outside.*] Until then it will be Dulcibella. 18

PRINCE. [*In a whisper*] Then good-bye, Camilla, until you lift your veil.

PRINCESS. Good-bye, Simon, until you raise your visor. [*The* KING *and* QUEEN *come in arm-in-arm, followed by* CARLO *and* DULCIBELLA *also arm-in-arm. The* CHANCELLOR *precedes them, walking backwards, at a loyal angle.*]

PRINCE. [*Supporting the* CHANCELLOR *as an*

26. swoon (swo͞on) v.: Faint.

18 **Discussion** Who will be most surprised after the wedding?

257

accident seems inevitable] Careful! [*The* CHANCELLOR *turns indignantly round.*]

KING. Who and what is this? More accurately who and what are all these?

CARLO. My attendant, Carlo, Your Majesty. He will, with Your Majesty's permission, prepare me for the ceremony. [*The* PRINCE *bows.*]

KING. Of course, of course!

QUEEN. [*To* DULCIBELLA] Your maid, Dulcibella, is it not, my love? [DULCIBELLA *nods violently.*] I thought so. [*To* CARLO] She will prepare Her Royal Highness. [*The* PRINCESS *curtsies.*]

KING. Ah, yes. Yes. *Most* important.

PRINCESS. [*Curtsying*] I beg pardon, Your Majesty, if I've done wrong, but I found the gentleman wandering—

KING. [*Crossing to her*] Quite right, my dear, quite right. [*He pinches her cheek, and takes advantage of this kingly gesture to say in a loud whisper*] We've pulled it off! [*They sit down; the* KING *and* QUEEN *on their thrones,* DULCIBELLA *on the* PRINCESS'*s throne.* CARLO *stands behind* DULCIBELLA, *the* CANCELLOR *on the right of the* QUEEN, *and the* PRINCE *and* PRINCESS *behind the long seat on the left.*]

CHANCELLOR. [*Consulting documents*] H'r'm! Have I Your Majesty's authority to put the final test to His Royal Highness?

QUEEN. [*Whispering to* KING] Is this safe?

KING. [*Whispering*] Perfectly, my dear. I told him the answer a minute ago. [*Over his shoulder to* CARLO] Don't forget. *Dog.* [*Aloud*] Proceed, Your Excellency. It is my desire that the affairs of my country should ever be conducted in a strictly constitutional manner.

CHANCELLOR. [*Oratorically*[27]] By the constitution of the country, a suitor to Her Royal Highness's hand cannot be deemed successful until he has given the correct answer to a riddle. [*Conversationally*] The last suitor answered incorrectly, and thus failed to win his bride.

KING. By a coincidence he fell into the moat.

CHANCELLOR. [*To* CARLO] I have now to ask Your Royal Highness if you are prepared for the ordeal?

CARLO. [*Cheerfully*] Absolutely.

CHANCELLOR. I may mention, as a matter, possibly, of some slight historical interest to our visitor, that by the constitution of the country the same riddle is not allowed to be asked on two successive occasions.

KING. [*Startled*] What's that?

CHANCELLOR. This one, it is interesting to recall, was propounded[28] exactly a century ago, and we must take it as a fortunate omen[29] that it was well and truly solved.

KING. [*To* QUEEN] I may want my sword directly.

CHANCELLOR. The riddle is this. What is it which has four legs and mews like a cat?

CARLO. [*Promptly*] A dog.

KING. [*Still more promptly*] Bravo, bravo! [*He claps loudly and nudges the* QUEEN, *who claps too.*]

CHANCELLOR. [*Peering at his documents*] According to the records of the occasion to

27. oratorically (ôr′ ə tôr′ i k′l ē) *adv.*: In a lofty, high-sounding way.
28. propounded (prə pound′ ′d) *v.*: Proposed; put forward for consideration.
29. omen (ō′ mən) *n.*: A thing or happening supposed to foretell a future event.

which I referred, the correct answer would seem to be—

PRINCESS. [*To* PRINCE] Say something, quick!

CHANCELLOR. —not dog, but—

PRINCE. Your Majesty, have I permission to speak? Naturally His Royal Highness could not think of justifying himself on such an occasion, but I think that with Your Majesty's gracious permission, I could—

KING. Certainly, certainly.

PRINCE. In our country, we have an animal to which we have given the name "dog," or, in the local dialect of the more mountainous districts, "doggie." It sits by the fireside and purrs.

CARLO. That's right. It purrs like anything.

PRINCE. When it needs milk, which is its staple food, it mews.

CARLO. [*Enthusiastically*] Mews like nobody's business.

PRINCE. It also has four legs.

CARLO. One at each corner.

PRINCE. In some countries, I understand, this animal is called a "cat." In one distant country to which His Royal Highness and I penetrated, it was called by the very curious name of "hippopotamus."

CARLO. That's right. [*To the* PRINCE] Do you remember that ginger-colored hippopotamus which used to climb on to my shoulder and lick my ear?

PRINCE. I shall never forget it, sir. [*To the* KING] So you see, Your Majesty—

KING. Thank you. I think that makes it perfectly clear. [*Firmly to the* CHANCELLOR] You are about to agree?

CHANCELLOR. Undoubtedly, Your Majesty. May I be the first to congratulate His Royal Highness on solving the riddle so accurately?

KING. You may be the first to see that all is in order for an immediate wedding.

CHANCELLOR. Thank you, Your Majesty. [*He bows and withdraws. The* KING *rises, as do the* QUEEN *and* DULCIBELLA.]

KING. [*To* CARLO] Doubtless, Prince Simon, you will wish to retire and prepare yourself for the ceremony.

CARLO. Thank you, sir.

PRINCE. Have I Your Majesty's permission to attend His Royal Highness? It is the custom of his country for Princes of the royal blood to be married in full armor, a matter which requires a certain adjustment—

KING. Of course, of course. [CARLO *bows to the* KING *and* QUEEN *and goes out. As the* PRINCE *is about to follow, the* KING *stops him.*] Young man, you have a quality of quickness which I admire. It is my pleasure to reward it in any way which commends itself to you.

PRINCE. Your Majesty is ever gracious. May I ask for my reward *after* the ceremony? [*He catches the eye of the* PRINCESS, *and they give each other a secret smile.*]

KING. Certainly. [*The* PRINCE *bows and goes out. To* DUCIBELLA] Now, young woman, make yourself scarce. You've done your work excellently, and we will see that you and your —what was his name?

DULCIBELLA. Eg, Your Majesty.

KING. —that you and your Eg are not forgotten.

DULCIBELLA. Coo! [*She curtsies and goes out.*]

Master Teacher Note Have students write newspaper accounts of the wedding and the reactions of the King and Queen. A group of students could prepare a newspaper with all kinds of information about this kingdom—the replacement of the drawbridge, the marriage of Dulcibella and Eg, and any other imaginative accounts of the kingdom.

Enrichment Have artistic students draw scenes from the play or sketch the clothing each of the characters would wear.

Reader's Response Have you ever used reverse psychology on anyone? Has anyone ever used it on you? If so was it successful? Explain.

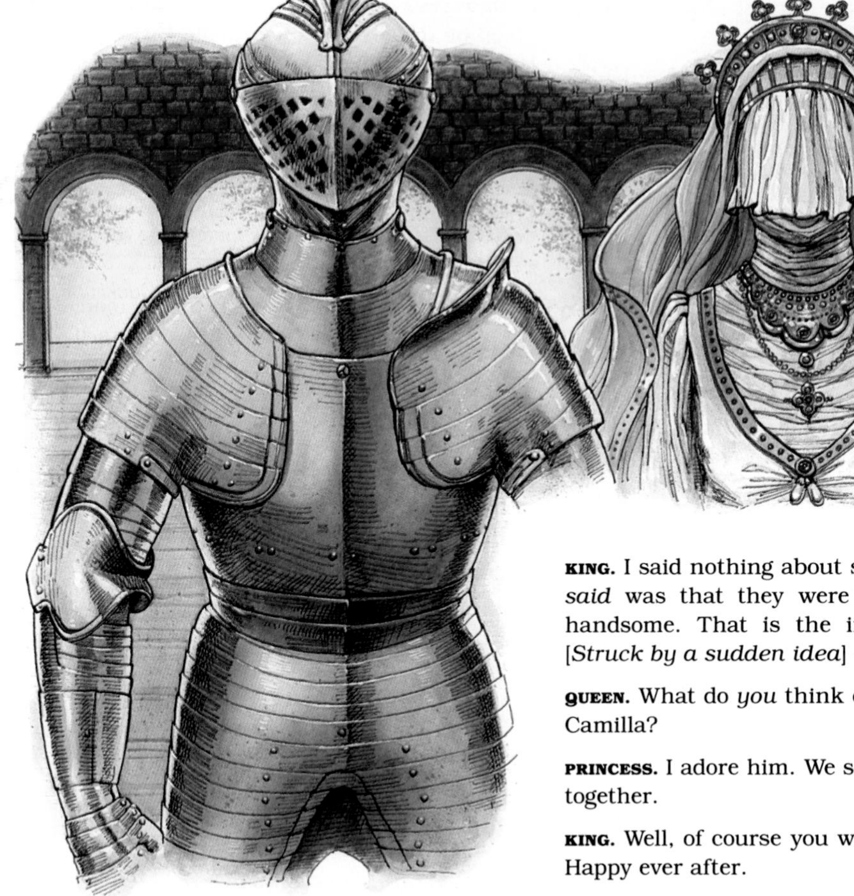

PRINCESS. [*Calling*] Wait for me, Dulcibella!

KING. [*To* QUEEN] Well, my dear, we may congratulate ourselves. As I remember saying to somebody once, "You have not lost a daughter, you have gained a son." How does he strike you?

QUEEN. Stupid.

KING. They made a very handsome pair, I thought, he and Dulcibella.

QUEEN. Both stupid.

KING. I said nothing about stupidity. What I *said* was that they were both extremely handsome. That is the important thing. [*Struck by a sudden idea*] Or isn't it?

QUEEN. What do *you* think of Prince Simon, Camilla?

PRINCESS. I adore him. We shall be so happy together.

KING. Well, of course you will. I told you so. Happy ever after.

QUEEN. Run along now and get ready.

PRINCESS. Yes, mother. [*She throws a kiss to them and goes out.*]

KING. [*Anxiously*] My dear, have we been wrong about Camilla all this time? It seemed to me that she wasn't looking *quite* so plain as usual just now. Did *you* notice anything?

QUEEN. [*Carelessly*] Just the excitement of the marriage.

KING. [*Relieved*] Ah, yes, that would account for it.

Closure and Extension

ANSWERS TO THINKING ABOUT THE SELECTION

Recalling

1. The godmother promised the princess dazzling beauty.
2. Great-Aunt Malkin promised "a wedding-day surprise."
3. The Prince is impressed that Camilla is able to jump across the castle moat.
4. The Princess is impressed that the Prince was able to jump the moat on his first try.
5. Camilla's godmother had predicted that the first person to whom the Princess seemed lovely would be the man she will marry. When Carlo says "You're very lovely," Camilla realizes he is the Prince.

Interpreting

6. Great-Aunt Malkin has promised "a wedding-day surprise." On her wedding day, Camilla's true beauty will be revealed, and everyone who thought her plain will be surprised to discover their mistake.
7. Their true beauty is evident only to others of their own kind. Among the ignorant, both are considered ugly. When the Princess finds someone who shares her characteristics of bravery, humility, and love of fun, her inner beauty is revealed.
8. Students should realize that Milne does not intend this statement seriously. Just as the King is ignorant of his daughter's beauty, he is ignorant of what makes a happy marriage. The exchanges between Camilla and Simon prove that compatibility is an essential ingredient of a happy marriage.

Applying

9. Answers will differ. Some students

THINKING ABOUT THE SELECTION

Recalling

1. What has the godmother on the Queen's side promised the princess at the christening?
2. What has Great-Aunt Malkin promised?
3. Why is the prince impressed when he first meets the princess?
4. Why is the princess impressed when she first meets the prince?
5. How does the princess know that the young man who says he is Carlo is Prince Simon before he even tells her?

Interpreting

6. The king says Camilla's beauty "has eluded everybody who has seen her." How does this relate to Great-Aunt Malkin's promise?
7. In the fairy tale "The Ugly Duckling" by Hans Christian Andersen, a young swan in a group of ducks feels ugly. Only when it finds swans does it realize that it is beautiful. How is the swan similar to the Princess in the play?
8. The King tells the Princess: "It doesn't matter how you marry or who you marry, as long as you get married. Because you'll be happy ever after in any case." Do you think the playwright expects you to take this statement seriously? Explain your answer.

Applying

9. Would you have liked to receive Great-Aunt Malkin's gift? Explain your answer.

ANALYZING LITERATURE

Understanding the One-Act Play

The **one-act play,** a form of drama with a single act, is in some ways like a short story. Because of its short length, it has only a few vivid characters and a plot that develops quickly. Like *The Ugly Duckling,* it usually has a single theme, presented through dialogue, and a single set.

1. Who are the main characters in this play?
2. Summarize the plot.
3. Describe the setting.
4. What span of time is covered in the play?
5. What is revealed about the idea of beauty?
6. What is the theme of the play?

CRITICAL THINKING AND READING

Recognizing Parody

A **parody** is a humorous mimicking of a serious piece of literature. *The Ugly Duckling* pokes gentle fun at the elements of the traditional fairy tale, although it takes one element seriously.

1. How are the King and Queen in this play different from traditional characters in a fairy tale? How does this difference add to the humor?
2. How are the Prince and Princess in this play different from traditional fairy-tale characters? How does this difference add to the humor?
3. How do the drawbridge and other details of setting in this play differ from those you would expect to find in a traditional fairy tale? How does this difference add to the humor?
4. In fairy tales, the suitor often has to win the hand of the princess. What makes the tournament in this play humorous? What makes the answering of the riddle humorous?
5. Many fairy tales center on a trick. How does the trick in this play contribute to the humor?
6. Does Milne expect you to take the theme of this play seriously? Explain your answer.

THINKING AND WRITING

Writing to Cast the Characters

Pretend that you are a movie producer who is going to produce *The Ugly Duckling.* Choose an actor who is appropriate for a major part. List reasons why this person could play the role well. Then draft a letter asking this actor to play the part and including your reasons. When you revise your letter, make sure your reasons could persuade this actor to accept the role.

(Answers begin on p. 260.)

might say that they could not endure being considered ugly until their wedding day. Others might think the reward of finding the ideal mate worth such a burden.

ANSWERS TO ANALYZING LITERATURE

1. The main characters are Camilla and Simon.
2. To marry off their "unbeautiful" daughter, the King and Queen plan to trick Prince Simon using a maid and a riddle ceremony, while he has a similar plot using his attendant. Camilla and Simon meet on their own and fall in love. The riddle ceremony is performed with the maid and attendant, and Simon and Camilla happily prepare for their wedding.
3. The play is set in the throne room of a castle "once upon a time."
4. The span of time is about half a day.
5. All but Camilla and Simon regard beauty as physical appearance only. The Princess and the Prince, however, regard personality as the true test of a person's beauty.
6. Answers may differ, but students should suggest that a person's true beauty is revealed when his or her character is appreciated.

ANSWERS TO CRITICAL THINKING AND READING

1. Traditional fairy-tale kings and queens are often idealized mother and father figures—or their exact opposites. In the play, the King and Queen are neither ideal parents nor villains. They are well-intentioned but ineffectual matchmakers. They love their daughter, but fail to recognize her true beauty. Their rather unregal behavior (such as the King's dozing with a handkerchief over his face) contributes to the play's humor.
2. Traditional fairy-tale princes and princesses are usually physically attractive and self-assured. In the play, the Prince and Princess are plain. The Prince is bashful. Students should note other untraditional details such as the Princess's penchant for leaping the moat. Such unexpected details add to the play's humor.
3. The drawbridge in the play makes a terrible noise and takes a long time to open and close. Students might note other unexpected details, such as the uncomfortable thrones. Such details allow for humorous sound effects and staging.
4. The suitors participating in the tournament would rather die than win the honor of marrying the ugly princess. The humor of the riddle lies in its answer being so obvious. The humor is compounded when Carlo stupidly answers incorrectly and the Prince fabricates a ludicrous explanation of why the wrong answer is right.
5. The humor arises from the complications surrounding the King and Queen's plan to have Dulcibella impersonate Camilla. The King and Queen are convinced their ruse was successful when, in fact, they have been tricked by the Prince and Camilla.
6. Answers will differ. However, students should realize that comedy often has a serious message.

THINKING AND WRITING

Publishing Student Writing You might want to have your students mail their letters to the actors they chose. Each student should address the letter to the actor in care of the film company that produced the actor's last film.

GUIDE FOR READING

Back There

Rod Serling (1924–1975) was one of television's most respected writers. He began his career as a radio dramatist, but in the early 1950's he started writing for television. He is credited with bringing the maturity and quality of stage drama to the television screen. His imaginative series, *The Twilight Zone,* combined elements of science fiction, fantasy, suspense, and horror. The television play "Back There" is an episode of *The Twilight Zone* in which a character travels back in time.

Staging

A play is written to be performed on stage before a live audience. Television plays, although they are not always performed before a live audience, must still have the appropriate **staging** to make the performance believable. Staging includes costumes, props, backdrops, and objects that characterize the time and place in which the scenes of the play are set.

Look For

As you read "Back There," try to visualize the stage as if you were watching the play on television. The scenery descriptions and stage directions will give you a sense of what the characters and the setting look like. How does staging affect the plot?

Writing

You may have seen or read other stories in which the characters go back in time. Imagine that you could go back in time. Write briefly about where you would go and why.

Vocabulary

Knowing the following words will help you as you read "Back There."

anachronism (ə nak′ rə niz′ əm) *n.*: Anything that is out of its proper time in history (p. 264)
deference (def′ ər əns) *n.*: Courteous respect (p. 264)
miscreants (mis′ krē ənts) *n.*: Criminals (p. 268)
clairvoyant (kler voi′ ənt) *adj.*: Having the ability to see what cannot be seen; keenly perceptive (p. 268)
incarcerated (in kär′sər āt′ əd) *v.*: Jailed; imprisoned (p. 269)
proffered (präf′ ərd) *adj.*: Having been offered (p. 270)
meticulously (mə tik′ yo͞o ləs lē) *adj.*: Extremely careful about details; impeccably (p. 274)
thesis (thē′sis) *n.*: Statement of position or proposition (p. 274)

Focus

More About the Author Throughout his career, Serling maintained that it is a dramatist's responsibility to make people think as well as to entertain them. Do you agree or disagree with Serling? What TV shows exemplify both points of view?

Literary Focus Ask students to imagine that they are in a theater. The curtain goes up on a room furnished only with a table and two chairs. On the table are a typewriter and a gun. Conjecture with the class about the characters and plot of the play. What has the audience learned even before one actor has entered the scene?

Look For Point out that stage directions in *Back There* appear in italic type within brackets. You might add that a dramatist may choose to write very precise stage directions, as in *Back There*, or leave more to the director's imagination. As they read, ask students to think about why Serling has written such precise stage directions.

Writing/Prior Knowledge As a lead-in to the writing assignment, ask students to think of movies or books that take place in earlier periods of history. Would students like to have lived at any of those earlier times?

If they prefer, students may complete the writing assignment by imagining that they live in the future and telling why they would like to visit the 1990's.

Vocabulary These words may be unfamiliar to some students: *aftermath* (p. 263), *securities* (p. 263), *abyss* (p. 263), *rationale* (p. 271).

Spelling Tip *Chron* is a combining form from *chronos*, the Greek word for time. The same form appears in *chronic* and *chronicle*.

Objectives

1. To appreciate the importance of staging in a play
2. To recognize the playwright's purpose
3. To write about staging the play

Support Material

Teaching Portfolio
Teacher Backup, pp. 377–379
Grammar in Action Worksheet, *Using Participles and Participial Phrases*, pp. 380–381
Usage and Mechanics Worksheet, p. 382
Vocabulary Check, p. 383
Analyzing Literature Worksheet, *Appreciating Staging*, p. 384
Critical Thinking and Reading Worksheet, *Understanding the Playwright's Purpose*, p. 385
Selection Test, pp. 386–387

Back There

Rod Serling

CHARACTERS

PETER CORRIGAN, a young man
JACKSON, member of the Washington Club
MILLARD, member of the Washington Club
WHITAKER, member of the Washington Club
WILLIAM, attendant at the Washington Club
ATTENDANT ONE, at the Washington Club
ATTENDANT TWO, at the Washington Club
MRS. LANDERS, landlady of a rooming house
LIEUTENANT
LIEUTENANT'S WIFE
POLICE CAPTAIN
POLICEMAN
POLICE OFFICER
JONATHAN WELLINGTON
LANDLADY
NARRATOR

ACT I

Scene 1

[Exterior of club at night. Near a large front entrance of double doors is a name plaque in brass which reads "The Washington Club, Founded 1858." In the main hall of the building is a large paneled foyer with rooms leading off on either side. An attendant, WILLIAM, *carrying a tray of drinks, crosses the hall and enters one of the rooms.*
1 *There are four men sitting around in the aftermath of a card game.* PETER CORRIGAN *is the youngest, then two middle-aged men named* WHITAKER *and* MILLARD, *and* JACKSON, *the oldest, a white-haired man in his sixties, who motions the tray from the attendant over to the table.]*

JACKSON. Just put it over here, William, would you?

WILLIAM. Yes, sir. *[He lays the tray down and walks away from the table.]*

CORRIGAN. Now what's your point? That if it were possible for a person to go back in time
there'd be nothing in the world to prevent 2
him from altering the course of history—is that it?

MILLARD. Let's say, Corrigan, that you go back in time. It's October, 1929. The day before the stock market crashed.[1] You know on the following morning that the securities are going to tumble into an abyss. Now using

1. **stock market crashed:** In October 1929, stocks suddenly depreciated in value, leading to a national financial disaster.

Presentation

Motivation/Prior Knowledge With the class, peruse the headlines of a recent newspaper. Ask students to imagine they have the power to change history by simply crossing out and changing one headline. Which would they pick? What changes would they make? Tell students they are about to read a play about someone who tried to change history.

Purpose-Setting Question Which of your own beliefs or attitudes does this play make you question?

Master Teacher Note Tell students that Serling's earlier works for television were critical of society for condoning prejudice, exploitation, and unethical business practices. Tired of battling networks and sponsors who feared that his works would offend audiences, Serling switched to fantasy writing. In fantasy, he expressed his ideas in a subtle way, so that they would be acceptable to commercial television but would still send a message to his audience. Tell the students to look for subtle forms of social criticism in *Back There.*

Thematic Idea Other fantasy/science fiction selections with which you may wish to group *Back There* are *Rain, Rain, Go Away* on page 13, *The Rule of Names* on page 69, *Crime on Mars* on page 137, and *Let Me Hear You Whisper,* on page 277.

Robert MacNeil's Essay, "The Trouble With Television," on page 463, criticizes the medium for providing only escapist entertainment and avoiding important issues and ideas.

1 **Literary Focus** What information about the play does the set give you?

2 **Reading Strategy** Ask students what Corrigan's line foreshadows.

3 **Reading Strategy** Ask students what Corrigan's line tells us about the significance of the play's title.

4 **Critical Thinking and Reading** Ask students with whom they agree—Corrigan or Millard.

5 **Reading Strategy** Suggest that students think about the purpose of Whitaker's joking warning.

6 **Critical Thinking and Reading** Ask students how they would describe the way Corrigan treats William? How would they feel toward Corrigan if they were William?

7 **Reading Strategy** The author emphasizes the date here. By putting together the foreshadowing earlier in the scene with what you've learned about American history, you might be able to predict what will happen in Scene 3. (What important event occurred on April 14, 1865?)

ESL Teaching Strategy Some students may not be sufficiently acquainted with the details of Abraham Lincoln's assassination to understand the use of foreshadowing in this play. Review the historical facts with them if necessary.

that prior knowledge, there's a hundred things you can do to protect yourself.

3 **CORRIGAN.** But I'm an anachronism back there. I don't really belong back there.

MILLARD. You could sell out the day before the crash.

CORRIGAN. But what if I did and that started the crash earlier? Now history tells us that on October 24th, 1929, the bottom dropped out of the stock market. That's a fixed date.
4 October 24th, 1929. It exists as an event in the history of our times. It *can't* be altered.

MILLARD. And I say it can. What's to prevent it? What's to prevent me, say, from going to a broker[2] on the morning of October 23rd?

CORRIGAN. Gentlemen, I'm afraid I'll have to leave this time travel to H. G. Wells.[3] I'm much too tired to get into any more metaphysics[4] this evening. And since nobody has ever gone back in time, the whole blamed thing is much too theoretical. I'll probably see you over the weekend.

5 **WHITAKER.** Don't get lost back in time now, Corrigan.

CORRIGAN. I certainly shall not. Good night, everybody.

VOICES. Good night, Pete. Good night, Corrigan. See you tomorrow.

[CORRIGAN *walks out into the hall and heads toward the front door.*]

WILLIAM. [*Going by*] Good night, Mr. Corrigan.

2. broker (brō′ kər) *n.*: A person who acts as an agent for people who are buying and selling stocks and bonds.

3. H.G. Wells: Herbert George Wells, 1866–1946, an English novelist and social critic best known for his science-fiction, particularly his novel *The Time Machine* about traveling in time.

4. metaphysics (met′ ə fiz′ iks) *n.*: Philosophy that goes beyond or transcends the physical or material world.

CORRIGAN. Good night, William. [*Then he looks at the elderly man a little more closely.*] Everything all right with you, William? Looks like you've lost some weight.

WILLIAM. [*With a deference built of a forty-year habit pattern*] Just the usual worries, sir. The stars and my salary are fixed. It's the cost of living that goes up. 6

[CORRIGAN *smiles, reaches in his pocket, starts to hand him a bill.*]

WILLIAM. Oh no, sir, I couldn't.

CORRIGAN. [*Forcing it into his hand*] Yes, you can, William. Bless you and say hello to your wife for me.

WILLIAM. Thank you so much, sir. [*A pause*] Did you have a coat with you?

CORRIGAN. No. I'm rushing the season a little tonight, William. I felt spring in the air. Came out like this.

WILLIAM. [*Opening the door*] Well, April *is* spring, sir.

CORRIGAN. It's getting there. What is the date, William?

WILLIAM. April 14th, sir. 7

CORRIGAN. April 14th. [*Then he turns and grins at the attendant.*] 1965—right?

WILLIAM. I beg your pardon, sir? Oh, yes, sir. 1965.

CORRIGAN. [*Going out*] Good night, William. Take care of yourself. [*He goes out into the night.*]

Scene 2

[*Exterior of the club. The door closes behind* CORRIGAN. *He stands there near the front entrance. The light from the street light illuminates the steps. There's the sound of chimes from the distant steeple*

Commentary

Piecing together the clues dropped by the author enhances enjoyment of the play. The following background information will help students pick up on the clues: Abraham Lincoln was assassinated at Ford's Theatre in Washington, D.C., on April 14, 1865, five days after the end of the Civil War. The assassin was John Wilkes Booth, a talented but emotionally unbalanced young actor who had been sympathetic with the Southern cause in the Civil War. Having learned that Lincoln was to attend a performance of the play "Our American Cousin," Booth entered the president's private box a few minutes after 10 P.M., and shot Lincoln through the head. Booth then leaped to the stage below, escaped through a back door, and fled on horseback, even though he had broken his leg in the leap. He was hunted down and shot in a barn near Port Royal, Virginia for his crime.

ock. CORRIGAN *looks at his wristwatch, ɔlding it out toward the light so it can be ·en more clearly. Suddenly his face takes ı a strange look. He shuts his eyes and ıbs his temple. Then he looks down at his ·rist again. This time the light has ıanged. It's a wavery, moving light, differ-ıt from what it had been.* CORRIGAN *looks cross toward the light again. It's a gas-ght*[5] *now. He reacts in amazement. The*

chimes begin to chime again, this time eight times. He once again looks at the watch, but instead of a wristwatch there is just a fringe of lace protruding from a coat. 10
There is no wristwatch at all. He grabs his wrist, pulling at the lace and coat. He's dressed now in a nineteenth-century costume. He looks down at himself, looks again toward the gaslight that flickers, and then slowly backs down from the steps staring at the building from which he's just come. The plaque reads "Washington 11
Club." He jumps the steps two at a time,

. **gaslight:** A lamp, used in the nineteenth century, ıat produces light by burning gas.

8 **Discussion** What might Corrigan see that puzzles him?

9 **Literary Focus** Ask students what effect the "wavery, moving light" creates. What information does it communicate to the audience?

10 **Literary Focus** Ask students if it would be possible to create a similar transformation in a live theater production of the play? How could this be done? Would it seem as real to the audience?

11 **Literary Focus** Ask students what has changed in the set? What is missing from the plaque? (Why is there no date?)

12 **Literary Focus** How do these stage directions make an unbelievable situation seem believable to the audience?

13 **Discussion** Why do Corrigan's words seem nonsensical to Mrs. Landers?

slams against the front door, pounding on it. After a long moment the door opens. An ATTENDANT, *half undressed, stands there peering out into the darkness.*]

ATTENDANT ONE. Who is it? What do you want?

CORRIGAN. I left something in there.

[*He starts to push his way in and the* ATTENDANT *partially closes the door on him.*]

ATTENDANT ONE. Now here you! The Club is closed this evening.

CORRIGAN. The devil it is. I just left here a minute ago.

ATTENDANT ONE. [*Peers at him*] You did what? You drunk, young man? That it? You're drunk, huh?

CORRIGAN. I am not drunk. I want to see Mr. Jackson or Mr. Whitaker, or William. Let me talk to William. Where is he now?

ATTENDANT ONE. Who?

CORRIGAN. William. What's the matter with you? Where did *you* come from? [*Then he looks down at his clothes.*] What's the idea of this? [*He looks up. The door has been shut. He pounds on it again, shouting.*] Hey! Open up!

VOICE. [*From inside*] You best get away from here or I'll call the police. Go on. Get out of here.

[CORRIGAN *backs away from the door, goes down to the sidewalk, stands there, looks up at the gaslight, then up and down the street, starts at the sound of noises. It's the*
12 *clip-clop of horses' hooves and the rolling, squeaky sound of carriage wheels. He takes a few halting, running steps out into the street. He bites his lip, looks around.*]

CORRIGAN. [*Under his breath*] I'll go home. That's it. Go home. I'll go home. [*He turns and starts to walk and then run down the street, disappearing into the night.*]

Scene 3

[*Hallway of rooming house. There is the sound of a doorbell ringing.* MRS. LANDERS, *the landlady, comes out from the dining room and goes toward the door.*]

MRS. LANDERS. All right. All right. Have a bit of patience. I'm coming. [*Opening door*] Yes?

CORRIGAN. Is this 19 West 12th Street?

MRS. LANDERS. That's right. Whom did you wish to see?

CORRIGAN. I'm just wondering if . . .

[*He stands there trying to look over her shoulder.* MRS. LANDERS *turns to look behind her and then suspiciously back toward* CORRIGAN.]

MRS. LANDERS. Whom did you wish to see, young man?

CORRIGAN. I . . . I used to live here. It's the oldest building in this section of town.

MRS. LANDERS. [*Stares at him*] How's that?

CORRIGAN. [*Wets his lips*] What I mean is . . . as I remember it . . . it was the oldest— 13

MRS. LANDERS. Well now really, young man. I can't spend the whole evening standing here talking about silly things like which is the oldest building in the section. Now if there's nothing else—

CORRIGAN. [*Blurting it out*] Do you have a room?

MRS. LANDERS. [*Opens the door just a little bit wider so that she can get a better look at him; looks him up and down and appears satisfied*] I have a room for acceptable boarders. Do you come from around here?

CORRIGAN. Yes. Yes. I do.

4 **MRS. LANDERS.** Army veteran?

CORRIGAN. Yes. Yes, as a matter of fact I am.

MRS. LANDERS. [*Looks at him again up and down*] Well, come in. I'll show you what I have.

5 [*She opens the door wider and* CORRIGAN *enters. She closes it behind him. She looks expectantly up toward his hat and* CORRIGAN *rather hurriedly and abruptly removes it. He grins, embarrassed.*]

CORRIGAN. I'm not used to it.

MRS. LANDERS. Used to what?

CORRIGAN. [*Points to the hat in his hand*] The hat. I don't wear a hat very often.

6 **MRS. LANDERS.** [*Again gives him her inventory look, very unsure of him now*] May I inquire as to what your business is?

CORRIGAN. I'm an engineer.

MRS. LANDERS. Really. A professional man. Hmmm. Well, come upstairs and I'll show you.

[*She points to the stairs that lead off the hall and* CORRIGAN *starts up as an army officer and his wife come down them.*]

17 **MRS. LANDERS.** [*Smiling*] Off to the play?

LIEUTENANT. That's right, Mrs. Landers. Dinner at The Willard and then off to the play.

18 **MRS. LANDERS.** Well, enjoy yourself. And applaud the President for me!

LIEUTENANT. We'll certainly do that.

LIEUTENANT'S WIFE. Good night, Mrs. Landers.

MRS. LANDERS. Good night, my dear. Have a good time. This way, Mr. Corrigan.

[*The* LIEUTENANT *and* CORRIGAN *exchange a nod as they pass on the stairs. As they go up the steps,* CORRIGAN *suddenly stops and* MRS. LANDERS *almost bangs into him.*]

MRS. LANDERS. Now what's the trouble?

CORRIGAN. [*Whirling around*] What did you say?

MRS. LANDERS. What did I say to whom? When?

CORRIGAN. To the lieutenant. To the officer. What did you just say to him?

[*The* LIEUTENANT *has turned. His wife tries to lead him out, but he holds out his hand to stop her so that he can listen to the conversation from the steps.*]

CORRIGAN. You just said something to him about the president.

LIEUTENANT. [*Walking toward the foot of the steps*] She told me to applaud him. Where might your sympathies lie? 19

MRS. LANDERS. [*Suspiciously*] Yes, young man. Which army *were* you in?

CORRIGAN. [*Wets his lips nervously*] The Army of the Republic,[6] of course.

LIEUTENANT. [*Nods, satisfied*] Then why make such a thing of applauding President Lincoln? That's his due, we figure. 20

MRS. LANDERS. That and everything else, may the good Lord bless him.

CORRIGAN. [*Takes a step down the stairs, staring at the* LIEUTENANT] You're going to a play tonight?

[*The* LIEUTENANT *nods.*]

LIEUTENANT'S WIFE. [*At the door*] We may or we may not, depending on when my husband makes up his mind to get a carriage in time to have dinner and get to the theater.

---

6. Army of the Republic: The northern army, also known as the Federal Army in the United States Civil War.

14 Reading Strategy When a character's words have different meaning for the audience than the other characters, the playwright is using a form of dramatic irony. What is ironic about this conversation?

15 Clarification In the nineteenth century, it was considered impolite for a gentleman to keep his hat on indoors, especially in the presence of a lady.

16 Clarification The word inventory usually means a list of items. In this context, Mrs. Landers is mentally listing or evaluating Corrigan's character traits in order to figure him out.

17 Reading Strategy For members of the audience who have not yet guessed what is about to take place, this is another clue. What was the role of the play in the event that occurred on April 14, 1865?

18 Reading Strategy Here is yet another clue. Who was president in 1865?

19 Discussion What do the lieutenant and Mrs. Landers want to know? Which army would Mrs. Landers think Corrigan was in?

20 Critical Thinking and Reading Now Serling leaves little doubt about what lies ahead. Why do you think he provided several clues before mentioning Lincoln's name?

CORRIGAN. What theater? *What* play?

LIEUTENANT. Ford's Theater, of course.

CORRIGAN. [*Looking off, his voice intense*] Ford's Theater. Ford's Theater.

LIEUTENANT. Are you all right? I mean do you feel all right?

CORRIGAN. [*Whirls around to stare at him*]
21 What's the name of the play?

LIEUTENANT. [*Exchanges a look with his wife*] I beg your pardon?

CORRIGAN. The play. The one you're going to tonight at Ford's Theater. What's the name of it?

LIEUTENANT'S WIFE. It's called "Our American Cousin."

CORRIGAN. [*Again looks off thoughtfully*] "Our American Cousin" and Lincoln's going to be there. [*He looks from one to the other, first toward the landlady on the*
22 *steps, then down toward the soldier and*
his wife.] And it's April 14, 1865, isn't it? Isn't it April 14th, 1865? [*He starts down the steps without waiting for an answer. The* LIEUTENANT *stands in front of him.*]

23 **LIEUTENANT.** Really, sir, I'd call your actions most strange.

[CORRIGAN *stares at him briefly as he goes by,*
24 *then goes out the door, looking purposeful and intent.*]

Scene 4

[*Alley at night. On one side is the stage door with a sign over it reading "Ford's Theater."* CORRIGAN *turns the corridor into the alley at a dead run. He stops directly under the light, looks left and right, then vaults over the railing and pounds on the stage door.*]

CORRIGAN. [*Shouting*] Hey! Hey, let me in! President Lincoln is going to be shot tonight!

[*He continues to pound on the door and shout.*]

ACT II

Scene 1

[*Police station at night. It's a bare receiving*
room with a POLICE CAPTAIN *at a desk. A long* 25
bench on one side of the room is occupied by sad miscreants awaiting disposition.[7] *There is a line of three or four men standing in front of the desk with several policemen in evidence. One holds onto* CORRIGAN *who has a bruise over his eye and his coat is*
quite disheveled. The POLICE CAPTAIN *looks up* 26
to him from a list.]

CAPTAIN. Now what's this one done? [*He peers up over his glasses and eyes* CORRIGAN *up and down.*] Fancy Dan with too much money in his pockets, huh?

CORRIGAN. While you idiots are sitting here, 27
you're going to lose a President!

[*The* CAPTAIN *looks inquiringly toward the* POLICEMAN.]

POLICEMAN. That's what he's been yellin' all the way over to the station. And that's what the doorman at the Ford Theater popped him on the head for. [*He nods toward* CORRIGAN.] Tried to pound his way right through the stage door. Yellin' some kind of crazy things about President Lincoln goin' to get shot.

CORRIGAN. President Lincoln *will* be shot! Tonight. In the theater. A man named Booth.

CAPTAIN. And how would you be knowin' this? I suppose you're clairvoyant or some-

---

7. disposition (dis′ pə zish′ ən) *n.*: The settlement of affairs.

21 **Clarification** Lincoln was shot in the head by the actor, John Wilkes Booth, at Ford's Theater in Washington, D.C. a few minutes after 10 p.m. during a performance of the play, *Our American Cousin.*

22 **Critical Thinking and Reading** What is Serling's purpose in repeating all this information here? What are some of the differences between watching television and being in a theater that might make this repetition necessary in a TV drama but not in a play?

23 **Discussion** What would you think of Corrigan's actions if you were Mrs. Landers, the Lieutenant, or the Lieutenant's wife?

24 **Reading Strategy** Where do you predict Corrigan will go?

25 **Literary Focus** What words would you use to describe the atmosphere created by this set? What are the details that contribute to the atmosphere?

26 **Discussion** What has happened to Corrigan?

27 **Discussion** Do you think the police are acting like idiots? Would you believe Corrigan if you were one of them?

thing. Some kind of seer or wizard or something.

CORRIGAN. I only know what I know. If I told you *how* I knew, you wouldn't believe me. Look, keep me here if you like. Lock me up.

CAPTAIN. [*Motions toward a* TURNKEY,[8] *points to cell block door*] Let him sleep it off.

[*The* TURNKEY *grabs* CORRIGAN's *arm and starts to lead him out of the room.*]

28 **CORRIGAN.** [*Shouting as he's led away*] Well you better hear me out. Somebody better get to the President's box at the Ford Theater.
29 Either keep him out of there or put a cordon[9] of men around him. A man named John Wilkes Booth is going to assassinate him tonight!

30 [*He's pushed through the door leading to the cell block. A tall man in cape and black moustache stands near the open door at the other side. He closes it behind him, takes a step into the room, then with a kind of very precise authority, he walks directly over to the* CAPTAIN's *table, shoving a couple of people aside as he does so with a firm gentleness. When he reaches the* CAPTAIN's *table he removes a card from his inside pocket, puts it on the table in front of the* CAPTAIN.]

WELLINGTON. Wellington, Captain. Jonathan Wellington.

[*The* CAPTAIN *looks at the card, peers at it over his glasses, then looks up toward the tall man in front of him. Obviously the man's manner and dress impresses him. His tone is respectful and quiet.*]

CAPTAIN. What can I do for you, Mr. Wellington?

WELLINGTON. That man you just had incarcerated. Mr. Corrigan I believe he said his name was.

CAPTAIN. Drunk, sir. That's probably what he is.

WELLINGTON. Drunk or . . . [*He taps his head* 31
meaningfully.] Or perhaps, ill. I wonder if he could be remanded in my custody. He might well be a war veteran and I'd hate to see him placed in jail.

CAPTAIN. Well, that's real decent of you, Mr. Wellington. You say you want him remanded in *your* custody?

WELLINGTON. Precisely. I'll be fully responsible for him. I think perhaps I might be able to help him.

CAPTAIN. All right, sir. If that's what you'd like. But I'd be careful of this one if I was you! There's a mighty bunch of crackpots running the streets these days and many of them his like, and many of them dangerous too, sir. [*He turns toward* TURNKEY.] Have Corrigan brought back out here. This gentleman's going to look after him. [*Then he turns to* WELLINGTON.] It's real decent of you, sir. Real decent indeed.

WELLINGTON. I'll be outside. Have him brought out to me if you would.

CAPTAIN. I will indeed, sir.

[WELLINGTON *turns. He passes the various people who look at him and make room for him. His walk, his manner, his positiveness suggest a commanding figure and everyone reacts accordingly. The* CAPTAIN *once again busies himself with his list and is about to check in the next prisoner, when a young* POLICE OFFICER *alongside says:*]

POLICE OFFICER. Begging your pardon, Captain.

CAPTAIN. What is it?

POLICE OFFICER. About that Corrigan, sir.

---

8. turnkey (turn′ kē′) *n.*: Jailer.
9. cordon (kôr′ dən) *n.*: A line or circle.

28 Literary Focus If this were a short story instead of a play, how would the author indicate that the character is shouting these lines?

29 Discussion What words would you use to describe Corrigan's feelings at this point in the play?

30 Literary Focus What can you tell about this character from the stage directions? What details in the stage directions give you this information?

31 Discussion What does Wellington mean when he taps his head?

32 **Critical Thinking and Reading** With which character does Serling want the audience to sympathize—the young police officer or the captain? How can you tell? What character trait of the captain's is Serling making fun of?

33 **Literary Focus** By the actions described in the stage directions, what do you predict the young police officer is going to do?

34 **Clarification** The term psychiatrist was not used until the end of the nineteenth century.

35 **Discussion** Why is Corrigan so concerned about the time?

36 **Reading Strategy** Has Corrigan ever mentioned what time the assassination would take place? How then does Wellington know that "there's time"? What do you think was Wellington's real reason for taking Corrigan out of jail?

CAPTAIN. What about him?

POLICE OFFICER. Wouldn't it be wise, sir, if—

CAPTAIN. [*Impatiently*] If what?

POLICE OFFICER. He seemed so positive, sir. So sure. About the President, I mean.

CAPTAIN. [*Slams on the desk with vast impatience*] What would you have us do? Send all available police to the Ford Theater? And on what authority? On the word of some demented fool who probably left his mind someplace in Gettysburg.[10] If I was you, mister, I'd be considerably more thoughtful at sizing up situations or you'll not advance one-half grade the next twenty years. Now be good enough to stand aside and let me get on with my work.

32 **POLICE OFFICER.** [*Very much deterred by all this, but pushed on by a gnawing sense of disquiet*] Captain, it wouldn't hurt.

CAPTAIN. [*Interrupting with a roar*] It wouldn't hurt if what?

POLICE OFFICER. I was going to suggest, sir, that if perhaps we place extra guards in the box with the President—

CAPTAIN. The President has all the guards he needs. He's got the whole Federal Army at his disposal and if they're satisfied with his security arrangements, then I am too and so should you. Next case!

[*The young* POLICE OFFICER *bites his lip and looks away, then stares across the room thoughtfully. The door opens and the* TURNKEY *leads* CORRIGAN *across the room and over to the door. He opens it and points out.* CORRIGAN *nods and walks outside. The door closes behind him. The young* POLICE OFFICER *looks briefly at the* CAPTAIN, *then puts his*
33 *cap on and starts out toward the door.*]

Scene 2

[*Lodging-house,* WELLINGTON'S *room.* WELLINGTON *is pouring wine into two glasses.* CORRIGAN *sits in a chair, his face in his hands. He looks up at the proffered drink and takes it.*]

WELLINGTON. Take this. It'll make you feel better. [CORRIGAN *nods his thanks, takes a healthy swig of the wine, puts it down, then looks up at the other man.*] Better?

CORRIGAN. [*Studying the man*] Who are you anyway?

WELLINGTON. [*With a thin smile*] At the moment I'm your benefactor[11] and apparently your only friend. I'm in the Government service, but as a young man in college I dabbled in medicine of a sort.

CORRIGAN. Medicine?

WELLINGTON. Medicine of the mind.

CORRIGAN. [*Smiles grimly*] Psychiatrist.

WELLINGTON. [*Turning to him*] I don't know the term. 3

CORRIGAN. What about the symptoms?

WELLINGTON. They *do* interest me. This story you were telling about the President being assassinated.

CORRIGAN. [*Quickly*] What time *is* it? 3

WELLINGTON. There's time. [*Checks a pocket watch*] A quarter to eight. The play won't start for another half hour. What gave you the idea that the President would be assassinated? 3

CORRIGAN. I happen to know, that's all.

WELLINGTON. [*Again the thin smile*] You have a premonition?

CORRIGAN. I've got a devil of a lot more than a

10. Gettysburg (get′ iz burg′) *n.*: A town in southern Pennsylvania; site of a crucial Civil War battle.

11. benefactor (ben′ ə fak′ tər) *n.*: A person who helps or takes care of another person.

Grammar in Action

A **participle** is a form of a verb that acts as an adjective: an *inspired* guess, no *running* water. A **participial phrase** consists of a participle and the words that modify it.

Writers use participial phrases to vary their sentence patterns and to add meaning to sentences. When writing stage instructions, participial phrases are often used.

The following stage directions begin with participial phrases.

CAPTAIN. [Interrupting with a roar]
CORRIGAN. [Studying the man]
WELLINGTON. [Turning to him]
WELLINGTON. [Smiling again]
LANDLADY. [Peering into the room]

If a participial phrase appears at the beginning of a sentence, it must be followed by a comma as in the following example:

Half struggling in the process, Corrigan reaches out to grab Wellington.

Student Activity 1. In the play, find three additional examples of stage directions that begin with participial phrases.

premonition. Lincoln *will* be assassinated. [*Then quickly*] Unless somebody tries to prevent it.

WELLINGTON. *I* shall try to prevent it. If you can convince me that you're neither drunk nor insane.

CORRIGAN. [*On his feet*] If I told you what I was, you'd be convinced I *was* insane. So all I'm *going* to tell you is that I happen to know for a fact that a man named John Wilkes Booth will assassinate President Lincoln in his box at the Ford Theater. I don't know what time it's going to happen . . . that's something I forgot—but—

WELLINGTON. [*Softly*] Something you forgot?

CORRIGAN. [*Takes a step toward him*] Listen, please—[*He stops suddenly, and begins to waver. He reaches up to touch the bruise over his head.*]

WELLINGTON. [*Takes out a handkerchief and hands it to* CORRIGAN] Here. That hasn't been treated properly. You'd best cover it.

CORRIGAN. [*Very, very shaky, almost faint, takes the handkerchief, puts it to his head and sits back down weakly*] That's . . . that's odd. [*He looks up, still holding the handkerchief.*]

WELLINGTON. What is?

CORRIGAN. I'm so . . . I'm so faint all of a sudden. So weak. It's almost as if I were—

WELLINGTON. As if you were what?

CORRIGAN. [*With a weak smile*] As if I'd suddenly gotten drunk or some—[*He looks up, desperately trying to focus now as his vision starts to become clouded.*] I've never. . . I've never felt like this before. I've never—[*His eyes turn to the wine glass on the table. As his eyes open wide, he struggles to his feet.*] You . . . you devil! You drugged me, didn't you! [*He reaches out to grab* WELLINGTON, *half struggling in the process.*] You drugged me, didn't you!

WELLINGTON. I was forced to, my young friend. You're a very sick man and a sick man doesn't belong in jail. He belongs in a **37**
comfortable accommodation where he can sleep and rest and regain his . . . [*He smiles a little apologetically.*] his composure, his rationale. Rest, Mr. Corrigan. I'll be back soon.

[*He turns and starts toward the door.* CORRIGAN *starts to follow him, stumbles to his knees, supports himself on one hand, looks up as* WELLINGTON *opens the door.*]

CORRIGAN. Please . . . please, you've got to believe me. Lincoln's going to be shot tonight.

WELLINGTON. [*Smiling again*] And *that's* odd! Because . . . perhaps I'm *beginning* to be- **38**
lieve you! Good night, Mr. Corrigan. Rest well. [*He turns and goes out of the room, closing the door behind him. We hear the sound of the key being inserted, the door* **39**
locked.]

[CORRIGAN *tries desperately to rise and then weakly falls over on his side. He crawls toward the door. He scrabbles at it with a weak hand.*]

CORRIGAN. [*Almost in a whisper*] Please . . . please . . . somebody . . . let me out. I wasn't kidding . . . I know . . . *the President's going to be assassinated!* [*His arm, supporting him, gives out and he falls to his face, then in a last effort, he turns himself over so that he's lying on his back.*]

[*There is a sound of a heavy knocking on the door. Then a* LANDLADY's *voice from outside.*]

LANDLADY. There's no need to break it open, Officer. I've got an extra key. Now if you don't mind, stand aside.

37 Discussion Do you believe Wellington is telling the truth about his motivation for drugging Corrigan? What do you think is his true motivation?

38 Discussion Why is Wellington beginning to believe Corrigan?

39 Reading Strategy Where is Wellington going?

Student Activity 2. Write five complete sentences beginning with the participial phrases italicized in the examples. Be sure to add a comma after the phrase, and then write a complete sentence. Example: *Interrupting* with a roar, the captain dismisses the young officer's suggestion.

Student Activity 3. Write three original sentences, beginning each with a participial phrase.

40 Reading Strategy If there is no one there by the name of Wellington, what might be Wellington's real name?

41 Literary Focus Why couldn't the identity of Wellington be revealed in the same way in a live production on a stage in a theater? If you were rewriting this play as a script for a live production, how would you reveal Wellington's identity to the audience?

[There's the sound of the key inserted in the lock and the door opens. The young POLICE OFFICER *from earlier is standing there with an angry-faced* LANDLADY *behind him. The* POLICE OFFICER *gets down on his knees, props up* CORRIGAN'S *head.]*

POLICE OFFICER. Are you all right? What happened?

CORRIGAN. What time is it? *[He grabs the* OFFICER, *almost pulling him over.]* You've got to tell me what time it is.

POLICE OFFICER. It's ten-thirty-five. Come on, Corrigan. You've got to tell me what you know about this. You may be a madman or a drunk or I don't know what—but you've got me convinced and I've been everywhere from the Mayor's office to the Police Commissioner's home trying to get a special guard for the President.

CORRIGAN. Then go yourself. Find out where he's sitting and get right up alongside of him. He'll be shot from behind. That's the way it happened. Shot from behind. And then the assassin jumps from the box to the stage and he runs out of the wings.

POLICE OFFICER. *[Incredulous]* You're telling me this as if, as if it has already happened.

CORRIGAN. It *has* happened. It happened a hundred years ago and I've come back to see that it *doesn't* happen. *[Looking beyond the* POLICE OFFICER*]* Where's the man who brought me in here? Where's Wellington?

LANDLADY. *[Peering into the room]* Welling-
40 ton? There's no one here by that name.

CORRIGAN. *[Waves a clenched fist at her, still holding the handkerchief]* Don't tell me there's no one here by that name. He brought me in here. He lives in this room.

LANDLADY. There's no one here by that name.

CORRIGAN. *[Holds the handkerchief close to his face, again waving his fist]* I tell you the man who brought me here was named—

[He stops abruptly, suddenly caught by something he sees on the handkerchief. His eyes slowly turn to stare at it in his hand. On the border are the initials J.W.B.] 4

CORRIGAN. J.W.B.?

LANDLADY. Of course! Mr. John Wilkes Booth who lives in this room and that's who brought you here.

CORRIGAN. He said his name was Wellington! And *that's* why he drugged me. *[He grabs the* POLICE OFFICER *again.]* He gave me wine and he drugged me. He didn't want me to stop him. He's the one who's going to do it. Listen, you've got to get to that theater. You've got to stop him. John Wilkes Booth! He's going to kill Lincoln. Look, get out of here now! Will you stop him? Will you—

[He stops abruptly, his eyes look up. All three people turn to look toward the window. There's the sound of crowd noises building, suggestive of excitement, and then almost a collective wail, a mournful, universal chant that comes from the streets, and as the sound builds we suddenly hear intelligible words that are part of the mob noise.]

VOICES. The President's been shot. President Lincoln's been assassinated. Lincoln is dying.

[The LANDLADY *suddenly bursts into tears. The* POLICE OFFICER *rises to his feet, his face white.]*

POLICE OFFICER. Oh my dear God! You were right. You *did* know. Oh . . . my . . . dear . . . God!

[He turns almost trance-like and walks out of the room. The LANDLADY *follows him.*

Primary Source

Serling's criticisms of television as a medium that values profit over social responsibility and artistic integrity earned him the title, television's "angry young man." He asked, "How do you put on a meaningful drama or documentary that is adult, incisive, probing, when every fifteen minutes the proceedings are interrupted by twelve dancing rabbits with toilet paper?"

When *The Twilight Zone* appeared, he was accused of conforming to commercialism. Serling's defense was that his attitude had not changed; he had merely embedded his social criticisms in fantasy. His themes were more oblique, but no less pointed. "The writer's role," he maintained, "is to be a menacer of [the] public's conscience."

As you read this play, decide whether you accept Serling's defense of "The Twilight Zone."

CORRIGAN *rises weakly and goes to the window, staring out at the night and listening to the sounds of a nation beginning its mourning. He closes his eyes and puts his head against the window pane and with fruitless, weakened smashes, hits the side of the window frame as he talks.*]

CORRIGAN. I tried to tell you. I tried to warn you. Why didn't anybody listen? Why? Why didn't anyone listen to me?

[*His fist beats a steady staccato*[12] *on the window frame.*]

12. **staccato** (stə kät′ ō) *n.*: Abrupt, distinct elements of sound.

Scene 3

[*The Washington Club at night.* CORRIGAN *is pounding on the front door of the Washington Club.* CORRIGAN *is standing there in mod-* 43 *ern dress once again. The door opens. An* ATTENDANT *we've not seen before appears.*]

ATTENDANT TWO. Good evening, Mr. Corrigan. Did you forget something, sir? 44

[CORRIGAN *walks past the* ATTENDANT, *through the big double doors that lead to the card room as in Act I. His three friends are in the middle of a discussion. The fourth man at the table, sitting in his seat, has his back to* 45 *the camera.*]

Humanities Note

Fine art, *Assassination of Abraham Lincoln by Booth at Ford's Theatre,* by an anonymous American artist, depicts Booth making his escape after fatally shooting the President. The style is impressionistic, depending more on light and color than on form to create a dramatic effect. The audience, all leaning or pointing in the same direction, leads the viewer's eye from the president's box, draped with flags, to the figure of Booth running across the stage.

History tells us that Booth broke his leg by catching his foot in the draped flag as he leaped from the box. As he ran, he brandished a dagger, shouting the words, "Sic semper tyrannis," Latin for "Thus always to tyrants."

Ask students how they would interpret this painting if they were unfamiliar with the subject matter.

42 **Discussion** Think back to the debate between Millard and Corrigan in Act I. Who seems to have been proven right by the events of this scene?

43 **Literary Focus** What is the effect of Corrigan's beating his fist on the window frame in the previous scene and pounding on the door in this scene?

44 **Critical Thinking and Reading** Look back at the beginning of Act I. What is similar about the beginning of that scene and this one? What effect does this similarity have on the audience?

45 **Critical Thinking and Reading** How does the author want the audience to react upon seeing William, the attendant from Act I, transformed into a wealthy gentleman? How does he elicit this reaction?

46 **Discussion** Explain what has happened to William? Who was his great-grandfather?

47 **Critical Thinking and Reading** Has the "new" William ever been a servant, or has he been wealthy all his life? What has happened to the William from Act I? Did he ever exist? Where is he now? Why doesn't the author attempt to answer these questions for the audience?

48 **Critical Thinking and Reading** How do William's and Corrigan's attitudes toward one another differ in this act from Act I? To what does William owe his social equality with Corrigan? What social value does Serling seem to be poking fun at?

49 **Discussion** Why doesn't Corrigan want to play cards?

50 **Enrichment** After each episode of *The Twilight Zone*, Serling himself took the part of the narrator, adding a final comment that called the audience's attention to the theme of the drama.

51 **Discussion** Was history altered, in this play, or not?

52 **Critical Thinking and Reading** Why does Serling tell you, the audience, that the thesis of the play should be "taken as you will"?

Reader's Response The author invites you to take the thesis as you will. How do you take it? Do you think that, if time travel were possible, history could be altered, or do you think something would stop the time traveler from changing the course of important events? What are the reasons for your response?

MILLARD. [*Looking up*] Hello, Pete. Come on over and join tonight's bull session. It has to do with the best ways of amassing a fortune. What are your tried-and-true methods?

CORRIGAN. [*His voice intense and shaky*] We were talking about time travel, about going back in time.

JACKSON. [*Dismissing it*] Oh that's old stuff. We're on a new track now. Money and the best ways to acquire it.

CORRIGAN. Listen . . . listen, I want to tell you something. This is true. If you go back into the past you can't change anything. [*He takes another step toward the table.*] Understand? You can't change anything.

[*The men look at one another, disarmed by the intensity of* CORRIGAN's *tone.*]

JACKSON. [*Rises, softly*] All right, old man, if you say so. [*Studying him intensely*] Are you all right?

CORRIGAN. [*Closing his eyes for a moment*] Yes . . . yes, I'm all right.

JACKSON. Then come on over and listen to a lot of palaver[13] from self-made swindlers. William here has the best method.

CORRIGAN. William?

46 [*He sees the attendant from Act I but now meticulously dressed, a middle-aged millionaire obviously, with a totally different manner, who puts a cigarette in a holder with manicured hands in the manner of a man totally accustomed to wealth.* WILLIAM *looks up and smiles.*]

WILLIAM. Oh yes. My method for achieving security is by far the best. You simply inherit it. It comes to you in a beribboned box. I was telling the boys here, Corrigan. My great-grandfather was on the police force here in Washington on the night of Lincoln's assassination. He went all over town trying to warn people that something might happen. [*He holds up his hands in a gesture.*] How he figured it out, nobody seems to know. It's certainly not recorded any place. But because there was so much publicity, people never forgot him. He became a police chief, then a councilman, did some wheeling and dealing in land and became a millionaire. What do you say we get back to our bridge, gentlemen?

[JACKSON *takes the cards and starts to shuffle.* WILLIAM *turns in his seat once again.*]

WILLIAM. How about it, Corrigan? Take a hand?

CORRIGAN. Thank you, William, no. I think I'll . . . I think I'll just go home.

[*He turns very slowly and starts toward the exit. Over his walk we hear the whispered, hushed murmurings of the men at the table.*]

VOICES. Looks peaked, doesn't he? Acting so strangely. I wonder what's the matter with him.

[CORRIGAN *walks into the hall and toward the front door.*]

NARRATOR'S VOICE. Mr. Peter Corrigan, lately returned from a place "Back There"; a journey into time with highly questionable results. Proving, on one hand, that the threads of history are woven tightly and the skein of events cannot be undone; but, on the other hand, there are small fragments of tapestry that *can* be altered. Tonight's thesis, to be taken as you will, in *The Twilight Zone!*[14]

---

13. palaver (pə lav′ ər) *n.*: Idle chatter.

14. *The Twilight Zone:* Television program on which *Back There* was originally produced.

Closure and Extension

ANSWERS TO THINKING ABOUT THE SELECTION
Recalling

1. Millard tries to convince Corrigan that if we could go back in time, we could alter history.
2. Students might cite Whitaker's warning, "Don't get lost back in time now, Corrigan."
3. Corrigan is jailed for causing a disturbance at Ford's Theater.
4. Wellington is John Wilkes Booth. He prevents Corrigan from preventing Lincoln's assassination.
5. Wellington and the police officer believe Corrigan. Others think he is insane.

Interpreting

6. He thinks they will believe he is insane.

THINKING ABOUT THE SELECTION

Recalling

1. Of what does Millard try to convince Corrigan as the play begins?
2. What statement in Scene 1 foreshadows, or hints at, what happens to Corrigan?
3. Why is Corrigan jailed?
4. Explain who Wellington is and describe his role in the play.
5. What effect do Corrigan's warnings have?

Interpreting

6. Why does Corrigan refuse to tell people the truth about where he's from?
7. The stage directions repeatedly feature Wellington with a thin smile. What is the writer trying to indicate about Wellington?
8. Why do you think certain elements of history were altered in the play, while others were not? Explain. What does the author want to emphasize?
9. How do the events in this play prove "that the threads of history are woven tightly and the skein of events cannot be undone"? How do they also prove that "there are small fragments of tapestry that can be altered"?

Applying

10. Imagine a future in which we can freely journey through time. Discuss the complications such journeys might cause in our lives.

ANALYZING LITERATURE

Appreciating Staging

Staging includes the costumes, props, lighting and sound effects that are used to make the scenes believable. Positioning of props, and the movements of the actors are also part of staging.

The staging of "Back There" changes as Corrigan goes back in time. As the setting changes from 1965 to 1865, the staging reflects that change.

1. What changes in the staging indicate that Corrigan is back in time?
2. How many times does the staging change?
3. Sound effects help characterize the 1865 setting. Find two examples of such sound effects.
4. Act I ends outside of Ford's Theater. As Act II begins, how does the staging change help us understand what happened to Corrigan outside the theater?

CRITICAL THINKING AND READING

Recognizing the Playwright's Purpose

Rod Serling's purpose as a television dramatist was to express viewpoints as well as to entertain. Serling thought television should function as an art form in which writers could explore attitudes and draw conclusions. He is noted for bringing a strong moral sense to his art.

In "Back There," the narrator concludes that if time travel were possible, history could not be changed.

1. What qualities of the play make it entertaining?
2. How does Serling's play function as an art form?
3. What purpose does the narration that ends the play serve?
4. Explain how Serling is or is not successful in expressing viewpoints and entertaining his audience in "Back There."

THINKING AND WRITING

Writing About Staging

Imagine that you have an opportunity to write an episode of *The Twilight Zone* similar to "Back There." Take a recent historical event with which you are familiar and create a character who travels back to that event. Make a list of the props, costumes, sound effects, and lighting you would need to stage the event. Revise your list; then prepare a final draft as if your stage crew would be purchasing these items for your production.

(Answers begin on p. 274.)

7. The writer indicates that Wellington is insincere.
8. Students may answer that the author is more interested in criticizing society than theorizing about history. He emphasizes the point that social and economic positions are controlled by twists of fate and not by a person's intrinsic worth.
9. The assassination is not prevented, but William's future is altered.

Applying

10. Students might suggest that even a seemingly insignificant event can have far-reaching implications. Thus, the mere presence of a time traveler would be sufficient to radically alter the course of history.

Challenge More advanced students may enjoy entertaining the notion, known, in science fiction, as "parallel universes." According to this theory, history may be changed, but every time an event is altered, an additional universe is created. The alternate universes exist side by side, and one can move from one to another.

ANSWERS TO ANALYZING LITERATURE

1. The light changes, the street lamp becomes a gaslight, Corrigan's watch disappears, he is wearing a nineteenth-century costume, the date has vanished from the plaque.
2. The staging changes six times.
3. Students should cite the sound of chimes, the clip-clop of horses' hooves, and the rolling, squeaky sound of carriage wheels.
4. Seeing Corrigan in a police station leads the audience to infer that he has been arrested for disturbing the peace.

ANSWERS TO CRITICAL THINKING AND READING

1. Students may respond that the play creates suspense, stimulates the imagination, takes the audience into a fantasy world, surprises the audience at the end.
2. Students may respond that Serling condemns the materialistic values and snobbishness of the club members and the narrow-mindedness of the police chief.
3. Television audiences are subject to frequent distractions. Serling's narrations compensate by making sure that the audience has not missed the point of the drama.
4. Some students may find the drama successful in this respect. Others may find the play too preachy to be entertaining, while still others may feel that the viewpoints are expressed too indirectly to be grasped by most television audiences.

THINKING AND WRITING

For help with this assignment, students can refer to Lesson 7, Writing About Setting, in the Handbook of Writing About Literature.

Writing Across the Curriculum You might wish to have students research and write essays on how history might have changed had Lincoln's assassination been prevented. Possible topics of research are Andrew Johnson, Ulysses S. Grant, William Seward, and the Reconstruction. You might inform a social studies teacher of this assignment.

Focus

More About the Author Zindel claims never to have been to the theater until he was in his twenties. He uses this statement to argue that he was genetically conditioned to be a playwright. Have students debate the logic of his statement and discuss other ways that his experiences might have prepared him to write plays.

Literary Focus If students have read "The Adventure of the Speckled Band," remind them that have studied one kind of conflict—external conflict. Ask students to give examples of internal conflicts in other stories or plays that they have read.

Look For Remind students that conflict is an element of any story's plot and that it leads to a climax and a resolution. Tell students to look for these moments in Zindel's play; being aware of them will help them understand Helen's conflict better.

Writing/Prior Knowledge As your students brainstorm, write their lists on the chalkboard. From each list, have students discuss which ideas can be clustered under a single larger idea, such as *Advances Beneficial to Health* or *Advances Hazardous to People's Safety.* They might try writing a topic sentence for a paragraph on different topics.

Vocabulary Have your more advanced students use dictionaries to find the etymologies of these words. Then have them discuss the debt owed by English to other languages. They should then discuss ways in which the study of a foreign language could help enlarge their vocabulary.

Spelling Tip A few words in American English like *macabre* end in *-re* instead of *-er*. Some of the more common ones are *acre, massacre,* and *mediocre.*

GUIDE FOR READING

Let Me Hear You Whisper

Paul Zindel (1936–   ) was born in Staten Island, New York, where he later taught high-school chemistry for ten years. After the publication of his young-adult novels *The Pigman* (1968) and *My Darling, My Hamburger* (1969), Zindel turned to writing full time. He wrote several plays, including *The Effects of Gamma Rays on Man-in-the-Moon Marigolds*. In the television play *Let Me Hear You Whisper,* Zindel focuses on some controversies associated with science.

Conflict in Drama

Conflict is a struggle between opposing sides or forces. In a play, the characters *act out* the conflict, and ultimately their actions result in a resolution, or outcome. External conflict is a struggle between a character and an outside force, such as another person, nature, or fate. Internal conflict is a struggle within the character's own mind. A character can express internal conflict—as well as external conflict—through actions, facial expressions, and dialogue.

Look For

As you read *Let Me Hear You Whisper,* look for indications of what the main character, Helen, experiences. Try to understand the reasons for her conflict and the way she resolves it.

Writing

Science has found the answers to many problems. However, sometimes, it creates problems. Brainstorm with your classmates to form two lists. Label one list *Advances Brought About Through Science.* Label the second list *Problems Caused by Science.*

Vocabulary

Knowing the following words will help you as you read *Let Me Hear You Whisper.*

predecessor (pred′ ə ses′ ər) *n.*: Someone who comes before another in a position (p. 278)

incessantly (in ses′ 'nt lē) *adv.*: Without interruption (p. 279)

compulsory (kəm pul′ sər ē) *adj.*: Required (p. 280)

enunciated (i nun′ sē āt′ əd) *v.*: Spoken clearly (p. 282)

macabre (mə käb′ rə) *adj.*: Gruesome, suggesting the horror of death (p. 291)

benevolent (bə nev′ ə lənt) *adj.*: Kindly (p. 291)

gyrations (jī rā′ shənz) *n.*: Circling or spiral movements (p. 293)

Objectives

1 To understand conflict in drama
2 To understand controversy
3 To appreciate specialized vocabulary
4 To write a response to a critical comment about a play

Support Material

Teaching Portfolio

Teacher Backup, pp. 389–392
Grammar in Action Worksheet, *Using Compound Sentences,* pp. 393–394, *Understanding Sentence Fragments,* pp. 395–396
Usage and Mechanics Worksheet, p. 397
Vocabulary Check, p. 398
Analyzing Literature Worksheet, *Understanding Conflict in Drama,* p. 399
Critical Thinking and Reading Worksheet, *Understanding Controversy;* p. 400
Selection Test, pp. 401–402

Let Me Hear You Whisper

Paul Zindel

CHARACTERS

Helen . . . . A cleaning lady
Miss Moray . . . Her briskly efficient supervisor
Dr. Crocus . . . . A dedicated lady of science
Mrs. Fridge . . . . Her assistant
Danielle . . . . . . A talky lady porter 1
A Dolphin . . . . . . The subject of an experiment

[The play is set in the laboratory of a building near the Hudson River in lower Manhattan—the home of American Biological Association Development For The Advancement of Brain Analysis.]

Scene 1

[Curtain rises on DR. CROCUS *and* MRS. FRIDGE, *conducting an experiment on the* DOLPHIN in the laboratory. The DOLPHIN *is in a long narrow tank with little room to move. A head sling lifting its blowhole out of the water*
2 *and several electrodes implanted in its brain further the impression of a trapped and sad animal.* DR. CROCUS *is observing closely as* MRS. FRIDGE *presses various buttons on cue. An oscilloscope is bleeping in the background.]*

DR. CROCUS. Pain.

[MRS. FRIDGE *presses a button. No response from* DOLPHIN.]

Pleasure.

[Another button]

Anger.

[Another]

Fear.

[There has been no satisfactory response from the DOLPHIN, *but an automatic recorder starts to play a charming melody. When the accompanying vocal commences, however, it is an eerily precise enunciation of the words.]*

RECORD.

Let me call you sweetheart,
I'm in love with you.
Let me hear you whisper,
That you love me, too.

[Disappointed at the lack of response, DR. CROCUS *crosses toward* MRS. FRIDGE.]

DR. CROCUS. Resistance to electrodic impulses. Possibly destroyed tissue. Continue impulse and auditory suggestion at intervals of seven minutes until end of week. If no response by Friday, termination. 3,4

[DOLPHIN'*s special discomfort at this word is unnoticed by others.* DR. CROCUS *and* MRS. FRIDGE *head toward elevator on other side of the stage. The elevator doors open and* MISS MORAY *emerges with* HELEN.]

Presentation

Motivation/Prior Knowledge Discuss the word *vivisection* with the students. Ask them how they feel about conducting experiments on animals. What are the benefits? What are the drawbacks? How do they think the scientists who conduct the experiments feel about what they are doing?

Thematic Idea Another selection that deals with the effects of technology is "Flowers for Algernon" (page 201).

Purpose-Setting Question What is Helen's problem and how does she resolve it?

1 **Discussion** Discuss the names of the character. Ask students why one character's name is a type of ell, one a flower, and one something cold. Ask students to describe these three characters solely on the basis of what their names mean.

2 **Enrichment** Impress upon the students the importance of carefully reading the stage directions. Explain how they help you visualize the actors' movements and emotions.

3 **Discussion** Discuss how scientific and nonfeeling the doctor appears. Does the dolphin understand what the doctor is saying?

4 **Master Teacher Note** Ask students the playwright's purpose in using euphemisms such as "termination." What grim reality is he masking in his characters' thoughts? This can lead to a discussion of euphemistic language in business and government. For example, "reduction in force" might be used instead of "You're fired!" or "excursion beyond their borders" instead of "They invaded Country X!"

5 **Discussion** What euphemism is used here? What is Helen's job?

6 **Enrichment** Discuss the use of acronyms. Explain that an acronym is a pronounceable word formed from the beginning letters in words that make up a phrase, as in C.A.R.E. (Cooperative for American Relief Everywhere) and MASH (Mobile Army Surgical Hospital). Elicit from students why acronyms are a part of our spoken language as well as our written language, whereas abbreviations are usually limited to our written language.

You might also mention to students that there was a popular song in the 1950's in which a monkey and owl spoke all day to each other saying, "Abadaba, dabadaba, dabadabadoo," which meant, "I love you."

7 **Discuss** Why would the personnel department ask such a question of an employee? What does Helen's response suggest about her?

MISS MORAY. Dr. Crocus. Mrs. Fridge. I'm so glad we've run into you. I want you to meet Helen.

HELEN. Hello.

[DR. CROCUS *and* MRS. FRIDGE *nod and get on elevator.*]

5 **MISS MORAY.** Helen is the newest member of our Custodial Engineering Team. So if you two "coaches" have any suggestions we'll be most grateful. We want everything to be perfect, don't we, Helen?

HELEN. I do the best I can.

MISS MORAY. Exactly. The doctor is one of the most remarkable . . . [*The elevator doors close and* MRS. FRIDGE *and* DR. CROCUS *are gone.*] Remarkable.

HELEN. She looked remarkable. [HELEN *looks like a peasant, kerchief and all. As they walk,* HELEN *begins to remove the kerchief and she would like to fold it properly, for that to be her only activity, but she is distracted by a shopping bag she carries, a bulky coat, and the voice of* MISS MORAY.]

6 **MISS MORAY.** Dr. Crocus is the guiding heart here at the American Biological Association Development For The Advancement of Brain Analysis. We call it ABADABA, for short.

HELEN. I guess you have to. [*They stop at a metal locker.*]

MISS MORAY. This will be your locker and your key. Mrs. Fridge has been with ABADABA only three months and already she's a much endeared part of our little family. Your equipment is in this closet.

[*She opens a closet next to the locker.*]

HELEN. I have to bring my own hangers, I suppose . . .

MISS MORAY. Although it was somewhat embarrassing to me, it was Mrs. Fridge's inventorial excellence that uncovered what Margaurita—your predecessor—did and why she had to leave us. She'd been drinking portions of the ethyl alcohol—there's a basin under the sink for rag rinsing—the undenatured ethyl alcohol, and she almost burned out her esophagus. [*Pause*] I wouldn't have minded so much if she had only asked. Didn't you find Personnel pleasant?

HELEN. They asked a lot of crazy questions.

MISS MORAY. For instance.

HELEN. They wanted to know how I felt watching TV.

MISS MORAY. What do you mean, *how you felt?*

HELEN. They wanted to know what went on in my head when I'm watching television in 7
my living room and the audience laughs. They asked if I ever thought the audience was laughing at *me.*

MISS MORAY. [*Laughing*] My, oh, my! What did you tell them?

HELEN. I don't have a TV.

MISS MORAY. I'm sorry.

HELEN. I'm not.

MISS MORAY. Yes. Now, it's really quite simple. That's our special soap solution. One tablespoon to a gallon of hot water for ordinary cleaning, if I may suggest. I so much prefer to act as an assist to the Custodial Engineering Staff. New ideas. Techniques. I try to keep myself open.

[*Her mouth pauses wide open.* HELEN *has been busy familiarizing herself with the contents of the closet. She has culminated a series of small actions which have put things in order for her, by running water into a pail which fits into a metal stand on wheels.*]

HELEN. She left a dirty mop.

MISS MORAY. I beg your pardon?

HELEN. The one that drank. She left a dirty mop.

MISS MORAY. How ugly. I'll report it first thing in the morning. It may seem like a small point but if she ever tries to use us as a reference, she may be amazed at the specificity of our files.

HELEN. It's not that dirty.

MISS MORAY. I'll start you in the main laboratory area. We like it done first. The specimen section next. By that time we'll be well toward morning and if there are a few minutes left you can polish the brass strip. [*She points to brass strip which runs around halfway between ceiling and floor.*] Margaurita never once got to the brass strip.

[HELEN *has completed her very professional preparations and looks impatient to get moving.*]

Ready? Fine.

[*They start moving toward Dolphin area,* MISS MORAY *thumbing through papers on a clipboard.*]

You were with one concern for fourteen years, weren't you? Fourteen years with the Metal Climax Building. That's next to the Radio City Music Hall, isn't it, dear?

HELEN. Uh huh . . .

MISS MORAY. They sent a marvelous letter of recommendation—how you washed the corridor on the seventeenth floor . . . and the Metal Climax Building is a very long building. My! Fourteen years on the seventeenth floor. You must be very proud. Why did you leave?

HELEN. They put in a rug.

[MISS MORAY *leads* HELEN *into the laboratory area as* DANIELLE *enters.*]

MISS MORAY. Danielle, Helen will be taking Margaurita's place. Danielle is the night porter for the fifth through ninth floors. Duties you might find distasteful. 8

DANIELLE. Hiya!

HELEN. Hello. [HELEN *looks over the place.*]

MISS MORAY. By the way Danielle . . . there's a crock on nine you missed and the technicians on that floor have complained about the odor . . . [*Back to* HELEN] you can be certain we'll assist in every way possible.

HELEN. Maybe you could get me some hangers . . . ?

DANIELLE. I'll be glad to do anything. Just say the word and . . .

HELEN. What's behind there? [*Opening the Dolphin area*]

MISS MORAY. What? Oh, that's a dolphin, dear. But don't you worry about anything except the floor. Dr. Crocus prefers us not to touch either the equipment or the animals. That was another shortcoming of Margaurita's. Recently the doctor was . . . experimenting . . . with a colony of mice in that cage . . . [*She indicates cage.*] . . . and she was incessantly feeding them popcorn.

DANIELLE. Kinda a nice lady, though. Lived in the East Village.[1]

MISS MORAY. Yes, she did live in the East Village.

HELEN. [*Attention still on* DOLPHIN] Do you keep him cramped up in that all the time? 9

---

1. East Village: A neighborhood in Manhattan in New York City.

8 **Discuss** Ask students what kinds of jobs they think a porter might have to do that would be less appealing than that of a cleaning lady.

9 **Literary Focus** Note Helen's immediate affection and concern for the dolphin. Her involvement results in conflict.

10 **Master Teacher Note** Ask students if they would work for a company that so rigidly controls employees. Have students assess pros and cons of working for a "benevolent" employer that controls workers' lives "for their own good." Do you lose your freedom of choice?

MISS MORAY. We have a natatorium[2] for it to exercise in at Dr. Crocus's discretion.

HELEN. He really looks cramped.

MISS MORAY. [*Closing the Dolphin area*] Well, you must be anxious to begin. I'll make myself available at the reception desk in the hall for a few nights in case any questions arise. Although my hunch is, that before you know it, I'll be coming to *you* with questions . . . coffee break at 2 and 6 A.M. Lunch at 4 A.M. All clear?

HELEN. I don't need a coffee break.

MISS MORAY. I beg your pardon?

HELEN. I said I don't need a coffee break.

MISS MORAY. Helen, we all need Perk-You-Ups. All of us. Perhaps you never liked them at the Metal Climax Building, but you'll learn to love them here. Perk-You-Ups make the employees much more efficient. Besides, Helen—

HELEN. I don't want one.

10 **MISS MORAY.** They're compulsory. Oh, Helen, I know, you're going to fit right in with our little family. You're such a *nice* person.

[*She exits.* HELEN *immediately gets to work moving her equipment into place and getting down on her hands and knees to scrub the floor.* DANIELLE *spots a ceiling bulb out and prepares to remove it by using a long stick with a grip on the end of it designed to unscrew bulbs one cannot reach.*]

DANIELLE. Margaurita wasn't half as bad as Miss Moray thought she was.

HELEN. I'm sure she wasn't.

DANIELLE. She was twice as bad. [*She laughs. Pause*] You live in the city? . . .

2. natatorium (nāt′ ə tôr′ ē əm) *n.*: An indoor swimming pool.

HELEN. Yes.

DANIELLE. That's nice. . . . my husband died two years ago.

HELEN. That's too bad.

DANIELLE. Yeah, two years in June. He blew up.

HELEN. Oh, I'm sorry.

DANIELLE. When you want that water changed, just lemme know. I'll take care of it.

HELEN. Thanks, but I just like to get the temperature right so my hands don't get boiled. You must miss your husband.

DANIELLE. Biggest mistake I ever made, getting married . . . you married?

HELEN. No.

DANIELLE. Good, if a woman ain't suited for it, she shouldn't do it.

HELEN. I didn't say I wasn't suited for it.

DANIELLE. My husband was set in his ways, too.

HELEN. If you'll excuse me, I have to get my work done.

DANIELLE. Guess I'd better see about that crock on nine. You don't like to talk, do you?

HELEN. I'm used to working alone and that's the way I get my work done.

[DANIELLE *exits. Not realizing she's already gone*]

What do you mean, your husband blew up?

[*But* DANIELLE *is gone. She glances at the curtain shielding the* DOLPHIN, *then continues scrubbing. After a beat, the record begins to play.*]

RECORD.

Let me call you sweetheart,
I'm in love with you.
Let me hear you whisper,
That you love me, too.

[HELEN *eyes the automatic machinery with suspicion, but goes on working. When the song is finished she looks at the curtain again and again until her curiosity makes her pull the curtain open and look at the* DOLPHIN. *He is looking right back at her. She becomes uncomfortable and starts to close the curtain again. She decides to leave it part-way open so she can still see the* DOLPHIN *while she scrubs. She glances out of the corner of her eye after a few moments of scrubbing and notices the* DOLPHIN *is looking at her. She pretends to look away and sings* Let Me Call You Sweetheart *to herself —missing a word or two here and there —but her eyes return to the* DOLPHIN. *She becomes uncomfortable again under his stare and crawls on her hands and knees to the other side of the room. She scrubs there for a moment or two and then shoots a look at the* DOLPHIN. *It is still looking at her. She tries to ease her discomfort by playing peek-a-boo with the* DOLPHIN *for a moment. There is no response and she resumes*

11 **Enrichment** Again, point out the importance of stage directions in a play. Explain how they will help you picture what the characters are doing. You might ask the following questions whose answers appear in information given in the stage directions.

1. How does Helen feel about all the automatic machinery around the dolphin?
2. How does Helen feel about the dolphin?
3. What children's game does Helen try to play with the dolphin?
4. How does the dolphin respond to Helen?

scrubbing and humming. The DOLPHIN *then lets out a bubble or two and moves in the tank to bring his blowhole to the surface. (Any sounds he does make, including words, are like a haunting whisper and never enunciated so they are absolute.)*]

DOLPHIN. Youuuuuuuuuuuu. [HELEN *hears the sound, assumes she is mistaken, and goes on with her work.*] Youuuuuuuuuuuu.

[HELEN *has heard the sound more clearly this time. She is puzzled, contemplates a moment, and then decides to get up off the floor. She closes the curtain on the* DOLPHIN*'s tank and is quite disturbed. The elevator door suddenly opens and* MISS MORAY *enters.*]

MISS MORAY. What is it, Helen?

HELEN. The fish is making some kinda funny noise.

MISS MORAY. Mammal, Helen. It's a mammal.

HELEN. The mammal's making some kinda funny noise.

MISS MORAY. Mammals are supposed to make funny noises.

HELEN Yes, Miss Moray.

[HELEN *hangs awkwardly a moment and then continues scrubbing.* MISS MORAY *exits officiously to another part of the floor. A moment later, from behind the curtains, the* DOLPHIN *is heard.*]

DOLPHIN. Youuuuuuuuuuuuu.

[HELEN *is quite worried.*] Youuuuuuuuuuuuu.

[*She apprehensively approaches the curtain, and opens it, when* DANIELLE *barges in. She goes to get her reaching pole and* HELEN *hurriedly returns to scrubbing the floor.*]

DANIELLE. Bulb out on ten.

HELEN. What do they have that thing for?

DANIELLE. What thing?

HELEN. That.

DANIELLE. Yeah, he's something, ain't he? They're tryin' to get it to talk.

HELEN. Talk?

DANIELLE. Uh-huh, but this one don't. They had one last year that used to laugh. It'd go heh heh heh heh heh heh heh. I'd be in here doing something and it'd start heh heh heh heh heh hehing. He died a year ago May. Then they got another one that used to say "Yeah, it's four o'clock." Everybody took pictures of that one. All the magazines.

HELEN. What'd it say "four o'clock" for?

DANIELLE. Nobody knows.

HELEN. It just kept saying "Yeah, it's four o'clock!"

DANIELLE. Until it died of pneumonia. [*Pause*] They talk outta their blowholes, when they can talk, that is. Did you see the blowhole?

HELEN. No.

DANIELLE. Come on and take a look. Look at it.

HELEN. I don't want to look at any blowhole.

DANIELLE. You can see it right there.

[HELEN *gets up and goes to the tank. As she and* DANIELLE *stand at the tank, their backs are to one of the entrances, and they don't see* MISS MORAY *open the door and watch them.*]

This one don't say anything at all. It bleeps, beeps, barks and blatts out of the mouth, but it don't talk out of the blowhole. They been playing that record every seven minutes for months and it can't learn beans.

MISS MORAY. Helen?

[HELEN *and* DANIELLE *turn around.*]

282

Helen, would you mind stepping over here a moment?

HELEN. Yes, Miss Moray.

DANIELLE. I was just showing her something.

MISS MORAY. Have you attended to the crock on nine?

DANIELLE. Yes, Ma'am.

MISS MORAY. Then hadn't we better get on with our duties? [MISS MORAY *guides* HELEN *aside putting her arm around her as though taking her into great confidence. She even whispers.*] Helen, I have to talk to you. Frankly, I need your help.

HELEN. She was just showing me . . .

MISS MORAY. It's something about Danielle I need your assistance with. I'm sure you've noticed that she . . .

HELEN. Yes?

MISS MORAY. Well, that she's the type of person who will do anything to breed idle chatter. Yes, an idle chatter breeder. How many times we've told her, "Danielle, this is a scientific atmosphere you're employed in and from Dr. Crocus all the way down to the
12 most insignificant member of the Custodial Engineering Staff we would appreciate a minimum of subjective intercourse." So—if you can help, Helen—and I'm sure you can, enormously—we'd be so grateful. This is science—and science means progress. You do want progress, don't you, dear?

HELEN. Yes, Miss Moray.

MISS MORAY. I knew you did.

DANIELLE. I just wanted to show her the blowhole.

MISS MORAY. I'm sure that's all it was, Danielle. [DANIELLE *exits.*]

Helen, why don't you dust for a while? Vary your labors.

[*She swings open a shelf area to reveal rather hideously preserved specimens.* HELEN *looks ready to gag as she sees the jars of all sizes. Various animals and parts of animals are visible in their formaldehyde baths.*]

A feather duster—here—is marvelous for dusting though a damp rag may be necessary for the glass surfaces. But whatever—do be careful. Margaurita once dropped a jar of assorted North Atlantic eels.

[MISS MORAY *smiles and exits in the elevator, leaving Helen alone. She is most uncomfortable in the environment. The sound of music and voice from beyond the walls falls over.*]

RECORD.

Let me call you sweetheart,
I'm in love with you.
Let me hear you whisper, 13
That you love me, too.

Scene 2

[*It is the next evening.* HELEN *gets off the elevator carrying a few hangers and still wearing her kerchief and coat. She looks around for anyone, realizes she is alone, and then proceeds to her locker. She takes her coat off and hangs it up.* HELEN *pushes her equipment into the lab. The curtain on the* DOLPHIN*'s tank has been closed. She sets her items up, then goes to the tank and pulls the curtain open a moment. The* DOLPHIN *is looking at her. She closes the curtain and starts scrubbing. The thought of the* DOLPHIN *amuses her a moment, relieving the tension she feels about the mammal, and she appears to be in good spirits as she*

12 **Discussion** What does this short lecture tell you about Miss Moray?

13 **Reading Strategy** Summarize the play up to this point and predict what Helen will do.

starts humming Let Me Call You Sweetheart *and scrubs in rhythm to it. She sets a one-two-three beat for the scrub brush.*

This mood passes quickly and she opens the curtain so she can watch the DOLPHIN *as she works. She and the* DOLPHIN *stare at each other and* HELEN *appears to be more curious than worried.*

Finally, she decides to try to imitate the sound she heard it make the night before.]

HELEN. Youuuuuuuuuuuuu. [*She pauses, watches for a response.*] Youuuuuuuu-uuuuu. [*Still no response. She returns her attention to her scrubbing for a moment. Then:*]

Polly want a cracker?
Polly want a cracker?

[*She wrings out a rag and resumes work.*]

Yeah, it's four o'clock. Yeah, it's four o'clock. [*When her expectation is unfulfilled, she is slightly disappointed. Then:*] Polly want a cracker at four o'clock?

[*She laughs at her own joke, then is reminded of the past success with laughter in working with dolphins. She can't resist trying it, so she goes to the* DOLPHIN*'s tank and notices how sad it looks. She is diverted from her initial intention by a guilty feeling of leaving the scrubbing. She bends down and looks directly into the* DOLPHIN*'s face. He lets out a bubble at her. She sticks her tongue out at him. She makes an exaggerated smile, and is very curious about what his skin feels like. She reaches her hand in and just touches the top of his head. He squirms and likes it, but she's interested in drying off her finger. She even washes it in her soap solution. She returns to scrubbing for a minute, then can't resist more fully petting the* DOLPHIN. *This time he reacts even more enthusiastically. She is half afraid and half happy. She returns to scrubbing. Then, at the tank:*]

Heh heh heh heh heh heh heh heh heh. [*Beat*] Heh heh heh heh. [*Beat*] Heh heh heh heh heh heh . . .

[MISS MORAY *enters. She sees what's going on. Then says, with exaggerated praise*]

MISS MORAY. Look how nicely the floor's coming along tonight! There's not a streak! Not a streak! You must have a special rinsing technique, Helen. You do, don't you? Why, you certainly do. I can smell something.

HELEN. Just a little . . . vinegar in the rinse water.

MISS MORAY. You brought that vinegar yourself just so the floors . . . they are sparkling, Helen. Sparkling! [*Jotting down in a pad*] This is going in your file, dear—and from now on, I'm going to requisition vinegar as a staple in the Custodial Engineering Department's supply list. [*She pauses—looks at the* DOLPHIN*—then at* HELEN.] It's marvelous, Helen, how well you've adjusted . . .

HELEN. Thank you, Miss Moray.

MISS MORAY. Not everyone does, you know. Just last week I had a problem with a porter on five, who became too fond of a St. Bernard they . . . worked on . . . and . . . [*Pause*] well, Helen a lot of people can't seem—

HELEN. [*Still scrubbing*] What do you mean, *worked on?*

MISS MORAY. Well . . . well, even Margaurita. She had fallen in love with the mice. All three hundred of them. She seemed shocked when she found out Dr. Crocus was . . .

using . . . them at the rate of twenty or so a day in connection with electrode implanting. She noticed them missing after a while and when I told her they'd been decapitated, she seemed terribly upset. It made one wonder if she'd thought we'd been sending them away on vacations or something. But, I'm sure you understand—you have such insight. [*She is at the tank.*] It's funny isn't it? To look at these mammals, you'd never sus-
4 pect they were such rapacious carnivori . . .[3]

HELEN. What do they want with it?

[*The* Let Me Call You Sweetheart *record commences playing but* MISS MORAY *talks over it.*]

MISS MORAY. Well, they may have an intelligence equal to our own. And if we can teach them our language—or learn theirs—we'll be able to communicate. [*Raising her voice higher over record*] Wouldn't that be won- 15
derful, Helen? To be able to communicate?

HELEN. I can't understand you.

MISS MORAY. [*Louder*] Communicate! Wouldn't it be wonderful?

HELEN. Oh, yeah.

MISS MORAY. [*With a cutting device*] When

---

3. rapacious (rə pā′ shəs) **carnivori** (kär nə vôr′ ī): Greedy flesh-eating mammals.

14 Literary Focus Have students explore the irony of this situation: a love song being taught to a creature Miss Moray characterizes as a "rapacious carnivore."

15 Discussion Discuss humor in the conversation about communication.

16 Discussion Who appears more logical—Helen or the scientists? Why?

17 Discussion Why does Miss Moray warn Helen not to become too involved with the dolphin?

Margaurita found out they were using this . . . on the mice, she almost fainted. No end of trouble.

HELEN. They chopped the heads off three hundred mice?

16 **MISS MORAY.** Now, Helen, you wanted progress, remember?

HELEN. That's horrible.

MISS MORAY. Helen, over a thousand individual laboratories did the same study last year.

HELEN. A thousand labs chopping off three hundred mice heads. Three hundred thousand mice heads chopped off? That's a lot of mouse heads. Couldn't one lab cut off a couple and then spread the word?

17 **MISS MORAY.** Now, Helen, this is exactly what I mean. You will do best not to become fond of the subject animals. When you're here a little longer you'll learn—well, there are some things in this world you have to accept on faith.

[*She exits. After a moment, the* DOLPHIN *starts in again.*]

DOLPHIN. Whisper . . .

HELEN. What?

DOLPHIN. Whisper to me . . .

[DANIELLE *barges in, pushing a hamper.*]

DANIELLE. Hi, Helen.

HELEN. Hello.

DANIELLE. [*Emptying wastes into hamper*] Miss Moray said she's got almond horns for our Perk-You-Up tonight.

HELEN. That thing never said anything to anybody?

DANIELLE. What thing?

HELEN. That mammal fish.

DANIELLE. Nope.

HELEN. Not one word?

DANIELLE. Nope.

HELEN. Nothing that sounded like "Youuuuuuuuuuuuu."

DANIELLE. What?

HELEN. "Youuuuuuuuuuuuu?" Or "Whisper?"

DANIELLE. I don't know what you're talking about. I got here an hour too early so I sat down by the docks. You can see the moon in the river.

[*The record goes on again, and* DANIELLE *exits without the hamper.*]

RECORD.

> Let me call you sweetheart,
> I'm in love with you.
> Let me hear you whisper,
> That you love me, too.

[HELEN *opens the curtain to see the* DOLPHIN. *It is staring at her. It is as though the* DOLPHIN *is trying to tell her something, and she can almost suspect this from the intensity of its stare. She goes to her locker, unwraps a sandwich she brought, and takes a slice of ham from it. She approaches the tank and offers the ham. The* DOLPHIN *moves and startles her, but the ham falls to the bottom of the tank.*]

DOLPHIN. Hear . . .

HELEN. Huh?

DOLPHIN. Hear me . . .

[DANIELLE *bursts back in carrying a crock, and Helen darts to her scrubbing.*]

DANIELLE. Ugh. This—gotta rinse this one out. Full of little gooey things.

HELEN. What do they eat?

Grammar in Action

A **compound sentence** consists of two or more independent clauses. In most cases, the independent clauses are joined by a comma and one of the coordinating conjunctions (*and, but, for, nor, or, so, yet*). Sometimes a semicolon joins independent clauses in a compound sentence. Remember that an independent clause can stand alone as a sentence. In other words, it has a subject and a verb. When the clause does not have a subject and a verb, it is a dependent (or subordinate) clause; compound sentences contain no subordinate clauses.

Compound sentences are useful for combining related ideas. When two actions occur simultaneously or as a result of each other, a compound sentence is an efficient way of expressing the relationship between the actions. Two actions occur as a result of each other in the following sentence from *Let Me Hear You Whisper:*

"It is as though the DOLPHIN is trying to tell her something, and she can almost suspect this from the intensity of its stare."

The compound sentence captures the close relationship between the dolphin's stare and Helen's perceptions.

Student Activity 1. Find the compound sentence in the following passage and explain why it is compound. "She goes to her

DANIELLE. What?

HELEN. What do dolphins eat?

DANIELLE. Fish.

HELEN. What kind of fish?

DANIELLE. These. [*She opens a freezer chest packed with fish.*] Fly 'em up from Florida. [DANIELLE *is at* DOLPHIN*'s tank.*] Hiya, fella! How are ya? That reminds me. Gotta get some formaldehyde jars set up by Friday.

[*She exits with hamper.* HELEN *returns to the* DOLPHIN, *apprehensive about leaving the piece of ham at the bottom of the tank. She begins to reach her hand into the tank.*]

HELEN. You wouldn't bite Helen, would you? Helen's got to get that ham out of there. I wouldn't hurt you. You know that. Helen knows you talk. You do talk to Helen, don't you? Hear . . . hear me . . .

DOLPHIN. Hear . . .

HELEN. That's a good boy. That's a goodie goodie boy.

DOLPHIN. Hear me . . .

HELEN. Oh, what a pretty boy. Such a pretty boy.

[*At this point, the elevator doors zip open and* MISS MORAY *enters.*]

MISS MORAY. What are you doing, Helen?

[HELEN *looks ready to cry.*]

HELEN. I . . . uh . . .

MISS MORAY. Never mind. Go on with your work. [MISS MORAY *surveys everything, and then sits on a stool and calms herself. As* HELEN *scrubs:*] You know, Helen, you're such a sympathetic person. You have pets, I imagine? Cats? Lots of cats?

8 **HELEN.** They don't allow them in my building.

MISS MORAY. Then plants. I'm sure you have hundreds of lovely green things crawling up the windows?

HELEN. If there were green things crawling up my windows I'd move out.

MISS MORAY. No plants, either?

HELEN. Two gloxinias.[4]

MISS MORAY. Gloxinias! Oh, such trumpets! Such trumpets!

HELEN. They never bloom. My apartment's too cold.

MISS MORAY. Oh, that is a shame. [*Pause*] You live alone, don't you, Helen?

HELEN. [*Almost hurt*] Yes. I live alone.

MISS MORAY. But you have friends, of course. Other . . . custodial colleagues, perhaps . . . clubs, you belong to . . . social clubs . . . activities?

HELEN. [*Continuing to scrub*] I'm used to . . . being alone.

MISS MORAY. Nothing . . . ?

HELEN. I took a ceramic course . . . once.

MISS MORAY. Isn't that nice. A ceramic course . . . [*Pause*] Oh, Helen, you're such a nice person. So nice. [*Pause*] It does seem unjust that so much more than that is required. You must feel overwhelmed by this environment here . . . of oscilloscopes and sonar and salinity meters. To have so many personal delicacies and then be forced to behold the complexity of an electronic and chemical world must be devastating. Nevertheless, I can't— 19

[DANIELLE *rushes in with several large jars on a wheeled table.*]

---

4. gloxinias (gläk sin′ ē əz) *n.*: A tropical plant with colorful, trumpet-shaped flowers.

18 Discussion What type of life does Helen lead outside of work?

19 Discussion What is Miss Moray discovering about Helen?

locker, unwraps a sandwich she brought, and takes a slice of ham from it. She approaches the tank and offers the ham. The DOLPHIN moves and startles her, but the ham falls to the bottom of the tank."

Student Activity 2. Write a brief plot summary of the play. Use compound sentences in your summary.

DANIELLE. 'Scuse me, but I figure I'll get the formaldehyde set up tonight so I'll only have to worry about the dissection stuff tomorrow.

MISS MORAY. Very good, Danielle.

DANIELLE. I'm gonna need a twenty-liter one for the lungs and there ain't any on this floor.

HELEN. [*Noticing the* DOLPHIN *is stirring*] What's the formaldehyde for?

MISS MORAY. That's what I'm trying to tell you, Helen . . . to make it easier on you. The experiment series on . . . the dolphin will . . . terminate . . . on Friday. Dr. Crocus left the orders with us tonight. That's why it has concerned me that you've apparently grown . . . fond . . . of the mammal.

HELEN. They're gonna kill it?

DANIELLE. Gonna sharpen the hand saws now. Won't have any trouble getting through the skull on this one, no sir. Everything's gonna be perfect. [*She exits.*]

HELEN. What for? Because it didn't say anything? Is that what they're killing it for?

MISS MORAY. [*So sweetly*] Of course, you wanted to be kind. You didn't know what harm you might have caused . . . what delicate rhythm you may have disturbed in the experiment. Helen, no matter how lovely our intentions, no matter how lonely we are and how much we want people or animals . . . to like us . . . we have no right to endanger the genius about us. Now, we've spoken about this before. And this time, we're going to remember, aren't you? Get your paraphernalia ready. In a minute you're going upstairs to the main specimen room.

[HELEN *is dumbfounded as* MISS MORAY *exits in the direction* DANIELLE *went.* HELEN *gathers her equipment and looks at the* DOLPHIN, *which is staring desperately at her.*]

DOLPHIN. Help. Please help me.

[MISS MORAY *returns, pauses a moment and then takes the mop to relieve* HELEN*'s burden.*]

MISS MORAY. Come, Helen. Let me help you up to the main specimen room.

[*As they get into the elevator, the record plays again.*]

RECORD.

Let me call you sweetheart,
I'm in love with you.
Let me hear you whisper . . .

Scene 3

[*At rise,* MISS MORAY *is walking with* DR. CROCUS *and* MRS. FRIDGE *to the elevator. She is jotting items down on a clipboard.*]

MISS MORAY. You can be assured the Custodial Engineering Staff is anxious to contribute in every nontechnical way possible. Every nontechnical way. [*The elevator doors open and* HELEN *gets off.*] Just a moment, Helen. I'd like to talk with you. [*To the others as they get on*] If you think of anything else between now and morning please don't hesitate to call. Extra scalpels, dissection scissors, autoclaved glassware . . . pleasant dreams.

[*The doors close on* DR. CROCUS *and* MRS. FRIDGE, *and* MISS MORAY *turns to* HELEN.]

I hope you're well this evening.

HELEN. When they gonna kill it?

MISS MORAY. [*Going with her to her locker*] Don't say kill, Helen. You make it sound like murder. Besides, you won't have to go into the dolphin area at all this evening.

HELEN. When they gonna do it?

MISS MORAY. They'll be back, but don't worry. I've decided to let you go before they start so . . . you won't have to be in the building when . . .

HELEN. What do they do?

MISS MORAY. [*A hesitating laugh*] Why, what do you mean, what do they do?

HELEN. How do they kill it?

MISS MORAY. Nicotine mustard, Helen. Nicotine mustard. It's very humane. They inject it.

HELEN. Just 'cause it don't talk they've got to kill it?

MISS MORAY. There's that word again.

HELEN. Maybe he's a mute.

MISS MORAY. Do you have all your paraphernalia?

HELEN. Some human beings are mute, you know. Just because they can't talk we don't kill them.

MISS MORAY. It looks like you're ready to open a new box of steel wool.

HELEN. Maybe he can type with his nose. Did they try that?

MISS MORAY. Now, now, Helen . . .

HELEN. Miss Moray, I don't mind doing the dolphin area.

MISS MORAY. Absolutely not! I'm placing it off limits for your own good. You're too emotionally involved.

HELEN. I'm not emotionally involved.

MISS MORAY. Trust me, Helen. Trust me.

HELEN. Yes, Miss Moray.

[MISS MORAY *exits and* HELEN *makes a beeline for the Dolphin area which is closed off by portable walls. She opens the area enough to slide in. The lights are out and moonlight from the window casts many shadows.*]

DOLPHIN. Help. [HELEN *moves slowly toward the tank.*] Help me. [HELEN *opens the curtain. The* DOLPHIN *and she look at each other.*] Help me.

HELEN. You don't need me. Just say something to them. Whatever you want. Say "help." Anything. They just need to hear you say something . . . [*She waits for a response, which doesn't come.*] You want me to tell 'em? I'll tell them. I'll just say I heard you say "help." O.K.? I'll go tell them. [*She starts to leave the area, turning back to give opportunity for a response.*]

DOLPHIN. Nooooooooooooo. [HELEN *stops. Moves back toward tank*] Nooooooooooooo. 20

HELEN. They're gonna kill you! [*Puzzled,* HELEN *moves a bit closer to the tank. Pause*]

DOLPHIN. Boooooooooooook.

HELEN. What? [*There is a long pause. No response. She moves closer.*]

DOLPHIN. Boooooooooooook.

HELEN. Book?

DOLPHIN. Boooooooooooook.

HELEN. Boooooooooooook? What book?

[DANIELLE *charges through a door and snaps on the light.*]

DANIELLE. Uh oh. Miss Moray said she don't want you in here. Said you have to not be in the lab and I'm not to talk to you about what they're gonna do because I make you nauseous.

[HELEN *goes to* DR. CROCUS*'s desk in the lab and begins to look at various books on it.*]

20 **Discussion** Why do you think the dolphin refuses to talk to the scientists, even to save his life?

21 **Discussion** Discuss how these stage directions create humor.

HELEN. Do you know anything about a book, Danielle?

DANIELLE. She's gonna be mad. What book?

HELEN. Something to do with . . . [*She indicates the* DOLPHIN.]

DANIELLE. Hiya, fella! [*To* HELEN] Do I really make you nauseous?

HELEN. About the dolphin . . .

DANIELLE. You talking about the experiment folder? They got an experiment folder they write in.

HELEN. Where?

DANIELLE. I don't know.

HELEN. Find it, please.

DANIELLE. I don't know where she keeps that stuff. Sometimes she puts it in the top and other times she puts it in the bottom.

HELEN. Please find it. Please. [*She steps outside the area.*]

DANIELLE. I'll try. I'll try, but I got other things to do, you know. Can't spend time looking for what ain't any of my business anyway. I never knew I made anybody nauseous.

[DANIELLE *rummages through the desk mumbling to herself and finally finds the folder. She hands the folder out to* HELEN *as the elevator doors spring open and* MISS MORAY *enters.* DANIELLE *exits quickly through a door in the Dolphin area as* HELEN *conceals the folder.*]

MISS MORAY. Helen?

HELEN. Yes, Miss Moray?

MISS MORAY. Would you feel better if we talked about it?

HELEN. About what?

MISS MORAY. Helen, you're such a nice person. I understand just what you're going through. Really, I do. And . . . well, I'm going to tell you something I've never told anyone else . . . my first week at ABADABA, I fell in love with an animal myself. An alley cat. Pussy Cat. That's what I called it—Pussy Cat.

HELEN. Did they cut the head off it?

[MISS MORAY *removes a plastic covering from an object on a shelf to reveal an articulated*[5] *cat skeleton. As she talks she sets it in view and gently dusts it with the feather duster.*] 2

MISS MORAY. I sense a touch of bitterness in your voice, Helen, and don't think I wasn't bitter when I saw what had happened to Pussy Cat.

HELEN. I'll bet it didn't sit well with Pussy Cat either.

MISS MORAY. But when I thought about it for awhile, I had to realize that I was just being selfish. Before . . . what happened to Pussy Cat happened I was the only one benefiting from her—whereas now she's borrowed at least once a month. Last week she went to an anatomy seminar at St. Vincent's Medical School.

HELEN. It's nice you let her out once in a while.

MISS MORAY. In life, she was unnoticed and worthless except to me. Now she belongs to the ages. [*Then solemnly*] I hope that's some comfort to you.

HELEN. Oh, it's very comforting.

MISS MORAY. Well, Perk-You-Up time will be here soon.

5. **articulated** (är tik′ yə lāt′ əd) *adj.*: Connected by joints.

Grammar in Action

Sentence fragments are incomplete sentences, or parts of sentences that are punctuated as if they were whole sentences. Sentence fragments do not usually express a complete thought—they do not have both subjects and verbs. Although you should avoid using fragments in your writing, fragments are acceptable in some cases. Fragments are especially frequent in dialogue and drama, where the writer wants to capture the way people normally speak.

Sentence fragments work well in dialogue because they quicken the pace of conversation by eliminating words or phrases that are implied by the speaker and understood by the listener. Whereas in formal compositions fragments might confuse the reader, in dialogue, fragments give the reader a sense of people actually speaking to each other. Read the following exchange between Helen and Miss Moray:

MISS MORAY. Would you feel better if we talked about it?
HELEN. About what?

"About what" is a fragment because it does not contain a subject and a verb, yet both Miss Moray and the reader understand what Helen means.

HELEN. Yes, Miss Moray.

MISS MORAY. We have lady fingers.

HELEN. Oh, good.

2 **MISS MORAY.** Such a strange thing to call a confectionary, isn't it? It's almost macabre.

HELEN. Miss Moray . . .

MISS MORAY. Yes, Helen?

HELEN. I was wondering . . .

MISS MORAY. Yes?

HELEN. I was wondering why they wanna talk with . . .

MISS MORAY. Now now now! I was the same way about Pussy Cat. Right up to the final moment I kept asking "What good is vivisection?"[6] "What good is vivisection?"

HELEN. What good is vivisection?

MISS MORAY. A *lot* of good, believe me.

HELEN. Like what?

MISS MORAY. Well, like fishing, Helen. If we could communicate with dolphins, they might be willing to herd fish for us. The fishing industry would be revolutionized. Millions of fish being rounded into nets by our little mammal friends.

HELEN. Is that all?

MISS MORAY. All? Heavens, no. They'd be a blessing to the human race. A blessing.

HELEN. What kind?

MISS MORAY. Oh. Why, oceanography. They would be worshipped in oceanography. Checking the Gulf Stream . . . taking water temperatures, depths, salinity readings. To say nothing of the contributions they could make in marine biology, navigation. Linguistics! Oh, Helen, it gives me the chills.

HELEN. It'd be good if they talked?

MISS MORAY. God's own blessing. God's own blessing.

[MISS MORAY *exits and* HELEN *returns to scrubbing for a moment. When she feels safe she sets the folder in front of her and begins reading. Commence fantasy techniques to establish the ensuing events are going on in* HELEN*'s mind concerning the benevolent utilization of dolphins. Relate to what* MISS MORAY *had told her about uses. Sound: Sonar beeping underwater. It has the urgency of a beating heart. Sweet strains of* Let Me Call You Sweetheart *in. Projection: Underwater shot, dolphins and other fish gliding by. All voices echo. Doors open and* MISS MORAY, DR. CROCUS *and* MRS. FRIDGE *appear phantasmagorically.*][7] 23

And if we could make friends with them, talk to them, they might be willing to herd all those fish for us . . .

DR. CROCUS. [*Lovingly*] All right, little mammal friends—today we want swordfish. Fat meaty ones suitable for controlled portion sizing. Go and get 'em! [*Projection of dolphins swimming, a school of large fish panicking in the water*]

MRS. FRIDGE. My dear dolphin friends. My dear, dear dolphin friends. We're most curious about seismographic readings at the bottom of the Mariana Trench. But do be careful. We're unsure of the weather above that area.

[*Projection of dolphins racing, deep underwater shots, sounding bell noises*]

MISS MORAY. [*Sweetly*] Our linguistics lesson today will consider the most beautiful word

---

6. vivisection (viv′ ə sek′ shən) *n.*: Surgical operations performed on living animals to study the structure and function of living organs.

7. phantasmagorically (fan taz′ mə gôr′ ik lē) *adv.*: In a rapidly changing way, as in a dream.

22 **Literary Focus** Discuss the irony of Miss Moray saying that it's macabre to call a confectionary "lady fingers."

23 **Discussion** In the scene that follows, discuss the fantasy of the use of dolphins to help people. Bring out how each person speaks of things that are completely out of character.

Student Activity 1. Find three more examples of sentence fragments from the play. Rewrite them in complete sentences, and then explain why the fragments you rewrote work better as fragments rather than complete sentences.

Student Activity 2. Think about how often you answer questions in fragments rather than complete sentences. Watch a couple minutes of television or listen to a conversation between or among people. Note each time you hear a sentence fragment.

in the English language: Love. Love is a strong, complex emotion or feeling causing one to appreciate and promote the welfare of another. Do you have a word like it in dolphinese? A word similar to love?
[*The fantasy disappears, leaving* MISS MORAY *and* HELEN *in the reality of the play.*]
It has a nice sheen.

HELEN. What?

MISS MORAY. It has a nice sheen. The floor. Up here where it's dried.

HELEN. Thank you. Miss Moray . . . ?

MISS MORAY. Yes, dear?

HELEN. You sure it would be good for us if . . . dolphins talked?

MISS MORAY. Helen, are you still thinking about that! Perhaps you'd better leave now. It's almost time.

HELEN. No! I'm almost finished.

[DANIELLE *opens the Dolphin area and yells over* HELEN*'s head to* MISS MORAY.]

DANIELLE. I got everything except the head vise.

MISS MORAY. I beg your pardon?

DANIELLE. The vise for the head. I can't find it. They can't saw through the skull bone without the head vise.

MISS MORAY. Did you look on five? They had it there for . . . what they did to the St. Bernard . . . they had.

[*The record plays again and the others try to talk over it.*]

RECORD.

Let me call you sweetheart,
I'm in love with you.
Let me hear you whisper,
That you love me, too.

DANIELLE. Can't hear you.

MISS MORAY. The St. Bernard. They used it for the St. Bernard.

DANIELLE. On five?

MISS MORAY. That's what I said.

DANIELLE. I looked on five. I didn't see any head vise.

MISS MORAY. You come with me. It must have been staring you in the face. Just staring you right in the face.

[DANIELLE *tiptoes over the wet portion of the floor and she and* MISS MORAY *get on the elevator.*]

We'll be right back, Helen.

[*The doors close and* HELEN *hurries into the Dolphin area. She stops just within the door and it is obvious that she is angry. There is a pause as she looks at the silhouette of the tank behind the closed curtain. Then:*]

DOLPHIN. Boooooooooooook.

[HELEN *charges to the curtain, pulls it open and prepares to reprimand the* DOLPHIN.]

HELEN. I looked at your book. I looked at your book all right!

DOLPHIN. Boooooooooooook.

HELEN. And you want to know what I think? I don't think much of you, that's what I think.

DOLPHIN. Boooooooooooook.

HELEN. Oh, shut up. Book book book book book. I'm not interested. You eat yourself silly—but to get a little fish for hungry humans is just too much for you. Well, I'm going to tell 'em you can talk.

[DOLPHIN *moves in the tank, lets out a few warning bubbles.*]

You don't like that, eh? Well, I don't like lazy selfish people, mammals or animals.

[*She starts away from the tank half intending to go and half watching for a reaction. The* DOLPHIN *looks increasingly desperate and begins to make loud blatt and beep sounds. He struggles a bit in the tank, starting to splash water.*]

Oh, you'd do anything to avoid a little work, wouldn't you?

[*In its most violent gyrations to date, the* DOLPHIN *blasts at her.*]

DOLPHIN. Boooooooooooook!

HELEN. Cut it out, you're getting water all over the floor.

DOLPHIN. Boooooooooooook!

[HELEN *is a little scared and stops moving toward the door. As she stops, the* DOLPHIN *calms down. She waits a moment and then moves closer to the tank again. They experience a sustained visual exchange.* HELEN'*s anger and fear subside into frustration. When it appears the* DOLPHIN *is going to say nothing else,* HELEN *starts to leave the room. She turns around and looks back at the* DOLPHIN. *Then she looks at the folder on the desk. She is going to leave again when she decides to go to the folder once more. She picks it up, opens it, closes it, and sets it down again.*]

HELEN. I guess you don't like us. [*Pause*] I guess you don't like us enough to . . . die rather than help us . . .

DOLPHIN. Hate.

24 **HELEN.** [*Picking up the folder and skimming reflexively*] Yes.

DOLPHIN. Hate.

HELEN. I guess you do hate us . . . [HELEN *stops. She returns to the folder. Reading*] Military implications . . . plants mines in enemy waters . . . useful as antipersonnel self-directing weapons . . . war . . . deliver atomic warheads . . . war . . . nuclear torpedoes . . . attach bombs to submarines or surface vessels . . . terrorize enemy waters, beaches . . . war . . . war . . . war . . .

[HELEN'*s voice becomes echoed in the middle of the last speech, theatrical effects creep-* 25
ing in to establish fantasy sequence like the first, except now the characters enter and appear sinister. Their requests are all war oriented.]

MISS MORAY. [*Demanding*] And if we could talk to them, we'd get them to herd fish all right. One way or another they'd do exactly as they were told!

[Let Me Call You Sweetheart *plays in background in a discordant version with projection of dolphins swimming.*]

DR. CROCUS. All right, you dolphins. Today we want you to herd fish. Herd all the fish you can away from the enemy's waters. Remove their food supply. Detonate underwater poison bombs and foul the enemy coastline. Make the water unfit for life of any kind.

[*A map is imposed over projection of dolphins.*]

MRS. FRIDGE. Enemy fleets are located here and here and here. You'll have twenty-seven hours to attach the nuclear warheads before automatic detonation. Our objective: total annihilation.

[*Projection of dolphins racing off, deep underwater shots, frogman examining ship's hulls, planting mines.*]

MISS MORAY. [*Fanatically*] Our linguistics lesson today will consider the most basic word in the English language: HATE. Hate is a

24 Discussion Why does Helen think the dolphin won't speak?

25 Discussion Contrast this fantasy scene with the previous one. Discuss with students uses for dolphins. Could they be used for war?

26 **Humanities Note** Can dolphins speak? Can they imitate human sounds? Can they communicate with people? Ask students for information they have gained about dolphins' intelligence and communication skills from visits to aquariums like Sea World, reading, and TV programs like the *Flipper* series, filmed in the Florida Keys in the 1960's and often rerun.

strong emotion which means abhorrence, anger, animosity, detestation, hostility, malevolence, malice, malignity, odium, rancor, revenge, repugnance, and dislike. Do you have a word like it in dolphinese? If you don't, we'll teach you every nuance of ours. Every nuance of the word *hate.*

[*The fantasy sequence evaporates leaving* HELEN *alone on stage with the* DOLPHIN. *She sadly closes the folder and moves slowly to the tank a bit ashamed about the way she had reprimanded the* DOLPHIN. *They look sadly at each other. She reaches out her hand and just pets his head gently.*]

HELEN. They're already thinking about ways to use you for . . . war . . . is that why you can't talk to them? What did you talk to me for? You won't talk to them but you . . . you talk to me because . . . you want something . . . there's something . . . I can do? Something you want me to do?

DOLPHIN. Hamm . . .

HELEN. What?

DOLPHIN. Hamm . . .

HELEN. Ham? I thought you ate fish.

26 **DOLPHIN.** [*Moving with annoyance*] Ham . . . purrrrr.

HELEN. Ham . . . purrrrr? I don't know what you're talking about?

DOLPHIN. [*Even more annoyed*] Ham . . . purrrrr.

HELEN. Ham . . . purrrr. What's a purrrrr?

[HELEN *is most upset and recalls that* MISS MORAY *is due back. Confused and scared she returns to scrubbing the floor just as the doors of the elevator open revealing* MISS MORAY, DANIELLE *and* MRS. FRIDGE. DANIELLE *pushes a dissection table loaded with shiny instruments toward the lab.*]

MISS MORAY. Clean the vise up, Danielle. Immediately.

DANIELLE. I didn't leave the blood on it.

MISS MORAY. I'm not accusing you. I just said whoever was the porter the night they did you know what to the St. Bernard was . . . [*To* MRS. FRIDGE] it's the first dirty vise since I've led the Custodial Engineering Department! Is the good doctor in yet?

MRS. FRIDGE. She's getting the nicotine mustard on eighteen. I'll have to see if she needs assistance.

MISS MORAY. I'll come with you. Oh, Helen. You can go now. It's time. [*She smiles and the elevator doors close on* MRS. FRIDGE *and* MISS MORAY.]

DANIELLE. [*Pushing the dissection table into the Dolphin area*] I never left a dirty head vise. She's trying to say I left it like that. I know what she's getting at.

HELEN. Did you ever hear of Ham . . . purrrrr?

DANIELLE. Wait'll I get my hands on Kazinski. Kazinski does the fifth floor and he should be cleaning this, not me. It's all caked up.

HELEN. Would you listen a minute? Ham . . . purrrrr. Do you know what a ham . . . purrrrr is?

DANIELLE. The only hamper I ever heard of is out in the hall.

[HELEN *looks toward an exit indicated by* DANIELLE.]

Five scalpels, large clamps . . . small clamps . . . bone saws . . . scissors . . . dissection needles, two dozen . . . Kazinski left the high-altitude chamber dirty once and I got blamed for that, too. And that had mucus all over it. [DANIELLE *exits.*]

HELEN. [*Rushing to the* DOLPHIN] You want me to do something with the hamper. What? To get it? To put—You want me to put you in it? . . . But what'll I do with you? Where can I take you?

DOLPHIN. Sea . . .

HELEN. See? See what?

DOLPHIN. Sea . . . ham . . . purrrrr . . .

HELEN. See ham—I *saw* the hamper.

DOLPHIN. Sea . . .

HELEN. See what? What do you want me to see? [*She walks about the room, mumbling, looking for what the* DOLPHIN *could want her to see. Finally, she looks out the window.*]

DOLPHIN. Sea . . . sea . . .

HELEN. See? . . . The sea! That's what you're talking about! [*There is almost an atmosphere of celebration.*] The river . . . to the sea!

[*She darts into the hall and returns with hamper, pushes it next to the* DOLPHIN. *She pulls closed the curtain as . . .* MISS MORAY *gets off the elevator.* MISS MORAY *looks very calm. Everything is under control and on schedule from her point of view. She then notices that* HELEN *is not there, though her mop and pail are. She wonders if* HELEN *has gone and just carelessly left the items out.*]

MISS MORAY. [*Sweetly*] Helen? [*When there is no response she starts into the Dolphin area.*] Helen? [HELEN *is not there, though her coat is still hanging in her locker. She is a little concerned at this point. For a second she assumes it is unlikely* HELEN *would be in there, since it was strictly placed off limits, but then she decides to investigate. She notices the closed curtain in front of the tank.*] Helen? Are you there? [*Pause*] Helen? Helen? [MISS MORAY *moves to the curtain and pulls it open. There is Helen with her arms around the front part of the* DOLPHIN, *lifting it a good part of the way out of the water.*]

Helen, what do you think you're hugging?

[HELEN *gets so scared she drops the* DOLPHIN *back into the tank, splattering* MISS MORAY *with water.* MISS MORAY *lets out a scream just as* DR. CROCUS *and* MRS. FRIDGE *enter.*]

MRS. FRIDGE. Is anything wrong, Miss Moray?

[MISS MORAY *is unable to answer at first.*]

Is anything wrong?

MISS MORAY. [*Not wishing to admit an irregularity.*] No . . . nothing wrong. Nothing at all.

[*She hurriedly composes herself, not wanting to hang any dirty wash of the Custodial Engineering Department.*]

Just a little spilled water. Right, Helen? Just a little spilled water. Get those sponges, Helen. Immediately!

[HELEN *and* MISS MORAY *grab sponges from the lab sink and begin to get up some of the water around the tank.* DR. CROCUS *begins to occupy herself with filling a hypodermic syringe while* MRS. FRIDGE *expertly gets all equipment into place.* DANIELLE *enters.*]

MRS. FRIDGE. Danielle, get the formaldehyde jars into position, please.

DANIELLE. I didn't spill anything. Don't try to blame *that* on me.

MISS MORAY. I didn't say you did.

DANIELLE. You spilled something?

MISS MORAY. Just do as Mrs. Fridge tells you. Hurry, Danielle, you're so slow.

DANIELLE. I'm tired of getting blamed for Kazinski.

27 Discussion What mood do these stage directions create?

28 Humanities Note Ask students to characterize Miss Moray, who openly ridicules Helen to her face. Why is she so insensitive to others? Elicit from students other characters in films, plays, or TV programs who have no regard for the feelings of others. Present Archie Bunker in *All in the Family*, who tells his wife to "stifle" herself.

29 Reading Strategy Have students summarize the play up to this point and predict what Helen plans to do.

30 Discussion Discuss Helen's passionate outburst with the students. Is being nice being a coward?

MRS. FRIDGE. Would you like to get an encephalogram during the death process, Dr. Crocus?

DR. CROCUS. Why not?

[MRS. FRIDGE *begins to implant electrodes into the* DOLPHIN*'s head. The* DOLPHIN *commences making high pitched distress signals which send shivers up and down* HELEN*'s back.*]

MISS MORAY. That'll do it. No harm done. Step outside, Helen. [*To the* DOCTOR] I do hope everything is satisfactory, doctor. [DR. CROCUS *looks at her, gives no reaction.*] The Custodial Engineering Staff has done everything in its power . . . [*She is still ignored.*] Come, Helen. I'll see you to the elevator.

27 [HELEN *looks at the* DOLPHIN *as* MRS. FRIDGE *is sticking the electrodes into its head. Its distress signals are pathetic, and* HELEN *is terrified.*]

Let's go now.

[MISS MORAY *leads her out to the hall.* MISS MORAY *is trying to get control of herself, to resist yelling at* HELEN, *as she gets on her coat and kerchief.*]

You can leave that.

HELEN. I never left a dirty mop. Never. [HELEN *gives the mop a quick rinse and puts the things in their place. Cuts to the lab door and the sounds coming out of it show where her attention is.*]

28 **MISS MORAY.** Well, I hardly know what to say. Frankly, Helen, I'm deeply disappointed. I'd hoped that by being lenient with you—and heaven knows I have been—that you'd develop a heightened loyalty to our team. I mean, do you think for one minute that putting vinegar in rinse water really is more effective? If you ask me, it streaks. Streaks.

HELEN. [*Bursting into tears and going to the elevator*] Leave me alone.

MISS MORAY. [*Softening as she catches up to her*] You really are a nice person, Helen. A very nice person. But to be simple and nice in a world where great minds are giant-stepping the micro- and macrocosms, well—one would expect you'd have the humility to yield in unquestioning awe. I truly am very fond of you, Helen, but you're fired. Call Personnel after 9. And I was going to bring you in hangers. I want you to know that. [*As* MISS MORAY *heads back toward the Dolphin area, the record starts to play.*]

RECORD.

Let me call you sweetheart,
I'm in love with you.
Let me hear you whisper . . .

[*The record is roughly interrupted. What* HELEN *is contemplating at that moment causes the expression on her face to turn from sadness to thought to strength to anger—and as the elevator doors open—to fury. Instead of getting on the elevator, she whirls around and marches back to the Dolphin area.* MISS MORAY, MRS. FRIDGE, DANIELLE, *and* DR. CROCUS *(with hypodermic needle poised to stick the* DOLPHIN) *turn and look at her with surprise.*]

HELEN. Who do you think you are? Who do you think you *are?* I think you're murderers, that's what I think.

MISS MORAY. Doctor, I assure you this is the first psychotic outburst the Custodial Engineering Department has ever had.

HELEN. I'm very tired of being a nice person, Miss Moray. You kept telling me how nice I was and now I know what you meant. [*Pause*] I'm going to report the bunch of you to the ASPCA—or somebody. Because . . . I've decided I don't like you cutting the heads off mice and sawing through skulls of St. Bernards . . . and if being a nice person is just not saying anything and letting you pack of butchers run around doing whatever you want, then I don't want to be nice any more. You gotta be very stupid people to need an animal to talk before you know just from looking at it that it's saying something . . . that it knows what pain feels like. I'd like to see you all with a few electrodes stuck in your heads. I really would. [HELEN *starts crying, though her features won't give way to weakness.*] Being nice isn't any good. [*Looking at* DOLPHIN] They just kill you off if you do that. And that's being a coward. You gotta talk back against what's wrong or you can't ever stop it. At least you've gotta try. [*She bursts into tears.*]

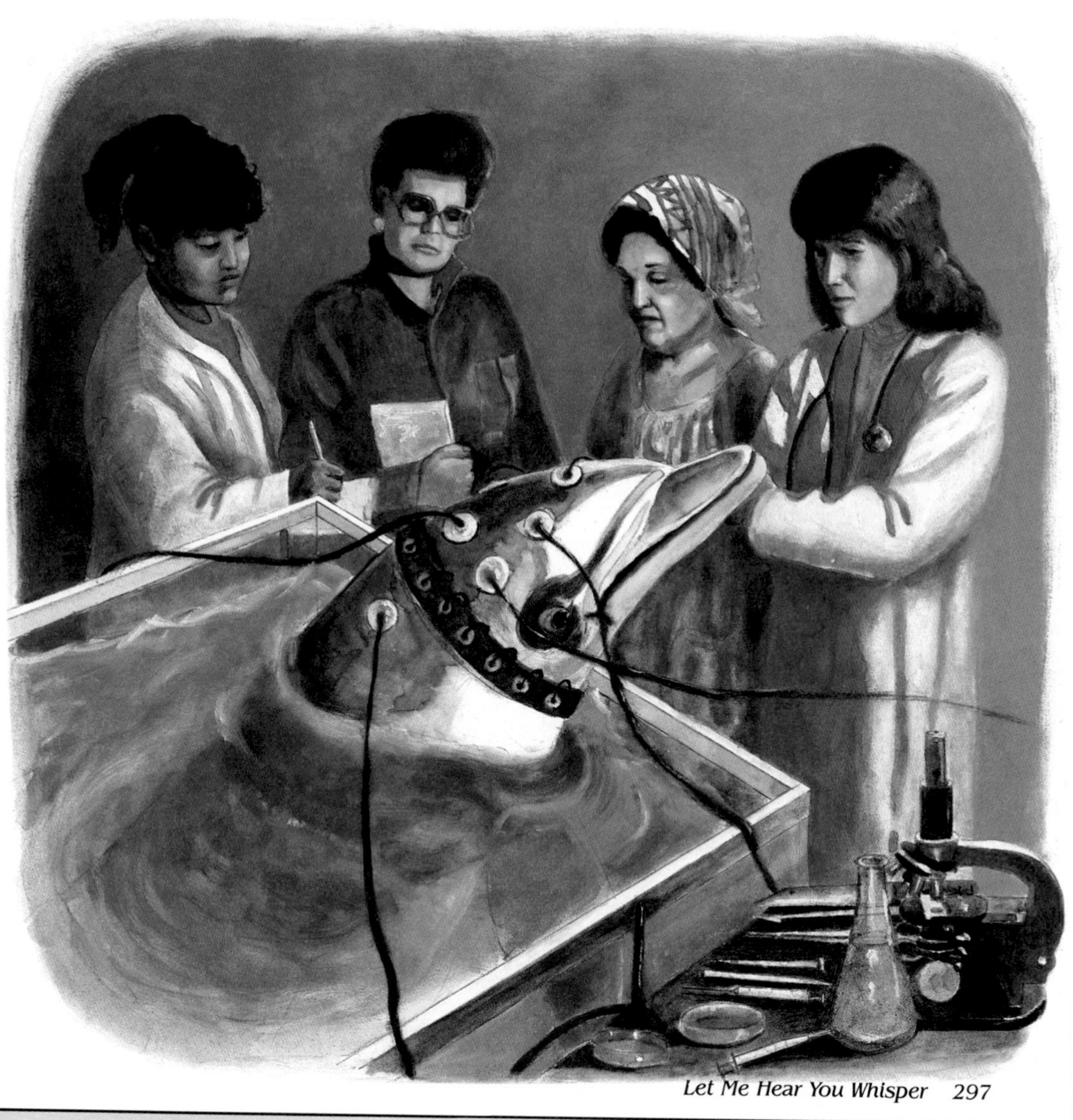

31 Critical Thinking and Reading Ask students why the dolphin, which can speak, refuses to do so. Is it believable that (1) the dolphin knows of the scientists warlike purposes for the use of its intelligence? (2) the dolphin is willing to sacrifice itself rather than to be used as an instrument of destruction?

32 Discussion Note the sarcasm in the last line. How has Helen changed through this episode?

33 Discussion Ask students if the play ends satisfyingly. Will the dolphin be saved? Are the scientists moved by its message of love or excited by its ability to speak? Is Helen right to leave? Should the play end here or proceed in another fashion?

Teaching to Ability Levels Have your **more advanced** students read excerpts from Thoreau's essay on "Civil Disobedience." You might read these excerpts aloud to your **less advanced** students. Tell of Thoreau's challenge of the government's use of tax monies, his willingness to be imprisoned for his principles, and his brief imprisonment.

Ask students how people can stand up for their rights and fight powerful groups. Emphasize the importance of being willing to pay the consequences of a morally correct position.

Enrichment You might wish to assign research reports on experiments that are currently being done with dolphins. Students could write to marine biology labs or aquariums, such as Sea World in San Diego, California.

Reader's Response What is your position on using animals for scientific research? Explain.

MISS MORAY. Nothing like this has ever happened with a member of the Custodial Engineering . . . Helen, dear . . .

HELEN. Get your hands off me. [*Yelling at the* DOLPHIN] You're a coward, that's what you
31 are. [*She turns and starts to leave. A sound comes from the* DOLPHIN*'s tank.*]

DOLPHIN. [*Whispering*] Looooooooooooveeeeeee. [*Everyone turns to stare at the* DOLPHIN, *and freezes for a second.*] Love.

DR. CROCUS. Get the recorder going. [*The laboratory becomes a bustle of activity concerning the utterance of the* DOLPHIN. *Plans for dissection are obviously canceled and* HELEN *has a visual exchange with the* DOLPHIN. *Then she continues toward the elevator.*]

DOLPHIN. Love . . .

DR. CROCUS. Is the tape going?

MRS. FRIDGE. Yes, Doctor.

MISS MORAY. I'm enormously embarrassed about the incident, Doctor. Naturally, I've taken steps to see this won't . . .

MRS. FRIDGE. He's opening the blowhole sphincter.

DOLPHIN. Love . . .

DR. CROCUS. That scrub woman's got something to do with this. Get her back in here.

MISS MORAY. She won't be any more trouble. I fired her.

DOLPHIN. Love . . .

DR. CROCUS. Just get her. [*To* MRS. FRIDGE.] You're sure the machine's recording?

MISS MORAY. Doctor, I'm afraid you don't understand. That woman was hugging the mammal . . .

DR. CROCUS. Try to get another word out of it.

MISS MORAY. The water on the floor was her fault. [*The record starts.*]

DR. CROCUS. Try the fear button.

MISS MORAY. She could have damaged the rib cage if I hadn't stopped her.

DR. CROCUS. One more word . . . try anger.

MISS MORAY. The last thing in the world I want is for our problems in Custodial Engineering to . . .

DR. CROCUS. [*Furious*] Will you shut up and get her back here?

[MISS MORAY *appears stunned momentarily.*]

MISS MORAY. Immediately, Doctor. [*She hurries to* HELEN *waiting for the elevator.*] Helen? Oh, Helen? [*She goes to* HELEN, *who refuses to pay any attention to her.*] Don't you want to hear what the dolphin has to say? He's so cute! Dr. Crocus thinks that his talking might have something to do with you. Wouldn't that be exciting? [*Pause*] Please, Helen. The doctor . . .

HELEN. Don't talk to me, do you mind?

MISS MORAY. It was only in the heat of argument that I distorted the ineffectiveness of the vinegar and . . . of course, you won't be discharged. All right? Please, Helen, you'll embarrass me . . .

[*The elevator doors open and* HELEN *gets on to face* MISS MORAY. *She looks at her a moment and then lifts her hand to press the button for the ground floor.*]

Don't you dare . . . Helen, the team needs you, don't you see? Everyone says the corridors have never looked so good. Ever. Helen, please. What will I do if you leave?

HELEN. Why don't you put in a rug? 32

[*She presses the button. The elevator doors close.*]

Closure and Extension

ANSWERS TO THINKING ABOUT THE SELECTION

Recalling

1. According to Miss Moray, the purpose is to communicate with dolphins to teach them to herd fish for humans and to perform underwater experiments.
2. The dolphin begins speaking to her when they are alone together.
3. He wants her to remove him from his tank, put him in a hamper, and release him in the sea.
4. Helen is caught by Miss Moray and fired. The dolphin, out of desperation, begins speaking to the scientists.
5. Dr. Crocus realizes that Helen is responsible for getting the dolphin to speak.

Interpreting

6. Both Helen and Miss Moray are conscientious workers and have a soft spot in their hearts for animals. Miss Moray, however, long ago learned to hide her feelings and convince herself that experiments on animals, however cruel, promote human progress. Helen, on the other hand, allows her sensitivity to show and refuses to yield her compassion. Students should also note Miss Moray's ag-

THINKING ABOUT THE SELECTION

Recalling

1. According to Miss Moray, what is the purpose of the experiment on the dolphin?
2. How does Helen learn the dolphin can talk?
3. In what way does the dolphin want Helen to help him?
4. What are the results of Helen's trying to rescue the dolphin?
5. For what reason does the doctor want Helen to come back at the end of the play?

Interpreting

6. Compare and contrast Helen and Miss Moray.
7. Miss Moray uses many euphemisms, words that hide the true meaning of things. For example, she calls the cleanup crew the "custodial engineering team." Find three other euphemisms. What euphemism disguises the true nature of the experiment?
8. The researchers use a love song to teach the dolphin to talk. What contrast is shown by having the researchers use a love song?
9. Why does the dolphin talk to Helen instead of the researchers? What does this suggest about the theme of this play?
10. Explain the title of the play.

Applying

11. Imagine you are Helen. What would you have done in her place? Explain your answer.

ANALYZING LITERATURE

Understanding Conflict in Drama

In a play, the characters *act out* the **conflict,** or struggle between opposing sides or forces. A character must rely on actions, facial expressions, and dialogue to express conflict, especially internal conflict.

In *Let Me Hear You Whisper,* there is both external and internal conflict. You learn about Helen's conflict through her dialogue, actions, and facial expressions.

1. What conflict does Helen have with the scientific laboratory?
2. What evidence in the play helps you recognize this conflict?
3. What is Helen's conflict with the dolphin?
4. What helps you recognize this conflict?
5. How are Helen's conflicts resolved?

CRITICAL THINKING AND READING

Understanding Controversy

Controversy occurs when two sides hold opposing views. *Let Me Hear You Whisper* presents the controversial issue of using animals for scientific experimentation. One side of this controversy believes such experimentation yields beneficial results for human beings. The other side believes such experimentation is cruel to animals and violates animals' rights. Take a side on this issue and discuss it with your classmates.

UNDERSTANDING LANGUAGE

Appreciating Specialized Vocabulary

Professional people often use words that seem difficult to people outside the profession. In *Let Me Hear You Whisper,* for example, all of the technical terms would be understood by workers in a scientific laboratory. Use a dictionary to find the meaning of the following technical terms.

1. salinity
2. autoclave
3. seismograph
4. electroencephalogram

THINKING AND WRITING

Writing a Response to Critical Comment

Paul Zindel has said, "In each of my plays, there is an attempt to find some grain of truth, something to hang onto." Brainstorm about what "grain of truth" you found in *Let Me Hear You Whisper.* Then use these ideas to write a letter to Paul Zindei, explaining what "grain of truth" you found in the play. Revise your letter for clarity and proofread it.

(Answers begin on p. 298.)

gressive tenacity in contrast to Helen's timidity preceding the play's climax.

7. Miss Moray's other euphemisms include "our little family" for ABADABA's staff, "experimenting" for vivisection, "subjective intercourse" for conversation, "worked on" and "using" for decapitated, and "terminate" for kill or die. Perhaps her most chilling euphemism for the experiment is "progress."
8. The emotions expressed in the song are in stark contrast to the insensitivity of the researchers toward the dolphin's suffering.
9. The dolphin refuses to talk to the researchers because he realizes they are insensitive and cruel and that their aim in communicating with dolphins is to exploit them for warfare. In Helen, the dolphin sees a sympathetic, compassionate soul who may be able to help him escape. The dolphin's actions suggest that the play's theme involves speaking out against evil.
10. The title expresses the researcher's desire to hear the dolphin speak. It also expresses the dolphin's desire to hear that he will be treated with love as an equal to human beings.

Applying

11. Answers will differ. They might agree with Zindel's theme as stated by Helen: "You gotta talk back against what's wrong or you can't ever stop it." Such talking back may take the form of political activism, letters to the editor, or protest marches.

ANSWERS TO ANALYZING LITERATURE

1. Helen opposes their cruel experiments and their goal of exploiting dolphins for use in war.
2. Helen's many exchanges with Miss Moray reveal the conflict.
3. Helen struggles with the dolphin to convince him to save himself by speaking to the researchers.
4. Helen's exchanges with the dolphin reveal the conflict.
5. Helen resolves to speak out publicly against the laboratory, thus resolving her internal conflict. Her external conflict with the laboratory, however, remains unresolved. Helen's conflict with the dolphin is resolved when he says "love" to Dr. Crocus.

ANSWERS TO UNDERSTANDING LANGUAGE

1. saltiness
2. a container for sterilizing instruments by superheated steam under pressure
3. an instrument that records the intensity and duration of earthquakes
4. a tracing of the changes in the electrical impulses of the brain

Challenge What other fields use specialized vocabularies? What are some words from another specialized vocabulary?

THINKING AND WRITING

Publishing Student Writing Make a bulletin board display of the letters to Paul Zindel.

Writing Across the Curriculum Using ideas from class discussions and from research in the library, have students write an essay in which they either support or argue against the use of animals in scientific experiments. You might wish to inform the science department of this writing assignment.

Enrichment The story of Anne Frank is compelling and has great appeal to students. For further reading, you might recommend these and other works by or about Anne Frank: *Anne Frank: The Diary of a Young Girl. Anne Frank's Tales from the Secret Annex* (Washington Square Press, 1983), *Anne Frank Remembered* by Miep Gies (Simon and Schuster, 1987). Miep Gies is the woman who helped hide the Frank family.

Master Teacher Note For background information about life and events during World War II, you might have students conduct interviews with people who live during the period. Veterans of the war could offer first-hand experiences. Others, who were not in the armed forces, might provide insight into how civilians aided the war effort.

ANNE FRANK: THE STORY BEHIND THE PLAY

The Diary of Anne Frank, the play by Frances Goodrich and Albert Hackett, is based on a real diary written by a young girl during World War II. Anne Frank was born in Frankfurt, Germany, on June 12, 1929, before World War II began. She had a normal, happy childhood until Adolf Hitler and his political party, the Nazis, gained control of the government of Germany in 1933.

Persecution of the Jews

The Nazis persecuted their political opponents and other groups. One group they particularly singled out was the Jews. Adolf Hitler blamed the Jews for the problems of the world. He had the Nazis round up German Jews and send them to prison camps, called concentration camps. Many Jews escaped from Germany to other countries to avoid this persecution. Even more, though, stayed behind.

Anne Frank's family was Jewish. They left their home in Germany in 1933 and moved to the Netherlands. In Amsterdam Mr. Frank reestablished his business, and Mrs. Frank set up their new household. Anne and her older sister, Margot, attended school and made new friends. Anne was known as a lively chatterbox who seemed to be a normal but not a particularly gifted child. World War II, however, affected the lives of millions of people on both sides of the fighting, and Anne Frank was no exception.

Amsterdam after a German bombing

World War II

World War II officially began on September 1, 1939, when Germany, which had already occupied Czechoslovakia and taken over Austria, invaded Poland. Britain and France declared war on Germany two days later. Hitler's forces attacked Denmark, Norway, and Luxembourg; and by May 1940, they invaded and defeated the Netherlands, where the Franks were now living.

German forces continued to move through Europe and occupied Belgium and France. It was not until May 1945 that Germany was defeated and surrendered to the Allied powers, which included Great Britain, the Soviet Union, and the United States.

The Holocaust

Meanwhile during the war, everywhere the German army went, Jews were persecuted. Jews had to register with government authorities and wear yellow stars on their clothing to identify themselves as Jews. Nazis seized their property and businesses.

People being rounded up to be sent to concentration camps by the Nazis

Millions of Jews throughout Europe were sent to concentration camps. There they were starved and put to death. About six million Jews died in what became known as the Holocaust, the systematic extermination of people by the Nazis. Gypsies, Slavs, political prisoners, and disabled people were also included in this systematic extermination.

In 1942, however, most Jews were unaware of the extent of the danger they faced. Most simply thought they would be temporarily imprisoned. To avoid this fate, the Frank family went into what they thought would be temporary hiding in the attic of a warehouse and office building that had been part of Mr. Frank's business in Amsterdam.

On her thirteenth birthday, Anne had received a diary as a gift. When her family went into hiding, she began to write regularly and often in her diary. The play *The Diary of Anne Frank,* which you are about to read, is based on this diary, which Mr. Frank recovered when he returned to the secret attic after the war.

Master Teacher Note Many writers have been motivated by isolation or feelings of alienation. Show students Art Transparency 7, *The Silent Seasons—Fall* by Will Barnet in the Teaching Portfolio. Ask students to describe the girl's expression as she peers out the window. What might have prompted her expression? What might she be thinking? Might she be isolated from the world outside her window? Tell students that Anne Frank, secluded with her family in an attic during the Nazi reign, was motivated to keep a diary by isolation and by the family's experiences.

Focus

More About the Authors Frances Goodrich and Albert Hackett began working together in 1927, were married in 1931, and ended their writing careers in 1962 with a script for the screenplay based on their drama, *The Diary of Anne Frank.* Both had been actors. Hackett had started acting at age six and worked in both vaudeville and silent films. After Goodrich graduated from Vassar, she took to the road as an actor and in 1913 first appeared on Broadway. Ask students to discuss in what ways being a former actor can help in writing a play.

Literary Focus Explain that in this play all but the first and last scenes occur in flashback and dramatize events described in Anne's actual diary. The two "envelope" scenes depict Mr. Frank's state of mind before and after he has read his daughter's words. Tell students to look for the change in Mr. Frank by the end.

Look For Remind students that Anne is only thirteen when the play begins and, like all teenagers, she is undergoing changes as her personality matures. Thus, *mercurial* is a vocabulary word for them to keep in mind as they assess Anne's relationships with the characters in the play.

Writing/Prior Knowledge Ask students to keep a diary for one week. Have them write every day about the people and places around them and their activities. Emphasize that what they write is private. After the week, have students discuss how they feel about keeping a personal record of their lives. Did they find, as Anne did, that a diary is like a friend and confidant?

Vocabulary The following words may not be known by your **less advanced** students: *aggravating* (p. 322), *rebellious* (p. 323), *finicky* (p. 326), *improvised* (p. 336), *precious* (p. 337), *jubilation* (p. 339).

Teaching to Ability Levels Suggest to your **more advanced** students that they read *A Tribute to Anne Frank,* edited by Anna Steenmeijer. The book contains letters and photographs representing the most poignant and meaningful responses to Anne Frank's diary.

Objectives

1 To understand the use of flashback in a play
2 To make predictions about the outcome of a play
3 To write a letter as a character in the play

GUIDE FOR READING

The Diary of Anne Frank, Act I

Frances Goodrich (1890–1984) and **Albert Hackett** (1900–) spent two years writing *The Diary of Anne Frank,* which is based on *The Diary of a Young Girl* by Anne Frank. As part of their background work, Goodrich and Hackett visited with Anne's father, Otto Frank. Goodrich and Hackett's play won the Pulitzer Prize, the Drama Critics Circle Award, and the Tony Award for best play of the 1955–1956 season. *The Diary of Anne Frank* shows the unconquerable spirit of a young girl.

Flashback

Most of this play is presented as a flashback. A **flashback** is a technique that writers use to present events that happened at an earlier time. The writer inserts a scene that presents the earlier action as though it were taking place in the present. *The Diary of Anne Frank* begins in 1945 as Mr. Frank returns to the warehouse where he and his family hid from the Nazis. When Mr. Frank starts to read Anne's diary, however, the time changes back to 1942. The events of 1942 are presented as though they were taking place in the present. Using a flashback lets the authors show you how Mr. Frank is affected now by what has happened in the past.

Look For

As you read the first act of this play, look for the ways Anne's reactions to being in hiding change as the act progresses.

Writing

Put yourself in Anne's place. Freewrite about what you would miss most if you had to go into hiding.

Vocabulary

Knowing the following words will help you as you read *The Diary of Anne Frank,* Act I.

conspicuous (kən spik' yo͞o wəs) *adj.*: Noticeable (p. 307)
mercurial (mər kyo͝or' ē əl) *adj.*: Quick or changeable in behavior (p. 307)
unabashed (un ə bash' əd) *adj.*: Unashamed (p. 311)
insufferable (in suf'ər ə b'l) *adj.*: Unbearable (p. 317)
meticulous (mə tik'yo͞o ləs) *adj.*: Extremely careful about details (p. 326)
fatalist (fā'tə list) *n.*: One who believes that all events are determined by fate and cannot be changed (p. 334)
ostentatiously (äs' tən tā' shəs lē) *adv.*: Showily (p. 339)

The Diary of Anne Frank

Frances Goodrich and Albert Hackett

CHARACTERS

Mr. Frank	**Mr. Van Daan**	**Margot Frank**	**Mr. Kraler**
Miep	**Peter Van Daan**	**Anne Frank**	**Mr. Dussel**
Mrs. Van Daan	**Mrs. Frank**		

ACT I

Scene 1

[The scene remains the same throughout the play. It is the top floor of a warehouse and office building in Amsterdam, Holland. The sharply peaked roof of the building is outlined against a sea of other rooftops, stretching away into the distance. Nearby is the belfry[1] *of a church tower, the Westertoren, whose carillon*[2] *rings out the hours. Occasionally faint sounds float up from below: the voices of children playing in the street, the tramp of marching feet, a boat whistle from the canal.*

The three rooms of the top floor and a small attic space above are exposed to our view. The largest of the rooms is in the center, with two small rooms, slightly raised, on either side. On the right is a bathroom, out of sight. A narrow steep flight of stairs at the back leads up to the attic. The rooms are sparsely furnished with a few chairs, cots, a table or two. The windows are painted over, or covered with makeshift blackout curtains.[3] *In the main room there is a sink, a gas ring for cooking and a woodburning stove for warmth.*

The room on the left is hardly more than a closet. There is a skylight in the sloping ceiling. Directly under this room is a small steep stairwell, with steps leading down to a door. This is the only entrance from the building below. When the door is opened we see that it has been concealed on the outer side by a bookcase attached to it.

The curtain rises on an empty stage. It is late afternoon November, 1945. 1

The rooms are dusty, the curtains in rags. Chairs and tables are overturned.

The door at the foot of the small stairwell swings open. MR. FRANK *comes up the steps into view. He is a gentle, cultured European in his middle years. There is still a trace of a German accent in his speech.*

He stands looking slowly around, making a supreme effort at self-control. He is weak, ill. His clothes are threadbare.

1. belfry (bel′ frē) *n.*: The part of a tower that holds the bells.

2. carillon (kar′ ə län′) *n.*: A set of stationary bells, each producing one note of the scale.

3. blackout curtains: Draperies that conceal all lights that might otherwise be visible to enemy air raiders at night.

Presentation

Motivation/Prior Knowledge Explain to students that this play is based on a diary kept by Anne Frank while she and her family were in hiding from the Nazis in Amsterdam, the Netherlands, during World War II. Discuss the Holocaust and the extermination of eleven million people, including six million Jews. Mention that Holland was an occupied country and that there was an underground resistance which, in addition to trying to undermine the Nazi occupation, also gave assistance to Jews.

Thematic Idea Another selection that deals with the theme of a teenager's response to war is "The Drummer Boy of Shiloh" (page 151); with the theme of the need for acceptance is "Flowers for Algernon" (page 201); and with the theme of courage is "Harriet Tubman: Guide to Freedom" (page 383).

Purpose-Setting Question How does Anne relate to the different people in the play?

1 **Discussion** Discuss when the play takes place. Point out that the play opens about six months after the end of World War II.

Support Material

Teaching Portfolio

Teacher Backup, pp. 403–406

Grammar in Action Worksheets, *Using Simple Sentences*, pp. 407–408; *Connecting Ideas of Equal Weight*, pp. 409–410; *Understanding Infinitive Verbs*, pp. 411–412; *Understanding Imperative Sentences*, pp. 413–414

Usage and Mechanics Worksheet, p. 415

Vocabulary Check, p. 416

Critical Thinking and Reading Worksheet, *Predicting Outcomes*, p. 417

Language Worksheet, *Recognizing Words From German*, p. 418

Selection Test, pp. 419–420

Library of Video Classics, *The Diary of Anne Frank*

2 Discussion How do the sounds from the street contrast with Mr. Frank's feelings?

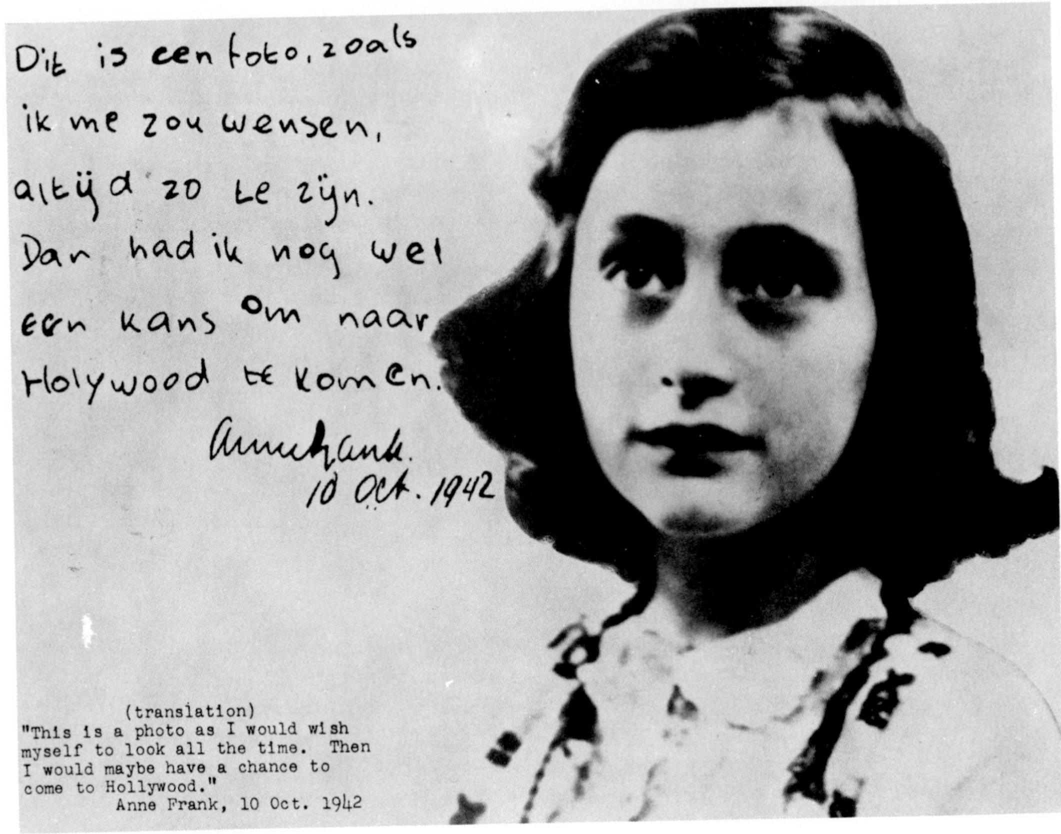

Anne Frank and her opinion of this photo

After a second he drops his rucksack[4] on the couch and moves slowly about. He opens the door to one of the smaller rooms, and then abruptly closes it again, turning away. He goes to the window at the back, looking off at the Westertoren as its carillon strikes the hour of six, then he moves restlessly on.

2 *From the street below we hear the sound of a barrel organ[5] and children's voices at play. There is a many-colored scarf hanging from a nail.* MR. FRANK *takes it, putting it around his neck. As he starts back for his rucksack, his eye is caught by something lying on the floor. It is a woman's white glove. He holds it in his hand and suddenly all of his self-control is gone. He breaks down, crying.*

We hear footsteps on the stairs. MIEP GIES *comes up, looking for* MR. FRANK. MIEP *is a Dutch girl of about twenty-two. She wears a coat and hat, ready to go home. She is*

4. **rucksack** (ruk' sak') *n.*: A knapsack.
5. **barrel organ** *n.*: A mechanical musical instrument played by turning a crank.

pregnant. Her attitude toward MR. FRANK *is protective, compassionate.]*

MIEP. Are you all right, Mr. Frank?

MR. FRANK. [*Quickly controlling himself*] Yes, Miep, yes.

MIEP. Everyone in the office has gone home . . . It's after six. [*Then pleading*] Don't stay up here, Mr. Frank. What's the use of torturing yourself like this?

MR. FRANK. I've come to say good-bye . . . I'm leaving here, Miep.

MIEP. What do you mean? Where are you going? Where?

MR. FRANK. I don't know yet. I haven't decided.

MIEP. Mr. Frank, you can't leave here! This is your home! Amsterdam is your home. Your business is here, waiting for you . . . You're needed here . . . Now that the war is over, there are things that . . .

MR. FRANK. I can't stay in Amsterdam, Miep. It has too many memories for me. Everywhere there's something . . . the house we lived in . . . the school . . . that street organ playing out there . . . I'm not the person you used to know, Miep. I'm a bitter old man. [*Breaking off*] Forgive me. I shouldn't speak to you like this . . . after all that you did for us . . . the suffering . . .

MIEP. No. No. It wasn't suffering. You can't say we suffered. [*As she speaks, she straightens a chair which is overturned.*]

MR. FRANK. I know what you went through, you and Mr. Kraler. I'll remember it as long as I live. [*He gives one last look around.*] Come, Miep. [*He starts for the steps, then remembers his rucksack, going back to get it.*]

MIEP. [*Hurrying up to a cupboard*] Mr. Frank, did you see? There are some of your papers here. [*She brings a bundle of papers to him.*] We found them in a heap of rubbish on the floor after . . . after you left.

MR. FRANK. Burn them. [*He opens his rucksack to put the glove in it.*]

MIEP. But, Mr. Frank, there are letters, notes . . .

MR. FRANK. Burn them. All of them.

MIEP. Burn *this?* [*She hands him a paperbound notebook.*]

MR. FRANK. [*Quietly*] Anne's diary. [*He opens the diary and begins to read.*] "Monday, the
sixth of July, nineteen forty-two." [*To* MIEP] 3
Nineteen forty-two. Is it possible, Miep? . . . Only three years ago. [*As he continues his reading, he sits down on the couch.*] "Dear Diary, since you and I are going to be great
friends, I will start by telling you about 4, 5
myself. My name is Anne Frank. I am thirteen years old. I was born in Germany the twelfth of June, nineteen twenty-nine. As my family is Jewish, we emigrated to Holland when Hitler came to power."

[*As* MR. FRANK *reads on, another voice joins
his, as if coming from the air. It is* ANNE'S 6
VOICE.]

MR. FRANK AND ANNE. "My father started a business, importing spice and herbs. Things went well for us until nineteen forty. Then the war came, and the Dutch capitulation,[6] followed by the arrival of the Germans. Then things got very bad for the Jews."

[MR. FRANK'S VOICE *dies out.* ANNE'S VOICE *continues alone. The lights dim slowly to darkness. The curtain falls on the scene.*]

---

6. capitulation (kə pich′ ə lā′ shən) *n.*: Surrender.

3 Literary Focus Discuss the playwright's technique for getting into the flashback. Point out that as Mr. Frank starts to read Anne's diary, the time goes back three years and Anne starts to tell the story.

4 Discussion What does the diary mean to Anne?

5 Literary Focus Explain that the diary was considered by Anne as a confidante, an imaginary friend to whom she could confess her most private thoughts and emotions. There is no attempt by the author to control the content of her entries. This fact is important to the reader, whose perspective must be adjusted accordingly.

6 Enrichment Have students look at the picture of Anne on the preceding page. What does her inscription on the photo tell you about Anne?

7 **Discussion** Discuss Anne's attitude. Bring out that, even under stressful conditions, Anne could still have fun.

ANNE'S VOICE. You could not do this and you could not do that. They forced Father out of his business. We had to wear yellow stars.[7] I had to turn in my bike. I couldn't go to a Dutch school any more. I couldn't go to the movies, or ride in an automobile, or even on a streetcar, and a million other things. But
7 somehow we children still managed to have
fun. Yesterday Father told me we were going into hiding. Where, he wouldn't say. At five o'clock this morning Mother woke me and told me to hurry and get dressed. I was to put on as many clothes as I could. It would look too suspicious if we walked along carrying suitcases. It wasn't until we were on our way that I learned where we were going. Our hiding place was to be upstairs in the building where Father used to have his business. Three other people were coming in with us . . . the Van Daans and their son Peter . . . Father knew the Van Daans but we had never met them . . .

[*During the last lines the curtain rises on the scene. The lights dim on.* ANNE'S VOICE *fades out.*]

7. **yellow stars:** Stars of David, which are six-pointed stars that are symbols of Judaism. The Nazis ordered all Jews to wear them sewn to their clothing so that Jews could be easily identified.

Front view and rear view of the building where the Franks and their friends hid

Grammar in Action

Usually writers vary their sentence patterns in order to achieve a lively and interesting style. However, sometimes a writer may purposely choose to use several short, **simple sentences** in succession in order to emphasize the content of each sentence; then each detail or event is treated as equally important.

Notice the style of writing in the following passage from *The Diary of Anne Frank:*

> **ANNE'S VOICE.** You could not do this and you could not do that. They forced Father out of his business. We had to wear yellow stars. I had to turn in my bike. I couldn't go to a Dutch school any more. I couldn't go to the movies, or ride in an automobile, or even on a streetcar, and a million other things. But somehow we children still managed to have fun.

The short, precise sentences, void of detail, emphasize each action and create a vivid impression of the starkness of her life.

Scene 2

[*It is early morning, July, 1942. The rooms are bare, as before, but they are now clean and orderly.*

MR. VAN DAAN, *a tall, portly*[8] *man in his late forties, is in the main room, pacing up and down, nervously smoking a cigarette. His clothes and overcoat are expensive and well cut.*

MRS. VAN DAAN *sits on the couch, clutching her possessions, a hatbox, bags, etc. She is a pretty woman in her early forties. She wears a fur coat over her other clothes.*

PETER VAN DAAN *is standing at the window of the room on the right, looking down at the street below. He is a shy, awkward boy of sixteen. He wears a cap, a raincoat, and long Dutch trousers, like "plus fours."*[9] *At his feet is a black case, a carrier for his cat.*

The yellow Star of David is conspicuous on all of their clothes.]

MRS. VAN DAAN. [*Rising, nervous, excited*] Something's happened to them! I know it!

MR. VAN DAAN. Now, Kerli!

MRS. VAN DAAN. Mr. Frank said they'd be here at seven o'clock. He said . . .

MR. VAN DAAN. They have two miles to walk. You can't expect . . .

MRS. VAN DAAN. They've been picked up. That's what's happened. They've been taken . . .

[MR. VAN DAAN *indicates that he hears someone coming.*]

MR. VAN DAAN. You see?

[PETER *takes up his carrier and his schoolbag, etc., and goes into the main room as* MR. FRANK *comes up the stairwell from below.* MR. FRANK *looks much younger now. His movements are brisk, his manner confident. He wears an overcoat and carries his hat and a small cardboard box. He crosses to the* VAN DAANS. *shaking hands with each of them.*]

MR. FRANK. Mrs. Van Daan, Mr. Van Daan, Peter. [*Then, in explanation of their lateness*] There were too many of the Green Police[10] on the streets . . . we had to take the long way around.

[*Up the steps come* MARGOT FRANK, MRS. FRANK, MIEP *(not pregnant now) and* MR. KRALER. *All of them carry bags, packages, and so forth. The Star of David is conspicuous on all of the* FRANKS' *clothing.* MARGOT *is eighteen, beautiful, quiet, shy.* MRS. FRANK *is a young mother, gently bred, reserved. She, like* MR. FRANK, *has a slight German accent.* MR. KRALER *is a Dutchman, dependable, kindly.*

As MR. KRALER *and* MIEP *go upstage to put down their parcels,* MRS. FRANK *turns back to call* ANNE.]

MRS. FRANK. Anne?

[ANNE *comes running up the stairs. She is thirteen, quick in her movements, interested in everything, mercurial in her emotions. She wears a cape, long wool socks and carries a schoolbag.*]

MR. FRANK. [*Introducing them*] My wife, Edith. Mr. and Mrs. Van Daan . . . their son, Peter . . . my daughters, Margot and Anne.

[MRS. FRANK *hurries over, shaking hands with them.*]

[ANNE *gives a polite little curtsy as she shakes* MR. VAN DAAN'S *hand. Then she imme-*

---

8. portly (pôrt′ lē) *adj.*: Large, heavy, and dignified.
9. plus fours *n.*: Loose knickers.

10. Green Police: The Nazi police who wore green uniforms.

Student Activity. Write a paragraph describing a highly dramatic situation. You would like to emphasize each action or event that takes place. An example of such a situation might be try outs for a school play or athletic team or a particularly rigid structure at a summer camp. Try to pattern your sentences after those of Anne Frank in the example. Use several short, simple sentences to emphasize the importance of each.

8 **Clarification** Explain the necessity of rationing here and abroad. During the war there was a worldwide shortage of consumer products. This was caused by the diversion of many raw materials into war goods. It was also caused by the impossibility of transporting materials through customary land, sea, and air channels now blocked by hostile forces. As supplies were limited, governments (including that of the United States) issued to their citizens ration books containing coupons for different types of commodities. Ration books were intended to limit the quantity of available supplies and to provide equal distribution among the people. However, it was possible in some instances to get extra ration books by illegal means.

Mr. and Mrs. Van Daan and Victor Kraler in happier times

diately starts off on a tour of investigation of her new home, going upstairs to the attic room.

MIEP *and* MR. KRALER *are putting the various things they have brought on the shelves.*]

MR. KRALER. I'm sorry there is still so much confusion.

MR. FRANK. Please. Don't think of it. After all, we'll have plenty of leisure to arrange everything ourselves.

MIEP. [*To* MRS. FRANK] We put the stores of food you sent in here. Your drugs are here . . . soap, linen here.

MRS. FRANK. Thank you, Miep.

MIEP. I made up the beds . . . the way Mr. Frank and Mr. Kraler said. [*She starts out.*] Forgive me. I have to hurry. I've got to go to the other side of town to get some ration books[11] for you. 8

MRS. VAN DAAN. Ration books? If they see our names on ration books, they'll know we're here.

MR. KRALER. There isn't anything . . .

MIEP. Don't worry. Your names won't be on them. [*As she hurries out*] I'll be up later.

11. ration books (rash′ ən books′) *n.*: Books of stamps given to ensure even distribution of scarce items, especially in wartime. Stamps as well as money must be given to obtain an item that is scarce.

MR. FRANK. Thank you, Miep.

MRS. FRANK. [*To* MR. KRALER] It's illegal, then, the ration books? We've never done anything illegal.

MR. FRANK. We won't be living here exactly according to regulations.

[*As* MR. KRALER *reassures* MRS. FRANK, *he takes various small things, such as matches, soap, etc., from his pockets, handing them to her.*]

MR. KRALER. This isn't the black market,[12] Mrs. Frank. This is what we call the white market . . . helping all of the hundreds and hundreds who are hiding out in Amsterdam.

[*The carillon is heard playing the quarter-hour before eight.* MR. KRALER *looks at his watch.* ANNE *stops at the window as she comes down the stairs.*]

ANNE. It's the Westertoren!

MR. KRALER. I must go. I must be out of here and downstairs in the office before the workmen get here. [*He starts for the stairs leading out.*] Miep or I, or both of us, will be up each day to bring you food and news and find out what your needs are. Tomorrow I'll get you a better bolt for the door at the foot of the stairs. It needs a bolt that you can throw yourself and open only at our signal. [*To* MR. FRANK] Oh . . . You'll tell them about the noise?

MR. FRANK. I'll tell them.

MR. KRALER. Good-bye then for the moment. I'll come up again, after the workmen leave.

MR. FRANK. Good-bye, Mr. Kraler.

MRS. FRANK. [*Shaking his hand*] How can we thank you?

[*The others murmur their good-byes.*]

MR. KRALER. I never thought I'd live to see the day when a man like Mr. Frank would have to go into hiding. When you think— 9

[*He breaks off, going out.* MR. FRANK *follows him down the steps, bolting the door after him. In the interval before he returns,* PETER *goes over to* MARGOT, *shaking hands with her. As* MR. FRANK *comes back up the steps,* MRS. FRANK *questions him anxiously.*]

MRS. FRANK. What did he mean, about the noise?

MR. FRANK. First let us take off some of these clothes.

[*They all start to take off garment after garment. On each of their coats, sweaters, blouses, suits, dresses, is another yellow Star of David.* MR. *and* MRS. FRANK *are underdressed quite simply. The others wear several things, sweaters, extra dresses, bathrobes, aprons, nightgowns, etc.*]

MR. VAN DAAN. It's a wonder we weren't arrested, walking along the streets . . . Petronella with a fur coat in July . . . and that cat of Peter's crying all the way.

ANNE. [*As she is removing a pair of panties*] A cat?

MRS. FRANK. [*Shocked*] Anne, please!

ANNE. It's all right. I've got on three more—

[*She pulls off two more. Finally, as they have all removed their surplus clothes, they look to* MR. FRANK, *waiting for him to speak.*]

MR. FRANK. Now. About the noise. While the men are in the building below, we must have complete quiet. Every sound can be heard down there, not only in the workrooms, but in the offices too. The men come at about eight-thirty, and leave at about five-thirty. 10

---

12. black market: An illegal way of buying scarce items without ration stamps.

9 Discussion From Mr. Kraler's brief appearance, what conclusions can you draw about his personality?

10 Discussion Discuss the conditions under which the Franks and the Van Daans must live. Ask students how they would feel living under such conditions.

11 **Discussion** What does this reveal about Mr. Frank's character?

So, to be perfectly safe, from eight in the morning until six in the evening we must move only when it is necessary, and then in stockinged feet. We must not speak above a whisper. We must not run any water. We cannot use the sink, or even, forgive me, the w.c.[13] The pipes go down through the work-rooms. It would be heard. No trash . . .

[MR. FRANK *stops abruptly as he hears the sound of marching feet from the street below. Everyone is motionless, paralyzed with fear.* MR. FRANK *goes quietly into the room on the right to look down out of the window.* ANNE *runs after him, peering out with him. The tramping feet pass without stopping. The tension is relieved.* MR. FRANK, *followed by* ANNE, *returns to the main room and resumes his instructions to the group.*]

. . . No trash must ever be thrown out which might reveal that someone is living up here . . . not even a potato paring. We must burn everything in the stove at night. This is the way we must live until it is over, if we are to survive.

[*There is silence for a second.*]

MRS. FRANK. Until it is over.

MR. FRANK. [*Reassuringly*] After six we can move about . . . we can talk and laugh and have our supper and read and play games . . . just as we would at home. [*He looks at his watch.*] And now I think it would be wise if we all went to our rooms, and were settled before eight o'clock. Mrs. Van Daan, you and your husband will be upstairs. I regret that there's no place up there for Peter. But he will be here, near us. This will be our common room, where we'll meet to talk and eat and read, like one family.

MR. VAN DAAN. And where do you and Mrs. Frank sleep?

13. **w.c.:** water closet; bathroom.

MR. FRANK. This room is also our bedroom.

MRS. VAN DAAN. That isn't right. We'll sleep here and you take the room upstairs. } [*Together*]

MR. VAN DAAN. It's your place. }

MR. FRANK. Please. I've thought this out for weeks. It's the best arrangement. The only arrangement. 11

MRS. VAN DAAN. [*To* MR. FRANK] Never, never can we thank you. [*Then to* MRS. FRANK] I don't know what would have happened to us, if it hadn't been for Mr. Frank.

MR. FRANK. You don't know how your husband helped me when I came to this country . . . knowing no one . . . not able to speak the language. I can never repay him for that. [*Going to* VAN DAAN] May I help you with your things?

MR. VAN DAAN. No. No. [*To* MRS. VAN DAAN] Come along, *liefje*.[14]

MRS. VAN DAAN. You'll be all right, Peter? You're not afraid?

PETER. [*Embarrassed*] Please, Mother.

[*They start up the stairs to the attic room above.* MR. FRANK *turns to* MRS. FRANK.]

MR. FRANK. You too must have some rest, Edith. You didn't close your eyes last night. Nor you, Margot.

ANNE. I slept, Father. Wasn't that funny? I knew it was the last night in my own bed, and yet I slept soundly.

MR. FRANK. I'm glad, Anne. Now you'll be able to help me straighten things in here. [*To* MRS. FRANK *and* MARGOT] Come with me . . . You and Margot rest in this room for the time being.

14. ***liefje*** (lēf hyə): Dutch for "little love."

Primary Source

The following excerpt from the June 8, 1989 edition of *The New York Times* discusses the authenticity of Anne Frank's diary:

"After years of detective work, the Dutch Government has for the first time proved the authenticity of Anne Frank's diary down to the last detail . . . " "One of the main reasons why we used scientific evidence to unravel all the facts about the diary was to expose the falsehoods of neo-Nazi and rightist groups in Europe and the United States," said David Barnouw, the co-editor of *The Diary of Anne Frank: The Critical Edition*, who is a researcher at the Netherlands State Institute for War Documentation. "Ever since her book first came out after the war, individuals and groups have made statements and issued anti-Semitic pamphlets claiming it was a hoax."

. . . Miss Frank's handwriting was closely analyzed by experts, as were specimens of her writing and those by 78 of her classmates. The experts took into account that sometimes Miss Frank used normal cursive lettering and sometimes a disconnected printing style. This is a common characteristic "applicable to the writing of young people," the experts said. Samples of her writing are included in the book to support their conclusion that the diary was indeed written by Anne Frank alone.

[*He picks up their clothes, starting for the room on the right.*]

MRS. FRANK. You're sure . . . ? I could help . . . And Anne hasn't had her milk . . .

MR. FRANK. I'll give it to her. [*To* ANNE *and* PETER] Anne, Peter . . . it's best that you take off your shoes now, before you forget.

[*He leads the way to the room, followed by* MARGOT.]

MRS. FRANK. You're sure you're not tired, Anne?

ANNE. I feel fine. I'm going to help Father.

MRS. FRANK. Peter, I'm glad you are to be with us.

PETER. Yes, Mrs. Frank.

[MRS. FRANK *goes to join* MR. FRANK *and* MARGOT.]

[*During the following scene* MR. FRANK *helps* MARGOT *and* MRS. FRANK *to hang up their clothes. Then he persuades them both to lie down and rest. The* VAN DAANS *in their room above settle themselves. In the main room* ANNE *and* PETER *remove their shoes.* PETER *takes his cat out of the carrier.*]

ANNE. What's your cat's name?

PETER. Mouschi.

ANNE. Mouschi! Mouschi! Mouschi! [*She picks up the cat, walking away with it.* To PETER] I love cats. I have one . . . a darling little cat. But they made me leave her behind. I left some food and a note for the neighbors to take care of her . . . I'm going to miss her terribly. What is yours? A him or a her?

PETER. He's a tom. He doesn't like strangers. [*He takes the cat from her, putting it back in its carrier.*]

ANNE. [*Unabashed*] Then I'll have to stop being a stranger, won't I? Is he fixed?

Star of David patch that the Nazis forced Jews to wear

PETER. [*Startled*] Huh?

ANNE. Did you have him fixed?

PETER. No.

ANNE. Oh, you ought to have him fixed—to keep him from—you know, fighting. Where did you go to school?

PETER. Jewish Secondary.

ANNE. But that's where Margot and I go! I never saw you around.

PETER. I used to see you . . . sometimes . . .

ANNE. You did?

PETER. . . . In the school yard. You were always in the middle of a bunch of kids. [*He takes a penknife from his pocket.*]

ANNE. Why didn't you ever come over?

PETER. I'm sort of a lone wolf. [*He starts to rip off his Star of David.*]

ANNE. What are you doing?

The Forensic Science Laboratory report also point out that the paper, ink and glue in the diary and some of her accompanying loose sheets all existed in the early 1940's, before Miss Frank and her family were betrayed in their hiding place in Amsterdam and sent away to concentration camps.

The glue and fibers used in the binding of the diaries were analyzed by infrared spectrometry. Both were found in common use when Miss Frank wrote her diary. After 1950, a different kind of synthetic glue came into use. Similarly, the paper used in the diary was examined by X-ray fluorescence and found to have been manufactured between 1939 and 1942.

12 Clarification Explain that the Star of David is the symbol of Judaism and of Israel. It consists of two triangles that interlace and form a six-pointed star. The star appears on the flag of Israel.

PETER. Taking it off.

ANNE. But you can't do that. They'll arrest you if you go out without your star.

[*He tosses his knife on the table.*]

PETER. Who's going out?

ANNE. Why, of course! You're right! Of course we don't need them any more. [*She picks up his knife and starts to take her star off.*] I wonder what our friends will think when we don't show up today?

PETER. I didn't have any dates with anyone.

ANNE. Oh, I did. I had a date with Jopie to go and play ping-pong at her house. Do you know Jopie de Waal?

PETER. No.

ANNE. Jopie's my best friend. I wonder what she'll think when she telephones and there's no answer? . . . Probably she'll go over to the house . . . I wonder what she'll think . . . we left everything as if we'd suddenly been called away . . . breakfast dishes in the sink . . . beds not made . . . [*As she pulls off her star, the cloth underneath shows clearly the color and form of the star.*] Look! It's still there!

[PETER *goes over to the stove with his star.*]

What're you going to do with yours?

PETER. Burn it.

ANNE. [*She starts to throw hers in, and cannot.*] It's funny, I can't throw mine away. I don't know why.

PETER. You can't throw . . . ? Something they branded you with . . . ? That they made you wear so they could spit on you?

12 ANNE. I know. I know. But after all, it *is* the Star of David, isn't it?

[*In the bedroom, right,* MARGOT *and* MRS. FRANK *are lying down.* MR. FRANK *starts quietly out.*]

PETER. Maybe it's different for a girl.

[MR. FRANK *comes into the main room.*]

MR. FRANK. Forgive me, Peter. Now let me see. We must find a bed for your cat. [*He goes to a cupboard.*] I'm glad you brought your cat. Anne was feeling so badly about hers. [*Getting a used small washtub*] Here we are. Will it be comfortable in that?

PETER. [*Gathering up his things*] Thanks.

MR. FRANK. [*Opening the door of the room on the left*] And here is your room. But I warn you, Peter, you can't grow any more. Not an inch, or you'll have to sleep with your feet out of the skylight. Are you hungry?

PETER. No.

MR. FRANK. We have some bread and butter.

PETER. No, thank you.

MR. FRANK. You can have it for luncheon then. And tonight we will have a real supper . . . our first supper together.

PETER. Thanks. Thanks. [*He goes into his room. During the following scene he arranges his possessions in his new room.*]

MR. FRANK. That's a nice boy, Peter.

ANNE. He's awfully shy, isn't he?

MR. FRANK. You'll like him, I know.

ANNE. I certainly hope so, since he's the only boy I'm likely to see for months and months.

[MR. FRANK *sits down, taking off his shoes.*]

MR. FRANK. Annele,[15] there's a box there. Will you open it?

---

15. Annele (än′ ə lə): Nickname for *Anne.*

Grammar in Action

Writers can emphasize ideas by putting them in the same grammatical form. By using the same grammatical form within a sentence or a series of sentences, writers connect ideas or equal weight for the reader.

For example, consider the following passage from *The Diary of Anne Frank.*

MR. FRANK. It'll be hard, I know. But always remember this, Anneke. There are no walls, there are no bolts, no locks that anyone can put on your mind. Miep will bring us books. We will read history, poetry, mythology.

What pattern do you find in the sentence "There are no walls, there are no books . . ."? What pattern do you see in the sentences, "Miep will bring us books. We will read history, poetry, mythology"?

Student Activity 1. Rewrite each of the following sentences, connecting ideas by placing them in the same grammatical form.

[He indicates a carton on the couch. ANNE *brings it to the center table. In the street below there is the sound of children playing.]*

ANNE. *[As she opens the carton]* You know the way I'm going to think of it here? I'm going to think of it as a boarding house. A very peculiar summer boarding house, like
13 the one that we—*[She breaks off as she pulls out some photographs.]* Father! My movie stars! I was wondering where they were! I was looking for them this morning . . . and Queen Wilhelmina![16] How wonderful!

MR. FRANK. There's something more. Go on. Look further. *[He goes over to the sink, pouring a glass of milk from a thermos bottle.]*

ANNE. *[Pulling out a pasteboard-bound book]* A diary! *[She throws her arms around her father.]* I've never had a diary. And I've always longed for one. *[She looks around the room.]* Pencil, pencil, pencil, pencil. *[She starts down the stairs.]* I'm going down to the office to get a pencil.

MR. FRANK. Anne! No! *[He goes after her, catching her by the arm and pulling her back.]*

ANNE. *[Startled]* But there's no one in the building now.

MR. FRANK. It doesn't matter. I don't want you ever to go beyond that door.

ANNE. *[Sobered]* Never . . . ? Not even at nighttime, when everyone is gone? Or on Sundays? Can't I go down to listen to the radio?

MR. FRANK. Never. I am sorry, Anneke.[17] It isn't safe. No, you must never go beyond that door.

[For the first time ANNE *realizes what "going into hiding" means.]*

ANNE. I see.

MR. FRANK. It'll be hard, I know. But always
remember this, Anneke. There are no walls, 14
there are no bolts, no locks that anyone can put on your mind. Miep will bring us books. We will read history, poetry, mythology. *[He gives her the glass of milk.]* Here's your milk. *[With his arm about her, they go over to the couch, sitting down side by side.]* As a matter of fact, between us, Anne, being here has certain advantages for you. For instance, you remember the battle you had with your mother the other day on the subject of overshoes? You said you'd rather die than wear overshoes? But in the end you had to wear them? Well now, you see, for as long as we are here you will never have to wear overshoes! Isn't that good? And the coat that you inherited from Margot, you won't have to wear that any more. And the piano! You won't have to practice on the piano. I tell you, this is going to be a fine life for you!

*[*ANNE'S *panic is gone.* PETER *appears in the doorway of his room, with a saucer in his hand. He is carrying his cat.]*

PETER. I . . . I . . . I thought I'd better get some water for Mouschi before . . .

MR. FRANK. Of course.

[As he starts toward the sink the carillon begins to chime the hour of eight. He tiptoes to the window at the back and looks

---

16. Queen Wilhelmina (kwēn′ wil′ hel mē′ nə): Queen of Holland from 1890 to 1948.

17. Anneke (än′ ə kə): Nickname for *Anne*.

13 Discussion What does this dialogue reveal about Anne?

14 Discussion In your own words, tell what Mr. Frank is saying.

1. There was no love, there wasn't any beauty either.
2. Some applauded, *bravo* was shouted by others.
3. Sharon will bring food. Records will be brought by Jack.
4. When my friend finds I'm gone, I wonder what she will think. What she will feel makes me wonder, too.

Student Activity 2. Write a paragraph in which you tell what things you think cannot be taken from a person's mind or spirit. Connect ideas of equal weight by placing them in the same grammatical form.
(For more practice with sentences, see *Grammar in Action Practice Book*, page 39.)

15 Discussion How long have the Franks been in hiding?

down at the street below. He turns to PETER, *indicating in pantomime that it is too late.* PETER *starts back for his room. He steps on a creaking board. The three of them are frozen for a minute in fear. As* PETER *starts away again,* ANNE *tiptoes over to him and pours some of the milk from her glass into the saucer for the cat.* PETER *squats on the floor, putting the milk before the cat.* MR. FRANK *gives* ANNE *his fountain pen, and then goes into the room at the right. For a second* ANNE *watches the cat, then she goes over to the center table, and opens her diary.*

In the room at the right, MRS. FRANK *has sat up quickly at the sound of the carillon.* MR. FRANK *comes in and sits down beside her on the settee, his arm comfortingly around her.*

Upstairs, in the attic room, MR. *and* MRS. VAN DAAN *have hung their clothes in the closet and are now seated on the iron bed.* MRS. VAN DAAN *leans back exhausted.* MR. VAN DAAN *fans her with a newspaper.*

ANNE *starts to write in her diary. The lights dim out, the curtain falls.*

In the darkness ANNE'S VOICE *comes to us again, faintly at first, and then with growing strength.*]

ANNE'S VOICE. I expect I should be describing what it feels like to go into hiding. But I really don't know yet myself. I only know it's funny never to be able to go outdoors . . . never to breathe fresh air . . . never to run and shout and jump. It's the silence in the nights that frightens me most. Every time I hear a creak in the house, or a step on the street outside, I'm sure they're coming for us. The days aren't so bad. At least we know that Miep and Mr. Kraler are down there below us in the office. Our protectors, we call them. I asked Father what would happen to them if the Nazis found out they were hiding us. Pim said that they would suffer the same fate that we would . . . Imagine! They know this, and yet when they come up here, they're always cheerful and gay as if there were nothing in the world to bother them . . . Friday, the twenty-first of August, nineteen forty-two. Today I'm going to tell you our general news. Mother is unbearable. She insists on treating me like a baby, which I loathe. Otherwise things are going better. The weather is . . .

[*As* ANNE'S VOICE *is fading out, the curtain rises on the scene.*]

Scene 3

[*It is a little after six o'clock in the evening, two months later.*

MARGOT *is in the bedroom at the right, studying.* MR. VAN DAAN *is lying down in the attic room above.*

The rest of the "family" is in the main room. ANNE *and* PETER *sit opposite each other at the center table, where they have been doing their lessons.* MRS. FRANK *is on the couch.* MRS. VAN DAAN *is seated with her fur coat, on which she has been sewing, in her lap. None of them are wearing their shoes.*

Their eyes are on MR. FRANK, *waiting for him to give them the signal which will release them from their day-long quiet.* MR. FRANK, *his shoes in his hand, stands looking down out of the window at the back, watching to be sure that all of the workmen have left the building below.*

After a few seconds of motionless silence, MR. FRANK *turns from the window.*]

MR. FRANK. [*Quietly, to the group*] It's safe now. The last workman has left.

[*There is an immediate stir of relief.*]

ANNE. [*Her pent-up energy explodes.*] WHEE!

Grammar in Action

An **infinitive** is the form of a verb that comes after the word *to;* it can act as a noun, adjective, or adverb. Infinitives are not to be confused with prepositional phrases beginning with *to.* Prepositional phrases beginning with *to* end with nouns *(to class);* infinitives begin with *to* and end with a verb *(to give).* An infinitive can be expanded to form an **infinitive phrase,** an infinitive with a modifier or complement, all acting together as a single part of speech. For example, on page 315, Margot says, "I have to help with supper." "To help with supper" is an infinitive phrase.

The frequent use of infinitives in *The Diary of Anne Frank* enhances the poignancy of the story because of the limitations expressed in these verbs. Anne wants "to be able to go outdoors . . . to breathe fresh air . . . to run and shout and jump." Instead she has "to go into hiding . . . to be dignified."

Student Activity 1. In the following sentences from the play, identify whether the phrase is an infinitive or a prepositional phrase:

MRS. FRANK. [*Startled, amused*] Anne!

MRS. VAN DAAN. I'm first for the w.c.

[*She hurries off to the bathroom.* MRS. FRANK *puts on her shoes and starts up to the sink to prepare supper.* ANNE *sneaks* PETER'S *shoes from under the table and hides them behind her back.* MR. FRANK *goes in to* MARGOT'S *room.*]

MR. FRANK. [*To* MARGOT] Six o'clock. School's over.

[MARGOT *gets up, stretching.* MR. FRANK *sits down to put on his shoes. In the main room* PETER *tries to find his.*]

PETER. [*To* ANNE] Have you seen my shoes?

ANNE. [*Innocently*] Your shoes?

PETER. You've taken them, haven't you?

ANNE. I don't know what you're talking about.

PETER. You're going to be sorry!

ANNE. Am I?

[PETER *goes after her.* ANNE, *with his shoes in her hand, runs from him, dodging behind her mother.*]

16 **MRS. FRANK.** [*Protesting*] Anne, dear!

PETER. Wait till I get you!

ANNE. I'm waiting!

[PETER *makes a lunge for her. They both fall to the floor.* PETER *pins her down, wrestling with her to get the shoes.*]

Don't! Don't! Peter, stop it. Ouch!

MRS. FRANK. Anne! . . . Peter!

[*Suddenly* PETER *becomes self-conscious. He grabs his shoes roughly and starts for his room.*]

ANNE. [*Following him*] Peter, where are you going? Come dance with me.

PETER. I tell you I don't know how.

ANNE. I'll teach you.

PETER. I'm going to give Mouschi his dinner.

ANNE. Can I watch?

PETER. He doesn't like people around while he eats.

ANNE. Peter, please.

PETER. No! [*He goes into his room.* ANNE *slams his door after him.*]

MRS. FRANK. Anne, dear, I think you shouldn't play like that with Peter. It's not dignified.

ANNE. Who cares if it's dignified? I don't want to be dignified.

[MR. FRANK *and* MARGOT *come from the room on the right.* MARGOT *goes to help her mother.* MR. FRANK *starts for the center table to correct* MARGOT'S *school papers.*]

MRS. FRANK. [*To* ANNE] You complain that I don't treat you like a grownup. But when I do, you resent it.

ANNE. I only want some fun . . . someone to laugh and clown with . . . After you've sat still all day and hardly moved, you've got to have some fun. I don't know what's the matter with that boy.

MR. FRANK. He isn't used to girls. Give him a little time.

ANNE. Time? Isn't two months time? I could cry. [*Catching hold of* MARGOT] Come on, Margot . . . dance with me. Come on, please.

MARGOT. I have to help with supper.

16 Discussion How would you describe Anne's and Peter's feelings toward each other? Have they changed since they first met?

1. He turns to Peter.
2. Anne starts to write in her diary.
3. For a second Anne watches the cat, then she goes over to the center table, and opens her diary.
4. Today I'm going to tell you our general news.
5. You're going to be sorry.

Student Activity 2. Write a diary entry of your own in which you discuss significant events of the day or of the past few days as well as your hopes for the future. Use infinitives in your entry.

17 **Discussion** Discuss Mr. Van Daan's emphasis on Peter's lessons. What does this reveal about Mr. Van Daan's attitude toward the future? How does this attitude compare with Anne's comment about not wanting to forget how to dance?

Anne and her father, Otto Frank

ANNE. You know we're going to forget how to dance . . . When we get out we won't remember a thing.

[*She starts to sing and dance by herself.* MR. FRANK *takes her in his arms, waltzing with her.* MRS. VAN DAAN *comes in from the bathroom.*]

MRS. VAN DAAN. Next? [*She looks around as she starts putting on her shoes.*] Where's Peter?

ANNE. [*As they are dancing*] Where would he be!

17 **MRS. VAN DAAN.** He hasn't finished his lessons, has he? His father'll kill him if he catches him in there with that cat and his work not done.

[MR. FRANK *and* ANNE *finish their dance. They bow to each other with extravagant formality.*]

Anne, get him out of there, will you?

ANNE. [*At* PETER'S *door*] Peter? Peter?

PETER. [*Opening the door a crack*] What is it?

ANNE. Your mother says to come out.

PETER. I'm giving Mouschi his dinner.

MRS. VAN DAAN. You know what your father says. [*She sits on the couch, sewing on the lining of her fur coat.*]

PETER. For heaven's sake, I haven't even looked at him since lunch.

MRS. VAN DAAN. I'm just telling you, that's all.

ANNE. I'll feed him.

PETER. I don't want you in there.

MRS. VAN DAAN. Peter!

PETER. [*To* ANNE] Then give him his dinner and come right out, you hear?

[*He comes back to the table.* ANNE *shuts the door of* PETER'S *room after her and disappears behind the curtain covering his closet.*]

MRS. VAN DAAN. [*To* PETER] Now is that any way to talk to your little girl friend?

PETER. Mother . . . for heaven's sake . . . will you please stop saying that?

MRS. VAN DAAN. Look at him blush! Look at him!

PETER. Please! I'm not . . . anyway . . . let me alone, will you?

MRS. VAN DAAN. He acts like it was something to be ashamed of. It's nothing to be ashamed of, to have a little girl friend.

PETER. You're crazy. She's only thirteen.

MRS. VAN DAAN. So what? And you're sixteen. Just perfect. Your father's ten years older than I am. [*To* MR. FRANK] I warn you, Mr. Frank, if this war lasts much longer, we're going to be related and then . . .

MR. FRANK. *Mazeltov!*[18]

MRS. FRANK. [*Deliberately changing the conversation*] I wonder where Miep is. She's usually so prompt.

[*Suddenly everything else is forgotten as they hear the sound of an automobile coming to a screeching stop in the street below. They are tense, motionless in their terror. The car starts away. A wave of relief sweeps over them. They pick up their occupations again.* ANNE *flings open the door of* PETER'S *room, making a dramatic entrance. She is dressed in* PETER'S *clothes.* PETER *looks at her in fury. The others are amused.*]

ANNE. Good evening, everyone. Forgive me if I don't stay. [*She jumps up on a chair.*] I have a friend waiting for me in there. My friend Tom. Tom Cat. Some people say that we look alike. But Tom has the most beautiful whiskers, and I have only a little fuzz. I am hoping . . . in time . . .

PETER. All right, Mrs. Quack Quack!

ANNE. [*Outraged—jumping down*] Peter!

PETER. I heard about you . . . How you talked so much in class they called you Mrs. Quack Quack. How Mr. Smitter made you write a composition . . . "'Quack, quack,' said Mrs. Quack Quack."

ANNE. Well, go on. Tell them the rest. How it was so good he read it out loud to the class and then read it to all his other classes!

PETER. Quack! Quack! Quack . . . Quack . . . Quack . . .

[ANNE *pulls off the coat and trousers.*]

ANNE. You are the most intolerable, insufferable boy I've ever met!

[*She throws the clothes down the stairwell.* PETER *goes down after them.*]

PETER. Quack, quack, quack!

MRS. VAN DAAN. [*To* ANNE] That's right, Anneke! Give it to him!

ANNE. With all the boys in the world . . . Why I had to get locked up with one like you! . . .

---

18. *mazeltov* (mä′ z'l tōv′): "Good luck" in Hebrew and Yiddish.

Edith Frank, Anne's mother

PETER. Quack, quack, quack, and from now on stay out of my room!

[*As* PETER *passes her,* ANNE *puts out her foot, tripping him. He picks himself up, and goes on into his room.*]

MRS. FRANK. [*Quietly*] Anne, dear . . . your hair. [*She feels* ANNE'S *forehead.*] You're warm. Are you feeling all right?

ANNE. Please, Mother. [*She goes over to the center table, slipping into her shoes.*]

MRS. FRANK. [*Following her*] You haven't a fever, have you?

ANNE. [*Pulling away*] No. No.

MRS. FRANK. You know we can't call a doctor here, ever. There's only one thing to do . . . watch carefully. Prevent an illness before it comes. Let me see your tongue.

ANNE. Mother, this is perfectly absurd.

MRS. FRANK. Anne, dear, don't be such a baby. Let me see your tongue. [*As* ANNE *refuses,* MRS. FRANK *appeals to* MR. FRANK.] Otto . . . ?

MR. FRANK. You hear your mother, Anne.

[ANNE *flicks out her tongue for a second, then turns away.*]

MRS. FRANK. Come on—open up! [*As* ANNE *opens her mouth very wide*] You seem all right . . . but perhaps an aspirin . . .

MRS. VAN DAAN. For heaven's sake, don't give that child any pills. I waited for fifteen minutes this morning for her to come out of the w.c.

ANNE. I was washing my hair!

MR. FRANK. I think there's nothing the matter with our Anne that a ride on her bike, or a visit with her friend Jopie de Waal wouldn't cure. Isn't that so, Anne?

[MR. VAN DAAN *comes down into the room. From outside we hear faint sounds of bombers going over and a burst of ack-ack.*][19]

MR. VAN DAAN. Miep not come yet?

MRS. VAN DAAN. The workmen just left, a little while ago.

MR. VAN DAAN. What's for dinner tonight?

MRS. VAN DAAN. Beans.

MR. VAN DAAN. Not again!

MRS. VAN DAAN. Poor Putti! I know. But what can we do? That's all that Miep brought us.

[MR. VAN DAAN *starts to pace, his hands behind his back.* ANNE *follows behind him, imitating him.*]

ANNE. We are now in what is known as the "bean cycle." Beans boiled, beans en casserole, beans with strings, beans without strings . . .

[PETER *has come out of his room. He slides into his place at the table, becoming immediately absorbed in his studies.*]

MR. VAN DAAN. [*To* PETER] I saw you . . . in there, playing with your cat.

MRS. VAN DAAN. He just went in for a second, putting his coat away. He's been out here all the time, doing his lessons.

MR. FRANK. [*Looking up from the papers*] Anne, you got an excellent in your history paper today . . . and very good in Latin.

ANNE. [*Sitting beside him*] How about algebra?

MR. FRANK. I'll have to make a confession. Up until now I've managed to stay ahead of you in algebra. Today you caught up with me. We'll leave it to Margot to correct.

ANNE. Isn't algebra *vile,* Pim!

MR. FRANK. Vile!

MARGOT. [*To* MR. FRANK] How did I do?

ANNE. [*Getting up*] Excellent, excellent, excellent, excellent!

MR. FRANK. [*To* MARGOT] You should have used the subjunctive[20] here . . .

MARGOT. Should I? . . . I thought . . . look here . . . I didn't use it here . . .

[*The two become absorbed in the papers.*]

ANNE. Mrs. Van Daan, may I try on your coat?

MRS. FRANK. No, Anne.

MRS. VAN DAAN. [*Giving it to* ANNE] It's all right . . . but careful with it.

[ANNE *puts it on and struts with it.*]

My father gave me that the year before he died. He always bought the best that money could buy.

ANNE. Mrs. Van Daan, did you have a lot of boy friends before you were married?

MRS. FRANK. Anne, that's a personal question. It's not courteous to ask personal questions.

MRS. VAN DAAN. Oh I don't mind. [*To* ANNE] Our house was always swarming with boys. When I was a girl we had . . .

---

19. ack-ack (ak′ ak′) *n.*: Slang for an antiaircraft gun's fire.

20. subjunctive (səb juŋk′ tiv) *n.*: A particular form of a verb.

MR. VAN DAAN. Oh, God. Not again!

MRS. VAN DAAN. [*Good-humored*] Shut up!

[*Without a pause, to* ANNE. MR. VAN DAAN *mimics* MRS. VAN DAAN. *speaking the first few words in unison with her.*]

One summer we had a big house in Hilversum. The boys came buzzing round like bees around a jam pot. And when I was sixteen! . . . We were wearing our skirts very short those days and I had good-looking legs. [*She pulls up her skirt, going to* MR. FRANK.] I still have 'em. I may not be as pretty as I used to be, but I still have my legs. How about it, Mr. Frank?

MR. VAN DAAN. All right. All right. We see them.

MRS. VAN DAAN. I'm not asking you. I'm asking Mr. Frank.

PETER. Mother, for heaven's sake.

MRS. VAN DAAN. Oh, I embarrass you, do I? Well, I just hope the girl you marry has as good. [*Then to* ANNE] My father used to worry about me, with so many boys hanging round. He told me, if any of them gets fresh, you say to him . . . "Remember, Mr. So-and-So, remember I'm a lady."

ANNE. "Remember, Mr. So-and-So, remember I'm a lady." [*She gives* MRS. VAN DAAN *her coat.*]

MR. VAN DAAN. Look at you, talking that way in front of her! Don't you know she puts it all down in that diary?

MRS. VAN DAAN. So, if she does? I'm only telling the truth!

[ANNE *stretches out, putting her ear to the floor, listening to what is going on below. The sound of the bombers fades away.*]

MRS. FRANK. [*Setting the table*] Would you mind, Peter, if I moved you over to the couch?

ANNE. [*Listening*] Miep must have the radio on.

[PETER *picks up his papers, going over to the couch beside* MRS. VAN DAAN.]

MR. VAN DAAN. [*Accusingly, to* PETER] Haven't you finished yet?

PETER. No.

MR. VAN DAAN. You ought to be ashamed of yourself.

PETER. All right. All right. I'm a dunce. I'm a hopeless case. Why do I go on?

MRS. VAN DAAN. You're not hopeless. Don't talk that way. It's just that you haven't anyone to help you, like the girls have. [*To* MR. FRANK] Maybe you could help him, Mr. Frank?

MR. FRANK. I'm sure that his father . . . ?

MR. VAN DAAN. Not me. I can't do anything with him. He won't listen to me. You go ahead . . . if you want.

MR. FRANK. [*Going to* PETER] What about it, Peter? Shall we make our school coeducational?

MRS. VAN DAAN. [*Kissing* MR. FRANK] You're an angel, Mr. Frank. An angel. I don't know why I didn't meet you before I met that one there. Here, sit down, Mr. Frank . . . [*She forces him down on the couch beside* PETER.] Now, Peter, you listen to Mr. Frank.

MR. FRANK. It might be better for us to go into Peter's room.

[PETER *jumps up eagerly, leading the way.*]

MRS. VAN DAAN. That's right. You go in there, Peter. You listen to Mr. Frank. Mr. Frank is a highly educated man.

[*As* MR. FRANK *is about to follow* PETER *into his room,* MRS. FRANK *stops him and wipes the lipstick from his lips. Then she closes the door after them.*]

ANNE. [*On the floor, listening*] Shh! I can hear a man's voice talking.

MR. VAN DAAN. [*To* ANNE] Isn't it bad enough here without your sprawling all over the place?

[ANNE *sits up.*]

MRS. VAN DAAN. [*To* MR. VAN DAAN] If you didn't smoke so much, you wouldn't be so bad-tempered.

MR. VAN DAAN. Am I smoking? Do you see me smoking?

MRS. VAN DAAN. Don't tell me you've used up all those cigarettes.

MR. VAN DAAN. One package. Miep only brought me one package.

MRS. VAN DAAN. It's a filthy habit anyway. It's a good time to break yourself.

MR. VAN DAAN. Oh, stop it, please.

MRS. VAN DAAN. You're smoking up all our money. You know that, don't you?

MR. VAN DAAN. Will you shut up?

[*During this,* MRS. FRANK *and* MARGOT *have studiously kept their eyes down. But* ANNE, *seated on the floor, has been following the discussion interestedly.* MR. VAN DAAN *turns to see her staring up at him.*]

And what are you staring at?

ANNE. I never heard grownups quarrel before. I thought only children quarreled.

MR. VAN DAAN. This isn't a quarrel! It's a discussion. And I never heard children so rude before.

ANNE. [*Rising, indignantly*] *I,* rude!

MR. VAN DAAN. Yes!

MRS. FRANK. [*Quickly*] Anne, will you get me my knitting?

[ANNE *goes to get it.*]

I must remember, when Miep comes, to ask her to bring me some more wool. 19

MARGOT. [*Going to her room*] I need some hairpins and some soap. I made a list. [*She goes into her bedroom to get the list.*]

MRS. FRANK. [*To* ANNE] Have you some library books for Miep when she comes?

ANNE. It's a wonder that Miep has a life of her own, the way we make her run errands for us. Please, Miep, get me some starch. Please take my hair out and have it cut. Tell me all the latest news, Miep. [*She goes over, kneeling on the couch beside* MRS. VAN DAAN] Did you know she was engaged? His name is Dirk, and Miep's afraid the Nazis will ship him off to Germany to work in one of their war plants. That's what they're doing with some of the young Dutchmen . . . they pick them up off the streets—

MR. VAN DAAN. [*Interrupting*] Don't you ever get tired of talking? Suppose you try keeping still for five minutes. Just five minutes.

[*He starts to pace again. Again* ANNE *follows him, mimicking him.* MRS. FRANK *jumps up and takes her by the arm up to the sink, and gives her a glass of milk.*]

MRS. FRANK. Come here, Anne. It's time for your glass of milk.

MR. VAN DAAN. Talk, talk, talk. I never heard such a child. Where is my . . . ? Every eve-

18 **Discussion** What effect has living in hiding begun to have on the people?

19 **Discussion** What effect does Mrs. Frank have on the quarrel?

20 Discussion Discuss how Anne is still able to fantasize and plan for the future. What does this show about her character?

ning it's the same talk, talk, talk. [*He looks around.*] Where is my . . . ?

MRS. VAN DAAN. What're you looking for?

MR. VAN DAAN. My pipe. Have you seen my pipe?

MRS. VAN DAAN. What good's a pipe? You haven't got any tobacco.

MR. VAN DAAN. At least I'll have something to hold in my mouth! [*Opening* MARGOT'S *bedroom door*] Margot, have you seen my pipe?

MARGOT. It was on the table last night.

[ANNE *puts her glass of milk on the table and picks up his pipe, hiding it behind her back.*]

MR. VAN DAAN. I know. I know. Anne, did you see my pipe? . . . Anne!

MRS. FRANK. Anne, Mr. Van Daan is speaking to you.

ANNE. Am I allowed to talk now?

MR. VAN DAAN. You're the most aggravating . . . The trouble with you is, you've been spoiled. What you need is a good old-fashioned spanking.

ANNE. [*Mimicking* MRS. VAN DAAN] "Remember, Mr. So-and-So, remember I'm a lady." [*She thrusts the pipe into his mouth, then picks up her glass of milk.*]

MR. VAN DAAN. [*Restraining himself with difficulty*] Why aren't you nice and quiet like your sister Margot? Why do you have to show off all the time? Let me give you a little advice, young lady. Men don't like that kind of thing in a girl. You know that? A man likes a girl who'll listen to him once in a while . . . a domestic girl, who'll keep her house shining for her husband . . . who loves to cook and sew and . . .

ANNE. I'd cut my throat first! I'd open my veins! I'm going to be remarkable! I'm going to Paris . . .

MR. VAN DAAN. [*Scoffingly*] Paris!

ANNE. . . . to study music and art.

MR. VAN DAAN. Yeah! Yeah!

ANNE. I'm going to be a famous dancer or singer . . . or something wonderful.

[*She makes a wide gesture, spilling the glass of milk on the fur coat in* MRS. VAN DAAN'S *lap.* MARGOT *rushes quickly over with a towel.* ANNE *tries to brush the milk off with her skirt.*]

MRS. VAN DAAN. Now look what you've done . . . you clumsy little fool! My beautiful fur coat my father gave me . . .

ANNE. I'm so sorry.

MRS. VAN DAAN. What do you care? It isn't yours . . . So go on, ruin it! Do you know what that coat cost? Do you? And now look at it! Look at it!

ANNE. I'm very, very sorry.

MRS. VAN DAAN. I could kill you for this. I could just kill you!

[MRS. VAN DAAN *goes up the stairs, clutching the coat.* MR. VAN DAAN *starts after her.*]

MR. VAN DAAN. Petronella . . . *liefje! Liefje!* . . . Come back . . . the supper . . . come back!

MRS. FRANK. Anne, you must not behave in that way.

ANNE. It was an accident. Anyone can have an accident.

MRS. FRANK. I don't mean that. I mean the answering back. You must not answer back. They are our guests. We must always show the greatest courtesy to them. We're all living under terrible tension.

[*She stops as* MARGOT *indicates that* VAN DAAN *can hear. When he is gone, she continues.*]

That's why we must control ourselves . . . You don't hear Margot getting into arguments with them, do you? Watch Margot. She's always courteous with them. Never familiar. She keeps her distance. And they respect her for it. Try to be like Margot.

1

ANNE. And have them walk all over me, the way they do her? No, thanks!

MRS. FRANK. I'm not afraid that anyone is going to walk all over you, Anne. I'm afraid for other people, that you'll walk on them. I don't know what happens to you, Anne. You are wild, self-willed. If I had ever talked to my mother as you talk to me . . .

ANNE. Things have changed. People aren't like that any more. "Yes, Mother." "No, Mother." "Anything you say, Mother." I've got to fight things out for myself! Make something of myself!

MRS. FRANK. It isn't necessary to fight to do it. Margot doesn't fight, and isn't she . . . ?

ANNE. [*Violently rebellious*] Margot! Margot! Margot! That's all I hear from everyone . . . how wonderful Margot is . . . "Why aren't you like Margot?"

2

MARGOT. [*Protesting*] Oh, come on, Anne, don't be so . . .

ANNE. [*Paying no attention*] Everything she does is right, and everything I do is wrong! I'm the goat around here! . . . You're all against me! . . . And you worst of all!

[*She rushes off into her room and throws herself down on the settee, stifling her sobs.* MRS. FRANK *sighs and starts toward the stove.*]

MRS. FRANK. [*To* MARGOT] Let's put the soup on the stove . . . if there's anyone who cares to eat. Margot, will you take the bread out?

[MARGOT *gets the bread from the cupboard.*]

I don't know how we can go on living this way . . . I can't say a word to Anne . . . she flies at me . . .

MARGOT. You know Anne. In half an hour she'll be out here, laughing and joking.

MRS. FRANK. And . . . [*She makes a motion upwards, indicating the* VAN DAANS.] . . . I told your father it wouldn't work . . . but no . . . no . . . he had to ask them, he said . . . he owed it to him, he said. Well, he knows now that I was right! These quarrels! . . . This bickering!

MARGOT. [*With a warning look*] Shush. Shush.

[*The buzzer for the door sounds.* MRS. FRANK *gasps, startled.*]

MRS. FRANK. Every time I hear that sound, my heart stops!

MARGOT. [*Starting for* PETER'S *door*] It's Miep. [*She knocks at the door.*] Father?

[MR. FRANK *comes quickly from* PETER'S *room.*]

MR. FRANK. Thank you, Margot. [*As he goes down the steps to open the outer door*] Has everyone his list?

MARGOT. I'll get my books. [*Giving her mother a list*] Here's your list.

[MARGOT *goes into her and* ANNE'S *bedroom on the right.* ANNE *sits up, hiding her tears, as* MARGOT *comes in.*]

Miep's here.

[MARGOT *picks up her books and goes back.* ANNE *hurries over to the mirror, smoothing her hair.*]

21 Discussion Compare and contrast how Mrs. Frank views each of her daughters.

22 Discussion How does Anne feel about Margot? How does she feel she compares to Margot?

Aerial view of Amsterdam, Holland. The house where Anne Frank hid is tinted

MR. VAN DAAN. [*Coming down the stairs*] Is it Miep?

MARGOT. Yes. Father's gone down to let her in.

MR. VAN DAAN. At last I'll have some cigarettes!

MRS. FRANK. [*To* MR. VAN DAAN] I can't tell you how unhappy I am about Mrs. Van Daan's coat. Anne should never have touched it.

MR. VAN DAAN. She'll be all right.

MRS. FRANK. Is there anything I can do?

MR. VAN DAAN. Don't worry.

[*He turns to meet* MIEP. *But it is not* MIEP *who comes up the steps. It is* MR. KRALER, *followed by* MR. FRANK. *Their faces are grave.* ANNE *comes from the bedroom.* PETER *comes from his room.*]

MRS. FRANK. Mr. Kraler!

MR. VAN DAAN. How are you, Mr. Kraler?

MARGOT. This is a surprise.

MRS. FRANK. When Mr. Kraler comes, the sun begins to shine.

MR. VAN DAAN. Miep is coming?

MR. KRALER. Not tonight.

[KRALER *goes to* MARGOT *and* MRS. FRANK *and* ANNE, *shaking hands with them.*]

MRS. FRANK. Wouldn't you like a cup of coffee? . . . Or, better still, will you have supper with us?

MR. FRANK. Mr. Kraler has something to talk over with us. Something has happened, he says, which demands an immediate decision.

MRS. FRANK. [*Fearful*] What is it?

[MR. KRALER *sits down on the couch. As he talks he takes bread, cabbages, milk, etc., from his briefcase, giving them to* MARGOT *and* ANNE *to put away.*]

MR. KRALER. Usually, when I come up here, I try to bring you some bit of good news. What's the use of telling you the bad news when there's nothing that you can do about it? But today something has happened . . . Dirk . . . Miep's Dirk, you know, came to me just now. He tells me that he has a Jewish friend living near him. A dentist. He says he's in trouble. He begged me, could I do anything for this man? Could I find him a hiding place? . . . So I've come to you . . . I know it's a terrible thing to ask of you, living as you are, but would you take him in with you?

MR. FRANK. Of course we will.

MR. KRALER. [*Rising*] It'll be just for a night or two . . . until I find some other place. This happened so suddenly that I didn't know where to turn.

MR. FRANK. Where is he?

MR. KRALER. Downstairs in the office.

MR. FRANK. Good. Bring him up.

MR. KRALER. His name is Dussel . . . Jan Dussel.

MR. FRANK. Dussel . . . I think I know him.

MR. KRALER. I'll get him.

[*He goes quickly down the steps and out.* MR. FRANK *suddenly becomes conscious of the others.*]

MR. FRANK. Forgive me. I spoke without consulting you. But I knew you'd feel as I do.

MR. VAN DAAN. There's no reason for you to consult anyone. This is your place. You have a right to do exactly as you please. The only thing I feel . . . there's so little food as it is . . . and to take in another person . . . 23

[PETER *turns away, ashamed of his father.*]

MR. FRANK. We can stretch the food a little. It's only for a few days.

MR. VAN DAAN. You want to make a bet?

MRS. FRANK. I think it's fine to have him. But, Otto, where are you going to put him? Where?

PETER. He can have my bed. I can sleep on the floor. I wouldn't mind.

MR. FRANK. That's good of you, Peter. But your room's too small . . . even for *you*.

ANNE. I have a much better idea. I'll come in here with you and Mother, and Margot can take Peter's room and Peter can go in our room with Mr. Dussel.

MARGOT. That's right. We could do that.

MR. FRANK. No, Margot. You mustn't sleep in that room . . . neither you nor Anne. Mouschi has caught some rats in there. Peter's brave. He doesn't mind.

ANNE. Then how about *this?* I'll come in here with you and Mother, and Mr. Dussel can have my bed.

MRS. FRANK. No. No. *No!* Margot will come in here with us and he can have her bed. It's the only way. Margot, bring your things in here. Help her, Anne.

[MARGOT *hurries into her room to get her things.*]

ANNE. [*To her mother*] Why Margot? Why can't I come in here?

23 Discussion Contrast Mr. Frank's reaction to another person living with them to Mr. Van Daan's. How does Peter react to his father's reaction?

24 **Clarification** More than any other European country occupied by the Nazis, the Netherlands is remarkable for the resistance shown by her citizens. The Dutch were particularly resentful of the anti-Semitic legislation enacted by Hitler and sought at first to counteract it by open opposition, such as workers' strikes and violent propaganda in print. The sympathizers were finally forced underground where they secretly worked for the destruction of the occupational forces.

MRS. FRANK. Because it wouldn't be proper for Margot to sleep with a . . . Please, Anne. Don't argue. Please.

[ANNE *starts slowly away.*]

MR. FRANK. [*To* ANNE] You don't mind sharing your room with Mr. Dussel, do you, Anne?

ANNE. No. No, of course not.

MR. FRANK. Good.

[ANNE *goes off into her bedroom, helping* MARGOT. MR. FRANK *starts to search in the cupboards.*]

Where's the cognac?

MRS. FRANK. It's there. But, Otto, I was saving it in case of illness.

MR. FRANK. I think we couldn't find a better time to use it. Peter, will you get five glasses for me?

[PETER *goes for the glasses.* MARGOT *comes out of her bedroom, carrying her possessions, which she hangs behind a curtain in the main room.* MR. FRANK *finds the cognac and pours it into the five glasses that* PETER *brings him.* MR. VAN DAAN *stands looking on sourly.* MRS. VAN DAAN *comes downstairs and looks around at all the bustle.*]

MRS. VAN DAAN. What's happening? What's going on?

MR. VAN DAAN. Someone's moving in with us.

MRS. VAN DAAN. In here? You're joking.

MARGOT. It's only for a night or two . . . until Mr. Kraler finds him another place.

MR. VAN DAAN. Yeah! Yeah!

[MR. FRANK *hurries over as* MR. KRALER *and* DUSSEL *come up.* DUSSEL *is a man in his late fifties, meticulous, finicky . . . bewildered now. He wears a raincoat. He carries a briefcase, stuffed full, and a small medicine case.*]

MR. FRANK. Come in, Mr. Dussel.

MR. KRALER. This is Mr. Frank.

DUSSEL. Mr. Otto Frank?

MR. FRANK. Yes. Let me take your things. [*He takes the hat and briefcase, but* DUSSEL *clings to his medicine case.*] This is my wife Edith . . . Mr. and Mrs. Van Daan . . . their son, Peter . . . and my daughters, Margot and Anne.

[DUSSEL *shakes hands with everyone.*]

MR. KRALER. Thank you, Mr. Frank. Thank you all. Mr. Dussel, I leave you in good hands. Oh . . . Dirk's coat.

[DUSSEL *hurriedly takes off the raincoat, giving it to* MR. KRALER. *Underneath is his white dentist's jacket, with a yellow Star of David on it.*]

DUSSEL. [*To* MR. KRALER] What can I say to thank you . . . ?

MRS. FRANK. [*To* DUSSEL] Mr. Kraler and Miep . . . They're our life line. Without them we couldn't live.

MR. KRALER. Please. Please. You make us seem very heroic. It isn't that at all. We simply don't like the Nazis. [*To* MR. FRANK, *who offers him a drink*] No, thanks. [*Then going on*] We don't like their methods. We don't like . . .

MR. FRANK. [*Smiling*] I know. I know. "No one's going to tell us Dutchmen what to do with our damn Jews!" 24

MR. KRALER. [*To* DUSSEL] Pay no attention to Mr. Frank. I'll be up tomorrow to see that they're treating you right. [*To* MR. FRANK] Don't trouble to come down again. Peter will bolt the door after me, won't you, Peter?

PETER. Yes, sir.

MR. FRANK. Thank you, Peter. I'll do it.

MR. KRALER. Good night. Good night.

GROUP. Good night, Mr. Kraler. We'll see you tomorrow, etc., etc.

[MR. KRALER *goes out with* MR. FRANK, MRS. FRANK *gives each one of the "grownups" a glass of cognac.*]

MRS. FRANK. Please, Mr. Dussel, sit down.

[MR. DUSSEL *sinks into a chair.* MRS. FRANK *gives him a glass of cognac.*]

DUSSEL. I'm dreaming. I know it. I can't believe my eyes. Mr. Otto Frank here! [*To* MRS. FRANK] You're not in Switzerland then? A woman told me . . . She said she'd gone to your house . . . the door was open, everything was in disorder, dishes in the sink. She said she found a piece of paper in the wastebasket with an address scribbled on it . . . an address in Zurich. She said you must have escaped to Zurich.

ANNE. Father put that there purposely . . . just so people would think that very thing!

DUSSEL. And you've been *here* all the time?

MRS. FRANK. All the time . . . ever since July.

[ANNE *speaks to her father as he comes back.*]

ANNE. It worked, Pim . . . the address you left! Mr. Dussel says that people believe we escaped to Switzerland.

MR. FRANK. I'm glad. . . . And now let's have a little drink to welcome Mr. Dussel.

[*Before they can drink,* MR. DUSSEL *bolts his drink.* MR. FRANK *smiles and raises his glass.*]

To Mr. Dussel. Welcome. We're very honored to have you with us.

MRS. FRANK. To Mr. Dussel, welcome.

[*The* VAN DAANS *murmur a welcome. The "grownups" drink.*]

MRS. VAN DAAN. Um. That was good.

MR. VAN DAAN. Did Mr. Kraler warn you that you won't get much to eat here? You can imagine . . . three ration books among the seven of us . . . and now you make eight.

[PETER *walks away, humiliated. Outside a street organ is heard dimly.*]

DUSSEL. [*Rising*] Mr. Van Daan, you don't realize what is happening outside that you should warn me of a thing like that. You don't realize what's going on . . .

[*As* MR. VAN DAAN *starts his characteristic pacing,* DUSSEL *turns to speak to the others.*]

Right here in Amsterdam every day hundreds of Jews disappear . . . They surround a block and search house by house. Children come home from school to find their parents gone. Hundreds are being deported . . . people that you and I know . . . the Hallensteins . . . the Wessels . . .

MRS. FRANK. [*In tears*] Oh, no. No!

DUSSEL. They get their call-up notice . . . come to the Jewish theater on such and such a day and hour . . . bring only what you can carry in a rucksack. And if you refuse the call-up notice, then they come and drag you from your home and ship you off to Mauthausen.[21] The death camp!

MRS. FRANK. We didn't know that things had got so much worse.

DUSSEL. Forgive me for speaking so.

---

21. Mauthausen (mou tou' zən): A village in Austria that was the site of a Nazi concentration camp.

25 Critical Thinking and Reading Contrast Mr. Dussel's report of life in Holland to that of Mr. Kraler's.

Dr. Albert Dussel

ANNE. [*Coming to* DUSSEL] Do you know the de Waals? . . . What's become of them? Their daughter Jopie and I are in the same class. Jopie's my best friend.

DUSSEL. They are gone.

ANNE. Gone?

DUSSEL. With all the others.

ANNE. Oh, no. Not Jopie!

[*She turns away, in tears.* MRS. FRANK *motions to* MARGOT *to comfort her.* MARGOT *goes to* ANNE, *putting her arms comfortingly around her.*]

MRS. VAN DAAN. There were some people called Wagner. They lived near us . . . ?

MR. FRANK. [*Interrupting, with a glance at* ANNE] I think we should put this off until later. We all have many questions we want to ask . . . But I'm sure that Mr. Dussel would like to get settled before supper.

DUSSEL. Thank you. I would. I brought very little with me.

MR. FRANK. [*Giving him his hat and briefcase*] I'm sorry we can't give you a room alone. But I hope you won't be too uncomfortable. We've had to make strict rules here . . . a schedule of hours . . . We'll tell you after supper. Anne, would you like to take Mr. Dussel to his room?

ANNE. [*Controlling her tears*] If you'll come with me, Mr. Dussel? [*She starts for her room.*]

DUSSEL. [*Shaking hands with each in turn*] Forgive me if I haven't really expressed my gratitude to all of you. This has been such a shock to me. I'd always thought of myself as Dutch. I was born in Holland. My father was born in Holland, and my grandfather. And now . . . after all these years . . . [*He breaks off.*] If you'll excuse me.

[DUSSEL *gives a little bow and hurries off after* ANNE. MR. FRANK *and the others are subdued.*]

ANNE. [*Turning on the light*] Well, here we are.

[DUSSEL *looks around the room. In the main room* MARGOT *speaks to her mother.*]

MARGOT. The news sounds pretty bad, doesn't it? It's so different from what Mr. Kraler tells us. Mr. Kraler says things are improving. 25

MR. VAN DAAN. I like it better the way Kraler tells it.

[*They resume their occupations, quietly.* PETER *goes off into his room. In* ANNE'S *room,* ANNE *turns to* DUSSEL.]

ANNE. You're going to share the room with me.

DUSSEL. I'm a man who's always lived alone. I haven't had to adjust myself to others. I hope you'll bear with me until I learn.

ANNE. Let me help you. [*She takes his brief-case.*] Do you always live all alone? Have you no family at all?

DUSSEL. No one. [*He opens his medicine case and spreads his bottles on the dressing table.*]

ANNE. How dreadful. You must be terribly lonely.

DUSSEL. I'm used to it.

ANNE. I don't think I could ever get used to it. Didn't you even have a pet? A cat, or a dog?

DUSSEL. I have an allergy for fur-bearing animals. They give me asthma.

ANNE. Oh, dear. Peter has a cat.

DUSSEL. Here? He has it here?

ANNE. Yes. But we hardly ever see it. He keeps it in his room all the time. I'm sure it will be all right.

DUSSEL. Let us hope so. [*He takes some pills to fortify himself.*]

ANNE. That's Margot's bed, where you're going to sleep. I sleep on the sofa there. [*Indicating the clothes hooks on the wall*] We cleared these off for your things. [*She goes over to the window.*] The best part about this room . . . you can look down and see a bit of the street and the canal. There's a houseboat . . . you can see the end of it . . . a bargeman lives there with his family . . . They have a baby and he's just beginning to walk and I'm so afraid he's going to fall into the canal some day. I watch him. . . .

DUSSEL. [*Interrupting*] Your father spoke of a schedule.

ANNE. [*Coming away from the window*] Oh, yes. It's mostly about the times we have to be quiet. And times for the w.c. You can use it now if you like.

DUSSEL. [*Stiffly*] No, thank you.

ANNE. I suppose you think it's awful, my talking about a thing like that. But you don't know how important it can get to be, especially when you're frightened . . . About this room, the way Margot and I did . . . she had it to herself in the afternoons for studying, reading . . . lessons, you know . . . and I took the mornings. Would that be all right with you?

DUSSEL. I'm not at my best in the morning.

ANNE. You stay here in the mornings then. I'll take the room in the afternoons.

DUSSEL. Tell me, when you're in here, what happens to me? Where am I spending my time? In there, with all the people?

ANNE. Yes.

DUSSEL. I see. I see.

ANNE. We have supper at half past six.

DUSSEL. [*Going over to the sofa*] Then, if you don't mind . . . I like to lie down quietly for ten minutes before eating. I find it helps the digestion.

ANNE. Of course. I hope I'm not going to be too much of a bother to you. I seem to be able to get everyone's back up.

26 **Discussion** How does Anne react to Mr. Dussel's statement about having no family?

27 **Discussion** Have students note how Anne can occupy herself with life outside the attic. What does this show about Anne's character?

28 Reading Strategy Have students summarize the play up to this point and predict how Anne and Mr. Dussel will get along.

29 Literary Focus Explain that the reader knows the thoughts and feelings of only Anne, the main character. The reader does not know what Mr. Dussel thinks or feels. Instead, the reader learns about Mr. Dussel only by what he says or does and by what Anne thinks of him. What do Anne's thoughts tell you about Mr. Dussel?

[DUSSEL *lies down on the sofa, curled up, his back to her.*]

28 **DUSSEL.** I always get along very well with children. My patients all bring their children to me, because they know I get on well with them. So don't you worry about that.

[ANNE *leans over him, taking his hand and shaking it gratefully.*]

ANNE. Thank you. Thank you, Mr. Dussel.

[*The lights dim to darkness. The curtain falls on the scene.* ANNE'S VOICE *comes to us faintly at first, and then with increasing power.*]

29 **ANNE'S VOICE.** . . . And yesterday I finished Cissy Van Marxvelt's latest book. I think she is a first-class writer. I shall definitely let my children read her. Monday the twenty-first of September, nineteen forty-two. Mr. Dussel and I had another battle yesterday. Yes, Mr. Dussel! According to him, nothing, I repeat . . . nothing, is right about me . . . my appearance, my character, my manners. While he was going on at me I thought . . . sometime I'll give you such a smack that you'll fly right up to the ceiling! Why is it that every grownup thinks he knows the way to bring up children? Particularly the grownups that never had any. I keep wishing that Peter was a girl instead of a boy. Then I would have someone to talk to. Margot's a darling, but she takes everything too seriously. To pause for a moment on the subject of Mrs. Van Daan. I must tell you that her attempts to flirt with father are getting her nowhere. Pim, thank goodness, won't play.

[*As she is saying the last lines, the curtain rises on the darkened scene.* ANNE'S VOICE *fades out.*]

Scene 4

[*It is the middle of the night, several months later. The stage is dark except for a little light which comes through the skylight in* PETER'S *room.*

Everyone is in bed. MR. *and* MRS. FRANK *lie on the couch in the main room, which has been pulled out to serve as a makeshift double bed.*

MARGOT *is sleeping on a mattress on the floor in the main room, behind a curtain stretched across for privacy. The others are all in their accustomed rooms.*

From outside we hear two drunken soldiers singing "Lili Marlene." *A girl's high giggle is heard. The sound of running feet is heard coming closer and then fading in the distance. Throughout the scene there is the distant sound of airplanes passing overhead.*

A match suddenly flares up in the attic. We dimly see MR. VAN DAAN. *He is getting his bearings. He comes quickly down the stairs, and goes to the cupboard where the food is stored. Again the match flares up, and is as quickly blown out. The dim figure is seen to steal back up the stairs.*

There is quiet for a second or two, broken only by the sound of airplanes, and running feet on the street below.

Suddenly, out of the silence and the dark, we hear ANNE *scream.*]

ANNE. [*Screaming*] No! No! Don't . . . don't take me!

[*She moans, tossing and crying in her sleep. The other people wake, terrified.* DUSSEL *sits up in bed, furious.*]

DUSSEL. Shush! Anne! Anne, for God's sake, shush!

ANNE. [*Still in her nightmare*] Save me! Save me!

Grammar in Action

An **imperative sentence** gives an order or a direction and ends with either a period or an exclamation mark. Most imperative sentences begin with a verb. When imperative sentences begin with a verb and have no subject, the understood subject is *you*. However, sometimes imperative sentences have subjects. When they do, they sound like questions. But unlike questions, they end with a period or exclamation mark instead of a question mark. The subject in the following imperative sentence is somebody: "Will somebody answer the phone!"

Imperative sentences in The Diary of Anne Frank reinforce the sense of urgency in the play. Notice that the understood subject of each of the following imperative sentences from the play is *you*. You should also see the sense of urgency in these lines.

ANNE. No! No! Don't . . . don't take me!
DUSSEL. Shush! Anne! Anne, for God's sake, shush!
ANNE. [Still in her nightmare] Save me! Save me!
DUSSEL. Quiet! Quiet! You want someone to hear?

Imperative sentences are recognizable because they give orders or directions.

[*She screams and screams.* DUSSEL *gets out of bed, going over to her, trying to wake her.*]

DUSSEL. For God's sake! Quiet! Quiet! You want someone to hear?

[*In the main room* MRS. FRANK *grabs a shawl and pulls it around her. She rushes in to* ANNE, *taking her in her arms.* MR. FRANK *hurriedly gets up, putting on his overcoat.* MARGOT *sits up, terrified.* PETER'S *light goes on in his room.*]

MRS. FRANK. [*To* ANNE, *in her room*] Hush, darling, hush. It's all right. It's all right. [*Over her shoulder to* DUSSEL] Will you be kind enough to turn on the light, Mr. Dussel? [*Back to* ANNE] It's nothing, my darling. It was just a dream.

[DUSSEL *turns on the light in the bedroom.* MRS. FRANK *holds* ANNE *in her arms. Gradually* ANNE *comes out of her nightmare still trembling with horror.* MR. FRANK *comes into the room, and goes quickly to the window, looking out to be sure that no one outside has heard* ANNE'S *screams.* MRS. FRANK *holds* ANNE, *talking softly to her. In the main room* MARGOT *stands on a chair, turning on the center hanging lamp. A light goes on in the* VAN DAANS' *room overhead.* PETER *puts his robe on, coming out of his room.*]

DUSSEL. [*To* MRS. FRANK, *blowing his nose*] Something must be done about that child, Mrs. Frank. Yelling like that! Who knows but there's somebody on the streets? She's endangering all our lives.

MRS. FRANK. Anne, darling.

DUSSEL. Every night she twists and turns. I don't sleep. I spend half my night shushing her. And now it's nightmares!

[MARGOT *comes to the door of* ANNE'S *room, followed by* PETER. MR. FRANK *goes to them, indicating that everything is all right.* PETER *takes* MARGOT *back.*]

MRS. FRANK. [*To* ANNE] You're here, safe, you see? Nothing has happened. [*To* DUSSEL] Please, Mr. Dussel, go back to bed. She'll be herself in a minute or two. Won't you, Anne?

DUSSEL. [*Picking up a book and a pillow*] Thank you, but I'm going to the w.c. The one place where there's peace!

[*He stalks out.* MR. VAN DAAN, *in underwear and trousers, comes down the stairs.*]

MR. VAN DAAN. [*To* DUSSEL] What is it? What happened?

DUSSEL. A nightmare. She was having a nightmare!

MR. VAN DAAN. I thought someone was murdering her.

DUSSEL. Unfortunately, no.

[*He goes into the bathroom.* MR. VAN DAAN *goes back up the stairs.* MR. FRANK, *in the main room, sends* PETER *back to his own bedroom.*]

MR. FRANK. Thank you, Peter. Go back to bed.

[PETER *goes back to his room.* MR. FRANK *follows him, turning out the light and looking out the window. Then he goes back to the main room, and gets up on a chair, turning out the center hanging lamp.*]

MRS. FRANK. [*To* ANNE] Would you like some water? [ANNE *shakes her head.*] Was it a very bad dream? Perhaps if you told me . . . ?

ANNE. I'd rather not talk about it. 31

MRS. FRANK. Poor darling. Try to sleep then. I'll sit right here beside you until you fall.

30 Literary Focus What do Mr. Dussel's speech and actions tell you about him? Is Anne's opinion of him justified? Point out that, although we see the characters from Anne's point of view, the very revealing nature of the dialogue itself attests to the validity of the narrator's opinion.

31 Discussion How does Anne feel toward her mother? What was her mother's reaction toward Anne?

Student Activity 1. Find five more imperative sentences from the play. Explain what makes them imperative.

Student Activity 2. Imagine that you are directing a scene from The Diary of Anne Frank. Write stage directions and directions for characters. Use imperative sentences in your directions.

asleep. [*She brings a stool over, sitting there.*]

ANNE. You don't have to.

MRS. FRANK. But I'd like to stay with you . . . very much. Really.

ANNE. I'd rather you didn't.

MRS. FRANK. Good night, then.

[*She leans down to kiss* ANNE. ANNE *throws her arm up over her face, turning away.* MRS. FRANK, *hiding her hurt, kisses* ANNE'S *arm.*]

You'll be all right? There's nothing that you want?

ANNE. Will you please ask Father to come.

MRS. FRANK. [*After a second*] Of course, Anne dear.

[*She hurries out into the other room.* MR. FRANK *comes to her as she comes in.*]

Sie verlangt nach Dir![22]

MR. FRANK. [*Sensing her hurt*] Edith, *Liebe, schau . . .*[23]

MRS. FRANK. *Es macht nichts! Ich danke dem lieben Herrgott, dass sie sich wenigstens an Dich wendet, wenn sie Trost braucht! Geh hinein, Otto, sie ist ganz hysterisch vor Angst.*[24] [*As* MR. FRANK *hesitates*] *Geh zu ihr.*[25]

[*He looks at her for a second and then goes to get a cup of water for* ANNE. MRS. FRANK *sinks down on the bed, her face in her hands, trying to keep from sobbing aloud.* MARGOT *comes over to her, putting her arms around her.*]

She wants nothing of me. She pulled away when I leaned down to kiss her.

MARGOT. It's a phase . . . You heard Father . . . Most girls go through it . . . they turn to their fathers at this age . . . they give all their love to their fathers.

MRS. FRANK. You weren't like this. You didn't shut me out.

MARGOT. She'll get over it . . .

[*She smooths the bed for* MRS. FRANK *and sits beside her a moment as* MRS. FRANK *lies down. In* ANNE'S *room* MR. FRANK *comes in, sitting down by* ANNE. ANNE *flings her arms around him, clinging to him. In the distance we hear the sound of ack-ack.*]

ANNE. Oh, Pim. I dreamed that they came to get us! The Green Police! They broke down the door and grabbed me and started to drag me out the way they did Jopie.

MR. FRANK. I want you to take this pill.

ANNE. What is it?

MR. FRANK. Something to quiet you.

[*She takes it and drinks the water. In the main room* MARGOT *turns out the light and goes back to her bed.*]

MR. FRANK. [*To* ANNE] Do you want me to read to you for a while?

ANNE. No. Just sit with me for a minute. Was I awful? Did I yell terribly loud? Do you think anyone outside could have heard?

---

22. *Sie verlangt nach Dir* (sē fer′ läŋt′ näk dir′): German for "She is asking for you."
23. *Liebe, schau* (lē′ bə′ shou): German for "Dear, look."
24. *Es macht . . . vor Angst* (es mäkt nichts ich dän′ kə dəm lē′ bən här′ gôt däs sē sich ven ig stəns än dish ven′ dət ven sē träst broukt gē hē nīn ät tō sē ist gänz hi ste′ rik fär äŋst): German for "It's all right. I thank dear God that at least she turns to you when she needs comfort. Go in, Otto, she is hysterical because of fear."
25. *Geh zu ihr* (gē tsoo ēr): German for "Go to her."

MR. FRANK. No. No. Lie quietly now. Try to sleep.

ANNE. I'm a terrible coward. I'm so disappointed in myself. I think I've conquered my fear . . . I think I'm really grown-up . . . and then something happens . . . and I run to you like a baby . . . I love you, Father. I don't love anyone but you.

MR. FRANK. [*Reproachfully*] Annele!

ANNE. It's true. I've been thinking about it for a long time. You're the only one I love.

MR. FRANK. It's fine to hear you tell me that you love me. But I'd be happier if you said you loved your mother as well . . . She needs your help so much . . . your love . . .

ANNE. We have nothing in common. She doesn't understand me. Whenever I try to explain my views on life to her she asks me if I'm constipated. 32

MR. FRANK. You hurt her very much just now. She's crying. She's in there crying.

ANNE. I can't help it. I only told the truth. I didn't want her here . . . [*Then, with sud-*

32 Discussion What does Mr. Frank feel is his role as a parent? How does Anne feel about showing her true self? How does she feel people will perceive her?

Scene along a canal in Amsterdam after a bombing raid

33 Enrichment Note the first thing that each person would want after the war. Ask students what would be the first thing they would want after being in hiding for four months.

34 Clarifications Explain the story of Hanukkah. The Hebrew word *hanukkah* means dedication. Hanukkah is a celebration of God's deliverance of the Jews in 165 B.C. That year, the Jews won their first struggle for religious freedom by defeating the Syrians, who wanted them to give up Judaism. The Jews held festivities in the temple in Jerusalem, and rededicated it to God. After cleaning the temple of Syrian idols, they found only one small container of oil with which to light their holy lamps. But miraculously, the container provided them with oil for eight days.

den change] Oh, Pim, I was horrible, wasn't I? And the worst of it is, I can stand off and look at myself doing it and know it's cruel and yet I can't stop doing it. What's the matter with me? Tell me. Don't say it's just a phase! Help me.

MR. FRANK. There is so little that we parents can do to help our children. We can only try to set a good example . . . point the way. The rest you must do yourself. You must build your own character.

ANNE. I'm trying. Really I am. Every night I think back over all of the things I did that day that were wrong . . . like putting the wet mop in Mr. Dussel's bed . . . and this thing now with Mother. I say to myself, that was wrong. I make up my mind, I'm never going to do that again. Never! Of course I may do something worse . . . but at least I'll never do *that* again! . . . I have a nicer side, Father . . . a sweeter, nicer side. But I'm scared to show it. I'm afraid that people are going to laugh at me if I'm serious. So the mean Anne comes to the outside and the good Anne stays on the inside, and I keep on trying to switch them around and have the good Anne outside and the bad Anne inside and be what I'd like to be . . . and might be . . . if only . . . only . . .

[*She is asleep.* MR. FRANK *watches her for a moment and then turns off the light, and starts out. The lights dim out. The curtain falls on the scene.* ANNE'S VOICE *is heard dimly at first, and then with growing strength.*]

ANNE'S VOICE. . . . The air raids are getting worse. They come over day and night. The noise is terrifying. Pim says it should be music to our ears. The more planes, the sooner will come the end of the war. Mrs. Van Daan pretends to be a fatalist. What will be, will be. But when the planes come over, who is the most frightened? No one else but Petronella! . . . Monday, the ninth of November, nineteen forty-two. Wonderful news! The Allies have landed in Africa. Pim says that we can look for an early finish to the war. Just for fun he asked each of us what was the first thing we wanted to do when we got out of here. Mrs. Van Daan longs to be home with her own things, her needle-point chairs, the Beckstein piano her father gave her . . . the best that money could buy. Peter would like to go to a movie. Mr. Dussel wants to get back to his dentist's drill. He's afraid he is losing his touch. 3
For myself, there are so many things . . . to ride a bike again . . . to laugh till my belly aches . . . to have new clothes from the skin out . . . to have a hot tub filled to overflowing and wallow in it for hours . . . to be back in school with my friends . . .

[*As the last lines are being said, the curtain rises on the scene. The lights dim on as* ANNE'S VOICE *fades away.*]

Scene 5

[*It is the first night of the Hanukkah*[26] *celebration.* MR. FRANK *is standing at the head of the table on which is the Menorah.*[27] *He lights the Shamos,*[28] *or servant candle, and holds it as he says the blessing. Seated*

26. Hanukkah (khä' noo kä') *n.*: A Jewish celebration that lasts eight days.
27. menorah (mə nō' rə) *n.*: A candle holder with nine candles, used during Hanukkah.
28. shamos (shä' məs) *n.*: The candle used to light the others in a menorah.

listening is all of the "family," dressed in their best. The men wear hats, PETER *wears his cap.*]

MR. FRANK. [*Reading from a prayer book*] "Praised be Thou, oh Lord our God, Ruler of the universe, who has sanctified us with Thy commandments and bidden us kindle the Hanukkah lights. Praised be Thou, oh Lord our God, Ruler of the universe, who has wrought wondrous deliverances for our fathers in days of old. Praised be Thou, oh Lord our God, Ruler of the universe, that Thou has given us life and sustenance and brought us to this happy season." [MR. FRANK *lights the one candle of the Menorah as he continues.*] "We kindle this Hanukkah light to celebrate the great and wonderful deeds wrought through the zeal with which God filled the hearts of the heroic Maccabees, two thousand years ago. They fought against indifference, against tyranny and oppression, and they restored our Temple to us. May these lights remind us that we should ever look to God, whence cometh our help." Amen.

ALL. Amen.

[MR. FRANK *hands* MRS. FRANK *the prayer book.*]

MRS. FRANK. [*Reading*] "I lift up mine eyes unto the mountains, from whence cometh my help. My help cometh from the Lord who made heaven and earth. He will not suffer thy foot to be moved. He that keepeth thee will not slumber. He that keepeth Israel doth neither slumber nor sleep. The Lord is thy keeper. The Lord is thy shade upon thy right hand. The sun shall not smite thee by day, nor the moon by night. The Lord shall keep thee from all evil. He shall keep thy soul. The Lord shall guard thy going out and thy coming in, from this time forth and forevermore." Amen.

ALL. Amen.

[MRS. FRANK *puts down the prayer book and goes to get the food and wine.* MARGOT *helps her.* MR. FRANK *takes the men's hats and puts them aside.*]

DUSSEL. [*Rising*] That was very moving.

ANNE. [*Pulling him back*] It isn't over yet!

MRS. VAN DAAN. Sit down! Sit down!

ANNE. There's a lot more, songs and presents.

DUSSEL. Presents?

MRS. FRANK. Not this year, unfortunately.

MRS. VAN DAAN. But always on Hanukkah everyone gives presents . . . everyone!

DUSSEL. Like our St. Nicholas' Day.[29]

[*There is a chorus of "no's" from the group.*]

MRS. VAN DAAN. No! Not like St. Nicholas! What kind of a Jew are you that you don't know Hanukkah?

MRS. FRANK. [*As she brings the food*] I remember particularly the candles . . . First one, as we have tonight. Then the second night you light two candles, the next night three . . . and so on until you have eight candles burning. When there are eight candles it is truly beautiful.

MRS. VAN DAAN. And the potato pancakes.

MR. VAN DAAN. Don't talk about them!

MRS. VAN DAAN. I make the best *latkes* you ever tasted!

---

29. St. Nicholas' Day: December 6, the day Christian children in Holland receive gifts.

MRS. FRANK. Invite us all next year . . . in your own home.

MR. FRANK. God willing!

MRS. VAN DAAN. God willing.

MARGOT. What I remember best is the presents we used to get when we were little . . . eight days of presents . . . and each day they got better and better.

MRS. FRANK. [*Sitting down*] We are all here, alive. That is present enough.

ANNE. No, it isn't. I've got something . . .[*She rushes into her room, hurriedly puts on a little hat improvised from the lamp shade, grabs a satchel bulging with parcels and comes running back.*]

MRS. FRANK. What is it?

ANNE. Presents!

MRS. VAN DAAN. Presents!

DUSSEL. Look!

MR. VAN DAAN. What's she got on her head?

PETER. A lamp shade!

ANNE. [*She picks out one at random.*] This is for Margot. [*She hands it to* MARGOT, *pulling her to her feet.*] Read it out loud.

MARGOT. [*Reading*]
"You have never lost your temper.
You never will, I fear,
You are so good.
But if you should,
Put all your cross words here."

[*She tears open the package.*] A new crossword puzzle book! Where did you get it?

ANNE. It isn't new. It's one that you've done. But I rubbed it all out, and if you wait a little and forget, you can do it all over again.

MARGOT. [*Sitting*] It's wonderful, Anne. Thank you. You'd never know it wasn't new.

[*From outside we hear the sound of a streetcar passing.*]

ANNE. [*With another gift*] Mrs. Van Daan.

MRS. VAN DAAN. [*Taking it*] This is awful . . . I haven't anything for anyone . . . I never thought . . .

MR. FRANK. This is all Anne's idea.

MRS. VAN DAAN. [*Holding up a bottle*] What is it?

ANNE. It's hair shampoo. I took all the odds and ends of soap and mixed them with the last of my toilet water.

MRS. VAN DAAN. Oh, Anneke!

ANNE. I wanted to write a poem for all of them, but I didn't have time. [*Offering a large box to* MR. VAN DAAN] Yours, Mr. Van Daan, is *really* something . . . something you want more than anything. [*As she waits for him to open it*] Look! Cigarettes!

MR. VAN DAAN. Cigarettes!

ANNE. Two of them! Pim found some old pipe tobacco in the pocket lining of his coat . . . and we made them . . . or rather, Pim did.

MRS. VAN DAAN. Let me see . . . Well, look at that! Light it, Putti! Light it.

[MR. VAN DAAN *hesitates.*]

ANNE. It's tobacco, really it is! There's a little fluff in it, but not much.

[*Everyone watches intently as* MR. VAN DAAN *cautiously lights it. The cigarette flares up. Everyone laughs.*]

PETER. It works!

MRS. VAN DAAN. Look at him.

Margot and Anne Frank

MR. VAN DAAN. [*Spluttering*] Thank you, Anne. Thank you.

[ANNE *rushes back to her satchel for another present.*]

ANNE. [*Handing her mother a piece of paper*] For Mother, Hanukkah greeting.

[*She pulls her mother to her feet.*]

MRS. FRANK. [*She reads*]
"Here's an I.O.U. that I promise to pay.
Ten hours of doing whatever you say.
Signed, Anne Frank." [MRS. FRANK, *touched, takes* ANNE *in her arms, holding her close.*]

DUSSEL. [*To* ANNE] Ten hours of doing what you're told? *Anything* you're told?

ANNE. That's right.

DUSSEL. You wouldn't want to sell that, Mrs. Frank?

MRS. FRANK. Never! This is the most precious gift I've ever had!

[*She sits, showing her present to the others.* ANNE *hurries back to the satchel and pulls out a scarf, the scarf that* MR. FRANK *found in the first scene.*]

ANNE. [*Offering it to her father*] For Pim.

MR. FRANK. Anneke . . . I wasn't supposed to have a present! [*He takes it, unfolding it and showing it to the others.*]

ANNE. It's a muffler . . . to put round your neck . . . like an ascot, you know. I made it myself out of odds and ends . . . I knitted it in the dark each night, after I'd gone to bed. I'm afraid it looks better in the dark!

MR. FRANK. [*Putting it on*] It's fine. It fits me perfectly. Thank you, Annele.

[ANNE *hands* PETER *a ball of paper; with a string attached to it.*]

ANNE. That's for Mouschi.

PETER. [*Rising to bow*] On behalf of Mouschi, I thank you.

ANNE. [*Hesitant, handing him a gift*] And . . . this is yours . . . from Mrs. Quack Quack. [*As he holds it gingerly in his hands*] Well . . . open it . . . Aren't you going to open it?

PETER. I'm scared to. I know something's going to jump out and hit me.

ANNE. No. It's nothing like that, really.

MRS. VAN DAAN. [*As he is opening it*] What is it, Peter? Go on. Show it.

ANNE. [*Excitedly*] It's a safety razor!

DUSSEL. A what?

ANNE. A razor!

MRS. VAN DAAN. [*Looking at it*] You didn't make that out of odds and ends.

ANNE. [*To* PETER] Miep got it for me. It's not new. It's second-hand. But you really do need a razor now.

DUSSEL. For what?

ANNE. Look on his upper lip . . . you can see the beginning of a mustache.

DUSSEL. He wants to get rid of that? Put a little milk on it and let the cat lick it off.

PETER. [*Starting for his room*] Think you're funny, don't you.

DUSSEL. Look! He can't wait! He's going in to try it!

PETER. I'm going to give Mouschi his present!

[*He goes into his room, slamming the door behind him.*]

MR. VAN DAAN. [*Disgustedly*] Mouschi, Mouschi, Mouschi.

[*In the distance we hear a dog persistently barking.* ANNE *brings a gift to* DUSSEL.]

ANNE. And last but never least, my roommate, Mr. Dussel.

DUSSEL. For me? You have something for me?

[*He opens the small box she gives him.*]

ANNE. I made them myself.

DUSSEL. [*Puzzled*] Capsules! Two capsules!

ANNE. They're ear-plugs!

DUSSEL. Ear-plugs?

ANNE. To put in your ears so you won't hear me when I thrash around at night. I saw them advertised in a magazine. They're not real ones . . . I made them out of cotton and candle wax. Try them . . . See if they don't work . . . see if you can hear me talk . . .

DUSSEL. [*Putting them in his ears*] Wait now until I get them in . . . so.

ANNE. Are you ready?

DUSSEL. Huh?

ANNE. Are you ready?

DUSSEL. Good God! They've gone inside! I can't get them out! [*They laugh as* MR. DUSSEL *jumps about, trying to shake the plugs out of his ears. Finally he gets them out. Putting them away*] Thank you, Anne! Thank you!

[*Together*]

MR. VAN DAAN. A real Hanukkah!

MRS. VAN DAAN. Wasn't it cute of her?

MRS. FRANK. I don't know when she did it.

MARGOT. I love my present.

ANNE. [*Sitting at the table*] And now let's have the song, Father . . . please . . . [*To* DUSSEL] Have you heard the Hanukkah song, Mr. Dussel? The song is the whole thing! [*She sings.*] "Oh, Hanukkah! Oh Hanukkah! The sweet celebration . . ."

MR. FRANK. [*Quieting her*] I'm afraid, Anne, we shouldn't sing that song tonight. [*To* DUSSEL] It's a song of jubilation, of rejoicing. One is apt to become too enthusiastic.

ANNE. Oh, please, please. Let's sing the song. I promise not to shout!

MR. FRANK. Very well. But quietly now . . . I'll keep an eye on you and when . . .

[*As* ANNE *starts to sing, she is interrupted by* DUSSEL, *who is snorting and wheezing.*]

DUSSEL. [*Pointing to* PETER] You . . . You!

[PETER *is coming from his bedroom, ostentatiously holding a bulge in his coat as if he were holding his cat, and dangling* ANNE'S *present before it.*]

How many times . . . I told you . . . Out! Out!

MR. VAN DAAN. [*Going to* PETER] What's the matter with you? Haven't you any sense? Get that cat out of here.

PETER. [*Innocently*] Cat?

MR. VAN DAAN. You heard me. Get it out of here!

PETER. I have no cat. [*Delighted with his joke, he opens his coat and pulls out a bath towel. The group at the table laugh, enjoying the joke.*]

DUSSEL. [*Still wheezing*] It doesn't need to be the cat . . . his clothes are enough . . . when he comes out of that room . . .

MR. VAN DAAN. Don't worry. You won't be bothered any more. We're getting rid of it.

DUSSEL. At last you listen to me. [*He goes off into his bedroom.*]

MR. VAN DAAN. [*Calling after him*] I'm not doing it for you. That's all in your mind . . . all of it! [*He starts back to his place at the table.*] I'm doing it because I'm sick of seeing that cat eat all our food. 36

PETER. That's not true! I only give him bones . . . scraps . . .

MR. VAN DAAN. Don't tell me! He gets fatter every day! Damn cat looks better than any of us. Out he goes tonight!

PETER. No! No!

ANNE. Mr. Van Daan, you can't do that! That's Peter's cat. Peter loves that cat.

MRS. FRANK. [*Quietly*] Anne.

PETER. [*To* MR. VAN DAAN] If he goes, I go.

MR. VAN DAAN. Go! Go!

MRS. VAN DAAN. You're not going and the cat's not going! Now please . . . this is Hanukkah . . . Hanukkah . . . this is the time to celebrate . . . What's the matter with all of you? Come on, Anne. Let's have the song.

35 **Discussion** Contrast the happy celebration of Hanukkah and the conditions under which the two families are living.

36 **Discussion** At what other time did Mr. Van Daan voice his concern about the scarcity of food?

37 Discussion Note how quickly the scene goes from one of happiness to one of horror. Who or what do you think caused the crash downstairs?

ANNE. [*Singing*]

"Oh, Hanukkah! Oh, Hanukkah!
The sweet celebration."

MR. FRANK. [*Rising*] I think we should first blow out the candle . . . then we'll have something for tomorrow night.

MARGOT. But, Father, you're supposed to let it burn itself out.

MR. FRANK. I'm sure that God understands shortages. [*Before blowing it out*] "Praised be Thou, oh Lord our God, who hast sustained us and permitted us to celebrate this joyous festival."

37 [*He is about to blow out the candle when suddenly there is a crash of something falling below. They all freeze in horror, motionless. For a few seconds there is complete silence.* MR. FRANK *slips off his shoes. The others noiselessly follow his example.* MR. FRANK *turns out a light near him. He motions to* PETER *to turn off the center lamp.* PETER *tries to reach it, realizes he cannot and gets up on a chair. Just as he is touching the lamp he loses his balance. The chair goes out from under him. He falls. The iron lamp shade crashes to the floor. There is a sound of feet below, running down the stairs.*]

MR. VAN DAAN. [*Under his breath*] God Almighty!

[*The only light left comes from the Hanukkah candle.* DUSSEL *comes from his room.* MR. FRANK *creeps over to the stairwell and stands listening. The dog is heard barking excitedly.*]

Do you hear anything?

MR. FRANK. [*In a whisper*] No. I think they've gone.

MRS. VAN DAAN. It's the Green Police. They've found us.

MR. FRANK. If they had, they wouldn't have left. They'd be up here by now.

MRS. VAN DAAN. I know it's the Green Police. They've gone to get help. That's all. They'll be back!

MR. VAN DAAN. Or it may have been the Gestapo,[30] looking for papers . . .

MR. FRANK. [*Interrupting*] Or a thief, looking for money.

MRS. VAN DAAN. We've got to do something . . . Quick! Quick! Before they come back.

MR. VAN DAAN. There isn't anything to do. Just wait.

[MR. FRANK *holds up his hand for them to be quiet. He is listening intently. There is complete silence as they all strain to hear any sound from below. Suddenly* ANNE *begins to sway. With a low cry she falls to the floor in a faint.* MRS. FRANK *goes to her quickly, sitting beside her on the floor and taking her in her arms.*]

MRS. FRANK. Get some water, please! Get some water!

[MARGOT *starts for the sink.*]

MR. VAN DAAN. [*Grabbing* MARGOT] No! No! No one's going to run water!

MR. FRANK. If they've found us, they've found us. Get the water. [MARGOT *starts again for the sink.* MR. FRANK, *getting a flashlight*] I'm going down.

[MARGOT *rushes to him, clinging to him.* ANNE *struggles to consciousness.*]

MARGOT. No, Father, no! There may be someone there, waiting . . . It may be a trap!

---

30. Gestapo (gə stä' pō) *n.*: The secret police force of the German Nazi state, known for its terrorism and atrocities.

MR. FRANK. This is Saturday. There is no way for us to know what has happened until Miep or Mr. Kraler comes on Monday morning. We cannot live with this uncertainty.

MARGOT. Don't go, Father!

MRS. FRANK. Hush, darling, hush.

[MR. FRANK *slips quietly out, down the steps and out through the door below.*]

Margot! Stay close to me.

[MARGOT *goes to her mother.*]

MR. VAN DAAN. Shush! Shush!

[MRS. FRANK *whispers to* MARGOT *to get the water.* MARGOT *goes for it.*]

MRS. VAN DAAN. Putti, where's our money? Get our money. I hear you can buy the Green Police off, so much a head. Go upstairs quick! Get the money!

MR. VAN DAAN. Keep still!

MRS. VAN DAAN. [*Kneeling before him, pleading*] Do you want to be dragged off to a concentration camp? Are you going to stand there and wait for them to come up and get you? Do something, I tell you!

MR. VAN DAAN. [*Pushing her aside*] Will you keep still!

[*He goes over to the stairwell to listen.* PETER *goes to his mother, helping her up onto the sofa. There is a second of silence, then* ANNE *can stand it no longer.*]

ANNE. Someone go after Father! Make Father come back!

PETER. [*Starting for the door*] I'll go.

MR. VAN DAAN. Haven't you done enough?

[*He pushes* PETER *roughly away. In his anger against his father* PETER *grabs a chair as if to hit him with it, then puts it down, burying his face in his hands.* MRS. FRANK *begins to pray softly.*]

ANNE. Please, please, Mr. Van Daan. Get Father.

MR. VAN DAAN. Quiet! Quiet!

[ANNE *is shocked into silence.* MRS. FRANK *pulls her closer, holding her protectively in her arms.*]

MRS. FRANK. [*Softly, praying*] "I lift up mine eyes unto the mountains, from whence cometh my help. My help cometh from the Lord who made heaven and earth. He will not suffer thy foot to be moved . . . He that keepeth thee will not slumber . . ."

[*She stops as she hears someone coming. They all watch the door tensely.* MR. FRANK *comes quietly in.* ANNE *rushes to him, holding him tight.*]

MR. FRANK. It was a thief. That noise must have scared him away.

MRS. VAN DAAN. Thank God!

MR. FRANK. He took the cash box. And the radio. He ran away in such a hurry that he didn't stop to shut the street door. It was swinging wide open. [*A breath of relief sweeps over them.*] I think it would be good to have some light.

MARGOT. Are you sure it's all right?

MR. FRANK. The danger has passed.

[MARGOT *goes to light the small lamp.*]

Don't be so terrified, Anne. We're safe.

DUSSEL. Who says the danger has passed? Don't you realize we are in greater danger than ever?

MR. FRANK. Mr. Dussel, will you be still!

[MR. FRANK *takes* ANNE *back to the table,*

Reader's Response What traditions or celebrations do you feel strengthened by?

Master Teacher Note Ask the class if the play is more effective limiting locale to the hideaway rather than allowing us to see Miep and Mr. Kraler functioning in the outside world. Why? How would the play change if we could see the office, the thief, the Nazis? What is the impact of our hearing but never seeing the Nazis?

Enrichment You might consider recommending that students see the French film *Peppermint Soda* if it is ever shown locally, or try to bring it into class for viewing. We urge you to preview the film in case there is any material in it to which individuals in your class might be sensitive. The film shows two Jewish teenagers in a girl's school where classmates are primarily Christian.

Enrichment Students may be encouraged to write poetry in tribute to Anne and those who died in concentration camps.

making her sit down with him, trying to calm her.]

DUSSEL. [*Pointing to* PETER] Thanks to this clumsy fool, there's someone now who knows we're up here! Someone now knows we're up here, hiding!

MRS. VAN DAAN. [*Going to* DUSSEL] Someone knows we're here, yes. But who is the someone? A thief! A thief! You think a thief is going to go to the Green Police and say . . . I was robbing a place the other night and I heard a noise up over my head? You think a thief is going to do that?

DUSSEL. Yes. I think he will.

MRS. VAN DAAN. [*Hysterically*] You're crazy!

[*She stumbles back to her seat at the table.* PETER *follows protectively, pushing* DUSSEL *aside.*]

DUSSEL. I think some day he'll be caught and then he'll make a bargain with the Green Police . . . if they'll let him off, he'll tell them where some Jews are hiding!

[*He goes off into the bedroom. There is a second of appalled silence.*]

MR. VAN DAAN. He's right.

ANNE. Father, let's get out of here! We can't stay here now . . . Let's go . . .

MR. VAN DAAN. Go! Where?

MRS. FRANK. [*Sinking into her chair at the table*] Yes. Where?

MR. FRANK. [*Rising, to them all*] Have we lost all faith? All courage? A moment ago we thought that they'd come for us. We were sure it was the end. But it wasn't the end. We're alive, safe.

[MR. VAN DAAN *goes to the table and sits.* MR. FRANK *prays.*]

"We thank Thee, oh Lord our God, that in Thy infinite mercy Thou hast again seen fit to spare us." [*He blows out the candle, then turns to* ANNE.] Come on, Anne. The song! Let's have the song!

[*He starts to sing.* ANNE *finally starts falteringly to sing, as* MR. FRANK *urges her on. Her voice is hardly audible at first.*]

ANNE. [*Singing*]
"Oh, Hanukkah! Oh, Hanukkah!
The sweet . . . celebration . . ."

[*As she goes on singing, the others gradually join in, their voices still shaking with fear.* MRS. VAN DAAN *sobs as she sings.*]

GROUP.
"Around the feast . . . we . . . gather
In complete . . . jubilation . . .
Happiest of sea . . . sons
Now is here.
Many are the reasons for good cheer."

[DUSSEL *comes from the bedroom. He comes over to the table, standing beside* MARGOT, *listening to them as they sing.*]

"Together
We'll weather
Whatever tomorrow may bring."

[*As they sing on with growing courage, the lights start to dim.*]

"So hear us rejoicing
And merrily voicing
The Hanukkah song that we sing.
Hoy!"

[*The lights are out. The curtain starts slowly to fall.*]

"Hear us rejoicing
And merrily voicing
The Hanukkah song that we sing."

[*They are still singing, as the curtain falls.*]

Closure and Extension

ANSWERS TO THINKING ABOUT THE SELECTION
Recalling

1. At first, Anne is unaffected and considers the hiding place "a very peculiar summer boarding house."
2. While the workers are in the building, there had to be complete quiet. There could be no noise from 8:00 A.M. to 6:00 P.M. They could move only in their stockinged feet and could not speak above a whisper. They could not run any water.
3. Her father's command that she must never go beyond the door of their hiding place makes Anne realize the severity of their confinement.
4. Margot, Anne, and Peter do school assignments under the guidance of Mr. Frank. Mrs. Frank and Mrs. Van Daan do sewing, embroidery, and prepare dinners. They all celebrate Hanukkah. The families cannot make any noise for fear of people becoming aware that they are hiding upstairs. They are never allowed to leave the attic to go outside. When a thief enters the warehouse, his noise fills everyone with fear. They think the intruder is the Green Police.
5. Anne wants to be able to ride her bike, to laugh, to have new clothes, to have a hot bath, and to

THINKING ABOUT THE SELECTION

Recalling

1. How does going into hiding affect Anne at first?
2. Explain the special precautions the two families take in order to prevent discovery.
3. When does Anne realize what going into hiding really means?
4. In what ways do the families try to live their lives normally? Which events intrude, showing that their lives are not normal?
5. What are Anne's dreams for her future? What fears are revealed through her nightmares?
6. What special meaning does Hanukkah have for the families? How does Anne make the celebration particularly special?

Interpreting

7. Compare and contrast Peter and Anne. How do their differences account for the reaction of each to removing the yellow star?
8. Compare and contrast Margot and Anne. How does the difference between the two characters account for each's relationship with Mrs. Frank?
9. Mr. Frank tells Anne, "There are no walls, there are no bolts, no locks that anyone can put on your mind." Explain this statement. How does Anne prove its truth?
10. Describe the mood at the end of Act I. What event has caused this mood?

Applying

11. Like the Franks and Van Daans, many people turn to traditions and celebrations to give them courage in times of trouble. How do such traditions help us through difficult times?
12. Does the fact that Anne Frank was a real person make this play more meaningful for you? Explain your answer.

ANALYZING LITERATURE

Appreciating the Use of Flashback

The play opens with Mr. Frank returning to the warehouse apartment in 1945 after the war. Once he has begun reading the diary, the action flashes back to 1942.

1. From whose point of view are the events seen at the beginning of the play?
2. During the flashback, to what character does the point of view shift?
3. Why is using a flashback more effective than having Mr. Frank simply tell what had happened in 1942?

CRITICAL THINKING AND READING

Predicting Outcomes

As you read, you continually make predictions about what will happen next. You make predictions based on clues authors provide and on your own experiences and those about which you have read.

As you make the following predictions, give two clues from Act I on which you base your predictions.

1. Choose two characters from this play. How do you think being in hiding will affect the relationship of these characters?
2. What do you think will happen to Anne?

THINKING AND WRITING

Writing as a Character in the Play

Pretend you are either Anne or Peter. Write a letter to Jopie or to another friend about what life in hiding is like. Before you start writing, list several topics you want to include. The topics might be how you spend your day, how your relationships with people have changed, and so forth. When you have finished your letter, make sure your spelling and punctuation are correct.

(Answers begin on p. 342.)

be back in school with her friends. Her nightmare was that the Green Police broke down the door and grabbed her.

6. Hanukkah is a time of celebration. It is a way of renewing your faith in God. Anne has managed to surprise the group by finding appropriate Hanukkah presents for each one.

Interpreting

7. Peter is gentle and well-mannered. He is shy and at times withdrawn. Anne is intelligent, honest, and eager for perfection. However, at times she can be difficult and temperamental. Peter impulsively rips the Star of David off his shirt and burns it. Anne has stronger feelings about what the star stands for and can't burn it.
8. Margot is quiet, courteous, and distant. Anne is boisterous, self-assertive, and engaging. Their mother prefers Margot's character to Anne's. Anne feels she is not understood and has nothing in common with her mother.
9. The statement means that, even though they are virtually prisoners in the attic, they can go anywhere through books. Anne is eager for intellectual activity and Mr. Frank is a great source of intellectual stimulation for her.
10. Everyone is fearful that the intruder will go to the Green Police and tell of their hiding. Yet they try to renew their faith and courage by continuing to celebrate Hanukkah.

Applying

11. Answers will differ. Suggested Response: Traditions help us get through difficult times by giving people a sense of security. The idea of sharing long-established values prevents a sense of rootlessness.
12. Answers will differ. Suggested Response: Yes. Students should note that Anne provides firsthand observations on the barbarism of the Nazis.

Challenge Why might Miep and Mr. Kraler hide news of the Jews' real situation in Amsterdam?

ANSWERS TO ANALYZING LITERATURE

1. The events are seen from Mr. Frank's point of view.
2. During the flashback, it shifts to Anne's point of view.
3. The flashback technique shows us the effect that reading the diary has on Mr. Frank. It also reveals Anne's character more directly.

ANSWERS TO CRITICAL THINKING AND READING

1. Answers will differ. Suggested Response: Noting how Anne teases Peter, students might predict that they will never become close friends. Others, noting their ages and need for companionship, might predict that Anne and Peter will grow close. Just make sure that students support their predictions with appropriate clues.
2. Answers will differ. Suggested Response: Students should note the solitary appearance of Anne's father in Scene 1 and the entire group's fear of imminent discovery by the end of Act I. Most students should correctly predict that Anne is taken prisoner and sent to a concentration camp.

THINKING AND WRITING

Publishing Student Writing Make an Anne Frank bulletin board. Display some of the letters.

Literary Focus Point out that characters change as a result of conflicts, both external and internal. Review the conflicts that emerged in Act I, such as the Jews' conflict against Nazism, individual conflicts between characters, and Anne's internal conflict to overcome fear and have "the good Anne outside and the bad Anne inside." Explain that the resolution of these conflicts will suggest the play's theme.

Look For Suggest that students use a chart to keep track of the changes in the characters in Act II. Such a chart should list all the characters, briefly describing each character's personality as revealed in Act I. There should be spaces where students can note changes in personality.

Writing/Prior Knowledge Before students freewrite, review the myth of Pandora in which she releases all the evils of the world from the box she was forbidden to open. What remained in the box was hope, which she eventually releases too. Have students imagine what the world would be like if Pandora had kept hope locked in the box.

Vocabulary The following words may not be known by your **less advanced** students: *disgruntled* (p. 345), *foreboding* (p. 348), *animation* (p. 354), *pandemonium* (p. 362), *liberated* (p. 363), *remorse* (p. 364).

Spelling Tip When you add the suffix *-ly* to a word that ends in *l*, like *ineffectual,* the *l* is kept: *ineffectually*.

GUIDE FOR READING

The Diary of Anne Frank, Act II

Characters and Theme

Act II begins a little more than a year after the end of Act I. The passage of time, along with the characters' living so closely together and always in fear, has changed the characters. Observing the changes in the characters can help you to understand the theme of the play.

When Anne Frank wrote the diary from which this play was created, she may not have set out to present a **theme,** or general observation about life. Nevertheless, the events in the play do point to a strong theme.

Look For

As you read Act II, notice the changes in the characters. Which have changed most? Which have changed least? Which have changed for the better? Which for the worse? How have these changes affected their relationships? What role does hope play in their lives?

Writing

O.S. Marden has written: "There is no medicine like hope, no incentive so great, and no tonic so powerful as expectation of something tomorrow." Freewrite for five minutes about hope. Think about a time when you or someone you know faced a difficult situation. What part did hope play in the situation? What enables people who face difficult circumstances to have hope in the future?

Vocabulary

Knowing the following words will help you as you read *The Diary of Anne Frank,* Act II.

inarticulate (in' är tik' yə lit) *adj.*: Speechless or unable to express oneself (p. 347)
apprehension (ap' rə hen' shən) *n.*: A fearful feeling about the future; dread (p. 349)
intuition (in'too wish'ən) *n.*: Ability to know immediately, without reasoning (p. 354)
sarcastic (sär kas' tik) *adj.*: Speaking with sharp mocking intended to hurt another (p. 355)
indignant (in dig' nənt) *adj.*: Filled with anger over some meanness or injustice (p. 356)
inferiority complex (in fir'ē ôr'ə tē käm' pleks) *n.*: Tendency to belittle oneself (p. 356)
stealthily (stel' thi lē') *adv.*: In a secretive or sneaky manner (p. 359)
ineffectually (in'i fek'choo wə lē) *adv.*: Without producing the desired effect (p. 365)

Objectives

1. To understand the relationship between characters and theme in a play
2. To find support for a character's opinion
3. To write a letter to the editor

Support Material

Teaching Portfolio
Teacher Backup, pp. 421–423
Grammar in Action Worksheets, *Using Contractions,* pp. 424–425, *Understanding Ellipses,* p. 426–427
Usage and Mechanics Worksheet, p. 428
Vocabulary Check, p. 429
Analyzing Literature Worksheet, *Understanding Characters and Theme,* p. 430
Critical Thinking and Reading Worksheet, *Finding Support for Opinions,* p. 431
Selection Test, pp. 432–433

ACT II

Scene 1

[*In the darkness we hear* ANNE'S VOICE, *again reading from the diary.*]

ANNE'S VOICE. Saturday, the first of January, nineteen forty-four. Another new year has begun and we find ourselves still in our hiding place. We have been here now for one year, five months and twenty-five days. It seems that our life is at a standstill.

[*The curtain rises on the scene. It is late afternoon. Everyone is bundled up against the cold. In the main room* MRS. FRANK *is taking down the laundry which is hung across the back.* MR. FRANK *sits in the chair down left, reading.* MARGOT *is lying on the couch with a blanket over her and the many-colored knitted scarf around her throat.* ANNE *is seated at the center table, writing in her diary.* PETER, MR. *and* MRS. VAN DAAN *and* DUSSEL *are all in their own rooms, reading or lying down.*

As the lights dim on, ANNE'S VOICE *continues, without a break.*]

ANNE'S VOICE. We are all a little thinner. The Van Daans' "discussions" are as violent as ever. Mother still does not understand me. But then I don't understand her either. 1 There is one great change, however. A change in myself. I read somewhere that girls of my age don't feel quite certain of themselves. That they become quiet within and begin to think of the miracle that is taking place in their bodies. I think that what is happening to me is so wonderful . . . not only what can be seen, but what is taking place inside. Each time it has happened I have a feeling that I have a sweet secret. [*We hear the chimes and then a hymn being played on the carillon outside.*] And in spite of any pain, I long for the time when I shall feel that secret within me again.

The Westertoren Church tower as seen through the window of the attic hiding place

[*The buzzer of the door below suddenly sounds. Everyone is startled,* MR. FRANK *tiptoes cautiously to the top of the steps and listens. Again the buzzer sounds, in* MIEP'S *V-for-Victory signal.*[1]]

MR. FRANK. It's Miep!

[*He goes quickly down the steps to unbolt the door.* MRS. FRANK *calls upstairs to the* VAN DAANS *and then to* PETER.]

MRS. FRANK. Wake up, everyone! Miep is here!

[ANNE *quickly puts her diary away.* MARGOT *sits up, pulling the blanket around her shoulders.* MR. DUSSEL *sits on the edge of his bed, listening, disgruntled.* MIEP *comes up the steps, followed by* MR. KRALER. *They bring flowers, books, newspapers, etc.* ANNE *rushes to* MIEP, *throwing her arms affectionately around her.*]

---

1. V-for-Victory signal: Three short rings and one long one (the letter *V* in Morse code).

Presentation

Motivation/Prior Knowledge Impress on students the fact that over one year has elapsed between the end of Act I and the events of Act II. What do they think has happened to the various conflicts in that time? Do they think the characters have learned to control their bickering? Their fears? Is it likely that Anne succeeded in putting "the good Anne outside and the bad Anne inside"?

Purpose-Setting Question What does Anne learn about herself as the play develops?

1 **Enrichment** In Act II, readers will see significant areas of development in Anne's maturity. Not unique among people her age are the "growing pains" that signify the end of childhood and the beginning of adulthood. This uncomfortable period of adolescence is the subject of many articles and books. Have students discuss other books they have read dealing with the problems of adolescence. The works of Judy Blume would be a good starting point.

2 Discussion Explain and discuss the examples of irony in this scene: colorful flowers and a band playing outside contrast with the life-threatening situation faced by all the characters.

Miep . . . *and* Mr. Kraler . . . What a delightful surprise!

MR. KRALER. We came to bring you New Year's greetings.

MRS. FRANK. You shouldn't . . . you should have at least one day to yourselves. [*She goes quickly to the stove and brings down teacups and tea for all of them.*]

ANNE. Don't say that, it's so wonderful to see them! [*Sniffing at* MIEP'S *coat*] I can smell the wind and the cold on your clothes.

MIEP. [*Giving her the flowers*] There you are. [*Then to* MARGOT, *feeling her forehead*] How are you, Margot? . . . Feeling any better?

MARGOT. I'm all right.

ANNE. We filled her full of every kind of pill so she won't cough and make a noise.

2 [*She runs into her room to put the flowers in water.* MR. *and* MRS. VAN DAAN *come from upstairs. Outside there is the sound of a band playing.*]

MRS. VAN DAAN. Well, hello, Miep. Mr. Kraler.

MR. KRALER. [*Giving a bouquet of flowers to* MRS. VAN DAAN] With my hope for peace in the New Year.

PETER. [*Anxiously*] Miep, have you seen Mouschi? Have you seen him anywhere around?

MIEP. I'm sorry, Peter. I asked everyone in the neighborhood had they seen a gray cat. But they said no.

[MRS. FRANK *gives* MIEP *a cup of tea.* MR. FRANK *comes up the steps, carrying a small cake on a plate.*]

MR. FRANK. Look what Miep's brought for us!

MRS. FRANK. [*Taking it*] A cake!

MR. VAN DAAN. A cake! [*He pinches* MIEP'S *cheeks gaily and hurries up to the cupboard.*] I'll get some plates.

[DUSSEL, *in his room, hastily puts a coat on and starts out to join the others.*]

MRS. FRANK. Thank you, Miepia. You shouldn't have done it. You must have used all of your sugar ration for weeks. [*Giving it to* MRS. VAN DAAN] It's beautiful, isn't it?

MRS. VAN DAAN. It's been ages since I even saw a cake. Not since you brought us one last year. [*Without looking at the cake, to* MIEP] Remember? Don't you remember, you gave us one on New Year's Day? Just this time last year? I'll never forget it because you had "Peace in nineteen forty-three" on it. [*She looks at the cake and reads*] "Peace in nineteen forty-four!"

MIEP. Well, it has to come sometime, you know. [*As* DUSSEL *comes from his room*] Hello, Mr. Dussel.

MR. KRALER. How are you?

MR. VAN DAAN. [*Bringing plates and a knife*] Here's the knife, *liefje.* Now, how many of us are there?

MIEP. None for me, thank you.

MR. FRANK. Oh, please. You must.

MIEP. I couldn't.

MR. VAN DAAN. Good! That leaves one . . . two . . . three . . . seven of us.

DUSSEL. Eight! Eight! It's the same number as it always is!

MR. VAN DAAN. I left Margot out. I take it for granted Margot won't eat any.

ANNE. Why wouldn't she!

MRS. FRANK. I think it won't harm her.

MR. VAN DAAN. All right! All right! I just didn't want her to start coughing again, that's all.

DUSSEL. And please, Mrs. Frank should cut the cake.

MR. VAN DAAN. What's the difference? } [*Together*]

MRS. VAN DAAN. It's not Mrs. Frank's cake, is it, Miep? It's for all of us. } [*Together*]

DUSSEL. Mrs. Frank divides things better.

MRS. VAN DAAN. [*Going to* DUSSEL] What are you trying to say? } [*Together*]

MR. VAN DAAN. Oh, come on! Stop wasting time! } [*Together*]

MRS. VAN DAAN. [*To* DUSSEL] Don't I always give everybody exactly the same? Don't I?

MR. VAN DAAN. Forget it, Kerli.

MRS. VAN DAAN. No. I want an answer! Don't I?

DUSSEL. Yes. Yes. Everybody gets exactly the same . . . except Mr. Van Daan always gets a little bit more.

[VAN DAAN *advances on* DUSSEL, *the knife still in his hand.*]

MR. VAN DAAN. That's a lie!

[DUSSEL *retreats before the onslaught of the* VAN DAANS.]

MR. FRANK. Please, please! [*Then to* MIEP] You see what a little sugar cake does to us? It goes right to our heads!

MR. VAN DAAN. [*Handing* MRS. FRANK *the knife*] Here you are, Mrs. Frank.

MRS. FRANK. Thank you. [*Then to* MIEP *as she goes to the table to cut the cake*] Are you sure you won't have some?

MIEP. [*Drinking her tea*] No, really, I have to go in a minute.

[*The sound of the band fades out in the distance.*]

PETER. [*To* MIEP] Maybe Mouschi went back to our house . . . they say that cats . . . Do you ever get over there . . . ? I mean . . . do you suppose you could . . . ?

MIEP. I'll try, Peter. The first minute I get I'll try. But I'm afraid, with him gone a week . . .

DUSSEL. Make up your mind, already someone has had a nice big dinner from that cat!

[PETER *is furious, inarticulate. He starts toward* DUSSEL *as if to hit him.* MR. FRANK *stops him.* MRS. FRANK *speaks quickly to ease the situation.*]

MRS. FRANK. [*To* MIEP] This is delicious, Miep!

MRS. VAN DAAN. [*Eating hers*] Delicious!

MR. VAN DAAN. [*Finishing it in one gulp*] Dirk's in luck to get a girl who can bake like this!

MIEP. [*Putting down her empty teacup*] I have to run. Dirk's taking me to a party tonight.

ANNE. How heavenly! Remember now what everyone is wearing, and what you have to eat and everything, so you can tell us tomorrow.

MIEP. I'll give you a full report! Good-bye, everyone!

MR. VAN DAAN. [*To* MIEP] Just a minute. There's something I'd like you to do for me.

[*He hurries off up the stairs to his room.*]

MRS. VAN DAAN. [*Sharply*] Putti, where are you going? [*She rushes up the stairs after him, calling hysterically.*] What do you want? Putti, what are you going to do?

MIEP. [*To* PETER] What's wrong?

PETER. [*His sympathy is with his mother.*] Father says he's going to sell her fur coat. She's crazy about that old fur coat.

3 **Discussion** What does this reveal about Mrs. Van Daan?

4 **Discussion** What does this reveal about Mr. Van Daan's relationship with his wife? Why did he sell her coat?

DUSSEL. Is it possible? Is it possible that anyone is so silly as to worry about a fur coat in times like this?

PETER. It's none of your darn business . . . and if you say one more thing . . . I'll, I'll take you and I'll . . . I mean it . . . I'll . . .

[*There is a piercing scream from* MRS. VAN DAAN *above. She grabs at the fur coat as* MR. VAN DAAN *is starting downstairs with it.*]

MRS. VAN DAAN. No! No! No! Don't you dare take that! You hear? It's mine!

[*Downstairs* PETER *turns away, embarrassed, miserable.*]

My father gave me that! You didn't give it to me. You have no right. Let go of it . . . you hear?

[MR. VAN DAAN *pulls the coat from her hands and hurries downstairs.* MRS. VAN DAAN *sinks to the floor, sobbing. As* MR. VAN DAAN *comes into the main room the others look away, embarrassed for him.*]

MR. VAN DAAN. [*To* MR. KRALER] Just a little —discussion over the advisability of selling this coat. As I have often reminded Mrs. Van Daan, it's very selfish of her to keep it when people outside are in such desperate need of clothing . . . [*He gives the coat to* MIEP.] So if you will please to sell it for us? It should fetch a good price. And by the way, will you get me cigarettes. I don't care what kind they are . . . get all you can.

MIEP. It's terribly difficult to get them, Mr. Van Daan. But I'll try. Good-bye.

[*She goes.* MR. FRANK *follows her down the steps to bolt the door after her.* MRS. FRANK *gives* MR. KRALER *a cup of tea.*]

MRS. FRANK. Are you sure you won't have some cake, Mr. Kraler?

MR. KRALER. I'd better not.

MR. VAN DAAN. You're still feeling badly? What does your doctor say?

MR. KRALER. I haven't been to him.

MRS. FRANK. Now, Mr. Kraler! . . .

MR. KRALER. [*Sitting at the table*] Oh, I tried. But you can't get near a doctor these days . . . they're so busy. After weeks I finally managed to get one on the telephone. I told him I'd like an appointment . . . I wasn't feeling very well. You know what he answers . . . over the telephone . . . Stick out your tongue! [*They laugh. He turns to* MR. FRANK *as* MR. FRANK *comes back.*] I have some contracts here . . . I wonder if you'd look over them with me . . .

MR. FRANK. [*Putting out his hand*] Of course.

MR. KRALER. [*He rises*] If we could go downstairs . . . [MR. FRANK *starts ahead;* MR. KRALER *speaks to the others.*] Will you forgive us? I won't keep him but a minute. [*He starts to follow* MR. FRANK *down the steps.*]

MARGOT. [*With sudden foreboding*] What's happened? Something's happened! Hasn't it, Mr. Kraler?

[MR. KRALER *stops and comes back, trying to reassure* MARGOT *with a pretense of casualness.*]

MR. KRALER. No, really. I want your father's advice . . .

MARGOT. Something's gone wrong! I know it!

MR. FRANK. [*Coming back, to* MR. KRALER] If it's something that concerns us here, it's better that we all hear it.

MR. KRALER. [*Turning to him, quietly*] But . . . the children . . . ?

Primary Source

Co-editor of *The Diary of Anne Frank: Critical Edition* David Barnouw discusses the second version of Anne Frank's diary in a June 8, 1989 article of *The New York Times*.

"To make her diary even more creative, she changed certain names in her second draft. For example, instead of calling her family Frank, she changed it to Robin; she became Anne Robin. And she attached other fictional names to people who were hiding from the Germans.

After her father returned from Auschwitz, he decided to publish the diary. He included some of the events that she had recorded in her "Tales." He restored the Frank family name that Anne had fictionalized, retained the fictional names that she had devised for other people, pared some of the criticism by Anne of her mother (who had also died in a concentration camp), and deleted some of the entries about her awakening sexual interest.

Some of Mr. Frank's deletions included minor entries on such things as French irregular verbs, washing her hair, hurting her little toe, breaking a vacuum cleaner. References to menstruation were omitted . . .

The bookcase moved aside to show the stairs leading to the attic hiding place; the bookcase hiding the stairs

MR. FRANK. What they'd imagine would be worse than any reality.

[*As* MR. KRALER *speaks, they all listen with intense apprehension.* MRS. VAN DAAN *comes down the stairs and sits on the bottom step.*]

MR. KRALER. It's a man in the storeroom . . . I don't know whether or not you remember him . . . Carl, about fifty, heavy-set, near-sighted . . . He came with us just before you left.

MR. FRANK. He was from Utrecht?

MR. KRALER. That's the man. A couple of weeks ago, when I was in the storeroom, he closed the door and asked me . . . how's Mr. Frank? What do you hear from Mr. Frank? I told him I only knew there was a rumor that you were in Switzerland. He said he'd heard that rumor too, but he thought I might know something more. I didn't pay any attention to it . . . but then a thing happened yesterday . . . He'd brought some invoices to the office for me to sign. As I was going through them, I looked up. He was standing staring at the bookcase . . . your bookcase. He said he thought he remembered a door there . . . Wasn't there a door there that used to go up to the loft? Then he told me he wanted more money. Twenty guilders[2] more a week.

2. guilders (gil′ dərz) *n.*: The monetary unit of Holland.

The critical edition discloses understandable motives behind Mr. Frank's deletions: his strong attachment to his dead daughter; his awareness that with publication of the diary he would be achieving her dearest wish—to become a famous writer one day; and his feelings of respect, first and foremost, toward his wife and others about whom Miss Frank had made unkind remarks during the occupation."

MR. VAN DAAN. Blackmail!

MR. FRANK. Twenty guilders? Very modest blackmail.

MR. VAN DAAN. That's just the beginning.

DUSSEL. [*Coming to* MR. FRANK] You know what I think? He was the thief who was down there that night. That's how he knows we're here.

MR. FRANK. [*To* MR. KRALER] How was it left? What did you tell him?

MR. KRALER. I said I had to think about it. What shall I do? Pay him the money? . . . Take a chance on firing him . . . or what? I don't know.

DUSSEL. [*Frantic*] For God's sake don't fire him! Pay him what he asks . . . keep him here where you can have your eye on him.

MR. FRANK. Is it so much that he's asking? What are they paying nowadays?

MR. KRALER. He could get it in a war plant. But this isn't a war plant. Mind you. I don't know if he really knows . . . or if he doesn't know.

MR. FRANK. Offer him half. Then we'll soon find out if it's blackmail or not.

DUSSEL. And if it is? We've got to pay it, haven't we? Anything he asks we've got to pay!

MR. FRANK. Let's decide that when the time comes.

MR. KRALER. This may be all my imagination. You get to a point, these days, where you suspect everyone and everything. Again and again . . . on some simple look or word, I've found myself . . .

[*The telephone rings in the office below.*]

MRS. VAN DAAN. [*Hurrying to* MR. KRALER] There's the telephone! What does that mean, the telephone ringing on a holiday?

MR. KRALER. That's my wife. I told her I had to go over some papers in my office . . . to call me there when she got out of church. [*He starts out.*] I'll offer him half then. Good-bye . . . we'll hope for the best!

[*The group calls their good-byes half-heartedly.* MR. FRANK *follows* MR. KRALER, *to bolt the door below. During the following scene,* MR. FRANK *comes back up and stands listening, disturbed.*]

DUSSEL. [*To* MR. VAN DAAN] You can thank your son for this . . . smashing the light! I tell you, it's just a question of time now.

[*He goes to the window at the back and stands looking out.*]

MARGOT. Sometimes I wish the end would come . . . whatever it is.

MRS. FRANK. [*Shocked*] Margot!

[ANNE *goes to* MARGOT, *sitting beside her on the couch with her arms around her.*]

MARGOT. Then at least we'd know where we were.

MRS. FRANK. You should be ashamed of yourself! Talking that way! Think how lucky we are! Think of the thousands dying in the war, every day. Think of the people in concentration camps.

ANNE. [*Interrupting*] What's the good of that? What's the good of thinking of misery when you're already miserable? That's stupid!

MRS. FRANK. Anne!

[*As* ANNE *goes on raging at her mother,* MRS. FRANK *tries to break in, in an effort to quiet her.*]

ANNE. We're young, Margot and Peter and I! You grownups have had your chance! But

Grammar in Action

A **contraction** is a combination of two words in which one or more omitted letters is replaced by an apostrophe. Contractions are usually to be avoided in expository and formal types of writing. They are much more common in fiction, especially fiction that contains dialogue. Contractions create more realistic dialogue because people use contractions in speech. As shortened forms of words or phrases, contractions are used for convenience and to save time.

The use of contractions in the following excerpt gives strength and speed to Anne's outburst.

What's the good of that? What's the good of thinking of misery when you're already miserable? That's stupid!

Notice how different Anne's exclamations would have sounded had she said "What is the good of that? What is the good of thinking of misery when you are already miserable? That is stupid!" The second version sounds flat and void of the emotional intensity of the original version.

look at us . . . If we begin thinking of all the horror in the world, we're lost! We're trying to hold onto some kind of ideals . . . when everything . . . ideals, hopes . . . everything, are being destroyed! It isn't our fault that the world is in such a mess! We weren't around when all this started! So don't try to take it out on us! [*She rushes off to her room, slamming the door after her. She picks up a brush from the chest and hurls it to the floor. Then she sits on the settee, trying to control her anger.*]

MR. VAN DAAN. She talks as if we started the war! Did we start the war?

[*He spots* ANNE'S *cake. As he starts to take it,* PETER *anticipates him.*]

PETER. She left her cake.

[*He starts for* ANNE'S *room with the cake. There is silence in the main room.* MRS. VAN DAAN *goes up to her room, followed by* VAN DAAN. DUSSEL *stays looking out the window.* MR. FRANK *brings* MRS. FRANK *her cake. She eats it slowly, without relish.* MR. FRANK *takes his cake to* MARGOT *and sits quietly on the sofa beside her.* PETER *stands in the doorway of* ANNE'S *darkened room, looking at her, then makes a little movement to let her know he is there.* ANNE *sits up, quickly, trying to hide the signs of her tears.* PETER *holds out the cake to her.*]

You left this.

ANNE. [*Dully*] Thanks.

[PETER *starts to go out, then comes back.*]

PETER. I thought you were fine just now. You know just how to talk to them. You know just how to say it. I'm no good . . . I never can think . . . especially when I'm mad . . . That Dussel . . . when he said that about Mouschi . . . someone eating him . . . all I could think is . . . I wanted to hit him. I wanted to give him such a . . . a . . . that he'd . . . That's what I used to do when there was an argument at school . . . That's the way I . . . but here . . . And an old man like that . . . it wouldn't be so good.

ANNE. You're making a big mistake about me.
I do it all wrong. I say too much. I go too far. I 6
hurt people's feelings . . .

[DUSSEL *leaves the window, going to his room.*]

PETER. I think you're just fine . . . What I want to say . . . if it wasn't for you around here, I don't know. What I mean . . .

[PETER *is interrupted by* DUSSEL'S *turning on the light.* DUSSEL *stands in the doorway, startled to see* PETER. PETER *advances toward him forbiddingly.* DUSSEL *backs out of the room.* PETER *closes the door on him.*]

ANNE. Do you mean it, Peter? Do you really mean it?

PETER. I said it, didn't I?

ANNE. Thank you, Peter!

[*In the main room* MR. *and* MRS. FRANK *collect the dishes and take them to the sink, washing them.* MARGOT *lies down again on the couch.* DUSSEL, *lost, wanders into* PETER'S *room and takes up a book, starting to read.*]

PETER. [*Looking at the photographs on the wall*] You've got quite a collection.

ANNE. Wouldn't you like some in your room? I could give you some. Heaven knows you spend enough time in there . . . doing heaven knows what . . .

PETER. It's easier. A fight starts, or an argument . . . I duck in there.

ANNE. You're lucky, having a room to go to. His lordship is always here . . . I hardly ever get a minute alone. When they start in on

5 **Discussion** Is Anne's attitude about the horrors happening in the world a typical attitude of youth? Do young people today feel the same way about their elders?

6 **Discussion** How does Anne characterize herself? How would you characterize Anne? What accounts for the difference?

Student Activity 1. Write out the full words of the following contractions:

1. weren't	6. that's
2. isn't	7. wouldn't
3. we'd	8. you've
4. would've	9. you're
5. what's	10. I'd

Student Activity 2. Rewrite Anne's speech that starts at the bottom of page 350 eliminating the contractions by writing out the words. How does this version of Anne's speech differ from the original version in terms of mood and tone?

7 Discussion Discuss Anne's changing attitude toward her father. What does this indicate about Anne?

8 Discussion What does this show about Anne's changing relationship with her father? Do you think she would have said this in Act I?

Anne's bedroom wall in the hiding place and the photographs she hung there

me, I can't duck away. I have to stand there and take it.

PETER. You gave some of it back just now.

ANNE. I get so mad. They've formed their opinions . . . about everything . . . but we . . . we're still trying to find out . . . We have problems here that no other people our age have ever had. And just as you think you've solved them, something comes along and bang! You have to start all over again.

PETER. At least you've got someone you can talk to.

ANNE. Not really. Mother . . . I never discuss
anything serious with her. She doesn't understand. Father's all right. We can talk 7
about everything . . . everything but one
thing. Mother. He simply won't talk about
her. I don't think you can be really intimate
with anyone if he holds something back, do
you?

PETER. I think your father's fine.

ANNE. Oh, he is, Peter! He is! He's the only
one who's ever given me the feeling that I 8
have any sense. But anyway, nothing can
take the place of school and play and friends

Primary Source

David Barnouw, co-editor of *The Diary of Anne Frank: The Critical Edition,* said the following about Anne Frank's diary in a June 8, 1989 article in *The New York Times:*

"We decided to publish it all—her mistakes, additions and deletions. She rewrote her diary in 1944 so people can compare it with her original. Why? She heard a broadcast beamed from London by the Dutch Government-in-exile. The Education Minister advised people in German-occupied Holland to keep diaries as a record of what went on under the Nazis.

Anne took the words personally. So in the second version, she made improvements in content and language. She thought the diary could become a kind of detective story. She added 'Tales From the Secret Annex' to her diary. In fact, the title of her diary in the original Dutch edition is 'The Annex.'"

. . . The American novelist Philip Roth became interested in the diary and those who have challenged it five years ago after a visit to the Anne Frank Foundation, which runs the museum at the house where Anne hid with her family for two years above a former office annex at 263 Prinsengracht, Amsterdam.

of your own age . . . or near your age . . . can it?

PETER. I suppose you miss your friends and all.

ANNE. It isn't just . . . [*She breaks off, staring up at him for a second.*] Isn't it funny, you and I? Here we've been seeing each other every minute for almost a year and a half, and this is the first time we've ever really talked. It helps a lot to have someone to talk to, don't you think? It helps you to let off steam.

PETER. [*Going to the door*] Well, any time you want to let off steam, you can come into my room.

ANNE. [*Following him*] I can get up an awful lot of steam. You'll have to be careful how you say that.

PETER. It's all right with me.

ANNE. Do you mean it?

PETER. I said it, didn't I?

[*He goes out.* ANNE *stands in her doorway looking after him. As* PETER *gets to his door he stands for a minute looking back at her. Then he goes into his room.* DUSSEL *rises as he comes in, and quickly passes him, going out. He starts across for his room.* ANNE *sees him coming, and pulls her door shut.* DUSSEL *turns back toward* PETER'S *room.* PETER *pulls his door shut.* DUSSEL *stands there, bewildered, forlorn.*

The scene slowly dims out. The curtain falls on the scene. ANNE'S VOICE *comes over in the darkness . . . faintly at first, and then with growing strength.*]

ANNE'S VOICE. We've had bad news. The people from whom Miep got our ration books have been arrested. So we have had to cut down on our food. Our stomachs are so empty that they rumble and make strange noises, all in different keys. Mr. Van Daan's is deep and low, like a bass fiddle. Mine is high, whistling like a flute. As we all sit 9
around waiting for supper, it's like an orchestra tuning up. It only needs Toscanini[3] to raise his baton and we'd be off in the Ride of the Valkyries.[4] Monday, the sixth of March, nineteen forty-four. Mr. Kraler is in the hospital. It seems he has ulcers. Pim says we are his ulcers. Miep has to run the business and us too. The Americans have landed on the southern tip of Italy. Father looks for a quick finish to the war. Mr. Dussel is waiting every day for the warehouse man to demand more money. Have I been skipping too much from one subject to another? I can't help it. I feel that spring is coming. I feel it in my whole body and soul. I feel utterly confused. I am longing . . . so longing . . . for everything . . . for friends . . . for someone to talk to . . . someone who understands . . . someone young, who feels as I do . . .

[*As these last lines are being said, the curtain rises on the scene. The lights dim on.* ANNE'S VOICE *fades out.*]

Scene 2

[*It is evening, after supper. From outside we hear the sound of children playing. The "grownups," with the exception of* MR. VAN DAAN, *are all in the main room.* MRS. FRANK *is* 10
doing some mending, MRS. VAN DAAN *is reading a fashion magazine.* MR. FRANK *is going over business accounts.* DUSSEL, *in his dentist's jacket, is pacing up and down, impa-*

3. Toscanini (täs' kə nē' nē): Arturo Toscanini, a famous Italian orchestral conductor.
4. Ride of the Valkyries (val' ki rēs): a stirring selection from an opera by Richard Wagner, a German composer.

9 **Enrichment** Discuss the use of similes in Anne's writing. Explain that a simile takes two essentially unlike things and draws an imaginative comparison between them using the word *like* or *as.* Anne compares the rumbling noises in their stomachs to musical instruments. Have students suggest other similes for the rest of the people in the Frank and Van Daan families.

10 **Master Teacher Note** Discuss the stage directions with students. Point out that stage directions in plays should be read carefully. They help the reader picture what the characters are doing. Question students on what each character is doing.

Discussing the changes Miss Frank made in her entries, Mr. Roth observed: "This brilliant young girl revised her diary because she discovered that she had become a much better writer. The fact that she rewrote it is one sign that, had she survived, she would have achieved an important literary career."

11 Discussion How is Margot's relationship with Anne changing?

tient to get into his bedroom. MR. VAN DAAN *is upstairs working on a piece of embroidery in an embroidery frame.*

In his room PETER *is sitting before the mirror, smoothing his hair. As the scene goes on, he puts on his tie, brushes his coat and puts it on, preparing himself meticulously for a visit from* ANNE. *On his wall are now hung some of* ANNE'S *motion picture stars.*

In her room ANNE *too is getting dressed. She stands before the mirror in her slip, trying various ways of dressing her hair.* MARGOT *is seated on the sofa, hemming a skirt for* ANNE *to wear.*

In the main room DUSSEL *can stand it no longer. He comes over, rapping sharply on the door of his and* ANNE'S *bedroom.*]

ANNE. [*Calling to him*] No, no, Mr. Dussel! I am not dressed yet.

[DUSSEL *walks away, furious, sitting down and burying his head in his hands.* ANNE *turns to* MARGOT.]

How is that? How does that look?

MARGOT. [*Glancing at her briefly*] Fine.

ANNE. You didn't even look.

MARGOT. Of course I did. It's fine.

ANNE. Margot, tell me, am I terribly ugly?

MARGOT. Oh, stop fishing.

11 **ANNE.** No. No. Tell me.

MARGOT. Of course you're not. You've got nice eyes . . . and a lot of animation, and . . .

ANNE. A little vague, aren't you?

[*She reaches over and takes a brassiere out of* MARGOT'S *sewing basket. She holds it up to herself, studying the effect in the mirror. Outside,* MRS. FRANK, *feeling sorry for* DUSSEL, *comes over, knocking at the girls' door.*]

MRS. FRANK. [*Outside*] May I come in?

MARGOT. Come in, Mother.

MRS. FRANK. [*Shutting the door behind her*] Mr. Dussel's impatient to get in here.

ANNE. [*Still with the brassiere*] Heavens, he takes the room for himself the entire day.

MRS. FRANK. [*Gently*] Anne, dear, you're not going in again tonight to see Peter?

ANNE. [*Dignified*] That is my intention.

MRS. FRANK. But you've already spent a great deal of time in there today.

ANNE. I was in there exactly twice. Once to get the dictionary, and then three-quarters of an hour before supper.

MRS. FRANK. Aren't you afraid you're disturbing him?

ANNE. Mother, I have some intuition.

MRS. FRANK. Then may I ask you this much, Anne. Please don't shut the door when you go in.

ANNE. You sound like Mrs. Van Daan! [*She throws the brassiere back in* MARGOT'S *sewing basket and picks up her blouse, putting it on.*]

MRS. FRANK. No. No. I don't mean to suggest anything wrong. I only wish that you wouldn't expose yourself to criticism . . . that you wouldn't give Mrs. Van Daan the opportunity to be unpleasant.

ANNE. Mrs. Van Daan doesn't need an opportunity to be unpleasant!

MRS. FRANK. Everyone's on edge, worried about Mr. Kraler. This is one more thing . . .

ANNE. I'm sorry, Mother. I'm going to Peter's room. I'm not going to let Petronella Van Daan spoil our friendship.

[MRS. FRANK *hesitates for a second, then goes out, closing the door after her. She gets a pack of playing cards and sits at the center table, playing solitaire. In* ANNE'S *room* MARGOT *hands the finished skirt to* ANNE. *As* ANNE *is putting it on,* MARGOT *takes off her high-heeled shoes and stuffs paper in the toes so that* ANNE *can wear them.*]

MARGOT. [*To* ANNE] Why don't you two talk in the main room? It'd save a lot of trouble. It's hard on Mother, having to listen to those remarks from Mrs. Van Daan and not say a word.

ANNE. Why doesn't she say a word? I think it's ridiculous to take it and take it.

MARGOT. You don't understand Mother at all, do you? She can't talk back. She's not like you. It's just not in her nature to fight back.

ANNE. Anyway . . . the only one I worry about is you. I feel awfully guilty about you. [*She sits on the stool near* MARGOT, *putting on* MARGOT'S *high-heeled shoes.*]

MARGOT. What about?

ANNE. I mean, every time I go into Peter's room, I have a feeling I may be hurting you. [MARGOT *shakes her head.*] I know if it were me, I'd be wild. I'd be desperately jealous, if it were me.

MARGOT. Well, I'm not.

ANNE. You don't feel badly? Really? Truly? You're not jealous?

MARGOT. Of course I'm jealous . . . jealous that you've got something to get up in the morning for . . . But jealous of you and Peter? No.

[ANNE *goes back to the mirror.*]

ANNE. Maybe there's nothing to be jealous of. Maybe he doesn't really like me. Maybe I'm just taking the place of his cat . . . [*She picks up a pair of short white gloves, putting them on.*] Wouldn't you like to come in with us?

MARGOT. I have a book.

[*The sound of the children playing outside fades out. In the main room* DUSSEL *can stand it no longer. He jumps up, going to the bedroom door and knocking sharply.*]

DUSSEL. Will you please let me in my room!

ANNE. Just a minute, dear, dear Mr. Dussel. [*She picks up her mother's pink stole and adjusts it elegantly over her shoulders, then gives a last look in the mirror.*] Well, here I go . . . to run the gauntlet.[5]

[*She starts out, followed by* MARGOT.]

DUSSEL. [*As she appears—sarcastic*] Thank you so much.

[DUSSEL *goes into his room.* ANNE *goes toward* PETER'S *room, passing* MRS. VAN DAAN *and her parents at the center table.*]

MRS. VAN DAAN. My God, look at her!

[ANNE *pays no attention. She knocks at* PETER'S *door.*]

I don't know what good it is to have a son. I never see him. He wouldn't care if I killed myself.

[PETER *opens the door and stands aside for* ANNE *to come in.*]

Just a minute, Anne. [*She goes to them at the door.*] I'd like to say a few words to my son. Do you mind?

[PETER *and* ANNE *stand waiting.*]

---

5. to run the gauntlet (gônt′ lit): Formerly, to pass between two rows of men who struck at the offender with clubs as he passed; here, a series of troubles or difficulties.

12 Discussion What do you learn about Mrs. Frank's character? Compare her character to that of Mrs. Van Daan.

13 Discussion How does Margot react to Peter and Anne's relationship?

14 Critical Thinking and Reading Compare Mrs. Van Daan's reaction to Peter and Anne's relationship to that of Mrs. Frank's. Which of the mothers' attitudes is more traditional?

15 Discussion How has Anne changed since the beginning of the play?

Peter, I don't want you staying up till all hours tonight. You've got to have your sleep. You're a growing boy. You hear?

MRS. FRANK. Anne won't stay late. She's going to bed promptly at nine. Aren't you, Anne?

ANNE. Yes, Mother . . . [*To* MRS. VAN DAAN] May we go now?

MRS. VAN DAAN. Are you asking me? I didn't know I had anything to say about it.

MRS. FRANK. Listen for the chimes, Anne dear.

[*The two young people go off into* PETER'S *room, shutting the door after them.*]

MRS. VAN DAAN. [*To* MRS. FRANK] In my day it was the boys who called on the girls. Not the girls on the boys.

MRS. FRANK. You know how young people like
14 to feel that they have secrets. Peter's room is the only place where they can talk.

MRS. VAN DAAN. Talk! That's not what they called it when I was young.

[MRS. VAN DAAN *goes off to the bathroom.* MARGOT *settles down to read her book.* MR. FRANK *puts his papers away and brings a chess game to the center table. He and* MRS. FRANK *start to play. In* PETER'S *room,* ANNE *speaks to* PETER, *indignant, humiliated.*]

ANNE. Aren't they awful? Aren't they impossible? Treating us as if we were still in the nursery.

[*She sits on the cot.* PETER *gets a bottle of pop and two glasses.*]

PETER. Don't let it bother you. It doesn't bother me.

ANNE. I suppose you can't really blame them . . . they think back to what *they* were like at our age. They don't realize how much more advanced we are . . . When you think what wonderful discussions we've had! . . . Oh, I forgot. I was going to bring you some more pictures.

PETER. Oh, these are fine, thanks.

ANNE. Don't you want some more? Miep just brought me some new ones.

PETER. Maybe later. [*He gives her a glass of pop and, taking some for himself, sits down facing her.*]

ANNE. [*Looking up at one of the photographs*] I remember when I got that . . . I won it. I bet Jopie that I could eat five ice-cream cones. We'd all been playing ping-pong . . . We used to have heavenly times . . . we'd finish up with ice cream at
the Delphi, or the Oasis, where Jews were 15
allowed . . . there'd always be a lot of boys . . . we'd laugh and joke . . . I'd like to go back to it for a few days or a week. But after that I know I'd be bored to death. I think more seriously about life now. I want to be a journalist . . . or something. I love to write. What do you want to do?

PETER. I thought I might go off some place . . . work on a farm or something . . . some job that doesn't take much brains.

ANNE. You shouldn't talk that way. You've got the most awful inferiority complex.

PETER. I know I'm not smart.

ANNE. That isn't true. You're much better than I am in dozens of things . . . arithmetic and algebra and . . . well, you're a million times better than I am in algebra. [*With sudden directness*] You like Margot, don't you? Right from the start you liked her, liked her much better than me.

PETER. [*Uncomfortably*] Oh, I don't know.

[*In the main room* MRS. VAN DAAN *comes from*

the bathroom and goes over to the sink, polishing a coffee pot.]

ANNE. It's all right. Everyone feels that way. Margot's so good. She's sweet and bright and beautiful and I'm not.

PETER. I wouldn't say that.

ANNE. Oh, no, I'm not. I know that. I know quite well that I'm not a beauty. I never have been and never shall be.

PETER. I don't agree at all. I think you're pretty.

ANNE. That's not true!

PETER. And another thing. You've changed . . . from at first, I mean.

ANNE. I have?

PETER. I used to think you were awful noisy.

ANNE. And what do you think now, Peter? How have I changed?

PETER. Well . . . er . . . you're . . . quieter.

[*In his room* DUSSEL *takes his pajamas and toilet articles and goes into the bathroom to change.*]

ANNE. I'm glad you don't just hate me.

PETER. I never said that.

ANNE. I bet when you get out of here you'll never think of me again.

PETER. That's crazy.

ANNE. When you get back with all of your friends, you're going to say . . . now what did I ever see in that Mrs. Quack Quack.

PETER. I haven't got any friends.

ANNE. Oh, Peter, of course you have. Everyone has friends.

PETER. Not me. I don't want any. I get along all right without them.

ANNE. Does that mean you can get along without me? I think of myself as your friend.

PETER. No. If they were all like you, it'd be different.

[*He takes the glasses and the bottle and puts them away. There is a second's silence and then* ANNE *speaks, hesitantly, shyly.*]

ANNE. Peter, did you ever kiss a girl?

PETER. Yes. Once.

ANNE. [*To cover her feelings*] That picture's crooked.

[PETER *goes over, straightening the photograph.*]

Was she pretty?

PETER. Huh?

ANNE. The girl that you kissed.

PETER. I don't know. I was blindfolded. [*He comes back and sits down again.*] It was at a party. One of those kissing games.

ANNE. [*Relieved*] Oh. I don't suppose that really counts, does it?

PETER. It didn't with me.

ANNE. I've been kissed twice. Once a man I'd never seen before kissed me on the cheek when he picked me up off the ice and I was crying. And the other was Mr. Koophuis, a friend of Father's who kissed my hand. You wouldn't say those counted, would you?

PETER. I wouldn't say so.

ANNE. I know almost for certain that Margot would never kiss anyone unless she was engaged to them. And I'm sure too that Mother never touched a man before Pim. But I don't know . . . things are so different now . . . What do you think? Do you think a
girl shouldn't kiss anyone except if she's 17

16 Discussion Do you think Anne is being realistic about her looks or is she looking for Peter to disagree?

17 Discussion How does Anne's fear and uncertainty affect her relationship with Peter? How would you feel in the same circumstance?

18 **Discussion** Why does Anne suddenly kiss Mrs. Van Daan? Why does this kiss confirm Mrs. Van Daan's suspicions?

Peter Van Daan

engaged or something? It's so hard to try to think what to do, when here we are with the whole world falling around our ears and you think . . . well . . . you don't know what's going to happen tomorrow and . . . What do you think?

PETER. I suppose it'd depend on the girl. Some girls, anything they do's wrong. But others . . . well . . . it wouldn't necessarily be wrong with them.

[*The carillon starts to strike nine o'clock.*]

I've always thought that when two people . . .

ANNE. Nine o'clock. I have to go.

PETER. That's right.

ANNE. [*Without moving*] Good night.

[*There is a second's pause, then* PETER *gets up and moves toward the door.*]

PETER. You won't let them stop you coming?

ANNE. No. [*She rises and starts for the door.*] Sometimes I might bring my diary. There are so many things in it that I want to talk over with you. There's a lot about you.

PETER. What kind of thing?

ANNE. I wouldn't want you to see some of it. I thought you were a nothing, just the way you thought about me.

PETER. Did you change your mind, the way I changed my mind about you?

ANNE. Well . . . You'll see . . .

[*For a second* ANNE *stands looking up at* PETER, *longing for him to kiss her. As he makes no move she turns away. Then suddenly* PETER *grabs her awkwardly in his arms, kissing her on the cheek.* ANNE *walks out dazed. She stands for a minute, her back to the people in the main room. As she regains her poise she goes to her mother and father and* MARGOT, *silently kissing them. They murmur their good nights to her. As she is about to open her bedroom door, she catches sight of* MRS. VAN DAAN. *She goes quickly to her, taking her face in her hands and kissing her first on one cheek and then on the other. Then she hurries off into her room.* MRS. VAN DAAN *looks after her, and then looks over at* PETER'S *room. Her suspicions are confirmed.*]

MRS. VAN DAAN. [*She knows.*] Ah hah!

[*The lights dim out. The curtain falls on the scene. In the darkness* ANNE'S VOICE *comes faintly at first and then with growing strength.*]

ANNE'S VOICE. By this time we all know each other so well that if anyone starts to tell a story, the rest can finish it for him. We're having to cut down still further on our meals. What makes it worse, the rats have been at work again. They've carried off some of our precious food. Even Mr. Dussel wishes now that Mouschi was here. Thursday, the twentieth of April, nineteen forty-four. Invasion fever is mounting every day. Miep tells us that people outside talk of nothing else. For myself, life has become much more pleasant. I often go to Peter's room after supper. Oh, don't think I'm in love, because I'm not. But it does make life more bearable to have someone with whom you can exchange views. No more tonight. P.S. . . . I must be honest. I must confess that I actually live for the next meeting. Is there anything lovelier than to sit under the skylight and feel the sun on your cheeks and have a darling boy in your arms? I admit now that I'm glad the Van Daans had a son and not a daughter. I've outgrown another dress. That's the third. I'm having to wear Margot's clothes after all. I'm working hard on my French and am now reading *La Belle Nivernaise.*[6]

[*As she is saying the last lines—the curtain rises on the scene. The lights dim on, as* ANNE'S VOICE *fades out.*]

Scene 3

[*It is night, a few weeks later. Everyone is in bed. There is complete quiet. In the* VAN DAAN'S *room a match flares up for a moment and then is quickly put out.* MR. VAN DAAN, *in bare feet, dressed in underwear and trousers, is dimly seen coming stealthily down the stairs and into the main room, where* MR. *and* MRS. FRANK *and* MARGOT *are sleeping. He goes to the food safe and again lights a match. Then he cautiously opens the safe, taking out a half-loaf of bread. As he closes the safe, it creaks. He stands rigid.* MRS. FRANK *sits up in bed. She sees him.*]

MRS. FRANK. [*Screaming*] Otto! Otto! *Komme schnell!*[7]

[*The rest of the people wake, hurriedly getting up.*]

MR. FRANK. *Was ist los? Was ist passiert?*[8]

[DUSSEL, *followed by* ANNE, *comes from his room.*]

MRS. FRANK. [*As she rushes over to* MR. VAN DAAN] *Er stiehlt das Essen!*[9]

DUSSEL. [*Grabbing* MR. VAN DAAN] You! You! Give me that.

MRS. VAN DAAN. [*Coming down the stairs*] Putti . . . Putti . . . what is it?

DUSSEL. [*His hands on* VAN DAAN'S *neck*] You dirty thief . . . stealing food . . . you good-for-nothing . . .

MR. FRANK. Mr. Dussel! For God's sake! Help me, Peter!

[PETER *comes over, trying, with* MR. FRANK, *to separate the two struggling men.*]

PETER. Let him go! Let go!

[DUSSEL *drops* MR. VAN DAAN, *pushing him away. He shows them the end of a loaf of bread that he has taken from* VAN DAAN.]

DUSSEL. You greedy, selfish . . . !

[MARGOT *turns on the lights.*]

MRS. VAN DAAN. Putti . . . what is it?

---

6. ***La Belle Nivernaise:*** A story by Alphonse Daudet, a French author.

7. ***Komme schnell*** (käm′ ə shnel): German for "Come quick!"

8. ***Was ist los? Was ist passiert?*** (väs ist los väs ist päs′ ērt): German for "What's the matter? What happened?"

9. ***Er stiehlt das Essen!*** (er stēlt däs es′ ən): German for "He steals food!"

19 **Discussion** How does Anne really feel about Peter? Is she seriously in love with him? How does her relationship with Peter affect her daily life?

20 **Discussion** How has Mrs. Frank's attitude changed? Why is she angry at Mr. Van Daan? Make sure students realize her rage toward him is not just for stealing the bread, but for stealing what should have gone to the children.

21 **Discussion** Mrs. Van Daan was accused of giving Mr. Van Daan more than his fair share of food earlier in Act II. Judging from what she says here, do you think Mr. Dussel was correct in his accusation? How does Mrs. Frank's view of marriage differ from that of Mrs. Van Daan?

22 **Discussion** How would you define Mr. Frank's role in this argument? Is this role typical of him?

[*All of* MRS. FRANK'S *gentleness, her self-control, is gone. She is outraged, in a frenzy of indignation.*]

MRS. FRANK. The bread! He was stealing the bread!

DUSSEL. It was you, and all the time we thought it was the rats!

MR. FRANK. Mr. Van Daan, how could you!

MR. VAN DAAN. I'm hungry.

20 **MRS. FRANK.** We're all of us hungry! I see the children getting thinner and thinner. Your own son Peter . . . I've heard him moan in his sleep, he's so hungry. And you come in the night and steal food that should go to them . . . to the children!

21 **MRS. VAN DAAN.** [*Going to* MR. VAN DAAN *protectively*] He needs more food than the rest of us. He's used to more. He's a big man.

[MR. VAN DAAN *breaks away, going over and sitting on the couch.*]

MRS. FRANK. [*Turning on* MRS. VAN DAAN] And you . . . you're worse than he is! You're a mother, and yet you sacrifice your child to this man . . . this . . . this . . .

MR. FRANK. Edith! Edith!

[MARGOT *picks up the pink woolen stole, putting it over her mother's shoulders.*]

MRS. FRANK. [*Paying no attention, going on to* MRS. VAN DAAN] Don't think I haven't seen you! Always saving the choicest bits for him! I've watched you day after day and I've held my tongue. But not any longer! Not after this! Now I want him to go! I want him to get out of here!

Together:

MR. FRANK. Edith!

MR. VAN DAAN. Get out of here?

MRS. VAN DAAN. What do you mean?

MRS. FRANK. Just that! Take your things and get out!

MR. FRANK. [*To* MRS. FRANK] You're speaking in anger. You cannot mean what you are saying.

MRS. FRANK. I mean exactly that!

[MRS. VAN DAAN *takes a cover from the* FRANKS' *bed, pulling it about her.*]

MR. FRANK. For two long years we have lived here, side by side. We have respected each other's rights . . . we have managed to live in peace. Are we now going to throw it all away? I know this will never happen again, will it, Mr. Van Daan?

MR. VAN DAAN. No. No.

MRS. FRANK. He steals once! He'll steal again!

[MR. VAN DAAN, *holding his stomach, starts for the bathroom.* ANNE *puts her arms around him, helping him up the step.*]

22 **MR. FRANK.** Edith, please. Let us be calm. We'll all go to our rooms . . . and afterwards we'll sit down quietly and talk this out . . . we'll find some way . . .

MRS. FRANK. No! No! No more talk! I want them to leave!

MRS. VAN DAAN. You'd put us out, on the streets?

MRS. FRANK. There are other hiding places.

MRS. VAN DAAN. A cellar . . . a closet. I know. And we have no money left even to pay for that.

MRS. FRANK. I'll give you money. Out of my own pocket I'll give it gladly. [*She gets her purse from a shelf and comes back with it.*]

MRS. VAN DAAN. Mr. Frank, you told Putti you'd never forget what he'd done for you when you came to Amsterdam. You said you could never repay him, that you . . .

MRS. FRANK. [*Counting out money*] If my husband had any obligation to you, he's paid it, over and over.

MR. FRANK. Edith, I've never seen you like this before. I don't know you.

MRS. FRANK. I should have spoken out long ago.

DUSSEL. You can't be nice to some people.

MRS. VAN DAAN. [*Turning on* DUSSEL] There would have been plenty for all of us, if *you* hadn't come in here!

3 **MR. FRANK.** We don't need the Nazis to destroy us. We're destroying ourselves.

[*He sits down, with his head in his hands.* MRS. FRANK *goes to* MRS. VAN DAAN.]

MRS. FRANK. [*Giving* MRS. VAN DAAN *some money*] Give this to Miep. She'll find you a place.

ANNE. Mother, you're not putting *Peter* out. Peter hasn't done anything.

MRS. FRANK. He'll stay, of course. When I say I must protect the children, I mean Peter too.

[PETER *rises from the steps where he has been sitting.*]

PETER. I'd have to go if Father goes.

[MR. VAN DAAN *comes from the bathroom.* MRS. VAN DAAN *hurries to him and takes him to the couch. Then she gets water from the sink to bathe his face.*]

MRS. FRANK. [*While this is going on*] He's no father to you . . . that man! He doesn't know what it is to be a father!

PETER. [*Starting for his room*] I wouldn't feel right. I couldn't stay.

MRS. FRANK. Very well, then. I'm sorry.

ANNE. [*Rushing over to* PETER] No, Peter! No!

[PETER *goes into his room, closing the door after him.* ANNE *turns back to her mother, crying.*]

I don't care about the food. They can have mine! I don't want it! Only don't send them away. It'll be daylight soon. They'll be caught . . .

MARGOT. [*Putting her arms comfortingly around* ANNE] Please, Mother!

MRS. FRANK. They're not going now. They'll stay here until Miep finds them a place. [*To* MRS. VAN DAAN] But one thing I insist on! He must never come down here again! He must never come to this room where the food is stored! We'll divide what we have . . . an equal share for each!

[DUSSEL *hurries over to get a sack of potatoes from the food safe.* MRS. FRANK *goes on, to* MRS. VAN DAAN]

You can cook it here and take it up to him.

[DUSSEL *brings the sack of potatoes back to the center table.*]

MARGOT. Oh, no. No. We haven't sunk so far that we're going to fight over a handful of rotten potatoes.

DUSSEL. [*Dividing the potatoes into piles*] Mrs. Frank, Mr. Frank, Margot, Anne, Peter, Mrs. Van Daan, Mr. Van Daan, myself . . . Mrs. Frank . . .

[*The buzzer sounds in* MIEP'S *signal.*]

MR. FRANK. It's Miep! [*He hurries over, getting his overcoat and putting it on.*]

MARGOT. At this hour?

MRS. FRANK. It is trouble.

23 Discussion What does Mr. Frank mean by this statement? Can Mrs. Frank's reaction and those of the others be blamed on their long confinement? Why?

24 Clarification D-Day, under the command of General Dwight Eisenhower, took place on June 6, 1944. During the night, about 176,000 soldiers crossed the English Channel. At dawn, battleships opened fire on the beaches at Normandy, France. At 6:30 A.M., troops from the United States, Britain, Canada, and France stormed ashore on a sixty-mile (one hundred-kilometer) front in the largest seaborne invasion in history.

MR. FRANK. [*As he starts down to unbolt the door*] I beg you, don't let her see a thing like this!

MR. DUSSEL. [*Counting without stopping*] . . . Anne, Peter, Mrs. Van Daan, Mr. Van Daan, myself . . .

MARGOT. [*To* DUSSEL] Stop it! Stop it!

DUSSEL. . . . Mr. Frank, Margot, Anne, Peter, Mrs. Van Daan, Mr. Van Daan, myself, Mrs. Frank . . .

MRS. VAN DAAN. You're keeping the big ones for yourself! All the big ones . . . Look at the size of that! . . . And that! . . .

[DUSSEL *continues on with his dividing.* PETER, *with his shirt and trousers on, comes from his room.*]

MARGOT. Stop it! Stop it!

[*We hear* MIEP'S *excited voice speaking to* MR. FRANK *below.*]

MIEP. Mr. Frank . . . the most wonderful news! . . . The invasion has begun!

MR. FRANK. Go on, tell them! Tell them!

[MIEP *comes running up the steps ahead of* MR. FRANK. *She has a man's raincoat on over her nightclothes and a bunch of orange-colored flowers in her hand.*]

24 **MIEP.** Did you hear that, everybody? Did you hear what I said? The invasion has begun! The invasion!

[*They all stare at* MIEP, *unable to grasp what she is telling them.* PETER *is the first to recover his wits.*]

PETER. Where?

MRS. VAN DAAN. When? When, Miep?

MIEP. It began early this morning . . .

[*As she talks on, the realization of what she has said begins to dawn on them. Everyone goes crazy. A wild demonstration takes place.* MRS. FRANK *hugs* MR. VAN DAAN.]

MRS. FRANK. Oh, Mr. Van Daan, did you hear that?

[DUSSEL *embraces* MRS. VAN DAAN. PETER *grabs a frying pan and parades around the room, beating on it, singing the Dutch National Anthem.* ANNE *and* MARGOT *follow him, singing, weaving in and out among the excited grown-ups.* MARGOT *breaks away to take the flowers from* MIEP *and distribute them to everyone. While this pandemonium is going on* MRS. FRANK *tries to make herself heard above the excitement.*]

MRS. FRANK. [*to* MIEP] How do you know?

MIEP. The radio . . . The B.B.C.![10] They said they landed on the coast of Normandy![11]

PETER. The British?

MIEP. British, Americans, French, Dutch, Poles, Norwegians . . . all of them! More than four thousand ships! Churchill spoke, and General Eisenhower! D-Day they call it!

MR. FRANK. Thank God, it's come!

MRS. VAN DAAN. At last!

MIEP. [*Starting out*] I'm going to tell Mr. Kraler. This'll be better than any blood transfusion.

MR. FRANK. [*Stopping her*] What part of Normandy did they land, did they say?

MIEP. Normandy . . . that's all I know now . . . I'll be up the minute I hear some more! [*She goes hurriedly out.*]

MR. FRANK. [*To* MRS. FRANK] What did I tell you? What did I tell you?

---

10. B.B.C.: British Broadcasting Corporation.
11. Normandy (nôr′ mən dē): A region in Northwest France, on the English channel.

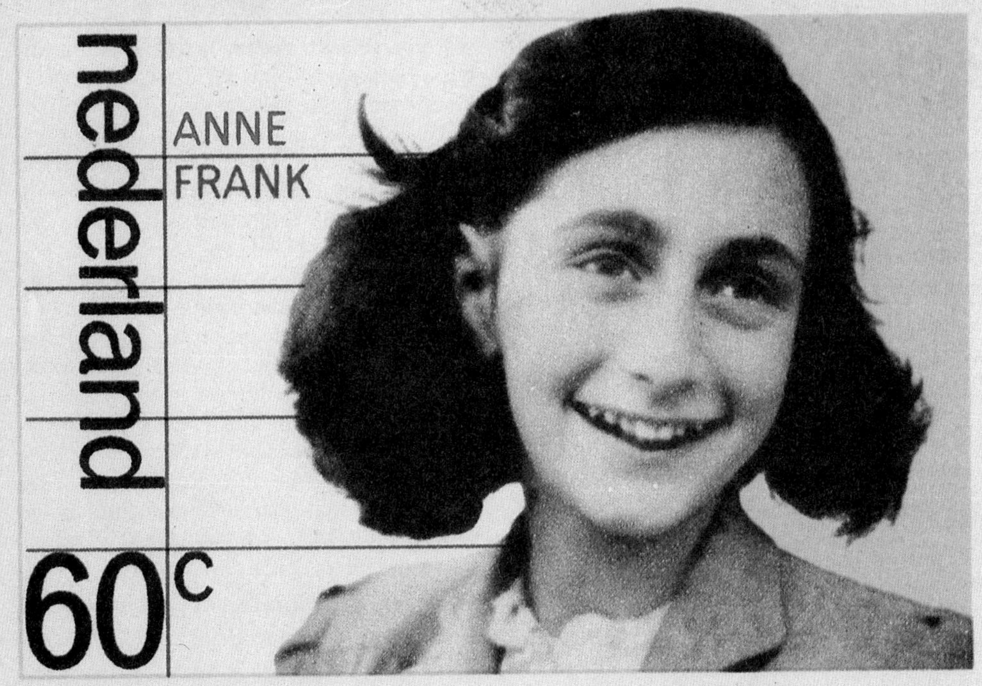

Postage stamp of Anne Frank issued in 1979

[MRS. FRANK *indicates that he has forgotten to bolt the door after* MIEP. *He hurries down the steps.* MR. VAN DAAN, *sitting on the couch, suddenly breaks into a convulsive*[12] sob. Everybody looks at him, bewildered.]

MRS. VAN DAAN. [*Hurrying to him*] Putti! Putti! What is it? What happened?

MR. VAN DAAN. Please, I'm so ashamed.

[MR. FRANK *comes back up the steps.*]

DUSSEL. Oh, for God's sake!

MRS. VAN DAAN. Don't, Putti.

MARGOT. It doesn't matter now!

MR. FRANK. [*Going to* MR. VAN DAAN] Didn't you hear what Miep said? The invasion has come! We're going to be liberated! This is a time to celebrate! [*He embraces* MRS. FRANK *and then hurries to the cupboard and gets the cognac and a glass.*]

MR. VAN DAAN. To steal bread from children! 25

MRS. FRANK. We've all done things that we're ashamed of.

ANNE. Look at me, the way I've treated Mother . . . so mean and horrid to her.

MRS. FRANK. No, Anneke, no.

[ANNE *runs to her mother, putting her arms around her.*]

12. convulsive (kən vul′ siv) *adj.*: Having an involuntary contraction or spasm of the muscles; shuddering.

25 Discussion Note how Mrs. Frank is forgiving Mr. Van Daan for stealing the bread. What made her change her attitude?

26 **Discussion** Discuss Anne's desire to live on after her death. Was she able to do this? How does she live on?

27 **Enrichment** Besides *The Diary of a Young Girl*, there is another book by Anne Frank titled *The Works of Anne Frank.* This is a collection of short stories, essays, and reminiscences that also includes her diary. All of the stories were written during her confinement in the attic. Students might wish to read some of her other works.

ANNE. Oh, Mother, I was. I was awful.

MR. VAN DAAN. Not like me. No one is as bad as me!

DUSSEL. [*To* MR. VAN DAAN] Stop it now! Let's be happy!

MR. FRANK. [*Giving* MR. VAN DAAN *a glass of cognac*] Here! Here! *Schnapps! L'chaim!*[13]

[VAN DAAN *takes the cognac. They all watch him. He gives them a feeble smile.* ANNE *puts up her fingers in a V-for-Victory sign. As* VAN DAAN *gives an answering V-sign, they are startled to hear a loud sob from behind them. It is* MRS. FRANK, *stricken with remorse. She is sitting on the other side of the room.*]

MRS. FRANK. [*Through her sobs*] When I think of the terrible things I said . . .

[MR. FRANK, ANNE *and* MARGOT *hurry to her, trying to comfort her.* MR. VAN DAAN *brings her his glass of cognac.*]

MR. VAN DAAN. No! No! You were right!

MRS. FRANK. That I should speak that way to you! . . . Our friends! . . . Our guests! [*She starts to cry again.*]

DUSSEL. Stop it, you're spoiling the whole invasion!

[*As they are comforting her, the lights dim out. The curtain falls.*]

ANNE'S VOICE. [*Faintly at first and then with growing strength*] We're all in much better spirits these days. There's still excellent news of the invasion. The best part about it is that I have a feeling that friends are coming. Who knows? Maybe I'll be back in school by fall. Ha, ha! The joke is on us! The warehouse man doesn't know a thing and we are paying him all that money! . . . Wednesday, the second of July, nineteen forty-four. The invasion seems temporarily to be bogged down. Mr. Kraler has to have an operation, which looks bad. The Gestapo have found the radio that was stolen. Mr. Dussel says they'll trace it back and back to the thief, and then, it's just a matter of time till they get to us. Everyone is low. Even poor Pim can't raise their spirits. I have often been downcast myself . . . but never in despair. I can shake off everything if I write. But . . . and that is the great question . . . will I ever be able to write well? I want to so much. I want to go on living even after my death. Another birthday has gone by, so now I am fifteen. Already I know what I want. I have a goal, an opinion.

[*As this is being said—the curtain rises on the scene, the lights dim on, and* ANNE'S VOICE *fades out.*]

Scene 4

[*It is an afternoon a few weeks later . . . Everyone but Margot is in the main room. There is a sense of great tension.*

Both MRS. FRANK *and* MR. VAN DAAN *are nervously pacing back and forth,* DUSSEL *is standing at the window, looking down fixedly at the street below.* PETER *is at the center table, trying to do his lessons.* ANNE *sits opposite him, writing in her diary.* MRS. VAN DAAN *is seated on the couch, her eyes on* MR. FRANK *as he sits reading.*

The sound of a telephone ringing comes from the office below. They all are rigid, listening tensely. MR. DUSSEL *rushes down to* MR. FRANK.]

13. ***Schnapps! L'chaim!*** (shnäps' lə khä' yim): German for "a drink" and a Hebrew toast meaning "To life."

DUSSEL. There it goes again, the telephone! Mr. Frank, do you hear?

MR. FRANK. [*Quietly*] Yes. I hear.

DUSSEL. [*Pleading, insistent*] But this is the third time, Mr. Frank! The third time in quick succession! It's a signal! I tell you it's Miep, trying to get us! For some reason she can't come to us and she's trying to warn us of something!

MR. FRANK. Please. Please.

MR. VAN DAAN. [*To* DUSSEL] You're wasting your breath.

DUSSEL. Something has happened, Mr. Frank. For three days now Miep hasn't been to see us! And today not a man has come to work. There hasn't been a sound in the building!

MRS. FRANK. Perhaps it's Sunday. We may have lost track of the days.

MR. VAN DAAN. [*To* ANNE] You with the diary there. What day is it?

DUSSEL. [*Going to* MRS. FRANK] I don't lose track of the days! I know exactly what day it is! It's Friday, the fourth of August. Friday, and not a man at work. [*He rushes back to* MR. FRANK, *pleading with him, almost in tears.*] I tell you Mr. Kraler's dead. That's the only explanation. He's dead and they've closed down the building, and Miep's trying to tell us!

MR. FRANK. She'd never telephone us.

DUSSEL. [*Frantic*] Mr. Frank, answer that! I beg you, answer it!

MR. FRANK. No.

MR. VAN DAAN. Just pick it up and listen. You don't have to speak. Just listen and see if it's Miep.

DUSSEL. [*Speaking at the same time*] For God's sake . . . I ask you.

MR. FRANK. No. I've told you, no. I'll do nothing that might let anyone know we're in the building.

PETER. Mr. Frank's right.

MR. VAN DAAN. There's no need to tell us what side you're on.

MR. FRANK. If we wait patiently, quietly, I believe that help will come.

[*There is silence for a minute as they all listen to the telephone ringing.*]

DUSSEL. I'm going down.

[*He rushes down the steps.* MR. FRANK *tries ineffectually to hold him.* DUSSEL *runs to the tower door, unbolting it. The telephone stops ringing.* DUSSEL *bolts the door and comes slowly back up the steps.*]

Too late.

[MR. FRANK *goes to* MARGOT *in* ANNE'*s bedroom.*]

MR. VAN DAAN. So we just wait here until we die.

MRS. VAN DAAN. [*Hysterically*] I can't stand it! I'll kill myself! I'll kill myself!

MR. VAN DAAN. For God's sake, stop it!

[*In the distance, a German military band is heard playing a Viennese waltz.*]

MRS. VAN DAAN. I think you'd be glad if I did! I think you want me to die!

MR. VAN DAAN. Whose fault is it we're here?

[MRS. VAN DAAN *starts for her room. He follows, talking at her.*]

We could've been safe somewhere . . . in America or Switzerland. But no! No! You wouldn't leave when I wanted to. You couldn't leave your things. You couldn't leave your precious furniture.

28 **Discussion** How does Anne's imagination help her survive her confinement?

29 **Discussion** Contrast Anne's attitude toward religion with that of Peter's. Does suffering cause Anne to lose faith in God?

30 **Discussion** Does it seem possible for her to truly believe this? How do you think you would feel under the same circumstances?

MRS. VAN DAAN. Don't touch me!

[*She hurries up the stairs, followed by* MR. VAN DAAN. PETER, *unable to bear it, goes to his room.* ANNE *looks after him, deeply concerned.* DUSSEL *returns to his post at the window.* MR. FRANK *comes back into the main room and takes a book, trying to read.* MRS. FRANK *sits near the sink, starting to peel some potatoes.* ANNE *quietly goes to* PETER'S *room, closing the door after her.* PETER *is lying face down on the cot.* ANNE *leans over him, holding him in her arms, trying to bring him out of his despair.*]

28 **ANNE.** Look, Peter, the sky. [*She looks up through the skylight.*] What a lovely, lovely day! Aren't the clouds beautiful? You know what I do when it seems as if I couldn't stand being cooped up for one more minute? I *think* myself out. I think myself on a walk in the park where I used to go with Pim. Where the jonquils and the crocus and the violets grow down the slopes. You know the most wonderful part about *thinking* yourself out? You can have it any way you like. You can have roses and violets and chrysanthemums all blooming at the same time . . . It's funny . . . I used to take it all for granted . . . and now I've gone crazy about everything to do with nature. Haven't you?

PETER. I've just gone crazy. I think if something doesn't happen soon . . . if we don't get out of here . . . I can't stand much more of it!

29 **ANNE.** [*Softly*] I wish you had a religion, Peter.

PETER. No, thanks! Not me!

ANNE. Oh, I don't mean you have to be Orthodox[14] . . . or believe in heaven and hell and purgatory[15] and things . . . I just mean some religion . . . it doesn't matter what. Just to believe in something! When I think of all that's out there . . . the trees . . . and flowers . . . and seagulls . . . when I think of the dearness of you, Peter . . . and the goodness of the people we know . . . Mr. Kraler, Miep, Dirk, the vegetable man, all risking their lives for us every day . . . When I think of these good things, I'm not afraid any more . . . I find myself, and God, and I . . .

[PETER *interrupts, getting up and walking away.*]

PETER. That's fine! But when I begin to think, I get mad! Look at us, hiding out for two years. Not able to move! Caught here like . . . waiting for them to come and get us . . . and all for what?

ANNE. We're not the only people that've had to suffer. There've always been people that've had to . . . sometimes one race . . . sometimes another . . . and yet . . .

PETER. That doesn't make me feel any better!

ANNE. [*Going to him*] I know it's terrible, trying to have any faith . . . when people are doing such horrible . . . But you know what I sometimes think? I think the world may be going through a phase, the way I was with Mother. It'll pass, maybe not for hundreds of years, but some day . . . I still believe, in spite of everything, that people are really good at heart. 3

PETER. I want to see something now . . . Not a thousand years from now! [*He goes over, sitting down again on the cot.*]

ANNE. But, Peter, if you'd only look at it as

14. Orthodox (ôr′ thə däks′) *adj.*: Strictly observing the rites and traditions of Judaism.

15. purgatory (pʉr′ gə tôr′ ē) *n.*: A state or place of temporary punishment.

Grammar in Action

Writers make use of a special punctuation mark known as an **ellipsis** or three dots (. . .). The ellipsis indicates the omission of a word or words. It is used by writers for special effects: to show a character's forgetfulness, to show a character's mind jumping from one thought to another without completing the first, to show a voice trailing off, to indicate a pause between thoughts.

Notice the use of the ellipsis in the following passages from *The Diary of Anne Frank:*

ANNE. Oh, I don't mean you have to be Orthodox . . . or believe in heaven and hell and purgatory and things . . . I just mean some religion . . . it doesn't matter what. Just to believe in something! When I think of all that's out there . . . the trees . . . and flowers . . . and seagulls . . . when I think of the dearness of you, Peter . . . and the goodness of the people we know . . . Mr. Kraler, Miep, Dirk, the vegetable man, all risking their lives for us every day . . . When I think of these good things, I'm not afraid any more . . . I find myself, and God, and I . . .

PETER. That's fine! But when I begin to think, I get mad! Look at us, hiding out for two years. Not able to move! Caught part of a great pattern . . . that we're just a little minute in the life . . . [*She breaks off.*] Listen to us, going at each other like a couple of stupid grownups! Look at the sky now. Isn't it lovely?

[*She holds out her hand to him.* PETER *takes it and rises, standing with her at the window looking out, his arms around her.*]

Some day, when we're outside again, I'm going to . . .

[*She breaks off as she hears the sound of a car, its brakes squealing as it comes to a sudden stop. The people in the other rooms also become aware of the sound. They listen tensely. Another car roars up to a screeching stop.* ANNE *and* PETER *come from* PETER'S *room.* MR. *and* MRS. VAN DAAN *creep down the stairs.* DUSSEL *comes out from his room. Everyone is listening, hardly breathing. A doorbell clangs again and again in the building below.* MR. FRANK *starts quietly down the steps to the door.* DUSSEL *and* PETER *follow him. The others stand rigid, waiting, terrified.*

In a few seconds DUSSEL *comes stumbling back up the steps. He shakes off* PETER'S *help and goes to his room.* MR. FRANK *bolts the door below, and comes slowly back up the steps. Their eyes are all on him as he stands there for a minute. They realize that what they feared has happened.* MRS. VAN DAAN *starts to whimper.* MR. VAN DAAN *puts her gently in a chair, and then hurries off up the stairs to their room to collect their things.* PETER *goes to comfort his mother. There is a sound of violent pounding on a door below.*]

31 **MR. FRANK.** [*Quietly*] For the past two years we have lived in fear. Now we can live in hope.

[*The pounding below becomes more insistent. There are muffled sounds of voices, shouting commands.*]

MEN'S VOICES. *Auf machen! Da drinnen! Auf machen! Schnell! Schnell! Schnell!*[16] *etc., etc.*

[*The street door below is forced open. We hear the heavy tread of footsteps coming up.* MR. FRANK *gets two school bags from the shelves, and gives one to* ANNE *and the other to* MARGOT. *He goes to get a bag for* MRS. FRANK. *The sound of feet coming up grows louder.* PETER *comes to* ANNE, *kissing her good-bye, then he goes to his room to collect his things. The buzzer of their door starts to ring.* MR. FRANK *brings* MRS. FRANK *a bag. They stand together, waiting. We hear the thud of gun butts on the door, trying to break it down.*

ANNE *stands, holding her school satchel, looking over at her father and mother with a soft, reassuring smile. She is no longer a child, but a woman with courage to meet whatever lies ahead.*

The lights dim out. The curtain falls on the scene. We hear a mighty crash as the door is shattered. After a second ANNE'S *voice is heard.*]

ANNE'S VOICE. And so it seems our stay here is over. They are waiting for us now. They've allowed us five minutes to get our things. We can each take a bag and whatever it will hold of clothing. Nothing else. So, dear Diary, that means I must leave you behind. Good-bye for a while. P.S. Please, please, Miep, or Mr. Kraler, or anyone else. If you should find this diary, will you please keep it safe for me, because some day I hope . . .

---

16. Auf machen! . . . Schnell! (o͝of mäk ən dä dri nən o͝of mäk ən shnel shnel shnel): German for "Open up, you in there, open up, quick, quick, quick."

31 Discussion What does Mr. Frank mean by this statement?

here like . . . waiting for them to come and get us . . . and all for what?

ANNE. We're not the only people that've had to suffer. There've always been people that've had to . . . sometimes one race . . . sometimes another . . . and yet . . .

Writers use the ellipsis for a special purpose—to capture the flavor or conversation or thought. However, excessive use of the ellipsis could indicate a lack of understanding of its use, or it could indicate laziness on the part of the writer.

Student Activity. Make up an interior monologue (thoughts of a character) in which he or she jumps from one idea to another. Use the ellipsis to indicate incomplete thoughts, shifts from one thought to another, or forgotten ideas. A good topic might be a teenager thinking about what to wear to the next school dance or a student tardy to his or her class for the fifth time thinking about what to say to the teacher.

32 **Discussion** What does Mr. Frank mean by this statement?

Enrichment Encourage students to read *The Diary of a Young Girl.* Have them compare it to the play.

Enrichment Have students find critical reviews about the play when it was first performed on Broadway in 1955.

Enrichment The movie *Shoah* (meaning *annihilation* in Hebrew) includes interviews with concentration camp survivors. The interviews are also in book form. You might read some of the passages to your students, if the film is unavailable for viewing.

Also, have the class assume that Anne survived. Ask members of the class to take on the role of Anne and perform a monologue in which she discusses her life in the camp and her views on fellow inmates and Nazi officials. Consider whether she will still declare that people are good at heart.

Enrichment *The Diary of Anne Frank* is a collaboration. With a partner, have students write a continuation of Act II, Scene 4. In it describe what happens immediately after the "mighty crash" when the Nazis break into the hideout.

Reader's Response What do you find most admirable about Anne?

[Her voice stops abruptly. There is silence. After a second the curtain rises.]

Scene 5

[It is again the afternoon in November, 1945. The rooms are as we saw them in the first scene. MR. KRALER *has joined* MIEP *and* MR. FRANK. *There are coffee cups on the table. We see a great change in* MR. FRANK. *He is calm now. His bitterness is gone. He slowly turns a few pages of the diary. They are blank.]*

MR. FRANK. No more. *[He closes the diary and puts it down on the couch beside him.]*

MIEP. I'd gone to the country to find food. When I got back the block was surrounded by police . . .

MR. KRALER. We made it our business to learn how they knew. It was the thief . . . the thief who told them.

*[*MIEP *goes up to the gas burner, bringing back a pot of coffee.]*

MR. FRANK. *[After a pause]* It seems strange to say this, that anyone could be happy in a concentration camp. But Anne was happy in the camp in Holland where they first took us. After two years of being shut up in these rooms, she could be out . . . out in the sunshine and the fresh air that she loved.

MIEP. *[Offering the coffee to* MR. FRANK*]* A little more?

MR. FRANK. *[Holding out his cup to her]* The news of the war was good. The British and Americans were sweeping through France. We felt sure that they would get to us in time. In September we were told that we were to be shipped to Poland . . . The men to one camp. The women to another. I was sent to Auschwitz.[17] They went to Belsen.[18] In January we were freed, the few of us who were left. The war wasn't yet over, so it took us a long time to get home. We'd be sent here and there behind the lines where we'd be safe. Each time our train would stop . . . at a siding, or a crossing . . . we'd all get out and go from group to group . . . Where were you? Were you at Belsen? At Buchenwald?[19] At Mauthausen? Is it possible that you knew my wife? Did you ever see my husband? My son? My daughter? That's how I found out about my wife's death . . . of Margot, the Van Daans . . . Dussel. But Anne . . . I still hoped . . . Yesterday I went to Rotterdam. I'd heard of a woman there . . . She'd been in Belsen with Anne . . . I know now.

[He picks up the diary again, and turns the pages back to find a certain passage. As he finds it we hear ANNE'S VOICE.*]*

ANNE'S VOICE. In spite of everything, I still believe that people are really good at heart. *[*MR. FRANK *slowly closes the diary.]*

MR. FRANK. She puts me to shame. 32

[They are silent.]

17. Auschwitz (ou' shvitz): A Nazi concentration camp in Poland, notorious as an extermination center.

18. Belsen (bel' z'n): A village in what is now West Germany that with the village of Bergen was the site of Bergen-Belsen, a Nazi concentration camp and extermination center.

19. Buchenwald (bo͞o' k'n wôld): A notorious Nazi concentration camp and extermination center in central Germany.

Closure and Extension

ANSWERS TO THINKING ABOUT THE SELECTION
Recalling

1. The people from whom Miep had gotten the ration books have been arrested, and so the refugees are particularly hungry.
2. Answers will differ. Some examples include Mr. Van Daan's attempt to sell his wife's fur coat, Peter's resentment over Dussel's remark about the boy's lost cat, news of the workman's blackmail of Mr. Kraler, Mrs. Van Daan's disapproval of her son's growing affection for Anne, and Mr. Van Daan's theft of food.
3. News of the D-Day invasion of Normandy and expectations of imminent liberation give the group hope.

   Mr. Kraler tells the group that he thinks one of the workmen is trying to blackmail him and knows that there are people hiding in the attic.
4. Mrs. Frank wants to turn out the Van Daans because she discovered Mr. Van Daan stealing bread that should have gone to the children.

   Mrs. Frank has always been shown to be concerned about the health and well-being of the children.
5. The Gestapo traces the stolen radio back to the thief, who re-

THINKING ABOUT THE SELECTION

Recalling

1. Why is Miep's cake such a treat? How does it also reveal rising tensions?
2. Give two other indications that tensions in the hideout are rising.
3. What gives the families hope? What troubling information does Mr. Kraler bring?
4. Why does Mrs. Frank want to turn out the Van Daans? How has the playwright prepared you for this aspect of her character?
5. What role does the thief play in the events?

Interpreting

6. How does Anne's friendship with Peter help her live through difficult times?
7. What does Mr. Frank mean when he says the people in hiding are Mr. Kraler's ulcers?
8. How does the families' behavior prove Mr. Frank's statement: "We don't need the Nazis to destroy us. We're destroying ourselves"?
9. How can Anne believe that "In spite of everything . . . people are really good at heart"?
10. Explain the meaning of Mr. Frank's last line: "She puts me to shame."

Applying

11. How might Anne's speech on page 351, beginning "We're young . . . ," express the attitudes of young people today?
12. How is Anne's diary a portrait of courage?

ANALYZING LITERATURE

Understanding Characters and Theme

The **theme** is the insight into life revealed by a work of literature. Sometimes a theme is stated directly. At other times you may have to figure out the theme by analyzing what the characters do and say. In this play the way characters cope with adversity reveals something about life.

1. How does Anne change during the the play?
2. What do the changes in the characters reveal about human beings in adversity?
3. What does the play reveal about hope?
4. What does it reveal about courage?

CRITICAL THINKING AND READING

Finding Support for Opinions

Opinions should be supported by reasons or evidence. For example, Anne tells Peter that he is wrong when he says she knows just how to talk to the adults. One piece of evidence that supports Anne's opinion is that she made her mother cry.

Anne wrote: "In spite of everything, I still believe that people are really good at heart."

1. Find three pieces of evidence in the play that support Anne's opinion about people.
2. Find three pieces of evidence in your own life that support Anne's opinion about people.

THINKING AND WRITING

Writing a Letter to the Editor

Imagine that it is the anniversary of Anne Frank's death. Write a letter to the editor of your local paper in which you explain why you feel it is good that the play based on her diary is read and performed regularly today

First, make an outline of points you want to include. Explain what the theme of the play is and why it is still an important one to consider.

Write a first draft of your letter. Then read it carefully. Make any needed revisions.

Finally, write a final draft of your letter, being careful to follow the correct form for a business letter. When you finish, reread your letter to make sure the spelling and punctuation are correct.

(Answers begin on p. 368.)

Challenge Even in the midst of crises, life goes on. How does Anne keep her spirits up?

ANSWERS TO ANALYZING LITERATURE

1. At first Anne is boisterous, mercurial, and self-assertive in ways that annoy others. By the play's end, Anne has learned to control her outbursts. She has established goals for herself, has found faith and courage, and displays a tolerance and concern for others.
2. The play suggests that human beings need faith, hope, and courage, as well as compassion for others, in order to endure adversity.
3. Human beings need hope in order to survive adversity.
4. Human beings need courage in times of adversity.

ANSWERS TO CRITICAL THINKING AND READING

1. Suggested answer: Evidence includes Miep's and Mr. Kraler's willingness to risk their lives for those in hiding; Mr. Frank's willingness to allow Dussel to join the group despite the inconvenience; Mr. Van Daan's realization that he was wrong to steal the bread; Mrs. Frank's admission that she was wrong to threaten the Van Daans with expulsion.
2. Answers will differ.

THINKING AND WRITING

Publishing Student Writing Send some of the better-written letters to the school newspaper.

Writing Across the Curriculum You might want students to do a research report on D-Day. Have them prepare outlines and discuss them with you. Then have them write their reports. History teachers might provide guidance for students on conducting their research.

veals the location of the hideout to the Nazis.

Interpreting

6. Peter provides her with the security she craves, and now this confidence in his affection for her enables her to be less defensive with the other occupants.
7. Ulcers can be caused by stress and aggravation. Mr. Frank feels that Mr. Kraler's ulcers were caused by constantly worrying about their safety.
8. Mr. Frank refers to the fact that living in confinement, compounded by the strain and tension of war, causes problems among people which might otherwise never occur.
9. Anne's successful struggle to achieve courage, hope, and compassion allows her to believe that people are really good at heart.
10. The implication is that Mr. Frank has lost his faith. Reading his daughter's entries restores his own faith in humanity.

Applying

11. Suggested answer: Like Anne in this speech, some young people think they can ignore the world's evils and on the strength of their hopes and ideals make the world a better place.
12. Anne's diary is an enduring testimonial to the power of courage and positivism to prevail over despair.

FOCUS ON READING

After discussing semantic mapping, you might model a semantic map by acting as "class secretary" and recording ideas suggested by the class on the board or on an overhead projector.

Mapping

Making a semantic map is a good way to remember and understand what you read. **Semantic mapping** is an easy, uncomplicated method of organizing information in graphic form. It is an excellent study technique that helps you to see how things are related to one another and provides a graphic pattern that is easy to remember. Creating and filling out a semantic map helps you understand, make your own assumptions, and evaluate information.

Steps

The first step in making a map is to decide what is the important information in the material you read. You must identify the major concepts or events that you want to organize. With a play you may want to make a map that organizes the plot, setting, and characters. You may choose to map the character traits of several characters or to show the development of one or more characters.

Once you have chosen your information, you should organize it into main ideas and relevant details. Now determine what type of diagram is best suited to organizing this information. The shape of the map should make it easy to see how everything is related. Different colors can be used to indicate these relationships. When your map is constructed, fill in all the information that you can recall. Then skim to find the information you couldn't remember and to check your facts. After skimming, fill in any blanks. Periodically review your map to recall the information.

The map on page 371 was constructed to give an overview of the play *The Diary of Anne Frank*. Look at it to understand what a semantic map is like and to see how the different parts of the plot structure relate to one another.

Note that this map is similar to an outline because everything is written concisely and is organized into main ideas or events and details. Events are listed in the order in which they occurred and under the appropriate part of the plot structure. You could have expanded this map by including sub-details under the details.

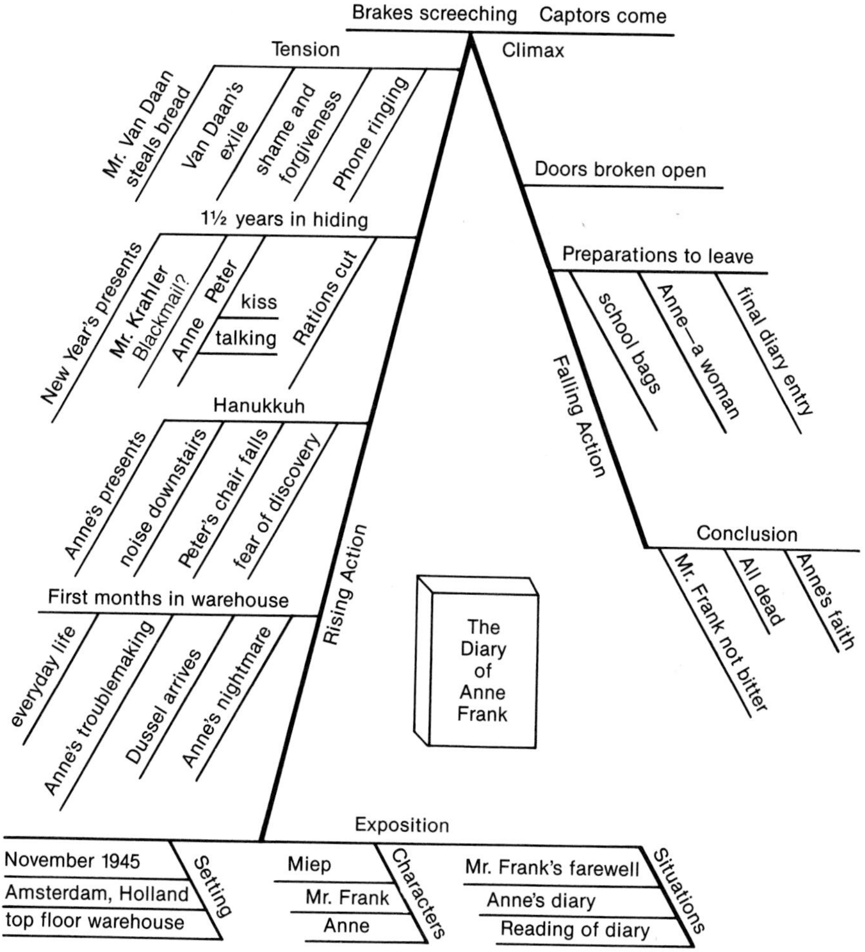

Activity

Now you are going to create your own map. Select a play. Brainstorm with your classmates to list the three most appropriate character traits for each of the major characters. Brainstorm some more to decide how you could organize this information so that your map would show which characters were most similar and which least alike. When you have created and filled in your map, compare it with those of your classmates.

ANSWERS TO THE ACTIVITY

Maps will differ. You might ask several students to reproduce their maps on the board or on transparencies for a class discussion.

The writing assignments on page 372 have students writing creatively, while those on page 373 have them thinking about drama and writing critically.

YOU THE WRITER

Guidelines for Evaluating Assignment 1

1. Does the dialogue illustrate how the main character confronts conflict?
2. Are there quotation marks and paragraph breaks to indicate a change of speaker?
3. Is the scene complete? Does it progress logically?
4. Is the dialogue free from grammar, usage, and mechanics errors?

Guidelines for Evaluating Assignment 2

1. Does the dialogue illustrate how the main character confronts conflict?
2. Are there quotation marks and paragraph breaks to indicate a change of speaker?
3. Is the scene complete? Does it progress logically?
4. Is the dialogue free from grammar, usage, and mechanics errors?

Guidelines for Evaluating Assignment 3

1. Does the description include the changes in the scene needed for a musical presentation?
2. Are there adequate details about the set, lighting, costumes, and musical numbers?
3. Does the introductory sentence explain which play the scene comes from?
4. Is the description free from grammar, usage, and mechanics errors?

YOU THE WRITER

Assignment

1. As an apprentice costume designer, you have been asked to create a costume for a minor character in one of the plays that you have read. Write a description of your design.

Prewriting. Review the plays, and select a minor character. Then brainstorm about the kind of costume this character might wear, noticing each item.

Writing. Write the first draft of a description of a costume you would create. Provide detailed descriptions of each part of the costume. Include appropriate items from head to toe.

Revising. Make sure you have arranged your description so that it covers each item from head to toe.

Assignment

2. Your local community theater is producing a version of "Back There" entitled "Out There." The director wants you to adapt the plot so that a character travels to the future. Write a scene from the adapted play.

Prewriting. Review "Back There." Brainstorm about what the main character will encounter in the future. Think of an episode around which the plot will revolve.

Writing. Develop the scene of the play that includes the main episode of the plot. Through dialogue, illustrate how the main character confronts conflict.

Revising. Make sure your dialogue logically illustrates the experience of the main character. Polish your scene by proofreading for spelling, grammar, and punctuation errors.

Assignment

3. Imagine one of the plays that you have read as a musical. Choose one scene from the play, and write a short description of the set, lighting, costumes, musical score, and songs that the characters might sing in this particular scene.

Prewriting. Freewrite until you have made some notes about adapting the scene. Then make notes about musicals that you have seen or read about.

Writing. Use your freewriting notes as the basis for your description. Describe how you would change this scene if the play were a musical. Include details about set, lighting, costumes, and musical numbers.

Revising. Make certain that your introductory sentence explains which play the scene you have adapted comes from. Have you provided adequate support for your ideas?

YOU THE CRITIC

Assignment **1.** Write a summary of the plot of a play to appear on a theatrical poster. Your sentences will be printed on the poster as an enticement to come see this play.

Prewriting. Choose one of the plays that you have read. Prepare a semantic map of the plot.

Writing. Use your map as the basis for writing your summary. Make certain that each sentence in your summary reveals why the play is interesting or intriguing.

Revising. Make certain that you have arranged events in chronological order.

Assignment **2.** What makes a hero or a villain? Choose one character from the plays that you have read. Write an evaluation of this character, describing why he or she is mostly good or mostly evil.

Prewriting. Review the plays that you have read, and select one character. List the characteristics and personality traits of that character.

Writing. Write your character evaluation, using your prewriting list as a basis for your essay. Make certain to explain your reasons for identifying this character as a villain or a hero. Include a discussion of clues that the playwright gives you.

Revising. Make certain that your opinions are supported by reasons and examples from the play. Check your evaluation for spelling, grammar, and punctuation errors.

Assignment **3.** *Theater Scoop Magazine* has sent an interviewer to opening night. The interviewer asks you about the play that you just saw. Write a short essay to explain your reaction to one of the plays.

Prewriting. Choose a play you found particularly interesting. Freewrite, exploring your reactions to it. Group your notes into negative and positive reactions.

Writing. Write your reaction to the play, including reasons for your opinions. Write your negative reactions in one paragraph and your positive reactions in another. Prepare an introduction and a conclusion that summarize your overall impressions of the play.

Revising. Make certain that you have written a strong introduction and conclusion and have provided reasons for your opinions. Are your opinions adequately supported by details from the play? Check your paragraphs for spelling, grammar, and punctuation errors.

YOU THE CRITIC

Guidelines for Evaluating Assignment 1

1. Has the student adequately summarized the plot?
2. Does the summary accomplish its purpose—enticing people to see the play?
3. Are the events arranged in chronological order?
4. Is the summary free from grammar, usage, and mechanics errors?

Guidelines for Evaluating Assignment 2

1. Does the evaluation show why a character could be judged a hero or a villain?
2. Does it back up its evaluation with reasons and examples?
3. Does it include a discussion of clues the playwright provides?
4. Is the evaluation free from grammar, usage, and mechanics errors?

Guidelines for Evaluating Assignment 3

1. Does the essay contain one paragraph of negative reaction and one paragraph of positive reaction?
2. Is there an introduction and a conclusion that summarize the student's overall impressions of the play?
3. Does the student adequately provide supported reasons for his or her opinions?
4. Is the essay free from grammar, usage, and mechanics errors?

MIRACLE OF NATURE
Thomas Moran
Three Lions

NONFICTION

Do you enjoy reading newspaper articles on sporting events? Do you take pleasure in reviews of performances you have seen? Do you particularly like stories of the lives of real people, both from the past and the present? Many people do. Newspaper articles, reviews, autobiographies, biographies—all are types of nonfiction.

Nonfiction deals with actual people, places, events, and topics based on real life. Autobiographies and biographies deal with the lives of real people, while essays provide a writer with room to express his or her thoughts and feelings on a particular subject. Nonfiction may inform, describe, persuade, or it may simply amuse.

In this unit you will encounter many types of nonfiction. The topics, too, will be varied; for example, a baseball player, a forest fire, shooting stars, and television.

Humanities Note

Fine art, *Miracle of Nature,* Thomas Moran. Thomas Moran (1837-1926) was a British-born American landscape painter. Moran studied wood engraving as a young man and toured the museums of France and Germany. Upon arrival in the United States, he worked for a time as an illustrator in Philadelphia. Moran was asked to accompany the official geographical expedition to Yellowstone as the recording artist in 1871. He went on this and other expeditions to what were to become America's great national parks. Thomas Moran's visual records of the fantastic natural beauties of the America West were instrumental in the establishment of the National Parks Commission in 1916.

The deep appreciation Thomas Moran had for nature is reflected in his painting *Miracle of Nature.* He recognized the spiritual and uplifting qualities in nature and translated them visually to the viewer. This sensitivity to nature, coupled with Moran's supreme command of color and light, made him the right person to record the natural phenomena of the west for the news-eager American public. Paintings such as this not only made the tales of the sights of the western territories believable, but they were also an invaluable lobbying tool for the men who fought to preserve these beauties as national treasures.

Reading Actively Based on research into the techniques of meaningful reading, the strategies outlined on this page will help students read nonfiction actively. Through this systematic approach, students interact with the text—questioning, predicting, clarifying, and summarizing what they read.

The strategies outlined here are similar to those on page 2 for reading short stories. One difference is the author's purpose. For nonfiction, students should question the author's purpose, his or her reason for writing, instead of characters' motives. The purpose is sometimes stated directly in a thesis statement and is supported through main ideas in the body of the essay.

For further practice with this process, you might have students use the selection in the Teaching Resource Portfolio, "The Seeing See Little," by Helen Keller, pages 448–451, which they can annotate themselves. Also, encourage students to continue to use these strategies when reading the other nonfiction selections.

Teaching to Ability Levels If your **less advanced** students have trouble understanding any of these elements, you might have them review the instruction on the appropriate pages or look up the necessary terms in the Handbook of Literary Terms and Techniques on page 824.

READING ACTIVELY

Nonfiction

What are active readers? Active readers are people who bring their own experiences to what they read. They filter the information the author provides through what they already know. They become actively involved with the writing as they pause to ask questions about the information and to predict where the information is leading. By interacting with the writing in this way, active readers gain a greater understanding of it.

You, too, can become an active reader by using the following strategies.

Question

Ask questions about the information. What does the author reveal about the topic? Do conclusions seem based on the information given? In addition, question the author's purpose. Is the author trying to persuade you to act or to think a certain way?

Predict

Think about what you already know about the topic. Where is the information leading? Make predictions about the conclusions you think the author will reach based on this information. As you read, you will find out whether your predictions are accurate.

Clarify

As you read, try to find the answers to your questions and check the accuracy of your predictions. In this way, you will monitor, or guide, your own reading and so gain the fullest understanding of the information presented. If there is a word you do not know, look it up in a dictionary. If there is information that seems inaccurate, check it in a reference book.

Summarize

Every now and then, pause to summarize, or review, the information the author has presented so far. What important points has the author made? How has the author supported these points?

Pull It Together

Determine the main idea of the entire selection. What did you find out about the topic? What are your reactions to the information the author had presented?

On the following pages, you will find a model of how to read an essay actively.

from One Writer's Beginnings

Eudora Welty

Learning stamps you with its moments. Childhood's learning is made up of moments. It isn't steady. It's a pulse.

In a children's art class, we sat in a ring on kindergarten chairs and drew three daffodils that had just been picked out of the yard; and while I was drawing, my sharpened yellow pencil and the cup of the yellow daffodil gave off whiffs just alike. That the pencil doing the drawing should give off the same smell as the flower it drew seemed part of the art lesson—as shouldn't it be? Children, like animals, use all their senses to discover the world. Then artists come along and discover it the same way, all over again. Here and there, it's the same world. Or now and then we'll hear from an artist who's never lost it.

In my sensory[1] education I include my physical awareness of the *word.* Of a certain word, that is; the connection it has with what it stands for. At around age six, perhaps, I was standing by myself in our front yard waiting for supper, just at that hour in a late summer day when the sun is already below the horizon and the risen full moon in the visible sky stops being chalky and begins to take on light. There comes the moment, and I saw it then, when the moon goes from flat to round. For the first time it met my eyes as a globe. The word "moon" came into my mouth as though fed to me out of a silver spoon. Held in my mouth the moon became a word. It had the roundness of a Concord grape Grandpa took off his vine and gave me to suck out of its skin and swallow whole, in Ohio.

Questions: What is the meaning of the title? Will the selection tell about this writer's youth? Will it tell how she became a writer?

Questions: What does this mean? Isn't a pulse steady? Perhaps she means that there are intense moments of learning followed by slack periods followed again by intense moments.

Clarification: Here is one of the writer's intense moments of learning. She is learning through her sense of smell.

Prediction: Perhaps the author will discuss how she learns through each of her senses.

Clarification: She *does* discuss what she learned through the sense of taste. How unusual to taste a word! The image of the grape suggests the richness of the word *moon.*

1. **sensory** (sen′ sər ē) *adj.*: Of receiving sense impressions.

Presentation

Motivation/Prior Knowledge You might lead the class in a discussion of memories. What are some of their vivid memories? What things that they remember have had an impact on their lives? Are they big events, small events, or both? What are their first memories?

Master Teacher Note To give students the opportunity to share their questions and ideas with the rest of the class, consider having them read the selection aloud. Oral reading allows students to discuss the annotations more completely, leading to better understanding and comprehension.

Thematic Idea Another selection that deals with memories that have had an impact on the author's life is "Christmas Day in the Morning," on page 21.

Purpose-Setting Question What influence do the memories described by the author have on her life?

Objectives

1. To learn how to read nonfiction actively
2. To understand informal essays
3. To compare and contrast opinions
4. To trace word histories
5. To write about the beginnings of a career

Support Material

Teaching Portfolio

Teacher Backup, pp. 445–447
Reading Actively, pp. 448–451
Grammar in Action Worksheet, *Understanding Complex Sentences,* pp. 452–453
Usage and Mechanics Worksheet, p. 454
Critical Thinking and Reading Worksheet, *Comparing and Contrasting Opinions,* p. 455
Language Worksheet, *Tracing Word Histories,* p. 456
Selection Test, pp. 457–458

Enrichment Your memory is very important to the learning process. Without remembering the past, you would be unable to learn anything new because all that you experience would be forgotten immediately. Therefore, all situations would be new and unfamiliar. Without memory, all of the emotions you experienced in the past, both happy and sad would be lost forever. What other difficulties would people face if they had no memories? What are some of the techniques that people use to remember things?

Grammar in Action

Complex sentences signal mature, sophisticated writing. Writing complex sentences is a skill that can be learned through studying grammar, but it is best learned by reading complex sentences of writers and writing them ourselves.

A complex sentence is made up of one independent clause and one or more subordinate clauses. Study the following complex sentence taken from *One Writer's Beginnings:*

> Though I was always waked for eclipses and indeed carried to the window as an infant in arms and shown Halley's Comet in my sleep, and though I'd been taught at our diningroom table about the solar system and knew the earth revolved around the sun, and our moon around us, I never found out the moon didn't come up in the west until I was a writer and Hershel Brickell, the literary critic, told me after I misplaced it in a story.

This complex sentence begins with two subordinate clauses, both beginning with the subordinating conjunction *though.* The independent clause (I never found out the moon didn't come up in the west) is followed by two more subordinate clauses, beginning with

This love did not prevent me from living for years in foolish error about the moon. The new moon just appearing in the west was the rising moon to me. The new should be rising. And in early childhood the sun and moon, those opposite reigning powers, I just as easily assumed rose in east and west respectively in their opposite sides of the sky, and like partners in a reel[2] they advanced, sun from the east, moon from the west, crossed over (when I wasn't looking) and went down on the other side. My father couldn't have known I believed that when bending behind me and guiding my shoulder, he positioned me at our telescope in the front yard and, with careful adjustment of the focus, brought the moon close to me.

Clarification: Here she learns through her sense of sight, but the knowledge she gains is in error.

Question: What will she learn from her mistake?

The night sky over my childhood Jackson was velvety black. I could see the full constellations in it and call their names; when I could read, I knew their myths. Though I was always waked for eclipses and indeed carried to the window as an infant in arms and shown Halley's Comet[3] in my sleep, and though I'd been taught at our diningroom table about the solar system and knew the earth revolved around the sun, and our moon around us, I never found out the moon didn't come up in the west until I was a writer and Herschel Brickell, the literary critic, told me after I misplaced it in a story. He said valuable words to me about my new profession: "Always be sure you get your moon in the right part of the sky."

Summary: As a child, Welty learned of the world through her senses.

Question: What does Brickell's remark indicate?

2. reel (rēl) *n.*: A lively Scottish dance.
3. Halley's Comet: A famous comet that reappears every 75 years.

Pulling It Together: Young children, like artists, learn through their senses. Good writers use sensory details to enrich their work. However, they must be certain the details are accurate.

Eudora Welty (1909–) was born and raised in Jackson, Mississippi, and this environment has formed the backdrop for most of her writing. After college she returned to Mississippi where her first full-time job for the Works Progress Administration took her all over the state, writing articles and taking photographs. Welty's first published short story appeared in 1936, and since then her reputation has grown steadily. In 1973 she was awarded a Pulitzer Prize for her novel *The Optimist's Daughter.*

the subordinating conjunctions *until* and *after.* The subject and verb in each clause is expanded with a number of prepositional phrases: *for eclipses, to the window, as an infant, in arms, in my sleep, at our diningroom table, about the solar system, around the sun, around us, in the west, in a story.*

Student Activity. Write a complex sentence in the pattern of Welty's example. Begin it with two subordinate clauses, each starting with the subordinating conjunction *although,* and end it with subordinate clauses beginning with *until* and *after.* A good way to start might be: Although I am only an eighth grader at this school and indeed care about my education. . . . Compare your sentence with those of your classmates.

More About the Author Eudora Welty has lived her entire life in the same house in Jackson, Mississippi. She has traveled widely in her lifetime, but her writing remains closely connected to the spirit and texture of the South.

Reader's Response What does Welty's remark "Learning stamps you with its moments" mean to you? Describe an outstanding "learning moment" from your life.

Closure and Extension

(Questions begin on p. 380.)

ANSWERS TO THINKING ABOUT THE SELECTION

Recalling

1. Welty notices that the sharpened pencil is giving off the same odor as the daffodils she is drawing.
2. Children, animals, and artists are alike because they all discover the world through all of their senses.
3. Welty believed that the moon always rose in the west. This seems logical to her because she thinks that the moon followed the sun's pattern, but in the opposite side of the sky.
4. She learns that the moon is round at about the age of six, standing in her front yard as the sun is setting and the moon is also in the sky. The moon also becomes round as a word. She made the connection between the object and the word.

Interpreting

5. Answers will differ. Suggested Response: She thinks that it is appropriate for the two objects to smell alike because, for it to be a part of art, one object used to record another object should have some sort of direct connection.
6. Answers will differ. Suggested Response: The meaning of the advice is that it is important not to have any misconceptions about life to be an effective writer. You cannot write about truth if you are inaccurate about the truth.

Applying

7. Answers will differ. Students may respond in agreement and support their opinion with images such as the rising sun indicating a new day and a growing person indicating a "new" person. If they disagree, they should also support their answer with concrete images.
8. Answers will differ. Students who

(Answers begin on p. 379.)

agree with the statement might support their answers by using the first paragraph from the essay and stating that by maintaining a childlike sense of wonder, an artist can record experiences from a fresh and untainted perspective. Students who disagree might support their answers by stating that artists are better able to record their perceptions accurately from the perspective of someone who has experienced things from many different vantage points.

ANSWERS TO ANALYZING LITERATURE

1. The topic of the essay is the effect of certain memories of the author's life on her learning. Welty expresses the opinion that, while these memories are important and lasting, they must nonetheless be free of misconceptions to be of any value in writing.
2. Suggested Response: You get the impression that the author is keenly aware of her natural surroundings and approaches her art with all of her senses aware. Students could use the first two paragraphs of the essay to support this particular answer.

Challenge How might the experiences related by the author in this essay be important to her as a photographer?

ANSWERS TO CRITICAL THINKING AND READING

1. Suggested Response: This statement contrasts sharply with Welty's feelings about words. Welty believes that words are closely linked with what they stand for while Glasow seems to view them with suspicion.
2. Suggested Response: This statement also contrasts with what Welty believes. Butler places no value at all on words while Welty sees them as inextricably linked with what they stand for.
3. Suggested Response: This statement reflects a sentiment about words that is the opposite of Welty's feelings. Hesse feels that words hide the meaning of what they stand for while Welty believes words are closely connected with what they stand for.
4. Suggested Response: Huxley's statement compares favorably to how Welty feels about words. He also seems to feel that words are connected very closely to experience.

ANSWERS TO UNDERSTANDING LANGUAGE

1. lunar: Anything caused by or affecting the moon.
2. lunacy: Insanity or wild and irresponsible behavior.
3. lunation: The elapsed time between two successive new moons.
4. lunarian: A supposed inhabitant of the moon or someone who makes a study of the moon.

All of these words are related because they contain the root *lun,* which is derived from the Latin word *luna,* meaning "moon."

THINKING AND WRITING

For help with this assignment, students can refer to Lesson 20, "Writing a Personal Essay," in the Handbook of Writing About Literature.

THINKING ABOUT THE SELECTION

Recalling

1. Explain the similarity Welty notices between the sharpened pencil and the daffodil.
2. According to Welty, how are children, animals, and artists alike?
3. What error does Welty make about the moon? Why does this error seem logical to her?
4. At what point does Welty learn that the moon is round? In what other way does the moon become round for her?

Interpreting

5. Why does Welty think it appropriate for the flower and the pencil to smell alike?
6. Explain the meaning of Herschel Brickell's advice.

Applying

7. Do you agree with Welty that the new should be rising? Explain your answer.
8. Do you think it necessary for an artist to see the world with a childlike sense of wonder? Explain your answer.

ANALYZING LITERATURE

Understanding the Informal Essay

An essay is a brief work of nonfiction in which a writer explores a topic and expresses an opinion or conclusion. It can be thought of as a kind of thinking aloud on paper. In an informal essay, writers use a conversational tone, injecting their personality into their observations.

1. What is the topic of this essay? What opinion does the writer express about this topic?
2. What impression do you form of Eudora Welty on the basis of this essay? Find evidence in the selection to support your answer.

CRITICAL THINKING AND READING

Comparing and Contrasting Opinions

An **opinion** is a personal view or a judgment or belief that rests on grounds insufficient to prove it true. People can consider the same topic and form different opinions. For example, Welty reached a special awareness of the meaning of words.

Compare and contrast Welty's understanding of words with those of the following writers.

1. Ellen Glasow: "I haven't much opinion of words . . . They're apt to set fire to a dry tongue, that's what I say."
2. Samuel Butler: "Words are like money; there is nothing so useless, unless in actual use."
3. Hermann Hesse: "Words are really a mask. They rarely express the true meaning; in fact they tend to hide it."
4. Aldous Huxley: "Words form the thread on which we string our experiences."

UNDERSTANDING LANGUAGE

Tracing Word Histories

Words have histories, just as people do. The word *lunatic,* for example, is based on *luna,* the Latin word for moon. A lunatic was thought to be moonstruck, or caused to go crazy by the influence of the moon.

Explain the meaning of each word. How does each relate to the Latin word for moon?

1. lunar
2. lunacy
3. lunation
4. lunarian

THINKING AND WRITING

Writing About Beginnings

Eudora Welty chose to write about a writer's beginnings. Think about another field—art, sports, teaching, medicine, or the like. Select a career. Then list the traits you think are necessary to be successful in that career. Using your list to guide you, write an essay entitled, "A ___________'s Beginnings." In your essay explain how you think a young person comes to realize these traits. Revise your essay, making sure you have organized your information in a logical fashion. Proofread your essay and share it with your classmates.

Biographies and Personal Accounts

MANY BRAVE HEARTS
Charles Demuth
Hirshhorn Museum and Sculpture Garden, Smithsonian Institution

Humanities Note

Fine art, *Many Brave Hearts,* by Charles Demuth. Charles Demuth (1883–1935) was a modern American watercolor painter. Born into an artistic family, Demuth was encouraged to pursue a childhood interest in art. He later attended the School of Industrial Art and the Pennsylvania Academy of the Fine Arts, both in Philadelphia. He also went to Paris where he studied Cubism. When he returned to New York, his art attracted the attention of gallery owner Alfred Stieglitz who championed Demuth and other innovative American artists. Demuth is remembered today for his aesthetic and sensitive watercolors of a variety of subjects.

Many Brave Hearts is a freely developed and illustrative painting. It demonstrates the exquisite technical skill with which Demuth handles the temperamental medium of watercolor. As in all of Demuth's paintings, the colors have a lush, velvety surface texture. The composition is balanced and harmonious with a jaunty air. Although Demuth often chose titles for his works that suggested a narrative or storytelling dimension, he felt that they conveyed their own meaning even without the aid of a title.

Publishing Student Writing Ask for student volunteers to read their essays aloud. Have students in the audience compare the essays read with their own and record similar traits needed for different careers.

Focus

More About the Author Ann Petry believes that it is impossible to understand the present without a knowledge of the past. Ask students to discuss how knowledge of black history would be helpful to Petry, a black writer.

Literary Focus You might point out that biographies are often, but not always, written about people who are known for some achievement. Ask students if they know of biographies about people who have well-known achievements and people who have not.

Look For Remind students that a biographical subject frequently has a dominant character trait that the biography emphasizes. For Harriet Tubman, it is her determination to go on in the face of great odds. This trait is shown in different ways throughout this selection.

Writing/Prior Knowledge You might present Martin Luther King, Jr. as an example of a person who showed great courage while facing many dangers. Ask students to discuss the dangers he faced and how he responded to them. Then have students invent a character and complete the freewriting assignment.

Vocabulary Point out that five of these words are adjectives. You might give students sentences with adjectives omitted and let them insert the appropriate adjectives from this list.

Spelling Tip Many adjectives like *fastidious* end in *dious,* including *studious, melodious,* and *invidious.*

GUIDE FOR READING

Harriet Tubman: Guide to Freedom

Ann Petry (1912–) worked as a newspaper reporter in New York City after college. Her first book, *The Street,* was set in Harlem, in northern New York City. Her short stories have appeared in magazines. Growing up in Old Saybrook, Connecticut, Petry decided that Harriet Tubman stood for everything indomitable, or not easily discouraged, in the human spirit. The following selection is from *Harriet Tubman: Conductor of the Underground Railroad.*

Biography

A **biography** is an account of a person's life as written by another person. A biography tells you about events in the person's life, focusing on his or her achievements and the difficulties that the person had to overcome. The biographer must create a living, believable character and stick to the known facts about the person. Usually an author chooses as a subject of a biography someone who has achieved something significant.

Look For

As you read "Harriet Tubman: Guide to Freedom," look for descriptions of Tubman that show that her spirit is not easily discouraged. Why would someone choose to write a biography about her?

Writing

In the selection you are about to read, Harriet Tubman shows great courage while facing many dangers. Imagine a situation in which a character faces danger with courage. Freewrite about this experience, describing what happens and how the character feels.

Vocabulary

Knowing the following words will help you as you read "Harriet Tubman: Guide to Freedom."

incentive (in sen′ tiv) *n.*: Something that stirs up people or urges them on (p. 385)
disheveled (di shev′′ld) *adj.*: Untidy; messy (p. 385)
guttural (gut′ ər əl) *adj.*: Made in back of the throat (p. 386)
mutinous (myo͞ot′′n əs) *adj.*: Rebelling against authority (p. 387)
cajoling (kə jōl′ iŋ) *v.*: Coaxing gently (p. 389)
indomitable (in däm′ it ə b′l) *adj.*: Not easily discouraged (p. 389)
fastidious (fas tid′ ē əs) *adj.*: Not easy to please (p. 390)

Objectives

1 To understand biography
2 To separate subjective from objective details
3 To use Latin roots
4 To write a biographical sketch

Support Material

Teaching Portfolio

Teacher Backup, pp. 459–462
Grammar in Action Worksheets, *Understanding Subject–Verb Agreement,* pp. 463–464, *Understanding Subordinate Clauses,* pp. 465–466
Usage and Mechanics Worksheet, p. 467
Vocabulary Check, p. 468
Analyzing Literature Worksheet, *Understanding Biography,* p. 469
Critical Thinking and Reading Worksheet, *Separating Subjective from Objective Details,* p. 470
Selection Test, pp. 471–472

Harriet Tubman: Guide to Freedom

Ann Petry

Along the Eastern Shore of Maryland, in Dorchester County, in Caroline County, the masters kept hearing whispers about the man named Moses, who was running off
1 slaves. At first they did not believe in his existence. The stories about him were fantastic, unbelievable. Yet they watched for him. They offered rewards for his capture.

They never saw him. Now and then they heard whispered rumors to the effect that he was in the neighborhood. The woods were searched. The roads were watched. There was never anything to indicate his whereabouts. But a few days afterward, a goodly number of slaves would be gone from the plantation. Neither the master nor the overseer had heard or seen anything unusual in
2 the quarter. Sometimes one or the other would vaguely remember having heard a whippoorwill call somewhere in the woods, close by, late at night. Though it was the wrong season for whippoorwills.

Sometimes the masters thought they had heard the cry of a hoot owl, repeated, and would remember having thought that the intervals between the low moaning cry were wrong, that it had been repeated four times in succession instead of three. There was never anything more than that to suggest that all was not well in the quarter. Yet when morning came, they invariably discovered that a group of the finest slaves had taken to their heels.

Unfortunately, the discovery was almost always made on a Sunday. Thus a whole day was lost before the machinery of pursuit could be set in motion. The posters offering rewards for the fugitives could not be printed until Monday. The men who made a living hunting for runaway slaves were out of reach, off in the woods with their dogs and
their guns, in pursuit of four-footed game, or 3
they were in camp meetings[1] saying their prayers with their wives and families beside them.

Harriet Tubman could have told them that there was far more involved in this matter of running off slaves than signaling the would-be runaways by imitating the call of a whippoorwill, or a hoot owl, far more
involved than a matter of waiting for a clear 4
night when the North Star was visible.

In December 1851, when she started out with the band of fugitives that she planned to take to Canada, she had been in the vicinity of the plantation for days, planning the trip, carefully selecting the slaves that she would take with her.

She had announced her arrival in the

1. **camp meetings** *n.*: Religious meetings held outdoors or in a tent.

Presentation

Motivation/Prior Knowledge Have students imagine they are slaves in the old South who have an opportunity to escape. If caught, they would be whipped and sold further South, where they would be treated more harshly. What would they choose? Why?

Master Teacher Note Tubman would announce her arrival among the slaves by singing the spiritual "Go down, Moses." Find a recording of this spiritual (Paul Robeson, Vanguard Label, # 79193) and play it for the students.

Purpose-Setting Question Tubman is described as "indomitable"—not easily discouraged. What details make Tubman seem indomitable in spirit?

Thematic Idea Another selection that deals with the theme of humanity helping humanity is "The Diary of Anne Frank" (page 303). You can show the similarity between Tubman leading slaves to freedom and the Dutch hiding the Jews from the Gestapo during World War II.

1 **Enrichment** Moses was the Biblical leader who brought the Israelites out of slavery in Egypt and led them to the Promised Land, received the Ten Commandments from God, and gave laws to the people.

2 **Clarification** The slave *quarter* was the section of the plantation where the slaves lived.

3 **Discussion** Have students discuss how these slave hunters were different from bounty hunters—men who pursued for money men on the "wanted list."

4 **Enrichment** Tell students that the North Star—Polaris—is a star almost directly above the northern end of the earth's axis. Tubman waited for the North Star to be guided by its bright light.

Humanities Note

Fine art, Harriet Tubman Series, #7, by Jacob Lawrence. Jacob Lawrence (1917–), an Afro-American, grew up in Harlem during the Depression. He has become one of the most important Afro-American artists of our time.

Lawrence's background, one of poverty in the inner city, helped to foster his great admiration for Harriet Tubman. Lawrence saw her story as a perfect example of people's ability to raise themselves from any depth. He created the Harriet Tubman Series of paintings to commemorate her life as the most famous and successful organizer of the Underground Railroad. Three works from this series (Numbers 7, 16, and 10) are used with this selection.

As you discuss this painting, emphasize that by simplifying the forms of his subject matter and exaggerating essential details, Lawrence was able to produce qualities that could not be expressed through realistic imitation.

1. What suggests the quality of strength in this painting?
2. How does Lawrence use color, shape, and arrangement to convey this feeling of strength?
3. Even though the subject of this painting was a real person, why do you suppose Lawrence chose to paint her in such an unrealistic style?

5 **Discussion** Why was singing this song forbidden? Ask students to discuss other examples from history of songs, speeches, or writing that were forbidden for fear they would incite disturbances.

6 **Literary Focus** What qualities or traits does Harriet Tubman show?

7 **Clarification** Explain to students that slaves could expect harsher treatment further South.

HARRIET TUBMAN SERIES, #7
Jacob Lawrence
Hampton University Museum

quarter by singing the forbidden spiritu-
5 al [2]—"Go down, Moses, 'way down to Egypt
Land"—singing it softly outside the door of
a slave cabin, late at night. The husky voice was beautiful even when it was barely more than a murmur borne on the wind.

Once she had made her presence known, word of her coming spread from cabin to cabin. The slaves whispered to each other, ear to mouth, mouth to ear, "Moses is here." "Moses has come." "Get ready. Moses is back again." The ones who had agreed to go North with her put ashcake and salt herring in an old bandanna, hastily tied it into a bundle, and then waited patiently for the signal that meant it was time to start.

There were eleven in this party, including one of her brothers and his wife. It was the largest group that she had ever conducted, but she was determined that more and more slaves should know what freedom was like.

She had to take them all the way to Canada. The Fugitive Slave Law[3] was no longer a great many incomprehensible words written down on the country's lawbooks. The new law had become a reality. It was Thomas Sims, a boy, picked up on the streets of Boston at night and shipped back to Georgia. It was Jerry and Shadrach, arrested and jailed with no warning.

She had never been in Canada. The
route beyond Philadelphia was strange to
her. But she could not let the runaways who
accompanied her know this. As they walked 6
along she told them stories of her own first
flight, she kept painting vivid word pictures
of what it would be like to be free.

But there were so many of them this time. She knew moments of doubt when she was half-afraid, and kept looking back over her shoulder, imagining that she heard the sound of pursuit. They would certainly be pursued. Eleven of them. Eleven thousand dollars' worth of flesh and bone and muscle
that belonged to Maryland planters. If they
were caught, the eleven runaways would be
whipped and sold South, but she—she 7
would probably be hanged.

They tried to sleep during the day but they never could wholly relax into sleep. She

---

2. **forbidden spiritual:** In 1831 a slave named Nat Turner encouraged an unsuccessful slave uprising in Virginia, by talking about the Biblical story of the Israelites' escape from Egypt. Afterwards, the singing of certain spirituals was forbidden, for fear of encouraging more uprisings.

3. **Fugitive Slave Law:** This part of the Compromise of 1850 held that escaped slaves, even if found in free states, could be returned to their masters. As a result, fugitives were not safe until they were in Canada.

Grammar in Action

Subject–verb agreement refers to the way subjects and verbs work together in sentences. A verb must agree with its subject in *number*. In terms of grammar, the *number* of a word can be either singular (one) or plural (more than one). Only nouns, pronouns, and verbs have number. Most nouns are made plural by adding *-s* or *-es* to the singular form. The plural of *moment*, for example, is *moments*. Verbs, on the other hand, are singular when *-s* or *-es* is added to them.

A singular subject must have a singular verb; similarly, a plural subject must have a plural verb. In the following passage from "Harriet Tubman: Guide to Freedom," subjects and verbs could tell by the positions they assumed, by their restless movements. And they walked at night. Their progress was slow. It took them three nights of walking to reach the first stop. She had told them about the place where they would stay, promising warmth and good food, holding these things out to them as an incentive to keep going.

When she knocked on the door of a farmhouse, a place where she and her parties of runaways had always been welcome, always been given shelter and plenty to eat, there was no answer. She knocked again, softly. A voice from within said, "Who is it?" There was fear in the voice.

She knew instantly from the sound of the voice that there was something wrong. She said, "A friend with friends," the password on the Underground Railroad.

The door opened, slowly. The man who stood in the doorway looked at her coldly, looked with unconcealed astonishment and fear at the eleven disheveled runaways who were standing near her. Then he shouted, "Too many, too many. It's not safe. My place was searched last week. It's not safe!" and slammed the door in her face.

She turned away from the house, frowning. She had promised her passengers food and rest and warmth, and instead of that, there would be hunger and cold and more walking over the frozen ground. Somehow she would have to instill courage into these eleven people, most of them strangers, would have to feed them on hope and bright dreams of freedom instead of the fried pork and corn bread and milk she had promised them.

They stumbled along behind her, half-dead for sleep, and she urged them on, though she was as tired and as discouraged as they were. She had never been in Canada but she kept painting wondrous word pictures of what it would be like. She managed to dispel their fear of pursuit, so that they would not become hysterical, panic-stricken. Then she had to bring some of the fear back, so that they would stay awake and keep walking though they drooped with sleep.

Yet during the day, when they lay down deep in a thicket, they never really slept, because if a twig snapped or the wind sighed in the branches of a pine tree, they jumped to their feet, afraid of their own shadows, shivering and shaking. It was very cold, but they dared not make fires because someone would see the smoke and wonder about it.

She kept thinking, eleven of them. Eleven thousand dollars' worth of slaves. And she had to take them all the way to Canada. Sometimes she told them about Thomas Garrett, in Wilmington. She said he was their friend even though he did not know them. He was the friend of all fugitives. He called them God's poor. He was a Quaker and his speech was a little different from that of other people. His clothing was different, too. He wore the wide-brimmed hat that the Quakers wear.

She said that he had thick white hair, soft, almost like a baby's, and the kindest eyes she had ever seen. He was a big man and strong, but he had never used his strength to harm anyone, always to help people. He would give all of them a new pair of shoes. Everybody. He always did. Once they reached his house in Wilmington, they would be safe. He would see to it that they were.

She described the house where he lived, told them about the store where he sold shoes. She said he kept a pail of milk and a loaf of bread in the drawer of his desk so that he would have food ready at hand for any of God's poor who should suddenly appear before him, fainting with hunger. There was a hidden room in the store. A whole wall

8 **Literary Focus** What challenge does Harriet Tubman face?

9 **Critical Thinking and Reading** Help students to see that this kind of detail, giving information about Tubman's feelings and thoughts, is a subjective detail. Such subjective details are interspersed with factual information.

agree; the subjects are underlined once, while verbs are underlined twice:

> There were eleven in this party, including one of her brothers and his wife. It was the largest group that she had ever conducted, but she was determined that more and more slaves should know what freedom was like.

Had the passage begun "there was eleven in this party," and concluded "she were determined," subjects and verbs would not agree because *eleven* is plural and *was* is singular; similarly, *she* is singular and *were* is plural.

Student Activity 1. Locate two more examples of subject-verb agreement in the selection. Explain why the subjects and verbs agree.

Student Activity 2. Write three of your own sentences in which subjects and verbs agree in number.

Humanities Note

Fine art, *Harriet Tubman Series, #16,* by Jacob Lawrence. Lawrence's paintings in the Tubman Series reflect a deep personal involvement in the ideals demonstrated in the life of Harriet Tubman and the plight of all Afro-Americans.

Point out that a strong element in the composition of this painting is repetition.

1. What part of the selection does this painting illustrate?
2. How does the artist show the element of repetition in this painting?
3. What repetitions would have been seen, heard, or felt by a slave fleeing on the Underground Railroad?

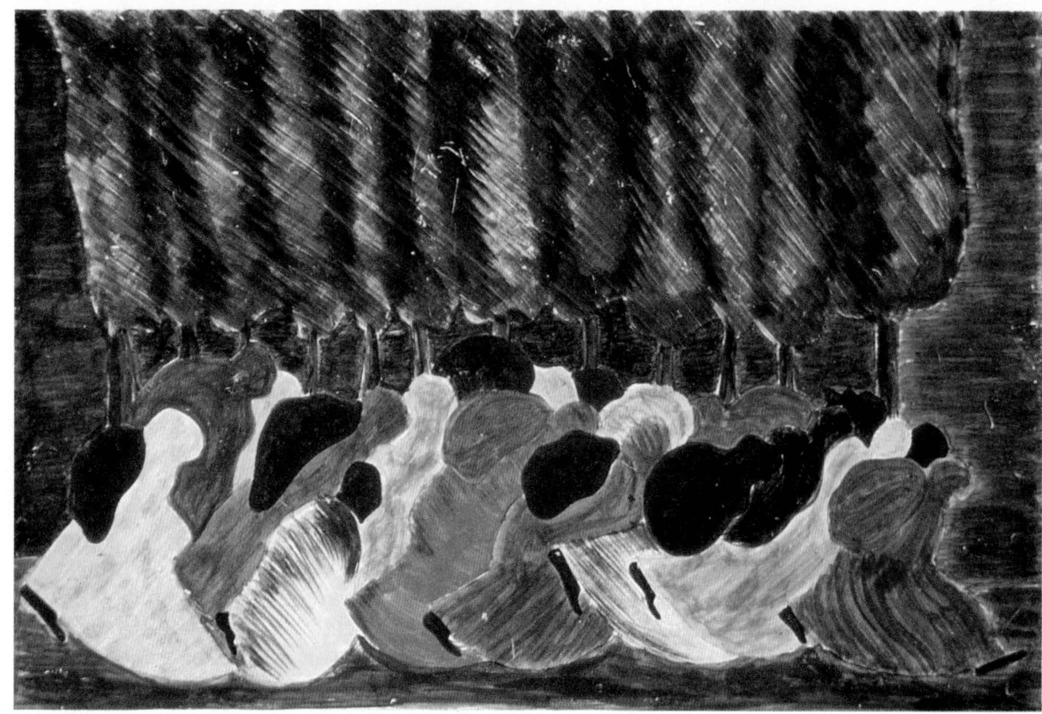

HARRIET TUBMAN SERIES, #16
Jacob Lawrence
Hampton University Museum

swung open, and behind it was a room where he could hide fugitives. On the wall there were shelves filled with small boxes —boxes of shoes—so that you would never guess that the wall actually opened.

While she talked, she kept watching them. They did not believe her. She could tell by their expressions. They were thinking. New shoes, Thomas Garrett, Quaker, Wilmington—what foolishness was this? Who knew if she told the truth? Where was she taking them anyway?

That night they reached the next stop—a farm that belonged to a German. She made the runaways take shelter behind trees at the edge of the fields before she knocked at the door. She hesitated before she approached the door, thinking, suppose that he, too, should refuse shelter, suppose—Then she thought, Lord, I'm going to hold steady on to You and You've got to see me through—and knocked softly.

She heard the familiar guttural voice say, "Who's there?"

She answered quickly, "A friend with friends."

He opened the door and greeted her warmly. "How many this time?" he asked.

"Eleven," she said and waited, doubting, wondering.

He said, "Good. Bring them in."

He and his wife fed them in the lamplit kitchen, their faces glowing, as they offered food and more food, urging them to eat,

Grammar in Action

Writers vary their sentences by beginning some with subordinate clauses. A **subordinate clause** begins with a subordinating conjunction such as *after, because, as if, in order that, when, though,* and others. The subordinating conjunction is followed by a clause which contains a subject and a verb, but because the clause begins with a subordinating conjunction, it cannot stand alone as a sentence. It must be connected to an independent clause. When a subordinate clause appears at the beginning of the sentence, it must be followed by a comma. If a subordinate clause appears after the independent clause, usually there is no comma.

Read the following sentences beginning with subordinate clauses taken from "Harriet Tubman: Guide to Freedom":

Once she had made her presence known, word of her coming spread from cabin to cabin.

If they were caught, the eleven runaways would be whipped and sold South, but she—she would probably be hanged.

saying there was plenty for everybody, have more milk, have more bread, have more meat.

They spent the night in the warm kitchen. They really slept, all that night and until dusk the next day. When they left, it was with reluctance. They had all been warm and safe and well-fed. It was hard to exchange the security offered by that clean, warm kitchen for the darkness and the cold of a December night.

Harriet had found it hard to leave the warmth and friendliness, too. But she urged them on. For a while, as they walked, they seemed to carry in them a measure of contentment; some of the serenity and the cleanliness of that big warm kitchen lingered on inside them. But as they walked farther and farther away from the warmth
and the light, the cold and the darkness
entered into them. They fell silent, sullen,
10 suspicious. She waited for the moment
when some one of them would turn mutinous. It did not happen that night.

Two nights later she was aware that the
feet behind her were moving slower and
11 slower. She heard the irritability in their
voices, knew that soon someone would refuse to go on.

She started talking about William Still and the Philadelphia Vigilance Committee.[4] No one commented. No one asked any questions. She told them the story of William and Ellen Craft and how they escaped from Georgia. Ellen was so fair that she looked as though she were white, and so she dressed up in a man's clothing and she looked like a wealthy young planter. Her husband, William, who was dark, played the role of her slave. Thus they traveled from Macon, Georgia, to Philadelphia, riding on the trains, staying at the finest hotels. Ellen pretended to be very ill—her right arm was in a sling, and her right hand was bandaged, because she was supposed to have rheumatism. Thus she avoided having to sign the register at the hotels for she could not read or write. They finally arrived safely in Philadelphia, and then went on to Boston.

No one said anything. Not one of them seemed to have heard her.

She told them about Frederick Douglass, the most famous of the escaped slaves, of his eloquence, of his magnificent appearance. Then she told them of her own first vain effort at running away, evoking the memory of that miserable life she had led as a child, reliving it for a moment in the telling.

But they had been tired too long, hungry too long, afraid too long, footsore too long. One of them suddenly cried out in despair, "Let me go back. It is better to be a slave than to suffer like this in order to be free."

She carried a gun with her on these
trips. She had never used it—except as a
threat. Now as she aimed it, she experienced
a feeling of guilt, remembering that time,
years ago, when she had prayed for the
death of Edward Brodas, the Master, and 12
then not too long afterward had heard that
great wailing cry that came from the throats
of the field hands, and knew from the
sound that the Master was dead.

One of the runaways said, again, "Let me go back. Let me go back," and stood still, and then turned around and said, over his shoulder, "I am going back."

She lifted the gun, aimed it at the despairing slave. She said, "Go on with us or die." The husky low-pitched voice was grim.

He hesitated for a moment and then he joined the others. They started walking again. She tried to explain to them why none of them could go back to the plantation. If a

---

4. Philadelphia Vigilance Committee: A group of citizens who helped escaped slaves. Its secretary was a free black man named William Still.

10 **Reading Strategy** Have students predict what Tubman will do now.

11 **Discussion** What might Tubman do if someone refuses to go on?

12 **Discussion** Tubman feels guilty about this childhood experience. What connection in her mind do you think she made as a child?

When she knocked on the door of a farmhouse, a place where she and her parties of runaways had always been welcome, always been given shelter and plenty to eat, there was no answer.

Once they reached his house in Wilmington, they would be safe.

While she talked, she kept watching them.

Notice in the above examples that each sentence begins with a subordinating conjunction *(once, if, when, while)*, which is followed by a clause containing a subject and a verb. After each subordinate clause, there is a comma.

Subordinate clauses can be added to the beginning or end of a sentence in order to combine ideas and to make the sentences longer and more interesting.

Student Activity 1. Find four other subordinate clauses in "Harriet Tubman: Guide to Freedom."

Student Activity 2. Write four of your own sentences that begin with a subordinating clause. Be sure that you follow the clause with a comma.

Humanities Note

Fine art, Harriet Tubman Series, #10, by Jacob Lawrence. In this painting, Jacob Lawrence uses strong, hard-edged shapes of intense color in a unique, personal style. He often uses these dramatic elements to create symbols of oppression and protest.

1. What symbols can you find in this painting?
2. What message might the artist be communicating with these symbols?

3 **Discussion** What methods might have been used to force a captured runaway to turn traitor?

14 **Discussion** What does Tubman mean by these words?

HARRIET TUBMAN SERIES, #10
Jacob Lawrence
Hampton University Museum

13 runaway returned, he would turn traitor, the master and the overseer would force him to turn traitor. The returned slave would disclose the stopping places, the hiding places, the cornstacks they had used with the full knowledge of the owner of the farm, the name of the German farmer who had fed them and sheltered them. These people who had risked their own security to help runaways would be ruined, fined, imprisoned.

14 She said, "We got to go free or die. And freedom's not bought with dust."

This time she told them about the long agony of the Middle Passage on the old slave ships, about the black horror of the holds, about the chains and the whips. They too knew these stories. But she wanted to remind them of the long hard way they had come, about the long hard way they had yet to go. She told them about Thomas Sims, the boy picked up on the streets of Boston and sent back to Georgia. She said when they got him back to Savannah, got him in prison there, they whipped him until a doctor who was standing by watching said, "You will kill him if you strike him again!" His master said, "Let him die!"

Thus she forced them to go on. Sometimes she thought she had become nothing but a voice speaking in the darkness, cajoling, urging, threatening. Sometimes she told them things to make them laugh, sometimes she sang to them, and heard the eleven voices behind her blending softly with hers, and then she knew that for the moment all was well with them.

She gave the impression of being a short, muscular, indomitable woman who could never be defeated. Yet at any moment she was liable to be seized by one of those curious fits of sleep, which might last for a few minutes or for hours.[5]

Even on this trip, she suddenly fell asleep in the woods. The runaways, ragged, dirty, hungry, cold, did not steal the gun as they might have, and set off by themselves, or turn back. They sat on the ground near her and waited patiently until she awakened. They had come to trust her implicitly, totally. They, too, had come to believe her repeated statement, "We got to go free or die." She was leading them into freedom, and so they waited until she was ready to go on.

Finally, they reached Thomas Garrett's house in Wilmington, Delaware. Just as Harriet had promised, Garrett gave them all new shoes, and provided carriages to take them on to the next stop.

By slow stages they reached Philadelphia, where William Still hastily recorded their names, and the plantations whence they had come, and something of the life they had led in slavery. Then he carefully hid what he had written, for fear it might be discovered. In 1872 he published this record 16
in book form and called it *The Underground Railroad.* In the foreword to his book he said: "While I knew the danger of keeping strict records, and while I did not then dream that in my day slavery would be blotted out, or that the time would come when I could publish these records, it used to afford 17
me great satisfaction to take them down, fresh from the lips of fugitives on the way to freedom, and to preserve them as they had given them."

William Still, who was familiar with all the station stops on the Underground Railroad, supplied Harriet with money and sent her and her eleven fugitives on to Burlington, New Jersey.

Harriet felt safer now, though there were danger spots ahead. But the biggest part of her job was over. As they went farther and farther north, it grew colder; she was aware of the wind on the Jersey ferry and aware of the cold damp in New York. From New York 18
they went on to Syracuse, where the temperature was even lower.

In Syracuse she met the Reverend J. W. Loguen, known as "Jarm" Loguen. This was the beginning of a lifelong friendship. Both Harriet and Jarm Loguen were to become friends and supporters of Old John Brown.[6]

From Syracuse they went north again, into a colder, snowier city—Rochester. Here they almost certainly stayed with Frederick Douglass, for he wrote in his autobiography:

"On one occasion I had eleven fugitives at the same time under my roof, and it was necessary for them to remain with me until

---

5. sleep . . . hours: When she was about 13, Harriet accidentally received a severe blow on the head. Afterwards, she often lost consciousness, and could not be woken until the episode was over.

6. John Brown: White abolitionist (1800–1859) who was hanged for leading a raid on the arsenal at Harpers Ferry, Virginia, as part of a slave uprising.

15 Reading Strategy Have students summarize what has happened so far and predict the outcome of the journey.

16 Enrichment Explain to students that the Underground Railroad was a system in the United States before the Civil War that was set up by certain opponents of slavery to help fugitive slaves escape to free states and Canada. The system involved designated hiding places along the journey in which the opponents used passwords to hide runaway slaves.

17 Discussion Have students discuss what would happen if William Still's records of runaway slaves were discovered.

18 Discussion Point out to students that this cold climate was unfamiliar to the slaves. What effect might it have on them?

19 **Clarification** Point out that none of these rights was granted to slaves in the United States.

Reader's Response Tubman says that "freedom is not bought with dust." Substitute the word freedom with another appropriate noun.

I could collect sufficient money to get them to Canada. It was the largest number I ever had at any one time, and I had some difficulty in providing so many with food and shelter, but, as may well be imagined, they were not very fastidious in either direction, and were well content with very plain food, and a strip of carpet on the floor for a bed, or a place on the straw in the barnloft."

Late in December, 1851, Harriet arrived in St. Catharines, Canada West (now Ontario), with the eleven fugitives. It had taken almost a month to complete this journey; most of the time had been spent getting out of Maryland.

That first winter in St. Catharines was a terrible one. Canada was a strange frozen land, snow everywhere, ice everywhere, and a bone-biting cold the like of which none of them had ever experienced before. Harriet rented a small frame house in the town and set to work to make a home. The fugitives boarded with her. They worked in the forests, felling trees, and so did she. Sometimes she took other jobs, cooking or cleaning house for people in the town. She cheered on these newly arrived fugitives, working herself, finding work for them, finding food for them, praying for them, sometimes begging for them.

Often she found herself thinking of the beauty of Maryland, the mellowness of the soil, the richness of the plant life there. The climate itself made for an ease of living that could never be duplicated in this bleak, barren countryside.

In spite of the severe cold, the hard work, she came to love St. Catharines, and the other towns and cities in Canada where black men lived. She discovered that freedom meant more than the right to change jobs at will, more than the right to keep the money that one earned. It was the right to vote and to sit on juries. It was the right to be elected to office. In Canada there were black men who were county officials and members of school boards. St. Catharines had a large colony of ex-slaves, and they owned their own homes, kept them neat and clean and in good repair. They lived in whatever part of town they chose and sent their children to the schools.

When spring came she decided that she would make this small Canadian city her home—as much as any place could be said to be home to a woman who traveled from Canada to the Eastern Shore of Maryland as often as she did.

In the spring of 1852, she went back to Cape May, New Jersey. She spent the summer there, cooking in a hotel. That fall she returned, as usual, to Dorchester County, and brought out nine more slaves, conducting them all the way to St. Catharines, in Canada West, to the bone-biting cold, the snow-covered forests—and freedom.

She continued to live in this fashion, spending the winter in Canada, and the spring and summer working in Cape May, New Jersey, or in Philadelphia. She made two trips a year into slave territory, one in the fall and another in the spring. She now had a definite crystallized purpose, and in carrying it out, her life fell into a pattern which remained unchanged for the next six years.

Closure and Extension

ANSWERS TO THINKING ABOUT THE SELECTION

Recalling

1. She announced her arrival by singing the forbidden spiritual "Go down, Moses."
2. It was smart of Tubman to plan escapes on Saturday nights because it was difficult to start slave hunting on Sunday. Because businesses were closed, posters could not be printed until Monday. Slave hunters were not available on Sundays because they were either hunting game or in camp meetings.
3. No fugitive was allowed to turn back because the master and overseer would force him or her to turn traitor, revealing hiding places and people who had helped him or her.

Interpreting

4. Moses was an appropriate name for Tubman because in the Biblical story Moses led the enslaved Israelites out of Egypt to freedom.
5. Tubman never told the fugitives she was afraid because that would encourage their fear; she needed to instill courage in them to keep going.
6. Tubman was a "guide to freedom" because she inspired trust in the slaves to follow her in the

THINKING ABOUT THE SELECTION

Recalling

1. How did Harriet Tubman announce her arrival in the slave quarter?
2. Why was it smart of Tubman to plan escapes on Saturday nights?
3. Why was no fugitive allowed to turn back?

Interpreting

4. Why was Moses an appropriate name for Harriet Tubman?
5. Why did Tubman never tell any of the fugitives that she was afraid?
6. In what sense was Tubman a "guide to freedom"? In what sense was she a "conductor on the railroad"?

Applying

7. Like the Israelites escaping Egypt, the slaves escaped to freedom. What other groups today have made similar escapes? What qualities do such people have?

ANALYZING LITERATURE

Understanding Biography

A biography, or account of a person's life written by another person, often focuses on the achievements of the person's life. The writer may tell you about the difficulties the person overcame.

1. How do you think the author wants you to feel about her subject—Harriet Tubman?
2. Find three details of Tubman's life that help create this impression.
3. For what reasons do you think Tubman is a good subject for a biography?

CRITICAL THINKING AND READING

Recognizing Subjective Details

Writers often include both objective and subjective details in a biography. **Objective details** are true-to-life descriptions that do not include personal feelings or judgments. For example, the writer says, "There were eleven in this party, including one of her brothers and his wife."

Subjective details are descriptions that tell you a person's feelings, attitudes, or judgments instead of external facts. An example is, ". . . she was determined that more and more slaves should know what freedom was like."

Identify which of the following contain subjective and which contain objective details.

1. "She knew moments of doubt when she was half-afraid, and kept looking back over her shoulder, imagining that she heard the sound of pursuit."
2. "In December 1851, when she started out with the band of fugitives that she planned to take to Canada, she had been in the vicinity of the plantation for days. . . ."

UNDERSTANDING LANGUAGE

Using Latin Roots

A **root** is a word or word part to which other parts may be added to make new words. The root *duct* comes from the Latin word *ducere*, meaning "to lead." For example, the word *conduct* means "to lead or direct an orchestra."

Explain how the root *duct* gives meaning to these English words.

1. educate 2. deduct 3. production

THINKING AND WRITING

Writing a Biography

Choose a person whom you admire. Select one incident in the person's life that portrays the qualities you most associate with that person. The incident may be one in which the person overcame an obstacle. Freewrite about this incident. Using the information from your freewriting, write a biographical sketch. Revise your sketch, making sure you have portrayed your subject vividly. Proofread your sketch.

(Answers begin on p. 390.)

journey North even when she was not sure of the route. She conducted the slaves from stop to stop on the Underground Railroad.

Applying

7. Answers will differ. Suggested Responses: Other groups today who have made similar escapes are dissidents from the Soviet Union, refugees from Vietnam and Cambodia. Such people probably possess courage, tenacity, endurance, and strong faith.

ANSWERS TO ANALYZING LITERATURE

1. The author probably wants you to admire and respect Tubman for her courage and endurance.
2. Three details of Tubman's life that help create this impression are that Tubman would not let the runaways know that the route beyond Philadelphia was strange to her, that she urged the runaways on even when she herself was tired and discouraged, and that she threatened deserters with a gun.
3. Suggested Response: Tubman is a good subject for a biography because she risked danger and her life for an unselfish goal.

Challenge What aspects of this biography are factual and can be verified and which do you think the author developed as what *probably* happened in certain situations?

ANSWERS TO CRITICAL THINKING AND READING

1. subjective detail
2. objective detail

ANSWERS TO UNDERSTANDING LANGUAGE

1. *educate*–to lead someone to develop knowledge, skill, mind or character, especially by schooling or study
2. *deduct*–to lead away; that is, to bring from or out
3. *production*–the act of bringing forth

THINKING AND WRITING

Publishing Student Writing This the kind of writing activity that can be shared—in groups, on a bulletin board, in a booklet.

Students might enjoy reading each other's biographical sketches. Prepare a bulletin board display of their written sketches. Students might contribute pictures of their subjects to be displayed with their written sketches.

Focus

More About the Author Izenberg has a Ph.D. from Harvard University, with postdoctoral education in psychoanalysis. Ask students what factors might motivate someone interested in the study of the human personality to write about a celebrated sports figure.

Literary Focus Point out that a memoir can be written by a close friend or relative of the subject without relying on interviews and anecdotes from other people. Usually, however, a memoir is supplemented with anecdotes from other people. Ask the students who they think the writer chose to interview about Roberto Clemente.

Look For Discuss with students how the writer could get interesting information from the people he interviews. What if a person being interviewed could not remember any significant information, or was not willing to talk?

Writing/Prior Knowledge You might have students list some qualities in others that they admire and value. Then help them brainstorm for people who demonstrate these qualities. They may then complete the writing assignment.

Vocabulary Have your **less advanced** students read these words aloud so that you can be sure they can read them.

Spelling Tip *Crypt* is one of a small group of words in which *y* sounds like a short *i*. Other words in this group include *myth, gyp, gypsy,* and *gypsum.*

GUIDE FOR READING

Roberto Clemente: A Bittersweet Memoir

Jerry Izenberg (1930–), a graduate of Rutgers University, is a sportswriter and reporter. He is a syndicated sports columnist based at the *Newark Star Ledger,* whose daily column appears in newspapers around the country. He has written seven books and written or directed thirty-one television specials. In the following selection from *Great Latin Sports Figures,* published in 1976, he portrays the inspiration of Roberto Clemente, the former All-Star right fielder and record-making hitter for the Pittsburgh Pirates.

Memoir

A **memoir** is a biographical piece usually written by a relative or personal friend of the subject. The writer has based this memoir about Roberto Clemente on interviews and anecdotes.

An interview is a planned meeting at which writers obtain information about a topic from someone who is knowledgeable about it. Izenberg gathered first-hand information about Roberto Clemente through interviews with people who had known him well.

Answers to interview questions often provide anecdotes—brief stories about noteworthy incidents—that give information and show the person in a different light.

Look For

As you read "Roberto Clemente: A Bittersweet Memoir," look for the information gained from others through interviews and the anecdotes that help create this strong, personal memoir. Why does Clemente's life serve as an inspiration to others?

Writing

List five well-known people about whom you might like to write a memoir. Note the field or career of each person, for example, Alice Walker—American writer.

Vocabulary

Knowing the following words will help you as you read "Roberto Clemente: A Bittersweet Memoir."

delineate (di lin′ ē āt′) *v.*: Describe in detail (p. 393)
brace (brās) *n.*: A pair of like things (p. 393)
conjectured (kən jek′ chərd) *v.*: Guessed from very little evidence (p. 394)
banked (baŋkt) *v.*: Tilted an airplane to the side when turning, making one wing higher than the other (p. 395)
crypt (kript) *n.*: An underground vault or room, used as a burial place (p. 397)
prospect (präs′ pekt) *n.*: A likely candidate (p. 399)

Objectives

1 To understand the memoir
2 To identify primary and secondary sources
3 To do an interview
4 To write a memoir

Support Material

Teaching Portfolio
Teacher Backup, pp. 473–475
Grammar in Action Worksheet, *Using Dashes,* pp. 476–477
Usage and Mechanics Worksheet, p. 478
Vocabulary Check, p. 479
Analyzing Literature Worksheet, *Understanding the Memoir,* p. 480
Language Worksheet, *Using Prefixes and Suffixes to Determine Meaning,* p. 481
Selection Test, pp. 482–483

Roberto Clemente: A Bittersweet Memoir

Jerry Izenberg

*I saw him play so often. I watched the
grace of his movements and the artistry of
his reflexes from who knows how many
press boxes. None of us really appreciated
how pure an athlete he was until he was
gone. What follows is a personal retracing
of the steps that took Roberto Clemente
from the narrow, crowded streets of his
1 native Carolina to the local ball parks in
San Juan and on to the major leagues. But
it is more. It is a remembrance formed as I
stood at the water's edge in Puerto Rico
and stared at daybreak into the waves
that killed him. It is all the people I
met in Puerto Rico who knew him and
loved him. It is the way an entire island
in the sun and a Pennsylvania city in the
smog took his death. . . .*

The record book will tell you that Roberto Clemente collected 3,000 hits during his major-league career. It will say that he came to bat 9,454 times, that he drove in 1,305 runs, and played 2,433 games over an eighteen-year span.

But it won't tell you about Carolina, Puerto Rico; and the old square; and the narrow, twisting streets; and the roots that produced him. It won't tell you about the Julio Coronado School and a remarkable woman named María Isabella Casares, whom he called "Teacher" until the day he died and who helped to shape his life in times of despair and depression. It won't tell you about a man named Pedron Zarrilla, who found him on a country softball team and put him in the uniform of the Santurce club and who nursed him from promising young athlete to major-league superstar.

And most of all, those cold numbers
won't begin to delineate the man Roberto
Clemente was. To even begin to understand
what this magnificent athlete was all about, 2
you have to work backward. The search
begins at the site of its ending.

The car moves easily through the predawn streets of San Juan. A heavy all-night rain has now begun to drive, and there is that postrain sweetness in the air that holds the promise of a new, fresh, clear dawn. This is a journey to the site of one of Puerto Rico's deepest tragedies. This last says a lot. Tragedy is no stranger to the sensitive emotional people who make this island the human place it is.

Shortly before the first rays of sunlight, the car turns down a bumpy secondary road and moves past small shantytowns, where the sounds of the children stirring for the long walk toward school begin to drift out on the morning air. Then there is another turn, between a brace of trees and onto the hard-

Presentation

Motivation/Prior Knowledge Ask students to discuss what types of people will risk their own lives and put themselves in dangerous situations in order to help others.

Purpose-Setting Question Discuss the meaning of *bittersweet*—pleasant with overtones of sadness. Ask students why is this a "bittersweet memoir"? What aspects of it are bitter, and what aspects of it are sweet?

1 **Literary Focus** What prompted Izenberg to write this memoir?

2 **Critical Thinking and Reading** What is the author's attitude about Clemente?

3 Discussion Ask students their opinion of this definition of friendship. What are their definitions of friendship?

4 Discussion Why did Vigereaux think a celebrity like Clemente would be more effective in getting help than, for example, he himself would?

5 Discussion What does this passage suggest about the economic status of the people who were donating?

6 Clarification The black market is a system for selling goods illegally, especially in violation of rationing. Products sold on the black market may not reach the people for whom they were intended, and often are more expensive than they should be.

packed dirt and sand, and although the light has not yet quite begun to break, you can sense the nearness of the ocean. You can hear its waves, pounding harshly against the jagged rocks. You can smell its saltiness. The car noses to a stop, and the driver says, "From here you must walk. There is no other way." The place is called Puente Maldonado and the dawn does not slip into this angry place. It explodes in a million lights and colors as the large fireball of the sun begins to nose above the horizon.

"This is the nearest place," the driver tells me. "This is where they came by the thousands on that New Year's Eve and New Year's Day. Out there," he says, gesturing with his right hand, "out there, perhaps a mile and a half from where we stand. That's where we think the plane went down."

The final hours of Roberto Clemente were like this. Just a month or so before, he had agreed to take a junior-league baseball team to Nicaragua and manage it in an all-star game in Managua. He had met people and made friends there. He was not a man who made friends casually. He had always said that the people you wanted to
3 give your friendship to were the people for whom you had to be willing to give something in return—no matter what the price.

Two weeks after he returned from that trip, Managua, Nicaragua exploded into flames. The earth trembled and people died. It was the worst earthquake anywhere in the Western Hemisphere in a long, long time.

Back in Puerto Rico, a television personality named Luis Vigereaux heard the news and was moved to try to help the victims. He needed someone to whom the people
4 would listen, someone who could say what had to be said and get the work done that had to be done and help the people who had to be helped.

"I knew," Luis Vigereaux said, "that Roberto was such a person, perhaps the only such person who would be willing to help."

And so the mercy project, which would eventually claim Roberto's life, began. He appeared on television. But he needed a staging area. The city agreed to give him Sixto Escobar Stadium.

"Bring what you can," he told them. "Bring medicine . . . bring clothes . . . bring food . . . bring shoes . . . bring yourself to help us load. We need so much. Whatever you bring, we will use."

And the people of San Juan came. They walked through the heat and they drove old
cars and battered little trucks, and the 5
mound of supplies grew and grew. Within two days, the first mercy planes left for Nicaragua.

Meanwhile, a ship had been chartered and loaded. And as it prepared to steam away, unhappy stories began to drift back from Nicaragua. Not all the supplies that had been flown in, it was rumored, were getting through. Puerto Ricans who had flown the planes had no passports, and Nicaragua was in a state of panic.

"We have people there who must be protected. We have black-market types who must not be allowed to get their hands on
these supplies," Clemente told Luis Vige- 6
reaux. "Someone must make sure—particularly before the ship gets there. I'm going on the next plane."

The plane they had rented was an old DC-7. It was scheduled to take off at 4 P.M. on December 31, 1972. Long before take-off time, it was apparent that the plane needed more work. It had even taxied onto the runway and then turned back. The trouble, a mechanic who was at the air-strip that day conjectured, "had to do with both port [left side] engines. We worked on them most of the afternoon."

The departure time was delayed an hour, and then two, and then three. Across town, a man named Rudy Hernandez, who had been a teammate of Roberto's when they were rookies in the Puerto Rican League and who had later pitched for the Washington Senators, was trying to contact Roberto by telephone. He had just received a five-hundred-dollar donation, and he wanted to know where to send it. He called Roberto's wife, Vera, who told him that Roberto was going on a trip and that he might catch him at the airport. She had been there herself only moments before to pick up some friends who were coming in from the States, and she had left because she was fairly sure that the trouble had cleared and Roberto had probably left already.

"I caught him at the airport and I was surprised," Rudy Hernandez told me. "I said I had this money for Nicaraguan relief and I wanted to know what to do with it. Then I asked him where he was going."

"Nicaragua," Clemente told him.

"It's New Year's Eve, Roberto. Let it wait."

"Who else will go?" Roberto told him. "Someone has to do it."

At 9 P.M., even as the first stirrings of the annual New Year's Eve celebration were beginning in downtown San Juan, the DC-7 taxied onto the runway, received clearance, rumbled down the narrow concrete strip, and pulled away from the earth. It headed out over the Atlantic and banked toward Nicaragua, and its tiny lights disappeared on the horizon.

Just ninety seconds later, the tower at San Juan International Airport received this message from the pilot: "We are coming back around."

Just that.

Nothing more.

And then there was a great silence.

"It was almost midnight," recalls Rudy Hernandez, a former teammate of Roberto's. "We were having this party in my restaurant, and somebody turned on the radio and the announcer was saying that Roberto's plane was feared missing. And then, because my place is on the beach, we saw these giant floodlights crisscrossing the waves, and we heard the sound of the helicopters and the little search planes."

Drawn by a common sadness, the people of San Juan began to make their way toward the beach, toward Puente Maldonado. A cold rain had begun to fall. It washed their faces and blended with the tears.

They came by the thousands, and they watched for three days. Towering waves

7 Discussion What does this response show about Roberto?

8 **Discussion** Why do some people react strangely during times of great sorrow or rejoicing?

9 **Critical Thinking and Reading** Point out that Maria Casares can give first-hand information about Clemente.

10 **Discussion** What is Izenberg's impression of Maria Casares as a teacher?

11 **Critical Thinking and Reading** Roberto comes to Maria Casares with a problem. What does this show about their relationship?

boiled up and made the search virtually impossible. The U.S. Navy sent a team of expert divers into the area, but the battering of the waves defeated them too. Midway through the week, the pilot's body was found in the swift-moving currents to the north. On Saturday bits of the cockpit were sighted.

And then—nothing else.

"I was born in the Dominican Republic," Rudy Hernandez said, "but I've lived on this island for more than twenty years. I have never seen a time or a sadness like that. The streets were empty, the radios silent, except for the constant bulletins about Roberto. Traffic? Forget it. All of us cried. All of us who knew him and even those who didn't, wept that week.

8 "Manny Sanguillen, the Pittsburgh catcher, was down here playing winter ball, and when Manny heard the news he ran to the beach and he tried to jump into the ocean with skin-diving gear. I told him, man, there's sharks there. You can't help. Leave it to the experts. But he kept going back. All of us were a little crazy that week.

"There will never be another like Roberto."

Who was he . . . I mean really?

Well, nobody can put together all the pieces of another man's life. But there are so many who want the world to know that it is not as impossible a search as you might think.

He was born in Carolina, Puerto Rico. Today the town has about 125,000 people, but when Roberto was born there in 1934, it was roughly one sixth its current size.

9 María Isabella Casares is a schoolteacher. She has taught the children of Carolina for thirty years. Most of her teaching has been done in tenth-grade history classes. Carolina is her home, and its children are her children. And among all of those whom she calls her own (who are all the children she taught), Roberto Clemente was something even more special to her.

"His father was an overseer on a sugar plantation. He did not make much money," she explained in an empty classroom at Julio Coronado School. "But then, there are no rich children here. There never have been. Roberto was typical of them. I had known him when he was a small boy because my father had run a grocery store in Carolina, and Roberto's parents used to shop there."

10 There is this thing that you have to know about Maria Isabella Casares before we hear more from her. What you have to know is that she is the model of what a teacher should be. Between her and her students even now, as back when Roberto attended her school, there is this common bond of mutual respect. Earlier in the day, I had watched her teach a class in the history of the Abolition Movement in Puerto Rico. I don't speak much Spanish, but even to me it was clear that this is how a class should be, this is the kind of person who should teach, and these are the kinds of students such a teacher will produce.

With this as a background, what she has to say about Roberto Clemente carries much more impact.

"Each year," she said, "I let my students choose the seats they want to sit in. I remember the first time I saw Roberto. He was a very shy boy and he went straight to the back of the room and chose the very last seat. Most of the time he would sit with his eyes down. He was an average student. But there was something very special about him. 11 We would talk after class for hours. He wanted to be an engineer, you know, and perhaps he could have been. But then he began to play softball, and one day he came to me and said, 'Teacher, I have a problem.'

"He told me that Pedron Zarrilla, who was one of our most prominent baseball

Grammar in Action

Dashes are punctuation marks that indicate an abrupt break in thought. Like commas, semicolons, and parentheses, dashes signal pause, but dashes signal a more striking, dramatic pause. Dashes are frequently used in punctuating fast-paced, dramatic sentences to capture the quick verbal exchange of the speakers. However, dashes do not necessarily indicate fast-paced dialogue. Dashes can also reflect the way we speak everyday.

In "Roberto Clemente: A Bittersweet Memoir," Izenberg uses dashes both to emphasize important ideas and to capture the dramatic pauses used by the people he interviewed. Perhaps one of the most dramatic and effective uses of the dash in the selection occurs when Izenberg describes the disappointment of the search after Clemente's plane crashed: "And then–nothing else."

Another example of how Izenberg uses the dash occurs when he quotes Maria Isabella Casares. Casares emphasizes important information, when Izenberg sets off by dashes.

> "He was like a son to me. This is why I want to tell you about him. This is why you must make people—particularly our

people, had seen him play, and that Pedron wanted him to sign a professional contract with the Santurce Crabbers. He asked me what he should do.

"I have thought about that conversation many times. I believe Roberto could have been almost anything, but God gave him a gift that few have, and he chose to use that gift. I remember that on that day I told him, 'This is your chance, Roberto. We are poor people in this town. This is your chance to do something. But if in your heart you prefer not to try, then, Roberto, that will be your problem—and your decision.' "

There was and there always remained a closeness between this boy-soon-to-be-a-man and his favorite teacher.

"Once, a few years ago, I was sick with a very bad back. Roberto, not knowing this, had driven over from Rio Piedras, where his house was, to see me."

"Where is the teacher?" Roberto asked Mrs. Casares' stepdaughter that afternoon.

"Teacher is sick, Roberto. She is in bed."

"Teacher," Roberto said, pounding on the bedroom door "get up and put on your clothes. We are going to the doctor whether you want to or not."

"I got dressed," Mrs. Casares told me, "and he picked me up like a baby and carried me in his arms to the car. He came every day for fifteen days, and most days he had to carry me, but I went to the doctor and he treated me. Afterward, I said to the doctor that I wanted to pay the bill.

" 'Mrs. Casares', he told me, 'please don't start with that Clemente, or he will kill
2 me. He has paid all your bills, and don't you dare tell him I have told you.'

"Well, Roberto was like that. We had been so close. You know, I think I was there the day he met Vera, the girl he later married. She was one of my students, too. I was working part-time in the pharmacy and he was already a baseball player by then, and one day Vera came into the store.

" 'Teacher,' Roberto asked me, 'who is that girl?'

" 'That's one of my students,' I told him. 'Now don't you dare bother her. Go out and get someone to introduce you. Behave yourself.'

"He was so proper, you know. That's just what he did, and that's how he met her, and they were married here in Carolina in the big church on the square."

On the night Roberto Clemente's plane disappeared, Mrs. Casares was at home, and a delivery boy from the pharmacy stopped by and told her to turn on the radio and sit down. "I think something has happened to someone who is very close with you, Teacher, and I want to be here in case you need help."

María Isabella Casares heard the news. She is a brave woman, and months later, standing in front of the empty crypt in the cemetery at Carolina where Roberto Clemente was to have been buried, she said, "He was like a son to me. This is why I want to tell you about him. This is why you must make people—particularly our people, our Puerto Rican children—understand what he was. He was like my son, and he is all our sons in a way. We must make sure that the children never forget how beautiful a man he was."

The next person to touch Roberto Clemente was Pedron Zarrilla, who owned the Santurce club. He was the man who discovered Clemente on the country softball team, 13
and he was the man who signed him for a four-hundred-dollar bonus.

"He was a skinny kid," Pedron Zarrilla recalls, "but even then he had those large, powerful hands, which we all noticed right away. He joined us, and he was nervous. But I watched him, and I said to myself, 'this kid can throw and this kid can run, and this kid

12 **Literary Focus** What characteristics of Clemente does Mrs. Casares highlight in this anecdote?

13 **Literary Focus** Why do you think Izenberg chose to interview Zarilla about Clemente?

people, our Puerto Rican children—understand what he was . . ."

In "Roberto Clemente: A Bittersweet Memoir," Izenberg captures the natural speech of the people he interviewed—what they said and how they said it—by using dashes.

Student Activity 1. Locate three more examples of the use of dashes in the selection. Explain why dashes work well in the examples you found.

Student Activity 2. Write a short description of someone you know who has made an important achievement. Use dashes in your description.

14 Clarification Point out that, because of the physical demands of sports, an athlete usually retires earlier than people in other fields and takes up some other occupation.

15 Discussion What does Zarilla mean when he says he knew they were going to lose Clemente?

can hit. We will be patient with him.' The season had been through several games before I finally sent him in to play."

Luis Olmo remembers that game. Luis Olmo had been a major-league outfielder
14 with the Brooklyn Dodgers. He had been a splendid ballplayer. Today he is in the insurance business in San Juan. He sat in his office and recalled very well that first moment when Roberto Clemente stepped up to bat.

"I was managing the other team. They had a man on base and this skinny kid comes out. Well, we had never seen him, so we didn't really know how to pitch to him. I decided to throw him a few bad balls and see if he'd bite.

"He hit the first pitch. It was an outside fast ball, and he never should have been able to reach it. But he hit it down the line for a double. He was the best bad-ball hitter I have ever seen, and if you ask major-league pitchers who are pitching today, they will tell you the same thing. After a while it got so that I just told my pitchers to throw the ball down the middle because he was going to hit it no matter where they put it, and at least if he decided not to swing, we'd have a strike on him.

"I played in the big leagues. I know what I am saying. He was the greatest we ever had . . . maybe one of the greatest anyone ever had. Why did he have to die?"

Once Pedron Zarrilla turned him loose, there was no stopping Roberto Clemente. As Clemente's confidence grew, he began to get better and better. He was the one the crowds came to see out at Sixto Escobar Stadium.

"You know, when Clemente was in the lineup," Pedron Zarrilla says, "there was always this undercurrent of excitement in the ball park. You knew that if he was coming to bat, he would do something spectacular. You knew that if he was on first base, he was going to try to get to second base. You knew that if he was playing right field and there was a man on third base, then that man on third base already knew what a lot of men on third base in the majors were going to find out—you don't try to get home against Roberto Clemente's arm."

"I remember the year that Willie Mays came down here to play in the same outfield with him for the winter season. I remember the wonderful things they did and I remember that Roberto still had the best of it.

"Sure I knew we were going to lose him. I knew it was just a matter of time. But I was
only grateful that we could have him if only 1
for that little time."

The major-league scouts began to make their moves. Olmo was then scouting, and he tried to sign him for the Giants. But it was the Dodgers who won the bidding war. The Dodgers had Clemente, but in having him, they had a major problem. He had to be hidden.

This part takes a little explaining. Under the complicated draft rules that baseball used at that time, if the Dodgers were not prepared to bring Clemente up to their major-league team within a year (and because they were winning with proven players, they couldn't), then Clemente could be claimed by another team.

They sent him to Montreal with instructions to the manager to use him as little as possible, to hide him as much as possible, and to tell everyone he had a sore back, a sore arm, or any other excuse the manager could give. But how do you hide a diamond when he's in the middle of a field of broken soda bottles?

In the playoffs that year against Syracuse, they had to use Clemente. He hit two doubles and a home run and threw a man out at home the very first try.

The Pittsburgh Pirates had a man who saw it all. They drafted him at the season's end.

And so Roberto Clemente came to Pittsburgh. He was the finest prospect the club had had in a long, long time. But the Pirates of those days were spectacular losers, and even Roberto Clemente couldn't turn them around overnight.

"We were bad, all right," recalls Bob Friend, who later became a great Pirate pitcher. "We lost over a hundred games, and it certainly wasn't fun to go to the ball park under those conditions. You couldn't blame the fans for being noisy and impatient. Branch Rickey, our general manager, had promised a winner. He called it his five-year plan. Actually, it took ten."

When Clemente joined the club, it was Friend who made it his business to try to make him feel at home. Roberto was, in truth, a moody man, and the previous season hadn't helped him any.

"I will never forget how fast he became a superstar in this town," says Bob Friend. "Later he would have troubles because he was either hurt or thought he was hurt, and some people would say that he was loafing. But I know he gave it his best shot and he helped make us winners."

The first winning year was 1960, when the Pirates won the pennant and went on to beat the Yankees in the seventh game of the World Series. Whitey Ford, who pitched against him twice in that Series, recalls that Roberto actually made himself look bad on an outside pitch to encourage Whitey to come back with it. "I did," Ford recalls, "and he unloaded. Another thing I remember is the way he ran out a routine ground ball in the last game, and when we were a little slow covering, he beat it out. It was something most people forget, but it made the Pirates' victory possible."

The season was over. Roberto Clemente had hit safely in every World Series game. He had batted over .300. He had been a superstar. But when they announced the Most Valuable Player Award voting, Roberto had finished a distant third.

"I really don't think he resented the fact that he didn't win it," Bob Friend says. "What hurt—and in this he was right—was how few votes he got. He felt that he simply wasn't being accepted. He brooded
about that a lot. I think his attitude became 18
one of 'Well, I'm going to show them from now on so that they will never forget.'

"And you know, he sure did."

Roberto Clemente went home and married Vera. He felt less alone. Now he could go on and prove what it was he had to prove. And he was determined to prove it.

"I know he was driven by thoughts like that," explains Buck Canel, a newspaper writer who covers all sports for most of the hemisphere's Spanish-language papers. "He would talk with me often about his feelings. You know, Clemente felt strongly
about the fact that he was a Puerto Rican 19
and that he was a black man. In each of these things he had pride.

"On the other hand, because of the early

16 Critical Thinking and Reading Have students paraphrase this statement. What does it mean?

17 Reading Strategy Have students summarize the events leading up to Clemente's joining the Pittsburgh Pirates.

18 Discussion Discuss what this tells you about Clemente's character.

19 Discussion What kind of difficulties might Roberto face as a Puerto Rican and a black man in major league baseball in the United States?

20 Discussion Do you agree or disagree with this statement? Give reasons for your answer.

21 Reading Strategy Have students summarize Clemente's major achievements as a baseball player.

22 Discussion An ideal in ancient Greece was for the young hero to die at the height of his powers. Why? Ask students their opinions about the ideal of dying before one's "powers" begin to fade. What other abilities in an older person can take the place of youthful powers?

23 Discussion Roberto Clemente was a national hero and role model for the people of Puerto Rico. What are other examples of national heroes?

Reader's Response In your eyes, was Roberto Clemente a hero? Explain.

language barriers, I am sure that there were times when he *thought* people were laughing at him when they were not. It is difficult for a Latin-American ballplayer to understand everything said around him when it is said at high speed, if he doesn't speak English that well. But, in any event, he wanted very much to prove to the world that he was a superstar and that he could do things that in his heart he felt he had already proven."

In later years, there would be people who would say that Roberto was a hypochondriac (someone who *imagined* he was sick or hurt when he was not). They could have been right, but if they were, it made the things he did even more remarkable. Because I can testify that I saw him throw his body into outfield fences, teeth first, to
20 make remarkable plays. If he thought he was hurt at the time, then the act was even more courageous.

His moment finally came. It took eleven years for the Pirates to win a World Series berth again, and when they did in 1971, it was Roberto Clemente who led the way. I will never forget him as he was during that 1971 series with the Orioles, a Series that the Pirates figured to lose, and in which they, in fact, dropped the first two games down in Baltimore.

When they got back to Pittsburgh for the middle slice of the tournament, Roberto Clemente went to work and led this team. He was a superhero during the five games that followed. He was the big man in the Series. He was the MVP. He was everything he had ever dreamed of being on a ball field.

Most important of all, the entire country saw him do it on network television, and never again—even though nobody knew it would end so tragically soon—was anyone ever to doubt his ability.

The following year, Clemente ended the season by collecting his three thousandth hit. Only ten other men had ever done that in the entire history of baseball.

"It was a funny thing about that hit," Willie Stargell, his closest friend on the Pirates, explains. "He had thought of taking himself out of the lineup and resting for the playoffs, but a couple of us convinced him that there had to be a time when a man had to do something for himself, so he went on and played and got it. I'm thankful that we
convinced him, because, you know, as things turned out, that number three thousand was his last hit. 21

"When I think of Roberto now, I think of the kind of man he was. There was nothing phony about him. He had his own ideas about how life should be lived, and if you didn't see it that way, then he let you know in so many ways, without words, that it was best you each go your separate ways.

"He was a man who chose his friends carefully. His was a friendship worth having. I don't think many people took the time and the trouble to try to understand him, and I'll admit it wasn't easy. But he was worth it.

"The way he died, you know, I mean on that plane carrying supplies to Nicaraguans who'd been dying in that earthquake, well, I wasn't surprised he'd go out and do something like that. I wasn't surprised he'd go. I just never thought what happened could happen to him.

"But I know this. He lived a full life. And if he knew at that moment what the Lord had decided, well, I really believe he would have said, 'I'm ready.'"

He was thirty-eight years old when he died. He touched the hearts of Puerto Rico in a way that few people ever could. He touched a lot of other hearts, too. He touched hearts that beat inside people of all colors of skin.

He was one of the proudest of The Proud People.

Closure and Extension

ANSWERS TO THINKING ABOUT THE SELECTION

Recalling

1. María Casares was Clemente's teacher and the person to whom he went for guidance. Pedron Zarilla was the owner of the Santurce ball club who asked Clemente to join.
2. Clemente was the Most Valuable Player in 1971. He collected three thousand hits in his career.
3. Clemente believed that friends "were the people to whom you had to be willing to give something in return—no matter what the price."
4. Luis Vigereaux enlisted Clemente's aid to encourage people to donate help to the Nicaraguans. Clemente was flying supplies to the people who needed them in Nicaragua when he died.
5. Clemente's friends remember most that he was a man of principle, determination, pride, and true friendship.

Interpreting

6. You can infer that Clemente was a kind and caring friend.
7. This piece is called a "bittersweet memoir" because it highlights Clemente's personality and achievements and describes the tragedy of his death.

THINKING ABOUT THE SELECTION

Recalling

1. What roles do María Casares and Pedron Zarrilla play in Clemente's childhood?
2. Name two achievements of Roberto Clemente's baseball career.
3. Explain Clemente's view of friendship.
4. Why did Luis Vigereaux try to enlist Clemente's aid? How was Clemente trying to help when he died?
5. What do Roberto Clemente's friends remember most about him?

Interpreting

6. What inference do you make about Clemente based on his treatment of Mrs. Casares when she was ill?
7. Why is this called a "bittersweet memoir"?

Applying

8. How is Clemente a model for others?

ANALYZING LITERATURE

Understanding the Memoir

A **memoir,** or biographical piece often written by a relative or personal friend of the subject, can be about a well-known person or about someone important to the writer. A memoir can be one person's recollection, or based on interviews and anecdotes of several people.

An interview is a planned meeting at which writers obtain information about a topic from someone knowledgeable about it. Anecdotes are brief stories about noteworthy incidents.

1. List the people the writer interviewed.
2. What two anecdotes did María Casares tell about Roberto that no one else could tell?

CRITICAL THINKING AND READING

Identifying Primary Sources

A **primary source** is the original or direct source. For example, the wife of a famous ballplayer would be a primary source of information about him. A **secondary source** is one that is based on primary sources. For example, a writer interviewing the friends of a famous ballplayer would be a secondary source.

Which of the following could give you primary-source information about Clemente?

1. María Casares
2. Jerry Izenberg
3. Manny Sanguillen
4. Rudy Hernandez

SPEAKING AND LISTENING

Doing an Interview

Before the **interview,** make an appointment for the meeting, research your topic, and prepare a list of simple and direct questions.

During the interview, listen attentively, take careful notes, and ask unprepared follow-up questions when a point needs to be made clearer. Immediately afterwards, look over your notes and pinpoint facts that need to be checked.

Think of a well-known person, and interview three classmates about their opinions about that person. Ask them to recall any anecdotes that show what that person means to them.

THINKING AND WRITING

Writing a Memoir

Write a memoir of someone you know well, based on your own knowledge of him or her. First freewrite about that person, including any details about his or her appearance or behavior. Include any anecdotes that help reveal this person's character. Then use this information in your memoir. Revise your memoir, making sure you have created a vivid portrait. Proofread your memoir and share it with your classmates.

(Answers begin on p. 400.)

Challenge If Izenberg had used old newspaper stories for information on Clemente, would he have been using primary or secondary sources?

SPEAKING AND LISTENING

Point out to students that when they interview a person, they should be prepared to ask follow-up questions. Such questions might be to verify the time period, the people involved, or whether a person's behavior was typical. Discuss what other kinds of follow-up questions they might ask.

THINKING AND WRITING

For help with this assignment, students can refer to Lesson 20, "Writing a Personal Essay," in the Handbook of Writing About Literature.

Publishing Student Writing Students might enjoy reading each other's memoirs. Consider breaking them into small groups in which they can read their essays aloud.

Applying

8. Answers will differ. Suggested response: Clemente is a model or inspiration to others in that he strove to achieve renown; once he achieved it, he was caring toward others and courageous.

ANSWERS TO ANALYZING LITERATURE

1. The writer interviewed Luis Vigereaux, a television personality; Rudy Hernandez, a teammate; María Casares, a former teacher; Pedron Zarrilla, who discovered and signed up Clemente in the Santurce club; Luis Olmo, an outfielder with the Brooklyn Dodgers; Bob Friend, a Pittsburgh Pirates teammate; Whitey Ford, a Yankee baseball player; Buck Canel, a newspaper sportswriter; and Willie Stargell, Clemente's closest friend on the Pittsburgh Pirates.
2. María Casares told one anecdote about Clemente asking her for advice about joining the Santurce baseball club, and one about Clemente getting proper care for her when she was sick.

ANSWERS TO CRITICAL THINKING AND READING

Those who could give primary-source information about Clemente are María Casares, Manny Sanguillen, and Rudy Hernandez.

Focus

More About the Author Maya Angelou writes about an experience from her own childhood. Discuss the pros and cons of writing about a childhood experience from the vantage point of an adult years later.

Literary Focus Have students discuss why a person might write his or her autobiography.

Look For An autobiographical excerpt usually focuses on a significant event in a person's life. In this excerpt, Angelou describes an experience that changed her feelings in a positive way. What might make an event significant?

Writing/Prior Knowledge Before students write, have them list people who are special to them. They may then choose one to freewrite about.

Vocabulary Have your **less advanced** students use these words in sentences, so you can be sure they understand their meaning.

Spelling Tip *Taut* is one of a group of words in which the *au* sounds like the *a* in *ball*. Other words in this group include *haul, maul, Paul,* and *Saul*. *Taut* should not be confused with its homophone *taught*.

Maya Angelou (1928–   ) was born Marguerite Johnson in St. Louis, Missouri. She and her older brother Bailey were raised by their grandmother, who owned a country store in Stamps, Arkansas. Angelou later became a journalist, a civil rights worker, and an author. In *I Know Why the Caged Bird Sings,* the first of four books of autobiography, she vividly recalls a woman from her childhood who influenced her life.

An **autobiography** is a person's own account of his or her life. Usually in an autobiography, a writer uses the first-person pronoun "I" to write about his or her experiences. You experience the writer's story through his or her eyes—knowing not only what he or she observes and recalls, but also what he or she thinks and feels about the experience. Unlike biography, autobiography provides you with information about the subject from the subject.

As you read this excerpt from *I Know Why the Caged Bird Sings,* look for the way in which Mrs. Flowers changes Maya's life. What does Maya learn from her?

Think of someone you consider special. Freewrite about that person, describing what they were like and what they did that made them special.

Knowing the following words will help you as you read this excerpt from *I Know Why the Caged Bird Sings*.

fiscal (fis′ kəl) *adj.*: Having to do with finances (p. 403)
troubadours (tro͞o′ bə dôrz′) *n.*: Traveling singers, usually accompanying themselves on stringed instruments (p. 403)
taut (tôt) *adj.*: Tightly stretched (p. 405)
voile (voil) *n.*: A light cotton fabric (p. 405)
benign (bi nīn′) *adj.*: Kindly (p. 406)
infuse (in fyo͞oz′) *v.*: To put into (p. 406)
couched (koucht) *v.*: Put into words; expressed (p. 407)
wormwood (wʉrm′ wood′) *n.*: A plant that produces a bitter oil (p. 408)

Objectives

1 To understand autobiography
2 To infer the author's purpose
3 To write an autobiographical sketch

Support Material

Teaching Portfolio
Teacher Backup, pp. 485–487
Grammar in Action Worksheet, *Using Vivid Adjectives,* pp. 488–489
Usage and Mechanics Worksheet, p. 490
Vocabulary Check, p. 491
Critical Thinking and Reading Worksheet, *Inferring the Author's Purpose,* p. 492
Language Worksheet, *Choosing the Meaning That Fits the Context,* p. 493
Selection Test, pp. 494–495
Library of Video Classics
I Know Why the Caged Bird Sings

from I Know Why the Caged Bird Sings

Maya Angelou

We lived with our grandmother and uncle in the rear of the Store (it was always
1 spoken of with a capital *s*), which she had owned some twenty-five years.

Early in the century, Momma (we soon stopped calling her Grandmother) sold lunches to the sawmen in the lumberyard (east Stamps) and the seedmen at the cotton gin (west Stamps). Her crisp meat pies and cool lemonade, when joined to her miraculous ability to be in two places at the same time, assured her business success. From being a mobile lunch counter, she set up a stand between the two points of fiscal interest and supplied the workers' needs for a few years. Then she had the Store built in the heart of the Negro area. Over the years it became the lay center of activities in town. On Saturdays, barbers sat their customers in the shade on the porch of the Store, and troubadours on their ceaseless crawlings through the South leaned across its benches and sang their sad songs of The Brazos[1] while they played juice harps[2] and cigar-box guitars.

The formal name of the Store was the Wm. Johnson General Merchandise Store. Customers could find food staples, a good variety of colored thread, mash[3] for hogs, corn for chickens, coal oil for lamps, light
bulbs for the wealthy, shoestrings, hair 2
dressing, balloons, and flower seeds. Anything not visible had only to be ordered.

Until we became familiar enough to belong to the Store and it to us, we were locked up in a Fun House of Things where the attendant had gone home for life. . . .

Weighing the half-pounds of flour, excluding the scoop, and depositing them dust-free into the thin paper sacks held a simple kind of adventure for me. I developed an eye for measuring how full a silver-looking ladle of flour, mash, meal, sugar or
corn had to be to push the scale indicator 3
over to eight ounces or one pound. When I was absolutely accurate our appreciative customers used to admire: "Sister Henderson sure got some smart grandchildrens." If I was off in the Store's favor, the eagle-eyed women would say, "Put some more in that sack, child. Don't you try to make your profit offa me."

---

1. The Brazos (bräz′ əs): An area in central Texas near the Brazos River.

2. juice (jew's) **harps:** Small musical instruments held between the teeth and played by plucking.

3. mash *n.*: A moist grain mixture fed to farm animals.

Presentation

Motivation/Prior Knowledge Ask students if they can think of a time when someone special to them did something nice for them. How did they feel? Maya Angelou writes about a similar incident in her life.

Thematic Idea Another selection that deals with the theme of a gift of personal attention is "Thank You, M'am" on page 169.

Purpose-Setting Question What effect does the kindness and attention of Mrs. Flowers have on Marguerite?

Master Teacher Note The title *I Know Why the Caged Bird Sings* is a line from the poem "Sympathy" by Paul Laurence Dunbar, who sympathizes with the caged bird who sings out of misery to be free. In this selection, the writer describes an experience that helped free her of her feelings of inferiority.

1 **Discussion** Why do you think the Store "was always spoken of with a capital *s*"?

2 **Discussion** How does "light bulbs for the wealthy" contrast with the other items mentioned? What do these items tell you about the lives of these customers?

3 **Literary Focus** A writer of an autobiography speaks in the first person. Angelou also uses "we" in the first paragraph. What effect does this have?

4 Literary Focus Throughout an autobiography, the writer describes thoughts and feelings as well as facts. What thoughts and feelings does Angelou express here?

5 Discussion The writer compares the Store to an unopened present. Why? She also compares it to a person who is tired. Why?

Then I would quietly but persistently punish myself. For every bad judgment, the fine was no silver-wrapped kisses, the sweet chocolate drops that I loved more than anything in the world, except Bailey. And maybe canned pineapples.
4 My obsession with pineapples nearly drove me mad. I dreamt of the days when I would be grown and able to buy a whole carton for myself alone.

Although the syrupy golden rings sat in their exotic cans on our shelves year round, we only tasted them during Christmas. Momma used the juice to make almost-black fruit cakes. Then she lined heavy soot-encrusted iron skillets with the pineapple rings for rich upside-down cakes. Bailey and I received one slice each, and I carried mine around for hours, shredding off the fruit until nothing was left except the perfume on my fingers. I'd like to think that my desire for pineapples was so sacred that I wouldn't allow myself to steal a can (which was possible) and eat it alone out in the garden, but I'm certain that I must have weighed the possibility of the scent exposing me and didn't have the nerve to attempt it.

Until I was thirteen and left Arkansas for good, the Store was my favorite place to be. Alone and empty in the mornings, it looked like an unopened present from a stranger. Opening the front doors was pulling the ribbon off the unexpected gift. The light would come in softly (we faced north), easing itself over the shelves of mackerel, salmon, tobacco, thread. It fell flat on the big vat of lard and by noontime during the summer the grease had softened to a thick soup. Whenever I walked into the Store in the afternoon, I sensed that it

Grammar in Action

Sentences come alive when the writer uses **vivid adjectives** to enhance the meaning. Adjectives describe nouns and pronouns, and without them, language would be dull and uninteresting. The best writers use specific words to call an image to the reader's mind. Look at the following sentences from "I Know Why the Caged Bird Sings:

Although the *syrupy golden* rings sat in their *exotic* cans on our shelves year round, we only tasted them during Christmas. Momma used the juice to make *almost-black* fruit cakes. Then she lined *heavy soot-encrusted* iron skillets with the pineapple rings for *rich* upside-down cakes.

. . . She was *thin* without the *taut* look of *wiry* people, and her *printed voile* dresses and *flowered* hats were as right for her as *denim* overalls for a farmer.

Her skin was a *rich black* that would have peeled like a plum if snagged, . . .

SYMBOLS
Benny Andrew
Museum of Art, Wichita State University

was tired. I alone could hear the slow pulse of its job half done. But just before bedtime, after numerous people had walked in and out, had argued over their bills, or joked about their neighbors, or just
6 dropped in "to give Sister Henderson a 'Hi y'all,'" the promise of magic mornings returned to the Store and spread itself over the family in washed life waves. . . .

When Maya was about ten years old, she returned to Stamps from a visit to St. Louis with her mother. She had become depressed and withdrawn.

For nearly a year, I sopped around the house, the Store, the school and the church, like an old biscuit, dirty and inedible. Then I met, or rather got to know, the lady who threw me my first lifeline.

Mrs. Bertha Flowers was the aristocrat[4] of Black Stamps. She had the grace of control to appear warm in the coldest weather, and on the Arkansas summer days it seemed she had a private breeze which swirled around, cooling her. She was thin without the taut look of wiry people, and her printed voile dresses and flowered hats were as right for her as denim overalls for a farmer. She was our side's answer to the richest white woman in town.

Her skin was a rich black that would have peeled like a plum if snagged, but then no one would have thought of getting close enough to Mrs. Flowers to ruffle her dress, let alone snag her skin. She didn't encourage familiarity. She wore gloves too.

---

4. aristocrat (ə ris′ tə krat) *n.*: A person belonging to the upper class.

6 **Clarification** "Sister" can mean any woman, often used colloquially as a familiar term of address.

Humanities Note

Fine art, The African-American artist and educator Benny Andrews was born in Georgia in 1930. From a very early age he knew he wanted to be an artist. Through hard work and a well deserved scholarship, Andrews was able to attend the Art Institute of Chicago. His unique style is a combination of painting and collage.

Symbols (1971) is a monumental painting which measures thirty-six feet long. Andrews fills this canvas with symbols of the daily struggles of African-American in our society. In creating this composition, Andrews drew upon his own life experience as well as the reality of our times. His insight and creativity make *Symbols* an important contribution to contemporary American art. The works of Benny Andrews are in many prestigious collections including that of the Museum of Modern Art.

You might want to use the following questions to discuss the art:

1. Why do you think Andrews chose to make *Symbols* so large?
2. What do you suppose the tree in the center, filled with children, symbolizes?
3. Choose another symbol from this painting and discuss your ideas about it.

One *summer* afternoon, *sweet-milk* fresh in my memory, . . .

She smiled that *slow dragging* smile . . .

Notice how clear and precise each of the above adjectives is. It is quite easy to picture "syrupy golden rings," "almost-black fruitcakes," and "heavy soot-encrusted iron skillets."

Student Activity 1. Rewrite each of the example sentences substituting your own descriptive words. Try to keep your sentence structure as close to the writer's as possible, but you may change the meaning of each sentence.

Student Activity 2. Write a description of a person. Use vivid adjectives to make this person come alive for readers.

7 Literary Focus What does this assessment of Mrs. Flowers tell you about her character?

8 Discussion Mrs. Flowers says that speaking words gives them deeper meaning. Do you agree with these statements about words?

9 Discussion What attitude is Mrs. Flowers trying to instill in Marguerite about property?

10 Literary Focus An autobiography includes a description of the writer's thoughts and feelings as well as facts.

I don't think I ever saw Mrs. Flowers laugh, but she smiled often. A slow widening of her thin black lips to show even, small white teeth, then the slow effortless closing. When she chose to smile on me, I always wanted to thank her. The action was so graceful and inclusively benign.

7 She was one of the few gentlewomen I have ever known, and has remained throughout my life the measure of what a human being can be. . . .

One summer afternoon, sweet-milk fresh in my memory, she stopped at the Store to buy provisions. Another Negro woman of her health and age would have been expected to carry the paper sacks home in one hand, but Momma said, "Sister Flowers, I'll send Bailey up to your house with these things."

She smiled that slow dragging smile, "Thank you, Mrs. Henderson. I'd prefer Marguerite, though." My name was beautiful when she said it. "I've been meaning to talk to her, anyway." They gave each other age-group looks.

Momma said, "Well, that's all right then. Sister, go and change your dress. You going to Sister Flowers's. . . ."

There was a little path beside the rocky road, and Mrs. Flowers walked in front swinging her arms and picking her way over the stones.

She said, without turning her head, to me, "I hear you're doing very good school work, Marguerite, but that it's all written. The teachers report that they have trouble getting you to talk in class." We passed the triangular farm on our left and the path widened to allow us to walk together. I hung back in the separate unasked and unanswerable questions.

"Come and walk along with me, Marguerite." I couldn't have refused even if I wanted to. She pronounced my name so nicely. Or more correctly, she spoke each word with such clarity that I was certain a foreigner who didn't understand English could have understood her.

"Now no one is going to make you talk—possibly no one can. But bear in mind, language is man's way of communicating with his fellow man and it is language alone which separates him from the lower animals." That was a totally new idea to me, and I would need time to think about it.

"Your grandmother says you read a lot. Every chance you get. That's good, but not good enough. Words mean more than what is set down on paper. It takes the human voice to infuse them with the shades of deeper meaning." 8

I memorized the part about the human voice infusing words. It seemed so valid and poetic.

She said she was going to give me some books and that I not only must read them, I must read them aloud. She suggested that I try to make a sentence sound in as many different ways as possible.

"I'll accept no excuse if you return a book to me that has been badly handled." My imagination boggled at the punishment I would deserve if in fact I did abuse a book of Mrs. Flowers'. Death would be too kind and brief. 9

The odors in the house surprised me. Somehow I had never connected Mrs. Flowers with food or eating or any other common experience of common people. There must have been an outhouse, too, but my mind never recorded it. 1

The sweet scent of vanilla had met us as she opened the door.

"I made tea cookies this morning. You

see, I had planned to invite you for cookies
11 and lemonade so we could have this little
chat. The lemonade is in the icebox."

It followed that Mrs. Flowers would have ice on an ordinary day, when most families in our town bought ice late on Saturdays only a few times during the summer to be used in the wooden ice cream freezers.

She took the bags from me and disappeared through the kitchen door. I looked around the room that I had never in my wildest fantasies imagined I would see. Browned photographs leered or threatened from the walls and the white, freshly done curtains pushed against themselves and against the wind. I wanted to gobble up the room entire and take it to Bailey, who would help me analyze and enjoy it.

"Have a seat, Marguerite. Over there by the table." She carried a platter covered with a tea towel. Although she warned that she hadn't tried her hand at baking sweets for some time, I was certain that like everything else about her the cookies would be perfect.

They were flat round wafers, slightly browned on the edges and butter-yellow in the center. With the cold lemonade they were sufficient for childhood's lifelong diet. Remembering my manners, I took nice little ladylike bites off the edges. She said she had made them expressly for me and that she had a few in the kitchen that I could take home to my brother. So I jammed one whole cake in my mouth and the rough crumbs scratched the insides of my jaws, and if I hadn't had to swallow, it would have been a dream come true.

As I ate she began the first of what we later called "my lessons in living." She said
that I must always be intolerant of igno-
12 rance but understanding of illiteracy. That
some people, unable to go to school, were more educated and even more intelligent than college professors. She encouraged me to listen carefully to what country people called mother wit. That in those homely sayings was couched the collective wisdom of generations.

When I finished the cookies she brushed off the table and brought a thick, small book from the bookcase. I had read *A Tale of Two Cities* and found it up to my standards as a romantic novel. She opened the first page and I heard poetry for the first time in my life.

"It was the best of times and the worst of times . . ." Her voice slid in and curved down through and over the words. She was nearly singing. I wanted to look at the pages. Were they the same that I had read? Or were there notes, music, lined on the pages, as in a hymn book? Her sounds began cascading gently. I knew from listening to a thousand preachers that she was nearing the end of her reading, and I hadn't really heard, heard to understand, a single word.

"How do you like that?"

It occurred to me that she expected a response. The sweet vanilla flavor was still on my tongue and her reading was a wonder in my ears. I had to speak.

I said, "Yes, ma'am." It was the least I could do, but it was the most also.

"There's one more thing. Take this book of poems and memorize one for me. Next time you pay me a visit, I want you to recite."

I have tried often to search behind the sophistication of years for the enchantment I so easily found in those gifts. The essence escapes but its aura[5] remains. To be allowed, no, invited, into the private lives of strangers, and to share their joys and fears,

5. aura (ôr′ ə) *n.*: An atmosphere or quality.

11 **Discussion** The writer mentions an icebox instead of a refrigerator. What other examples can you find of life during this time period of the 1930's?

12 **Discussion** What advice does Mrs. Flowers give Marguerite? What do these statements tell you about the character of Mrs. Bertha Flowers? Do you agree with these statements?

13 Discussion What do you think is the reason that Mrs. Flowers paid special attention to Marguerite?

14 Reading Strategy Have students summarize the episode with Mrs. Flowers. Why was it so significant to Marguerite?

Reader's Response Angelou writes, "Childhood's logic never asks to be proved (all conclusions are absolute)." Describe a "conclusion" from your childhood.

was a chance to exchange the Southern bitter wormwood for a cup of mead with Beowulf[6] or a hot cup of tea and milk with Oliver Twist. When I said aloud, "It is a far far better thing that I do, than I have ever done . . ."[7] tears of love filled my eyes at my selflessness.

On that first day, I ran down the hill and into the road (few cars ever came along it) and had the good sense to stop running before I reached the Store.

I was liked, and what a difference it made. I was respected not as Mrs. Henderson's grandchild or Bailey's sister but for just being Marguerite Johnson.

Childhood's logic never asks to be proved (all conclusions are absolute). I didn't question why Mrs. Flowers had singled me 13
out for attention, nor did it occur to me that Momma might have asked her to give me a little talking to. All I cared about was that she had made tea cookies for *me* and read to *me* from her favorite book. It was enough to 14
prove that she liked me.

6. Beowulf (bā' ə wool̇f'): The hero of an old Anglo-Saxon epic. People in this poem drink mead, (mēd), a drink made with honey and water.

7. "It is . . . than I have ever done": A speech from *A Tale of Two Cities* by Charles Dickens.

THINKING ABOUT THE SELECTION

Recalling

1. According to Mrs. Flowers, for what two reasons is language so important?
2. Although Marguerite reads a great deal, what does she *not* do? According to Mrs. Flowers, why is reading a great deal not enough?
3. What does Mrs. Flowers tell Marguerite as the first of her "lessons in living"?
4. What does Mrs. Flowers want Marguerite to do with the book of poems she gives her?
5. What does Mrs. Flowers's making cookies and reading to Marguerite prove to Marguerite?

Interpreting

6. The word *sopped* means "to have been wet, like a piece of bread soaked in gravy." What does the use of the word "sopped" tell you about how Marguerite feels about herself before meeting with Mrs. Flowers?
7. Why does Mrs. Flowers tell Marguerite to read aloud and in as many different ways as possible?
8. After listening to *A Tale of Two Cities*, why does Marguerite write, "I said, 'Yes, ma'am.' It was the least I could do, but it was the most also"?
9. How do you think Marguerite changes as a result of her meetings with Mrs. Flowers?

Closure and Extension

ANSWERS TO THINKING ABOUT THE SELECTION

Recalling

1. Language is a person's way of communicating with other humans and language separates humans from the lower animals.
2. Marguerite does not speak much. Reading a great deal is not enough because "Words mean more than what is set down on paper. It takes the human voice to infuse them with the shades of deeper meaning."
3. As her first lesson in living, Mrs. Flowers tells Marguerite that she "must always be intolerant of ignorance but understanding of illiteracy. That some people, unable to go to school, were more educated and even more intelligent than college professors," and that she should listen to "mother wit" for the "collective wisdom of generations."
4. Mrs. Flowers wants Marguerite to memorize and recite a poem for her.
5. It proves to Marguerite that Mrs. Flowers likes her.

Interpreting

6. The word *sopped*, implying soggy or used, tells you that Marguerite

10. Why has Mrs. Flowers remained "the measure of what a human being can be"?

Applying

11. Mrs. Flowers throws Marguerite a "lifeline" by inviting her to her house for lemonade and cookies and reading with her. In what other ways do people give others "lifelines"?

ANALYZING LITERATURE

Understanding Autobiography

An **autobiography** is the story of a person's life, written by that person. Through the writer's eyes, you see events unfold and come to understand his or her feelings and thoughts. The writer's view influences the telling of each incident. For example, Marguerite says, "I wanted to gobble up the room entire and take it to Bailey, who would help me analyze and enjoy it."

1. What does Marguerite tell you about the Store that only she could tell you?
2. What does Marguerite tell you about Mrs. Flowers that only she could tell you?

CRITICAL THINKING AND READING

Inferring the Author's Purpose

The autobiographer writes for a certain purpose, or reason. For example, authors may write autobiographies to entertain you, to preserve their memories, to inform you of their accomplishments, or for some other purpose. When you read, you usually infer, or draw conclusions about, the author's purpose. Of course, you can never get inside the author's mind, so your inference remains simply an intelligent guess.

Considering who the author is can help you infer his or her purpose. For example, a famous politician may want to emphasize in her autobiography that her policies improved people's lives. Therefore she will emphasize those incidents from her career that highlight this favorable effect, rather than those incidents that point out her drawbacks.

1. Why do you think Maya Angelou wrote about Mrs. Flowers? Explain the reason for your answer.
2. How is the author's purpose evident? Explain the reason for your answer.

THINKING AND WRITING

Writing an Autobiographical Sketch

Choose an incident in your life that is important to you. First, freewrite about this incident. Then, using this information, write an autobiographical account of it. Use the first-person point of view. Revise your writing, making sure you have presented the information clearly. Proofread your autobiography and share it with your classmates.

(Answers begin on p. 408.)

2. Marguerite tells you that when Mrs. Flowers smiled she wanted to thank her, since "the action was so graceful and inclusively benign," and that she was one of the few gentlewomen Marguerite has ever known.

ANSWERS TO CRITICAL THINKING AND READING

1. Suggested Response: Angelou probably wrote about Mrs. Flowers to explain a childhood experience that changed her life in a positive way.
2. The author's purpose to explain is evident in the following passages:
   a. the paragraph stating that she was depressed until she got to know "the lady who threw me my first lifeline." In this way you expect that she is going to relate an incident to you.
   b. the statement at the end of the incident saying "I was liked, and what a difference it made." In this way you know that the incident had a positive effect on Marguerite's life.

THINKING AND WRITING

For help with this assignment, students can refer to Lesson 20, "Writing a Personal Essay," in the Handbook of Writing About Literature.

Publishing Student Writing You might prepare a class book of autobiographical sketches. Ask for volunteers to organize the sketches and put together the book.

feels unhappy and negative about herself.

7. She wants Marguerite to read aloud to begin speaking more, and to read in as many different ways as possible to understand their deeper meaning.
8. Marguerite knew that saying something to be polite was the least she could do, but saying "Yes, ma'am" was also the most she could do.
9. Suggested Response: As a result of her meetings with Mrs. Flowers, Marguerite probably feels better about herself and speaks more.
10. Throughout Marguerite's life, Mrs. Flowers continued to be an example of graciousness and dignity in a human being.

Applying

11. Answers will differ. Suggested Response: Other ways in which people can give others "lifelines" are spending time with them doing things that they like, making or giving them a present they like, or showing or telling them something helpful to them.

ANSWERS TO ANALYZING LITERATURE

1. Suggested Response: Marguerite tells you that the Store was her favorite place to be; that the Store seemed tired in the afternoons; and that just before bedtime, the "promise of magic mornings" returned to the Store.

Focus

More About the Author Twain was strongly influenced by the Mississippi River while growing up. Discuss how the place in which an author lives can affect his or her writing.

Literary Focus Point out that, as in fiction, conflict in autobiography can be external or internal. Ask students for examples of external and internal conflicts.

Look For What kinds of conflicts can a person have on a job? This excerpt is about Twain's conflict on the job.

Writing/Prior Knowledge In this selection, what Twain expects to be a conflict with the captain turns out not to be. Ask students for examples of situations that they expected to be conflicts but were not.

Vocabulary For less advanced students first put these words in context and have students guess the meaning.

GUIDE FOR READING

Cub Pilot on the Mississippi

Mark Twain (1835–1910) was the pen name of Samuel Langhorne Clemens. A phrase used by boatmen in taking river soundings, *mark twain* means "two fathoms deep." Twain was known for his humorous writing and for novels of growing up like *The Adventures of Tom Sawyer.* Born in Florida, Missouri, he grew up in Hannibal on the Mississippi River. The influence the river had on Twain is evident in the following excerpt from *Life on the Mississippi,* published in 1883. In this excerpt, Twain tells of his experience steamboating.

Conflict in Autobiography

In autobiographical accounts, writers often describe how they have dealt with **conflicts,** or struggles. The conflicts they describe may be external or internal. An **external conflict** is one that takes place between the writer and a person or a natural force. An **internal conflict** is one that exists in the writer's mind, such as the struggle to make a difficult decision or to overcome an overwhelming fear. The outcome of a conflict is called its resolution. In "Cub Pilot on the Mississippi," Twain tells of the conflicts he faced as an apprentice —a person learning a trade while working for a master craftsman.

Look For

As you read "Cub Pilot on the Mississippi," look for the reasons behind the conflict Twain has with one of the pilots—a person who steers ships—and the way he resolves it. What do you learn about the life of a cub pilot from this excerpt?

Writing

Imagine some conflicts that a person could experience. Identify which are external conflicts with outside forces or other people, and which are internal conflicts within the person.

Vocabulary

Knowing the following words will help you as you read "Cub Pilot on the Mississippi."

furtive (fər′ tiv) *adj.*: Sly or done in secret (p. 412)
pretext (prē′ tekst) *n.*: A false reason or motive given to hide a real intention (p. 413)
intimation (in′ tə mā′ shən) *n.*: Hint or suggestion (p. 415)
indulgent (in dul′ jənt) *adj.*: Very mild and tolerant, not strict or critical (p. 416)
emancipated (i man′ sə pā′ təd) *v.*: Freed from the control or power of another (p. 418)

Objectives

1 To understand conflict in autobiography
2 To separate fact from opinion
3 To use contrast (context) clues
4 To write about conflict

Support Material

Teaching Portfolio
Teacher Backup, pp. 497–500
Grammar in Action Worksheets, *Appreciating Dialect*, pp. 501–502; *Using Precise, Carefully Selected Verbs*, pp. 503–504
Usage and Mechanics Worksheet, p. 505
Vocabulary Check, p. 506
Analyzing Literature Worksheet, *Understanding Conflicts*, p. 507
Language Worksheet, *Using Contrast Clues*, p. 508
Selection Test, pp. 509–510

Cub Pilot on the Mississippi

Mark Twain

THE GREAT MISSISSIPPI STEAMBOAT RACE, 1870
Currier and Ives
The Granger Collection

During the two or two and a half years of
my apprenticeship[1] I served under many
1 pilots, and had experience of many kinds of
steamboatmen and many varieties of steamboats. I am to this day profiting somewhat by that experience; for in that brief, sharp schooling, I got personally and familiarly acquainted with about all the different types of human nature that are to be found in fiction, biography, or history.

The fact is daily borne in upon me that the average shore-employment requires as

---

1. **apprenticeship** (ə pren′ tis ship) *n.*: The time spent by a person working for a master craftsman in a craft or trade in return for instruction and, formerly, support.

Presentation

Humanities Note

Fine art, *The Great Mississippi Steamboat Race,* 1879, by Currier and Ives. Nathaniel Currier (1813–1888) and James Merrit Ives (1824–1895) built an enormously successful printmaking business, satisfying a demand for affordable, popular prints. With their own stable of artists, they created a pictorial record of the post-Civil War days.

Accompanying this print is the following information: ". . . from New Orleans to St. Louis, July 1870. Between the *R.E. Lee,* Capt. John W. Cann and the *Natchez,* Capt. Leathers. Won by the *R.E. Lee.* Time: 3 days, 18 hours, and 30 min., Distance: 1210 mi."

Explain to the students that although Currier and Ives prints are not usually considered great artistic work, they did capture the feeling, the tempo, and the look of the Mississippi.

1. What information about steamboats can you get from this print?
2. Describe what you might see if you were standing on the upper deck of one of the steamboats in this picture.

Motivation/Prior Knowledge Have students imagine that they worked for a difficult boss. What would they do about it?

Purpose-Setting Question How might the conflict be different if it had been described by Brown, the cub pilot's boss, or the Captain?

1 **Enrichment** At the time Twain wrote this, the river was an important means of transportation, used to ship not only cargo but also passengers. Transportation took much longer at that time, although the pace of life in general was much slower than today.

2 Discussion Where in today's society would you be likely to meet a varied assortment of people to enjoy "people watching"?

3 Discussion Point out that Twain frequently uses exaggeration to provide humor. What details might be exaggerated in this description?

4 Enrichment A century ago, an apprentice had to tolerate almost any action of his master, since he was under a legal agreement to him. In medieval times, organizations called guilds gave the master powerful control over the lives of his apprentices. Today, *apprentice* is a more informal term. More than 90 trades offer apprenticeship training in about 300 skilled occupations; conditions of the work often are regulated by agreements between unions and employers.

much as forty years to equip a man with this sort of an education. When I say I am still profiting by this thing, I do not mean that it has constituted me a judge of men—no, it has not done that, for judges of men are born, not made. My profit is various in kind and degree, but the feature of it which I value most is the zest which that early experience has given to my later reading. When I find a well-drawn character in fiction or
2 biography I generally take a warm personal interest in him, for the reason that I have known him before—met him on the river.

The figure that comes before me oftenest, out of the shadows of that vanished time, is that of Brown, of the steamer *Pennsylvania.* He was a middle-aged, long, slim,
3 bony, smooth-shaven, horse-faced, ignorant, stingy, malicious, snarling, fault-hunting, mote[2]-magnifying tyrant. I early got the habit of coming on watch with dread at my heart. No matter how good a time I might have been having with the off-watch below,
4 and no matter how high my spirits might be when I started aloft, my soul became lead in my body the moment I approached the pilothouse.

I still remember the first time I ever entered the presence of that man. The boat had backed out from St. Louis and was "straightening down." I ascended to the pilothouse in high feather, and very proud to be semiofficially a member of the executive family of so fast and famous a boat. Brown was at the wheel. I paused in the middle of the room, all fixed to make my bow, but Brown did not look around. I thought he took a furtive glance at me out of the corner of his eye, but as not even this notice was repeated, I judged I had been mistaken. By this time he was picking his way among some dangerous "breaks" abreast the woodyards; therefore it would not be proper to interrupt him; so I stepped softly to the high bench and took a seat.

There was silence for ten minutes; then my new boss turned and inspected me deliberately and painstakingly from head to heel for about—as it seemed to me—a quarter of an hour. After which he removed his countenance[3] and I saw it no more for some seconds; then it came around once more, and this question greeted me: "Are you Horace Bigsby's cub?[4]"

"Yes, sir."

After this there was a pause and another inspection. Then: "What's your name?"

I told him. He repeated it after me. It was probably the only thing he ever forgot; for although I was with him many months he never addressed himself to me in any other way than "Here!" and then his command followed.

"Where was you born?"

"In Florida, Missouri."

A pause. Then: "Dern sight better stayed there!"

By means of a dozen or so of pretty direct questions, he pumped my family history out of me.

The leads[5] were going now in the first crossing. This interrupted the inquest.[6] When the leads had been laid in he resumed:

"How long you been on the river?"

I told him. After a pause:

"Where'd you get them shoes?"

---

2. mote (mōt) *n.*: A speck of dust or other tiny particle.

3. countenance (koun′ tə nəns) *n.*: Face.
4. cub (kub) *n.*: Beginner.
5. leads (lēdz) *n.*: Weights that were lowered to test the depth of the river.
6. inquest (in′ kwest) *n.*: Investigation.

Grammar in Action

Dialect is the form of language peculiar to a particular region or social group. By using dialect, writers can capture the flavor of a particular area.

Dialect may contain special vocabulary words or may violate standard rules of grammar. For example, look at the following dialect from "Cub Pilot on the Mississippi."

Where was you born?

Dern sight better stayed there!

Where'd you get them shoes?

I'll learn you to swell yourself up and blow around here . . .

I'm deuced glad of it! Hark ye, never mention that I said that.

Student Activity 1. Rewrite each of the examples above following the rules of standard grammar. Which sentences seem more appropriate for this selection—the ones you have rewritten or the original ones? Why?

I gave him the information.

"Hold up your foot!"

I did so. He stepped back, examined the shoe minutely and contemptuously, scratching his head thoughtfully, tilting his high sugar-loaf hat well forward to facilitate the operation, then ejaculated, "Well, I'll be dod derned!" and returned to his wheel.

What occasion there was to be dod derned about it is a thing which is still as much of a mystery to me now as it was then. It must have been all of fifteen minutes —fifteen minutes of dull, homesick silence —before that long horse-face swung round upon me again—and then what a change! It was as red as fire, and every muscle in it was working. Now came this shriek: "Here! You going to set there all day?"

I lit in the middle of the floor, shot there by the electric suddenness of the surprise. As soon as I could get my voice I said apologetically: "I have had no orders, sir."

5 "You've had no *orders!* My, what a fine bird we are! We must have *orders!* Our father was a *gentleman*—and *we've* been to *school.* Yes, *we* are a gentleman, *too,* and got to have *orders!* ORDERS, is it? ORDERS is what you want! Dod dern my skin, *I'll* learn you to swell yourself up and blow around *here* about your dod-derned *orders!* G'way from the wheel!" (I had approached it without knowing it.)

I moved back a step or two and stood as in a dream, all my senses stupefied by this frantic assault.

"What you standing there for? Take that ice-pitcher down to the texas-tender![7] Come, move along, and don't you be all day about it!"

The moment I got back to the pilothouse Brown said: "Here! What was you doing down there all this time?"

"I couldn't find the texas-tender; I had to go all the way to the pantry."

"Derned likely story! Fill up the stove."

I proceeded to do so. He watched me like a cat. Presently he shouted: "Put down that shovel! Derndest numskull I ever saw —ain't even got sense enough to load up a stove." 6

All through the watch this sort of thing went on. Yes, and the subsequent watches were much like it during a stretch of months. As I have said, I soon got the habit of coming on duty with dread. The moment I was in the presence, even in the darkest night, I could feel those yellow eyes upon me, and knew their owner was watching for a pretext to spit out some venom on me. Preliminarily he would say: "Here! Take the wheel."

Two minutes later: "*Where* in the nation you going to? Pull her down! pull her down!"

After another moment: "Say! You going to hold her all day? Let her go—meet her! meet her!"

Then he would jump from the bench, snatch the wheel from me, and meet her himself, pouring out wrath upon me all the 7 time.

George Ritchie was the other pilot's cub. He was having good times now; for his boss, George Ealer, was as kind-hearted as Brown wasn't. Ritchie had steered for Brown the season before; consequently, he knew exactly how to entertain himself and plague me, all by the one operation. Whenever I took the wheel for a moment on Ealer's watch, Ritchie would sit back on the bench and play Brown, with continual ejaculations

---

7. texas tender: The waiter in the officers' quarters. On Mississippi steamboats, rooms were named after the states. The officers' area, which was the largest, was named after what was then the largest state, Texas.

5 Discussion Why is Brown so angry that Twain had formal schooling? Is he envious or is he insecure, fearing that Twain is better than he?

6 Literary Focus Have students paraphrase the conflict between Brown and Twain.

7 Discussion Ask students why a fault-finder might derive satisfaction from destructive criticism. How do they think this kind of personality should be handled —with sympathy or combativeness? Explain your answer.

Student Activity 2. Pick a particular area of the country. Using dialect, write a conversation between two people from this region. Read it aloud to your classmates.

Humanities Note

Fine art, *St. Louis from the River,* 1832, by George Catlin. George Catlin (1796–1872) was born in Wilkes-Barre, Pennsylvania. He practiced law and did some portrait painting until 1832, when he decided to devote himself to art and to becoming an artist-historian. While on an exploratory expedition among the Native American tribes of the Mississippi River region, Catlin went ashore whenever the boat stopped, to draw and paint what he saw. In this painting, Catlin provides a dramatic view of the *Yellowstone* steaming past St. Louis.

1. In what ways would a view of St. Louis today differ from this 1832 view?
2. How does the feeling of drama in Catlin's painting relate to feelings in this selection?

8 **Literary Focus** Have students paraphrase the conflict in Twain's mind.

Samuel Clemens as a Young Man, M. T. Papers

of "Snatch her! Snatch her! Derndest mudcat I ever saw!" "Here! Where are you going *now?* Going to run over that snag?" "Pull her *down!* Don't you hear me? Pull her *down!*" "There she goes! *Just* as I expected! I *told* you not to cramp that reef. G'way from the wheel!"

So I always had a rough time of it, no matter whose watch it was; and sometimes it seemed to me that Ritchie's good-natured badgering was pretty nearly as aggravating as Brown's dead-earnest nagging.

8 I often wanted to kill Brown, but this would not answer. A cub had to take everything his boss gave, in the way of vigorous comment and criticism; and we all believed that there was a United States law making it a penitentiary offense to strike or threaten a pilot who was on duty.

However, I could *imagine* myself killing Brown; there was no law against that; and that was the thing I used always to do the moment I was abed. Instead of going over my river in my mind, as was my duty, I threw business aside for pleasure, and killed Brown. I killed Brown every night for months; not in old, stale, commonplace ways, but in new and picturesque ones

Grammar in Action

Mark Twain's writing, like the man himself, is filled with energy. **Precise, carefully selected verbs** create that energy in his writing.

Look at his use of verbs in the following excerpt from "Cub Pilot on the Mississippi":

> His face *turned* red with passion; he *made* one bound, *hurled* me across the house with a sweep of his arm, *spun* the wheel down, and *began* to pour out a stream of vituperation upon me which *lasted* until he was out of breath.

In the above example Twain uses the following verbs: *turned, made, hurled, spun, began* and *lasted.* Of these verbs, *hurled* and *spun* are especially precise, creating a vivid picture of the action. Each of the verbs is followed by additional descriptive words which add to the action of the sentence.

—ways that were sometimes surprising for freshness of design and ghastliness of situation and environment.

Brown was *always* watching for a pretext to find fault; and if he could find no plausible pretext, he would invent one. He would scold you for shaving a shore, and for not shaving it; for hugging a bar, and for not hugging it; for "pulling down" when not invited, and for *not* pulling down when not invited; for firing up without orders, and for waiting *for* orders. In a word, it was his invariable rule to find fault with *everything* you did and another invariable rule of his was to throw all his remarks (to you) into the form of an insult.

9 One day we were approaching New Madrid, bound down and heavily laden. Brown was at one side of the wheel, steering; I was at the other, standing by to "pull down" or "shove up." He cast a furtive glance at me
10 every now and then. I had long ago learned what that meant; viz., he was trying to invent a trap for me. I wondered what shape it was going to take. By and by he stepped back from the wheel and said in his usual snarly way:

"Here! See if you've got gumption enough to round her to."

This was simply *bound* to be a success; nothing could prevent it; for he had never allowed me to round the boat to before; consequently, no matter how I might do the thing, he could find free fault with it. He stood back there with his greedy eye on me, and the result was what might have been foreseen: I lost my head in a quarter of a minute, and didn't know what I was about; I started too early to bring the boat around, but detected a green gleam of joy in Brown's eye, and corrected my mistake. I started around once more while too high up, but corrected myself again in time. I made other false moves, and still managed to save myself; but at last I grew so confused and anxious that I tumbled into the very worst blunder of all—I got too far *down* before beginning to fetch the boat around. Brown's chance was come.

His face turned red with passion; he made one bound, hurled me across the house with a sweep of his arm, spun the wheel down, and began to pour out a stream of vituperation[8] upon me which lasted till he was out of breath. In the course of this speech he called me all the different kinds of hard names he could think of, and once or twice I thought he was even going to swear—but he had never done that, and he didn't this time. "Dod dern" was the nearest he ventured to the luxury of swearing.

Two trips later I got into serious trouble. Brown was steering; I was "pulling down." My younger brother Henry appeared on the hurricane deck, and shouted to Brown to stop at some landing or other, a mile or so below. Brown gave no intimation that he had heard anything. But that was his way: he never condescended to take notice of an underclerk. The wind was blowing; Brown
was deaf (although he always pretended he 11
wasn't), and I very much doubted if he had heard the order. If I had had two heads, I would have spoken; but as I had only one, it seemed judicious to take care of it; so I kept still.

Presently, sure enough, we went sailing by that plantation. Captain Klinefelter appeared on the deck, and said: "Let her come around, sir, let her come around. Didn't Henry tell you to land here?"

"No, sir!"

"I sent him up to do it."

8. **vituperation** (vī to͞o′ pə rā′ shən) *n.*: Abusive language.

9 **Clarification** New Madrid is a town along the Mississippi River.

10 **Clarification** *Viz.* is Latin for "namely."

11 **Discussion** What is the possibility that Brown yelled loudly because he couldn't hear?

Student Activity 1. Find ten other precise verbs in "Cub Pilot on the Mississippi." Tell why you selected each one.

Student Activity 2. Think of a time when someone was extremely angry with you. Using Twain's description of the enraged steamboat pilot, write a description of that person and what he or she did to show rage and anger.

12 **Reading Strategy** Ask students to summarize this anecdote so far. You might have them predict what will happen as a result of this incident.

13 **Discussion** Ask students if they think that Twain's criticizing Brown for his grammar after a physical fight adds to the humor of this selection. They should give reasons for their answers.

"He *did* come up; and that's all the good it done, the dod-derned fool. He never said anything."

"Didn't *you* hear him?" asked the captain of me.

Of course I didn't want to be mixed up in this business, but there was no way to avoid it; so I said: "Yes, sir."

I knew what Brown's next remark would be, before he uttered it. It was: "Shut your mouth! You never heard anything of the kind."

I closed my mouth, according to instructions. An hour later Henry entered the pilothouse, unaware of what had been going on. He was a thoroughly inoffensive boy, and I was sorry to see him come, for I knew Brown would have no pity on him. Brown began, straightway: "Here! Why didn't you tell me we'd got to land at that plantation?"

"I did tell you, Mr. Brown."

"It's a lie!"

I said: "You lie, yourself. He did tell you."

Brown glared at me in unaffected surprise; and for as much as a moment he was entirely speechless; then he shouted to me: "I'll attend to your case in a half a minute!" then to Henry, "And you leave the pilothouse; out with you!"

It was pilot law, and must be obeyed. The boy started out, and even had his foot on the upper step outside the door, when Brown, with a sudden access of fury, 12 picked up a ten-pound lump of coal and sprang after him; but I was between, with a heavy stool, and I hit Brown a good honest blow which stretched him out.

I had committed the crime of crimes—I had lifted my hand against a pilot on duty! I supposed I was booked for the penitentiary sure, and couldn't be booked any surer if I went on and squared my long account with this person while I had the chance; consequently I stuck to him and pounded him with my fists a considerable time. I do not know how long, the pleasure of it probably made it seem longer than it really was; but in the end he struggled free and jumped up and sprang to the wheel: a very natural solicitude, for, all this time, here was this steamboat tearing down the river at the rate of fifteen miles an hour and nobody at the helm! However, Eagle Bend was two miles wide at this bank-full stage, and correspondingly long and deep: and the boat was steering herself straight down the middle and taking no chances. Still, that was only luck—a body *might* have found her charging into the woods.

Perceiving at a glance that the *Pennsylvania* was in no danger, Brown gathered up the big spyglass, war-club fashion, and ordered me out of the pilothouse with more than ordinary bluster. But I was not afraid of him now; so, instead of going, I tarried, and criticized his grammar. I reformed his ferocious speeches for him, and put them into good English, calling his attention to the advantage of pure English over the dialect of the collieries[9] whence he was extract- 13
ed. He could have done his part to admiration in a crossfire of mere vituperation, of course; but he was not equipped for this species of controversy; so he presently laid aside his glass and took the wheel, muttering and shaking his head; and I retired to the bench. The racket had brought everybody to the hurricane deck, and I trembled when I saw the old captain looking up from amid the crowd. I said to myself, "Now I *am* done for!" for although, as a rule, he was so fatherly and indulgent toward the boat's family, and so patient of minor shortcomings, he could be stern enough when the fault was worth it.

---

9. collieries (käl′ yər ēz) *n.*: Coal mines.

THE CHAMPIONS OF THE MISSISSIPPI
Currier & Ives

Humanities Note

Fine art, *The Champions of the Mississippi,* by Currier and Ives. Point out to students that, although Currier and Ives faithfully recorded the mood and many details of life on the Mississippi, they often fabricated scenes to convey a certain amount of pictorial information. This very atmospheric night scene would, no doubt, have been a steamboat pilot's nightmare.

1. What is the mood Currier and Ives create in this picture? How does this mood fit the story?
2. Why is this scene a probable fabrication? Consider the dangers of piloting a steamboat in a night race in the early 1800's.

I tried to imagine what he *would* do to a cub pilot who had been guilty of such a crime as mine, committed on a boat guard-deep[10] with costly freight and alive with passengers. Our watch was nearly ended. I thought I would go and hide somewhere till I got a chance to slide ashore. So I slipped out of the pilothouse, and down the steps, and around to the texas-door, and was in the act of gliding within, when the captain confronted me! I dropped my head, and he stood over me in silence a moment or two, then said impressively: "Follow me."

I dropped into his wake; he led the way to his parlor in the forward end of the texas. We were alone now. He closed the afterdoor, then moved slowly to the forward one and closed that. He sat down; I stood before him. He looked at me some little time, then said: "So you have been fighting Mr. Brown?"

I answered meekly: "Yes, sir."

"Do you know that that is a very serious matter?"

"Yes, sir."

"Are you aware that this boat was plowing down the river fully five minutes with no one at the wheel?"

"Yes, sir."

"Did you strike him first?"

"Yes, sir."

"What with?"

"A stool, sir."

"Hard?"

10. guard-deep: Here, a wooden frame protecting the paddle wheel.

14 Discussion Why does the Captain want Twain to thrash Brown on shore rather than on the boat?

15 Discussion Ask students if they are surprised at the Captain's reaction. Why?

16 Discussion Conflicts have resolutions. How is Twain's conflict with Brown resolved?

Master Teacher Note A group of your **more advanced** students might read *Life on the Mississippi*, from which this excerpt comes. They could report to the class on some of Twain's other experiences as a cub pilot.

Reader's Response What acquaints you with "the various types of human nature" the way the narrator was acquainted during his apprenticeship?

"Middling, sir."

"Did it knock him down?"

"He—he fell, sir."

"Did you follow it up? Did you do anything further?"

"Yes, sir."

"What did you do?"

"Pounded him, sir."

"Pounded him?"

"Yes, sir."

"Did you pound him much? that is, severely?"

"One might call it that, sir, maybe."

"I'm deuced glad of it! Hark ye, never mention that I said that. You have been guilty of a great crime; and don't you ever be guilty of it again, on this boat. *But*—lay for him ashore! Give him a good sound thrash-
14 ing, do you hear? I'll pay the expenses. Now go—and mind you, not a word of this to anybody. Clear out with you! You've been guilty of a great crime, you whelp!"[11]

I slid out, happy with the sense of a close
15 shave and a mighty deliverance; and I heard him laughing to himself and slapping his fat thighs after I had closed his door.

When Brown came off watch he went straight to the captain, who was talking with some passengers on the boiler deck, and demanded that I be put ashore in New Orleans—and added: "I'll never turn a wheel on this boat again while that cub stays."

The captain said: "But he needn't come round when you are on watch, Mr. Brown."

"I won't even stay on the same boat with him. *One* of us has got to go ashore."

"Very well," said the captain, "let it be yourself," and resumed his talk with the passengers.

During the brief remainder of the trip I 16
knew how an emancipated slave feels, for I was an emancipated slave myself. While we lay at landings I listened to George Ealer's flute, or to his readings from his two Bibles, that is to say, Goldsmith and Shakespeare, or I played chess with him—and would have beaten him sometimes, only he always took back his last move and ran the game out differently.

11. whelp (hwelp) *n.*: A young dog or puppy; here, a disrespectful young man.

THINKING ABOUT THE SELECTION

Recalling

1. Describe Mr. Brown when he meets the cub pilot, Twain.
2. What causes Twain's "serious trouble" with Mr. Brown? How is the trouble resolved?
3. Why does Twain feel like "an emancipated slave" at the end?
4. How does knowing the various kinds of steamboatmen profit Twain as a writer?

Interpreting

5. In what ways was Brown's treatment of the young Twain unfair?
6. Compare and contrast Brown's and Ritchie's treatment of Twain.
7. How does the Captain feel about Mr. Brown? What evidence supports your answer?

Applying

8. John Locke wrote: "It is easier for a tutor to command than to teach." Explain the mean-

Closure and Extension

ANSWERS TO THINKING ABOUT THE SELECTION

Recalling

1. Brown is middle-aged, long, slim, bony, smooth-shaven, and horse-faced.
2. Twain's "serious trouble" with Mr. Brown is caused by Brown's abusing Twain's brother Henry; Twain responds by fighting and beating Brown, and the captain privately tells Twain he will pay him to fight the captain on shore.
3. Twain feels like an emancipated slave because he is free of Brown's abuse.
4. It acquaints him with all the different types of human nature; he can use this knowledge to make his fiction true to life.

Interpreting

5. Brown's treatment of the young Twain was unfair in that he yelled at him for no cause—even when Twain did things correctly.
6. Suggested Responses: Brown's and Ritchie's treatment of Twain was similar in that it was full of berating and ejaculations; it was different in that Ritchie's was good-natured badgering, while Brown's was dead-earnest abuse.
7. The Captain does not like Mr. Brown. Evidence that supports this is that he says he is glad that Twain pounded Brown and offers to pay Twain for thrashing Brown on shore,

ing of this quotation. How does it relate to this selection?

ANALYZING LITERATURE
Understanding Conflicts

Conflicts may provide the main element of a plot, or sequence of action, in an autobiography. For example, "Cub Pilot on the Mississippi" is based on the conflict between Mark Twain as a cub pilot and Mr. Brown. The outcome of the conflict is its resolution; however, a conflict may not always be resolved.

1. Why are the cub pilot and Mr. Brown in conflict?
2. What conflict does the cub pilot experience in his mind?
3. How are both conflicts resolved?

CRITICAL THINKING AND READING
Separating Fact from Opinion

Autobiographies may contain both facts and opinions. **Facts** are statements that can be proved true with reliable sources, such as an encyclopedia or an expert. For example, the statement that cub pilots were apprentices on Mississippi River steamboats can be verified with historical records.

Opinions are beliefs or judgments. The writer's opinions are not subject to verification, because they are based on the writer's attitudes or beliefs. For example, it is Twain's opinion that Mr. Brown is a "mote-magnifying tyrant."

Identify which of the following is fact and which is opinion. Indicate what source you might use to verify each fact.

1. The cub's brother Henry was a thoroughly inoffensive boy.
2. A cub pilot was required to obey a steamboat pilot on duty.
3. The cub pilot was born in Florida, Missouri.
4. George Ealer was as kind-hearted as Brown was not.

UNDERSTANDING LANGUAGE
Using Contrast Clues

You can often figure out the meaning of a word by using **contrast clues,** or other words in the sentence that are the opposite to or quite different from the unfamiliar word. The following sentence provides two contrast clues for the word *stern:*

". . . although, as a rule, he was . . . fatherly and indulgent toward the boat's family . . . he could be stern enough when the fault was worth it."

The clues *fatherly* and *indulgent* suggest a contrast to *stern.*

Find the meaning of each underlined word by using the contrast clues.

1. He was as *miserly* as she was generous.
2. It was *trivial* to me, but important to Joe.

THINKING AND WRITING
Writing About Conflict

Robert Keith Miller has said that in *Life on the Mississippi,* Mark Twain writes about the conflicting feelings of being attracted to and repulsed, or disgusted, by the world of the steamboat pilot. Write an essay explaining the conflicting feelings in the selection. First list some aspects of life on the Mississippi that attract Mark Twain and some that repulse him. Then develop your essay, showing the conflict between Mark Twain and Mr. Brown. Revise your essay, making sure that you use examples to support your views. Proofread your essay and share it with your classmates.

(Answers begin on p. 418.)

ANSWERS TO UNDERSTANDING LANGUAGE

1. Suggested Response: You can figure out that *miserly* means greedy and stingy because it is presented as the oppoşite of *generous.*
2. Suggested Response: You can figure out that *trivial* means insignificant because it is presented as the opposite of *important.*

THINKING AND WRITING

Publishing Student Writing You might want to put together a booklet of the students' essays, or display them on the bulletin board.

Writing Across the Curriculum You might have students report on different aspects of the Mississippi River. If you do, you might notify the social studies department. Social studies teachers might provide guidance for students on conducting their research or offer them extra credit.

and that Twain hears the Captain chuckling after he closes the door.

Applying

8. Answers will differ. Suggested Responses: To command is simply to order; to teach involves providing with knowledge and insight through explanation and example. A person can perform something as ordered without any insight into it. In this selection, Brown simply orders and shouts commands; he does not explain or show how to do things to help the cub pilot gain any insight.

ANSWERS TO ANALYZING LITERATURE

1. The cub pilot and Mr. Brown are in conflict because Brown continually abuses and screams at the cub pilot, who does not like such abuse.
2. The conflict in the cub pilot's mind is that he wanted to thwart Brown, which was not permitted.
3. The conflicts are resolved when Twain fights and beats Brown, and the Captain privately condones Twain's behavior.

ANSWERS TO CRITICAL THINKING AND READING

1. Opinion
2. Fact; can be verified by the Captain or a record of the law
3. Fact; can be verified by birth records in Florida, Mo., or an encyclopedia
4. Opinion

Focus

More About the Author Douglas was a United States Supreme Court Justice who served on the bench from 1939 to 1975. As a child, he knew poverty and suffered from polio. Ask how this experience may have served to make him a climber of mountains and a supporter of the downtrodden and the individual.

Literary Focus The narrator in autobiography is the author, who speaks as "I." You might introduce your **more advanced** students to the term *first-person point of view,* and discuss the effects of this point of view.

Look For The narrator in autobiography relates what he recalls, feels, and observes. Remind students that these are subjective details. For your **less advanced** students, you might want to review the difference between subjective and objective details.

Writing/Prior Knowledge Ask students for examples of well-publicized challenges people have undertaken. Then have them complete the freewriting assignment.

Vocabulary To help your **less advanced** students understand these words, you might give them each word in context.

Spelling Tip The ending *-ious* occurs frequently in words like *precarious,* unlike *-eous,* which occurs mainly in scientific words. Other *-ious* words include: *spacious, gracious,* and *facetious.*

GUIDE FOR READING

from Of Men and Mountains

William O. Douglas (1898–1980) was born in Maine, Minnesota, but grew up in Yakima, Washington. He is best known as a U.S. Supreme Court Justice who served for more than thirty-six years, and as a champion of conservation, the official care of natural resources. After recovering from polio as a child, he was drawn to nature. The following selection is from *Of Men and Mountains,* an autobiographical account of his mountain-climbing adventures.

The Narrator in Autobiography

A **narrator** is a person or character who tells a story. In an **autobiography** the author is the narrator, who tells his or her experiences from the first-person point of view, speaking as "I." When you read about William O. Douglas's climb, you experience it through his eyes and mind—knowing what he recalls, feels, and observes about his experience.

Look For

As you read "Of Men and Mountains," look for the way Douglas re-creates his experience by telling you what he recalls, feels, and observes. Why does the young Douglas want to face the challenge of climbing Kloochman, a rock on the southern side of the Tieton Basin?

Writing

Why do some people enjoy a challenge? Freewrite, exploring your answer.

Vocabulary

Knowing the following words will help you as you read "Of Men and Mountains."

shunned (shund) *v.*: Deliberately avoided (p. 421)
precarious (pri ker′ ē əs) *adj.*: Insecure and dangerous (p. 421)
tortuous (tôr′ choo wəs) *adj.*: Winding with repeated twists and turns (p. 421)
bravado (brə va′ dō) *n.*: A show of bravery (p. 423)
laterally (lat′ ər əl ē) *adv.*: Toward the side (p. 425)
abyss (ə bis′) *n.*: A bottomless space (p. 426)
buoyant (boi′ ənt) *adj.*: Lighthearted (p. 427)

Objectives

1 To understand the narrator in autobiography
2 To recognize the effect of point of view
3 To appreciate words from Greek myths
4 To write from another point of view

Support Material

Teaching Portfolio

Teacher Backup, pp. 511–514
Grammar in Action Worksheets, *Using Semicolons,* pp. 515–516; *Understanding Repetition,* pp. 517–518
Usage and Mechanics Worksheet, p. 519
Vocabulary Check, p. 520
Analyzing Literature Worksheet, *Understanding the Narrator in Autobiography,* p. 521
Critical Thinking and Reading Worksheet, *Recognizing the Effect of Point of View,* p. 522
Selection Test, pp. 523–524

from Of Men and Mountains

William O. Douglas

It was in 1913 when Doug was 19 and I
1 was not quite 15 that the two of us made
this climb of Kloochman.[1] Walter Kohagen,
Doug, and I were camped in the Tieton Basin
at a soda spring. The basin was then in large
part a vast rich bottomland. We were traveling light, one blanket each. The night, I
recall, was so bitter cold that we took turns
refueling the campfire so that we could keep
our backs warm enough to sleep. We rose at
2 the first show of dawn, and cooked frying-
pan bread and trout for breakfast. We had
not planned to climb Kloochman, but somehow the challenge came to us as the sun
touched her crest.

After breakfast we started circling the
3 rock. There are fairly easy routes up Kloochman, but we shunned them. When we came
to the southeast face (the one that never has been conquered, I believe) we chose it. Walter decided not to make the climb, but to wait at the base of the cliff for Doug and me. The July day was warm and cloudless. Doug led. The beginning was easy. For 100 feet or so we found ledges six to twelve inches wide we could follow to the left or right. Some ledges ran up the rock ten feet or more at a gentle grade. Others were merely steps to another ledge higher up. Thus by hugging the wall we could either ease ourselves upward or hoist ourselves from one ledge to another.

When we were about 100 feet up the wall, the ledges became narrower and footwork more precarious. Doug suggested we take off our shoes. This we did, tying them behind us on our belts. In stocking feet we wormed up the wall, clinging like flies to the dark rock. The pace was slow. We gingerly tested each toehold and fingerhold for loose rock before putting our weight on it. At times we had to inch along sidewise, our stomachs pressed tightly against the rock, in order to gain a point where we could reach the ledge above us. If we got on a ledge that turned out to be a cul-de-sac,[2] the much more dangerous task of going down the rock wall would confront us. Hence we picked our route with care and weighed the advantages of several choices which frequently were given us. At times we could not climb easily from one ledge to another. The one above might be a foot or so high. Then we would have to reach it with one knee, slowly bring the other knee up, and then, delicately balancing on both knees on the upper ledge, come slowly to our feet by pressing close to the wall and getting such purchase[3] with our fingers as the lava rock permitted.

In that tortuous way we made perhaps

---

1. Kloochman: An oval-shaped lava rock on the southern side of the Tieton Basin in the Cascades. The final third of it consists of a sheer cliff rising straight up 1,200 feet or more.

2. cul-de-sac (kul′ də sak′) *n.*: A passage with only one outlet.

3. purchase (pur′ chəs) *n.*: A tight hold to keep from slipping.

Presentation

Motivation/Prior Knowledge Ask students if they have ever done any rock climbing. If not, have them imagine some of the dangers involved. What satisfactions and challenges does it give the climber? What are other examples of famous mountain climbs?

Master Teacher Note Bring in photographs of Kloochman Rock to show the class.

Thematic Idea Another selection that deals with the theme of courage is "Harriet Tubman; Guide to Freedom" on page 303.

Purpose-Setting Question What can meeting a challenge teach you about yourself and about living?

1 **Clarification** Doug is William O. Douglas's childhood friend; Doug is 19 and William is 15.

2 **Discussion** What equipment and gear would you need to go camping and rock climbing?

3 **Discussion** What does the fact that they shunned the easy routes tell you about the two boys?

600 feet in two hours. It was late forenoon when we stopped to appraise our situation. We were in serious trouble. We had reached the feared cul-de-sac. The two- or three-inch ledge on which we stood ended. There seemed none above us within Doug's reach. I was longer-legged than Doug; so perhaps I could have reached some ledge with my fingers if I were ahead. But it was impossible to change positions on the wall. Doug was ahead and there he must stay. The problem was to find a way to get him up.

Feeling along the wall, Doug discovered a tiny groove into which he could press the tips of the fingers of his left hand. It might help him maintain balance as his weight began to shift from the lower ledge to the upper one. But there was within reach not even a lip of rock for his right hand. Just out of reach, however, was a substantial crevice, one that would hold several men. How could Doug reach it? I could not boost him, for my own balance was insecure. Clearly, Doug would have to jump to reach it—and he would have but one jump. Since he was standing on a ledge only a few inches wide, he could not expect to jump for his handhold, miss it, and land safely. A slip meant he would go hurtling down some 600 feet onto the rocks. After much discussion and indecision, Doug decided to take the chance and go up.

He asked me to do him a favor: If he failed and fell, I might still make it, since I was longer-legged; would I give certain messages to his family in that event? I nodded.

"Then listen carefully. Try to remember my exact words," he told me. "Tell Mother

Grammar in Action

Writers combine sentences in order to show a close relation between the main idea of each clause. The **semicolon** can be used in place of a period and a capital letter or in place of a comma and a coordinating conjunction when the meaning of the second clause is closely tied to the meaning of the first. Look at the following examples in which William O. Douglas uses a semicolon to join two clauses:

I was longer-legged than Doug; so perhaps I could have reached some ledge with my fingers if I were ahead.

He asked me to do him a favor; if he failed and fell, I might still make it, since I was longer-legged; would I give certain messages to his family in that event?

I held my breath; my heart pounded.

There was no toehold; he would have to hoist himself by his arms alone.

We needed our toes, not our heels, on the rock; and we needed to have our stomachs pressed tightly against it.

that I love her dearly. Tell her I think she is the most wonderful person in the world. Tell her not to worry—that I did not suffer. Tell Sister that I have been a mean little devil but I had no malice towards her. Tell her I love her too—that some day I wanted to marry a girl as wholesome and cheery
4 and good as she.

"Tell Dad I was brave and died unafraid. Tell him about our climb in full detail. Tell Dad I have always been very proud of him, that some day I had planned to be a doctor too. Tell him I lived a clean life, that I never did anything to make him ashamed. . . . Tell Mother, Sister, and Dad I prayed for them."

Every word burned into me. My heart was sick, my lips quivered. I pressed my face against the rock so Doug could not see. I wept.

All was silent. A pebble fell from the ledge on which I squeezed. I counted seconds before it hit 600 feet below with a faint, faraway tinkling sound. Would Doug
5 drop through the same space? Would I follow? When you fall 600 feet do you die before you hit the bottom? Closing my eyes, I asked God to help Doug up the wall.

In a second Doug said in a cheery voice, "Well, here goes."

A false bravado took hold of us. I said he could do it. He said he would. He wiped first one hand then the other on his trousers. He placed both palms against the wall, bent his knees slowly, paused a split second, and jumped straight up. It was not much of a jump—only six inches or so. But that jump by one pressed against a cliff 600 feet in the air had daredevil proportions. I held my breath; my heart pounded. The suspense was over.

Doug made the jump, and in a second was hanging by two hands from a strong, wide ledge. There was no toehold; he would have to hoist himself by his arms alone. He did just that. His body went slowly up as if pulled by some unseen winch.[4] Soon he had the weight of his body above the ledge and was resting on the palms of his hands. He then put his left knee on the ledge, rolled over on his side, and chuckled as he said, "Nothing to it."

A greater disappointment followed. Doug's exploration of the ledge showed he was in a final cul-de-sac. There was no way up. There was not even a higher ledge he could reach by jumping. We were now faced with the nightmare of going down the sheer rock wall. We could not go down frontwards because the ledges were too narrow and the wall too steep. We needed our toes, not our heels, on the rock; and we needed to have our stomachs pressed tightly against it. Then we could perhaps feel our way. But as every rock expert knows, descent of a cliff without ropes is often much more difficult than ascent.

That difficulty was impressed on us by the first move. Doug had to leave the ledge he had reached by jumping. He dared not slide blindly to the skimpy ledge he had just left. I must help him. I must move up the wall and
stand closer to him. Though I could not 6
possibly hold his weight, I must exert sufficient pressure to slow up his descent and to direct his toe onto the narrow ledge from which he had just jumped.

I was hanging to the rock like a fly, twelve feet or more to Doug's left. I inched my way toward him, first dropping to a lower ledge and then climbing to a higher one, using such toeholds as the rock afforded and edging my way crabwise.

When I reached him I said, "Now I'll help."

Doug lowered himself and hung by his fingers full length. His feet were about six inches above the ledge from which he had

---

4. winch *n.*: A machine used for lifting.

4 **Discussion** Why do people make speeches such as this? How does this speech and its effect on the narrator add to the tension and suspense in this account?

5 **Reading Strategy** Have students summarize the situation the boys are in and predict what will happen as they continue.

6 **Discussion** Discuss why, in the face of danger, people often have a reserve of strength and courage to go on.

Notice how there is a complete sentence (independent clause) both before and after each semicolon, and the sentences are related to one another. Writers choose a semicolon when a period would make too abrupt a pause between the two sentences, and a comma with a coordinating conjunction (*and, but, or, nor*) wouldn't be appropriate to the meaning of the two sentences.

Student Activity. Create a fictional situation when you and a friend are in some kind of danger. Write a short narrative relating this event. Correctly use the semicolon at least twice in your narrative. Have one of your classmates read your narrative and check for the correct use of a semicolon.

7 **Discussion** Why is this analogy appropriate?

8 **Literary Focus** How does the narrative perspective affect the story?

9 **Discussion** How do you think the two friends felt about each other after this experience?

10 **Discussion** Why do you think they were determined to make the second climb?

jumped. He was now my responsibility. If he dropped without aid or direction he was gone. He could not catch and hold to the scanty ledge. I had little space for maneuvering. The surface on which I stood was not more than three inches wide. My left hand fortunately found an overhead crevice that gave a solid anchor in case my feet slipped.

I placed my right hand in the small of Doug's back and pressed upward with all my might. "Now you can come," I said.

He let go gently, and the full weight of his body came against my arm. My arm trembled under the tension. My left hand hung onto the crack in the rock like a grappling hook. My stomach pressed against the wall as if to find mucilage[5] in its pores. My toes dug in as I threw in every ounce of strength.

Down Doug came—a full inch. I couldn't help glancing down and seeing the rocks 600 feet below.

Down Doug moved another inch, then a third. My left hand seemed paralyzed. The muscles of my toes were aching. My right arm shook. I could not hold much longer.

Down came Doug a fourth inch. I thought he was headed for destruction. His feet would miss the only toehold within reach. I could not possibly hold him. He would plunge to his death because my arm was not strong enough to hold him. The messages he had given me for his family raced through my mind. And I saw myself, sick and ashamed, standing before them, testifying to my own inadequacy, repeating his last words.

"Steady, Doug. The ledge is a foot to your right." He pawed the wall with the toes of his foot, searching.

"I can't find it. Don't let go."

The crisis was on us. Even if I had been safely anchored, my cramped position would have kept me from helping him much more. I felt helpless. In a few seconds I would reach the physical breaking point and Doug would go hurtling off the cliff. I did not see how I could keep him from slipping and yet maintain my own balance.

I will never know how I did it. But I tapped some reserve and directed his right foot onto the ledge from which he had earlier jumped. I did it by standing for a moment on my left foot alone and then using my right leg as a rod to guide his right foot to the ledge his swinging feet had missed.

His toes grabbed the ledge as if they were
the talons of a bird. My right leg swung back 7
to my perch.

"Are you OK?" I asked.

"Yes," said Doug. "Good work."

My right arm fell from him, numb and
useless. I shook from exhaustion and for the
first time noticed that my face was wet with 8
perspiration. We stood against the rock in
silence for several minutes, relaxing and
regaining our composure.

Doug said: "Let's throw our shoes down.
It will be easier going." So we untied them
from our belts and dropped them to Walter 9
Kohagen, who was waiting at the rock field
below us.

Our descent was painfully slow but uneventful. We went down backwards, weaving a strange pattern across the face of the cliff as we moved from one side to the other. It was perhaps midafternoon when we reached the bottom, retrieved our shoes, and started around the other side of the rock. We left the southeast wall unconquered.

But, being young, we were determined to
climb the rock. So once more we started to 10
circle. When we came to the northwest wall,
we selected it as our route.

5. **mucilage** (myōō' s'l ij) *n.*: Any watery solution of gum, glue, etc. used as an adhesive.

Grammar in Action

A useful device for emphasizing an idea or creating a dramatic effect is **repetition.** Using the same word or group of words more than once or twice in a sentence, paragraph or group of paragraphs reinforces important ideas for the reader. Repetition can also enhance coherence in a literary work. Although if overused, repetition can make writing seem flat, unoriginal, and boring, there are times when repetition is especially appropriate.

Douglas's use of repetition in this excerpt from *Of Men and Mountains* is particularly appropriate. He is describing a slow, tension-filled process in which something happens repeatedly.

> Down Doug came—a full inch. I couldn't help glancing down and seeing the rocks 600 feet below.
>
> Down Doug moved another inch, then a third. My left hand seemed paralyzed. The muscles of my toes were aching. My right arm shook. I could not hold much longer.
>
> Down came Doug a fourth inch. I thought he was headed for destruction.

As Douglas recreates his mountain climbing effort, he painstakingly dramatizes the tortuous and slow procedure through the

Here, too, is a cliff rising 1,000 feet like some unfinished pyramid. But close examination shows numerous toe- and fingerholds that made the start at least fairly easy. So we set out with our shoes on.

Again it was fairly easy going for a hundred feet or so, when Doug, who was ahead, came to a ledge to which he could not step. On later climbs we would send the longer-legged chap ahead. And on other occasions Doug himself has used a rope to traverse this spot. But this day success of the climb depended at this point on Doug's short legs alone. The ledge to which he must move was up to his hips. There were few fingerholds overhead, and none firm enough to carry his whole weight. Only a few tiny cracks were within reach to serve as purchase for him. But Doug would not give up.

He hitched up his trousers, and grasped a tiny groove of rock with the tips of the fingers of his left hand, pressing his right hand flat against the smooth rock wall as if it had magical sticking power. Slowly he lifted his left knee until it was slightly over the ledge above him. To do so he had to stand tiptoe on his right foot. Pulling with his left hand, he brought his right knee up. Doug was now on both knees on the upper ledge. If he could find good purchase overhead for his hands, he was safe. His hands explored the wall above him. He moved them slowly over most of it without finding a hold. Then he reached straight above his head and cried out, "This is our lucky day."

He had found strong rough edges of rock, and on this quickly pulled himself up. His hands were on a ledge a foot wide. He lay down on it on his stomach and grasped my outstretched hand. The pull of his strong arm against the drop of 100 feet or more was as comforting an experience as any I can recall. In a jiffy I was at his side. We pounded each other on the shoulders and laughed.

My own most serious trouble was yet to come. For a while Doug and I were separated. I worked laterally along a ledge to the south, found easier going, and in a short time was 200 feet or more up the rock wall. I was above Doug, 25 feet or so, and 50 feet to his right. We had been extremely careful to test each toe- and finger-hold before putting our trust in it. Kloochman is full of treacherous rock. We often discovered thin ledges that crumbled under pressure and showered handfuls of rock and dust down below. Perhaps I was careless; but whatever the cause, the thin ledge on which I was standing gave way.

As I felt it slip, I grabbed for a hold above me. The crevasse[6] I seized was solid. But there I was, hanging by my hands 200 feet in the air, my feet pawing the rock. To make

6. crevasse (kri vas′) *n.*: A deep crack.

use of repetition. Tension builds as we read of Douglas's inch by inch descent.

Student Activity 1. As you read more from *Of Men and Mountains,* look for more examples of repetition. Take note of them and explain why repetition is appropriate in the examples you found.

Student Activity 2. Write a brief narrative in which you use repetition to emphasize an important idea or create tension.

11 **Discussion** Which words show fear? How does this affect the narrative?

matters worse, my camera had swung between me and the cliff when I slipped. It was a crude and clumsy instrument, a box type that I carried on a leather strap across my shoulders. Its hulk was actually pushing me from the cliff. I twisted in an endeavor to get rid of it, but it was firmly lodged between me and the wall.

I yelled to Doug for help. He at once started edging toward me. It seemed hours, though it was probably not over a few minutes. He shouted, "Hang on, I'll be there."

Hang on I did. My fingers ached beyond description. They were frozen to the rock. My exertion in pawing with my feet had added to the fatigue. The ache of my fingers extended to my wrists and then along my arms. I stopped thrashing around and hung like a sack, motionless. Every second seemed a minute, every minute an hour. I did not see how I could possibly hold.

I would slip, I thought, slip to sure death. I could not look down because of my position. But in my mind's eye I saw in sharp outline the jagged rocks that seemed to pull me toward them. The camera kept pushing my fingers from the ledge. I felt them move. They began to give way before the pull of a force too great for flesh to resist.

11 Fright grew in me. The idea of hanging helpless 200 feet above the abyss brought panic. I cried out to Doug but the words caught in my dry throat. I was like one in a nightmare who struggles to shout—who is then seized with a fear that promises to destroy him.

Then there flashed through my mind a family scene. Mother was sitting in the living room talking to me, telling me what a wonderful man Father was. She told me of his last illness and his death. She told me of his departure from Cleveland, Washington to Portland, Oregon for what proved to be a fatal operation. His last words to her were: "If I die it will be glory. If I live, it will be grace."

The panic passed. The memory of those words restored reason. Glory to die? I could not understand why it would be glory to die. It would be glory to live. But as Father said, it might take grace to live, grace from One more powerful than either Doug or I.

And so again that day I prayed. I asked God to save my life, to save me from destruction on this rock wall. I asked God to make my fingers strong, to give me strength to hang on. I asked God to give me courage, to make me unafraid. I asked God to give me guts, to give me power to do the impossible.

My fingers were as numb as flesh that is full of novocaine. They seemed detached from me, as if they belonged to someone else. My wrists, my shoulders, cried out for respite from the pain. It would be such welcome relief if they could be released from the weight that was on them.

Hang on? You can't hang on. You are a weakling. The weaklings die in the woods.

Weakling? I'll show you. How long must I hang on? All day? OK, all day then. I'll hang on, I'll hang on. O, help me hang on!

I felt someone pushing my left foot upwards. It was Doug. As if through a dream his voice was saying, "Your feet are 18 inches below your toehold." Doug found those toeholds for my feet.

I felt my shoes resting in solid cracks. I pulled myself up and leaned on my elbows on the ledge to which my hands had been glued. I flexed my fingers and bent my wrists to bring life back.

Doug came up abreast of me and said, "We're even Stephen now."

"Even Stephen?"

"Today each of us has saved the other's life."

It was shortly above the point where Doug saved my life that we discovered a classic path up Kloochman. It is a three-sided chimney chute,[7] a few feet wide, that leads almost to the top. There are several such chutes on Kloochman. In later years Cragg Gilbert and Louis Ulrich went up Devil's Chimney on the northeast face in a seven-hour nerve-wracking climb with ropes. Clarence Truitt and many others have gone up the chimney chute that Doug and I discovered. Then as now this chute was filled with loose rock that had to be cleared away. To negotiate the chute we took off our shoes and tied them to our belts. We climbed the chute in stocking feet, pressing our hands and feet against the opposing walls as we kept our backs to the abyss below us. This day we went up the chute with ease, stopping every eight feet or so to measure our progress.

The sun was setting when we reached the top. We were gay and buoyant. We talked about the glories of the scene in front of us. We bragged a bit about our skill in rock work—how we must be part mountain goat to have reached the top. We shouted and hallooed to the empty meadows far below us.

On Kloochman Rock that July afternoon both Doug and I valued life more because death had passed so close. It was wonderful to be alive, breathing, using our muscles, shouting, seeing.

We stayed briefly at the top. We went down as we came up, in stocking feet. We raced against darkness, propelled by the thought of spending the night on Kloochman's treacherous wall.

It was deep dusk when we rejoined Walter on the rock fields at the base. We put on our shoes and hurried on. We entered the woods at double-quick time, seeking the trail that led toward the South Fork of the Tieton. We saw the trail from the edge of a clearing as a faint, light streak in a pitch-black night. We had two ways of keeping on it. We had no matches or torch or flashlight. But we could feel the edges with our feet. And we could search out the strip of night sky over the path.

We finally decided that it would take too long to follow the trail to camp in this groping way. We'd take a short cut to Westfall Rocks, whose formless shape we could see against the sky. We took to the brush on our right, and kept our hands out in front to ward off boughs and branches. We crossed a marshy bog where we went in up to our knees. We came to soft earth where we went in up to our hips.

There were animals in the brush. We could hear them in the thickets, disturbed by our approach, and going out ahead of us. Thinking they might be bear, we paused to listen. "Cattle," said Doug.

We reached the Tieton River, which we knew could not be forded in many places in that stretch. So we took off our pants, shoes, and shirts and rolled them in bundles which we held on our heads. We waded out into the dark, cold, swift river, Doug in the lead. We had by accident picked one of the few good fords in the Tieton. We were never in water over our waists.

Then we dressed and located the road leading back to camp. As we started along it Doug said: "You know, Bill, there is power in prayer."

That night I prayed again. I knelt on a bed of white fir boughs beside the embers of a campfire and thanked God for saving Doug's life and mine, for giving us the strength to save each other. 13, 14

7. **chimney** (chim′ nē) **chute** (sho͞ot): A vertical passage the size of a chimney.

12 **Discussion** Ask students to describe a similar experience.

13 **Discussion** What is the meaning of this statement?

14 **Discussion** What impact do you think this experience had on the author?

Reader's Response What impressed you the most about Douglas's and his partner's mountain-climbing experience?

Closure and Extension

(Questions begin on p. 428)

ANSWERS TO THINKING ABOUT THE SELECTION

Recalling

1. The first serious problem is that the ledge on which they stood ended, and Doug must reach an upper ledge. He does this by jumping upward six inches.
2. William gets into the trouble of hanging onto the edge of a cliff by his fingers. Doug helps him find toeholds for his feet.
3. They feel exhilarated, proud, and thankful to God for saving their lives.

Interpreting

4. Courage, perseverance, and ingenuity enable the boys to get themselves out of difficulties.
5. Luck plays a significant role in saving the boys, when Doug reaches

(Answers begin on p. 427.)

above his head and finds strong rough edges of rock to help pull himself up, when William manages to keep his own balance while directing Doug's foot to the ledge, and when Doug finds toeholds for William's feet when William is hanging by his fingers.

6. Answers will differ. Suggested Response: "Of Men and Mountains" could be seen to juxtapose the two subjects, as if in opposition—men versus mountains.

Applying

7. Answers will differ, but may include the idea that the impossible is challenging, calling upon one to attempt it.

ANSWERS TO ANALYZING LITERATURE

Passages that are good examples of ideas, feelings, and observations that only the narrator would know are any of the six paragraphs on page 426 beginning "I would slip, I thought, slip to sure death" and ending with "It would be such welcome relief if they could be released from the weight that was on them."

ANSWERS TO CRITICAL THINKING AND READING

1. Doug might have described his own feelings of panic and fear as he watched and tried to help William.
2. An objective observer would have simply described the events, and would not have been able to describe the thoughts of Doug and William.

ANSWERS TO UNDERSTANDING LANGUAGE

1. arachnid–any of a large class of arthropods. In Greek mythology, Arachne was a girl turned into a spider by Athena for challenging the goddess to a weaving contest.
2. narcissus–any of a genus of the bulb plants of the amaryllis family. In Greek mythology, Narcissus was a beautiful youth who was made to pine away for love of his own reflection in a spring and was changed into the narcissus plant.
3. titan–any person or thing of great size or power. In Greek mythology, a Titan was any of a race of giant deities who were overthrown by the Olympian gods.
4. echo–the reflection of sound waves from a surface. In Greek mythology, Echo was a nymph who, because of her unreturned love for Narcissus, pined away until only her voice remained.
5. ocean–the great body of salt water that covers about 71% of the earth's surface. In Greek mythology, Oceanus was a Titan who was god of the sea before Poseidon and father of the Oceanids.
6. herculean–very powerful or courageous. In Greek mythology, Hercules, the son of Zeus and Alcmene, was renowned for feats of strength.
7. protean–very changeable, readily taking on different shapes and forms. In Greek mythology, Proteus was a sea god who could chang his own form or appearance at wil

Writing Across the Curriculu
Have students report on the im portance of, general effects of and steps involved in achievin physical fitness. You might wan to inform the physical educatio department of this assignment since teachers might provid guidance for students on con ducting their research.

THINKING ABOUT THE SELECTION

Recalling

1. What is the first serious problem that William and his friend Doug encounter? How do they solve this problem?
2. Describe the serious trouble that William gets into. How does he get out of this serious trouble?
3. How do the boys feel at the end of the climb?

Interpreting

4. What qualities enable the boys to get themselves out of difficulties when they are in trouble?
5. What role does luck play in saving the boys?
6. Explain the meaning of the title.

Applying

7. What is it about the impossible that makes people want to make it possible?

ANALYZING LITERATURE

Understanding Narrator in Autobiography

A **narrator** is the person telling his or her autobiography. A narrator tells a personal story from his or her own point of view. As a result, you find out what the narrator knows and feels and what the narrator guesses about the thoughts and feelings of others. For example, the narrator tells you his own thoughts and feelings as he is hanging by his fingers 200 feet in the air: "How long must I hang on? All day? OK, all day then. I'll hang on."

Find two passages in "Of Men and Mountains" that are good examples of ideas, feelings, and observations that only the narrator would know about the central character—himself.

CRITICAL THINKING AND READING

Recognizing the Effect of Point of View

When you read a selection written in the first person, you experience the events as the narrator experienced them. Although the experience is based on facts, what you read is subjective, that is, colored by the writer's views.

1. How might Doug have written the incident in which William almost falls?
2. How might the selection have been different if an objective observer had written it?

UNDERSTANDING LANGUAGE

Appreciating Words from Greek Myths

Many English words have their origins in Greek myths. The word *panic,* meaning "fear," comes from the name of the Greek god Pan, a noisy musician who was thought to play his pipes day and night in the woods. Long ago people thought Pan made the sounds that frightened travelers in the wilderness at night. The word *panic* soon came to describe their fear.

Use a dictionary to find the meaning and origin of the following words from Greek mythology.

1. arachnid
2. narcissus
3. titan
4. echo
5. ocean
6. herculean
7. protean

THINKING AND WRITING

Writing from Another Point of View

Select an event in this selection and retell it from Doug's point of view. What did Doug think about the event? What were his feelings? How will Doug's account be different from William's? Write your first draft of Doug's account. Revise it, making sure you have maintained a consistent point of view. Finally proofread your account and share it with your classmates.

Essays for Enjoyment

GIRL READING OUTDOORS
Fairfield Porter

Humanities Note

Fine Art; *Girl Reading Outdoors,* Fairfield Porter. Fairfield Porter (1907–1975), an American "Intimist" painter in the French style, was born in Winnetka, Illinois. He attended Harvard University for art history and studied painting at the Art Students League in New York City. In addition to his prolific career as a painter, Porter has taught art at many prestigious schools and universities and has written noteworthy books and articles on the subject of American art and artists.

The subject of the painting *Girl Reading Outdoors* is typical of the pleasant and familiar scenes that Fairfield Porter preferred to paint. The girl in the painting is obviously enjoying her reading. Although the influence of the Impressionists is apparent in this work, Porter's interpretation of the style is direct, rough, and more typically American. He uses color rather than modeling to delineate the features of the girl, the shadows of the house, and the shade from the sunlight. Fine details are sacrificed in the effort to capture the essence of the scene. Like fellow American artists, Edward Hopper and Winslow Homer, Fairfield Porter concentrated on the study of color in the harsh northeastern light.

Focus

More About the Author Almost all of Frank Dobie's work has been on the history of Texas. Some critics see him as a folklorist, others as a historian of this cowboy state. Ask the class whether they think folklore and history can appear together in one literary work, or must they be separate?

Literary Focus Ask students for examples of other narratives they have read—either fiction or nonfiction. Point out that a narrative essay contains the elements of a narrative but is true.

Look For For your **less advanced** students, you may first want to review and distinguish between subjective and objective details. This review may help students look for details.

Writing Ask students to brainstorm about what daily life might have been like for a woman on a ranch in the latter part of the nineteenth century. Then have them complete the freewriting assignment.

Vocabulary Your students may also find it helpful to know these expressions: as "paint bull calf" (p. 431), a young steer that is piebald, or covered with patches of two colors, or "drag drivers" (p. 433), the cowboys who rode at the back of a herd in a cattle drive.

GUIDE FOR READING

Sancho

J. Frank Dobie (1888–1964) grew up in the southwest Texas brush country. He pursued a writing and teaching career devoted to the folklore and history of his native state. Over the years he became, in his words, "a historian of the longhorns, the mustangs, the coyote, and the other characters of the West." In his book *The Longhorns*, he tells of some memorable Texas steers. He included the story of Sancho, which he heard from John Rigby, a trail boss on the Texas Range.

Narrative Essay

An essay is a short nonfiction composition exploring a topic. A **narrative essay** explores this topic by telling a true story. It discusses a topic of personal interest to the writer, giving the writer's view of the subject or personal experience with it. In "Sancho," the author J. Frank Dobie tells you about a Texas longhorn whose story he found unusual as well as interesting.

Look For

As you read "Sancho," look for details that make Sancho stand out from the herd. Why did the author choose to write about this Texas longhorn?

Writing

In this selection, Maria lives on a ranch in the latter part of the nineteenth century. Freewrite about what a day in her life might be like.

Vocabulary

Knowing the following words can help you as you read "Sancho."

dogie (dō′ gē) **calves**: Motherless calves or strays in a range herd; used chiefly in the West (p. 431)

vigorous (vig′ ər əs) *adj.*: Strong and energetic (p. 431)

yearling (yir′ liŋ) *n.*: An animal that is between one and two years old (p. 433)

Objectives

1 To understand a narrative essay
2 To put events in chronolgical order
3 To understand words from Spanish
4 To write a letter about Sancho

Support Material

Teaching Portfolio

Teacher Backup, pp. 525–528
Grammar in Action Worksheet, *Understanding Prepositional Phrases*, pp. 529–530
Usage and Mechanics Worksheet, p. 531
Vocabulary Check, p. 532
Analyzing Literature Worksheet, *Understanding a Narrative Essay*, p. 533
Critical Thinking and Readir Worksheet, *Putting Events Chronological Order*, p. 534
Selection Test, pp. 535–536

Sancho

J. Frank Dobie

A man by the name of Kerr had a little ranch on Esperanza Creek in Frio County, in the mesquite lands[1] south of San Antonio. He owned several good cow ponies, a few cattle, and a little bunch of goats that a dog guarded by day. At night they were shut up in a brush corral near the house. Three or four acres of land, fenced in with brush and poles, grew corn, watermelons and "kershaws"—except when the season was too drouthy.[2] A hand-dug well equipped with pulley wheel, rope and bucket furnished water for the establishment.

Kerr's wife was named María. They had no children. She was clean, thrifty, cheerful, always making pets of animals. She usually milked three or four cows and sometimes made cheese out of goat's milk.

Late in the winter of 1877, Kerr while riding over on the San Miguel found one of his cows dead in a bog-hole. Beside the cow was a mud-plastered little black-and-white paint bull calf less than a week old. It was too weak to run; perhaps other cattle had saved it from the coyotes. Kerr pitched his rope over its head, drew it up across the saddle in front of him, carried it home, and turned it over to María.

She had raised many dogie calves and numerous colts captured from mustang mares. The first thing she did now was to pour milk from a bottle down the orphan's throat. With warm water she washed the caked mud off its body. But hand-raising a calf is no end of trouble. The next day Kerr rode around until he found a thrifty brown cow with a young calf. He drove them to the
pen. By tying this cow's head up close to a 2
post and hobbling her hind legs, Kerr and María forced her to let the orphan suckle. She did not give a cup of milk at this first sucking. Her calf was kept in the pen next day, and the poor thing bawled herself hoarse. María began feeding her some prickly pear with the thorns singed off. After
being tied up twice daily for a month, she 3
adopted the orphan as a twin to her own offspring.

Now she was one of the household cows. Spring weeds came up plentifully and the guajilla brush put out in full leaf. When the brown cow came in about sundown and her two calves were released for their supper, it was a cheering sight to see them wiggle their tails while they guzzled milk.

The dogie was a vigorous little brute, and before long he was getting more milk than the brown cow's own calf. María called him Sancho, a Mexican name meaning "pet." She was especially fond of Sancho, and he grew to be especially fond of her.

---

1. **mesquite** (mes kēt′) **lands** *n.*: Areas in which grow certain thorny trees and shrubs, common in the southwest U.S. and in Mexico.
2. **drouthy** (drouth′ ē) *adj.*: Dried up due to drought—a lack of rain.

Presentation

Motivation/Prior Knowledge Ask students to imagine that they adopted a newly born animal whose mother was gone. What are some of the difficulties they might encounter?

Master Teacher Note Bring in a map of the Southwest for the students and trace the route of the cattle drive.

Thematic Idea Another selection that deals with an animal with some human characteristics is "Debbie" on page 439.

Purpose-Setting Question What is unusual about Sancho?

Thematic Idea Another selection that involves the theme of having the gift of loving animals is "Debbie" by James Herriot, page 439. Ask students what special qualities do such people have? Why are animals drawn to them?

1 **Literary Focus** Point out that a narrative essay tells a *true* story.

2 **Enrichment** Sancho is suckled by another cow and is adopted as an orphan. Similarly, tell students about Romulus and Remus, founders of Rome, who were left as infants to die in the Tiber, and were suckled by a she-wolf.

3 **Discussion** Discuss whether animals are inclined to adopt young not their own. You might tell students that the U.S. Government has done experiments encouraging adult birds of depleted species to hatch eggs not their own.

Humanities Note

Fine art, *In a Stampede,* 1888, by Frederic Remington. Frederic Remington (1861–1909) was born in Canton, New York. He attended the Yale School of Art and the Art Students' League. He worked primarily as an illustrator for magazines such as *Harper's Weekly* and *Outing*. Remington is best known for his small bronze sculptures of cowboys, Native Americans, and soldiers, and for his paintings of Western action.

In this illustration, the full front view of rampaging steer approaching with lowered horns and the cowboy trying to herd them with raised whip create strong dramatic tension.

1. What part of the story does this picture suggest?
2. What sounds might you hear in this scene?

IN A STAMPEDE
Illustration by Frederic Remington
The Granger Collection

She would give him the shucks wrapped around tamales. Then she began treating him to whole tamales, which are made of ground corn rolled around a core of
4 chopped-up meat, this banana-shaped roll, done up in a shuck, then being steam-boiled. Sancho seemed not to mind the meat. As everybody who has eaten them knows, Mexican tamales are highly seasoned with pepper. Sancho seemed to like the seasoning.

In southern Texas the little chiltipiquin peppers, red when ripe, grow wild in low, shaded places. Cattle never eat them, leaving them for the wild turkeys, mockingbirds and blue quail to pick off. Sometimes in the early fall wild turkeys used to gorge on them so avidly that their flesh became too peppery for human consumption. By eating tamales Sancho developed a taste for the little red peppers growing in the thickets along Esperanza Creek. In fact, he became a kind of chiltipiquin addict. He would hunt for the peppers.

Furthermore, the tamales gave him a tooth for corn in the ear. The summer after he became a yearling he began breaking through the brush fence that enclosed Kerr's corn patch. A forked stick had to be tied around his neck to prevent his getting through the fence. He had been branded and turned into a steer, but he was as strong as any young bull. Like many other pets, he was something of a nuisance. When he could not steal corn or was not humored with tamales, he was enormously contented with grass, mixed in summertime with the sweet mesquite beans. Now and then María gave him a lump of the brown *piloncillo* sugar, from Mexico, that all the border country used.

Every night Sancho came to the ranch pen to sleep. His bed ground was near a certain mesquite tree just outside the gate. He spent hours every summer day in the shade of this mesquite. When it rained and other cattle drifted off, hunting fresh pasturage, Sancho stayed at home and drank at the well. He was strictly a home creature.

In the spring of 1880 Sancho was three years old and past, white of horn and as blocky of build as a long-legged Texas steer ever grew. Kerr's ranch lay in a big unfenced range grazed by the Shiner brothers. That spring they had a contract to deliver three herds of steers, each to number 2500 head, in Wyoming. Kerr was helping the Shiners gather cattle, and, along with various other ranchers, sold them what steers he had.

Sancho was included. One day late in March the Shiner men road-branded him
7 Z and put him in the first herd headed north. 5
The other herds were to follow two or three days apart.

It was late in the afternoon when the "shaping up" of the herd was completed. It was watered and thrown out on open prairie ground to be bedded down. But Sancho had no disposition to lie down—there. He wanted to go back to that mesquite just outside the pen gate at the Kerr place on the Esperanza where he had without variation slept every night since he had been weaned. Perhaps he had in mind an evening tamale. He stood and roamed about on the south side of the herd. A dozen times during the night the men on guard had to drive him back. As reliefs were changed, word passed to keep an eye on that paint steer on the lower side.

When the herd started on next morning, Sancho was at the tail end of it, often stopping and looking back. It took constant attention from one of the drag drivers to keep
him moving. By the time the second night 6
arrived, every hand in the outfit knew Sancho, by name and sight, as being the stubbornest and gentlest steer of the lot. About dark one of them pitched a loop over his

4 Discussion Explain that tamales are a native Mexican food of minced meat and red peppers rolled in cornmeal, wrapped in corn husks, and cooked by baking or steaming. Ask students who have had tamales to describe their taste.

5 Clarification Tell students that branding was burning a mark with a hot iron on the skin of cattle to show ownership. Different cattle brands were used to distinguish which steer belonged to which owner.

6 Critical Thinking and Reading What words in this paragraph indicate chronological order?

7 **Reading Strategy** Have students summarize the events so far. Ask them to predict what kinds of events could happen.

8 **Discussion** What does Sancho's mimicking of human behavior indicate about his intelligence?

horns and staked him to a bush. This saved bothering with his persistent efforts to walk off.

Daily when the herd was halted to graze, spreading out like a fan, the steers all eating their way northward, Sancho invariably pointed himself south. In his lazy way he grabbed many a mouthful of grass while the herd was moving. Finally, in some brush up on the Llano, after ten days of trailing, he dodged into freedom. On the second day following, one of the point men of the second Shiner herd saw him walking south, saw his *7 Z* road brand, rounded him in, and set him traveling north again. He became the chief drag animal of this herd. Somewhere north of the Colorado there was a run one night, and when morning came Sancho was missing. The other steers had held together; probably Sancho had not run at all. But he was picked up again, by the third Shiner herd coming on behind.

He took his accustomed place in the drag and continued to require special driving. He picked up in weight. He chewed his cud peacefully and slept soundly, but whenever he looked southward, which was often, he raised his head as if memory and expectation were stirring. The boys were all person-
7 ally acquainted with him, and every night
one of them would stake him.

One day the cattle balked and milled at a bank-full river. "Rope Old Sancho and lead him in," the boss ordered, "and we'll point the other cattle after him." Sancho led like a horse. The herd followed. As soon as he was released, he dropped back to the rear. After this, however, he was always led to the front when there was high water to cross.

By the time the herd got into No Man's Land, beyond Red River, the sand-hill plums and the low-running possum grapes were
turning ripe. Pausing now and then to pick a
8 little of the fruit, Sancho's driver saw the pet
steer following his example.

Meantime the cattle were trailing, trailing, always north. For five hundred miles across Texas, counting the windings to find water and keep out of breaks, they had come. After getting into the Indian Territory, they snailed on across the Wichita, the South Canadian, the North Canadian, and the Cimarron. On into Kansas they trailed and across the Arkansas, around Dodge City, cowboy capital of the world, out of Kansas into Nebraska, over the wide, wide Platte, past the roaring cow town of Ogalla-la, up the North Platte, under the Black Hills, and then against the Big Horn Mountains. For two thousand miles, making ten or twelve miles a day, the Shiner herds trailed. They "walked with the grass." Slow, slow, they moved. "Oh, it was a long and lonesome go"—as slow as the long drawn-out notes of "The Texas Lullaby," as slow as the night herder's song on a slow-walking horse:

It's a whoop and a yea, get along
my little dogies,
For camp is far away.
It's a whoop and a yea and a-
driving the dogies,
For Wyoming may be your new
home.

When, finally, after listening for months, day and night, to the slow song of their motion, the "dogies" reached their "new home," Sancho was still halting every now and then to sniff southward for a whiff of the Mexican Gulf. The farther he got away from home, the less he seemed to like the change. He had never felt frost in September before. The Mexican peppers on the Esperanza were red ripe now.

The Wyoming outfit received the cattle. Then for a week the Texas men helped brand *C R* on their long sides before turning them loose on the new range. When San-

Grammar in Action

Writers effectively use **prepositional phrases** in order to construct vivid sentences with specific details. A prepositional phrase begins with a preposition (*in, on, around, near, through,* and others) and ends with a noun or pronoun that answers "who" or "what" of the preposition. Prepositional phrases modify nouns, pronouns, or verbs in the sentence. The prepositional phrase must appear close to the noun, pronoun, or verb that it describes.

Prepositional phrases provide description and show the relationship between a noun or a verb and the object of a preposition. Look at the following sentences that have been expanded with prepositional phrases:

> After getting into the Indian Territory, they snailed on across the Wichita, the South Canadian, the North Canadian, and the Cimarron. On into Kansas they trailed and across the Arkansas, around Dodge City, cowboy capital of the world, out of Kansas into Nebraska, over the wide, wide Platte, past the roaring cow town of Ogalla-la, up the North Platte, under the Black Hills, and then against the Big Horn Mountains.

THE AMERICAN COWBOY
Charlie Dye
Collection of Harold McCracken

Humanities Note

Fine art, *The American Cowboy,* by Charlie Dye. Charlie Dye (1906–1972) was born in Canon City, Colorado, and worked as a cowboy. He began pursuing his childhood love of sketching at the age of 21, and was influenced by the Western artist Charles Russell. In 1936 he moved to New York City to become a magazine illustrator. In 1960 he helped form the "Cowboy Artists of America" in Arizona.

Dye draws on his own experience as a cowboy herding cattle in this painting.

1. What part of the story does this painting illustrate?
2. Based on this painting, how do you think Dye felt about being a cowboy?

Student Activity 1. There are fourteen prepositional phrases in the example. Find each one.

Student Activity 2. Write your own description of a trip that you once took. Use a series of prepositional phrases in your description. Model your description after the example.

9 Clarification Tobacco juice would sting the eyes and keep the cowboys awake.

10 Literary Focus In a narrative essay, the writer gives his or her view of the subject or personal experience with it.

11 Discussion Discuss the strength of strong homing instincts in animals. Ask students for fictional and true-life examples of animals escaping from a new owner to return home.

12 Discussion What does Sancho's behavior tell you about his personality?

Reader's Response Describe an animal with which you are familiar who is part of a family the way Sancho was.

cho's time came to be branded in the chute,[3] one of the Texans yelled out, "There goes my pet. Stamp that *C R* brand on him good and deep." Another one said, "The line riders had better watch for his tracks."

And now the Shiner men turned south, taking back with them their saddle horses and chuck wagons—and leaving Sancho behind. They made good time, but a blue norther was whistling at their backs when they turned the remuda[4] loose on the Frio River. After the "Cowboys' Christmas Ball" most of them settled down for a few weeks of
winter sleep. They could rub tobacco juice in
9 their eyes during the summer when they
needed something in addition to night rides and runs to keep them awake.

Spring comes early down on the Esperanza. The mesquites were all in new leaf with that green so fresh and tender that the color seems to emanate into the sky. The bluebonnets and the pink phlox were sprinkling every hill and draw. The prickly pear was studded with waxy blossoms, and the glades were heavy with the perfume of white brush. It was a good season, and tallow weed and grass were coming together. It was time for the spring cow hunts and the putting up of herds for the annual drive north. The Shiners were at work.

"We were close to Kerr's cabin on Esper-
10 anza Creek," John Rigby told me, "when I looked across a pear flat and saw something that made me rub my eyes. I was riding with Joe Shiner, and we both stopped our horses."

"Do you see what I see?" John Rigby asked.

"Yes, but before I say, I'm going to read the brand," Joe Shiner answered.

They rode over. "You can hang me for a horse thief," John Rigby will tell, "if it wasn't that Sancho paint steer, four years
old now, the Shiner *7 Z* road brand and the 11
Wyoming *C R* range brand both showing on him as plain as boxcar letters."

The men rode on down to Kerr's.

"Yes," Kerr said, "Old Sancho got in about six weeks ago. His hoofs were worn
mighty nigh down to the hair, but he wasn't 12
lame. I thought María was going out of her senses, she was so glad to see him. She actually hugged him and she cried and then she begun feeding him hot tamales. She's made a batch of them nearly every day since, just to pet that steer. When she's not feeding him tamales, she's giving him *piloncillo*."

Sancho was slicking off and certainly did seem contented. He was coming up every night and sleeping at the gate, María said. She was nervous over the prospect of losing her pet, but Joe Shiner said that if that steer loved his home enough to walk back to it all the way from Wyoming, he wasn't going to drive him off again, even if he was putting up another herd for the *C R* owners.

As far as I can find out, Old Sancho lived right there on the Esperanza, now and then getting a tamale, tickling his palate with chili peppers in season, and generally staying fat on mesquite grass, until he died a natural death. He was one of the "walking Texas Longhorns."

---

3. chute (sho͞ot) *n.*: A narrow, high-walled device used to restrain cattle.
4. remuda (rə mo͞o′ də) *n.*: Group of extra saddle horses kept as a supply of remounts.

Closure and Extension

ANSWERS TO THINKING ABOUT THE SELECTION
Recalling

1. The Kerrs' ranch included several cow ponies, a few cattle, a little bunch of goats, three or four acres of land that grew corn, watermelons, and "kershaws," and a hand-dug well.

THINKING ABOUT THE SELECTION

Recalling

1. Describe the Kerrs' ranch.
2. How does Sancho become María's pet?
3. What is unusual about Sancho's eating habits?
4. Why does Sancho leave the ranch?
5. Describe Sancho's behavior on the drive.
6. What finally happens to Sancho? Why does Joe Shiner agree to this decision?

Interpreting

7. What does Sancho learn from his early experiences on the ranch that makes him different from the other longhorn cattle?
8. Dobie said that Sancho's story was the best range story he had ever heard. Why do you think he liked the story so much?
9. Dobie felt that Sancho was an animal worth remembering. Find three examples of Sancho's almost human personality.

Applying

10. Think about where María lived and what her daily life must have been like. Why would a pet be so important to her?

ANALYZING LITERATURE

Understanding a Narrative Essay

A **narrative essay** is a nonfiction composition in which the writer explores the subject by telling a true story. People write essays to present their observations, views, or opinions about a topic. Dobie knew the section of Texas where Sancho lived, and he had written and studied about cattle drives like the one described in "Sancho." Dobie was able to include details that help make Sancho vivid to readers.

1. List three details about the section of Texas where Sancho lived that Dobie includes.
2. List three details about cattle drives that Dobie includes in the essay.

CRITICAL THINKING AND READING

Putting Events in Chronological Order

Chronological order is the order in which events happen in time. Authors use certain words and phrases to place events in time, such as "the first thing she did" and "the next day" to signal time order.

Write the numbers of the following events in the order in which they happened. Then list the phrases that signal the order in which they should appear.

1. When he was a yearling, Sancho broke into the corn patch.
2. Sancho lived on the ranch until he died.
3. Sancho at three years old was a handsome Texas steer.

UNDERSTANDING LANGUAGE

Understanding Words from Spanish

Many Spanish words such as *tortilla, taco,* and *rodeo* have become part of the English language. The following words from "Sancho" came from the Spanish language. Look up the meaning of each in a dictionary. Also copy the spellings of the original Spanish words.

1. chili
2. corral
3. ranch
4. tamale

THINKING AND WRITING

Writing a Letter

Look over the freewriting you did before you began this selection. Use ideas from it and from the selection as the basis for a letter to a friend telling about Sancho's return. Revise your letter, making sure you have presented the information from María's point of view. Proofread your letter and share it with your classmates.

(Answers begin on p. 436.)

Challenge Ask students how they think Sancho might react if the Kerrs acquired another pet steer to live with Sancho.

ANSWERS TO ANALYZING LITERATURE

1. Three details about the section of Texas where Sancho lives are that it is on Esperanza Creek, in Frio County, and in the mesquite lands south of San Antonio.
2. Three details about cattle drives are that the cattle were branded before the journey, they were driven in herds, and the men took turns guarding the cattle at night.

ANSWERS TO CRITICAL THINKING AND READING

1. When he was a yearling
3. at three years old
2. until he died

ANSWERS TO UNDERSTANDING LANGUAGE

1. **chili**–From the Mexican Spanish *chilli.* The dried pod of red pepper, a very hot seasoning.
2. **corral**–From the Spanish *corro.* An enclosure for holding or capturing horses, cattle, or other animals.
3. **ranch**–From the Spanish *rancho.* A large farm for the raising of cattle, horses, or sheep in great numbers.
4. **tamale**–From the Mexican Spanish *tamal.* A native Mexican food of minced meat and red pepper rolled in cornmeal, wrapped in corn husks, and cooked by baking or steaming.

Writing Across the Curriculum
You might want to have students research and report on cattle drives across the United States. If you do, perhaps inform the social studies department about this assignment. Social studies teachers might provide guidance for students in conducting their research.

2. Kerr found Sancho next to a dead cow in a bog-hole, and brought him home to Maria.
3. Sancho likes to eat peppers and tamales.
4. Sancho was sold and put in a herd of steer headed for Wyoming.
5. Sancho is always wandering away from the herd and being brought back.
6. Sancho walks back to Kerr's ranch, where he is allowed to stay. Joe Shiner agrees to this decision because if Sancho loved his home enough to walk back to it from Wyoming, Joe wasn't going to drive him off again.

Interpreting

7. Sancho learns to like tamales and peppers, to sleep under the mesquite tree just outside the gate, and to stay at home and drink from the well.
8. He may have liked the story because it was amusing, true, and about one of his favorite subjects —a steer.
9. Sancho grew fond of Maria and peppers, tried to leave the herd to go back to the ranch, and eventually walked home all the way from Wyoming.

Applying

10. Suggested Response: Maria's day was filled with work, and she probably did not have many neighbors or friends. A pet would be important to her to help dispel loneliness, and to give affection.

Focus

More About the Author James Herriot is a veterinarian who writes mostly about the animals he encounters on his job. Ask students what other aspects of his job Herriot might write about.

Literary Focus Ask students what they think would make "real" characters interesting to read about.

Look For Have students brainstorm about what kinds of details would make a character come alive.

Writing/Prior Knowledge You might consider doing this writing activity as a class, rather than individually.

Vocabulary For your less advanced students, you may also want to review these words: wheedling (p. 440), malignant (p. 441), irreverent (p. 442), incredulously (p. 442), and feline (p. 442).

Spelling Tip The final consonant of one-syllable words ending in consonant-vowel-consonant, like *fret*, is doubled before a consonant suffix. Thus

fret + *ed* = fretted

Other words following this pattern include

big + *er* = bigger

wrap + *ed* = wrapped

GUIDE FOR READING

Debbie

James Herriot (1916–), who was born in Glasgow, Scotland, studied veterinary medicine. Since 1940 he has been a veterinarian in England, the setting for his true stories about being a "country vet." British veterinarians are not allowed to use any form of advertising. Since writing under his own name would be considered advertising, he chose James Herriot as his pen name. The incidents Herriot describes, such as the one in "Debbie," have filled more than ten books and have inspired a popular television series.

Characters in a Narrative Essay

The characters in a narrative essay are real people. In fact, sometimes the author even appears as a character. You learn about these characters in the same way you learn about characters in a piece of fiction. You can read about their actions, listen to their words, share their thoughts, or read descriptive details about them. Finally, you can learn much about a character by reading what other characters say or think about him or her.

Look For

As you read, look for the details that make the characters come alive for you. What impression do you form of James Herriot, Mrs. Ainsworth, Debbie, and Buster?

Writing

Many people enjoy reading Herriot's true stories because he provides an insider's view of the daily life of a veterinarian. List the questions you would like to ask James Herriot about his work with animals.

Vocabulary

Knowing the following words can help you as you read "Debbie."

fretted (fret′ əd) *adj.*: Decoratively arranged (p. 440)

sage (sāj) *n.*: A plant used to flavor food (p. 440)

wafted (waf′ təd) *v.*: Moved lightly through the air (p. 440)

knell (nel) *n.*: The sound of a bell slowly ringing, as for a funeral (p. 441)

privations (prī vā′ shənz) *n.*: Lack of common comforts (p. 441)

ornate (ôr nāt′) *adj.*: Having fancy decorations (p. 442)

goading (gōd ′iŋ): *v.*: Urging to action (p. 442)

Objectives

1 To understand characters in a narrative essay
2 To compare and contrast characters
3 To write an article comparing and contrasting

Support Material

Teaching Portfolio

Teacher Backup, pp. 537–539

Grammar in Action Worksheet, *Understanding Quotation Marks*, pp. 540–541

Usage and Mechanics Worksheet, p. 542

Vocabulary Check, p. 543

Critical Thinking and Reading Worksheet, *Comparing and Contrasting Characters*, p. 544

Language Worksheet, *Understanding Technical Words*, p. 545

Selection Test, pp. 546–547

Debbie

James Herriot

I first saw her one autumn day when I was called to see one of Mrs. Ainsworth's dogs, and I looked in some surprise at the furry black creature sitting before the fire.

"I didn't know you had a cat," I said.

The lady smiled. "We haven't, this is Debbie."

"Debbie?"

"Yes, at least that's what we call her. She's a stray. Comes here two or three times a week and we give her some food. I don't know where she lives but I believe she spends a lot of her time around one of the farms along the road."

"Do you ever get the feeling that she wants to stay with you?"

"No." Mrs. Ainsworth shook her head. "She's a timid little thing. Just creeps in, has some food then flits away. There's something so appealing about her but she doesn't seem to want to let me or anybody into her life."

I looked again at the little cat. "But she isn't just having food today."

"That's right. It's a funny thing but every now and again she slips through here into the lounge and sits by the fire for a few minutes. It's as though she was giving herself a treat."

"Yes . . . I see what you mean." There was no doubt there was something unusual in the attitude of the little animal. She was sitting bolt upright on the thick rug which
1 lay before the fireplace in which the coals glowed and flamed. She made no effort to curl up or wash herself or do anything other than gaze quietly ahead. And there was something in the dusty black of her coat, the half-wild scrawny look of her, that gave me a clue. This was a special event in her life, a rare and wonderful thing; she was lapping up a comfort undreamed of in her daily existence.

As I watched she turned, crept soundlessly from the room and was gone.

"That's always the way with Debbie," Mrs. Ainsworth laughed. "She never stays more than ten minutes or so, then she's off."

Mrs. Ainsworth was a plumpish, pleasant-faced woman in her forties and the kind of client veterinary surgeons dream of; well off, generous, and the owner of three cosseted[1] Basset hounds. And it only needed the habitually mournful expression of one of the dogs to deepen a little and I was round 2
there posthaste.[2] Today one of the Bassets had raised its paw and scratched its ear a couple of times and that was enough to send its mistress scurrying to the phone in great alarm.

So my visits to the Ainsworth home were frequent but undemanding, and I had ample opportunity to look out for the little cat that had intrigued me. On one occasion I spotted her nibbling daintily from a saucer at the 3
kitchen door. As I watched she turned and almost floated on light footsteps into the hall then through the lounge door.

---

1. cosseted (käs′ it əd) *adj.*: Pampered, indulged.
2. posthaste (pōst′ hāst′) *adv.*: With great quickness.

Presentation

Motivation/Prior Knowledge A veterinarian, in taking care of animals, comes to know their personalities. Ask students to describe the personality of an animal they have known. Remind them to look for the personalities of the animals in this essay.

Master Teacher Note James Herriot practices in Yorkshire, England. Bring in any photographs of the Yorkshire countryside that you can find and share them with the students.

Thematic Idea Another selection that deals with an animal with human characteristics is "Sancho" on page 431.

Purpose-Setting Question Do animals have feelings similar to those of humans?

Thematic Idea Another selection that involves the idea of animals behaving like people and showing fondness for humans is "Sancho," by Frank Dobie, on page 431. What qualities do such animals have? What qualities do the people have that draw the animals to them?

1 **Discussion** Ask students if they have ever witnessed similar humanlike behavior in animals. What do they think it means?

2 **Discussion** Why is Mrs. Ainsworth the "kind of client veterinary surgeons dream of"?

3 **Discussion** What kind of life do you think Debbie had?

4 **Literary Focus** What does Debbie's decision to roam free tell you about her? What are its advantages and disadvantages over a stable home?

5 **Discussion** Discuss the job of a veterinarian. What tasks and responsibilities are involved? What kind of person would make a good veterinarian? What kinds of inconvenience must he accept?

6 **Reading Strategy** Have students predict what might be wrong.

7 **Enrichment** In several works by the English novelist Charles Dickens (1812–1870), some towns —especially on Christmas—are portrayed as quaint, picturesque, colorful, and having a festive feeling of townspeople preparing for bountiful celebrations.

The three Bassets were already in residence, draped snoring on the fireside rug, but they seemed to be used to Debbie because two of them sniffed her in a bored manner and the third merely cocked a sleepy eye at her before flopping back on the rich pile.

Debbie sat among them in her usual posture; upright, intent, gazing absorbedly into the glowing coals. This time I tried to make friends with her. I approached her carefully but she leaned away as I stretched out my hand. However, by patient wheedling and soft talk I managed to touch her and gently stroked her cheek with one finger. There was a moment when she responded by putting her head on one side and rubbing back against my hand but soon she was ready to leave. Once outside the house she darted quickly along the road then through
4 a gap in a hedge and the last I saw was the little black figure flitting over the rain-swept grass of a field.

"I wonder where she goes," I murmured half to myself.

Mrs. Ainsworth appeared at my elbow. "That's something we've never been able to find out."

It must have been nearly three months before I heard from Mrs. Ainsworth, and in fact I had begun to wonder at the Bassets' long symptomless run when she came on the phone.

It was Christmas morning and she was apologetic. "Mr. Herriot, I'm so sorry to bother you today of all days. I should think
5 you want a rest at Christmas like anybody else." But her natural politeness could not hide the distress in her voice.

"Please don't worry about that," I said. "Which one is it this time?"

"It's not one of the dogs. It's . . . Debbie."

"Debbie? She's at your house now?"

"Yes . . . but there's something wrong. 6
Please come quickly."

Driving through the marketplace I thought again that Darrowby on Christmas Day was like Dickens come to life; the empty square with the snow thick on the cobbles and hanging from the eaves of the fretted
lines of roofs; the shops closed and the 7
colored lights of the Christmas trees winking at the windows of the clustering houses, warmly inviting against the cold white bulk of the fells[3] behind.

Mrs. Ainsworth's home was lavishly decorated with tinsel and holly, rows of drinks stood on the sideboard and the rich aroma of turkey and sage and onion stuffing wafted from the kitchen. But her eyes were full of pain as she led me through to the lounge.

Debbie was there all right, but this time everything was different. She wasn't sitting upright in her usual position; she was stretched quite motionless on her side, and huddled close to her lay a tiny black kitten.

I looked down in bewilderment. "What's happened here?"

"It's the strangest thing," Mrs. Ainsworth replied. "I haven't seen her for several weeks then she came in about two hours ago—sort of staggered into the kitchen, and she was carrying the kitten in her mouth. She took it through to the lounge and laid it on the rug and at first I was amused. But I could see all was not well because she sat as she usually does, but for a long time—over an hour—then she lay down like this and she hasn't moved."

I knelt on the rug and passed my hand over Debbie's neck and ribs. She was thinner than ever, her fur dirty and mudcaked. She did not resist as I gently opened her mouth. The tongue and mucous membranes

3. fells *n.*: Rocky or barren hills.

Grammar in Action

Quotation marks enclose the exact words of a speaker. When an introductory expression identifying the speaker appears before the quoted words, place a comma after this expression:

> Mrs. Ainsworth stated, "That's something we've never been able to find out."

When the expression identifying the speaker comes after the quoted words, place a comma, question mark, or exclamation mark before the final quotation mark.

> "I've never had a cat before," she said.
>
> "Oh, poor little thing!" she sobbed.
>
> "Is she dying?" Mrs. Ainsworth asked?

When the expression identifying the speaker appears in the middle of a quoted sentence, end the first part of the quoted sentence with a comma placed before the quotation mark; then place a comma at the end of the expression identifying the speaker.

were abnormally pale and the lips ice-cold against my fingers. When I pulled down her eyelid and saw the dead white conjunctiva[4] a knell sounded in my mind.

I palpated[5] the abdomen with a grim certainty as to what I would find and there was no surprise, only a dull sadness as my fingers closed around a hard lobulated[6] mass deep among the viscera.[7] Massive lymphosarcoma. Terminal and hopeless. I put my stethoscope on her heart and listened to the increasingly faint, rapid beat then I straightened up and sat on the rug looking sightlessly into the fireplace, feeling the warmth of the flames on my face.

Mrs. Ainsworth's voice seemed to come from afar. "Is she ill, Mr. Herriot?"

I hesitated. "Yes . . . yes, I'm afraid so. She has a malignant growth." I stood up. "There's absolutely nothing I can do. I'm sorry."

"Oh!" Her hand went to her mouth and she looked at me wide-eyed. When at last she spoke her voice trembled. "Well, you must put her to sleep immediately. It's the only thing to do. We can't let her suffer."

"Mrs. Ainsworth," I said. "There's no need. She's dying now—in a coma—far beyond suffering."

She turned quickly away from me and was very still as she fought with her emotions. Then she gave up the struggle and dropped on her knees beside Debbie.

"Oh, poor little thing!" she sobbed and stroked the cat's head again and again as the tears fell unchecked on the matted fur. "What she must have come through. I feel I ought to have done more for her."

For a few moments I was silent, feeling her sorrow, so discordant among the bright seasonal colors of this festive room. Then I spoke gently.

"Nobody could have done more than you," I said. "Nobody could have been kinder."

"But I'd have kept her here—in comfort. It must have been terrible out there in the cold when she was so desperately ill—I daren't think about it. And having kittens, too—I . . . I wonder how many she did have?"

I shrugged. "I don't suppose we'll ever know. Maybe just this one. It happens sometimes. And she brought it to you, didn't she?"

"Yes . . . that's right . . . she did . . . she did." Mrs. Ainsworth reached out and lifted the bedraggled black morsel. She smoothed her finger along the muddy fur and the tiny mouth opened in a soundless miaow. "Isn't it strange? She was dying and she brought her kitten here. And on Christmas Day."

I bent and put my hand on Debbie's heart. There was no beat.

I looked up. "I'm afraid she's gone." I lifted the small body, almost feather light, wrapped it in the sheet which had been spread on the rug and took it out to the car.

When I came back Mrs. Ainsworth was still stroking the kitten. The tears had dried on her cheeks and she was brighteyed as she looked at me.

"I've never had a cat before," she said.

I smiled. "Well, it looks as though you've got one now."

And she certainly had. That kitten grew rapidly into a sleek handsome cat with a boisterous nature which earned him the name of Buster. In every way he was the opposite to his timid little mother. Not for him the privations of the secret outdoor life; he stalked the rich carpets of the Ainsworth

---

4. conjunctiva (kän′ jəŋk tī′ və) *n.*: Lining of the inner surface of the eyelids.
5. palpated (pal′ pāt ed) *v.*: Examined by touching.
6. lobulated (läb′ yo͞o lāt′ əd) *adj.*: Subdivided.
7. viscera (vis′ ər ə) *n.*: Internal organs.

"When the cat came into the kitchen," said Mrs. Ainsworth, "we could see she was not well."

Student Activity 1. Punctuate each of the following items.

1. Where does Debbie go asked the doctor.
2. Oh, what a delight she is cried Mrs. Ainsworth.
3. She is very ill said Dr. Herriot and we can't let her suffer.
4. Mrs. Ainsworth said I can't imagine a nicer cat.

Student Activity 2. Write a passage in which two people speak about a special pet. Be sure to punctuate the dialogue correctly.

8 Discussion What other jobs require one to work on some holidays? What do you think is a good attitude to have toward this requirement?

9 Discussion It is unusual for a cat to retrieve a ball. What other behaviors would be unusual in a cat or a dog?

Reader's Response Describe an animal you know who has human-like characteristics like Debbie.

home like a king and the ornate collar he always wore added something more to his presence.

On my visits I watched his development with delight but the occasion which stays in my mind was the following Christmas Day, a year from his arrival.

8 I was out on my rounds as usual. I can't remember when I haven't had to work on Christmas Day because the animals have never got round to recognizing it as a holiday; but with the passage of the years the vague resentment I used to feel has been replaced by philosophical acceptance. After all, as I tramped around the hillside barns in the frosty air I was working up a better appetite for my turkey than all the millions lying in bed or slumped by the fire.

I was on my way home, bathed in a rosy glow. I heard the cry as I was passing Mrs. Ainsworth's house.

"Merry Christmas, Mr. Herriot!" She was letting a visitor out of the front door and she waved at me gaily. "Come in and have a drink to warm you up."

I didn't need warming up but I pulled in to the curb without hesitation. In the house there was all the festive cheer of last year and the same glorious whiff of sage and onion which set my gastric juices surging. But there was not the sorrow; there was Buster.

He was darting up to each of the dogs in turn, ears pricked, eyes blazing with devilment, dabbing a paw at them then streaking away.

Mrs. Ainsworth laughed. "You know, he plagues the life out of them. Gives them no peace."

She was right. To the Bassets, Buster's arrival was rather like the intrusion of an irreverent outsider into an exclusive London club. For a long time they had led a life of measured grace; regular sedate walks with their mistress, superb food in ample quantities and long snoring sessions on the rugs and armchairs. Their days followed one upon another in unruffled calm. And then came Buster.

He was dancing up to the youngest dog again, sideways this time, head on one side, goading him. When he started boxing with both paws it was too much even for the Basset. He dropped his dignity and rolled over with the cat in a brief wrestling match.

"I want to show you something." Mrs. Ainsworth lifted a hard rubber ball from the sideboard and went out to the garden, followed by Buster. She threw the ball across the lawn and the cat bounded after it over the frosted grass, the muscles rippling under the black sheen of his coat. He seized the ball in his teeth, brought it back to his mistress, dropped it at her feet and waited expectantly. She threw it and he brought it 9
back again.

I gasped incredulously. A feline retriever!

The Bassets looked on disdainfully. Nothing would ever have induced them to chase a ball, but Buster did it again and again as though he would never tire of it.

Mrs. Ainsworth turned to me. "Have you ever seen anything like that?"

"No," I replied. "I never have. He is a most remarkable cat."

She snatched Buster from his play and we went back into the house where she held him close to her face, laughing as the big cat purred and arched himself ecstatically against her cheek.

Looking at him, a picture of health and contentment, my mind went back to his mother. Was it too much to think that that dying little creature with the last of her strength had carried her kitten to the only haven of comfort and warmth she had ever known in the hope that it would be cared for there? Maybe it was.

But it seemed I wasn't the only one with

Closure and Extension

ANSWERS TO THINKING ABOUT THE SELECTION
Recalling

1. Mrs. Ainsworth calls him to check the health of her dogs.

such fancies. Mrs. Ainsworth turned to me and though she was smiling her eyes were wistful.

"Debbie would be pleased," she said.

I nodded. "Yes, she would . . . It was just a year ago today she brought him, wasn't it?"

"That's right." She hugged Buster to her again. "The best Christmas present I ever had."

THINKING ABOUT THE SELECTION

Recalling

1. Why does Herriot first visit Mrs. Ainsworth?
2. Describe Debbie and her life.
3. Explain the reason for Herriot's second visit.
4. How is the Ainsworth household different as a result of Buster?

Interpreting

5. What qualities does Mrs. Ainsworth show in her treatment of animals?

Applying

6. Mrs. Ainsworth receives an unexpected reward for her kindness to Debbie. She receives Buster. Why are unexpected rewards sometimes more valued than expected ones?

ANALYZING LITERATURE

Understanding Characters in an Essay

You can learn about characters by reading about their actions, by reading their words, by reading about their thoughts and feelings, by reading descriptive details about them, and by reading what other characters say or think about them.

Look back over "Debbie" and point out one example of information about Herriot that you found in each of the following ways.

1. By reading about his actions
2. By reading his words
3. By reading about his thoughts
4. By reading a descriptive detail
5. By reading what another character says or thinks about him

CRITICAL THINKING AND READING

Comparing and Contrasting Characters

When you **compare** characters, you discuss traits about each that are the same. When you **contrast** characters, you discuss traits that are different. Comparing and contrasting characters can help you to understand them better.

1. List traits that Debbie and Buster share.
2. List traits that differ between Debbie and Buster.
3. What was it about the presentation of Debbie that made her come alive for you?
4. What was it about the presentation of Buster that made him come alive for you?

THINKING AND WRITING

Comparing and Contrasting Cats

Using the lists of traits you wrote for Debbie and Buster, write an article for a pet journal comparing and contrasting the two cats. Describe one cat completely and follow that description with a complete description of the other cat. When you revise, check the organization of your article carefully. Finally, proofread your article and share it with your classmates.

(Answers begin on p. 442.)

2. She is a thin, black stray cat, muddy and bedraggled. She lives outdoors but occasionally visits Mrs. Ainsworth's home to be fed and simply to sit in front of the fire and enjoy its comforts; then she disappears again.
3. Mrs. Ainsworth calls him to examine Debbie, who is dying.
4. It is livelier and happier because Buster teases and plays with the dogs, runs about energetically, retrieves balls, and is affectionate with Mrs. Ainsworth.

Interpreting

5. Answers will differ. Suggested Response: Kindness, anxiety, responsibility, sympathy, playfulness, and appreciation.

Applying

6. Answers will differ. Suggested Response: Unexpected rewards sometimes are more valued than expected ones because they offer a delightful surprise, a reward for something that you would have done anyway.

ANSWERS TO ANALYZING LITERATURE

1. By his visiting sick animals on a holiday, you know that Herriot puts their welfare ahead of his own convenience.
2. By his telling Mrs. Ainsworth that nobody could have done more for Debbie than she did, you know that Herriot is kind.
3. By his description of his thoughts that he was working up a better appetite by visiting sick animals than by sleeping at home, you know that Herriot looks on the bright side of things.
4. By his description of himself as being "bathed in a rosy glow," you know that Herriot is healthy and energetic.
5. By Mrs. Ainsworth's invitation to him to come in to celebrate Christmas when the animals are not sick, you know that Herriot is a likable and friendly person.

ANSWERS TO CRITICAL THINKING AND READING

1. Debbie and Buster share the traits of being black, of having some degree of wildness, and of trusting Mrs. Ainsworth.
2. Debbie and Buster differ in that Debbie is sickly and undersized, timid, and likes to live outdoors. Buster is healthy and well fed, boisterous and playful, and lives indoors with Mrs. Ainsworth.
3. Answers will differ. Suggested Responses: The descriptions of Debbie's behavior in front of the fire, of bringing her kitten to Mrs. Ainsworth, of her bedraggled appearance and of her death make her come alive.
4. Answers will differ. Suggested Responses: The descriptions of Buster's playfulness with the dogs, his sleek and healthy appearance, and his affection for Mrs. Ainsworth make him come alive.

Challenge Name a real person or television character who shares Buster's main qualities.

THINKING AND WRITING

For help with this assignment, students can refer to Lesson 16, "Writing a Comparative Evaluation," in the Handbook of Writing About Literature.

Publishing Student Writing You might want to share students' articles by displaying them on a bulletin board or even sending the best ones to a pet journal.

Focus

More About the Author Jean Kerr is best known for *Please Don't Eat the Daisies,* a collection of wryly humorous essays about her life as a suburban housewife. What does the fact that Kerr can write humorously about the routine aspects of her life tell you about her?

Literary Focus You might point out to students that humor is often achieved through exaggeration, or overstatement; through describing a ridiculous situation in a serious way; and through describing the unexpected.

Look For In Kerr's description of her mother, a few traits seem pronounced. Ask students to think of a person they know. What is that person's most prominent character trait?

Writing/Prior Knowledge "Laugh and the world laughs with you; weep, and you weep alone." Have students discuss the meaning of this quotation before completing the freewriting assignment.

Vocabulary For your less advanced students, first use these words in context to help them guess the meaning.

Spelling Tip *Portentous* should not be confused with *pretentious* or other words ending in *-eious* or *-tious* like *gracious* or *contentious.*

GUIDE FOR READING

My Wild Irish Mother

Jean Kerr (1923–) was born in Scranton, Pennsylvania. She was eight years old when she decided that she wanted "to be able to sleep until noon," a goal she achieved partly by becoming a writer who begins each day "at the stroke of the noon whistle." Still, Jean Kerr has found time to write many humorous stories, essays, and plays—all works of "realistic comedy." The essay "My Wild Irish Mother," published in 1978, comes from a collection of her essays called *How I Got To Be Perfect.*

Humorous Essay

A **humorous essay** is a short nonfiction composition in which a writer presents a subject in a humorous way. In "My Wild Irish Mother," Kerr writes about her mother, a woman of Irish descent and spirit. Kerr reveals her mother's character in a series of anecdotes —brief, amusing incidents or stories that make a simple point. These anecdotes and the writer's skill make this essay like a funny Valentine: it talks of love while making you laugh.

Look For

As you read "My Wild Irish Mother," look for the humorous anecdotes and descriptive details that reveal Mother's character. What is Mother like? Why does Kerr consider her such a character?

Writing

Think of a person who would be an interesting subject for a humorous essay. It may be someone you know, someone you have read about, or someone you have seen on television or in the movies. Freewrite about that person, recalling amusing anecdotes that reveal his or her most outstanding character traits.

Vocabulary

Knowing the following words will help you as you read "My Wild Irish Mother."

conviction (kən vik′ shən) *n.*: Strong belief (p. 445)
indulgent (in dul′ jənt) *adj.*: Generous (p. 445)
protestations (prät′ is tā′ shənz) *n.*: Formal declarations or assertions (p. 447)
portentous (por′ ten′ təs) *adj.*: Pompous and self-consciously weighty (p. 447)
conspiratorial (kən spir′ ə tôr′ ē əl) *adj.*: Secretive (p. 448)
languorous (laŋ′ gər əs) *adj.*: Slow and lazy (p. 448)
beguiled (bi gīl′d′) *v.*: Charmed (p. 448)
credo (krē′ dō) *n.*: Set of personal beliefs (p. 449)

Objectives

1 To understand the humorous essay
2 To identify exaggeration
3 To find homophones
4 To write a humorous essay

Support Material

Teaching Portfolio
Teacher Backup, pp. 549–551
Grammar in Action Worksheet, *Using Sophisticated Sentences,* pp. 552–553
Usage and Mechanics Worksheet, p. 554
Vocabulary Check, p. 555
Critical Thinking and Reading Worksheet, *Identifying Exaggeration,* p. 556
Language Worksheet, *Finding Homophones,* p. 557
Selection Test, pp. 558–559

My Wild Irish Mother

Jean Kerr

I'm never going to write my autobiography and it's all my mother's fault. I didn't hate her, so I have practically no material. In
1 fact, the situation is worse than I'm pretending. We were crazy about her—and you know I'll never get a book out of that, much less a musical.

Mother was born Kitty O'Neill, in Kinsale, Ireland, with bright red hair, bright
2 blue eyes, and the firm conviction that it was wrong to wait for an elevator if you were only going up to the fifth floor. It's not just that she won't wait for elevators, which she really feels are provided only for the convenience of the aged and infirm. I have known her to reproach herself on missing one section of a revolving door. And I well remember a time when we missed a train from New York to Washington. I fully expected her to pick up our suitcases and announce, "Well, darling, the exercise will be good for us."

When I have occasion to mutter about the financial problems involved in maintaining six children in a large house, Mother
3 is quick to get to the root of the problem. "Remember," she says, "you take cabs a lot."

The youngest daughter of wealthy and indulgent parents, Mother went to finishing
4 schools in France and to the Royal Conservatory of Music in London. Thus, when she came to America to marry my father, her only qualifications for the role of housewife and mother were the ability to speak four languages, play three musical instruments, and make *blancmange*.[1] I, naturally, wasn't around during those first troubled months when Mother learned to cook. But my father can still recall the day she boiled corn on the cob, a delicacy unknown in Ireland at that time, for five hours until the cobs were tender. And, with a typical beginner's zeal, Mother "put up" twenty bushels of tomatoes for that first winter before it struck her that neither she nor Dad really liked canned tomatoes.

By the time I was old enough to notice things, Mother was an excellent cook. She would cook things she had no intention of eating. Where food is concerned, she is totally conservative. She will study the menu at an expensive restaurant with evident interest and then say, "Darling, where do you see lamb chops?" Or she will glance with real admiration at a man at a nearby table who seems actually to be consuming an order of cherrystone clams. "Aren't Americans marvelous?" she'll remark. "They will eat anything."

On the other hand she was always willing to prepare all manner of exotic dishes for Dad and the rest of us. In the old days the men who worked for my father frequently gave him gifts of game—venison, rabbit, and the like. Occasionally we children

---

1. **blancmange** (blə mänzh') *n.*: A sweet, molded jellylike dessert.

Presentation

Motivation/Prior Knowledge Imagine that you wanted readers to share the same feelings that you have for someone special in your life. What would you do to impart that feeling to readers?

Thematic Idea Another selection that deals with a humorous character is "The Day I Got Lost" on page 113.

Purpose-Setting Question Why did Jean Kerr write this humorous essay about her mother?

1 **Discussion** What does the writer suggest about one's relationship with one's mother and the ability to write an autobiography? Do you agree with this idea?

2 **Discussion** Why is Mother's "firm conviction" humorous in the context of the rest of the sentence?

3 **Discussion** Why is Mother's comment about cabs humorous?

4 **Clarification** A finishing school is a private school for girls that specializes in imparting social poise and polish.

Humanities Note

Fine art, *After the Meeting,* 1914, by Cecelia Beaux. Cecelia Beaux (1863–1942) was born in Philadelphia. She was a pupil of William Sartain, and studied at the Julien School and the Layar School in Paris. She won many art awards, including a gold medal at the Paris Exposition (1900), a gold medal from the American Academy of Arts and Letters, and the National Achievement Award (1934). She is remembered chiefly as a portraitist of children and women.

This painting portrays an elegant woman dressed fashionably in what resembles a Victorian style.

1. What do you imagine is happening in this picture?
2. What do you think is the personality of this subject?
3. How might this subject be like Mother?

AFTER THE MEETING, 1914
Cecelia Beaux
The Toledo Museum of Art

Grammar in Action

Instead of a series of short, choppy sentences, the style of an effective writer is often marked by longer, more sophisticated sentences. For example, look at the following sentence from "My Wild Irish Mother."

> I remember my brother Hugh, when he was about eight, sitting on the foot of Mother's bed and giving her a half-hour lecture which began with the portentous question, "Mom, how much do you know about the habits of the common housefly?"

A less mature writer might have written the above sentence as follows:

> I remember my brother Hugh. He was about eight. He was sitting on the foot of Mother's bed. He was giving her a half-hour lecture. The lecture began with a portentous question. The question was, "Mom, how much do you know about the habits of the common housefly?"

would protest. I recall becoming quite tearful over the prospect of eating deer, on the theory that it might be Bambi. But Mother was always firm. "Nonsense," she would say, "eat up, it's just like chicken."

But one night she went too far. I don't know where she got this enormous slab of meat; I don't think my father brought it home. It stood overnight in the icebox in some complicated solution of brine[2] and herbs. The next day the four of us were told that we could each invite a friend to dinner. Mother spent most of the day lovingly preparing her roast. That night there were ten of us around the dining-room table, and if Mother seemed too busy serving all the rest of us to eat anything herself, that was not at all unusual. At this late date I have no impression of what the meat tasted like. But I know that we were all munching away when Mother beamed happily at us and asked, "Well, children, how are you enjoying the bear?"

5 Forks dropped and certain of the invited guests made emergency trips to the bathroom. For once, all of Mother's protestations that it was just like chicken were unavailing. Nobody would touch another bite. She was really dismayed. I heard her tell Dad, "It's really strange, Tom—I thought all Americans liked bear."

6 Mother's education, as I have indicated, was rather one-sided. While she knew a great deal about such "useless" things as music and art and literature, she knew nothing whatever, we were quick to discover, about isosceles triangles[3] or watts and volts or the Smoot-Hawley Tariff.[4] As we were growing up, we made haste to repair these gaps.

One of the most charming things about Mother was the extraordinary patience with which she would allow us youngsters to "instruct" her. I remember my brother Hugh, when he was about eight, sitting on the foot of Mother's bed and giving her a half-hour lecture which began with the portentous question, "Mom, how much do you know about the habits of the common housefly?"

At that, it's remarkable how much of this unrelated information stayed with her. Just recently I was driving her to a train and she noticed, high up in the air, a squirrel that was poised on a wire that ran between two five-story buildings. "Look at that little squirrel 'way up on that wire," she said. "You know, if he gets one foot on the ground, he'll be electrocuted."

But if her knowledge of positive and negative electricity is a little sketchy, there is nothing sketchy about her knowledge of any subject in which she develops an interest. Mother always adored the theater and was a passionate playgoer from the time she was five years old. However, during the years when she was sobbing gently over *The Lily of Killarney* in Cork City, she was blissfully unaware of the menacing existence of American drama critics or the fact that their printed opinions had a certain measurable effect on the box office. Even when she came to America, she still had the feeling that five nights was probably an impressive run for a Broadway show.

Time passed, and my husband and I

---

2. brine (brīn) *n.*: Water full of salt and used for pickling.

3. isosceles triangles (ī säs′ ə lēz′ trī′ an′ g'ls) *n.*: Geometrical figures with three angles and three sides, two sides of which are equal in length.

4. Smoot-Hawley Tariff: A tax law that required people to pay high taxes or tariffs on goods imported into the country.

5 Discussion Different cultures appreciate different foods. What is an example of a food that one culture would like that another would not?

6 Discussion Why do you think such interests as music, art, and literature were sometimes considered "useless"?

Student Activity. Work with a group of three or four other students. Combine each of the following groups of sentences into one more mature sentence. Compare your combined sentences with the ones in "My Wild Irish Mother."

1. That night there were ten of us. We sat around the dining-room table. Mother may have seemed too busy to eat anything herself. This was because she was serving all the rest of us. This was not at all unusual.
2. She knew a great deal about such "useless" things as music and art and literature. We were quick to discover the following fact. She knew nothing whatever about isosceles triangles or watts and volts or the Smoot-Hawley Tariff.
3. Just recently I was driving her to a train. She noticed a squirrel. The squirrel was high up in the air. It was poised on a wire. The wire ran between two five-story buildings.

7 Discussion What was the real reason Kerr did not send her mother *The Sun's* notice?

8 Discussion Restate in your own words this statement.

9 Discussion What does the fact that people like to tell Mother their troubles tell you about Mother?

became involved in the theater. Mother began to get the facts. When, quite a few years ago, we were living in Washington and came up to New York for the opening of a revue[5] we had written, I promised Mother that I would send her all the reviews, special delivery, as soon as they appeared. In those days, before the demise[6] of *The Sun*, there were eight metropolitan dailies. Eventually we got hold of all the papers and I was able to assess the evidence. All but one of the morning papers were fine, and while there were certain quibbles in the afternoon papers, the only seriously negative notice appeared in *The Sun*. Ward Morehouse was then the critic on *The Sun* but happened to be out of town at the moment, and the review was written by his assistant, or, as I was willing to suppose, his office boy. So, with that special brand of feminine logic that has already made my husband prematurely gray, I decided to omit this particular notice in the batch I was sending to my mother, on the theory that (a) it wasn't written by the *real* critic, and (b) nobody in
7 Scranton, Pennsylvania, knew there was a paper called *The Sun* anyway. This was a serious miscalculation on my part, as I realized later in the day when I got Mother's two-word telegram. It read, "Where's Morehouse?"

Let me say that her interest in the more technical aspects of the theater continues unabated. Not long ago we were in Philadelphia, deep in the unrefined bedlam that surrounds any musical in its tryout stage. The phone rang. It was Mother. Without any preliminary word of greeting, she asked in hushed, conspiratorial tones, "Darling, have you pointed and sharpened?"

"Good Lord, Mother," I said, "what are you talking about?"

"I'm talking about the show, dear," she said, sounding like a small investor, which she was. "*Variety*[7] says it needs pointing and sharpening, and I think we should listen to them."

To the four low-metabolism types[8] she inexplicably produced, Mother's energy has always seemed awesome. "What do you think," she's prone to say, "do I have time to cut the grass before I stuff the turkey?" But her whirlwind activity is potentially less dangerous than her occasional moments of 8
repose. Then she sits, staring into space, clearly lost in languorous memories. The faint, fugitive smile that hovers about her lips suggests the gentle melancholy of one hearing Mozart played beautifully. Suddenly she leaps to her feet. "I know it will work," she says. "All we have to do is remove that wall, plug up the windows, and extend the porch."

It's undoubtedly fortunate that she has the thrust and the energy of a well-guided missile. Otherwise she wouldn't get a lick of work done, because everybody who comes to her house, whether to read the gas meter or to collect for UNICEF,[9] always stays at least 9
an hour. I used to think that they were one and all beguiled by her Irish accent. But I have gradually gleaned[10] that they are telling her the story of their invariably unhappy lives. "Do you remember my lovely huckleberry man?" Mother will ask. "Oh, *yes* you do—he had red hair and ears. Well, his brother-in-law sprained his back and hasn't

5. revue (ri vyōō') *n.*: A musical show with loosely connected skits, songs, and dances.
6. demise (di mīz') *n.*: A ceasing to exist; death.

7. *Variety:* A newspaper that specializes in show-business news.
8. low-metabolism types: Less energetic people.
9. UNICEF: United Nations International Children's Emergency Fund.
10. gleaned (glēn'd) *v.*: Found out gradually bit by bit.

WOMAN BEFORE AN AQUARIUM, 1921
Henry Matisse
The Art Institute of Chicago

worked in six months, and we're going to have to take a bundle of clothes over to those children." Or, again: "Do you remember that nice girl in the Scranton Dry Goods? Oh, yes you do, she was in lamp shades and she had gray hair and wore gray dresses. Well, she's having an operation next month and you must remember to pray for her." Mother's credo, by the way, is that if you want something, anything, don't just sit there—pray for it. And she combines a Job-like[11] patience in the face of the mysterious ways of the Almighty with a flash of Irish rebellion which will bring her to say—and I'm sure she speaks for many of us—"Jean,

11. Job-like (jōb′ līk) *adj.*: Similar to the man named Job in the Old Testament who endured much suffering but did not lose his faith in God.

Humanities Note

Fine art, *Woman Before an Aquarium,* 1921, by Henri Matisse. Henri Matisse (1869–1954) was a French painter who originally studied law. At age 20, while recuperating from an illness, he begain painting to pass the time. He was instantly taken with the idea of life as a painter: "I felt uplifted into a sort of paradise in which I felt wonderfully free." He became one of the greatest colorists of all time and an important member of the Fauves, a group of young painters who began exhibiting in Paris in 1905. The Fauves ("the wild beasts") owed their name to the shock created by their radically new style of painting using bold distortions and intense colors.

Matisse developed a unique style that radiated feelings of peace and harmony. He continually experimented with color to achieve his unique view of a subject.

1. Study the use of color in this painting. What mood does it create?
2. How does this woman compare with the description of Mother?

10 Discussion What does this paragraph say about Mother's effect on people?

11 Discussion Ask students for examples of books, musicals, or stories written about parents, such as "Life With Father" by Clarence Day.

Reader's Response Which anecdote did you find especially amusing?

what I am really looking for is a blessing that's *not* in disguise."

She does have a knack for penetrating disguises, whether it be small boys who claim that they have taken baths or middle-aged daughters who swear that they have lost five pounds. She has a way of cutting things to size, particularly books, which she gobbles up in the indiscriminate[12] way that a slot machine gobbles up quarters. The first time I had a collection of short pieces brought out in book form, I sent an advance copy to Mother. She was naturally delighted. Her enthusiasm fairly bubbled off the pages of the letter. "Darling," she wrote, "isn't it marvelous the way those old pieces of yours finally came to the surface like a dead body!"

I knew when I started this that all I could
do was list the things Mother says, because
it's not possible, really, to describe her. All
my life I have heard people break off their 10
lyrical descriptions of Kitty and announce
helplessly, "You'll just have to meet her."

However, I recognize, if I cannot describe, the lovely festive air she always
brings with her, so that she can arrive any
old day in July and suddenly it seems to be
Christmas Eve and the children seem hand- 11
somer and better behaved and all the adults
seem more charming and—

Well, you'll just have to meet her.

12. **indiscriminate** (in' dis krim' ə nit) *adj.*: Not based on careful choices; random.

THINKING ABOUT THE SELECTION

Recalling

1. What are Mother's three unlikely qualifications for the role of wife and mother?
2. Give two examples of Mother's unusual ideas about food.
3. Why does the writer finally stop listing her mother's qualities and comments and end the essay?

Interpreting

4. What do we mean when we call someone "a real character"? In what ways is Mother "a real character"?
5. Based on what you know about the mother and daughter from this essay, name one way in which they are alike and one way in which they differ.
6. The writer has borrowed the title of her essay from an old Irish love song, "My Wild Irish Rose." Knowing this, what meaning does the title of the essay convey?

Applying

7. Think of a song title that would be appropriate as the title of a humorous essay about the subject of your freewriting assignment. Explain why that song title would be appropriate for an essay about that person.

ANALYZING LITERATURE

Understanding the Humorous Essay

A **humorous essay** is a nonfiction composition that gives a writer's thoughtful but humorous view of a subject. Although the subject may be serious, its treatment is lighthearted and intended to make you laugh. Writers of humorous

Closure and Extension

ANSWERS TO THINKING ABOUT THE SELECTION

Recalling

1. Mother's unlikely qualifications for the role of wife and mother are her ability to speak four languages, play three musical instruments, and make *blancmange.*
2. Two examples of Mother's unusual ideas about food are her belief, based on seeing a person eat cherrystone clams, that Americans will eat anything; and that bear is just like chicken.
3. The writer finally ends the essay because she says it is impossible to describe her mother—you just have to meet her.

Interpreting

4. Answers will differ. Suggested Response: When we say someone is "a real character," we mean that they are an odd, eccentric, or noteworthy person. Mother is a real character in that she has an extraordinarily high energy level and unusual ideas about food, occasionally mixes up or misinterprets information in an amusing way, takes an avid interest in anyone who comes to the house, and has a knack for penetrating disguises.
5. Answers will differ. Suggested Response: They are alike in that they share a great interest in the theater and literature and that they both raised large families. They differ in that the writer is a "low-metabolism type" while Mother has inexhaustible energy.
6. Answers will differ. Suggested Response: The title implies that the writer loves her "wild Irish mother," and that her mother is like a rose in being beautiful, fresh, sweet, and natural.

Applying

7. Answers will differ, depending on the freewriting subject.

essays amuse their audiences in different ways. Some use amusing anecdotes as Jean Kerr does when she tells about her mother boiling the corn on the cob.

1. What is Kerr's attitude toward her mother? Find the statement that reveals this.
2. How do you think she wants you to feel about her mother? Explain your answer.
3. Name three examples of the ways she used to accomplish her purpose.

CRITICAL THINKING AND READING

Identifying Exaggeration

Writers often achieve comic effects through **exaggeration**—the act of making something appear greater, more important, or funnier than it really is. Kerr exaggerates, for example, when she tells you that her mother "has the thrust and the energy of a well-guided missile." Her exaggeration is a much funnier way of overstating a fact.

1. Find three examples of exaggeration in this essay.
2. Explain the effect of each of these examples.

UNDERSTANDING LANGUAGE

Finding Homophones

A **homophone** is a word that sounds like another word but is spelled differently and has a different meaning. For example, the words *cash* and *cache* are homophones. *Cash* refers to ready money, whereas *cache* refers to a place in which stores of supplies are hidden.

Complete each word analogy below by filling in the appropriate homophone.

1. write:right::red:__________
2. know:no::weight:__________
3. ewe:you::time:__________
4. roll:role::days:__________
5. four:for::deer:__________
6. meet:meat::bite:__________
7. eight:ate::hi:__________
8. son:sun::review:__________
9. one:won::morning:__________
10. reel:real::more:__________

THINKING AND WRITING

Writing a Humorous Essay

Choose one of the humorous events in the essay "My Wild Irish Mother." Rewrite this episode making the daughter the subject instead of the mother. Using the information about Jean Kerr in the essay, retell the event from the mother's point of view. When you have finished writing, make sure you have consistently had the mother tell the story about Jean Kerr. Revise your essay and read it aloud to your classmates. Try to tell it aloud in the mother's voice.

(Answers begin on p. 450.)

ANSWERS TO ANALYZING LITERATURE

1. Kerr loved her mother. She reveals this in the first paragraph: "We were crazy about her."
2. Answers will differ. Suggested Response: Kerr probably wants you to regard her mother as a lovable and special person who is also amusing.
3. Suggested Response:
   a. She says that Mother "put up" twenty bushels of tomatoes before it struck her that neither she nor Dad really liked canned tomatoes, as a way of humorously describing Mother's impulsiveness.
   b. She describes Mother's serving the bear to guests as a way of humorously depicting Mother's assumptions about American eating habits.
   c. She described Mother's being instructed by her children as a way of humorously depicting Mother's patient attitude toward her children.

ANSWERS TO CRITICAL THINKING AND READING

1. Answers will differ. Three examples of exaggeration are the following.
   a. "I have known her to reproach herself on missing one section of a revolving door."
   b. "And I well remember a time when we missed a train from New York to Washington. I fully expected her to pick up our suitcases and announce, "Well, darling, the exercise will be good for us.""
   c. "What do you think," she's prone to say, "do I have time to cut the grass before I stuff the turkey?"
2. Answers will differ. Following are suggested explanations of the effect of these examples.
   a. The effect is comic because Kerr's mother makes missing a section of a revolving door more important than it actually is.
   b. The effect is comic because Kerr imagines her mother making light of walking a very long journey.
   c. The effect is comic because the question is asked seriously about an unreasonable plan of action.

ANSWERS TO UNDERSTANDING LANGUAGE

1. read
2. wait
3. thyme
4. daze
5. dear
6. bight
7. high
8. revue
9. mourning
10. moor

Challenge The humorous character in this story has a great deal of energy. What is the relationship between humor and personal energy?

THINKING AND WRITING

Publishing Student Writing Ask for student volunteers to read their essays aloud. Have students in the audience record at least one noteworthy feature of each essay.

Writing Across the Curriculum You might want to have students research and report on the culture from which they descended—for example, the Italian culture if the student is part Italian. If you do, perhaps inform the social studies department of this assignment. Social studies teachers might provide guidance for students in conducting their research.

Focus

More About the Author Anais Nin has said that she wanted "to unmask the deeper self that lies hidden" [from the real world]. What does this statement tell you about the author? What are other reasons for writing?

Literary Focus Ask students what kinds of details they would include in describing a scene to someone who is blind.

Look For You may want to review with the students what sensory details are.

Writing/Prior Knowledge Ask students what types of people who have survived a natural disaster would make the best candidates to interview about their experience.

Teaching to Ability Levels for your **more advanced** students, you may want to review simile and metaphor. Explain that simile and metaphor are part of description. Students should look for them when reading this descriptive essay.

Vocabulary Have your **less advanced** students, use each of these words in a sentence to be sure that they understand the meanings.

Spelling Tip When the last letter of the prefix *dis, mis,* or *un* is the same as the first letter of the stem, as in *dissolution,* the letter is double in the new word. Other examples: *misspell, unnoticed, dissatisfaction.*

GUIDE FOR READING

Forest Fire

Anaïs Nin (1903–1977) was born in France but grew up in the United States. At age eleven, she began the writing that continued her whole life. Although she wrote novels and short stories, Nin was best known for her six published diaries spanning sixty years. "Forest Fire," from the fifth diary, illustrates how Nin looked at life "as an adventure and a tale." The incident she wrote about in "Forest Fire" happened when she was living in Sierra Madre, California.

Descriptive Essay

A **descriptive essay** is a short nonfiction composition in which an author describes or creates word pictures of a subject. Like most other kinds of essays, an author writes a descriptive essay to present his or her view of a subject. But in descriptive essays, authors achieve their purpose mainly by including images and details that show us how things look, sound, smell, taste, or feel. Such details work to allow you to share the writer's experience fully.

Look For

As you read "Forest Fire," look for specific details the writer uses to create vivid word pictures for you. What sensory impressions do these details create?

Writing

Imagine that you are a newspaper reporter. You are preparing to interview the people who have just survived a forest fire. They managed to put out the fire quickly and without much damage to their surroundings. Write a list of interview questions to ask these people about the fire and the precautions they took that helped lessen the effects of the fire. Write questions that begin with *who, what, when, where, why, how,* or *tell me about.*

Vocabulary

Knowing the following words will help you as you read "Forest Fire."

tinted (tint′ əd) *v.*: Colored (p. 453)

evacuees (i vak′ yo͞o wēz′) *n.*: People who leave a place, especially because of danger (p. 453)

pungent (pun′ jənt) *adj.*: Sharp and stinging to the smell (p. 454)

tenacious (tə nā′ shəs) *adj.*: Holding on firmly (p. 454)

dissolution (dis′ ə lo͞o′ shən) *n.*: The act of breaking down and crumbling (p. 454)

ravaging (rav′ ij iŋ) *adj.*: Severely damaging or destroying (p. 454)

Objectives

1 To understand the descriptive essay
2 To separate fact from opinion
3 To write a descriptive essay

Support Material

Teaching Portfolio

Teacher Backup, pp. 561–563
Usage and Mechanics Worksheet, p. 564
Vocabulary Check, p. 565
Analyzing Literature Worksheet, *Understanding Descriptive Essays,* p. 566
Language Worksheet, *Identifying Word Origins,* p. 567
Selection Test, pp. 568–569

Forest Fire

Anaïs Nin

A man rushed in to announce he had seen smoke on Monrovia Peak.[1] As I looked out of the window I saw the two mountains facing the house on fire. The entire rim burning wildly in the night. The flames, driven by hot Santa Ana winds[2] from the desert, were as tall as the tallest trees, the sky already tinted coral, and the crackling noise of burning trees, the ashes and the smoke were already increasing. The fire raced along, sometimes descending behind the mountain where I could only see the glow, sometimes descending toward us. I thought of the foresters in danger. I made coffee for the weary men who came down occasionally with horses they had led out, or with old people from the isolated cabins. They were covered with soot from their battle with the flames.

At six o'clock the fire was on our left side and rushing toward Mount Wilson. Evacuees from the cabins began to arrive and had to be given blankets and hot coffee. The streets were blocked with fire engines ready-
ing to fight the fire if it touched the houses.
1 Policemen and firemen and guards turned
away the sightseers. Some were relatives concerned over the fate of the foresters, or the pack station family. The policemen lighted flares, which gave the scene a theatrical, tragic air. The red lights on the police cars twinkled alarmingly. More fire engines arrived. Ashes fell, and the roar of the fire was now like thunder.

We were told to ready ourselves for evac- 2
uation. I packed the diaries. The saddest
spectacle, beside that of the men fighting
the fire as they would a war, were the animals, rabbits, coyotes, mountain lions, deer,
driven by the fire to the edge of the moun- 3
tain, taking a look at the crowd of people
and panicking, choosing rather to rush back
into the fire.

The fire now was like a ring around Sierra Madre,[3] every mountain was burning. People living at the foot of the mountain were packing their cars. I rushed next door to the Campion children, who had been left with a baby-sitter, and got them into the car. It was impossible to save all the horses. We parked the car on the field below us. I called up the Campions, who were out for the evening, and reassured them. The baby-sitter dressed the children warmly. I made more coffee. I answered frantic telephone calls.

All night the fire engines sprayed water over the houses. But the fire grew immense, angry, and rushing at a speed I could not
believe. It would rush along and suddenly
leap over a road, a trail, like a monster, 4
devouring all in its path. The firefighters cut
breaks in the heavy brush, but when the wind was strong enough, the fire leaped

1. **Monrovia** (mən rō′ vē ə) **Peak:** Mountain in southwest California.
2. **Santa** (san′ tə) **Ana** (an′ ə) **winds:** Hot desert winds from the east or northeast in southern California.

3. **Sierra** (sē er′ ə) **Madre** (mä′ drā): Mountain range.

Presentation

Motivation/Prior Knowledge Natural disasters can have a great impact on people's lives. Ask students for examples of any natural disaster they or their friends have lived through.

Master Teacher Note This essay derives some of its excitement from the theme—the race against time.

1. Discuss how quick thinking contributes to the excitement of the action.
2. Ask students to list three things they would do before making a "quick escape."

Purpose-Setting Question How is nature like a person or an animal?

Thematic Idea Another selection that deals with a natural disaster and its effect on people and animals is "Grass Fire," by Loula Grace Erdman on page 129. A selection that deals with a natural phenomenon is "Shooting Stars" on page 469.

1 **Discussion** What is it about natural disaster and human tragedy that excites curiosity?

2 **Discussion** What items would you take with you if you had to evacuate?

3 **Discussion** Why did the animals rush back into the fire to certain death rather than face the humans? What do you think was their previous experience with humans?

4 **Discussion** What other similarities can you think of between a fire and a monster?

5 Clarification *Backfiring* is starting a fire to stop an advancing forest fire by creating a burned area in its path.

6 Discussion Discuss how the reporter did not see the "human interest" in the writer saving her diaries.

7 Clarification People may stack sandbags around their homes to absorb water from the flood and prevent it from entering their homes.

8 Critical Thinking and Reading Ask students whether this is a fact or an opinion.

9 Discussion What are other examples of nature in its peaceful moments and in its furies?

Reader's Response Which image was the most vivid to you?

across them. At dawn one arm of the fire reached the back of our houses but was finally contained.

But high above and all around, the fire was burning, more vivid than the sun, throwing spirals of smoke in the air like the smoke from a volcano. Thirty-three cabins burned, and twelve thousand acres of forest still burning endangered countless homes below the fire. The fire was burning to the back of us now, and a rain of ashes began to fall and continued for days. The smell of the burn in the air, acid and pungent and tenacious. The dragon tongues of flames devouring, the flames leaping, the roar of destruction and dissolution, the eyes of the panicked animals, caught between fire and human beings, between two forms of death. They chose the fire. It was as if the fire had come from the bowels of the earth, like that of a fiery volcano, it was so powerful, so swift, and so ravaging. I saw trees become skeletons in one minute, I saw trees fall, I saw bushes turned to ashes in a second, I saw weary, ash-covered men, looking like men returned from war, some with burns, others overcome by smoke.

The men were rushing from one spot to another watching for recrudescence.[4] Some
5 started backfiring up the mountain so that
the ascending flames could counteract the descending ones.

As the flames reached the cities below, hundreds of roofs burst into flame at once. There was no water pressure because all the fire hydrants were turned on at the same time, and the fire departments were helpless to save more than a few of the burning homes.

The blaring loudspeakers of passing police cars warned us to prepare to evacuate in case the wind changed and drove the fire in our direction. What did I wish to save? I thought only of the diaries. I appeared on the porch carrying a huge stack of diary volumes, preparing to pack them in the car. A reporter for the Pasadena *Star News* was taking pictures of the evacuation. He came up, very annoyed with me. "Hey, lady, next
time could you bring out something more 6
important than all those old papers? Carry some clothes on the next trip. We gotta have human interest in these pictures!"

A week later, the danger was over.

Gray ashy days.

In Sierra Madre, following the fire, the
January rains brought floods. People are 7
sandbagging their homes. At four A.M. the streets are covered with mud. The bare, burnt, naked mountains cannot hold the rains and slide down bringing rocks and mud. One of the rangers must now take photographs and movies of the disaster. He asks if I will help by holding an umbrella over the cameras. I put on my raincoat and he lends me hip boots which look to me like seven-league boots.

We drive a little way up the road. At the third curve it is impassable. A river is rushing across the road. The ranger takes pictures while I hold the umbrella over the camera. It is terrifying to see the muddied
waters and rocks, the mountain disintegrat- 8
ing. When we are ready to return, the road before us is covered by large rocks but the ranger pushes on as if the truck were a jeep and forces it through. The edge of the road is being carried away.

I am laughing and scared too. The ranger is at ease in nature, and without fear. It is a wild moment of danger. It is easy to love
nature in its peaceful and consoling mo- 9
ments, but one must love it in its furies too, in its despairs and wildness, especially when the damage is caused by us.

---

4. recrudescence (rē′ kroo des′ əns) *n.*: A fresh outbreak of something that has been inactive.

THINKING ABOUT THE SELECTION

Recalling

1. Describe the setting—the time and place—of the forest fire.
2. How does the writer respond to the fire?
3. What are the effects of the forest fire?

Interpreting

4. Why is a fire so particularly dangerous in this setting?
5. What does the writer's choice of saving only her diaries tell you about her?

Applying

6. Imagine a natural disaster in your community. Develop a list of rules or guidelines for helping people survive the disaster.

ANALYZING LITERATURE

Understanding Descriptive Essays

Authors write descriptive essays to present their personal view of or experience with a subject. **Descriptive essays** usually contain two important elements: many specific details and figurative language—language that makes comparison between unlike things and that is not intended to be interpreted strictly or literally. For example, when Anaïs Nin describes the *angry fire,* she does not mean that the fire is really angry. She is saying that the fire has a wild, out-of-control quality that makes it like an angry person. Sometimes Nin uses the words *like* or *as, is* or *was.* At other times she gives the fire the qualities and movements of a living creature.

1. Find two examples of figurative language that contain the words *like* or *as* in the essay.
2. Find two examples of figurative language that describe something nonliving with the qualities of a living creature.
3. Find one descriptive detail you found especially effective, or strong. Explain your reasons for choosing this detail.

CRITICAL THINKING AND READING

Separating Fact and Opinion

Facts are statements about things that have either happened or are happening. This information can always be proved true or false using reliable sources. For example, that the forest fire occurred near Sierra Madre is a fact; it can be proved by checking newspaper accounts or local records. **Opinions,** on the other hand, cannot be proved true or false because they are based on the writer's personal beliefs or attitudes. For example, the statement that the forest is a beautiful place is an opinion. This information cannot be proved true or false.

Identify which of the following are facts and which are the writer's opinions. Be prepared to support your answers.

1. "I rushed next door to the Campion children . . . and got them into the car."
2. "The . . . lighted flares . . . gave the scene a theatrical, tragic air."
3. "It is easy to love nature in its peaceful and consoling moments, but one must love it in its furies too."

THINKING AND WRITING

Writing a Descriptive Essay

Write a descriptive essay that you could read as a radio news report. Write about the forest fire at Sierra Madre from a human-interest angle —that is, based on the feelings and reactions of the people the fire affected. Refer to the list of interview questions that you wrote. Write answers that people might give to them. Develop these answers into your account. When you finish your first draft, check to see that you included descriptive details and figurative language. Finally, proofread your essay and deliver it to your classmates.

Closure and Extension

ANSWERS TO THINKING ABOUT THE SELECTION

Recalling

1. The forest fire takes place in the Sierra Madre mountains. The writer begins reporting at night on the fire, which lasts for a week.
2. The writer responds to the fire by making coffee for the firefighters, packing to evacuate the area, helping the children next door to evacuate, and answering telephone calls.
3. The forest fire has these effects: people were evacuated; at least twelve thousand acres of forest and countless homes were burned; and once the January floods came, mudslides occurred down the mountains that were denuded of trees.

Interpreting

4. A fire is particularly dangerous in this setting because the mountains, bare of trees, "cannot hold the rains and slide down bringing rocks and mud."
5. It tells you that she values her writing more than any material object.

Applying

6. Answers will differ. Suggested Response:
   a. When a natural disaster occurs, have a telephone committee contact volunteers.
   b. Have volunteer groups of firefighters, police, and medical personnel come to the scene of a natural disaster.
   c. Have the community gather in a designated safe place that is equipped with supplies.

ANSWERS TO ANALYZING LITERATURE

1. Two examples of figurative language containing the words *like* or *as* are the following:
   a. "The flames, driven by hot Santa Ana winds from the desert, were as tall as the tallest trees . . ."
   b. "The fire was now like a ring around Sierra Madre . . ."
2. Answers will differ. Suggested Responses:
   a. "It would rush along and suddenly leap over a road, a trail, like a monster, devouring all in its path."
   b. "The dragon tongues of flames devouring . . ."
3. Answers will differ. Suggested Response:
   "It was as if the fire had come from the bowels of the earth, like that of a fiery volcano."

ANSWERS TO CRITICAL THINKING AND READING

1. Fact. This could be checked by interviewing the Campion children.
2. Opinion. Someone else might think the flares gave the scene a festive air.
3. Opinion. Someone else might think that nature in its furies is more enthralling.

Challenge What is a news reporter's responsibility when covering natural disasters? What roles does fact and opinion play in the media coverage?

THINKING AND WRITING

Publishing Student Writing

You might select several of the best essays and have students tape record them. You could then play the tapes for the class.

Focus

More About the Author Bernard DeVoto was an English professor who wrote histories of the American West and who made Mark Twain his major interest. What kind of influence would you expect these factors to have on DeVoto's writing?

Literary Focus An expository essay is informative, as opposed to a persuasive, descriptive, or humorous essay. Ask students for examples of topics that might be discussed in an expository essay.

Look For For your **less advanced** students, you may first want to review the concepts of main idea and supporting details on page 461.

Writing/Prior Knowledge The United States has been called a "melting pot" of cultures. Discuss what this means before having students do the writing assignment.

Vocabulary For your **less advanced** students, first give these words in context to help them guess their meaning.

GUIDE FOR READING

The Indian All Around Us

Bernard DeVoto (1897–1955) was born in Ogden, Utah, and became a respected critic, novelist, editor, and magazine columnist during his varied literary career. Above all, however, Bernard DeVoto was a historian. His book *Across the Wide Missouri,* one of a series of books about America's westward movement, received the Pulitzer Prize for history in 1948. In his essay "The Indian All Around Us," Bernard DeVoto explains the history of many Native American words that are familiar to people of the United States.

Expository Essay

An **expository essay** is a short nonfiction piece that explains or gives information about a topic. The word *expository,* in fact, simply means to give information about something or to explain what is difficult to understand. In expository essays, writers not only explain information but may also express a particular point of view or opinion on their topic.

Look For

As you read "The Indian All Around Us," look for the information the writer gives to help you understand his topic. What words come from the Native Americans? What do you learn about these words?

Writing

Work with a group of students. Select a culture, such as Spanish or German, from which many words have come into English. You may want to choose your own cultural heritage. In the center of a piece of paper, write the culture you have chosen and circle it. Think of a number of words that this culture has added to English. Include place names, foods, objects, games, and so forth. Write these words around the circled word, circling each one and drawing a line from it to the center of the word cluster.

Vocabulary

Knowing the following words will help you as you read "The Indian All Around Us."

versatile (vʉr′ sə t'l) *adj.*: Having many uses (p. 457)

tangible (tan′ jəb'l) *adj.*: Capable of being perceived or of being precisely identified (p. 457)

alkaloid (al′ kə loid′) *adj.*: Referring to certain bitter substances found chiefly in plants (p. 458)

gutturals (gut′ ər əlz) *n.*: Sounds produced in the throat (p. 460)

Objectives

1 To understand the expository essay
2 To identify the main idea and supporting details
3 To investigate word origins
4 To write an expository essay

Support Material

Teaching Portfolio

Teacher Backup, pp. 571–574
Grammar in Action Worksheet, *Using Commas*, pp. 575–576
Usage and Mechanics Worksheet, p. 577
Vocabulary Check, p. 578
Analyzing Literature Worksheet, *Understanding an Expository Essay*, p. 579
Critical Thinking and Reading Worksheet, *Identifying Main Idea*, p. 580
Selection Test, pp. 581–582
Art Transparency 9, *The Indian Trapper* by Frederic Remington

The Indian All Around Us

Bernard DeVoto

1 The Europeans who developed into the Americans took over from the Indians many things besides their continent. Look at a few: tobacco, corn, potatoes, beans (kidney, string and lima and therefore succotash), tomatoes, sweet potatoes, squash, popcorn and peanuts, chocolate, pineapples, hominy, Jerusalem artichokes, maple sugar. Moccasins, snowshoes, toboggans, hammocks, ipecac,[1] quinine, the crew haircut, goggles to prevent snow blindness—these are all Indian in origin. So is the versatile boat that helped the white man occupy the continent, the birch-bark canoe, and the custom canoeists have of painting designs on its bow.

PAINTED BUFFALO HIDE SHIELD
Jémez, New Mexico
Museum of the American Indian

A list of familiar but less important plants, foods and implements would run to several hundred items. Another long list would be needed to enumerate less tangible Indian contributions to our culture, such as arts, crafts, designs, ideas, beliefs, superstitions and even profanity. But there is something far more familiar, something that is always at hand and is used daily by every American and Canadian without awareness that it is Indian: a large vocabulary.

Glance back over the first paragraph. "Potato" is an Indian word, so is "tobacco," and if "corn" is not, the word "maize" is and we used it for a long time, as the English do still. Some Indians chewed tobacco, some used snuff, nearly all smoked pipes or cigars or cigarettes, and the white man gladly adopted all forms of the habit. But he spoke of "drinking" tobacco, instead of smoking it, for a long time. Squash, hominy, ipecac, quinine, hammock, chocolate, canoe are all common nouns that have come into the English—or rather the American—language from Indian languages. Sometimes the word has changed on the way, perhaps only a little as with "potato," which was something like "batata" in the original, or sometimes a great deal, as with "cocoa,"

1. **ipecac** (ip′ ə kák′) *n.*: A medicine made from certain dried roots.

Humanities Note

Fine art, *Painted Buffalo Hide Shield,* Jemez, New Mexico. Of the art created by the Plains Indians, the best known is painting on animal hides. The Plains Indians used earth pigments, especially yellow, brown, and red. The color green was made from vegetable matter, and black from burned wood or bone. The Indians used a thin glue of boiled hide scrapings as a binder. Their tool for applying the paint was a semiresilient pointed object, such as the spongy part of a bone.

A warrior highly prized his shield, which was believed to have magical powers. A warrior painted his shield, say some historians, with a design received in a vision and whose meaning only he knew.

1. What kind of design would you create for a shield?
2. What examples can you suggest of other weapons or tools decorated with designs?

Master Teacher Note Bring in and play a recording of native American music. Suggestions are "Authentic Music of the American Indians," Everest 3450; and "Music of the Plains Apache," Folkways 4252.

Purpose-Setting Question How has the native American culture affected our everyday lives?

Thematic Idea Another selection with the theme of other cultures' effects on American language is "A to Z in Foods as Metaphors" by Mimi Sheraton on page 491.

1 **Enrichment** Early European settlers in America were those who established Spanish missions in California in the 1500's, those who founded Jamestown, Virginia in 1607, and Pilgrims who founded Plymouth Colony in Massachusetts in 1620.

Master Teacher Note The English language has been influenced by the language of other cultures. Look at Art Transparency 8, "The Indian Trapper" by Frederic Remington in the Teaching Portfolio. Considering the way Indians lived and the help they gave some American settlers, what kinds of words would students expect to have come into common English use from Indian languages? In "The Indian All Around Us," the author discusses some of these words.

Motivation/Prior Knowledge Ask students to list all the geographical names from your state that reflect Native Americans.

Humanities Note

Fine art, *Painted Bowl: Deer Figure,* Mimbres, New Mexico. Southwestern Native American pottery was usually made by women. Each potter would dig her clay near her village, perhaps asking permission of the earth to do so. The potter decorated her bowls with the traditional patterns of her village.

The animal design in the center of this bowl probably represents a story. Notice how the potter skillfully matched the deer figure to the design around the rim.

1. What importance do you think deer had in the native American culture?
2. Create your own story to explain the decoration on this bowl.

2 **Discussion** What does this tell you about the lives of some native Americans?

PAINTED BOWL: DEER FIGURE
Mimbres, New Mexico
Museum of the American Indian

which began as, approximately, "cacahuatl."

Sometimes, too, we have changed the meaning. "Succotash" is a rendering of a Narraganset word that meant an ear of corn. The dish that the Indians ate was exactly what we call succotash today, though an Indian woman was likely to vary it as much as we do stew, by tossing in any leftovers she happened to have on hand. Similarly with "quinine." This is a modern word, made up by the scientists who first isolated the alkaloid substance from cinchona bark[2], but they derived it from the botanical name of the genus, which in turn was derived from the Indian name for it, "quinquina." The Indians, of course, used a decoction[3] made from the bark.

Put on your moccasins and take a walk in the country. If it is a cold day and you wear a mackinaw, your jacket will be as Indian as your footwear, though "mackinaw" originally meant a heavy blanket of fine quality and, usually, bright colors. On your walk you may smell a skunk, see a raccoon or possum, hear the call of a moose. Depending on what part of the country you are in, you may see a chipmunk, muskrat, woodchuck or coyote. The names of all these animals are Indian words. (A moose is "he who eats off," that is, who browses on leaves. A raccoon is "he who scratches with his hands.") You may see hickory trees or catalpas,[4] pecans or mesquite,[5] and these too are Indian words. At the right season and place you may eat persimmons or pawpaws or scuppernongs.[6] All the breads and most of the puddings we make from cornmeal originated with the Indians but we haven't kept many of the original names, except "pone."

On a Cape Cod beach you may see clammers digging quahogs,[7] or as a Cape Codder would say, "coehoggin'." The Pilgrims learned the name and the method of getting
at them from the Indians: they even learned 2
the technique of steaming them with seaweed that we practice at clambakes. The muskellunge[8] and the terrapin[9] were named for us by Indians. Your children may build a wigwam to play in—it was a brush hut or a lodge covered with bark—or they may ask you to buy them a tepee, which was original-

2. cinchona (sin kō′ nə) **bark** *n.*: bark from certain tropical South American trees.
3. decoction (di käk′ shən) *n.*: An extract or flavor produced by boiling.

4. catalpas (kə tal′ pəs) *n.*: American and Asiatic trees with large, heart-shaped leaves, trumpet-shaped flowers, and beanlike pods.
5. mesquite (mes kēt′) *n.*: Thorny trees or shrubs common in the southwest U.S. and in Mexico.
6. pawpaws, scuppernongs *n.*: Kinds of fruit.
7. quahogs (kwô′ hôgz) *n.*: Edible clams of the east coast of North America.
8. muskellunge (mus′ kə lunj) *n.*: A very large pike fish of the Great Lakes and upper Mississippi drainages.
9. terrapin (ter′ ə pin) *n.*: Several kinds of North American turtles.

Grammar in Action

Writers use **commas** to separate three or more words, phrases, or clauses in a **series.** The comma tells the reader to take a slight pause before reading the next item.

Notice the commas in the following sentences:

Series of Words:
Consider such rivers as the Arkansas, Ohio, Mohawk, Wisconsin, Rappahannock, Minnesota, Merrimack, Mississippi, Missouri and Suwannee.

Squash, hominy, ipecac, quinine, hammock, chocolate, canoe are all common nouns that have come into the English—or rather the American—language from Indian languages.

Series of Phrases:
Indian words have been used for names of mountains, of rivers, of towns.

Series of Clauses:
"Succotash" began as "musickwautash," "hominy" as

ly made of buffalo hide but can be canvas now. They may chase one another with tomahawks. And we all go to barbecues.

The people earliest in contact with the Indians found all these words useful, but some Indian sounds they found hard to pronounce, such as the *tl* at the end of many words in Mexico and the Southwest. That is why "coyotl" became "coyote" and "tomatl" our tomato. Or accidental resemblances to English words might deceive them, as with "muskrat." The animal does look like a rat and has musk glands, but the Indian word was "musquash," which means "it is red."

Some words were simply too long. "Succotash" began as "musickwautash," "hominy" as "rockahominy," and "mackinaw" as "michilimackinac." (The last, of course, was the name given to the strait, the fort,
3 the island, and ended as the name of a
blanket and a jacket because the fort was a trading post.) At that, these are comparatively short; remember the lake in Massachusetts whose name is Chargoggagoggmanchaugagoggchaubunagungamaugg.[10]

Twenty-six of our states have Indian names, as have scores of cities, towns, lakes, rivers and mountains. In Maine are Kennebec, Penobscot, Androscoggin, Piscataqua, Wiscasset and many others, from Arowsic to Sytopilock by way of Mattawamkeag. California, noted for its Spanish names, still is well supplied with such native ones as Yosemite, Mojave, Sequoia, Truckee, Tahoe, Siskiyou. Washington has Yakima, Walla Walla, Spokane, Snoqualmie, Wenatchee; and Florida has Okeechobee, Seminole, Manitee, Ocala and as many more as would fill a page. So with all the other states.

Consider such rivers as the Arkansas, Ohio, Mohawk, Wisconsin, Rappahannock, Minnesota, Merrimack, Mississippi, Missouri and Suwannee. Or such lakes as Ontario, Cayuga, Winnipesaukee, Memphremagog, Winnebago. Or such mountain ranges and peaks as Allegheny, Wichita, Wasatch, Shasta, Katahdin. Or cities: Milwaukee, Chattanooga, Sandusky.

The meaning of such names is not always clear. Tourist bureaus like to make up
translations like bower-of-the-laughing- 4
princess or land-of-the-sky-blue-water, but Indians were as practical-minded as anyone

JAR WITH ANIMAL HEAD HANDLE
Socorro County, New Mexico
Museum of the American Indian

10. **Char . . . maugg:** The translation is "You fish your side of the lake, we'll fish our side, and nobody fishes in the middle."

3 **Critical Thinking and Reading** What is the main idea in this paragraph? What are the supporting details?

4 **Discussion** Why might a tourist bureau like to make up such fanciful translations?

Humanities Note

Fine art, *Jar with Animal Head Handle,* Socorro County, New Mexico. Native Americans, before the arrival of Europeans and the wheel, made pottery by the coil method. After building a vessel, the potter smoothed the surface by rubbing and scraping with a special paddle. Each village had its own subtly different set of pottery shapes, painted designs, and colors. Patterns and designs were handed down from generation to generation, sometimes for hundreds of years. Much of our knowledge of ancient Native Americans comes from the study of designs painted on jars such as this.

1. Considering the design and color of this jar, what do you think it was used for?
2. What kind of design and colors do you think would be used for a jar intended for use in a funeral or a burial?

"rockahominy," and "mackinaw" as "mickilimackinac."

Some Indians chewed tobacco, some used snuff, nearly all smoked pipes or cigars or cigarettes. . . .

Student Activity. American English has been enriched by words from many other languages. Think about the words from other languages you hear every day in the area where you live. Perhaps these words are from Spanish, from French, or from the American Indian languages. Write a paragraph telling about these words. Be sure to use commas to separate items in a series.

5 **Discussion** What other languages are considered to have a beautiful sound? Which are known to sound guttural?

6 **Discussion** What do you think is the most valuable heritage native Americans have given our society?

Reader's Response Why do you think it is important to preserve original names?

else and usually used a word that would identify the place. Our unpoetic pioneers christened dozens of streams Mud Creek or Muddy River—and that is about what Missouri means. The Sauk or Kickapoo word that gave Chicago its name had something to do with a strong smell. There may be some truth in the contention of rival cities that it meant "place of the skunks," but more likely it meant "place where wild onions grow." Kentucky does not mean "dark and bloody ground" as our sentimental legend says, but merely "place of meadows," which shows that the blue grass impressed Indians, too. Niagara means "point of land that is cut in two." Potomac means "something brought." Since the thing brought was probably tribute, perhaps in wampum,[11] we would not be far off if we were to render it "place where we pay taxes."

5 Quite apart from their meaning, such words as Kentucky, Niagara and Potomac are beautiful just as sounds. Though we usually take it for granted, the beauty of our Indian place names impresses foreign visitors. But since some Indian languages abounded with harsh sounds or gutturals, this beauty is unevenly distributed. In New England such names as Ogunquit, Megantic and Naugatuck are commoner than such more pleasing ones as Housatonic, Narragansett and Merrimack. The Pacific Northwest is overbalanced with harsh sounds like Nootka, Klamath, Klickitat and Clackamas, though it has its share of more agreeable ones—Tillamook, for instance, and Umatilla, Willamette, Multnomah. (Be sure to pronounce Willamette right: accent the second syllable.)

Open vowels were abundant in the languages spoken in the southeastern states, so that portion of the map is thickly sown with delightful names. Alabama, Pensacola, Tuscaloosa, Savannah, Okefenokee, Chattahoochee, Sarasota, Ocala, Roanoke—they are charming words, pleasant to speak, pleasanter to hear. One could sing a child to sleep with a poem composed of just such names. In New York, if Skaneateles twists the tongue, Seneca glides smoothly from it and so do Tonawanda, Tuscarora, Oneonta, Saratoga, Genessee, Lackawanna, even Chautauqua and Canajoharie.

What is the most beautiful Indian place name? A surprising number of English writers have argued that question in travel books. No one's choice can be binding on anyone else. But there is a way of making a kind of answer: you can count the recorded votes. In what is written about the subject certain names appear repeatedly. Niagara and Tuscarora and Otsego are on nearly all the lists. So are Savannah and Potomac, Catawba, Wichita and Shenandoah.

But the five that are most often mentioned are all in Pennsylvania. That state has its Allegheny and Lackawanna, and many other musical names like Aliquippa, Towanda, Punxsutawney. But five others run away from them all. Wyoming (which moved a long way west and named a state)[12] and Conestoga and Monongahela seem to be less universally delightful than the two finalists, Juniata and Susquehanna. For 150 years, most of those who have written on the subject have ended with these two, and in the outcome Juniata usually takes second place. According to the write-in vote, then, the most beautiful place name in the United States is Susquehanna. It may be ungracious to remember that it first came into the language as "Saquesahannock."

11. wampum (wäm′ pəm) *n.*: Small beads made of shells and used by North American Indians as money and as ornaments.

12. which . . . state: The name Wyoming was originally given to a valley in Pennsylvania.

THINKING ABOUT THE SELECTION

Recalling

1. What is an important native American contribution to life in the United States that we use every day? Explain the importance of this contribution.
2. Name two reasons why some Indian words were changed before becoming part of English.

Interpreting

3. How would you interpret the title, "The Indian All Around Us"?
4. Why does the writer tell you to "put on your moccasins and take a walk in the country"?

Applying

5. What foods mentioned in the essay are a regular part of your diet?
6. Based on what you learned in this essay, what criteria could you apply when you are naming something?

ANALYZING LITERATURE

Understanding an Expository Essay

Expository essays are usually written to inform or to explain. But many expository essays do both. For example, "The Indian All Around Us" not only informs us that the Indian word *coyotl* was changed to the American word *coyote,* but it also explains the reason why: because people found the *tl* sound hard to pronounce.

Give three examples of this essay informing the reader.

CRITICAL THINKING AND READING

Identifying Main Ideas

In an expository essay, each paragraph usually has a main idea. Looking again at the fourth paragraph of "The Indian All Around Us," for example, the main idea of it is expressed in the first sentence: "Sometimes, too, we have changed the meaning." **Main ideas** are general statements that need supporting details, such as specific examples or reasons, to explain them. For example, DeVoto supports the main idea in the fourth paragraph with two specific examples —succotash and quinine.

Read the eleventh paragraph that begins "The meaning of such names."

1. What is the main idea of the paragraph?
2. List the supporting details that appear in the paragraph.

UNDERSTANDING LANGUAGE

Investigating Word Origins

If you look at a map of the United States, you will find many place names that have their origins in other languages as well as in the names of famous people. For example, the *Rio Grande* (river) comes from the Spanish words meaning "great river." The city of Lincoln, Nebraska, was named for President Abraham Lincoln.

1. Using a map of your own state, find five place names and identify their origins—the language or the famous person from which the name was taken.
2. In a dictionary, look up the meanings of three of the names you found.

THINKING AND WRITING

Writing an Expository Essay

Write an expository essay about the contributions a particular culture has made to life in the United States. Before you write, be sure that you have narrowed your topic to fit what you can say in a short essay. For example, you may want to narrow your topic to foods, a sport, or place names. Revise your essay, making sure you have supported your main ideas. Then proofread your essay and share it with your classmates.

Closure and Extension

ANSWERS TO THINKING ABOUT THE SELECTION

Recalling

1. An important native American contribution to life in the United States that we use every day is vocabulary. This contribution is important because it provides names for many fundamental aspects of our life.
2. Two reasons why some Indian words were changed before becoming part of English are that some of the Indian sounds, such as *tl* at the end of many words, are hard to pronounce; and that some words were simply too long.

Interpreting

3. Answers will differ. Suggested Response: The title implies that there are many Indian influences, some of which we may not be aware, that affect our everyday lives.
4. Answers will differ. Suggested Response: The moccasins you would wear, along with some other clothing, and many of the things you would see have names that come from the Indian.

Applying

5. Answers will differ.
6. Answers will differ. Suggested Response: When naming something, you could apply the criteria that the name should be easy to pronounce and not long, the name should reflect the meaning of the thing, and the sound of the name should be beautiful.

ANSWERS TO ANALYZING LITERATURE

Answers will differ. Suggested Responses:

a. Sometimes the original Indian word has changed over time.
b. Sometimes we have changed the meaning of the original Indian word.
c. "Twenty-six of our states have Indian names, as have scores of cities, towns, lakes, rivers and mountains."

ANSWERS TO CRITICAL THINKING AND READING

1. The main idea of the paragraph is "For place names, Indians usually used a practical word that would identify the place."
2. The supporting details in this paragraph are that the Indians christened many streams Mud Creek or Muddy River, which is what Missouri means; that the Indian "word that gave Chicago its name had something to do with a strong smell;" that Kentucky means "place of meadows"; that Niagara means "point of land that is cut in two"; and Potomac means "something brought."

Challenge Native Americans had the opportunity to name their natural surroundings. If you had been the first to see a river, mountain, or natural land formation in your area, what would you name it?

ANSWERS TO UNDERSTANDING LANGUAGE

1. Answers will differ, depending on the state.
2. Answers will differ, depending on answers to #1.

THINKING AND WRITING

Publishing Student Writing

Ask for student volunteers to read their essays aloud, in front of the class or perhaps in groups.

Focus

More About the Author How does Robert MacNeil's experience as a co-host of an in-depth news program make him a good critic of television? How might it detract from his credibility?

Literary Focus Point out to students that we often use persuasive techniques—arguments or reasons to support our views, plus emotive language—in our everyday lives. Ask students for instances when they have used persuasion.

Look For Ask students what are their own opinions about television. What reasons do they have for their views?

Writing/Prior Knowledge Have students list the different ways besides television in which they can be informed about the news or scientific advances and can be entertained. Have them think about the approximate amount of time they spend in those ways, as opposed to watching television. Then have them complete the writing assignment.

Vocabulary Have your **more advanced** students write single sentences in which they use each word with either an antonym or a group of words suggesting the opposite meaning. Example: The kaleidoscopic view seen from the window of the speeding train was more stimulating than the static view seen when the train was more stimulating than the static view seen when the train was stopped.

GUIDE FOR READING

The Trouble with Television

Robert MacNeil (1931–   ) was born in Montreal, Canada. He is a radio and television journalist. He has worked for NBC radio and for the British Broadcasting Corporation. In the mid-1970's, MacNeil came to public television station WNET to host his own news analysis program, which has grown into the highly regarded *MacNeil/Lehrer Newshour.* This differs from other news programs by offering more in-depth reports on important issues. In the following essay, MacNeil criticizes American television programming.

Persuasive Essay

A **persuasive essay** is a short nonfiction composition in which a writer presents his or her views in order to convince you to accept the author's opinion or to act a certain way. Since you may not share the writer's opinion, the writer usually offers arguments, or reasons, to support the position. Because you may not care enough to take any action, the writer tries to stir your concern and emotions so that you will act.

Look For

As you read "The Trouble with Television," look for ways MacNeil tries to persuade you about the value of television. Are the arguments convincing?

Writing

Write down the amount of time you spend watching different types of programs, such as news, science specials, situation comedies, quiz shows, and so on. Which programs do you get the most from? List possible alternatives to watching television.

Vocabulary

Knowing the following words will help you as you read "The Trouble with Television."

gratification (grat' ə fi kā' shən) *n.*: The act of pleasing or satisfying (p. 463)
diverts (də vʉrts') *v.*: Distracts (p. 463)
kaleidoscopic (kə lī' də skäp' ik) *adj.*: Constantly changing (p. 463)
usurps (yo͞o sʉrps') *v.*: Takes over (p. 463)
medium (mē' dē əm) *n.*: Means of communication; television (p. 464)
august (ô gust') *adj.*: Honored (p. 464)
pervading (pər vād' iŋ) *v.*: Spreading throughout (p. 465)
trivial (triv' ē əl) *adj.*: Of little importance (p. 465)

Objectives

1. To understand the persuasive essay
2. To recognize connotative language
3. To use combining forms
4. To write a persuasive essay

Support Material

Teaching Portfolio
Teacher Backup, pp. 583–585
Grammar in Action Worksheet, *Using Topic Sentences,* pp. 586–587
Usage and Mechanics Worksheet, p. 588
Vocabulary Check, p. 589
Analyzing Literature Worksheet, *Understanding the Persuasive Essay,* p. 590
Language Worksheet, *Choosing the Meaning that Fits the Context,* p. 591
Selection Test, pp. 592–593

The Trouble with Television

Robert MacNeil

It is difficult to escape the influence of television. If you fit the statistical averages, by the age of 20 you will have been exposed to at least 20,000 hours of television. You
1, 2 can add 10,000 hours for each decade you have lived after the age of 20. The only things Americans do more than watch television are work and sleep.

Calculate for a moment what could be done with even a part of those hours. Five thousand hours, I am told, are what a typical college undergraduate spends working
3 on a bachelor's degree. In 10,000 hours you could have learned enough to become an astronomer or engineer. You could have learned several languages fluently. If it appealed to you, you could be reading Homer[1] in the original Greek or Dostoevski[2] in Russian. If it didn't, you could have walked around the world and written a book about it.

The trouble with television is that it
4 discourages concentration. Almost anything interesting and rewarding in life requires some constructive, consistently applied effort. The dullest, the least gifted of us can achieve things that seem miraculous to those who never concentrate on anything. But television encourages us to apply no effort. It sells us instant gratification. It diverts us only to divert, to make the time pass without pain.

Television's variety becomes a narcotic,[3] not a stimulus.[4] Its serial, kaleidoscopic exposures force us to follow its lead. The viewer is on a perpetual guided tour: thirty minutes at the museum, thirty at the cathedral, then back on the bus to the next attraction—except on television, typically, the spans allotted are on the order of minutes or seconds, and the chosen delights are more often car crashes and people killing one another. In short, a lot of television usurps one of the most precious of all human gifts, the ability to focus your attention yourself, rather than just passively surrender it.

Capturing your attention—and holding it—is the prime motive of most television programming and enhances its role as a profitable advertising vehicle. Programmers
live in constant fear of losing anyone's 5
attention—anyone's. The surest way to

1. **Homer** (hō′ mər): Greek epic poet of the eighth century B.C.
2. **Dostoevski** (dôs′ tô yef′ skē): Fyodor (fyô′ dôr) Mikhailovich (mi khī′ lô vich) Dostoevski (1821–1881), Russian novelist.
3. **narcotic** (när kät′ ik) *n.*: Something that has a soothing effect.
4. **stimulus** (stim′ yə ləs) *n.*: Something that rouses to action.

Presentation

Motivation/Prior Knowledge Ask students to think about the influence television has had in their lives. How would they describe its place and its impact?

Master Teacher Note You may want to bring and share with students any cartoons you find that show people being influenced by television.

Thematic Idea Another selection that deals with the disadvantages of technology is "Dial Versus Digital" on page 477.

Purpose-Setting Question What reasons does the writer give for questioning the value of television in our society?

1 **Discussion** Ask students how true this is for them. Consider that mini portable televisions can be taken virtually anywhere and that there is widespread use of cable television, video cassette recorders, and closed-circuit television.

2 **Literary Focus** Persuasive essays are often written in the third person, but can be written in the first person, with the writer speaking as "I."

3 **Discussion** What else could be accomplished within 20,000 hours?

4 **Discussion** Ask students if this is always true. What about the use of television for educational or business purposes?

5 **Clarification** The reasons they fear losing anyone's attention is that advertising pays for much of television, and advertisers want to know that they are reaching a large audience.

Humanities Note

Fine art, *Afternoon Television,* 1965, by Maxwell Hendler. Maxwell Hendler (1938–) was born in St. Louis, Missouri. He studied at the University of California in Los Angeles and taught at California State University and the Art Center College of Design in Pasadena.

Hendler has exhibited his work, which has been labeled "realism," at the Ceeje Gallery in Los Angeles, the Metropolitan Museum of Art in New York, the Los Angeles County Museum of Art, and the Robert Miller Gallery in New York.

Although at first this picture seems to be an imitation of a camera image, the subject matter, attention to detail, and use of color and light seem to go beyond reality.

1. There are no people in this picture, except for the television image, and yet do you feel the presence of someone? Who might this person be?
2. What do you think the artist is saying about television in this painting?

6 **Clarification** David Sarnoff (1891–1971) was one of the first businessmen to see the full possibilities of using radio and television for entertainment. He was executive president of the Radio Corporation of America from 1930 to 1948 and was chairman of the board from 1947 to 1970.

AFTERNOON TELEVISION
Maxwell Hendler
The Metropolitan Museum of Art

avoid doing so is to keep everything brief, not to strain the attention of anyone but instead to provide constant stimulation through variety, novelty, action and movement. Quite simply, television operates on the appeal to the short attention span.

It is simply the easiest way out. But it has come to be regarded as a given, as inherent[5] in the medium itself: as an imperative, as though General Sarnoff, or one of 6
the other august pioneers of video, had be-

5. **inherent** (in hir′ ənt) *adj.*: Natural.

Grammar in Action

Good writers begin every paragraph with a **topic sentence,** stating the main idea or topic of the paragraph. Although the topic sentence is not necessarily the first sentence of the paragraph, it should be somewhere in the beginning of the paragraph. The sentences in the paragraph should relate closely to the topic sentence. Otherwise, the paragraph will lack clarity, focus, and coherence.

Although it is always important to use topic sentences, it is especially important when writing to persuade, as MacNeil does in "The Trouble with Television." The more focused your writing, the more persuasive it is likely to be. Your audience must have a clear idea of what you are "selling" them before they will be convinced. For example, MacNeil believes that television news communicates inefficiently. Here is his topic sentence: "In the case of news, this practice, in my view, results in inefficient communication." In the sentences following his topic sentence he supports his assertion.

queathed to us tablets of stone commanding that nothing in television shall ever require more than a few moments' concentration.

In its place that is fine. Who can quarrel with a medium that so brilliantly packages escapist entertainment as a mass-marketing tool? But I see its values now pervading this nation and its life. It has become fashionable to think that, like fast food, fast ideas are the way to get to a fast-moving, impatient public.

In the case of news, this practice, in my view, results in inefficient communication. I question how much of television's nightly news effort is really absorbable and understandable. Much of it is what has been aptly described as "machine gunning with scraps." I think its technique fights coherence.[6] I think it tends to make things ultimately boring and dismissable (unless they are accompanied by horrifying pictures) because almost anything is boring and dismissable if you know almost nothing about it.

I believe that TV's appeal to the short attention span is not only inefficient communication but decivilizing as well. Consider the casual assumptions that television tends to cultivate: that complexity must be avoided, that visual stimulation is a substitute for thought, that verbal precision is an anachronism.[7] It may be old-fashioned, but I was taught that thought is words, arranged in grammatically precise ways.

There is a crisis of literacy in this country. One study estimates that some 30 million adult Americans are "functionally illiterate" and cannot read or write well enough to answer a want ad or understand the instructions on a medicine bottle.

Literacy may not be an inalienable human right, but it is one that the highly literate Founding Fathers might not have found unreasonable or even unattainable. We are not only not attaining it as a nation, statistically speaking, but we are falling further and further short of attaining it. And, while I would not be so simplistic as to suggest that television is the cause, I believe it contributes and is an influence.

Everything about this nation—the structure of the society, its forms of family organization, its economy, its place in the world—has become more complex, not less. Yet its dominating communications instrument, its principal form of national linkage, is one that sells neat resolutions to human problems that usually have no neat resolutions. It is all symbolized in my mind by the hugely successful art form that television has made central to the culture, the thirty-second commercial: the tiny drama of the earnest housewife who finds happiness in choosing the right toothpaste.

When before in human history has so much humanity collectively surrendered so much of its leisure to one toy, one mass diversion? When before has virtually an entire nation surrendered itself wholesale to a medium for selling?

Some years ago Yale University law professor Charles L. Black, Jr. wrote: ". . . forced feeding on trivial fare is not itself a trivial matter." I think this society is being force fed with trivial fare, and I fear that the effects on our habits of mind, our language, our tolerance for effort, and our appetite for complexity are only dimly perceived. If I am wrong, we will have done no harm to look at the issue skeptically and critically, to consider how we should be resisting it. I hope you will join with me in doing so.

---

6. coherence (kō hir′ əns) *n.*: The quality of being connected in an intelligible way.

7. anachronism (ə nak′ rə niz′m) *n.*: Anything that seems to be out of its proper place in history.

7 **Discussion** What does this phrase mean?

8 **Discussion** Ask students for examples of television's lack of complexity. (One example is the use of the 10- to 90-second spot announcement by political candidates.)

Reader's Response What is your opinion of television? What advantages and disadvantages are there to television?

Closure and Extension

(Questions begin on page 466.)

ANSWERS TO THINKING ABOUT THE SELECTION

Recalling

1. When the average viewer reaches the age of twenty, he or she has watched at least 20,000 hours of television.
2. MacNeil believes the major trouble with television is that as a passive activity it discourages concentration.
3. MacNeil's three assumptions that contribute to television's "decivilizing" are the following:
   a. complexity must be avoided;
   b. visual stimulation is a substitute for thought; and
   c. verbal precision is an anachronism.

Interpreting

4. MacNeil is trying to persuade you to view television critically and to cut down on the amount of time you spend watching television.
5. Answers will differ. Suggested Response: MacNeil might prefer people to pursue further education, to be more active in general, and to devote more concentration and attention to what is around them.
6. Answers will differ. Suggested Response: He might institute longer program times, a more complex approach to more complicated issues, and greater verbal precision.

Student Activity 1. Evaluate the success of each of MacNeil's topic sentences in "The Trouble with Television."

Student Activity 2. Write a reaction to MacNeil's essay. Be sure to use clear, focussed, specific topic sentences.

(Answers begin on p. 465.)

Applying

7. Answers will differ. Suggested Response: Television could be improved by following the changes suggested in answers to Question 6, by using it for educational purposes, and by televising more cultural events. It is a valuable tool for society in that it reaches so many people and has great potential for educating.

ANSWERS TO CRITICAL THINKING AND READING

1. Answers will differ. Suggested Response: These words have a positive connotation and seem to suggest that studying for these professions would have been more beneficial than watching television.
2. Answers will differ. Suggested Response: This phrase has a negative connotation and seems to suggest that other activities—or even television programming—that require a longer attention span would be more beneficial.

ANSWERS TO UNDERSTANDING LANGUAGE

a. **teletype:** a telegraph in which the message is typed on a keyboard that sends electric signals to a machine that prints the words.
b. **telephone:** an instrument for sending sounds over distances by changing them into electric impulses that are sent through a wire and then changed back into sounds.
c. **telescope:** an instrument, containing lenses, for making distant objects seem nearer and larger.
d. **telex:** a teletypewriter with a telephone dial for making connections.

Challenge You might want to ask students to research and report on what the effect of violence on television is on our society.

THINKING ABOUT THE SELECTION

Recalling

1. When the average viewer reaches the age of twenty, how many hours of television has he or she watched?
2. According to MacNeil, what is the major trouble with television?
3. MacNeil states that television's appeal is "decivilizing." What three assumptions does he give that contribute to this decivilization?

Interpreting

4. What action is MacNeil trying to persuade you to take?
5. What do you think MacNeil would want people to do instead of watching television?
6. If MacNeil were the president of a commercial television network, what changes in the programming do you think he would make?

Applying

7. How do you think television could be improved? In what ways is it a valuable tool for society?

ANALYZING LITERATURE

Understanding the Persuasive Essay

A **persuasive essay** is nonfiction in which writers strive to make readers accept a certain way of thinking about an issue. Whether or not they are successful depends on how strong their reasons are and what facts they use.

1. Write down three points MacNeil makes that caused you to think again about watching television. Explain why each was effective.
2. Write down any points in the essay that are not persuasive. Explain why you think each is not effective.
3. Explain why MacNeil is or is not successful in persuading you to think carefully about and possibly change your television viewing habits.

CRITICAL THINKING AND READING

Recognizing Connotative Language

Persuasive writers often use words that provoke an emotional response in their readers. These words have certain **connotations,** or associated ideas and images, beyond their literal meanings. If the writer is supporting something, the words chosen will have positive connotations. If the writer opposes something, the words will be negative. For example, MacNeil states that television is a "narcotic," and that viewers "passively surrender" to it. Both of these words create negative images.

Explain what connotations the italicized words in the following sentences have for you.

1. "In 10,000 hours you could have learned enough to become an *astronomer* or *engineer*."
2. "Quite simply, television operates on the appeal to the short attention span. It is simply the *easiest way out*."

UNDERSTANDING LANGUAGE

Using Combining Forms

The combining form *tele* comes from Greek and means "far off." This form is often combined with other word parts to form new words. The word *television* consists of *tele* combined with *vision*. A television is the receiving set that receives pictures or visions from far off. Explain the meaning of each of the following words:

(a) teletype (c) telescope
(b) telephone (d) telex

THINKING AND WRITING

Writing a Persuasive Essay

Make a list of suggestions about programming that would make television viewing a more worthwhile experience. Write the suggestions in a letter to a television network or producer. When you have finished, check to be sure you have used the correct form for a business letter. Proofread it and prepare a final draft. Mail your letter if you wish.

Writing Across the Curriculum You might want to have students choose another aspect of modern technology and research it. They can report on how it affects our everyday lives and whether they think this effect is beneficial or not. Perhaps inform the social studies department of this assignment. Social studies teachers might provide guidance in conducting student research.

Essays in the Content Areas

PAUL HELLEU SKETCHING WITH HIS WIFE, 1889
John Singer Sargent
The Brooklyn Museum, Museum Collection Fund

Humanities Note

Fine Art; *Paul Helleu Sketching With His Wife,* 1889, by John Singer Sargent. John Singer Sargent (1856-1925) was born in Italy of American parents. Educated in a privileged, cosmopolitan fashion in the great cities of Europe, Sargent became one of the most influential and important portrait painters of his era. Members of high society and famous people were recorded by this virtuoso painter.

Paul Helleu, portrayed in this painting, was an important French painter and close friend of Sargent. This work was painted in New York at a time when Sargent was exploring the Impressionist technique. This sensitive rendering of the couple on a grassy bank was painted quickly, in the open air. The light on the grass is fragmented into colors that create a lively texture behind the figures. The light bathing the couple, however, seems to be more subtle and diffused, perhaps reflected from the water. Sargent painted his subjects with the poetry and charm that characterized American Impressionism. This was not to be his permanent style, rather it was a stage in his constantly evolving art.

Focus

More About the Author Hal Borland spent a great deal of time in the Southwest, the homeland of the Ute Indians. As a young man, Borland knew many Utes and learned much about nature from them. One of his works, *When the Legends Die,* tells the story of a young Indian boy brought up in the wilderness. After attending school and becoming a famous bronco rider, the young man returns to the wilderness to find happiness. Ask students to discuss the relationship between nature and personal fulfillment. How did the natural world help Borland to fulfill his potential as a writer?

Reading in the Content Areas Observation is an important skill to cultivate in life. Careful observation results in scientific discoveries, crime solving, and lifesaving. Think about all the professions that require people to observe things closely and accurately.

Look For Point out to students that this story combines observation and scientific knowledge. A naturalist must both observe and research in order to place observations in their correct context.

Writing/Prior Knowledge Have students think about how different this selection would have been if it were just observation with no background information. Then have them complete the freewriting assignment.

Vocabulary Most students will have no difficulty with these words. You might have them use each word in a sentence orally before reading the story.

GUIDE FOR READING

Shooting Stars

Hal Borland (1900–1978), born in Sterling, Nebraska, was a naturalist, a person who studies animals and plants. He worked as a reporter for the *Denver Post* and the *Brooklyn Times*. He was also a writer of documentary film scripts, radio scripts, and other nonfiction. Borland loved the outdoors. The National Audubon Society honored him by creating the Hál Borland Trail in Connecticut. Borland's essay "Shooting Stars" blends his fascination with nature and his ability to report facts in a clear, captivating manner.

Observation

One of the skills required of a naturalist is observation. **Observation** is the act of looking at or noticing an object or event carefully and objectively. When you observe, you try to concentrate only on what you see, not on what you feel, think, or conclude about it. Observing allows you to report or describe clearly and factually what happens.

Look For

As you read "Shooting Stars," notice the factual way in which the writer tends to report what he and others have observed. What do you learn about meteors as a result of these observations?

Writing

Choose an incident from nature to describe. First describe it objectively, or factually, reporting only what you see. Then describe it personally, including your own thoughts.

Vocabulary

horizon (hə rī′ zən) *n.*: The line that forms the apparent boundary between the earth and the sky (p. 469)
friction (frik′ shən) *n.*: The rubbing of the surface of one body against another (p. 469)
droves (drōvz) *n.*: Large numbers; crowds (p. 470)

Objectives

1 To observe an object carefully in order to describe it
2 To distinguish between observation and inference
3 To describe something without naming it
4 To investigate word origins

Support Material

Teaching Portfolio
Teacher Backup, pp. 595–597
Usage and Mechanics Worksheet, p. 598
Vocabulary Check, p. 599
Reading in the Content Areas Worksheet, *Understanding Observation,* p. 600
Critical Thinking and Reading Worksheet, *Recognizing Observation and Inference,* p. 601
Selection Test, pp. 602–603

Shooting Stars

Hal Borland

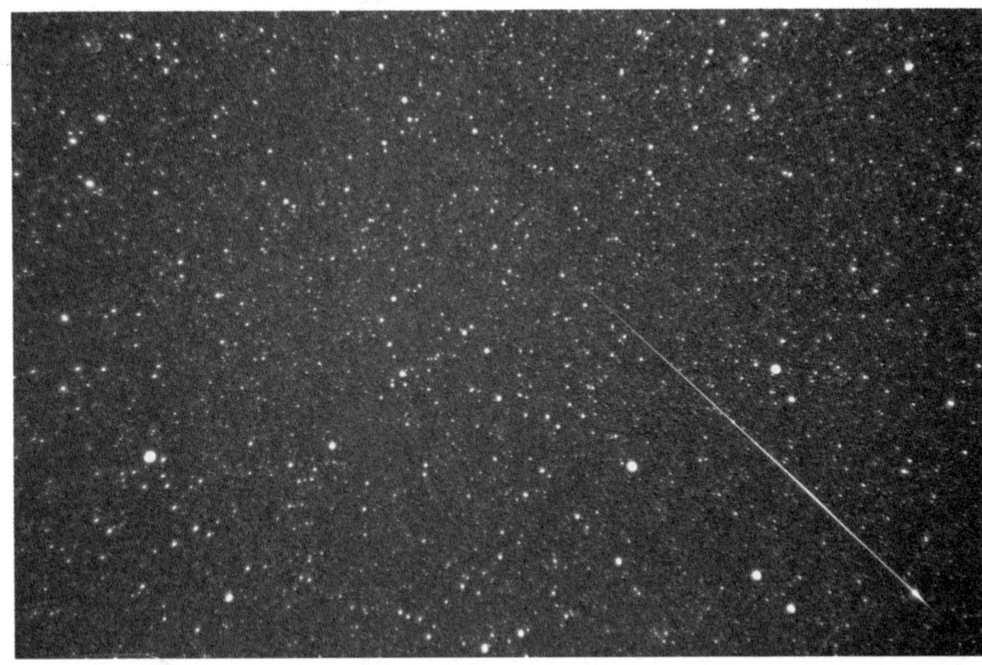

Most clear, dark nights you can see a shooting star, as we call it, if you keep looking. Those shooting stars are meteors. They are points of light that suddenly appear in the sky, like distant stars, race across the darkness, usually toward the horizon, and disappear.

For a long time nobody knew what a meteor was. But finally those who study stars and the sky decided that a meteor is a piece of a comet that exploded long ago. Those pieces are still wandering about the universe in huge, looping paths that follow the original comet's orbit. There are uncounted pieces of such comets out there in the depths of space. Periodically clusters of them come close to the earth's orbit, or path around the sun. Most meteors are small, probably only a few inches in diameter, but when they enter the earth's atmosphere the friction makes them white-hot. Then they look big as stars streaking across the darkness.

There are half a dozen meteor showers

Presentation

Motivation/Prior Knowledge Give students some background information on meteoroids, meteors, and meteorites. Meteoroids are chunks of stone or metal that orbit the sun. The streak of light produced by a burning meteoroid is called a meteor. A meteor that strikes Earth's surface is a meteorite. Ask those students who have seen meteors to describe what they saw. Have other students imagine what a meteor shower looks like. Is seeing a meteor or a meteor shower more frightening or exciting?

Thematic Idea Another selection that deals with a natural phenomenon is "Forest Fire" on page 453.

Purpose-Setting Question What role does observation play in this story?

1 **Discussion** Why might this be a problem in the city? What is Borland assuming about the observer's location here?

2 **Clarification** A comet is an object made of ice, gas, and dust that orbits the sun. The tail of a comet points away from the sun as the comet makes its way around the sun. Comets' tails have been observed since ancient times. In fact, the long tail streaming out behind the comet is the basis for its name, which comes from the Greek word for long-haired.

3 Clarification Constellations are groups of stars in which early peoples thought they saw imaginary figures of animals or people. Most of the constellations referred to today were named by the ancient Greeks after mythical heroes, heroines, and beasts such as Perseus, Andromeda, and Leo the lion.

4 Critical Thinking and Reading Evaluate Professor Olmstead's powers of observation. What do you think the relationship is between being a keen observer and being an astronomer?

5 Discussion Why do people watch for meteors? Why do the heavens fascinate people?

6 Critical Thinking and Reading What does this Indian legend probably refer to? Based on the author's background, how do you think he knows about the legend?

7 Enrichment A meteorite found recently in Antarctica appears to have come from the moon. It is made of materials very much like those brought back from the moon. Another meteorite found in Antarctica may have come from Mars. It is similar in composition to the Martian soil tested by *Viking I.*

Reader's Response Does "Shooting Stars" pique your interest in meteors? Explain.

each year. Each is named after the constellation from which it appears to come. The biggest of all, the Perseids, named for the
3 constellation of Perseus, occurs on the 10th, 11th, and 12th of August. The next largest, the Leonids, named for the constellation of Leo, comes on the nights of November 14, 15, and 16. Another, the Andromedids, which is not quite so big, comes from November 17 through 23. There are other meteor showers in December, January, April, May, and July, but none of them is as big as those in August and November.

Most people watching meteors will be satisfied if they see ten or twenty in an hour of watching. On special occasions, however, the meteors seem to come in droves. The most remarkable meteor shower I ever heard of was seen by a distinguished astronomer, Professor Denison Olmstead, of New Haven, Connecticut, on the night of November 12, 1833. He was watching the Leonids, which seem to come from directly overhead and race downward toward the horizon in all directions. He reported that meteors fell "like flakes of snow." He estimated that he
4 saw 240,000 meteors in nine hours that night. He said they ranged in size from mere streaks of light to "globes of the moon's diameter." If he had not been a notable astronomer whose accuracy was beyond question, such statements would seem ridiculous. But there is no reason to doubt what he reported. He had seen one of the most unusual meteor showers ever reported. What he watched should be called a meteor storm rather than a shower.

I once watched the August Perseids with an astronomer on a hilltop in open country, and in two hours we counted almost a thousand meteors. That was the most I ever saw at one time. And we were bitten by one mosquito for every meteor we saw. After that I tried watching for meteors in November, when there were no mosquitoes. But the most I ever saw in November was about one hundred meteors in two hours of watching.

The amazing thing about these meteor showers is that they come year after year. Professor Olmstead saw all those Leonids in November of 1833, but if you watch for meteors this year you almost certainly will see them on the same nights he saw them. They will come next year, the year after that, and for countless years more. Your grandfather saw them, and your grandchildren will see them if they look for them.

Occasionally a meteor reaches the earth. Then it is called a meteorite and it is valued as a sample of the vast mystery of the deep space in the sky. Scientists examine it, try to guess what it was to begin with, where it came from, what it is like out there. Nobody ever learned very much from the meteorites except that they often contain a great deal of nickel and iron.

Only a few large meteorites have struck the earth. The largest we know about fell in Arizona many centuries ago and made what is now called Meteor Crater, a hole about a mile across and 600 feet deep. Some Indian legends of the Southwest tell of a big fire that fell from the sky and ate a huge hole in the earth, so this big meteorite may have fallen since man first arrived in America, perhaps twenty-five thousand years ago.

Other big meteorites have fallen, in ancient times, in Texas, in Argentina, in northern Siberia, in South-West Africa, and in Greenland. A meteorite weighing more than thirty-six tons was found in Greenland and now can be seen in the Hayden Planetarium in New York City. Millions of meteors have flashed across the night sky, but only a few large meteorites have ever reached the earth. Never in all the centuries of written history has there been a report of anyone being struck by a meteorite.

THINKING ABOUT THE SELECTION

Recalling

1. What are meteors?
2. When do the biggest meteor showers occur?
3. Describe the most unusual meteor shower ever reported.
4. Why are meteorites valued so much?
5. What was the effect of the largest meteorite that fell to earth?

Interpreting

6. Why do you think scientists collect meteorites? What is it about meteors that stirs the imagination?

Applying

7. What is the difference between a scientific explanation and an explanation offered by a legend or myth? What can scientists learn from legends or myths?

READING IN THE CONTENT AREAS

Understanding Observation

Observation, or the act of looking at or noticing an object or event objectively, or factually, is a skill that scientists use to gain information. When observing, they try to concentrate only on the facts, not on their opinions.

You too can use observation to learn. By screening out your personal reactions, you can think only about the facts.

Take notes on one of the following situations, reporting the facts. Summarize what you observe.

a. the view outside your classroom window
b. students changing class

CRITICAL THINKING AND READING

Recognizing Observation and Inference

An **observation** is an act of noticing and recording facts and events. An **inference** is a reasonable conclusion you can draw from given facts or clues. When you see storm clouds overhead and note that they are gray and gathering quickly, you are observing the facts. When you remark that it looks as though it will storm soon, you are inferring based on what you see and know about storm clouds.

State whether the following sentences from "Shooting Stars" are observations or inferences.

1. "I once watched the August Perseids with an astronomer on a hilltop in open country, and in two hours we counted almost a thousand meteors."
2. "Some Indian legends of the Southwest tell of a big fire that fell from the sky and ate a huge hole in the earth, so this big meteorite may have fallen since man first arrived in America, perhaps twenty-five thousand years ago."

UNDERSTANDING LANGUAGE

Appreciating Words from Myths

Some scientific phenomena are named after myths. The Perseids meteor shower and the constellation of Perseus are named for Perseus, the son of Zeus who slew Medusa.

Find the origins, based on myths, of the following words.

1. Orion 2. Mercury 3. Mars 4. Venus

THINKING AND WRITING

Observing

Choose a common object such as a safety pin or a pencil sharpener. Observe it carefully, making notes. Then write a description of it, but do not name it. Revise to make sure you have described the object so precisely that someone reading it could guess what it is. Finally, read your description to your classmates and see if they can identify the object.

ANSWERS TO CRITICAL THINKING AND READING

1. observation
2. inference

ANSWERS TO UNDERSTANDING LANGUAGE

1. Orion is named for a handsome and great hunter in Greek mythology.
2. Mercury is named for the swift messenger of the gods in Roman mythology.
3. Mars is named for the god of war in Roman mythology.
4. Venus is named for the goddess of love in Roman mythology.

Challenge Discuss the importance of highly developed powers of observation in appreciating nature. Name some natural phenomena that require careful observation to be fully appreciated. What types of life might be missed altogether if people didn't observe carefully?

Writing Across the Curriculum You might want to have students research and report on the solar system. If you do, perhaps inform the science department of this assignment. Science teachers might provide guidance for students in conducting their research.

Closure and Extension

ANSWERS TO THINKING ABOUT THE SELECTION

Recalling

1. A meteor is a piece of a comet that exploded long ago.
2. August and November have the largest number of meteor showers.
3. In 1833, Professor Olmstead reported seeing 240,000 meteors in nine hours falling "like flakes of snow."
4. Meteorites are valued as samples of the "vast mystery of the deep space in the sky." Scientists try to find out information by studying them.
5. It made a hole in the earth one mile across and 600 feet deep.

Interpreting

6. Scientists collect meteorites to try and unlock the secrets of deep space. Meteors stir the imagination because they have traveled so far and have been seen for centuries.

Applying

7. Scientific explanation is based on careful observation, testing an hypothesis, and physical evidence. Legends and myths explain things imaginatively based on local culture and folklore. Answers will differ. Suggested response: Scientists can learn that some phenomenon occurred, where it occurred, and approximately how long ago it occurred.

GUIDE FOR READING

The Sounds of Richard Rodgers

Ellen Goodman (1941–   ) is a national columnist based at the *Boston Globe*. Her column is syndicated by the *Washington Post* Writers Groups and appears in more than 170 newspapers. Born in Newton, Massachusetts, Goodman graduated from Radcliffe College and is a former Nieman Fellow at Harvard University. In 1980 she received the Pulitzer Prize for distinguished commentary. "The Sounds of Richard Rodgers" shows her common-sense, realistic style of writing.

Setting a Purpose for Reading

A **purpose** is a reason for doing something. If you set a purpose before you read, you will read more efficiently. One way of setting a purpose is to get a general idea of what the selection is about, first by looking at the title. Then ask yourself basic questions about the topic of the essay. You might use the journalistic formula *who? what? when? where? why?* and *how?* For example: Who was Richard Rodgers? For what is he best known? When and where did he live? How did he achieve success? Why do we remember him?

Look For

As you read, look for answers to these questions: Who? What? When? Where? Why? and How?

Writing

Think of a famous composer of music, including rock and popular music. Freewrite about that composer and his or her music. Include your thoughts and any anecdotes you know about the composer.

Vocabulary

Knowing the following words will help you as you read "The Sounds of Richard Rodgers."

scores (skôrz) *n.*: The music for a stage production or film, apart from the lyrics and dialogue (p. 473)

esophagus (i saf′ ə gəs) *n.*: The tube through which food passes to the stomach (p. 473)

regimen (rej′ ə mən) *n.*: A regulated system of diet and exercise (p. 474)

legacy (leg′ ə sē) *n.*: Anything handed down, as from an ancestor (p. 474)

Focus

More About the Author Ellen Goodman writes about both famous people and her own friends and family. She portrays famous people with the same familiarity and warmth that characterize her more personal writing. Because she is a newspaper columnist, she tackles both controversial issues and amusing everyday-life experiences for a wide audience. Ask students to discuss how writing for a newspaper affects a writer's style. How is writing regularly for a widely-read paper different from writing a book?

Reading in the Content Areas Every journalist has a purpose for writing every article. The purpose of a piece is particularly evident when it is nonfiction and biographical. However, you can apply the *who? what? when? where? why?* and *how?* formula to all your reading with enlightening results.

Look For Your less advanced students may find it helpful to answer the questions *who? what? when? where? why?* and *how?* as they read the essay. Then ask students if any other questions are answered in the essay.

Writing/Prior Knowledge Have students discuss the meaning of this quotation by William Congreve: "Music has charms to soothe a savage breast, to soften rocks, or bend a knotted oak." Then have them complete the freewriting assignment. For extra credit, you might ask them to use their freewriting as the basis for a formal composition.

Vocabulary It would be helpful for students to know the following words also: *orchestrally, contagious* (p. 473); *intrigued, sustains,* and *spontaneously* (p. 474).

Objectives

1. To set a purpose for reading
2. To identify subjective and objective details
3. To appreciate music terms
4. To write about an artistic person

Support Material

Teaching Portfolio

Teacher Backup, pp. 605–607
Usage and Mechanics Worksheet, p. 608
Vocabulary Check, p. 609
Critical Thinking and Reading Worksheet, *Recognizing Subjective Details,* p. 610
Language Worksheet, *Appreciating Music Terms,* p. 611
Selection Test, pp. 612–613

The Sounds of Richard Rodgers[1]

Ellen Goodman

He came into our house with the first Victrola[2] . . . and stayed. By the time I was ten I knew every song on our boxed and 1 scratched "78" records: songs from *Oklahoma!* and *Carousel* and *South Pacific.* They were, very simply, the earliest tunes in a house that was more alive with the sound of politics than the sound of music.

As I grew older, I knew he was no Bee-
2 thoven[3] or Verdi,[4] or John Lennon[5] for that matter. By then his songs had been orchestrally overkilled into the sort of Muzak that kept you company in elevators or "on hold" at the insurance company line.

But the fact is that from the time I was a
3 child, to the time I sat with my own child watching the Trapp family escape again over the mountains,[6] there has always been a Richard Rodgers song in the background.

His work has been, very simply, our musical common exchange—as familiar and contagious as the composer ever hoped.

By the time he died, he was that rare man, someone who accomplished what he set out to do: "All I really want to do is to provide a hard-working man in the blouse business with a method of expressing him- 4
self. If he likes a tune, he can whistle it and it will make his life happier."

And, at seventy-seven, he was something even rarer, a man who remained centered in his work over six decades.

The numbers were overwhelming: 1,500 songs, 43 stage musical scores, 9 film scores, 4 television scores. He wrote music when he had a heart attack and music when he had cancer and music when he was learning to talk through his esophagus. He wrote music when his plays were huge successes and music when they were not; music when he needed the money and music when he didn't.

At fourteen, he composed his first song
and at sixty-seven he still wrote to a friend: 5
"I have a strong need to write some more music, and I just hope nothing stands in the way."

Yet when he was praised, he said, "I admit with no modesty whatever that not

---

1. Richard Rodgers (1902–1979): U.S. composer of musicals.

2. Victrola (vik trō′ lə) *n.*: A trademark for a phonograph.

3. Ludwig van Beethoven (lo͞ot′ viH vän bā′ tō vən) (1770–1827): German composer.

4. Giuseppe Verdi (jo͞o zep′ pe ver′ dē) (1813–1901): Italian operatic composer.

5. John Lennon (1940–1980): Leader of the British rock music group The Beatles, which achieved world renown in the 1960's and 1970's.

6. Trapp family . . . mountains: An Austrian family who fled over mountains to escape Hitler, dictator of Germany during World War II. The musical *The Sound of Music* is about their experiences.

Presentation

Motivation/Prior Knowledge Have students identify the most common type of music in their lives. Is it popular, rock, or classical? It should be the music that they hear most often at home and that they hear in their minds as well. Have students discuss the impact of this music on their lives. How important is it? How does it make them feel?

Master Teacher Note Obtain and play for students some of the examples of Richard Rodgers' music mentioned in the essay. For example, play selections from *Oklahoma* (Decca, DL-9017), or *Carousel* (Decca, DL-9020(M)), or *South Pacific* (Columbia, OS-2040) or *The King and I* (Capitol, TCL(M)/STCL(S) 1790 or RCA LOC/LSO-1092). Many of the songs should be familiar to students.

Thematic Idea Another Selection that deals with a creative personality is "Hokusai: The Old Man Mad About Drawing" on page 481.

Purpose-Setting Question What role does music play in people's lives?

1 **Clarification** The number "78" here refers to "revolutions per minute," or the speed at which the record turns on the turntable.

2 **Critical Thinking and Reading** What opinion does Goodman have of Richard Rodgers?

3 **Clarification** Goodman is referring here to the musical *The Sound of Music,* which is the story of the Trapp family set to music.

4 **Discussion** Why did Rodgers write music?

5 **Critical Thinking and Reading** Do you think all artists have this drive to create? Explain your answer.

6 **Discussion** How important to people are their jobs? What does a person's job tell you about that person? How does a person's feelings about a job influence that person's life?

7 **Clarification** It took Michelangelo four and a half years to complete the Sistine Chapel ceiling. He painted on the ceiling the history of the creation of the world, the fall of humanity, and the flood, according to the Bible.

8 **Discussion** Do you agree or disagree with Rodgers? Why?

9 **Discussion** What is the secret of Rodgers's success?

10 **Discussion** What does Goodman mean by this? What is Rodgers' legacy?

Reader's Response What does the word work mean to you?

many people can do it. But when they say, 'You're a genius,' I say, 'no, it's my job.' "

Music was his job. It is a curious phrase. Yet it seems to me, looking back over his career, how little attention we've paid re-
6 cently to the relationship between a life and "a job." For the past several years we've been more intrigued by life styles than by work styles, more curious about how someone sustains a marriage or a health regimen than how someone sustains an interest in his work.

The magazines we read are more focused on how we play than how we produce. We assume now that work is what we do for a living and leisure is how we enjoy living. When we meet people who do not understand this split, we label them "workaholics."

But Richard Rodgers was never seen in *People* magazine wearing his jog-togs. His "job" was writing music and his hobby was listening to it.

Usually we think of creative work as either inspired or tortured. We remember both Handel[7] writing "The Messiah" in three weeks and Michelangelo mounting the
7 scaffolding of the Sistine Chapel[8] year after year. Rodgers for his part once wrote a song in five minutes. But when asked about it, he said, "The song situation has probably been going around in my head for weeks. Sometimes it takes months. I don't believe that a writer does something wonderful spontane-
8 ously. I believe it's the result of years of living, or study, reading—his very personality and temperament."

The man knew something about the relationship between creativity and productivity. He knew something about the satisfactions of both, and managed to blend them. He could write music when handed the lyrics and write it before the lyrics. He could and would write a song to fit a scene. If Woody Allen is right in saying that "Eighty percent of life is showing up," well, Richard Rodgers showed up.

"Some Enchanted Evening" will never go into the annals of great classics. *The King and I* is not *Aida*.[9] Rodgers was a workaday artist and he knew it. But he also knew that for some people there is a fuzzy line between work and play, between what is hard and what is fun.

"I heard a very interesting definition of work from a lawyer. Work, he said, is any activity you'd rather not do. . . . I don't find it work to write music, because I enjoy it," said Rodgers. Yet he also said, "It isn't any easier than when I began, and by the same token it isn't any harder."

He was a man who was lucky in his work and lucky in his temperament. In an era when we tend to doubt the satisfactions that can come from work and tend to regard hard workers as a touch flawed in their capacity for pleasure, this composer showed what work can be: how it can sustain rather than drain, heighten rather than diminish, a full life. He leaves us a legacy in the sound of his life as well as his music.

---

7. George Frederick Handel (han' d'l) (1685–1759): English composer, born in Germany.

8. Michelangelo(mī' k'l an' jə lō') **. . . Sistine Chapel**: Italian sculptor, painter, architect and poet (1475–1564) who painted the ceiling of the Sistine Chapel, the principal chapel in the Vatican at Rome.

9. *The King . . . Aida*: *The King and I*, a musical by Rodgers and his partner Oscar Hammerstein (1895–1960), is not on the same level as *Aida*, an Italian opera by Verdi.

THINKING ABOUT THE SELECTION

Recalling

1. What was Rodgers' goal in life?
2. What is Rodgers' special talent? Give examples of how he used his abilities.
3. On what, according to Rodgers, is writing music or performing an artistic task based?

Interpreting

4. What is the difference between Muzak and music?
5. Why did Rodgers say that he wasn't a genius but simply someone doing his job?
6. The writer says that "We assume now that work is what we do for a living and leisure is how we enjoy living." What does this say about the way many people feel about their work? How was the way Rodgers felt about his work different?
7. How did Rodgers leave "a legacy in the sound of his life" as well as in his music?

Applying

8. What do you think is the relationship between creativity and productivity?

READING IN THE CONTENT AREAS

Setting a Purpose for Reading

Setting a purpose for reading can help you read more efficiently. One way of setting a purpose for reading is imagining you are a journalist acquiring information for an article. Reading this essay should give you the answers to the questions you asked before reading.

1. Who was Richard Rodgers?
2. For what is he best known?
3. When and where did he live?
4. How did he achieve success?
5. Why do we remember him?

CRITICAL THINKING AND READING

Recognizing Subjective Details

Writers often include both objective and subjective details in their descriptions. **Objective details** are factual statements that are free from personal feelings or opinions. For example, Ellen Goodman gives this objective detail about Richard Rodgers' work, "The numbers were overwhelming: 1,500 songs, 43 stage musical scores, 9 film scores, 4 television scores." **Subjective details** are based on a person's feelings, interests, or opinions rather than on outside facts. For example, Goodman includes this subjective detail: "As I grew older, I knew he was no Beethoven or Verdi, or John Lennon for that matter."

Find two objective details in the selection and two subjective details.

UNDERSTANDING LANGUAGE

Appreciating Music Terms

In writing about the composer Richard Rodgers, Goodman uses some music terms. Look up each of the following music terms in the dictionary, and then use each one in a sentence.

1. lyrics 2. opera 3. orchestrate

THINKING AND WRITING

Writing About an Artistic Person

Think of someone skilled at singing, dancing, painting, or playing a musical instrument. First answer *who, what, when, where, why,* and *how* about this person. Then use this information in an article about this person for the cultural section of a newspaper. Revise your article, keeping in mind the audience, and proofread it.

3. He lived from 1902–1979 in the United States.
4. He achieved success through hard work.
5. He is remembered because of his music and his satisfying life.

ANSWERS TO CRITICAL THINKING AND READING

Answers will differ. Suggested Response: Two objective details are that Rodgers composed his first song at fourteen and at sixty-seven still had a need to write music.

Two subjective details are that the author, by the time she was ten, knew every song on their Richard Rodgers records, and that while she was growing up there was always a Richard Rodgers song in the background.

ANSWERS TO UNDERSTANDING LANGUAGE

1–3. Answers will differ.

Challenge What can people do to make their jobs and their lives more rewarding? How can people fulfill themselves through their work?

Writing Across the Curriculum You might want to have students research and report on Richard Rodgers' musicals. If you do, perhaps inform the music department of this assignment. Music teachers might provide guidance for students in conducting their research.

Closure and Extension

ANSWERS TO THINK ABOUT THE SELECTION

Recalling

1. Rodgers wanted to write music that would make people happy.
2. Rodgers's special talent was enjoying his work. He used his abilities to write 1,500 songs, 43 stage musical scores, 9 film scores, and 4 television scores.
3. It is based on loving what you do.

Interpreting

4. Music is creative and dynamic, while Muzak is over-played and stale.
5. Rodgers said this because writing music to him was a job he loved.
6. Many people regard work as pure drudgery. Rodgers felt his work sustained and enriched him.
7. Rodgers left us a good example by his life.

Applying

8. The more creative the job, the more people can produce in their own field.

ANSWERS TO READING IN THE CONTENT AREAS

1. He was a composer.
2. He is best known for his songs from such musicals as *Oklahoma, Carousel, South Pacific,* and *The King and I.*

Focus

More About the Author Isaac Asimov is well known for his science fiction books and stories. But his nonfiction is noted for making scientific and technological material understandable to the general reader. He has also written on such nonscientific topics as the Bible and Shakespeare. Ask students to discuss how a writer can be so versatile. What do all kinds of writing have in common? What makes one kind of writing different from another?

Reading in the Content Areas In the course of your reading during the next week, note the kind of reading you are doing and the reason you are either scanning, skimming, or reading intensively. Note the reading rate you use most often.

Look For Your more advanced students might try skimming an article or story that they would otherwise read intensively. Have them note what they learned from the material by skimming. Then have them go back and read the material intensively. Have students notice the difference in detail between these two reading rates.

Writing/Prior Knowledge Have students think about the clocks they see every day. How many of them have dials and how many are digital? Have students comment on the transition from dial clocks to digital. Then have them complete the freewriting assignment.

Vocabulary Most students will have no difficulty with these words. You might have them use each word in a sentence orally before reading the story.

GUIDE FOR READING

Dial Versus Digital

Isaac Asimov (1920–   ) was born in the Soviet Union and came to the United States with his family in 1923. Asimov has written and edited more than four hundred books. His interests range from science to history, literature (especially science fiction), and humor —fields in which he has done research, teaching, writing, or editing. "Dial Versus Digital" shows a fascination with time and how time is measured.

Varying Rates of Reading

When you read, you can use **varying rates of reading:** scanning, skimming, or reading intensively. You can vary your rate of reading depending on your purpose. You **scan** to find specific facts or details. You **skim,** or look through without reading carefully, to get a general idea of what is written. You **read intensively,** that is, you read slowly and carefully, to get a clear understanding of what is written.

Look For

Skim "Dial Versus Digital" to get an overview of it. Then read it intensively—slowly and carefully—pausing frequently to question your understanding of what you have just read. Later, when you answer the questions that follow the essay, scanning it may prove helpful.

Writing

"Dial Versus Digital" discusses the replacement of dial clocks by digital clocks. What other object or activity can you think of that has been replaced by modern technology? List any such item that comes to mind.

Vocabulary

Knowing the following words will help you as you read "Dial Versus Digital."

digital (dij′ it′l) *adj.*: Giving a reading in digits, which are the numerals from 0 to 9 (p. 477)

hovering (huv′ər iŋ) *v.*: Staying suspended in the air (p. 478)

arbitrary (är′ bə trer′ ē) *adj.*: Based on one's preference or whim (p. 478)

Objectives

1 To vary your rate of reading
2 To find main ideas and identify supporting details
3 To use the prefix *counter-*
4 To write about technology

Support Material

Teaching Portfolio

Teacher Backup, pp. 615–617
Usage and Mechanics Worksheet, p. 618
Vocabulary Check, p. 619
Critical Thinking and Reading Worksheet, *Finding Main Ideas,* p. 620
Language Worksheet, *Using the Prefix counter,* p. 621
Selection Test, pp. 622–623
Art Transparency 8, *Study for Airport* by Theodore Roszak

Dial Versus Digital

Isaac Asimov

There seems no question but that the clock dial, which has existed in its present form since the seventeenth century and in earlier forms since ancient times, is on its way out. More and more common are the digital clocks that mark off the hours, minutes, and seconds in ever-changing numbers. This certainly appears to be an advance in technology. You will no longer have to interpret the meaning of "the big hand on the eleven and the little hand on
1 the five." Your digital clock will tell you at once that it is 4:55. And yet there will be a loss in the conversion of dial to digital, and no one seems to be worrying about it.

When something turns, it can turn in just one of two ways, clockwise or counterclockwise, and we all know which is which. Clockwise is the normal turning direction of the hands of a clock and counterclockwise is the opposite of that. Since we all stare at clocks (dial clocks, that is), we have no trouble following directions or descriptions that include those words. But if dial clocks disappear, so will the meaning of those words for anyone who has never stared at anything but digitals. There are no *good* substitutes for clockwise and counterclockwise. The nearest you can come is by a consideration of your hands. If you clench your fists with your thumbs pointing at your chest and

THE PERSISTENCE OF MEMORY 1931
Salvador Dali
The Museum of Modern Art

Presentation

Motivation/Prior Knowledge Give students some background on the history of clocks. The first mechanical clock was probably invented in China in the late 1000's. It is believed that the first mechanical clocks in Western civilization were developed in the late 1200's. By the mid-1300's, the dial and hour hand had been added. The pendulum was developed during the mid-1600's, when the minute and second hands became common. By the mid-1700's, most of the mechanisms in modern mechanical clocks had been invented. Digitial clocks have been used only since the 1970's. How do students envision the clock of the future?

Purpose-Setting Question What comment is the author making on modern technology in this story?

1 **Critical Thinking and Reading** What is Asimov's opinion of the conversion of dial clocks to digital? How do you know?

Humanities Note

Fine art, *The Persistence of Memory,* 1931 by Salvador Dali. Salvador Dali (1905–) was born in Spain but moved to the United States in 1940. He is best known as a leading member of the Surrealist movement, which developed after World War I. Surrealism is a kind of magic realism that explores the subconscious and shocks the viewer with impossible natural images.

In *The Persistence of Memory,* Dali has created a fantasy world. The painting leaves the viewer with the haunting feeling that there must be some sense in all the apparent madness.

1. If you had a dream similar to this painting, how would it make you feel?
2. In what ways does this painting illustrate the text?

Master Teacher Note Place Art Transparency 9, "Study for Airport" by Theodore Roszak in the Teaching Portfolio, on the overhead projector. Ask students what feeling this scene conveys, and why. How do they think the artist feels about technology?

In "Dial Versus Digital," the author expresses his views about one aspect of technology.

2 Discussion What is the relationship between the traditional clock face and language?

3 Discussion Do you think digital clocks will eventually cause confusion in schools because they introduce an "irregularity into the number system"? Why or why not?

4 Discussion What is the "odd conservatism" referring to? How would most people feel about 100 minutes to the hour? What is the tone of this essay? How serious is Asimov?

5 Critical Thinking and Reading Do you agree with Asimov about the drawbacks of converting to digital or decimal clocks? Why or why not? How would the conversion affect our descendants?

Reader's Response Do you prefer dial or digital? Why?

then look at your fingers, you will see that the fingers of your right hand curve counterclockwise from knuckles to tips while the fingers of your left hand curve clockwise. You could then talk about a "right-hand twist" and a "left-hand twist," but people don't stare at their hands the way they stare at a clock, and this will never be an adequate replacement.

Nor is this a minor matter. Astronomers define the north pole and south pole of any rotating body in such terms. If you are hovering above a pole of rotation and the body is rotating counterclockwise, it is the north pole; if the body is rotating clockwise, it is the south pole. Astronomers also speak of "direct motion" and "retrograde motion," by which they mean counterclockwise and clockwise, respectively.

Here is another example. Suppose you are looking through a microscope at some object on a slide or through a telescope at
2 some view in the sky. In either case, you might wish to point out something to a colleague and ask him or her to look at it, too. "Notice that object at eleven o'clock," you might say—or five o'clock or two o'clock. Everyone knows exactly where two, five, or eleven—or any number from one to twelve—is located on the clock dial, and can immediately look exactly where he is told. (In combat, pilots may call attention to the approach of an enemy plane or the location of antiaircraft bursts or the target, for that matter, in the same way.)

Once the dial is gone, location by "o'clock" will also be gone, and we have nothing to take its place. Of course, you can use directions instead: "northeast," "southwest by south," and so on. However, you will have to know which direction is north to begin with. Or, if you are arbitrary and decide to let north be straight ahead or straight up, regardless of its real location, it still remains true that very few people are as familiar with a compass as with a clock face.

Here's still another thing. Children learn to count and once they learn the first few numbers, they quickly get the whole idea. You go from 0 to 9, and 0 to 9, over and over again. You go from 0 to 9, then from 10 to 19, then from 20 to 29, and so on till you reach 90 to 99, and then you pass on to 100. It is a very systematic thing and once you learn it, you never forget it. Time is different! The early Sumerians couldn't handle fractions very well, so they chose 60 as their base because it can be divided evenly in a number of ways. Ever since, we have continued to use the number 60 in certain applications, the chief one being the measurement of time. Thus, there are 60 minutes in an hour.

If you are using a dial, this doesn't matter. You simply note the position of the 3
hands and they automatically become a measure of time: "half past five," "a quarter past three," "a quarter to ten," and so on. You see time as space and not as numbers. In a digital clock, however, time is measured *only* as numbers, so you go from 1:01 to 1:59 and then move directly to 2:00. It introduces an irregularity into the number system that is going to insert a stumbling block, and an unnecessary one, into education. Just think: 5.50 is halfway between 5 and 6
if we are measuring length or weight or 4
money or anything but time. In time, 5:50 is nearly 6, and it is 5:30 that is halfway between 5 and 6.

What shall we do about all this? I can 5
think of nothing. There is an odd conservatism among people that will make them fight to the death against making time decimal and having a hundred minutes to the hour. And even if we do convert to decimal time, what will we do about "clockwise," "counterclockwise," and locating things at "eleven o'clock"? It will be a pretty problem for our descendants.

THINKING ABOUT THE SELECTION

Recalling

1. For how long has the dial clock existed? By what is it being replaced?
2. In addition to showing time, what are two uses of the dial clock?
3. In what two ways do you see time if you are using a dial clock? In what way do you see time if you are using a digital clock?
4. Find three disadvantages of changing from dial to digital.

Interpreting

5. Why do you think many directions say to turn clockwise or counterclockwise?
6. The digital clock is a replacement for the dial clock. What did the dial clock replace?

Applying

7. Poll your classmates. How many have digital watches? How many have dial watches? How do you explain your findings?

READING IN THE CONTENT AREAS

Varying Your Rate of Reading

Varying rates of reading include reading intensively, or reading carefully to understand the meaning; scanning, or reading to locate specific information; and skimming, or looking over quickly without reading carefully.

Sometimes you **read intensively** for meaning, especially when reading a textbook. **Scanning** can be helpful when reading the newspaper or doing research to locate particular facts or details. **Skimming** is helpful for getting an idea of what a written work is about.

Indicate which rate of reading would be useful for the following tasks.

1. Looking through a magazine to find an article that interests you
2. Finding the author's date of birth in the encyclopedia entry
3. Reading a biography in preparation for an oral report on this person's life

CRITICAL THINKING AND READING

Finding Main Ideas

The **main idea** of each paragraph is the most important idea in it. Writers sometimes state the main idea directly in the topic sentence. However, when the main idea is not directly stated but is implied, you must discover it by making inferences from the **supporting details.**

1. Reread the second paragraph of the essay. What is the main idea?
2. What details support this main idea?

UNDERSTANDING LANGUAGE

Using the Prefix *Counter-*

The prefix *counter-* means "against." For example, a *counterattack* is an attack made against another attack.

Add the prefix *counter-* to the following words, and use each new word in a sentence.

1. clockwise
2. act
3. type
4. productive

THINKING AND WRITING

Writing About Technology

Write an article for a magazine called *Contemporary Life* about an object or activity in our culture that has been replaced by technology. You can choose your subject from the list you made earlier, or you can choose another. Explain how the object was used or the activity was done in the past, how it changed, and what is done now. Revise your article, supporting your main ideas. Proofread your article.

ANSWERS TO READING IN THE CONTENT AREAS

1. skimming
2. scanning
3. reading intensively

ANSWERS TO CRITICAL THINKING AND READING

1. The main idea is that the meaning of clockwise and counterclockwise will be lost if dial clocks disappear.
2. The supporting details are that there are no good substitutes for these words, and the example of the clenched fist seems cumbersome and absurd by comparison.

ANSWERS TO UNDERSTANDING LANGUAGE

1. counterclockwise. Students' sentences will differ.
2. counteract. Students' sentences will differ.
3. countertype. Students' sentences will differ.
4. counterproductive. Students' sentences will differ.

Challenge Have students describe a clock of the future that is neither dial nor digital. How does it work? What does it look like?

Writing Across the Curriculum
You might want to have students research and report on the history of time keeping, from sundials to atomic clocks. If you do, perhaps inform the social studies department of this assignment. Social studies teachers might provide guidance for students in conducting their research.

Closure and Extension

ANSWERS TO THINKING ABOUT THE SELECTION

Recalling

1. The dial clock has existed in its present form since the seventeenth century.
2. It shows people what clockwise and counterclockwise mean, and people identify locations based on the clock's face.
3. You see time as a direction and time as space. With a digital clock, time is seen only as numbers.
4. Three disadvantages are (1) the meaning of clockwise and counterclockwise will be lost, (2) locating objects using o'clocks will become meaningless, and (3) school children will be confused by the irregularity in the number system.

Interpreting

5. Directions use these terms because they are universally understood and clear.
6. The dial clock was a replacement for more primitive time-keeping devices, such as the sundial.

Applying

7. Answers will differ. Suggested Response: Digital watches are becoming more popular as they become more common in stores and as they become less expensive. Many people like their accuracy.

Focus

More About the Author Stephen Longstreet is himself a painter as well as an art critic and lecturer. He has written the introductions to more than a dozen books on famous painters and their work. Ask students to discuss the relationship between practicing an art and critiquing it. How is Longstreet uniquely qualified to be an art critic? Is every art critic a painter as well? What qualifies a person to be a critic of someone else's work?

Reading in the Content Areas Note taking is a valuable life skill. Journalists, doctors, and mechanics all must know how to take quick and accurate notes in order to do their jobs well. Students who learn to take good notes may find studying easier.

Look For Your students can be broken up into small groups to read and take notes on this essay. Have students compare notes with one another to sharpen their note-taking skill.

Writing/Prior Knowledge Have students discuss the meaning of this quotation: "Works of art are indeed always products of having-been-in-danger, or having-gone-to-the-very-end in an experience, to where man can go no further." Then have them complete the freewriting assignment.

Vocabulary Most students will have no difficulty with these words. You might have them use each word in a sentence orally before reading the story.

GUIDE FOR READING

Hokusai: The Old Man Mad About Drawing

Stephen Longstreet (1907-) is a writer of movie screenplays, art criticism, novels, television scripts, and detective stories. An accomplished artist, Longstreet studied painting in Paris, Rome, London, and Berlin. While living in Europe in the 1920's, he became acquainted with such famous artists as Marc Chagall, Henri Matisse, and Pablo Picasso. "Hokusai: The Old Man Mad About Drawing" combines Longstreet's interests in both writing and art.

Note Taking

Note taking is an important tool for learning. It is the jotting down of the important points of what you read. Taking notes can help you understand what you read and how it is organized, and can be an aid to writing an essay or a research paper.

Look For

As you read "Hokusai: The Old Man Mad About Drawing," look for the important points the author makes about the artist. What facts and details does he use to support his main ideas?

Writing

There are many different forms of art, dance, music, and literature. For example, two of the many forms of dance are ballet and folk dancing. Choose one of these arts: painting, dancing, singing, or writing. Then list all the forms of this art that come to mind.

Vocabulary

apprenticed (ə pren′ tist) *v.*: Contracted to learn a trade under a skilled worker (p. 481)

commissioned (kə mish′ ənd) *v.*: Ordered to make something (p. 481)

engulfing (in gulf′ iŋ) *v.*: Flowing over and swallowing (p. 481)

mania (mā′nē ə) *n.*: Uncontrollable enthusiasm (p. 482)

Objectives

1 To take notes
2 To find implied main ideas
3 To appreciate art terms
4 To write about art

Support Material

Teaching Portfolio

Teacher Backup, pp. 625–627
Usage and Mechanics Worksheet, p. 628
Vocabulary Check, p. 629
Reading in the Content Areas Worksheet, *Taking Notes,* p. 630
Language Worksheet, *Appreciating Art Terms,* p. 631
Selection Test, pp. 632–633

Hokusai: The Old Man Mad About Drawing

Stephen Longstreet

Of all the great artists of Japan, the one Westerners probably like and understand best is Katsushika Hokusai. He was a restless, unpredictable man who lived in as
1 many as a hundred different houses and changed his name at least thirty times. For a very great artist, he acted at times like P.T. Barnum[1] or a Hollywood producer with his curiosity and drive for novelty.

Hokusai was born in 1760 outside the city of Edo[2] in the province of Shimofusa. He was apprenticed early in life to a mirror maker and then worked in a lending library, where he was fascinated by the
2 woodcut illustrations of the piled-up books. At eighteen he became a pupil of Shunsho, a great artist known mainly for his prints of actors. Hokusai was soon signing his name as Shunro, and for the next fifteen years he, too, made actor prints, as well as illustrations for popular novels. By 1795 he was calling himself Sori and had begun working with the European copper etchings which had become popular in Japan. Every time Hokusai changed his name, he changed his style. He drew, he designed fine surimino (greeting prints), he experimented with pure landscape.

Hokusai never stayed long with a period or style, but was always off and running to something new. A great show-off, he painted with his fingers, toothpicks, a bottle, an eggshell; he worked left-handed, from the bottom up, and from left to right. Once he painted two sparrows on a grain of rice.
Commissioned by a shogun (a military ruler 3
in 18th century Japan) to decorate a door of the Temple of Dempo-ji, he tore it off its hinges, laid it in the courtyard, and painted wavy blue lines on it to represent running water, then dipped the feet of a live rooster in red seal ink and chased the bird over the painted door. When the shogun came to see the finished job, he at once saw the river Tatsuta and the falling red maple leaves of autumn. Another time Hokusai used a large broom dipped into a vat of ink to draw the full-length figure of a god, over a hundred feet long, on the floor of a courtyard.

When he was fifty-four, Hokusai began to issue books of his sketches, which he called *The Manga*. He found everything worth sketching: radish grinders, pancake women, street processions, jugglers, and wrestlers. And he was already over sixty
when he began his great series, *Thirty-six* 4
Views of Fuji, a remarkable set of woodcut prints that tell the story of the countryside around Edo: people at play or work, great waves engulfing fishermen, silks drying in

---

1. P.T. Barnum: Phineas Taylor Barnum (1810–1891), U.S. showman and circus operator.
2. Edo (ē′ dō): Now Tokyo.

Presentation

Motivation/Prior Knowledge Katsushika Hokusai is not the only artist to ever use unconventional tools and painting techniques. In the United States in the 1940's, artists such as Jackson Pollack were called action painters because of the paintings they produced and the way in which they produced them. Pollack, for example, laid his canvas on the floor and splattered paint on the surface as he walked around it. Have students think of other unconventional ways in which well-known works of art have been produced.

Master Teacher Note Since this essay is about Hokusai and his different styles of painting, bring in some other examples of his work. An excellent example of his landscape painting is *Ono Waterfall,* painted in his characteristic colors of blue, brown, and green. Point out to students that it was not until after his death that some of his prints were shown in the West. Hokusai's work influenced such famous Western painters as Whistler, Gauguin, and van Gogh.

Purpose-Setting Question How are creativity and courage related in this story?

1 **Discussion** What kind of man was Hokusai?

2 **Clarification** A woodcut is a picture made by carving an image into a block of wood. The uncut portions of the wood are coated with ink, and paper is pressed over the block to form the image on paper. The cutaway sections of the wood appear as white.

3 **Critical Thinking and Reading** Why might Hokusai be considered a man ahead of his time? How do you think he would fit into today's art world?

4 **Enrichment** It is thought that Hokusai's greatest work was done when he was past age sixty.

Thematic Idea Another selection that deals with a creative personality is "The Sounds of Richard Rodgers" on page 473.

THE GREAT WAVE OFF KANAGAWA
Katsushika Hokusai
The Metropolitan Museum of Art

the sun, lightning playing on great mountains, and always, somewhere, the ash-tipped top of Fuji.

5 Hokusai did thirty thousand pictures during a full and long life. When he was seventy-five he wrote:

> From the age of six I had a mania for drawing the shapes of things. When I was fifty I had published a universe of designs. But all I have done before the age of seventy is not worth bothering with. At seventy-five I have learned something of the pattern of nature, of animals, of plants, of trees, birds, fish, and insects. When I am eighty you will see real progress. At ninety I shall have cut my way deeply into the mystery of life itself. At a hundred I shall be a marvelous artist. At a hundred and ten everything I create, a dot, a line, will jump to life as never before. To 6 all of you who are going to live as long as I do, I promise to keep my word. I am writing this in my old age. I used to call myself Hokusai, but today I sign myself "The Old Man Mad About Drawing."

He didn't reach a hundred and ten, but he nearly reached ninety. On the day of his death, in 1849, he was cheerfully at work on a new drawing. 7

Humanities Note

Fine art, *The Great Wave Off Kanagawa,* 1929, by Katsushika Hokusai. Katsushika Hokusai (1760 –1849) was born in Edo, Japan. In 1778, he entered the studio of the master artist Katsukawa Shunsho and worked there for fifteen years. Under Shunsho, he learned the traditional Japanese artistic philosophy: everything in nature has an invariable form. It is within this tradition that Hokusai created his own unique, powerful images.

Prints such as *The Great Wave Off Kanagawa* were discovered by many nineteenth-century French Impressionist and Post-Impressionist painters. Hokusai's prints helped the French painters to see and interpret nature in new and very personal ways.

1. What rhythms and repetitions can you find in this picture?
2. What emotions do you feel when looking at this picture?

5 **Thematic Idea** How is Hokusai like Richard Rodgers, as he is described in the essay on page 473? What do the two men have in common?

6 **Discussion** Why did Hokusai feel that his work would only improve as he got older?

7 **Critical Thinking and Reading** Has this essay changed the way you look at senior citizens? How would a senior citizen feel after reading this essay?

Reader's Response Why might it be important for an artist to change the circumstances of his or her life frequently? How does change affect you?

Closure and Extension

ANSWERS TO THINKING ABOUT THE SELECTION

Recalling

1. Hokusai was born in Edo in 1760.
2. He worked for a mirror maker and in a lending library.
3. Hokusai made actor prints, copper etchings, greeting prints, sketches of everyday objects, woodcut prints, and drawings.
4. He drew thirty thousand pictures during his lifetime.
5. Hokusai was drawing the day he died.

Interpreting

6. He meant that he would only get better with age because he would continue to learn about nature and artistic technique.
7. This is an appropriate name because he had been obsessed with painting all his life. His drawing defined him and he loved to draw.

THINKING ABOUT THE SELECTION

Recalling

1. Where and when was Hokusai born?
2. What jobs did he have early in his life?
3. What types of art did Hokusai create?
4. How many pictures did Hokusai draw during his lifetime?
5. What was Hokusai doing the day he died?

Interpreting

6. What did Hokusai mean when he said, "At a hundred I shall be a marvelous artist"?
7. Hokusai called himself "The Old Man Mad About Drawing." Why is this name appropriate? Explain your answer.

Applying

8. According to the author, Westerners like and understand Hokusai best of all Japan's great artists. Why do you think this is?

READING IN THE CONTENT AREAS

Taking Notes

Note taking, or jotting down the important points of what you read, can help you understand what is written and how it is organized.

To take notes, you must be able to identify the main point, or important idea, of each paragraph. The writer may support the main point by giving details, examples, or quotes.

When you take notes, write in your own words, using words and phrases rather than complete sentences. Pay attention to words in italic, in boldface type, and in quotation marks. Notice words and phrases that may indicate main points; for example, *first, then, finally, most important, the reasons for, the result was.*

Reread the essay about Hokusai.

1. Take notes on the author's main points.
2. Compare your notes with your classmates'.

CRITICAL THINKING AND READING

Finding Implied Main Ideas

The **main idea** of each paragraph is the most important idea in it. Often the main idea is **implied** rather than stated. When this is the case, you must recognize it from the supporting details.

Look at the paragraph on page 481, beginning "When he was fifty-four." The implied main idea in this paragraph is that Hokusai continued to be a prolific painter throughout his life. The supporting details that tell you this are that Hokusai at age fifty-four issued books of numerous sketches.

Reread the paragraph on page 481, beginning "Hokusai never stayed long with a period."

1. What is the implied main idea?
2. What are the supporting details?

UNDERSTANDING LANGUAGE

Appreciating Art Terms

Every field has certain terms that are used to discuss it. Art terms describe the process of a particular art, the products of the type of art, or the materials used to create the art.

Use a dictionary to define the following art terms. Then use each one in a sentence.

a. woodcut prints
b. still lifes
c. lithographs
d. sketches

THINKING AND WRITING

Writing About Art

Look at Hokusai's print "Great Wave Off Kanagawa" on page 482. As you look at this work of art, freewrite about the thoughts and associations that come to mind. Then write several paragraphs describing the painting for someone who has never seen it. Include a description of its details, shapes, and colors.

Applying

8. Answers will differ. Suggested Response: Hokusai's paintings have universal appeal because they are beautifully executed studies of everyday objects and nature, and they have great emotional impact for the viewer.

ANSWERS TO READING IN THE CONTENT AREAS

1. Answers will differ. Suggested Response: Hokusai was born in 1760. He became interested in art while working in a library. He had many different styles over the years, and every time he changed his style, he changed his name. He used unconventional materials and techniques to paint. When he was over sixty, he began his greatest work: a series of woodcut prints that tell the story of country life. He felt that as he got older, he got better. He died drawing.
2. Students should note differences.

ANSWERS TO CRITICAL THINKING AND READING

1. The implied main idea is that Hokusai's experiments with his art worked, and he was a successful artist.
2. The supporting details are that the shogun recognized the river Tatsuta and falling red maple leaves on the temple door.

(Answers begin on p. 482.)

ANSWERS TO UNDERSTANDING LANGUAGE

Students' sentences will differ. Definitions are as follows:

a. Woodcut prints are prints done by carving a block of wood, inking the uncarved areas, and pressing paper down on the block. The carved, uninked areas show white on paper.
b. Still lifes are paintings of small, inanimate objects such as fruits, flowers, bottles, and books.
c. A lithograph is a print made by lithography, which is a process based on the repulsion between grease and water. A design is drawn on a metal plate with a grease pencil. When water and printing ink are applied, the greasy areas, which repel water, absorb the ink, but the wet parts do not.
d. A sketch is a simple, rough drawing or design, done quickly and without a lot of detail.

Challenge Name some other artists who have undertaken major projects late in life and achieved success. You can name painters, sculptors, dancers, singers, writers, or actors. Identify the artist and his or her accomplishment.

THINKING AND WRITING

For help with this assignment, students can refer to Lesson 20, "Writing a Personal Essay" in the Handbook of Writing About Literature.

Writing Across the Curriculum You might want to have students research and report on Japanese art. If you do, perhaps inform the art department of this assignment. Art teachers might provide guidance for students in conducting their research.

Focus

More About the Author Ursula K. Le Guin is a well-known writer of science fiction. In the introduction to one of her books, *The Left Hand of Darkness,* she says, "In reading a novel, any novel, we have to know perfectly well that the whole thing is nonsense, and then, while reading, believe every word of it." Ask students to discuss the difficulty of making the fantastic believable. Do they ever forget when they are reading fiction that it is make-believe? Have they ever read a totally unbelievable work of fiction?

Reading in the Content Areas Point out to students that making an outline can help you to understand someone else's writing, and it can also help you to organize your own thoughts for a written composition. When writing a lengthy or complex paper, it is helpful to make an outline to order your thoughts and to be sure you are including all the important points that will make your work most effective.

Look For Your less advanced students may find outlining a difficult skill to master. It may be helpful to preview Reading in the Content Areas on page 489 so that students can outline a part of the whole essay before outlining an entire work.

Writing/Prior Knowledge Have students discuss what they think is important in becoming a writer. What must a person do to become a writer? Then have them complete the freewriting assignment.

Vocabulary It would be helpful for students to know the following words also: *stenographer, illegible* (p. 485); *immense* (p. 486); *intervals, dimensions, objective, superficial, collaboration* (p. 487); *installments, grudgingly,* and *mutilate* (p. 488).

GUIDE FOR READING

Talking About Writing

Ursula K. Le Guin (1929-   ) was born in Berkeley, California, and grew up listening to Indian legends retold by her father, a scientist who worked with Native Americans. Le Guin's writing, which has been influenced also by Norwegian and Irish folk tales, includes imagined beings and invented places. Le Guin has won the Nebula Award of the Science Fiction Writers of America and the Hugo Award of the World Science Fiction Convention. In her speech "Talking About Writing," she expresses her love for writing.

Outlining

Outlining is the systematic listing of the most important points of a piece of writing. An outline lists the main points and supporting details in the order in which they occur.

I. First main topic
   A. First subtopic
      1. First supporting idea or detail
      2. Second supporting idea or detail
   B. Second Subtopic
II. Second main topic (The outline continues in the same way.)

Look For

As you read "Talking About Writing," pay attention to what the speaker believes are important points for writing.

Writing

In this selection, the speaker discusses her area of expertise —writing—and points to follow to succeed in it. Choose a skill or an area in which you have ability. Then list the points that you believe are important to follow to be successful in that skill or area.

Vocabulary

Knowing the following words will help you as you read "Talking About Writing."

snide (snīd) *adj.*: Intentionally mean (p. 485)
fluctuating (fluk' choo wāt' iŋ) *adj.*: Constantly changing; wavering (p. 485)
prerequisite (pri rek' wə zit) *n.*: An initial requirement (p. 486)
vicarage (vik' ər ij) *n.*: A place where the clergy live (p. 486)
premonition (prē mə nish' ən) *n.*: An omen; forewarning (p. 487)
communal (käm'yoon'l) *adj.*: Shared by members of a group or a community (p. 487)
axioms (ak' sē əmz) *n.*: Truths or principles that are widely accepted (p. 487)

Objectives

1 To make an outline
2 To sequence events
3 To write advice about performing a skill

Support Material

Teaching Portfolio
Teacher Backup, pp. 635–637
Usage and Mechanics Worksheet, p. 638
Vocabulary Check, p. 639
Reading in the Content Areas Worksheet, *Understanding Outlining,* p. 640
Language Worksheet, *Using Dictionary Terms,* p. 641
Selection Test, pp. 642–643

Talking About Writing

Ursula K. Le Guin

1 Tonight we are supposed to be talking about writing. I think probably the last person who ought to be asked to talk about writing is a writer. Everybody else knows so much more about it than a writer does.

I'm not just being snide; it's only common sense. If you want to know all about the sea, you go and ask a sailor, or an oceanographer, or a marine biologist, and they can tell you a lot about the sea. But if you go and ask the sea itself, what does it say? Grumble grumble swish swish. It is too busy being itself to know anything about itself.

Anyway, meeting writers is always so disappointing. I got over wanting to meet live writers quite a long time ago. There is this terrific book that has changed your life, and then you meet the author, and he has shifty eyes and funny shoes and he won't talk about anything except the injustice of the United States income tax structure toward people with fluctuating income, or how to breed Black Angus cows, or something.

2 Well, anyhow, I am supposed to talk about writing, and the part I really like will come soon, when *you* get to talk to *me* about writing, but I will try to clear the floor for that by dealing with some of the most basic questions.

People come up to you if you're a writer, and they say, I want to be a writer. How do I become a writer?

I have a two-stage answer to that. Very often the first stage doesn't get off the ground, and we end up standing around the ruins on the launching pad, arguing.

3 The first-stage answer to the question, how do I become a writer, is this: You learn to type.

The only alternative to learning to type is to have an inherited income and hire a fulltime stenographer. If this seems unlikely, don't worry. Touch typing is easy to learn. My mother became a writer in her sixties, and realizing that editors will not read manuscripts written lefthanded in illegible squiggles, taught herself touch typing in a few weeks; and she is not only a very good writer but one of the most original, creative typists I have ever read.

4 Well, the person who asked, How do I become a writer, is a bit cross now, and he mumbles, but that isn't what I meant. (And I say, I know it wasn't.) I want to write short stories, what are the rules for writing short stories? I want to write a novel, what are the rules for writing novels?

Now I say Ah! and get really enthusiastic. You can find all the rules of writing in the book called Fowler's *Handbook of English Usage*, and a good dictionary. There are only a very few rules of writing not covered in those two volumes, and I can summarize them thus: Your story may begin in longhand on the backs of old shopping lists, but when it goes to an editor, it should be typed, double-spaced, on one side of the paper only, with generous margins—especially the left-

Presentation

Motivation/Prior Knowledge Elicit from students the areas in which they excel. Then have them try to explain how someone else could excel in that area. Students should attempt to formulate rules that a person could follow to become a good history student, bowler, hiker, dancer, and so on. After certain students have attempted to formulate these rules, discuss the difficulty of making rules for someone who wants to succeed at something.

Master Teacher Note There are a number of essays and books that attempt to tell people how to become writers. Read to students excerpts from Alva Johnston's amusing essay "How to Become a Great Writer" in *A Subtreasury of American Humor.* Johnston relates how Edgar Rice Burroughs, who had failed in numerous endeavors, sought refuge from his problems in fantasizing. One of his fantasies became the *Tarzan of the Apes* series.

Purpose-Setting Question What roles do experience and self-knowledge play in someone's becoming a writer?

1 **Discussion** Why, in Le Guin's opinion, is a writer the last person who should be asked to talk about writing?

2 **Critical Thinking and Reading** What is the distinction Le Guin is drawing between talking about writing and answering questions about her writing from the audience?

3 **Discussion** Is this the answer you expected? Why or why not?

4 **Discussion** Why might the person who asked the question be annoyed with Le Guin's first-stage answer?

5 Discussion Why does Le Guin's second-stage answer arouse resentment even among writers?

6 Critical Thinking and Reading What value does Le Guin place on experience for a would-be fiction writer? Why?

7 Critical Thinking and Reading What is the most valuable thing for a writer to know? What evidence does Le Guin provide to support her opinion?

hand one—and not too many really grotty corrections per page.

Your name and its name and the page number should be on the top of every single page; and when you mail it to the editor it should have enclosed with it a stamped, self-addressed envelope. And those are the Basic Rules of Writing.

I'm not being funny. Those are the basic requirements for a readable, therefore publishable, manuscript. And, beyond grammar and spelling, they are the only rules of writing I know.

All right, that is stage one of my answer. If the person listens to all that without hitting me, and still says All right all right, but how *do* you become a writer, then we've got off the ground, and I can deliver stage two. How do you become a writer? Answer: You write.

5 It's amazing how much resentment and
disgust and evasion this answer can arouse. Even among writers, believe me. It is one of those Horrible Truths one would rather not face.

The most frequent evasive tactic is for the would-be writer to say, But before I have anything to say, I must get *experience.*

Well, yes; if you want to be a journalist. But I don't know anything about journalism, I'm talking about fiction. And of course fiction is made out of the writer's experience, his whole life from infancy on, everything he's thought and done and seen and read and dreamed. But experience isn't something you go and *get*—it's a gift, and the only prerequisite for receiving it is that you be open to it. A closed soul can have the
most immense adventures, go through a 6
civil war or a trip to the moon, and have nothing to show for all that "experience"; whereas the open soul can do wonders with nothing. I invite you to meditate on a pair of sisters, Emily and Charlotte. Their life experience was an isolated vicarage in a small, dreary English village, a couple of bad years at a girls' school, another year or two in Brussels, which is surely the dullest city in all Europe, and a lot of housework. Out of that seething mass of raw, vital, brutal, gutsy Experience they made two of the greatest novels ever written: *Jane Eyre* and *Wuthering Heights.*

Now of course they were writing from experience; writing about what they knew, which is what people always tell you to do; but what was their experience? What was it they knew? Very little about "life." They knew their own souls, they knew their own minds and hearts; and it was not a knowledge lightly or easily gained. From the time they were seven or eight years old, they
wrote, and thought, and learned the land- 7
scape of their own being, and how to describe it. They wrote with the imagination, which is the tool of the farmer, the plow you plow your own soul with. They wrote from

inside, from as deep inside as they could get by using all their strength and courage and intelligence. And that is where books come from. The novelist writes from inside. What happens to him outside, during most of his life, doesn't really matter.

I'm rather sensitive on this point, because I write science fiction, or fantasy, or about imaginary countries, mostly—stuff that, by definition, involves times, places, events that I could not possibly experience in my own life. So when I was young and would submit one of these things about space voyages to Orion or dragons or something, I was told, at extremely regular intervals, "You should try to write about things you know about." And I would say, But I do; I know about Orion, and dragons, and imaginary countries. Who do you think knows about my own imaginary countries, if I don't?

But they didn't listen, because they don't understand, they have it all backward. They think an artist is like a roll of photographic film, you expose it and develop it and there is a reproduction of Reality in two dimensions. But that's all wrong, and if any artist tells you "I am a camera," or "I am a mirror," distrust him instantly, he's fooling you, pulling a fast one. Artists are people who are not at all interested in the facts—only in the truth. You get the facts from outside. The truth you get from inside.

OK, how do you go about getting at that truth? You want to tell the truth. You want to be a writer. So what do you do?

You write.

Honestly, why do people ask that question? Does anybody ever come up to a musician and say, Tell me, tell me—How should I become a tuba player? No! it's too obvious. If you want to be a tuba player you get a tuba, and some tuba music. And you ask the neighbors to move away or put cotton in their ears. And probably you get a tuba teacher, because there are quite a lot of objective rules and techniques both to written music and to tuba performance. And then you sit down and you play the tuba, every day, every week, every month, year after year, until you are good at playing the tuba; until you can—if you desire—play the truth on the tuba.

It is exactly the same with writing. You sit down and you do it, and you do it, and you do it, until you have learned how to do it. 10

Of course, there are differences. Writing makes no noise, except groans, and it can be done anywhere, and it is done alone.

It is the experience or premonition of that loneliness, perhaps, that drives a lot of young writers into this search for rules. I envy musicians very much, myself. They get to play together, their art is largely communal; and there are rules to it, an accepted body of axioms and techniques, which can be put into words or at least demonstrated, and so taught. Writing cannot be shared, nor can it be taught as a technique, except on the most superficial level. All a writer's real learning is done alone, thinking, reading other people's books, or writing—practicing. A really good writing class or workshop can give us some shadow of what musicians have all the time—the excitement of a group working together, so that each member outdoes himself—but what comes out of that is not a collaboration, a joint accomplishment, like a string quartet or a symphony performance, but a lot of totally separate, isolated works, expressions of individual souls. And therefore there are no rules, except those each individual makes up for himself. 11

I know. There are lots of rules. You find them in the books about The Craft of Fiction and The Art of the Short Story and so on. I know some of them. One of them says: Never

8 **Discussion** Why is Le Guin sensitive on this point? What early experiences could have ruined her career as a writer?

9 **Critical Thinking and Reading** What is the difference between facts and truth? How does a writer tell the truth?

10 **Discussion** How is learning to write like learning to do anything else?

11 **Discussion** Why do young writers search for rules? What is the rule for writing according to Le Guin? Explain why you agree or disagree with her.

12 Critical Thinking and Reading What point is Le Guin making with her example of *War and Peace?*

13 Discussion What has a writer bought for his or her solitude? Why is it up to the individual writer to make up individual and unique rules?

14 Critical Thinking and Reading What advice is Le Guin really giving to those who want to become writers?

Reader's Response Le Guin says of the sea, "It is too busy being itself to know anything about itself." How does this apply to your life or the life of someone you know well?

begin a story with dialogue! People won't read it; here is somebody talking and they don't know who and so they don't care, so—Never begin a story with dialogue.

Well, there is a story I know, it begins like this:

"Eh bien, mon prince! so Genoa and
12 Lucca are now no more than private estates of the Bonaparte family!"

It's not only a dialogue opening, the first four words are in *French,* and it's not even a French novel. What a horrible way to begin a book! The title of the book is *War and Peace.*

There's another Rule I know: Introduce all the main characters early in the book. That sounds perfectly sensible, mostly I suppose it is sensible, but it's not a rule, or if it is somebody forgot to tell it to Charles Dickens. He didn't get Sam Weller into the Pickwick Papers for ten chapters—that's five months, since the book was coming out as a serial in installments.

Now you can say, all right, so Tolstoy can break the rules, so Dickens can break the rules, but they're geniuses; rules are made for geniuses to break, but for ordinary, talented, not-yet-professional writers to follow, as guidelines.

And I would accept this, but very very grudgingly, and with so many reservations that it amounts in the end to nonacceptance. Put it this way: if you feel you need rules and want rules, and you find a rule that appeals to you, or that works for you, then follow it. Use it. But if it doesn't appeal to you or doesn't work for you, then ignore it; in fact, if you want to and are able to, kick it in the teeth, break it, fold staple mutilate and destroy it.

See, the thing is, as a writer you are free. You are about the freest person that ever was. Your freedom is what you have bought with your solitude, your loneliness. You are in the country where *you* make up the rules, the laws. You are both dictator and obedient populace. It is a country nobody has ever explored before. It is up to you to make the maps, to build the cities. Nobody else in the world can do it, or ever could do it, or ever will be able to do it again.

Absolute freedom is absolute responsibility. The writer's job, as I see it, is to tell the truth. The writer's truth—nobody else's. It is not an easy job. One of the biggest implied lies going around at present is the one that hides in phrases like "self-expression" or "telling it like it is"—as if that were easy, anybody could do it if they just let the words pour out and didn't get fancy. The "I am a camera" business again. Well, it just doesn't work that way. You know how hard it is to say to somebody, just somebody you know, how you *really* feel, what you *really* think—with complete honesty? You have to trust them; and you have to *know yourself:* before you can say anything anywhere near the truth. And it's hard. It takes a lot out of you.

You multiply that by thousands; you remove the listener, the live flesh-and-blood friend you trust, and replace him with a faceless unknown audience of people who may possibly not even exist; and you try to write the truth to them, you try to draw them a map of your inmost mind and feelings, hiding nothing and trying to keep all the distances straight and the altitudes right and the emotions honest. . . . And you never succeed. The map is never complete, or even accurate. You read it over and it may be beautiful but you realize that you have fudged here, and smeared there, and left this out, and put in some stuff that isn't really there at all, and so on—and there is nothing to do then but say OK; that's done; now I come back and start a new map, and try to do it better, more truthfully. And all of

Closure and Extension

ANSWERS TO THINKING ABOUT THE SELECTION

Recalling

1. The first stage is learning how to type and using Fowler's *Handbook of English Usage* and a dictionary. The second stage is writing.
2. She compares writing to tuba playing.
3. She cannot encourage people to become writers and yet she is glad to know that she's not alone in wanting to write. She hopes would-be writers know the pitfalls of the process.
4. Le Guin says writers should follow their own rules or whatever works for them.

Interpreting

5. She means that a writer is too close to the process of writing to describe it clearly.
6. Experience is not important because it is not facts that are meaningful but inner truth.
7. The facts are objective and verifiable while the truth is subjective and based on the writer's personal observations and conclusions.

Applying

8. Answers will differ. Students may respond that experienced people are the best ones to ask because they know their professions so well that they have valuable advice to offer; or students may agree with Le Guin that experienced people are too close to their professions to describe them clearly. These people have become one with their careers and so cannot give sound objective advice to anyone else.

ANSWERS TO READING IN THE CONTENT AREAS

Answers will differ. The following is a sample outline of three paragraphs from the essay (p. 486, this, every time, you do alone—absolutely alone. The only questions that really matter are the ones you ask yourself.

You may have gathered from all this that I am not encouraging people to try to be writers. Well, I can't. You hate to see a nice young person run up to the edge of a cliff and jump off, you know. On the other hand, it is awfully nice to know that some other people are just as nutty and just as determined to jump off the cliff as you are. You just hope they realize what they're in for.

THINKING ABOUT THE SELECTION

Recalling

1. The speaker answers "How do I become a writer?" in two stages. What are they?
2. To what does the speaker compare writing?
3. How does the speaker feel about encouraging people to be writers?
4. What rules should writers follow?

Interpreting

5. What does the speaker mean by "I think probably the last person who ought to be asked to talk about writing is a writer"?
6. According to the author, why is experience not important to a writer of fiction?
7. How is telling the truth different from telling the facts?

Applying

8. Do you feel experienced people should not be asked about how to do their jobs? Explain.

READING IN THE CONTENT AREAS

Understanding Outlining

Outlining breaks down the most important points and their supporting details, following the order in which they are written. Begin an outline by listing the main point, or central idea, about each paragraph. The main points should be listed by roman numerals. Also note the supporting details of each main point. Supporting details may include details, examples, or quotations. Indent and label them with a capital letter.

Make an outline of three consecutive paragraphs from "Talking About Writing."

CRITICAL THINKING AND READING

Sequencing Events

Sequencing events is putting a series of events in a particular order. The events might be in chronological order—the order in which they happened. The events might be in order of the least important to the most important, or vice versa. Similar events may be grouped together.

1. What steps does the writer describe in answering the question "How do I become a writer?" How does she arrange these steps?
2. What steps does the writer describe in the process of becoming a tuba player? How does she arrange these steps?

THINKING AND WRITING

Writing Advice About Performing a Skill

Refer to the skill you wrote about earlier, or choose another skill. Freewrite about how to accomplish that skill. Then prepare a how-to list of steps for a younger relative. Revise your steps, arranging your details chronologically. Proofread your steps.

15 **Discussion** Is this an encouraging essay about writing for would-be writers? What makes it encouraging or discouraging?

(Answers begin on p. 488.)

column 2).

First Paragraph

I. Experience is not of primary importance to fiction writers.
A. It is what a person makes of experience that is important.
1. Experience is for journalists.
2. An open soul can interpret the most minimal experience.
B. Emily and Charlotte Brontë were not worldly and yet wrote two of the greatest novels ever written.

Second Paragraph

II. The Brontë sisters knew little about life.
A. They knew themselves.
1. They began writing at early ages.
2. They wrote with their imaginations.
3. They wrote from inside.
B. The novelist must write from inside.

Third Paragraph

III. Le Guin is convinced that experience is low-priority for a fiction writer.
A. Fiction involves times, places, and events that no one could experience in real life.
1. When she wrote fantasies as a student, she was told to write about things she knew about.
2. She wrote about space voyages and dragons.
B. She knew her own imagination better than anyone else.

ANSWERS TO CRITICAL THINKING AND READING

1. The writer describes two steps: (1) learning to type and using Fowler's handbook and a dictionary and (2) writing itself. She arranges the steps from the obvious and mechanical to the cerebral and creative.
2. The writer describes these steps: (1) get a tuba and tuba music, (2) get a tuba teacher, and (3) practice. She arranges the steps, once again, logically from the physical acquisition of materials to the actual playing.

Challenge Do you think anyone can become a writer? What makes writing so different from other occupations? What type of person might be more likely than another to become a writer? What characteristics does Le Guin suggest writers must have?

THINKING AND WRITING
Publishing Student Writing

Have students make lists of various occupations and the characteristics required for success in those fields. These lists could be compiled and presented to the school guidance counselor to be posted in the guidance office. The lists could also be published in the school newspaper.

Focus

Putting It Together The information on this page summarizes how the ideas, techniques, and structure in nonfiction interrelate to produce the overall effect. By following the systematic approach shown in these sample annotations, students will increase their reading comprehension and literary appreciation. Students should read actively and form their own questions and opinions about the purpose, techniques, support, and organization of the selection.

Remind students that, as they read actively, they should be able to see how the separate elements of nonfiction interrelate to produce an effective essay.

For further practice with these elements, use the selection "Manganar, U.S.A.," by Jeanne Wakatsuki Houston and James D. Houston, pages 649–652, in the Teaching Portfolio which students can annotate themselves. Encourage students to continue to use this strategy as they read other nonfiction selections.

PUTTING IT TOGETHER

Nonfiction

Nonfiction is based on real people and real events and presents factual information. A writer of nonfiction often sets out with a certain purpose in mind and directs the writing to a certain intended audience. For example, the writer may set out to explain, to persuade, or to entertain. The writer may direct the essay toward people already familiar with the subject or people who have little or no knowledge of it. You will gain more from reading nonfiction if you examine the techniques the writer uses to accomplish the purpose, the support the writer uses to back up the main idea, and the way the writer arranges the supporting information.

Purpose

By **purpose** we mean the writer's reason for writing. Usually a writer has both a general purpose and a specific purpose. For example, a writer may in general wish to give information about a topic, entertain readers, describe something, or even persuade readers to do something. In addition, the writer may want to make a specific point about the topic. This point, or main idea, may be stated in the topic sentence.

Techniques

Just as builders use tools to construct their buildings, writers use tools, or **techniques,** to accomplish their purpose. For example, writers may use vivid adjectives to describe a landscape or exaggeration to create humorous effects. They may use figurative language to create startling word pictures or words with strong connotations to stir up feelings and associations.

Support

Support is the information the writer uses to back up or clarify the main idea. This support may take several forms: facts, opinions, reasons, details, examples, or incidents. The better an idea is supported, the more likely the reader is to accept it.

Arrangement

The writer **arranges** the support to best accomplish the purpose. For example, the writer may arrange steps in chronological order, to show which should be done after the other. The writer may arrange reasons in order of importance, saving the most important reason for last and so building to a powerful conclusion.

On the following pages is a model of how an active reader might read an essay. As you read, pay close attention to the annotations.

Objectives

1. To understand an essay's purpose
2. To interpret metaphorical language
3. To identify mixed metaphors
4. To write about language arts

Support Material

Teaching Portfolio

Teacher Backup, pp. 645–648
Grammar in Action Worksheet, *Understanding Parenthetical Expressions,* pp. 649–650
Usage and Mechanics Worksheet, p. 655
Analyzing Literature Worksheet, *Understanding an Essay's Purpose,* p. 656
Critical Thinking and Reading Worksheet, *Interpreting Metaphorical Language,* p. 657
Selection Test, pp. 658–659

A to Z in Foods as Metaphors: Or, a Stew Is a Stew Is a Stew

Purpose: The title provides a clue to the main idea of the essay. It will most likely express an idea about foods and how we use foods as metaphors. What could the subtitle mean?

Mimi Sheraton

Cooking styles may vary from one country to another, but certain foods inspire the same symbolism and human characteristics with remarkable consistency. The perception of food as metaphor is apparently more consistent than the perception of food as ingredient.

Arrangement: The writer begins her essay by stating the main idea. What is the main idea?

The inspiration for some of this imagery is easier to find than others. It is not too hard to understand, for example, why the big, compact, plebeian-tasting cabbage is widely regarded as being stupid, a role it shares with the starchy, inexpensive staple the potato. A cabbage head in this country is considered to be as dull-witted as a krautkopf in Germany, and a potato head indicates a similar, stodgy-brained individual, never mind that both are delicious and can be prepared in elegant ways.

Support: Here the writer offers three examples to support the main idea. What are they?

Italians, on the other hand, consider the cucumber a symbol of ineptness, and to call a person a cetriolo is to cast him among the cabbages of the world.

Salt has been a highly regarded commodity throughout history, and so a valuable person is described as being the salt of the earth. Considering the bad press salt is getting these days, however, that remark may soon be taken as an insult.

It is difficult to understand why ham is the word for a bad actor who overacts. But no one has to explain why a pretty and delightful young woman is considered to be a peach, or why her adorable, accommodating brother is a lamb. With luck, he will not grow up to be a muttonhead, to be classified with the cabbage and potatoes. If he remains a lamb, he can

Techniques: Here the writer uses figurative language to make her points. What figurative expressions does she include? What is the meaning of these figurative expressions?

Presentation

Teaching to Ability Levels If your less advanced students have difficulty understanding any of these elements, you might have them review the instruction on the appropriate pages or look up the necessary terms in the Handbook of Literary Terms and Techniques.

Motivation/Prior Knowledge You might lead the class in a discussion of the use of metaphor and simile to describe people. Ask the class for examples of descriptions of people as animals or plants, such as "stubborn as a mule," "cunning as a fox," or expressions like "I'm in hot water." What do people really mean when they use these expressions? Why do people use expressions like these instead of saying exactly what they mean?

Master Teacher Note Have students read each annotation carefully and consider the questions raised as well as any questions of their own. Also, have them consider how each of the separate elements relates to the others.

Thematic Idea Another selection that uses metaphors to describe people is the poem by Julio Noboa Polanco, "Identity," on page 598. You might have students compare the use of food as metaphors with Polanco's use of plants as metaphors. A selection that deals with the theme of another culture's effect on American language is "The Indian All Around Us" by Bernard DeVoto on page 457.

Purpose-Setting Question What makes this topic interesting to people of all ages?

Master Teacher Note Consider having the class read this essay aloud. An oral reading of the selection and the accompanying annotations might help students' comprehension and afford the opportunity for class discussion. Encourage students to share their own thoughts and questions concerning the essay, as well as those questions raised in the annotations.

Humanities Note

Fine art, *Trading Cards*. Trading cards were conceived as an advertising device with the advent of lithography, a printing technique that allowed inexpensive mass reproduction of art and print. They were very popular in the years 1860 to 1900. Manufacturers included such cards in packaged food products such as cocoa, sugar, and coffee as advertising gimmicks to encourage sales. Merchants also handed out the trading cards to advertise their establishments. The cards were produced in sets, numbered to encourage collection of an entire series. Children and adults avidly collected and traded the cards. The popularity of trading cards as a form of advertising died in the early 1900's with the advent of the home magazine.

You might want to use the following questions to discuss the art:

1. Which card do you find the most amusing or interesting?
2. Would these cards have appealed to you if you were a consumer at the turn of the century?

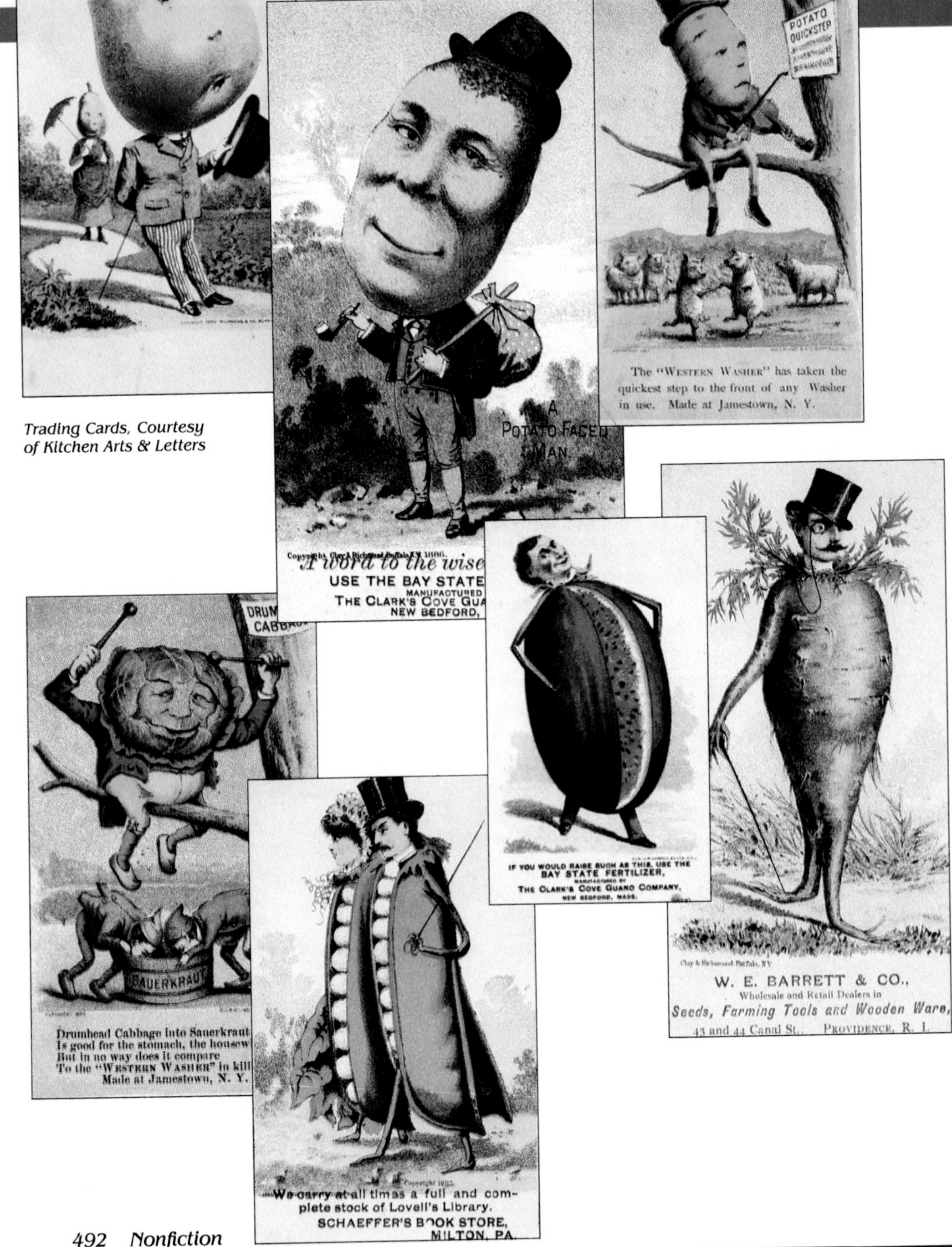

Trading Cards, Courtesy of Kitchen Arts & Letters

Grammar in Action

A word or phrase that is not essential to the meaning of a sentence is called a **parenthetical expression.** Writers may place a parenthetical expression in the middle of a sentence. When they do this, they place a comma before and after the expression.

Look at the parenthetical expressions in the following sentences:

All things sweet, *especially sugar and honey,* inspire dozens of terms of endearment in every language. . . .

. . . the lemon, *despite its sunny and piquant flavor,* is best known for its sourness. . . .

Italians, *on the other hand,* consider the cucumber a symbol of ineptness. . . .

Considering the bad press salt is getting these days, *however,* that remark may soon be taken as an insult.

What effect is created by the use of parenthetical expressions in the above examples?

be counted on to bring home the bacon that is the bread and dough.

All things sweet, especially sugar and honey, inspire dozens of terms of endearment in every language; but the lemon, despite its sunny and piquant flavor, is best known for its sourness and so describes such things as an automobile always in need of repairs. In many countries the nut is, inexplicably, the metaphor for craziness, though it is easier to explain why someone who is sprightly and hot-tempered is said to be peppery.

Support: Notice the examples here that support the main idea. What are these examples?

Cooked foods or dishes also inspire such comparisons. To be in the soup (it's hot) is to be in trouble and to be in a stew indicates one is troubled. Stews and soups with many ingredients are the consistent metaphors in many languages for big, complicated events and procedures.

In New York the most commonly heard of such expressions is tsimmes,[1] referring to the Eastern European Jewish stew of carrots, sweet potatoes, prunes, onions and, often, beef. To make a whole tsimmes out of something is to create an event of endlessly involved complications. In English, a tsimmes is a hodgepodge, which in turn is named for the stew derived from the French hochepot, which became hotchpotch or hotpot.

But a tsimmes is no more complicated than the New Orleans gumbo, also an event of dazzling complexities derived from the soup that may include okra, onions, peppers, shrimp, oysters, ham, sausage, chicken and at least a dozen other possibilities. Similarly used in their own countries are bouillabaisse,[2] the French soup of many fishes, and the Rumanian ghivetch, a baked or simmered stew that can be made with more than a dozen vegetables plus meat.

In Spain, to make an olla podrida[3] out of something is to make it as complex as that mixed boil of meats, poultry and onions. And though some Italians refer to a big mess as a big minestrone, the more popular metaphor is a pasticci,[4] a mess derived from the complicated preparations of the pastry chef,

Arrangement: Up until now, the writer has discussed individual foods. Here she shifts to cooked foods or dishes. What examples does she provide?

Master Teacher Note You might have students draw representations of some of the metaphors described in the essay. Using the illustration on page 492 as an example, have students imagine what a "cabbage head" looks like and draw it. They could also devise their own metaphors and illustrate them. You could collect these drawings and put together a book or display them on the class bulletin board.

---

1. **tsimmes** (tsim′ əs)
2. **bouillabaisse** (bo͞ol′ yə bās′)
3. **olla** (äl′ ə) **podrida** (pə drē′ də)
4. **pasticci** (päs tē′ chē)

Student Activity. Write a paragraph about one category of common expressions—for example, common expressions from baseball or from football or from cooking. Use commas to set off parenthetical expressions.

More About the Author Mimi Sheraton has written many articles about different foods and trends in how food is prepared and served. She has traveled extensively and experienced a variety of cultures. What might be some advantages and disadvantages in having a job similar to Sheraton's? Would students like such a job?

Reader's Response Which of the metaphors Sheraton describes have you yourself used or heard other people use?

or pasticcere.[5] In Denmark it is the sailor's hash or stew known as labskaus that signifies complications, and no wonder when you consider that such a dish contains meat and herring in the same pot.

Arrangement: The writer concludes by expanding on her main idea. What new idea does she introduce? What details support this main idea?

Putting It Together: People use foods to describe a variety of things from character traits to situations.

Some foods inspire conflicting metaphors. Fish is brain food, but a cold and unemotional person is a cold fish. You can beef up a program and make it better, but don't beef about the work that it involves or you will be marked a complainer. Instead of being given a promotion that is a plum you will be paid peanuts, even though you know your onions and are the apple of your boss's eye.

5. **pasticcere** (päs′ tē cher′ ē)

Mimi Sheraton (1926–) was born in Brooklyn, New York. As a food critic for *The New York Times*, she traveled all over the world to do research on food and how it is prepared. One of her popular books is *Mimi Sheraton's Favorite New York Restaurants*. Sheraton traces her interest in food to her childhood in Brooklyn, where good food and family situations were important.

Closure and Extension

ANSWERS TO THINKING ABOUT THE SELECTION

Recalling

1. Both the cabbage and the potato are used as metaphors for dull-witted people.
2. Valuable people are considered "the salt of the earth" because salt has been regarded as a valuable commodity throughout history.
3. The word *stew* expresses the idea of being troubled or a big complicated event or procedure. Three words from other languages that express this idea are *tsimmes, olla podrida,* and *labskaus.*
4. Fish is a conflicting metaphor because it is used to represent brain and an unemotional person. Beef is conflicting as a metaphor because it is used to represent bolstering or strengthening, as well as complaining. In both cases, the words represent two concepts whose meanings conflict.

THINKING ABOUT THE SELECTION

Recalling

1. Explain what the cabbage and the potato have in common.
2. Why are valuable people considered "the salt of the earth"?
3. What idea is expressed by the word *stew?* Find three other words from other languages that express this same idea.
4. Explain the conflicting metaphors expressed by fish and beef.

Interpreting

5. Why would you call a promotion a "plum"?
6. Why would knowledgeable people be said to "know their onions"?
7. Why might you call a loved one "the apple of my eye"?

Applying

8. What foods would you use to describe someone with great physical strength? Explain.

ANALYZING LITERATURE

Understanding an Essay's Purpose

Sometimes writers will directly state their purpose for writing. At other times you must infer, or draw a conclusion from given facts or clues, what the writer's purpose is. The clues may be given in statements, quotes, examples, or tone.

For instance, a writer may use colorful, descriptive language and an emotional attitude to persuade; factual language and a serious attitude to inform; and humorous descriptions and a light attitude to entertain. In "A to Z in Foods as Metaphors," the writer sets the purpose directly.

1. What direct statement does the writer make that sets the purpose for writing?
2. List three quotes or examples the writer gives to support her purpose.
3. What tone does the writer use? Give examples.
4. Based on the writer's direct statement, examples and tone, what is her purpose?

CRITICAL THINKING AND READING

Interpreting Metaphorical Language

A **metaphor** is a way of comparing two seemingly unlike objects to highlight a characteristic of one of the objects. Metaphors can produce images in your mind. Read the following metaphor to see the image created.

The wind-tossed field was an ocean of grain.

Explain the following metaphors.

1. She is the Rock of Gibraltar.
2. He is the guiding light of the department.
3. She is a wizard of the stock market.

UNDERSTANDING LANGUAGE

Identifying Mixed Metaphors

A **mixed metaphor** consists of two or more metaphors that do not fit together. An example is this sentence: The *wave* of protest was *nipped in the bud*. *Wave* and *nipped in the bud* do not fit together. It would be more appropriate to say: A *wave* of protest *washed over* the crowd. In this case, *wave* and *washed over* fit together.

The following sentences contain mixed metaphors. Rewrite each sentence to make the metaphor consistent and effective.

1. A *roar* of approval *sifted* through the audience.
2. An *onslaught* of insults *besieged* him daily.

THINKING AND WRITING

Writing About Language Arts

List five metaphors that are used to compare people or situations to animals. Working with a group of students, research the origins of these metaphors. Then write a brief explanation of each one. Turn these explanations into an essay on "Animals as Metaphors," patterning the style in "A to Z in Foods as Metaphors." Revise your essay, making sure you have adequately supported your main idea. Then proofread your essay and share it with your classmates.

(Answers begin on p. 494.)

2. These quotations support her purpose: "A cabbage head in this country is considered to be as dull-witted as a krautkopf in Germany"; "All things sweet, especially sugar and honey, inspire dozens of terms of endearment in every language . . ."; "But a tsimmes is no more complicated than the New Orleans gumbo, also an event of dazzling complexities . . ."
3. The tone is informal and conversational. Students can find examples to support this throughout the essay.
4. Her purpose is to informally convey the idea that people all over the world use foods to describe different things and situations.

ANSWERS TO CRITICAL THINKING AND READING

1. This means that she has a steadfast character and is not given to extremes in emotion.
2. This means that he is the leader and source of inspiration for the department.
3. This means that she is very good at what she does and accomplishes things that others cannot.

Challenge Write down five other uses of metaphors and their meanings.

ANSWERS TO UNDERSTANDING LANGUAGE

1. Suggested Response: A roar of approval burst from the audience.
2. Suggested Response: He was buried under an avalanche of insults.

THINKING AND WRITING

For help with this assignment, students can refer to Lesson 20, "Writing a Personal Essay," in the Handbook of Writing About Literature.

Publishing Student Writing Have all the groups work together and combine the individual essays into one, full-length essay on "Animals as Metaphors." Students can contribute art work to illustrate the essay, which can be submitted to the school or the community newspaper.

Interpreting

5. Answers will differ. Suggested Response: You would call a promotion a plum because plums are sweet, juicy, and delicious; a fruit that is desirable and enjoyable. A promotion is also desirable and enjoyable.
6. Answers will differ. Suggested Response: Knowledgeable people are said to "know their onions" because there are many different varieties of onions, which have similar tastes. So to "know your onions," you would have to be knowledgeable. Therefore, people who are knowledgeable in general are referred to this way.
7. Answers will differ. Suggested Response: A loved one might be referred to as the "apple of my eye" because of the universal appeal of the fruit. It is the favorite fruit of many people, so to be the "apple of one's eye" is also to be the favorite.

Applying

8. Answers will differ. Students might choose words pertaining to strong animals such as "beefy" or "ox-like."

ANSWERS TO ANALYZING LITERATURE

1. "Cooking styles may vary from one country to another, but certain foods inspire the same symbolism and human characteristics with remarkable consistency."

FOCUS ON READING

After reading and discussing the information about stating positions, have the students suggest stated positions on a controversial issue in music, sports, or school. Record them on the board or on a transparency. Discuss their merits.

After reading all of the "Understanding Persuasive Techniques" section, you might want to discuss the importance of a good summary.

Understanding Persuasive Techniques

Writers of nonfiction often use **persuasive techniques** to convince readers to accept their opinions or to take some action. Understanding the persuasive techniques is helpful in determining whether or not to agree with the author or take the action.

Stated Position

To evaluate persuasive writing, you need to identify the stated position, or major opinion, that the author wants you to accept. This position should be stated in the topic sentence and should be written so that it is easily understood. Unfamiliar terms used in the position statement should be defined so that the reader can clearly understand what the author is proposing. The stated position is an opinion that is held by a writer and that is open to debate. It cannot be a fact because facts are verifiable and cannot be argued over.

Examine the following sentences:

Hokusai is a Japanese artist who painted over thirty thousand pictures.
Hokusai is my favorite artist.
Hokusai should be considered the Westerners' favorite Japanese artist.

Both the first and second sentences are unacceptable as stated positions. The first is a fact, which is not debatable, while the second is merely someone's personal opinion. It, too, cannot be disputed. The third sentence, however, is a good stated position because it is an opinion that can be sensibly argued. Facts can be used to support or dispute it.

Major Points

Repeating the major points is another effective persuasive technique. Writers often restate their position, especially at the conclusion of their essay. Consequently, looking for ideas that are repeated will help you identify the stated position and major points.

Once you understand the stated position, you must identify the facts the author uses to support it. Evaluate them in terms of their quality and quantity. Use the following criteria. The supporting facts should be accurate, logical, and relevant to the argument. If an expert is quoted, the person should be an outstanding authority in the field. The quotation by Hokusai is convincing because it emphasizes what the author is saying and is by the artist himself.

Organization

Organization is important in persuasive writing. Facts should be introduced in an appropriate order. For example, it would be best to discuss the work and contributions of Hokusai in the order in which he made them, as this would be the easiest order to follow.

Support

Another persuasive technique is to use examples, comparisons, and descriptions to support the facts. Using forceful, vivid language that appeals to the emotions makes these descriptions and comparisons more effective. For example, Hokusai is compared with P. T. Barnum, which reminds the reader of the excitement and novelty of the circus and thus creates a vivid image of the artist.

Piling up the evidence by using a series of examples or descriptions adds weight to the point being made. For instance, the author piles up evidence when he describes the woodcut prints Hokusai made. He says the prints "tell the story of the countryside around Edo: people at play or work, great waves engulfing fishermen, silks drying in the sun, lightning playing on great mountains, and always, somewhere, the ash-tipped top of Fuji." Piling up evidence is not only convincing; it also is a concise way of conveying a lot of ideas.

Finally a writer should include sufficient supporting facts or reasons to make a strong argument. The more supporting facts a writer includes, the more convincing is the argument.

Activity

Read "The Trouble with Television" by Robert MacNeil and answer the following questions about this essay.

1. What is the stated position of the author? Is this position clearly expressed? Give reasons to support your answer.
2. List the facts the author uses to back up his position.
3. Does the author use descriptions and examples to back up his facts? Has he used a series of examples or descriptions to make a more convincing argument? If so, give examples.
4. Does the author use comparisons to clarify and make his supporting facts more convincing? If so, give examples.
5. Based on your previous answers, how would you evaluate this persuasive essay?

ANSWERS TO THE ACTIVITY

1. The author's position that television discourages concentration is clearly expressed. For support, the many facts and examples that the author gives might be cited.
2. Some facts are that television encourages passive behavior, television appeals to a short attention span, television news is inefficient communication, and television contributes to illiteracy.
3. The author uses a series of description and examples to back up his facts. One example is his statements about TV news; another is his evidence that TV is a narcotic.
4. The author uses a comparison to clarify his facts: he compares television to fast food.
5. Suggested response: the essay is very persuasive.

The writing assignments on page 498 have students writing creatively, while those on page 499 have them thinking about the essays and writing critically.

YOU THE WRITER

Guidelines for Evaluating Assignment 1

1. Does the essay begin with a description of the person and the skill in which the student is interested?
2. Does the student become the person and describe the creative process?
3. Are the sentences and ideas logically arranged?
4. Is the essay free from grammar, usage, and mechanics errors?

Guidelines for Evaluating Assignment 2

1. Does the essay build a case that agrees or disagrees with the basic premise of the scientist by using adequate support?
2. Does the introductory paragraph end with a thesis statement?
3. Is the essay organized logically?
4. Does the title suggest the main point?
5. Is the essay free from grammar, usage, and mechanics errors?

Guidelines for Evaluating Assignment 3

1. Does the introductory paragraph state the discipline in which the student chose to write?
2. Does the essay present reasons for the student's choice in a clear, logical way?
3. Is the vocabulary appropriate to the subject?
4. Is the essay free from grammar, usage, and mechanics errors?

YOU THE WRITER

Assignment

1. Choose an essay in which a person has a special gift or ability. Imagine what it would be like to be this person. Describe how it feels to paint, write music, and so on. Explain what motivates you and how creating something makes you feel.

Prewriting. Make word banks to collect the vocabulary you will need to write about your subject from the perspective of the creator.

Writing. Begin your own essay with a description of the person and the skill in which you are interested. Become that person and describe the creative process. Why do you write, paint, or write music, for example? Explain why you must do what you do.

Revising. Revise your essay. Add any information you think will strengthen it. Edit your sentences so that they are logically arranged.

Assignment

2. Choose one of the more scientific or technological essays in this unit and pretend you are a scientist researching a similar topic. As a scientist, do you agree or disagree with the basic premise of the essay? Explain why the essay is effective or why it is not.

Prewriting. List the scientific points in the essay. Use this list to build your argument for or against the premise of the essay.

Writing. Write the first draft of your own essay. Be sure to end your introductory paragraph with a thesis statement. Organize your ideas as you think a scientist would.

Revising. Revise your first draft. Check to see that your title suggests the main point and that this point is clearly made. Make sure your opinion is adequately supported.

Assignment

3. If you were a writer, about which of these subjects would you choose to write: science, music, math, art, or language arts? Why? What is it about the content area that appeals to you? Explain how you would go about writing an essay.

Prewriting. Freewrite about the content area that appeals to you. Explore why you would choose to write about a particular subject if you were a writer.

Writing. Write the first draft of your own essay. In your introductory paragraph, be sure to state the discipline in which you would write. Go on to discuss the reasons for your choice. Try to use the vocabulary appropriate to your subject.

Revising. Revise your first draft. Check to see that you have stated the reasons for your choice clearly and in logical order. Edit your sentences. Finally, proofread your final draft.

YOU THE CRITIC

Assignment

1. Choose two of the essays in this unit and compare or contrast their tones. Analyze the language in the essays and draw a conclusion about how the authors achieved their tones. Also discuss how the tone of each essay is appropriate for the subject.

Prewriting. Make word banks for each essay. List the key words that point to specific tones. Categorize them in logical order.

Writing. Begin your own essay with an explanation of tone. Examine one essay then the other. Compare or contrast their tones, using specific language from the essays. Summarize your main points in your last paragraph and reach a conclusion.

Revising. Read over your essay. Make sure your introduction provides an adequate explanation of tone. Check to see that you have compared or contrasted the tones of your chosen essays.

Assignment

2. Choose one of the essays and explore how the author makes his subject exciting and appealing. Analyze the language the author uses to make the subject of the essay come alive for the reader. Examine any other techniques, such as dialogue, that are used.

Prewriting. Brainstorm to form a list of the essay's appealing features. Organize the list to separate language and technique.

Writing. Begin your own essay with an introductory paragraph stating your premise. List and discuss the language that makes the essay exciting. Continue with a discussion of the author's technique. Summarize your main points and state a conclusion.

Revising. Read over your essay. Make sure your introduction arouses your reader's interest. Check to see that you have discussed both language and technique logically and cohesively.

Assignment

3. Choose one of the essays about a person and explain how the essay introduces the person to the reader. How does the author make the person interesting? What details are given to make the subject of the essay real to the reader?

Prewriting. Use a cueing technique to generate ideas about your topic. Jot down the questions *Who? What? Where? When?* and *Why?* Then answer each of the questions and explore how effectively the author presents information to answer each of the questions.

Writing. Present the subject, what he or she is famous for, where the person worked or works, when the person worked or works, and why the person does what he or she does. Continue with a discussion of how well you got to know the subject of the essay.

Revising. Revise your essay. Add any information you think will strengthen it. Edit your sentences so that they flow smoothly.

YOU THE CRITIC
Guidelines for Evaluating Assignment 1

1. Does the essay compare or contrast the tones of two essays?
2. Does the beginning of the essay provide an adequate explanation of the tone?
3. Does the paper clearly compare or contrast the tones by using specific language from the essays?
4. Is the essay free from grammar, usage, and mechanics errors?

Guidelines for Evaluating Assignment 2

1. Does the introductory paragraph state the student's premise about how the author makes his subject exciting, and does it arouse the reader's interest?
2. Is the language and technique which makes the essay exciting discussed logically and cohesively?
3. Does the final paragraph summarize the main points and state a conclusion based on evidence?
4. Is the essay free from grammar, usage, and mechanics errors?

Guidelines for Evaluating Assignment 3

1. Does the essay present the subject in all aspects of his or her life?
2. Has the student explained how well he or she got to know and relate to the subject through the selection?
3. Do the sentences flow smoothly?
4. Is the essay free from grammar, usage, and mechanics errors?

ABOVE VITEBSK, 1922
Marc Chagall
Three Lions

POETRY

Short stories, essays, autobiographies—all are examples of prose, the language that you hear in your daily life. Poetry, unlike prose, consists of language with a strong musical quality in which the words are highly charged with meaning. Usually poetry is written in lines, and these lines are grouped into stanzas.

Poetry is one of the oldest forms of literature. Before literature was written down, people told stories. They used rhythm and rhyme to help them remember the stories better. Ballads were actually stories in poetic form that were sung. Many narrative poems still use rhythm and rhyme to tell stories.

In addition to using rhythm and rhyme, poets use language in other special ways to appeal to a reader's senses and emotions. Because many poems are short, poets choose each word and phrase with care to create vivid images, or pictures, in the reader's mind.

The poems in this unit include narrative poems and poems in which language is used in unusual and creative ways.

Humanities Note

Fine art, *Above Vitebsk,* 1922, by Marc Chagall. The painter Marc Chagall (1887-1985) began his study of painting in his native Russia at schools in Vitebsk and St. Petersburg. His quest for knowledge and freedom in the arts took him to Berlin and then to Paris, where he was to spend most of his artistic life. In Paris he was exposed to all of the trends of modern art. These movements had little effect on Chagall's art. His fiercely independent style combines memories and dreams painted in a colorful, personal way.

Marc Chagall returned to Russia in 1914; the outbreak of World War I prevented him from leaving until 1922. During this period, Chagall looked to the Russian village life around him for subjects to express in his art. *Above Vitebsk* (1922) was one of the many paintings he produced in these years. This landscape is based on a view from a window of his rented room. Above the lanes of Vitebsk an image floats, cloud-like, defying gravity. The landscape in cool and pale colors is a sharp contrast to the bizarre image of the floating man. Chagall perhaps wanted to disrupt the placid order of the village with this fantastic shape above it. Chagall often introduced illogical images such as this into a composition for poetic emphasis.

Reading Actively The process outlined on this page will help students become more active readers of poetry.

You may want to explain to students that this process is similar to the one they have used in reading fiction. The special requirements of poetry, however, call for a few key differences in approach.

Since poetry tends to be more musical than prose, it is important to read a poem slowly and read it several times—aloud as well as silently. You may also want to tell students that the music of a poem often reinforces its meaning. A poem about a cavalry charge, for instance, might have a galloping rhythm.

Another strategy that you might want to highlight for students is paraphrasing. In its intensity, poetry can sometimes be intimidating. When students can put a poem in their own words, they will feel more at home with it. Caution them, however, that a paraphrase is not a substitute for a poem. Show them that, while paraphrasing is a useful technique, it also eliminates a poem's music.

After discussing each strategy with students, you may want to read "Mushrooms" with them and show how these approaches work in action. Tell them that the annotations accompanying the poem are only a sample and that their own questions might be different.

For further practice with the process, use the selection in the Teaching Portfolio, "Elizabeth Blackwell," pp. 682–685, which students can annotate themselves. Encourage them to continue using these strategies when reading other poems.

READING ACTIVELY

Poetry

Reading poetry demands getting actively involved. The poet Wallace Stevens has written: "In poetry, you must love the words, the ideas, and the images and rhythms with all your capacity to love anything at all."

Use the following strategies to help you read a poem actively and discover the poem's full meaning.

Question

Poetry makes us look at the world with new eyes. As you read, ask questions about the meaning of the words and the effect of the language. Stop to think about the vivid images, or word pictures. What do they make you see and feel?

Clarify

The words in poetry are often easy to read, but getting the sense of the words is more difficult. Stop to clarify or clear up any questions you may have. If the words do not make sense to you, perhaps the poet is using them figuratively and intends to play with your imagination.

Listen

Listen to the musical quality created by the use of rhythm and rhyme. What effect is created by the use of repetition and alliteration?

Summarize

If a poem tells a story, stop at appropriate points to summarize what has happened so far.

Paraphrase

Put the poem in your own words. By doing so, you will make its meaning your own.

Pull It Together

Ralph Waldo Emerson has written: "A poem is made up of thoughts, each of which filled the whole sky of the poet in its turn." After you have read a poem, bring all these thoughts together. What did the poem say to you?

Objectives

1 To learn how to read a poem actively
2 To understand personification
3 To learn how to read lines of poetry
4 To find synonyms in a poem
5 To write a poem using personification

Support Material

Teaching Portfolio

Teacher Backup, pp. 679–681
Grammar in Action Worksheet, *Understanding Punctuation in Poetry,* pp. 686–687
Usage and Mechanics Worksheet, p. 688
Analyzing Literature Worksheet, *Understanding Personification,* p. 689
Language Worksheet, *Finding Synonyms,* p. 690
Selection Test, pp. 691–692

Mushrooms

Question: Will this poem be about mushrooms?

Sylvia Plath

Overnight, very
Whitely, discreetly,
Very quietly

Our toes, our noses
Take hold on the loam,[1]
Acquire the air.

Questions: Who is the speaker? Could it be the mushrooms?

Nobody sees us,
Stops us, betrays us;
The small grains make room.

Listening: Notice the way in which the short lines create a quiet but insistent rhythm.

Soft fists insist on
Heaving the needles,
The leafy bedding,

Clarification: The mushrooms *do* seem to be speaking. The poet presents them as an army.

Even the paving.
Our hammers, our rams,[2]
Earless and eyeless,

Perfectly voiceless,
Widen the crannies,
Shoulder through holes. We

Clarification: These stanzas seem to describe how the caps of the mushrooms poke up through the ground.

Diet on water,
On crumbs of shadow,
Bland-mannered,[3] asking

---

1. **loam** (lōm) *n.*: Rich, dark soil.
2. **rams**: Heavy beams used to break down gates, walls, doors, and so forth.
3. **bland-mannered** (bland′ man′ ərd) *adj.*: Having a smooth, mild way of acting.

Presentation

Motivation/Prior Knowledge You might want to ask students whether they have seen mushrooms growing in the woods. Have them describe these plants. Then ask them what they think a mushroom would say if it could speak like a human. Tell them that the speakers in Sylvia Plath's poem *are* mushrooms.

Master Teacher Note If you want to develop the idea of extended personification, you may use the poem "Jetliner," page 536, with this selection. In that poem, a jetliner is compared to a runner.

Thematic Idea Another selection that deals with the theme of fantasy is "The Story-Teller" on page 615.

Purpose-Setting Question What makes this poem a drama rather than a mere description?

Master Teacher Note By encouraging students to interact with the text, you will help them to become active readers. Questioning and clarifying are strategies that students have already used in reading fiction.

Listening is an activity that is particularly suited to poetry, with its rhythms and rich texture of sounds. Students will gain more from a poem by reading it aloud and considering the relation of sound devices to meaning.

Paraphrasing is also a strategy that is especially appropriate for poetry. You may want to have students paraphrase shorter poems in their entirety. For longer poems, you can ask students to paraphrase difficult passages or key thematic statements.

As students first work with this process, you may have to coach them on how to formulate good questions, relate sound to meaning, and construct paraphrases.

Enrichment Another poem in which Sylvia Plath uses personification is "Mirror" (from *Crossing the Water,* by Sylvia Plath).

Personification is also a favorite device of the contemporary poet A.R. Ammons, who frequently converses with mountains, winds, and brooks in his work (see *Collected Poems 1951–1971.* New York: W.W. Norton & Co., 1972).

Question Consider telling students that a poem spoken by a character, whether a person or a mushroom, usually has more dramatic interest than a poem which is a description. When we hear or read a speech, we immediately want to know more about the speaker—or speakers, in this case.

Listen You might want to point out to students that the lines of this poem are unusually short, each containing two accented syllables. The short lines and small stanzas create an effect of creeping, insistent motion that imitates the advance of the mushrooms.

Grammar in Action

Traditionally, the first word in a line of **poetry** is capitalized. Some modern poets take poetic license to break this rule; however, this poem by Sylvia Plath and all except three of the other poems in this unit follow the traditional rule of capitalization.

Additionally, most poets start each line of poetry directly under the preceeding one. However, some poets establish their own pattern for where each line will begin.

Poets also establish their own internal and end punctuation. When you read poetry, pay close attention to the punctuation marks. It is not always necessary to pause at the end of a line. Rather, pause when the poet has indicated to do so with a punctuation mark. The rhythm and meaning of the poem depend on correct reading.

Student Activity 1. Peruse through the poetry section of this book and find the poems that do not follow the traditional rules of capitalization. Do the poets seem to have established their own rule for capitalization or not? Explain.

Little or nothing.
So many of us!
So many of us!

We are shelves, we are
Tables, we are meek,
We are edible,

Nudgers and shovers
In spite of ourselves.
Our kind multiplies:

We shall by morning
Inherit the earth.
Our foot's in the door.

Questions: Why does the speaker repeat these two lines? Perhaps the repetition intensifies the effect!

Paraphrase: The mushrooms move quietly and meekly, but their presence is felt because they multiply.

Pulling It Together: The mushrooms are like a quiet army that takes over the world.

Sylvia Plath (1932–1963) was born in Boston. She developed an early interest in writing and published her first poems when she was only seventeen. A brilliant student, Plath attended Cambridge University on a Fulbright scholarship. While in England, she met and married Ted Hughes, who was to become one of the foremost British poets of his generation. Plath's own work is often noted for its gothic undertones. Did you notice the violent images as you read "Mushrooms"?

Paraphrase The poet emphasizes the multiplying number of mushrooms by describing them in so many different ways in one small stanza.

Pulling It Together Allusion is the device by which a writer refers to a well-known passage from another work in order to point up a theme. In using the phrase "Inherit the earth," Plath is alluding to a phrase spoken by Jesus in the Bible. "Blessed are the meek: for they shall inherit the earth." (Matthew 5:5)

Of course Plath's allusion is ironic. Jesus was referring to those who are mild and deserving. There are no connotations of an insidious takeover, as there are in Plath's poem.

More About the Author Sylvia Plath wrote many of her last poems in a burst of inspiration, often at the rate of more than one a day. (These poems appear in her book *Ariel.*) Ask students what conditions might lead a poet to write so many good poems in such a short space of time.

Reader's Response What do the mushrooms symbolize to you?

Student Activity 2. Find the poems in this unit that do not begin each line directly under the preceding one. See if you can identify a pattern to each of them.

Student Activity 3. Read Sylvia Plath's poem twice. First pay close attention to the punctuation marks. Then reread it pausing at the end of each line and between each of the stanzas where there are no end punctuation marks. What has happened to the meaning and the rhythm of the poem? Find three other poems in this book where the poet has not used punctuation marks at the end of each line. Copy several of the lines according to the way they should be read, not the way the poet wrote them. Practice reading the poem without pausing at the end of each line. Be prepared to read the poem aloud in class.

Student Activity 4. Become a modern poet. Find a poem that you particularly like but that does not follow the traditional rules of capitalization, punctuation, and line placement. Write your own poem following the pattern of the one you have chosen.

Student Activity 5. Organize a bulletin board with poems you like. Some should follow the traditional poetry rules, others should vary. Point out the rules and the variations.

Closure and Extension

ANSWERS TO THINKING ABOUT THE SELECTION

Recalling

1. Their purpose is to take over the earth.
2. They will accomplish their purpose "Overnight."
3. No one notices because they are quiet, discreet, and small.

Interpreting

4. Suggested Response: These words create a sense of secret, silent activity. Another word that creates this effect is "Whitely."
5. Suggested Response: These words create a sense of violent, warlike action. A verb that creates this same effect is "Shoulder."
6. Suggested Response: This line calls up a picture of mushrooms sprouting everywhere.

Applying

7. Answers will differ. Suggested Response: It is easier to defend against a clearcut attack because you know who or what your opponent is. An insidious attack may surprise you with your guard down.

Challenge Why do you think the poet divided her poem into three-line stanzas rather than running all the lines together?

ANALYZING LITERATURE

1. The poet makes it seem as if the mushrooms are talking. She says they have "toes" and "noses" and that their "foot's in the door." She describes them as if they were an army.
2. Suggested Response: By having the mushrooms speak about their secret attempt to take over the earth, the poet makes their growth seem ominous and dramatic.

CRITICAL THINKING AND READING

1. There are ten sentences. One sentence ends in the middle of a line.
2. The following lines should be read without stopping at the end: 1, 3, 4, 10, 18, 21, 25, 28, and 31.

THINKING ABOUT THE SELECTION

Recalling

1. What is the mushrooms' purpose?
2. How long does it take them to accomplish their purpose?
3. Why does no one notice what the mushrooms are doing?

Interpreting

4. Explain the effect created by the words *discreetly, quietly,* and *voiceless.* Find one other word that also creates this impression.
5. Explain the effect created by the words *fists, hammers,* and *rams.* Find a verb that creates the same effect.
6. Explain the effect of the line: "Our kind multiplies."

Applying

7. The word *insidious* means "operating at a slow but relentless pace in a manner that is not readily apparent." Explain why an insidious attack can be even more dangerous than an open one.

ANALYZING LITERATURE

Understanding Personification

Personification is the process of giving human characteristics to nonhuman objects. For example, a gentle spring breeze can be personified as a child at play.

1. Explain how the poet personifies mushrooms.
2. Why is this use of personification effective?

CRITICAL THINKING AND READING

Reading Lines

The end of a line in poetry does not always signal the end of a sentence. Let the punctuation marks guide you. A period, question mark, or exclamation mark tells you to come to a full stop. A comma tells you to pause briefly, and a semicolon or colon tells you to take a slightly longer pause. If no punctuation mark appears at the end of a line, do not pause at all.

Answer each question below. Then read the poem aloud.

1. How many sentences are there in this poem? How many sentences end in the middle of a line?
2. Which lines should you read without stopping at the end?
3. Why do you think the poet used a colon at the end of line 30?
4. What effect is created by having you come to a full stop before reading the last line?

UNDERSTANDING LANGUAGE

Finding Synonyms

A **synonym** is a word that means the same or almost the same thing as another word. For example, the words *whole* and *complete* are synonyms, as are the words *injure* and *damage.* For each of the following words, find its synonym in the poem.

1. deceive
2. silently
3. carefully
4. mild

THINKING AND WRITING

Using Personification

A mushroom is a rapidly growing fungus that you may have eaten for dinner. By using personification, however, the poet makes you see this common food with new eyes. Select a fruit or vegetable that might appear as part of someone's dinner. For example, you might select the potato. Brainstorm to list as many qualities of this foodstuff as possible. Then, by using personification, write a poem making your classmates see this common food in a new light. When you revise, make sure you have given your foodstuff human traits that seem appropriate. Proofread your poem and share it with your classmates.

3. Suggested Response: She used a colon because the sentence in the next two lines illustrates the meaning of the sentence in line 30.
4. Suggested Response: Having to stop before reading the last line gives it more emphasis and makes it seem more ominous.

UNDERSTANDING LANGUAGE

1. deceive—betrays
2. silently—quietly
3. carefully—discreetly
4. mild—meek

THINKING AND WRITING

For help with this assignment, students can refer to Lesson 18, "Writing a Poem," in the Handbook of Writing About Literature.

Publishing Student Writing You may want to collect students' poems together in a booklet.

Writing Across the Curriculum Have students research and report on mushrooms. You might want to inform the science department of this assignment, so that science teachers can direct student research.

Narrative Poetry

HOLY MOUNTAIN III, 1945
Horace Pippin
Hirshhorn Museum and Sculpture Garden, Smithsonian Institution

Humanities Note

Fine art, *The Holy Mountain III,* 1945, by Horace Pippin. The Afro-American artist Horace Pippin (1888-1946) was born in West Chester, Pennsylvania. Pippin was a true primitive, or naive, painter; he had no formal art training. Wounded in World War I, he lost the use of his right arm. Unable to deny the urge to express himself through art, Pippin completed his first painting, at the age of forty-three, by guiding his lifeless arm with his left hand. His images of the people, fantasy scenes, and history are all painted from the heart.

Near the end of his life, Horace Pippin produced a series of four paintings entitled *The Holy Mountain.* They were inspired by the outbreak of World War II. His own memories of war were so vivid and horrible that he felt compelled to make an anti-war statement through his art. These paintings were a cry for world peace and love among mankind. *The Holy Mountain III* shows a good shepherd in an idyllic, flower-studded field. Animals, wild and tame, and children are all together in harmony in this field. In the background is a line of trees under which are darkness, graves, and figures of war. A viewer can easily give a narrative interpretation to the painting.

Focus

More About the Author As a professor of romance languages, Henry Wadsworth Longfellow studied the cultures and tongues of Europe. But as a poet, he was drawn to write about the heroic figures in the American past —Paul Revere and Hiawatha among them. You might ask the class why, with a background in European languages, he chose to write about American subjects.

Literary Focus At this point, perhaps, you may want to review the narrative elements, including plot, character, setting, and point of view.

Look for As background, you can tell students that the British were marching to Lexington and Concord to arrest several leaders of the colonists whom the British looked upon as rabblerousers. They also wanted to confiscate an arsenal of weapons the colonists had collected.

Writing/Prior Knowledge You might help students start their brainstorming by asking when Paul Revere lived, where he lived, what he did for a living, and so on. They can continue to brainstorm in groups.

Vocabulary Many of the words in the list help to set the mood of the poem. Your **more advanced** students might profit from writing sentences using the vocabulary words.

Spelling Tip The *ea* spelling of short *e* as in *tread* and *stealthy* is also found in *wealth, measure, read* (past tense).

GUIDE FOR READING

Paul Revere's Ride

Henry Wadsworth Longfellow (1807-1882) was born in Portland, in what is now the state of Maine. Longfellow published his first poem at the age of thirteen and two years later entered Bowdoin College, where he was a classmate of Nathaniel Hawthorne, who also became a famous writer. Longfellow's best-remembered works include the narrative poems "The Song of Hiawatha" and "Paul Revere's Ride." In "Paul Revere's Ride," he tells of a Revolutionary hero's historic ride.

The Narrative Poem

A **narrative poem** is a poem that tells a story. Like short stories, narrative poems have plot, setting, characters, dialogue, and theme. "Paul Revere's Ride" is set around Boston on the eve of the American Revolution. The main action is Revere's legendary midnight ride, during which he warned his fellow colonists of the approaching British army. His bravery gave the colonists time to get ready so they could turn back the British that night. The main characters are Paul Revere and his friend.

However, a poem is not a short story. A narrative poem is in poetic form, not in prose. It relies on rhythm and rhyme. It is usually organized in **stanzas,** groups of lines that form units in a poem, just as paragraphs are the units of a story.

Look For

As you read "Paul Revere's Ride," pay attention to the first time Paul Revere speaks because it will prepare you for what will happen in the rest of the poem. Why is his ride so important? How does it affect the fate of the colonists?

Writing

Most likely, you have heard of Paul Revere before this. Brainstorm with your classmates to list all the details you can recall about him.

Vocabulary

Knowing the following words will help you as you read "Paul Revere's Ride."

phantom (fan′ təm) *n.*: Ghostlike (p. 509)
tread (tred) *n.*: Step (p. 510)
stealthy (stel′ thē) *adj.*: Secret; quiet (p. 510)
somber (säm′ bər) *adj.*: Dark; gloomy (p. 510)
impetuous (im pech′ oo wəs) *adj.*: Impulsive (p. 511)
spectral (spek′ trəl) *adj.*: Ghostly (p. 511)
aghast (ə gast′) *adj.*: Horrified (p. 512)

Objectives

1 To understand the elements of a narrative poem
2 To understand a sequence of events
3 To participate in a choral reading
4 To summarize the events in a narrative poem

Support Material

Teaching Portfolio
Teacher Backup, pp. 693–695
Usage and Mechanics Worksheet, p. 696
Vocabulary Check, p. 697–698
Critical Thinking and Reading Worksheet, *Sequencing Events,* p. 699
Language Worksheet, *Using a Thesaurus,* p. 700
Selection Test, pp. 701–702
Art Transparency 10, *Paul Revere Gives the Alarm to the Countryside* by Charles Hoffbauer

Paul Revere's Ride

Henry Wadsworth Longfellow

Listen, my children, and you shall hear 1
Of the midnight ride of Paul Revere,
On the eighteenth of April, in Seventy-five;
Hardly a man is now alive 2
Who remembers that famous day and year.

He said to his friend, "If the British march 3
By land or sea from the town to-night,
Hang a lantern aloft in the belfry arch[1]
Of the North Church tower as a signal light,—
One, if by land, and two, if by sea;
And I on the opposite shore will be,
Ready to ride and spread the alarm
Through every Middlesex[2] village and farm,
For the country folk to be up and to arm."

Then he said, "Good night!" and with muffled oar
Silently rowed to the Charlestown[3] shore,
Just as the moon rose over the bay,
Where swinging wide at her moorings[4] lay
The Somerset, British man-of-war;[5]
A phantom ship, with each mast and spar[6] 4
Across the moon like a prison bar,
And a huge black hulk, that was magnified
By its own reflection in the tide.

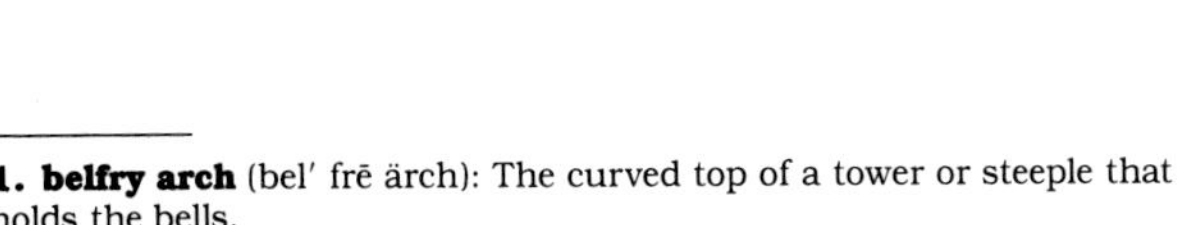

1. **belfry arch** (bel′ frē ärch): The curved top of a tower or steeple that holds the bells.
2. **Middlesex** (mid′ 'l seks′): A county in Massachusetts.
3. **Charlestown** (chärl′ stoun′): Part of Boston on the harbor.
4. **moorings** (moor′ iŋs) *n.*: The lines, cables, or chains that hold a ship to the shore.
5. **man-of-war**: An armed naval vessel; warship.
6. **mast and spar**: Poles used to support sails.

Presentation

Motivation/Prior Knowledge Paul Revere placed the cause of the colonists above his own safety. Elicit names of others in United States history who have placed the nation's welfare above their own. Nathan Hale ("I regret that I have but one life to give for my country.") could be one example.

Speaking and Listening Reading stanzas 10–12 aloud can demonstrate to students how pronounced the rhythm of the poem becomes as it imitates the pace of Revere's actual ride. You might read it yourself or choose a student who can read it dramatically.

Thematic Idea Another selection that deals with the theme of courage in the face of war is "Barbara Frietchie" on page 525.

Purpose-Setting Question What effect do poems such as this one have on people's understanding of their country's history, heroes, and ideals?

1 **Literary Focus** What effect does starting the poem with the word *listen* have on the reader?

2 **Discussion** The poem was actually written eighty years after Paul Revere's ride. How might that fact affect the telling of the story?

3 **Discussion** What is the effect of not mentioning the name of Revere's friend? On whom is the reader's attention focused?

4 **Discussion** How do these details help to build tension?

Master Teacher Note Have students look at Art Transparency 10, *Paul Revere Gives the Alarm to the Countryside* by Charles Hoffbauer, in the Teaching Portfolio. This painting illustrates the poem "Paul Revere's Ride," in which Revere on horseback alerts his countrymen of the approach of the British. Ask students what other works of literature and art were inspired by the events of the Revolutionary War.

5 Literary Focus Ask students the effect of the repetition of initial sounds as in *p*igeons-*p*erch, *r*afters-*r*ound, *m*ade-*m*asses-*m*oving, *s*hapes-*s*hade, *t*rembling-*t*all, *w*indow-*w*all.

6 Literary Focus What atmosphere does the description of the cemetery create?

Meanwhile, his friend, through alley and street,
Wanders and watches with eager ears,
Till in the silence around him he hears
The muster[7] of men at the barrack door,
The sound of arms, and the tramp of feet,
And the measured tread of the grenadiers,[8]
Marching down to their boats on the shore.

Then he climbed the tower of the Old North Church,
By the wooden stairs, with stealthy tread,
To the belfry-chamber overhead,
And startled the pigeons from their perch
On the somber rafters,[9] that round him made
5 Masses and moving shapes of shade,—
By the trembling ladder, steep and tall,
To the highest window in the wall,
Where he paused to listen and look down
A moment on the roofs of the town,
And the moonlight flowing over all.

Beneath, in the churchyard, lay the dead,
In their night-encampment on the hill,
Wrapped in silence so deep and still
6 That he could hear, like a sentinel's[10] tread,
The watchful night-wind, as it went
Creeping along from tent to tent,
And seeming to whisper, "All is well!"
A moment only he feels the spell
Of the place and the hour, and the secret dread
Of the lonely belfry and the dead;
For suddenly all his thoughts are bent
On a shadowy something far away,
Where the river widens to meet the bay,—
A line of black that bends and floats
On the rising tide, like a bridge of boats.

---

7. muster *v.*: An assembly of troops summoned for inspection, roll call, or service.
8. grenadiers (gren′ ə dirz′) *n.*: Members of a special regiment or corps.
9. rafters *n.*: The beams that slope from the ridge of a roof to the eaves and serve to support the roof.
10. sentinel (sen′ ti n'l) *n.*: A person who keeps guard.

Meanwhile, impatient to mount and ride,
Booted and spurred, with a heavy stride
On the opposite shore walked Paul Revere.
Now he patted his horse's side,
Now gazed at the landscape far and near,
Then, impetuous, stamped the earth,
And turned and tightened his saddle-girth;[11]
But mostly he watched with eager search
The belfry-tower of the Old North Church, 7
As it rose above the graves on the hill,
Lonely and spectral and somber and still.
And lo! as he looks, on the belfry's height
A glimmer, and then a gleam of light!
He springs to the saddle, the bridle[12] he turns,
But lingers and gazes, till full on his sight
A second lamp in the belfry burns!

A hurry of hoofs in a village street,
A shape in the moonlight, a bulk in the dark,
And beneath, from the pebbles, in passing, a spark
Struck out by a steed flying fearless and fleet:
That was all! And yet, through the gloom and the light,
The fate of a nation was riding that night;
And the spark struck out by that steed[13] in his flight, 8
Kindled the land into flame with its heat.

He has left the village and mounted the steep,[14]
And beneath him, tranquil and broad and deep,
Is the Mystic,[15] meeting the ocean tides;
And under the alders[16] that skirt its edge,
Now soft on the sand, now loud on the ledge,
Is heard the tramp of his steed as he rides.

7 Discussion What details in this stanza create a feeling of eagerness and tension?

8 Discussion What was the "spark" struck by that steed in his flight?

---

11. girth (gurth) *n.*: A band put around the belly of a horse for holding a saddle.
12. bridle (brīd' 'l) *n.*: A head harness for guiding a horse.
13. steed *n.*: A horse, especially a high-spirited riding horse.
14. steep *n.*: A slope or incline having a sharp rise.
15. Mystic (mis' tik): A river in Massachusetts.
16. alders (ôl' dərz) *n.*: Trees and shrubs of the birch family.

9 Critical Thinking and Reading What future events do these lines foreshadow?

It was twelve by the village clock,
When he crossed the bridge into Medford[17] town.
He heard the crowing of the cock,
And the barking of the farmer's dog,
And felt the damp of the river fog,
That rises after the sun goes down.

It was one by the village clock,
When he galloped into Lexington.[18]
He saw the gilded weathercock[19]
Swim in the moonlight as he passed,
And the meeting-house windows, blank and bare,
Gaze at him with a spectral glare,
9 As if they already stood aghast
At the bloody work they would look upon.

---

17. Medford (med′ fərd): A town outside of Boston.
18. Lexington (lek′ siŋ tən): A town in eastern Massachusetts, outside of Boston.
19. weathercock (weth′ ər käk′) *n.*: A weathervane in the form of a rooster.

It was two by the village clock,
When he came to the bridge in Concord[20] town.
He heard the bleating[21] of the flock,
And the twitter of birds among the trees,
And felt the breath of the morning breeze
Blowing over the meadows brown.
And one was safe and asleep in his bed
Who at the bridge would be first to fall,
Who that day would be lying dead,
Pierced by a British musket-ball.

You know the rest. In the books you have read,
How the British Regulars[22] fired and fled,— 10

20. Concord (kän′ kôrd): A town in eastern Massachusetts. The first battles of the Revolutionary War (April 19, 1775) were fought in Lexington and Concord.
21. bleating (blēt′ iŋ) *n.*: The sound made by sheep.
22. British Regulars: Members of the army of Great Britain.

10 **Discussion** The day after Revere's ride, colonists from Lexington and Concord fought the British troops. What details does the poet include about the tactics the colonists will use?

513

11 Discussion What was the midnight message of Paul Revere?

Reader's Response You have probably read about Paul Revere in social studies class. How does reading about him in a poem affect your understanding of his role in history?

How the farmers gave them ball for ball,
From behind each fence and farm-yard wall,
Chasing the red-coats down the lane,
Then crossing the fields to emerge again
Under the trees at the turn of the road,
And only pausing to fire and load.

So through the night rode Paul Revere;
And so through the night went his cry of alarm
To every Middlesex village and farm,—
A cry of defiance and not of fear,
A voice in the darkness, a knock at the door,
And a word that shall echo forevermore!
For, borne on the night-wind of the Past,
Through all our history, to the last,
In the hour of darkness and peril and need,
The people will waken and listen to hear
The hurrying hoof-beats of that steed,
11 And the midnight message of Paul Revere.

Closure and Extension

ANSWERS TO THINKING ABOUT THE SELECTION

Recalling

1. Paul Revere makes his ride on April 18, 1775, at midnight.
2. Revere and his friend agree that the friend would hang one lantern in the tower of North Church if the British marched by land and two lanterns if they came by sea. Revere, who would be waiting on the

THINKING ABOUT THE SELECTION

Recalling

1. When does Paul Revere make his ride? (lines 1–5)
2. What agreement does Revere make with his friend? (lines 6–14)
3. How many lamps does Paul Revere finally see in the belfry? (lines 70–72)
4. Through which towns does he ride? (lines 87–110) Name two things he passes in each.
5. Explain whether or not Paul Revere accomplished his purpose.

Interpreting

6. To what is the Somerset compared? (lines 15-23) What is the effect of this image?
7. From his position in the belfry-chamber, how does the friend feel at first? (lines 42–51)
8. What is the "shadowy something far away" that the friend suddenly sees? (lines 52–56)
9. How do lines 78 through 80 express the importance the poet places on the ride?

Applying

10. Do you think Revere's friend is also a hero? Explain your answer.

ANALYZING LITERATURE

Understanding a Narrative Poem

Although it is a poem, "Paul Revere's Ride" resembles a short story in several important ways. First, the poem has a **plot,** a sequence of events that take place and that present a conflict. Characters are introduced, and the setting is established. Next, the poem builds suspense as Revere and his friend wait. The poet writes first of one and then of the other, and the tension mounts. At last the signal appears, and the climax of the poem—the ride—begins.

1. What is the conflict in this narrative poem?
2. Describe Paul Revere's character.
3. How does the poet create suspense in his description of the friend's climb to the belfry-chamber?
4. Cite two specific details that describe the setting effectively. Explain why you chose each.

CRITICAL THINKING AND READING

Sequencing Events

Narrative poems present a **sequence of events,** or arrangement of actions. In the first stanza, the poet tells about Revere's agreement with his friend. That information prepares you for events that follow. Every other stanza builds on the information in the first two stanzas.

1. What does the friend do even before he climbs the belfry-tower?
2. How does stanza 7 relate to stanza 2?
3. How do stanzas 6 and 7 help build suspense?

SPEAKING AND LISTENING

Understanding Choral Reading

Poetry is especially effective when it is read aloud. A **choral reading** is a reading performed by a group, or chorus, of readers.

To perform a choral reading of "Paul Revere's Ride," divide the class into groups, each reading a stanza in turn. Or one group could read the stanzas that tell about Paul Revere; another could read those about his friend; a third could read the stanzas at the beginning and end, which contain the poet's own thoughts.

As you read, remember you are telling a story of adventure and heroism. Read each stanza with an appropriate tone of voice.

THINKING AND WRITING

Summarizing the Events in the Poem

Make a list of the main events in the poem. List them in the order in which they occur. Using this list as your guide, write a summary of the action. When you have finished, reread your summary, making sure you have covered all the important points. Proofread your summary.

(Answers begin on p. 514.)

opposite shore, would ride throughout the countryside and spread the alarm so the people could arm themselves.
3. Revere sees two lamps.
4. Revere rides through Medford, where he hears a cock crow, a farmer's dog bark, and he feels the damp of the river fog. He gallops into Lexington, where he sees the gilded weathercock and the blank meeting-house windows. Finally, he arrives at the bridge in Concord, where he hears sheep bleating and birds twittering, and he feels the morning breeze.
5. He accomplished his purpose. The colonists were warned, were able to prepare themselves, and defeated the British the next day.

Interpreting

6. The poet compares the *Somerset* to a ghost and its masts and spars to prison bars. The effect is an ominous, eerie feeling of possible danger.
7. The friend feels dread at being in the lonely tower at midnight with the dead below in the church cemetery.
8. The "shadowy something far away" that the friend sees are the boats of the British soldiers.
9. The poet states directly that the fate of a nation rested on the outcome of the ride.

Applying

10. Answers will differ. Suggested Response: Revere's friend was also a hero because he risked his life giving Revere information needed to give the alarm. If caught by the British, he would have been branded a traitor.

ANSWERS TO ANALYZING LITERATURE

1. The conflict involves Paul Revere's riding into the countryside without the British knowing so that he could alert the colonists that the British were coming.
2. Paul Revere was brave, impatient, impetuous, and dependable.
3. The poet creates suspense by using words such as *stealthily* to describe the way the friend climbed and by using *somber* and *masses* and *moving shapes of shade* to describe the rafters.
4. Answers will differ. Suggested Response: Lines 44-47, 53, 67, 82, 97–98 all give effective details describing the setting. The details add to the mood of danger and suspense.

ANSWERS TO CRITICAL THINKING AND READING

1. The friend wanders through Boston listening until he hears soldiers marching down to their boats.
2. Stanza 7 returns to describing Revere's actions, a continuation from stanza 2.
3. Stanzas 6 and 7 help build suspense by presenting the apprehensive friend making his way to the eerie belfry-tower and then switching to an impatient Revere on the shore waiting for his signal.

Speaking and Listening Some social studies teachers might be interested in having a choral reading of the poem presented to a social studies class.

Writing Across the Curriculum You may want to tell social studies teachers about the summaries of the poem your students write. They may want to have students compare them with information about the actual historical event.

Focus

More About the Author The author of this ballad is unknown. You might wish to take this opportunity to discuss the worldwide oral tradition, in which many anonymous ballads and other types of literature are handed on.

Literary Focus Common subjects of many ballads still sung today are events in United States history. "The Wreck of the Old '97" and "John Henry," which is included in this text on page 663, are two examples. You might suggest that students bring more historical ballads, either written or recorded, to class. You may also have students identify other common subjects of ballads.

Writing/Prior Knowledge You might want to lead students in a discussion of how reality can be stranger than fiction. For example, you might visit a small, little known, foreign village and be surprised to find your neighbor is staying in the next hotel room.

Vocabulary Your less advanced students may benefit from going over the vocabulary words and their definitions in class before reading the ballad.

GUIDE FOR READING

William Stafford

Ballad

A **ballad** is a narrative poem that tells a simple and dramatic story. It is usually intended to be sung or recited. Ballads generally have strong rhythms and rhymes. For example, read aloud these lines from "William Stafford":

> Through all its ups and downs
>   Some bitter days I saw,
> But never knew what misery was
>   Till I struck Arkansaw.

If you listen carefully as you read, you can hear the very regular rhythm. This regularity contributes to the musical, songlike quality of the ballad. The same is true of the ballad's strong rhymes: *saw/ Arkansaw.*

Many ballads were written by anonymous authors. They were passed along by word of mouth, often through singing, until someone finally wrote them down.

Look For

As you read "William Stafford," look for the ways it is similar to a song. What might the melody be like? Listen closely to the rhythms and rhymes. Finally, think about its story. Is it a sad story or a comical one? Or both?

Writing

Imagine an experience that was so unusual that it seemed "stranger than fiction." Or, imagine someone who seems larger than life. Freewrite about this experience or person, exploring what strikes you as strange or colorful.

Vocabulary

Knowing the following words will help you as you read "William Stafford."

sultry (sul′ trē) *adj.*: Hot and humid (p. 517)

crane (krān) *n.*: A large, slender bird with very long legs and neck (p. 518)

sassafras (sas′ ə fras′) *n.*: Dried root bark of the sassafras tree, usually used in cooking for flavoring (p. 518)

Objectives

1 To understand the features of a ballad
2 To identify sentences not in normal word order and rewrite them in normal order
3 To perform a dramatic reading in a selected tone
4 To write an evaluation of the ballad

Support Material

Teaching Portfolio

Teacher Backup, pp. 703–705
Usage and Mechanics Worksheet, p. 706
Vocabulary Check, p. 707
Critical Thinking and Reading Worksheet, *Reading Inverted Sentences*, p. 708
Language Worksheet, *Understanding Multiple Meanings of Words*, p. 709
Selection Test, pp. 710–711

William Stafford

Anonymous

My name is William Stafford,
Was raised in Boston Town;
For nine years as a rover
I roved the wide world 'round;
Through all its ups and downs
Some bitter days I saw,
But never knew what misery was
Till I struck Arkansaw. 1

I started on my journey,
'Twas the merry month of June;
I landed in New Jersey
One sultry afternoon.
Along came a walking skeleton
With long and lantern jaw.[1]
He asked me to his hotel
In the state of Arkansaw.

1. **lantern jaw:** A long, thin, projecting lower jaw.

Motivation/Prior Knowledge Have students imagine they are wanderers trying to exist in a strange place among strange people. Tell students that they will meet a wanderer who finds himself in a strange place among strange people in the ballad "William Stafford."

Master Teacher Note Point out to students that although this ballad tells of an unpleasant experience, William Stafford tells of the experience in a humorous tone. What might the tone he uses tell you about William Stafford?

Purpose-Setting Question What causes a person to change? Is it the influence of other people, events, or the environment? What causes changes in William Stafford?

1 **Clarification** You may want to have students speculate about why the correct spelling of *Arkansas* was not used in the poem.

2 **Master Teacher Note** Grant Wood is known for painting lean and hungry Americans. This ballad, which tells of lean and hungry people, has a lean and hungry quality to the writing. Encourage the class to compare the techniques that convey "leanness and hungriness" in the poem and in a Grant Wood painting. Consider using Wood's *American Gothic*.

3 **Discussion** What might the ballad be saying about the difficulty of changing one's life for the better?

Master Teacher Note Some students might like to draw a picture of Charles Tyler.

Reader's Response People can seem strange to you when you are outside of your familiar environment. Describe an experience with people (or a person) you encountered when you were away from home or outside of your familiar surroundings. What was strange about the person or people?

I followed up a great long rope
Into his boarding place,
Where hunger and starvation
Were printed on his face;
His bread it was corn dodger;[2]
His beef I could not chaw;[3]
He taxed me fifty cents for that
In the state of Arkansaw.

I rose the next morning early
To catch the early train.
He said, "Young man, you'd better stay.
I have some land to drain.
I'll give you fifty cents a day,
Your washing, board,[4] and all;
You'll find yourself a different lad
When you leave Arkansaw."

Six months I worked for this galoot;[5]
Charles Tyler was his name;
2 He was six feet seven in his boots
And thin as any crane.
His hair hung down like rat tails
Around his lantern jaw;
He was the photograph of all the gents
That's raised in Arkansaw.

He fed me on corn dodgers
As hard as any rock;
My teeth began to loosen;
My knees began to knock.
I got so thin on sassafras,
Could hide behind a straw,
3 So I sho' was a different lad
When I left Arkansaw.

---

2. corn dodger: A small cake of cornmeal, baked or fried hard.
3. chaw: Chew.
4. board: Meals.
5. galoot (gə loot′) *n.*: An awkward person.

Closure and Extension

ANSWERS TO THINKING ABOUT THE SELECTION
Recalling

1. Stafford has roamed the world.
2. Stafford winds up in Arkansas after meeting a man in New Jersey who invited him to his hotel in Arkansas.
3. The food consists of corn dodgers, which are small, hard, baked or

THINKING ABOUT THE SELECTION

Recalling

1. What has William Stafford done for nine years? (lines 1–8)
2. How does he wind up in "Arkansaw"? (lines 9–16)
3. Describe the food there. (lines 21–24)
4. Describe Charles Tyler. (lines 33–40)

Interpreting

5. Why does Stafford stay in "Arkansaw"?
6. In what ways is Stafford "a different lad" when he leaves?
7. Do you thing the anonymous poet expected listeners to take the ballad seriously? Explain.

Applying

8. What people find humorous in one age may not be found amusing in another. Work with your classmates to list the things people find humorous today. Then list the things people might laugh at fifty years from now.

ANALYZING LITERATURE

Understanding Features of a Ballad

Generally, ballads tell about the adventures of colorful, larger-than-life characters. Often the main character is either a great hero or a terrible villain. Events and situations are exaggerated, or stretched to a nearly unrealistic degree. In "William Stafford," exaggeration creates humorous effects. Look, for example, at the description of William's main food—and its effects on him:

He fed me on corn dodgers
As hard as any rock;
My teeth began to loosen;
My knees began to knock.

1. Find two other exaggerations you found especially effective in the ballad. Explain your reason for each choice.
2. In what ways is Tyler a larger-than-life villain?
3. How is this ballad both funny and sad?

CRITICAL THINKING AND READING

Reading Inverted Sentences

In a sentence that is in normal word order, the subject precedes the predicate: *The hikers tramped up the mountain trail.* In an inverted sentence, the order is reversed. Sometimes the direct object comes before the subject and the predicate. In this case the verb follows the subject as it does in normal word order as in this example: *Some bitter days I saw.* To rewrite the example in normal word order, you must put the subject first: *I saw some bitter days.*

Find two sentences in "William Stafford" in which the direct object comes before the subject. Rewrite them in normal word order.

SPEAKING AND LISTENING

Selecting a Voice for a Dramatic Reading

Poetry was sung or recited aloud long before it was written down. Remember that a ballad is a special kind of narrative poem that was meant to be sung or read aloud. Perform a dramatic reading of "William Stafford." Choose an appropriate **tone of voice.** For example, your tone might be **dramatic** (serious or suspenseful). Or, it might be **parodic** (comical or as if you were telling a joke). Then take turns reading aloud.

THINKING AND WRITING

Evaluating the Ballad

You have probably reached an opinion as to whether "William Stafford" is an effective ballad or not. List reasons why you think this ballad is successful or unsuccessful. Then write an essay in which you explain your opinion. Be sure that you support your opinion with specific references from the poem. When you revise, make sure you have organized your supporting information logically. Then proofread your essay and share it with your classmates.

(Answers begin on p. 518.)

fried cakes of cornmeal, unchewable beef, and sassafras tea, for which he is charged fifty cents.

4. Charles Tyler is six feet seven in his boots and thin as any crane. His hair hangs down like rat tails around his long, lantern jaw. He is a galoot, which means he is awkward and ungainly.

Interpreting

5. Stafford stays in Arkansas because Tyler offers him a job draining land.
6. Stafford's teeth have loosened, his knees are knocking, and he is so thin he can hide behind a straw by the time he leaves Arkansas.
7. Answers will differ. Suggested Response: It is not meant to be taken seriously because its tone is light. The purpose of the ballad is to amuse people.

Applying

8. Answers will differ. Suggested Response: People today laugh at situations, people, and events they consider ridiculous or comical. They often laugh at exaggerations. In fifty years people may laugh at our current fashions, food choices, hair styles, and so forth.

Challenge The ballad does not mention how Stafford and Tyler traveled from New Jersey to Arkansas. What means of transportation might they have used and what route might they have taken?

ANSWERS TO ANALYZING LITERATURE

1. Answers will differ. Suggested Response: Exaggerations exist in the description of Tyler as being thin as any crane and having hair that hangs down like rat tails. They are effective because they are vivid and easily pictured in your mind.
2. Tyler is a larger-than-life villain because no good qualities at all are mentioned and because his physical description makes him more of a caricature than a real man.
3. This ballad is funny because the exaggerations are cartoonlike rather than realistic, but it is also sad because Stafford's experience was so unpleasant.

ANSWERS TO CRITICAL THINKING AND READING

Two sentences with the direct object first are "His beef I could not chaw" and "Six months I worked for this galoot." In normal word order they would read: "I could not chaw his beef" and "I worked six months for this galoot."

Speaking and Listening Students can give dramatic readings of "William Stafford" or of other ballads they have brought to the class.

THINKING AND WRITING

For help with this assignment, students can refer to Lesson 13, "Writing About a Poem," in the Handbook of Writing About Literature.

Writing Across the Curriculum You might want to alert music teachers to your use of this ballad. Under a music teacher's guidance, some students could set the ballad to music and sing it to the class.

Focus

More About the Author The name **Joaquin Miller** is the pen name of Cincinnatus Miller. At the age of 17, Miller ran away to the California gold fields. Later, he helped establish a pony express route between Washington Territory and Idaho. When he was in London, he wore a sombrero and cowboy boots and smoked three cigars at once, causing society people of London to accept him as representative of Americans of the West. Ask students why society people of London might have been eager to meet and talk with Joaquin Miller.

Literary Focus Lead students in a discussion of the ways that poetry differs from prose. Have them offer examples of rhythm (perhaps tapping it out on their desks), rhyme, and refrain.

Look For As they notice the rhythm of the poem, your **more advanced** students may be interested in knowing that it is written in iambic tetrameter. Each line has four beats; the pattern is an unstressed syllable followed by a stressed one.

Writing/Prior Knowledge In a speech in 1872, Benjamin Disraeli, Prime Minister of Great Britain, said, "The secret of success is constancy to purpose." Discuss the meaning of this quotation with students. Then have them do the writing exercise.

Vocabulary Using the vocabulary words in sentences will help your **less advanced** students learn them.

Teaching to Ability Levels Ask your **less advanced** students what they know about Columbus's voyage. You might provide background information about the voyage to give the poem a context.

GUIDE FOR READING

Columbus

Joaquin Miller (1837–1913) was born near Liberty, Indiana, though he once claimed that his cradle was "a covered wagon pointed West." He lived in Oregon and California and worked as a teacher, lawyer, and journalist. Disappointed that poetry he had written was not well received, he left for England. In London, both he and his poetry won admiration. In 1886 he returned to America to live near Oakland, California, until his death. "Columbus," Miller's best-known poem, recounts the famous voyage of this daring explorer.

Elements of Poetry

Three basic elements of poetry are rhythm, rhyme, and refrain. **Rhythm** is the pattern of stressed and unstressed syllables in the lines of a poem. A poem's rhythm usually contributes to meaning. For example, the basic rhythm of "Columbus" is aggressive and forward-driving. It is a rhythm well suited to the poem's theme.

Rhyme is the repetition of sounds in words that appear close to one another in a poem. The commonest form of rhyme is **end rhyme,** which occurs at the end of two or more lines:

> This mad sea shows his teeth to-night.
> He curls his lip, he lies in wait,
> With lifted teeth as if to bite!

A **refrain** is a word, phrase, line, or group of lines that is repeated regularly in a poem. A refrain usually comes at the end of each stanza. Sometimes, as in "Columbus," the refrain recurs with small variations: "He said, 'Sail on! sail on! and on!' "

Look For

As you read "Columbus," listen to its rhythm. Look for the rhymes and see if they follow a regular pattern. Think, too, about the refrain. How does it convey the poem's theme?

Writing

Recall a person who kept trying until succeeding at some activity that seemed impossible at first. Freewrite for five minutes about this.

Vocabulary

Knowing the following words will help you as you read "Columbus."

mutinous (myōōt′ 'n əs) *adj.*: Rebellious (p. 522)
wan (wan) *adj.*: Pale (p. 522)
swarthy (swôr′ thē) *adj.*: Having a dark complexion (p. 522)
unfurled (un furld′) *adj.*: Unfolded (p. 522)

Objectives

1 To understand the use of rhythm and refrain
2 To make inferences about theme
3 To appreciate old-fashioned words
4 To write a poem about a historical figure

Support Material

Teaching Portfolio
Teacher Backup, pp. 713–715
Usage and Mechanics Worksheet, p. 716
Vocabulary Check, p. 717
Critical Thinking and Reading Worksheet, *Making Inferences About Theme,* p. 718
Language Worksheet, *Appreciating Old-fashioned Words,* p. 719
Selection Test, pp. 720–721

THE LANDING OF COLUMBUS, 1876
Currier and Ives
Museum of the City of New York

Columbus

Joaquin Miller

Behind him lay the gray Azores,[1]
Behind the Gates of Hercules;[2] 1
Before him not the ghost of shores;
Before him only shoreless seas.
The good mate said: "Now must we pray,
For lo! the very stars are gone.
Brave Adm'r'l, speak; what shall I say?"
"Why, say: 'Sail on! sail on! and on!'"

---

1. **Azores** (ā′ zôrz): A group of Portuguese islands in the North Atlantic west of Portugal.
2. **Gates of Hercules** (gāts uv hʉr′ kyə lēz′): Entrance to the Strait of Gibraltar, between Spain and Africa.

Presentation

Humanities Note

This illustration is a Currier and Ives lithograph. A lithograph is a print made with ink and stone or metal plates.

During the mid- and late-1800's, Currier and Ives published over 4,000 scenes of American life and history. Their pictures have been used for illustration and for decoration ever since.

1. In what way does this lithograph symbolize Columbus's monumental deed?
2. What details in this print capture the spirit of Columbus's "Sail on!"
3. Could the message of the refrain have been visually stated by a symbol, rather than by the illustration? If so, what might the symbol have been?

Motivation/Prior Knowledge Lead students in a discussion of the dangers faced by early explorers. These dangers included environmental forces, such as storms, drought, and cold. Other dangers were encountering hostile inhabitants, losing their way, and running out of supplies. Remind students that when Columbus began his voyage, he did not know what challenges or dangers were in store for him.

Master Teacher Note Ask the class what comparable challenges twentieth century people, undaunted by fear of the enormity of their undertaking, have faced. Who among these challengers have succeeded? Who have failed? What is the common denominator they share with Columbus?

Purpose-Setting Question Why does Columbus continue in the face of his crew's fear?

1 **Clarification** You may want to explain that the Gates of Hercules were named for Hercules, hero of Greek and Roman mythology, who performed great feats of strength and courage.

Thematic Ideas Another selection in this book that depicts events in the establishment of the United States is "Paul Revere's Ride," page 509.

Courage and perseverance in the face of danger is a theme that recurs throughout this book. "The Captain and His Horse" (page 47), "The Day the Sun Came Out" (page 107), "The Drummer Boy of Shiloh" (page 151), "The Diary of Anne Frank" (page 303), "Harriet Tubman: Guide to Freedom" (page 383), "Paul Revere's Ride" (page 509), "Barbara Frietchie" (page 525), "Staying Alive" (page 609), and "The Girl Who Hunted Rabbits" (page 635) involve courage in the face of danger.

2 Discussion What changes are taking place in the mate?

3 Discussion What attitude does the mate show in these lines?

4 Discussion Have students contrast the way that Columbus feels with the way that the sailors felt.

5 Literary Focus You may want to point out the metaphor used for the sea in these lines.

6 Critical Thinking and Reading What is being referred to in these lines?

Reader's Response Describe an occasion when perseverence brought success to you, and contrast that experience with one in which perseverence proved foolish.

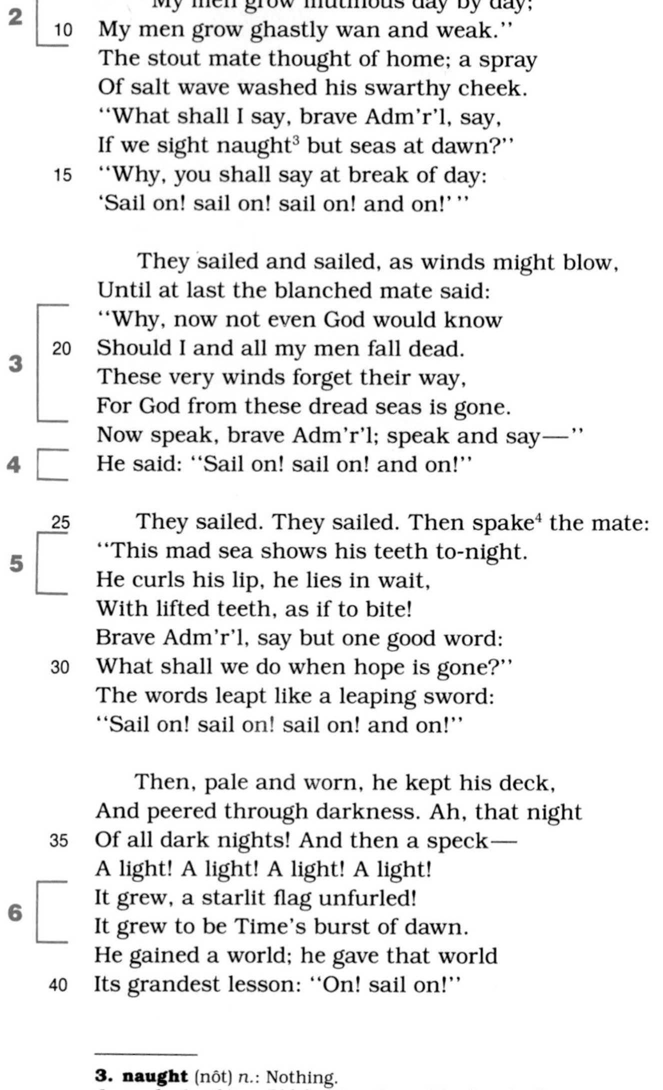

2 "My men grow mutinous day by day;
My men grow ghastly wan and weak."
The stout mate thought of home; a spray
Of salt wave washed his swarthy cheek.
"What shall I say, brave Adm'r'l, say,
If we sight naught[3] but seas at dawn?"
"Why, you shall say at break of day:
'Sail on! sail on! sail on! and on!' "

They sailed and sailed, as winds might blow,
Until at last the blanched mate said:
"Why, now not even God would know
3 Should I and all my men fall dead.
These very winds forget their way,
For God from these dread seas is gone.
Now speak, brave Adm'r'l; speak and say—"
4 He said: "Sail on! sail on! and on!"

They sailed. They sailed. Then spake[4] the mate:
5 "This mad sea shows his teeth to-night.
He curls his lip, he lies in wait,
With lifted teeth, as if to bite!
Brave Adm'r'l, say but one good word:
What shall we do when hope is gone?"
The words leapt like a leaping sword:
"Sail on! sail on! sail on! and on!"

Then, pale and worn, he kept his deck,
And peered through darkness. Ah, that night
Of all dark nights! And then a speck—
A light! A light! A light! A light!
6 It grew, a starlit flag unfurled!
It grew to be Time's burst of dawn.
He gained a world; he gave that world
Its grandest lesson: "On! sail on!"

3. **naught** (nôt) *n.*: Nothing.
4. **spake** (spāk) *v.*: Old-fashioned word for "spoke."

Closure and Extension

ANSWERS TO THINKING ABOUT THE SELECTION

Recalling

1. The "Brave Adm'r'l" is Christopher Columbus. He responds each time to the mate with "Sail on."
2. Increasingly bad sailing conditions frighten the mate: first, clouds so the stars disappear; second, high

THINKING ABOUT THE SELECTION

Recalling

1. Who is the "Brave Adm'r'l"? What does he say each time in response to the mate?
2. What seems to frighten the mate in each of the first four stanzas?

Interpreting

3. To what does the poet compare the sea in lines 26–28? What is the effect of this comparison?
4. What is the light sighted in the last stanza?
5. Interpret line 38.
6. What is the "grandest lesson"?
7. In what ways is this poem about the great value of determination and perseverance?

Applying

8. What is the difference between perseverance and stubbornness? Explain why you do or do not think there is a point at which perseverance becomes foolish and dangerous.

ANALYZING LITERATURE

Understanding Rhythm and Refrain

A poem's **rhythm** is the pattern of stressed and unstressed syllables it contains. A **refrain** is a phrase or line or group of lines that is repeated several times in the poem. A refrain reinforces and helps express the meaning of the poem. The rhythm of "Columbus" creates a feeling of action; the refrain states the poet's main theme.

1. What general mood or feeling does the rhythm create?
2. What larger meaning does the refrain have?
3. How do the rhythm and refrain work together to convey the theme of the poem?

CRITICAL THINKING AND READING

Making Inferences About Theme

Theme is the main idea expressed in a literary work. Sometimes the theme is openly stated. More often it is implied, and you must **infer** it—you must draw a conclusion about it based on all the elements of the work. One way to infer the theme of a poem is to consider its refrain. In "Columbus," the simple refrain "sail on! and on!" expresses the theme of the poem.

1. How does the refrain apply to the actual events?
2. How does the refrain show what Columbus was like?
3. To what does the poet refer in his final use of the refrain?

UNDERSTANDING LANGUAGE

Appreciating Old-fashioned Words

This poem contains several old-fashioned words, words rarely used in writing or speech. It is useful to understand these words, however, as you are likely to encounter them again in your reading of American and English literature. Two such words, *naught* and *spake*, are defined in the footnotes. Others are *lo!* (line 6) and *blanched* (line 18). Find the definitions of these in a dictionary. Then use each of the four old-fashioned words mentioned here in an original sentence.

THINKING AND WRITING

Writing a Poem About a Historical Figure

List historical people who interest you. Next to each name, note one key idea that you associate with that figure.

From your list select one historical figure, and write a line or two that expresses the main idea you noted about him or her. Using these lines as a refrain, write a narrative poem that tells about the person you have chosen. After you have written one draft of your poem, read it over and make any corrections and improvements you feel are necessary. When you have finished your second draft, proofread it and read your poem aloud to the class.

waves that wash his cheek and make the sailors mutinous and weak; third, strong winds; and fourth, the sea, which he compares to a mad dog showing his teeth.

Interpreting

3. The mate compares the sea to a mean dog. The effect of this comparison is to create an image of high seas with angry waves pounding the ship.
4. The light is the shore of the new world.
5. Line 38 refers to the hope and new beginning offered by what was to become the United States.
6. The "grandest lesson" is to persevere.
7. Without determination and perseverance, Columbus would not have succeeded in opening the Americas for people from other parts of the world. His sailors would have convinced him to turn back. The poem, therefore, is even more about determination and perseverance than it is about exploration.

Applying

8. Answers will differ. Suggested Response: The difference between perseverance and stubbornness is that perseverance implies a continuing to do something in spite of difficulties and obstacles while stubbornness implies an obstinate resistance to change. Students will probably decide that perseverance becomes foolish when the goal is trivial or when the danger outweighs its value.

(Answers begin on p. 522.)

ANSWERS TO ANALYZING LITERATURE

1. The rhythm creates a feeling of forward-moving action.
2. The larger meaning of the refrain relates to life in general; one should keep going and persevere in spite of difficulties.
3. The rhythm and refrain together portray the theme of the poem which is that perseverance and determination in moving ahead are of great value in life.

ANSWERS TO CRITICAL THINKING AND READING

1. The refrain illustrates Columbus's desire to continue sailing, despite his shipmates' doubts.
2. The refrain shows that Columbus was determined and brave.
3. The poet refers to the United States, which is urged to persevere also in order to fulfill its promise.

ANSWERS TO UNDERSTANDING LANGUAGE

1. *Naught* means "nothing." Sample sentence: I have naught but my good name.
2. *Spake* means "spoke." Sample sentence: He always spake the truth.
3. *Lo!* means "Look! See!" Sample sentence: Lo! the moon is full.
4. *Blanched* means "pale." Sample sentence: His blanched face indicated how frightened he was.

THINKING AND WRITING

For help with this assignment, students can refer to Lesson 18, "Writing a Poem," in the Handbook of Writing About Literature.

Publishing Student Writing You can collect your students' original poems in booklets for the students.

Writing Across the Curriculum You may want to have students do additional research to find diaries or journals of other explorers. If you do, inform the social studies department. Social studies teachers may guide students in their research.

Focus

More About the Author His Quaker upbringing led **John Greenleaf Whittier** to become heavily involved in matters of social conscience; he became an ardent abolitionist. You might want to ask students what abolitionists were seeking to abolish.

Literary Focus In discussing characters that stand for heroic qualities, you might want to have students list some qualities that authors could have characters represent, such as courage, honesty, loyalty, and so on.

Look for Whittier directly states the qualities that his characters possess, so students should not have any difficulty finding them.

Writing/Prior Knowledge You might have students brainstorm as a group to identify various figures from history who would make interesting subjects for this activity.

Vocabulary You may want to give **less advanced** students the vocabulary words in context. For example: As soon as the game was over, a *horde* of people left the stadium. As the soldier carrying the *banner* passed, the spectators all saluted.

GUIDE FOR READING

Barbara Frietchie

John Greenleaf Whittier (1807–1892) was born in Haverhill, Massachusetts. His poems are influenced by his Quaker upbringing and by his New England farm background. His most famous works express his political opinions, such as his opposition to slavery. Other works present the simple pleasures of country living. In the narrative poem "Barbara Frietchie," Whittier describes the courage and honor of people on both sides of the Civil War struggle.

Characters in Narrative Poems

In narrative poems, **characters** often stand for certain ideas or heroic qualities, which the poet wishes to celebrate. In order to understand a narrative poem, you must recognize the qualities that the characters in the poem represent. For example, in the poem about the Civil War that you are about to read, Barbara Frietchie, a Union supporter, is the subject, who represents human qualities that Whittier admires. He tells about her heroic action and Confederate General Stonewall Jackson's reaction to it to praise these qualities.

Look For

As you read, look for details about Barbara Frietchie and General Stonewall Jackson. How are they described? What are their actions? What human qualities did Whittier use them to represent?

Writing

Think of a person who has stood up for something he or she really believed in. It may be a figure from history or current events or someone you know, including yourself. What inspired that person? What actions did that person take? Did that person face disapproval or punishment from others? Freewrite for five minutes about this person's experience.

Vocabulary

Knowing the following words will help you as you read "Barbara Frietchie."

horde (hôrd) *n.*: Large moving group (p. 525)

banner (ban′ ər) *n.*: Flag (p. 526)

Objectives

1 To understand how authors create characters
2 To make inferences about characters
3 To choose meaning to fit context
4 To write a definition of a hero

Support Material

Teaching Portfolio

Teacher Backup, pp. 723–725
Grammar in Action Worksheet, *Understanding Verb Tense*, pp. 726–727
Usage and Mechanics Worksheet, p. 728
Vocabulary Check, p. 729–730
Analyzing Literature Worksheet, *Creating Characters*, p. 731
Language Worksheet, *Choosing Meaning to Fit Context*, p. 732
Selection Test, pp. 733–734

Barbara Frietchie

John Greenleaf Whittier

Up from the meadows rich with corn,
Clear in the cool September morn,

The clustered spires of Frederick[1] stand 1
Green-walled by the hills of Maryland.

Round about them orchards sweep,
Apple and peach tree fruited deep,

Fair as the garden of the Lord
To the eyes of the famished rebel horde,

On that pleasant morn of the early fall
When Lee[2] marched over the mountain wall;

Over the mountains winding down,
Horse and foot, into Frederick town.

Forty flags with their silver stars, 2
Forty flags with their crimson bars,

Flapped in the morning wind: the sun
Of noon looked down, and saw not one.

Up rose old Barbara Frietchie then, 3
Bowed with her fourscore[3] years and ten;

Bravest of all in Frederick town, 4
She took up the flag the men hauled down

In her attic window the staff she set,
To show that one heart was loyal yet.

---

1. **Frederick** (fred′ rik): A town in Maryland.
2. **Lee** (lē): Robert E. Lee, commander in chief of the Confederate army in the Civil War.
3. **fourscore** (fôr′ skôr′) *adj.*: Four times twenty; eighty.

Presentation

Motivation/Prior Knowledge Ask what are some of the ways in which people display their feelings about their country. Tell students that in this narrative poem, the poet writes about the way in which one woman showed her feelings about her country during the Civil War.

Clarification Confederate troops, in need of supplies, are invading Frederick, Maryland.

Master Teacher Note If your students have read "Paul Revere's Ride" (page 509) or "Columbus" (page 521), you may want to use this occasion to compare fictional and historical accounts of events. Your discussion could include a discussion of historical fiction.

Thematic Ideas You may want students to compare Frietchie's patriotism with that of Paul Revere, page 509. Notice that both were ordinary citizens—not members of the military.

Other selections in this text that present Civil War settings include a fictional account, "The Drummer Boy of Shiloh" on page 151, and accounts of actual events, including "Harriet Tubman: Guide to Freedom", on page 383 and "O Captain! My Captain!" on page 534.

Purpose-Setting Question Does the poet's presentation of the characters seem to favor either the North or the South in the poem?

1 **Discussion** What effect do these details about the setting have on the rebel troops?

2 **Enrichment** The Confederate flag was called the stars and bars, and the Union flag was and is called the stars and stripes.

3 **Literary Focus** How old is Barbara Frietchie?

4 **Discussion** Who had taken down the Union flag?

Humanities Note

Henri Cartier-Bresson was born in 1908 near Paris, France, and became a photographer in 1930. Cartier-Bresson usually photographs in black and white with a small hand-held camera. This Cartier-Bresson photograph is typical of his work, which captures the significance of events and characters by the arrangement of the people and objects.

You might ask students what details in this photograph make it look as though he could have taken it specifically to illustrate "Barbara Frietchie".

5 **Enrichment** In 1824 Thomas Jonathan Jackson was born in Clarksburg, Virginia, which is now in West Virginia. Although he was orphaned at an early age, he worked and studied hard and received an appointment to West Point. After his graduation Jackson served in the Mexican War. At the first Battle of Bull Run, he received the nickname Stonewall because he and his Confederate troops stood fast in the face of overwhelming odds. One of Robert E. Lee's most trusted generals, Jackson was accidentally shot by his own troops. He had gone out after dark to scout near Chancellorsville, Virginia, and some of his men mistook him for an enemy soldier. He died eight days later, on May 10, 1863.

© Henri Cartier-Bresson/Magnum

5 Up the street came the rebel tread,
Stonewall Jackson[4] riding ahead.

Under his slouched hat left and right
He glanced; the old flag met his sight.

"Halt!"—the dust-brown ranks stood fast.
"Fire!"—out blazed the rifle-blast.

It shivered the window, pane and sash;[5]
It rent the banner with seam and gash.

Quick, as it fell, from the broken staff
Dame Barbara snatched the silken scarf.

---

4. Stonewall Jackson (stōn′ wôl′ jak′ s'n): Nickname of Thomas Jonathan Jackson, Confederate general in the Civil War.
5. sash (sash) *n.*: The frame holding the glass panes of the window.

Grammar in Action

In both prose and poetry a writer may begin a story in one time, change to the past, and return to the present. This may present a difficult problem for the reader. However, close attention to the **verb tense** makes reading and understanding a passage easier.

John Greenleaf Whittier begins his famous patriotic poem in the present tense:

Up from the meadows rich with corn,
Clear in the cool September morn,

The clustered spires of Frederick *stand*
Green-walled by the hills of Maryland.

Round about them orchards *sweep,*
Apple and peach tree fruited deep.

The spires stand, the orchards sweep—this is in the present tense. However, Whittier changes into the past tense as he describes the action on the day Lee marched into town:

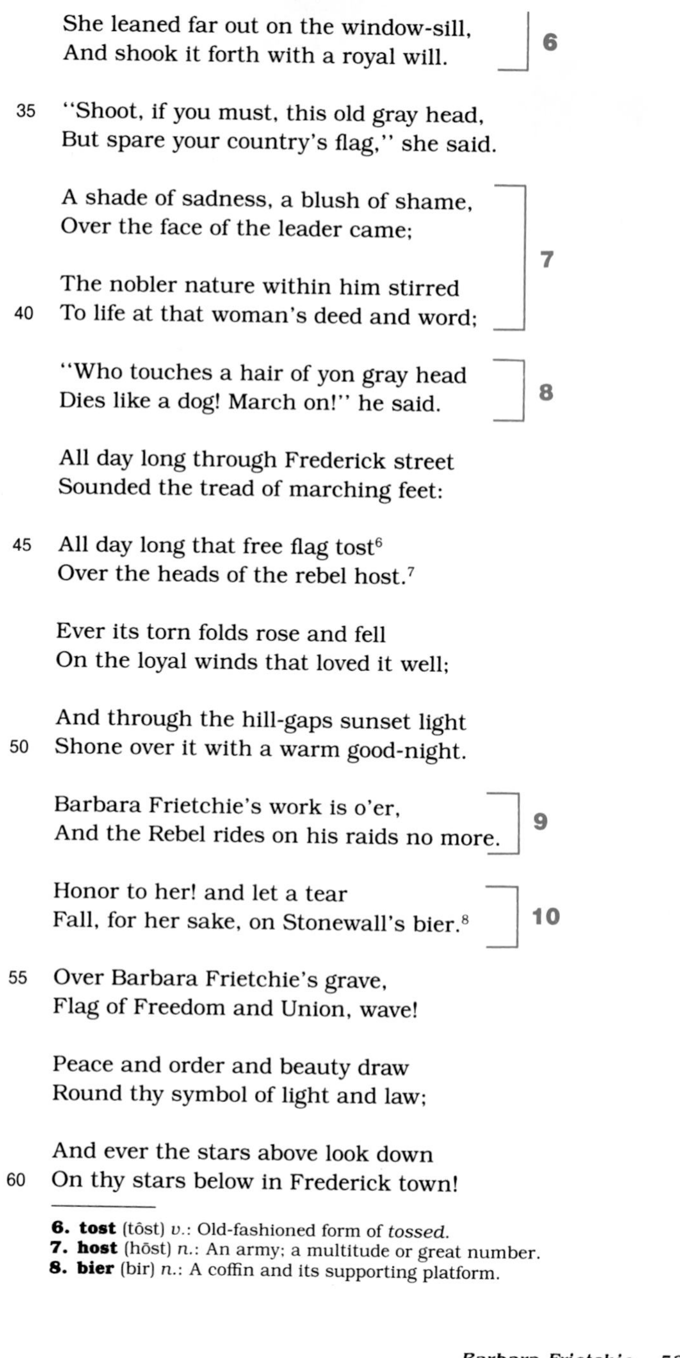

She leaned far out on the window-sill,
And shook it forth with a royal will. 6

"Shoot, if you must, this old gray head,
But spare your country's flag," she said.

A shade of sadness, a blush of shame,
Over the face of the leader came;

The nobler nature within him stirred
To life at that woman's deed and word; 7

"Who touches a hair of yon gray head
Dies like a dog! March on!" he said. 8

All day long through Frederick street
Sounded the tread of marching feet:

All day long that free flag tost[6]
Over the heads of the rebel host.[7]

Ever its torn folds rose and fell
On the loyal winds that loved it well;

And through the hill-gaps sunset light
Shone over it with a warm good-night.

Barbara Frietchie's work is o'er,
And the Rebel rides on his raids no more. 9

Honor to her! and let a tear
Fall, for her sake, on Stonewall's bier.[8] 10

Over Barbara Frietchie's grave,
Flag of Freedom and Union, wave!

Peace and order and beauty draw
Round thy symbol of light and law;

And ever the stars above look down
On thy stars below in Frederick town!

---

6. tost (tôst) *v.*: Old-fashioned form of *tossed.*
7. host (hōst) *n.*: An army; a multitude or great number.
8. bier (bir) *n.*: A coffin and its supporting platform.

6 Literary Focus What words in these lines give clues about Barbara Frietchie's character?

7 Literary Focus What details in these lines show Stonewall Jackson's character?

8 Literary Focus Ask the class what is revealed about Jackson's respect for the woman through this order to his soldiers? Would Jackson have shot or arrested anyone else bold enough to display the Union flag on principle—say, a younger woman or a man?

9 Literary Focus You may want to have students realize that the poet seems to put into sharp focus the actions of admirable individuals, without regard to which side of the conflict they support.

10 Critical Thinking and Reading What do you learn about Stonewall Jackson from the poem? What other information might you want to know about him?

Master Teacher Note You might encourage students to do research on the life of Stonewall Jackson and his tragic death.

Reader's Response What do you admire most about Barbara Freitchie?

Forty flags with their silver stars,
Forty flags with their crimson bars,

Flapped in the morning wind: the sun
Of noon *looked* down, and *saw* not one.

The flags flapped, the noon sun looked and saw—the poem is now in the past tense.

Student Activity 1. Find the line where the poem again shifts to the present tense.

Student Activity 2. List ten other verbs in the poem. Identify them as either present or past tense.

Student Activity 3. Using the present tense, write a passage describing an event. Then rewrite the passage in the past tense.

Closure and Extension

ANSWERS TO THINKING ABOUT THE SELECTION

Recalling

1. The poem takes place during the Civil War in Frederick, Maryland.
2. The Confederate Army arrives in town. Before they arrive, the men have taken down the Union flag and everyone has left the streets.
3. Stonewall Jackson has ordered the men to fire at the flag. Frietchie, grabbing the falling flag and shaking it out the window, says, "Shoot, if you must, this old gray head. But spare your country's flag."
4. Jackson feels sad and ashamed. His nobler nature stirs him to tell his men not to shoot Barbara Frietchie.

Interpreting

5. Barbara Frietchie represents the admirable qualities of patriotism and courage.
6. Stonewall Jackson represents understanding, compassion, and respect.
7. The last two lines express the hope that the qualities symbolized by Barbara Frietchie will be represented by Frederick and the United States.
8. The theme of this poem is that people's beliefs, patriotism, and courage deserve respect.

Applying

9. Answers will differ. Suggested Response: Other patriotic themes that could be used in poetry might be responsibilities of citizens in a democratic republic, freedom of religion, freedom of speech, the right to assemble peaceably, the right to petition the government for a redress of grievances, the right to due process of law, and other Bill of Rights guarantees. The purpose of a poem with a patriotic theme is to inspire people to feel patriotic.

ANSWERS TO ANALYZING LITERATURE

1. Whittier uses direct description in line 39.
2. Jackson's words in lines 41–42 show that he is used to giving orders and to being obeyed and that he respects Barbara Frietchie.

THINKING ABOUT THE SELECTION

Recalling

1. Describe the time and place of the poem.
2. Who arrives in the town? What has happened before their arrival?
3. Why do the soldiers fire their guns? What does Barbara Frietchie do after they fire?
4. What is Stonewall Jackson's reaction to what Barbara Frietchie does?

Interpreting

5. What admirable human qualities does Barbara Frietchie represent?
6. What admirable human qualities does Stonewall Jackson represent?
7. Explain the last two lines of the poem.
8. What is the theme of this poem?

Applying

9. This poem has a patriotic theme. What other patriotic themes might be suitable for poetry? What might be the purpose of a poem with a patriotic theme?

ANALYZING LITERATURE

Creating Characters

A writer can create a character in several ways. Whittier directly describes Barbara Frietchie as ninety years old, "bowed" with age, and "Bravest of all in Frederick town."

Whittier also uses other methods to develop the character of Barbara Frietchie. He recounts her actions and he quotes her speech. Finally he shows the reactions of others to her and to her actions.

1. What method of developing a character does Whittier use in line 39?
2. What do Jackson's words in lines 41–42 tell you about his character?

CRITICAL THINKING AND READING

Making Inferences About Characters

To **infer** is to draw a conclusion based on available information. If a person always takes responsibility and completes given tasks, then it is reasonable to infer that this person is dependable.

1. List Barbara Frietchie's actions.
2. What does she say to Stonewall Jackson?
3. What does Stonewall Jackson's reaction to Barbara Frietchie tell you about *her*?
4. What inferences do you make about Stonewall Jackson?

UNDERSTANDING LANGUAGE

Choosing Meaning to Fit Context

If you come across a word you do not know, first check its meaning in a dictionary. If a dictionary is unavailable, try to figure out the word's meaning by looking at its **context**—the words and sentences around it.

In line 32 the poet writes that Barbara "snatched the silken scarf." Suppose you did not know the definition of *snatched*. Earlier lines explain that Barbara had held a flag from a window and that the flag had fallen. From the context you might then conclude that *snatched* means "caught" or "grabbed quickly."

Reread the context of each word below. Using the context, define each word. Then check your definitions in a dictionary.

1. famished (line 8)
2. rent (line 30)
3. tread (line 44)

THINKING AND WRITING

Writing a Definition of a Hero

Think about the admirable qualities that Barbara Frietchie has. Then make a list of other heroic qualities. Organize your list in order of increasing importance. Using your list as a guide, write an essay in which you define a true hero. Read your definition over after you have written it and make any changes you feel are needed. Proofread it and share it with your classmates.

ANSWERS TO CRITICAL THINKING AND READING

1. Barbara Frietchie takes up the flag and hangs it out her attic window. She grabs the flag as it falls and shakes it out the window.
2. Frietchie says to shoot her if he must but not to shoot his country's flag.
3. Jackson's reaction tells you that Frietchie is worthy of admiration because of her courage.
4. Inferences about Jackson include that he is used to giving orders and having them obeyed and that he respects Frietchie's patriotism and courage.

ANSWERS TO UNDERSTANDING LANGUAGE

1. famished–hungry
2. rent–tore
3. tread–step; tramp

THINKING AND WRITING

Students could compare the heroic qualities they included in their compositions with those of their classmates. You might compile a class list of heroic qualities against which heroes of other selections could be measured.

Figurative Language and Imagery

THE BROOKLYN BRIDGE: VARIATION ON AN OLD THEME, 1939
Joseph Stella
Collection of Whitney Museum of American Art

Humanities Note

Fine art, *Brooklyn Bridge, Variation on an Old Theme,* 1939, by Joseph Stella. Joseph Stella (1877-1946) was an Italian-American painter who immigrated to the United States in 1923. He had trained at the Art Students League and New York School of Art, both in New York City. His subsequent travels to Europe exposed him to the beginning movements of Cubism and Futurism. He saw the artistic possibilities of this new "modern" outlook in art and began to explore it.

Brooklyn Bridge, Variation on an Old Theme relates to the spirit not to the actual details of the Brooklyn Bridge in New York City. Stella's imagery shows an assemblage of the dynamic motion, cable tension, shoreline views, sparkling lights, and low pitched hum of this busy bridge. The painting becomes the symbol of the American urban experience —fast, tense, and neon-colored. Stella was influenced by the rapid technological changes of the twentieth century. He responded to this unheaval with his innovative and aggressive images of the urban experience.

Focus

More About the Authors Considered an original and talented poet, **José Garcia Villa** received the Shelley Memorial Award from the Poetry Society of America in 1959 and was elected Philippines National Artist in 1973. What might winning prizes for his poetry in two countries show about Villa's poetry?

The longest poem in *Leaves of Grass* is "Song of Myself," which is considered **Walt Whitman's** greatest poem. Whitman wrote essays as well as poetry. While his poetry is romantic, his essays are realistic. During the Civil War, Whitman volunteered to work in military hospitals in Washington, D.C. After the war, he held several government jobs until a stroke forced him to retire to Camden, New Jersey, where he continued to write. What subjects might Whitman's varied jobs have given him for his poetry?

Although Japanese is his native language, **Naoshi Koriyama** has written poems in English because he is "interested to see how well one could write in a second language." You may want to point out some of the difficulties involved in writing poetry in a language other than your own. These difficulties include vocabulary, syntax, and especially differences in connotations and idioms.

GUIDE FOR READING

Lyric 17

José Garcia Villa (1914–) was born in Manila, Philippines, and emigrated to the United States in 1930. He attended the University of New Mexico and Columbia University in New York City. Villa has published several volumes of poetry as well as short stories. "Lyric 17" reflects the judgment of one critic, who said that Villa's poems come "straight from the poet's being, from his blood, from his spirit, as a fire breaks from wood, or as a flower grows from its soil."

O Captain! My Captain!

Walt Whitman (1819–1892) was born in Long Island, New York, and grew up in Brooklyn. He worked as a printer and journalist in and around New York City. In 1848 he began working on *Leaves of Grass,* a long poem about America. Because of its unusual style, commercial publishers refused to publish it; therefore Whitman printed a first edition with his own money. Since then the style of Whitman's poetry has greatly influenced poets around the world. Whitman's most popular poem is "O Captain! My Captain!," which was inspired by the tragic death of President Lincoln.

Jetliner

Naoshi Koriyama (1926–) was born on Kikai Island in the southern part of Japan. He studied at Kagoshima Normal School in Japan, at a foreign language School in Okinawa, and at the University of New Mexico and graduated from the State University of New York at Albany. A member of the Poetry Society of Japan, Koriyama now teaches courses in English and American literature in a Tokyo university. Although his native language is Japanese, he writes some poems, such as "Jetliner," in English.

Figurative Language and Imagery

Figurative language is meant to be interpreted *imaginatively,* not literally. For example, if we write that the sun is like a golden eye, if we call a famous person an institution, or if we say that the summer night seems to whisper—then we are using figurative language.

In "Lyric 17," for example, the poet states that a poem must be "musical as a sea-gull." Poetry is compared with music; but it is beautiful music, music that darts, swoops, and soars. The comparison enables the poet to express this idea in an immediate, brief, and memorable way. This is an example of a particular form of figurative language called a simile. A **simile** is a comparison between two basically unlike things, using the words *like* or *as.*

Two other figures of speech are metaphor and personification. A **metaphor,** like a simile, is a comparison between two things. A metaphor, however, does not use the words *like* or *as* but simply identifies the two things. For example, according to "Lyric 17," a poem "must be a brightness moving." It must *shine,* and it must *move.* This radiance in motion is a metaphor for good poetry.

Personification is a figure of speech in which an animal, idea, or inanimate object is given human characteristics. In "Jetliner," a jet about to take off is personified as an athlete at the start of a race.

Imagery is the use of vivid language to describe people, places, things, and ideas. You must be able to picture in your mind what authors mean by their imagery in order for their writing to be effective.

Look For

As you read the following poems, look for ways that figurative language and imagery create fresh and memorable pictures.

Writing

The writer William Faulkner once wrote: "I would say that music is the easiest means in which to express . . . but since words are my talent, I must try to express clumsily in words what the pure music would have done better." Freewrite about the meaning of this quotation. How does it relate to poetry?

Vocabulary

Knowing the following words will help you as you read these poems.

luminance (lo͞o′ mə nəns) *n.*: Brightness; brilliance (p. 532)

exulting (ig zult′ iŋ) *v.*: Rejoicing (p. 534)

tread (tred) *n.*: Step (p. 534)

Literary Focus Your less advanced students could benefit from a class discussion of the three types of figurative language discussed. During the discussion, you could elicit examples from the students of similes, metaphors, and personification and list them on the board.

Look For If the poems are read aloud in class, you might have students as a group discuss the figurative language and imagery they found after finishing the first reading.

Writing/Prior Knowledge You might want to play a moving musical selection in class while students are doing this writing exercise. Possible selections might be Debussy's "Clair de Lune," A Chopin prelude or nocturne, or a section of Stravinsky's "Rite of Spring."

Vocabulary Your less advanced students will benefit from pronouncing the vocabulary words in class and seeing them used in context. For example, "In the luminance of the moon, we could see the palm trees swaying," and "We were exulting over the team's victory in the tournament."

Objectives

1 To understand similes
2 To appreciate diction
3 To write similes
4 To understand metaphors
5 To understand personification
6 To analyze a simile or metaphor in writing

Support Material

Teaching Portfolio

Teacher Backup, pp. 735–738
Usage and Mechanics Worksheet, p. 739
Vocabulary Check, p. 740
Analyzing Literature Worksheet, *Understanding Similes, Metaphors, and Personification,* p. 741
Language Worksheet, *Appreciating Diction,* p. 742
Selection Test, pp. 743–744

Presentation

Motivation/Prior Knowledge You might discuss with the class what they think a poem should be. Put their ideas on the board. Note that "Lyric 17," the first poem they will read, is a poem about what a poem should be.

Master Teacher Note In Marianne Moore's poem "Poetry," she describes true poets as "literalists of the imagination" who can offer "imaginary gardens with real toads in them." Have the class discuss what she may have meant.

Purpose-Setting Question What does José García Villa think a poem should be?

1 **Discussion** Ask for views about whether a poem "must be able to hide what it seeks" or whether it should be direct in giving its insight.

Discussion Ask your students what quality they think every poet must have. Is it awareness of beauty? Sensitivity to the feelings of others? A love of words and phrasing?

Reader's Response What quality of poetry would you add to Garcia Villa's "Lyric 17"?

Lyric 17

José Garcia Villa

First, a poem must be magical,
Then musical as a sea-gull.
It must be a brightness moving
And hold secret a bird's flowering.
It must be slender as a bell,
And it must hold fire as well.
It must have the wisdom of bows
And it must kneel like a rose.
It must be able to hear
The luminance of dove and deer.
1 It must be able to hide
What it seeks, like a bride.
And over all I would like to hover
God, smiling from the poem's cover.

THINKING ABOUT THE SELECTION

Recalling

1. According to the poet, what must a poem be, first of all?
2. List ten other qualities that a poem must have.
3. Where does the poet imagine himself?

Interpreting

4. Look at the qualities the poet names. Which three do you consider the most important? Explain your answer.

Applying

5. The poet Emily Dickinson defined poetry as follows: "If . . . it makes my whole body so cold no fire can warm me, I know that is poetry." Explain the meaning of Dickinson's definition. How would you define poetry?

ANALYZING LITERATURE

Understanding Similes

A **simile** is a comparison between two basically unlike things that uses the word *like* or *as*. For example, José Garcia Villa uses a simile when he writes that a poem must be "Slender as a bell." The simile illustrates similarities between things we do not normally consider similar—a poem and a bell. But, through the simile, we see one way in which a poem and a bell *are* alike. The comparison connects the two things in a new way and extends our appreciation of *both*.

1. What simile occurs in line 2? What is the effect of this simile?
2. Explain the simile in line 8. What is the effect of this simile?
3. Explain the simile in lines 11–12. What is the effect of this simile?

Closure and Extension

ANSWERS TO THINKING ABOUT THE SELECTION

Recalling

1. A poem must be magical first of all.
2. Besides being magical, ten other qualities a poem must have include the following: being musical, being a moving brightness, holding secret a bird's flowering, being slender as a bell, holding fire, having the wisdom of bows, kneeling like a rose, able to hear the luminance of dove and deer, able to hide what it seeks, and having the poet's image hovering over it.
3. The poet imagines himself like God smiling from the poem's cover.

Interpreting

4. Answers will differ. Suggested Response: The three most important qualities of a poem are to be magical, musical, and slender as a bell. It should be magical because its subject or descriptions should surprise and delight the reader. It should be musical to please the ear. Finally, a poem should be slender as a bell, so that it concentrates its message and presents only the essence.

Applying

5. Answers will differ. Suggested Response: Emily Dickinson means

STILL LIFE: FLOWERS, 1855
Severin Roesen
The Metropolitan Museum of Art

UNDERSTANDING LANGUAGE

Appreciating Diction

José Garcia Villa has chosen his words with great care. For instance, in line 10 he says that a poem should *hear* the "luminance of dove and deer." This word choice is important. Normally, luminance is not something we hear, but *see*. The dove and the deer are quiet creatures that we usually see but do not hear. The poet suggests that true poetry shows us not only how to see, but also how to *hear* even quiet living things in nature.

1. Why do you think the author uses the word *flowering* in line 4?
2. Why do you think the author uses the word *kneel* in line 8?

THINKING AND WRITING

Writing Similes

Think again of your definition of poetry. Following the pattern of Villa's poem, write your own poem explaining the qualities you think poetry must have. Be sure to use similes to help clarify your points. When you revise, check that you have expressed the qualities of poetry in a vivid way. Then proofread your poem and read it aloud to your classmates.

Humanities Note

Fine art, *Still Life: Flowers* by Severin Roesen. Severin Roesen painted *Still Life: Flowers* in 1855. Born in Cologne, Germany, Roesen came to the United States in 1847 and lived here until his death in 1871. He is best known for his paintings of flowers and fruit, done in a Baroque style. You might ask students if they think *Still Life: Flowers* is an appropriate illustration for "Lyric 17". Why or why not?

THINKING AND WRITING

For help with this assignment, students can refer to Lesson 18, "Writing a Poem," in the Handbook of Writing About Literature.

Publishing Student Writing Students can choose poems from the class to submit to the school newspaper or literary magazine.

Writing Across the Curriculum You might want to inform the art teacher about the poems written by your students. The art teacher might be interested in having students illustrate their poems or in preparing illuminated manuscripts of them.

that poetry touches her deepest feelings. Students might define poetry as appealing to their emotions by using original images and rhythm.

ANSWERS TO ANALYZING LITERATURE

1. The simile in line 2 says a poem is as musical as a sea-gull. This simile makes one think about ways in which a sea-gull, with its raucous voice, is musical.
2. The simile in line 5 means that the poem's message must not waste words but should be presented in a clear as a bell manner.
3. In lines 11–12, the poet says a poem "must be able to hide / What it seeks, like a bride." The effect of this simile is to help one understand why the meaning of a poem is not always obvious.

ANSWERS TO UNDERSTANDING LANGUAGE

1. Answers will differ. Suggested Response: The author uses the word *flowering* in line 4 to relate two usually unrelated ideas so the reader would think of both birds and flowering in a new light.
2. Answers will differ. Suggested Response: The author uses the word *kneel* in line 8 to give the rose the human quality of humility.

Presentation

Motivation/Prior Knowledge Show pictures of Abraham Lincoln and discuss with your class why people felt he was such a great man. Then you could ask your students to imagine how people might react when someone greatly admired dies unexpectedly.

Master Teacher Note You might tell your students that poets, artists, and other creative people sometimes cope with extreme circumstances, such as war, natural disaster, or the assassination of a leader, by using their creative talents. This poem was written by Walt Whitman as he grieved over President Lincoln's assassination.

Purpose-Setting Question How did Walt Whitman feel about Abraham Lincoln?

1 **Discussion** Ask students what is meant by the first four lines. Be sure they know that the "fearful trip" refers to the Civil War, the "ship" refers to the nation, and the "prize" and the "port" refer to peace. When does the poem take place? What is the mood of the people? What has happened?

2 **Discussion** The second stanza presents the first reaction of the poet. What was Whitman's first reaction to Lincoln's death?

3 **Literary Focus** What other metaphor is used for Lincoln in the second stanza?

4 **Discussion** How is the poet's reaction different in the last stanza? How might this poem illustrate the various reactions that people would experience when faced with any unexpected tragic event?

Master Teacher Note You might ask students what other "fearful" trips in U.S. history the ship of state has taken and which leaders have led the nation through to a safe harbor. A possible technique might be to have one student name a leader and other students provide the "fearful" trip.

Literary Focus You might have students write tributes to other fallen leaders either in poetry or in prose form. You could ask them to concentrate on developing metaphors. If possible, the entire eulogy could be an extended metaphor as is this poem.

O Captain! My Captain!

Walt Whitman

1 O Captain! my Captain! our fearful trip is done,
The ship has weather'd every rack,[1] the prize we sought is won,
The port is near, the bells I hear, the people all exulting,
While follow eyes the steady keel,[2] the vessel grim and daring;
But O heart! heart! heart!
O the bleeding drops of red,
Where on the deck my Captain lies,
Fallen cold and dead.

2 O Captain! my Captain! rise up and hear the bells;
Rise up—for you the flag is flung—for you the bugle trills,
For you bouquets and ribbon'd wreaths—for you the shores a-crowding,
For you they call, the swaying mass, their eager faces turning;
3 Here Captain! dear father!
This arm beneath your head!
It is some dream that on the deck,
You've fallen cold and dead.

4 My Captain does not answer, his lips are pale and still,
My father does not feel my arm, he has no pulse nor will,
The ship is anchor'd safe and sound, its voyage closed and done,
From fearful trip the victor ship comes in with object won;
Exult O shores, and ring O bells!
But I with mournful tread,
Walk the deck my Captain lies,
Fallen cold and dead.

---

1. **rack** *n.*: A great stress.
2. **keel** *n.*: The chief structural beam extending along the entire length of the bottom of a boat or ship and supporting the frame.

ABRAHAM LINCOLN
William Willard
National Portrait Gallery, Smithsonian Institution

THINKING ABOUT THE SELECTION

Recalling

1. What has happened to the Captain? Why is this event especially unfortunate?
2. What other name does the poet call the Captain?

Interpreting

3. What pronoun does the poet use to modify the world Captain? What is the significance of the pronoun?
4. What effect has the event described in this poem had on the poet? How would you describe the mood of the poem?

Applying

5. Do you think the fate of a nation ever rests entirely on one person? Explain your answer.

ANALYZING LITERATURE

Understanding Metaphors

A **metaphor** is a direct comparison between two unlike things. Throughout "O Captain! My Captain!," Whitman compares President Lincoln to the captain of a ship. The metaphor conveys and reinforces the poet's feelings about President Lincoln—that he was a great leader of the country and a hero.

1. Walt Whitman wrote this poem in response to the assassination of President Lincoln in 1865. If the Captain is a metaphor for Lincoln, explain the metaphor of the ship.
2. What is the "fearful trip" that the ship has "weathered"?
3. Explain why you do or do not think that a ship's captain is an appropriate metaphor for any kind of leader.

Humanities Note

The portrait of Abraham Lincoln used to illustrate this poem was painted by William Willard. The painting now hangs in the National Portrait Gallery in the Smithsonian Institution, Washington, D.C. Ask students how the bright background might affect people's feelings when they look at the portrait. What qualities of character are captured in this portrait of a president who successfully led the nation through four years of a tragic war?

Closure and Extension

ANSWERS TO THINKING ABOUT THE SELECTION

Recalling

1. The Captain is dead. It is extremely unfortunate because he has just brought the ship safely through and the people are exulting.
2. The poet calls the Captain father.

Interpreting

3. The poet uses the pronoun *my* to refer to the Captain. This pronoun makes the Captain seem less distant and more personal.
4. At first the poet is unbelieving and then he is grief stricken. The mood of the poem is one of grief.

Applying

5. Answers will differ. Suggested Response: The fate of a nation never rests entirely on one person because others will use their leadership abilities and take over.

ANSWERS TO ANALYZING LITERATURE

1. The ship is a metaphor for the United States. It has weathered every rack (the Civil War), has been led by the Captain (Lincoln), and is anchored safely (at peace).
2. The "fearful trip" that the ship has "weathered" is the Civil War.
3. Answers will differ. Suggested Response: A ship's captain is an appropriate metaphor for almost any leader. The captain can be a gently guiding force or a harsh authoritarian one as the occasion demands. You could not, however, use a ship's captain for a metaphor if the leader was actually a ship's captain.

Challenge You might have your **more advanced** students think of other metaphors that could effectively express the same feelings that Whitman's poem does.

Presentation

Motivation/Prior Knowledge You might ask students for their impressions of jet airplanes based on flying experiences, on observations made at airports, or on the photograph on page 537.

Master Teacher Note List students' impressions of jets on the chalkboard. Ask students which items on the list may refer to human qualities. At this point, **less advanced** students may find it helpful to preview the questions under Analyzing Literature on page 537.

Thematic Idea Another poem that describes a machine in human terms is "Concrete Mixers" on page 587.

Purpose-Setting Question To what is the jetliner compared?

1 **Literary Focus** To what part of the runner's body is the jet compared in the first stanza?

2 **Literary Focus** To what part of the runner's body is the jetliner compared in the second stanza? What parts of the jetliner are being compared in this stanza?

3 **Literary Focus** To what part of the runner's body is the jetliner compared in this line? What human qualities or abilities are given to the jetliner because of this comparison?

4 **Literary Focus** To what parts of the runner's body is the jetliner compared? Which parts of the jetliner are compared?

5 **Discussion** What does the jetliner do in the last stanza? To what does Koriyama compare the arrangement of stars in the sky?

Speaking and Listening Select a student to read the poem aloud with expression. The student should imitate the speed of the jet in the speed of the reading.

Jetliner

Naoshi Koriyama

1 now he takes his mark
at the very farthest end of the runway
looking straight ahead, eager, intense
with his sharp eyes shining

2 he takes a deep, deep breath
with his powerful lungs
expanding his massive chest
his burning heart beating like thunders

then . . . after a few . . . tense moments . . . of pondering[1]
he roars at his utmost
3 and slowly begins to jog
kicking the dark earth hard
and now he begins to run
kicking the dark earth harder
then he dashes, dashes like mad, like mad
4 howling, shouting, screaming, and roaring

5 then with a most violent kick
he shakes off the earth's pull
softly lifting himself into the air
soaring higher and higher and higher still
piercing the sea of clouds
up into the chandelier[2] of stars

1. **pondering** (pän′ dər iŋ) *n.*: Thinking deeply; considering carefully.
2. **chandelier** (shan′ də lir′) *n.*: A lighting fixture hanging from a ceiling, with branches for several candles or electric bulbs.

Literary Focus This poem is an extended personification. Which words in the poem could apply both to a runner and to a jetliner?

Master Teacher Note Personification is often expressed by verbs. You might ask your **more advanced** students to look around their school, homes, and neighborhoods to find other objects that could be personified. They could then write a personification of each using appropriate verbs to create their comparisons. For example, a storm cloud might be compared to an angry, disapproving person by using the verb *glower* to describe what it does.

Students can then choose one of the personifications and write a poem using it as part of an extended personification.

THINKING ABOUT THE SELECTION

Recalling

1. Where does "he" take his mark? Where does "he" wind up?

Interpreting

2. Interpret lines 9–16. Describe what happened in this stanza. How is this poetic description different from a prose description?

Applying

3. What is it about flight that stirs the imagination? Explain your answer.

ANALYZING LITERATURE

Understanding Personification

Personification is a figure of speech in which an animal, object, or idea is given human qualities. Personification gives us new ways of thinking about things.

Through personification, the poet provides us with a kind of "double vision." We see both a jetliner *and* a runner at the same time. We imagine a great machine in human terms.

1. What are the "sharp eyes shining" in line 4?
2. What are the "powerful lungs" in line 6? What is the "massive chest" in line 7?
3. Find three other examples of figurative language in this poem.

THINKING AND WRITING

Writing About Figurative Language

Review the definitions of figurative language, simile, metaphor, and personification. Be sure you understand the differences between these terms. Choose a simile or a metaphor from "Jetliner," and write an analysis of it. What two things are compared? How does the simile or metaphor add to your appreciation of both elements? Revise, making sure your analysis is clear. Proofread your paper and share it with your classmates.

Closure and Extension

ANSWERS TO THINKING ABOUT THE SELECTION

Recalling

1. "He" takes his mark "at the very farthest end of the runway." "He" ends up in the sky, "piercing the sea of clouds up into the chandelier of stars."

Interpreting

2. After a few moments, the jetliner's engines roar, and it starts down the runway, picking up speed until it is roaring down the runway at full speed. Answers will differ. Suggested Response: This poetic description is different from a prose description because of the accelerating rhythm in which it is written, the extension of the personification, the arrangement of the words into lines.

Applying

3. Answers will differ. Suggested Response: Flight is still an adventurous activity. It still seems incredible that people can actually soar in the sky like birds.

ANSWERS TO ANALYZING LITERATURE

1. The "sharp eyes shining" in line 4 are the jetliner's headlights.
2. The "powerful lungs" in line 5 are the jet air inlets. The "massive chest" in line 8 is the jet engine.
3. Answers will differ. Suggested Response: Three other examples of figurative language in this poem are "his burning heart," "slowly begins to jog," "begins to run kicking the dark earth," and "howling, shouting, screaming, and roaring."

Challenge What other machines might you personify as a runner?

THINKING AND WRITING

For help with this assignment, students can refer to Lesson 6, "Writing About Figures of Speech" in the Handbook of Writing About Literature.

Publishing Student Writing Students might share their papers in small groups. Hearing other students' views can increase students' general understanding.

Focus

More About the Authors Besides working as an editor, **May Swenson** held positions as poet in residence at Purdue University, University of North Carolina at Greensboro, Lethbridge University in Canada, and University of California at Riverside. Swenson received numerous fellowships from the Guggenheim Foundation, Ford Foundation, and Rockefeller Foundation, among others. She received a National Institute of Arts and Letters award in 1960, a Brandeis University award in 1967, and the Shelley Memorial Award from the Poetry Society of America in 1968. You might want to ask your students why poets usually hold jobs doing something other than writing poetry. The need for fellowships and awards, which often include money as well as honor, should also become apparent to your students.

Phyllis McGinley praised the virtues of suburban living with humor. She also satirized the absurdities of life. She wrote two books of humorous essays, *The Province of the Heart* (1959) and *Sixpence in Her Shoe* (1964), as well as more than a dozen books for young people, including *The Horse Who Lived Upstairs* (1944) and *Sugar and Spice* (1960). McGinley once worked for an advertising agency. You might ask your students if they see any connection between writing advertising and writing poetry.

Alfred, Lord Tennyson's father was a clergyman in Lincolnshire, an area of England known for its lonely marshes. These marshes became the setting for many of Tennyson's poems. You might want to ask students how the message of poems written more than one hundred years ago can be as applicable today as when they were written.

GUIDE FOR READING

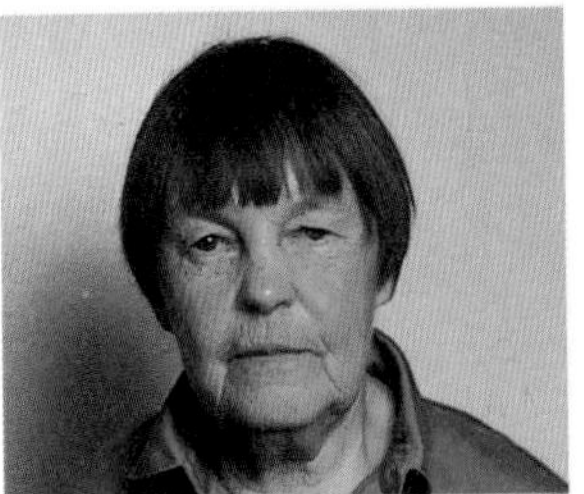

By Morning

May Swenson (1919–   ) was born in Logan, Utah, and attended Utah State University. At the age of thirty, after working as a newspaper reporter, she moved to New York City. There she worked as an editor and lectured at colleges and universities. Swenson's poems have appeared in many magazines including *The New Yorker, Harper's,* and *The Nation.* She has written that enjoyment of poetry is based on our common desire to get through "the curtains of things as they *appear,* to things as they *are.*" "By Morning" is an example of her precise observations of the everyday world.

Reflections Dental

Phyllis McGinley (1905–1978), born in Ontario, Oregon, began writing poetry when she was a schoolteacher in Utah. After several of her poems were accepted by New York magazines, she moved to New Rochelle, New York, to teach and to write. Her early poems were serious and even sad in tone. She turned to lighter subjects only after an editor urged her to avoid "the same sad song all . . . poets sing." *Times Three: Selected Verse from Three Decades, with Seventy New Poems* (1960) is the only book of light verse ever to be awarded the Pulitzer Prize.

Ring Out, Wild Bells

Alfred, Lord Tennyson (1809–1892) was born in Somersby, Lincolnshire, England. Tennyson studied at Cambridge but never received a degree. He was an enthusiastic reader and worked hard to perfect his own craft as a poet. He composed short lyrics as well as longer works, such as *Idylls of the King* (a series of twelve narrative poems based on the King Arthur legends) and *In Memoriam* (a poem in memory of his closest friend Arthur Henry Hallam). In 1850 Lord Tennyson was named poet laureate of England, serving in this capacity for more than forty years.

Objectives

1 To recognize and interpret imagery that appeals to the senses
2 To write a poem containing images
3 To understand how images create humor
4 To write a poem by following a pattern

Support Material

Teaching Portfolio

Teacher Backup, pp. 745–748
Usage and Mechanics Worksheet, p. 749
Vocabulary Check, p. 750–751
Analyzing Literature Worksheet, *Recognizing and Interpreting Imagery,* p. 752
Critical Thinking and Reading Worksheet, *Recognizing Denotations and Connotations of Words,* p. 753
Selection Test, pp. 754–755

Imagery

Imagery is language that appeals to the senses. Imagery is the use of words and phrases to describe something so that a mental picture, or **image,** of it is created in your mind. Most images are visual, but often a writer may use language to suggest how something sounds, smells, tastes, or feels.

Images occur in all forms of writing, but they occur especially in poetry. For example, in "By Morning," May Swenson describes cars as "fumbling sheep." Phyllis McGinley portrays the teeth of television announcers as "rows of hybrid corn." Lord Tennyson evokes the *sound* of "wild bells" ringing "across the snow."

Look For

As you read these poems, keep your eyes open for visual images, but also be aware of imagery that appeals to your other senses. What is the effect of the use of imagery?

Writing

Look out your classroom window. What do you see? What images come to mind? Freewrite about this scene.

Vocabulary

Knowing the following words will help you as you read these poems.

airily (er′ ə lē) *adv.*: Lightly (p. 540)

gracious (grā′ shəs) *adj.*: Here, kind and generous (p. 540)

fleece (flēs) *n.*: Soft, warm covering made of sheep's wool (p. 540)

gleeful (glē′ fəl) *adj.*: Merry (p. 542)

hybrid (hī′ brid) *adj.*: Here, grown from different varieties (p. 542)

crooner (kro͞on′ ər) *n.*: Singer (p. 542)

teem (tēm) *v.*: Swarm (p. 542)

strife (strīf) *n.*: Conflict (p. 544)

slander (slan′ dər) *n.*: Lies (p. 544)

Literary Focus You can point out that the figures of speech (similes, metaphors, and personification) that students studied in the last three poems help to create vivid imagery.

Look For Your more advanced students can identify the figures of speech (similes, metaphors, and personification) used to create some of the imagery they identify in these poems.

Writing/Prior Knowledge If the view out your classroom window is particularly barren, you could have students look around the classroom itself and freewrite about images that come to mind. You might want students to share some of their best images with their classmates.

Vocabulary Your less advanced students will benefit from pronouncing and discussing the definitions of the vocabulary words together in class.

By Morning

May Swenson

1 Some for everyone
plenty

and more coming

2 Fresh   dainty   airily arriving
everywhere at once

3 Transparent at first
each faint slice
slow   soundlessly tumbling

4 then quickly thickly a gracious fleece
will spread like youth   like wheat
over the city

5 Each building will be   a hill
all sharps made round

6 dark worn noisy narrows made still
wide   flat   clean   spaces

7 Streets will be   fields
cars be   fumbling sheep

8 A deep bright harvest will be seeded
in a night

By morning we'll be   children
feeding on manna[1]

9 a new loaf on every doorsill

---

1. **manna** (man′ ə) *n.*: In the Bible, food that was miraculously provided for the Israelites in the wilderness.

Presentation

Motivation/Prior Knowledge People often anticipate events they hope will happen the next day. What are some of the events people might anticipate in this way?

Master Teacher Note The poem has a design with empty spaces. You might ask students to speculate about the reason for these spaces. How should a reader treat these spaces when reading the poem aloud?

Thematic Idea Another selection that deals with the theme of how nature can transform one's surroundings is "Silver" on page 564.

Master Teacher Note To compare and contrast descriptions of winter, you may want to use "January" on page 576.

Purpose-Setting Question May Swenson's poem is a riddle because she does not include the name of her subject in the poem. What is the subject of the poem?

1 **Literary Focus** Who is going to receive whatever it is?

2 **Literary Focus** How will whatever it is arrive?

3 **Literary Focus** What are some of its qualities?

4 **Literary Focus** What three things is it being compared to in this stanza?

5 **Literary Focus** What image tells you how the buildings will be affected?

6 **Literary Focus** What does Swenson mean by "dark worn noisy narrows"?

7 **Literary Focus** How will it affect the streets and cars? What image does Swenson use to tell you this?

8 **Literary Focus** To what is the subject of the poem being compared here?

9 **Literary Focus** What is the subject of the poem? At what point do you first realize what its subject is?

Discussion How does Swenson's comparison of snow to wheat, to a harvest, to manna, and to a loaf on every doorstep add to the meaning of the poem? Do you think the meaning of the poem is restricted simply to a snowfall? Explain.

Challenge You might want your more advanced students to discuss the lack of punctuation in Swenson's poem. What effect does the lack of punctuation have on the poem?

THINKING ABOUT THE SELECTION

Recalling

1. Where is this poem set?
2. What will happen to the buildings?
3. What will the streets become?

Interpreting

4. What will arrive "everywhere at once"?
5. Why will sidewalks become "wide flat clean spaces"?
6. What is the poet actually describing?

Applying

7. How are we "children" *every* morning?

ANALYZING LITERATURE

Recognizing and Interpreting Imagery

Imagery can involve senses other than sight. A poet can describe a thing so that it evokes a sound, a smell, a taste, even a feeling (to the touch). Look, for instance, at Swenson's description:

dark worn noisy narrows made still

The poet imagines city sidewalks at nightfall. Once noisy and crowded, they are now still, empty, quiet. With one image, the poet involves our senses of sight, hearing, and even touch.

1. Find two visual images in the poem.
2. What images of touch and of sound occur?
3. What image of taste and smell occurs?

THINKING AND WRITING

Using Images to Compose a Poem

Recall an experience you have had that stimulated your senses—for example, a movie, a swim, a visit to a zoo. Jot down a list of images related to that experience. Using your list as a reference, compose a poem telling about the experience. When you have finished, make sure you have given a clear picture of your experience. Proofread and share your poem.

Closure and Extension

ANSWERS TO THINKING ABOUT THE SELECTION

Recalling

1. This poem is set in a city.
2. The sharp corners of buildings will be made round, so that they look like hills.
3. The streets will become fields full of fumbling sheep.

Interpreting

4. Snow will arrive everywhere at once.
5. Sidewalks will be wide, flat, clean spaces because they will be evenly covered with snow.
6. The poet is actually describing a snowfall.

Applying

7. Answers will differ. Suggested Response: We are children every morning because we start anew with energy renewed by rest, and we face a new day with the chance to see and do new things.

ANSWERS TO ANALYZING LITERATURE

1. Suggested responses are two of the following: "Transparent at first," "Then quickly thickly a gracious fleece," "Each building will be a hill/all sharps made round," "Streets will be fields/cars be fumbling sheep," and "a new loaf on every doorsill."
2. Images of touch are "thickly," "all sharps made round," and "feeding on manna." Images of sound are "soundlessly tumbling" and "noisy narrows."
3. The poem ends with the image of bread, which appeals to the senses of taste and smell.

THINKING AND WRITING

For help with this assignment, students can refer to Lesson 18, "Writing a Poem," in the Handbook of Writing About Literature.

Publishing Student Writing Select students to organize their classmates' writing into a magazine. If a copying machine is available, you may distribute copies of the magazine to each member of the class.

Writing Across the Curriculum You might inform the art department of your students' creative poetry writing. Art teachers might direct the students in illustrating or illuminating the manuscripts of their poems.

Presentation

Motivation/Prior Knowledge Have students imagine they are going to appear on television. Ask them what preparations they would make before their appearance. In "Reflections Dental" the poet writes about one preparation everyone appearing on television seems to have made.

Master Teacher Note To compare and contrast other poems with humorous themes, you may want to use Two Limericks on page 569 and "The Choice" on page 604.

Purpose-Setting Question What is something that everyone who appears on television seems to have in common?

1 **Literary Focus** What words create an image in your mind in these lines?

2 **Literary Focus** What is the metaphor in these lines?

3 **Discussion** Do you think the poet intends you to take the comment about announcers as absolutely true? What technique is the poet using to create humor in this comment?

4 **Discussion** What are examples of alliteration in these lines? How does the grouping of occupations add to the humor?

5 **Clarification** An M.C. is a master of ceremonies.

6 **Discussion** Why might the poet have used the word *treasures* to refer to teeth in this poem?

7 **Discussion** What metaphor does the poet use in these lines?

8 **Discussion** Why would anyone be pleased to see imperfections in someone else?

Reflections Dental

Phyllis McGinley

1 How pure, how beautiful, how fine
Do teeth on television shine!
2 No flutist flutes, no dancer twirls,
But comes equipped with matching pearls.
3 Gleeful announcers all are born
With sets like rows of hybrid corn.
4 Clowns, critics, clergy, commentators,
Ventriloquists and roller skaters,
5 M.C.s who beat their palms together,
The girl who diagrams the weather,
The crooner crooning for his supper—
6 All flash white treasures, lower and upper.
7 With miles of smiles the airwaves teem,
And each an orthodontist's[1] dream.

8 'Twould please my eye as gold a miser's—
One charmer with uncapped incisors.[2]

---

1. **orthodontist** (ôr' thə dän' tist) *n.*: A dentist who straightens teeth.
2. **incisors** (in sī' zərz) *n.*: The front teeth.

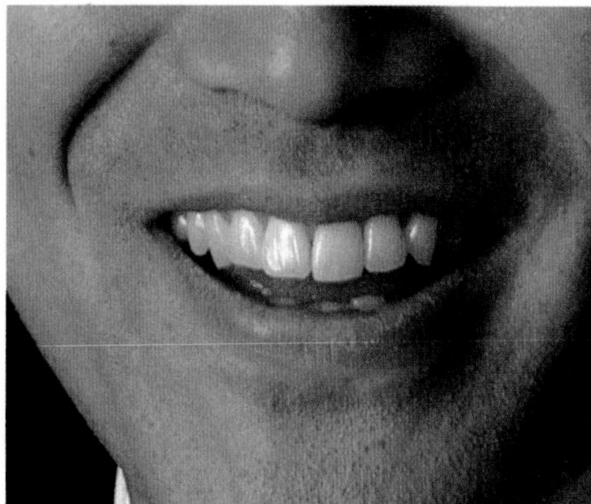

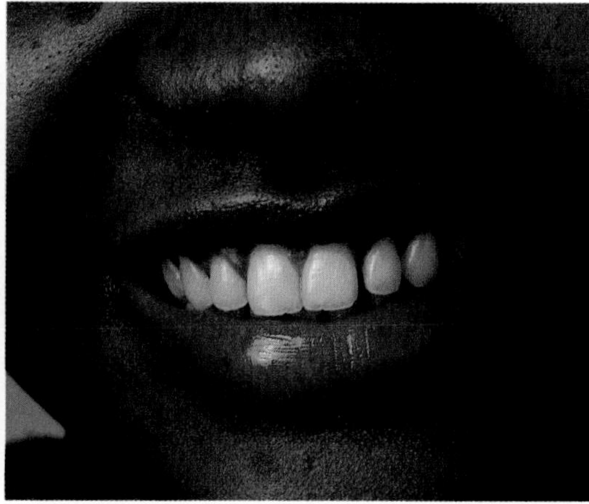

Reader's Response Would a "charmer with uncapped incisors" necessarily be as charming? Why?

THINKING ABOUT THE SELECTION

Recalling

1. What has the poet observed about people on television?
2. Name three groups of people that the poet mentions.
3. What are two things to which she compares teeth?

Interpreting

4. The poet uses alliteration, the repetition of initial consonant sounds, to help her poke fun at her topic. For example, look at the repetition of the *c* sound in line 7. Find two other examples of alliteration in the poem. Explain how each of these helps create a humorous effect.
5. A *reflection* is usually a serious thinking about or consideration of a topic. Why is the title of this poem humorous?

Applying

6. Why do you think some viewers expect people on television to look perfect?

ANALYZING LITERATURE

Understanding Humorous Images

Images can be humorous in themselves if they are presented or put together in surprising ways. They can also be funny if they are exaggerated. Phyllis McGinley pictures an endless line of gleaming teeth: "miles of smiles." This is both a comical exaggeration and an unusual view of the behavior of television personalities.

1. List two other exaggerations the author uses.
2. What unusual image combinations occur in lines 3 through 6?

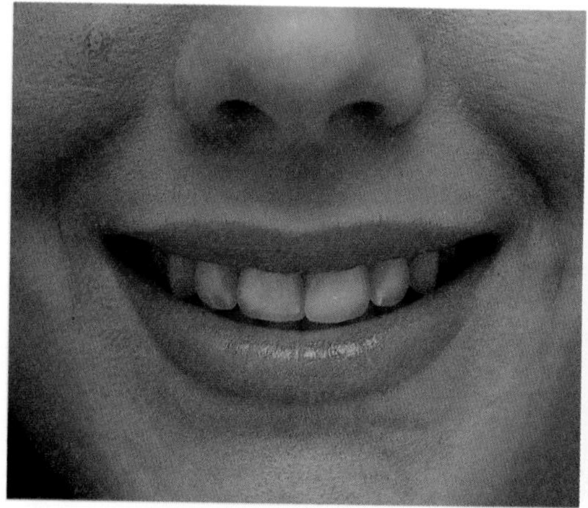

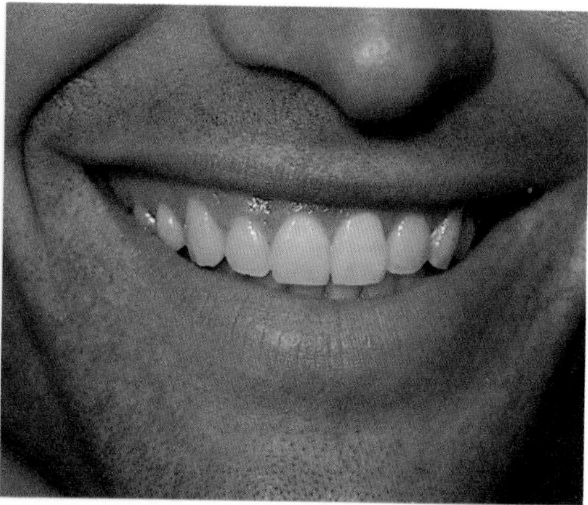

Closure and Extension

ANSWERS TO THINKING ABOUT THE SELECTION

Recalling

1. The poet has observed that people on television all have teeth that are straight, gleaming, and beautiful.
2. Answers will differ. Suggested Response: Groups of people mentioned by the poet can include three of the following—flutists, dancers, announcers, clowns, critics, clergy, commentators, ventriloquists, roller skaters, M.C.'s, girls who present the weather, and crooners.
3. McGinley compares teeth to matching pearls and to rows of hybrid corn.

Interpreting

4. Two examples of alliteration are "flutist flutes" in line 3 and "crooner crooning" in line 11. They help to create a humorous effect because there is no need to say that flutists flute or that croonists croon. Their titles alone indicate what they do.
5. The title is humorous because it includes a pun. *Reflections* can mean a serious consideration of a topic or it can also mean the throwing back of images from a shiny surface—in this case, shiny, white teeth.

Applying

6. Answers will differ. Suggested Response: Some viewers expect people on television to look perfect because they see television as representing the way they would like to be, not as they are.

ANSWERS TO ANALYZING LITERATURE

1. Two other exaggerations McGinley uses are "gleeful announcers" and "the airwaves teem." Announcers are not always "gleeful," and "teem" implies that they are swarming all over.
2. Unusual image combinations in lines 3 through 6 are flutists and dancers with matching pearls and gleeful announcers with sets of teeth like rows of hybrid corn.

Presentation

Motivation/Prior Knowledge Most New Year's resolutions are personal goals. Have students imagine that someone was going to make a list of New Year's resolutions for the whole world. What are some of the resolutions or goals that a person might include on such a list?

Master Teacher Note Your more advanced students might benefit from a discussion of the meter and rhyme pattern of "Ring Out, Wild Bells." The poem is in iambic (one unaccented syllable followed by one accented one) tetrameter (four beats per line) and has a rhyme scheme of *a b b a*.

Purpose-Setting Question What does Tennyson hope the new year will bring?

1 **Discussion** To what does this line refer?

2 **Discussion** In this line what wish is expressed for the new year?

3 **Discussion** What three improvements are asked for in this stanza?

4 **Discussion** To what aspect of life do these lines refer?

5 **Discussion** What is meant by this line?

Ring Out, Wild Bells

Alfred, Lord Tennyson

Ring out, wild bells, to the wild sky,
The flying cloud, the frosty light:
1 The year is dying in the night;
Ring out, wild bells, and let him die.

Ring out the old, ring in the new,
Ring, happy bells, across the snow:
The year is going, let him go;
2 Ring out the false, ring in the true.

3 Ring out the grief that saps[1] the mind,
For those that here we see no more;
Ring out the feud of rich and poor,
Ring in redress[2] to all mankind.

4 Ring out a slowly dying cause,
And ancient forms of party strife;
Ring in the nobler modes[3] of life,
With sweeter manners, purer laws.

Ring out the want, the care, the sin,
The faithless coldness of the times;
Ring out, ring out thy mournful rhymes,
But ring the fuller minstrel[4] in.

5 Ring out false pride in place and blood,
The civic[5] slander and the spite;
Ring in the love of truth and right,
Ring in the common love of good.

Ring out old shapes of foul disease;
Ring out the narrowing lust of gold;
Ring out the thousand wars of old,
Ring in the thousand years of peace.

---

1. **saps** (saps) *v.*: Drains; exhausts.
2. **redress** (rē′ dres) *n.*: The righting of wrongs.
3. **modes** (mōdz) *n.*: Ways; forms.
4. **fuller minstrel** (min′ strəl) *n.*: A singer of the highest rank.
5. **civic** (siv′ ik) *adj.*: Of a city.

THINKING ABOUT THE SELECTION

Recalling

1. This poem celebrates the new year. What does the poet wish to "ring out"? What does he wish to "ring in"?

Interpreting

2. How does the poet seem to feel about the past? Support your answer.
3. What does he hope for the future? Support your answer.
4. What is this poem about in addition to the passing of the old year? What is its theme?
5. Would you describe this poem as sad and pessimistic, or hopeful and optimistic? Find details to support your answer.

Applying

6. Why does the start of a new year often make people feel hopeful?

THINKING AND WRITING

Writing a Patterned Poem

Write a poem that expresses your wishes for the new year. Begin by rereading all or part of "Ring Out, Wild Bells." Take note of the *pattern* of Tennyson's poem, especially the way every negative thing is balanced by something positive. Compose two or three stanzas following Tennyson's example. Tell what you would like to "ring out" and "ring in." After you have finished, read over your stanzas and make any corrections or improvements you feel are needed. Share your poem with your classmates.

Closure and Extension

ANSWERS TO THINKING ABOUT THE SELECTION

Recalling

1. The poet wishes to ring out everything that is old and bad, such as the false, grief, the feud between rich and poor, a dying cause, party strife, want, care, sin, faithless coldness, mournful rhymes, false pride in station and family, civic slander, spite, disease, lust of gold, and the thousand wars of old. The poet wishes to ring in all that is good, such as the true, redress to all mankind, nobler modes of life, sweeter manners, purer laws, the fuller minstrel, love of truth and right, the common love of good, and the thousand years of peace.

Interpreting

2. The poet seems to find no virtues in the past, only those aspects that should be rung out, such as grief, a dying cause, and so on.
3. The poet hopes only good for the future, including redress for all mankind, sweeter manners, purer laws, and so on.
4. Answers will differ. Suggested Response: This poem is about improving society. The theme of the poem seems to be that human beings can improve their circumstances.
5. This poem is hopeful and optimistic because it implies that human beings can rid the world of grief, the feud between the rich and poor, party strife, and so on.

Applying

6. Answers will differ. Suggested Response: The start of a new year often makes people feel hopeful because it seems to offer the opportunity to start anew.

THINKING AND WRITING

For help with this assignment, students can refer to Lesson 18, "Writing a Poem," in the Handbook of Writing About Literature.

Publishing Student Writing If you have previously started booklets of your students' creative writing, you might make copies of the stanzas they write and add them to their booklets.

You might submit several of the better stanzas to the school newspaper or literary magazine.

Focus

More About the Authors As well as poetry, **Robert P. Tristram Coffin** wrote essays, novels, and biographies. He had more than forty of his books published. One of them, *Lost Paradise,* which was published in 1934, is his autobiography. As a professor, Coffin exercised great influence over other writers of his day. You might want to discuss with students why an author might write in so many different genres.

Many of **Sara Teasdale's** poems are about women who are facing death or who have been deserted by a loved one. When she wrote of moral or spiritual virtues, she compared them to the beauty of the natural world. Much of Teasdale's poetry, therefore, deals with nature. As well as writing her own poetry, Teasdale edited a volume of women's lyrics about love and a collection of poems for young people. You might ask students why the words of a poet who wrote over fifty years ago are still read today.

Evelyn Tooley Hunt says, "I like to write from the inside of some culture other than my own." She has done this by writing "Man With a Word," which first appeared in the *Chicago Jewish Forum* (although she is not Jewish,) by writing her own variation of haiku under the pen name of Tao-Li (although she is not Chinese,) and by writing "Taught Me Purple," which first appeared in *Negro Digest* (although she is not black.) You might ask your students if they think it is ever possible to adopt completely a culture not your own.

GUIDE FOR READING

The Secret Heart

Robert P. Tristram Coffin (1892–1955) was born in Brunswick, Maine, grew up on a farm, and got his early education in a rural schoolhouse. He attended Bowdoin College in Maine, Princeton University in New Jersey, and Oxford University in England. His poems often portray life on a farm or along the seacoast in Maine. Coffin illustrated many of his own books, including *Strange Holiness,* for which he won a Pulitzer Prize in 1936. Like many of Coffin's poems, "The Secret Heart" portrays the good in the world by describing the devoted love of a parent for his child.

Advice to a Girl

Sara Teasdale (1884–1933) was born in St. Louis, Missouri, and was educated at home and in private schools. Later she traveled extensively both in the United States and abroad. Teasdale's poetry was praised by critics and enjoyed by the public. In 1918 she won a Pulitzer Prize for a collection of poems entitled *Love Songs*. Generally, Teasdale's poems are short, graceful, and intense. She spent her last years in New York City, where her poems became simpler, more passionate, and deeply personal.

Taught Me Purple

Evelyn Tooley Hunt (1904–) was born in Hamburg, New York. In 1926 she graduated from William Smith College in Geneva, New York, where she had been an editor of the literary magazine. She received the Sidney Lanier Memorial Award for her first collection of poems, *Look Again, Adam,* published in 1961. Hunt's interest in different cultures is demonstrated in her writing. She is best known for her variations of haiku, a type of Asian poetry, which she writes under the pen name of Tao-Li. In "Taught Me Purple," Hunt writes of the lessons learned from a mother.

Objectives

1. To interpret symbols carefully
2. To paraphrase a poem
3. To write an analysis of a symbol

Support Material

Teaching Portfolio

Teacher Backup, pp. 757–760
Usage and Mechanics Worksheet, p. 761
Vocabulary Check, p. 762
Analyzing Literature Worksheet, *Interpreting Symbols Carefully,* p. 763
Language Worksheet, *Understanding Synonyms and Antonyms,* p. 764
Selection Test, pp. 765–766

Symbols

A **symbol** is any person, place, or thing that has a meaning in itself and that also *stands for* something else. A symbol can be another living thing, an object, a situation, or an action. Usually symbols stand for ideas or qualities. You are probably familiar with certain common symbols: a flag symbolizing a nation; a dove symbolizing peace; the five interlocking rings (each ring symbolizing a continent) symbolizing the Olympic Games.

Symbols are a kind of figurative language. Like simile, metaphor, and personification, a symbol enables a writer to express a complicated idea or a deep feeling in few words, sometimes in a single image. For example, "The Secret Heart" begins with the image of a lighted match held between two hands in the dark. In the course of the poem, that image is gradually developed into a symbol of love.

Look For

As you read these poems, look for images, objects, situations, and places that might be symbolic. Think first about the literal meaning of what is being described. Then consider the overall mood and meaning of the poem. What might the object represent? In what way does it relate to the theme of the poem?

Writing

Choose a symbol with which you are familiar. The symbol may be one that represents a place, a holiday, a product, or an idea. Freewrite for five minutes about what the symbol you have chosen means.

Vocabulary

Knowing the following words will help you as you read these poems.

sire (sīr) *n.*: Father (p. 548)
kindled (kin′ d'ld) *v.*: Ignited (p. 548)
semblance (sem′ bləns) *n.*: Likeness; image (p. 548)
tenement (ten′ ə mənt) *n.*: Here, a rundown apartment building (p. 551)
molding (mōl′ diŋ) *n.*: Ornamental woodwork that projects from the walls of a room (p. 551)

Literary Focus You might ask your students to think of other selections they have read in your class. Have them suggest symbols that appeared in these selections. Be sure students volunteering symbols can explain what each symbol represents and how they can tell it is being used symbolically.

Look For Your **less advanced** students might benefit from a class discussion of the symbols in these poems. Elicit from students how they can tell what each symbol represents and how each symbol is related to the theme of the poem.

Writing/Prior Knowledge Your less advanced students might benefit from a brainstorming session about possible symbols to use in this activity.

Vocabulary With the possible exception of *semblance,* your students should not find these words difficult.

Spelling Tip In words like *kindled, d* is regularly followed by *le* with these exceptions:

citadel	model
infidel	yodel

Presentation

Motivation/Prior Knowledge When a child is half asleep, ordinary objects may seem strange or threatening. Discuss with the class what types of everyday objects might look different to a young child who is half asleep in a dimly lit room.

Master Teacher Note You might want to point out to students that this poem is written in rhyming couplets. Have them notice Coffin's punctuation of the poem as well.

Thematic Idea Another selection that deals with the theme of the love between a father and a son is the short story "Christmas Day in the Morning" by Pearl Buck on page 21. If your students have read the story, you might ask them what kind of love there was between the father and son. Does love always have to be spoken? How might love that is shown be more special than love that is simply spoken?

Purpose-Setting Question What symbol appears in this poem and how is it related to the theme of the poem?

1 **Discussion** To what does the title of the poem refer?

2 **Reading Strategy** What prediction can you make about the subject of the rest of the poem from this first couplet?

3 **Discussion** What does this line mean?

4 **Discussion** Look at the photograph on page 549. Might a sleepy, young child see a heart glowing in the darkness?

5 **Discussion** What does the poet mean in this line?

6 **Discussion** Discuss how this line expresses an idea similar to the idea in line 16.

7 **Literary Focus** What does the symbol in this poem represent?

8 **Literary Focus** What new symbol is introduced in this couplet? To what does it refer?

1 The Secret Heart

Robert P. Tristram Coffin

2 Across the years he could recall
His father one way best of all.

In the stillest hour of night
The boy awakened to a light.

Half in dreams, he saw his sire
With his great hands full of fire.

The man had struck a match to see
If his son slept peacefully.

He held his palms each side the spark
3 His love had kindled in the dark.

4 His two hands were curved apart
In the semblance of a heart.

He wore, it seemed to his small son,
5 A bare heart on his hidden one,

A heart that gave out such a glow
No son awake could bear to know.

It showed a look upon a face
6 Too tender for the day to trace.

One instant, it lit all about,
7 And then the secret heart went out.

8 But it shone long enough for one
To know that hands held up the sun.

THINKING ABOUT THE SELECTION

Recalling

1. How does the boy best recall his father?
2. Why does the father strike a match? Where does he hold the match?

Interpreting

3. What do the two hands holding the flame seem to be? Is this image effective? Explain.
4. What do lines 16 and 18 mean?
5. Interpret the last two lines of the poem.

Applying

6. We say love fills us with warmth and unfriendliness leaves us feeling cold. Why are the sensations of warmth and cold appropriate for discussing love and unfriendliness?

ANALYZING LITERATURE

Interpreting Symbols Carefully

A symbol may mean something particular to the poet but not to everyone. Therefore it is important to think about a symbol in context (the words and ideas that surround it). For example, the image of "hands full of fire" could stand for many things. In "The Secret Heart," it becomes, for the boy, a symbol of his father's love.

1. How do the hands become a symbol of love?
2. In the last line, what does the sun symbolize?
3. Explain the meaning of the title of the poem.

Humanities Note

Certain portraits expose an inner quality of the subject, the subject's "secret heart." You might show your students portraits such as Van Gogh's *The Postman Rouline* and *A Woman in the Cafe Le Tambourin* and Picasso's *Woman in White.* Ask the class to speculate about the "secret heart" of each subject.

Closure and Extension

ANSWERS TO THINKING ABOUT THE SELECTION

Recalling

1. The boy best recalls his father standing with his great hands full of fire so that they resembled a glowing heart.
2. The father strikes a match so that he can see if his son is sleeping peacefully without turning on a light that might wake the boy. The father holds the match between his cupped palms.

Interpreting

3. The two hands holding the flame seem to be a bare heart (one that can be seen) on his hidden (actual internal) one. Answers will differ. Suggested Response: The image is effective because two hands glowing in the dark might well resemble a heart.
4. Answers will differ. Suggested Response: The glow is something "no son awake could bear to know" because the love it represented was too intense. The look upon the father's face was also so intensely loving that a person would avoid displaying an emotion so openly in the daylight.
5. Answers will differ. Suggested Response: Hands that are all-powerful could hold up the sun. Young children often think their parents are all-powerful.

Applying

6. Answers will differ. Suggested Response: Warmth and cold are appropriate for discussing love and unfriendliness because when warm, people can be comfortable. When people are cold, they cannot be comfortable. Therefore, love, a comforting relationship, is equated with warmth, and unfriendliness, an uncomfortable relationship, is equated with cold.

ANSWERS TO ANALYZING LITERATURE

1. This image becomes a symbol of love as the young boy sees that the hands form the shape of a heart. He sees the look of love on his father's face and the glowing heart becomes a symbol of the love his father feels for him.
2. The sun symbolizes the boy's whole world. Because his father's hands are holding it up, it becomes a symbol of his father's all-encompassing and all-powerful strength.
3. The title of the poem refers to the glowing heart that the boy saw but that was not seen by anyone else and was, therefore, the boy's secret.

Motivation/Prior Knowledge Imagine how people might feel if given advice about their personal lives that they did not want to hear. What might be their reactions?

Master Teacher Note You may want students to speculate about what the speaker is like, based on what the speaker says and the way it is said.

Thematic Idea Another selection that deals with the theme of love is "The Secret Heart," on page 548.

Purpose-Setting Question What advice does this poem contain?

1 **Discussion** Whom do you think the speaker is referring to?

2 **Discussion** Who has made the young girl angry?

3 **Literary Focus** What kind of figure of speech appears in this line? What is being compared in it?

4 **Literary Focus** What kind of figure of speech appears in this line? How is this figure of speech related to the one in line 5?

5 **Literary Focus** Why will the girl be blessed if she takes a long look into the crystal?

6 **Discussion** Why do you think the first two lines are repeated here?

Reader's Response Rephrase the narrator's advice in your own words.

Advice to a Girl

Sara Teasdale

1 No one worth possessing
Can be quite possessed;
Lay that on your heart,
2 My young angry dear;
3 This truth, this hard and precious stone,
Lay it on your hot cheek,
Let it hide your tear.
4 Hold it like a crystal
When you are alone
And gaze in the depths of the icy stone.
5 Long, look long and you will be blessed:
6 No one worth possessing
Can be quite possessed.

THINKING ABOUT THE SELECTION

Recalling

1. What is the advice the poet gives the girl?
2. To what does the poet compare the "truth"?
3. What does the poet tell the girl to do with the advice?

Interpreting

4. Why might the poet's "truth" be both precious and hard?
5. How do you think the girl is feeling? Support your answer with details from the poem.
6. Why do you think the poet begins and ends the poem with her words of advice?

Applying

7. Explain why you do or do not agree with the poet's advice.

THINKING AND WRITING

Paraphrasing a Poem

An effective way to clarify a poem for yourself is to **paraphrase** it—that is, restate it in your own words. You must be careful to paraphrase both accurately and *completely*. Reread "Advice to a Girl." Imagine that you are the speaker. Rewrite, or paraphrase, the poem as if you were writing a letter to a close friend. After you have finished, compare your letter with the poem to make sure you have paraphrased accurately and thoroughly. Proofread your letter and share it with your classmates.

Closure and Extension

ANSWERS TO THINKING ABOUT THE SELECTION

Recalling

1. The poet says, "No one worth possessing can be quite possessed"—not to be possessive because no worthwhile man will stand for it.
2. The poet compares the "truth" to a hard and precious stone that turns out to be a crystal ball.
3. The poet tells the girl to "Long, look long" at the advice, to consider it carefully.

Interpreting

4. It is precious because following it will improve her relationships with young men, hard because following it will be difficult.
5. Answers will differ. Suggested Response: The young girl is angry and hurt. The poet calls her "My young angry dear;" she has a "hot cheek"—a sign of anger; and the poet speaks of her tear.
6. Answers will differ. Suggested Response: She begins and ends with advice so the girl will remember it.

Applying

7. Answers will differ. Students might agree because no one likes to feel like a prisoner of someone.

Taught Me Purple

Evelyn Tooley Hunt

My mother taught me purple
    Although she never wore it. 1
Wash-gray was her circle,
    The tenement her orbit. 2

My mother taught me golden 3
    And held me up to see it,
Above the broken molding,
    Beyond the filthy street. 4

My mother reached for beauty
    And for its lack she died, 5
Who knew so much of duty
    She could not teach me pride. 6

SUMMER MILLINERY, 1915
Charles W. Hawthorne
Chrysler Museum

Presentation

Motivation/Prior Knowledge Lead the class in a discussion of the different ways in which things can be taught. How is learning by following someone's example different from learning by listening to someone giving an explanation?

Master Teacher Note A discussion of the meaning that various colors have for people might be in order here. You might want to explain to students how purple became known as the color of royalty. In ancient times, the purple dyes were extremely rare and costly so that only royalty could wear purple clothes.

Purpose-Setting Question What does the title of the poem mean?

1 **Literary Focus** How could the mother teach the child purple if she never wore it?

2 **Discussion** Where do the mother and child live?

3 **Literary Focus** To what do you think "golden" refers?

4 **Discussion** Where are the "broken molding" and "filthy street"?

5 **Literary Focus** For what does the mother yearn? Does she ever achieve what she wants?

6 **Discussion** Why is the mother unable to teach the child pride?

Humanities Note

Fine art, *Summer Millinery* by Charles Webster Hawthorne (1872–1930). Hawthorne founded and directed the Cape Cod School of Art at Provincetown, Massachusetts. Although many of his paintings are of people engaged in commercial fishing off the Massachusetts coast, this particular painting shows a black woman making a hat. You might want to see how many of your students are familiar with the term *millinery*.

In what way does the illustration capture the message or theme of the poem?

Challenge This poem presents a series of contrasting symbols. What are they, and to what do they refer?

Challenge You might want to have your more advanced students write poems using colors as symbols.

Reader's Response How is beauty beyond everyone's reach? How is it beyond your reach?

THINKING ABOUT THE SELECTION

Recalling

1. What two things does the poet say her mother taught her?
2. What lack causes the mother to die?

Interpreting

3. The colors purple, gray, and golden are used in this poem. What does each color symbolize?
4. Compare and contrast the mother's surroundings with her goals.
5. Why could the mother not teach the daughter pride?
6. What is the theme of this poem?

Applying

7. We often use colors to symbolize qualities. What does the color red usually symbolize? Why is this symbol effective?

THINKING AND WRITING

Writing About Symbolism

Write an essay analyzing the use of symbols in "Taught Me Purple." First think of the meaning of the symbols. Then consider their effect on the theme. Write a first draft of your essay. When you revise, make sure your analysis is clear and well organized. Proofread your essay and share it with your classmates.

Closure and Extension

ANSWERS TO THINKING ABOUT THE SELECTION

Recalling

1. The poet says her mother taught her purple and golden.
2. A lack of beauty causes the mother to die.

Interpreting

3. The color purple symbolizes the beauty and wealth the world has to offer. The color gray symbolizes the lack of beauty and wealth and life as mere drab existence. Golden is another symbol of what was possible in life beyond the restrictions of poverty.
4. The mother's surroundings were drab and poor. The surroundings were rundown and filthy. The mother's goals were beauty and an interesting life without poverty.
5. The mother was so busy doing her duty in her difficult circumstances that she never developed pride. Therefore, she never taught the child pride.
6. The theme of this poem is that despite poverty people can find beauty even in unlikely places.

Applying

7. The color red usually symbolizes the quality of courage. The red in the flag of the United States symbolizes courage. It is an effective symbol because its meaning is recognized by many people.

THINKING AND WRITING

Publishing Student Writing Your students' essays analyzing the use of symbols can be posted on the bulletin board or made available in a booklet. Students can then read others' papers to broaden their understanding of symbols.

If your students write the poems suggested in the Challenge activity, you might add them to booklets of creative writing they are collecting. Some of the better poems could also be submitted to the school newspaper or literary magazine.

Lyric Poetry

INVITATION TO THE SIDESHOW, (LA PARADE)
Georges Pierre Seurat
The Metropolitan Museum of Art

Humanities Note

Fine art, *Invitation to the Sideshow,* 1888, by Georges Seurat. Georges Seurat (1859-1891) was a French Post-Impressionist painter who invented Pointillism, a painting system of applying pure color in tiny dots which are visually blended when viewed from a distance. Seurat was educated in academic art at the École des Beaux-Arts in Paris. Although he admired the work of the Impressionists, he sought to establish his own, more ordered, style of painting. His Pointillist technique imbued his canvases with shimmering light and subtle, evocative atmosphere.

The painting, *Invitation to the Side Show,* is clearly a forerunner to more modern styles of painting. The picture plane is organized into rigid geometric shapes that sacrifice warmth for precision. The colors are somber but rich in tone. The artificial light seems to scintillate in a light mist, creating a mood of mystery. The subtle shading of the faces and the formal composition show the intense planning that went into this work. Although circus entertainers are a favorite Impressionist theme, Seurat's lyrical handling of the subject sets his art apart from Impressionism.

Master Teacher Note To introduce lyric poetry, place Art Transparency 11, *Spring* by Ben Shahn from the Teaching Portfolio, on the overhead projector. Explain that lyric poetry creates a mood, rather than tells a story. It expresses the poet's thoughts and feelings through descriptive words and musical rhythm. Discuss with students what mood this painting conveys. Discuss whether a painting, like this one, could be considered lyrical, and why.

Focus

More About the Author Tell students that **Lew Sarett** served as a woodsman, guide, and U.S. Ranger in the Northwest for several months each year over a long period of time. Ask them how such experience might be valuable for a nature poet.

Langston Hughes was involved in the Harlem Renaissance. Point out to students that Harlem became a cultural center for blacks who had come North during World War I (1914–1918) looking for jobs. Ask students to consider why a flowering of creativity might occur in a community of recently uprooted people living in a large city.

Tell students that **Robert Frost** lived in New England for most of his life, working as a farmer and schoolteacher until he became famous. Almost all of his poems have a New England setting. What advantages and disadvantages are there in getting to know and writing about one particular region?

Alice Walker's novel *The Color Purple* was made into a major motion picture. Ask students to consider what problems an author might face in adapting his or her novel for the movies.

GUIDE FOR READING

Four Little Foxes

Lew Sarett (1888–1954) first began working at age twelve to support his family in Chicago. It was then that he developed a love for nature, which is shown in poems like "Four Little Foxes." Among those who encouraged him to write poetry was Carl Sandburg. Some of Sarett's poems echo the rhythms of Native American music and folklore. "Much of whatever is joyous and significant in life, timeless, true, and peculiarly American," he wrote, "tends to be rooted in the wild earth of America.".

Harlem Night Song

Langston Hughes (1902–1967) was the first black American to earn his living as a writer and public speaker. Hughes was part of the Harlem Renaissance of the 1920's—a period of intense creativity among black writers and artists living in the northern part of New York City. In his poems, short stories, and songs, Hughes wrote about the sorrows and joys of ordinary black people. "Harlem Night Song" shows how Hughes incorporated some aspects of black music, especially jazz themes, into his songs and poems.

Blue-Butterfly Day

Robert Frost (1874–1963) was an unofficial poet laureate of the United States. Born in San Francisco, he moved to New England at age ten. He did not attend college, but worked in a Massachusetts textile mill and began writing poetry. Frost's poetry was awarded the Pulitzer Prize four times. He read his poem "The Gift Outright" at the 1961 inauguration of President John F. Kennedy. In poems like "Blue-Butterfly Day," Frost deals with the relationship between human beings and nature.

For My Sister Molly Who in the Fifties

Alice Walker (1944–), the youngest of eight children, grew up in Georgia, where her parents were sharecroppers. Her novel *The Color Purple* is based on true stories about her great-grandmother and on research Walker did at Spelman College. Besides being active in the civil rights movement in the 1960's Walker has written works that deal with black heritage. This interest can be seen in "For My Sister Molly Who in the Fifties," which is from *Revolutionary Petunias and Other Poems.*

Objectives

1 To understand the features of lyric poetry
2 To make inferences about the mood of a lyric poem
3 To write a lyric poem

Support Material

Teaching Portfolio

Teacher Backup, pp. 767–770
Usage and Mechanics Worksheet, p. 771
Vocabulary Check, p. 772
Critical Thinking and Reading Worksheet, *Making Inferences About Mood,* p. 773
Language Worksheet, *Recognizing Sensory Language,* p. 774
Selection Test, pp. 775–776

Lyric Poetry

Lyric poetry is poetry that expresses the poet's thoughts and feelings. It does not tell a story, as narrative poetry does, but creates a mood through vivid images—or pictures—descriptive words, and the musical quality of the lines. These means of creating mood help you remember the poet's thoughts and feelings, and "see" or "hear" the image the poet presents. Lyric poems may be made up of regular stanzas, like "Four Little Foxes," or they may have uneven stanzas, like "Harlem Night Song."

Originally, a lyric was a poem that was sung and accompanied by a lyre; today, lyric poetry reflects this musical heritage.

Look For

As you read these four poems, "see" the images and "hear" their musical quality. What is each poem about? What feelings does each poem arouse about its topic?

Writing

Many lyric poems use images, or pictures, from nature. These images may help create a mood, or show the poet's attitude toward nature or the relationship between people and nature. For example, the image of fresh snow on pine trees in winter may call up a peaceful feeling about nature. List five of your own vivid images of nature. They may appeal to the sense of sight, sound, smell, taste, or feeling.

Vocabulary

Knowing the following words will help you as you read these poems.

forbear (fôr ber′) *v.*: To refrain from (p. 556)

suckled (suk′ ′ld) *v.*: Sucked at the breast (p. 556)

rampant (ram′ pənt) *adj.*: Violent and uncontrollable (p. 556)

Literary Focus You may want to explain to students what is meant by the "musical quality" of lyric poetry. Poets no longer sing their songs to the accompaniment of a lyre, so they must create their own music from the sounds and stressed syllables of words. Read to students the following lines from Edgar Allan Poe's "Annabel Lee":

"It was many and many a year ago/In a kingdom by the sea./ That a maiden there lived whom you may know/By the name of Annabel Lee;—/And this maiden she lived with no other thought/ Than to love and be loved by me."

Poe creates the haunting music of these lines with end rhymes ("sea"-"Lee"-"me"; "ago"-"know"), repetitions ("many and many"; "a maiden there lived" and "this maiden she lived"), pleasing sounds (the long *a* sound in lines 2 and 3: m*a*iden-m*a*y-n*a*me), and a regular rhythmic pattern (lines of four beats and three beats alternating).

Look For Consider telling students that the musical quality of a poem and the images it paints are often related. For example, a poem with vivid descriptions of fast-moving horses may have a galloping rhythm. A poem that describes a quiet beach, however, might have a rhythm like the peaceful lapping of waves on the shore.

Writing/Prior Knowledge You may want to divide the class into small groups and have students discuss their images before completing the assignment.

Vocabulary Ask **less advanced** students to read aloud the words and definitions.

Have **more advanced** students find five synonyms for *rampant* in a thesaurus. Also have them look up the word *forebear* and distinguish it from its homonym *forbear.*

Presentation

Motivation/Prior Knowledge You might ask students if they have ever seen helpless, newborn animals. Have them describe these creatures. Then tell them that the poem they will read is about four newborn foxes.

Purpose-Setting Question How would the mood of this poem change if the first and last lines of each stanza were eliminated?

1 **Master Teacher Note** You might want to tell students that poets use vivid, specific language to make their thoughts and feelings memorable. Ask students why the specific verb *squirming* in line 3 is more effective than the general verb *moving* would be. Then have students find other specific verbs the poet uses to describe what the newborn foxes are doing. Ask students to explain how each of these verbs creates a vivid image.

2 **Discussion** How does the poet create the music of this stanza? What is the pattern of rhymes? How many accented syllables does each line have? Which words are repeated?

3 **Enrichment** Have students look at the photograph on page 557. Can you think of another scene that would go well with this poem?

Reader's Response When is everyone like the four little foxes in the poem? What circumstances can cause even grown people to be like the little foxes?

Four Little Foxes

Lew Sarett

Speak gently, Spring, and make no sudden sound;
1 For in my windy valley, yesterday I found
New-born foxes squirming on the ground—
Speak gently.

2 Walk softly, March, forbear the bitter blow;
Her feet within a trap, her blood upon the snow,
The four little foxes saw their mother go—
Walk softly.

Go lightly, Spring, oh, give them no alarm;
When I covered them with boughs to shelter them from harm,
The thin blue foxes suckled at my arm—
Go lightly.

Step softly, March, with your rampant hurricane;
Nuzzling one another, and whimpering with pain,
3 The new little foxes are shivering in the rain—
Step softly.

THINKING ABOUT THE SELECTION

Recalling

1. What happened to the newborn foxes' mother?
2. What does the poet do to protect the foxes?

Interpreting

3. To what two things does the phrase "bitter blow" in line 5 refer?
4. Why does the poet plead with nature rather than with people to protect the animals?
5. What two kinds of relationships between people and nature are presented in the poem?

Applying

6. What is it about helpless creatures that makes us want to protect them? What other helpless creatures arouse strong protective feelings in people?

ANALYZING LITERATURE

Understanding Lyric Poetry

Lyric poetry expresses the poet's thoughts and feelings about a topic through vivid images and musical language.

In "Four Little Foxes," the phrase "The thin blue foxes suckled at my arm—" creates the vivid image of helpless creatures so hungry that they turn to a stranger's arm for milk.

1. What feeling does the image "Her feet within a trap, her blood upon the snow" suggest?
2. What is the effect of the repetition of such phrases as "Speak gently"?
3. What seems to be the poet's feelings or attitude about the foxes, who are "Nuzzling one another, and whimpering with pain"? What feelings do you think the poet wants to stir up in readers? Explain your answer.

Closure and Extension

ANSWERS TO THINKING ABOUT THE SELECTION

Recalling

1. She was caught in a trap and died.
2. He covers them with boughs.

Interpreting

3. It can refer to any shock or calamity in general or, more specifically, to a violent storm with blowing winds.
4. Answers will differ. Suggested Response: The poet may feel that the animals are in the natural world and therefore at the mercy of natural forces. Some students may also say that humans have proved cruel—the trap that killed their mother is an example—and so the poet does not bother to plead with people.
5. Answers will differ. Suggested Response: People have both positive and negative relationships with nature. The poet helps the four little foxes, but someone else set a trap that killed their mother.

Applying

6. Students' answers will differ. Suggested Response: Their helplessness seems to stir up a very deep-rooted desire to protect such creatures. This desire is probably not as strong with respect to animals that are more distantly related to us, like insects. The type of animals we would most want to protect are probably small children, puppies, kittens, baby birds, and so forth.

Challenge If you were setting this poem to music, what instruments would you use? Explain.

ANALYZING LITERATURE

1. Answers will differ. Suggested Response: It suggests a feeling of sadness and even a touch of horror.
2. Answers will differ. Suggested Response: The repetition emphasizes the need to be gentle and reminds us of the dangers that these animals face. Especially insightful students will realize that it almost seems appropriate to whisper the repeated phrase.
3. Answers will differ. Suggested Response: The poet seems to feel a great sense of pity for them, as well as a wish to shelter them from harm. He urges "Spring" and "March" to be gentle with them, and he covers them "with boughs" to protect them. He seems to want to call up the same feeling in readers, because he describes the little foxes' pain and need so vividly.

Presentation

Motivation/Prior Knowledge Ask students whether they have ever walked through a large city at night. Have them describe the lights in the building, the crowds, and any other factors that made the city seem exciting or magical at night.

Master Teacher Note For comparison and contrast, you may want to use "The City Is So Big," page 586. García also describes the city at night but sees the city as threatening.

Purpose-Setting Question Why do you think the poet used lines and stanzas of different lengths?

1 **Discussion** Whom do you think Hughes is addressing? Explain.

2 **Master Teacher Note** You may want to tell students that the Harlem Renaissance, in which Hughes participated, also involved music. Duke Ellington, jazz composer, band leader, and pianist, was known for his performances in Harlem in the late 1920's.

Play for students Ellington's famous jazz composition "Take the A Train" (on the record *Sophisticated Ellington,* RCA, CPL 2–4098, or the two-record set *Duke Ellington— Carnegie Hall Concerts,* Prestige, 24074). The A train is a subway line that stops in Harlem. Ask whether the mood of this piece is similar to that of the poem and how jazz might have influenced Hughes.

Harlem Night Song

Langston Hughes

Come,
Let us roam the night together
1 Singing.

I love you.

Across
The Harlem[1] roof-tops
Moon is shining.
Night sky is blue.
Stars are great drops
Of golden dew.
2

Down the street
A band is playing.

I love you.

Come,
Let us roam the night together
Singing.

---

1. Harlem (här′ ləm) *n.*: Section of New York City, in the northern part of Manhattan.

THINKING ABOUT THE SELECTION

Recalling

1. What invitation does the poet give the friend?

Interpreting

2. What feeling do short lines give the poem?
3. Why does the speaker feel full of life?

Applying

4. Elizabeth Bowen wrote: "When you love someone all your saved up wishes start coming out." Do you agree that love makes people feel generous? Explain your answer.

CRITICAL THINKING AND READING

Making Inferences About Mood

An **inference about mood** is a reasonable conclusion you can draw about the overall feeling of a poem, based on clues.

Find three details that suggest a joyful mood.

Closure and Extension

ANSWERS TO THINKING ABOUT THE SELECTION

Recalling

1. "Let us roam the night together/ Singing."

Interpreting

2. Answers will differ. Suggested Response: The short lines make the poet's invitation seem urgent and direct and give a feeling of informality.
3. Answers will differ. Suggested Response: He feels full of life because the night is beautiful and he has the chance to be with someone he loves.

Applying

4. Answers will differ. Suggested Response: Love can make people feel generous because they are so happy that they want to share it.

ANSWERS TO CRITICAL THINKING AND READING

Among the details that contribute to a mood of joyfulness are these: the poet's repeated assertion that he loves his friend; the beautiful description of the night sky; the band playing music; and the repetition of the invitation to "roam the night," like a refrain in a song.

Blue-Butterfly Day

Robert Frost

It is blue-butterfly day here in spring,
And with these sky-flakes down in flurry on flurry
There is more unmixed color on the wing
Than flowers will show for days unless they hurry.

But these are flowers that fly and all but sing:
And now from having ridden out desire
They lie closed over in the wind and cling
Where wheels have freshly sliced the April mire.[1]

1. **mire** (mīr) *n.*: Deep mud.

THINKING ABOUT THE SELECTION

Recalling

1. In what season does the poem take place?
2. What happens to the butterflies at the end of the poem?

Interpreting

3. To what does the poet compare the butterflies in line 2? Why is this comparison especially appropriate for New England in the early part of this season?
4. In what way are the butterflies also like birds? In what way are they like flowers?
5. What is suggested by the last two lines of the poem? What contrast do you find between the beginning of the poem and the end?

Applying

6. The poet describes the butterflies as "flowers that fly and all but sing." How else might you describe butterflies?

THINKING AND WRITING

Writing a Lyric Poem

"Blue-Butterfly Day" is a lyric poem about spring. The images of the color and movement of the butterflies, the descriptive language, and the musical quality suggest a mood of quiet, thoughtful delight.

Choose one of the other seasons and write a lyric poem about it. Describe what mood you would like to create in your poem. Then freewrite about the season, including descriptive words and phrases that create the mood you have chosen and that express your thoughts and feelings. Use this information to write a lyric poem. When you revise, make sure you have maintained a consistent mood. Proofread your poem and share it with your classmates.

Presentation

Motivation/Prior Knowledge Ask students what qualities of butterflies make them seem so fascinating to many people. Have them describe butterflies they have seen. Then tell them that, in the poem they will read, Robert Frost describes butterflies in a magical way.

Thematic Idea Another selection you may want to use with this one is the haiku by Moritake on page 573. This delicate nature poem also describes a butterfly.

Purpose-Setting Question How does the poet make the butterflies seem magical and mysterious?

1 **Discussion** What rhyme scheme and rhythmic pattern does Frost use in this lyric poem? How do the regular rhymes and rhythms of the poem contribute to its mood?

2 **Master Teacher Note** This poem is set in New England during the early spring, when flowers have not yet blossomed and a last snowfall is still possible. Point out to students that the butterflies are a good symbol for this uncertain state of things suggesting both snow and flowers. Also, they are delicate, as this time of year itself seems to be.

Writing Across the Curriculum You might want to have students research and report on seasonal transitions in different regions of the country. Consider informing the science department of this assignment, so that they can provide guidance for students.

Closure and Extension

ANSWERS TO THINKING ABOUT THE SELECTION

Recalling

1. It takes place in early spring.
2. They close up their wings and rest on the mud.

Interpreting

3. Answers will differ. Suggested Response: He compares them to snowflakes. Snow can still fall in New England at this time of year.
4. Answers will differ. Suggested Response: They are like birds in that they can fly, and like flowers in that they are colorful.
5. Answers will differ. Suggested Response: The last two lines imply that the butterflies are tired of flying. They start by resembling flakes of snow, but end resembling flowers growing in the mud.

Applying

6. Answers will differ. Suggested Response: Encourage students to use their imaginations. Students might compare them to tiny kites or little circus aerialists with colorful capes.

Presentation

Motivation/Prior Knowledge You might ask students to think of an older sister, brother, or friend who has helped them. Have them describe what they learned from this person. Then tell them that the poem they are about to read is an expression of gratitude for an older sister's help.

1 **Master Teacher Note** You may want to tell students that some poems are patterned on lists. The items in such lists are often connected by means of repeated phrases and conjunctions like *and.*

In this poem, the list is made up of the poet's memories of her sister. Ask students to look for the words and phrases that the poet uses to link these memories. Also, have them consider the way in which the individual memories contribute to a portrait of the sister.

2 **Clarification** Tell students that the first sentence in contemporary poems sometimes begins with the title rather than the first line.

3 **Discussion** Why do you think the poet chose to begin the poem with this image?

4 **Discussion** How do the children seem to respond to Molly?

1 For My Sister Molly Who in the Fifties

Alice Walker

2 Once made a fairy rooster from
3 Mashed pctatoes
Whose eyes I forget
But green onions were his tail
And his two legs were carrot sticks
A tomato slice his crown.
Who came home on vacation
When the sun was hot
and cooked
and cleaned
4 And minded least of all
The children's questions
A million or more
Pouring in on her
Who had been to school
And knew (and told us too) that certain
Words were no longer good
And taught me not to say us for we
No matter what "Sonny said" up the
road.

FOR MY SISTER MOLLY WHO IN THE FIFTIES.
Knew Hamlet well and read into the night
And coached me in my songs of Africa
A continent I never knew
But learned to love
Because "they" she said could carry
A tune
And spoke in accents never heard
In Eatonton.[1]
Who read from *Prose and Poetry*
And loved to read "Sam McGee from Tennessee"
On nights the fire was burning low

---

1. **Eatonton** (ēt'n tən): A town in Georgia.

And Christmas wrapped in angel hair[2]
And I for one prayed for snow.

5 WHO IN THE FIFTIES
Knew all the written things that made
Us laugh and stories by
The hour   Waking up the story buds
Like fruit. Who walked among the flowers
And brought them inside the house
And smelled as good as they
And looked as bright.
Who made dresses, braided
Hair. Moved chairs about
Hung things from walls
Ordered baths
Frowned on wasp bites
6 And seemed to know the endings
Of all the tales
I had forgot.

2. angel hair: Fine, white, filmy Christmas tree decoration.

THINKING ABOUT THE SELECTION

Recalling

1. How does Molly act as a teacher to the children? Find three works she enjoys reading.
2. How does Molly take care of the house? How does she take care of the children?

Interpreting

3. Explain the title of this poem.
4. How does Molly reveal her creative spirit? How does she awaken the creative spirit in the children?
5. How do you know that being away at school has not separated Molly from the children?
6. What adjectives would you use to describe Molly?
7. What do the last three lines of the poem suggest about Molly?
8. How do you think the speaker feels about her sister Molly?

Applying

9. Think of a character in another work of literature who seems most like Molly. Explain how these characters are alike.
10. Think of an area in which you have expertise or experience. How might you interest a friend in this area?

5 **Discussion** Why do you think the poet uses a different kind of type for lines 21 and 35? How do the words from the title serve as connecting links in the poem?

6 **Discussion** What picture of Molly emerges from this list of memories?

Reader's Response If you were to write a poem to someone influential, who would it be? Explain why.

Closure and Extension

ANSWERS TO THINKING ABOUT THE SELECTION

Recalling

1. She answered their questions, told them that certain words were no longer "good," taught the poet the correct way to speak, and coached the poet in singing. Three works she enjoyed reading are *Hamlet, Prose and Poetry,* and "Sam McGee from Tennessee."
2. She cooked, cleaned, brought flowers into the house, moved chairs, and hung things from walls. She took care of the children by making dresses, braiding their hair, ordering baths, and frowning on wasp bites.

Interpreting

3. Answers will differ. Suggested Response: The title means that the poem was written for the poet's sister Molly, who did much to take care of her during the 1950's.
4. Answers will differ. Suggested Response: She reveals her creative spirit by making a "fairy rooster" from food, coaching her sister in singing, reading aloud in an entertaining way, bringing flowers into the house, making dresses, and hanging things from walls. She awakens the creative spirit in the children by reading to them, coaching them, and showing them by example how to be creative. Especially insightful students may see that she wakens their creative spirit by making them aware of the world beyond their home.
5. Answers will differ. Suggested Response: When she returns, she is still warm and generous toward them.
6. Answers will differ. Suggested Response: Creative, imaginative, generous, loving, capable, and intelligent.
7. Answers will differ. Suggested Response: These lines seem to indicate more than the fact that Molly remembered what the poet forgot. They symbolize Molly's role as family story-teller and leader.
8. Answers will differ. Suggested Response: She loves and admires her.

Applying

9. Answers will differ. Suggested Response: Students should choose a character with the same qualities that Molly demonstrates—generosity, intelligence, creativity, and so forth.
10. Answers will differ. Suggested Response: You can show your friend how enjoyable and valuable this pursuit is.

Focus

More About the Author Tell students that **Walter de la Mare** edited and wrote books for children in addition to his work for adults. Ask students what special talents a writer would need to be able to please adults and children alike.

Shel Silverstein lives in a houseboat that is usually anchored off Sausalito, California. In this floating home, he keeps a saxophone, trombone, guitar, piano, and camera. Ask students what the advantages of such a living situation would be. Also, have them design other types of houses that would be ideal for a writer.

Tell students that some of **William Shakespeare's** lyric poems, like "Blow, Blow, Thou Winter Wind," were written for plays. During the performance, these lyrics would be sung to music. Many of the actors were skilled singers, and the theater companies kept a variety of musical instruments. Ask students why Shakespeare and other playwrights of the time might have included such lyric poems in their plays. Also ask them how the presentation of these poems was in keeping with the original meaning of lyric poetry.

GUIDE FOR READING

Silver

Walter de la Mare (1873–1956), British poet and novelist, attended St. Paul's Cathedral Choir School in London. After graduation, for eighteen years he worked as a clerk; later a government grant allowed him to write full time. De la Mare believed that the world beyond human experience could best be understood through the imagination. His poems often stress the magical and the mysterious, as does "Silver," an enchanted look at a moonlit night.

Forgotten Language

Shel Silverstein (1932–) is a writer of children's books, a cartoonist, a folk singer, a composer, and an author of a one-act play, "The Lady or the Tiger" (1981). The critic William Cole has said that Silverstein's poems are "tender, funny, sentimental, philosophical, and ridiculous in turn, and they're for all ages." Youngsters delight in his poem's playful images, while older readers appreciate his observations about growing up. In "Forgotten Language" Silverstein vividly captures the magical moment called childhood.

Blow, Blow, Thou Winter Wind

William Shakespeare (1564–1616) was born in Stratford-upon-Avon, England. At eighteen he married Anne Hathaway; they had three children. In London he joined the Lord Chamberlain's Company, which performed plays at the Globe Theatre. Shakespeare wrote plays and poems that are among the best in the English language. They endure through the years because of his insight into human nature, his ability to lighten the tragic with the humorous, and his portrayal of kings and scoundrels with equal understanding. "Blow, Blow, Thou Winter Wind" is from his play *As You Like It*.

Sound Devices

Sound devices contribute to the musical quality of a poem. Including alliteration and repetition, sound devices are most noticeable when a poem is read aloud.

Alliteration is the repetition of a consonant at the beginning of words. For example, the phrase "casements catch" in "Silver" repeats the "k" sound at the beginning of each word.

There are various types of **repetition** in poetry. Parallel structure is the repetition of a grammatical structure. In "Forgotten Language" several of the beginning phrases, such as "Once I spoke," "Once I understood," are in parallel form. Like other sound devices, the repetition emphasizes the musical quality of the poem.

Look For

As you read the following three poems, look for alliteration and parallel structure. What effect does the use of these sound devices have on the poems?

Writing

Alliteration can add punch to ordinary speech as well as to poetry. "Pots and pans" and "sweet and sour" are examples of alliterative pairs of words used in everyday language. List other examples of alliteration that you hear or use in conversation.

Vocabulary

Knowing the following words will help you as you read these poems.

shoon (shōōn) *n.*: Old-fashioned word for *shoes* (p. 564)

keen (kēn) *adj.*: Having a sharp cutting edge (p. 566)

feigning (fān'iŋ) *v.*: Making a false show of (p. 566)

Literary Focus You might point out to students that alliteration is a kind of rhyme. Many years ago, poems written in an older version of English used patterns of alliteration rather than the end rhymes we are familiar with today.

The modern American poet Ezra Pound imitated these older patterns of alliteration in his poem "The Seafarer" (italics added): "*N*eareth *n*ightshade, s*n*oweth from *n*orth,/*Fr*ost *fr*oze the land, hail fell on earth then, . . ."

Tell students that poets' use of parallel structure in English has been strongly influenced by the King James Version of the *Bible*. To illustrate this point, you might want to read aloud the following passage from Ecclesiastes (3:1–2): "To every thing there is a season, and a time to every purpose under the heaven: A time to be born and a time to die; a time to plant; and a time to pluck up that which is planted . . ."

Look For You may want to advise students to listen for the effect of sound devices as you read each poem aloud.

Writing/Prior Knowledge Consider dividing the class into small groups to complete this assignment. Each group can then brainstorm to gather examples of alliteration.

Vocabulary Have **less advanced** students read aloud the words and definitions. Ask **more advanced** students to find other examples—besides *shoon*—of old-fashioned terms for clothes. One possible source for such words is the poem "The Highwayman," by Alfred Noyes.

Spelling Tip The *ei* spelling of long *a*, as in *feigning*, is also found in words like *weigh, neighbor, reign,* and *sleigh.*

Objectives

1 To understand alliteration
2 To understand parallel structure

Support Material

Teaching Portfolio

Teacher Backup, pp. 777–780
Usage and Mechanics Worksheet, p. 781
Vocabulary Check, p. 782
Analyzing Literature Worksheet, *Understanding Alliteration,* p. 783
Language Worksheet, *Understanding Poetic Language,* p. 784
Selection Test, pp. 785–786
Art Transparency 12, *Souvenir* by Marc Chagall

Presentation

Motivation/Prior Knowledge Ask students to describe the effect of moonlight on such environments as a city street or a country field. Tell them that de la Mare tries to capture the magical quality of moonlight in his poem "Silver."

Purpose-Setting Question How does the repetition of the word *silver* contribute to the mood?

Master Teacher Note Play the first movement of Beethoven's "Moonlight Sonata" (RCA LSC-4001) for students. Ask them what pictures the music brought to mind or what feelings it called up in them. Have them compare its mood to that of the poem.

1 **Discussion** Why is the title fitting for a poem about the moon?

2 **Discussion** Do you think this poem should be read loudly or softly? Explain.

3 **Discussion** Why do you think the poet chose to describe the moon as if it were a person? How might the poem be different if the poet did not make this comparison?

Closure and Extension

1 # Silver

Walter de la Mare

2 Slowly, silently, now the moon
3 Walks the night in her silver shoon;[1]
This way, and that, she peers, and sees
Silver fruit upon silver trees;
One by one the casements catch
Her beams beneath the silvery thatch;
Couched in his kennel, like a log,
With paws of silver sleeps the dog;
From their shadowy coat the white breasts peep
Of doves in a silver-feathered sleep;
A harvest mouse goes scampering by,
With silver claws, and silver eye;
And moveless fish in the water gleam,
By silver reeds in a silver stream.

1. **shoon** (shōōn) *n.*: Old-fashioned word for "shoes."

THINKING ABOUT THE SELECTION

Recalling

1. At what time does this poem take place?
2. Name three human activities the moon does.
3. Describe the "silver" scene.
4. What is the only animal that moves in the poem? What do the other animals do?

Interpreting

5. Describe the effect of the moon's walk.
6. Find four details that create a picture of stillness. What mood is created by this?
7. In what way does the poem seem magical?

Applying

8. Find three other examples of "magic" in nature. Explain the reason for your choices.

ANALYZING LITERATURE

Understanding Alliteration

Alliteration, the repetition of consonants at the beginning of words, is one sound device poets use to heighten the musical quality of their work. The repetition of the sounds is especially striking when the poem is recited aloud. Read "Silver" aloud before answering the following questions.

1. Find two examples of alliteration in lines 1–2.
2. Find three other examples in the poem of the repetition of the sound of *s*.
3. What effect is created by the repetition of the sound of *s*?

ANSWERS TO THINKING ABOUT THE SELECTION

Recalling

1. It takes place at night because the moon is shining.
2. It walks, peers, and sees.
3. It is a country scene, with fruit trees, a cottage, a stream, and various animals.
4. A harvest mouse is the only animal that moves. The other animals are sleeping, or at least not moving.

Interpreting

5. Answers will differ. Suggested Response: The effect of the moon's walk is to cast silver light on the earth.
6. Answers will differ. Suggested Response: Among the details that create a picture of stillness are the fruit hanging on "silver trees"; the dog sleeping "like a log"; the dove "in a silver-feathered sleep"; and the "moveless fish." A mood of hushed peacefulness is created.
7. Answers will differ. Suggested Response: The silence, stillness, and silver light make this seem like a magical fairy tale world.

Applying

8. Answers will differ. Suggested Response: Examples of magic in nature are the poking of a bud through the earth; the pattern of veins in a leaf; a snowflake; and the reflection of sunlight in water.

ANSWERS TO ANALYZING LITERATURE

1. *s* sound—*slowly, silently, silver; n* sound—*now, night*
2. Lines 3-4, 8, 10, 12, and 14.
3. Suggested Response: It creates a hushed, whispering effect.

Forgotten Language

Shel Silverstein

Once I spoke the language of the flowers,
Once I understood each word the caterpillar said,
Once I smiled in secret at the gossip of the starlings,[1]
And shared a conversation with the housefly
    in my bed. 1
Once I heard and answered all the questions
    of the crickets,
And joined the crying of each falling dying
    flake of snow, 2
Once I spoke the language of the flowers . . .
        How did it go?
        How did it go?

1. **starlings** (stär′ liŋs) *n.*: Dark-colored birds with short tails, long wings, and a sharp, pointed bill.

THINKING ABOUT THE SELECTION

Recalling

1. Name six languages from nature the poet once "understood."

Interpreting

2. When do you think the events in the poem took place?
3. Why are the snowflakes "crying"?
4. Explain the meaning of the lines "How did it go?" How would you answer this question?

Applying

5. In "Forgotten Language," the poet says that once he understood the language of flowers and animals. What other things might people forget as they grow older?

ANALYZING LITERATURE

Understanding Parallel Structure

Parallel structure is the repetition of a grammatical structure that allows the poet to emphasize important ideas and add to the musical quality of the poem. For example, the repetition of "Once I spoke," and "Once I understood," emphasizes the idea of time past.

1. Name the other beginning phrases that are in parallel form with "Once I spoke."
2. Which lines are not in parallel form with "Once I spoke"? Why do you think the poet chose to begin these lines in a different way?

Presentation

Motivation/Prior Knowledge Ask students which animal they would most want to communicate with, if they had the ability to understand the language of animals. Tell them that the poem they are about to read deals with this idea.

Master Teacher Note Look at Art Transparency 12, *Souvenir* by Marc Chagall, in the Teaching Portfolio. Have students discuss the experiences, in the shaded areas, that the person remembers upon seeing the flowers, palette, bottle, etc., in the painting. Ask students for examples of objects that bring a particular memory back to them.

Purpose-Setting Question What mood is created through use of parallel structure?

1 **Enrichment** Tell students that many scientists study the language of animals. Whales, for example, communicate over long distances by means of a kind of clicking noise.

2 **Master Teacher Note** You might want to tell students that poets may create patterns that include differences as well as similarities. Silverstein begins many of his sentences with the phrase "Once I. . . ." Ask students what words he uses to avoid repeating the word *language.*

ANSWERS TO ANALYZING LITERATURE

1. "Once I understood. . . ."; "Once I smiled. . . .; "Once I heard. . . ."
2. Lines 4, 6, 8, and 9 are not in parallel form with "Once I spoke. . . ." Suggested response: He probably changed the beginning of lines 4 and 6 to make the poem more interesting by varying the pattern. He broke the pattern in the last two lines to emphasize that he no longer knows this language.

Closure and Extension

ANSWERS TO THINKING ABOUT THE SELECTION

Recalling

1. He "understood" the speech of flowers, caterpillars, starlings, houseflies, crickets, and snowflakes.
2. The events in the poem probably took place during winter, since snowflakes are mentioned as falling.

Interpreting

3. Answers will differ. Suggested Response: He says that they are "crying" because they are "falling" and "dying."
4. Answers will differ. Suggested Response: The line has two possible meanings—1) What were the meanings of words in this language? 2) How did my memory of this language vanish? One possible answer to the second question is that as we become adults, we lose the close contact with nature that we enjoyed as children.

Applying

5. Answers will differ. Suggested Response: People sometimes lose a capacity for enjoying life and a sense of wonder at the world.

1 Blow, Blow, Thou Winter Wind

William Shakespeare

2 Blow, blow, thou winter wind.
Thou art not so unkind
As man's ingratitude.
Thy tooth is not so keen,
Because thou art not seen,
Although thy breath be rude.[1]
Heigh-ho! Sing, heigh-ho! unto the green holly.
Most friendship is feigning, most loving mere folly.
Then, heigh-ho, the holly!
This life is most jolly.

3 Freeze, freeze, thou bitter sky,
That dost not bite so nigh
As benefits forgot.
Though thou the waters warp,[2]
Thy sting is not so sharp
As friend remembered not.
Heigh-ho! Sing, heigh-ho! unto the green holly.
Most friendship is feigning, most loving mere folly.
Then, heigh-ho, the holly!
This life is most jolly.

1. **rude** *adj.*: Rough, harsh.
2. **warp** *v.*: Freeze.

Presentation

Motivation/Prior Knowledge Ask students to remember and describe a time when they felt extremely cold. Tell them that, in this poem, Shakespeare uses images of winter to describe feelings that are even more chilling than freezing weather.

Master Teacher Note You may want to contrast the hopeful feeling in Tennyson's poem "Ring Out, Wild Bells," page 544, with the bitterness and cynicism in this poem.

Purpose-Setting Question How does the poet make an abstract idea like "man's ingratitude" seem more concrete and specific?

1 **Enrichment** Consider playing for students some Elizabethan music, so that they better understand the flavor of this song. We particularly recommend the following records from the 7-record set of the New York Pro Musica's greatest works (Everest 6145/7): Record 2—"Thomas Morley"; Record 6—"Children's Songs of Shakespeare's Time." You may also want to use the record *Glenn Gould Plays William Byrd/Orlando Gibbons* (CBS 7464-39552-1).

2 **Discussion** What is the rhyme scheme of this stanza? Basing your answer on the rhyme scheme, what can you infer about the pronunciation of "wind" and "unkind" during Shakespeare's time?

3 **Master Teacher Note** You may want to explain briefly the dramatic context in which this poem appears. In *As You Like It,* a Duke of France loses his lands to his evil younger brother and goes to live in the forest of Arden with some faithful followers. Eventually, his lands are restored to him. While he lives in the forest, however, he says that he prefers winter's cold to the lying and flattery he found at court. This song, which is sung at the end of the second act, expresses the same idea.

You may want to encourage **more advanced** students to read Shakespeare's play.

Reader's Response Do you share the poet's views on friendship?

TRÈS RICHES HEURES DU DUC DE BERRY: FEBRUARY
Chantilly—Musée Conde
Girardon/Art Resource

Humanities Note

Fine art, *February* from *Les Très Riches Heures du Duc de Berry,* 1413–16, by Pol de Limbourg (?–1416) and his brothers. Pol de Limbourg and his two brothers were Flemings who had settled in France. They produced an illuminated manuscript called *Les Très Riches Heures* for the Duc de Berry, the brother of the French king. The most important pages of this manuscript are those depicting scenes typical of the various months of the year.

1. What do you think the women in the lower left-hand corner are doing?
2. What other winter activities can you identify?
3. Do you think this picture goes well with the poem? Explain.

THINKING ABOUT THE SELECTION

Recalling

1. What is more unkind than the winter wind? Why is the wind's "tooth . . . not so keen"?
2. What does the poet think of friendship? What does the poet think of love?
3. What is sharper than the sting of the bitter sky?

Interpreting

4. Explain what the poem suggests about the harshness of nature compared to the pain of human relationships?
5. Keeping in mind the poet's views of human relationships, what do the phrases "Sing, heigh-ho!" and "This life is most jolly" tell you about the poet's attitude?

Applying

6. Do you agree with the poet that ingratitude is painful? Explain your answer.

Closure and Extension

ANSWERS TO THINKING ABOUT THE SELECTION

Recalling

1. More unkind than the winter wind is "man's ingratitude." The wind's "tooth is not so keen" because the wind is invisible—it is not a human foe.
2. Most friends are secretly untrue, and love is just foolishness.
3. People's ingratitude is more painful.

Interpreting

4. Answers will differ. Suggested Response: The poem indicates that the harshness of nature is not as painful as people's cruelty.
5. Answers will differ. Suggested Response: If the poem is read by itself, the poet's attitude in these phrases seems to be ironical. Even though he is saying "This life is most jolly," he really means that it is bitter and cruel. However, especially insightful students may see that, in dramatic context, the words "This life. . . ." may refer to the life in the forest, which *is* "jolly" by contrast with the life in court.

Applying

6. Answers will differ. Suggested Response: Most students will say that it is painful, because it involves rejection and the violation of trust.

Focus

More About the Author The humorous poetry of **Morris Bishop** appeared in a volume entitled *The Best of Bishop: Light Verse from the New Yorker and Elsewhere* (1980). You might want to ask students why a professor engaged in serious scholarship would also want to write humorous verse.

Literary Focus Consider telling students that Edward Lear included many limericks in *A Book of Nonsense* (1846) and contributed to the popularity of the form. Lear always began his limericks with the statement that someone came from a certain place—for example, "There was a young lady of Wilts. . . ."

You might want to encourage students to read other light verse by Lear *(The Nonsense Books of Edward Lear.* New York: The New American Library, 1964).

Look For Suggest to students that surprise and exaggeration often play an important role in humor. Have students look for these elements in the limericks.

Writing/Prior Knowledge You might want to divide the class into small groups and have students tell their comical stories to each other before beginning the assignment.

Vocabulary Consider asking **less advanced** students to find three synonyms for the word *applaud* in a thesaurus.

Spelling Tip The spelling of *meets* should not be confused with *meats,* meaning "types of flesh from animals."

GUIDE FOR READING

Hog Calling

Morris Bishop (1893–1973) was born in Willard, New York, and lived most of his life in Ithaca, New York. He attended Cornell University and went on to teach there from 1921 to 1973. Bishop translated plays by Molière and edited numerous collections of short stories. His diverse writings include histories, critical biographies, and light verse such as "Hog Calling."

I Raised a Great Hullabaloo

Anonymous. No one knows for sure how limericks came into being. It is believed that they were originally passed down by word of mouth.

Limerick

A **limerick** is a kind of light or humorous verse. Limericks follow a pattern. Generally, every limerick has five lines: three long lines (the first, second, and fifth) that rhyme with each other, and two short lines (the third and fourth) that rhyme. The lines also follow a particular rhythm. Each of the three long lines has three accented, or stressed, syllables; each of the two short lines has two stressed syllables. The purpose of most limericks is to make you laugh.

Look For

As you read these limericks, look for what they have in common. Why do they make you laugh?

Writing

Recall a comical incident that you recently observed or experienced. What made it funny? Freewrite about what happened.

Vocabulary

Knowing the following words will help you as you read these limericks.

meets (mētz) *n.*: A series of races or competitions held during a period of days at a certain place (p. 569)

applaud (ə plôd′) *v.*: To show approval or enjoyment by clapping the hands or by cheering (p. 569)

awed (ôd) *v.*: A mixed feeling of reverence, fear, and wonder (p. 569)

appalling (ə pôl′ iŋ) *adj.*: Causing horror or shock (p. 569)

Objectives

1 To understand the features of a limerick
2 To write limericks

Support Material

Teaching Portfolio

Teacher Backup, pp. 787–789
Usage and Mechanics Worksheet, p. 790
Vocabulary Check, p. 791
Analyzing Literature Worksheet, *Understanding Limericks,* p. 792
Language Worksheet, *Using Rhythmic Language,* p. 793
Selection Test, pp. 794–795

HOG HEAVEN
Mike Patrick

Two Limericks

A bull-voiced young fellow of Pawling
Competes in the meets for hog-calling;
1 The people applaud,
And the judges are awed,
But the hogs find it simply appalling.
Morris Bishop

I raised a great hullabaloo[1]
When I found a large mouse in my stew,
Said the waiter, "Don't shout
And wave it about,
Or the rest will be wanting one, too!"
Anonymous

1. **hullabaloo** (hul′ ə bə lo͞o′) *n.*: Loud noise and confusion; hubbub.

Presentation

Motivation/Prior Knowledge You might ask students if they can recall a joke with a surprising twist at the end. Have several students tell their jokes. Then explain to students that the limericks they are about to read also have such "punch lines."

Thematic Idea Other selections you may want to teach with these poems are "Paul Bunyan of The North Woods," page 643; "Pecos Bill: The Cyclone," page 647; and "The Foggy Stew," page 669. Like many limericks, these folk tales are anonymous and use exaggeration to achieve humorous effects.

Purpose-Setting Question How is the humor in these limericks based on surprise and exaggeration?

1 **Master Teacher Note** You may want to show students how the form and rhythm of a limerick contribute to its humor.

Tell students that the first two lines—with three accented syllables each and the same end rhyme—introduce a silly situation. The third and fourth lines—with only two beats each and a different end rhyme—develop the humorous situation further. Returning to the form of the first two lines, the final line provides a surprising and funny twist.

The rhythm of a limerick is based on a pattern of two unstressed syllables followed by an accented one. This rhythm has a jaunty, humorous feeling.

Ask **less advanced** students to find the rhymes in these limericks. Have **more advanced** students find examples of two unstressed syllables preceding a stressed syllable.

Reader's Response Which limerick do you find more amusing? Why?

Humanities Note

Fine art, *Hog Heaven,* Mike Patrick. The American illustrator Mike Patrick gives us an amusing perspective of that barnyard clown, the pig. The humor of Patrick's rendering, obvious at once, is intensified by the title, Hog Heaven, which describes the feelings of the center of interest. The unusual point of view is a clever way to frame the portrait of bliss we see in this picture. Skillfully executed, this work reveals the artist's knowledge of animals as well as his keen sense of humor.

You might want to use the following questions to discuss the art:

1. Why is Hog Heaven an appropriate piece of art for this selection?
2. Is Patrick's representation of pigs consistent with the general conception of these animals?

Closure and Extension

ANSWERS TO THINKING ABOUT THE SELECTION
Recalling

1. He finds a mouse in his stew.
2. He takes part in hog-calling meets.

Interpreting

3. Answers will differ. Suggested Response: An embarrassed reply might have further enraged the customer. Instead, the waiter uses surprise and humor to get his point across—he wants the customer to stop making a fuss.
4. The people "applaud," showing that they approve, and the judges are very impressed. The hogs, however, think the young man is terrible.

Applying

5. Answers will differ. Suggested Response: Students may think of ridiculous situations involving a bowl of soup, a beard, and a bathtub. Particularly clever students may combine all the elements so that, for instance, a man taking a bath gets his beard in a bowl of soup.

ANALYZING LITERATURE

1. In "Hog Calling," the humorous twist is that the young man's talents are appreciated by everyone *except* those who really matter —the hogs.
2. The surprise is that the waiter acts as if it is a privilege to have a mouse in one's stew.

THINKING AND WRITING

For help with this assignment, students can refer to Lesson 18, "Writing a Poem" in the Handbook of Writing About Literature.

Publishing Student Writing You may want to collect students' work to create an anthology of limericks.

THINKING ABOUT THE SELECTION
Recalling

1. In "I Raised a Great Hullabaloo," what does the speaker find in his stew?
2. What does the "young fellow" in "Hog Calling" do?

Interpreting

3. In "I Raised a Great Hullabaloo," how does the waiter's reply show cleverness and presence of mind?
4. Contrast the responses of the people and the judges with those of the hogs in "Hog Calling."

Applying

5. Humorists have a talent for looking at the everyday and seeing the ridiculous. Allow yourself to be silly for a few minutes. What would be ridiculous about an everyday bowl of soup? What could be ridiculous about a person with a beard? What could be ridiculous about a bath tub?

ANALYZING LITERATURE
Understanding Limericks

Limericks are meant to be funny, even foolish. Their writers observe, then poke good-natured fun at, human weaknesses and silly behavior. Generally, the humor of a limerick is delivered in a kind of "punch line"—a surprising and comical twist that comes at the end.

1. Explain the comical twist at the end of "Hog Calling."
2. What is surprising about the last line of "I Raised a Great Hullabaloo"?

THINKING AND WRITING
Writing a Limerick

Now that you are in a silly mood, choose a topic for a limerick. A good way to start a limerick is to introduce a character by name: for example, "There once was a fellow named Mo." When you revise your limerick, make sure you have followed the correct pattern. Share your completed limerick with your classmates.

Facets of Nature

SHADOWS OF EVENING, 1921-23
Rockwell Kent
Collection of Whitney Museum of American Art

Humanities Note

Fine art, *Shadows of Evening,* by Rockwell Kent. Rockwell Kent (1882–1971), an American painter and graphic artist, originally studied architecture at Columbia University in New York City while attending night classes taught by the dynamic realist painter, Robert Henri. Kent began his career as an architectural draftsman but soon decided that fine art was more important to him. He embarked on an individualistic and rugged lifestyle that combined painting, writing, and travel with various menial jobs. A true nonconformist, Kent believed that each person should live his life as he pleased, and he practiced his belief.

Shadows of Evening (c. 1921–3), shows the realistic and romantic style of Rockwell Kent. In this depiction of evening in rugged country, Kent reveals the beauty of the scene in his highly individualistic way. Views of the dramatic and harsh landscape of the northern seacoast are Kent's trademark.

Master Teacher Note To introduce the theme of nature in poetry, have students look at Art Transparency 13, *Morning Light* by Oscar Bleumner, in the Teaching Portfolio. Explain that in writing poems inspired by aspects of nature, poets often use sensory language—descriptive words that express what they feel, see, smell, hear, or touch. Ask students to imagine that they are in this scene. What sensory language would they use to describe what they experienced? What might a poet emphasize in describing this scene?

GUIDE FOR READING

Haiku

Matsuo Bashō (1644–1694) of Japan is generally regarded as the greatest of all haiku poets. At the age of eight, he entered the service of a nobleman in Iga, in southern Japan. There he is believed to have composed his first poem when he was only nine. Later he lived for a time in a monastery. By the age of thirty, he had founded a school for the study of haiku, and he was revered as a master of the art. **Moritake** (1452–1540) was a priest as well as one of the leading Japanese poets of the sixteenth century.

Haiku

Haiku is a special type of poetry from Japan. A haiku consists of seventeen syllables arranged in three lines. The first line has five syllables, the second has seven, and the third has five. Haiku developed from an older thirty-one-syllable form, but it became an independent form in the latter part of the sixteenth century. It has remained the most popular of Japanese poetic forms.

Generally in a haiku, the poet describes a fleeting moment in nature—usually something he has observed and that has moved him. Through the haiku's simple image or series of images, the poet tries to arouse in the reader the same sensation that he experienced.

Look For

As you read each haiku, keep in mind that a haiku is a kind of "snapshot": an attempt to capture a fleeting moment of beauty in nature. Visualize, or picture, these two "snapshots." What is the poet describing? What emotion is he capturing?

Writing

List some scenes in nature that stay in your memory. Choose one and freewrite about how you felt and thought when you were in those surroundings.

Vocabulary

Haiku uses seemingly simple words that suggest vivid images, as do the following words from the haiku by Bashō.

slashing (slash′iŋ) *v.*: Cutting with a sweeping stroke (p. 573)

screech (skrēch) *n.*: A shrill, high-pitched shriek or sound (p. 573)

Focus

More About the Authors The poet **Matsuo Bashō** was born a *samurai* (warrior). At the age of twenty-two he abandoned this honored status to devote himself wholly to writing poetry. What advantages are there of a poet's being able to spend all of his or her time writing poetry instead of having to work at a job at the same time?

F. Arakida Moritake was a Shinto priest. The word *Shinto* means the way of the gods. The gods, called *kami,* are believed to live in rocks, trees, rivers, mountains, and so on. Prayers and offerings are offered to the kami at shrines in homes and along the roadsides. About thirty-three million people practice Shinto, which is the oldest surviving religion in Japan. Why might being a Shinto priest inspire a person to write haiku?

Literary Focus It is not always possible to translate exactly a haiku written in Japanese into English. The strict rule requiring five syllables in the first and third lines and seven syllables in the second line makes it difficult to translate them from one language to another. If you have any bilingual students, they might attempt to write the same haiku in both languages, keeping the syllable count as it should be.

Look For Another question you might want to have students ask themselves as they read is what mood the poet has created in the haiku. Each of these two haiku presents quite a different mood.

Writing/Prior Knowledge You might bring in photographs of scenes from nature and have students use them to inspire their freewriting.

Vocabulary After having your students study the vocabulary words listed, you might want them to list other simple words that describe aspects of nature and that create vivid images.

Objectives

1 To understand haiku
2 To write a haiku

Support Material

Teaching Portfolio

Teacher Backup, pp. 797–799
Usage and Mechanics Worksheet, p. 800
Vocabulary Check, p. 801
Analyzing Literature Worksheet, *Understanding Haiku,* p. 802
Language Worksheet, *Choosing Words,* p. 803
Selection Test, pp. 804–805

Two Haiku

1 The lightning flashes!
And slashing through the darkness,
A night-heron's[1] screech.
Bashō

The falling flower
I saw drift back to the branch
Was a butterfly.
Moritake

Japanese Lacquered Box (19th century)
Inside Top Cover (detail)
The Metropolitan Museum of Art

1. **night-heron** (nīt′ her′ ən) *n.*: A large wading bird with a long neck and long legs that is active at night.

THINKING ABOUT THE SELECTION

Recalling

1. What is the subject in the haiku by Bashō?
2. What is the subject in the haiku by Moritake?

Interpreting

3. How does the image in Bashō's haiku change by the third line?
4. How does the image in Moritake's haiku change by the third line?

Applying

5. Choose one of these two haiku and another poem about nature in this book. Compare and contrast the two views of nature. For example, you might compare and contrast Bashō's haiku with Frost's "Blue-Butterfly Day."

THINKING AND WRITING

Writing a Haiku

A haiku presents a moment in nature. It has three lines with five syllables in the first line, seven syllables in the second line, and five syllables in the third line.

Choose one of your freewritten impressions and observations about nature. Try to communicate your impression in a single image or two. Write a haiku to describe the image. As you write, keep in mind the emotion or sensation you felt. Try to involve at least two of your senses. Revise your haiku, making sure you have followed the correct form for a haiku. Proofread it and prepare a final draft that you illustrate. Place your illustrated haiku on the bulletin board.

Presentation

Motivation/Prior Knowledge You might bring in a Japanese teacup, scroll, or picture of a garden and have students describe its characteristics. Elicit the fact that attention to detail is characteristic of Japanese art forms. Explain that haiku describes a detail or a moment in nature.

Master Teacher Note Haiku are a good example of the idea that "less is more." In only three short lines, a haiku can portray the essence of a sudden and intense moment observed in the natural world. It can also make the reader feel the emotion or sensation that the poet felt. How can a haiku poet accomplish so much with so little? First, in many haiku seemingly unrelated images are brought together in ways that surprise and delight. Second, the poet tries to involve more than one of our senses at the same time. Third, a haiku tries to contain in a very condensed form a sequence of events.

1. To which of our senses does each haiku appeal?
2. What emotions does each haiku express?
3. What sequence of events occurs in Moritake's haiku?

Purpose-Setting Question What moments in nature are described?

1 **Discussion** Ask how signs or sounds of alarm complement one another in the Bashō haiku.

Reader's Response Were the images these Haiku poets used familiar to you? Did you feel like you had seen the pictures they presented before?

Closure and Extension

ANSWERS TO THINKING ABOUT THE SELECTION

Recalling

1. The subject is lightning flashing and a night heron screeching.
2. The subject of Moritake's haiku is a butterfly landing on a branch.

Interpreting

3. The visual image of the lightning becomes a sound—the night heron's screech.
4. The falling flower has been recognized as a butterfly.

Applying

5. Answers will differ. A suggested response might include contrasting the poet's mistaking the butterfly for a flower in the haiku and simply comparing the butterflies to flowers that fly in a metaphor in "Blue-Butterfly Day." Another contrast is the number of butterflies—one in Moritake's haiku and many in the Frost poem. One similarity is the subject matter—a butterfly compared to a flower.

Focus

More About the Authors In 1982 **John Updike** won the Pulitzer Prize for fiction for *Rabbit Is Rich,* a continuation of the story that started with *Rabbit Run* and *Rabbit Redux.* Much of Updike's fiction is about middleclass suburban life. Updike is known for his careful attention to details in his writing. The poem "January" shows how careful choice of words and attention to line and stanza lenth all work together to describe a day in the month of January. You might ask students what words they might use to describe a day in the month of January. You might write the list of words on the board and see if any duplicate those used by Updike

Langston Hughes's early poetry advocated humor and self-control as defenses against unjust social and economic conditions. His later works reflected the increased demand for social justice. In 1960 Langston Hughes won the Spingarn Medal, a gold medal with a figure of justice on it that is awarded by the National Association for the Advancement of Colored People for highest achievement in the recipient's field.

The **Tewa Indians** believe their people ascended from the underworld from the center of the cosmos, a lake in Colorado. As Pueblos, living in a dry climate, dependent upon scarce water for their crops, the rhythms of nature were of utmost importance to them. Their religious observances and their poetry both reflect this. You could ask students in what ways their religious observances and poetry might show this concern with nature.

Because **N. Scott Momaday** spent his boyhood on a number of different reservations in the Southwest, he gained a vast knowledge of Native American history and culture. N. Scott Momaday has had two books of poems published and considers himself primarily a poet. You might ask your students for ways in which living in a number of different places among different people might help an author with his or her writing.

GUIDE FOR READING

January

John Updike (1932–) was born in Shillington, Pennsylvania. In 1954 he graduated from Harvard, where he won numerous writing honors, and then studied art in England for a year. From 1955 to 1957 he was a cartoonist and staff writer for *The New Yorker,* where many of his short stories appeared. Also a distinguished essayist and respected poet, Updike is well known for such novels as *Rabbit Run* (1960) and *Rabbit Redux* (1971). In "January" he uses stark language to portray the coldness of a winter day.

Winter Moon

Langston Hughes (1902–1967) was born in Joplin, Missouri, and grew up in Lincoln, Illinois, and Cleveland, Ohio. He left Columbia University after a year to travel and write. In 1925 he met the poet Vachel Lindsay, who helped Hughes publish his first poetry collection, *The Weary Blues* (1926). Hughes also wrote two autobiographical works and humorous sketches about black city life called *The Best of Simple* (1961). "Winter Moon" depicts the moon as it might appear on a city night.

Song of the Sky Loom

The **Tewa Indians** were among the many Native Americans who flourished on the North American continent before the first European explorers arrived. The Tewa expressed their close relationship with nature through poetry. Native American poetry, like "Song of the Sky Loom," was not written; rather, it was chanted or sung along with music, dance, and colorful costumes. Native Americans believed this kind of poetry had magical power, and they performed it hoping to cause some good for the community.

New World

N. Scott Momaday (1934–), a Kiowa Indian, was born in Lawton, Oklahoma. His parents were teachers. Momaday was educated on Indian reservations and in 1952 entered the University of New Mexico. Today he is professor of English at Stanford University, California. He is best known for *The Way to Rainy Mountain* (1969). In 1968 his novel *House Made of Dawn* was awarded the Pulitzer Prize. In poems like "New World," Momaday reveals the Native American's rapport with nature.

Sensory Language

Sensory language, or language that appeals to the senses—sight, hearing, smell, touch, and taste—is an important part of any kind of descriptive writing. A description of the visible features of a landscape, of a sound (or of a silence), of the taste or smell of an exotic food, of the way a fabric feels—all these involve the writer's use of sensory language.

For example, in "January" John Updike gives you images of "Fat snowy footsteps" and "trees of lace," word pictures that appeal to your sense of sight. N. Scott Momaday imagines winds that "lean upon mountains" and foxes that "stiffen in cold," images that appeal to your sense of touch. These examples of sensory language are used to create pictures in your imagination and help you experience what the poet describes.

Look For

As you read these poems, experience the poets' sensory language. Remember that an image, though usually visual, can also engage your senses of hearing, smell, taste, and touch. Look for words and phrases that appeal to the different senses. How do these poems make you feel—cold, wind-tossed, hungry, etc.?

Writing

Recall an experience in nature. Where were you? What do you remember seeing, hearing, smelling, tasting, and touching? Freewrite about the sensory impressions you remember from that experience.

Vocabulary

Knowing the following words will help you as you read these poems.

fittingly (fit′ iŋ lē) *adv.*: Properly (p. 579)
glistens (glis′ 'nz) *v.*: Shines (p. 580)
borne (bôrn) *v.*: Carried (p. 580)
low (lō) *v.*: Make the typical sound that a cow makes (p. 580)
hie (hī) *v.*: Hurry (p. 580)
recede (ri sēd′) *v.*: Move farther away (p. 581)

Literary Focus At this point your students may need to be told that sensory language can include figures of speech. Sensory language often creates images and, to be effective, uses vivid language. In other words, figures of speech, imagery, vivid language, and sensory language are overlapping categories, not discrete ones. You might want to have your students find, in this or other books or magazines, examples of sensory language that appeals to each of the five senses. They could then present them to the class.

Look For Your **less advanced** students might benefit from going back over these poems, identifying words and phrases that have sensory appeal and indicating whether each example contains a figure of speech, imagery, or vivid language.

Writing/Prior Knowledge Students, especially **less advanced** ones, might benefit from discussing their experiences with nature in groups before they start to write about them.

Vocabulary You might want to discuss with your students the spelling of the word *borne* in "New World" and the meaning of the word *low* as it is used in "New World."

Spelling Tip Note that the ending of *recede* is regular, as in *precede, secede, impede,* etc. Only four words end differently: *exceed, proceed, succeed, supersede.*

Objectives

1 To recognize sensory language
2 To use sensory language in writing a description
3 To write a poem creating a vivid image
4 To paraphrase a poem
5 To give a choral reading

Support Material

Teaching Portfolio
Teacher Backup, pp. 807–810
Grammar in Action Worksheet, *Understanding Verb Tense,* pp. 811–812
Usage and Mechanics Worksheet, p. 813
Vocabulary Check, p. 814
Analyzing Literature Worksheet, *Recognizing Sensory Language,* p. 815
Language Worksheet, *Writing Sensory Language,* p. 816
Selection Test, pp. 817–818
Art Transparency 14, *Aurora Borealis,* by Frederic Church

Presentation

Motivation/Prior Knowledge You might discuss with the class how they would describe the month of January. List their words and phrases on the board. Then tell them they will see how someone else described the month of January in a poem.

Master Teacher Note The length of the lines and stanzas of "January" are as descriptive of the month as are the words of the poem. You may want to analyze the poem's meter and ask students how it adds to the description of the month of January. Updike used iambic diameter in this poem; that is, two sets of iambs —an unaccented syllable followed by an accented one—per line.

Purpose-Setting Question What sensory language does John Updike use to describe the month of January?

1 **Discussion** What else is short here besides "the days"?

2 **Discussion** What object from the natural world is mentioned here?

3 **Discussion** What two natural phenomena does Updike mention here?

4 **Discussion** What two natural phenomena does Updike mention here?

5 **Discussion** What two natural phenomena does Updike mention here?

6 **Critical Thinking and Reading** How does the image of the radiator purring contrast with the other images in the poem?

Reader's Response Are the images in Updike's poem similar to your perceptions of the month of January?

January

John Updike

1 The days are short,
The sun a spark
Hung thin between
2 The dark and dark.

Fat snowy footsteps
Track the floor.
3 Milk bottles burst
Outside the door.

The river is
4 A frozen place
Held still beneath
The trees of lace.

5 The sky is low.
The wind is gray.
The radiator
6 Purrs all day.

WINTER TWILIGHT NEAR ALBANY, NEW YORK, 1858
George Henry Boughton
Courtesy of The New York Historical Society

THINKING ABOUT THE SELECTION

Recalling

1. How does Updike describe the sun?
2. What happens to the milk bottles? Why?
3. What image of the river is delicate?
4. How does the poet describe the sky?
5. What sound fills the air at the poem's end?

Interpreting

6. Explain the image "dark and dark" in line 4.
7. Why do the trees appear to be made of "lace"?
8. Why did Updike write such short lines?

Applying

9. The poet uses the color gray to describe wind in winter. What colors do you associate with the other seasons? Explain your choices.

ANALYZING LITERATURE

Recognizing Sensory Language

"January" gives the poet's impressions of the month. For example, he refers to the sun as "a spark/ Hung thin . . ." This image of the sun as a mere spark barely hanging in the sky between morning and night expresses the poet's feeling.

1. To what sense does "purrs all day" appeal?
2. What does "fat snowy footsteps" mean?
3. To what senses does the last stanza appeal?
4. What impression do you form from this poem?

THINKING AND WRITING

Using Sensory Language

List impressions of your favorite month. Include impressions experienced through all your senses. Using this list, write a description of the month. Include sensory language, but do not state the name of the month. Check your description and make sure it portrays the month clearly. Then read your description to your classmates and let them guess which month you have described.

Closure and Extension

ANSWERS TO THINKING ABOUT THE SELECTION

Recalling

1. Updike describes the sun as a spark that "Hung thin between/The dark and dark."
2. The milk bottles burst. They burst because the milk in them froze.
3. The delicate image of the river is its being "Held still beneath / The trees of lace."
4. The poet describes the sky as "low"—heavy with clouds.
5. The purring of the radiator fills the air at the end of the poem.

Interpreting

6. The "dark and dark" refers to the shortness of the day which starts with early morning darkness and ends in late afternoon with darkness.
7. The trees appear to be made of lace because each branch and twig is covered with snow.
8. Updike wrote such short lines to imitate the shortness of January's days.

Applying

9. Answers will differ. A possible student response would be pink for spring because of the pink blossoms on so many trees then, green for summer because the leaves are covering the trees then, and orange for fall because the leaves have turned color then.

ANSWERS TO ANALYZING LITERATURE

1. "Purrs all day" appeals to the sense of hearing.
2. "Fat snowy footsteps" suggests that the snow is deep and heavy. Boots or shoes look several sizes larger than they really are when covered with snow.
3. The last stanza appeals to the sense of sight ("sky is low" and "wind is gray"), the sense of touch ("wind" and heat from the "radiator"), and the sense of hearing ("radiator / Purrs all day").
4. Answers will differ. Suggested Response: The impression is that January is a rather unpleasant month with short days; snowy, cold, cloudy, and gray.

Challenge Instead of writing a prose description of a month as called for in the Thinking and Writing section, you might want your **more advanced** students to write their descriptions in poetry form. Have them consider the month they have chosen when they decide on line and stanza length and meter for their poem.

Thematic Idea Another selection that deals with the theme of winter is "By Morning" by May Swenson on page 540.

Enrichment Students might be asked to write contrasting images similar to that used by Updike in the last stanza of "January." They could write images of a hot day contrasted with a method of cooling off, or images of a rainy day contrasted with a method of drying off, and so on.

THINKING AND WRITING

Publishing Student Writing

Student descriptions—or poems—can be displayed on the class bulletin board or collected in a booklet of student writing.

Presentation

Motivation/Prior Knowledge Bring to class pictures of the moon in its various phases. Tell students they are going to read a poem about one of these phases.

Master Teacher Note Students might benefit from a class discussion about what constitutes a poem. Langston Hughes's poem "Winter Moon" is extremely short. Discuss with students why it is still considered a poem.

Master Teacher Note Another poem that presents an image of the moon is "Silver" by Walter de la Mare on page 564. Students might want to compare poems and to speculate about the phase of the moon represented in that poem.

Purpose-Setting Question What phase of the moon is Hughes describing?

1 **Language** What two adjectives does Hughes use to describe the moon in this line?

2 **Discussion** To what senses does this description appeal? How is it similar to line 1? How is it different from line 1?

Closure and Extension

ANSWERS TO THINKING ABOUT THE SELECTION

Recalling

1. The poet describes a new moon.

Interpreting

2. "How thin and sharp" is the repeated phrase. The effect is emphasis and perhaps a feeling of mystery.
3. The poet sees a new moon.
4. The thinness, sharpness, and shape like a curved crook are qualities of the moon that seem to appeal to the poet.
5. The poet's tone seems to be that of a surprised exclamation.

Applying

6. Answers will differ. Suggested Response: the full moon's radiance, the appearance of features on the moon.
7. Answers will differ. Suggested Response: Although the moon is visible, we have not known exactly of what it was made or how it controlled the tides until recently. Therefore, there has always been an element of mystery surrounding the moon.

THINKING AND WRITING

Publishing Student Writing

Student poems could be duplicated if a copying machine is available. Each student could add them to their individual booklets of student writing.

Writing Across the Curriculum You might want to tell science teachers about your students' investigation of the moon's phases in case they wish to conduct similar investigations in their classes.

Winter Moon

Langston Hughes

1 How thin and sharp is the moon tonight!
2 How thin and sharp and ghostly white
Is the slim curved crook of the moon tonight!

THINKING ABOUT THE SELECTION

Recalling

1. What precisely does the poet describe?

Interpreting

2. What phrase is repeated? What effect does the poet achieve by repeating this phrase?
3. The moon goes through several phases during a month. What phase of the moon does the poet see?
4. What qualities of the moon seem to appeal to the poet? Look at the exclamation mark at the end of the third line.
5. What is the poet's *tone,* or attitude toward what he sees?

Applying

6. What are some of your own impressions of the moon?
7. Notice the word *ghostly* in line 2. What is it about the moon that has suggested mystery to people throughout the ages?

THINKING AND WRITING

Writing a Poem

Reread "Winter Moon." Notice the pattern of the lines. Line 1 is a complete sentence. Lines 2 and 3, which make a second complete sentence, repeat the idea of line 1—but add to it.

Choose an aspect of nature that you freewrote about earlier. Write three lines about it, following the pattern of "Winter Moon." Revise your poem, making sure you have created a vivid picture. Proofread your poem and share it with your classmates.

Song of the Sky Loom

Tewa Indian

Oh our Mother the Earth, oh our Father the Sky, 1
Your children are we, and with tired backs 2
We bring you the gifts that you love. 3
Then weave for us a garment of brightness;
May the warp[1] be the white light of morning,
May the weft[2] be the red light of evening, 4
May the fringes be the falling rain,
May the border be the standing rainbow.
Thus weave for us a garment of brightness
That we may walk fittingly where birds sing, 5
That we may walk fittingly where grass is green,
Oh our Mother the Earth, oh our Father the Sky! 6

---

1. **warp** (wôrp) *n.*: The threads running lengthwise in a loom.
2. **weft** (weft) *n.*: The threads carried horizontally by the shuttle back and forth across the warp in weaving.

THINKING ABOUT THE SELECTION

Recalling

1. Who are the Mother, Father and children?
2. What do the children bring? What do they want?

Interpreting

3. How is one's climate like a "garment"?
4. Explain the title of the poem.

Applying

5. Do you consider a close relationship to nature important? Explain your answer.

CRITICAL THINKING AND READING

Paraphrasing a Poem

Paraphrasing a poem, or restating it in your own words, can help you understand it. In "Song of the Sky Loom," the first three lines might be paraphrased: "Dear Mother Earth and Father Sky, we, your children, honor you with gifts."

1. How would you paraphrase lines 5 to 11?
2. What is the theme of this poem?

Presentation

Motivation/Prior Knowledge The Pueblo Indians (of which the Tewa were a group) have practiced weaving since about 700 A.D. Native Americans of Southwestern United States are still known for the beauty of their weaving. You might want to bring in pictures of actual artifacts woven by Native Americans, such as baskets, rugs, and wall hangings.

Purpose-Setting Question To what does the title refer?

1 **Discussion** Who is the audience to whom this poem is addressed?

2 **Discussion** Who offers this poem?

3 **Discussion** What might be the gifts offered? What might "tired backs" have to do with the gifts?

4 **Discussion** What is really being requested? What metaphor appears in these lines?

5 **Discussion** Why are these gifts being requested?

6 **Discussion** Why is the first line repeated at the end of the poem?

ANSWERS TO CRITICAL THINKING AND READING

1. Answers will differ. Suggested Response: May the day be started with sunshine and end with a beautiful sunset. May there be rain around the edges followed by a beautiful rainbow. Thus we will have a beautiful and bountiful environment with singing birds and green grass.
2. The theme is that if we show nature the proper respect and care, we will be rewarded with the kind of environment we need to live.

Closure and Extension

ANSWERS TO THINKING ABOUT THE SELECTION

Recalling

1. The Mother is the Earth; the Father is the Sky; the children are the Tewa Indians.
2. The children bring gifts that will be loved by Mother Earth and Father Sky. The children want a garment, or environment, of brightness, with white light of morning, red light of evening, falling rain, and rainbows so that there will be birds singing and green grass.

Interpreting

3. One's climate is all around one, affecting the environment and the way the environment looks.
4. The title refers to the metaphor of weaving for the creation of their climate, much of which seems to come from the sky.

Applying

5. Answers will differ. Suggested Response: We need pure water, fertile soil, and fresh air to survive, making a close relationship to nature essential.

Presentation

Motivation/Prior Knowledge You might ask your students to imagine that they are the first humans to view the world after it was created. What sights would they see first? What sounds would they hear? What animals would they see? List your students' suggestions on the chalkboard.

Master Teacher Note You might want to discuss this poem as an account of the creation of the Earth and compare it to the Book of Genesis in the Bible and any other accounts of the creation you may have available.

Master Teacher Note Spectacular natural phenomena have been the subject of much poetry, art, and photography. Place Art Transparency 14, *Aurora Borealis* by Frederic Church, located in the Teaching Portfolio, on the overhead projector. Ask students what other majestic, awe-inspiring natural scenes have been captured in poetry, art, or photography.

In "New World," the poet addresses what could be the beginning of the world or of a new day.

Purpose-Setting Question To what does the title of this poem refer?

1 **Discussion** To whom is this poem addressed?

2 **Discussion** Keeping in mind the Biblical account of creation, why do you think the poet talks of rain in this stanza? Why is it appropriate for him to mention pollen here?

3 **Discussion** What geographical phenomenon does Momaday mention here?

4 **Discussion** What form of plant life does the poet mention here?

New World

N. Scott Momaday

1.

1 First Man,
behold:
the earth
glitters
with leaves;
the sky
glistens
with rain.
Pollen[1]
is borne
on winds
that low
2 and lean
upon
mountains.
Cedars
blacken
the slopes—
and pines.

2.

At dawn
eagles
hie and
hover
above
the plain
where light
3 gathers
in pools.
Grasses
4 shimmer
and shine.

---

1. pollen (päl′ ən) *n.*: The yellow, powderlike male cells formed in the stamen of a flower.

Grammar in Action

In both prose and poetry, writers must be careful to keep the **verb tense** consistent within a passage. In this poem Scott Momaday uses the present tense to express his ideas. Notice the verbs he uses in the first stanza: *behold, glitters, glistens, is borne, low, lean, blacken.* These verbs are all in the same tense because the author wants to say that the events all occur at once, now, in the present. The meaning of the poem is dependent upon the idea that these actions all occur now and will continue to occur; they didn't happen only in the past, nor will they happen only in the future. The use of the present tense in this poem is crucial.

Shadows
withdraw
and lie 5
away
like smoke.

3.

At noon
turtles
enter
slowly
into 6
the warm
dark loam.[2]
Bees hold
the swarm.
Meadows
recede
through planes 7
of heat
and pure
distance.

4.

At dusk 8
the gray
foxes
stiffen
in cold; 9
blackbirds
are fixed
in the
branches.
Rivers
follow 10
the moon,
the long
white track
of the
full moon.

2. loam (lōm) *n.*: Rich, dark soil.

5 Literary Focus What two things are being compared in this simile?

6 Discussion What forms of life does Momaday mention here?

7 Discussion What type of geographical features are mentioned here?

8 Discussion What span of time has elapsed?

9 Discussion How do the living creatures here compare with those mentioned in the previous stanza?

10 Discussion What geographical features are described?

Student Activity 1. List all of the verbs in the remaining three stanzas. In what tense are they?

Student Activity 2. Reconstruct this poem by changing all of the verbs to past tense. Begin as follows:

First man,
beheld:
the earth
glittered
with leaves;

Continue through the entire poem.

Student Activity 3. Write your own contrasting poem. Begin as follows:

Present man,
behold:
the earth

Continue telling how the earth is now.

Closure and Extension

ANSWERS TO THINKING ABOUT THE SELECTION

Recalling

1. The poet speaks to "First Man."
2. The poem takes place anywhere in the world on any day. It may be the poem takes place on the day of the world's creation and it might take place in the poet's environment —the Southwest.
3. The poem moves from before daybreak, through dawn, noon, and dusk.

Interpreting

4. Three details that suggest newness in the first stanza are addressing the poem to "First Man," the use of the words *glitters* and *glistens,* and the mention of pollen from which new plants arise.
5. In the second stanza, the impression is of graceful eagles hovering above a flat plain shining with light. In the third stanza, the impression is of slow-moving turtles burrowing into rich, black soil, while bees swarm, and the heat extends as far as one can envision. In the last stanza, cold comes with the darkness and even the "foxes stiffen in cold," blackbirds huddle on the branches, and rivers seem to follow the full moon's "long white track."
6. The title could mean that each new day seems to dawn on a new world that is fresh and alive. On the other hand, the title might refer to the creation of the world in the first place.

Applying

7. The world is new every day because we see it after resting and after it has been hidden by the darkness of night. An awakening seems like a rebirth. People are new every day because they greet the new day rested and ready to start anew. When we speak of renewing ourselves, we mean wiping out all the disappointments and failures of the past and meeting the new with a rested, peaceful mind and body.

THINKING ABOUT THE SELECTION

Recalling

1. To whom does the poet speak?
2. Where and when does the poem take place?
3. Explain the progression of time throughout the poem.

Interpreting

4. Find three details that suggest newness in the first stanza. Why are these details appropriate in this stanza?
5. What impression is created in the second stanza? In the third? In the last? Explain which details in each stanza help create this impression.
6. Explain the two meanings suggested by the title.

Applying

7. In what way is the world new every day? In what way are people new every day? What do we mean when we speak of renewing ourselves?

SPEAKING AND LISTENING

Giving a Choral Reading

The earliest poetry was chanted or sung aloud. Even today, poems gain in force and meaning when read aloud. A choral reading is one performed by a group, or *chorus,* of readers.

Give a choral reading of "New World." Your teacher may split the class into four groups, each reading one section of the poem in turn. Read with a tone of voice that communicates wonder at the beauty of the natural world seen for the first time.

Speaking and Listening Students may wish to present their choral reading of "New World" to another class, possibly even to an elementary class. You might want to have them prepare choral readings of several poems and present a program for another class.

Challenge You might have students write their own poems about nature. They might divide their poems into stanzas representing different times of day as Momaday did, or they might divide their poems into stanzas representing months or seasons.

Perceptions

HOUSES OF MURNAU AT OBERMARKT, 1908
Wassily Kandinsky
Lugano-Thyssen-Bornemisza Collection
Art Resource

Humanities Note

Fine art, *Houses of Murnau at Obermarkt,* Wassily Kandinsky. Wassily Kandinsky (1866–1944) was a Russian painter who began as a legal expert in his native country. The bright peasant folk art of Russia and Impressionist paintings he saw on a visit to France convinced Kandinsky that his true interest was in art. He went to Munich, Germany, where he studied painting at the Academy under Franz Stuck. Kandinsky is important to modern art as the first European artist to paint in a totally abstract fashion. A dynamic personality, he greatly influenced his contemporaries with his writings on modern art, his teachings, and his work.

Kandinsky was not immediately committed to abstraction in art. He arrived at this stage through a series of evolutionary phases in his work. His initial paintings were Impressionistic. As his focus changed, his style became what he termed "improvisational." These works of vibrant color and simple form are related to Fauvism (a movement in art based on the exaltation of pure color). The painting *Houses of Murnau at Obermarkt* falls into this category. Painted in 1908, just two years before his first completely nonobjective work, his direction is apparent. He uses a recognizable subject, but he has simplified the forms into geometric shapes and used colors that have no basis in reality. Kandinsky's innovative genius changed the course of twentieth-century art.

Master Teacher Note To introduce the theme of perceptions in poetry, show Art Transparency 15, *La chiave dei campi* by René Magritte, in the Teaching Portfolio. Tell students that the way one views the world can affect the way one thinks about it. Discuss the fact that the broken shards of glass from the window reflect the trees, grass, and sky seen from the window. What statement do they think the artist is making? Explain that poets sometimes write poems in free verse—a nontraditional approach using irregular rhythms and varied line lengths. Why might free verse be appropriate for a poem about this painting?

Focus

More About the Authors *My Aunt Otilia's Spirits,* by **Richard García,** has been published in a bilingual edition that is printed in both English and Spanish. How might authors who can write in more than one language and who are familiar with more than one culture help other people to improve their understanding of cultures other than their own?

Patricia Hubbell Born in Bridgeport, Connecticut, Patricia Hubbell was raised in, and still lives in, Easton, Connecticut. Easton is a small town of about 6,000 people in southeastern Connecticut. How might living in a small town near a large metropolitan area help a poet see ordinary city sights in new and creative ways?

May Swenson has lectured and given readings at more than thirty American colleges and universities. Swenson has received a Guggenheim Fellowship, the William Rose Benét Prize of the Poetry Society of America, a Ford Foundation grant, a Rockefeller Writing fellowship, and many others. Often literary honors and awards involve money as well as prestige. Why might it be especially important for a poet to receive awards of money? Speaking of poetry, Swenson has said "by bringing into play the sensual apparatus of the reader, the poem causes him to realize the content eye-wise, ear-wise, taste, touch, and muscle-wise. . . . The analyzing intellect . . . applied alone . . . can . . . bypass initial curiosity and individual exploration, resulting in little more than a mechanistic contact with the poem." What do you think Swenson means by this statement?

GUIDE FOR READING

The City Is So Big

Richard García (1941–) writes poetry for adults and children. He has published *Selected Poetry* (1973) and a contemporary folk tale for children. *My Aunt Otilia's Spirits* (1978). Garcia is the director of the Poets in the Schools program in Marin County, California. Born in San Francisco, California, he has also lived in Mexico and Israel. In "The City Is So Big" he describes the city as a child might see it.

Concrete Mixers

Patricia Hubbell (1928–) is a freelance journalist as well as a poet. She was born in Bridgeport, Connecticut, and attended the University of Connecticut. Her books include *The Apple Vendor's Fair* (1963), *8 A.M. Shadows* (1965), and *Catch Me a Wind* (1968). In "Concrete Mixers," she imagines these machines as elephants.

Southbound on the Freeway

May Swenson (1919–1989) was born in Logan, Utah, and attended Utah State University. After working for a while as a newspaper reporter, she moved to New York City, where she found employment as an editor and as a lecturer at colleges and universities. Her poems have been published in such magazines as *The New Yorker, Harper's,* and *The Nation.* Swenson believed that poetry is based on the desire to see things as they are, rather than as they appear. In "Southbound on the Freeway," however, she portrays an aspect of our culture as it might appear to an alien creature.

Objectives

1 To understand free verse
2 To read free verse
3 To write free verse

Support Material

Teaching Portfolio
Teacher Backup, pp. 819–822
Usage and Mechanics Worksheet, p. 823
Vocabulary Check, p. 824
Analyzing Literature Worksheet, *Understanding Free Verse,* p. 825
Critical Thinking and Reading Worksheet, *Reading Free Verse,* p. 826
Selection Test, pp. 827–828

Free Verse

Free verse is poetry with irregular rhythms and varied line lengths. It is "free" of the traditional forms of poetry. Since it is written in a way that is similar to ordinary speech, if it uses rhyme, the rhymes are loose and also irregular.

A poem written in free verse may be long or short. It may or may not have stanzas. The stanzas may be long or short, or both. Sometimes, as in "Southbound on the Freeway," the stanzas may be regular. In general, the lines in free verse are organized according to the flow of the poet's thoughts, ideas, and images. For example, "Concrete Mixers" is arranged according to the natural pauses one makes when speaking normally.

They rid the trunk-like trough of concrete,
Direct the spray to the bulging sides,
Turn and start the monsters moving.

Look For

As you read these poems, *listen* to them as if a friend were talking to you. Do most of the pauses sound natural and conversational?

Writing

You will read three poems about machinery in the modern world and will see technology in a new way. Freewrite about the new technology people encounter every day.

Vocabulary

Knowing the following words will help you as you read these poems.

ponderous (pän′ dər əs) *adj.*: Heavy, massive (p. 587)
perch (purch) *v.*: Rest upon (p. 587)
trough (trôf) *n.*: Long, narrow container for holding water or food for animals (p. 587)
bellow (bel′ ō) *v.*: Roar powerfully (p. 587)

Literary Focus Although free verse does not exhibit the traditional forms of poetry, it is still poetry, not prose. You might want to have your students list elements that they think free verse might have, which distinguishes it from prose.

Look For As your students read these three poems, have them see if these poems contain any of the elements they listed as necessary in free verse.

Writing/Prior Knowledge You might want to have **less advanced** students brainstorm in groups to list examples of new technology about which they could write.

Vocabulary Your **less advanced** students might benefit from pronouncing and discussing the meaning of each of the vocabulary words before the students read the poems.

Presentation

Humanities Note

Fine art, *City at the Sea,* 1933, by Helmut Kies. Helmut Kies was born and educated in Austria. Ask students what they think the mood of the painting is. Is the mood the same as that in the poem? If not, how does it differ?

Motivation/Prior Knowledge Discuss with students their impressions of a big city. List some of the images on the chalkboard.

Master Teacher Note The speaker in this poem seems to be intimidated by the city. You might ask students why this is so.

Purpose-Setting Question What images of the city are expressed?

1 **Literary Focus** What kind of figurative language does the poet use in his image of bridges?

2 **Literary Focus** What kind of figurative language does the poet use to describe train windows?

3 **Discussion** What impressions are given here of the city?

The City Is So Big

Richard García

The city is so big
1 Its bridges quake with fear
I know, I have seen at night

The lights sliding from house to house
2 And trains pass with windows shining
Like a smile full of teeth

I have seen machines eating houses
And stairways walk all by themselves
3 And elevator doors opening and closing
And people disappear.

THINKING ABOUT THE SELECTION

Recalling

1. What has the speaker seen the bridges doing?
2. What do the passing trains resemble?

Interpreting

3. Describe the mood of this poem. Find five details that help create this mood.
4. Interpret lines 7–10. Explain how each of the three details is possible.

Applying

5. This poem presents one side of living in a big city. Discuss with your classmates the pros and cons of city living.

ANALYZING LITERATURE

Understanding Free Verse

Poetry that is written in free verse often follows its own form. In attempting to capture the sounds of natural speech, free verse often abandons any precise rhythmic pattern and regular rhyme scheme.

1. Read the poem aloud. How would you describe its rhythm?
2. What do you notice about the length of the lines?
3. How do these two features add to the mood of the poem?

Closure and Extension

ANSWERS TO THINKING ABOUT THE SELECTION

Recalling

1. The speaker has seen the bridges quake with fear.
2. The passing trains have windows that resemble smiles full of teeth.

Interpreting

3. The mood is one of apprehension and fear. Details that help to create this mood are "bridges quake with fear," train windows like a smile full of teeth, "machines eating houses," stairways walking by themselves, and people disappearing behind elevator doors.
4. Line 7 refers to equipment used to knock buildings down, which could be seen as "eating houses." Line 8 refers to escalators, which move along apparently by themselves. Lines 9 and 10 tell of people going inside elevators when the doors open and then having disappeared the next time the doors open.

Applying

5. Answers will differ. Pros may include excitement, and the availability of theaters, museums, stores, and sporting events. Cons may include crime, crowded living arrangements, and the lack of open spaces.

ANSWERS TO ANALYZING LITERATURE

1. The rhythm seems irregular and hurried due to lack of punctuation.
2. The lines in the first stanza are all short. The first two lines of second and third stanzas are longer; each ends with a short line.
3. The hurried rhythm and breathlessness caused by the lack of punctuation marks and the longer lines that begin stanzas 2 and 3 add to the mood of fear.

Concrete Mixers

Patricia Hubbell

CITY AT THE SEA
Helmut Kies
Three Lions

The drivers are washing the concrete mixers;
Like elephant tenders[1] they hose them down.
Tough gray-skinned monsters standing ponderous, 1
Elephant-bellied and elephant-nosed,
Standing in muck up to their wheel-caps, 2
Like rows of elephants, tail to trunk.
Their drivers perch on their backs like mahouts,[2]
Sending the sprays of water up.
They rid the trunk-like trough of concrete, 3
Direct the spray to the bulging sides,
Turn and start the monsters moving.
        Concrete mixers
        Move like elephants
        Bellow like elephants
        Spray like elephants
    Concrete mixers are urban elephants, 4
    Their trunks are raising a city.

---

1. **elephant tenders**: People in charge of elephants.
2. **mahouts** (mə hout″s) *n.*: Elephant drivers or keepers.

THINKING ABOUT THE SELECTION

Recalling

1. What scene is being described in this poem?
2. What do the concrete mixers accomplish?

Interpreting

3. An extended metaphor is a figurative comparison carried throughout a poem. Describe how the two items here are alike.

Applying

4. Advertisers often use animal metaphors to describe cars. Tell what impression the advertiser is trying to create about two cars named for animals.

CRITICAL THINKING AND READING

Reading Free Verse

Let punctuation marks help you when you read free verse. Pause at commas and take a slightly longer pause at semicolons. Stop when you come to periods, question marks, and exclamation marks. If a line does not have a punctuation mark at the end of it, read on to the next line without pausing.

1. The punctuation marks in lines 1 through 11 tell you that these lines should be read one by one, pausing or stopping at the end of each. Given the subject, why do you suppose the poet chose this "step-by-step" arrangement?
2. How should lines 12 through 15 be read? Why?

Presentation

Motivation/Prior Knowledge Tell students that in "Concrete Mixers" the poet has chosen to use an extended metaphor. Explain that an extended metaphor is a comparison between unlike items. Ask them to what they think a concrete mixer might be compared.

Purpose-Setting Question What image of concrete mixers does the poet present?

1 **Literary Focus** What metaphor is introduced here?

2 **Literary Focus** What words are used in these lines to continue the metaphor? Why are these words appropriate?

3 **Discussion** What are the drivers doing throughout the poem?

4 **Discussion** What do the concrete mixers do for the city?

Enrichment You might have your **more advanced** students think of other vehicles that they could compare to animals. These might include a bus, a jeep, a helicopter, a fire truck, a train, or a subway.

ANSWERS TO CRITICAL THINKING AND READING

1. Answers will differ. Suggested Response: the poet may have chosen this "step-by-step" arrangement of lines to indicate the way both cement mixers and elephants seem to be solid and predictable.
2. Lines 12 through 15 should be read without pause because there are no punctuation marks at the ends of the lines. This adds a feeling of movement or action to the poem.

Closure and Extension

ANSWERS TO THINKING ABOUT THE SELECTION

Recalling

1. The drivers of concrete mixers are washing the trucks.
2. They help to build the city.

Interpreting

3. Concrete mixers and elephants are alike because they are both large, gray, slow-moving, bellowing, spraying, and round in the middle with trunk-like parts. The drivers are sitting on top of the concrete mixers, washing them with hoses, just as the elephant tenders would do to elephants.

Applying

4. Answers will differ. Suggested Response: Jaguars, Cougars, Lynxes, Mustangs, Colts, and Pintos suggest speed and sleekness; Rabbits suggest speed and compactness.

Presentation

Motivation/Prior Knowledge Lead a discussion about point of view. Elicit from students that different people will interpret events in different ways, depending on their point of view. Tell students the speaker in this poem has an unusual view of what he or she sees.

Master Teacher Note If your students are from rural areas, you might want to show them pictures of elaborate freeway systems. An alternative would be to have those who have visited California describe the freeways they saw there.

Purpose-Setting Question Why is the point of view of the speaker in this poem unusual?

1 **Discussion** From where does the tourist come?

2 **Discussion** What are the creatures referred to here?

3 **Discussion** What are the transparent parts?

4 **Discussion** What are their feet?

5 **Discussion** What are the measuring tapes?

6 **Discussion** What is the special one?

7 **Discussion** What are the soft shapes?

Literary Focus Why do you think the poet chose to write this poem in couplets, stanzas of two lines each?

Reader's Response Choose a subject and describe it as if you were a visitor from outer space seeing the subject for the first time.

Southbound on the Freeway

May Swenson

1 A tourist came in from Orbitville,
parked in the air, and said:

2 The creatures of this star
are made of metal and glass.

3 Through the transparent parts
you can see their guts.

4 Their feet are round and roll
on diagrams—or long

5 measuring tapes—dark
with white lines.

They have four eyes.
The two in the back are red.

Sometimes you can see a five-eyed
one, with a red eye turning

on the top of his head.
6 He must be special—

the others respect him,
and go slow,

when he passes, winding
among them from behind.

They all hiss as they glide,
like inches, down the marked

7 tapes. Those soft shapes,
shadowy inside

the hard bodies—are they
their guts or their brains?

THINKING ABOUT THE SELECTION

Recalling

1. Who is the tourist in this poem?
2. According to the title, what does the tourist see?

Interpreting

3. Part of the humor in this poem comes from the tourist misinterpreting what he or she sees. How does the tourist misinterpret the creatures of this star?
4. What is the five-eyed creature? In what way is the tourist's analysis of the five-eyed creature actually correct?
5. Explain the question that the tourist asks. How would you answer this question?

Applying

6. Put yourself in the place of this tourist. For example, if this tourist were to see a parking lot, he or she might interpret it as a hotel. How might this tourist interpret a drive-through window at a fast-food restaurant? How might this tourist interpret a drive-in movie? List three other items and explain how this tourist might misinterpret them.

THINKING AND WRITING

Writing Free Verse

Imagine the tourist from Orbitville parked in the air above a football game. Freewrite about what the tourist would see and how the tourist might interpret what he or she sees. Then use your freewriting as the basis for writing a poem in free verse. When you revise your poem, make sure you have consistently described the game from the tourist's point of view. Then proofread your poem and share it with your classmates.

Challenge You might have students write poems about people on earth seeing the tourist from outer space and misinterpreting what he or she is.

Thematic Idea The short story "Rain, Rain, Go Away" by Isaac Asimov, page 13, is also about extraterrestrials.

Enrichment You might have students write poems about the Sakkaro family as seen by the Wrights in "Rain, Rain, Go Away."

Another possibility might be to have artistic students illustrate the poems they write for the Thinking and Writing activity.

THINKING AND WRITING

For help with this assignment, students can refer to Lesson 18, "Writing a Poem," in the Handbook of Writing About Literature.

Publishing Student Writing If a copying machine is available, students' poems could be added to booklets of creative writing kept by each student. If no copying machines are available, students' poems might be displayed on a bulletin board.

Writing Across the Curriculum You might want to tell the art teachers if you plan to have students illustrate poems they have written. They might want to guide students in illustrating their poems.

Closure and Extension

ANSWERS TO THINKING ABOUT THE SELECTION

Recalling

1. The tourist is someone from outer space.
2. According to the title, the tourist sees the southbound lane of a freeway.

Interpreting

3. The tourist thinks the automobiles are the living creatures of this star.
4. The five-eyed creature is a police car or an ambulance. The tourist is correct in saying that the other cars respect it and go slow when he passes.
5. The tourist asks whether the soft shapes inside are the creature's guts or brains. Students will probably respond that the soft shapes inside are the brains of the creature.

Applying

6. Answers will differ. Possible responses might be that a drive-through window at a fast-food restaurant might be where the creatures eat; a drive-in movie might be the creatures' school. Three other possibilities might be a school misinterpreted as a zoo; a gas station misinterpreted as a hospital; and a ship misinterpreted as a large fish.

Focus

More About the Author The poet **Maxine Kumin** received an American Academy and Institute of Arts and Letters award in 1980 and became a consultant in poetry to the Library of Congress in 1981. Why do you think the Library of Congress would hire a consultant in poetry?

Literary Focus Concrete poetry should not be noteworthy only for its shape. In the case of "400-Meter Free Style," for example, the description of a swimmer's movements that Kumin gives is a complete and accurate one about swimming such a race. Why do you think it is important for poets not to depend completely upon the shape of a concrete poem to communicate to readers?

Look For You may want to lead **less advanced** students in a group discussion of the meaning of the poem's shape.

Writing/Prior Knowledge For your **less advanced** students, you might want to make listing physical actions a group activity before students draw the shape of the action.

Vocabulary You might want to go over the vocabulary words and the footnoted words with your **less advanced** students before they read the poem.

Spelling Tip Note that there is no rule to determine whether *-ence* or *-ance* is correct. If a word ends in *-ance,* however, like *extravagance,* then parallel forms like *extravagant* use the same letter.

GUIDE FOR READING

400-Meter Free Style

Maxine Kumin (1925–) was born in Philadelphia, Pennsylvania. She attended Radcliffe College and taught there and at Tufts University, both in Massachusetts. Kumin has written novels, essays, and children's books, as well as several volumes of poetry. In 1973 she was awarded the Pulitzer Prize for *Up Country: Poems of New England.* In her poem "400-Meter Free Style," Kumin describes a swim race not only in words but also in shape.

Concrete Poetry

Concrete poetry is poetry in which the shape of the poem on the page resembles the subject of the poem. With concrete poetry, poets experiment with the way a poem *looks* on the page. They arrange the words so as to form a concrete, or actual, shape that is recognizable. Poems have been written in many shapes, including hearts, trees, wings, and even falling rain.

For example, the arrangement of the lines of "400-Meter Free Style" may confuse you at first. If so, just think about the poem's subject: a swimmer in a race.

Look For

As you read this concrete poem, look at its shape and consider its subject. Based on the title, what is the topic of this poem? What shape do you see as you look at the lines?

Writing

Imagine a simple physical action—a motion, a gesture, a series of movements; for example, the leap of a dancer, the downhill racing of a skier, or the uphill rocky scrambling of a mountain climber. On a blank sheet of paper, draw a simple shape of the action that you imagine.

Vocabulary

Knowing the following words will help you as you read "400-Meter Free Style."

catapults (kat′ ə pultz′) *v.*: Launches (p. 591)
cunningly (kun′ iŋ lē) *adv.*: Skillfully (p. 591)
extravagance (ik strav′ ə gəns) *n.*: Waste (p. 591)
compensation (käm′ pən sā′ shən) *n.*: Here, equal reaction (p. 591)
nurtures (nʉr′ chərz) *v.*: Nourishes (p. 591)
tick (tik) *v.*: Operate smoothly (p. 593)
expended (ik spend′ id) *v.*: Used up (p. 593)
plum (plum) *adj.*: Here, first-class (p. 593)

Objectives

1 To understand concrete poetry
2 To write a concrete poem

Support Material

Teaching Portfolio
Teacher Backup, pp. 829–830
Usage and Mechanics Worksheet, p. 831
Vocabulary Check, p. 832
Analyzing Literature Worksheet, *Understanding Concrete Poetry,* p. 833
Language Worksheet, *Choosing the Meaning That Fits the Context,* p. 834
Selection Test, pp. 835–836

400-Meter Free Style

Maxine Kumin

The gun full swing the swimmer catapults and cracks
s
i
x
feet away onto that perfect glass he catches at 1
a
n
d
throws behind him scoop[1] after scoop cunningly moving
t
h
e
water back to move him forward. Thrift is his wonderful
s
e 2
c
ret; he has schooled out all extravagance. No muscle
r
i
p
ples without compensation wrist cock[2] to heel snap to
h
i
s
mobile mouth that siphons[3] in the air that nurtures
h
i 3
m
at half an inch above sea level so to speak.
T
h
e
astonishing whites of the soles of his feet rise
a
n
d

1. **scoop** (skōōp) *n.*: The amount taken up, in this case with a cupped hand.
2. **wrist cock:** The tilted position of the wrist.
3. **siphons** (sī' fənz) *v.*: Draws; pulls.

Presentation

Motivation/Prior Knowledge You might lead the class in a discussion of swimming and swimming in races. If none of your students have personal experiences with competing in or watching swimming races, perhaps they have watched Olympic swimming races on television. Elicit information about how the swimmers take their mark, dive into the water, and flip to turn as they reach the end of the pool.

Master Teacher Note In the writing activity on page 590, your students listed actions that could become the subject of concrete poems. You might want to point out to students that objects can also be the subjects of concrete poems. Students might brainstorm in groups to list objects and the characteristics about them that they might include in concrete poems.

Purpose-Setting Question How does making a poem concrete add to its effect on the reader?

1 **Discussion** To what does "that perfect glass" refer?

2 **Discussion** What does the poet mean by this sentence?

3 **Discussion** What is the swimmer doing with his mouth?

salute us on the turns. He flips, converts, and is gone
a
l
l
in one. We watch him for signs. His arms are steady at
t
h
e
catch, his cadent[4] feet tick in the stretch, they know
t
h
e
lesson well. Lungs know, too; he does not list[5] for
a
i
r
he drives along on little sips carefully expended 4
b
u
t
that plum red heart pumps hard cries hurt how soon
i
t
s
near one more and makes its final surge TIME 4:25:9

---

4. cadent (kā′ dənt) *adj.*: Rhythmic; beating.
5. list (list) *v.*: Wish; crave.

4 **Discussion** Explain why the swimmer's air supply is described as "little sips carefully expended"?

Reader's Response What object or activity can you think of that could be described in the shape of its motion?

Closure and Extension

ANSWERS TO THINKING ABOUT THE SELECTION

Recalling

1. The poet mentions the swimmer's arm movements, breathing technique, and kicking.
2. In lines 3–6, the poet admires the thrift of the swimmer's motion, with no unnecessary movement, with only movements that produce the desired result.
3. The swimmer's heart hurts as he nears the end of the race and makes his final surge to the finish.

Interpreting

4. At the end the poet moves "inside" the swimmer by talking about his heart hurting and by mentioning his thoughts.
5. The shape of the poem shows the laps of the pool that the swimmer swims.
6. By finishing the poem with the swimmer's racing time, the poet makes the race in the poem appear to be actually taking place as you read it.

Applying

7. Answers will differ. Suggested Response: the swimmer's training and discipline can be helpful in daily living because the swimmer is used to finishing difficult tasks, trying his hardest despite discomfort, and constantly working to improve his performance.

ANSWERS TO ANALYZING LITERATURE

1. Answers will differ. Suggested Response: it takes longer to read aloud because you have to concentrate on when to go to the left of each line.
2. Answers will differ. Suggested Response: You have to concentrate on how to read the poem in the same way the swimmer has to concentrate on how to move in order to win the race.

THINKING ABOUT THE SELECTION

Recalling

1. What three aspects of the swimmer's movements does the poet mention?
2. In lines 3 through 6, what does the poet admire about the swimmer's motion?
3. What hurts the swimmer?

Interpreting

4. Until the last four lines, the poet confines her observations to the swimmer's external movement. How does the poet move "inside" the swimmer at the end?
5. What does the shape of the poem show?
6. What is the effect of ending the poem with the swimmer's racing time?

Applying

7. How can the swimmer's training and discipline be helpful in daily living?

ANALYZING LITERATURE

Understanding Concrete Poetry

A **concrete poem** gives you another element—shape—to think about. The shape of a concrete poem not only reinforces the subject; it may also give you another way of understanding its meaning. Both the title and the shape tell you that "400-Meter Free Style" is about the idea of a swimming race.

In a concrete poem, punctuation may occur in places other than at the end of a line, and words may be placed other than horizontally. This may make the poem more difficult to read, but is meant to surprise you by the way the poem looks and sounds.

1. Read the poem aloud. What do you notice about your reading of a poem in this shape?
2. How might reading this poem aloud require the kind of concentration and effort that the swimmer has?

THINKING AND WRITING

Writing a Concrete Poem

Write a short concrete poem. Your subject can be the physical action and shape that you created earlier, or you may choose a person, a place, an event, or some form of movement. Think of a shape that in some way relates to your subject. For instance, if you wanted to write about the destruction of a fire, you could shape your poem like a flame. Draw the shape.

Freewrite about the subject you chose. Use this information to write your lines of poetry. Then fit the lines to the shape.

THINKING AND WRITING

For help with this assignment, students can refer to Lesson 18, "Writing a Poem," in the Handbook of Writing About Literature.

Publishing Student Writing These concrete poems could be included in a class booklet of the students' creative writing or could be displayed on a bulletin board.

Choices

ON THE PROMENADE
August Macke
Three Lions

Humanities Note

Fine art, *On The Promenade* by August Macke. August Macke (1887-1914) was a German Expressionist artist who received his academic training at the Dusseldorf Academy and the Arts and Crafts School. He is placed in the Blue Rider (*Blaue-Reiter*) Movement, a vital and influential movement by a group of German painters concerned with the spiritualism of nature in modern art. Macke's art involved spontaneous, happy, and colorful studies of the human figure. His death, on the front in World War I, was a severe loss to the world of modern art.

The painting *On The Promenade* is a study of the effect of people on a landscape. The simplified elongated figures appear in a park setting broken into geometric shapes and lit with fresh, pleasant color. Linear patterns produce a curving rhythm and give a sense of movement to the canvas. A woman's white parasol and a man's jaunty straw hat add compositional interest. The scene is a pleasant, harmonious observation of city life, just the sort of scene that Macke liked to paint.

Master Teacher Note To introduce the theme of choices in poetry, show students Art Transparency 16, *Wood's Edge* by Henri Rousseau, in the Teaching Portfolio. Explain to students that the speaker in a poem—the person who addresses the reader—has a great impact on the effect of the poem. The speaker can be the poet or some other character. Discuss what the woman in the painting might be thinking as she stands in the middle of the road, poised at the edge of the woods. If she were the speaker in a poem about choices, what might she say? Based on her appearance, how might she say it? What choice might she make?

Focus

More About the Author The poet **Julio Noboa Polanco** has worked as a leadership trainer with the Latino Institute in Chicago. He has also been an editor for *The Rican, Journal of Puerto Rican Thought,* where a number of his poems have been published. He writes poetry both in Spanish and in English. If there are any bilingual students in your class, you might invite them to tell what it is like to speak, write, and think in two languages. They might also answer their classmates' questions about the experience of bilingualism.

Robert Frost's first published book, *A Boy's Will,* did not appear until he was thirty-nine years old, and it was published in England, where he lived for several years. Much of Frost's life was shadowed by loneliness, family sorrows, depression, and fear of mental unbalance. You might wish to discuss with your class whether happiness or unhappiness is more likely to inspire literary creativity.

GUIDE FOR READING

Identity

Julio Noboa Polanco (1949–) was born in The Bronx, New York, of Puerto Rican parents. The family moved to Chicago, and "Identity" was written while the poet was an eighth grader at a school on the west side of Chicago. As a bilingual poet who values his parents' Hispanic heritage, Julio Noboa Polanco has developed an interest in the variety of cultures in the world and has received a Bachelor's Degree in Anthropology as well as a Master's Degree in Education. Currently living in San Antonio, Texas, he administers a dropout prevention program in a barrio school in the city.

The Road Not Taken

Robert Frost (1874–1963) was born in San Francisco. In 1885, following the death of his father, his family moved to New England. There Frost attended school in Lawrence, Massachusetts, and then went on to Dartmouth and Harvard colleges. His experiences as a farmer and schoolteacher provided the material for many of his most famous poems. For twelve years, Frost met with little success in getting his poetry published. However, in 1913 and 1914 he put together two of his major collections, *A Boy's Will* and *North of Boston,* and these works brought him critical acclaim. Between 1913 and 1962, he won the Pulitzer Prize four times. In 1960 Congress gave him a special gold medal "in recognition of his poetry, which has enriched the culture of the United States and the philosophy of the world."

The Speaker

If you read a poem carefully, you will notice that someone–a speaker—is addressing you. Sometimes the speaker is the poet. Other times, however, the speaker is a character the poet has created. This character may be a man or a woman, a child, an animal, or even an inanimate object to whom the poet has chosen to give human qualities. For example, the poet may create a princess, a boxer, a baseball player, a cat, or even mushrooms that speak—all tell their own story from their unique point of view.

Look For

As you read, look for the speaker in each poem. What is the speaker like? How does the speaker reveal the world through his or her unique point of view?

Writing

In the poems you are about to read, each speaker makes a choice. George Moore has written, "The difficulty in life is the choice." Freewrite about choice. What is it? What types of choices do people have to make every day? Why do people find making a choice so difficult?

Vocabulary

Knowing the following words will help you as you read these poems.

harnessed (här′ nisd) *v.*: Tied (p. 598)

abyss (ə bis′) *n.*: Great depth (p. 598)

shunned (shund) *v.*: Avoided (p. 598)

fertile (fʉr′ t′l) *adj.*: Rich; productive (p. 598)

musty (mus′ tē) *adj.*: With a stale, damp smell (p. 598)

stench (stench) *n.*: Bad smell (p. 598)

diverged (də vʉrjd′) *v.*: Branched off (p. 600)

Literary Focus To make the distinction between the speaker and the poet unmistakably clear, you might read a few of the poems in *Spoon River Anthology* or, with **more advanced** students, passages from Browning's dramatic monologues. Since at least some students think of poetry as nothing more than direct self-expression, you might discuss why poets might choose to create speakers who are clearly distinguishable from themselves.

Look For You can help **less advanced** students by suggesting that they imagine a person standing before them and speaking each poem directly to them. They are more likely to get a sense of the speaker's personality.

Writing/Prior Knowledge A class discussion on the subject of choice will help students get started with this exercise. You might begin by asking students to suggest some of the more difficult choices people sometimes have to make.

Vocabulary When discussing "Identity," you may wish to question students on the suggestions and associations they see in these words (excluding *diverged*) and others. The vocabulary of Frost's poem is not likely to require discussion.

Spelling Tip Note that a one-syllable word in which the last three letters are consonant-vowel-consonant doubles the final consonant before adding a suffix beginning with a vowel: *shunned.*

Objectives

1 To hear the speaker's voice
2 To interpret differences in metaphors

Support Material

Teaching Portfolio

Teacher Backup, pp. 837–839
Usage and Mechanics Worksheet, p. 840
Vocabulary Check, p. 841
Analyzing Literature Worksheet, *Hearing the Speaker's Voice,* p. 842
Language Worksheet, *Finding Synonyms,* p. 843
Selection Test, pp. 844–845

Presentation

Motivation/Prior Knowledge Ask your students, "What do we mean by identity? Is it just one's name and the various numbers assigned to us by computers?" Lead them to see that learning who one really is presents a problem with which poets and other thinkers have long grappled.

Master Teacher Note Polanco has said the following about his poem: "The whole poem is essentially a search for my individuality—finding myself as a person, as opposed to being one of the crowd." Before reading the poem, you might wish to discuss how people go about finding themselves and separating themselves from the crowd.

Purpose-Setting Question What has the speaker decided about his own identity?

1 **Discussion** The "them" is the crowd, whom the speaker likens to flowers harnessed to a pot of dirt. In contrast, there is the "I" of the poem, likened to a weed. By questioning, lead your students to see the contrast established in these stanzas. Ask them to point out the implications of the two figurative comparisons.

2 **Clarification** This stanza consists of two incomplete sentences. You can help your students' comprehension by suggesting that they imagine each sentence beginning with the phrase *It would be better* . . . Ask how this stanza continues the image of the speaker as a weed.

3 **Discussion** Ask the students what is undesirable about being a pleasant-smelling flower? Then direct students' attention to the last two lines, especially the words *handled, plucked,* and *greedy.*

Identity

Julio Noboa Polanco

1 Let them be as flowers,
always watered, fed, guarded, admired,
but harnessed to a pot of dirt.

I'd rather be a tall, ugly weed,
clinging on cliffs, like an eagle
wind-wavering above high, jagged rocks.

2 To have broken through the surface of stone,
to live, to feel exposed to the madness
of the vast, eternal sky.
To be swayed by the breezes of an ancient sea,
carrying my soul, my seed, beyond the mountains of time
or into the abyss of the bizarre.

3 I'd rather be unseen, and if
then shunned by everyone,
than to be a pleasant-smelling flower,
growing in clusters in the fertile valley,
where they're praised, handled, and plucked
by greedy, human hands.

4 I'd rather smell of musty, green stench
than of sweet, fragrant lilac.
If I could stand alone, strong and free,
I'd rather be a tall, ugly weed.

4 **Discussion** Have students restate in their own words the meaning of the last two lines.

Challenge Return to the purpose-setting question and encourage your students to answer it with the ideas developed in the poem.

Reader's Response What does Polanco's poem mean to you? Do you ever share the narrator's desires?

SEASHORE AT PALAVAS, 1854
Gustave Courbet
Musée Fabre, Montpellier

THINKING ABOUT THE SELECTION

Recalling

1. According to the speaker, what benefits do flowers have? What two drawbacks make beings like flowers unattractive?
2. What would the speaker rather be? What benefit makes this choice extremely attractive to the speaker?

Interpreting

3. Explain what the speaker is really choosing between in this poem.
4. Which choice would be the easier to make? Support your answer.
5. What do you think is the theme of this poem? Explain how the title of the poem relates to the theme.

Applying

6. Provide three examples of how people make the choice the speaker makes in their daily lives.

ANALYZING LITERATURE

Hearing the Speaker's Voice

Hearing the speaker's voice when you read can help you understand the poem. In "Identity" the speaker is an individual who has made a choice about what kind of person to be.

1. Find three adjectives you think describe the speaker. Explain your reason for selecting each adjective.
2. Name three people from history or current affairs you think the speaker would admire. Explain the reason for each choice.
3. Look at the art that accompanies this poem. In what way does the figure in the painting capture the identity of the speaker?

Humanities Note

Fine art, *Seashore at Palavas*, 1854, by Gustave Courbet. Courbet (1819–1877) was a French painter who advanced the realist movement in art. He believed that art should show the people and events of the time realistically and honestly. In politics, he was sympathetic to the revolutionary movements of his day and spent time in prison for his political activities. His paintings influenced later art movements, such as naturalism and impressionism.

1. Which says more to you about the meaning of individualism and personal identity, the poem or the painting? Give reasons for your opinion.
2. What does a painting such as this express that a poem cannot?

Closure and Extension

ANSWERS TO THINKING ABOUT THE SELECTION

Recalling

1. Flowers are watered, fed, guarded, and admired. The drawbacks are that they are harnessed to a pot of dirt, and that they are plucked by greedy hands.
2. The speaker would rather be a tall, ugly weed clinging to a cliff. The benefit is that he could be independent, strong, and free.

Interpreting

3. The speaker is choosing between conformity and independence.
4. Answers will differ. Suggested Response: Conformity would be the easier choice; conformity brings support, protection, approval, and praise.
5. Answers will differ. Suggested Response: Individuality and independence are preferable to conformity within a group. The title denotes what individuality and independence can enhance and confirm—one's identity.

Applying

6. Answers will differ. Suggested Response: Choosing not to follow fads in clothing, music, behavior, and career ambitions are examples.

ANSWERS TO ANALYZING LITERATURE

1. Answers will differ. Suggested Response: Independent, nonconformist, unpopular, private, and unattractive are three possibilities. Such adjectives are implicit in the image of the speaker as an isolated, ugly weed alone on a cliff.
2. Answers will differ. Suggested Response: Possibilities include Christ, Socrates, Joan of Arc, Abraham Lincoln, Martin Luther King, and Mother Teresa.
3. Like the speaker in the poem, the figure in the painting is alone, removed from the crowd, and exposed to "the breezes of an ancient sea."

Presentation

Motivation/Prior Knowledge It is quite common for people to wonder what their lives might have been like had they made different choices at crucial moments. *What might have been* teases our imaginations. Suggest that your students imagine how their lives might have been had some moment of the past been different.

Master Teacher Note At some point in your discussion of this poem, you may wish to point out that if the last stanza were dropped there would be no strong reason for believing that the poem is anything other than a literal account of the speaker's choosing one path in the woods instead of another. What is said in the fourth stanza makes it clear that the poem is symbolic of a choice in life that determines the course of one's experience and excludes the course that might have been.

Purpose-Setting Question What does this poem reveal about the important choices in life that people must make?

1 **Clarification** The syntax of these lines may seem difficult to some. A paraphrase like the following may help **less advanced** students: And—feeling sorry that I could not travel both and still remain one person—I stood for a long time. Ask students to summarize the situation presented in this stanza.

2 **Discussion** Compare the two roads as the speaker describes them. How different are they?

3 **Discussion** Ask your **less advanced** students to paraphrase what the speaker says about the road not taken.

The Road Not Taken

Robert Frost

Two roads diverged in a yellow wood,
1 And sorry I could not travel both
And be one traveler, long I stood
And looked down one as far as I could
To where it bent in the undergrowth;

2 Then took the other, as just as fair,
And having perhaps the better claim,
Because it was grassy and wanted wear;
Though as for that, the passing there
Had worn them really about the same,

3 And both that morning equally lay
In leaves no step had trodden black.
Oh, I kept the first for another day!
Yet knowing how way leads on to way,
I doubted if I should ever come back.

4 I shall be telling this with a sigh
Somewhere ages and ages hence:
Two roads diverged in a wood, and I—
I took the one less traveled by,
And that has made all the difference.

4 **Critical Thinking and Reading** Which details indicate that the diverging roads are symbolic of choices that change forever the course of one's life? What might a reader infer from the pause in the speaker's voice at the end of line 18?

Challenge Why might Frost have decided against titling his poem "The Road Taken"? Wouldn't this title be just as appropriate?

THINKING ABOUT THE SELECTION

Recalling

1. At the beginning of the poem the speaker is faced with a choice between two roads. Which choice does he make?
2. What reason does the speaker give for making this choice? Which lines tell you that he is not certain his reason is valid?
3. What does the speaker hope to be able to do later? Which lines tell you that he doubts he will be able to do this?

Interpreting

4. Find two details suggesting that the speaker feels this decision is significant.
5. What do the roads seem to symbolize? Find details from the poem to support your answer.
6. Explain the theme of the poem.

Applying

7. An old proverb states that opportunity is a short-lived visitor. Another old saying says that opportunity never knocks twice. How do these sayings relate to the poem? Do you agree with the sayings? Why or why not?

CRITICAL THINKING AND READING

Interpreting Differences in Metaphors

Many writers have used metaphors to describe life. Read each of the common metaphors below. Explain how each suggests a specific attitude toward life. For example, one common metaphor says that life is just a bowl of cherries. This metaphor suggests an optimistic view. However, the comedian Rodney Dangerfield has responded to this metaphor by saying that life is just a bowl of pits. His metaphor suggests a more pessimistic outlook.

1. Life is a long, hard road.
2. Life is a journey of discovery.
3. Life is a merry-go-round.
4. Life is an endless feast.

Closure and Extension

ANSWERS TO THINKING ABOUT THE SELECTION

Recalling

1. He chooses the road that has "perhaps the better claim."
2. His reason is that the chosen road is grassy and not worn down by passersby. Lines 9 and 10 indicate he is not certain that his reason is valid.
3. He hopes to be able to take the other road in the future. Lines 14 and 15 express his doubt that he will ever do so.

Interpreting

4. He shall be telling about his choice in the future, and he says that the road he took "has made all the difference."
5. The roads symbolize the irreversible, life-changing choices that people make. Lines 14 and 15 indicate that such choices are irreversible; the last line indicates that they are life-changing.
6. Answers will differ. Suggested Response: The theme is basically that people make choices that establish a particular course for their lives and that the course that might have been can never be known.

Applying

7. The ideas contained in these sayings are similar to those of the poem. However, Frost's poem emphasizes the sadness of never knowing what might have been had a different choice been made. The sayings emphasize the need to act and to make positive choices. It is possible to agree or to disagree with the sayings. Students should offer good examples from real life to support their opinions.

ANSWERS TO CRITICAL THINKING AND READING

1. This metaphor suggests the attitude that life is unpleasant and difficult.
2. This metaphor suggests the attitude that life pleases and surprises with what we learn as we live.
3. This metaphor suggests the attitude that life is continually amusing.
4. This metaphor suggests the attitude that life is a series of pleasures.

Focus

More About the Authors The poems of **Dorothy Parker** are usually commentaries on love and the relationship between the sexes. They can be found in the volume *Not So Deep as a Well.* She was the coauthor, with Elmer Rice, of the play *Close Harmony.* Her place in the history of modern literature is based on her contribution to the development of modern urbane humor. You might wish to discuss with your class the question what causes some people to take a sharply satirical, and even sarcastic, attitude toward certain aspects of life.

Adrien Stoutenburg's poetry has appeared in *The New Yorker, Saturday Review, The Nation, Commonweal,* and other notable periodicals. Her biographies include one of Freud, *Explorer of the Unconscious.* Besides being a writer, she is an amateur artist and sculptor; she plays the piano, guitar, and harmonica. You may wish to discuss with your students how a variety of interests can benefit a writer.

GUIDE FOR READING

The Choice

Dorothy Parker (1893–1967) was born in West End (now part of Long Branch), New Jersey, and lived mostly in New York City. She began her literary career in 1916 as a magazine writer. For several years she was the regular book reviewer for *The New Yorker.* Today she is best remembered for her stories and poems, which are distinguished for their wit and sarcasm. Like "The Choice," Dorothy Parker's writing in general expresses a gentle cynicism toward life and its disappointments.

Journey to the Interior

Adrien Stoutenburg (1916–   ) was born in Darfur, Minnesota, and has lived in Mexico, New Mexico, and California. At various times she has worked as a librarian, journalist, editor, and freelance writer. Stoutenburg has written biographies and numerous other books for children, but she is best known for her poetry. She has won the Commonwealth Club of California Silver Medal and the Lamont Poetry Award from the Academy of American Poets.

Objectives

1. To understand tone
2. To understand the speaker and tone in relation to each other
3. To appreciate concrete words

Support Material

Teaching Portfolio

Teacher Backup, pp. 847–849
Usage and Mechanics Worksheet, p. 850
Vocabulary Check, p. 851
Analyzing Literature Worksheet, *Understanding Speaker and Tone,* p. 852
Language Worksheet, *Appreciating Concrete Words,* p. 853
Selection Test, pp. 854–855
Art Transparency 17, *The Upstairs,* by Charles Sheeler

Tone

The **tone** of any piece of writing is the attitude the writer takes toward the subject and audience. Just as you can hear someone's tone of voice in speech, you can infer it when reading. Tone is present in all writing, and many tones are possible. Usually, the speaker in a poem expresses the tone. The tone of a work may be formal or informal, serious or comic, angry or playful, sad or joyful.

Look For

As you read these two poems, listen for the speaker's tone of voice. How would you read these poems aloud to reflect the tone?

Writing

We all have to make many decisions living in our complex world. Some decisions are personal—affecting only the individual—while others are public—affecting other people. Freewrite about the tools we need to make wise decisions. In what way does education help us? In what way does sharing things with others help us?

Vocabulary

Knowing the following words will help you as you read these poems.

billowing (bil′ ō iŋ) *adj.*: Large; spread-out (p. 604)
smoldering (smōl′ dər iŋ) *adj.*: Here, fiery (p. 604)
lilting (lilt′ iŋ) *adj.*: With a light, graceful rhythm (p. 604)
sheen (shēn) *n.*: Shininess (p. 604)
garnets (gär′ nits) *n.*: Deep red gems (p. 606)
tenure (ten′ yər) *n.*: Time of residence (p. 606)
snickers (snik′ ərz) *v.*: Laughs in a mean way (p. 606)

Literary Focus You may wish to emphasize, especially with **less advanced** students, that tone can be thought of as tone of voice, a more familiar concept. To illustrate how words on a page can convey tone, write on the board *Hello* and *Hey! What's up?*, or some other popular expression of greeting. Ask your class how these two greetings differ in tone. Most should see that the former is neutral or flat in tone, the latter lively and upbeat.

Look For You may want to tell your students that volunteers will be invited to recite these poems in whatever tone of voice they feel is appropriate.

Writing/Prior Knowledge To help students get started, you can give them an example, such as the question whether to take a part-time job after school or participate in an extracurricular activity or spend most of one's after-school time in studying. How do you choose among these possibilities?

Vocabulary These words, as well as others in the poems, are richly connotative. As you discuss the poems, you may wish to have your students discuss the suggestions and associations they see in the words.

Presentation

Motivation/Prior Knowledge You might begin by presenting to your students a hypothetical choice comparable to the one in the poem, for example, a woman must choose between a partner who can offer her wealth, monetary security, and luxuries and a partner who sweeps her off her feet. How does one make such a choice? What is the basis of the decision?

Master Teacher Note The tone of this poem is quite complex, and some students may have difficulty finding adjectives to describe it. With **less advanced** students, it may be prudent to accept as correct any descriptions of the tone that are not fundamentally mistaken. You may need to point out that the speaker uses one tone when she speaks of the first man, another tone when she speaks of the second, and a third—cynical—tone in the last line.

Purpose-Setting Question What does the speaker think of the choice she has made? What do you think of it?

1 **Discussion** The speaker is talking about the lover she could have had. What kind of man is he? What can you infer about the speaker?

2 **Discussion** She is now addressing the lover she chose. How does the tone of voice of these lines differ from that of the first four? What does line 8 suggest about her response to the second man?

3 **Literary Focus** You may wish to point out that these four lines parallel the first four of the preceding stanza. You might also note that the next four lines of stanza 2 parallel the second group of four in stanza 1.

4 **Literary Focus** How does the tone of the poem change here?

The Choice

Dorothy Parker

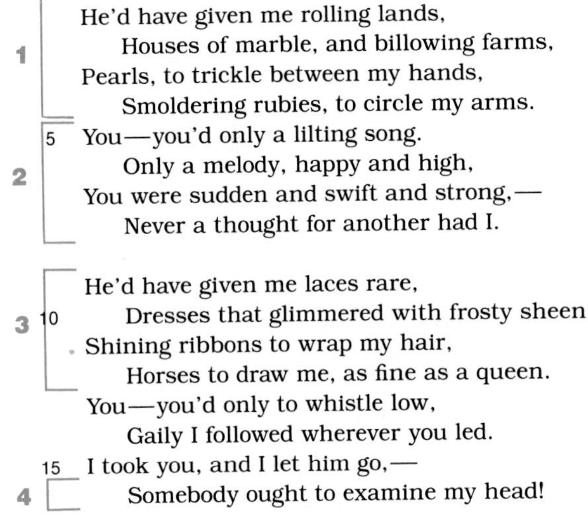

He'd have given me rolling lands,
1 Houses of marble, and billowing farms,
Pearls, to trickle between my hands,
Smoldering rubies, to circle my arms.
You—you'd only a lilting song.
2 Only a melody, happy and high,
You were sudden and swift and strong,—
Never a thought for another had I.

He'd have given me laces rare,
3 Dresses that glimmered with frosty sheen,
Shining ribbons to wrap my hair,
Horses to draw me, as fine as a queen.
You—you'd only to whistle low,
Gaily I followed wherever you led.
I took you, and I let him go,—
4 Somebody ought to examine my head!

Master Teacher Note To compare and contrast humorous poems, you may want to use "Reflections Dental" on page 542 and Two Limericks on page 569.

THINKING ABOUT THE SELECTION

Recalling

1. What did the first man have to offer?
2. How did the second man differ from the first?
3. Whom did the speaker choose?

Interpreting

4. The speaker uses many image-producing words. Compare and contrast the imagery describing the two men.
5. Why is the last line surprising?
6. The last line tells you something about the character of the speaker. Until the last line, has her practical nature or romantic nature been speaking? Which side speaks in the last line?

Applying

7. Do you think decision making should be based on only practical considerations such as money and comfort? Explain your answer.

ANALYZING LITERATURE

Understanding Tone

Tone is the writer's attitude toward the subject. It may be angry, affectionate, comic, serious, sad, and so on.

1. What attitude toward romantic love does the speaker present?
2. How would you describe the tone of the poem?

Challenge Does this poem present strong evidence that practical and material values should play a stronger role than romantic feelings in a person's life?

Reader's Response Have you ever made a choice similar to the one the narrator made? If not, perhaps someone you know has. Describe the circumstances and consequences of the choice.

Closure and Extension

ANSWERS TO THINKING ABOUT THE SELECTION

Recalling

1. The first man could offer material wealth—lands, houses, and jewels.
2. The second man had only great personal appeal.
3. She chose the second man.

Interpreting

4. The imagery used for the first man is that of material wealth. The imagery used for the second is that of music. The two kinds of imagery are in sharp contrast.
5. It is surprising because all that precedes strongly implies that the speaker is deeply in love with the second man.
6. Her romantic nature is expressed in the first fifteen lines, her practical nature in the last line.

Applying

7. Answers will differ. Suggested Response: No, decisions should not always be based only on practical considerations. Moral values, personal inclinations, circumstances, and the distinctive aspects of every situation are some of the considerations that must usually affect a decision.

ANSWERS TO ANALYZING LITERATURE

1. For the first fifteen lines, romantic love is presented as a powerful, irresistible force that dominates the speaker's life. In the last line, the speaker implies that it is silly or stupid.
2. The tone is intensely romantic, until the last line, when it becomes biting, ironic, and humorous.

Presentation

Motivation/Prior Knowledge You might suggest that your students imagine that they have been living in an unspoiled rural place that is now about to be developed. How would they feel about such a change? This poem explores such a situation.

Master Teacher Note Be prepared to clarify, especially with **less advanced** students, the dramatic situation of the poem. The "here" of the poem is a rural place once inhabited by coyotes, grizzlies, and condors—creatures long since gone. The speaker and her family or friends are preparing to leave before the engineers arrive. They will be journeying to a locale—a desert—not yet of interest to the engineers.

Purpose-Setting Question What feelings are conveyed by the speaker's voice?

1 **Discussion** It is uncertain who the "you" is—possibly someone who will accompany the "we" on their journey, or maybe anyone who might have once been a future inhabitant of the place now being left. Ask your students what is about to occur and what has already occurred.

2 **Discussion** Ask your students to summarize what the speaker intends to do in the brief time that remains. The metaphors and similes in this stanza are descriptive in purpose; they emphasize the red markings on the hummingbirds, the brown of the madronas (evergreen trees), the smell of the bay trees, and the sound of the owls. You may wish to help your **less advanced** students see the purpose of these images.

3 **Discussion** Your **more advanced** students can be asked to summarize the main idea of these stanzas: The creatures that once inhabited the place could not stop humans from moving in. **Less advanced** students should be guided by questions and suggestions to grasp the idea. You may wish to analyze the figurative language in the stanza. Like that of the preceding stanza, it is mainly descriptive in intent.

Journey to the Interior

Adrien Stoutenburg

You will not live here,
nor your children,
nor the old, laughing coyotes
1 who once sang in these hills.
We are leaving here soon,
as the grizzly left, and the condor.
(Who has seen such claws or wings?)

There is a moment yet,
before the engineers arrive,
to watch hummingbirds
strung with garnets,
2 madronas brown as the wrists of Indians,
bay trees that smell like green candles,
and listen again for the silence
that made a darkness for owls
with horned mouths
speaking like the E string of a guitar.

The termite with his sad drill
opposed our tenure
but could not defeat us,
nor the bats strumming their teeth
3 within the wall where the telephone snickers—
(they have always been there,

in strange cradles,
a tiny echo of dark wires)—
nor the wood borer[1] on the sill
with his attic dream.

1. **wood borer**: An insect or worm that bores holes in wood.

Our trunks are ready,
a funeral of hinges and locks,
stuffed with snapshots, rose pips,[2] pencils,
4 and cool clothing for the desert—
the compass at hand,
the water bag hanging from the bumper
like a leaky, gray pillow.

2. rose pips: Pieces of roots with which to start new rose bushes.

THINKING ABOUT THE SELECTION

Recalling

1. What once sang in the hills? What animals have departed?
2. Who will soon arrive?
3. What obstacles had the people overcome?

Interpreting

4. Why are the people leaving? What will be lost once the engineers arrive?
5. What obstacle are the people unable to overcome?
6. What choice has been made?
7. Explain the title of the poem.

Applying

8. What other choices can people in a similar situation make?

ANALYZING LITERATURE

Understanding Speaker and Tone

The **speaker** is the voice the poet has chosen to present the poem. The **tone** of the poem expresses the poet's attitude or point of view toward the subject.

1. What can you tell about what the speaker likes from the first two stanzas?
2. What do stanzas 3 and 4 tell you about the speaker?
3. What can you tell about the speaker from the things that are packed in the trunks?
4. What descriptive words in the last stanza help set the tone of the poem?

UNDERSTANDING LANGUAGE

Appreciating Concrete Words

Concrete words are words that name or describe things that we can perceive through our senses. Many concrete words are nouns: *stone, whisper, mist, garlic, shadow.* Since concrete words are specific, immediate, and precise, writers tend to use them in description. For example, Adrien Stoutenburg writes of "bay trees that smell like green candles." The concrete words *bay trees* and *green candles* help make the description specific and sharp. They evoke a precise picture that we can envision clearly.

Find three more concrete words in the poem. First define each one. Then tell how each strengthens the overall imagery of the poem.

4 **Discussion** Ask the students What is now about to happen? Discuss the striking metaphor in line 30. Help students to see that packing and closing the trunks is like a funeral—a sad, solemn farewell to a portion of life that has died.

Challenge Ask students to find lines and passages where they get an especially clear sense of the speaker's tone of voice. Have them describe the tone. You might also ask that they read the lines and passages aloud as they feel they should be read.

Master Teacher Note The place in which one lives can arouse strong feelings. Place Art Transparency 17, *The Upstairs* by Charles Sheeler from the Teaching Portfolio, on the overhead projector. Ask students to describe what feeling the painting conveys. What are other examples of literature involving one's home?

In "Journey to the Interior," the speaker is leaving the home he loves.

Closure and Extension

ANSWERS TO THINKING ABOUT THE SELECTION

Recalling

1. Coyotes once sang there. Grizzlies and condors, and probably the coyotes as well, have departed.
2. Engineers will arrive.
3. The people overcame the problems caused by termites, bats, and wood borers.

Interpreting

4. The people are leaving because engineers, or possibly industrial operations, are arriving. The present ecology will be ruined.
5. The people are unable to overcome development and the changes it will bring.
6. The people have chosen to move to a desert in the interior of the land.
7. Answers will differ. Suggested Response: The people are journeying to a desert in the interior of the land, retreating from engineers and developers who destroy the natural surroundings.

Applying

8. Answers will differ. Suggested Response: People can choose to take legal or political action against those who intend to develop unspoiled land.

ANSWERS TO ANALYZING LITERATURE

1. You can tell that the speaker likes nature and its creatures.
2. They suggest that the speaker was determined to establish a life there in spite of difficulties.
3. The speaker has been attached to the place (snapshots), wishes to take part of it with her (rose pips), may be a writer (pencils), and is prepared to live in the outdoors.
4. The word *funeral* and the simile "like a leaky, gray pillow" help establish the sad tone.

ANSWERS TO UNDERSTANDING LANGUAGE

Concrete words include *coyotes, grizzly, condor, claws, wings, hummingbirds, garnets, owls, E string, termite, drill, bats, teeth, wood borer, hinges, locks, compass, water bag, bumper, and pillow.* Answers will differ as to how such words strengthen the overall imagery. However, they all evoke a picture of the ecology of the place or of the presence of the people who are about to depart.

Focus

More About the Author David Wagoner's themes include survival, anger at those who destroy nature, and delight in the oddities of people. The tone of his poetry is sometimes lighthearted and sometimes serious, but rarely solemn. "Staying Alive" is one of several mock instruction manuals he has written. It may be interpreted both literally, as advice for anyone lost in the woods, and figuratively, as advice for anyone anywhere who wants to stay alive. You might invite students to speculate aloud about the idea of a poem in the form of a manual of instructions. What might such a poem be like? Do they find the idea of a poem in such a form appealing or not?

Literary Focus Figurative language will seem a less intimidating topic if you point out that people use figurative language in ordinary speech quite frequently. "It's raining cats and dogs," "This coffee is like mud," "The test was a breeze" are just a few figurative expressions which people use every day. Invite your class to give their own examples of figurative language. To clarify their grasp of the distinction between the literal and the figurative, have them restate the figurative expressions in literal terms.

Look For Since understanding poetry on the literal level is often challenging enough for younger students, encourage yours to seek a clear understanding of Wagoner's poem on this level first. Then they can consider the figurative level.

Writing/Prior Knowledge Help students get started by offering a few examples of difficult situations—a building in flames, an earthquake, a tornado or other violent storm, becoming lost at sea in a small boat, or some other situation about which your class can brainstorm.

GUIDE FOR READING

Staying Alive

David Wagoner (1926–) was born in Massillon, Ohio. He attended Pennsylvania State University and Indiana University and currently teaches English at the University of Washington in Seattle. He is respected not only as a poet, but also as a novelist. Collections of his verse include *Riverbed* (1972), *Sleeping in the Woods* (1974), and *Travelling Light* (1976). "Staying Alive," his most famous poem, has been called "one of the best American poems since World War II."

Figurative and Literal Language

Figurative language is language that appeals to the imagination. **Literal language,** on the other hand, is language that is to be interpreted in accordance with actual or strict meaning of the words.

We might, for example, describe an athlete in literal terms: "He ran with great speed and agility, eluding would-be tacklers on all sides." Or we might make the description figurative: "He ran like a jagged wind cutting through a field of limp, high grass." Both sentences describe the same thing. Yet the second description —the figurative one—is an image that appeals to our imagination.

Poems should be read both literally and figuratively. That is, first understand a poem's literal meaning. Then look for any additional meaning. Literally, "Staying Alive" is about how to survive in the woods. However, the poem contains helpful advice for all of us.

Look For

As you read "Staying Alive," first look for what the poem says literally about survival in the woods. What other meaning does the poem have? How might the instructions be applied to life in general?

Writing

Working with a group of your classmates, list rules for "staying alive" in a life-threatening situation.

Vocabulary

Knowing the following words will help you as you read "Staying Alive."

nuzzling (nuz′ liŋ) *v.*: Rubbing with the nose (p. 610)

uncanny (un kan′ ē) *adj.*: Strange (p. 610)

hoarse (hôrs) *adj.*: Sounding harsh (p. 610)

Vocabulary Since the vocabulary of "Staying Alive" presents few difficulties, the poem offers opportunities to pause and discuss the connotations of Wagoner's well-chosen words.

Objectives

1 To understand figurative language
2 To write an interpretation of a poem

Support Material

Teaching Portfolio

Teacher Backup, pp. 857–859
Usage and Mechanics Worksheet, p. 860
Vocabulary Check, p. 861
Analyzing Literature Worksheet, *Understanding Literature Worksheet,* p. 862
Language Worksheet, *Finding Figurative Language,* p. 863
Selection Test, pp. 864–865

Staying Alive

David Wagoner

Staying alive in the woods is a matter of calming down
At first and deciding whether to wait for rescue,
Trusting to others,
Or simply to start walking and walking in one direction
Till you come out—or something happens to stop you.
By far the safer choice
Is to settle down where you are, and try to make a living
Off the land, camping near water, away from shadows.
Eat no white berries;
1 Spit out all bitterness. Shooting at anything
Means hiking further and further every day
To hunt survivors;
It may be best to learn what you have to learn without a gun,
Not killing but watching birds and animals go
In and out of shelter
At will. Following their example, build for a whole season:
Facing across the wind in your lean-to,[1]
You may feel wilder,
But nothing, not even you, will have to stay in hiding.
If you have no matches, a stick and a fire-bow[2]
Will keep you warmer,
Or the crystal[3] of your watch, filled with water, held up to the sun
Will do the same in time. In case of snow
Drifting toward winter,
Don't try to stay awake through the night, afraid of freezing—

---

1. lean-to (lēn' too') *n.*: A rough shelter with a sloping roof.
2. stick and a fire-bow: A way of starting a fire in which the string of the bow is wrapped around a stick and the bow is pulled back and forth rapidly, twirling the stick and thus creating sparks.
3. crystal (kris' t'l) *n.*: The transparent covering over the face of a watch.

Presentation

Motivation/Prior Knowledge The idea of staying alive—of maintaining one's existence—is not an idea that most people think about constantly. Nevertheless, there are times when almost everyone feels the need to think about self-protection against life's dangers. Ask your students to imagine themselves on their own in a hostile environment—a jungle, a mountain slope, or the like—with no one to offer help. What basic rules for survival would they follow?

Master Teacher Note Explain that "Staying Alive" is literally about survival when lost in the woods, but that by the end of the poem a careful reader should see that much of the speaker's advice can be modified or adapted to other situations or to life in general. This secondary level of meaning is the figurative level.

Thematic Idea Other selections that deal with the theme of courage in the face of adversity are "The Captain and His Horse" on page 47 and *The Pearl* on page 695.

Purpose-Setting Question What rules or principles for survival in the woods could you adapt to your own life?

1 **Discussion** Suggest that your students list at least several of the items of advice presented in these nineteen lines. Ask your **less advanced** students to point out passages that seem unclear to them. Then discuss these passages so that readers can paraphrase them.

2 Clarification The watch crystal filled with water could serve as a magnifying glass with which to start a fire. Lines 23-28 mean that people have a deep-rooted instinct that prevents them from falling asleep in bitter cold and thus freezing to death. By questioning and discussion, lead your students to understand the meaning of these passages. Again, have them list, in their own words, the suggestions and advice presented here.

3 Discussion These twenty lines contain half a dozen pieces of advice. What are they? What does the speaker mean by "Think of yourself by time and not by distance"? What does he mean by "Remember the stars/And moss when your mind runs into circles"?

4 Discussion Ask students to paraphrase these lines so that they can answer the question "What does the speaker mean by staying alive"?

The bottom of your mind knows all about zero;
2 It will turn you over
And shake you till you waken. If you have trouble sleeping
Even in the best of weather, jumping to follow
With eyes strained to their corners
The unidentifiable noises of the night and feeling
Bears and packs of wolves nuzzling your elbow,
Remember the trappers
Who treated them indifferently and were left alone.
If you hurt yourself, no one will comfort you
Or take your temperature,
So stumbling, wading, and climbing are as dangerous as flying.
But if you decide, at last, you must break through
In spite of all danger,
Think of yourself by time and not by distance, counting
Wherever you're going by how long it takes you;
No other measure
Will bring you safe to nightfall. Follow no streams: they run
Under the ground or fall into wilder country.
3 Remember the stars
And moss when your mind runs into circles. If it should rain
Or the fog should roll the horizon[4] in around you,
Hold still for hours
Or days if you must, or weeks, for seeing is believing
In the wilderness. And if you find a pathway,
Wheel-rut, or fence-wire,
Retrace it left or right: someone knew where he was going
Once upon a time, and you can follow
Hopefully, somewhere,
Just in case. There may even come, on some uncanny evening,
A time when you're warm and dry, well fed, not thirsty,
Uninjured, without fear,
4 When nothing, either good or bad, is happening.
This is called staying alive. It's temporary.
What occurs after
Is doubtful. You must always be ready for something to come bursting
Through the far edge of a clearing, running toward you,
Grinning from ear to ear
And hoarse with welcome. Or something crossing and hovering

4. horizon (hə rī′ z'n) *n.*: The line where the sky seems to meet the earth.

Overhead, as light as air, like a break in the sky,
Wondering what you are.
Here you are face to face with the problem of recognition.
Having no time to make smoke, too much to say,
You should have a mirror
With a tiny hole in the back for better aiming, for reflecting
Whatever disaster you can think of, to show
The way you suffer.
These body signals have universal meaning: If you are lying
Flat on your back with arms outstretched behind you,
5 You say you require
Emergency treatment; if you are standing erect and holding
Arms horizontal, you mean you are not ready;
If you hold them over
Your head, you want to be picked up. Three of anything
Is a sign of distress. Afterward if you see
No ropes, no ladders,
No maps or messages falling, no searchlights or trails blazing,
Then, chances are, you should be prepared to burrow
Deep for a deep winter.

5 Discussion The speaker here describes the possibility of rescue by an airplane. What should the person in distress do to attract the potential rescuer? What signals should the person know? Paraphrase the last two lines. What do they imply about the fate of the person who will not be rescued by plane?

Challenge Tell your class that though they may never be lost in the woods they may nevertheless someday find themselves in some life-threatening situation. Moreover, dangers and hazards—even if not life-threatening—are always present in life. What generally useful advice for staying alive in ordinary circumstances does this poem present? Encourage your class to list six common-sense rules for living that come to mind as a result of reading and discussing the poem.

Reader's Response How can "Staying Alive" apply to situations where people are not literally "in the woods"?

THINKING ABOUT THE SELECTION

Recalling

1. What situation does the poet imagine?
2. What decision must you make in this situation?
3. What, according to the poet, is the safest choice?
4. How can a watch crystal filled with water take the place of matches?
5. Why is it a good idea to keep track of time rather than distance when traveling?

Interpreting

6. How does the poet define "staying alive"?
7. What instructions for living are contained in lines 16, 26, and 34?
8. How might the poet's advice about "Shooting at anything" apply to life generally?
9. To stay alive means to *survive*. Given the poet's definition of "staying alive," what would you say is his view of life?

Applying

10. What is the difference between surviving and living? Is it enough to merely survive? Explain your answer.

ANALYZING LITERATURE

Understanding Figurative Language

To begin to understand any poem, you must try to comprehend its literal meaning first. For example, David Wagoner writes that in the woods, one should "Eat no white berries;/Spit out all bitterness." He means this literally: white berries are usually poisonous, as are many bitter-tasting things. Once you have understood this literal content, think further about the possible figurative meaning of these lines. What else might the poet mean by the suggestion that one ought to "spit out all bitterness"? Not only in the woods, but in life generally, one should avoid bitterness.

1. Give three examples of the poet's advice on survival in the woods.
2. How might any single piece of advice be extended to life in general?
3. How do you interpret lines 46 through 50?
4. How do you interpret the last six lines?
5. The first line begins "Staying alive in the woods . . .," yet the title is simply, "Staying Alive." What does this difference suggest about the true subject of this poem?

THINKING AND WRITING

Writing an Interpretation of a Poem

Write a simple outline of the literal content of this poem. Then jot down a few of the poem's suggestions for how to live life in general. Using your notes as a guide, write an essay in which you interpret the poem as completely as you can. Include specific references to the poem in your writing. Revise your essay to make sure you have organized your information logically. Proofread your essay and share it with your classmates.

Closure and Extension

ANSWERS TO THINKING ABOUT THE SELECTION

Recalling

1. He imagines the situation of a person's being lost in the woods.
2. You must decide whether to stay where you are and wait to be rescued or to start walking until you find a way out.
3. The safer choice is to stay where you are and prepare for staying alive there.
4. It can be used like a magnifying glass to start a fire.
5. Answers will differ. Suggested Response: Physical distance and direction may be deceiving, whereas time can be estimated by the sun, so that you can know when to settle down and prepare for the night.

Interpreting

6. "Staying alive" is defined as calming down and making the best of any possibly dangerous or threatening situation.
7. Line 16 advises one to prepare a shelter for at least a whole season, such as winter. Line 26 advises not to worry about freezing to death during sleep. Line 34 advises one not to worry about, and to ignore, fearful animals.
8. The general advice here is not to approach life with aggressive hostility, but rather to observe and learn.
9. The poet seems to view life not as offering happiness but rather as presenting the challenge of just surviving by means of skill and resourcefulness.

Applying

10. Answers will differ. Suggested Response: Surviving means maintaining physical existence, or life as a biological process. To most, living means not just surviving but moreover enjoying life in a way appropriate to human beings. Most students will rightly feel that survival is not enough—people deserve and expect more.

ANSWERS TO ANALYZING LITERATURE

1. The following are just some of the suggestions the poet gives: stay where you are and learn to live off the land; do not eat white berries or anything bitter; do not use a gun; build a shelter for a whole season; treat potentially fierce animals indifferently; measure travel by time, not distance; do not follow streams; in rain or fog, stay where you are.
2. Answers will differ. Suggested Response: The advice about being indifferent to fierce animals can be extended to life in general by saying that one should not allow oneself to be irrationally fearful of the dangerous people in the world; try to ignore them.
3. Lines 46–50 mean that one should not proceed in any endeavor if a clear purpose and direction cannot be perceived.
4. These lines may be interpreted to mean that in times of trouble you may get no help from others and therefore must prepare to survive on your own for a long and difficult time.
5. The true subject of the poem is survival in general.

THINKING AND WRITING

For help with this assignment, students can refer to Lesson 13, "Writing About a Poem," in the Handbook of Writing About Literature.

PUTTING IT TOGETHER

Poetry

The poet A. E. Housman has written: "I could no more define poetry than a terrier can define a rat." Although like Housman you may not be able to define poetry, you probably can recognize a poem when you read one. You can fully appreciate it by putting all its elements together.

Types of Poetry

The most common **types of poetry** are the narrative poem and the lyric poem. A narrative poem tells a story, while a lyric poem expresses strong personal feelings about a subject.

Figurative Language

Figurative language consists of words used beyond their usual dictionary meaning. The words take on more imaginative implications. Three common types of figurative language are simile, metaphor, and personification. A **simile** is a figurative comparison between two basically unlike items. It uses the word *like* or *as* to make the comparison. A **metaphor** is a figurative comparison that does not use the word *like* or *as*. **Personification** means giving human qualities to nonhuman objects.

Imagery

Imagery refers to the use of language to create vivid word pictures. Usually these words have a sensory appeal.

Sound

Poetry has a musical quality created by the **sound** of the words, the use of rhythm and rhyme, and the use of repetition and alliteration. Onomatopoeia, or the use of words to imitate sounds, also helps create this musical effect.

Theme

Most poems provide an insight into life. As you read, ask yourself what **theme** the poem reveals.

On the following pages is a poem with annotations in the side column showing the elements of poetry that an active reader might note while reading.

Focus

Putting It Together This lesson will help students to review what they have learned about poetry. Then they may test their knowledge in reading Mark Van Doren's poem "The Story-Teller."

Poetry Review with students the idea that poetry is language at its most concentrated and intense. Tell students that the intensity of a poem requires a method of reading different from that they would use for a newspaper article or even a short story. To fully enjoy a poem, they may want to read it several times, both quietly and aloud.

Types of Poetry You might want to tell students that a lyric poem often suggests a story even though it is an expression of the poet's thoughts and emotions. In reading such a poem, for instance, they might want to consider the events that led the poet to write it.

Figurative Language Point out to students that simile and metaphor both make use of surprise. By comparing a woman to a silken tent or fog to a cat, a poet can startle readers into seeing the world with fresh eyes.

Imagery Remind students that imagery can appeal to other senses—hearing, touch, taste, and smell—as well as sight. Poets use imagery so that a reader can experience what they are describing.

Sound Suggest to students that poets use repetition, alliteration, and onomatopoeia to create sound patterns that are pleasing in themselves and to reinforce the meaning of the poem.

Theme Consider telling students that the theme of the poem is not always stated directly. A reader must sometimes infer the poet's insight into life from the poem as a whole, taking into account the imagery, figurative language, and sound devices.

Objectives

1 To appreciate a poem by putting the elements of it together
2 To understand rhyme
3 To define poetry
4 To find antonyms in a poem
5 To retell a story

Support Material

Teaching Portfolio

Teacher Backup, pp. 867–869
Usage and Mechanics Worksheet, p. 872
Analyzing Literature Worksheet, *Understanding Rhyme,* p. 873
Critical Thinking and Reading Worksheet, *Defining Poetry,* p. 874
Selection Test, pp. 875–876
Art Transparency 18, *The Fantasy World,* by Alain Thomas

MODEL

GREEN VIOLINIST, 1923–24
Marc Chagall
Solomon R. Guggenheim Museum

The Story-Teller

Mark Van Doren

Title: The title indicates that the poem will be about a storyteller. What special insight about a storyteller will the poem provide?

He talked, and as he talked
Wallpaper came alive;
Suddenly ghosts walked,
And four doors were five;

Figurative Language: The poet is using language figuratively here. Certainly wallpaper doesn't come alive and ghosts don't walk. What does the use of figurative language indicate about the magic of the storyteller?

Presentation

Humanities Note

Fine Art, *Green Violinist*, 1923–24, by Marc Chagall. Mark Chagall (1897–1985) was born in Russia. He studied painting at the Pen Academy in his native town of Vitebsk, at the Imperial School of Fine Art in St. Petersburg, and with the famous stage designer, Leon Bakst. In France, where he was to live for most of his life, he was exposed to all of the new trends in modern art. Chagall studied each but developed his own unique style that remains unclassifiable.

Green Violinist was painted in France in the years 1923–24. Haunted by memories of his life in Russia, Chagall painted images of this small village and its people, over and over. The dreamlike image of a violinist appears in many of his paintings. This painting appeals directly to the viewers' emotions with its bright colors and nostalgic vision.

You might use the following for discussion.

1. Describe the details of this painting.
2. What qualities of "The Story-Teller" are evident in *The Green Violinist?*

Motivation/Prior Knowledge Consider asking students to recall a time when they heard a well-told story. Have them briefly describe the occasion and explain why the storyteller was effective. Then tell them that the poem they will read is about the art of storytelling.

Purpose-Setting Question How does the poet use surprise to communicate his theme?

Master Teacher Note Look at Art Transparency 18, *The Fantasy World* by Alain Thomas, in the Teaching Portfolio. Ask students what aspects of this painting seem fantastic or other worldly. What are other examples of fantasy or magic in literature or the movies?

"The Story-Teller" describes the magical effects of a story well told.

Thematic Idea You might want to use the essay "Talking About Writing," page 485, with this selection. In this piece, Ursula K. Le Guin tells how she discovers within herself the ideas for her tales of fantasy and science fiction.

Clarification When sailboats tack, they travel against the wind in a zigzag pattern. This maneuver is usually associated with brisk movements. Lines 7–8 therefore combine opposites, just as line 5 does.

Enrichment The images in lines 9–12 are surreal, meaning that they show ordinary objects in unusual combinations. Trains, of course, do not ordinarily climb trees or drip like honey. Surreal images, however, can make the world seem strange and magical.

Putting it Together For further practice with these elements, use the selection in the Teaching Portfolio, "The Bad Dream," pages 870–871, which students can annotate themselves. Encourage students to continue to use this strategy as they read other poetry selections.

Master Teacher Note You might want to point out to students that this poem about storytelling does not tell a story itself. Instead, it suggests the magic of the storyteller's art through a series of images. Ask students to consider why the poet chose this strategy rather than describing an actual storytelling session.

More About the Author The poet **Mark Van Doren** taught literature at Columbia University from 1920 to 1959. Ask students why they think many poets today teach at universities.

Reader's Response How can a person telling a story or a person speaking in general bring material alive? Do you know someone who has such a talent?

Sound: Notice the regular pattern of rhyme. How does this regular pattern fit the subject matter?

Calendars ran backward,
And maps had mouths;
Ships went tackward[1]
In a great drowse;[2]

Imagery: What effect is created by the odd images? To what senses do these images appeal?

Trains climbed trees,
And soon dripped down
Like honey of bees
On the cold brick town.

Theme: The poem provides an important insight into the magic of storytelling. What is this insight?

He had wakened a worm
In the world's brain,
And nothing stood firm
Until day again.

---

1. **tackward** (tak′ wərd) *adv.*: Against the wind.
2. **drowse** (drouz) *n.*: Sluggishness; doze.

Mark Van Doren (1894–1972) was a Pulitzer Prize-winning poet. Among his collections of poetry are *Collected Works* and *Good Morning: Last Poems by Mark Van Doren.* An English professor, Van Doren also wrote critical studies of major writers.

THINKING ABOUT THE SELECTION

Recalling

1. Find seven magical things that the storyteller is able to accomplish.
2. According to the last line, when do things return to normal?

Interpreting

3. What is the *worm* referred to in line 13? What is the *world's brain* in line 14?
4. Interpret lines 15–16.
5. Express the theme of this poem.

Applying

6. Why do you think that people like stories? Use details from life to support your answer.

ANALYZING LITERATURE

Understanding Rhyme

Rhyme is created by words sounding alike. In a poem, rhyme often occurs at the end of lines. The rhyme pattern of a poem helps give it a musical quality.

1. Look at the first stanza. Which words at the end of lines rhyme?
2. Look at the second stanza. Which words at the end of lines rhyme?
3. What conclusion do you draw about the rhyme pattern of this poem?

CRITICAL THINKING AND READING

Defining Poetry

Defining means giving the distinguishing characteristics of something. Read each definition of poetry below. Explain which one you think best captures the essential meaning of a poem.

1. Samuel Johnson: "Poetry is the art of uniting pleasure with truth."
2. Edgar Allan Poe: "Poetry is the rhythmical creation of beauty in words."
3. Gwyn Thomas: "Poetry is trouble dunked in tears."

UNDERSTANDING LANGUAGE

Finding Antonyms

An **antonym** is a word that means the opposite or nearly the opposite of another word. For example, the words *peaceful* and *warlike* are antonyms, as are the words *quiet* and *noise*. For each of the following words, find its antonym in the poem.

1. forward
2. listened
3. dead
4. slowly

THINKING AND WRITING

Retelling a Story

Think about the best story you have ever heard. What made this story come alive for you. Brainstorm, listing all the qualities that made this story special. Then retell the story in your own words. When you revise make sure you have included the features that made this story magical for you. Proofread your story and share it with your classmates.

Closure and Extension

ANSWERS TO THINKING ABOUT THE SELECTION

Recalling

1. The story-teller accomplishes the following magic things—wallpaper comes alive; ghosts walk; four doors turn into five; calendars go backward; maps have mouths; ships sail against the wind very lazily (this maneuver is usually brisk); trains climb trees and drip down like honey.
2. Things return to normal at dawn.

Interpreting

3. Answers will differ. Suggested Response: The "worm" might stand for the story-teller's ability to undermine the ordinary world and make it seem strange and mysterious. The "world's brain" might be either the everyday world or our usual ideas about it.
4. Answers will differ. Suggested Response: The story-teller made the world seem like a strange place where anything could happen. Not until the next day did the world appear normal again.
5. Answers will differ. Suggested Response: A well-told story can make the world seem surprising, miraculous, and alive with possibilities.

Applying

6. Answers will differ. Suggested Response: People like the excitement, glamor, and romance of stories. Listening to ghost stories around a campfire, people can experience an enjoyable shiver of fear.

Challenge What makes a person a good story-teller?

ANALYZING LITERATURE

1. The first stanza contains the following end rhymes: talked-walked, alive-five.
2. The second stanza contains the following end rhymes: backward-tackward, mouths-drowse (an approximate rhyme).
3. Each stanza has the rhyme scheme *abab.*

CRITICAL THINKING AND READING

Answers will differ. Suggested response: Most students will probably choose #1 or #2, especially since "The Story-Teller" does not seem at all like "trouble dunked in tears." Students who remember that "The Story-Teller" has a theme will probably choose #1, because it makes allowance for "truth" in a poem. No matter which definition they select, students should be able to justify their choice.

UNDERSTANDING LANGUAGE

1. forward: backward
2. listened: talked
3. dead: alive
4. slowly: suddenly

THINKING AND WRITING
Publishing Student Writing

You may want to publish and distribute a class magazine containing all the stories.

Focus on Reading

After discussing inferences, give the students these statements and ask them to make some valid inferences.

1. Joanne works hard at her job in a fast-food restaurant after school every day.
   (Valid inference: Joanne probably earns a fair amount of money.)
2. Jean attends the School of American Ballet.
   (Valid inference: She must be a good dancer.)
3. Carl got a 62 in a math test.
   (Valid inference: If he does not improve, he might not pass the course.)

Ask the students who, besides readers of literature, might make inferences.

FOCUS ON READING

Making Inferences

Reading actively is essential to enjoy and understand poetry because most poems are made up of only a few words. Poets often imply or suggest things rather than state them outright. You may have to make inferences, or intelligent guesses, to understand what a poet is saying in a poem. An **inference** is a conclusion based on evidence such as facts or clues provided by the author. It often requires using the reader's background knowledge and experience. To arrive at sound inferences, you must carefully weigh both types of evidence to determine if they support the inference that is being made. If the evidence does not support the inference, then you should discard it and make a different inference.

Character

Making inferences can help you understand the characters. Reread "O Captain! My Captain!" on page 534. Who is the Captain referred to in the poem? If you had read this poem when Walt Whitman wrote it, you would immediately know that the Captain was Abraham Lincoln. Since you cannot do that, you will have to find out when the poet wrote the poem and use your background knowledge to determine that Lincoln had just been assassinated. Now you have sufficient evidence to prove that Lincoln is the Captain.

What kind of man is this Captain, and what is the poet's attitude toward him? Like a detective, you need to search for clues. The poet calls him "my Captain" and "dear father," which indicates that the poet greatly respects and loves him. The reference to the poet's "mournful tread" and the terrible aching of his heart reinforces the idea that he loves the man. The greatness of the Captain is shown by the exulting eager crowds, the ringing bells and bugle trills, and the fact that the ship reached shore safely. Clearly, the evidence indicates that the Captain is a great, heroic man, loved and respected by the poet.

Plot

Now make inferences to understand the plot. Knowing that the Captain is Lincoln will help you. First you need to know what the ship represents. This is where your background knowledge will help you.

Remember that Lincoln was President during the Civil War, which was a time when the Union was threatened. The Southerners wanted to form their own Confederacy of states and break away from the Union. Therefore, you can figure out that the ship was the Union and the racks it weathered were the assaults from different groups of people and the forces of the war.

Now you need to find out why the voyage is over and why the people exult. Keeping in mind that the ship is the Union, you can see that "the prize we sought" is to keep the Union together. The voyage is over because "the prize . . . is won"—the Union has stayed together. And when you win a prize or succeed in doing something really important, you cheer and celebrate. Keeping the Union together makes the crowds exult and ring bells. Thus you can see that this poem is a tribute to Lincoln. It is telling how the poet and most Americans felt when the Civil War was over and President Lincoln had been shot for defending the Union. Using both evidence from the poem and your background knowledge has enabled you to make inferences that help explain the poem.

Mood

To understand the mood of a poem, you have to make inferences based on the words the poet uses and the way the events are described. The mood of "O Captain! My Captain!" is one of somber rejoicing. The poet rejoices because the Union is saved but mourns because the leader most responsible for saving it is dead.

Activity

Choose one of the narrative poems in this book. Reread it.

1. Make one inference about the main character. Find evidence to back up your inference.
2. Make one inference about the plot. Find evidence to back up your inference.
3. Make one inference about mood. Find evidence to back up your inference.

ANSWERS TO THE ACTIVITY

1. A suggested response might be in "Paul Revere's Ride" p. 509. Revere showed courage and patriotism. Riding past the *Somerset* showed courage. Patriotism is indicated by the second stanza.
2. A suggested response might be that Paul Revere's actions were important to the American patriots' success against the British. Evidence is in the first stanza and the concluding lines (126-130).

The writing assignments on page 620 have students writing creatively, while those on page 621 have them thinking about the poetry and writing critically.

YOU THE WRITER

Guidelines for Evaluating Assignment 1

1. Does the student use first-person and have this character describe himself or herself?
2. Does each line of the poem begin with the words "I am."
3. Are there vivid details?
4. Is the poem free from grammar, usage, and mechanics errors?

Guidelines for Evaluating Assignment 2

1. Has the student written a different ending to a poem?
2. Is the alternate ending in the original poem's realm of possibility?
3. If the original poem had a rhyme and rhythm pattern, did the student stay within it?
4. Is the poem free from grammar, usage, and mechanics errors?

Guidelines for Evaluating Assignment 3

1. Does the poem describe how the character chosen would feel if transported to the present?
2. Does the poem begin with a description of the character?
3. Does the poem describe how the character's courage would help him or her survive in the present?
4. Is the poem free from grammar, usage, and mechanics errors?

YOU THE WRITER

Assignment

1. Imagine that you are one of the characters in one of the poems. Write a poem describing yourself.

Prewriting. Use a cueing technique to generate ideas about your character. Jot down the questions *Who? What? Where? When?* and *Why?* Then answer each of these questions.

Writing. Write the first draft of your poem. Use a first-person speaker and have this character describe himself or herself. Begin each line of your poem with the words "I am."

Revising. Read over your poem. Make sure your speaker has included vivid details.

Assignment

2. Choose one of the poems and write a different ending for it. You can describe a happier or sadder ending, but you must stay within the plot and time frame of the poem.

Prewriting. Brainstorm for a list of possible alternative endings. They must all be in the realm of possibility for the poem. After you have your list, brainstorm for details for each item on your list.

Writing. Write your new ending. If the poem you have chosen has a regular rhyme and rhythm pattern, be sure to stay within this pattern.

Revising. Check to see that your details are consistent with the poem. Add anything else that would strengthen your ending.

Assignment

3. Choose a character from a poem set in an earlier time and place, and place him or her in a modern-day setting. Write a poem describing how the character would feel transported to our technological age. Explore how the character would react to such things as the automobile, space shuttle, and computer.

Prewriting. Freewrite about your character transported to the present time. Explore any aspect of this idea that comes to mind.

Writing. Begin your poem with a description of your character. Go on to develop situations in which to place your character. Then describe his or her feelings and reactions. Describe how the character's courage would enable him or her to meet the challenges of a new age.

Revising. Revise your poem. Be sure your character acts consistently throughout. Check to see that you have included sufficient details. Edit your sentences. Proofread your final draft.

YOU THE CRITIC

Assignment

1. Choose a narrative poem from this unit and evaluate its plot, setting, characters, dialogue, and theme. Explain why the poem is or is not, in your opinion, effective. End your essay with an overall opinion of the poem's literary merit.

Prewriting. Prepare an outline of the poem. Be sure to include plot, setting, characters, dialogue, and theme.

Writing. Using your outline as a guide, write an evaluation of the poem. Discuss plot, setting, characters, dialogue, and theme. Finish with your general review of the poem's worth. Base your opinion on how effectively each of the elements was handled.

Revising. Check to see that you have evaluated the poem on the five basic elements. Be sure your opinion is supported by evidence from the poem itself. Add any information that you think will strengthen your opinion.

Assignment

2. The growth of character is a common literary theme. Choose one poem and show how the main character develops. Describe what the character goes through. Decide if the character has changed and, if so, in what way.

Prewriting. Choose a character from a poem. Freewrite, describing the character at the beginning of the poem and at the end.

Writing. Begin your essay by identifying and describing the character. Show how the character developed in the course of the poem. Organize your thoughts in an order-of-importance pattern. Discuss how the character has changed.

Revising. Be sure you have made your points clearly. If you feel the character has changed, verify your evidence to support your opinion.

Assignment

3. Choose two poems and compare and contrast the settings. In what ways are the settings alike and in what ways are they different?

Prewriting. Freewrite about the settings of the poems. Let your mind roam freely through the settings, exploring any detail that comes to mind.

Writing. Write the first draft of an essay. Begin by describing each setting in detail. Go on to describe how the two settings you have chosen are alike or how they are different from each other. Use evidence from the poems themselves to support your thesis.

Revising. Revise your first draft. Be sure you have consistently compared or contrasted the settings. Check the accuracy of your details.

YOU THE CRITIC
Guidelines for Evaluating Assignment 1

1. Does the evaluation explain why the poem is effective?
2. Does the evaluation discuss the five basic elements: plot, setting, characters, dialogue, theme?
3. Are the opinions supported by evidence from the poem?
4. Does the evaluation conclude with a general review of the poem's worth?
5. Is the evaluation free from grammar, usage, and mechanics errors?

Guidelines for Evaluating Assignment 2

1. Does the essay begin by identifying and describing the character?
2. Does the essay show how the character developed in the poem?
3. Does the essay conclude with a discussion, supported by evidence, of how the character changed?
4. Is the essay organized in an order-of-importance pattern?
5. Is the essay free from grammar, usage, and mechanics errors?

Guidelines for Evaluating Assignment 3

1. Does the comparison begin by describing each setting in detail?
2. Does the comparison explain how the two settings are alike and how they are different from each other?
3. Does the student use evidence from the poems to support his or her thesis?
4. Is the essay free from grammar, usage, and mechanics errors?

WOODCUTTER ON A ROCK, 1891
Winslow Homer
Private Collection

AMERICAN MYTHS, LEGENDS, AND FOLKTALES

Myths, legends, and folktales are similar types of stories. They originated long ago when stories were all told orally, long before writing was invented. Their authors are unknown. Myths often explain early people's ideas about nature. Myths involve stories about gods, goddesses, and other supernatural beings, as well as the adventures of great heroes and heroines who serve as models for the way people in a particular culture are expected to behave. Legends differ from myths because they often involve heroes and heroines who may actually have existed. Folktales present the customs and beliefs of a culture but do not generally involve gods and goddesses. All cultures have their own myths, legends, and folktales. The ones in this unit are American. Some were told in early Native American cultures, while others are more recent.

Humanities Note

Fine art, *Woodcutter on a Rock,* by Winslow Homer. The painter and illustrator Winslow Homer (1836–1910) is one of America's best known artists. Influenced at a young age by his mother, a talented watercolor painter, Homer wanted to become an artist. Without any formal training, he worked as an illustrator, an occupation he pursued for most of his life. Success in this field enabled him to paint. He is known today for the marine, genre, and landscape paintings, which he produced in great number during his lifetime.

Woodcutter on a Rock, c. 1891, is a watercolor painted in the Adirondack region of New York State. Homer often spent time in this area camping, fishing, and hunting. His years as an illustrator gave him the keen sense of observation and quick sketching ability necessary to handle the difficult medium of watercolor. During the end of the nineteenth century, Homer became increasingly interested in the effects of atmosphere. The attention he has given to the sky in this painting is an example of his exploration in this area. The sky provides a dramatic backdrop for the figure of the woodsman in the foreground. The figure seems to represent American ruggedness and a connection with the land.

623

Master Teacher Note Elicit from students some myths, legends, or folktales that they have known since childhood. Some of the stories that students may tell may be regional or ethnic in origin and therefore unknown to other students. However, such responses would provide you with an excellent opportunity to reinforce the definition of folklore and show how different peoples made up different types of stories to suit their own purposes. If students do know stories from their own regional or ethnic backgrounds, ask them to explain how the stories may have been used or why they were told in the first place. Have students discuss what problem or mystery might have been explained in the story.

Next, have students discuss why people in the northeast may never have heard a Zuñi Indian legend, for example. Or, have them discuss why people in a landlocked state may never have heard the story told in *The Foggy Stew.* Lead students to understand that myths, legends, and folktales arose for a reason. Be sure they realize that these stories were not created by these writers in recent times but were recorded as stories handed down orally for many years.

READING ACTIVELY

American Myths, Legends, and Folktales

Background

Myths, legends, and folktales are three kinds of folklore. Folklore records the customs, traditions, and beliefs of a people and also consists of arts and crafts, dances, games, fairy tales, nursery rhymes; proverbs, riddles, songs, and superstitions. American folklore is as old as the country itself. Like its European counterpart, American folklore has been passed down orally from generation to generation. People have always told stories to entertain, to explain the mysterious, and to teach lessons or prove points. The stories recorded here are stories that were first heard around campfires or first told to pass the time on long winter nights or on wagons heading west.

Although the divisions are often blurred, there are distinct characteristics that make myths, legends, and folktales different from one another. Myths often explain how the world and its phenomena were created. Legends are rooted in historical events, even though they often have their heroes perform superhuman deeds. They are set in real and familiar environments and in relatively recent times. Folktales are fictional stories about animals or people that have been passed down from generation to generation orally. Often, they are not set in any particular time or place, and they often teach a lesson through the actions of the characters.

Reading Strategy

You may find colloquial language and clichés in American myths, legends, and folktales difficult to understand. Remember that in each tale, the flavor of the people who first told the story comes through. Identify the source of the story or the region of the country from which it comes. It will help you to understand the action and characters if you know whether it's an American Indian tale, a southern story, or a western story, for example. Think about why the story was probably first told.

Finally, interact with the literature by using the active reading strategies: question, predict, clarify, summarize, and pull together. The strategy that you may find particularly useful here is the questioning strategy. Ask yourself what the purpose of the story was when it was first told. Ask yourself why events are so exaggerated and why the characters have superhuman powers over nature and the elements. Using this strategy when you read will give you deeper insight into myths, legends, and folktales.

Themes

You will encounter the following themes.

- courage and bravery
- power over nature
- quick thinking to solve a problem
- superhuman strength and achievements
- exaggerated accomplishments

Characters

Become familiar with the following folk characters.

Indian boy—the boy who brought fire to his people

Indian girl—a maiden who hunts rabbits and encounters supernatural beings

Paul Bunyan—a lumberjack who could change the face of the earth and control the elements

Pecos Bill—a powerful cowboy who could control animals and nature and who created some of the most famous natural phenomena in the West

John Henry—a steel-driving man who could dig a tunnel faster than a steam drill

Stormalong—an ingenious sailor who blew his sailing ship out of the fog and doldrums into open water and safety

Johnny Appleseed—a frontiersman who traveled the Midwest planting apple trees

Davy Crockett—a real-life frontiersman and politician who became a folk hero

Reading Actively You may want to have students distinguish between myths, legends, and folktales in their own words. What makes them different from one another? What makes each unique? You might point out that folklore includes the arts and crafts, dances, traditions, games, proverbs, riddles, songs, or superstitions that people may have learned from their grandparents or great-grandparents.

Reading Strategy Students may want to review the active reading strategies before beginning American myths, legends, and folktales. They may use any or all of the strategies depending on the length and difficulty of the selection. The questioning strategy may be particularly useful for this type of material since the central issue is why the work was written.

Focus

More About the Myth The lives of Nez Percé Indians changed dramatically after horses were introduced into their lives. The Nez Percé were unique among Native Americans in learning how to breed horses selectively. At one time they had one of the largest horse herds on the North American continent. You might ask students what specific changes would have taken place in the lives of the Nez Percé once they had horses.

Literary Focus A myth is a culture's attempt to explain something, in familiar terms, that cannot be explained by reason. Many people are not comfortable with anything they do not understand. They devise explanations to make sense out of an often bewildering world. These explanations often take the form of myths. Ask students to recall other myths they may know, for instance, Greek or Roman myths.

Look For Your more advanced students might also look for the various aspects of the Nez Percé culture that are revealed in the myth.

Writing/Prior Knowledge You might give specific topics to less advanced students. The topics could include why volcanoes erupt, why earthquakes occur, why birds fly south in the fall, or why the sun rises every morning.

Vocabulary You might have more advanced students write an original sentence for each of the vocabulary words.

Spelling Tip Note that *tipi* is an alternate spelling for *tepee.*

GUIDE FOR READING

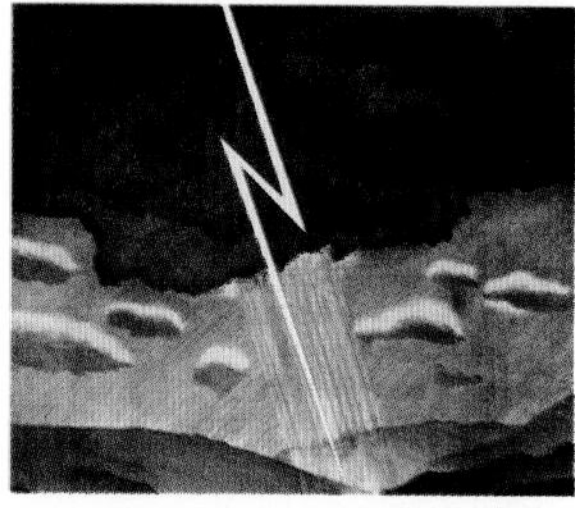

The Origin of Fire

The **Nez Percé** (nez′ pər sā′) were a powerful North American Indian tribe in Idaho, Oregon, and Washington. Their name, French for "pierced nose," was given them by a French interpreter who saw some of them wearing decorative shells in their noses.

"The Origin of Fire" is related by **Ella Elizabeth Clark** (1896–), born in Summertown, Tennessee, who has collected tales of the Pacific Northwest Indians.

Myth

A **myth** is an ancient story often involving supernatural beings that explains a natural phenomenon. For example, a myth may explain the origin of fire, the eruption of a volcano, or the shape of a lake. A myth explains these occurrences in familiar terms. It also reveals the culture itself: its beliefs, ideals, and gods.

Look For

As you read "The Origin of Fire," look for the explanation the Nez Percés provide for the origin of fire. Why is fire so important to people?

Writing

Do you ever wonder about how a river began, or why a nearby mountain has a certain shape, or why some dogs' tails curl? Think of something you see and wonder about, which a myth could explain. Brainstorm and write down your ideas for a possible imaginative explanation.

Vocabulary

Knowing the following words will help you as you read "The Origin of Fire."

fragrant (frā′ grənt) *adj.*: Covered with the odor of something (p. 627)
hurtling (hʉrt′ 'liŋ) *v.*: Moving quickly and forcefully (p. 627)
tipis (tē′ pēz′) *n.*: Cone-shaped tents made of animal skins (p. 627)
abalone (ab′ ə lō′ nē) **shell:** An oval shell with a pearly lining (p. 628)

Objectives

1 To understand myths
2 To understand cause and effect
3 To write an original myth

Support Material

Teaching Portfolio
Teacher Backup, pp. 895–897
Usage and Mechanics Worksheet, p. 898
Vocabulary Check, p. 899
Analyzing Literature Worksheet, *Understanding a Myth*, p. 900
Language Worksheet, *Appreciating Homographs*, p. 901
Selection Test, pp. 902–903

The Origin of Fire 1

Ella E. Clark

Long ago the Nez Percé had no fire. They could see fire in the sky sometimes, but it belonged to the Great Power. He kept it in great black bags in the sky. When the bags bumped into each other, there was a crashing, tearing sound, and through the hole that was made fire sparkled.

People longed to get it. They ate fish and meat raw as the animals do. They ate roots and berries raw as the bears do. The women grieved when they saw their little ones shivering and blue with cold. The medicine men beat on their drums in their efforts to bring fire down from the sky, but no fire came.

At last a boy just beyond the age for the sacred vigil[1] said that he would get the fire. People laughed at him. The medicine men angrily complained, "Do you think that you can do what we are not able to do?"

But the boy went on and made his plans. The first time that he saw the black fire bags drifting in the sky, he got ready. First he bathed, brushing himself with fir branches until he was entirely clean and was fragrant with the smell of fir. He looked very handsome.

With the inside bark of cedar he wrapped an arrowhead and placed it beside his best and largest bow. On the ground he placed a beautiful white shell that he often
wore around his neck. Then he asked his 2
guardian spirit[2] to help him reach the cloud with his arrow.

All the people stood watching. The medicine men said among themselves, "Let us have him killed, lest he make the Great Power angry."

But the people said, "Let him alone. Perhaps he can bring the fire down. If he does not, then we can kill him."

The boy waited until he saw that the largest fire bag was over his head, growling and rumbling. Then he raised his bow and shot the arrow straight upward. Suddenly,
all the people heard a tremendous crash, 3
and they saw a flash of fire in the sky. Then the burning arrow, like a falling star, came hurtling down among them. It struck the boy's white shell and there made a small flame.

Shouting with joy, the people rushed
forward. They lighted sticks and dry bark 4
and hurried to their tipis to start fires with

1. **vigil** (vij′ əl), *n.*: Here, a religious period marking a young person's passage to adulthood.

2. **guardian** (gârd′ ē ən) **spirit:** A supernatural being that protects a person.

Presentation

Motivation/Prior Knowledge Have students imagine that something happened one day that had never happened before and that there was no apparent explanation for it. Perhaps dogs started to speak like people or trees began to grow on the moon. How would people react? How do you think people would try to explain such events? Their explanations might take the form of stories or myths.

Thematic Idea A selection that explains natural phenomenon in a scientific way is "Shooting Stars" by Hal Borland, on page 469. You could have students compare and contrast these two selections. How might earlier peoples have explained shooting stars before there was a scientific explanation?

Purpose-Setting Question What do the Nez Percé acquire in this myth?

1 **Literary Focus** The title is a straightforward statement of what the myth is explaining. You could point this out to your **less advanced** students. Do the myths that they are familiar with have similar titles?

2 **Discussion** Why do you think the boy wore a shell around his neck? What other things do you think his guardian spirit does?

3 **Literary Focus** You might want to point out to the students the supernatural aspects of this action. Ask students if they think that use of supernatural actions or beings is necessary in all myths.

4 **Critical Thinking and Reading** What is the cause for this celebration? What might be some of the other effects?

Humanities Note

Fine art: *Lightning,* 1973, by David Hockney. Born in 1937, Hockney is Britain's best known contemporary painter and graphic artist. He is known as a painter of difficult effects such as sunlight dancing on pool water and reflections in glass.

Lightning is a lithograph from the *Weather Series* completed in 1973. The stark bolt of lightning, striking toward a stylized landscape from the dark mass of clouds, demonstrates Hockney's polished technique and strong sense of design. Although the subject is a fearsome display of a force in nature, the work maintains the aloof, observant quality that pervades Hockney's art.

1. Do you think the lightning bolt looks realistic? Why or why not?
2. Discuss whether this was the kind of sight the Nez Percé saw when fire came to the ground.

5 **Discussion** Why do you think no one could use the boy's bow? What does this indicate about him?

Reader's Response How do you think you would have reacted to the boy?

Enrichment The Nez Percé Indians now live on a reservation in north central Idaho. In 1877, fighting broke out with U.S. troops, who wanted to move the tribe to this reservation. The leader of the Nez Percé, Chief Joseph, led his people on a long and difficult march toward Canada. During the march, the Nez Percé frequently clashed with U.S. troops. Although they were outnumbered, Joseph's warriors managed to win several battles. However, the hardships of the one thousand mile retreat forced Joseph to surrender only forty miles from the border. His surrender speech was a powerful and moving statement about the nobility of his people and the horrors of war.

LIGHTNING, 1973
David Hockney
Gemini Gel

them. Children and old people ran around, laughing and singing.

When the excitement had died down, people asked about the boy. But he was nowhere to be seen. On the ground lay his shell, burned so that it showed the fire colors. Near it lay the boy's bow. People tried to shoot with it, but not even the strongest man and the best with bow and arrow could bend it.

The boy was never seen again. But his abalone shell is still beautiful, still touched with the colors of flame. And the fire he brought from the black bag is still in the center of each tipi, the blessing of every home.

Closure and Extension

ANSWERS TO THINKING ABOUT THE SELECTION
Recalling

1. The difficulties they faced included eating fish, meat, roots, and berries raw and people shivering with cold

THINKING ABOUT THE SELECTION

Recalling

1. What two difficulties or problems did the Nez Percé have before they had fire?
2. What was the medicine men's reaction to the boy's plan to bring down fire?
3. How did the boy bring down the fire?
4. After the excitement had died down, what did the people find?
5. Besides the origin of fire, what other natural phenomenon does the myth explain?

Interpreting

6. What were the great black bags in the sky?
7. What do you think happened to the boy after he captured the fire? Explain your answer.

Applying

8. The boy in this myth attempts to do what others consider impossible. What qualities might a person have who tries to do what others believe he or she cannot do?

ANALYZING LITERATURE

Understanding a Myth

A **myth** is an ancient story attempting to explain an aspect of the world, such as a custom or natural phenomenon. You can learn much about a culture from myths. In fact, researchers often gain valuable insights about cultures from studying myths. For example, "The Origin of Fire" tells you that when the Nez Percé bathed, they brushed themselves with fir branches to be clean and fragrant.

1. What job did the medicine men have?
2. What weapons did the Nez Percé use?
3. Who did the Nez Percé believe guided them?
4. In what did the Nez Percé live?
5. What does this myth—about how the Nez Percé get their fire—tell you about who or what they believed was responsible for the mysteries in their world?

CRITICAL THINKING AND READING

Understanding Cause and Effect

A **cause** makes something occur. An **effect** is the outcome of the cause.

Myths are a culture's attempts to explain the unknown; myths present imaginative causes for effects that seem unexplainable. "The Origin of Fire" is the Nez Percé's attempt to explain how they first came to use fire in their homes.

To identify an effect, ask yourself "What happened?" Ask "Why did this happen?" to identify its cause.

1. What causes the following events?
   a. The abalone shell was burned with color.
   b. The boy disappears.
2. What are the effects of the following events?
   a. The medicine men beat on their drums to bring fire down from the sky.
   b. The boy shot his arrow into the largest fire bag.
3. How do the causes science offers for natural phenomena differ from the causes offered by myths?

THINKING AND WRITING

Writing a Myth

Make up a myth that explains the topic you thought about before reading "The Origin of Fire." Your myth could explain your topic in terms of life as it was long ago or in terms of modern technology. List and describe the characters in your myth. Sketch out the plot—what will happen in the myth. Then write the story, using dialogue when needed. Reread your myth to see if it offers an imaginative explanation of the topic you chose.

(Answers begin on p. 628.)

2. The medicine men reacted by getting angry that someone was going to try to do something that they had failed to do. They were also afraid of angering the Great Power.
3. The boy brought down the fire by shooting an arrow straight into a thunder cloud. The thunder cloud set the arrow on fire and the arrow fell to earth.
4. The people found that the boy was nowhere around and his shell was burned so that it showed the fire colors.
5. The myth also explains why an abalone shell is beautifully colored.

Interpreting

6. The great black bags were thunder clouds.
7. Answers will differ. They might include that the boy was sent by the Great Power to get fire for the people. The fact that he was successful, that he disappeared, and that no one could use his bow support this answer.

Applying

8. Answers will differ. Suggested Response: Qualities might include bravery, intelligence, determination, foresight. Answers such as foolishness and stubbornness are also acceptable if the act to be attempted seems especially foolhardy.

ANSWERS TO ANALYZING LITERATURE

1. One job of the medicine men was to beat on drums to bring fire from the skies.
2. They used bows and arrows as weapons.
3. They believed the Great Power guided them.
4. They lived in tipis.
5. The myth tells you that they believed supernatural beings and powers, such as the Great Power and the boy, were responsible for the mysteries in their world.

ANSWERS TO CRITICAL THINKING AND READING

1. a. The burning arrow striking the shell caused it to be burned with color.
   b. Bringing fire to the people was the cause of the boy's disappearance.
2. a. The medicine men beating on their drums had no effect.
   b. The effect of the arrow being shot into the fire bag was that the arrow caught fire and returned to earth.
3. The causes science offers differ because they are based on observation, study, and experimentation while causes offered in myths are based on magic and supernatural occurrences.

Challenge What do you think the people's attitude toward the Great Power was? What feelings did they have about it?

THINKING AND WRITING

Writing Across the Curriculum

You might want to have students research and report on the scientific causes for thunder and lightning. If you do, perhaps inform the science department of this assignment. Science teachers might provide assistance and guidance for students in conducting their research.

Focus

More About the Author Carl Sandburg always wanted to be a poet of the ordinary person. He succeeded, becoming one of the best-known and widely read poets in America. His subjects were the people themselves and his tone was upbeat. What kinds of writing would you expect from such a person?

Literary Focus Humor is the main characteristic of many yarns. It helps to suspend the listener's belief and creates interest in the tale.

Look For You might also have your students look for the states that are mentioned. In what region of the country do most of these yarns seem to take place?

Writing/Prior Knowledge You might have your **less advanced** students reread the definition of a yarn to be sure that they understand the activity. You might also offer other suggestions for topics.

Vocabulary If some of your **less advanced** students are having trouble, you might have them pronounce each word aloud.

Spelling Tip The word *flue* should not be confused with its homophone *flew*.

GUIDE FOR READING

from The People, Yes

Carl Sandburg (1878–1967), born in Galesburg, Illinois, is best known for his poetry. Sandburg became a journalist, an author of children's books, and a historian, and also wrote and sang his own songs and ballads. He won the Pulitzer Prize in 1940 for his biography of Abraham Lincoln, and in 1950 for his *Complete Poems*. Sandburg's poetry celebrates the lives of ordinary people. In "The People, Yes," he uses the words, style, and rhythms of common speech to celebrate the tall tales of the American people.

Yarn

A **yarn** is a tale or story filled with exaggeration. The subject of a yarn is the tallest, fastest, strongest, longest, or most unusual of its kind. The yarnteller describes characteristics or actions that the listener knows are impossible but which, with only a small leap of the imagination, are fun to imagine as true.

Look For

As you read this selection from "The People, Yes," look for the feats or qualities that are exaggerated. Notice that this selection presents the *subjects* of various yarns, some of them well known. With which of these yarns are you familiar?

Writing

Have you ever used exaggeration to add effect to a story? Perhaps you were telling about how fast the roller coaster sped, or how far you swam. Brainstorm and write down your ideas for subjects or experiences that you could exaggerate in a yarn.

Vocabulary

Knowing the following words will help you as you read this selection from "The People, Yes."

shingled (shiŋ′ g'ld) *v.*: Covered the roof with shingles (p. 631)
mutineers (myo͞ot′ 'n irz′) *n.*: People on a ship who revolt against their officers (p. 631)
runt (runt) *n.*: The smallest animal in a litter (p. 631)
flue (flo͞o) *n.*: The pipe in a chimney that leads smoke outside (p. 631)
hook-and-eye: A fastening device in which a metal hook catches on to a loop (p. 631)

Objectives

1 To understand and identify yarns
2 To appreciate compound words
3 To write a yarn

Support Material

Teaching Portfolio

Teacher Backup, pp. 905–907
Usage and Mechanics Worksheet, p. 908
Vocabulary Check, p. 909
Analyzing Literature Worksheet, *Understanding a Yarn*, p. 910
Language Worksheet, *Appreciating Compound Words*, p. 911
Selection Test, pp. 912–913

from The People, Yes

Carl Sandburg

They have yarns
Of a skyscraper so tall they had to put hinges
1 On the two top stories so to let the moon go by,
Of one corn crop in Missouri when the roots
Went so deep and drew off so much water
The Mississippi riverbed that year was dry,
2 Of pancakes so thin they had only one side,
Of "a fog so thick we shingled the barn and six feet out on the fog,"
Of Pecos Pete straddling a cyclone in Texas and riding it to the west coast where "it rained out under him,"
Of the man who drove a swarm of bees across the Rocky Mountains and the Desert "and didn't lose a bee,"
Of a mountain railroad curve where the engineer in his cab can touch the caboose and spit in the conductor's eye,
Of the boy who climbed a cornstalk growing so fast he would have starved to death if they hadn't shot biscuits up to him,
Of the old man's whiskers: "When the wind was with him his whiskers arrived a day before he did,"
Of the hen laying a square egg and cackling, "Ouch!" and of hens laying eggs with the dates printed on them,
Of the ship captain's shadow: it froze to the deck one cold winter night,
Of mutineers on that same ship put to chipping rust with rubber hammers,
Of the sheep counter who was fast and accurate: "I just count their feet and divide by four," 3
Of the man so tall he must climb a ladder to shave himself,
Of the runt so teeny-weeny it takes two men and a boy to see him,
Of mosquitoes: one can kill a dog, two of them a man,
Of a cyclone that sucked cookstoves out of the kitchen, up the chimney flue, and on to the next town,
Of the same cyclone picking up wagon-tracks in Nebraska and dropping them over in the Dakotas,
Of the hook-and-eye snake unlocking itself into forty pieces, each piece two inches long, then in nine seconds flat snapping itself together again,
Of the watch swallowed by the cow—when they butchered her a year later the watch was running and had the correct time,
Of horned snakes, hoop snakes that roll themselves where they want to go, and rattlesnakes carrying bells instead of rattles on their tails,
Of the herd of cattle in California getting lost in a giant redwood tree that had hollowed out,
Of the man who killed a snake by putting its tail in its mouth so it swallowed itself, 4
Of railroad trains whizzing along so fast they reach the station before the whistle,
Of pigs so thin the farmer had to tie knots in

Presentation

Motivation/Prior Knowledge Have students imagine that they are listening to a championship yarn-telling match. Two speakers are swapping tales, each one more fabulous and incredible than the one before. Would students enjoy such an event? What kinds of tales might be told?

Master Teacher Note The images evoked in this selection are taken from a wide range of the American landscape. Students might appreciate some of the images more if they saw photographs of the actual places or things. For example, photos of the Mississippi River, a redwood forest, the Rocky Mountains, a cyclone, the landscape of Nebraska, or some of the other states mentioned could be helpful.

Purpose-Setting Question What similar characteristics do all of these yarns have?

1 **Discussion** *The People, Yes* was published in 1936. How would the teller of this yarn feel if he or she saw cities today? Why was the yarn just as effective in 1936 when the buildings were not nearly as tall as they are today?

2 **Literary Focus** Point out that these yarns can be visualized. Ask students to try to visualize this image. Is it possible to imagine a one-sided pancake? Why?

3 **Dicussion** What is humorous about this method?

4 **Literary Focus** You might point out the form used to present brief, one-sentence versions of these yarns. This technique is used to summarize the different kinds of yarns and to give the reader an idea of the types of people who told them. Do the short passages make you want to hear the yarns in their entirety? Do they create an interest in hearing more yarns?

5 **Reading Strategy** Have students summarize the yarns. Which yarn is the most incredible? Which is the most believable? Which yarn forms the funniest image?

Reader's Response Which of these yarns would you like to hear or read? Why?

Humanities Note

Fine art, *Baseball Player and Circus Performers*, John Zielenski. The American illustrator John Zielenski has used bizarre symbolism in *Baseball Players and Circus Performers.* Zielenski's symbolism is reminiscent of surrealism, a modern art technique that depicts the workings of the unconscious mind. The incongruities of this piece are puzzling and prompt the viewer to think more carefully and look more closely. The fact that the viewer is prompted to wonder about the artist's meaning is an indication that the work is a success.

You might *want to* use the following questions to discuss the art:

1. Why do you think the baseball diamond is in a circus tent?
2. What symbols can you identify in *Baseball Player and Circus Performers?*

BASEBALL PLAYER AND CIRCUS PERFORMERS
John Zielinski
Sal Barracca & Associates

their tails to keep them from crawling
through the cracks in their pens,
Of Paul Bunyan's big blue ox, Babe, measuring between the eyes forty-two
ax-handles and a plug of Star tobacco
exactly,
Of John Henry's hammer and the curve of
5 its swing and his singing of it as "a
rainbow round my shoulder."

Closure and Extension

ANSWERS TO THINKING ABOUT THE SELECTION
Recalling

1. Two of the yarns that exaggerate height are the yarn about the skyscraper that had to be hinged to let the moon go by and the yarn about the man so tall that he had to climb a ladder to shave.
2. Three yarns that involve cyclones are the yarn of Pecos Bill, who straddled a cyclone, the yarn about the cyclone that sucked cookstoves out of the kitchen, and the yarn about the same cyclone that sucked up wagon tracks.
3. Yarns involving fantastic speed include the yarn about the boy who climbed the cornstalk, the yarn about the hook-and-eye snake, the yarn about the railroad trains that reach the station before their whistles.
4. Yarns involving snakes include the yarn about the hook-and-eye snake; the yarn about the horned snakes, the hoop snakes, and the rattlesnakes with bells instead of rattles; and the yarn about the man who killed a snake by putting its tail in its mouth so it swallowed itself.

THINKING ABOUT THE SELECTION

Recalling

1. Find two yarns that involve exaggerated heights.
2. Find three yarns that involve cyclones.
3. Find two yarns that involve fantastic speed.
4. Find three yarns that involve snakes.

Interpreting

5. What does the statement "When the wind was with him his whiskers arrived a day before he did" tell you about the length of the man's whiskers?
6. Why is being made to chip rust with rubber hammers an effective punishment?
7. What did John Henry mean when he described the swing of his hammer as "a rainbow around my shoulder"?
8. Who are the people ("they") who told these yarns? What do these yarns suggest about these people?
9. Upon what characteristics of people, animals, or nature are these yarns built?

Applying

10. Why do you think people take pleasure in spinning yarns?

ANALYZING LITERATURE

Understanding a Yarn

A **yarn** is a tale or story that is exaggerated or incredible. Yarns usually start with everyday situations that then become so exaggerated as to be fantastic. For example, corn crops might have deep roots (true), but not actually so deep that the Mississippi riverbed would go dry (exaggerated).

1. What might a yarn exaggerate about the following topics?
   a. cats fighting
   b. a river overflowing
2. "The People, Yes" tells you about the way of life of Americans on the frontier. Find two yarns that reveal the dangers of nature. Find two yarns that reveal the need for hard work.

UNDERSTANDING LANGUAGE

Appreciating Compound Words

A **compound word** is formed by joining two words. Some words, such as *airplane,* are closed compounds because two words are joined together directly. Others, such as *babysit,* are hyphenated compounds. Still others, such as *major league,* are open compounds —although they are not actually joined, the two words are considered to mean one thing. You can usually learn the meaning of a compound word by breaking it into its parts.

1. Write the parts of the following compound words. Then write a sentence using each word correctly. Check the meaning in a dictionary.
   a. skyscraper
   b. riverbed
   c. pancakes
   d. ax handle
   e. West Coast
2. Add a second word to each of the following words to make a compound word. Check the dictionary if you need to.
   a. snow b. night c. bee

THINKING AND WRITING

Writing a Yarn

Refer to the list of subjects and experiences that you developed earlier. First freewrite about these subjects, including details that are as wild and exaggerated as you like. Then use these ideas to add eight lines to "The People, Yes" telling about some yarns that people could have in the 1980's and 1990's. Revise your writing, making sure you have used exaggeration effectively. Finally, proofread your work and share it with your classmates.

(Answers begin on p. 632.)

ANSWERS TO ANALYZING LITERATURE

1. a. Answers will differ. Suggested Response: A yarn might exaggerate the cats' claws, the speed with which they attack each other, and the noise they make.
   b. Answers will differ. Suggested Response: A yarn about a river overflowing might exaggerate the extent of the flooding, the depth of the river, or the appearance of the area after the waters subsided.
2. Yarns that reveal the dangers of nature include these: the night it was so cold the captain's shadow froze; the cyclone that sucked cookstoves out of the chimney; and mosquitoes so strong that two of them could kill a man. Yarns that reveal the need for hard work include the tale of the man who drove a swarm of bees across the Rockies and the desert and didn't lose a bee; and the story of John Henry and his hammer.

Challenge What might be some topics for yarns about life in the 1980's?

ANSWERS TO UNDERSTANDING LANGUAGE

1. a. sky, scraper
   b. river, bed
   c. pan, cake
   d. ax, handle
   e. west, coast

Students' sentences will differ.

2. Answers will differ. Suggested Response:
   a. snowstorm
   b. nightmare
   c. beehive

Writing Across the Curriculum
You might want to have students set their new yarns to music. They can use well known tunes, such as "Oh Susanna," for this purpose. If you inform the music department, music teachers might provide guidance in setting the words to music. You could then ask for student volunteers to sing their songs, in groups or solo.

Interpreting

5. This statement tells you that the whiskers were extremely long.
6. It is an effective punishment because rubber hammers would chip rust very slowly, if at all.
7. John Henry meant that he swung his hammer with such great speed and force that to anyone watching it would appear as a rainbow.
8. They were the American working people, who take pride in their work and their abilities to thrive on the frontier. Answers will differ. Suggested Response: The yarns suggest that the people enjoy fantastic stories about common things, that they have a good imagination and a sense of humor, that they want to glorify the qualities and attitudes that are admirable and necessary in their lives.
9. The yarns are built on the basic skills and character traits necessary to the people who live and work on the frontier.

Applying

10. Answers will differ. Suggested Response: People may like to spin yarns because they want to glorify their lives and work, and they enjoy using their imaginations. People who enjoy telling stories also enjoy holding their audiences's attention by stretching the facts as far as they can.

Focus

More About the Legend Zuñi Indians are descendants of the cliff-dwelling Anasazi Indians. Their first contact with outsiders was in 1539, when a Spanish expedition discovered six of their villages. Today, many Zuñi Indians still live in adobe and stone houses. They raise livestock and produce fine jewelry from coral, silver, and turquoise.

Literary Focus You might want to point out to students that, unlike myths, legends are not meant to explain natural phenomena. Also, they usually have some basis, however slight, in fact.

Look For You might have your more advanced students look for the clues to what Zuñi life was like at the time of the story.

Writing/Prior Knowledge You might want to explain that a journal entry can vary in length, tone, and detail. It should contain the experience and the writer's reaction to it. Encourage students to include colorful details.

Vocabulary You might have your more advanced students create a sentence that includes at least three of the vocabulary words.

Spelling Tip The ending *-ious,* as in *voracious,* is much more common than *-eous,* which is used often in technical and scientific terms like *gaseous, cutaneous,* or *vitreous.*

GUIDE FOR READING

The Girl Who Hunted Rabbits

The **Zuñi Indians** live in a harsh and unforgiving land, in northwestern New Mexico near Arizona. The early Zuñis were farmers. Their territory, governed by the United States after 1848, is parched by sun in summer and swept by wind and snow in winter. Yet there is beauty in the land: towering cliffs flaming red in the sunset; deep, cool canyons; and wide-open vistas. "The Girl Who Hunted Rabbits" tells of a courageous girl who faces the harsh elements to bring food home to her family.

Legend

A **legend** is an imaginative story believed to be based on an actual person or event, rather than on the supernatural. The story is passed from generation to generation, often by word of mouth. With retelling, the character's actions or the event may become more fantastic. The character becomes larger than life—a hero or heroine.

Legends also give you information about the people who tell them. "The Girl Who Hunted Rabbits" tells you how the Zuñis lived and some of the gods they believed in.

Look For

As you read "The Girl Who Hunted Rabbits," look for the dangers the girl faces. How is she finally saved from the demon?

Writing

Think of a time when a person did something brave. Freewrite, describing what happened. Describe how the brave person may have felt.

Vocabulary

Knowing the following words will help you as you read "The Girl Who Hunted Rabbits."

procured (prō kyoord') *adv.*: Obtained by some effort (p. 635)

sinew (sin' yoo) **n.**: A tendon, a band of fibrous tissue that connects muscles to bones or to other parts and can also be used as thread for sewing (p. 636)

mantle (man't'l) *n.*: Sleeveless cloak or cape (p. 636)

unwonted (un wun' tid) *adj.*: Not usual (p. 636)

bedraggled (bi drag' 'ld) *adj.*: Dirty and wet (p. 638)

voracious (vô rā' shəs) *adj.*: Eager to devour large quantities of food (p. 639)

devoured (di vourd') *v.*: Ate greedily (p. 639)

Objectives

1 To understand legends
2 To make inferences from legends
3 To choose meaning to fit a word's context
4 To retell a legend

Support Material

Teaching Portfolio
Teacher Backup, pp. 915–918
Grammar in Action Worksheets, *Using Conjunctions,* pp. 919–920; *Understanding Prepositional Phrases,* pp. 921–922
Usage and Mechanics Worksheet, p. 923
Vocabulary Check, p. 924
Critical Thinking and Reading Worksheet, *Making Inferences from a Legend,* p. 925
Language Worksheet, *Choosing Meaning to Fit Context,* p. 926
Selection Test, pp. 927–928

The Girl Who Hunted Rabbits

Zuñi Indian Legend

It was long ago, in the days of the ancients, that a poor maiden lived at "Little Gateway of Zuñi River." You know there are
1 black stone walls of houses standing there on the tops of the cliffs of lava, above the narrow place through which the river runs, to this day.

In one of these houses there lived this poor maiden alone with her feeble old father and her aged mother. She was unmarried, and her brothers had all been killed in wars, or had died gently; so the family lived there helplessly, so far as many things were concerned, from the lack of men in their house.

It is true that in making the gardens—the little plantings of beans, pumpkins, squashes, melons, and corn—the maiden was able to do very well; and thus mainly on the products of these things the family were supported. But, as in those days of our ancients we had neither sheep nor cattle, the hunt was depended upon to supply the meat; or sometimes it was procured by barter[1] of the products of the fields to those who hunted mostly. Of these things this little family had barely enough for their own subsistence; hence, they could not procure their supplies of meat in this way.

Long before, it had been a great house, for many were the brave and strong young men who had lived in it; but the rooms were now empty, or at best contained only the leavings of those who had lived there, much used and worn out.

One autumn day, near wintertime, snow fell, and it became very cold. The maiden had gathered brush and firewood in abundance, and it was piled along the roof of the 2
house and down underneath the ladder which descended from the top. She saw the young men issue forth the next morning in great numbers, their feet protected by long stockings of deerskin, the fur turned inward, and they carried on their shoulders and stuck in their belts stone axes and rabbit sticks. As she gazed at them from the roof, she said to herself, "O that I were a man and could go forth, as do these young men, hunting rabbits! Then my poor old mother and father would not lack for flesh with which to duly season their food and nourish their lean bodies." Thus ran her thoughts, and before night, as she saw these same young men coming in, one after another, some of them bringing long strings of rabbits, others short ones, but none of them empty-handed, she decided that she would set forth on the morrow to try what luck she might find in the killing of rabbits herself.

It may seem strange that, although this maiden was beautiful and young, the youths did not give her some of their rabbits. But

1. **barter** (bär' tər), *v.*: To exchange goods.

Presentation

Motivation/Prior Knowledge Ask students if they have ever heard a story in which the main character is placed in a desperate situation with seemingly no way out. When all appears lost, some unforeseen character or situation presents itself and the main character is saved. How do students feel about such stories? Have they ever experienced anything similar to this in real life?

Master Teacher Note The legend is set in northwestern New Mexico. To give your students a better idea of the rugged nature of the landscape, it might be helpful to show them photographs of the area.

Thematic Idea Another selection that deals with the theme of a woman's sacrifice and courage is "Grass Fire" on page 129.

Purpose-Setting Question What elements of the story make it a legend and not a factual tale?

1 **Literary Focus** By referring directly to the reader, the author presents the story as if it were being told by a storyteller. Tales and legends such as this were passed on in the oral tradition. Ask students how this style affects the way they read the legend.

2 **Enrichment** The houses that Zuñi Indians lived in were called Pueblos and consisted of one or more flat-roofed structures built of stone or adobe. (Adobe is a sun-dried brick made out of clay.) The houses were arranged in terraces with few doors on the ground level. The people used ladders to reach the doors on the roofs.

3 **Reading Strategy** You might have students summarize what they discover about the way Zuñis lived at the time of this legend. What did Zuñis eat? What were the roles of men and women? What types of shelter did they live in?

4 **Discussion** How do her parents feel about their daughter hunting? What do their preparations indicate about their feelings toward her?

their feelings were not friendly, for no one of them would she accept as a husband, although one after another of them had offered himself for marriage.

Fully resolved, the girl that evening sat down by the fireplace, and turning toward her aged parents, said, "O my mother and father, I see that the snow has fallen, whereby easily rabbits are tracked, and the young men who went out this morning returned long before evening heavily laden with strings of this game. Behold, in the other rooms of our house are many rabbit sticks, and there hang on the walls stone axes, and with these I might perchance strike down a rabbit on his trail, or, if he runs into a log, split the log and dig him out. So I have thought during the day, and have decided to go tomorrow and try my fortunes in the hunt."

"*Naiya*, my daughter," quavered the feeble, old mother, "you would surely be very cold, or you would lose your way, or grow so tired that you could not return before night, and you must not go out to hunt rabbits."

"Why, certainly not," insisted the old man, rubbing his lean knees and shaking his head over the days that were gone. "No, no; let us live in poverty rather than that you should run such risks as these, O my daughter."

But, say what they would, the girl was determined. And the old man said at last, "Very well! You will not be turned from your course. Therefore, O daughter, I will help
3, you as best I may." He hobbled into another
room, and found there some old deerskins
4 covered thickly with fur; and drawing them
out, he moistened and carefully softened them, and cut out for the maiden long stockings, which he sewed up with sinew and the fiber of the yucca[2] leaf. Then he selected for her from among the old possessions of his brothers and sons, who had been killed or perished otherwise, a number of rabbit sticks and a fine, heavy stone ax. Meanwhile, the old woman busied herself in preparing a lunch for the girl, which was composed of little cakes of cornmeal, spiced with pepper and wild onions, pierced through the middle, and baked in the ashes. When she had made a long string of these by threading them like beads on a rope of yucca fiber, she laid them down not far from the ladder on a little bench, with the rabbit sticks, the stone ax, and the deerskin stockings.

That night the maiden planned and planned, and early on the following morning, even before the young men had gone out from the town, she had put on a warm, short-skirted dress, knotted a mantle over her shoulder and thrown another and larger one over her back, drawn on the deerskin stockings, had thrown the string of corncakes over her shoulder, stuck the rabbit sticks in her belt, and carrying the stone ax in her hand sallied[3] forth eastward through the Gateway of Zuñi and into the plain of the valley beyond, called the Plain of the Burnt River, on account of the black, roasted-looking rocks along some parts of its sides. Dazzlingly white the snow stretched out before her—not deep, but unbroken—and when she came near the cliffs with many little canyons in them, along the northern side of the valley, she saw many a trail of rabbits running out and in among the rocks and between the bushes.

Warm and excited by her unwonted exercise, she did not heed a coming snowstorm, but ran about from one place to another, following the trails of the rabbits, sometimes up into the canyons where the forests of pine and cedar stood, and where

2. yucca (yuk′ ə), *n.*: A desert plant with stiff leaves and white flowers.

3. sallied (sal′ ēd), *v.*: Set out energetically.

Grammar in Action

Conjunctions connect individual words or groups of words, holding the sentence together. There are three categories of conjunctions: **coordinating, correlative** and **subordinating.** Coordinating conjunctions connect words of a similar kind. For example, two or more verbs can be connected by a coordinating conjunction. Similarly, coordinating conjunctions connect larger groups of words, such as prepositional phrases, or even entire sentences. Examples of coordinating conjunctions are *and, but, for, nor, or, so,* and *yet.* Notice how the coordinating conjunctions in the following sentence from "The Girl Who Hunted Rabbits" hold the sentence together:

> It was little work to split these logs, *for* they were small, as you know, *and* to dig out the rabbits *and* slay them by a blow of the hand on the nape of the neck, back of the ears; *and* as she killed each rabbit she raised it reverently to her lips, *and* breathed from its nostrils its expiring breath *and,* tying its legs together, placed it on the string . . ."

Correlative conjunctions also connect the same kinds of words or groups of words, but unlike coordinating conjunctions, correlative conjunctions come in pairs—*both . . . and, either . . .*

INDIAN GIRL (1917)
Robert Henri
Indianapolis Museum of Art

here and there she had the good fortune sometimes to run two, three, or four rabbits into a single hollow log. It was little work to split these logs, for they were small, as you know, and to dig out the rabbits and slay them by a blow of the hand on the nape of the neck, back of the ears; and as she killed each rabbit she raised it reverently to her lips, and breathed from its nostrils its expiring breath[4] and, tying its legs together, placed it on the string, which after a while began to grow heavy on her shoulders. Still she kept on, little heeding the snow which was falling fast; nor did she notice that it was growing darker and darker, so intent was she on the hunt, and so glad was she to capture so many rabbits. Indeed, she followed the trails until they were no longer visible, as the snow fell all around her, thinking all the while, "How happy will be my poor old father and mother that they shall now have flesh to eat! How strong will 5
they grow! And when this meat is gone, that which is dried and preserved of it also, lo! another snowstorm will no doubt come, and I can go out hunting again."

At last the twilight came, and, looking

4. **expiring** (ik spīr′ ing) **breath:** Air breathed out as the rabbit dies.

5 **Literary Focus** You might point out to students that the legend to this point could easily have been a true story.

Humanities Note

Fine art, *Indian Girl*, Robert Henri. Robert Henri (1865–1929) was an innovative painter and teacher of art. As a founding member of the "Ashcan" school of American painting (so called because of its unglamorous subject matter), Henri worked with "the Eight," a group of free-thinking painters whose work was a radical departure from the approved academic style of American painting. Their paintings of the ordinary life around them were initially scorned as "mundane" and "ugly" but eventually won public acclaim.

Indian Girl was one of the fourteen canvases produced by Henri on a trip to Santa Fe. The canvases chronicle his admiration and respect for Native Americans. Each of these paintings displays an Indian blanket as a decorative motif. In *Indian Girl*, the flat abstract design of the blanket curiously enhances the living presence of the girl. The color palette, while not harmonious, is given continuity by repetition of the soft, vibrant reds.

This painting affirms Henri's desire to show the world "his people." He did so again and again in his numerous portraits of poor, foreign, and minority peoples.

You might want to use the following questions to discuss the art:

1. Is this how you pictured the girl in the selection? Explain.
2. How does Henri's painting affect your interpretation of the selection?

or, neither . . . nor, not only . . . but also, whether . . . or.

Subordinating conjunctions connect two ideas by making one idea dependent on the other. Some examples of frequently used subordinating conjunctions are *after, although, as if, because, before, since, though, unless, until, whenever,* and *while.* In the following sentence from "The Girl Who Hunted Rabbits," the subordinating conjunction *although* connects the dependent clause to the main idea: "But their feelings were not friendly, for no one of them would she accept as a husband, although one after another of them had offered himself for marriage."

Student Activity. Locate five more examples of conjunctions in the selection and identify each one as either coordinating, correlative, or subordinating.

6 Discussion Do you think the girl would have been this fortunate in real life or is her good fortune one of the events that was changed in the retelling of the legend? Support your answer.

around, she found that the snow had fallen deeply, there was no trail, and that she had lost her way. True, she turned about and started in the direction of her home, as she supposed, walking as fast as she could through the soft, deep snow. Yet she reckoned not rightly, for instead of going eastward along the valley, she went southward across it, and entering the mouth of the Descending Plain of the Pines, she went on and on, thinking she was going homeward, until at last it grew dark and she knew not which way to turn.

"What harm," thought she, "if I find a sheltered place among the rocks? What harm if I remain all night, and go home in the morning when the snow has ceased falling, and by the light I shall know my way?"

So she turned about to some rocks which appeared, black and dim, a short distance away. Fortunately, among these rocks is the cave which is known as Taiuma's[5] Cave. This she came to, and peering into that black hole, she saw in it, back some distance, a little glowing light. "Ha, ha!" thought she, "perhaps some rabbit hunters like myself, belated yesterday, passed the night here and left the fire burning. If so, this is greater good fortune than I could have looked for." So, lowering the string of rabbits which she carried on her shoulder, and throwing off her mantle, she crawled in, peering well into the darkness, for fear of wild beasts; then, returning, she drew in the string of rabbits and the mantle.

Behold! there was a bed of hot coals
buried in the ashes in the very middle of the
cave, and piled up on one side were frag-
6 ments of broken wood. The girl, happy in
her good fortune, issued forth and gathered
more sticks from the cliffside, where dead
pines are found in great numbers, and bringing them in little armfuls one after another, she finally succeeded in gathering a store sufficient to keep the fire burning brightly all the night through. Then she drew off her snow-covered stockings of deerskin and the bedraggled mantles, and, building a fire, hung them up to dry and sat down to rest herself. The fire burned up and glowed brightly, so that the whole cave was as light as a room at night when a dance is being celebrated. By and by, after her clothing had dried, she spread a mantle on the floor of the cave by the side of the fire, and, sitting down, dressed one of her rabbits and roasted it, and, untying the string of corncakes her mother had made for her, feasted on the roasted meat and cakes.

She had just finished her evening meal, and was about to recline and watch the fire for awhile, when she heard away off in the distance a long, low cry of distress—*"Ho-o-o-o thlaia-a!"*

"Ah!" thought the girl, "someone, more belated than myself, is lost; doubtless one of the rabbit-hunters." She got up, and went nearer to the entrance of the cavern.

"Ho-o-o-o thlaia-a!" sounded the cry, nearer this time. She ran out, and, as it was repeated again, she placed her hand to her mouth, and cried, as loudly as possible, *"Li-i thlaia-a!"* ("Here!")

The cry was repeated near at hand, and presently the maiden, listening first, and then shouting, and listening again, heard the clatter of an enormous rattle. In dismay and terror she threw her hands into the air, and, crouching down, rushed into the cave and retreated to its farthest limits, where she sat shuddering with fear, for she knew that one of the Cannibal Demons of those days, perhaps the renowned Atahsaia[6] of

---

5. **Taiuma's** (tī o͞o′ məz).

6. **Atahsaia** (ah′tə sī′ ə).

Grammar in Action

Prepositional phrases begin with a preposition and end with a noun or pronoun called the object of the preposition. A prepositional phrase can act as an adjective and modify a noun or pronoun. It can also act as an adverb and modify a verb, adjective, or adverb. A prepositional phrase that acts as an adjective is called an adjective phrase. It modifies a noun or pronoun by telling what kind or which one. A prepositional phrase that acts as an adverb modifying a verb, adjective or adverb is an adverb phrase. Adverb phrases point out where, when, in what manner, or to what extent.

The following sentence from "The Girl Who Hunted Rabbits" has several prepositional phrases.

> Behold! there was a bed *of hot coals* buried *in the ashes in the very middle of the cave,* and piled up *on one side* were fragments *of broken wood.*

Of hot coals and *of broken wood* are adjective phrases, modifying bed and fragments respectively, while *in the ashes, in the very middle, of the cave,* and *on one side* are adverb the east, had seen the light of her fire through the cave entrance, with his terrible staring eyes, and assuming it to be a lost wanderer, had cried out, and so led her to guide him to her place of concealment.

7 On came the Demon, snapping the twigs under his feet and shouting in a hoarse, loud voice, *"Ho lithlsh tâ ime!"* ("Ho, there! So you are in here, are you?") *Kothl!* clanged his rattle, while, almost fainting with terror, closer to the rock crouched the maiden.

The old Demon came to the entrance of the cave and bawled out, "I am cold, I am hungry! Let me in!" Without further ado, he stooped and tried to get in; but, behold! the entrance was too small for his giant shoulders to pass. Then he pretended to be wonderfully civil, and said, "Come out, and bring me something to eat."

"I have nothing for you," cried the maiden. "I have eaten my food."

"Have you no rabbits?"

"Yes."

"Come out and bring me some of them."

But the maiden was so terrified that she dared not move toward the entrance.

"Throw me a rabbit!" shouted the old Demon.

The maiden threw him one of her precious rabbits at last, when she could rise and go to it. He clutched it with his long, horny hand, gave one gulp and swallowed it. Then he cried out, "Throw me another!" She threw him another, which he also immediately swallowed; and so on until the poor maiden had thrown all the rabbits to the voracious old monster. Every one she threw him he caught in his huge, yellow-tusked mouth, and swallowed, hair and all, at one gulp.

"Throw me another!" cried he, when the last had already been thrown to him.

So the poor maiden was forced to say, "I have no more."

"Throw me your overshoes!" cried he.

She threw the overshoes of deerskin, and these like the rabbits he speedily devoured. Then he called for her moccasins, and she threw them; for her belt, and she threw it; and finally, wonderful to tell, she threw even her mantle, and blanket, and her overdress, until, behold, she had nothing left!

Now, with all he had eaten, the old Demon was swollen hugely at the stomach, and, though he tried and tried to squeeze himself through the mouth of the cave, he could not by any means succeed. Finally, lifting his great flint ax, he began to shatter the rock about the entrance to the cave, and slowly but surely he enlarged the hole and the maiden now knew that as soon as he could get in he would devour her also, and she almost fainted at the sickening thought. Pound, pound, pound, pound, went the great ax of the Demon as he struck the rocks. 8

In the distance the two war-gods were sitting in their home at the Shrine amid the Bushes beyond Thunder Mountain, and though far off, they heard thus in the middle of the night the pounding of the Demon's hammer ax against the rocks. And of course they knew at once that a poor maiden, for the sake of her father and mother, had been out hunting—that she had lost her way and, finding a cave where there was a little fire, entered it, rebuilt the fire, and rested herself; that, attracted by the light of her fire, the Cannibal Demon had come and besieged her retreat,[7] and only a little time hence would he so enlarge the entrance to the cave that he could squeeze even his great overfilled paunch through it and come at the maiden to destroy her. So, catching up their wonderful weapons, these two

7. besieged (bi sējd') **her retreat:** Attacked her place of refuge.

7 **Literary Focus** The legend now takes on a fantastic element. This element is made believable by setting the story in the time of the "ancients."

8 **Reading Strategy** You might have students, based on what they know about legends, predict the outcome to this seemingly hopeless situation.

phrases. *In the ashes, in the very middle, of the cave* are all adverb phrases telling where the coal was buried; *on one side* is an adverb phrase modifying piled.

Student Activity. Determine whether the prepositional phrases in the following sentence from the story are adjective or adverb phrases:

> In dismay and terror she threw her hands into the air, and, crouching down, rushed into the cave and retreated to its farthest limits, where she sat shuddering with fear, for she knew that one of the Cannibal Demons of those days, perhaps the renowned Atahsaia of the east, had seen the light of her fire through the cave entrance, with his terrible staring eyes, and assuming it to be a lost wanderer, had cried out, and so led her to guide him to her place of concealment.

Explain what each modifies and what information each gives.

9 Discussion What qualities does the girl display that make her worthy of the war-gods' help?

10 Critical Thinking and Reading The war-gods "slay" the rabbits that they had taken from the Cannibal Demon's belly. The girl had hunted and killed these rabbits the day before. What power does this indicate in the war-gods?

11 Critical Thinking and Reading Based on the two incidents in the legend, have students make inferences about the cultural meaning of the girl breathing on the hands of the gods.

Reader's Response Legends are often changed as they are passed on from generation to generation. If you were to retell this legend, what, if anything, would you change? Why?

war-gods flew away into the darkness and in no time they were approaching the Descending Plain of the Pines.

Just as the Demon was about to enter the cavern, and the maiden had fainted at seeing his huge face and gray shock of hair and staring eyes, his yellow, protruding tusks, and his horny, taloned hand, they came upon the old beast. Each one hitting him a blow with his war club, they "ended his daylight," and then hauled him forth into the open space. They opened his huge paunch and withdrew from it the maiden's garments, and even the rabbits which had been slain. The rabbits they cast away among the soap-weed plants that grew on the slope at the foot of the cliff. The garments they spread out on the snow, and cleansed and made them perfect, even more perfect than they had been before. Then, flinging the huge body of the giant Demon down into the depths of the canyon, they turned them about and, calling out gentle words to the maiden, entered and restored her. She, seeing in them not their usual ugly persons, but handsome youths, was greatly comforted; and bending low, and breathing upon their hands, thanked them over and
9 over for the rescue they had brought her. But she crouched herself low with shame that her garments were but few, when, behold! the youths went out and brought in to her the garments they had cleaned, restoring them to her.

Then, spreading their mantles by the door of the cave, they slept there that night, in order to protect the maiden, and on the morrow wakened her. They told her many things, and showed her many things which she had not known before, and counseled her thus, "It is not fearful that a maiden should marry; therefore, O maiden, return unto thy people in the Village of the Gateway of the River of Zuñi. This morning we will slay rabbits unnumbered for you, and start you on your way, guarding you down the snow-covered valley. When you are in sight of your home we will leave you, telling you our names."

So, early in the morning the two gods went forth, flinging their sticks among the soap-weed plants. Behold! as though the soap-weed plants were rabbits, so many lay killed on the snow before these mighty hunters. And they gathered together great numbers of these rabbits, a string for each one of the party. When the Sun had risen clearer in the sky, and his light sparkled on the snow around them, they took the rabbits to the maiden and presented them, saying, "We will carry each one of us a string of these rabbits." Then taking her hand, they led her out of the cave and down the valley, until, beyond on the high black mesas[8] at the Gateway of the River of Zuñi, she saw the smoke rise from the houses of her village. Then turned the two war-gods to her, and they told her their names. And again she bent low, and breathed on their hands. Then, dropping the strings of rabbits which they had carried close beside the maiden, they swiftly disappeared.

Thinking much of all she had learned, she continued her way to the home of her father and mother. As she went into the town, staggering under her load of rabbits, the young men and the old men and women and children beheld her with wonder; and no hunter in that town thought of comparing himself with the Maiden Hunter of Zuñi River. The old man and the old woman, who had mourned the night through and sat up anxiously watching, were overcome with happiness when they saw their daughter had returned.

---

8. mesas (mā′ səz), *n.*: Small mountains with flat tops and steep sides.

Closure and Extension

ANSWERS TO THINKING ABOUT THE SELECTION

Recalling

1. The reasons the girl goes hunting are that there was no one else to get meat for the family, as her brothers are dead and her father is too old to hunt. Also, the male hunters did not give her any of their rabbits because she has refused to marry them.
2. Her parents resist because they think she will get lost or become too tired to return.
3. She becomes lost because she remains out hunting during a heavy snowstorm and her tracks become covered.
4. His plan once he discovered he could not enter the cave was to have her bring food out to him.
5. The girl is rescued by two war-gods who see her plight, rush to her aid, and kill the Cannibal Demon.

THINKING ABOUT THE SELECTION

Recalling

1. For what reasons does the girl go hunting?
2. Why do the girl's parents at first resist her plans?
3. How does the girl become lost?
4. Explain the Cannibal Demon's plan to get the girl out of the cave.
5. How is the girl rescued?
6. How do the villagers regard the girl when she returns?

Interpreting

7. Why do the girl's parents help her when they really do not want her to go?
8. Why does the war god help the girl?
9. Why does the girl see the two "usually ugly" war gods as handsome youths?
10. What does the girl learn from the war gods? Do you think what she learns will affect the way she behaves in the future? Explain your answer.

Applying

11. In this legend the girl demonstrates bravery. Select one other character you have read about who is brave. Compare and contrast the girl and this character.

ANALYZING LITERATURE

Understanding a Legend

Legends are imaginative stories that are based on real people or real events. As the story is passed from generation to generation it often changes. Sometimes the retelling may result in downplaying the factual and highlighting the imaginative. "The Girl Who Hunted Rabbits" is probably based on a real incident.

1. What details of the legend could be based on fact?
2. What parts seem purely imaginative?

CRITICAL THINKING AND READING

Making Inferences from a Legend

An **inference** is a reasonable conclusion that can be drawn from evidence. In "The Girl Who Hunted Rabbits" you can infer that Zuñi girls were not expected to hunt based on the girl's statement, "O that I were a man and could go forth, as do these young men, hunting rabbits!"

1. Find evidence in this legend that suggests that young girls were expected to get married.
2. Find evidence that the Zuñi placed high value on children taking care of their parents.

UNDERSTANDING LANGUAGE

Choosing Meaning to Fit Context

Context is the surrounding words and ideas that can help you understand the meaning of an unfamiliar word.

From the context of the following sentences, figure out the meanings of the words in italics.

1. "But, as in those days of our ancients, we had neither sheep nor cattle, the hunt was depended upon to supply the meat; or sometimes it was *procured* by barter of the products of the fields to those who hunted mostly."
2. "Of these things this little family had barely enough for their own *subsistence;* hence, they could not procure their supplies of meat in this way."

THINKING AND WRITING

Retelling a Legend

Imagine you are the girl in this legend. Think about your feelings when the demon tried to devour you. Retell this episode from the girl's point of view. Use the pronoun *I* to identify yourself as the girl. Revise, making sure you have told events through the girl's eyes. Finally, proofread your story and share it with your classmates.

6. The villagers regard her with wonder and think that she is a great hunter. Her parents are overjoyed at her return.

Interpreting

7. Her parents help her because they realize that she will go even if they do not want her to. Therefore, they want to help her as best they can because they care for her.
8. The war-gods help the girl because they know that she is hunting for the sake of her parents and became lost as a result.
9. Answers will differ. Suggested Responses: The war-gods chose to appear before her as handsome youths so that she would not be frightened. Also, they might be ugly only during war, and since they were not at war, they did not appear ugly. They later tell her not to be afraid to marry, and make themselves handsome so that she will not be afraid to do so. Possibly, the girl's happiness and gratitude over being saved by the war-gods affects her view of them.
10. The maiden learned many things that she had not known before, including the gods' names and the fact that she should marry. A suggested response is that she will be affected by what she has learned because she was "thinking much of all she had learned," as she returned to the village and the people looked on her with wonder.

(Answers begin on p. 640.)

Applying

11. Answers will differ depending on the character the student chooses. Be sure that they contrast their characters with the maiden, as well as compare them.

ANSWERS TO ANALYZING LITERATURE

1. The details that were probably based on fact include any of the details concerning the girl, her family, the hunt, and the village.
2. The parts which seem purely imaginative are those about the Cannibal Demon and the two war-gods.

ANSWERS TO CRITICAL THINKING AND READING

1. The evidence that girls were expected to marry includes the following points: the other hunters would not give her rabbits because she had refused to marry them; and the war-gods advise her that "It is not fearful that a maiden should marry."
2. The evidence that suggests that the Zuñi placed high value on children caring for their parents is the maiden's willingness to risk her life so her parents would have meat and her unwillingness to marry and leave her parents.

Challenge Find evidence in this legend that indicates that women did not normally hunt rabbits.

ANSWERS TO UNDERSTANDING LANGUAGE

1. **procured:** Obtained by some effort.
2. **subsistence:** Barest needs in terms of food, clothing, and shelter needed to sustain life.

Writing Across the Curriculum You might want to have students research and report on the way of life and the history of the Zuñi Indians. If you assign this, perhaps inform the social studies department. Social studies teachers might provide guidance and assistance for students in conducting their research.

Focus

More About the Tale Some historians suggest that the legend of Paul Bunyan can be traced to French-Canadian lumberjacks who may have related old French folktales about giants. It is possible that these tales were transformed in the New World, and developed into the legend of Paul Bunyan. The first references to Paul Bunyan in print were stories written by James McGillivray for a Detroit newspaper in 1910. These stories were based on tales he had heard from Michigan lumberjacks.

Literary Focus Point out to students that authentic folktales last because they continue to appeal to people through the years. For folktales to be considered authentic, they must have at least two versions. For example, the tale Cinderella has more than a thousand versions developed over hundreds of years in many different countries.

Look For You might have your **less advanced** students make a list of these traits as they read the passage.

Writing/Prior Knowledge Have students discuss the importance of heroes in society. Why do people look up to and admire professional athletes, actors and actresses, cartoon characters, and other such figures? What characteristics do these people have that make them admirable?

Vocabulary The words for this selection are fairly easy to grasp, and students should have little difficulty with them.

Spelling Tip *Shanties* is the plural of *shanty.* If the final *y* is preceded by a consonant, the *y* usually changes to *i* when a suffix is added.

Example: *carry* *carried*
merry *merriment*

GUIDE FOR READING

Paul Bunyan of the North Woods

Paul Bunyan is a legendary frontiersman—a gigantic lumberjack known for his tremendous strength and fantastic logging feats. According to folklore, Paul Bunyan invented the idea of logging in the Pacific Northwest. He created the Great Lakes—to provide drinking water for his enormous blue ox, Babe.

Folktales about Paul Bunyan have been recorded by numerous writers, among them **Carl Sandburg** (1878–1967). (For more information on Carl Sandburg, see also page 630.)

Folktale

Folktales, like legends and myths, are stories that have been passed down orally, but today have been preserved in written form. They are not about gods and goddesses but often involve a hero who performs amazing feats of strength or daring or solves problems. Folktales often may last because they highlight qualities that a culture values.

Look For

As you read "Paul Bunyan of the North Woods," look for the traits about Paul Bunyan—strength, size, and cleverness—that make people enjoy hearing tales about him. Notice that this selection summarizes several folktales about Paul Bunyan. Which of the tales about him do you like the most?

Writing

Create an imaginary hero, such as the greatest football player or the most brilliant scientist. Brainstorm and write down your ideas about folktales that you could tell about that person.

Vocabulary

Knowing the following words will help you as you read "Paul Bunyan of the North Woods."

lumberjack (lum′ bər jak′) *n.*: A person employed to cut down timber (p. 643)
shanties (shan′ tēz) *n.*: Huts or shacks in which loggers lived (p. 643)
granite (gran′ it) *adj.*: Made of a type of very hard rock (p. 643)
hobnailed (häb′ nāld′) *adj.*: Having short nails put on the soles to provide greater traction (p. 643)
commotion (kə mō′ shən) *n.*: Noisy movement (p. 644)
bellowing (bel′ ō iŋ) *adv.*: Roaring (p. 644)

Objectives

1 To understand folktales
2 To make generalizations about folktales
3 To understand homophones
4 To respond to a critical comment

Support Material

Teaching Portfolio
Teacher Backup, pp. 929–931
Usage and Mechanics Worksheet, p. 932
Vocabulary Check, p. 933
Critical Thinking and Reading Worksheet, *Making Generalizations About a Folktale,* p. 934
Language Worksheet, *Appreciating Homophones,* p. 935
Selection Test, pp. 936–937

Paul Bunyan of the North Woods

Carl Sandburg

Who made Paul Bunyan, who gave him birth as a myth, who joked him into life as the Master Lumberjack, who fashioned him forth as an apparition[1] easing the hours of men amid axes and trees, saws and
1 lumber? The people, the bookless people, they made Paul and had him alive long before he got into the books for those who read. He grew up in shanties, around the hot stoves of winter, among socks and mittens drying, in the smell of tobacco smoke and the roar of laughter
2 mocking the outside weather. And some of Paul came overseas in wooden bunks below decks in sailing vessels. And some of Paul is old as the hills, young as the alphabet.

The Pacific Ocean froze over in the winter of the Blue Snow and Paul Bunyan had long teams of oxen hauling regular white snow over from China. This was the winter Paul gave a party to the Seven Axmen. Paul fixed a granite floor sunk two hundred feet deep for them to dance on. Still, it tipped and tilted as the dance went on. And because the Seven Axmen refused to take off their hobnailed boots, the sparks from the nails of their dancing feet lit up the place so that Paul didn't light the kerosene lamps. No women being on the Big Onion river at that time the Seven Axmen had to dance

PAUL BUNYAN CARRYING A TREE ON HIS SHOULDER AND AN AX IN HIS HAND
The Bettmann Archive

---

1. apparition (ap'ə rish'ən), *n.*: A strange figure appearing suddenly or in an extraordinary way.

Presentation

Humanities Note

Paul Bunyan has been depicted in many paintings and statues.

1. How does this painting compare with the student's image of Paul?
2. What kind of man has the artist drawn?
3. Why is he laughing? Does his laughter imply his ease in carrying the enormous tree? Or does it show his overall good nature?

Motivation/Prior Knowledge Have students discuss what they know about Paul Bunyan and his companion, Babe the blue ox. What impressions do they have of Paul?

Master Teacher Note Have students recall comic strip or cartoon heroes. What qualities do they share with Paul Bunyan? What common themes are in the stories?

Purpose-Setting Question What character traits are exaggerated in these tales?

1 **Discussion** What does the author mean by "bookless people"?

2 **Critical Thinking and Reading** You might have students infer who might be the people that the author is discussing. What do they all seem to have in common?

3 Literary Focus One of the reasons that folktales survive is that they continue to appeal to listeners and readers. You might point out to students that people have always admired someone who, when faced with a problem, solves it no matter how difficult. How is this ability helpful in life?

4 Discussion What qualities of this yarn are repetitious? How does the repetitive nature of these folktales affect your reading of them?

5 Literary Focus The style is informal, as if the tale is being told orally. This style reflects the oral heritage in which all such stories originate.

Enrichment The lumber industry has played an important role in the development of our country since colonial times. Prior to the twentieth century, life for the men who cut down the trees was difficult. Lumberjacks lived in isolated logging camps in the wilderness. These camps offered few comforts and the men spent most of their time working and sleeping. It was their reputation as strong, skilled, and courageous workers that led to the creation of many of the legends of their exploits. While some of the legends are true, others, such as the legends of Paul Bunyan, are humorous tall tales.

Reader's Response What contemporary figures can you think of who might someday have heroic status because they embody our cultural values?

with each other, the one left over in each set taking Paul as a partner. The commotion of the dancing that night brought on an earthquake and the Big Onion river moved over three counties to the east.

3 One year when it rained from St. Patrick's Day till the Fourth of July, Paul Bunyan got disgusted because his celebration on the Fourth was spoiled. He dived into Lake Superior and swam to where a solid pillar of water was coming down. He dived under this pillar, swam up into it and climbed with powerful swimming strokes, was gone about an hour, came splashing down, and as the rain stopped, he explained, "I turned the dam thing off." This is told in the Big North Woods and on the Great Lakes, with many particulars.

Two mosquitoes lighted on one of Paul Bunyan's oxen, killed it, ate it, cleaned the bones, and sat on a grub shanty picking their teeth as Paul came along. Paul sent to Australia for two special bumblebees to kill these mosquitoes. But the bees and the mosquitoes intermarried; their children had stingers on both ends. And things kept getting worse till Paul brought a big boatload of sorghum[2] up from Louisiana and while all the bee-mosquitoes were eating at the sweet sorghum he floated them down to the Gulf of Mexico. They got so fat that it was easy to drown them all between New Orleans and Galveston.

Paul logged on the Little Gimlet in Oregon one winter. The cookstove at that camp covered an acre of ground. They fastened the side of a hog on each snowshoe and four men used to skate on the griddle while the cook flipped the pancakes. The eating table was three miles long; elevators carried the cakes to the ends of the table where boys on bicycles rode back and forth on a path down the center of the table dropping the cakes where called for. 4

Benny, the Little Blue Ox of Paul Bunyan, grew two feet every time Paul looked at him, when a youngster. The barn was gone one morning and they found it on Benny's back; he grew out of it in a night. One night he kept pawing and bellowing for more pancakes, till there were two hundred men at the cook-shanty stove trying to keep him fed. About breakfast time Benny broke loose, tore down the cook-shanty, ate all the pancakes piled up for the loggers' breakfast. And after that Benny made his mistake; he ate the red hot stove; and that finished him. This is only one of the hot-stove stories told in the North Woods. 5

2. sorghum (sor'gəm), *n.*: Tropical grasses bearing flowers and seeds that are grown for use as grain or syrup.

Closure and Extension

ANSWERS TO THINKING ABOUT THE SELECTION

Recalling

1. Bunyan showed his cleverness in the tale where he got rid of the bee-mosquitoes.
2. Bunyan used his strength when he swam up the pillar of water to turn off the rain.
3. Bunyan solved the problem of serving pancakes by using elevators to carry the pancakes to the ends of the table, where boys on bicycles picked them up, rode down the center of the tables, and delivered pancakes where they were called for.

THINKING ABOUT THE SELECTION

Recalling

1. How did Paul Bunyan show his cleverness?
2. How did Paul Bunyan use his strength?
3. How did Paul Bunyan solve the problem of serving pancakes at a table three miles long?
4. How often did Benny, the Little Blue Ox of Paul Bunyan, grow when a youngster?

Interpreting

5. Interpret the following statement: "And some of Paul is old as the hills, young as the alphabet"?
6. What qualities and abilities seem to be valued in this selection?

Applying

7. Explain how Paul's qualities of strength, cleverness, and size might be valuable for real lumberjacks.

ANALYZING LITERATURE

Understanding a Folktale

Before **folktales** were preserved in written form, they were simply stories retold whenever a group of people with the same interests gathered. Many times, the storyteller would claim to have witnessed the tale in order to make it seem more authentic. The tales that people chose to recount indicate something about what their lives were like. For example, this selection shows you the rugged lives that loggers lived.

1. Find three other details that indicate the ruggedness of the loggers' lives.
2. Find two details that indicate the need for courage.
3. Think about the landscape of the Pacific Northwest. Why would the people telling these folktales make Paul so big?

CRITICAL THINKING AND READING

Making Generalizations About a Folktale

A **generalization** is a general idea or statement derived from particular instances. For example, if every book you have read by a certain author is about science fiction, you can generalize that the author is a science-fiction writer.

1. What generalization do you make about the folktales based on "Paul Bunyan of the North Woods"?
2. Give the particular instances on which this generalization is based.

UNDERSTANDING LANGUAGE

Appreciating Homophones

Homophones are words that have the same sound, but differ in spelling and meaning. For example, *bough* sounds like *cow* and means "the branch of a tree." A homophone of *bough* is *bow,* which sounds the same, but is spelled differently and means "to bend the head or body in respect."

Write the homophone for each of the following words.

1. meet
2. site
3. pane
4. know

THINKING AND WRITING

Writing a Response to Critical Comment

A writer has said that the Paul Bunyan folktales were told matter-of-factly, as if by an eyewitness of commonly known events. This gives the tales a feeling of truthfulness. Choose which tales in this selection are told in a matter-of-fact manner. Then write an essay for your classmates explaining in what ways they seem matter-of-fact. Use examples to support your view. Revise your paragraphs to make sure your opinion is stated clearly. Finally, proofread your essay and share it with your classmates.

(Answers begin on p. 644.)

4. Benny grew every time Bunyan looked at him.

Interpreting

5. Suggested Response: Some of the material that was the source of the stories about Paul was very old and some was added more recently.
6. Answers will differ. Suggested Responses: qualities include strength, resolve, cleverness, the ability to eat a great deal, and the ability to enjoy oneself under difficult conditions.

Applying

7. Answers will differ. Suggested Responses: The qualities of strength and size are important for the handling and transportation of large trees. Cleverness is important for solving difficult problems in remote areas with limited resources.

ANSWERS TO ANALYZING LITERATURE

1. Answers will differ. Suggested Responses: The Seven Axmen wore hobnailed boots; there were no women in the area for the party; the mosquitoes were so ferocious that they could kill an ox; and the weather was sometimes severe (the winter of the Blue Snow, the year it rained from St. Patrick's Day until July Fourth).
2. Answers will differ. Suggested Response: Details include the harsh weather and the ferocious mosquitoes.
3. Answers will differ. Suggested Response: Largeness of many things found in the Northwest, such as the mountains, the trees, and the rugged, wild areas. Largeness can also be associated with strength.

Challenge Why would the work of a lumberjack be a likely topic out of which tall tales emerge?

ANSWERS TO CRITICAL THINKING AND READING

1. Answers will differ. Suggested Response: A generalization about folktales based on "Paul Bunyan of the North Woods" is that folktales are humorous, exaggerated stories glorifying the values necessary for living and working on the American frontier.
2. Answers will differ. Suggested Response: The aspect of humor is found in the tale of the three-mile-long table, among others. The aspect of exaggeration can be found in all of the tales, including the tale when the winter was so cold that the Pacific Ocean froze over. Values, including solving difficult problems, are shown in the tale of the ferocious mosquitoes.

Challenge What generalization do you make about yarns and tall tales based on the excerpt from *The People, Yes* and "Paul Bunyan of the North Woods"?

ANSWERS TO UNDERSTANDING LANGUAGE

1. meat
2. sight
3. pain
4. no

THINKING AND WRITING

Publishing Student Writing Ask for student volunteers to read their essays aloud. Have students in the audience record one important feature of each essay. Finally, using these notes, along with their own essays as a guide, have the class discuss their impressions of Paul Bunyan of the North Woods.

Focus

More About the Tale The folktales of Pecos Bill originated in a magazine article written by an American journalist named Edward O'Reilly in 1923. The author patterned his hero after other frontier folk heroes such as Paul Bunyan. How might a folktale about a cowboy differ from one about a lumberjack?

Literary Focus Point out to students that folk heroes like Pecos Bill are endowed with all of the qualities considered valuable on the frontier. In these tales, the conflicts the hero encounters tend to test these skills. By triumphing, the folk hero reaffirms the value of such skills.

Look For Your more advanced students might look for the human characteristics attributed to the cyclone that make it a more interesting and entertaining adversary.

Writing/Prior Knowledge You might have your less advanced students work in small groups to help one another brainstorm for ideas.

Vocabulary Have your more advanced students write original sentences using each of the vocabulary words.

Spelling Tip The adjective ending *-ible,* meaning "capable of," as in words like *invincible,* is the less common spelling of the ending. Most adjectives take *-able.*

GUIDE FOR READING

Pecos Bill: The Cyclone

Pecos Bill is a legendary American cowboy. He is credited with the invention of branding, roping, and the six-shooter, and is said to have taught broncos how to buck. The tales tell that Pecos Bill was born in Texas in the 1830's. One of the most famous tales about Pecos Bill tells of the time he rode a cyclone in Oklahoma.

That exploit is recounted by **Harold W. Felton** (1902–), born in Neola, Iowa, who collected folklore of the West.

Conflict in a Folktale

A **conflict** is a struggle between opposing sides or forces. A conflict can be that of a person against another person, nature, fate, or society; or it can be between two opposing forces within a person.

The hero in a folktale may be in conflict with the fastest runner, the hardest worker, the best shot, the most courageous person, or the quickest thinker. Folktales are full of conflicts and competitions, such as shooting and boxing matches and encounters with nature, that the heroes win because of their extraordinary daring, skill, or strength.

Look For

As you read "Pecos Bill: The Cyclone," look for how Pecos Bill, the greatest of the cowboys, deals with conflicts in ways that are different from those of an average human being. Why is he able to win each of these conflicts?

Writing

Conflicts in folktales often involve a human being who is pitted against some overwhelming force or obstacle. Brainstorm and write down your ideas about the types of conflicts you could write a folktale about.

Vocabulary

Knowing the following words will help you as you read "Pecos Bill: The Cyclone."

usurped (yo͞o sʉrpt') *v.*: To take power or authority away from (p. 649)

invincible (in vin' sə b'l) *adj.*: Unbeatable (p. 651)

futile (fyo͞ot' 'l) *adj.*: Useless, hopeless (p. 651)

inexplicable (in eks' pli kə b'l) *adj.*: Without explanation (p. 652)

skeptics (skep' tiks) *n.*: Persons who doubt (p. 652)

Objectives

1 To understand conflict in folktales
2 To identify reasons
3 To appreciate words from Spanish
4 To write a description of a conflict

Support Material

Teaching Portfolio

Teacher Backup, pp. 939–942
Grammar in Action Worksheet, *Using Precise Words,* pp. 943–944
Usage and Mechanics Worksheet, p. 945
Vocabulary Check, p. 946
Analyzing Literature Worksheet, *Understanding Conflict in a Folktale,* p. 947
Critical Thinking and Reading Worksheet, *Identifying Reasons,* p. 948
Selection Test, pp. 949–950

Pecos Bill: The Cyclone

Harold W. Felton

One of Bill's greatest feats, if not the greatest feat of all time, occurred unexpectedly one Fourth of July. He had invented the Fourth of July some years before. It was a great day for the cowpunchers.[1] They had taken to it right off like the real Americans they were. But the celebration had always ended on a dismal note. Somehow it seemed to be spoiled by a cyclone.

Bill had never minded the cyclone much. The truth is he rather liked it. But the other celebrants ran into caves for safety. He invented cyclone cellars for them. He even named the cellars. He called them "'fraid holes." Pecos wouldn't even say the word "afraid." The cyclone was something like he was. It was big and strong too. He always stood by musing[2] pleasantly as he watched it.

The cyclone caused Bill some trouble, though. Usually it would destroy a few hundred miles of fence by blowing the postholes away. But it wasn't much trouble for him to fix it. All he had to do was to go and get the postholes and then take them back and put the fence posts in them. The holes were rarely ever blown more than twenty or thirty miles.

In one respect Bill even welcomed the cyclone, for it blew so hard it blew the earth away from his wells. The first time this happened, he thought the wells would be a total loss. There they were, sticking up several hundred feet out of the ground. As wells they were useless. But he found he could cut them up into lengths and sell them for postholes to farmers in Iowa and Nebraska. It was very profitable, especially after he invented a special posthole saw to cut them with. He didn't use that type of posthole himself. He got the prairie dogs to dig his for him. 3 He simply caught a few gross[3] of prairie dogs and set them down at proper intervals. The prairie dog would dig a hole. Then Bill would put a post in it. The prairie dog would get disgusted and go down the row ahead of the others and dig another hole. Bill fenced all of Texas and parts of New Mexico and Arizona in this manner. He took a few contracts and fenced most of the Southern Pacific right of way too. That's the reason it is so crooked. He had trouble getting the prairie dogs to run a straight fence.

As for his wells, the badgers dug them. The system was the same as with the prairie dogs. The labor was cheap so it didn't make much difference if the cyclone did spoil some of the wells. The badgers were digging all of the time anyway. They didn't seem to care whether they dug wells or just badger holes.

One year he tried shipping the prairie dog holes up north, too, for postholes. It was not successful. They didn't keep in storage

1. **cowpunchers** (kou' pun chərz), *n.*: Cowboys.
2. **musing** (myo͞oz' ing), *adv.*: Thinking deeply.

3. **gross** (grōs), *n.*: Twelve dozen.

Presentation

Motivation/Prior Knowledge You might have students visualize someone actually climbing onto and riding a tornado. What would that person look like? What similar actions are portrayed in cartoons like "Bugs Bunny"?

Thematic Idea To compare folk heroes in conflict with natural phenomena, you might use Davy Crockett's Tussle with a Bear, page 681.

Purpose-Setting Question What is the conflict in this folktale?

1 **Clarification** The cyclone in this folktale is more commonly known as a tornado. Tornadoes are powerful, twisting storms with winds that reach speeds of more than 300 miles per hour. The winds are the most violent that occur on earth and often cause great destruction and death. About 700 tornadoes are reported annually in the United States, with most striking the Midwest and the states that border the Gulf of Mexico. One of the largest and fastest tornadoes in history went through Missouri, Illinois, and Indiana on March 18, 1925, leaving 689 people dead. It measured up to a mile wide and traveled at about sixty miles per hour over a distance of 220 miles.

2 **Discussion** Why won't Bill even say the word "afraid"?

3 **Critical Thinking and Reading** What is the reason that Bill does not use the same postholes as other men?

Master Teacher Note Like other authentic folktales, "Pecos Bill: The Cyclone" has more than one version. Another version of this story has Pecos Bill riding the cyclone to win a bet. There are also several variations of other tales, including the death of Bill. According to one, he laughed himself to death listening to a man from Boston who asked silly questions about the West.

4 **Discussion** What is the purpose of setting the story during "those days"? How does this compare with other folktales, such as that of Paul Bunyan?

5 **Reading Strategy** You might have students question when these references to "old days" might be. Why does the writer refer to other incidents?

6 **Literary Focus** The conflict is now established between Bill and the biggest and most terrible, original cyclone.

and they couldn't stand the handling in shipping. After they were installed they seemed to wear out quickly. Bill always thought the difference in climate had something to do with it.

It should be said that in those days there was only one cyclone. It was the
4 first and original cyclone, bigger and more terrible by far than the small cyclones of today. It usually stayed by itself up north around Kansas and Oklahoma and didn't bother anyone much. But it was attracted by the noise of the Fourth of July celebration and without fail managed to put in an appearance before the close of the day.

On this particular Fourth of July, the celebration had gone off fine. The speeches were loud and long. The contests and games were hard fought. The high point of the day was Bill's exhibition with Widow Maker, which came right after he showed off Scat and Rat. People seemed never to tire of seeing them in action. The mountain lion was almost useless as a work animal after
5 his accident, and the snake had grown old and somewhat infirm, and was troubled with rheumatism in his rattles. But they too enjoyed the Fourth of July and liked to make a public appearance. They relived the old days.

Widow Maker had put on a good show, bucking as no ordinary horse could ever buck. Then Bill undertook to show the gaits[4] he had taught the palomino.[5] Other mustangs[6] at that time had only two gaits. Walking and running. Only Widow Maker could pace. But now Bill had developed and taught him other gaits. Twenty-seven in all. Twenty-three forward and three reverse. He was very proud of the achievement. He showed off the slow gaits and the crowd was eager for more.

He showed the walk, trot, canter, lope, jog, slow rack, fast rack, single foot, pace, stepping pace, fox trot, running walk and the others now known. Both men and horses confuse the various gaits nowadays. Some of the gaits are now thought to be the same, such as the rack and the single foot. But with Widow Maker and Pecos Bill, each one was different. Each was precise and to be distinguished from the others. No one had ever imagined such a thing.

Then the cyclone came! All of the people except Bill ran into the 'fraid holes. Bill was annoyed. He stopped the performance. The remaining gaits were not shown. From that day to this horses have used no more than the gaits Widow Maker exhibited that day. It is unfortunate that the really fast gaits were not shown. If they were, horses might be much faster today than they are.

Bill glanced up at the cyclone and the quiet smile on his face faded into a frown. He saw the cyclone was angry. Very, very angry indeed.

The cyclone had always been the center of attention. Everywhere it went people would look up in wonder, fear and amazement. It had been the undisputed master of the country. It had observed Bill's rapid climb to fame and had seen the Fourth of July celebration grow. It had been keeping an eye on things all right.

In the beginning, the Fourth of July crowd had aroused its curiosity. It liked nothing more than to show its superiority and power by breaking the crowd up sometime during the day. But every year the crowd was larger. This preyed on the cyclone's mind. This year it did not come to watch. It deliberately came to spoil the celebration. Jealous of Bill and of his success,

---

4. gaits (gātz), *n.*: Any of the various foot movements of a horse.
5. palomino (pal'ə mē' nō), *n.*: A light tan or golden brown horse with a cream-colored mane and tail.
6. mustangs (mus' taŋz), *n.*: Wild horses of the American plains.

Grammar in Action

Writers have all the words in the English language at their disposal. The more specific or **precise** the **word** they choose, the more vivid will be the word picture they create.

Consider the precise words in the following passage:

> Other mustangs at that time had only two gaits. Walking and running. Only Widow Maker could *pace*. But now Bill had developed and taught him other gaits. Twenty-seven in all. Twenty-three forward and three reverse. . . . He showed the *walk, trot, canter, lope, jog, slow rack, fast rack, single foot, pace, stepping pace, fox trot, running walk* and the others now known . . . Each was precise and to be distinguished from the others.

Notice all the words that describe types of walks. What does each word mean precisely?

Student Activity 1. Working with a group of five students, compile a list of words that name types of walking.

it resolved to do away with the whole institution of the Fourth of July once and for all. So much havoc and destruction would be wrought that there would never be another Independence Day Celebration. On that day, in future years, it would circle around the horizon leering[7] and gloating. At least, so it thought.

The cyclone was resolved, also, to do away with this bold fellow who did not hold it in awe and run for the 'fraid hole at
7 its approach. For untold years it had been the most powerful thing in the land. And now, here was a mere man who threatened its position. More! Who had usurped its position!

When Bill looked at the horizon and saw the cyclone coming, he recognized the anger and rage. While a cyclone does not often smile, Bill had felt from the beginning that it was just a grouchy fellow who never had a pleasant word for anyone. But now, instead of merely an unpleasant character, Bill saw all the viciousness of which an angry cy-
8 clone is capable. He had no way of knowing that the cyclone saw its kingship tottering and was determined to stop this man who threatened its supremacy.

But Bill understood the violence of the onslaught even as the monster came into view. He knew he must meet it. The center of the cyclone was larger than ever before. The fact is, the cyclone had been training for this fight all winter and spring. It was in best form and at top weight. It headed straight for Bill intent on his destruction. In an instant it was upon him. Bill had sat quietly and silently on the great pacing mustang. But his mind was working rapidly. In the split second between his first sight of the monster and the time for action he had made his plans. Pecos Bill was ready! Ready and waiting!

Green clouds were dripping from the cyclone's jaws. Lightning flashed from its eyes as it swept down upon him. Its plan was to envelope Bill in one mighty grasp. Just as it was upon him, Bill turned Widow
Maker to its left. This was a clever move for 9
the cyclone was right-handed, and while it had been training hard to get its left in shape, that was not its best side. Bill gave rein to his mount. Widow Maker wheeled and turned on a dime which Pecos had, with great foresight[8] and accuracy, thrown to the ground to mark the exact spot for this maneuver. It was the first time that anyone had thought of turning on a dime. Then he urged the great horse forward. The cyclone, filled with surprise, lost its balance and rushed forward at an increased speed. It went so fast that it met itself coming back. This confused the cyclone, but it did not confuse Pecos Bill. He had expected that to happen. Widow Maker went into his twenty-first gait and edged up close to the whirlwind. Soon they were running neck and neck.

At the proper instant Bill grabbed the cyclone's ears, kicked himself free of the stirrups and pulled himself lightly on its back. Bill never used spurs on Widow Maker. Sometimes he wore them for show and because he liked the jingling sound they made. They made a nice accompaniment for his cowboy songs. But he had not been singing, so he had no spurs. He did not have his rattlesnake for a quirt.[9] Of course there
was no bridle. It was man against monster! 10
There he was! Pecos Bill astride a raging cyclone, slick heeled and without a saddle!

7. **leering** (lir'ing), *adv.*: Looking with malicious triumph.

8. **foresight** (fôr' sīt), *n.*: The act of seeing beforehand.

9. **quirt** (kwurt), *n.*: A short-handled riding whip with a braided rawhide lash.

7 **Discussion** Why does the cyclone have thoughts and actions like humans? How does this affect the conflict?

8 **Reading Strategy** Have students summarize the reasons that the cyclone is angry with Bill. How do these reasons heighten the conflict?

9 **Discussion** How is this description similar to the description of a boxing match?

10 **Literary Focus** You might want to point out that this sentence directly states the conflict.

Student Activity 2. Working with a group of five students, compile a list of words that name types of dancing.

Student Activity 3. Working with a group of five students, compile a list of words that name types of running.

11 **Discussion** Does this illustration represent Pecos Bill accurately? Is this how you imagined him? Support your answer with details from the illustration.

11

The cyclone was taken by surprise at this sudden turn of events. But it was undaunted. It was sure of itself. Months of training had given it a conviction that it was invincible. With a mighty heave, it twisted to its full height. Then it fell back suddenly, twisting and turning violently, so that before it came back to earth, it had turned around a thousand times. Surely no rider could ever withstand such an attack. No rider ever had. Little wonder. No one had ever ridden a cyclone before. But Pecos Bill did! He fanned the tornado's ears with his hat and dug his heels into the demon's flanks and yelled, "Yipee-ee!"

The people who had run for shelter began to come out. The audience further enraged the cyclone. It was bad enough to be disgraced by having a man astride it. It was unbearable not to have thrown him. To have all the people see the failure was too much! It got down flat on the ground and rolled over and over. Bill retained his seat throughout this ruse.[10] Evidence of this desperate but futile stratagem[11] remains today. The great Staked Plains, or as the Mexicans call it, *Llano Estacado* is the result. Its small, rugged mountains were covered with trees at the time. The rolling of the cyclone destroyed the mountains, the trees, and almost everything else in the area. The destruction was so complete, that part of the country is flat and treeless to this day. When the settlers came, there were no landmarks to guide them across the vast unmarked space, so they drove stakes in the ground to mark the trails. That is the reason it is called "Staked Plains." Here is an example of the proof of the events of history by

---

10. ruse (rōōz), *n.*: Trick.
11. stratagem (stra′ tə jəm), *n.*: Plan for defeating an opponent.

651

12 Critical Thinking and Reading This folktale explains the geographical peculiarity of the Staked Plains, as "The Origin of Fire" explained how Indians first got fire. What other things is Bill given credit for inventing or creating in this folktale?

13 Discussion What does Bill's reaction indicate about his character?

14 Literary Focus The outcome of the conflict of this and most folktales is the same. The hero succeeds in overcoming a seemingly invincible foe. What qualities of frontier life are illustrated in Bill's victory?

15 Discussion Do you agree with this logic? How is the writer's argument flawed?

Reader's Response The folktale about Pecos Bill could only have originated in an area where cyclones are a common problem. What natural phenomena might inspire a folktale in your region of the country? Your region may have its own tales. If so, what are they?

12 careful and painstaking research. It is also an example of how seemingly inexplicable geographical facts can be explained.

It was far more dangerous for the rider when the cyclone shot straight up to the sky. Once there, the twister tried the same thing it had tried on the ground. It rolled on the sky. It was no use. Bill could not be unseated. He kept his place, and he didn't have a sky hook with him either.

13 As for Bill, he was having the time of his life, shouting at the top of his voice, kicking his opponent in the ribs and jabbing his thumb in its flanks. It responded and went on a wild bucking rampage over the entire West. It used all the bucking tricks known to the wildest broncos as well as those known only to cyclones. The wind howled furiously and beat against the fearless rider. The rain poured. The lightning flashed around his ears. The fight went on and on. Bill enjoyed himself immensely. In spite of the elements he easily kept his place. . . .

14 The raging cyclone saw this out of the corner of its eye. It knew then who the victor was. It was twisting far above the Rocky Mountains when the awful truth came to it. In a horrible heave it disintegrated! Small pieces of cyclone flew in all directions. Bill still kept his seat on the main central portion until that rained out from under him. Then he jumped to a nearby streak of lightning and slid down it toward earth. But it was raining so hard that the rain put out the lightning. When it fizzled out from under him, Bill dropped the rest of the way. He lit in what is now called Death Valley. He hit quite hard, as is apparent from the fact that he so compressed the place that it is still two hundred and seventy-six feet below sea level. The Grand Canyon was washed out by the rain, though it must be understood that this happened after Paul Bunyan had given it a good start by carelessly dragging his ax behind him when he went west a short time before.

The cyclones and the hurricanes and the tornadoes nowadays are the small pieces that broke off of the big cyclone Pecos Bill rode. In fact, the rainstorms of the present day came into being in the same way. There are always skeptics, but even they will recognize the logic of the proof of this event. They will recall that even now it almost always rains on the Fourth of July. That is because the rainstorms of today still retain some of the characteristics of the giant cyclone that met its comeuppance at the hands of Pecos Bill.

Bill lay where he landed and looked up at the sky, but he could see no sign of the cyclone. Then he laughed softly as he felt the warm sand of Death Valley on his back. . . .

It was a rough ride though, and Bill had resisted unusual tensions and pressures. When he got on the cyclone he had a twenty-dollar gold piece and a bowie knife[12] in his pocket. The tremendous force of the cyclone was such that when he finished the ride he found that his pocket contained a plugged nickel[13] and a little pearl-handled penknife. His two giant six-shooters were compressed and transformed into a small water pistol and a popgun.

It is a strange circumstance that lesser men have monuments raised in their honor. Death Valley is Bill's monument. Sort of a monument in reverse. Sunk in his honor, you might say. Perhaps that is as it should be. After all, Bill was different. He made his own monument. He made it with his hips, as is evident from the great depth of the valley. That is the hard way.

---

12. bowie (bō' ē) **knife:** A strong, single-edged hunting knife named after James Bowie (1799–1836), U.S. soldier.

13. plugged nickel: Fake nickel.

Closure and Extension

ANSWERS TO THINKING ABOUT THE SELECTION

Recalling

1. Pecos Bill used prairie dogs to dig postholes. He fenced all of Texas, parts of New Mexico and Arizona, and the Southern Pacific right of way with this method. Bill also used badgers to dig wells for him. He also trained his horse, Widow Maker, to use twenty-seven different gaits.
2. The cyclone wants to spoil the celebration because it is jealous of Pecos Bill and his success. The cyclone had been the center of attention and the most powerful thing in the land. Now it is threatened by Pecos Bill and his Fourth of July celebration.
3. As the cyclone was just about to envelope him, Pecos Bill turned his horse to his left, wheeled on a dime, and was astride it.
4. The cyclone disintegrates into small cyclones when it realizes Bill is the victor.
5. The Staked Plains, Death Valley, and the Grand Canyon were caused by Bill or the cyclone.

Interpreting

6. The cyclone and Bill are similar in that they are both big and strong; they both are the center of attention; and they both like to display their superiority.

THINKING ABOUT THE SELECTION

Recalling

1. Before riding the cyclone, what feats had Pecos Bill performed?
2. Why does the cyclone want to spoil the Fourth of July celebration?
3. How does Pecos Bill get astride the cyclone?
4. What happens when the cyclone realizes that Pecos Bill is the victor?
5. What natural wonders or geographical sites are caused by Pecos Bill or the cyclone?

Interpreting

6. How is the cyclone similar to Pecos Bill?
7. How can Pecos Bill tell that the cyclone is very angry?
8. Bill laughs when he sees the cyclone is gone. What does this tell you about Bill?
9. Why does the writer call Death Valley a "monument in reverse" to Pecos Bill?

Applying

10. Bill makes his plans for this battle in "the split second between his first sight of the monster and the time for action." Do you believe anyone can think that quickly? Support your answer with examples of quick (or slow) thinking that you know about.

ANALYZING LITERATURE

Understanding Conflict in a Folktale

A **conflict,** or struggle between opposing sides or forces, is usually what a folktale is about. Often the hero of a folktale is thrown into conflict with another person or a natural force. After a significant struggle, the hero emerges as the winner.

1. What is the conflict in this folktale?
2. Write down your idea for a variation of this conflict.

CRITICAL THINKING AND READING

Identifying Reasons

A **reason** is the information that explains or justifies a decision, an action, or a conclusion. A reason may be a fact, an opinion, a situation, or an occurrence. For example, in "Pecos Bill: The Cyclone," the reason for Bill's welcoming the cyclone is that it blew the earth away from his wells, which Bill then sold for postholes.

Give the reasons for the following situations from "Pecos Bill: The Cyclone."

1. The cyclone wants to do away with Pecos Bill.
2. The cyclone is in top form.
3. The cyclone disintegrates.

UNDERSTANDING LANGUAGE

Appreciating Words from Spanish

Many words in English come from the Spanish language. For example, *chaps* comes from the Spanish *chaperejos,* meaning "leather trousers worn by cowboys to protect their legs."

Look up the original meanings of the following words from Spanish in an English dictionary. Then use each one in a sentence.

1. palomino 2. canyon 3. mustang 4. lasso

THINKING AND WRITING

Writing a Description of a Conflict

Choose one of the ideas about types of conflict that you wrote down earlier. Freewrite about how Pecos Bill might handle this conflict. Then use this information to write a description of the conflict and Pecos Bill's solving of it. Imagine that you are writing for a group of young children who are hearing about Pecos Bill for the first time. Revise your description, making sure you have used exaggeration effectively. Finally, proofread your description and share it with your classmates.

(Answers begin on p. 652.)

7. Bill can tell that the cyclone is angry because he can see that its center is larger than ever before and can see green clouds dripping from the cyclone's jaws and lightning flashing from its eyes.
8. Answers will differ. Suggested Response: His laughter tells you that Bill enjoys taking on and overcoming such challenges and that this feat has not affected him that greatly. It might also indicate that he finds humor in overcoming these challenges.
9. The writer calls Death Valley a monument in reverse because most monuments rise up from the ground so that they can be seen. Death Valley is cut into the ground to a great depth.

Applying

10. Answers will differ. Suggested Response: Some thoughts can be made in split seconds, such as those associated with sporting events when athletes make quick decisions. Other thoughts cannot be made so quickly, especially those involving many factors and possible outcomes, such as strategies for battles, and decisions that affect many lives.

ANSWERS TO ANALYZING LITERATURE

1. The conflict in this folktale is a struggle between Pecos Bill and the original cyclone.
2. Answers will differ. Suggested responses: A conflict between Bill and the cyclone in which Bill is trying to harness the cyclone's power for his own purposes or in which Bill is trying to stop the cyclone from destroying something, a conflict between Bill and the original earthquake, a conflict between Bill and the largest bear in the West.

ANSWERS TO CRITICAL THINKING AND READING

1. The reasons that the cyclone wants to get rid of Pecos Bill include that it is jealous of Bill and his success, and it feels threatened by him.
2. The cyclone is in top form because it has been training all through the winter and spring in anticipation of this conflict.
3. The cyclone disintegrates because it realizes that it cannot defeat and destroy Pecos Bill.

Challenge Ask your **less advanced** students to give the reasons that Pecos Bill welcomed the cyclone before their encounter in this tale.

ANSWERS TO UNDERSTANDING LANGUAGE

1. **palomino:** A cream, golden, or light-chestnut horse that has a silvery-white or ivory mane and tail.
2. **canyon:** A long, narrow valley between high cliffs, often with a stream flowing through it.
3. **mustang:** A small wild or half-wild horse of the southwest plains of the United States.
4. **lasso:** A long rope or leather thong with a sliding noose at one end, used to catch cattle or wild horses.

Sentences will differ for each of the above words.

THINKING AND WRITING

Publishing Student Writing You might want to put together a collection of Pecos Bill folktales created by the class. Each student could have his or her tale on a page with original artwork. You could also have some students design and create front and back covers for the collection.

Focus

More About the Legend This legend may be based on a true incident. The only differences between the legend and the actuality were the length of the contest between John Henry and a steam drill, and the way he died. The contest was arranged to last thirty-five minutes rather than the entire day and the real John Henry was said to have been killed by a falling rock after he beat the engine. Why do you think these details were changed as the story was told?

Literary Focus You might want to point out to your students that as the frontier of the United States disappeared, the frontier folk hero began to be replaced by another type of folk hero. These heroes retained the extraordinary gifts of the frontiersmen, but could now be found working in factories, in mines, and on the railroad. This change reflected the change of the United States into an industrial nation.

Look For You might have students look for the qualities that John Henry has in common with ordinary people as well as his extraordinary qualities.

Writing/Prior Knowledge If some of your students are having trouble with this activity, you might suggest examples of groups of people who are sometimes held as heroes. These include sports figures and actors.

Vocabulary Students should not have any difficulty understanding and pronouncing these vocabulary words.

GUIDE FOR READING

Hammerman

Hammerman was the nickname for a black laborer named John Henry, who in the early 1870's helped construct the Big Bend Tunnel along the Chesapeake and Ohio Railroad in West Virginia. At the time, the workers used long-handled hammers to pound steel drills into rocks. One day a man arrived with a steam-powered drill, which he claimed could drill holes faster than twenty men using hammers.

This folktale is retold by **Adrien Stoutenburg** (1916–), a poet, biographer, and writer, who was born in Darfur, Minnesota.

Folk Hero

A **folk hero** is an extraordinary person who appears in folktales. Folktales glorify the hero for his or her wonderful qualities, which are far superior to those of most "folk," or ordinary, common people. There may be many tales about a hero, each focusing on a different aspect, such as strength, daring, or cunning. John Henry is an example of a folk hero.

Look For

As you read "Hammerman," look for John Henry's extraordinary qualities. What makes him stand out from ordinary people?

Writing

John Henry is one example of a folk hero. Brainstorm and write down your ideas about people, real or imaginary, who could be folk heroes in our society today.

Vocabulary

Knowing the following words will help you as you read "Hammerman."

whirl (hwurl) *adj.*: To drive with a rotating motion (p. 655)
hefted (hef′ tid) *v.*: Lifted; tested the weight of (p. 657)

Objectives

1. To understand a folk hero
2. To make inferences about characters
3. To dramatize a folktale
4. To write another adventure of John Henry

Support Material

Teaching Portfolio

Teacher Backup, pp. 951–953
Usage and Mechanics Worksheet, p. 954
Vocabulary Check, p. 955
Critical Thinking and Reading Worksheet, *Making Inferences About Characters*, p. 956
Language Worksheet, *Choosing Effective Synonyms*, p. 957
Selection Test, pp. 958–959
Art Transparency 19, *John Henry's Hand*, by Fred Becker

Hammerman

Adrien Stoutenburg

People down South still tell stories about John Henry, how strong he was, and how he could whirl a big sledge[1] so lightning-fast you could hear thunder behind it. They even say he was born with a hammer in his hand. John Henry himself said it, but he probably didn't mean it exactly as it sounded.

The story seems to be that when John Henry was a baby, the first thing he reached out for was a hammer, which was hung nearby on the cabin wall.

John Henry's father put his arm around his wife's shoulder. "He's going to grow up to be a steel-driving man. I can see it plain as rows of cotton running uphill."

As John Henry grew a bit older, he practiced swinging the hammer, not hitting at things, but just enjoying the feel of it whooshing against the air. When he was old enough to talk, he told everyone, "I was born with a hammer in my hand."

John Henry was still a boy when the
1 Civil War started, but he was a big, hard-muscled boy, and he could outwork and outplay all the other boys on the plantation.

"You're going to be a mighty man, John Henry," his father told him.

2 "A man ain't nothing but a man," young John Henry said. "And I'm a natural man, born to swing a hammer in my hand."

At night, lying on a straw bed on the floor, John Henry listened to a far-off train whistling through the darkness. Railroad tracks had been laid to carry trainloads of Southern soldiers to fight against the armies of the North. The trains had a lonesome,
longing sound that made John Henry want 3
to go wherever they were going.

When the war ended, a man from the North came to John Henry where he was working in the field. He said, "The slaves are free now. You can pack up and go wherever you want, young fellow."

"I'm craving to go where the trains go," said John Henry.

The man shook his head. "There are too many young fellows trailing the trains around now. You better settle down to doing what you know, like handling a cotton hook or driving a mule team."

John Henry thought to himself, there's a big hammer waiting for me somewhere, because I know I'm a steel-driving man. All I have to do is hunt 'til I find it.

That night, he told his folks about a dream he had had.

"I dreamed I was working on a railroad somewhere," he said, "a big, new railroad called the C. & O., and I had a mighty hammer in my hand. Every time I swung it, it made a whirling flash around my shoulder. And every time my hammer hit a spike,[2] the sky lit up from the sparks."

1. **sledge** (slej), *n.*: A heavy hammer, usually held with both hands.

2. **spike** (spīk), *n.*: A long, thick metal nail used for splitting rock.

Presentation

Motivation/Prior Knowledge You might ask students if they have ever known about anyone who competed directly against a machine instead of another person. Have them imagine what it might be like. Do they think it is possible to defeat machines?

Master Teacher Note The legend of John Henry represents to many the struggle between workers and the machines designed to replace them. This aspect of the folktale is just as applicable today as it was in the late 1800's. You might want to point this out to students and ask them if they are familiar with any situations, such as the introduction of robots to factory assembly lines, where machines threaten the jobs of people. Have students discuss whether this theme will remain important in the future.

Thematic Ideas Another selection that deals with technological changes is "Dial Versus Digital" on page 477. Another selection that deals with the same legend is the traditional folk song, "John Henry," on page 663.

Purpose-Setting Question What does this tale suggest about humans and machines?

1 **Clarification** The Civil War began in 1861.

2 **Critical Thinking and Reading** What inferences can students make about the character and qualities of John Henry based on what they have read?

3 **Discussion** Have you ever heard anything that evoked a specific feeling like the wail of a train whistle did for John?

Enrichment Railroads remain a vital form of transportation. They are second only to airplanes in speed, and only ships are capable of carrying heavier loads over long distances. If all of the world's railroad tracks were laid end to end, they would stretch about 800,000 miles. Railroads in the United States played an important role in industrial development and the settlement of the West.

Master Teacher Note Have students look at Art Transparency 19, *John Henry's Hand* by Fred Becker, in the Teaching Portfolio. Discuss with students what the hand could symbolize. What are examples of symbols that could stand for strength or for determination?

"John Henry" is a ballad glorifying the strength, pride, and determination of John Henry.

Humanities Note

Fine art, *Hammer in His Hand,* by Palmer Hayden. The Afro-American painter Palmer Hayden (1890–1973) was a leading artist of the Harlem Renaissance, a black art movement in the 1920's. Hayden first supported his painting career with menial jobs. As his art gained recognition, he won the support of a patron who sponsored a trip to Paris. Like many Black artists, he found an accepting audience for his art in Europe. This encouragement led to his continued interest in painting the pulse of life in Harlem and other Afro-American subjects.

The painting, *Hammer in His Hand,* was one of a group done about John Henry. Completed in 1954, these canvases are considered to be his finest work. John Henry is shown as a handsome, vital, strong young man who is at peace with himself and is filled with a sense of well-being. He is confidently striding along the tracks with his heavy hammer easily balanced on his shoulders. The scene behind the figure—river, sky, and softly diffused light—speaks of Hayden's landscape painting skill. Paintings such as this helped awaken America's awareness of the value of Afro-American myth and legend.

1. What details of the legend are depicted in the painting?
2. What seems to be John Henry's attitude?

4 **Reading Strategy** You might have students summarize the events that led to John Henry's working on the railroad. What events made this seem inevitable?

HAMMER IN HIS HAND
Palmer C. Hayden
Museum of African American Art

"I believe it," his father said. "You were born to drive steel."

"That ain't all of the dream," John Henry said. "I dreamed that the railroad was going to be the end of me and I'd die with the hammer in my hand."

The next morning, John Henry bundled up some food in a red bandanna handkerchief, told his parents good-by, and set off
4 into the world. He walked until he heard the clang-clang of hammers in the distance. He followed the sound to a place where gangs of men were building a railroad. John Henry watched the men driving steel spikes down into the crossties[3] to hold the rails in place. Three men would stand around a spike, then each, in turn, would swing a long hammer.

John Henry's heart beat in rhythm with the falling hammers. His fingers ached for the feel of a hammer in his own hands. He walked over to the foreman.

"I'm a natural steel-driving man," he said. "And I'm looking for a job."

3. **crossties** (krôs' tīz), *n.*: Beams laid crosswise under railroad tracks to support them.

"How much steel-driving have you done?" the foreman asked.

"I was born knowing how," John Henry said.

The foreman shook his head. "That ain't good enough, boy. I can't take any chances. Steel-driving's dangerous work, and you might hit somebody."

"I wouldn't hit anybody," John Henry said, "because I can drive one of those spikes all by myself."

The foreman said sharply, "The one kind of man I don't need in this outfit is a bragger. Stop wasting my time."

John Henry didn't move. He got a stubborn look around his jaw. "You loan me a hammer, mister, and if somebody will hold the spike for me, I'll prove what I can do."

The three men who had just finished driving in a spike looked toward him and laughed. One of them said, "Anybody who would hold a spike for a greenhorn[4] don't want to live long."

"I'll hold it," a fourth man said.

John Henry saw that the speaker was a small, dark-skinned fellow about his own age.

The foreman asked the small man, "D'you aim to get yourself killed, Li'l Willie?"

Li'l Willie didn't answer. He knelt and set a spike down through the rail on the crosstie. "Come on, big boy," he said.

John Henry picked up one of the sheepnose hammers lying in the cinders. He hefted it and decided it was too light. He picked up a larger one which weighed twelve pounds. The handle was lean and limber and greased with tallow[5] to make it smooth.

Everyone was quiet, watching, as he stepped over to the spike.

John Henry swung the hammer over his shoulder so far that the hammer head hung down against the back of his knees. He felt a thrill run through his arms and chest.

"Tap it down gentle, first," said Li'l Willie.

But John Henry had already started to swing. He brought the hammer flashing down, banging the spike squarely on the head. Before the other men could draw a
breath of surprise, the hammer flashed 6
again, whirring through the air like a giant hummingbird. One more swing, and the spike was down, its steel head smoking from the force of the blow.

The foreman blinked, swallowed, and blinked again. "Man," he told John Henry, "you're hired!"

That's the way John Henry started steel-driving. From then on, Li'l Willie was always with him, setting the spikes, or placing the drills[6] that John Henry drove with his hammer. There wasn't another steel-driving man in the world who could touch John Henry for speed and power. He could hammer every which way, up or down or sidewise. He could drive for ten hours at a stretch and never miss a stroke.

After he'd been at the work for a few years, he started using a twenty-pound hammer in each hand. It took six men, working fast, to carry fresh drills to him. People would come for miles around to watch John Henry.

Whenever John Henry worked, he sang. Li'l Willie sang with him, chanting the rhythm of the clanging hammer strokes.

Those were happy days for John Henry. One of the happiest days came when he met a black-eyed, curly-haired girl called Polly Ann. And, on the day that Polly Ann said

4. **greenhorn** (grēn′ hôrn), *n.*: An inexperienced person; a beginner.
5. **tallow** (tal′ ō), *n.*: Solid fat obtained from sheep or cattle.

6. **drills** (drilz), *n.*: Pointed tools used for making holes in hard substances.

5 **Literary Focus** Point out that John Henry knows he has the strength and skill to drive steel even before he tries, despite the danger and difficulty involved. How did Henry's father know this as well? How does this help to glorify his deeds?

6 **Literary Focus** What qualities does John Henry exhibit by this action?

7 Critical Thinking and Reading You might have students make inferences about the character of John Henry based on this event. Are these qualities extraordinary or do all people possess them? Support your answer.

8 Reading Strategy You might have students question why this dream continues to recur in the tale.

9 Critical Thinking and Reading What do the statements of both men and the fact that they go together indicate about the characters of John and Willie? What do they indicate about their friendship?

7 she would marry him, John Henry almost burst his throat with singing.

8 Every now and then, John Henry would remember the strange dream he had had years before, about the C. & O. Railroad and dying with a hammer in his hand. One night, he had the dream again. The next morning, when he went to work, the steel gang gathered round him, hopping with excitement.

"The Chesapeake and Ohio Railroad wants men to drive a tunnel through a mountain in West Virginia!" they said.

"The C. & O. wants the best hammermen there are!" they said. "And they'll pay twice as much as anybody else."

9 Li'l Willie looked at John Henry. "If they want the best, John Henry, they're goin' to need you."

John Henry looked back at his friend. "They're going to need you, too, Li'l Willie. I ain't going without you." He stood a minute, looking at the sky. There was a black thundercloud way off, with sunlight flashing behind it. John Henry felt a small chill between his shoulder blades. He shook himself, put his hammer on his shoulder, and said, "Let's go, Willie!"

When they reached Summers County where the Big Bend Tunnel was to be built, John Henry sized up the mountain standing in the way. It was almost solid rock.

"Looks soft," said John Henry. "Hold a drill up there, Li'l Willie."

Li'l Willie did. John Henry took a seventy-pound hammer and drove the drill in with one mountain-cracking stroke. Then he settled down to working the regular way, pounding in the drills with four or five strokes of a twenty-pound sledge. He worked so fast that his helpers had to keep buckets of water ready to pour on his hammers so they wouldn't catch fire.

Polly Ann, who had come along to West Virginia, sat and watched and cheered him on. She sang along with him, clapping her hands to the rhythm of his hammer, and the sound echoed around the mountains. The songs blended with the rumble of dynamite where the blasting crews were at work. For every time John Henry drilled a hole in the mountain's face, other men poked dynamite and black powder into the hole and then lighted a fuse to blow the rock apart.

One day the tunnel boss Cap'n Tommy Walters was standing watching John Henry, when a stranger in city clothes walked up to him.

"Howdy, Cap'n Tommy," said the stranger. "I'd like to talk to you about a steam engine[7] I've got for sale. My engine can drive a drill through rock so fast that not even a crew of your best men can keep up with it."

"I don't need any machine," Cap'n Tommy said proudly. "My man John Henry can out-drill any machine ever built."

"I'll place a bet with you, Cap'n," said the salesman. "You race your man against my machine for a full day. If he wins, I'll give you the steam engine free."

Cap'n Tommy thought it over. "That sounds fair enough, but I'll have to talk to John Henry first." He told John Henry what the stranger had said. "Are you willing to race a steam drill?" Cap'n Tommy asked.

John Henry ran his big hands over the handle of his hammer, feeling the strength in the wood and in his own great muscles.

"A man's a man," he said, "but a machine ain't nothing but a machine. I'll beat that steam drill, or I'll die with my hammer in my hand!"

"All right, then," said Cap'n Tommy. "We'll set a day for the contest."

---

7. steam engine: Here, a machine that drives a drill by means of steam power.

Polly Ann looked worried when John Henry told her what he had promised to do.

"Don't you worry, honey," John Henry said. It was the end of the workday, with the sunset burning across the mountain, and the sky shining like copper. He tapped his chest. "I've got a man's heart in here. All a machine has is a metal engine." He smiled and picked Polly Ann up in his arms, as if she were no heavier than a blade of grass.

10 On the morning of the contest, the slopes around the tunnel were crowded with people. At one side stood the steam engine, its gears and valves and mechanical drill gleaming. Its operators rushed around, giving it final spurts of grease and oil and shoving fresh pine knots into the fire that fed the steam boiler.

11 John Henry stood leaning on his hammer, as still as the mountain rock, his shoulders shining like hard coal in the rising sun.

"How do you feel, John Henry?" asked Li'l Willie. Li'l Willie's hands trembled a bit as he held the drill ready.

"I feel like a bird ready to bust out of a nest egg," John Henry said. "I feel like a rooster ready to crow. I feel pride hammering at my heart, and I can hardly wait to get started against that machine." He sucked in the mountain air. "I feel powerful free, Li'l Willie."

Cap'n Tommy held up the starting gun. For a second everything was as silent as the dust in a drill hole. Then the gun barked, making a yelp that bounced against mountain and sky.

John Henry swung his hammer, and it rang against the drill.

12 At the same time, the steam engine gave a roar and a hiss. Steam whistled through its escape valve. Its drill crashed down, gnawing into the granite.

John Henry paid no attention to anything except his hammer, nor to any sound except the steady pumping of his heart. At the end of an hour, he paused long enough to ask, "How are we doing, Li'l Willie?"

Willie licked his lips. His face was pale with rock dust and with fear. "The machine's ahead, John Henry."

John Henry tossed his smoking hammer aside and called to another helper, "Bring me two hammers! I'm only getting warmed up."

He began swinging a hammer in each hand. Sparks flew so fast and hot they singed his face. The hammers heated up until they glowed like torches.

"How're we doing now, Li'l Willie?" John Henry asked at the end of another hour.

Li'l Willie grinned. "The machine's drill busted. They have to take time to fix up a new one. You're almost even now, John Henry! How're you feeling?"

"I'm feeling like sunrise," John Henry took time to say before he flashed one of his hammers down against the drill. "Clean out the hole, Willie, and we'll drive right down to China."

Above the clash of his hammers, he heard the chug and hiss of the steam engine starting up again and the whine of its rotary drill biting into rock. The sound hurt John Henry's ears. 13

"Sing me a song, Li'l Willie!" he gasped. "Sing me a natural song for my hammers to sing along with."

Li'l Willie sang, and John Henry kept his hammers going in time. Hour after hour, he kept driving, sweat sliding from his forehead and chest.

The sun rolled past noon and toward the west.

"How're you feeling, John Henry?" Li'l Willie asked.

"I ain't tired yet," said John Henry and

10 **Discussion** Who do you think the people are going to root for, John Henry or the machine? Support your answer.

11 **Literary Focus** The image of John Henry standing "as still as a mountain rock" heightens the impression of his being extra ordinary or larger than life. What image do students have of his physical appearance—his height, weight, and frame?

12 **Discussion** What image is created by this description and the one several paragraphs earlier of the steam drill? How does it contrast with descriptions of John Henry?

13 **Discussion** Why does the sound of the drill hurt John Henry's ears?

14 Critical Thinking and Reading Compare John Henry's statement to his actions. What does this indicate about his character?

15 Critical Thinking and Reading Have the class make inferences about the qualities that are revealed by John Henry's sacrifice. What qualities of all workers are being glorified in this tale?

Reader's Response John Henry remarks that "a machine ain't nothing but a machine." How would such a comment be received in our technology-oriented society?

14 stood back, gasping, while Willie put a freshly sharpened drill into the rock wall. "Only, I have a kind of roaring in my ears."

"That's only the steam engine," Li'l Willie said, but he wet his lips again. "You're gaining on it, John Henry. I reckon you're at least two inches ahead."

John Henry coughed and slung his hammer back. "I'll beat it by a mile, before the sun sets."

At the end of another hour, Li'l Willie called out, his eyes sparkling, "You're going to win, John Henry, if you can keep on drivin'!"

John Henry ground his teeth together and tried not to hear the roar in his ears or the racing thunder of his heart. "I'll go until I drop," he gasped. "I'm a steel-driving man and I'm bound to win, because a machine ain't nothing but a machine."

The sun slid lower. The shadows of the crowd grew long and purple.

"John Henry can't keep it up," someone said.

"The machine can't keep it up," another said.

Polly Ann twisted her hands together and waited for Cap'n Tommy to fire the gun to mark the end of the contest.

"Who's winning?" a voice cried.

"Wait and see," another voice answered.

There were only ten minutes left.

"How're you feeling, John Henry?" Li'l Willie whispered, sweat dripping down his own face.

John Henry didn't answer. He just kept slamming his hammers against the drill, his mouth open.

Li'l Willie tried to go on singing. "Flash that hammer—uh! Wham that drill—uh!" he croaked.

Out beside the railroad tracks, Polly beat her hands together in time, until they were numb.

The sun flared an instant, then died behind the mountain. Cap'n Tommy's gun cracked. The judges ran forward to measure the depth of the holes drilled by the steam engine and by John Henry. At last, the judges came walking back and said something to Cap'n Tommy before they turned to announce their findings to the crowd.

Cap'n Tommy walked over to John Henry, who stood leaning against the face of the mountain.

"John Henry," he said, "you beat that steam engine by four feet!" He held out his hand and smiled.

John Henry heard a distant cheering. He held his own hand out, and then he staggered. He fell and lay on his back, staring up at the mountain and the sky, and then he saw Polly Ann and Li'l Willie leaning over him.

"Oh, how do you feel, John Henry?" Polly Ann asked.

"I feel a bit tuckered out," said John Henry.

"Do you want me to sing to you?" Li'l Willie asked.

"I got a song in my own heart, thank you, Li'l Willie," John Henry said. He raised up on his elbow and looked at all the people and the last sunset light gleaming like the edge of a golden trumpet. "I was a steel-driving man," he said, and lay back and closed his eyes forever. 15

Down South, and in the North, too, people still talk about John Henry and how he beat the steam engine at the Big Bend Tunnel. They say, if John Henry were alive today, he could beat almost every other kind of machine, too.

Maybe so. At least, John Henry would die trying.

Closure and Extension

ANSWERS TO THINKING ABOUT THE SELECTION

Recalling

1. John Henry dreamed that he was working on a railroad, swinging a mighty hammer so hard that it made a whirling flash around his shoulder. Every time the hammer hit a spike, the sky lit up from the sparks. He also dreamed that the railroad would be the end of him and that he would die with a hammer in his hand.
2. He wins his first job by borrowing a hammer and driving a spike into the ground with only two blows.
3. Willie helps John by holding the spikes and the drills for him and by singing along with him.
4. A salesman makes a bet that his steam-powered drill can outdri John Henry in a day's work. John

THINKING ABOUT THE SELECTION

Recalling

1. Describe John Henry's dream.
2. Explain how John Henry wins his first job hammering steel.
3. How does Li'l Willie help John Henry with his work?
4. What events bring about John Henry's death?

Interpreting

5. Why is Li'l Willie willing to hold the spike for John Henry—a dangerous task—when no one else will?
6. Interpret the sentence: "A man's a man, but a machine ain't nothing but a machine."
7. What is the goal and the purpose of the quest?
8. What clues in the tale hint at the outcome?

Applying

9. Ever since the invention of machines, some people have felt threatened by them. Why? What machines today cause this reaction?

ANALYZING LITERATURE

Understanding the Folk Hero

A **folk hero** is an extraordinary person whose qualities are glorified in folktales. The fantastic qualities glorified in the folk hero give you an idea of the characteristics valued on the frontier.

1. What qualities of John Henry are glorified in the following sentences from "Hammerman"?
   a. "He brought the hammer flashing down, banging the spike squarely on the head . . . One more swing, and the spike was down, its steel head smoking from the force of the blow."
   b. "It took six men, working fast, to carry fresh drills to him."
2. What do these qualities say about the type of person who was admired on the frontier?

CRITICAL THINKING AND READING

Making Inferences About Characters

Inferences are conclusions drawn from evidence in a story. You make inferences about a character's traits and personality from clues given in the character's words and actions.

For example, L'il Willie goes with John Henry to work on the railroad, joins him in his competition against the machine, and sings to John Henry to urge him along. From these actions you can conclude that L'il Willie is a loyal friend.

What inferences about John Henry's character can you draw from the following?

1. '"I feel like a rooster ready to crow. I feel pride hammering at my heart, and I can hardly wait to get started against that machine."'
2. "I'll go until I drop."

SPEAKING AND LISTENING

Dramatizing a Folktale

Prepare and dramatize a skit based on "Hammerman" for your class. List the cast of characters and devise simple dialogue and stage directions. Choose the cast and director from your classmates. After you rehearse, perform the skit for your class.

THINKING AND WRITING

Writing Another Adventure

Brainstorm and write down your ideas for other adventures that John Henry could have had. Select one to write about for your class. First freewrite about the adventure, including descriptions of John Henry, the challenge that confronts him, and what happens. Use this information to write about the adventure, including dialogue when necessary. Revise your story, making sure you have used the qualities that John Henry exhibits in "Hammerman." Read the adventure aloud to your class.

agrees to the bet and races the machine all day. He beats the machine but dies from the effort.

Interpreting

5. Answers will differ. Suggested Response: Willie holds the drill for John when no one else will because he sees something special in John. Students might also suggest that this action adds to the larger-than-life quality of the story.
6. Answers will differ. Suggested Response: A man has some qualities that machines lack, such as heart, determination, and courage.
7. Answers will differ. Suggested Response: John decides to pit himself against the machine because of his great pride and love for his work. He feels that he should prove the superiority of humans over machine and is willing to die in the effort.
8. Clues that hint the outcome include John's dream, the chill John feels when he decides to take the job with the C. & O., Polly Ann's worry about the steam drill bet, and the roaring in John's ears as he was racing the machine.

Applying

9. Answers will differ. Suggested Response: People have always felt threatened by machines because they perceive them as a threat to their jobs, and therefore a threat to their income and to their sense of worth. It is difficult for people to accept the idea that a mindless, heartless machine might be superior to humans. New machines today

(Answers begin on p. 660.)

that cause this reaction could be computers or robots on assembly lines.

ANSWERS TO ANALYZING LITERATURE

1. a. Qualities that are glorified are strength, speed, and accuracy.
   b. Glorified qualities include power, speed, tirelessness, and hard work.
2. These qualities indicate that the type of person admired on the frontier worked hard, had strength and endurance, and took great pride in doing the job well.

Challenge How do the qualities of John Henry compare and contrast with those of Pecos Bill?

ANSWERS TO CRITICAL THINKING AND READING

1. Inferences about John Henry's character include a great pride in and enthusiasm for his work, as well as determination.
2. Inferences about John Henry's character include a strong will, a willingness to sacrifice, and a tremendous pride.

Speaking and Listening You might want to arrange to have the class perform their skit in front of the entire school. Additional skits dramatizing some of the other folk tales, myths, and legends from this unit could be added to include the entire class.

You might have students make their own costumes and design their own scenery for their dramatic presentations of the folk tale. If you choose to do this, you might inform the art department. Art teachers might provide guidance and materials for the completion of this assignment.

THINKING AND WRITING

Publishing Student Writing You might display the additional adventures of John Henry on the bulletin board so that all class members can read them.

Focus

More About the Legend American folk music has been influenced by folk music from Great Britain, Europe, and Africa. The songs of Native American Indians also have an important part in this heritage. For example, the ballad and stanza form of "John Henry" may have been influenced by early American colonists from Great Britain, while the vocal style may have been influenced by African slaves.

Literary Focus The oral tradition has been in existence from earliest humanity. Even today, those societies that do not have a written language have a folk culture that is passed along orally.

Look For It might be helpful for some students to tap their feet or clap their hands to keep time rhythmically as they read this song. Perhaps you or a student volunteer would be willing to read the song aloud to this accompaniment.

Writing/Prior Knowledge You might have your more advanced students develop this assignment into a modern folk story for extra credit.

Vocabulary Students will probably have little trouble pronouncing and understanding these vocabulary words.

GUIDE FOR READING

John Henry

John Henry, also called Hammerman in folk tales, was a black laborer who helped build the Big Bend Tunnel on the Chesapeake & Ohio Railroad in West Virginia in the early 1870's. He was a huge man, capable of deeds that ordinary workers could only dream of doing, and he did race a steam drill.

John Henry appears in songs, poems, and folktales, sometimes as a dockworker. He is always the "superworker"—able to work all day and night, amazing others with his incredible feats.

Oral Tradition

Oral tradition is the developing and passing down by word of mouth stories, beliefs, and customs from generation to generation. Ballads, legends, myths, yarns, and folktales are all part of our oral tradition. They have been written down to be remembered.

This version about John Henry is a ballad—a song or poem in short stanzas that tells a story in simple words. A refrain, a phrase or verse repeated at intervals, emphasizes a point and adds to the poem's rhythmic quality.

Look For

As you read "John Henry," look for the ballad's refrain: "Lawd, Lawd," and the repetition of the last line of the stanza. Imagine that you are pounding spikes on a railroad or drilling a tunnel and that you are singing this ballad in time with the swinging of your hammer.

Writing

Today computers and humans play chess against each other. Think of other contests that could take place between a human and a modern machine. Describe what the competition would be about and how it might take place.

Vocabulary

Knowing the following words will help you as you read "John Henry."

drive (drīv) *v.*: To force by hitting (p. 663)

yonder (yän′ dər) *adj.*: In the distance (p. 665)

flagged (flagd) *v.*: Signaled to a train to stop so a passenger can board (p. 666)

Objectives

1 To understand the oral tradition
2 To share other ballads about folk heroes
3 To compare and contrast two selections

Support Material

Teaching Portfolio

Teacher Backup, pp. 961–963
Usage and Mechanics Worksheet, p. 964
Vocabulary Check, p. 965
Analyzing Literature Worksheet, *Understanding the Oral Tradition,* p. 966
Language Worksheet, *Determining Word Meaning from Latin Roots,* p. 967
Selection Test, pp. 968–969

John Henry

Traditional

John Henry was a lil baby,
Sittin' on his mama's knee,
Said: 'The Big Bend Tunnel on the C. & O. road
Gonna cause the death of me,
Lawd, Lawd, gonna cause the death of me.'

Cap'n says to John Henry,
'Gonna bring me a steam drill 'round,
Gonna take that steam drill out on the job,
Gonna whop that steel on down,
Lawd, Lawd, gonna whop that steel on down.

John Henry tol' his cap'n,
Lightnin' was in his eye:
'Cap'n, bet yo' las' red cent on me,
Fo' I'll beat it to the bottom or I'll die,
Lawd, Lawd, I'll beat it to the bottom or I'll die.'

Sun shine hot an' burnin',
Wer'n't no breeze a-tall,
Sweat ran down like water down a hill,
That day John Henry let his hammer fall,
Lawd, Lawd, that day John Henry let his hammer fall.

John Henry went to the tunnel,
An' they put him in the lead to drive,
The rock so tall an' John Henry so small,
That he lied down his hammer an' he cried,
Lawd, Lawd, that he lied down his hammer an' he cried. 1

Presentation

Motivation/Prior Knowledge Have students imagine that they were witnesses to the contest between John Henry and the steam drill recounted in "Hammerman." What would they tell others about John Henry? What would they say about the contest? How would they portray the struggle?

Master Teacher Note You might want to play an audio recording of "John Henry" for your students. There are many recordings of this song, including one on the record "California Blues," issued on the Fantasy record label, number 24723.

Thematic Idea To compare and contrast selections from the American folk music heritage, you may want to use the Tewa Indian prayer "Song of the Sky Loom" on page 579.

Purpose-Setting Question What kind of people might have been responsible for the creation of this song?

1 **Discussion** How is this action inconsistent with the other qualities John Henry demonstrates?

Humanities Note

Fine art: *A Man Ain't Nothin' But a Man* by Palmer Hayden. For information about the artist, refer to the Humanities Note on page 656.

This painting, *A Man Ain't Nothin' But a Man,* is one of a group done about John Henry. The style is the same as that of *Hammer in His Hand* on page 656. This group is considered to be Hayden's finest work. Each work in the group depicts a scene from the legend of John Henry. Here John Henry is shown holding a hammer and smiling at his boss, having just accepted the bet pitting himself against a machine.

1. What are the similarities and differences between this painting and the one of John Henry on page 656?
2. Do you think that John Henry was driven by fate to accept the bet or was he acting foolishly or with too much pride?

A MAN AIN'T NOTHIN' BUT A MAN
Palmer C. Hayden

John Henry started on the right hand,
The steam drill started on the lef'—
'Before I'd let this steam drill beat me down,
I'd hammer my fool self to death,
Lawd, Lawd, I'd hammer my fool self to death.'

John Henry had a lil woman,
Her name were Polly Ann,
John Henry took sick an' had to go to bed,
Polly Ann drove steel like a man,
Lawd, Lawd, Polly Ann drove steel like a man.

John Henry said to his shaker,[1]
'Shaker, why don' you sing?
I'm throwin' twelve poun's from my hips on down,
Jes' listen to the col' steel ring,
Lawd, Lawd, jes' listen to the col' steel ring.'

Oh, the captain said to John Henry,
'I b'lieve this mountain's sinkin' in.'
John Henry said to his captain, oh my!
'Ain' nothin' but my hammer suckin' win',
Lawd, Lawd, ain' nothin' but my hammer suckin' win'.'

John Henry tol' his shaker,
'Shaker, you better pray,
For, if I miss this six-foot steel,
Tomorrow'll be yo' buryin' day,
Lawd, Lawd, tomorrow'll be yo' buryin' day.'

John Henry tol' his captain,
'Look yonder what I see—
Yo' drill's done broke an' yo' hole's done choke,
An' you cain' drive steel like me,
Lawd, Lawd, an' you cain' drive steel like me.'

The man that invented the steam drill,
Thought he was mighty fine.
John Henry drove his fifteen feet,
An' the steam drill only made nine,
Lawd, Lawd, an' the steam drill only made nine.

---

1. **shaker** (shā' kər), *n.*: Person who sets the spikes and places the drills for a steel-driver to hammer.

2 Critical Thinking and Reading You might want to point out that this is the third stanza that foreshadows the death of John Henry. How do these repeated references to his death affect the mood of the song?

3 Literary Focus The folk ballad, like other forms of folk stories, exaggerates the qualities of its characters. You might want to point out that John Henry's wife is also portrayed as a larger-than-life character because of the fact that women did not drive steel in the 1800's.

4 **Discussion** Why do all the women want to visit the spot where John Henry died? What does this indicate about the extent of his fame?

Reader's Response Did you enjoy the prose or poetry version of the John Henry tale? Why?

The hammer that John Henry swung,
It weighed over nine pound;
He broke a rib in his lef'-han' side,
An' his intrels[2] fell on the groun',
Lawd, Lawd, an' his intrels fell on the groun'.

All the womens in the Wes',
When they heared of John Henry's death,
Stood in the rain, flagged the eas'-boun' train,
Goin' where John Henry fell dead,
Lawd, Lawd, goin' where John Henry fell dead. 4

John Henry's lil mother,
She was all dressed in red,
She jumped in bed, covered up her head,
Said she didn' know her son was dead,
Lawd, Lawd, didn' know her son was dead.

Dey took John Henry to the graveyard,
An' they buried him in the san',
An' every locomotive come roarin' by,
Says, 'There lays a steel-drivin' man,
Lawd, Lawd, there lays a steel-drivin' man.'

2. **intrels: entrails** (en' trālz), *n.*: Inner organs.

THINKING ABOUT THE SELECTION

Recalling

1. At what point in his life does John Henry make his prediction about his own death?
2. What happens in the contest between John Henry and the steam drill?
3. Which one wins the contest?
4. What injuries does John Henry suffer?
5. What tribute do trains give John Henry when they roll by his grave?

Interpreting

6. Why does John Henry say that if he misses the six-foot steel, tomorrow will be his shaker's burying day?
7. Why does John Henry's mother react as she does to the news of her son's death?
8. State what we learn from this tale about John Henry that explains why he is a folk hero.

Applying

9. What jobs today are as dangerous as driving steel was in John Henry's day? Give two examples, and explain why they are dangerous.

ANALYZING LITERATURE

Understanding the Oral Tradition

Oral tradition is the passing down by word of mouth stories, beliefs, and customs from generation to generation. Ballads, for example, are usually sung long before they are ever written down. A ballad's refrain—phrase or verse repeated at intervals—emphasizes a point and sounds like a chorus. In the first stanza of "John Henry," the refrain "Lawd, Lawd, gonna cause the death of me" adds the phrase "Lawd, Lawd," and repeats the line before it.

A ballad passed down in the oral tradition may have several different versions. It may often include the dialect, or particular manner of speaking, of its creators. For example, "Gonna whop that steel on down" is the way black laborers in the South in the late 1800's might have said, "I will hammer that spike into the ground." To get the full flavor of the dialect, you should read the ballad aloud.

Read "John Henry" aloud. Then answer the following questions.

1. What lines contain a refrain?
2. What are two other examples of dialect from "John Henry"?
3. What feelings for John Henry does this ballad arouse?

SPEAKING AND LISTENING

Sharing Other Ballads About Folk Heroes

John Henry is not the only folk hero about whom ballads have been written. Working with a group of students, think of a ballad you know about another American folk hero, or find one in the library. Read it aloud to the class.

THINKING AND WRITING

Comparing and Contrasting Selections

Compare and contrast "John Henry" with "Hammerman." First list the similarities and differences between the two selections. Consider the characters, situations, form of literature, and descriptions. Then use this information to write an essay for a school literary magazine. Revise your essay, making sure you use examples to support your views. Proofread your essay and share it with your classmates.

Closure and Extension

ANSWERS TO THINKING ABOUT THE SELECTION

Recalling

1. He is a little baby when he makes the prediction.
2. The steam drill breaks down during the contest.
3. John Henry wins the contest.
4. He breaks a rib on his left side, and his entrails fall on the ground.
5. The locomotives say, "There lays a steel-drivin' man."

Interpreting

6. He says this because if he misses, his hammer will strike the shaker and kill him.
7. Answers will differ. Suggested Responses: John's mother was surprised at the news, she was extremely upset, and she cannot believe that it is true.
8. Answers will differ. Suggested Response: John Henry possessed great strength and will power, along with pride in his work and a willingness to sacrifice. These qualities made him a folk hero because they are the qualities that all workers strive to have.

Applying

9. Answers will differ but should be supported by evidence. Suggested Response: Working on bridges or other tall structures, such as oil platforms in the ocean, is dangerous because you can fall off them. Being a test pilot is dangerous because the aircraft can malfunction and crash. Working in certain mines is dangerous because mines can collapse, trapping and suffocating the miners.

ANSWERS TO ANALYZING LITERATURE

1. Students can choose any two of the following lines: numbers 5, 10, 15, 20, 25, 30, 35, 40, 45, 50, 55, 60, 65, 70, 75, 80.
2. The poem is virtually all written in dialect. Two examples are: "Cap'n, bet yo' las' red cent on me," and "I'm throwin' twelve poun's from my hips on down."
3. Answers will differ. Suggested Response: Feelings of respect, admiration, sympathy, and sorrow are aroused.

Speaking and Listening If you use this assignment, perhaps inform the school librarian. The librarian might help with guidance for research.

THINKING AND WRITING

For help with this assignment, students can refer to Lesson 16, "Writing a Comparative Evaluation," in the Handbook of Writing About Literature.

Publishing Student Writing If your school does not have a literary magazine, you might consider choosing a number of the essays for display on the class bulletin board.

Focus

More About the Tale In another tale about Stormalong's seamanship, Stormalong suggested that the sides of his enormous ship be soaped up so that it could squeeze through the English Channel. The soap was scraped off by the cliffs of Dover, leaving them white to this day.

Literary Focus You might want to use some incidents from the previous selections in this unit as examples of the exaggeration. Ask students to provide examples of their own from television, movies, or books.

Look For It may be helpful to preview the Analyzing Literature questions on pge 673 if any of your **less advanced** students are having difficulty understanding exaggeration.

Writing/Prior Knowledge You might suggest that students exaggerate an actual experience, such as something they did with friends, a school function, or a family vacation. This approach might help them get started. Remind them that it is important that they exaggerate freely.

Vocabulary You might have your **less advanced** students read these words aloud so that you can be sure they can pronounce them.

Spelling Tip The /ou/ sound in *prowl* can also be spelled *ou,* as in *cloud,* but the two spellings should not be confused.

GUIDE FOR READING

The Foggy Stew

Alfred Bulltop Stormalong was a gigantic sea captain in New England folklore. In some stories he stood over four fathoms (twenty-four-feet!) tall and picked his teeth with an eighteen-foot oar. His ship was so huge that its deck had to be traveled on horseback. The masts were hinged in order to let the sun and moon pass by. Young sailors who climbed its rigging returned with gray beards.

"The Foggy Stew," by **Harold Felton** (1902–), relates one of Stormalong's fantastic deeds before he became a captain.

Exaggeration in a Folk Tale

Exaggeration is overstatement. It is often used in tall tales, folktales, and legends for humorous effect. For instance, a story may be about a rainstorm so heavy that people have to wear scuba gear to walk outside. Rainstorms in actuality can be heavy, but a rainstorm so heavy as to require scuba gear is exaggerated. In "The Foggy Stew" the famous sailor Stormalong comes up against a fog so thick that fish are swimming in it.

Look For

As you read "The Foggy Stew," look for exaggeration. What effect is caused by the use of exaggeration?

Writing

Freewrite about another exaggerated situation. Let your mind wander freely, creating the most outrageous of details.

Vocabulary

Knowing the following words will help you as you read "The Foggy Stew."

notions (nō′ shənz) *n.:* Small, useful, household items (p. 669)
becalmed (bi kämd′) *v.:* Made motionless, as a sailing ship when there is no wind (p. 669)
galley (gal′ ē) *n.:* Cooking area on a ship (p. 669)
starboard (stär′ bərd) *adj.:* The right side of a ship, as one faces forward (p. 669)
poached (pōcht) *adj.:* Cooked gently in near-boiling water (p. 671)
prow (prou) *n.:* The frontmost part of a ship (p. 672)
promoted (prə mōt′ id) *v.:* Given a higher position (p. 672)

Objectives

1 To understand exaggeration
2 To interpret the storyteller's purpose
3 To write with exaggeration in a folk tale

Support Material

Teaching Portfolio
Teacher Backup, pp. 971-973
Usage and Mechanics Worksheet, p. 974
Vocabulary Check, p. 975
Critical Thinking and Reading Worksheet, *Interpreting the Storyteller's Purpose,* p. 976
Language Worksheet, *Understanding Comparison of Adjectives,* p. 977
Selection Test, pp. 978-979

The Foggy Stew

Harold W. Felton

The *Lady of the Sea* was in the China trade. She was fully loaded with timber, metal goods, cotton cloth and notions. When she cast off the wind filled her sails, and soon the land was left far behind.

On the outward voyage the ship became becalmed in the doldrums.[1] For days she lay silent in a fog, with never a cat's paw of wind.[2]

The fog grew thicker. "It's the worst fog I
1 ever saw," declared Captain Hardstone.

There seemed to be no sun or moon or stars. There seemed to be no day or night. Nothing but a gray curtain of fog. There seemed to be no fore or aft,[3] no up or down.

"The only way you can tell up from
down," said the captain, "is to drop some-
2 thing. When it hits your foot, you can tell
that way is down."

The fog got thicker still. "This ain't no pea soup fog," said the captain. "It's thicker than that."

"Speaking of pea soup, that's an uncommon good smell coming from the galley,"
3 said Stormalong.

"So it is. But it ain't pea soup. It's plum duff,[4]" said the captain. "A heaven-touched mixture of flour, water, and prunes."

"What's that?" asked Stormalong.

"Plum duff," said the captain.

"No. I know what plum duff is. I mean, what's that noise?"

Captain Hardstone cocked his head to listen better. "It's a kind of a flutterin' sound," he said.

"It's fish. That's what it is. It's fish! There are fish swimming in the fog!" said Stormalong.

"Fish?" the captain was puzzled.

Stormalong listened again. Then slowly the facts came to his mind, and as they did, he put them into words. "This fog is so thick a man can't tell where the water stops and the fog begins. So it stands to reason that a fish, which is no ways as smart as a man, can't tell either."

"Yes, sir, it stands to reason. It certainly
does," the captain muttered, still wondering
how this strange fact could be true, as it
undoubtedly was, and at the same time
admiring Stormy for his quick logic and 4
clear explanation.

Stormy continued. "They smell the plum duff cooking. It smells so good, they are swimming for it."

When he heard his own words, Stormy got an idea. Peering through the fog, he was dimly able to see a school of salmon[5] nosing around the cracks at the edge of the galley door.

Softly he glided to the starboard porthole
of the galley. "Cookie, are you there?" he 5
whispered.

---

1. doldrums (dol' drəmz), *n.*: Parts of the ocean near the equator where there is a lack of wind.
2. cat's paw of wind: A light wind that barely ruffles the water.
3. fore or aft: Front or back.
4. duff (duf), *n.*: A thick flour pudding boiled in a cloth bag.

5. school of salmon: A large number of salmon swimming together.

Presentation

Motivation/Prior Knowledge Have students imagine what it might be like to be in the midst of a fog so thick they could barely see three feet away. How would they feel? Would they be able to find their way around? How does fog affect their perceptions?

Purpose-Setting Question What is the effect of the exaggeration on the mood of the story?

1 **Enrichment** Fog is tiny droplets of water that collect together in the air. Fog forms from water vapor, evaporated water from the earth. The air can only hold a certain amount of water vapor. When the water vapor exceeds the maximum amount that the air can hold, the excess condenses and changes into small droplets of water. This condensation is fog. Fog is very similar to clouds except that clouds do not touch the earth's surface.

2 **Literary Focus** You might want to point out that, although this is an exaggeration, it helps the reader to imagine the thickness of the fog. Have you ever exaggerated weather conditions such as rain, snow, or wind?

3 **Discussion** What images do names like Stormalong and Hardstone evoke? Why do these men have such unusual names?

4 **Reading Strategy** You might have students summarize what other qualities are highlighted.

5 **Reading Strategy** You might have students predict what Stormalong has in mind.

Master Teacher Note You might want to point out to students that, as the stories about Paul Bunyan, Pecos Bill, and John Henry reflect the occupations of the people who created them, so Stormalong reflects the strong tie with the ocean that many people in New England had. You might show students photographs of ports in New England such as New Bedford or Nantucket as they appeared during the 1800's.

Thematic Idea Other selections that use exaggeration extensively are "Davy Crockett's Dream," p. 679 and "Tussle with a Bear," p. 681.

New England Folk Art of the 1800's: The Little Navigator *from the Whaling Museum and Old Dartmouth Historical Society; New Bedford, Massachusetts. All other wood carvings from the Shelburne Museum, Shelburne, Vermont.*

670

"Yes," the cook answered. "I shut the galley door so as to try to keep some of the fog out."

"You're keeping the salmon out too," Stormy told him.

"What?" The wonder in the cook's voice made it clear that he was not following Stormy.

"There are salmon sniffing at the galley door. They smell your plum duff cooking."

"Most everybody likes my plum duff," the cook said with pride in his voice. There was a pause. "But—fish! I never heard of fish caring one way or another about plum duff. As a matter of fact, I never heard of fish sniffing around a galley door!"

"Just take my word for it," said Stormy. "Listen. Put some plum duff in a big cooking pot, the biggest one you've got."

"Well, I don't know what you've got in mind. But I'll do what you say," the cook answered.

When the pot was ready, Stormalong opened the galley door. The salmon swam inside. They swam directly toward the plum duff in the pot.

Stormy followed closely behind them. Fortunately the salmon were so intent on the delicious-smelling plum duff, they ignored all signs of danger and forgot caution. They swam right into the waiting pot and greedily began to munch at the tasty plum duff.

Stormy stepped forward and slammed the lid on the pot. "Got 'em!" he declared.

6 The salmon were poached in the pot full of fog, and all the sailors agreed they had never had better poached salmon. And the plum duff was the perfect dessert for such a delicious meal.

Stormalong met the captain after dinner on the quarter deck. There was a happy, contented look in Captain Hardstone's eyes. "I do declare, that was the best poached salmon I ever put a tooth to. I tell you it makes a big difference when fish are fresh caught."

But the contentment did not last. A man can't remember a pleasant meal forever. Work must be done, and the captain was restless at the long delay in the fog. He tried to peer through the gray curtain that enveloped the ship, examining every quarter for a sign of a breeze.

But the sails hung limp, with no flap or flutter. She was a silent ship on a silent sea—as quiet as an eel swimming in oil.

"I certainly would admire to see a sign of a breeze," Captain Hardstone said. "I'd welcome any wind able to move, even enough to ripple up a fly's eyelashes would give me hope." 7

"Maybe I can help," said Stormalong.

"Poached salmon is fine, and I like it. I would enjoy eating a good many meals of it. But it's wind I want, boy." Captain Hardstone moved to the rail and stared over it into the gray fog. The captain was now a solemn man.

"That's what I mean," said Stormy. He turned and walked to the stern of the ship. Facing the bow, he planted his feet firmly on the planks that were wet from the dripping fog. He squared his shoulders, took a deep breath, and blew.

The slack sails fluttered a small flutter. "There's a show of a breeze," Captain Hardstone cried.

Stormy took another deep breath. His chest expanded and three buttons popped off and danced across the wet planks.

"What are you doing there, boy?" the captain shouted.

Stormy didn't answer. He blew again. The sails bent out.

"Never seen anything like it before," the captain exclaimed. "Man and boy, I never seen—"

6 **Literary Focus** What is exaggerated in this paragraph?

7 **Discussion** Is this statement an exaggeration? Support your answer. Why might such a small amount of wind give the captain hope?

Reader's Response Describe a situation in which your quick thinking or the quick thinking of someone you know helped solve a problem.

SABLE ISLAND: THE SAILOR'S GRAVE YARD
John Frost
Abby Aldrich Rockefeller Folk Art Center
Williamsburg, Virginia

His words were lost in the breeze as Stormy blew again. A small white crest began to trail along each side of the prow, as the *Lady of the Sea* moved slowly through the water.

The ship picked up speed. The prow pushed the seas aside.

Captain Hardstone and the crew watched with amazement as Stormy blew the fog away. He blew the ship right out of the doldrums and into the trade winds.[6]

When the breeze of nature caught the sails, Stormy stopped his blowing. To tell the truth, his face was red, and he sat down because he needed a rest. But he soon caught his breath and grinned, well satisfied with what he had done.

"Hip, hip!" the captain cried.

"Hooray!" the crew replied.

"Stormalong!"

"Stormalong!"

Captain Hardstone promoted Stormy and made him boatswain.[7] When he blew his boatswain's whistle he blew it so loud the echo would dry the sailors' laundry on a rainy day.

---

6. **trade winds:** Either of two winds blowing in the same direction toward the equator.

7. **boatswain** (bō′ sən), *n.*: An officer of a ship in charge of the rigging and anchors. He calls the crew to duty with his whistle.

THINKING ABOUT THE SELECTION

Recalling

1. Where does the ship become becalmed?
2. What problems does the heavy fog create for Captain Hardstone and his crew?
3. How does Stormalong take advantage of the heavy fog?
4. Why is the captain still discontented after the salmon dinner?
5. How does Stormalong solve the captain's problem?
6. What is Stormalong's reward?

Interpreting

7. Do you agree with Captain Hardstone that Stormalong has quick logic and a clear explanation about the fish swimming in the fog? Give reasons for your answer.
8. What does Stormalong's calm reaction to his getting the ship moving tell you about him?
9. What qualities of Stormalong does this folk tale glorify?

Applying

10. Captain Hardstone promotes Stormalong because his quick thinking and reactions were helpful. Think of examples of people from history or current affairs whose quick thinking and reactions were helpful.

ANALYZING LITERATURE

Understanding Exaggeration

Exaggeration, or overstatement, is often used for comic effect by treating the impossible as if it were real. Exaggeration can be expressed in a statement or through a description of an unbelievable situation.

1. Indicate which of the following statements contain exaggeration.
   a. "A man can't remember a pleasant meal forever."
   b. '"This fog is so thick a man can't tell where the water stops and the fog begins."'
   c. "When he blew his boatswain's whistle he blew it so loud the echo would dry the sailors' laundry on a rainy day."
   d. "To tell the truth, his face was red, and he sat down because he needed a rest."
2. Find three examples of exaggeration you found especially effective. Explain your reason for selecting each.

CRITICAL THINKING AND READING

Interpreting the Storyteller's Purpose

A writer's purpose is his or her reason for writing. A writer may write to inform, entertain, or persuade. You must infer, or recognize, the writer's purpose from clues that are given. Sometimes the writer may use factual language and a serious tone, or attitude, to inform; exaggeration and a light tone to entertain; and strong, definite language and an emotional tone to persuade.

1. What tone, or attitude, does the writer use in "The Foggy Stew"?
2. What kind of language does the writer use?
3. What do you think is the writer's purpose in "The Foggy Stew"?
4. Do you think the author may have had more than one purpose? Explain your answer.

THINKING AND WRITING

Writing with Exaggeration in a Folktale

Choose one of the ideas for an exaggerated situation that you thought of earlier and write a folktale about it for your classmates. First freewrite about the situation, including a description of your hero—like Stormalong or your own invention—what happens, and how your hero deals with the situation. Make sure you exaggerate your descriptions to create humor. Then write a folktale using the exaggerated situation. Revise each, making sure your writing is entertaining. Proofread your story and read it to your class.

8. Answers may differ. Suggested Response: His nonchalant reaction indicates that this feat was not extraordinary for him and that he is capable of other great tasks. It also may reflect the quality of modesty.
9. Answers will differ. Suggested Response: Qualities include quick thinking, logic, modesty, cleverness, and strength.

Applying

10. Answers will differ. They might include Paul Revere or various sports figures who must think quickly to succeed.

Challenge Why were the qualities of quick thinking and reactions important to sailors in the 1800's?

ANSWERS TO ANALYZING LITERATURE

1. a. This statement is generally not an exaggeration.
   b. This statement is exaggerated.
   c. This statement is exaggerated.
   d. This statement is not exaggerated.
2. Students have many examples to choose from in the folktale, and they should support each example.

ANSWERS TO CRITICAL THINKING AND READING

1. The writer uses a light tone.
2. The writer uses exaggerated, informal language.
3. The writer's purpose is to entertain and to highlight some of the qualities valued by the people of New England.
4. Answers will differ. Suggested Response: Yes. Most folk tales have the dual purpose of entertainment and instruction.

Writing Across the Curriculum
You might have students research and write a report on the primary routes traveled by sailing ships during the 1800's. The report could include a map of these routes and of the trade winds. If you make this assignment, perhaps inform the social studies department. Social studies teachers might provide guidance for students in conducting their research.

Closure and Extension

ANSWERS TO THINKING ABOUT THE SELECTION

Recalling

1. The ship was becalmed in the doldrums.
2. The fog gives the impression that there is no night or day, sun or moon, fore or aft, nor up or down.
3. Stormalong takes advantage of the fog by catching some salmon who lost their way and swam into the galley.
4. The captain is still discontented because there is still no wind to move the ship.
5. Stormalong solves the problem by standing at the back of the ship and blowing into the sails, moving the ship to the trade winds.
6. Stormalong's reward is a promotion to boatswain.

Interpreting

7. Students should disagree because his logic does not include the law of gravity and the fact that fish cannot swim out of the water. In a fantastic folktale, however, his explanations seem logical.

Focus

More About the Legend The tales of Johnny Appleseed became widely known following the publication of an article by W.D. Haley, called "Johnny Appleseed, a Pioneer Hero," in *Harper's New Monthly Magazine* in 1871. Although many stories, novels, and poems were written about John Chapman's deeds, none has ever been proven true.

Literary Focus You might point out to students that characterization is important in literature because all readers are interested in what other people are like. Readers usually identify as hero the character who possesses the character traits they admire most.

Look For You might want students to jot down on a piece of paper the two lists of traits.

Writing/Prior Knowledge If some of your **less advanced** students have trouble thinking of people, you might suggest that they list the accomplishments of people such as Jerry Lewis, who devotes his time to raising money to support research on muscular dystrophy.

Vocabulary Have your **more advanced** students use each vocabulary word in an original sentence.

Spelling Tip The silent *g* in *gnarled* is also found in words like *gnaw*. Other silent initial consonants include *k (knife, knave)*, *p (psalm, psaltery)*, and *w (wring, wretch)*.

GUIDE FOR READING

Johnny Appleseed

Johnny Appleseed (1774–1845) was a real-life frontiersman —John Chapman. Chapman was born in Leominster, Massachusetts. His life was so extraordinary that he became a folklore hero. In stories about him that blend truth and fantasy, he scattered apple seeds throughout Pennsylvania along the Allegheny River. His apple orchards spread through Ohio to northern Indiana!

This poem about him was written by the poet and editor **Rosemary Carr Benét** (1898–1962).

Characterization

Characterization is the way a writer shows you what a character is like. A writer can give you an idea of a character's personality through a description of his or her appearance and actions, through dialogue, or through direct statements. In "Johnny Appleseed," the writer portrays the character through his appearance and actions.

Look For

As you read "Johnny Appleseed," look for his character traits. Which traits might describe the real-life man? Which belong solely to the legendary hero?

Writing

Think of people you have heard about who have selflessly given of their time and abilities to others in some beneficial way. List these people and their accomplishments.

Vocabulary

Knowing the following words will help you as you read "Johnny Appleseed."

gnarled (närld) *adj.*: Knotty and twisted, as the trunk of an old tree (p. 675)
ruddy (rud′ ē) *adj.*: Healthy color (p. 675)
encumber (in kum′ bər) *v.*: Weigh down (p. 675)
tendril (ten′ drəl) *n.*: Thin shoot from a plant (p. 676)
stalking (stôk′ iŋ) *adj.*: Secretly approaching (p. 676)
lair (ler) *n.*: Den of a wild animal (p. 676)

Objectives

1 To understand characterization
2 To make inferences about characters
3 To complete word analogies
4 To compare and contrast the character

Support Material

Teaching Portfolio
Teacher Backup, pp. 981–983
Usage and Mechanics Worksheet, p. 984
Vocabulary Check, p. 985
Analyzing Literature Worksheet, *Understanding Characterization*, p. 986
Critical Thinking and Reading Worksheet, *Making Inferences About Characters*, p. 987
Selection Test, pp. 988–989

Johnny Appleseed

Rosemary Carr Benét

Of Jonathan Chapman
Two things are known,
That he loved apples,
That he walked alone.

1 At seventy-odd
He was gnarled as could be,
But ruddy and sound
As a good apple tree.

For fifty years over
Of harvest and dew,
2 He planted his apples
Where no apples grew.

The winds of the prairie
Might blow through his rags,
But he carried his seeds
In the best deerskin bags.

From old Ashtabula
To frontier Fort Wayne,
He planted and pruned
And he planted again.

He had not a hat
To encumber his head.
3 He wore a tin pan
On his white hair instead.

He nested with owl,
And with bear-cub and possum,

JOHN CHAPMAN, 1871
The Granger Collection

Presentation

Humanities Note

Colored engraving, *John Chapman,* 1871. This engraving of John Chapman, known as Johnny Appleseed, was done a quarter century after Chapman's death. As students read the poem and look at the engraving, you might discuss how legends grow.

1. What details of this illustration reflect details of the poem?
2. Why might an illustration like this show a man with characteristics different from those described in the poem?

Motivation/Prior Knowledge Have students imagine what it might be like to meet Johnny Appleseed in person. How would he appear? What would his personality be like?

Master Teacher Note You might ask students how easy it is today for one person to make "a difference."

Purpose-Setting Question What actions or qualities of Johnny Appleseed have made him into a folk hero?

Enrichment The apple is one of the most important and popular fruits that grow on trees. There are thousands of varieties of apples that have been eaten by humans since prehistoric times. Apple trees are part of the rose family and can be grown anywhere but the hottest and coldest regions on earth.

1 **Literary Focus** What do the first two stanzas reveal about Johnny Appleseed's character?

2 **Discussion** Why do you think he did this? What characteristics does a person need to accomplish such a task?

3 **Critical Thinking and Reading** You might have students make inferences about Johnny's character based on this stanza.

Challenge How do you think society would view a person like Johnny Appleseed today?

4 **Discussion** Why does the author compare Johnny to an apple?

5 **Discussion** Do you think that this is a "marvelous story"? Do you think that Johnny Appleseed is or is not a folk hero? Support your answers.

Reader's Response If there were a modern John Chapman, what might he plant, where, and why?

And knew all his orchards
Root, tendril and blossom.

A fine old man,
4 As ripe as a pippin,[1]
His heart still light,
And his step still skipping.

The stalking Indian,
The beast in its lair
Did no hurt
While he was there.

For they could tell,
As wild things can,
That Jonathan Chapman
Was God's own man.

Why did he do it?
We do not know.
He wished that apples
Might root and grow.

He has no statue.
He has no tomb.
He has his apple trees
Still in bloom.

Consider, consider,
Think well upon
5 The marvelous story
Of Appleseed John.

---

1. **pippin** (pip′ in), *n.*: An apple.

THINKING ABOUT THE SELECTION

Recalling

1. What are the two things that the speaker says are known about John Chapman?
2. Describe Chapman's life on the frontier.
3. What kind of relationship does Chapman have with animals?
4. What monument to Chapman stands today?

Interpreting

5. What is Chapman's most important possession?
6. How does Chapman feel about nature?

Applying

7. What areas in today's world would benefit from having someone provide help in growing food? Explain what those areas might need.

ANALYZING LITERATURE

Understanding Characterization

Characterization is the way a writer presents a character. A character's personality can be shown through his or her appearance, actions, and thoughts; through dialogue; or through the writer's direct statements about him or her.

1. Find a detail that shows that Chapman did not care about his appearance.
2. Find a detail that shows that Chapman did not care to live in town.
3. Find details that indicate Chapman's health.

CRITICAL THINKING AND READING

Making Inferences About Characters

An **inference** is a reasonable conclusion you draw from given evidence. You can make inferences about a character from his or her appearance and actions. For example, from "He nested with owl, and with bear-cub and possum" you can infer that Johnny Appleseed liked animals.

What can you infer from the following?

1. Although he wore rags, he carried his apple seeds in the best deerskin bags.
2. He has no tombstone or memorial, but the apple trees he planted still thrive.

UNDERSTANDING LANGUAGE

Completing Word Analogies

A **word analogy** shows a relationship that two pairs of words have in common. The relationship may be in terms of similar meaning, size, volume, use, appearance, or other aspect. On tests, word analogies are usually written with colons:

gnarled: straight :: roundabout: direct

This is stated: Gnarled is to straight as roundabout is to direct. The relationship is that of opposites.

To complete word analogy problems, determine the relationship in the given pair of words. Then look for a pair with the same relationship.

Select the pair of words that has the same relationship as the italicized pair.

1. *harvest: crop* ::
   a. fertilize: field
   b. reap: grain
   c. preserve: fruit
2. *prune: tree* ::
   a. trim: hair
   b. hem: dress
   c. plant: seed

THINKING AND WRITING

Comparing and Contrasting

Write down what you know about John Chapman. Also write down what you know about Johnny Appleseed. Then list the similarities and differences between the actual man and the legend he became. Use these lists to write an essay comparing and contrasting the two for your school literary magazine. Revise your essay, making sure you state your points clearly and support them with examples. Proofread your work and share it with your classmates.

Closure and Extension

ANSWERS TO THINKING ABOUT THE SELECTION

Recalling

1. The two things known about Chapman are that he loved apples and that he walked alone.
2. His life is a simple one. He dresses in rags, carries seeds with him, and plants wherever he goes. He sleeps out of doors and only knows and cares for his apple orchards. He lived this way for about fifty years.
3. Chapman has a close relationship with animals, as he sleeps among owls, bears, and possums.
4. Chapman's monuments are the apple orchards that he planted and that remain today.

Interpreting

5. Apple seeds are Chapman's most important possession.
6. Chapman feels very close to nature. He sleeps out-of-doors, knows animals and their ways, and cares deeply about his apple orchards.

Applying

7. Answers will differ. Suggested Response: African nations experiencing famine conditions would need help in getting enough water to grow food.

ANSWERS TO ANALYZING LITERATURE

1. Details that show he did not care about his appearance include his wearing rags for clothes and a tin pan for a hat.
2. The details that show he did not care to live in town are that he walked alone and that he nested with animals.
3. Details that show that he was in good health are that he was seventy but ruddy and sound, that he was ripe as an apple, and that his heart was still light.

ANSWERS TO CRITICAL THINKING AND READING

1. You can infer that Chapman cared more for his appleseeds than he did for his own comfort and appearance.
2. You can infer that Chapman was not interested in fame or recognition but in the lasting quality of his apple orchards.

ANSWERS TO UNDERSTANDING LANGUAGE

1. b
2. a

THINKING AND WRITING

For help with this assignment, students can refer to Lesson 16, "Writing a Comparative Evaluation," in the Handbook of Writing About Literature.

Publishing Student Writing You might divide the students into groups. The members of a group could pool their lists and decide which characteristics of the man were real and which were fictitious. The groups could decide what John Chapman might have really been like and what characteristics were created as the legend of Johnny Appleseed grew.

Focus

More About the Legend Books and magazines elevated Crockett to a legendary status even before his death. After his death the tales lost all basis in reality. Tales were told of his riding up Niagara Falls on the back of an alligator and escaping from a tornado by sliding down a streak of lightning. One publication, the *Davy Crockett Almanac,* was especially popular and is among the forerunners of comic books.

Literary Focus The etymology of the word *yarn* may interest students. The expression, "to spin a yarn," means to tell a tale. Just as yarn is made by drawing out and twisting fibers of material such as wool, a tall tale is made by stretching out, extending or exaggerating the original facts of a story.

Look For Suggest that students be aware of understatement as well as exaggeration as a source of humor in Davy Crockett's stories. Point out to them, for example, the lines "This started my temper a trifle" (p. 679–680), and "The bear got a notion that the dog was unfriendly to him" (p. 681).

Writing/Prior Knowledge More advanced students may write a letter to a friend in which they exaggerate their ordinary experiences to make the letter more interesting **Less advanced** students may prefer to describe a routine daily experience, e.g. walking to school; then add exaggeration to make the experience more entertaining.

Vocabulary Students may need help with the following words: **varmints** (p. 679), **sallied** (p. 681).

Spelling Tip Students may use a mnemonic to remember the first *c* in *acquaintance:* you recognize *acquaintances* when you c (see) them.

GUIDE FOR READING

Davy Crockett's Dream
Tussle With a Bear

Davy Crockett (1786–1836) was a Tennessee frontiersman with both refined and wild qualities. As a civilized man, he served in the U.S. Army, the Tennessee militia, and Congress. As America's first comic superman, he personifies the untamed, comic spirit of the western frontier. In 1836 he died heroically at the Alamo, fighting Mexican troops for Texan independence. "Davy Crockett's Dream" and "Tussle with a Bear" are entries from his Almanacs that reflect the humor and peculiarity of his boisterous character.

Yarn

A yarn is an exaggerated, or overstated, story that captures the spirit and language of the times in which it was told. Yarns were commonly told on the American frontier for entertainment; a good yarn teller could hold an audience spellbound for hours. A yarn can be about any subject. It may include several anecdotes about the hero, mixing fact with imagination and exaggeration.

Look For

As you read these yarns from *The Crockett Almanacs,* imagine that Davy Crockett is telling them aloud. Look for the language and the exaggeration he uses to hold your interest. What is the effect of each yarn?

Writing

Davy Crockett's yarns brought humor to tiresome frontier life. Crockett stretched and exaggerated his routine experiences to make people laugh. Write about ways in which you or people you are familiar with color ordinary experiences. Also explore the reasons why people do so.

Vocabulary

Knowing the following words will help you as you read these two yarns from *The Crockett Almanacs.*

parson (pär′sən) *n.*: A clergyman (p. 681)

acquaintance (ə kwānt′ ′ns) *n.*: A person one has met (p. 681)

disposition (dis′pə zish′ən) *n.*: One's nature or temperament (p. 683)

caper (kā′pər) *n.*: Slang term for criminal act (p. 683)

Objectives

1 To understand yarns
2 To recognize exaggeration
3 To appreciate dialect
4 To create a yarn

Support Material

Teaching Portfolio

Teacher Backup, pp. 991–993
Usage and Mechanics Worksheet, p. 994
Vocabulary Check, p. 995
Analyzing Literature Worksheet, *Understanding a Yarn,* p. 996
Language Worksheet, *Appreciating Dialect,* p. 997
Selection Test, pp. 998–999

Davy Crockett's Dream

Davy Crockett

One day when it was so cold that I was afeard to open my mouth, lest I should freeze my tongue, I took my little dog named Grizzle and cut out for Salt River Bay to kill something for dinner. I got a good ways from
1 home afore I knowed where I was, and as I had swetted some before I left the house my hat froze fast to my head, and I like to have put my neck out of joint in trying to pull it off. When I sneezed the icicles crackled all up and down the inside of my nose, like when you walk over a bog in winter time. The varmints was so scarce that I couldn't find one, and so when I come to an old log
2 hut that had belonged to some squatter that had ben reformed out by the nabors, I stood my rifle up agin one of the door posts and went in. I kindled up a little fire and told
3 Grizzle I was going to take a nap. I piled up a heap of chestnut burs for a pillow and straitened myself out on the ground, for I can curl closer than a rattle-snake and lay straiter than a log. I laid with the back of my head agin the hearth, and my eyes looking up chimney so that I could see when it was noon by the sun, for Mrs. Crockett was always rantankerous[1] when I staid out over the time. I got to sleep before Grizzle had done warming the eend of his nose, and I had swallowed so much cold wind that it laid hard on my stomach, and as I laid gulping and belching the wind went out of me and roared up chimney like a young whirlwind. So I had a pesky dream, and kinder thought, till I waked up, that I was floating down the Massassippy in a holler tree, and I hadn't room to stir my legs and arms no more than they were withed together with young saplings. While I was there and want able to help myself a feller called Oak Wing that lived about twenty miles off, and that I had give a most almighty licking once, cum and looked in with his blind eye that I had gouged out five years before, and I saw him looking in one end of the hollow log, and he axed me if I wanted to get out. I telled him to tie a rope to one of my legs and draw me out as soon as God would let him and as much sooner as he was a mind to. But he said he wouldn't do it that way, he would ram me out with a pole. So he took a long pole and rammed it down agin my head as if he was ramming home the cattridge in a cannon. This didn't make me budge an inch, but it pounded my head down in between my shoulders till I look'd like a turcle with his head drawn in. This started my temper a

1. **rantankerous** (ran′ tăn′ kər əs) *adj.*: Dialect for "cantankerous," meaning "wildly and noisily upset."

Presentation

Motivation/Prior Knowledge You might lead the class in a discussion about all of the yarns covered in the previous selections. Based on what they have learned so far, what do students expect these tales to be like? What qualities will be glorified in the character of this frontiersman? What might some of his adventures include?

Purpose-Setting Question What events in these tales are exaggerations and which may be real?

Master Teacher Note To give your students a better idea of the widespread popularity that the legend of Davy Crockett enjoys today, you might play them the recording, "Davy Crockett, King of the Wild Frontier," from the soundtrack of the Walt Disney movie of the same name that was popular in the 1950's. The album, number CL666, was issued by Columbia. You might also tell them about the popular television series that was based on his life.

Thematic Idea Another selection whose subject was an actual person who became a part of folklore is "Paul Revere's Ride" on page 509.

1 **Critical Thinking and Reading** What parts of this passage are realistic? What parts are exaggerated? Try reading the passage without the exaggerations. How does exaggeration enhance the passage?

2 **Clarification** A squatter is a person who lives on land that he has no rights to.

3 **Literary Focus** Chestnut burs are hard and prickly. In what way is Davy Crockett boasting by claiming that he used them for a pillow? What does this tell you about his audience? What kinds of human qualities do you think they admired?

trifle, and I ript and swore till the breath boiled out of the end of the log like the steam out of the funnel pipe of a steemboat. Jest then I woke up, and seed my wife pulling my leg, for it was enermost sundown and she
4 had cum arter me. There was a long icicle hanging to her nose, and when she tried to kiss me, she run it right into my eye. I telled her my dreem, and sed I would have revenge on Oak Wing for pounding my head. She said it was all a dreem and that Oak was not to blame; but I had a very diffrent idee of the matter. So I went and talked to him, and telled him what he had done to me in a dreem, and it was settled that he should
make me an apology in his next dreem, and 5
that wood make us square,[2] for I don't like to be run upon when I'm asleep, any more than I do when I'm awake.

2. square: Even.

THINKING ABOUT THE SELECTION

Recalling

1. Give three examples of details that Crockett exaggerates.
2. What is Crockett's goal, and does he accomplish it by the end of the tale?
3. Where is Crockett in his dream?
4. Approximately how long does Crockett oversleep?
5. What does Crockett decide will settle his differences with Oak Wing?

Interpreting

6. At the end of the tale, Crockett and Oak Wing come to a fantastic and humorous settlement. What does their agreement tell you about respect in frontier life?
7. Explain how Crockett's dialect affects his tale. Had he written his tale in standard English, what would have been lost?

Applying

8. Crockett's audience must be careful not to take him literally. What other examples of writing should you examine carefully before taking at face value?

ANALYZING LITERATURE

Understanding a Yarn

A **yarn** is an exaggerated story that captures the spirit and language of the times in which it was told. A yarn is told for entertainment; it does not have a "lesson." Through descriptions of fantastic events or heroic feats, a yarn can help you imagine what life was like at that time.

1. In what ways do you think the information you learn about Davy Crockett from a biographical account differs from the information you learn about him from a yarn?
2. Are there any ways in which the information would be similar? Explain your answer.

CRITICAL THINKING AND READING

Recognizing Exaggeration

In his yarn, Crockett takes an ordinary event and transforms it into a bizarre experience. Through exaggerated comparisons and elaborate language, Crockett inflates the actions of his story to capture his audience. For example, to convince his readers of the extreme cold he encountered, he said: "I had swallowed so much cold wind that it laid hard on my stomach, and as I laid gulping and belching the wind went out of me and roared up chimney like a young whirlwind." By comparing his breath to a whirlwind out of a chimney, Crockett stretches the facts of his adventures out of proportion to amaze his audience.

1. Cite other examples of exaggerations of facts that lead to fantastic descriptions.
2. Do these exaggerations enhance or detract from Crockett's tales? Explain.

4 **Literary Focus** Notice that Crockett did not write in standard English, but in the dialect of the Tennessee frontier. Try rereading this passage as if it had been written in standard English. What is lost? How does the use of dialect enhance the yarn?

5 **Literary Focus** Because a yarn's main purpose is to entertain, humor is one of its main elements. What makes this sentence humorous?

Reader's Response After reading this yarn, do you think you would have enjoyed living on the frontier in Davy Crockett's day? What might you find attractive about this life? What would you find unappealing?

ESL Teaching Strategy The many nonstandard spellings and pronunciations in this selection may present difficulties for students with limited English proficiency. A group of students may want to compile a list of all the nonstandard words in the selection with their standard spellings for use by any student having difficulty with the dialect.

Closure and Extension

ANSWERS TO THINKING ABOUT THE SELECTION

Recalling

1. He says the weather was so cold that his hat froze to his head, he fell asleep before his dog could warm his nose, and his breath went up the chimney like a whirlwind.
2. Crockett's goal was to shoot something for dinner, which he failed to do.
3. He is floating down the Mississippi River in a hollow tree.
4. He overslept about five or six hours; he meant to get up by noon; when his wife wakes him up it is almost sundown.
5. The next time Oak Wing has a dream, he must apologize for his actions in Crockett's dream.

Interpreting

6. Students may answer that respect for an individual's rights was valued highly.
7. Students may answer that the use of dialect makes it seem like Crockett is actually speaking to us. The standard English version would have been less colorful and less entertaining.

Applying

8. Students may mention persuasive writing such as propaganda or advertising copy, or figurative writing found in poetry or fiction.

ANSWERS TO ANALYZING LITERATURE

Understanding a Yarn

1. A biographical account provides the reader with more accurate, factual information. A yarn may give the reader a more vivid picture of a character's personality and sense of humor.
2. A biographer may attempt to convey to readers the personality traits that come across directly in a yarn.

ANSWERS TO CRITICAL THINKING AND READING

Recognizing Exaggeration

1. Some examples are "I was afeard to open my mouth, lest I should

Tussle with a Bear

Davy Crockett

I salled out from hum, one rainy arternoon, to go down to Rattle-snake Swamp to git a squint at a turkey-buzzard, for thar war a smart chance of them down that way, and I had hered how thar war to be a Methodist parson at my house on the next day, and my wife wanted me to git sumthing nice for his tooth. She said it would help out his sarment[1] almighty much. So I took my dog and rifle and sallied out rite away. I had got down about as fur as where the wood opens at the Big Gap, when I seed it war so dark and mucilaginous[2] that I coodn't hardly see at all. I went on, howsever, and intarmined[3] in my own mind, to keep on, tho I shood run afoul of an earthquake, for thar is no more give back to me than thar is to a flying bullet when a painter stares it rite in the face. I war going ahead like the devil on a gambler's trail, when, all at once, or I might say, all at twice, for it war done in double quick time, I felt sumthing ketch me around the middle, and it squeezed me like it war an old acquaintance. So I looked up and seed pretty quick it war no relation of mine. It was a great bear that war hugging me like a brother, and sticking as close to me as a turcle to his shell. So he squeezed an idee into my hed that if I got him as ded as common, and his hide off of his pesky body, he would do as well for the parson as any thing else. So I felt pretty well satisfied when I cum to think I had my Sunday's dinner so close to me. But when he railly seemed to be cuming closer and closer, I telled him to be patient for he wood git into me arter he war cooked; but he didn't seem to take a hint, and to tell the truth, I begun to think that although there war to be won dinner made 5
out between us, it war amazing uncertain which of us would be the dinner and which would be the eater. So I seed I ought to hav ben thinking about other matters. I coodn't get my knife out, and my rifle had dropped down. He put up won of his hind claws agin my side, and I seed it war cuming to the *scratch* amazing sudden. So I called to my dog, and he cum up pretty slow till he seed what war the matter, and then he jumped a rod rite towards the bear. The bear got a 6
notion that the dog was unfriendly to him, before he felt his teeth in his throat, and when Rough begun to gnaw his windpipe, 7
the varmint ment there should be no love lost. But the bear had no notion of loosening his grip on me. He shoved his teeth so near my nose that I tried to cock it up out of his way, and then he drew his tongue across my 8
throat to mark out the place where he should put in his teeth. All this showed that he had no regard for my feelings. He shook

1. **sarment** (sär′mənt) *n.*: Dialect term for "sermon."
2. **mucilaginous** (myo͞o′ si läj′ ə nəs) *adj.*: Thick and sticky.
3. **intarmined** (in tär′ mənd) *v.*: Dialect for "determined."

1 **Clarification** Ask the students how they would translate the following words from this passage from dialect to standard English: *salled, hum, arternoon, git, thar, war, hered, sumthing.*

2 **Clarification** Crockett is referring to the Cumberland Gap, a natural pass through the Appalachian mountains at the meeting point of Virginia, Kentucky, and Tennessee. The Cumberland Gap is narrow and has steep sides about five hundred feet high. This scenic area is now Cumberland Gap National Historical Park, one of the country's largest historical parks.

3 **Discussion** "Give back" is dialect for giving up; "painter" is dialect for panther. What does Davy Crockett want his audience to think about him?

4 **Reading Strategy** Crockett uses colorful language to make this passage humorous and vivid. Look for examples of simile, ("like the devil on a gambler's trail"); play on words, ("all at once, or I might say, all at twice"); understatement, ("it war no relation of mine"); and exaggeration ("sticking as close to me as a turcle to his shell").

5 **Reading Strategy** How does Crockett make a dangerous situation seem funny?

6 **Clarification** A rod is 16.5 feet or 5.029 meters. Could a dog jump this far?

7 **Discussion** How do people usually choose names for pets? What does the name Crockett chose for his dog tell you about the qualities he admired in pets?

8 **Discussion** What is Crockett's purpose in speaking of the bear as though he were acting intelligently, or as if he could have regard for someone's feelings?

freeze my tongue" (p. 679), ". . . my hat froze fast to me head, and I like to have put my neck out of joint in trying to pull it off" (p. 679), "When I sneezed the icicles crackled all up and down the inside of my nose . . ." (p. 679), or "There was a long icicle hanging to her nose . . ." (p. 680).

2. Students might respond that the exaggerations enhance the tale be making ordinary experiences both amazing and amusing.

Challenge Some students will find it interesting to read an article on Davy Crockett in an encyclopedia and compare and contrast the information they learn from the article with what they have learned about Davy Crockett from his yarns.

9 Reading Strategy Identify each place in this passage at which listeners would laugh if the tale were being told aloud. If Crockett could give you advice on how to spin a good yarn, how might he tell you to end your tale?

Reader's Response Not all people have the same sense of humor. How do you respond to Davy Crockett's humor? Do you find his tale to be funny? If so, why? If not, why not?

Enrichment Bret Harte (1836–1902) helped shape a movement in American fiction called local color writing, a style that tries to capture the feeling of a particular place and people, including their natural form of speech. More advanced students might enjoy Harte's tales of the California gold rush days in his collection of stories, *The Luck of Roaring Camp and Other Sketches,* or Harte's humorous poem, "Plain Language from Truthful James."

off the dog three or four times, like nothing at all, and once he trod on his head; but Rough stood up to his lick log and bit at him, but the varmint's hairs set his teeth on
9 edge. All this passed in quicker time than a blind hoss can run agin a post, when he can't see whar to find it. The varmint made a lounge and caught hold of my rite ear, and so I made a grab at his ear too, and caught it between my teeth. So we held on to each others' ears, till my teeth met through his ear. Then I tripped him down with one leg, and the cretur's back fell acrost a log, and I war on top of him. He lay so oncomfortable that he rolled off the log, and loosened his grip so much that I had a chance to get hold of my nife, and Rough dove into him at the same time. Seeing thar war two of us, he

DAVY CROCKETT, WITH THE HELP OF HIS DOG, FIGHTING A BEAR
Cover of the Crockett Almanac, 1841
The Granger Collection

thought he would use one paw for each one. The varmint cocked one eye at me as much as to ax me stay whar I war till he could let go of me with one paw, and finish the dog. No man can say I am of a contrary disposition, though it come so handy for me to feel the haft of my big butcher, as soon as my rite hand war at liberty, that I pulled it out. The way it went into the bowels of the varmint war nothing to nobody. It astonished him most mightily. He looked as if he thought it war a mean caper, and he turned pale. If he didn't die in short time arterwards, then the Methodist parson eat him alive, that's all. When I cum to strip, arter the affair war over, the marks of the bear's claws war up and down on my hide to such a rate that I might have been hung out for an American flag. The stripes showed most beautiful.

THINKING ABOUT THE SELECTION

Recalling

1. What did Crockett intend to hunt when he left home?
2. Describe Crockett's struggle with the bear.
3. What help does Crockett get during his struggle with the bear?
4. Crockett describes himself in superhuman terms. Give examples from the tale.
5 What does Crockett compare his body to after he has killed the bear?

Interpreting

6. Are Crockett's actions heroic? Explain.
7. What effect do Crockett's exaggerations and outrageous comparisons have on the mood?
8. What does Crockett's final remark, "The stripes showed most beautiful," indicate about his feelings about killing the bear?

Applying

9. Crockett's accounts of his outrageous experiences helped shape his image as a frontier hero. Give examples of how you shape your image.

UNDERSTANDING LANGUAGE

Appreciating Dialect

Dialect is the pronunciation, grammar, spelling, and vocabulary used by a particular group of people in a region. Dialect adds humor to the yarns and makes the settings seem authentic. An example of dialect is "I salled out from hum, one rainy arternoon, to go down to Rattle-snake Swamp to git a squint at a turkey-buzzard, for thar war a smart chance of them down that way . . ." In standard English we might say: I set out from home to Rattle-snake Swamp, where I had a good chance of shooting a turkey.

Rewrite the following sentences in standard English:

1. "I went on, howsever, and intarmined in my own mind, to keep on, tho I shood run afoul of an earthquake, for thar is no more give back to me than thar is to a flying bullet when a painter stares it rite in the face."
2. "He put up won of his hind claws agin my side, and I seed it war cuming to the *scratch* amazing sudden."

THINKING AND WRITING

Creating a Yarn

Think of an adventurous experience you have had and write about it in the same style as Davy Crockett. Exaggerate the details of your story by using fantastic descriptions and comparisons. Like Davy Crockett, reveal something about your character by the end of your story. Revise your yarn, making sure it is well organized. Proofread your yarn and share it with classmates.

Closure and Extension

ANSWERS TO THINKING ABOUT THE SELECTION

Recalling

1. He intended to hunt for a turkey-buzzard.
2. The bear squeezed Crockett, scratched him, bit his ear. Crockett bit the bear's ear, tripped him. Crockett killed the bear with his knife.
3. Crockett's dog jumps at the bear and bites him.
4. Suggested answers: Crockett bit the bear; tripped him; didn't feel the scratches.
5. He compares it to the American flag.

Interpreting

6. His fearlessness may seem heroic to some; boastful and clownish to others.
7. They lighten the mood of the tale, making it amusing rather than frightening.
8. Crockett was proud of his victory.

Applying

9. Ask students how they would like others to see them. Then ask them how they might project this image.

ANSWERS TO UNDERSTANDING LANGUAGE

Appreciating Dialect

Students' rewritten passages should be similar to the following:

1. I went on, however, and made up my mind to continue, even if there should be an earthquake, for I don't give up any more than a flying bullet would if it were headed for a panther.
2. He put one of his hind claws against my side, and I saw he was about to scratch.

ANSWERS TO THINKING AND WRITING

Creating a Yarn

For help with this assignment, students can refer to Lesson 17, "Writing a Short Story," in the Handbook of Writing About Literature.

Writing Across the Curriculum Have students write reports on other frontier figures such as Daniel Boone, Mary Jemison, or James Bowie. You might inform a social studies teacher of this assignment.

Challenge Some students might want to try writing their yarns in dialect.

American Myths, Legends and Folk Tales

Johnny Appleseed
NEW YORK
VERMONT
NEW HAMPSHIRE
MAINE
MASS.
CONN.
R.I.
N.J.
PENN.
MARYLAND
DEL.
WEST VIRGINIA
VIRGINIA
OHIO
INDIANA
ILLINOIS
MICHIGAN
KENTUCKY
TENNESSEE
NORTH CAROLINA
SOUTH CAROLINA
GEORGIA
ALABAMA
MISSISSIPPI
FLORIDA
Mississippi River
JOHN HENRY
Davy Crockett
STORMALONG
Atlantic Ocean
of Mexico
N
E
S
W

Focus on Reading

Bring in various types of maps and show them to the class. You might even use them as a quick quiz after you have presented the material in the "Using a Map" section to the class. You might ask the social studies teachers for some samples.

FOCUS ON READING

Using a Map

Sometimes writers present information through various types of maps. They may want to show the locations of their settings, the distances their characters have traveled, or geographical features of an area, such as mountain ranges and bodies of water. To be able to understand and appreciate this information, it is necessary to know how to use a map.

Information

Before using a map, you should know what kind of information the map presents. A **road map** shows the highways, cities, county and state boundaries, and recreational areas. A **population** or **historical map** is used to show information about population, political boundaries, industry, and farm production. **Physical maps** indicate the geographical features of an area. The map on pages 684–685 illustrates the continental United States and the locations of the folktales and heroes you have read about.

Layout

Next you need to understand how maps are laid out. The top part of the map is the north and the bottom part is south. The area to the right is east while that to the left is west.

Keys

Most maps contain keys, or legends, which are located at the bottom right or left of the map. These keys provide important information to help you interpret a map. The map on pages 684–685 provides a scale of distance at the bottom left. This scale tells you approximately what measurement equals a number of miles.

Use the map on pages 684–685 to locate Pennsylvania. Remember that this is where Johnny Appleseed was famous for planting apple seeds. To help someone find Pennsylvania, you could explain that it borders the state of New Jersey. You could also specify that it is in the northeast region of the map. You could further explain Pennsylvania's location by identifying the states surrounding it. Knowing how to use a map will help give you a sense of where the places you read about are located.

Activity

In each of the following numbered items, identify the folk hero. Then use the American Myths, Legends, and Folktales map to determine in which part of the country the tales or heroes originated.

1. He planted apple orchards in three northern states.
2. According to legend, he created the Great Lakes to provide water for his blue ox.
3. He was born in this state and rode a legendary cyclone in Oklahoma.
4. With superhuman strength, he built a railroad.
5. He wrote about his fantastic frontier experiences in almanacs named after himself.
6. He wrote a poem about yarns.
7. She was a Zuñi Indian.
8. According to folklore, he was a sea captain.
9. A boy from this Indian tribe brought fire to his people.

Activity

Use the American Myths, Legends, and Folktales map to answer the following questions.

1. Where were the Davy Crockett tales set?
2. Pecos Bill rode the legendary cyclone
   a. north of Kansas
   b. south of Mexico
   c. west of Louisiana
3. What country borders Texas?
4. The Zuñi Indian girl hunted rabbits in New Mexico, east of which state?
5. John Henry built the famous railroad in which state?

ANSWERS TO THE ACTIVITIES

Activity 1

1. Johnny Appleseed; Pennsylvania, Ohio, Indiana
2. Paul Bunyan; Pacific northwest
3. Pecos Bill; Texas
4. John Henry; West Virginia
5. Davy Crockett; Tennessee
6. Carl Sandburg; Illinois
7. The girl who hunted rabbits; New Mexico
8. Alfred Bulltop Stormalong; New England
9. Nez Perce; Idaho, Oregon, Washington

Activity 2

1. Tennessee
2. a
3. New Mexico or Oklahoma or Mississippi
4. Arizona
5. West Virginia

The writing assignments on page 688 have students writing creatively, while those on page 689 have them thinking about the myths, legends, and folktales and writing critically.

YOU THE WRITER
Guidelines for Evaluating Assignment 1

1. Does the myth provide an imaginative explanation for some natural occurrence?
2. Are there descriptive details in the myth?
3. Are the events and details arranged chronologically to tell a story?
4. Is the myth free from grammar, usage, and mechanics errors?

Guidelines for Evaluating Assignment 2

1. Is the legend based on a contemporary figure who is presented in a vivid way?
2. Does the legend tell about the contemporary figure's exploits in a vivid manner?
3. Does the student use exaggeration to make the exploit seem larger than life?
4. Is the legend free from grammar, usage, and mechanics errors?

Guidelines for Evaluating Assignment 3

1. Does the tall tale about a wagon train present exaggerated events?
2. Has the student included dialect to give the tale a regional flavor?
3. Has the student created vivid characters?
4. Is the tall tale free from grammar, usage, and mechanics errors?

YOU THE WRITER

Assignment

1. Many myths deal with the origin of some natural occurrence. Write a myth explaining an event in nature.

Prewriting. First brainstorm to list natural occurrences such as a sunset, a waterfall, or a volcanic eruption. Select one of these events and jot down as many details about it as you can.

Writing. Write the first draft of a myth, providing an imaginative explanation for the natural occurrence you have chosen. Be sure to include descriptive details in your myth. Proceed in chronological order.

Revising. Revise your myth, making sure you have provided an imaginative explanation. Proofread your myth and share it with your classmates.

Assignment

2. Many legends are based on real-life people. Create a character for a legend based on a contemporary figure.

Prewriting. Brainstorm to list contemporary figures who might be the subject of future legends. For example, you might list famous athletes, astronauts, or even computer experts. Select one of these figures, and freewrite about his or her deeds.

Writing. Write the first draft of a legend, using your figure as a folk hero and telling about one of his or her exploits. Use exaggeration to make the exploit seem larger than life.

Revising. Have you made the exploit seem larger than life? Revise your legend, making sure it presents your character in a vivid way. Proofread your legend and prepare a final draft.

Assignment

3. Imagine you are living in the early 1800's and you are traveling across the country by wagon train. Write a tall tale to entertain your fellow travelers sitting around the campfire at night.

Prewriting. Create a story map, showing the plot, characters, and setting of your tale.

Writing. Write the first draft of your tall tale. Since this tale is "tall," make sure you exaggerate events. Also include dialect to give your tale a regional flavor.

Revising. When you revise, make sure you have created vivid characters and have used exaggeration to describe them and their deeds. Have you included dialect? Check your spelling and punctuation, paying special attention to your use of quotation marks.

YOU THE CRITIC

Assignment

1. Write an essay explaining how one of the folkheroes you have read about presents traits considered especially "American."

Prewriting. Choose a folk hero from one of the selections in this unit. List words and phrases describing this hero. From the list select the trait that you think most characterizes this hero.

Writing. Write the first draft of your essay. Begin with a topic sentence explaining how this folk hero portrays a special aspect of the American character. Support your main idea with details from the selection.

Revising. When you revise, make sure you have provided adequate support for your main idea. Proofread your essay and prepare a final draft.

Assignment

2. Write an essay comparing and contrasting a mythical explanation with a scientific explanation.

Prewriting. Thumb through the selections you have read and list mythical explanations for events in nature. Do some research to find a scientific explanation of the same event.

Writing. Write the first draft of your essay, comparing and contrasting a mythical and a scientific explanation. Organize your essay so that one paragraph deals with the mythical explanation and the next deals with the scientific explanation.

Revising. When you revise, make sure you have organized your information logically. Proofread your essay and prepare a final draft.

Assignment

3. What is it about myths, legends, and folktales that stirs our imagination? Write an essay explaining the appeal of this type of literature.

Prewriting. Freewrite, exploring the appeal of myths, legends, and folktales. Review your freewriting, underlining important ideas and starring especially effective use of language.

Writing. Write the first draft of an essay explaining the appeal of myths, legends, and folktales. Support your main idea with examples or reasons drawn from real life.

Revising. When you revise your essay, make sure you have presented your main idea in a clear fashion. Have you supported it with examples or reasons? Proofread your essay and prepare a final draft.

YOU THE CRITIC
Guidelines for Evaluating Assignment 1

1. Does the essay begin with a topic sentence explaining how the chosen folk hero portrays a trait considered especially American?
2. Is the main idea supported by details from the selection?
3. Is there adequate support for the reasons?
4. Is the essay free from grammar, usage, and mechanics errors?

Guidelines for Evaluating Assignment 2

1. Does the comparison examine the similarities and differences between the mythical and the scientific explanation?
2. Is the comparison organized by the block method?
3. Is the information organized logically within the paragraphs?
4. Is the comparison free from grammar, usage, and mechanics errors?

Guidelines for Evaluating Assignment 3

1. Does the essay explain the appeal of myths, legends, and folk tales?
2. Is the main idea supported by examples or reasons drawn from real life?
3. Are the ideas presented in a clear, organized fashion?
4. Is the essay free from grammar, usage, and mechanics errors?

MESA AND CACTI
Diego Rivera
Detroit Institute of Arts

THE NOVEL

A novel is a work of fiction; that is, an author creates it from his or her imagination. Like the short story, a novel includes the elements of plot, characters, setting, theme, and point of view. However, a novel is considerably longer than the short story, allowing the writer to develop elements such as setting, plot, and character more fully. A novel usually takes place in more than one setting. Typically, the plot, or sequence of events, in a novel is more complicated than that of a short story and often includes conflicts in addition to the main conflict. Characters in a novel are usually more complex because the author has room to develop them more thoroughly.

Readers can gain greater insights about life and about a particular time and place from a novel than they can from most short stories. In *The Pearl* you will read about a time and place unfamiliar to most readers.

Humanities Note

Diego Rivera (1886–1951) is perhaps the most well known Mexican artist. He received his formal training in Paris but returned to his native land to use his art for the glory of the Mexican people. Rivera is most notable for his murals, found around the world, which are monuments to his people and the workers of the world.

"Mesa and Cacti" is a landscape painting of terrain typical of Mexico. The handlike shapes of the cacti are counterbalanced by the mountains on the horizon. The picture plane is unified by the soft coloring of the composition. The skill of this rendering attests to the formal training Rivera underwent in Europe.

You might want to ask the following questions to discuss the art:

1. What is the atmosphere of this painting?
2. What emotion does this landscape evoke?

Reading Actively Have students keep a notebook containing any thoughts and comments they have while reading. Tell them to stop periodically to summarize what has happened so far. After students have finished reading each section of the novel, you might ask them to share any thoughts, comments, or summaries with others.

Enrichment Because it is shorter than most novels, *The Pearl* is often classified as a novella, or novelette.

READING ACTIVELY

The Novel

On a sailing trip in 1940, John Steinbeck heard a folk tale about a fisherman who suffered great misfortune after he discovered a magnificent pearl. Inspired by the legend, Steinbeck wrote *The Pearl* four years later. Like many important novels, *The Pearl* can be interpreted on several different levels. To present his multilevel theme, Steinbeck chose to write this novel as a parable, or allegory. A parable is a short work, usually fictitious, that illustrates a lesson, often about good and evil. In his preface to *The Pearl,* Steinbeck wrote: "If the story is a parable, perhaps everyone takes his own meaning from it." Some readers see *The Pearl* as a parable about human greed, while others find it a parable about social oppression.

Steinbeck often wrote about the struggle between the wealthy and the poor, between the strong and the weak, and between different cultures. To understand *The Pearl,* you should know that when the legend originated in the early 1900's, Indians of Mexico had been oppressed by people of Spanish descent for over three hundred years. In many cases, Indians were not allowed to attend school or own land. While Spanish culture was forced upon the Indians, many retained elements of tribal customs, just as Juana does when she combines Catholic Hail Marys with ancient prayers.

Reading Strategies

To increase your understanding of *The Pearl,* read the background and biographical information carefully. Understanding the significance of culture in the story will clarify some events in the plot. For example, many Mexican Indians believed that they were meant to remain in their birthplace. Therefore, leaving La Paz is an enormous step for Kino. It might also help you to appreciate the style in which Steinbeck wrote *The Pearl.* Keep in mind that he used very little dialogue and created simple rather than complex characters so that his novel would read like a parable. Finally, interact with the literature, using the active reading strategies for questioning, predicting, clarifying, summarizing, and pulling together.

Themes

You will encounter the following themes in *The Pearl.*

- The struggle for survival
- Oppression and social class
- Corruption by material wealth and possessions

The Pearl

LA MOLENDERA, 1924
Diego Rivera
Museo de Art Moderno

Humanities Note

Fine art, *La Molendera,* by Diego Rivera. Rivera (1886-1951), a Mexican artist, studied art in Paris. Uncomfortable with the radical movements in the Parisian art world, Rivera returned to his native land. After an extended tour of his country, he took steps to bring art embodying the spirit of the Revolution to the Mexican people. He is celebrated today for the murals he created worldwide that have become monuments to both the Mexican people and to workers.

La Molendera means The Grinder. It is a decorative painting of a woman making tortillas. This plain, sturdy woman, absorbed in the act of preparing this humble bread, becomes almost god-like in her simplicity. She is typical of the earthy folk images that populate Rivera's art. He paints them in a stylized fashion that harks back to the art of the Aztec and Mayan civilizations. Diego Rivera's art was a dynamic force that created a distinctly Mexican style in painting.

GUIDE FOR READING

The Pearl, Chapters 1–3

John Steinbeck (1902–1968) grew up in the Salinas Valley of California. As an accomplished writer, he has novels, short stories, and newspaper articles to his credit. After college, he spent five years drifting and writing; he even joined a hobo camp to study the lives of its people. Steinbeck's fiction, such as his Pulitzer Prize-winning novel *The Grapes of Wrath,* shows sympathy for underprivileged people who are exploited by society. In *The Pearl* he depicts the tragic plight of socially oppressed people.

Characters in a Parable

A **parable** is a short tale that illustrates a universal truth, a belief that appeals to all people of all civilizations. Characters in a parable are seldom complex and three-dimensional; instead, they tend to be flat, representing qualities rather than real-life people. In a parable, the characters, their experiences, and the lessons they learn are meant to parallel human experience.

Look For

As you read the first three chapters of *The Pearl,* look for what Kino learns in this parable. What universal truth does the parable reveal?

Writing

Imagine that you suddenly found a priceless treasure. How would your life change? Freewrite about your imagined experience, describing your thoughts and feelings.

Vocabulary

Knowing the following words will help you as you read the first three chapters of *The Pearl.*

feinted (fānt'id) *v.*: Made a pretense of attack (p. 697)
scorpion (skôr'pē ən) *n.*: Any of a group of poisonous arachnids found in warm regions (p. 697)
plaintively (plān'tiv lē) *adv.*: Sorrowfully; mournfully (p. 697)
avarice (av'ər is) *n.*: Greediness (p. 700)
alms (ämz) *n.*: Money given to poor people (p. 700)
indigent (in'di jənt) *adj.*: Needy; poor (p. 700)
bulwark (bo͞ol'wərk) *n.*: Protection; defense (p. 703)
undulating (undyo͞o lāt'iŋ) *adj.*: Wavy in form (p. 704)
semblance (sem'bləns) *n.*: Deceptive appearance (p. 706)
dissembling (di sem'b liŋ) *v.*: Concealing true feelings with a false appearance (p. 711)

Focus

More about the Author John Steinbeck was born in California. His knowledge of the Salinas River Valley farms and people was gained first-hand and provides the setting for many of his stories. He often used his books to point out injustice in society and to voice his concern for the oppressed. Elicit from students why Steinbeck was sympathetic to the oppressed and distressed.

Literary Focus Being attentive to characterization is critical in *The Pearl.* The characters in this novel are allegorical; that is, they are symbolic representations of humanity. As the reader observes the words and actions of the characters, sees their thoughts and secret hopes, and watches their interactions with nature, an image emerges of Steinbeck's view of humankind.

Look For The readers must make inferences as they read in order to understand character traits and feelings. These inferences are made through the information given about the character; sometimes, however, inferences might be made about a character through descriptions of nature. These descriptions often give the reader important clues to a character's development.

Writing/Prior Knowledge Have students consider what they would do with a new-found treasure; have them also consider possible drawbacks in having found it. Have them include these drawbacks in their freewriting. When students have completed the freewriting, have them consider whether the negative repercussions could make them want to give the treasure up.

Vocabulary Have your **less advanced** students read the words and their definitions. Have them participate in a discussion that allows them to use the words and demonstrate understanding of their meanings.

Objectives

1 To understand characterization when reading a novel
2 To appreciate words derived from Spanish
3 To write from Juana's point of view

Support Material

Teaching Portfolio

Teacher Backup, pp. 1013–1016
Grammar in Action Worksheets, *Using Dashes*, pp. 1017–1018, *Understanding Intensive and Reflexive Pronouns*, pp. 1019–1020
Usage and Mechanics Worksheet, p. 1021
Vocabulary Check, p. 1022
Analyzing Literature Worksheet, *Understanding Characterization and Point of View*, p. 1023
Language Worksheet, *Appreciating Words From Spanish*, p. 1024
Selection Test, pp. 1025–1026

The Pearl

John Steinbeck

"In the town they tell the story of the great pearl—how it was found and how it was lost again. They tell of Kino, the fisherman, and of his wife, Juana, and of the baby, Coyotito. And because the story has been told so often, it has taken root in every
1 man's mind. And, as with all retold tales that are in people's hearts, there are only good and bad things and black and white things and good and evil things and no in-between anywhere.

"If this story is a parable, perhaps everyone takes his own meaning from it and reads his own life into it. In any case, they say in the town that . . ."

Chapter 1

Kino awakened in the near dark. The stars still shone and the day had drawn only a pale wash of light in the lower sky to the east. The roosters had been crowing for some time, and the early pigs were already
2 beginning their ceaseless turning of twigs and bits of wood to see whether anything to eat had been overlooked. Outside the brush house in the tuna[1] clump, a covey of little birds chittered and flurried with their wings.

Kino's eyes opened, and he looked first at the lightening square which was the door and then he looked at the hanging box where Coyotito slept. And last he turned his head to Juana, his wife, who lay beside him on the mat, her blue head shawl over her nose and over her breasts and around the small of her back. Juana's eyes were open too. Kino could never remember seeing them closed when he awakened. Her dark eyes made little reflected stars. She was looking at him as she was always looking at him when he awakened.

Kino heard the little splash of morning waves on the beach. It was very good—Kino closed his eyes again to listen to his music. Perhaps he alone did this and perhaps all of his people did it. His people had once been great makers of songs so that everything they saw or thought or did or heard became
a song. That was very long ago. The songs 3
remained; Kino knew them, but no new songs were added. That does not mean that there were no personal songs. In Kino's head there was a song now, clear and soft, and if he had been able to speak of it, he would have called it the Song of the Family.

His blanket was over his nose to protect him from the dank air. His eyes flicked to a rustle beside him. It was Juana arising, almost soundlessly. On her hard bare feet she went to the hanging box where Coyotito slept, and she leaned over and said a little reassuring word. Coyotito looked up for a moment and closed his eyes and slept again.

Juana went to the fire pit and uncovered a coal and fanned it alive while she broke little pieces of brush over it.

---

1. tuna (tōō′ nə) *adj.*: Prickly-pear cactus.

Presentation

Motivation/Prior Knowledge Have students consider their impressions of a pearl, perhaps its beauty, its simultaneous simplicity and complexity, and its value. You might want to have students consider other stories they have read in which the pearl was a symbol, for example, the character Pearl in Hawthorne's *The Scarlet Letter.*

Purpose-Setting Question Throughout the novel Steinbeck creates sympathy for the plight of Kino. How does Steinbeck create this sympathy? What does the reader find out about Kino in the first three chapters?

1 **Enrichment** You might want to tell students that parables present stories that teach religious truths, moral lessons or general truths by using realistic events. What are examples of other parables? Have students discuss some possible themes in parables —harmony with nature, love and family, material possessions and greed.

2 **Literary Focus** In this paragraph Steinbeck has Kino awaken to the sounds of animals. Through this initial description, a mood or climate is conveyed. What is the atmosphere that his description suggests?

3 **Discussion** Theme, mood, and harmony with the world are suggested by these ancient songs. When Kino is in harmony with his world the song is melodic. What does the reader learn about Kino in this paragraph?

Master Teacher Note The story *The Pearl* was a result of Steinbeck's ecological explorations in the Sea of Cortez. While there he was told a legend of an Indian boy who found a pearl of great size and who was imprisoned by it until he could finally rid himself of it. *The Pearl,* as it is known today, was first published in 1945 in the *Woman's Home Companion* under the title "The Pearl of the World." Prior to publication, the novel was referred to as "The Pearl of La Paz" and "The Pearl of Peace." Have students consider the novel's titles as they read; and have them analyze the pearl's meaning.

Master Teacher Note To further discussion of the culture in which Kino and Juana live, you may want to place Art Transparency 20, *Flower Day* by Diego Rivera, on the overhead projector. Encourage students to find details in the painting that give them information about the culture. You may want to start your discussion of symbolism in *The Pearl* by discussing the symbolism apparent in this painting.

Humanities Note

Fine art, *Peasant with Sombrero*, Diego Rivera (1886–1957), Rivera trained in Mexico City. He was influenced by, among others, Cezanne, Gauguin, and Picasso. Rivera, a famous mural painter, was also a political activist. The subject matter of his murals was often the oppression suffered by Native Mexicans.

The man portrayed in this reproduction could represent the character Kino. Have students notice the positioning of the sombrero and the man's expression. Does the man appear to be at ease and looking forward to the task at hand? What might the man's eyes and the lines and shadows in the man's face reveal about his character? Has he had an easy life? As they read, have students identify points in the story when Kino most resembles the man in the painting.

4 **Clarification** Steinbeck often lived and worked with the people of a specific locale. Doing this helped him gain a better understanding to develop the characters and settings for his novels. For example, he traveled with migrants from Oklahoma to California in preparation for his novel *The Grapes of Wrath,* and he lived and worked in the Gulf of California among the Indians prior to his writing *The Pearl.*

5 **Literary Focus** What is Kino feeling? How does the reader know?

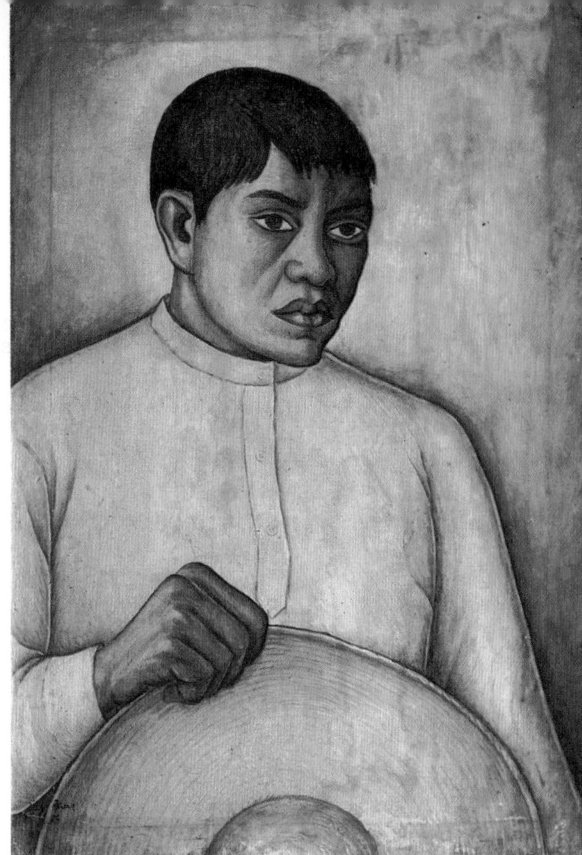

PEASANT WITH SOMBRERO (PEON), 1926
Diego Rivera
Galeria Arvil, Mexico City

Now Kino got up and wrapped his blanket about his head and nose and shoulders. He slipped his feet into his sandals and went outside to watch the dawn.

Outside the door he squatted down and gathered the blanket ends about his knees. He saw the specks of Gulf[2] clouds flame high
4 in the air. And a goat came near and sniffed
at him and stared with its cold yellow eyes. Behind him Juana's fire leaped into flame and threw spears of light through the chinks of the brush-house wall and threw a wavering square of light out the door. A late moth blustered in to find the fire. The Song
of the Family came now from behind Kino. 5
And the rhythm of the family song was the grinding stone where Juana worked the corn for the morning cakes.

The dawn came quickly now, a wash, a glow, a lightness, and then an explosion of fire as the sun arose out of the Gulf. Kino looked down to cover his eyes from the glare. He could hear the pat of the corncakes in the house and the rich smell of them on the

2. Gulf: The Gulf of California, a body of water between Baja California—a Mexican peninsula—and the main part of Mexico.

696 *The Novel*

cooking plate. The ants were busy on the ground, big black ones with shiny bodies, and little dusty quick ants. 6 Kino watched with the detachment of God while a dusty ant frantically tried to escape the sand trap an ant lion had dug for him. A thin, timid dog came close and, at a soft word from Kino, curled up, arranged its tail neatly over its feet, and laid its chin delicately on the pile. It was a black dog with yellow-gold spots where its eyebrows should have been.
7 It was a morning like other mornings and yet perfect among mornings.

Kino heard the creak of the rope when Juana took Coyotito out of his hanging box and cleaned him and hammocked him in her shawl in a loop that placed him close to her breast. Kino could see these things without looking at them. Juana sang softly an ancient song that had only three notes and yet endless variety of interval. And this was part of the family song too. It was all part. Sometimes it rose to an aching chord that caught the throat, saying this is safety, this is warmth, this is the *Whole*.

Across the brush fence were other brush houses, and the smoke came from them too, and the sound of breakfast, but those were other songs, their pigs were other pigs, their wives were not Juana. Kino was young and strong and his black hair hung over his brown forehead. His eyes were warm and fierce and bright and his mustache was thin and coarse. He lowered his blanket from his nose now, for the dark poisonous air was gone and the yellow sunlight fell on the house. Near the brush fence two roosters bowed and feinted at each other with squared wings and neck feathers ruffed out. It would be a clumsy fight. They were not game chickens. Kino watched them for a moment, and then his eyes went up to a flight of wild doves twinkling inland to the hills. The world was awake now, and Kino arose and went into his brush house.

As he came through the door Juana stood up from the glowing fire pit. She put Coyotito back in his hanging box and then she combed her black hair and braided it in two braids and tied the ends with thin green ribbon. Kino squatted by the fire pit and rolled a hot corncake and dipped it in sauce and ate it. And he drank a little pulque[3] and that was breakfast. That was the only breakfast he had ever known outside of feast days and one incredible fiesta on cookies that had nearly killed him. When Kino had finished, Juana came back to the fire and ate her breakfast. They had spoken once, 8 but there is not need for speech if it is only a habit anyway. Kino sighed with satisfaction —and that was conversation.

The sun was warming the brush house, breaking through its crevices in long streaks. And one of the streaks fell on the hanging box where Coyotito lay, and on the ropes that held it.

It was a tiny movement that drew their eyes to the hanging box. Kino and Juana froze in their positions. Down the rope that hung the baby's box from the roof support a scorpion moved slowly. His stinging tail was straight out behind him, but he could whip it up in a flash of time.

Kino's breath whistled in his nostrils and he opened his mouth to stop it. And then the startled look was gone from him and the rigidity from his body. In his mind a new song had come, the Song of Evil, the 9 music of the enemy, of any foe of the family, a savage, secret, dangerous melody, and underneath, the Song of the Family cried plaintively.

The scorpion moved delicately down the rope toward the box. Under her breath Juana repeated an ancient magic to guard 10 against such evil, and on top of that she

---

3. pulque (po͞ol′ kā) *n.*: A milky drink made from the juice of the agave, a family of Mexican desert plant.

6 Discussion The scene with Kino and the ants tells us about the protagonist. What can you infer about Kino from the statement that "Kino watched with the detachment of God . . ."?

7 Reading Strategy Summarize the events of the morning that make it like every other morning.

8 Literary Focus The essence of the relationship between Kino and Juana is found here. Why was there "not need for speech" in their relationship?

9 Discussion Kino now translates his intuitions and apprehension into the "Song of Evil." What do you think is meant by this phrase?

10 Discussion Juana mutters a "Hail Mary" and whispers the old magic. What do these two behaviors tell you about Juana and the way she lives?

11 **Critical Thinking and Reading** Comment on the behaviors of both Juana and Kino regarding the bite of the scorpion. What important differences does the reader see in these characters?

12 **Literary Focus** Based on what the reader already knows about Juana, why is it surprising that she is requesting a doctor?

13 **Discussion** Juana's demand that Coyotito be seen by a doctor elicits a strong reaction from neighbors and people of the village. Discuss what the village people have said, and speculate on its importance.

muttered a Hail Mary[4] between clenched teeth. But Kino was in motion. His body glided quietly across the room, noiselessly and smoothly. His hands were in front of him, palms down, and his eyes were on the scorpion. Beneath it in the hanging box Coyotito laughed and reached up his hand toward it. It sensed danger when Kino was almost within reach of it. It stopped, and its tail rose up over its back in little jerks and the curved thorn on the tail's end glistened.

Kino stood perfectly still. He could hear Juana whispering the old magic again, and he could hear the evil music of the enemy. He could not move until the scorpion moved, and it felt for the source of the death that was coming to it. Kino's hand went forward very slowly, very smoothly. The thorned tail jerked upright. And at that moment the laughing Coyotito shook the rope and the scorpion fell.

Kino's hand leaped to catch it, but it fell past his fingers, fell on the baby's shoulder, landed and struck. Then, snarling, Kino had it, had it in his fingers, rubbing it to a paste in his hands. He threw it down and beat it into the earth floor with his fist, and Coyotito screamed with pain in his box. But Kino beat and stamped the enemy until it
11 was only a fragment and a moist place in the dirt. His teeth were bared and fury flared in his eyes and the Song of the Enemy roared in his ears.

But Juana had the baby in her arms now. She found the puncture with redness starting from it already. She put her lips down over the puncture and sucked hard and spat and sucked again while Coyotito screamed.

Kino hovered; he was helpless, he was in the way.

The screams of the baby brought the neighbors. Out of their brush houses they poured—Kino's brother Juan Tomás and his fat wife Apolonia and their four children crowded in the door and blocked the entrance, while behind them others tried to look in, and one small boy crawled among legs to have a look. And those in front passed the word back to those behind—"Scorpion. The baby has been stung."

Juana stopped sucking the puncture for a moment. The little hole was slightly enlarged and its edges whitened from the sucking, but the red swelling extended farther around it in a hard lymphatic[5] mound. And all of these people knew about the scorpion. An adult might be very ill from the sting, but a baby could easily die from the poison. First, they knew, would come swelling and fever and tightened throat, and then cramps in the stomach, and then Coyotito might die if enough of the poison had gone in. But the stinging pain of the bite was going away. Coyotito's screams turned to moans.

Kino had wondered often at the iron in his patient, fragile wife. She, who was obedient and respectful and cheerful and patient, she could arch her back in child pain with
hardly a cry. She could stand fatigue and 12
hunger almost better than Kino himself. In the canoe she was like a strong man. And now she did a most surprising thing.

"The doctor," she said. "Go to get the doctor."

The word was passed out among the neighbors where they stood close packed in the little yard behind the brush fence. And they repeated among themselves, "Juana
wants the doctor." A wonderful thing, a 13
memorable thing, to want the doctor. To get

4. **Hail Mary:** A prayer to the Virgin Mary, the mother of Jesus, used in the Roman Catholic Church.

5. **lymphatic** (lim fat′ ik) *adj.*: Containing the clear liquid of inflamed body tissues.

Primary Source

Steinbeck recorded a sketch of the germ-anecdote out of which he constructed *The Pearl* in *The Sea of Cortex* (1941).

An event which happened at La Paz in recent years is typical of such places. An Indian boy by accident found a pearl of great size, an unbelievable pearl. He knew its value was so great that he need never work again. In his one pearl he had the ability to be drunk as long as he wished, to marry any one of a number of girls, and to make many more a little happy too. In his great pearl lay salvation, for he could in advance purchase masses sufficient to pop him out of Purgatory like a squeezed watermelon seed. In addition he could shift a number of dead relatives a little nearer Paradise. He went to La Paz with his pearl in his hand and his future clear into eternity in his heart. He took his pearl to a broker and was offered so little that he grew angry, for he knew he was cheated. Then he carried his pearl to another broker and was offered the same amount. After a few more visits he came to know that he could not sell his pearl for more. He took it to the beach and hid it under a stone, and that night he was clubbed into

DELFINA AND DIMAS
Diego Rivera
Private Collection

him would be a remarkable thing. The doctor never came to the cluster of brush houses. Why should he, when he had more than he could do to take care of the rich people who lived in the stone and plaster houses of the town.

"He would not come," the people in the yard said.

"He would not come," the people in the door said, and the thought got into Kino.

"The doctor would not come," Kino said to Juana.

She looked up at him, her eyes as cold as the eyes of a lioness. This was Juana's first baby—this was nearly everything there was in Juana's world. And Kino saw her determination and the music of the family sounded in his head with a steely tone.

"Then we will go to him," Juana said, and with one hand she arranged her dark
blue shawl over her head and made of one 14
end of it a sling to hold the moaning baby and made of the other end of it a shade over his eyes to protect him from the light. The people in the door pushed against those behind to let her through. Kino followed her. They went out of the gate to the rutted path and the neighbors followed them.

Humanities Note

Fine art, *Delfina and Dimas,* Diego Rivera. The woman in this painting could represent Juana, her baby, and perhaps the special relationship between mother and child. Ask students how this painting represents that relationship. What is the role of the mother? What is the need of the child?

Point out to students that the mother's arms form a circle. Ask students to consider where circles begin and end, and to discuss their symbolic meaning. What do circles symbolize? Have students discuss the relationship or connection between this art selection and the plot of the story.

14 **Literary Focus** Objects function symbolically to reveal themes and characters. Juana's shawl is her badge of womanliness and maternity. Have students note its use here and throughout the novel.

unconsciousness and his clothing was searched. The next night he slept at the house of a friend and his friend and he were injured and bound and the whole house searched. Then he went inland to lose his pursuers and he was waylaid and tortured. But he was very angry now and he knew what he must do. Hurt as he was he crept back to La Paz in the night and he skulked like a hunted fox to the beach and took out his pearl from under the stone. Then he cursed it and threw it as far as he could into the channel. He was a free man again with his soul in danger and his food and shelter insecure. And he laughed a great deal about it.

15 **Discussion** Throughout the story, Steinbeck provides many examples of the old and new residing side-by-side yet never blending. Note Steinbeck's contrast of the lives of the rich and the poor.

16 **Discussion** Explain Steinbeck's reference to beggars as "experts in financial analysis."

17 **Literary Focus** The reader is introduced to the doctor through the eyes of four beggars. Why does Steinbeck refer to the beggars as "these endless searchers after perfect knowledge of their fellow men"? What are the first impressions given of the doctor?

18 **Discussion** What is the significance of Kino taking his hat off in such an instance?

The thing had become a neighborhood affair. They made a quick soft-footed procession into the center of the town, first Juana and Kino, and behind them Juan Tomás and Apolonia, her big stomach jiggling with the strenuous pace, then all the neighbors with the children trotting on the flanks. And the yellow sun threw their black shadows ahead of them so that they walked on their own shadows.

They came to the place where the brush houses stopped and the city of stone and plaster began, the city of harsh outer walls and inner cool gardens where a little water
15 played and the bougainvillaea[6] crusted the walls with purple and brick-red and white. They heard from the secret gardens the singing of caged birds and heard the splash of cooling water on hot flagstones. The procession crossed the blinding plaza and passed in front of the church. It had grown now, and on the outskirts the hurrying newcomers were being softly informed how the baby had been stung by a scorpion, how the father and mother were taking it to the doctor.

And the newcomers, particularly the
16 beggars from the front of the church who were great experts in financial analysis, looked quickly at Juana's old blue skirt, saw the tears in her shawl, appraised the green ribbon on her braids, read the age of Kino's blanket and the thousand washings of his clothes, and set them down as poverty people and went along to see what kind of drama might develop. The four beggars in front of the church knew everything in the town. They were students of the expressions
17 of young women as they went in to confession, and they saw them as they came out and read the nature of the sin. They knew every little scandal and some very big crimes. They slept at their posts in the shadow of the church so that no one crept in for consolation without their knowledge. And they knew the doctor. They knew his ignorance, his cruelty, his avarice, his appetites, his sins. They knew his clumsy operations and the little brown pennies he gave sparingly for alms. They had seen his corpses go into the church. And, since early Mass was over and business was slow, they followed the procession, these endless searchers after perfect knowledge of their fellow men, to see what the fat lazy doctor would do about an indigent baby with a scorpion bite.

The scurrying procession came at last to the big gate in the wall of the doctor's house. They could hear the splashing water and the singing of caged birds and the sweep of the long brooms on the flagstones. And they could smell the frying of good bacon from the doctor's house.

Kino hesitated a moment. This doctor was not of his people. This doctor was of a race which for nearly four hundred years had beaten and starved and robbed and despised Kino's race, and frightened it too, so that the indigene[7] came humbly to the door. And as always when he came near to one of this race, Kino felt weak and afraid and angry at the same time. Rage and terror went together. He could kill the doctor more easily than he could talk to him, for all of the doctor's race spoke to all of Kino's race as though they were simple animals. And as Kino raised his right hand to the iron ring knocker in the gate, rage swelled in him,
and the pounding music of the enemy beat 18
in his ears, and his lips drew tight against his teeth—but with his left hand he reached to take off his hat. The iron ring pounded against the gate. Kino took off his hat and stood waiting. Coyotito moaned a

6. **bougainvillaea** (bo͞o′ gən vil′ ē ə) *n.*: A tropical vine with large, colorful flowers.

7. **indigene** (in′ di jēn′) *n.*: A native.

Grammar in Action

Dashes are used to set off explanations, summaries, or interruptions within a clause. They may also be used to set off appositives and modifiers which are lengthy, already punctuated, or dramatic. Look at Steinbeck's use of dashes:

Summary: They tell the story of the great pearl—how it was found and how it was lost again. (page 695)

Interruption: It was very good—Kino closed his eyes again to listen to his music. (page 695)

Explanation: Kino sighed with satisfaction —and that was conversation. (page 697)

Apossitive. And those in front passed the word back to those behind—"Scorpion." (page 698)

Student Activity 1. On the above pages locate the sentences containing dashes. Why did Steinbeck use a dash in each case?

Student Activity 2. Insert dashes where needed in the following sentences.

little in Juana's arms, and she spoke softly to him. The procession crowded close the better to see and hear.

After a moment the big gate opened a few inches. Kino could see the green coolness of the garden and little splashing fountain through the opening. The man who looked out at him was one of his own race. Kino spoke to him in the old language. "The little one—the firstborn—has been poisoned by the scorpion," Kino said. "He requires the skill of the healer."

The gate closed a little, and the servant refused to speak in the old language. "A little moment," he said. "I go to inform myself," and he closed the gate and slid the bolt home. The glaring sun threw the bunched shadows of the people blackly on the white wall.

In his chamber the doctor sat up in his high bed. He had on his dressing gown of red watered silk that had come from Paris, a little tight over the chest now if it was buttoned. On his lap was a silver tray with a silver chocolate pot and a tiny cup of eggshell china, so delicate that it looked silly when he lifted it with his big hand, lifted it with the tips of thumb and forefinger and spread the other three fingers wide to get them out of the way. His eyes rested in puffy little hammocks of flesh and his mouth drooped with discontent. He was growing very stout, and his voice was hoarse with the fat that pressed on his throat. Beside
19 him on a table was a small Oriental gong and a bowl of cigarettes. The furnishings of the room were heavy and dark and gloomy. The pictures were religious, even the large tinted photograph of his dead wife, who, if Masses willed and paid for out of her own estate could do it, was in Heaven. The doctor had once for a short time been a part of the great world and his whole subsequent life was memory and longing for France. "That," he said, "was civilized living"—by which he meant that on a small income he had been able to keep a mistress and eat in restaurants. He poured his second cup of chocolate and crumbled a sweet biscuit in his fingers. The servant from the gate came to the open door and stood waiting to be noticed.

"Yes?" the doctor asked.

"It is a little Indian with a baby. He says a scorpion stung it."

The doctor put his cup down gently before he let his anger rise.

"Have I nothing better to do than cure insect bites for 'little Indians'? I am a doctor, not a veterinary."

"Yes, *Patron*,"[8] said the servant.

"Has he any money?" the doctor demanded. "No, they never have any money. I, I alone in the world am supposed to work for nothing—and I am tired of it. See if he has any money!" 20

At the gate the servant opened the door a trifle and looked out at the waiting people. And this time he spoke in the old language.

"Have you money to pay for the treatment?"

Now Kino reached into a secret place somewhere under his blanket. He brought out a paper folded many times. Crease by crease he unfolded it, until at last there came to view eight small misshapen seed pearls,[9] as ugly and gray as little ulcers, flattened and almost valueless. The servant took the paper and closed the gate again, but this time he was not gone long. He opened the gate just wide enough to pass the paper back.

"The doctor has gone out," he said. "He was called to a serious case." And he shut the gate quickly out of shame.

And now a wave of shame went over the whole procession. They melted away. The

---

8. *Patron* (pä trōn'): Spanish for "master."
9. seed pearls: Very small pearls, often imperfect.

19 Critical Thinking and Reading Contrast the differences in the descriptions given of the doctor's house and Kino's house.

20 Literary Focus What do these events tell the reader about the character of the doctor?

1. Out of their brush houses they poured Kino's brother, his fat wife, and their four children crowded in the door and blocked the entrance.
2. Kino heard music in his head the Song of the Family, the Song of Evil, the Song of the Enemy.
3. Coyotito was Juana's first baby this was nearly everything there was in Juana's world.
4. The songs were all in Kino and in his people every song that had ever been made, even the ones forgotten.
5. A vision hung in the air to the north of the city the vision of a mountain that was over two hundred miles away.
6. . . . there were not many buyers really there was only one, and he kept these agents in separate offices to keep a semblance of competition.
7. All manner of people grew interested in Kino people with things to sell and people with favors to ask.
8. It was in the pearl the picture glowing there.

21 Clarification Steinbeck uses the neighbors and village people in a way similar to that of the Chorus in Greek drama. The Chorus informed the audience of how common people viewed an event. They frequently gave a foreshadowing of what was about to happen. Have students share what the procession might tell the reader in this passage.

22 Critical Thinking and Reading In this incident Kino strikes a crushing blow with his fist. In a previous incident Kino crushes the scorpion with his hand in a similar style. What does this tell us about Kino and his patterns of behavior? Contrast the reactions and temperament of Juana in dealing with similar frustrations.

23 Master Teacher Note Steinbeck uses animals in the story in a variety of ways. In this paragraph Steinbeck describes how creatures of the sea live together and yet strive for their own survival. Have students note Steinbeck's use of animals as symbols. Have them suggest what is implied in the description of the hungry dogs and pigs.

24 Discussion Steinbeck's description of the Gulf has meaning for the way in which the story is developing. What do you think is meant by "There was no certainty in seeing, no proof that what you saw was there or was not there"?

25 Discussion The canoe is meant as a symbol. What does it represent?

beggars went back to the church steps, the
21 stragglers moved off, and the neighbors departed so that the public shaming of Kino would not be in their eyes.

For a long time Kino stood in front of the gate with Juana beside him. Slowly he put his suppliant hat on his head. Then, with-
22 out warning, he struck the gate a crushing blow with his fist. He looked down in wonder at his split knuckles and at the blood that flowed down between his fingers.

Chapter 2

The town lay on a broad estuary,[1] its old yellow plastered buildings hugging the beach. And on the beach the white and blue canoes that came from Nayarit[2] were drawn up, canoes preserved for generations by a hard shell-like waterproof plaster whose making was a secret of the fishing people. They were high and graceful canoes with curving bow and stern and a braced section midships where a mast could be stepped to carry a small lateen sail.[3]

The beach was yellow sand, but at the water's edge a rubble of shell and algae took its place. Fiddler crabs bubbled and sputtered in their holes in the sand, and in the shallows little lobsters popped in and out of
23 their tiny homes in the rubble and sand. The sea bottom was rich with crawling and swimming and growing things. The brown algae waved in the gentle currents and the green eel grass swayed and little sea horses clung to its stems. Spotted botete, the poison fish, lay on the bottom in the eel-grass beds, and the bright-colored swimming crabs scampered over them.

On the beach the hungry dogs and the hungry pigs of the town searched endlessly for any dead fish or sea bird that might have floated in on a rising tide.

Although the morning was young, the hazy mirage was up. The uncertain air that magnified some things and blotted out others hung over the whole Gulf so that all sights were unreal and vision could not be trusted; so that sea and land had the sharp clarities and the vagueness of a dream. Thus it might be that the people of the Gulf trust things of the spirit and things of the imagination, but they do not trust their eyes to show them distance or clear outline or any optical exactness. Across the estuary
from the town one section of mangroves 24
stood clear and telescopically defined, while another mangrove clump was a hazy black-green blob. Part of the far shore disappeared into a shimmer that looked like water. There was no certainty in seeing, no proof that what you saw was there or was not there. And the people of the Gulf expected all places were that way, and it was not strange to them. A copper haze hung over the water, and the hot morning sun beat on it and made it vibrate blindingly.

The brush houses of the fishing people were back from the beach on the right-hand side of the town, and the canoes were drawn up in front of this area.

Kino and Juana came slowly down to the beach and to Kino's canoe, which was the one thing of value he owned in the world. It was very old. Kino's grandfather
had brought it from Nayarit, and he had 25
given it to Kino's father, and so it had come to Kino. It was at once property and source of food, for a man with a boat can guarantee a woman that she will eat something. It is

1. **estuary** (es' cho͞o er' ē) *n.*: An inlet formed where a river enters the ocean.
2. **Nayarit** (nä' yä rēt'): A state of western Mexico across the Gulf of California from Baja California.
3. **stepped . . . lateen** (la tēn') **sail:** Raised and fixed in place to carry a triangular sail attached to a long rod.

the bulwark against starvation. And every year Kino refinished his canoe with the hard shell-like plaster by the secret method that had also come to him from his father. Now he came to the canoe and touched the bow tenderly as he always did. He laid his diving rock and his basket and the two ropes in the sand by the canoe. And he folded his blanket and laid it in the bow.

Juana laid Coyotito on the blanket, and she placed her shawl over him so that the hot sun could not shine on him. He was quiet now, but the swelling on his shoulder had continued up his neck and under his ear and his face was puffed and feverish. Juana went to the water and waded in. She gathered some brown seaweed and made a flat damp poultice[4] of it, and this she applied
26 to the baby's swollen shoulder, which was as good a remedy as any and probably better than the doctor could have done. But the remedy lacked his authority because it was simple and didn't cost anything. The stomach cramps had not come to Coyotito. Perhaps Juana had sucked out the poison in time, but she had not sucked out her worry over her firstborn. She had not prayed directly for the recovery of the baby—she had prayed that they might find a pearl with which to hire the doctor to cure the baby, for the minds of people are as unsubstantial as the mirage of the Gulf.

Now Kino and Juana slid the canoe down the beach to the water, and when the bow floated, Juana climbed in, while Kino pushed the stern in and waded beside it until it floated lightly and trembled on the little breaking waves. Then in coordination Juana and Kino drove their double-bladed paddles into the sea, and the canoe creased the water and hissed with speed. The other pearlers were gone out long since. In a few moments Kino could see them clustered in the haze, riding over the oyster bed.

Light filtered down through the water to the bed where the frilly pearl oysters lay fastened to the rubbly bottom, a bottom strewn with shells of broken, opened oysters. This was the bed that had raised the King of Spain to be a great power in Europe in past years, had helped to pay for his wars, and had decorated the churches for his soul's sake. The gray oysters with ruffles like skirts on the shells, the barnacle-crusted oysters with little bits of weed clinging to the skirts and small crabs climbing over them. An accident could happen to these oysters, a grain of sand could lie in the folds of muscle and irritate the flesh until in self-protection the flesh coated the grain with a layer of smooth cement. But once
started, the flesh continued to coat the for- 27
eign body until it fell free in some tidal flurry or until the oyster was destroyed. For centuries men had dived down and torn the oysters from the beds and ripped them open, looking for the coated grains of sand. Swarms of fish lived near the bed to live near the oysters thrown back by the searching men and to nibble at the shining inner shells. But the pearls were accidents, and the finding of one was luck, a little pat on the back by God or the gods or both.

Kino had two ropes, one tied to a heavy stone and one to a basket. He stripped off his shirt and trousers and laid his hat in the bottom of the canoe. The water was oily smooth. He took his rock in one hand and his basket in the other, and he slipped feet first over the side and the rock carried him to the bottom. The bubbles rose behind him until the water cleared and he could see. Above, the surface of the water was an

---

4. poultice (pōl' tis) *n.*: An absorbent mass applied to a sore or inflamed part of the body.

26 Critical Thinking and Reading Steinbeck shows Juana's resourcefulness in applying primitive medicine. Have students compare this with the previous references to Kino and Juana's belief that only the doctor could cure their child.

27 Enrichment The pearl, the central image of the novel, is described as an accident of nature. Finding one is lucky or like "a little pat on the back . . . by the gods." Some critics feel that this novel is making a statement about the need to leave nature as undisturbed as possible in order to preserve the balance of nature. Ask students what they think of this viewpoint. Do they agree or disagree? Ask them to consider their response as they continue to read. Have students consider the same question when they have completed reading *The Pearl*.

28 **Literary Focus** What can you infer about Kino and his people based on the songs that are described in this paragraph?

29 **Enrichment** Kino and Juana are superstitious. Have students discuss present day superstitions, for example, walking under a ladder and a black cat crossing one's path.

undulating mirror of brightness, and he could see the bottoms of the canoes sticking through it.

Kino moved cautiously so that the water would not be obscured with mud or sand. He hooked his foot in the loop on his rock and his hands worked quickly, tearing the oysters loose, some singly, others in clusters. He laid them in his basket. In some places the oysters clung to one another so that they came free in lumps.

28 Now, Kino's people had sung of everything that happened or existed. They had made songs to the fishes, to the sea in anger and to the sea in calm, to the light and the dark and the sun and the moon, and the songs were all in Kino and in his people —every song that had ever been made, even the ones forgotten. And as he filled his basket the song was in Kino, and the beat of the song was his pounding heart as it ate the oxygen from his held breath, and the melody of the song was the gray-green water and the little scuttling animals and the clouds of fish that flitted by and were gone. But in the song there was a secret little inner song, hardly perceptible, but always there, sweet and secret and clinging, almost hiding in the countermelody, and this was the Song of the Pearl That Might Be, for every shell thrown in the basket might contain a pearl. Chance was against it, but luck and the gods might be for it. And in the canoe above him Kino knew that Juana was making the magic of prayer, her face set rigid and her muscles hard to force the luck, to tear the luck out of the gods' hands, for she needed the luck for the swollen shoulder of Coyotito. And because the need was great and the desire was great, the little secret melody of the pearl that might be was stronger this morning. Whole phrases of it came clearly and softly into the Song of the Undersea.

Kino, in his pride and youth and strength, could remain down over two minutes without strain, so that he worked deliberately, selecting the largest shells. Because they were disturbed, the oyster shells were tightly closed. A little to his right a hummock[5] of rubbly rock stuck up, covered with young oysters not ready to take. Kino moved next to the hummock, and then, beside it, under a little overhang, he saw a very large oyster lying by itself, not covered with its clinging brothers. The shell was partly open, for the overhang protected this ancient oyster, and in the liplike muscle Kino saw a ghostly gleam, and then the shell closed down. His heart beat out a heavy rhythm and the melody of the maybe pearl shrilled in his ears. Slowly he forced the oyster loose and held it tightly against his breast. He kicked his foot free from the rock loop, and his body rose to the surface and his black hair gleamed in the sunlight. He reached over the side of the canoe and laid the oyster in the bottom.

Then Juana steadied the boat while he climbed in. His eyes were shining with excitement, but in decency he pulled up his rock, and then he pulled up his basket of oysters and lifted them in. Juana sensed his excitement, and she pretended to look away. It is not good to want a thing too much. It sometimes drives the luck away. You must want it just enough, and you must be very tactful with God or the gods. But Juana stopped breathing. Very deliberately Kino opened his short strong knife. He looked speculatively at the basket. Perhaps it would be better to open *the* oyster last. He took a small oyster from the basket, cut the muscle, searched the folds of flesh, and threw it in the water. Then he seemed to see the great oyster for the first time. He squatted in the bottom of the canoe, picked up the shell 29

5. hummock (hum′ ək) *n.*: A low, rounded hill.

and examined it. The flutes were shining black to brown, and only a few small barnacles adhered to the shell. Now Kino was reluctant to open it. What he had seen, he knew, might be a reflection, a piece of flat shell accidentally drifted in or a complete illusion. In this Gulf of uncertain light there
30 were more illusions than realities.

But Juana's eyes were on him and she could not wait. She put her hand on Coyotito's covered head. "Open it," she said softly.

Kino deftly slipped his knife into the edge of the shell. Through the knife he could feel the muscle tighten hard. He worked the blade leverwise and the closing muscle parted and the shell fell apart. The liplike flesh writhed up and then subsided. Kino lifted the flesh, and there it lay, the great pearl,
31 perfect as the moon. It captured the light and refined it and gave it back in silver incandescence.[6] It was as large as a sea gull's egg. It was the greatest pearl in the world.

Juana caught her breath and moaned a little. And to Kino the secret melody of the maybe pearl broke clear and beautiful, rich and warm and lovely, glowing and gloating
32 and triumphant. In the surface of the great pearl he could see dream forms. He picked the pearl from the dying flesh and held it in his palm, and he turned it over and saw that its curve was perfect. Juana came near to
33 stare at it in his hand, and it was the hand he had smashed against the doctor's gate, and the torn flesh of the knuckles was turned grayish white by the sea water.

Instinctively Juana went to Coyotito where he lay on his father's blanket. She lifted the poultice of seaweed and looked at the shoulder. "Kino," she cried shrilly.

He looked past his pearl, and he saw that the swelling was going out of the baby's shoulder, the poison was receding from its body. Then Kino's fist closed over the pearl and his emotion broke over him. He put back his head and howled. His eyes rolled up and he screamed and his body was rigid. The men in the other canoes looked up, startled, and then they dug their paddles into the sea and raced toward Kino's canoe.

6. **incandescence** (in′ kan des′ əns) *n.*: State of gleaming or shining brilliantly.

Chapter 3

A town is a thing like a colonial animal. A town has a nervous system and a head and shoulders and feet. A town is a thing separate from all other towns, so that there
are no two towns alike. And a town has a 34
whole emotion. How news travels through a town is a mystery not easily to be solved. News seems to move faster than small boys can scramble and dart to tell it, faster than women can call it over the fences.

Before Kino and Juana and the other fishers had come to Kino's brush house, the nerves of the town were pulsing and vibrating with the news—Kino had found the Pearl of the World. Before panting little boys could strangle out the words, their mothers knew it. The news swept on past the brush houses, and it washed in a foaming wave into the town of stone and plaster. It came to the priest walking in his garden, and it put a thoughtful look in his eyes and a memory of certain repairs necessary to the church. He wondered what the pearl would be worth. And he wondered whether he had baptized
Kino's baby, or married him for that matter. 35
The news came to the shopkeepers, and they looked at men's clothes that had not sold so well.

The news came to the doctor where he sat with a woman whose illness was age, though neither she nor the doctor would admit it. And when it was made plain who Kino was, the doctor grew stern and

30 Discussion The description of the Gulf focuses on illusion. There are other references to illusion in this novel—the pearl fisherman dreams of the great pearl, the doctor dreams of Paris and his youth, and the priest dreams of a great church. Have students discuss Steinbeck's use of illusion. Why is it so effective?

31 Discussion What figures of speech does Steinbeck use to describe the pearl?

32 Enrichment Based on what you know about Kino, what dreams does he have for the pearl? What do these dreams represent?

33 Discussion What is Steinbeck conveying in his description of the pearl in Kino's beaten and bruised hand?

34 Clarification In this paragraph Steinbeck implies that every part of a complex structure relates to the whole. What happens in one part impacts on all of the other parts. Ask students to speculate what implications this might have for the finding of the pearl.

35 Reading Strategy Summarize the reactions of the priest and the doctor.

Humanities Note

Fine art, *Two Mexican Women and a Child,* Diego Rivera. Have students consider why the artist included the bowl in this scene. Students should notice that while a visitor is present the mother continues to hold the baby close to her. Have students identify and discuss the consistency in symbolism between this painting and the prior one.

Rivera's murals often dealt with the theme of oppression. Have students select references to the theme of oppression in the story.

36 **Discussion** Have students suggest what is meant by this statement.

37 **Discussion** What wishes do the pearl buyers have for the great pearl? How will it help to change their lives?

TWO MEXICAN WOMEN AND A CHILD
Diego Rivera
The Fine Arts Museum of San Francisco

judicious at the same time. "He is a client of mine," the doctor said. "I am treating his child for a scorpion sting." And the doctor's eyes rolled up a little in their fat hammocks and he thought of Paris. He remembered the room he had lived in there as a great and luxurious place, and he remembered the hard-faced woman who had lived with him as a beautiful and kind girl, although she had been none of these three. The doctor looked past his aged patient and saw himself sitting in a restaurant in Paris and a waiter was just opening a bottle of wine.

The news came early to the beggars in front of the church, and it made them giggle a little with pleasure, for they knew that
36 there is no almsgiver in the world like a poor man who is suddenly lucky.

37 Kino had found the Pearl of the World. In the town, in little offices, sat the men who bought pearls from the fishers. They waited in their chairs until the pearls came in, and then they cackled and fought and shouted and threatened until they reached the lowest price the fisherman would stand. But there was a price below which they dared not go, for it had happened that a fisherman in despair had given his pearls to the church. And when the buying was over, these buyers sat alone and their fingers played restlessly with the pearls, and they wished they owned the pearls. For there were not many buyers really—there was only one, and he kept these agents in separate offices to give a semblance of competition. The news came to these men, and their eyes squinted and their fingertips burned a little, and each one thought how the patron could not live forever and someone had to take his place. And each one thought how

with some capital he could get a new start.

All manner of people grew interested in Kino—people with things to sell and people with favors to ask. Kino had found the Pearl of the World. The essence of pearl mixed with essence of men and a curious dark residue was precipitated.[1] Every man suddenly became related to Kino's pearl, and Kino's pearl went into the dreams, the
38 speculations, the schemes, the plans, the futures, the wishes, the needs, the lusts, the hungers, of everyone, and only one person stood in the way and that was Kino, so that he became curiously every man's enemy. The news stirred up something infinitely black and evil in the town; the black distillate[2] was like the scorpion, or like hunger in the smell of food, or like loneliness when love is withheld. The poison sacs of the town began to manufacture venom, and the town swelled and puffed with the pressure of it.

But Kino and Juana did not know these things. Because they were happy and excited they thought everyone shared their joy. Juan Tomás and Apolonia did, and they were the world too. In the afternoon, when the sun had gone over the mountains of the Peninsula to sink in the outward sea, Kino squatted in his house with Juana beside him. And the brush house was crowded with neighbors. Kino held the great pearl in his hand, and it was warm and alive in his hand. And the music of the pearl had merged with the music of the family so that one beautified the other. The neighbors looked at the pearl in Kino's hand and they wondered how such luck could come to any man.

And Juan Tomás, who squatted on Kino's right hand because he was his brother, asked, "What will you do now that you have become a rich man?"

Kino looked into his pearl, and Juana cast her eyelashes down and arranged her shawl to cover her face so that her excitement could not be seen. And in the incandescence of the pearl the pictures formed of the things Kino's mind had considered in the past and had given up as impossible. In the pearl he saw Juana and Coyotito and himself standing and kneeling at the high altar, and they were being married now that they could pay. He spoke softly, "We will be married—in the church."

In the pearl he saw how they were dressed—Juana in a shawl stiff with newness and a new skirt, and from under the long skirt Kino could see that she wore shoes. It was in the pearl—the picture glowing there. He himself was dressed in new white clothes, and he carried a new hat 39
—not of straw but of fine black felt—and he too wore shoes—not sandals but shoes that laced. But Coyotito—he was the one—he wore a blue sailor suit from the United States and a little yachting cap such as Kino had seen once when a pleasure boat put into the estuary. All of these things Kino saw in the lucent[3] pearl and he said, "We will have new clothes."

And the music of the pearl rose like a chorus of trumpets in his ears.

Then to the lovely gray surface of the pearl came the little things Kino wanted: a harpoon to take the place of one lost a year ago, a new harpoon of iron with a ring in the end of the shaft; and—his mind could hardly make the leap—a rifle—but why not, since he was so rich. And Kino saw Kino in the pearl, Kino holding a Winchester carbine. It was the wildest day-dreaming and very pleasant. His lips moved hesitantly

---

1. precipitated (prē sip′ ə tāt′ əd) *v.*: Formed abrubtly.

2. distillate (dis′ tə lāt′) *n.*: The essence of anything; here, the atmosphere of the town.

3. lucent (lo͞o′ sənt) *adj.*: Shining.

38 Literary Focus People's feelings and attitudes toward Kino are changing; he is resented because he has something they want. Have students discuss how these changes are affecting the whole town.

39 Discussion Ask students to consider Kino's dreams of what he will do with his wealth—being married in church, buying a rifle, and sending his son to school. What do these dreams tell us about how poor Kino and his people are? Which of the dreams do you think would be the greatest achievement for him?

40 **Reading Strategy** Have students summarize Kino's dreams. What is the significance of the word *transfigured*?

41 **Discussion** Why does Kino not recognize the priest's song of evil?

over this—"A rifle," he said. "Perhaps a rifle."

It was the rifle that broke down the barriers. This was an impossibility, and if he could think of having a rifle whole horizons were burst and he could rush on. For it is said that humans are never satisfied, that you give them one thing and they want something more. And this is said in disparagement, whereas it is one of the greatest talents the species has and one that has made it superior to animals that are satisfied with what they have.

The neighbors, close pressed and silent in the house, nodded their heads at his wild imaginings. And a man in the rear murmured, "A rifle. He will have a rifle."

But the music of the pearl was shrilling with triumph in Kino. Juana looked up, and her eyes were wide at Kino's courage and at his imagination. And electric strength had come to him now the horizons were kicked out. In the pearl he saw Coyotito sitting at a little desk in a school, just as Kino had once seen it through an open door. And Coyotito was dressed in a jacket, and he had on a white collar and a broad silken tie. Moreover, Coyotito was writing on a big piece of paper. Kino looked at his neighbors fiercely. "My son will go to school," he said, and the neighbors were hushed. Juana caught her breath sharply. Her eyes were bright as she watched him, and she looked quickly down at Coyotito in her arms to see whether this might be possible.

But Kino's face shone with prophecy. "My son will read and open the books, and my son will write and will know writing.
40 And my son will make numbers, and these things will make us free because he will know—he will know and through him we will know." And in the pearl Kino saw himself and Juana squatting by the little fire in the brush hut while Coyotito read from a great book. "This is what the pearl will do," said Kino. And he had never said so many words together in his life. And suddenly he was afraid of his talking. His hand closed down over the pearl and cut the light away from it. Kino was afraid as a man is afraid who says, "I will," without knowing.

Now the neighbors knew they had witnessed a great marvel. They knew that time would now date from Kino's pearl, and that they would discuss this moment for many years to come. If these things came to pass, they would recount how Kino looked and what he said and how his eyes shone, and they would say, "He was a man transfigured. Some power was given to him, and there it started. You see what a great man he has become, starting from that moment. And I myself saw it."

And if Kino's planning came to nothing, those same neighbors would say, "There it started. A foolish madness came over him so that he spoke foolish words. God keep us from such things. Yes, God punished Kino because he rebelled against the way things are. You see what has become of him. And I myself saw the moment when his reason left him."

Kino looked down at his closed hand and the knuckles were scabbed over and tight where he had struck the gate.

Now the dusk was coming. And Juana looped her shawl under the baby so that he hung against her hip, and she went to the fire hole and dug a coal from the ashes and broke a few twigs over it and fanned a flame alive. The little flames danced on the faces of the neighbors. They knew they should go to their own dinners, but they were reluctant to leave.

The dark was almost in, and Juana's
fire threw shadows on the brush walls when 41
the whisper came in, passed from mouth to mouth. "The Father is coming—the priest

Grammar in Action

Pronouns ending in *-self* or *-selves* are either **intensive** or **reflexive.** Intensive pronouns emphasize another noun or pronoun in the sentence. Reflexive pronouns refer back to the subject of the clause. Consider Steinbeck's sentences:

Intensive: He *himself* was dressed in new white clothes.

Reflexive: The doctor looked past his aged patient and saw *himself* sitting in a restaurant in Paris.

Reflexive: Kino was already making a hard skin for *himself* against the world.

These pronouns should never be used as subjects of their own clauses. It is incorrect to say "My wife and myself found the greatest pearl."

Student Activity 1. Identify the pronouns in italics as either intensive or reflexive.

1. "So the doctor knew," he said, but he said it for *himself*.

is coming." The men uncovered their heads and stepped back from the door, and the women gathered their shawls about their faces and cast down their eyes. Kino and Juan Tomás, his brother, stood up. The priest came in—a graying, aging man with an old skin and a young sharp eye. Children, he considered these people, and he treated them like children.

"Kino," he said softly, "thou art named after a great man—and a great Father of the Church."[4] He made it sound like a benediction. "Thy namesake tamed the desert and sweetened the minds of thy people, didst thou know that? It is in the books."

Kino looked quickly down at Coyotito's head, where he hung on Juana's hip. Some day, his mind said, that boy would know what things were in the books and what things were not. The music had gone out of Kino's head, but now, thinly, slowly, the melody of the morning, the music of evil, of the enemy sounded, but it was faint and weak. And Kino looked at his neighbors to see who might have brought this song in.

But the priest was speaking again. "It has come to me that thou hast found a great fortune, a great pearl."

Kino opened his hand and held it out, and the priest gasped a little at the size and beauty of the pearl. And then he said, "I hope thou wilt remember to give thanks, my son, to Him who has given thee this treasure, and to pray for guidance in the future."

Kino nodded dumbly, and it was Juana who spoke softly. "We will, Father. And we will be married now. Kino has said so." She looked at the neighbors for confirmation, and they nodded their heads solemnly.

The priest said, "It is pleasant to see that your first thoughts are good thoughts. God bless you, my children." He turned and left quietly, and the people let him through.

But Kino's hand had closed tightly on the pearl again, and he was glancing about
suspiciously, for the evil song was in his 42
ears, shrilling against the music of the pearl.

The neighbors slipped away to go to their houses, and Juana squatted by the fire and set her clay pot of boiled beans over the little flame. Kino stepped to the doorway and looked out. As always, he could smell the smoke from many fires, and he could see the hazy stars and feel the damp of the night air so that he covered his nose from it. The thin dog came to him and threshed[5] itself in
greeting like a windblown flag, and Kino 43
looked down at it and didn't see it. He had broken through the horizons into a cold and lonely outside. He felt alone and unprotected, and scraping crickets and shrilling tree frogs and croaking toads seemed to be carrying the melody of evil. Kino shivered a little and drew his blanket more tightly against his nose. He carried the pearl still in his hand, tightly closed in his palm, and it was warm and smooth against his skin.

Behind him he heard Juana patting the cakes before she put them down on the clay cooking sheet. Kino felt all the warmth and security of his family behind him, and the Song of the Family came from behind him like the purring of a kitten. But now, by saying what his future was going to be like, he had created it. A plan is a real thing, and things projected are experienced. A plan once made and visualized becomes a reality along with other realities—never to be destroyed but easily to be attacked. Thus
Kino's future was real, but having set it up, 44
other forces were set up to destroy it, and

42 Discussion Explain what is happening to Kino when the priest leaves. What is meant by having the two songs "shrilling" against each other?

43 Literary Focus What does this paragraph tell us about the way Kino is changing?

44 Discussion What are the forces referred to in this paragraph?

4. Father of the Church: Eusebius Kino, a Spanish missionary and explorer in the seventeenth century.

5. threshed (threshd) *v.*: Tossed.

2. And in the pearl Kino saw *himself* and Juana squatting by the little fire in the brush hut while Coyotito read from a great book.
3. And I *myself* saw the moment when his reason left him.
4. The thin dog came to him and threshed *itself* in greeting like a windblown flag.
5. Then Kino must have thought to *himself* that he imagined the sound.

Student Activity 2. Add intensive or reflexive pronouns to the following sentences.

1. Kino would buy a rifle for ________ when he sold the pearl.
2. The townspeople wondered among ________ if the money would go to Kino's head.
3. The doctor helped ________ to the chocolate and cheese.
4. Juana knew that she ________ had to care for the injured baby.
5. While they didn't discuss it among ________, the agents knew exactly how much they would offer for the pearl.

45 **Literary Focus** Throughout the novel the doctor is portrayed as evil. The reader knows the doctor was in when Kino first visited, but the doctor now tells Kino that he has come as quickly as he could. Based on what the reader already knows about the doctor, what might one suspect are the doctor's motives and how valid might his advice be?

46 **Discussion** The symbolism of the shawl is used in this paragraph. Have students discuss what it represents.

this he knew, so that he had to prepare to meet the attack. And this Kino knew also—that the gods do not love men's plans, and the gods do not love success unless it comes by accident. He knew that the gods take their revenge on a man if he be successful through his own efforts. Consequently Kino was afraid of plans, but having made one, he could never destroy it. And to meet the attack, Kino was already making a hard skin for himself against the world. His eyes and his mind probed for danger before it appeared.

Standing in the door, he saw two men approach; and one of them carried a lantern which lighted the ground and the legs of the men. They turned in through the opening of Kino's brush fence and came to his door. And Kino saw that one was the doctor and the other the servant who had opened the gate in the morning. The split knuckles on Kino's right hand burned when he saw who they were.

The doctor said, "I was not in when you came this morning. But now, at the first chance, I have come to see the baby."

Kino stood in the door, filling it, and hatred raged and flamed in back of his eyes, and fear too, for the hundreds of years of subjugation[6] were cut deep in him.

"The baby is nearly well now," he said
45 curtly.

The doctor smiled, but his eyes in their little lymph-lined hammocks did not smile.

He said, "Sometimes, my friend, the scorpion sting has a curious effect. There will be apparent improvement, and then without warning—pouf!" He pursed his lips and made a little explosion to show how quick it could be, and he shifted his small black doctor's bag about so that the light of the lamp fell upon it, for he knew that Kino's race love the tools of any craft and trust them. "Sometimes," the doctor went on in a liquid tone, "sometimes there will be a withered leg or a blind eye or a crumpled back. Oh, I know the sting of the scorpion, my friend, and I can cure it."

Kino felt the rage and hatred melting toward fear. He did not know, and perhaps this doctor did. And he could not take the chance of pitting his certain ignorance against this man's possible knowledge. He was trapped as his people were always trapped, and would be until, as he had said, they could be sure that the things in the books were really in the books. He could not take a chance—not with the life or with the straightness of Coyotito. He stood aside and let the doctor and his man enter the brush hut.

Juana stood up from the fire and backed away as he entered, and she covered the baby's face with the fringe of her shawl. And
when the doctor went to her and held out his 46
hand, she clutched the baby tight and looked at Kino where he stood with the fire shadows leaping on his face.

Kino nodded, and only then did she let the doctor take the baby.

"Hold the light," the doctor said, and when the servant held the lantern high, the doctor looked for a moment at the wound on the baby's shoulder. He was thoughtful for a moment and then he rolled back the baby's eyelid and looked at the eyeball. He nodded his head while Coyotito struggled against him.

"It is as I thought," he said. "The poison has gone inward and it will strike soon. Come look!" He held the eyelid down. "See—it is blue." And Kino, looking anxiously, saw that indeed it was a little blue.

6. subjugation (sub′ jə gā′ shən) *n.*: Act of being brought under control.

And he didn't know whether or not it was always a little blue. But the trap was set. He couldn't take the chance.

The doctor's eyes watered in their little hammocks. "I will give him something to try to turn the poison aside," he said. And he handed the baby to Kino.

Then from his bag he took a little bottle of white powder and a capsule of gelatine. He filled the capsule with the powder and closed it, and then around the first capsule he fitted a second capsule and closed it. Then he worked very deftly. He took the baby and pinched its lower lip until it opened its mouth. His fat fingers placed the capsule far back on the baby's tongue, back of the point where he could spit it out, and then from the floor he picked up the little pitcher of pulque and gave Coyotito a drink, and it was done. He looked again at the baby's eyeball and he pursed his lips and seemed to think.

At last he handed the baby back to Juana, and he turned to Kino. "I think the poison will attack within the hour," he said. "The medicine may save the baby from hurt, but I will come back in an hour. Perhaps I am in time to save him." He took a deep breath and went out of the hut, and his servant followed him with the lantern.

Now Juana had the baby under her shawl, and she stared at it with anxiety and fear. Kino came to her, and he lifted the shawl and stared at the baby. He moved his hand to look under the eyelid, and only then saw that the pearl was still in his hand. Then he went to a box by the wall, and from it he brought a piece of rag. He wrapped the pearl in the rag, then went to the corner of the brush house and dug a little hole with his fingers in the dirt floor, and he put the pearl in the hole and covered it up and concealed the place. And then he went to the fire where Juana was squatting, watching the baby's face.

The doctor, back in his house, settled into his chair and looked at his watch. His people brought him a little supper of chocolate and sweet cakes and fruit, and he stared at the food discontentedly.

In the houses of the neighbors the subject that would lead all conversations for a long time to come was aired for the first time to see how it would go. The neighbors showed one another with their thumbs how big the pearl was, and they made little caressing gestures to show how lovely it was. From now on they would watch Kino and Juana very closely to see whether riches turned their heads, as riches turn all people's heads. Everyone knew why the doctor had come. He was not good at dissembling and he was very well understood.

Out in the estuary a tight woven school of small fishes glittered and broke water to escape a school of great fishes that drove in to eat them. And in the houses the people could hear the swish of the small ones and the bouncing splash of the great ones as the 49
slaughter went on. The dampness arose out of the Gulf and was deposited on bushes and cacti and on little trees in salty drops. And the night mice crept about on the ground and the little night hawks hunted them silently.

The skinny black puppy with flame spots over his eyes came to Kino's door and looked in. He nearly shook his hind quarters loose when Kino glanced up at him, and he subsided when Kino looked away. The puppy did not enter the house, but he watched with frantic interest while Kino ate his beans from the little pottery dish and wiped it clean with a corncake and ate the cake and washed the whole down with a drink of pulque.

47 **Literary Focus** Kino knows that Coyotito is well. Why does Kino allow himself to be controlled by the doctor?

48 **Discussion** Again Steinbeck uses symbolism in the shawl. Compare this reference to the preceding one.

49 **Critical Thinking and Reading** Compare and contrast the events taking place outside Kino's hut to those inside.

50 Literary Focus How does this description support previous comments about the doctor?

51 Reading Strategy Summarize the doctor's behavior in these paragraphs.

Kino was finished and was rolling a cigarette when Juana spoke sharply. "Kino." He glanced at her and then got up and went quickly to her for he saw fright in her eyes. He stood over her, looking down, but the light was very dim. He kicked a pile of twigs into the fire hole to make a blaze, and then he could see the face of Coyotito. The baby's face was flushed and his throat was working and a little thick drool of saliva issued from his lips. The spasm of the stomach muscles began, and the baby was very sick.

Kino knelt beside his wife. "So the doctor knew," he said, but he said it for himself as well as for his wife, for his mind was hard and suspicious and he was remembering the white powder. Juana rocked from side to side and moaned out the little Song of the Family as though it could ward off the danger, and the baby vomited and writhed in her arms. Now uncertainty was in Kino, and the music of evil throbbed in his head and nearly drove out Juana's song.

The doctor finished his chocolate and nibbled the little fallen pieces of sweet
50 cake. He brushed his fingers on a napkin, looked at his watch, arose, and took up his little bag.

The news of the baby's illness traveled quickly among the brush houses, for sickness is second only to hunger as the enemy of poor people. And some said softly, "Luck, you see, brings bitter friends." And they nodded and got up to go to Kino's house. The neighbors scuttled with covered noses through the dark until they crowded into Kino's house again. They stood and gazed, and they made little comments on the sadness that this should happen at a time of joy, and they said, "All things are in God's hands." The old women squatted down beside Juana to try to give her aid if they could and comfort if they could not.

Then the doctor hurried in, followed by his man. He scattered the old women like chickens. He took the baby and examined it and felt its head. "The poison it has worked," he said. "I think I can defeat it. I will try my best." He asked for water, and in the cup of it he put three drops of ammonia, and he pried open the baby's mouth and poured it down. The baby spluttered and screeched under the treatment, and Juana watched him with haunted eyes. The doctor spoke a little as he worked. "It is lucky that I know about the poison of the scorpion, otherwise—" and he shrugged to show what could have happened.

But Kino was suspicious, and he could not take his eyes from the doctor's open bag, and from the bottle of white powder there. Gradually the spasms subsided and the baby relaxed under the doctor's hands. And then Coyotito sighed deeply and went to sleep, for he was very tired with vomiting.

The doctor put the baby in Juana's arms. "He will get well now," he said. "I have won the fight." And Juana looked at him with adoration.

The doctor was closing his bag now. He said, "When do you think you can pay this bill?" He said it even kindly.

"When I have sold my pearl I will pay you," Kino said.

"You have a pearl? A good pearl?" the doctor asked with interest.

And then the chorus of the neighbors broke in. "He has found the Pearl of the
World," they cried, and they joined forefin- 51
ger with thumb to show how great the pearl was.

"Kino will be a rich man," they clamored. "It is a pearl such as one has never seen."

The doctor looked surprised. "I had not heard of it. Do you keep this pearl in a safe place? Perhaps you would like me to put it in my safe?"

Kino's eyes were hooded now, his cheeks were drawn taut. "I have it secure," he said.

"Tomorrow I will sell it and then I will pay you."

The doctor shrugged, and his wet eyes never left Kino's eyes. He knew the pearl would be buried in the house, and he thought Kino might look toward the place where it was buried. "It would be a shame to have it stolen before you could sell it," the doctor said, and he saw Kino's eyes flick involuntarily to the floor near the side post of the brush house.

When the doctor had gone and all the neighbors had reluctantly returned to their houses, Kino squatted beside the little glowing coals in the fire hole and listened to the night sound, the soft sweep of the little waves on the shore and the distant barking of dogs, the creeping of the breeze through the brush house roof and the soft speech of his neighbors in their houses in the village. For these people do not sleep soundly all night; they awaken at intervals and talk a little and then go to sleep again. And after a while Kino got up and went to the door of his house.

He smelled the breeze and he listened for any foreign sound of secrecy or creeping, and his eyes searched the darkness, for the music of evil was sounding in his head and he was fierce and afraid. After he had probed the night with his senses he went to the place by the side post where the pearl was buried, and he dug it up and brought it
52 to his sleeping mat, and under his sleeping mat he dug another little hole in the dirt floor and buried the pearl and covered it up again.

And Juana, sitting by the fire hole, watched him with questioning eyes, and when he had buried his pearl she asked, "Who do you fear?"

Kino searched for a true answer, and at last he said, "Everyone." And he could feel a shell of hardness drawing over him.

After a while they lay down together on the sleeping mat, and Juana did not put the baby in his box tonight, but cradled him in her arms and covered his face with her head shawl. And the last light went out of the embers in the fire hole.

But Kino's brain burned, even during his sleep, and he dreamed that Coyotito could read, that one of his own people could tell him the truth of things. And in his dream, Coyotito was reading from a book as large as a house, with letters as big as dogs, and the words galloped and played on the 53
book. And then darkness spread over the page, and with the darkness came the music of evil again, and Kino stirred in his sleep; and when he stirred, Juana's eyes opened in the darkness. And then Kino awakened, with the evil music pulsing in him, and he lay in the darkness with his ears alert.

Then from the corner of the house came a sound so soft that it might have been simply a thought, a little furtive movement, a touch of a foot on earth, the almost inaudible purr of controlled breathing. Kino held his breath to listen, and he knew that whatever dark thing was in his house was holding its breath too, to listen. For a time no sound at all came from the corner of the brush house. Then Kino might have thought he had imagined the sound. But Juana's hand came creeping over to him in warning, and then the sound came again! the whisper of a foot on dry earth and the scratch of fingers in the soil.

And now a wild fear surged in Kino's breast, and on the fear came rage, as it always did. Kino's hand crept into his breast where his knife hung on a string, and then he sprang like an angry cat, leaped striking and spitting for the dark thing he knew was in the corner of the house. He felt cloth, struck at it with his knife and missed, and struck again and felt his knife go through cloth, and then his head crashed with

52 Literary Focus Kino's character gradually changes in this novel. Explain why "a shell of hardness" seemed to enclose him at this point.

53 Discussion Consider the dream that Kino had. What do you think this dream means?

54 **Critical Thinking and Reading** Contrast the differing viewpoints of Juana and Kino. In view of what you have read so far, do you think Juana is right? How might the pearl destroy the family?

Reader's Response How can material wealth, while making health and happiness affordable, breed evil. What kinds of feelngs does wealth arouse?

lightning and exploded with pain. There was a soft scurry in the doorway, and running steps for a moment, and then silence.

Kino could feel warm blood running from his forehead, and he could hear Juana calling to him. "Kino! Kino!" And there was terror in her voice. Then coldness came over him as quickly as the rage had, and he said, "I am all right. The thing has gone."

He groped his way back to the sleeping mat. Already Juana was working at the fire. She uncovered an ember from the ashes and shredded little pieces of cornhusk over it and blew a little flame into the cornhusks so that a tiny light danced through the hut. And then from a secret place Juana brought a little piece of consecrated[7] candle and lighted it at the flame and set it upright on a fireplace stone. She worked quickly, crooning as she moved about. She dipped the end of her head shawl in water and swabbed the blood from Kino's bruised forehead. "It is nothing," Kino said, but his eyes and his voice were hard and cold and a brooding hate was growing in him.

54 Now the tension which had been growing in Juana boiled up to the surface and her lips were thin. "This thing is evil," she cried harshly. "This pearl is like a sin! It will destroy us," and her voice rose shrilly. "Throw it away, Kino. Let us break it between stones. Let us bury it and forget the place. Let us throw it back into the sea. It has brought evil. Kino, my husband, it will destroy us." And in the firelight her lips and her eyes were alive with her fear.

But Kino's face was set, and his mind and his will were set. "This is our one chance," he said. "Our son must go to school. He must break out of the pot that holds us in."

"It will destroy us all," Juana cried. "Even our son."

"Hush," said Kino. "Do not speak any more. In the morning we will sell the pearl, and then the evil will be gone, and only the good remain. Now hush, my wife." His dark eyes scowled into the little fire, and for the first time he knew that his knife was still in his hands, and he raised the blade and looked at it and saw a little line of blood on the steel. For a moment he seemed about to wipe the blade on his trousers but then he plunged the knife into the earth and so cleansed it.

The distant roosters began to crow and the air changed and the dawn was coming. The wind of the morning ruffled the water of the estuary and whispered through the mangroves, and the little waves beat on the rubbly beach with an increased tempo. Kino raised the sleeping mat and dug up his pearl and put it in front of him and stared at it.

And the beauty of the pearl, winking and glimmering in the light of the little candle, cozened[8] his brain with its beauty. So lovely it was, so soft, and its own music came from it—its music of promise and delight, its guarantee of the future, of comfort, of security. Its warm lucence promised a poultice against illness and a wall against insult. It closed a door on hunger. And as he stared at it Kino's eyes softened and his face relaxed. He could see the little image of the consecrated candle reflected in the soft surface of the pearl, and he heard again in his ears the lovely music of the undersea, the tone of the diffused green light of the sea bottom. Juana, glancing secretly at him, saw him smile. And because they were in some way one thing and one purpose, she smiled with him.

And they began this day with hope.

---

7. **consecrated** (kän si krāt əd) *adj.*: Holy.

8. **cozened** (kuz′ ənd) *v.*: Deceived.

Closure and Extension

ANSWERS TO THINKING ABOUT THE SELECTION

Recalling

1. Kino's Song of the Family is a personal song, soft and clear, made up of the familiar sounds of the home he loved. The Song of Evil is another personal song—a savage, secret, dangerous melody that Kino hears when he or his family is threatened.
2. Coyotito is bitten by the scorpion.
3. Juana wants the great pearl to pay for the expenses for medical care for Coyotito. She feels that wanting something too much will drive the luck away.
4. The people secretly envy Kino's good fortune. The priest and the doctor suddenly treat Kino with respect.

Interpreting

5. The doctor has no interest in treat-

THINKING ABOUT THE SELECTION

Recalling

1. Compare Kino's Song of the Family with the Song of Evil.
2. What harm comes to Coyotito?
3. Why does Juana wish for a great pearl? Why does she feel that it is "not good to want a thing too much"?
4. How do people's attitudes toward Kino change after he finds "the Pearl of the World"?

Interpreting

5. What is the doctor's attitude toward Kino and his people?
6. Explain how the news of Kino's find stirs up something "infinitely black and evil in the town."
7. In what ways does luck bring Kino and Juana "bitter friends"?
8. By the end of Chapter 3, what changes have come about in Kino?
9. How does Juana's attitude toward the pearl change?

Applying

10. The narrator writes, "For it is said that humans are never satisfied, that you give them one thing and they want something more." Do you agree that this is a universal trait in human beings? Explain your answer.

ANALYZING LITERATURE

Understanding Characters in a Parable

A **parable** is a short tale told to illustrate a universal truth. In parables, characters tend to be simple and flat rather than complex and three-dimensional. Characters in parables represent traits in people. For example, the doctor in *The Pearl* represents greed.

1. Explain what traits are represented by Kino, Juana, and Coyotito.
2. Consider the narrator's comment: "In tales that are in people's hearts, there are only good and bad things and black and white things and good and evil things and no in-between anywhere." What does this statement suggest about the stories people know by heart?
3. Do you agree that there are only good and evil things and no in-between? Explain your answer.

UNDERSTANDING LANGUAGE

Appreciating Words from Spanish

The English language has many words that come from Spanish. For example, *coyote*, meaning "a small animal related to the wolf," comes from the Mexican Nahuatl (Indian) language.

Look in a dictionary for the definition and the language of origin for each of the following words. Then use each word correctly in a sentence.

1. pulque
2. plaza
3. hammocks
4. fiesta

THINKING AND WRITING

Writing from Juana's Point of View

Choose an incident in the story and rewrite it from Juana's point of view. First, review Chapters 1 through 3, concentrating on aspects of Juana's character. Next, imagine that you are Juana and freewrite about the incident, describing your thoughts, feelings, and actions. Then use this information to rewrite the incident from her point of view. Revise your description to make sure that it suits Juana's character. Proofread for errors in spelling, grammar, and punctuation.

(Answers begin on p. 714)

ANSWERS TO UNDERSTANDING LANGUAGE

Sentences will differ. Definitions and origins follow:

1. *Pulque* is a fermented milky drink made from the juice of a species of agave. (Mexican-Spanish from Nahuatl)
2. A plaza is a public square in a city or town. (Spanish, from Latin)
3. Hammocks are hanging cots or lounges made of netting or canvas that hang from two trees or another kind of support. (Spanish, from Taino)
4. A fiesta is a religious feast or holiday, especially in Spanish-speaking countries. (Spanish, from Latin)

Challenge To create an image of sound is more difficult than to create a visual image. That is why Steinbeck often uses metaphors or similes to describe sounds. Choose a sound not presented in this novel and try writing a description of it in words. Read your description to the class—without mentioning outright what sound is being described—and see if the class can recognize the sound.

THINKING AND WRITING

Publishing Student Writing *The Pearl* takes place over a three-day period. Display students' writing from Juana's point of view as a journal entry of day 1. You might want to have students write a journal entry from the point of view of Juana or another character for each of the three days.

Writing Across the Curriculum Edward F. Ricketts, a marine biologist, was a close friend of John Steinbeck. It was with Ricketts that Steinbeck explored marine life in the Sea of Cortez. Have students research their exploration and write an essay. You might want to notify social studies or geography teachers, so they could guide students in researching Ricketts and Steinbeck's exploration. Students could write an essay about their findings.

ing patients who cannot pay his fees. The doctor views Kino and his people with contempt—as uneducated people who cannot afford his services.

6. The news of the pearl stirs up everyone's desires and the only person who stands in the way of the pearl fulfilling them is Kino, so that he becomes everyone's enemy.
7. The townspeople envy them, the greedy doctor and priest come to visit, and an intruder invades their hut in the night.
8. Hate is growing in Kino and he is determined to sell the pearl to improve his family's life.
9. Juana wants to get rid of the pearl.

Applying

10. Answers will differ, but should be supported by explanation or example.

ANSWERS TO ANALYZING LITERATURE

1. Answers will differ. Suggested response: Kino represents ambition, Juana maternal love and safety, and Coyotito innocence and hope.
2. Answers will differ, but should be supported by explanation or examples.
3. Answers will differ, but explantions should be supported by examples.

Literary Focus Before students proceed with chapters 4, 5, and 6, have them review the plot to this point. Have them discuss the conflicts—both internal and external—between primitive and modern societies, between Kino's desires and his traditions, and between Kino and the townspeople. Have students comment about how these conflicts relate to the theme.

Look For As students read, encourage them to be attentive to both the internal and external conflicts, that is, the opposing forces within a character and those outside the character. Have students find relationships between the events and their causes, and the events and their outcomes.

Writing/Prior Knowledge Before students begin the freewriting activity, have them consider the answers to the following questions. What was their intended outcome? What obstacles prevented the outcome from happening? What were the reactions of others? Given an opportunity to strive for the same outcomes, how might they proceed differently?

Vocabulary Have your **less advanced** students read the words and their definitions. Have them participate in a discussion that allows them to use the words and demonstrate understanding of their meanings.

GUIDE FOR READING

The Pearl, Chapters 4–6

Plot and Theme

Plot is the sequence of related events or incidents that makes up a literary work. Plot usually involves **conflict, climax,** and **resolution.** Conflict, a struggle between opposing forces, can occur between people, between nature and people, or within a person. The climax is the story's highest point of interest, after which the action turns and begins to resolve. In the resolution, the characters solve the conflict, and the reader learns the outcome of the plot.

Theme is the central idea of a story, or the general insight into life that a story conveys. Writers of parables use plot to help express theme. Carefully examining the events in a parable will increase your understanding of its theme.

Look For

As you read Chapters 4–6 of *The Pearl,* look for the major events of the story. Notice the sequence in which they occur and the clues they give you to the theme.

Writing

Do you agree that wisdom can be gained from tragedy? Freewrite, exploring your answer.

Vocabulary

Knowing the following words will help you as you read Chapters 4–6 of *The Pearl.*

benign (bi nīn′) *adj.*: Good natured; harmless (p. 720)
spurned (spʉrnd) *v.*: Kicked; rejected (p. 721)
lethargy (leth′ər jē) *n.*: Laziness or indifference (p. 724)
edifice (ed′i fis) *n.*: Imposing structure (p. 728)
leprosy (lep′rə sē) *n.*: An infectious, disfiguring disease (p. 729)
waning (wān′iŋ) *adj.*: Shrinking to a new moon (p. 730)
covert (kuv′ərt) *n.*: A hiding place (p. 731)
sentinel (sen′ti nəl) *n.*: Guard (p. 732)
goading (gōd iŋ) *n.*: Urging (p. 733)
monolithic (man′ə lith′ik) *adj.*: Formed from a single block (p. 735)
escarpment (e skarp′mənt) *n.*: A long cliff (p. 736)
intercession (in′tər sesh′ən) *n.*: A prayer said on behalf of another person (p. 739)
malignant (mə lig′nənt) *adj.*: Harmful; likely to cause death (p. 742)

Objectives

1 To understand plot and theme when reading the novel
2 To recognize cause and effect when reading a novel
3 To appreciate the use of vivid verbs
4 To respond to literary criticism

Support Material

Teaching Portfolio

Teacher Backup, pp. 1027–1029
Grammar in Action Worksheets, *Understanding Gerunds*, pp. 1030–1031; *Understanding Participles*, pp. 1032–1033; *Using Specific Verbs*, pp. 1034–1035
Usage and Mechanics Worksheet, p. 1036
Vocabulary Check, p. 1037
Critical Thinking and Reading Worksheet, *Recognizing Cause and Effect*, p. 1038
Language Worksheet, *Appreciating Vivid Verbs*, p. 1039
Selection Test, pp. 1040–1041

Chapter 4

It is wonderful the way a little town keeps track of itself and of all its units. If every single man and woman, child and baby, acts and conducts itself in a known pattern and breaks no walls and differs with no one and experiments in no way and is not sick and does not endanger the ease and peace of mind or steady unbroken flow of the
1 town, then that unit can disappear and never be heard of. But let one man step out of the regular thought or the known and trusted pattern, and the nerves of the townspeople ring with nervousness and communication travels over the nerve lines of the town. Then every unit communicates to the whole.

Thus, in La Paz,[1] it was known in the early morning through the whole town that Kino was going to sell his pearl that day. It was known among the neighbors in the brush huts, among the pearl fishermen; it was known among the Chinese grocery-store owners; it was known in the church, for the altar boys whispered about it. Word
2 of it crept in among the nuns; the beggars in front of the church spoke of it, for they would be there to take the tithe[2] of the first fruits of the luck. The little boys knew about it with excitement, but most of all the pearl buyers knew about it, and when the day had come, in the offices of the pearl buyers, each man sat alone with his little black velvet tray, and each man rolled the pearls about with his fingertips and considered his part in the picture.

It was supposed that the pearl buyers were individuals acting alone, bidding
3 against one another for the pearls the fishermen brought in. And once it had been so. But this was a wasteful method, for often, in the excitement of bidding for a fine pearl, too great a price had been paid to the fishermen. This was extravagant and not to be countenanced.[3] Now there was only one pearl buyer with many hands, and the men who sat in their offices and waited for Kino knew what price they would offer, how high they would bid, and what method each one would use. And although these men would not profit beyond their salaries, there was excitement among the pearl buyers, for there was excitement in the hunt, and if it be a man's function to break down a price, then he must take joy and satisfaction in breaking it as far down as possible. For every man
in the world functions to the best of his 4
ability, and no one does less than his best, no matter what he may think about it. Quite apart from any reward they might get, from any word of praise, from any promotion, a pearl buyer was a pearl buyer, and the best and happiest pearl buyer was he who bought for the lowest prices.

The sun was hot yellow that morning, and it drew the moisture from the estuary and from the Gulf and hung it in shimmering scarves in the air so that the air vibrated and vision was insubstantial. A vision hung in the air to the north of the city—the vision of a mountain that was over two hundred miles away, and the high slopes of this mountain were swaddled with pines and a great stone peak arose above the timber line.

And the morning of this day the canoes lay lined up on the beach; the fishermen did not go out to dive for pearls, for there would be too much happening, too many things to see when Kino went to sell the great pearl.

In the brush houses by the shore Kino's neighbors sat long over their breakfasts, and they spoke of what they would do if they had found the pearl. And one man said that

---

1. La Paz: City in southern Baja California.
2. tithe (tīth) *n.*: One tenth of one's income; here, a small amount given to charity.

3. countenanced (kounʹ tə nənsd) *v.*: Approved; supported.

Presentation

Motivation/Prior Knowledge Have students consider what they have learned about the pearl thus far. Have them consider the images which have formed in their minds of the pearl. Consider the description of how a pearl is formed and Steinbeck's use of irony—in order to get the beautiful pearl, an oyster must be killed. Have students speculate whether or not they think this might be a foreshadowing.

Purpose-Setting Question Understanding the goals and desires and conflicts of a character are important in understanding story plot, climax, and resolution. How do the events in Kino's life and his character relate to the plot of the story?

1 **Discussion** In previous chapters Steinbeck has compared the town to a living organism. How is Kino changing and what effect does this have on the town?

2 **Reading Strategy** Summarize the climate in the town.

3 **Reading Strategy** Summarize the climate in the pearl buyers' offices. What are the implications for their attitudes?

4 **Enrichment** Steinbeck has become philosophical here about the nature of man. Have students tell whether they agree or disagree with his statement that "every man in the world functions to the best of his ability . . ."

Master Teacher Note *The Pearl* was not favorably received when it was first published. In one review Maxwell Geismar wrote that ". . . the quality that has marked Steinbeck's work as a whole is . . . the sense of black and white things and good and bad things—that is to say, the sense of a fabulist or a propagandist rather than the insight of an artist." You might want to read this to students and have them consider whether they agree or disagree after they have completed the reading.

Humanities Note

Fine art, *Group,* by Jesus Guerrero Galvan. This painting differs in style and content from Rivera's. Have students discuss the differences. While the style and content of the artist's paintings vary, both approaches effectively relate to the story's content.

Have students identify and discuss the interactions that are taking place in the painting and the relationships between these interactions and the details of the story.

5 **Discussion** Kino's neighbors say they would use the money from the pearl for the benefit of others. Kino has not planned to do this. Have students discuss whether they feel Steinbeck is making a judgment of right or wrong in this paragraph.

6 **Critical Thinking and Reading** There is an obvious cause-and-effect relationship here between wealth and destruction. How does this cause-and-effect relationship relate to the theme?

7 **Discussion** Based on what is described and what the reader knows about the story thus far, what are Juana's and Kino's expectations for the day? What do they anticipate the day will be like?

GROUP
Jesus Guerrero Galván
Collection IBM Corporation, Armonk, New York

he would give it as a present to the Holy Father in Rome. Another said that he would buy Masses for the souls of his family for a thousand years. Another thought he might take the money and distribute it among the poor of La Paz; and a fourth thought of all
5 the good things one could do with the money from the pearl, of all the charities, benefits, of all the rescues one could perform if one had money. All of the neighbors hoped that sudden wealth would not turn Kino's head, would not make a rich man of him, would not graft onto him the evil limbs of greed and hatred and coldness. For Kino was a well-liked man; it would be a shame if the pearl destroyed him. "That good wife Juana," they said, "and the beautiful baby
Coyotito, and the others to come. What a 6
pity it would be if the pearl should destroy them all."

For Kino and Juana this was the morning of mornings of their lives, comparable only to the day when the baby had been born. This was to be the day from which all other days would take their arrangement.
Thus they would say, "It was two years 7
before we sold the pearl," or, "It was six weeks after we sold the pearl." Juana, considering the matter, threw caution to the winds, and she dressed Coyotito in the clothes she had prepared for his baptism, when there would be money for his bap-

tism. And Juana combed and braided her hair and tied the ends with two little bows of red ribbon, and she put on her marriage skirt and waist.[4] The sun was quarter high when they were ready. Kino's ragged white clothes were clean at least, and this was the last day of his raggedness. For tomorrow, or even this afternoon, he would have new clothes.

The neighbors, watching Kino's door through the crevices in their brush houses, were dressed and ready too. There was no self-consciousness about their joining Kino and Juana to go pearl selling. It was expected, it was an historic moment, they would be crazy if they didn't go. It would be almost a sign of unfriendship.

Juana put on her head shawl carefully, and she draped one long end under her right elbow and gathered it with her right hand so that a hammock hung under her arm, and in this little hammock she placed Coyotito, propped up against the head shawl so that he could see everything and perhaps remember. Kino put on his large straw hat and felt it with his hand to see that it was properly placed, not on the back or side of
8 his head, like a rash, unmarried, irresponsible man, and not flat as an elder would wear it, but tilted a little forward to show aggressiveness and seriousness and vigor. There is a great deal to be seen in the tilt of a hat on a man. Kino slipped his feet into his sandals and pulled the thongs up over his heels. The great pearl was wrapped in an old soft piece of deerskin and placed in a little leather bag, and the leather bag was in a pocket in Kino's shirt. He folded his blanket carefully and draped it in a narrow strip over his left shoulder, and now they were ready.

Kino stepped with dignity out of the
9 house, and Juana followed him, carrying Coyotito. And as they marched up the freshet-washed[5] alley toward the town, the neighbors joined them. The houses belched people; the doorways spewed out children. But because of the seriousness of the occasion, only one man walked with Kino, and that was his brother, Juan Tomás.

Juan Tomás cautioned his brother. "You must be careful to see they do not cheat you," he said.

And, "Very careful," Kino agreed.

"We do not know what prices are paid in other places," said Juan Tomás. "How can we know what is a fair price, if we do not know what the pearl buyer gets for the pearl in another place?"

"That is true," said Kino, "but how can we know? We are here, we are not there."

As they walked up toward the city the crowd grew behind them, and Juan Tomás, in pure nervousness, went on speaking.

"Before you were born, Kino," he said, 10
"the old ones thought of a way to get more money for their pearls. They thought it would be better if they had an agent who took all the pearls to the capital and sold them there and kept only his share of the profit."

Kino nodded his head. "I know," he said. "It was a good thought."

"And so they got such a man," said Juan Tomás, "and they pooled their pearls, and they started him off. And he was never heard of again and the pearls were lost. Then they got another man, and they started him off, and he was never heard of again. And so they gave the whole thing up and went back to the old way."

"I know," said Kino. "I have heard our father tell of it. It was a good idea, but it was 11
against religion, and the Father made that very clear. The loss of the pearl was a

4. **waist** (wāst) *n.*: Blouse.

5. **freshet** (fresh' it) **-washed** *adj.*: Washed by a stream.

8 **Enrichment** You can learn much about Kino's people through information presented about the wearing of hats. Select an item of clothing worn by people today. Tell what that item of clothing might tell about our culture.

9 **Discussion** How does this procession differ from the first one?

10 **Discussion** What does this conversation between Kino and his brother tell the reader about their relationship?

11 **Humanities Note** This paragraph is reminiscent of Milton's sonnet, "On His Blindness." Have students read the sonnet and then discuss Kino's statement that "But each one must remain faithful to his post. . . ." in light of Milton's idea that "They also serve who only stand and wait."

12 Literary Focus What does this statement tell us about the priest?

13 Discussion What is the defensive behavior in response to?

14 Reading Strategy The pearl buyers are preparing for Kino's visit. Tell how they are doing this. What do their actions tell the reader? What do you think might happen?

punishment visited on those who tried to leave their station. And the Father made it clear that each man and woman is like a soldier sent by God to guard some part of the castle of the Universe. And some are in the ramparts and some far deep in the darkness of the walls. But each one must remain faithful to his post and must not go running about, else the castle is in danger from the assaults of Hell."

12 "I have heard him make that sermon," said Juan Tomás. "He makes it every year."

The brothers, as they walked along, squinted their eyes a little, as they and their grandfathers and their great-grandfathers had done for four hundred years, since first the strangers came with argument and authority and gunpowder to back up both. And in the four hundred years Kino's people had learned only one defense—a slight slitting
13 of the eyes and a slight tightening of the lips and a retirement. Nothing could break down this wall, and they could remain whole within the wall.

The gathering procession was solemn, for they sensed the importance of this day, and any children who showed a tendency to scuffle, to scream, to cry out, to steal hats and rumple hair, were hissed to silence by their elders. So important was this day that an old man came to see, riding on the stalwart shoulders of his nephew. The procession left the brush huts and entered the stone and plaster city where the streets were a little wider and there were narrow pavements beside the buildings. And as before, the beggars joined them as they passed the church; the grocers looked out at them as they went by; the little saloons lost their customers and the owners closed up shop and went along. And the sun beat down on the streets of the city and even tiny stones threw shadows on the ground.

The news of the approach of the procession ran ahead of it, and in their little dark offices the pearl buyers stiffened and grew alert. They got out papers so that they could be at work when Kino appeared, and they put their pearls in the desks, for it is not good to let an inferior pearl be seen beside a beauty. And word of the loveliness of Kino's pearl had come to them. The pearl buyers' offices were clustered together in one narrow street, and they were barred at the windows, and wooden slats cut out the light so that only a soft gloom entered the offices.

A stout slow man sat in an office waiting. His face was fatherly and benign, and his eyes twinkled with friendship. He was a caller of good mornings, a ceremonious shaker of hands, a jolly man who knew all jokes and yet who hovered close to sadness, for in the midst of a laugh he could remember the death of your aunt, and his eyes could become wet with sorrow for your loss. This morning he had placed a flower in a vase on his desk, a single scarlet hibiscus, and the vase sat beside the black velvet-lined pearl tray in front of him. He was shaved close to the blue roots of his beard, and his hands were clean and his nails polished. His door stood open to the morning, and he hummed under his breath while his right hand practiced legerdemain.[6] He rolled a coin back and forth over his knuckles and made it appear and disappear, made it spin and sparkle. The coin winked into sight and as quickly slipped out of sight, and the man did not even watch his own performance. The fingers did it all mechanically, precisely, while the man hummed to himself and peered out the door. Then he heard the tramp of feet of the approaching crowd, and the fingers of his right hand worked faster and faster until, as the figure of Kino filled

6. legerdemain (lej′ ər də mān′) *n.*: Trickery; tricks with the hand.

Grammar in Action

Gerunds are verb forms ending in *-ing* used as nouns. They may assume any noun function. Consider Steinbeck's sentences:

Object of preposition: In the excitement of *bidding* for a fine pearl, too great a price had been paid to the fisherman.

Direct Object: He felt the *creeping* of fate.

Subject: . . . The *whispering* went back through the crowd.

Appositive: . . . Kinos' people had learned only one defense —a slight *slitting* of the eyes and a slight *tightening* of the lips. . . .

Because gerunds are nouns, nouns and pronouns immediately preceding them must be in the possessive form:

There was no self-consciousness about *their* joining Kino . . .
Kino's finding the pearl was the talk of the town.

the doorway, the coin flashed and disappeared.

"Good morning, my friend," the stout man said. "What can I do for you?"

Kino stared into the dimness of the little office, for his eyes were squeezed from the outside glare. But the buyer's eyes had become as steady and cruel and unwinking as a hawk's eyes, while the rest of his face smiled in greeting. And secretly, behind his desk, his right hand practiced with the coin.

"I have a pearl," said Kino. And Juan Tomás stood beside him and snorted a little at the understatement. The neighbors peered around the doorway, and a line of little boys clambered on the window bars and looked through. Several little boys, on their hands and knees, watched the scene around Kino's legs.

"You have a pearl," the dealer said. "Sometimes a man brings in a dozen. Well,
15 let us see your pearl. We will value it and give you the best price." And his fingers worked furiously with the coin.

Now Kino instinctively knew his own dramatic effects. Slowly he brought out the leather bag, slowly took from it the soft and dirty piece of deerskin, and then he let the great pearl roll into the black velvet tray, and instantly his eyes went to the buyer's face. But there was no sign, no movement,
16 the face did not change, but the secret hand behind the desk missed in its precision. The coin stumbled over a knuckle and slipped silently into the dealer's lap. And the fingers behind the desk curled into a fist. When the right hand came out of hiding, the forefinger touched the great pearl, rolled it on the black velvet; thumb and forefinger picked it up and brought it near to the dealer's eyes and twirled it in the air.

Kino held his breath, and the neighbors held their breath, and the whispering went back through the crowd. "He is inspecting it—No price has been mentioned yet—They have not come to a price."

Now the dealer's hand had become a personality. The hand tossed the great pearl 17
back in the tray, the forefinger poked and insulted it, and on the dealer's face there came a sad and contemptuous smile.

"I am sorry, my friend," he said, and his shoulders rose a little to indicate that the misfortune was no fault of his.

"It is a pearl of great value," Kino said.

The dealer's fingers spurned the pearl so that it bounced and rebounded softly from the side of the velvet tray.

"You have heard of fool's gold," the dealer said. "This pearl is like fool's gold. It is too large. Who would buy it? There is no market for such things. It is a curiosity only. I am sorry. You thought it was a thing of value, and it is only a curiosity."

Now Kino's face was perplexed and worried. "It is the Pearl of the World," he cried. "No one has ever seen such a pearl."

"On the contrary," said the dealer, "it is large and clumsy. As a curiosity it has interest; some museum might perhaps take it to place in a collection of seashells. I can give you, say, a thousand pesos."[7]

Kino's face grew dark and dangerous. "It 18
is worth fifty thousand," he said. "You know it. You want to cheat me."

And the dealer heard a little grumble go
through the crowd as they heard his price. 19
And the dealer felt a little tremor of fear.

"Do not blame me," he said quickly. "I am only an appraiser. Ask the others. Go to their offices and show your pearl—or better let them come here, so that you can see there is no collusion.[8] Boy," he called. And when his servant looked through the rear

---

7. pesos (pā′ sōz) *n.*: Mexican unit of money.
8. collusion (kə lo͞o′ zhən) *n.*: A secret agreement for an illegal purpose.

15 Discussion How does the pearl buyer attempt to minimize and devalue Kino's pearl?

16 Literary Focus The student must be attentive to detail in this paragraph if they are not to be misled later on in the story. What do the words and actions of the dealer tell the reader about the pearl?

17 Literary Focus What has the dealer's hand told the reader about the dealer?

18 Literary Focus Based on what we have seen of Kino thus far, what do you think Kino has learned about this modern culture and the people that operate within it?

19 Discussion The crowd is more distanced and quiet than it has been on previous occasions. What is the significance of this?

Student Activity 1. Locate the gerunds in each of the following sentences and explain how each gerund is used.

1. He must take joy and satisfaction in breaking it down as far as possible.
2. Juan Tomás, in pure nervousness, continued speaking.
3. But each one must remain faithful to his post and must not go running about.
4. The buyer's eyes had become as steady and cruel and unwinking as a hawk's eyes, while the rest of his face smiled in greeting.
5. When the right hand came out of hiding, the forefinger touched the great pearl.
6. He felt a little tugging at his back.
7. She knew she could help him best by being silent and by being near.

Student Activity 2. Some words like *morning* and *evening* may not seem like gerunds because their verb forms have become obsolete. Use your dictionary to find the original verbs from which morning and evening were derived.

20 Discussion The coin becomes a symbol. What does the coin represent?

21 Reading Strategy Summarize the behavior of the three pearl buyers. How could their reactions have been predicted from previous actions?

22 Literary Focus There is a strong message here related to the theme of the story. What is the message and how does it relate to the theme?

door, "Boy, go to such a one, and such another one and such a third one. Ask them to step in here and do not tell them why. Just say that I will be pleased to see them." And his right hand went behind the desk
20 and pulled another coin from his pocket, and the coin rolled back and forth over the knuckles.

Kino's neighbors whispered together. They had been afraid of something like this. The pearl was large, but it had a strange color. They had been suspicious of it from the first. And after all, a thousand pesos was not to be thrown away. It was comparative wealth to a man who was not wealthy. And suppose Kino took a thousand pesos. Only yesterday he had nothing.

But Kino had grown tight and hard. He felt the creeping of fate, the circling of wolves, the hover of vultures. He felt the evil coagulating[9] about him, and he was helpless to protect himself. He heard in his ears the evil music. And on the black velvet the great pearl glistened, so that the dealer could not keep his eyes from it.

The crowd in the doorway wavered and broke and let the three pearl dealers through. The crowd was silent now, fearing to miss a word, to fail to see a gesture or an expression. Kino was silent and watchful. He felt a little tugging at his back, and he turned and looked in Juana's eyes, and when he looked away he had renewed strength.

The dealers did not glance at one another nor at the pearl. The man behind the desk said, "I have put a value on this pearl. The
21 owner here does not think it fair. I will ask you to examine this—this thing and make an offer. Notice," he said to Kino, "I have not mentioned what I have offered."

The first dealer, dry and stringy, seemed now to see the pearl for the first time. He took it up, rolled it quickly between thumb and forefinger, and then cast it contemptuously back into the tray.

"Do not include me in the discussion," he said dryly. "I will make no offer at all. I do not want it. This is not a pearl—it is a monstrosity." His thin lips curled.

Now the second dealer, a little man with a shy soft voice, took up the pearl, and he examined it carefully. He took a glass from his pocket and inspected it under magnification. Then he laughed softly.

"Better pearls are made of paste," he said. "I know these things. This is soft and chalky, it will lose its color and die in a few months. Look—." He offered the glass to Kino, showed him how to use it, and Kino, who had never seen a pearl's surface magnified, was shocked at the strange-looking surface.

The third dealer took the pearl from Kino's hands. "One of my clients likes such things," he said. "I will offer five hundred pesos, and perhaps I can sell it to my client for six hundred."

Kino reached quickly and snatched the pearl from his hand. He wrapped it in the deerskin and thrust it inside his shirt.

The man behind the desk said, "I'm a fool, I know, but my first offer stands. I still offer one thousand. What are you doing?" he asked, as Kino thrust the pearl out of sight.

"I am cheated," Kino cried fiercely. "My
pearl is not for sale here. I will go, perhaps 22
even to the capital."

Now the dealers glanced quickly at one another. They knew they had played too hard; they knew they would be disciplined for their failure, and the man at the desk said quickly, "I might go to fifteen hundred."

But Kino was pushing his way through the crowd. The hum of talk came to him dimly, his rage blood pounded in his ears,

9. coagulating (kō ag′ yo͞o lāt′ iŋ) *v.*: Becoming solid.

and he burst through and strode away. Juana followed, trotting after him.

When the evening came, the neighbors in the brush houses sat eating their corncakes and beans, and they discussed the great theme of the morning. They did not know, it seemed a fine pearl to them, but they had never seen such a pearl before, and surely the dealers knew more about the value of pearls than they. "And mark this," they said. "Those dealers did not discuss these things. Each of the three knew the pearl was valueless."

"But suppose they had arranged it before?"

"If that is so, then all of us have been cheated all of our lives."

Perhaps, some argued, perhaps it would have been better if Kino took the one thousand five hundred pesos. That is a great deal of money, more than he has ever seen. Maybe Kino is being a pigheaded fool. Suppose he should really go to the capital and find no buyer for his pearl. He would never live that down.

And now, said other fearful ones, now that he had defied them, those buyers will not want to deal with him at all. Maybe Kino has cut off his own head and destroyed himself.

And others said, Kino is a brave man, and a fierce man; he is right. From his courage we may all profit. These were proud of Kino.

In his house Kino squatted on his sleeping mat, brooding. He had buried his pearl under a stone of the fire hole in his house, and he stared at the woven tules[10] of his sleeping mat until the crossed design danced in his head.
23 He had lost one world and had not gained another. And Kino was afraid. Never in his life had he been far from home. He was afraid of strangers and of strange places. He was terrified of that monster of strangeness they called the capital. It lay over the water and through the mountains, over a thousand miles, and every strange terrible mile was frightening. But Kino had lost his old world and he must clamber on to a new one. For his dream of the future was real and never to be destroyed, and he had said "I will go," and that made a real thing too. To determine to go and to say it was to be halfway there.

Juana watched him while he buried his pearl, and she watched him while she cleaned Coyotito and nursed him, and Juana made the corncakes for supper.

Juan Tomás came in and squatted down beside Kino and remained silent for a long time, until at last Kino demanded, "What else could I do? They are cheats."

Juan Tomás nodded gravely. He was the elder, and Kino looked to him for wisdom. "It is hard to know," he said. "We do know that we are cheated from birth to the overcharge 24
on our coffins. But we survive. You have defied not the pearl buyers, but the whole structure, the whole way of life, and I am afraid for you."

"What have I to fear but starvation?" Kino asked.

But Juan Tomás shook his head slowly. "That we must all fear. But suppose you are correct—suppose your pearl is of great value—do you think then the game is over?"

"What do you mean?" 25

"I don't know," said Juan Tomás, "but I am afraid for you. It is new ground you are walking on, you do not know the way."

"I will go. I will go soon," said Kino.

"Yes," Juan Tomás agreed. "That you must do. But I wonder if you will find it any different in the capital. Here, you have friends and me, your brother. There, you will have no one."

10. tules (to͞o′ lēz) *n.*: Grasslike plants.

23 **Literary Focus** The sentence "He had lost one world and had not gained another" is a very important one that Steinbeck does not explicitly follow up on as the story continues. Consider what Kino's hopes are—being married in the church and education. These would give him entry into the modern world, yet the modern world is not letting him in so easily. Have students discuss the significance of this, especially in relation to what Kino has lost by his recent quest.

24 **Critical Thinking and Reading** What do you think might be the effects of Kino's defiance of the whole system?

25 **Discussion** What do you think Juan Tomás believes Kino should do? Do you think that Juan Tomás feels that the dealer is lying?

26 Literary Focus How does this event relate to the theme? In both instances, the intruder has been unidentified. What do you think Steinbeck is saying?

"What can I do?" Kino cried. "Some deep outrage is here. My son must have a chance. That is what they are striking at. My friends will protect me."

"Only so long as they are not in danger or discomfort from it," said Juan Tomás. He arose, saying, "Go with God."

And Kino said, "Go with God," and did not even look up, for the words had a strange chill in them.

Long after Juan Tomás had gone Kino sat brooding on his sleeping mat. A lethargy had settled on him, and a little gray hopelessness. Every road seemed blocked against him. In his head he heard only the dark music of the enemy. His senses were burningly alive, but his mind went back to the deep participation with all things, the gift he had from his people. He heard every little sound of the gathering night, the sleepy complaint of settling birds, the love agony of cats, the strike and withdrawal of little waves on the beach, and the simple hiss of distance. And he could smell the sharp odor of exposed kelp[11] from the receding tide. The little flare of the twig fire made the design on his sleeping mat jump before his entranced eyes.

Juana watched him with worry, but she knew him and she knew she could help him best by being silent and by being near. And as though she too could hear the Song of Evil, she fought it, singing softly the melody of the family, of the safety and warmth and wholeness of the family. She held Coyotito in her arms and sang the song to him, to keep the evil out, and her voice was brave against the threat of the dark music.

Kino did not move nor ask for his supper. She knew he would ask when he wanted it. His eyes were entranced, and he could sense the wary, watchful evil outside the brush house; he could feel the dark creeping things waiting for him to go out into the night. It was shadowy and dreadful, and yet it called to him and threatened him and challenged him. His right hand went into his shirt and felt his knife; his eyes were wide; he stood up and walked to the doorway.

Juana willed to stop him; she raised her hand to stop him, and her mouth opened with terror. For a long moment Kino looked out into the darkness and then he stepped outside. Juana heard the little rush, the grunting struggle, the blow. She froze with terror for a moment, and then her lips drew back from her teeth like a cat's lips. She set Coyotito down on the ground. She seized a stone from the fireplace and rushed outside, but it was over by then. Kino lay on the ground, struggling to rise, and there was no one near him. Only the shadows and the strike and rush of waves and the hiss of distance. But the evil was all about, hidden behind the brush fence, crouched beside the house in the shadow, hovering in the air. 2

Juana dropped her stone, and she put her arms around Kino and helped him to his feet and supported him into the house. Blood oozed down from his scalp and there was a long deep cut in his cheek from ear to chin, a deep, bleeding slash. And Kino was only half conscious. He shook his head from side to side. His shirt was torn open and his clothes half pulled off. Juana sat him down on his sleeping mat and she wiped the thickening blood from his face with her skirt. She brought him pulque to drink in a little pitcher, and still he shook his head to clear out the darkness.

"Who?" Juana asked.

"I don't know," Kino said. "I didn't see."

Now Juana brought her clay pot of water and she washed the cut on his face while he stared dazed ahead of him.

"Kino, my husband," she cried, and his

11. kelp *n.*: Seaweed.

MEXICAN PEASANT WITH SOMBRERO AND SERAPE
Diego Rivera
Harry Ransom Humanities Research Center
The University of Texas at Austin

eyes stared past her. "Kino, can you hear me?"

"I hear you," he said dully.

"Kino, this pearl is evil. Let us destroy it before it destroys us. Let us crush it between two stones. Let us—let us throw it back in the sea where it belongs. Kino, it is evil, it is evil!"

And as she spoke the light came back in Kino's eyes so that they glowed fiercely and his muscles hardened and his will hardened.

"No," he said. "I will fight this thing. I will win over it. We will have our chance." His fist pounded the sleeping mat. "No one shall take our good fortune from us," he said. His eyes softened then and he raised a gentle hand to Juana's shoulder. "Believe me," he said. "I am a man." And his face grew crafty.

"In the morning we will take our canoe and we will go over the sea and over the mountains to the capital, you and I. We will not be cheated. I am a man."

"Kino," she said huskily, "I am afraid. A man can be killed. Let us throw the pearl back into the sea."

"Hush," he said fiercely. "I am a man. Hush." And she was silent, for his voice was
command. "Let us sleep a little," he said. 27
"In the first light we will start. You are not afraid to go with me?"

"No, my husband."

His eyes were soft and warm on her then, his hand touched her cheek. "Let us sleep a little," he said.

Humanities Note

Fine art, *Mexican Peasant with Sombrero and Serape,* Diego Rivera. This painting represents the guarded, suspicious aspects of Kino's personality. Have students notice how, throughout the story, the art selections reflect developments in the plot. Here, the Kino figure appears to be guarded, suspicious, and brooding, as if possessed by the pearl. Have students discuss how this mood is different from Kino's personality before he found the pearl.

27 **Discussion** What does Juana's reaction tell the reader about their people and their beliefs?

28 Enrichment Do you think that Juana is justified in throwing away the pearl? Do you agree or disagree with her decision?

29 Literary Focus How does the description of Kino tell the reader that he has changed?

30 Discussion What does this paragraph tell the reader about Juana and Kino, their people and beliefs?

Chapter 5

The late moon arose before the first rooster crowed. Kino opened his eyes in the darkness, for he sensed movement near him, but he did not move. Only his eyes searched the darkness, and in the pale light of the moon that crept through the holes in the brush house Kino saw Juana arise silently from beside him. He saw her move toward the fireplace. So carefully did she work that he heard only the lightest sound when she moved the fireplace stone. And then like a shadow she glided toward the door. She paused for a moment beside the hanging box where Coyotito lay, then for a second she was black in the doorway, and then she was gone.

And rage surged in Kino. He rolled up to his feet and followed her as silently as she had gone, and he could hear her quick footsteps going toward the shore. Quietly he tracked her, and his brain was red with anger. She burst clear out of the brush line and stumbled over the little boulders toward the water, and then she heard him coming and she broke into a run. Her arm was up to
28 throw when he leaped at her and caught her arm and wrenched the pearl from her. He struck her in the face with his clenched fist and she fell among the boulders, and he kicked her in the side. In the pale light he could see the little waves break over her, and her skirt floated about and clung to her legs as the water receded.

Kino looked down at her and his teeth were bared. He hissed at her like a snake, and Juana stared at him with wide unfright-
29 ened eyes, like a sheep before the butcher. She knew there was murder in him, and it was all right; she had accepted it, and she would not resist or even protest. And then the rage left him and a sick disgust took its place. He turned away from her and walked up the beach and through the brush line. His senses were dulled by his emotion.

He heard the rush, got his knife out and lunged at one dark figure and felt his knife go home, and then he was swept to his knees and swept again to the ground. Greedy fingers went through his clothes, frantic figures searched him, and the pearl, knocked from his hand, lay winking behind a little stone in the pathway. It glinted in the soft moonlight.

Juana dragged herself up from the rocks on the edge of the water. Her face was a dull pain and her side ached. She steadied herself on her knees for a while and her wet skirt clung to her. There was no anger in her for Kino. He had said, "I am a man," and that meant certain things to Juana. It meant that he was half insane and half god. It meant that Kino would drive his strength against a mountain and plunge his strength against the sea. Juana, in her woman's soul, knew that the mountain would stand while the man broke himself; that the sea would surge while the man drowned in it. 30
And yet it was this thing that made him a man, half insane and half god, and Juana had need of a man; she could not live without a man. Although she might be puzzled by these differences between man and woman, she knew them and accepted them and needed them. Of course she would follow him, there was no question of that. Sometimes the quality of woman, the reason, the caution, the sense of preservation, could cut through Kino's manness and save them all. She climbed painfully to her feet, and she dipped her cupped palms in the little waves and washed her bruised face with the stinging salt water, and then she went creeping up the beach after Kino.

A flight of herring clouds had moved over the sky from the south. The pale moon dipped in and out of the strands of clouds so that Juana walked in darkness for a moment and in light the next. Her back was bent with pain and her head was low. She went through the line of brush when the moon was covered, and when it looked through she saw the glimmer of the great pearl in the path behind the rock. She sank to her knees and picked it up, and the moon went into the darkness of the clouds again. Juana remained on her knees while she considered whether to go back to the sea and finish her job, and as she considered, the light came again, and she saw two dark figures lying in the path ahead of her. She leaped forward and saw that one was Kino and the other a stranger with dark shiny fluid leaking from his throat.

Kino moved sluggishly, arms and legs stirred like those of a crushed bug, and a thick muttering came from his mouth. Now, in an instant, Juana knew that the old life was gone forever. A dead man in the path and Kino's knife, dark bladed beside him, convinced her. All of the time Juana had
31 been trying to rescue something of the old peace, of the time before the pearl. But now it was gone, and there was no retrieving it. And knowing this, she abandoned the past instantly. There was nothing to do but to save themselves.

Her pain was gone now, her slowness. Quickly she dragged the dead man from the pathway into the shelter of the brush. She went to Kino and sponged his face with her wet skirt. His senses were coming back and he moaned.

"They have taken the pearl. I have lost it. Now it is over," he said. "The pearl is gone."

Juana quieted him as she would quiet a sick child. "Hush," she said. "Here is your pearl. I found it in the path. Can you hear me now? Here is your pearl. Can you understand? You have killed a man. We must go away. They will come for us, can you understand? We must be gone before the daylight comes."

"I was attacked," Kino said uneasily. "I struck to save my life."

"Do you remember yesterday?" Juana asked. "Do you think that will matter? Do you remember the men of the city? Do you think your explanation will help?"

Kino drew a great breath and fought off his weakness. "No," he said. "You are right." And his will hardened and he was a man again.

"Go to our house and bring Coyotito," he said, "and bring all the corn we have. I will drag the canoe into the water and we will go."

He took his knife and left her. He stumbled toward the beach and he came to his canoe. And when the light broke through again he saw that a great hole had been knocked in the bottom. And a searing rage came to him and gave him strength. Now the darkness was closing in on his family; now the evil music filled the night, hung over the
mangroves, skirled[1] in the wave beat. The 32
canoe of his grandfather, plastered over and over, and a splintered hole broken in it. This was an evil beyond thinking. The killing of a man was not so evil as the killing of a boat. For a boat does not have sons, and a boat cannot protect itself, and a wounded boat does not heal. There was sorrow in Kino's rage, but this last thing had tightened him beyond breaking. He was an animal now, for hiding, for attacking, and he lived only to preserve himself and his family. He was not conscious of the pain in his head. He leaped up the beach, through the brush line toward his brush house, and it did not occur to him to take one of the canoes of his neighbors. Never once did the

---

1. skirled (skurld) *v.*: Made a shrill, piercing sound.

31 Literary Focus When Juana "abandoned the past," the future was determined for her and her family. One might argue that the climax of the novel has been reached, for the ending is now inevitable. How might the killing of the man lying beside Kino be considered the climax of the novel?

32 Reading Strategy In previous references the reader has seen the importance of the canoe—it has served as a symbol of the family and its heritage. What predictions might you make regarding the destruction of the canoe?

33 Discussion Less than twenty-four hours have elapsed since Kino and Juana awoke and longingly anticipated the events of this day. Unlike their expectations, the day has been filled with destruction. Recount the events of the day. Discuss the changes that have occurred in both Juana's and Kino's lives in the course of this time.

34 Discussion Again Steinbeck keeps the intruders unnamed. Why do you think Juana refers to them as "the dark ones"?

35 Reading Strategy Based on what the reader knows about Juan Tomás, how do you think Kino, Juana, and Coyotito will be received by him?

thought enter his head, any more than he could have conceived breaking a boat.

33 The roosters were crowing and the dawn was not far off. Smoke of the first fires seeped out through the walls of the brush houses, and the first smell of cooking corncakes was in the air. Already the dawn birds were scampering in the bushes. The weak moon was losing its light and the clouds thickened and curdled to the southward. The wind blew freshly into the estuary, a nervous, restless wind with the smell of storm on its breath, and there was change and uneasiness in the air.

Kino, hurrying toward his house, felt a surge of exhilaration. Now he was not confused, for there was only one thing to do, and Kino's hand went first to the great pearl in his shirt and then to his knife hanging under his shirt.

He saw a little glow ahead of him, and then without interval a tall flame leaped up in the dark with a crackling roar, and a tall edifice of fire lighted the pathway. Kino broke into a run; it was his brush house, he knew. And he knew that these houses could burn down in a very few moments. And as he ran a scuttling figure ran toward him —Juana, with Coyotito in her arms and Kino's shoulder blanket clutched in her hand. The baby moaned with fright, and Juana's eyes were wide and terrified. Kino could see the house was gone, and he did not question Juana. He knew, but she said, "It was torn up and the floor dug—even the baby's box turned out, and as I looked they put the fire to the outside."

34 The fierce light of the burning house lighted Kino's face strongly. "Who?" he demanded.

"I don't know," she said. "The dark ones."

The neighbors were tumbling from their houses now, and they watched the falling sparks and stamped them out to save their own houses. Suddenly Kino was afraid. The light made him afraid. He remembered the man lying dead in the brush beside the path, and he took Juana by the arm and drew her into the shadow of a house away from the light, for light was danger to him. For a moment he considered and then he worked among the shadows until he came to the house of Juan Tomás, his brother, and he slipped into the doorway and drew Juana after him. Outside, he could hear the squeal of children and the shouts of the neighbors, for his friends thought he might be inside the burning house.

The house of Juan Tomás was almost exactly like Kino's house; nearly all the brush houses were alike, and all leaked light and air, so that Juana and Kino, sitting in the corner of the brother's house, could see the leaping flames through the wall. They saw the flames tall and furious, they saw the roof fall and watched the fire die down as quickly as a twig fire dies. They heard the cries of warning of their friends, and the shrill, keening[2] cry of Apolonia, wife of Juan Tomás. She, being the nearest woman relative, raised a formal lament for the dead of the family.

Apolonia realized that she was wearing her second-best head shawl and she rushed to her house to get her fine new one. As she rummaged in a box by the wall, Kino's voice said quietly, "Apolonia, do not cry out. We are not hurt."

"How do you come here?" she demanded.

"Do not question," he said. "Go now to Juan Tomás and bring him here and tell no one else. This is important to us, Apolonia." 35

She paused, her hands helpless in front

2. **keening** (kēn′ iŋ) *adj.*: Wailing for the dead.

Grammar in Action

Sometimes a verb form acts as an adjective. This form of the verb is called a **participle.** The present participle ends in *-ing*; the past participle usually ends in *-ed*, *-t*, or *-n*. Using participles adds action and drama to your writing. Notice the participles in these sentences:

. . . She washed her *bruised* face with the *stinging* salt water. . . .

A *searing* rage came to him and gave him strength.

. . . A *wounded* boat does not heal.

Notice also that participles can be used to compress your writing. The third sentence might have read:

A boat *that has been wounded* does not heal.

Student Activity 1. Locate the participles in the following sentences.

1. He struck her in the face with his clenched fist.

of her, and then, "Yes, my brother-in-law," she said.

In a few moments Juan Tomás came back with her. He lighted a candle and came to them where they crouched in a corner and he said, "Apolonia, see to the door, and do not let anyone enter." He was older, Juan Tomás, and he assumed the authority. "Now, my brother," he said.

"I was attacked in the dark," said Kino. "And in the fight I have killed a man."

"Who?" asked Juan Tomás quickly.

"I do not know. It is all darkness—all darkness and shape of darkness."

36 "It is the pearl," said Juan Tomás. "There is a devil in this pearl. You should have sold it and passed on the devil. Perhaps you can still sell it and buy peace for yourself."

And Kino said, "Oh, my brother, an insult has been put on me that is deeper than my life. For on the beach my canoe is broken, my house is burned, and in the brush a dead man lies. Every escape is cut off. You must hide us, my brother."

And Kino, looking closely, saw deep worry come into his brother's eyes and he forestalled him in a possible refusal. "Not for long," he said quickly. "Only until a day has passed and the new night has come. Then we will go."

"I will hide you," said Juan Tomás.

"I do not want to bring danger to you," Kino said. "I know I am like a leprosy. I will go tonight and then you will be safe."

"I will protect you," said Juan Tomás, and he called, "Apolonia, close up the door. Do not even whisper that Kino is here."

37 They sat silently all day in the darkness of the house, and they could hear the neighbors speaking of them. Through the walls of the house they could watch their neighbors raking through the ashes to find the bones. Crouching in the house of Juan Tomás, they heard the shock go into their neighbors' minds at the news of the broken boat. Juan Tomás went out among the neighbors to divert their suspicions, and he gave them theories and ideas of what had happened to Kino and to Juana and to the baby. To one he said, "I think they have gone south along the coast to escape the evil that was on them." And to another, "Kino would never leave the sea. Perhaps he found another boat." And he said, "Apolonia is ill with grief."

And in that day the wind rose up to beat the Gulf and tore the kelps and weeds that lined the shore, and the wind cried through the brush houses and no boat was safe on the water. Then Juan Tomás told among the neighbors, "Kino is gone. If he went to the sea, he is drowned by now." And after each trip among the neighbors Juan Tomás came back with something borrowed. He brought a little woven straw bag of red beans and a gourd full of rice. He borrowed a cup of dried peppers and a block of salt, and he brought in a long working knife, eighteen inches long and heavy, as a small ax, a tool and a weapon. And when Kino saw this knife his eyes lighted up, and he fondled the blade and his thumb tested the edge.

The wind screamed over the Gulf and turned the water white, and the mangroves plunged like frightened cattle, and a fine sandy dust arose from the land and hung in a stifling cloud over the sea. The wind drove off the clouds and skimmed the sky clean and drifted the sand of the country like snow.

Then Juan Tomás, when the evening approached, talked long with his brother. "Where will you go?"

"To the north," said Kino. "I have heard that there are cities in the north."

"Avoid the shore," said Juan Tomás. "They are making a party to search the

36 Discussion Based on what the reader knows about the pearl, do you think the pearl can bring Juana and Kino peace?

37 Discussion How does Juan Tomás protect his brother and Juana?

2. Kino's arms and legs stirred like those of a crushed bug.
3. The canoe of his grandfather, plastered over and over, now had a splintered hole in it.
4. A tall flame leaped up in the dark with a crackling roar.
5. And as he ran a scuttling figure ran toward him.
6. The fierce light of the burning house lighted Kino's face strongly.
7. Juana and Kino could see the leaping flames.

Student Activity 2. Use participles to combine or compress the following sentences. Then, compare your sentences with Steinbeck's on the above pages.

1. They heard the shock go into their neighbors' minds at the news of the boat which had been broken.
2. He brought a little straw bag of red beans. The straw bag was woven.
3. He borrowed a cup of peppers and a block of salt. The peppers had been dried.
4. The mangroves plunged like cattle which had been frightened.
5. A fine sandy dust arose from the land and hung over the sea in a cloud which was stifling.

38 Discussion How is this description of the pearl different from previous descriptions?

39 Discussion Kino now identifies the pearl as becoming part of his soul. The importance of the pearl has heightened. What might this tell the reader about Kino's determination to keep the pearl and all that it stands for?

40 Discussion Steinbeck has used animal imagery in a variety of ways throughout the novel. How is this imagery used here?

shore. The men in the city will look for you. Do you still have the pearl?"

38 "I have it," said Kino. "And I will keep it. I might have given it as a gift, but now it is my misfortune and my life and I will keep it." His eyes were hard and cruel and bitter.

Coyotito whimpered and Juana muttered little magics over him to make him silent.

"The wind is good," said Juan Tomás. "There will be no tracks."

They left quietly in the dark before the moon had risen. The family stood formally in the house of Juan Tomás. Juana carried Coyotito on her back, covered and held in by her head shawl, and the baby slept, cheek turned sideways against her shoulder. The head shawl covered the baby, and one end of it came across Juana's nose to protect her from the evil night air. Juan Tomás embraced his brother with the double embrace and kissed him on both cheeks. "Go with God," he said, and it was like a death. "You will not give up the pearl?"

39 "This pearl has become my soul," said Kino. "If I give it up I shall lose my soul. Go thou also with God."

Chapter 6

The wind blew fierce and strong, and it pelted them with bits of sticks, sand, and little rocks. Juana and Kino gathered their clothing tighter about them, and covered their noses and went out into the world. The sky was brushed clean by the wind and the stars were cold in a black sky. The two walked carefully, and they avoided the center of the town where some sleeper in a doorway might see them pass. For the town closed itself in against the night, and anyone who moved about in the darkness would be noticeable. Kino threaded his way around the edge of the city and turned north, north by the stars, and found the rutted sandy road that led through the brushy country toward Loreto[1] where the miraculous Virgin has her station.[2]

Kino could feel the blown sand against his ankles and he was glad, for he knew there would be no tracks. The little light from the stars made out for him the narrow road through the brushy country. And Kino could hear the pad of Juana's feet behind him. He went quickly and quietly, and Juana trotted behind him to keep up.

Some ancient thing stirred in Kino. Through his fear of dark and the devils that haunt the night, there came a rush of exhilaration; some animal thing was moving in him so that he was cautious and wary and dangerous; some ancient thing out of the past of his people was alive in him. The wind was at his back and the stars guided him. 4
The wind cried and whisked in the brush, and the family went on monotonously, hour after hour. They passed no one and saw no one. At last, to their right, the waning moon arose, and when it came up the wind died down, and the land was still.

Now they could see the little road ahead of them, deep cut with sand-drifted wheel tracks. With the wind gone there would be footprints, but they were a good distance from the town and perhaps their tracks might not be noticed. Kino walked carefully in a wheel rut, and Juana followed in his path. One big cart, going to the town in the morning, could wipe out every trace of their passage.

All night they walked and never changed their pace. Once Coyotito awakened, and Juana shifted him in front of her and soothed him until he went to sleep again.

---

1. Loreto (lō rā' tō): A town on the western coast of Baja California.
2. station: Religious shrine.

And the evils of the night were about them. The coyotes cried and laughed in the brush, and the owls screeched and hissed over their heads. And once some large animal lumbered away, crackling the undergrowth as it went. And Kino gripped the handle of the big working knife and took a sense of protection from it.

The music of the pearl was triumphant in Kino's head, and the quiet melody of the
41 family underlay it, and they wove themselves into the soft padding of sandaled feet in the dust. All night they walked, and in the first dawn Kino searched the roadside for a covert to lie in during the day. He found his place near to the road, a little clearing where deer might have lain, and it was curtained thickly with the dry brittle trees that lined the road. And when Juana had seated herself and had settled to nurse the baby, Kino went back to the road. He broke a branch and carefully swept the footprints where they had turned from the roadway. And then, in the first light, he heard the creak of a wagon, and he crouched beside the road and watched a heavy two-wheeled cart go by, drawn by slouching oxen. And when it had passed out of sight, he went back to the roadway and looked at the rut and found that the footprints were gone. And again he swept out his traces and went back to Juana.

She gave him the soft corncakes Apolonia had packed for them, and after a while she slept a little. But Kino sat on the ground and stared at the earth in front of him. He watched the ants moving, a little column of them near to his foot, and he put his foot in their path. Then the column climbed over his instep and continued on its way, and Kino left his foot there and watched them move over it.

The sun arose hotly. They were not near
42 the Gulf now, and the air was dry and hot so that the brush cricked[3] with heat and a good resinous smell[4] came from it. And when Juana awakened, when the sun was high, Kino told her things she knew already.

"Beware of that kind of tree there," he said, pointing. "Do not touch it, for if you do and then touch your eyes, it will blind you. And beware of the tree that bleeds. See, that one over there. For if you break it the red blood will flow from it, and it is evil luck." And she nodded and smiled a little at him, for she knew these things.

"Will they follow us?" she asked. "Do you think they will try to find us?"

"They will try," said Kino. "Whoever finds us will take the pearl. Oh, they will try."

And Juana said, "Perhaps the dealers
were right and the pearl has no value. Per- 43
haps this has all been an illusion."

Kino reached into his clothes and brought out the pearl. He let the sun play on it until it burned in his eyes. "No," he said, "they would not have tried to steal it if it had been valueless."

"Do you know who attacked you? Was it the dealers?"

"I do not know," he said. "I didn't see them."

He looked into his pearl to find his vision. "When we sell it at last, I will have a rifle," he said, and he looked into the shining surface for his rifle, but he saw only a
huddled dark body on the ground with shin- 44
ing blood dripping from its throat. And he said quickly, "We will be married in a great church." And in the pearl he saw Juana with her beaten face crawling home through the night. "Our son must learn to read," he

---

3. **cricked** (krikt) *v.*: Twisted.
4. **resinous** (rez′ 'n əs) **smell:** Odor of the pitchy substance that is discharged from some trees, such as evergreens.

41 **Discussion** How is the music of the pearl triumphant? Why does Kino believe it is triumphant?

42 **Literary Focus** Kino's explanations to Juana convey a certain attitude about her. Is this consistent with the way she has been portrayed throughout?

43 **Discussion** Juana wonders if the value of the pearl has been an illusion. Certainly the pearl and all that it represents has been an illusion to Kino and those in the town closely connected with it. Discuss Steinbeck's use of illusion. Have students comment on other stories they have read that were based on illusion.

44 **Literary Focus** Steinbeck now helps the reader to see the signs of illusion and reality. How does he do this?

45 Critical Thinking and Reading What causes the trackers to hunt for Kino?

46 Discussion Discuss the animal imagery. How is Kino similar to prey?

said frantically. And there in the pearl Coyotito's face, thick and feverish from the medicine.

And Kino thrust the pearl back into his clothing, and the music of the pearl had become sinister in his ears, and it was interwoven with the music of evil.

The hot sun beat on the earth so that Kino and Juana moved into the lacy shade of the brush, and small gray birds scampered on the ground in the shade. In the heat of the day Kino relaxed and covered his eyes with his hat and wrapped his blanket about his face to keep the flies off, and he slept.

But Juana did not sleep. She sat quiet as a stone and her face was quiet. Her mouth was still swollen where Kino had struck her, and big flies buzzed around the cut on her chin. But she sat as still as a sentinel, and when Coyotito awakened she placed him on the ground in front of her and watched him wave his arms and kick his feet, and he smiled and gurgled at her until she smiled too. She picked up a little twig from the ground and tickled him, and she gave him water from the gourd she carried in her bundle.

Kino stirred in a dream, and he cried out in a guttural voice, and his hand moved in symbolic fighting. And then he moaned and sat up suddenly, his eyes wide and his nostrils flaring. He listened and heard only the cricking heat and the hiss of distance.

"What is it?" Juana asked.

"Hush," he said.

"You were dreaming."

"Perhaps." But he was restless, and when she gave him a corncake from her store he paused in his chewing to listen. He was uneasy and nervous; he glanced over his shoulder; he lifted the big knife and felt its edge. When Coyotito gurgled on the ground Kino said, "Keep him quiet."

"What is the matter?" Juana asked.

"I don't know."

He listened again, an animal light in his eyes. He stood up then, silently; and crouched low, he threaded his way through the brush toward the road. But he did not step into the road; he crept into the cover of a thorny tree and peered out along the way he had come.

And then he saw them moving along. His body stiffened and he drew down his head and peeked out from under a fallen branch. In the distance he could see three figures, two on foot and one on horseback. But he knew what they were, and a chill of fear went through him. Even in the distance he could see the two on foot moving slowly along, bent low to the ground. Here, one would pause and look at the earth, while the other joined him. They were the trackers, 45
they could follow the trail of a bighorn sheep in the stone mountains. They were as sensitive as hounds. Here, he and Juana might have stepped out of the wheel rut, and these people from the inland, these hunters, could follow, could read a broken straw or a little tumbled pile of dust. Behind them, on a horse, was a dark man, his nose covered with a blanket, and across his saddle a rifle gleamed in the sun.

Kino lay as rigid as the tree limb. He barely breathed, and his eyes went to the place where he had swept out the track. Even the sweeping might be a message to the trackers. He knew these inland hunters. In a country where there was little game they managed to live because of their ability 46
to hunt, and they were hunting him. They scuttled over the ground like animals and found a sign and crouched over it while the horseman waited.

The trackers whined a little, like excited dogs on a warming trail. Kino slowly drew his big knife to his hand and made it ready. He knew what he must do. If the trackers found the swept place, he must leap for the horseman, kill him quickly and take the rifle. That was his only chance in the world. And as the three drew nearer on the road, Kino dug little pits with his sandaled toes so that he could leap without warning, so that his feet would not slip. He had only a little vision under the fallen limb.

Now Juana, back in her hidden place, heard the pad of the horse's hoofs, and Coyotito gurgled. She took him up quickly and put him under her shawl and gave him her breast and he was silent.

When the trackers came near, Kino could see only their legs and only the legs of the horse from under the fallen branch. He saw the dark horny feet of the men and their ragged white clothes, and he heard the creak of leather of the saddle and the clink
47 of spurs. The trackers stopped at the swept place and studied it, and the horseman stopped. The horse flung his head up against the bit and the bit-roller clicked under his tongue and the horse snorted. Then the dark trackers turned and studied the horse and watched his ears.

Kino was not breathing, but his back arched a little and the muscles of his arms and legs stood out with tension and a line of sweat formed on his upper lip. For a long moment the trackers bent over the road, and then they moved on slowly, studying the ground ahead of them, and the horseman moved after them. The trackers scuttled along, stopping, looking, and hurrying on. They would be back, Kino knew. They would be circling and searching, peeping, stooping, and they would come back sooner or later to his covered track.

He slid backward and did not bother to cover his tracks. He could not; too many little signs were there, too many broken twigs and scuffed places and displaced stones. And there was a panic in Kino now, a panic of flight. The trackers would find his trail, he knew it. There was no escape, except in flight. He edged away from the road and went quickly and silently to the hidden place where Juana was. She looked up at him in question.

"Trackers," he said. "Come!"

And then a helplessness and a hopelessness swept over him, and his face went black and his eyes were sad. "Perhaps I should let them take me."

Instantly Juana was on her feet and her hand lay on his arm. "You have the pearl," she cried hoarsely. "Do you think they would take you back alive to say they had
stolen it?" 48

His hand strayed limply to the place where the pearl was hidden under his clothes. "They will find it," he said weakly.

"Come," she said. "Come!"

And when he did not respond, "Do you think they would let me live? Do you think they would let the little one here live?"

Her goading struck into his brain; his lips snarled and his eyes were fierce again. "Come," he said. "We will go into the mountains. Maybe we can lose them in the mountains."

Frantically he gathered the gourds and the little bags that were their property. Kino carried a bundle in his left hand, but the big knife swung free in his right hand. He parted the brush for Juana and they hurried to the west, toward the high stone mountains. They trotted quickly through the tangle of the undergrowth. This was panic flight. Kino did not try to conceal his passage as he trotted, kicking the stones, knocking the telltale leaves from the little trees. The high sun streamed down on the dry creaking

47 **Discussion** How do these sounds create the mood of this scene?

48 **Discussion** Discuss the dialogue between Kino and Juana. What do their words convey?

Humanities Note

Fine art, *Cactus on the Plains (Hands)*, 1931, by Diego Rivera. This painting shows rugged terrain. Ask students to identify and discuss the relationship between this painting and the plot. What event in the novel might take place here? Have students discuss how the landscape shown differs from the environment Kino and Juana live in each day. Have students support their answers with specific details from the story.

CACTUS ON THE PLAINS (HANDS), 1931
Diego Rivera
Edsel and Eleanor Ford House
Grosse Pointe Shores, Michigan

earth so that even the vegetation ticked in protest. But ahead were the naked granite mountains, rising out of erosion rubble and standing monolithic against the sky. And Kino ran for the high place, as nearly all animals do when they are pursued.

This land was waterless, furred with the cacti which could store water and with the great-rooted brush which could reach deep into the earth for a little moisture and get along on very little. And underfoot was not soil but broken rock, split into small cubes, great slabs, but none of it water-rounded. Little tufts of sad dry grass grew between
49 the stones, grass that had sprouted with one single rain and headed,[5] dropped its seed, and died. Horned toads watched the family go by and turned their little pivoting dragon heads. And now and then a great jackrabbit, disturbed in his shade, bumped away and hid behind the nearest rock. The singing heat lay over this desert country, and ahead the stone mountains looked cool and welcoming.

And Kino fled. He knew what would happen. A little way along the road the trackers would become aware that they had missed the path, and they would come back, searching and judging, and in a little while they would find the place where Kino and Juana had rested. From there it would be easy for them—these little stones, the fallen leaves and the whipped branches, the scuffed places where a foot had slipped. Kino could see them in his mind, slipping along the track, whining a little with eagerness, and behind them, dark and half disinterested, the horseman with the rifle. His work would come last, for he would not take them
50 back. Oh, the music of evil sang loud in Kino's head now, it sang with the whine of heat and with the dry ringing of snake rattles. It was not large and overwhelming now, but secret and poisonous, and the pounding of his heart gave it undertone and rhythm.

The way began to rise, and as it did the rocks grew larger. But now Kino had put a little distance between his family and the trackers. Now, on the first rise, he rested. He climbed a great boulder and looked back over the shimmering country, but he could not see his enemies, not even the tall horseman riding through the brush. Juana had squatted in the shade of the boulder. She raised her bottle of water to Coyotito's lips; his little dried tongue sucked greedily at it. She looked up at Kino when he came back; she saw him examine her ankles, cut and scratched from the stones and brush, and she covered them quickly with her skirt. Then she handed the bottle to him, but he shook his head. Her eyes were bright in her tired face. Kino moistened his cracked lips with his tongue.

"Juana," he said, "I will go on and you will hide. I will lead them into the mountains, and when they have gone past, you will go north to Loreto or to Santa Rosalia.[6] Then, if I can escape them, I will come to you. It is the only safe way."

She looked full into his eyes for a moment. "No," she said. "We go with you." 51

"I can go faster alone," he said harshly. "You will put the little one in more danger if you go with me."

"No," said Juana.

"You must. It is the wise thing and it is my wish," he said.

"No," said Juana.

He looked then for weakness in her face,

5. **headed** (hed′ əd) *v.*: Grew to maturity.

6. **Santa Rosalia** (san′ tə rō za′ lē ə): A town on the western coast of Baja California.

49 Reading Strategy Summarize the description of the terrain. How is the terrain fitting with the development of the story? How might this act as a foreshadowing?

50 Discussion How is this description of the music of evil different from any other?

51 Discussion What does this conversation tell the reader about Juana? How is she changing?

52 **Discussion** Why is their flight no longer one of "panic"?

53 **Reading Strategy** Steinbeck uses symbolism to convey meaning throughout the story *The Pearl.* Summarize what the message of this paragraph is; be attentive to the symbolism, particulary in the last sentence.

for fear or irresolution,[7] and there was none. Her eyes were very bright. He shrugged his shoulders helplessly then, but he had taken
52 strength from her. When they moved on it was no longer panic flight.

The country, as it rose toward the mountains, changed rapidly. Now there were long outcroppings of granite with deep crevices between, and Kino walked on bare unmarkable stone when he could and leaped from ledge to ledge. He knew that wherever the trackers lost his path they must circle and lose time before they found it again. And so he did not go straight for the mountains any more; he moved in zigzags, and sometimes he cut back to the south and left a sign and then went toward the mountains over bare stone again. And the path rose steeply now, so that he panted a little as he went.

The sun moved downward toward the bare stone teeth of the mountains, and Kino set his direction for a dark and shadowy cleft in the range. If there were any water at all, it would be there where he could see, even in the distance, a hint of foliage. And if there were any passage through the smooth stone range, it would be by this same deep cleft. It had its danger, for the trackers would think of it too, but the empty water bottle did not let that consideration enter. And as the sun lowered, Kino and Juana struggled wearily up the steep slope toward the cleft.

High in the gray stone mountains, under a frowning peak, a little spring bubbled out of a rupture in the stone. It was fed by shade-preserved snow in the summer, and now and then it died completely and bare rocks and dry algae were on its bottom. But nearly always it gushed out, cold and clean and lovely. In the times when the quick rains fell, it might become a freshet and send its column of white water crashing down the mountain cleft, but nearly always it was a lean little spring. It bubbled out into a pool and then fell a hundred feet to another pool, and this one, overflowing, dropped again, so that it continued, down and down, until it came to the rubble of the upland, and there it disappeared altogether. There wasn't much left of it then anyway, for every time it fell over an escarpment the thirsty air drank it, and it splashed from the pools to the dry vegetation. The animals from miles around came to drink from the little pools, and the wild sheep and the deer, the pumas and raccoons, and the mice—all came to drink. And the birds which spent
the day in the brushland came at night to 53
the little pools that were like steps in the mountain cleft. Beside this tiny stream, wherever enough earth collected for roothold, colonies of plants grew, wild grape and little palms, maidenhair fern, hibiscus, and tall pampas grass[8] with feathery rods raised above the spike leaves. And in the pool lived frogs and water-skaters, and waterworms crawled on the bottom of the pool. Everything that loved water came to these few shallow places. The cats took their prey there, and strewed feathers and lapped water through their bloody teeth. The little pools were places of life because of the water, and places of killing because of the water, too.

The lowest step, where the stream collected before it tumbled down a hundred feet and disappeared into the rubbly desert, was a little platform of stone and sand. Only a pencil of water fell into the pool, but it was enough to keep the pool full and to keep the ferns green in the underhang of the cliff, and wild grape climbed the stone mountain

7. **irresolution** (ir rez′ ə lo͞o′ shən) *n.*: Indecisiveness.

8. **pampas** (pam′ pəs) **grass:** Grass that grows on treeless plains in certain areas of the south.

and all manner of little plants found comfort here. The freshets had made a small sandy beach through which the pool flowed, and bright green watercress grew in the damp sand. The beach was cut and scarred and padded by the feet of animals that had come to drink and to hunt.

54 The sun had passed over the stone mountains when Kino and Juana struggled up the steep broken slope and came at last to the water. From this step they could look out over the sunbeaten desert to the blue Gulf in the distance. They came utterly weary to the pool, and Juana slumped to her knees and first washed Coyotito's face and then filled her bottle and gave him a drink. And the baby was weary and petulant,[9] and he cried softly until Juana gave him her breast, and then he gurgled and clucked against her. Kino drank long and thirstily at the pool. For a moment, then, he stretched out beside the water and relaxed all his muscles and watched Juana feeding the baby, and then he got to his feet and went to the edge of the step where the water slipped over, and he searched the distance carefully. His eyes set on a point and he became rigid. Far down the slope he could see the two trackers; they were little more than dots or scurrying ants and behind them a larger ant.

Juana had turned to look at him and she saw his back stiffen.

"How far?" she asked quietly.

"They will be here by evening," said Kino. He looked up the long steep chimney of the cleft where the water came down. "We must go west," he said, and his eyes searched the stone shoulder behind the cleft. And thirty feet up on the gray shoulder he saw a series of little erosion caves. He slipped off his sandals and clambered up to them, gripping the bare stone with his toes, and he looked into the shallow caves. They were only a few feet deep, wind-hollowed scoops, but they sloped slightly downward and back. Kino crawled into the largest one and lay down and knew that he could not be seen from the outside. Quickly he went back to Juana.

"You must go up there. Perhaps they will not find us there," he said.

Without question she filled her water bottle to the top, and then Kino helped her up to the shallow cave and brought up the packages of food and passed them to her. And Juana sat in the cave entrance and watched him. She saw that he did not try to erase their tracks in the sand. Instead, he climbed up the brush cliff beside the water, clawing and tearing at the ferns and wild grape as he went. And when he had climbed a hundred feet to the next bench, he came down again. He looked carefully at the smooth rock shoulder toward the cave to see that there was no trace of passage, and last he climbed up and crept into the cave beside Juana.

"When they go up," he said, "we will slip away, down to the lowlands again. I am afraid only that the baby may cry. You must see that he does not cry." 55

"He will not cry," she said, and she raised the baby's face to her own and looked into his eyes and he stared solemnly back at her.

"He knows," said Juana.

Now Kino lay in the cave entrance, his chin braced on his crossed arms, and he watched the blue shadow of the mountain move out across the brushy desert below until it reached the Gulf, and the long twilight of the shadow was over the land.

The trackers were long in coming, as though they had trouble with the trail Kino had left. It was dusk when they came at last

9. petulant (pech′ ə lənt) *adj.*: Impatient; irritable.

54 Discussion Kino is becoming more and more like a hunted animal. What images does Steinbeck use to convey this?

55 Discussion What does this conversation between Kino and Juana tell the reader?

56 **Critical Thinking and Reading** Why does Kino decide to get the rifle from one of the trackers?

57 **Enrichment** What do you think Juana and Kino feel as Kino departs?

58 **Discussion** In previous chapters Juana combines prayer and magic. Does it seem fitting that she would say both of these now? Why or why not?

to the little pool. And all three were on foot now, for a horse could not climb the last steep slope. From above they were thin figures in the evening. The two trackers scurried about on the little beach, and they saw Kino's progress up the cliff before they drank. The man with the rifle sat down and rested himself, and the trackers squatted near him, and in the evening the points of their cigarettes glowed and receded. And then Kino could see that they were eating, and the soft murmur of their voices came to him.

Then darkness fell, deep and black in the mountain cleft. The animals that used the pool came near and smelled men there and drifted away again into the darkness.

He heard a murmur behind him. Juana was whispering, "Coyotito." She was begging him to be quiet. Kino heard the baby whimper, and he knew from the muffled sounds that Juana had covered his head with her shawl.

Down on the beach a match flared, and in its momentary light Kino saw that two of the men were sleeping, curled up like dogs, while the third watched, and he saw the glint of the rifle in the match light. And then the match died, but it left a picture on Kino's eyes. He could see it, just how each man was, two sleeping curled up and the third squatting in the sand with the rifle between his knees.

Kino moved silently back into the cave. Juana's eyes were two sparks reflecting a low star. Kino crawled quietly close to her and he put his lips near to her cheek.

56 "There is a way," he said.

"But they will kill you."

"If I get first to the one with the rifle," Kino said, "I must get to him first, then I will be all right. Two are sleeping."

Her hand crept out from under her shawl and gripped his arm. "They will see your white clothes in the starlight."

"No," he said. "And I must go before moonrise."

He searched for a soft word and then gave it up. "If they kill me," he said, "lie quietly. And when they are gone away, go to Loreto."

Her hand shook a little, holding his wrist.

"There is no choice," he said. "It is the only way. They will find us in the morning." 57

Her voice trembled a little. "Go with God," she said.

He peered closely at her and he could see her large eyes. His hand fumbled out and found the baby, and for a moment his palm lay on Coyotito's head. And then Kino raised his hand and touched Juana's cheek, and she held her breath.

Against the sky in the cave entrance Juana could see that Kino was taking off his white clothes, for dirty and ragged though they were, they would show up against the dark night. His own brown skin was a better protection for him. And then she saw how he hooked his amulet[10] neck-string about the horn handle of his great knife, so that it hung down in front of him and left both hands free. He did not come back to her. For a moment his body was black in the cave entrance, crouched and silent, and then he was gone.

Juana moved to the entrance and looked out. She peered like an owl from the hole in the mountain, and the baby slept under the blanket on her back, his face turned sideways against her neck and shoulder. 58 She could feel his warm breath against her skin, and Juana whispered her combination of

---

10. amulet (am' yə lit) *adj.*: Charm worn to protect against evil.

Grammar in Action

Using **specific verbs** that are both colorful and vivid will make your meaning clear and your sentences interesting. Study the following pairs of sentences. The first uses a common, less specific verb; the second is Steinbeck's.

The wind hit them with bits of sticks. . . .
[The wind] *pelted* them with bits of sticks . . .

Kino found his way around the edge of the city . . .
Kino *threaded* his way around the edge of the city . . .

Pelted tells us that they were hit repeatedly; *threaded* tells us Kino moved in a winding, complicated manner.

Student Activity 1. Choose verbs from the list to complete the following sentences.

hissed, gurgled, scampered
lumbered, gripped, burned
screeched

prayer and magic, her Hail Marys and her ancient intercession, against the black unhuman things.

The night seemed a little less dark when she looked out, and to the east there was a lightening in the sky, down near the horizon where the moon would show. And, looking down, she could see the cigarette of the man on watch.

Kino edged like a slow lizard down the smooth rock shoulder. He had turned his neck-string so that the great knife hung down from his back and could not clash against the stone. His spread fingers gripped the mountain, and his bare toes found support through contact, and even his chest lay against the stone so that he would not slip. For any sound, a rolling pebble or a sigh, a little slip of flesh on rock, would rouse the watchers below. Any sound that was not
59 germane[11] to the night would make them alert. But the night was not silent; the little tree frogs that lived near the stream twittered like birds, and the high metallic ringing of the cicadas filled the mountain cleft. And Kino's own music was in his head, the music of the enemy, low and pulsing, nearly asleep. But the Song of the Family had become as fierce and sharp and feline as the snarl of a female puma. The family song was alive now and driving him down on the dark enemy. The harsh cicada seemed to take up its melody, and the twittering tree frogs called little phrases of it.

And Kino crept silently as a shadow down the smooth mountain face. One bare foot moved a few inches and the toes touched the stone and gripped, and the other foot a few inches, and then the palm of one hand a little downward, and then the other hand, until the whole body, without seeming to move, had moved. Kino's mouth was open so that even his breath would make no sound, for he knew that he was not invisible. If the watcher, sensing movement, looked at the dark place against the stone which was his body, he could see him. Kino must move so slowly he would not draw the watcher's eyes. It took him a long time to reach the bottom and to crouch behind a little dwarf palm. His heart thundered in his chest and his hands and face were wet with sweat. He crouched and took great slow long breaths to calm himself.

Only twenty feet separated him from the enemy now, and he tried to remember the ground between. Was there any stone which might trip him in his rush? He kneaded his legs against cramp and found that his muscles were jerking after their long tension. And then he looked apprehensively to the east. The moon would rise in a few moments
now, and he must attack before it rose. He 60
could see the outline of the watcher, but the sleeping men were below his vision. It was the watcher Kino must find—must find quickly and without hesitation. Silently he drew the amulet string over his shoulder and loosened the loop from the horn handle of his great knife.

He was too late, for as he rose from his crouch the silver edge of the moon slipped above the eastern horizon, and Kino sank back behind his bush.

It was an old and ragged moon, but it threw hard light and hard shadow into the mountain cleft, and now Kino could see the seated figure of the watcher on the little beach beside the pool. The watcher gazed full at the moon, and then he lighted another cigarette, and the match illumined his dark face for a moment. There could be no waiting now; when the watcher turned his

---

11. germane (jər mān′) *adj.*: Truly related.

59 Literary Focus Note the vivid description of nature. How does this emphasize Kino's predicament?

60 Reading Strategy Summarize these paragraphs. Tell the importance of time and timing.

1. When Coyotito ________ on the ground Kino said, "Keep him quiet."
2. The owls ________ and ________ over Kino's head.
3. He let the sun play on the pearl until it ________ in his eyes.
4. Some large animal ________ away, crackling the undergrowth as it went.
5. Small gray birds ________ on the ground in the shade.
6. Kino ________ the handle of the big working knife.

Student Activity 2. Rewrite the following sentences, substituting a more specific, vivid verb for the verb underlined.

1. The two trackers *moved* about on the little beach.
2. Her voice *shook* a little.
3. She *watched* like an owl from the hole in the mountain.
4. Kino *moved* like a slow lizard down the smooth rock shoulder.
5. His heart *beat* in his chest.
6. The match *lit up* his dark face for a moment.

61 Enrichment Coyotito's name means "little coyote." What do you think the significance might be of the trackers thinking Coyotito's cry is that of a coyote pup?

62 Literary Focus Discuss the role of sound in the resolution of the conflict between Kino and the trackers.

63 Reading Strategy Based on what you know about Kino, what might you predict has happened?

64 Discussion Reread Steinbeck's description of Kino and Juana as they return to their village. How has their relationship changed? What does Steinbeck mean when he writes that "they had gone through pain and had come out on the other side"? Does it mean that Kino and Juana will be all right now that the experience is over? Why or why not?

head, Kino must leap. His legs were as tight as wound springs.

And then from above came a little murmuring cry. The watcher turned his head to listen and then he stood up, and one of the sleepers stirred on the ground and awakened and asked quietly, "What is it?"

"I don't know," said the watcher. "It sounded like a cry, almost like a human—like a baby."

The man who had been sleeping said,
61 "You can't tell. Some coyote bitch with a litter. I've heard a coyote pup cry like a baby."

The sweat rolled in drops down Kino's forehead and fell into his eyes and burned them. The little cry came again and the watcher looked up the side of the hill to the dark cave.

"Coyote maybe," he said, and Kino heard the harsh click as he cocked the rifle.

"If it's a coyote, this will stop it," the watcher said as he raised the gun.

Kino was in midleap when the gun crashed and the barrel-flash made a picture on his eyes. The great knife swung and crunched hollowly. It bit through neck and deep into chest, and Kino was a terrible machine now. He grasped the rifle even as he wrenched free his knife. His strength and his movement and his speed were a machine. He whirled and struck the head of the
62 seated man like a melon. The third man scrabbled away like a crab, slipped into the pool, and then he began to climb frantically, to climb up the cliff where the water penciled down. His hands and feet threshed in the tangle of the wild grapevine, and he whimpered and gibbered as he tried to get up. But Kino had become as cold and deadly as steel. Deliberately he threw the lever of the rifle, and then he raised the gun and aimed deliberately and fired. He saw his enemy tumble backward into the pool, and Kino strode to the water. In the moonlight he could see the frantic frightened eyes, and Kino aimed and fired between the eyes.

And then Kino stood uncertainly. Something was wrong, some signal was trying to get through to his brain. Tree frogs and cicadas were silent now. And then Kino's
brain cleared from its red concentration and 63
he knew the sound—the keening, moaning, rising hysterical cry from the little cave in the side of the stone mountain, the cry of death.

Everyone in La Paz remembers the return of the family; there may be some old ones who saw it, but those whose fathers and whose grandfathers told it to them remember it nevertheless. It is an event that happened to everyone.

It was late in the golden afternoon when the first little boys ran hysterically in the town and spread the word that Kino and Juana were coming back. And everyone hurried to see them. The sun was settling toward the western mountains and the shadows on the ground were long. And perhaps that was what left the deep impression on those who saw them.

The two came from the rutted country road into the city, and they were not walking
in single file, Kino ahead and Juana behind, 64
as usual, but side by side. The sun was behind them and their long shadows stalked ahead, and they seemed to carry two towers of darkness with them. Kino had a rifle across his arm and Juana carried her shawl like a sack over her shoulder. And in it was a small limp heavy bundle. The shawl was crusted with dried blood, and the bundle swayed a little as she walked. Her face was hard and lined and leathery with fatigue and with the tightness with which she fought fatigue. And her wide eyes stared inward on herself. She was as remote and as removed as Heaven. Kino's lips were thin

Primary Source

In *Twentieth Century Views,* Harry Morris draws the following comparisons and contrasts between *The Pearl* and the legend from which it sprang:

> We see in Steinbeck's source all the major elements of his expanded version: the Mexican peasant, the discovered pearl, the belief that the pearl will make the finder free, the corrupt brokers, the attacks, the flight, the return, and the disposal of the pearl. But there are also additions and alterations. The episodes of the doctor and the priest are added; the motives for retaining the pearl are changed. While the additions add perhaps some realism at the same time that they increase the impact of the allegory, the alterations tend to diminish the realistic aspects of the hero. Kino becomes almost unbelievably sophisticated. The boy wants only to be drunk forever; Kino wants his son educated. The boy wants to buy prayers for his own soul and for the souls of his relatives in Purgatory; Kino distrusts the priest who asks that the church be remembered when

and his jaws tight, and the people say that he carried fear with him, that he was as dangerous as a rising storm. The people say that the two seemed to be removed from human experience; that they had gone through pain and had come out on the other side; that there was almost a magical protection about them. And those people who had rushed to see them crowded back and let them pass and did not speak to them.

Kino and Juana walked through the city as though it were not there. Their eyes glanced neither right nor left nor up nor down, but stared only straight ahead. Their legs moved a little jerkily, like well-made wooden dolls, and they carried pillars of black fear about them. And as they walked through the stone and plaster city brokers peered at them from barred windows and servants put one eye to a slitted gate and mothers turned the faces of their youngest children inward against their skirts. Kino and Juana strode side by side through the stone and plaster city and down among the brush houses, and the neighbors stood back and let them pass. Juan Tomás raised his hand in greeting and did not say the greeting and left his hand in the air for a moment uncertainly.

In Kino's ears the Song of the Family was as fierce as a cry. He was immune and terrible, and his song had become a battle cry. They trudged past the burned square
65 where their house had been without even looking at it. They cleared the brush that edged the beach and picked their way down the shore toward the water. And they did not look toward Kino's broken canoe.

And when they came to the water's edge they stopped and stared out over the Gulf. And then Kino laid the rifle down, and he dug among his clothes, and then he held the
66 great pearl in his hand. He looked into its surface and it was gray and ulcerous. Evil faces peered from it into his eyes, and he saw the light of burning. And in the surface of the pearl he saw the frantic eyes of the man in the pool. And in the surface of the

THE SOB
David Alfaro Siqueiros, 1939
The Museum of Modern Art, New York

Humanities Note

Fine art, *The Sob,* David Alfaro Siqueiros. The artist is a Mexican-born painter (1896). Like Rivera he became famous through painting murals. He is responsible for many politically inspired, technically innovative, murals that he executed in Mexico and in the United States.

The quality, source, and direction of light used by artists creates contrast and establishes a mood. Ask students to interpret the painting. What is its mood? What elements of the painting create the mood? Do students feel the painting would be more or less effective if the figure's eyes were shown? Have students identify and discuss the elements and events of the story this painting might relate to.

65 **Critical Thinking and Reading** What has caused Kino and Juana to return to La Paz?

66 **Critical Thinking and Reading** Contrast the description of the pearl at this point with its earlier descriptions. What does this contrast say about material wealth?

the pearl is sold, closes his fist only more tightly about the pearl, determined instead to buy a rifle. The boy's desires are primitive; they are consonant with his origins and his intellect, crafty and wise as he may be. Kino's wants are sophisticated; he sees in the pearl not the objects that can be bought, but beyond. Coyotito's education will make the Indians free, a social, political, and economic sophistication; new clothes and a church wedding will give Kino and Juana position and respectability, again a social sophistication. With the rifle all other things were possible . . . Later, ironically, all that the rifle gives to Kino is the power to destroy human life; and in this irony, the symbolic import of the pearl-rifle fusion gives to the allegory the very complication that . . . is lacking. The pearl is not clearly good or evil, black or white.

pearl he saw Coyotito lying in the little cave with the top of his head shot away. And the pearl was ugly; it was gray, like a malignant growth. And Kino heard the music of the pearl, distorted and insane. Kino's hand shook a little, and he turned slowly to Juana and held the pearl out to her. She stood
67 beside him, still holding her dead bundle over her shoulder. She looked at the pearl in his hand for a moment and then she looked into Kino's eyes and said softly, "No, you."

And Kino drew back his arm and flung
68 the pearl with all his might. Kino and Juana watched it go, winking and glimmering under the setting sun. They saw the little splash in the distance, and they stood side by side watching the place for a long time.

And the pearl settled into the lovely green water and dropped toward the bottom. The waving branches of the algae called to it and beckoned to it. The lights on its surface were green and lovely. It settled down to the sand bottom among the fernlike plants. Above, the surface of the water was a green mirror. And the pearl lay on the floor of the sea. A crab scampering over the bottom raised a little cloud of sand, and when it settled the pearl was gone.

And the music of the pearl drifted to a whisper and disappeared.

THINKING ABOUT THE SELECTION

Recalling

1. What do the pearl dealers tell Kino about his pearl? Explain Kino's decision after visiting the pearl dealers.
2. For what reason does Kino fear the trackers? What sound does Kino hear after he kills the trackers?
3. What does Kino do with the pearl at the end of the story?

Interpreting

4. Why does Kino hear "evil music" after the pearl dealer names his price?
5. Compare and contrast reactions to Kino's turning down the 1500 pesos.
6. What does Kino mean at the end of Chapter 4 when he says: "I am a man."
7. What does Kino mean when he says: "This pearl has become my soul. If I give it up I shall lose my soul"?
8. When Kino hands Juana the pearl to dispose of, why does she insist that he throw it away?

Applying

9. Do you agree with Kino's decision to go to the capital to sell his pearl instead of accepting one of the pearl dealers' offers? Give reasons for your answer.
10. If Kino and Juana had never found the pearl, their life probably would not have changed. Do you think any good came of their discovery? Give reasons for your answer.

67 **Discussion** Why do you think Juana wants Kino to throw the pearl away?

68 **Enrichment** What do you think lies ahead for Kino and Juana now that they have thrown the pearl away? Discuss their future in light of the tragedy they have experienced.

69 **Literary Focus** The conflict in the novel is parallel to the sounds in the novel. Trace the changes in sounds and compare these to the action of the conflict. What is meant by the last line of the novel, "And the music of the pearl drifted to a whisper and disappeared"?

Reader's Response Of *The Pearl,* Steinbeck says, "If this story is a parable, perhaps everyone takes his own meaning from it and reads his own life into it." What meaning do you take from *The Pearl?* How do you read your life into the allegory?

Closure and Extension

ANSWERS TO THINKING ABOUT THE SELECTION

Recalling

1. They say the pearl is like "fool's gold" and that it is too big and no one would buy it. Kino decides to go to the capital to try to sell it for more money.
2. Kino has killed one of the "dark ones"; he is afraid the trackers will seek revenge and in doing so will kill him and get the pearl. Kino hears the cry of death after he kills the trackers.
3. Kino throws the pearl into the Gulf.

Interpreting

4. He feels that the pearl dealer is cheating him.
5. The neighbors are divided in regard to what they think Kino should do—some think he is being cheated by the pearl buyers, others think that Kino is fighting the established procedures. The comments of the pearl buyers influence their views regarding the value of the pearl.
6. Answers will differ. Suggested response: Kino means that as a man and the head of his family he will do anything in his determination to protect them and improve their lives.
7. Answers will differ. Suggested response: Kino means that he has identified so strongly with his dreams that the pearl can fulfill that his self-image would be damaged if he gave up his dreams.
8. She wants him to prove that he no longer wants it.

Applying

9. Answers will differ. Some students might say that if Kino had taken the 1500 pesos that were offered him, less harm would have come his way; others might say that by not allowing himself to be cheated by the pearl buyers Kino made a powerful—and perhaps admirable statement—about his rejection of that dishonest system.
10. Answers will differ. Some students might say that since Kino and Juana are still young and can have more children, it will help them in the future to know how greed can change other people and themselves.

ANSWERS TO ANALYZING LITERATURE

1. The major events include the visit with the pearl buyers, the intruder striking a blow at Kino, Juana being struck by Kino for attempting to

ANALYZING LITERATURE

Understanding Plot and Theme

Plot, the sequence of related events or incidents that make up a literary work, usually involves conflict, climax, and resolution. The first conflict in *The Pearl* is the problem caused by Coyotito's scorpion sting. The sting generates the conflicts that follow throughout the plot. The climax, or the story's highest point of interest, comes near the end of the novel. It is followed by the resolution, when the characters resolve the conflict, and the writer reveals the outcome of the plot.

Theme is the universal truth or message the author conveys. A novel may have several themes. Analyzing the plot can often lead you to a better understanding of these themes.

1. List the major events that make up the plot in Chapters 4 through 6 of *The Pearl.*
2. What is the major conflict in *The Pearl?*
3. What is the climax of *The Pearl?*
4. How is the conflict resolved?
5. In their minds, Kino and Juana hear the "song" of the family, of evil, and of the pearl. How does the writer use these "songs" to give clues to the theme?
6. When Kino and Juana set out to sell the pearl, what do they feel? How does what they feel reveal theme?
7. What do you think is the main theme of *The Pearl?* What minor themes can you identify?

CRITICAL THINKING AND READING

Recognizing Cause and Effect

When writing about cause and effect, you attempt to explain relationships. A **cause** makes something occur; an **effect** is the outcome of the cause.

To identify an effect, ask yourself, "What happened?" To identify its cause, ask, "Why?"

1. What causes the following events?
   a. Kino decides to go to the capital.
   b. The watcher shoots into the cave.
2. What are the effects of the following events?
   a. Juana returns the pearl to Kino after it has been knocked from his hand in the pathway by the beach.
   b. Kino kills a man in self-defense.

UNDERSTANDING LANGUAGE

Appreciating Vivid Verbs

Vivid verbs can help you see, hear, smell, taste, and feel what the characters do and experience in the story. For example, in *The Pearl,* "The coyotes cried and laughed in the brush, the owls screeched and hissed over their heads. And once some large animal lumbered away, crackling the undergrowth as it went." Such vivid verbs can make the action in a story come alive.

The following vivid verbs are from the last three chapters of *The Pearl.* Use each word correctly in a sentence.

1. spewed
2. spurned
3. glinted
4. whisked

THINKING AND WRITING

Responding to Literary Criticism

It has been said of Steinbeck, "He wanted to be an individualist; he admired individualists; yet he also had a strong social conscience and a strong sense of right and wrong."

Write an essay explaining how this quotation is true of Steinbeck's writing in *The Pearl.* First list the ways in which Steinbeck shows his admiration for individualists, or people who choose to go their own way. Then describe his strong social conscience—his caring for people who are downtrodden—and his strong sense of right and wrong. Then use this information to write your essay. Revise your essay to include examples that support your statements. Proofread for errors in spelling, grammar, and punctuation.

(Answers begin on p. 742)

throw the pearl back into the Gulf, Kino killing the man on the path, their flight to Loreto, running from the trackers, the killing of the three trackers, the death of Coyotito, the return to La Paz, and the throwing of the pearl back into the Gulf.

2. The conflict is between Kino's desire to have the pearl and all that it represents—entrance into the modern world—and people in the modern world wanting this same pearl. On an allegorical level this simple man is attempting to gain entrance into the modern world that is filled with destruction and greed while the people of the modern world people resist the simplicity and mysticism of the primitive man.
3. Once Juana abandoned the past, the future was determined for her and her family. At this point the climax of the story has been reached and the ending is now inevitable.
4. The conflict is resolved when the pearl is thrown back into the Gulf.
5. The songs tell the reader how Kino feels; they describe Kino's comfort level with the opposing forces.
6. When Kino and Juana set out to sell the pearl, they are hopeful about making their fortune. This feeling turns out to be ironic because they are disappointed—the pearl buyers try to cheat them. It helps reveal theme by showing the conflict between their desire to improve their lives and the obstacles they encounter.
7. Many interpretations have been made regarding the central idea of the story or its insight about life—for the possibility of gaining the privileges of the modern world, Kino gives up his soul and his heritage; it is about the search for happiness and one's need to choose between the simple, natural life and the sophisticated, opulent life.

ANSWERS TO CRITICAL THINKING AND READING

1. a. Kino feels cheated by the pearl buyers.
   b. The watcher hears the sound of what he thinks is a coyote pup.
2. a. Because Kino still has the pearl, Juana, Kino, and Coyotito must flee from the people who envy and hate him.
   b. Juana, Kino, and Coyotito take flight to Loreto.

ANSWERS TO UNDERSTANDING LANGUAGE

Sentences will differ.

Challenge In the opening paragraph, this story is referred to as a parable, and it states that everyone finds his or her own meaning to that parable. Write a paragraph on what the story means to you.

THINKING AND WRITING

Publishing Student Writing Have students read their essays to the class, encouraging discussion on the different viewpoints. Students might want to design the page in the magazine where their essays would appear. Display their designed pages and essays.

Writing Across the Curriculum You might want to notify social studies teachers and then have students read John Steinbeck's nonfiction book, *America and Americans.* Have them write an essay telling how their viewpoints of Americans are the same as, or different from, Steinbeck's.

FOCUS ON READING

Making Generalizations

A general statement drawn from specific facts or cases is called a **generalization.** For a generalization to be considered valid, or true, it must apply to more than one case. Form generalizations based on the information provided in order to read with deeper insight and greater appreciation.

Evaluating Generalizations

Evaluate a generalization you form by determining whether your generalization is based on one or more than one situation. Remember that a sound generalization must apply to a number of situations, but it does not have to apply to all cases.

Overgeneralizations

An **overgeneralization** is a generalization that is invalid because it is too broad. There are words that signal overgeneralizations. Some of these words are *always, everyone, all, must, no one,* and *never*. Using these words may make a generalization too broad. On the other hand, using qualifying words such as *several, many, most, usually, often,* and *sometimes* will help you avoid making overgeneralizations.

Activity

Think about *The Pearl.* Decide which of the following generalizations are sound and which are overgeneralizations. Explain your answers.

1. All Mexican Indians are fishers.
2. Scorpion stings can sometimes be fatal.
3. Wealth always leads to tragedy.
4. Buyers usually try to buy pearls at the lowest prices.
5. Envy leads some people to violence.

You should have selected sentences 2,4, and 5 as sound. The facts in the novel support them, and they apply to a broad number of cases. Sentences 1 and 3 are too broad. From this novel, which centers on the experience of two people, you cannot conclude that all Mexican Indians are fishers or that wealth always leads to tragedy.

FOCUS ON READING

Ask the class to define *generalization*. Then, have students suggest some generalizations about *The Pearl.* Record their generalizations on the board or on a transparency. After the class has read and discussed this section, have them decide if their generalizations are valid generalizations, overgeneralizations, or hasty generalizations.

ACTIVITY ANSWERS

1. overgeneralization
2. sound
3. overgeneralization
4. sound
5. sound

You might ask the students to pinpoint the words that signaled the overgeneralizations.

Hasty Generalizations

A **hasty generalization** is a generalization that is made prematurely because it is based on insufficient evidence. For example, imagine that on your first visit to a school, you heard some students shouting in the hallways. You then said, "Students in this school are unruly." Your generalization would be hasty, since you were basing it on only one experience. Perhaps the students are normally well behaved, but you caught them on a bad day.

Guidelines

- Make sure you understand the main idea and supporting details of the material.
- Be certain the conclusions you draw are adequately supported by facts or evidence.
- Make sure the generalization you draw applies to many different cases or situations.
- Avoid using the words *always* or *must,* that do not allow for any exceptions and that make the generalizations too broad.

Activity

Read each of the following sentences based on *The Pearl.* Tell whether or not the generalization is sound. Explain your answers.

1. All pearl dealers are greedy and evil.
2. Sudden wealth can mean new and unforeseen problems for the recipients.
3. At the time of this novel, many Mexican pearl divers had to work very hard to earn a living.
4. All pearl divers have to work very hard to earn a living.
5. Some pearl dealers do not offer fair prices to divers.
6. The more money people have, the more money they want.
7. Sudden wealth makes other people both envious and suspicious.
8. No one ever gained happiness from sudden wealth.

Activity

You can make some generalizations based on the information John Steinbeck includes in *The Pearl.*

1. What generalizations can you make about the lives of pearl divers in Mexico in the early 1900's? Support your generalizations with evidence from the novel.
2. What generalizations can you make about the lives of Mexican Indians in the 1900's? Cite evidence from the novel to support your generalizations.

ACTIVITY ANSWERS

1. not sound
2. sound
3. sound
4. not sound
5. sound
6. not sound
7. not sound
8. not sound

ACTIVITY ANSWERS
Suggested responses

1. Many Mexican pearl divers lived in miserable conditions. The pearl divers in the village lived in huts, had to cook over open fires, and had virtually no medical care.
2. Mexican Indians were treated as inferior in the 1900's. They were exploited by the Spanish people. Students might cite the last paragraph on page 700 as evidence; ". . . all of the doctor's race spoke to all of Kino's race as though they were simple animals."

The writing assignments on page 746 have students write creatively, while those on page 747 have them think about the novel and write critically.

YOU THE WRITER
Guidelines for Evaluating Assignment 1

1. Is the dialogue between a character from the novel and the student interesting and believable?
2. Does the dialogue focus on one topic?
3. Is the language consistent with the way this character speaks in the novel?
4. Is the dialogue free from grammar, usage, and mechanics errors?

Guidelines for Evaluating Assignment 2

1. Does the description explain which scene the student intends to film in the introductory sentence?
2. Is there a description of the studio or on-location set?
3. Does the student explain how he or she intends to film the powerful scene?
4. Has the student used vivid sensory details for the description?
5. Is the description free from grammar, usage, and mechanics errors?

Guidelines for Evaluating Assignment 3

1. Does the student write an original ending to *The Pearl?*
2. Does the ending differ significantly from the novel's original ending?
3. Does the student's ending result logically from the previous events?
4. Is the ending free from grammar, usage, and mechanics errors?

YOU THE WRITER

Assignment

1. Imagine that you meet one of the characters in *The Pearl*. Which character would you like to meet? What would you discuss? What would you like to ask? Write a dialogue between you and this character.

Prewriting. List all the characters in the novel. Circle the name of the character you would most like to meet. Freewrite about what you would like to talk about.

Writing. Write your dialogue. Try to focus your dialogue around one topic. Use appropriate language that is consistent with the way this character speaks in the novel.

Revising. Make certain that your dialogue is believable and interesting. Have you used quotation marks to indicate when each speaker is talking?

Assignment

2. You are a world-renowned film producer and have been hired to film *The Pearl*. Select one powerful scene from the novel. Write a description of how you will film the scene—either at an on-location shoot or a studio set.

Prewriting. Skim through the novel to find a scene you would like to film. Brainstorm about how you would film it effectively, and jot down notes about the setting.

Writing. Use your prewriting notes to write a description of your studio or on-location set. Make certain that you explain which scene you are going to film in your introductory sentence.

Revising. Make certain that you have explained what you are going to film and how you plan to do so. Have you used vivid sensory details?

Assignment

3. Rewrite the ending of *The Pearl,* providing an outcome different from the one in the novel.

Prewriting. Write a summary in which you explain what happens and identify who is involved.

Writing. Write your own ending to the novel, using your summary as a guideline. Make certain that your ending differs significantly from the novel's ending.

Revising. Although your ending is new, it should result logically from the previous events. Ask a friend to read your ending and tell you whether it is logical.

YOU THE CRITIC

Assignment

1. Write an essay comparing and contrasting two characters in the novel.

Prewriting. Prepare a chart showing the similarities and differences between the two characters.

Writing. Write the first draft of your essay. Begin by showing how the characters are alike. Then show how they differ. Finally, explain how their similarities and differences affect their relationship.

Revising. When you revise, make sure you have included enough details to reveal the similarities and differences.

Assignment

2. Imagine that you are in a book club that meets every week. Interpret the theme of *The Pearl* for club members. Write a summary of the novel's theme that you will present to the club.

Prewriting. Skim the novel to remind you of its theme. In your own words, jot down your thoughts about the theme of the novel.

Writing. Use your prewriting notes as the basis for your interpretation. Write an introduction and a conclusion. Include evidence from the novel that supports your interpretation.

Revising. Make certain that your interpretation includes a strong introduction, a conclusion, and details and examples to support your interpretation.

Assignment

3. As the new book reviewer for the *Sunday Pen and Ink,* you will review *The Pearl.* Write a review that discusses your positive and negative reactions. Discuss why you would or would not recommend the novel to your readers.

Prewriting. Make two lists of your impressions, one noting what you liked about the novel and the other noting what you did not like.

Writing. Write your book review. Begin by stating the title and author of the novel; then give your negative reactions in one paragraph and your positive reactions in the other. Summarize your feelings about the novel in your conclusion.

Revising. Make certain that your book review has a strong introduction and conclusion. Does it include examples from the novel that support your opinions?

YOU THE CRITIC

Guidelines for Evaluating Assignment 1

1. Does the comparison begin by showing how the two characters are alike?
2. Does it then show how they differ?
3. Does the comparison explain the effect the similarities and differences have on their relationship?
4. Has the student included enough details to reveal the similarities and differences?
5. Is the essay free from grammar, usage, and mechanics errors?

Guidelines for Evaluating Assignment 2

1. Does the introduction of the essay present an interpretation of the theme on the novel?
2. Does the body of the essay include evidence from the novel that supports the student's interpretation?
3. Does the interpretation include a strong conclusion?
4. Is the essay free from grammar, usage, and mechanics errors?

Guidelines for Evaluating Assignment 3

1. Does the book review begin by stating the title and the author of the novel?
2. Does the review contain a paragraph that gives the student's negative reactions?
3. Does the review contain a para--graph that gives the student's positive reactions?
4. Does the paper conclude with a summarization of the student's feelings and a recommendation?
5. Is the essay free from grammar, usage, and mechanics errors?

Using the Handbook The lessons in the Handbook of Writing About Literature may be used for direct instruction in the writing process, specifically the process of writing about literature. In addition, students may use these lessons for reference and support when they are doing the Thinking and Writing assignments with the selections. References to appropriate lessons are suggested on the Annotated Teacher's Edition page with the assignment.

HANDBOOK OF WRITING ABOUT LITERATURE

Motivation for Writing Have students imagine that they are building a birdhouse for a shop project. Ask them to imagine the steps they would follow in building the birdhouse. (Elicit various answers. Suggested Response:
1. draw sketch of birdhouse;
2. list materials needed;
3. gather materials.)

Note that in the writing process, one goes through a similar procedure before actually writing. Tell the class that in this lesson they will learn more about this part of the writing process.

SECTION 1: UNDERSTANDING THE WRITING PROCESS

Lesson 1: Prewriting

The writing process can be divided into five stages, as follows:
1. *Prewriting:* planning the writing project
2. *Drafting:* writing your ideas in sentences and paragraphs
3. *Revising:* making improvements in your draft
4. *Proofreading:* checking for errors in spelling and mechanics
5. *Publishing,* or *sharing:* allowing others to read your writing

In this lesson you will learn about the steps involved in prewriting.

STEP 1: ANALYZE THE SITUATION

A writing situation can be analyzed in six parts: topic, purpose, audience, voice, content, and form. As you begin thinking about a writing project, ask yourself the following questions about these six parts.
1. *Topic* (the subject you will be writing about): What, exactly, is this subject? Can you state it in a sentence? Is your subject too broad or too narrow?
2. *Purpose* (what you want your writing to accomplish): Is your purpose to explain? to describe? to persuade? to tell a story? What do you want the reader to take away from the writing?
3. *Audience* (the people who will be reading or listening to your work): What are the backgrounds of these people? Do they already know a great deal about your subject, or will you have to provide basic information?
4. *Voice* (the way your writing will sound to the reader): What impression do you want to make on your readers? What tone should the writing have? Should it be formal or informal? Should it be cool and reasoned or charged with emotion?
5. *Content* (the subject and all the information provided about the subject): How much do you already know about the subject? What will you have to find out? Will you have to do some research? What people, books, magazines, newspapers, or other sources should you consult?
6. *Form* (the shape that the writing will take, including its organization and length): What will the final piece of writing look like? How long will it be? Will it be a single paragraph or several paragraphs? Will it take some special form such as verse or drama? In what order will the content be presented?

The answers to some of these questions will usually be obvious from the start. For example, your teacher may assign you a particular topic and may require that your writing be of a specified length or form. However, the answers to many of these questions will be up to you to decipher. Writing always involves making decisions, setting goals, and then making a plan for achieving these goals.

STEP 2: MAKE A PLAN

Your answers to the questions listed under Step 1 will help you determine what your plan of action will be. For example, if you discover that you are undecided about your topic, your plan of action will have to include clarifying what your topic will be. Your plan of action might also include doing research to find out more about your topic. Depending on what you need to know before you begin writing, choose one or more of the prewriting techniques described in the next section to help you.

STEP 3: GATHER INFORMATION

The following are some techniques for gathering ideas and information for use in your writing.

1. *Freewriting:* Think about your topic, and as you do so, write down everything that comes to your mind. Do not pause to think about proper spelling, grammar, or punctuation. Just write, nonstop, for one to five minutes. Then read your freewriting to find ideas that you can use in your paper.
2. *Clustering:* Write your topic in the middle of a piece of paper and circle it. Then, in the space around your topic, write down ideas that are related to it and circle these ideas. Draw lines to show how the ideas are connected to each other and to the main topic. This technique is especially useful for broadening or narrowing a topic. If your topic is too broad, you might use one of the related ideas as a new main topic. If your topic is too narrow, you might include some of the related ideas in your main topic.
3. *Analyzing:* Divide your topic into parts. Then think about each part separately and write down your thoughts about it in your notes. Also think about how the parts relate to each other and how they relate to the topic as a whole.
4. *Questioning:* Make a list of questions about your topic in your notes. Begin your questions with the words *who, what, when, where, why,* and *how.* Then do some research to find the answers to your questions.
5. *Using outside sources:* Consult books, magazines, newspapers, pamphlets, and reference works such as encyclopedias and atlases. Talk to people who are knowledgeable about your topic. Record in your notes any information that you gather from these sources.
6. *Making charts* or *lists:* Create charts or lists of information related to your topic. For example, you might list all the parts or characteristics of your topic, or you might make a time line or a pros-and-cons chart.

STEP 4: ORGANIZE YOUR NOTES

To make sense of the information you have gathered, you will need to put it into some kind of logical order. The following are ways to organize your notes.

1. *Chronological order,* or *time order:* the order in which events occur
2. *Spatial order:* the order in which objects appear in space, as from left to right, top to bottom, or near to far
3. *Degree order:* in increasing or decreasing order, as of size, importance, or familiarity

After you have organized your notes, make a rough outline for your paper.

CASE STUDY: PREWRITING

Mia's English teacher asked the class to write a paragraph on the topic of animals. Mia knew that the topic was too broad for a one-paragraph composition, so she tried clustering to narrow the topic. See her chart on the next page.

Since Mia had two cats of her own, she decided that the topic of her paper would be *Why Cats Make Good Pets.* Her purpose would be to explain why it is worthwhile to own a cat, and her audience would be her classmates and her teacher. She decided that her tone would be informal, since a very formal, serious tone would not suit her topic.

Mia's next plan of action was to gather ideas about why she thought cats made good house pets. She made a list in her notes of the reasons why she believed this:

- They don't take up the whole chair like big dogs.

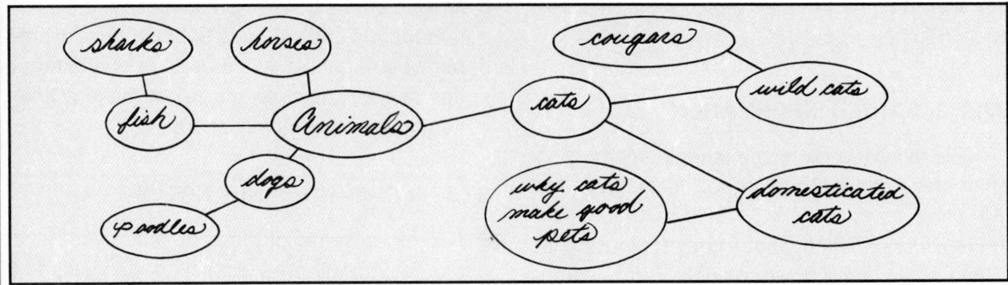

- They don't make a lot of noise.
- You don't have to walk them.
- They clean themselves and don't have to be bathed.
- They're easy to clean up after.
- They're cuddly.
- They can play with each other and not be too mad at you when you're out all day.

Mia made a rough outline for her paper. She showed in the outline that she would first introduce her topic, then would give three reasons why cats make good house pets, and finally would conclude with a summarizing sentence. She also decided that she would organize her three reasons by degree, from least to most important.

ACTIVITIES AND ASSIGNMENTS

A. Answer the following questions about the case study:

1. How did Mia analyze the writing situation? What was her plan of action after she had analyzed it?
2. Why did Mia use the clustering technique? How did it help her?
3. Why did Mia make a list in her notes?

B. Choose one of the following topics or think of one of your own:

School	Weekends
Hobbies	Writing

Prepare to write a paragraph on the topic by following these steps.

1. Analyze the writing situation by answering the questions listed in this lesson.
2. Make a plan of action for gathering information and ideas to use in your paper. Use one of the prewriting techniques described in this lesson to gather information. Record this information in your notes.
3. Organize your notes and make a rough outline for your paragraph. Save your notes and outline in a folder.

Lesson 2: Drafting and Revising

CHOOSING A METHOD FOR DRAFTING

Drafting is the second stage in the writing process. After you have gathered information and made a rough outline, the next step is to put your ideas down on paper. As you draft, keep the following points in mind:

1. Choose a drafting method that feels right to you. There are many different ways of writing a draft. Some writers like to work from a detailed outline and to write very slowly and carefully. Other writers prefer to make only a very brief outline and to write quickly. Then they go back over their work and take care of the details. Whichever method works best for you is the method you should use.
2. Do not expect your first draft to be a finished product. Drafting gives you the chance to work out your ideas on paper. At this stage you should not worry about proper spelling, grammar, punctuation, and so on. You can take care of these details later.
3. Refer to your prewriting notes and to your outline as you write. Work from your notes and outline, keeping your audience and your purpose in mind.
4. Be flexible. Do not be afraid to discard old ideas as better ones come to mind. You may need to stop in the middle of your draft and do some more prewriting to develop your new ideas.
5. Write as many rough drafts as you need. You may have to make several attempts at drafting before you come up with a draft that is satisfactory. If you write a draft that does not seem to have a well-defined purpose or doesn't contain enough information to support your main idea, go back to the prewriting stage. Define your purpose more clearly, review your notes to discard irrelevant ideas, and gather any additional ideas and facts that you need.

REVISING YOUR DRAFT

Once you have a draft that pleases you, you

CHECKLIST FOR REVISION

Topic and Purpose

☐ Is my topic clear?
☐ Does my writing have a specific purpose?
☐ Does my writing achieve its purpose?

Audience

☐ Will everything that I have written be clear to my audience?
☐ Will my audience find the writing interesting?
☐ Will my audience respond in the way that I would like?

Voice and Word Choice

☐ Is the impression that my writing conveys the one I intended it to convey?
☐ Is my language appropriately formal or informal?
☐ Have I avoided vague, undefined terms?
☐ Have I avoided jargon that my audience will not understand?
☐ Have I avoided clichés?
☐ Have I avoided slang, odd connotations, euphemisms, and gobbledygook except for novelty or humor?

Content/Development

☐ Have I avoided including unnecessary or unrelated ideas?
☐ Have I developed my topic completely?
☐ Have I supplied examples or details that support the statements I have made?
☐ Are my sources of information unbiased, up-to-date, and authoritative?

Form

☐ Have I followed a logical method of organization?
☐ Have I used transitions, or connecting words, to make the organization clear?
☐ Does the writing have a clear introduction, body, and conclusion?

Motivation for Writing Before students begin drafting, have them gather together and review all of their prewriting notes. That way, they will have all of their information at hand and can proceed more efficiently with drafting.

can begin refining and polishing it. This process of reworking a draft is known as *revising.* As you revise, ask yourself the questions in the following Checklist for Revision. If your answer to any of the questions is "no," revise your draft until you can answer "yes."

Editorial Symbols

Use the following symbols to edit, or revise, your draft:

SYMBOL	MEANING	EXAMPLE
	move text	She however was not at home.
	delete	I also went, too.
^	insert	of our car
	close up; no space	every where
⊙	insert period	ran I
	insert comma	mice, bats and rats
	add apostrophe	theyre here
	add quotation marks	The Tell-Tale Heart
	transpose	to clearly see
¶	begin paragraph	crash. The man
/	make lower case	the Basketball player
═	capitalize	president Truman

CASE STUDY: DRAFTING AND REVISING

Mia used her prewriting notes from the preceding lesson to begin drafting her paragraph. Here is her first draft:

> Cats are grate housepets. They don't bark, you can take care of them easy and they're cuddly. I love my two cats.

Mia stopped writing and looked at her draft. She had given the three reasons why she thought cats were good pets, and now she had nothing more to say. She set a goal for her next draft: to give examples that would support each of her reasons.

Mia wrote several more drafts. Here is the last draft that she wrote, which she revised using standard editorial symbols:

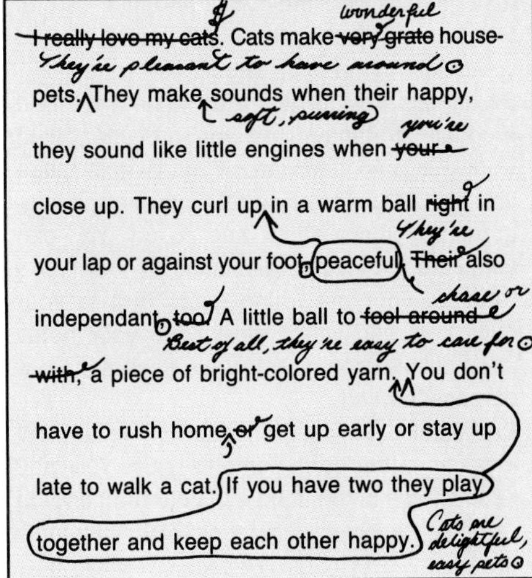
I really love my cats. Cats make very grate house-
pets. They're pleasant to have around. They make soft, purring sounds when their happy,
they sound like little engines when your you're close up. They curl up in a warm ball right in
your lap or against your foot, peaceful. Their They're also
independant, too. A little ball to fool around chase or with, a piece of bright-colored yarn. Best of all, they're easy to care for. You don't
have to rush home or get up early or stay up
late to walk a cat. If you have two they play
together and keep each other happy. Cats are delightful, easy pets.

ACTIVITIES AND ASSIGNMENTS

A. Answer the following questions about the revised draft in the case study:

1. Why hasn't Mia corrected all of her grammar and spelling errors? When will these errors be corrected?
2. Why did Mia delete material in the first two sentences?

3. Why did Mia add the sentence "They're pleasant to have around"?
4. Why did Mia change the words "fool around with"?
5. What transitional words did Mia add to indicate that she was about to tell the last reason why cats are good house pets?
6. Why did Mia move the original last sentence in her paragraph?
7. Why did Mia add a new last sentence?
8. What other revisions did Mia make? Why did she make them?

B. Using your prewriting notes from the last lesson, write a draft of a paragraph on your topic. Then revise your draft. Follow these steps:

1. Read over your outline to see how your paragraph will be organized. Then write a thesis statement of one or two sentences to introduce your topic.
2. Write the rest of your draft, based on your outline and your prewriting notes. Make sure that you support your statements with evidence from your notes. Do not worry about spelling and mechanics at this point.
3. Write a conclusion that sums up the main point of your paragraph.
4. Revise your draft, using the Checklist for Revision in this lesson. If you answer "no" to any of the questions on the checklist, use standard editorial symbols to make the necessary corrections.

755

Motivation for Writing Ask students to continue to think of the writing process as being similar to building a birdhouse. Have them think what remains to be done after putting together the various parts of the birdhouse. (Elicit various answers. Suggested response: You might want to sand and paint the birdhouse. You also need to attach it to a tree or other location where birds will use it.)

Note that in some ways the step of proofreading and publishing is similar to the steps in building a birdhouse. Tell the class that they will find out in much greater detail about proofreading and publishing in this lesson.

Lesson 3: Proofreading and Publishing

PROOFREADING YOUR FINAL DRAFT

Before a draft is ready to be shared with a reader, it must be checked for errors in grammar and usage, spelling, punctuation, capitalization, and manuscript form. This process of final checking is called *proofreading*. When you proofread, ask yourself the questions in the checklist at the left. If your answer to any of the questions is "no," make the necessary corrections on your revised draft.

If you need to check your spelling or to review rules for mechanics, refer to a dictionary, writing textbook, or handbook of style.

CHECKLIST FOR PROOFREADING

Grammar and Usage

- ☐ Are all of my sentences complete? That is, have I avoided sentence fragments?
- ☐ Does each of my sentences express only one complete thought? That is, have I avoided run-on sentences?
- ☐ Do the verbs I have used agree with their subjects?
- ☐ Have all the words in my paper been used correctly? Am I sure about the meanings of all of these words?
- ☐ Is the person or thing being referred to by each pronoun clear?
- ☐ Have I used adjectives and adverbs correctly?

Spelling

- ☐ Am I absolutely sure that each word has been spelled correctly?

Punctuation

- ☐ Does every sentence end with a punctuation mark?
- ☐ Have I correctly used commas, semicolons, colons, hyphens, dashes, parentheses, quotation marks, and apostrophes?

Capitalization

- ☐ Have I capitalized any words that should not be capitalized?
- ☐ Should I capitalize any words that I have not capitalized?

Manuscript Form

- ☐ Have I indented the first line(s) of my paragraph(s)?
- ☐ Have I written my name and the page number in the top right-hand corner of each page?
- ☐ Have I double-spaced the manuscript?
- ☐ Is my draft neat and legible?

PUBLISHING OR SHARING YOUR WORK

After you have proofread your revised draft, you are ready to share your writing with other people. When you write for school, you generally submit your work to your teachers. However, there are many other ways to share, or publish, your writing. The following is a list of possibilities:

1. Share your work in a small discussion group.
2. Read your work aloud to the class.
3. Share copies of your writing with members of your family or with friends.
4. Display your work on the class bulletin board.
5. Save your work in a folder for later publication. At the end of the year, work from the entire class can be bound together into a booklet.
6. Submit your writing to the school literary magazine, or start a literary magazine for your school or for your class.
7. Submit your writing to your school or community newspaper.
8. Enter your writing in literary contests for student writers.
9. Submit your writing to a magazine that publishes work by young people.

CASE STUDY: PROOFREADING AND PUBLISHING

After revising her final draft, Mia made a fresh, clean copy for proofreading. She read the Checklist for Proofreading in this lesson and applied each question to her revised draft. Here is Mia's paragraph, with the proofreading corrections that she made, marked with editorial symbols:

> ¶ Cats make wonderful house pets. They're pleasant to have around. They make soft, purring sounds when ~~their~~ they're happy; they sound like little engines when you're close up. They curl up peacefully in a warm ball in your lap or against your foot. They're also independent— all they need is a little ball to chase or a piece of brightly colored yarn. Best of all, they're easy to care for. If you have two they play together and keep each other happy. You don't have to rush home, get up early, or stay up late to walk a cat. Cats are delightful, easy pets.

Mia made a clean final copy of her paragraph. Then she read it aloud to a few of her classmates in a small discussion group.

ACTIVITIES AND ASSIGNMENTS

A. Answer the following questions about the case study:

1. What errors in spelling did Mia correct during proofreading?
2. Why did Mia change "peaceful" to "peacefully"?
3. What sentence fragment did Mia correct? How did she do this?
4. What punctuation error did Mia correct?
5. What error in manuscript form did Mia make? How did she correct it?
6. Are there any changes you think should still be made in Mia's paragraph? Explain.

B. Make a clean copy of your revised paragraph from the preceding lesson. Then use the Checklist for Proofreading to correct any errors in grammar and usage, spelling, punctuation, capitalization, and manuscript form that remain in your draft.

Make a final copy of your paragraph, and share this copy with your classmates and with your teacher.

Motivation for Writing Tell students that you are going to read a short poem from the poetry unit. Tell them to listen while you read for the things in the poem that they can see, taste, feel, smell or hear. Then read "January," by John Updike, on page 576 or "Concrete Mixers," by Patricia Hubbell, on page 587.

After you have finished reading, have students briefly note the things in the poem that appealed to any of the five senses.

Then explain that the next lesson will show them more about how to write about things that appeal to the senses in a literary work.

SECTION 2: UNDERSTANDING THE PARTS OF A LITERARY WORK: ANALYSIS AND INTERPRETATION

Lesson 4: Writing About Images

WHAT IS AN IMAGE?

An *image* is a word or phrase that appeals to one of the five senses. These senses include sight, hearing, touch, taste, and smell. Consider this line from William Melvin Kelley's short story "A Good Long Sidewalk":

> The barbershop was warm enough to make Carlyle Bedlow sleepy, and smelled of fragrant shaving soap.

In this line Kelley uses images that appeal to the senses of touch ("the barbershop was warm") and smell ("fragrant shaving soap").

WHY DO WRITERS USE IMAGES?

Writers use images for two purposes:

1. To portray scenes that include people, places, and things, and
2. To create feelings, or moods.

Look again at the line from William Kelley's short story. Notice that the images in the line help to create a picture of the barbershop. They create a mood of relaxation and coziness.

Now consider the use of images in the following passage from Maya Angelou's autobiography *I Know Why the Caged Bird Sings:*

> Throughout the year, until the next frost, we took our meals from the smokehouse . . . and from the shelves of canned foods. There were choices on the shelves that could set a hungry child's mouth to watering. Green beans, snapped always the right length, collards, cabbage, juicy red tomato preserves that came into their own on steaming buttered biscuits, and sausage, beets, berries, and every fruit grown in Arkansas.

The images in this passage:

1. Create a picture of jars of colorful, delicious-tasting, fragrant foods sitting on pantry shelves, waiting to be enjoyed, and
2. Create feelings of pleasure and happiness.

CASE STUDY: WRITING ABOUT IMAGES

Prewriting

Tenetia's English teacher asked the class to write an analysis of a favorite poem. Tenetia chose to write about the use of images in the following poem:

DRIVING TO TOWN LATE TO MAIL A LETTER

Robert Bly

It is a cold and snowy night. The main
street is deserted.
The only things moving are swirls of snow.
As I lift the mailbox door, I feel its
cold iron.
There is a privacy I love in this snowy
night.
Driving around, I will waste more time.

Tenetia checked to see if there were any words she needed to look up in the dictionary. There weren't. She then read the poem again, paying close attention to its images. Next she made a list of the images in the poem:

- Images of sight:
  - Dark, "snowy night"
  - "street is deserted"
  - "swirls of snow" moving around
  - Speaker mailing letter in mailbox
  - Speaker's car waiting
- Images of sound:
  - Silence—no people, only silent snow

- Images of touch:
  "cold iron" of mailbox door
  Softness of "swirls of snow"
  Coldness of night
- Images of taste:
  None
- Images of smell:
  None

Then Tenetia asked herself, "What picture do these images create and what mood do they suggest?" She wrote her responses in her prewriting notes:

- Picture created by images in the poem:
  Cold, snowy, deserted corner of town at night by a mailbox
  Speaker has parked a car by the mailbox to mail a letter
  Snow swirling around
- Mood created by the images:
  Alone but not lonely
  What the speaker calls "a privacy I love"

Tenetia decided to write about how Bly used images to create a mood of wonderful privacy. She made the following rough outline of her paper:

- Introduction:
  Tell what poem I'm writing about.
  State my purpose (to show that Bly uses images to create a mood of wonderful privacy).
- Body:
  Describe the images of sight, sound, and touch in the poem.
- Conclusion:
  Point out how the last two lines sum up the mood created by the poem's images.

Drafting and Revising

Using her outline and her prewriting notes, Tenetia wrote a draft of her analysis. Then she carefully revised and proofread her work. At right is her rough draft with the handwritten corrections that she made.

¶ In the poem "Driving to Town Late to Mail a Letter," Robert Bly uses images to create a mood of wonderful privacy, the images of sight show the speaker, who has driven downtown late at night to mail a letter. The "main street is deserted" for workers and shoppers have gone home. However the lively "swirls of snow" keeps the scene from being lonley.

Also, images of touch ~~also~~ reinforce the pleasure of this mood the speaker calls "the privacy I love". The swirling snow suggests a soft, pleasant touch. The cold night air seems refreshing and energizing, but not chilling. Not even the "cold iron" of the mailbox door is unpleasant in this setting. Instead the cold iron suggests strenth. The speaker's privacy is enhanced by the snow's softness and ~~charged~~ by the bracing cold.

The night's silence, too, emphasises the privacy. No sounds ~~intrude. Moreover, this is~~ the magical silence of noiseless snow. Little wonder the speaker loves this privacy. When he says Driving around, I will waste more time, the reader realizes it can not be the speaker who judges this mood a waste of time. It must be those who are not poets.

759

Proofreading and Publishing

After making a clean final copy of her paper, Tenetia proofread it carefully. As she did so, she caught several punctuation errors and one spelling error. She corrected these. Then she shared her paper with a small group of classmates. First she read the poem to them, and then she read her analysis.

ACTIVITIES AND ASSIGNMENTS

A. Study the corrections Tenetia made in her paragraph. Identify each of the following:

1. Places where Tenetia corrected errors in spelling
2. A place where Tenetia corrected an error in subject and verb agreement
3. A place where Tenetia eliminated unnecessary repetition
4. A place where Tenetia fixed a sentence fragment
5. Places where Tenetia corrected errors in punctuation
6. Errors in punctuation and spelling that were not corrected on Tenetia's revised draft (Hint: Check her use of quotation marks.)

B. Choose one of the poems from the poetry unit of your anthology. Then write a short paper about its images and the mood that the images create. Follow these steps:

1. Read the poem carefully. Look up any words that you don't know and write out their definitions.
2. Make a chart showing the images of sight, sound, touch, taste, and smell used in the poem.
3. Make notes telling what picture is created by the images and what mood, or feeling, the images convey.
4. Write an introduction that gives the name of the poem and tells what mood is created by the images.
5. In the body of your paper, explain what images are used in the poem.
6. Write a conclusion that sums up the poem's mood.
7. Revise and proofread your paragraph carefully. Add any important details that you left out. Delete any unnecessary words. Proofread for errors in organization, grammar, spelling, usage, punctuation, and capitalization.
8. Make a clean final copy to be handed in.

Lesson 5: Writing About Sound

SOUND AND MEANING

Sometimes when you hear a writer's words read aloud, you discover a new dimension of meaning. The sounds made by the words are part of what the writer wants to communicate. For example, note how the following poem sounds when read aloud:

WINTER OCEAN

John Updike

Many-maned scud-thumper, tub
of male whales, maker of worn wood,
shrub-ruster, sky-mocker, rave!
portly pusher of waves, wind-slave.

The sound of the poem gives the reader a strong sense of the choppy violence and power of an ocean in winter. In both prose and poetry, sound and meaning are often closely related.

TECHNIQUES INVOLVING SOUND

Writers use many techniques to enrich the way their writing sounds. The chart below lists some common literary devices of sound.

Read the entries for the terms in the Sound Devices chart below in the Handbook of Literary Terms. Then read the following case study.

CASE STUDY: WRITING ABOUT SOUND

Arthur's English class was studying the use of sound in poetry. For an assignment to write about sound in a poem, Arthur chose the following poem, which he had enjoyed reading:

A LAZY THOUGHT

Eve Merriam

There go the grownups
To the office,
To the store,
Subway rush,
Traffic crush;
Hurry, scurry,
Worry, flurry.

No wonder
Grownups
Don't grow up
Any more.

It takes a lot
Of slow
To grow.

SOUND DEVICES	
Onomatopoeia: words that sound like what they mean, such as "whoosh" or "buzz"	*Assonance:* repetition of vowel sounds, as in "the flat sad face of a rather fat man"
Euphony: flowing, pleasant sounds, as in "graceful lilies floating by"	*Meter:* a regular rhythmical pattern, as in "The soup is on the stove"
Cacophony: harsh, jarring sounds, as in this line from the Updike poem: "shrub-ruster, sky-mocker, rave!"	*Parallelism:* repetition of groups of words with similar grammatical structures, as in "over the river and through the woods" (Both are prepositional phrases.)
Alliteration: repetition of initial consonant sounds, as in "*b*right *b*eauty"	*Repetition:* a repeated sound, word, phrase, or sentence. Examples of repetition include rhyme, consonance, assonance, and parallelism.
Consonance: repetition of internal consonant sounds, as in "Don*k*eys, tur*k*eys, and mon*k*eys all gathered around."	

Motivation for Writing Have students listen carefully to the sounds in the classroom around them and outside the classroom doors and windows. Have them describe, using the most precise words they can think of, the exact sounds they hear and the circumstances under which the sounds are made.

Then explain that in this lesson they will learn more about how to write about sounds.

Prewriting

Arthur read the poem aloud several times, listening carefully to its sounds. Then, to gather information, he made a copy of the poem and marked it as follows:

1. He underlined examples of onomatopoeia.
2. He circled the rhyming words.
3. He underlined, twice, all the repeated sounds he could find.
4. In the margins he noted examples of alliteration, consonance, assonance, parallelism, and repeated words.
5. He marked the stresses and feet in the first and last stanzas to show the meter of the poem.

Here is Arthur's marked copy of "A Lazy Thought":

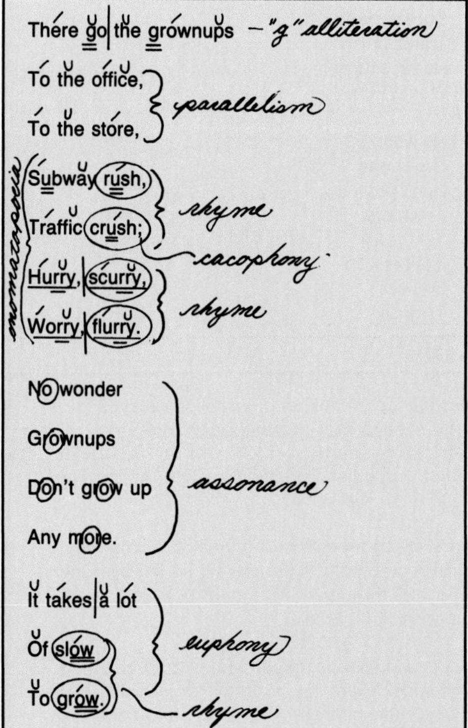

Arthur made some further notes about the meter and the rhyme in the poem:

- Meter: The first stanza has a heavy, drumming meter that echoes the footsteps of the grownups going to work.
- Rhyme: The first stanza has lots of rhyme, which accentuates the abrupt rhythm of the grownups rushing. The second stanza doesn't rhyme—makes the reader stop and listen to the poet. The third stanza rhymes and gives the poem a smooth ending.

Arthur reviewed the poem and his notes. Then he made the following generalizations about the poem:

- First stanza: sounds rushed, like the grownups' world
- Last stanza: sounds lazy and a slow, like kids' time

Next Arthur made a rough outline for his composition. He decided to organize his information by topic—he would discuss one sound device at a time and give examples of each.

Drafting and Revising

Arthur used his prewriting notes and his outline to write a draft of his composition. Here is the beginning of his unrevised first draft:

> In her poem "A Lazy Thought," Eve Merriam uses many sound devices, especially meter and repetition, to show what time is like for rushing grownups contrasted with the lazy pleasent, slow time of others. First of all, the fast-paced meter in the first stanza emphasizes the frantic pace of grownups. Lines 2–7 start with heavy beats and each have two stressed beats. The rhythm of the first stanza is like the grownups pounding footsteps. In contrast, the last stanza has a lovely rhythm. Each line begins with a soft beat. And it is followed by a gentley accented beat. The repetition of sounds emphasize the same contrast, between grownup time and kid time. Onomatopoia, for example, lets the reader hear the "rush,/ . . . crush;/

Hurry, scurry,/Worry, flurry" of the grownups. In addition, the assonance and rhyme in the last two stanzas, with the repeated long *o* sounds, contrast with the rushing feeling and emphasize slowness.

Arthur finished his draft and then revised it.

Proofreading and Publishing

Arthur carefully proofread his revised draft. Then he made a clean final copy of his composition and shared it with a small group of his classmates before handing it in to his teacher.

ACTIVITIES AND ASSIGNMENTS

A. Finish writing Arthur's rough draft. Then revise the entire draft, making sure that all of the ideas are expressed clearly and are supported with examples. Finally, proofread the draft and make a final copy of it. Share the composition with a small group of your classmates.

B. Write a two-paragraph composition on the use of sound in one of the following poems: "By Morning," on page 540; "Ring Out, Wild Bells," on page 544; "Four Little Foxes," on page 556; or "Silver," on page 564. Follow these steps:

1. Select a poem and read it aloud several times. Listen to the way the poem sounds, and think about how the sounds affect the poem's meaning.
2. Make a copy of the poem. If the poem is particularly long, copy only one or two stanzas.
3. Mark the copy as Arthur did in the case study, showing examples of onomatopoeia, rhyme, repeated sounds, alliteration, consonance, assonance, parallelism, and repeated words.
4. Read the entry for Meter in the Handbook of Literary Terms and Techniques. Then choose one stanza of the poem and mark its stresses and feet.
5. Organize your notes and make a rough outline for your composition. In the introduction, tell what poem you are writing about and explain that you are going to discuss the poet's use of sound. In the body of your composition, discuss each device of sound in turn, giving at least one example of each. Conclude your composition with a summary of your main point.
6. Revise and proofread your composition. Then make a final copy of it, and share this copy with your classmates and with your teacher.

Motivation for Writing Write the following line of poetry by Robert Burns on the board: "My love is like a red, red rose."

Ask students to put the poet's meaning in their own words. (Accept various answers.) Ask students what they like about the way the poet expresses himself in this phrase.

Then explain that in this lesson they will learn more about the kind of expressions, called figures of speech, used by the poet.

Lesson 6: Writing About Figures of Speech

WHAT IS A FIGURE OF SPEECH?

Sometimes a writer uses words to convey more than just a literal meaning. When a word or group of words is used in a special, nonliteral way, it is called a *figure of speech*. In the opening lines of the excerpt from *One Writer's Beginnings,* on page 377, Eudora Welty uses several figures of speech:

> Learning stamps you with its moments. Childhood's learning is made up of moments. It isn't steady. It's a pulse.

Learning doesn't literally "stamp" anyone, nor is it really a "pulse." These are figures of speech used to describe, vividly and imaginatively, the process of learning.

The following are some of the most frequently used figures of speech.

FIGURES OF SPEECH
Hyperbole: exaggeration for emphasis:
"My brother makes the best chocolate chip cookies in the world."
Personification: speaking or writing about a nonhuman subject as though it were human:
"That wallpaper pattern reaches right out and grabs you!"
Simile: a comparison of two very different things, using *like* or *as*:
"Your thoughtful gift was like sunshine on a cold winter's day."
Metaphor: writing or speaking of one thing as though it were something very different:
"The engine of my mother's new car purrs."

WHY WRITERS USE FIGURES OF SPEECH

Figures of speech can be much more vivid and interesting than literal language. For example, here is one way to describe how someone feels after a long day at work:

> Feeling very tired, Maria took a nap.

The statement is accurate, but not very striking. Here is an example of a figure of speech—a simile—used to describe the same subject:

> Feeling like someone who had just run the Boston Marathon, Maria collapsed on the couch.

The comparison in the second sentence helps the reader to feel Maria's exhaustion.

HOW WRITERS CREATE FIGURES OF SPEECH

To create a hyperbole, a writer first thinks of a subject and then of a particular quality of that subject.

> Subject: myself
> Quality: energetic

Then the writer writes a sentence that exaggerates the quality:

> Today I could run around the world.

Personifications, similes, and metaphors are slightly more challenging to write. Again the writer begins with a subject and with a particular quality of that subject.

> Subject: publishing the school newspaper
> Quality: satisfying

Then the writer chooses a second subject that shares the same quality:

> Second subject: making a slam dunk

Finally, the writer uses the second subject to describe the first:

> Publishing the school newspaper is as satisfying as making a slam dunk.

CASE STUDY: WRITING ABOUT FIGURES OF SPEECH

Mario's English teacher asked the class to write a paragraph about the figures of speech in a favorite poem. Mario decided to write about Sylvia Plath's "Mushrooms," on page 503.

Prewriting

Mario read the poem several times. Then he listed the following figures of speech in his prewriting notes:

- Personification: Mushrooms are personified throughout the poem. Specific examples include:
  "discreetly" (line 2)
  "Our toes, our noses" (line 4)
  "fists" (line 10)
  "Our hammers, our rams" (line 14)
  "We/Diet on water" (line 19)
  "Bland-mannered" (line 21)
  "we are meek" (line 26)
  "Nudgers and shovers" (line 28)
  "We shall . . . /Inherit the earth" (lines 31–32)
  "Our foot's in the door" (line 33)
- Metaphor: Personification is a type of metaphor. Other examples of metaphors include:
  "crumbs of shadow" (line 20)
  "We are shelves, we are/Tables" (lines 25–26)

Now that Mario had gathered enough information for his paragraph, he needed to organize it. He made the following rough outline:

- Introduction: Tell what poem I'm writing about. Introduce topic: figures of speech in the poem.
- Body: Give examples of personification and then examples of metaphor. Tell how each gives poem deeper meaning.
- Conclusion: Sum up main idea of paragraph—say that figures of speech make this poem especially vivid and imaginative.

Drafting and Revising

Mario wrote a draft of his paragraph, based on his outline and his prewriting notes. Then he revised his draft, making sure that his points were clear. He made a fresh copy of his revised draft for proofreading.

Proofreading and Publishing

Mario proofread his paragraph, correcting his errors in grammar, usage, spelling, and punctuation. Then he made a final copy and shared this copy with his parents before turning it in to his English teacher.

ACTIVITIES AND ASSIGNMENTS

A. Use Mario's notes and outline to write a paragraph about the figures of speech in Sylvia Plath's "Mushrooms," on page 503. Follow these steps:

1. Read the poem several times. Then reread Mario's prewriting notes. Write a topic sentence that introduces the main point of the paragraph.
2. Draft the rest of the paragraph. First discuss the use of personification in the poem and give examples. Then discuss how metaphor is used and cite specific examples.
3. Write a conclusion of one or two sentences, summarizing the main idea of your paragraph.
4. Revise your paragraph, using the Checklist for Revision on page 769. Then proofread your work carefully and make a clean final copy. Share your final copy with a small group of your classmates and with your teacher.

B. Write a paragraph about the figures of speech in one of the following poems: "Harlem Night Song," on page 558; "Blue-Butterfly Day," on page 559; "Silver," on page 564; "January," on page 576; "Winter Moon," on page 578; "The City Is So Big," on page 586; "Concrete Mixers," on page 587; or "The Story-Teller," on page 615. Follow these steps:

1. Select a poem and read it several times. Then copy the poem by hand onto a separate sheet of paper. This will help you to become familiar with the exact words and punctuation used by the poet.
2. On the copy, underline all the examples of figures of speech that you can find. List them in your notes under the following headings: *Hyperbole, Personification, Simile,* and *Metaphor.*
3. Decide which figure of speech you think is the most important to the meaning of the poem. Begin your rough draft with a topic sentence that gives the title and author of the poem and introduces the central figure of speech.
4. Make an outline for the rest of your paragraph that shows the order in which you will present your information. Then finish your draft. Conclude with a summary of the main point of your paragraph.
5. Revise your draft. Make sure that all of your ideas are clear. Also check to see that your statements are supported by examples from the poem.
6. Proofread your paragraph for errors in spelling and mechanics. Then make a clean final copy for sharing with your classmates and with your teacher.

Lesson 7: Writing About Setting

WHAT IS SETTING?

The *setting* of a literary work is the time and place in which the action occurs. Setting is revealed by details that describe furniture, scenery, customs, transportation, clothing, dialects, weather, time of day, and time of year. Writers use images of sight, sound, touch, taste, and smell to create vivid settings.

The following passage is from the opening of Dorothy M. Johnson's short story, "The Day the Sun Came Out," on page 107. To create the setting for the story, the author uses details about transportation, scenery, historical time, economic conditions, and weather as well as images of sight and sound.

> We left the home place behind, mile by slow mile, heading for the mountains, across the prairie where the wind blew forever.
>
> At first there were four of us with the one-horse wagon and its skimpy load. Pa and I walked, because I was a big boy of eleven. My two little sisters romped and trotted until they got tired and had to be boosted up into the wagon bed.
>
> That was no covered Conestoga, like Pa's folks came West in, but just an old farm wagon, drawn by one weary horse, creaking and rumbling westward to the mountains, toward the little woods town where Pa thought he had an old uncle who owned a little two-bit sawmill.

THE FUNCTIONS OF A SETTING

A writer may use setting to serve one or more functions in a literary work. The chart on uses of setting in the right column lists some of the possible functions of setting.

CASE STUDY: WRITING ABOUT SETTING

Nora's English teacher asked the class to write about the setting in a literary work. Nora decided to write about the setting of "Paul Revere's Ride," on page 509.

USES OF SETTING
To create a mood: A description of an open wagon traveling across a huge expanse of windy prairie creates a lonely mood. Details about a sunny, fragrant field of flowers might create a happy, carefree mood.
To show the reader a different way of life: For example, through details about customs, furniture, and transportation, a reader can get a sense of what life was like in a different time in history or of how people live in a foreign country.
To make the action seem more real: Through vivid details and images, the reader is transported to the scene of the action. The reader can imagine the setting almost as if he or she were participating in the story.
To be the source of the conflict, or struggle, in a work: A character fighting a snowstorm, the heat of a desert, or a high mountain is in conflict with an element of the setting.
To symbolize an idea: For example, the ocean might symbolize the immense power of nature as compared to the puny strength of one person, or a springtime setting might symbolize new life and growth.

Prewriting

First Nora read the poem several times. Then she listed some of the details that helped to create the poem's setting:

- Time: midnight; April 18, 1775
- Historical Setting: just before the outbreak of the American Revolution
- Images of sight:

Motivation for Writing Ask students to think of a time and place in their lives when they felt especially happy. After a minute or so, ask for volunteers to describe their time and place. Then note that the class has been discussing what in a literary work is called a setting—the time and place in which a story takes place.

Note that in this lesson they will describe settings in works they have read and learn how a setting functions.

"Just as the moon rose over the bay" (line 17)
"A phantom ship, with each mast and spar/Across the moon like a prison bar" (lines 20–21)
"moonlight flowing over all" (line 41)

- Images of sound:
  "muffled oar" (line 15)
  "Silently rowed" (line 16)
  "his friend . . . /Wanders and watches with eager ears,/Til in the silence around him he hears" (lines 24–26)
  "startled the pigeons from their perch" (line 34)
  "Beneath . . . lay the dead/ . . . /Wrapped in silence so deep and still/That he could hear . . . /The watchful nightwind" (lines 42–46)

Nora looked over the information she had gathered from the poem and thought about what function the setting served. She decided that it did two things: (1) It showed the reader what Boston was like in 1775, and (2) it created a mood.

Nora thought the second function was more important, so she decided that the topic of her composition would be how setting created a mood in "Paul Revere's Ride." To gather more ideas about this mood, Nora did some freewriting:

> The mood of the poem is one of waiting—there is a great deal of suspense, as if the setting—including the moon, the bay, the houses, etc.—is holding its breath in anticipation. The reader feels this tension, and when Paul Revere starts his ride, there is a sharp contrast—the silence is broken. The fact that the action takes place at midnight is important to the setting because midnight is a time of stillness.

Next Nora wrote a topic sentence for her composition:

> The setting of Henry Wadsworth Longfellow's "Paul Revere's Ride" creates a mood of stillness and anticipation.

Nora made an outline for her composition that showed the order in which she would present her information.

Drafting and Revising

Nora wrote a draft of her composition. When she reread her draft, she decided that she needed more specific examples to support her ideas. As she revised her paper, she added these examples.

Proofreading and Publishing

Nora proofread her composition, correcting errors in grammar, spelling, and punctuation. Then she made a clean copy of her paper and shared this copy with her classmates and with her teacher.

ACTIVITIES AND ASSIGNMENTS

A. Using Nora's prewriting notes from the case study, write a one- or two-paragraph composition about the setting of "Paul Revere's Ride." Follow these steps:

1. Read the poem carefully at least twice. Then read Nora's notes and add to your own notes any important details that she left out.
2. Make an outline for your compositition. You may use Nora's topic sentence in your paper, or you may write your own.
3. Write a draft of your composition, based on your notes and your outline. Then revise your draft, making sure that it is clear and well organized.
4. Proofread your revised draft for errors in grammar, usage, spelling, punctuation, capitalization, and manuscript form. Then make a clean final copy of your composition, and share this copy with a small group of your classmates.

B. Select one of the following short stories for a one- or two-paragraph composition on setting: "The Land and the Water," on page 119; "Grass Fire," on page 129; "Crime on Mars," on page 137; "The Tell-Tale Heart," on page 145; or "The Drummer Boy of Shiloh," on page 151. Follow these steps when writing your paper:

1. Read the story once, and then freewrite about the impression the setting has made on you. Then read the story again, and list in your notes specific details from the story that help to create the setting.
2. Decide what you think is the most important function of the setting. Write a topic sentence that tells the title and author of the story and that introduces this function of the setting. Then make a rough outline for the rest of your composition.
3. Write a draft of your paper. Then revise the draft, using the Checklist for Revision on page 769.
4. Proofread your revised draft carefully. When you are certain that you have corrected all your errors, make a clean final copy. Share your composition with a small group of your classmates before handing it in to your teacher.

Motivation for Writing Write the following opening sentence of a story on the board: "The King died in battle."

Ask students to give brief suggestions as to where the story might go from there. (Accept various answers.) Then note that students have been discussing the plot of a literary work—what happens in a narrative, how it happens, and also why it happens.

Tell students that in this lesson they will learn the various parts of a plot and the techniques an author uses to keep up interest in the plot.

Lesson 8: Writing About Plot

WHAT IS PLOT?

Plot is what happens and how it happens in a narrative. A *narrative* is any work that tells a story, such as a short story, a novel, a drama, or a narrative poem. To understand a narrative work, a reader must first understand its plot.

THE PARTS OF A PLOT

The following is a list of events that might take place in a simple plot:

> A boy passes a pet store and sees a dog that he would like to own. The boy has no money, and his parents will not buy him the dog because they do not think that he is responsible enough to take care of it. The boy gets a job after school and earns enough money to buy the dog. The boy asks his parents if he can buy the dog with the money he has earned. The boy's parents see that he is responsible enough to earn the money for the dog, so they give him permission to buy it. The boy buys the dog.

These events may be grouped into parts of the plot as follows:

1. *Inciting incident:* The inciting incident is an event that gives rise to the conflict. In the example, this event takes place when the boy sees the dog in the window of the pet store.
2. *Development:* In this part of the plot, events occur as a result of the central conflict. The development in the example includes all the events that occur while the boy is struggling to earn money to buy the dog.
3. *Climax:* The climax is the high point of interest or suspense in a story. In the example, the climax occurs when the boy asks his parents for permission to buy the dog. The reader wonders whether the boy's hard work will pay off.
4. *Resolution:* When the conflict ends, the plot has reached its resolution. In the example, the resolution occurs when the boy finally gets his dog.

Most narratives also have an *introduction,* or *exposition,* which is the section at the beginning of the work that introduces the setting and the major characters. Some narratives also have a *denouement,* which is made up of the events that take place after the resolution. In this section, the writer answers any questions about the plot that remain in the reader's mind.

A writer may use other variations on the standard plot form as well. For example, in some narratives the inciting incident occurs before the opening of the story. If the example had opened with the boy already working, the inciting incident would have occurred before the start of the narrative.

Sometimes the climax and the resolution are the same event. This would have been the case in the example if the boy had gone to ask his parents whether he could buy the dog and had found that they had already bought it for him.

A standard plot may be represented in diagram form as follows:

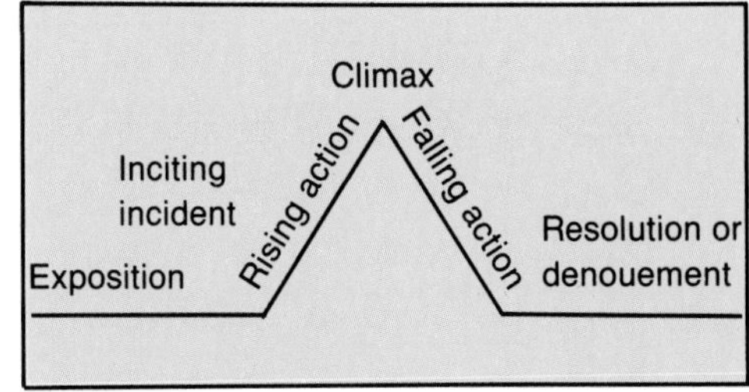

SPECIAL TECHNIQUES OF PLOT

Writers often use the following techniques to make their plots more interesting:

1. *Suspense:* This is the excitement or tension that keeps the reader interested in the plot of a narrative. A writer creates suspense by raising questions in the reader's mind about what will happen next.
2. *Foreshadowing:* This is a hint, or clue, about something that will happen later in the story.
3. *Flashback:* This is a section of a story that interrupts the normal sequence of events to tell about something that happened in the past.
4. *Surprise ending:* This is a conclusion to a story that the reader does not expect.

CONFLICT

Conflict is a struggle between opposing forces. Every plot must contain some kind of conflict—otherwise there would be no action. Although a story might have several different conflicts, short narratives usually have one central conflict involving the main character.

Conflicts can be external or internal. An *external conflict* takes place between a person or a group and some outside force. The outside force might be another person, a group, or a nonhuman obstacle such as a hurricane or a difficult homework assignment. An *internal conflict* takes place within a character's mind. For example, a character may struggle against the temptation to tell a lie.

Read the entries for Conflict and Plot in the Handbook of Literary Terms. Then read the following case study.

CASE STUDY: WRITING ABOUT PLOT

Gabe's English teacher asked the class to write a paragraph about plot. Gabe had enjoyed reading Shirley Jackson's "Charles," on page 79, so he decided to write about the plot of this short story.

Prewriting

First Gabe reread the story, paying special attention to details of the plot. Then he made the following chart of the parts of the plot:

- Introduction: The narrator introduces the main character, her son Laurie, who has just started kindergarten.
- Inciting incident: Laurie announces that there is a boy at school named Charles who is very fresh and who was spanked by the teacher.
- Development: Laurie comes home from school every day with a new story about Charles. Laurie's parents become increasingly curious about this little boy.
- Climax and resolution: The narrator goes to a PTA meeting, hoping to meet Charles's mother. She asks Laurie's teacher about Charles, and the teacher says that there is no Charles in the class. (The reader and the narrator realize at once that Laurie is the one who has been misbehaving.)

Next Gabe looked for special plot techniques in the story. He made another list in his notes, as follows:

- Suspense: During the development, the reader wonders along with the narrator what Charles is really like and what his mother would be like.
- Foreshadowing: Laurie's story of how the entire class stayed after school with Charles sounds fishy. Also, at the beginning of the narrator's conversation with the teacher, the teacher says, "We had a little trouble adjusting, the first week or so, but now he's a fine little helper."
- Surprise ending: Charles turns out to be Laurie.

Gabe used his notes to make a rough outline for his paragraph.

Drafting and Revising

Gabe worte a draft of his paragraph, based

on his prewriting notes. Then he revised the draft to improve its wording and organization.

Proofreading and Publishing

Gabe proofread his paragraph carefully and made a clean final copy of it. Then he shared his paragraph with his parents and with his teacher.

ACTIVITIES AND ASSIGNMENTS

A. Using Gabe's notes from the case study, write a paragraph about the plot of "Charles." Read the story carefully, review Gabe's notes, and write a topic sentence that tells how the plot makes the story interesting to read. Make an outline for the rest of your paragraph. Then finish your draft, revise it, and proofread it. Share your work with your classmates and with your teacher.

B. Choose one of the following short stories for a paragraph on plot: "Rain, Rain, Go Away," on page 13; "Christmas Day in the Morning," on page 21; "The Adventure of the Speckled Band," on page 27; "The Captain and His Horse," on page 47; "A Retrieved Reformation," on page 61; or "The Rule of Names," on page 69. Follow these steps:

1. Read the story twice. In your notes, list the events of the plot under the following headings: *Introduction, Inciting Incident, Development, Climax, Resolution, and Denouement*. Also make a list of the special plot techniques used in the story.
2. Write a topic sentence that tells the title and author of the story and that introduces the reason why you think the plot makes the story worth reading. Make a rough outline for the rest of the paragraph.
3. Finish the draft of your paragraph. Then revise and proofread your draft. Share your final copy with your classmates and with your teacher.

Lesson 9: Writing About Character

TYPES OF CHARACTER

The people and animals who take part in the action of a literary work are called *characters*. Some characters play very important roles in the plot. These are the *major characters*. Other characters play lesser roles and are known as *minor characters*. Normally a narrative focuses on the actions of a single major character, the *protagonist*. Sometimes there is another major character, called the *antagonist,* who is in conflict with the protagonist.

CHARACTERIZATION

A writer reveals what a character is like and how the character changes through the process of *characterization*. There are two primary methods of characterization: direct and indirect. In *direct characterization,* the writer simply tells the reader what the character is like. A statement such as "Sheila was a cheerful conspirator in many harmless pranks" is an example of direct characterization.

In *indirect characterization,* the writer shows what a character is like by describing what the character looks like, by telling what the character says and does, and by telling what other characters say about and do in response to the character. Some of these methods of characterization are very subtle. Tiny details that the writer provides about a character may contain important clues to the character's personality.

ELEMENTS OF CHARACTER

To analyze a character, a reader must think about many factors. These factors appear in the following list:

1. *Appearance:* What does the character look like? What kinds of clothing does the character wear? What do these aspects of appearance reveal about the character?
2. *Personality:* Does the character tend to be emotional or rational? shy or outgoing? skillful or clumsy? happy or depressed? caring or cold? honest or dishonest? a leader or a follower?
3. *Background:* Where did the character grow up? What experiences has he or she had? Is the character experienced or naive? What is the character's social status? How has the character been educated? What does the character do for a living? What are the character's hobbies or skills?
4. *Motivation:* What makes the character act as he or she does? What does the character like and dislike? What are the character's wishes, goals, desires, dreams, and needs?
5. *Relationships:* How is the character related to other characters in the narrative? How does he or she interact with these characters? What happens as a result of these interactions?
6. *Conflict:* Is the character involved in some conflict? If so, is this an internal conflict—one that takes place within the character's mind—or an external conflict—a struggle between the character and some outside force? Is the conflict ever resolved? If so, how?
7. *Change:* Does the character change in the course of the narrative? Does he or she learn or grow? In other words, is the character static (unchanging) or dynamic (changing)?

CASE STUDY: WRITING ABOUT CHARACTER

Ben's English class learned about the methods used by writers to characterize the people and animals in their works. Then his teacher asked the class to write a paragraph about the characterization of the protagonist in a short story. Ben decided to write about the main character in Juan A. A. Sedillo's "Gentleman of Río en Medio," on page 93.

Motivation for Writing Have students take a few minutes to think of a person they know well and to jot down a few notes about the person that they feel will help others to know him or her.

Then ask for volunteers to share their character with the class. During the discussion you might note which aspects of the character are revealed: appearance, personal traits, background, reasons for his or her behavior, and so on.

Now tell the class that in this lesson they will learn more about the different elements that go in to making a character.

Prewriting

Ben read the short story once. He did some freewriting to gather ideas about the main character, Anselmo:

> This character is very proud. He has lots of dignity. I would really trust him. He is a man of principle, although sometimes his principles seem a little strange . . . he refused to take more money for the land—he would only stick to the original bargain.

Ben read the story a second time and listed in his notes some specific examples from the story to support the ideas he had gathered in his freewriting. Then he made a rough outline for his paragraph.

Drafting and Revising

Ben wrote a draft of his paragraph, based on his prewriting notes and his outline. Then he revised his draft, using standard editorial symbols. Here is Ben's draft and the revisions that he made in it:

> ~~What a great guy!~~ The protagenist in Juan A. A. Sedillo's short story, "Gentleman of Rio en Medio," is a very honest and principaled character. Never tries to cheat any body—he just wants to do the right thing. ~~You can tell~~ this ~~cause of~~ the way he ~~won't~~ take more than the original ~~agreed on~~ price. Anselmo is also a very proud man his clothes are old and ragged but he wears them like a gentleman. For example, he takes off his gloves, which have no fingers left in them, very slow and dignified. He is very civilized too. He doesn't ~~jump right into~~ business. ~~He~~ discusses the weather first. This strange old man truly is a gentleman.

Proofreading and Publishing

Ben made a fresh copy of his draft and proofread it for errors in grammar, usage, spelling, and punctuation. Then he made a final copy of his paragraph and shared this copy with his class discussion group.

ACTIVITIES AND ASSIGNMENTS

A. Answer the following questions about the case study:

1. Why did Ben delete the first sentence in his rough draft?
2. What spelling errors did Ben correct?
3. Why did Ben add "Anselmo" to the beginning of the second sentence? Why did he not simply add "He"?
4. Why did Ben change "You can tell" to "The reader knows"?
5. What run-on sentence did Ben correct? How did he do this?
6. Why did Ben change "jump right into" to "talk about . . . right away"?
7. What other changes did Ben make? Why did he make them?

B. Choose one of the following short stories for a paragraph on character: "The House Guest," on page 85; "Raymond's Run," on page 97; "The Day the Sun Came Out," on page 107; or "The Day I Got Lost," on page 113. Follow these steps when planning and writing your paragraph:

1. Read the story and select a major character to write about. Freewrite about your impression of the character. Focus your freewriting on the character's outstanding qualities.
2. Reread the story and make a list of specific details from the story that reveal the character. After each detail, write down what it tells you about that character.
3. Look over your prewriting notes and decide what you think is the most interesting aspect of the character. Write a topic sentence that introduces this aspect as the main idea of your paragraph.
4. Organize your notes. For each idea you want

774

to convey about the character, make sure that you have specific details from the story to support it. Then make a rough outline for your paragraph.

5. Write a draft of your paragraph, referring to your prewriting notes and to your outline as you write. Make sure to conclude with a sentence that summarizes the main point of your paper.
6. Use the Checklist for Revision, on page 769, to revise your rough draft. Then proofread your revised draft for errors in grammar, usage, spelling, punctuation, capitalization, and manuscript form.
7. Share the final copy of your paragraph with a small group of classmates before turning it in to your teacher.

Motivation for Writing Ask the class to imagine an argument between two brothers or sisters over who gets to use the family computer. Then ask how that argument might be viewed by three different people: (1) one of the two children; (2) a friend of the older child; and (3) a friend of the children's parents.

Elicit the fact that each of the three will see the argument somewhat differently. The two children obviously disagree; the older child's friend will probably see things the way the older child does; and perhaps the parents' friend will be able to see things from a more objective viewpoint.

Now tell the class that when a writer tells a story, he or she creates a narrator who also sees the story from a particular point of view. Note that in this lesson the class will find out more about the different possible points of view from which a story can be told.

Lesson 10: Writing About Point of View

WHAT IS NARRATION?

The act of telling a story is called *narration*. Literary works that tell stories are called *narratives*. Short stories, novels, plays, and narrative poems are types of narratives.

The writer of a narrative creates a voice to tell the story. This voice is the *narrator*. The type of narrator a story has determines the story's point of view.

WHAT IS POINT OF VIEW?

Point of view is the perspective from which a narrative is told. Imagine that a friend is telling you about a basketball game in which she played. Because your friend is a character in her own story, she will refer to herself as "I" and will describe what happened as she herself experienced it. Such a narrative, in which the narrator participates in the action, is told from the *first-person point of view*.

Now imagine that your friend is telling you a made-up story about a boy who wants a pet skunk. In this case the narrator will not refer to herself as "I" but will use third-person pronouns such as *he, her, them,* and *their* to refer to the characters in the story. This type of narrative, in which the narrator tells the story from outside the action, is told from the *third-person point of view*.

Once a writer has decided whether to use the first-person or the third-person point of view, he or she must then decide how much the narrator will know about the thoughts and feelings of each character in the story. A story told from the first-person point of view is almost always *limited*. The narrator knows only what is going on inside his or her own mind. A *first-person limited narrator* can report the words and actions of the other characters but not their thoughts or feelings.

A story told from the third-person point of view can also be limited. A *third-person limited narrator* can tell the reader what *one* of the characters is thinking and feeling but only what the other characters say and do.

A third-person narrator who knows what every character is thinking is called *omniscient,* or "all-knowing." A story told from the third-person omniscient point of view will include details not only about the words and actions of all its characters but also about their thoughts and feelings.

WHY WRITERS USE POINT OF VIEW

The point of view from which a story is told affects the way the reader experiences the narrative. For example, a story told from the point of view of a small child will be quite different from one told from the point of view of a college student. Even if the events of the stories are the same, the two points of view will give them completely different flavors.

CASE STUDY: WRITING ABOUT NARRATION AND POINT OF VIEW

Joyce's English teacher asked the class to write a paragraph about the point of view in a short story. Joyce selected Pearl S. Buck's "Christmas Day in the Morning," on page 21.

Prewriting

Joyce read the story and then thought about the point of view from which it was told. She knew that the voice telling the story had not referred to itself as "I," so the point of view was definitely not first-person. Next she asked herself whether the point of view was limited or omniscient. She recalled that the narrator had been able to tell about the thoughts and feelings of one of the characters, Rob. However, the voice related only the actions and words of the other characters in the story. Joyce decided that "Christmas Day in the Morning" was told from the third-person limited point of view.

Joyce did some freewriting to gather ideas about the story's point of view. Then she made a rough outline to organize her notes.

Drafting and Revising

Joyce used her notes and her outline to write the following draft of her paragraph:

> The point of view of Pearl S. Buck's short story, "Christmas Day in the Morning," is third-person limited. Because the narrator can look inside the head of the protagonist, Rob—none of the other characters. I guess she used this point of view to show how Rob saw things, both as an old man and as a fifteen-year-old kid. Even though so many years have past, Rob has similar feelings about Christmas, he has learned the true meaning of Christmas: love. He wants to show his love to his wife as he did to his pa. Also the point of view makes the flash-back which takes place in Rob's mind possible.

Joyce revised her paragraph and made a fresh copy of it for proofreading.

Proofreading and Publishing

Joyce proofread her revised draft for errors in grammar, spelling, and punctuation. Then she made a final copy of her paragraph and shared it with her family before turning it in to her teacher.

ACTIVITIES AND ASSIGNMENTS

A. Revise and proofread Joyce's rough draft. Follow these steps:

1. Find Joyce's topic sentence. Does it express clearly the main point of her paragraph? If not, change it as necessary.
2. Read the rest of Joyce's paragraph. Is it well organized? Are there any sentences that should be moved? Are the main ideas supported by evidence from the story? Make the necessary revisions.
3. Has Joyce used appropriate langauge, avoiding slang and informal expressions? Correct any errors in word choice that you find in her paragraph.
4. When you have finished revising the paragraph, make a clean copy of it for proofreading. Then use the Checklist for Proofreading on page 772.
5. Make a final copy of the paragraph, and share this copy with your classmates and with your teacher.

B. Select one of the following short stories for a paragraph on point of view: "The Adventure of the Speckled Band," on page 27; "The Captain and His Horse," on page 47; "The House Guest," on page 85; "Raymond's Run," on page 97; "The Drummer Boy of Shiloh," on page 151; or "Grass Fire," on page 129. Follow these steps:

1. Read the story once and determine the point of view from which the story is told. Then read the story a second time, keeping in mind the question, "Why did the writer use this point of view?"
2. Freewrite about the point of view, or list ways in which the point of view contributes to the effect of the story. Then write a topic sentence that tells the most important way in which the point of view makes the story effective.
3. Make an outline for your paragraph that shows how you will organize your information.
4. Following your outline, write a draft of the paragraph. First write your topic sentence. Then write the body of your paragraph, supporting your main idea with evidence from the story. Finally, write a conclusion that summarizes the main point of your paragraph.
5. Revise your draft, making sure that all your ideas are clear.
6. Proofread your paragraph for errors in grammar, usage, spelling, punctuation, capitalization, and manuscript form. Make a clean final copy of your paragraph for sharing with your classmates and with your teacher.

Motivation for Writing Ask students who has heard any of Aesop's fables. Request a volunteer to tell one of the fables (for example, the story of the hare and the tortoise).

At the end of the story, point out that the author has included what is called a moral. (In the story of the tortoise and the hare, the moral is usually stated: "Slow and steady wins the race.")

Point out that the moral is one way of stating the theme of a story—the main idea of the work. Note that in this lesson students will learn more about how writers present themes in a story and how to identify a theme when it is not clearly stated.

Lesson 11: Writing About Theme

WHAT IS THEME?

The central idea or insight into life provided by a literary work is called its *theme.* The theme usually reveals an important point about human beings or about life. A statement of theme is a sentence that tells what message a writer wants to convey through a work.

Consider the theme of this poem by an unknown author:

The lightning bug has wings of gold,
The goldbug wings of flame;
The bedbug has no wings at all,
But it gets there just the same.

The poem is about bugs, but it also has a meaning beyond what it says about bugs. One way of stating the poem's theme is, "A person doesn't have to be wealthy or beautiful to make it through life."

Not every literary work has a theme. A complex mystery novel, for example, might be intended merely to entertain. It might contain no deeper meaning beyond the level of the plot.

HOW WRITERS PRESENT THEMES

In some cases a writer simply states the theme of a work. For example, in a short story, a character may make a statement that expresses the theme. A theme that is stated directly is said to be *explicit*.

In other cases, there is no statement of theme included in the work itself. The reader must infer the theme from clues in the work, such as what happens to the characters and how the conflicts are resolved. A theme that is not stated directly is *implicit,* or *implied*.

IDENTIFYING THE THEME OF A LITERARY WORK

It is not always easy to discover an implicit theme in a literary work. You might have to read a work several times to figure out what message the writer wants to communicate. The following list contains questions about several elements of a work that will help you to identify the theme:

1. *Title:* What does the title mean? Does it contain a clue to the theme of the work?
2. *Characters:* What is each of the characters like? Which characters are arrogant? Which are honest? Which are foolish? What happens to each of the characters as a result of his or her personality or actions? What does each character learn from his or her experiences? What can the reader learn from the experiences of the characters?
3. *Conflict:* How is the central conflict in the work resolved, or ended? Does the resolution contain a message about a particular moral or ethical issue?

Some literary works contain more than one theme. One reader might read a work and come to a certain understanding of its meaning, while another reader might read the same work and derive a completely different meaning. Both interpretations would be valid if they could be supported by evidence in the work.

CASE STUDY: WRITING ABOUT THEME

Marita's English teacher asked the class to select a short story and to write a paragraph about its theme. Marita decided to write about "The Ninny," by Anton Chekhov, on page 159.

Prewriting

Marita read the short story twice. Then she thought about the theme of the work. She tried to state the theme in a single sentence, as follows:

> The governess in "The Ninny" is spineless and won't stand up for her rights.

Marita read her sentence and realized that it was too narrow. It did not tell what important message the story conveyed to its readers. She rewrote her sentence as follows:

> People who are spineless can be taken advantage of by stronger, dishonest people.

Marita rewrote her sentence several more times before she had a statement she was satisfied with. Then she read the story again and made notes of specific details that supported the theme. Next she organized her notes and made a rough outline for her paragraph.

Drafting and Revising

Marita used her notes and her outline to write a draft of her paragraph. Then she revised her draft, using standard editorial symbols. Here is Marita's first draft, with her revisions:

¶The theme of Anton Chekhov's "The Ninny" can be ~~put;~~ *stated as follows:* "By refusing to stand up for your rights, you make your life very difficult and risk being taken advantage of." In the story, the narrator plays a trick on his spineless gov~~e~~*e*rness. He ~~says~~ *asks her to* come into ~~my~~ *his* study. He ~~is very forceful and~~ tells her *very forcefully* that he is deducting (from her money) *pay* for every Sunday and holiday and ~~because Kolya tore~~ *for "allowing" his son to tear* his coat. *He even lies about agreements that they made.* The young woman doesn't protest, ~~she just looks sad. You can tell that she's upset.~~ *her eyes merely fill up with tears.* Finally the ~~boss~~ *narrator* tells her that he's *been playing a trick* ~~only kidding~~ and ~~she gets~~ *gives her* the full amount. ~~How can anyone be so meek?~~ *As she leaves, he wonders why anyone would make life so hard by being meek.*

Proofreading and Publishing

Marita proofread her paragraph carefully. Then she made a clean final copy and shared it with her class discussion group.

ACTIVITIES AND ASSIGNMENTS

A. Answer the following questions about the case study:

1. Why did Marita change "put" to "stated as follows"?
2. What spelling error did Marita correct?
3. How did Marita revise the original sentence "He says come into my study"? Why did she change it?
4. Why did Marita change "because Kolya tore" to "for 'allowing' his son to tear"?
5. Why did Marita change "she just looks sad" to "her eyes merely fill up with tears" and delete the sentence "You can tell that she's upset"?
6. Why did she change "boss" to "narrator"?
7. How did Marita revise the last sentence of her paragraph? Why is her new sentence a better conclusion to her paper?
8. What other changes did Marita make? Why did she make them?
9. Are there any changes that you think should still be made in Marita's paragraph? What are these changes?

B. Choose one of the following short stories for a one- or two-paragraph composition on theme: "The Six Rows of Pompons," on page 163; "Thank You, M'am," on page 169; "The Gift-Giving," on page 175; "The Man Without a Country," on page 185; or "Flowers for Algernon," on page 201. Follow these steps when planning and writing your composition:

1. Read the short story once and write down a sentence that explains what you think the story means. Then reread the story and look for evidence to support your statement of theme. List this evidence in your prewriting notes.
2. Organize your notes in a logical order. Then make an outline for your composition.
3. Write a draft of your composition from your notes and your outline. First write a topic sentence that tells the title and author of the

story and briefly describes the theme. Then write the body of your paper, giving specific details from the story that support your topic statement. Conclude with a sentence that summarizes the main point of your paper.

4. Revise your draft. Make sure that all of your points are clear and that they are supported by examples from the story.
5. Proofread your composition for errors in grammar and usage, spelling, punctuation, capitalization, and manuscript form.
6. Make a clean final copy of your composition. Share it with a small group of your classmates before handing it in to your teacher.

SECTION 3: UNDERSTANDING THE WORK AS A WHOLE: INTERPRETATION AND SYNTHESIS

Lesson 12: Writing About a Short Story

There are many elements that must be covered when writing about a short story as a whole. The following list of elements and questions about them will help you to gather information for a composition about a short story.

1. *Author:* Who is the author of the story?
2. *Title:* What is the story's title? Does this title suggest the story's subject or theme?
3. *Setting:* What are the time and place of the story? What mood is created by the setting? Does the setting determine the action or conflict of the story?
4. *Point of view:* Is the story written from the first-person or third-person point of view? Is the narrator limited or omniscient?
5. *Central conflict:* What is the central conflict of the story? Is this conflict internal or external? If the conflict is external, is it between two people, between a person and nature, between a person and society, or between a person and a supernatural force?
6. *Plot:* What are the major events of the story? What happens in the introduction? What is the inciting incident? What happens during the development? What is the climax of the story? How is the central conflict resolved? What, if anything, happens after the resolution? That is, does the story have a denouement?

   What special plot devices are used in the story? Does the story make use of foreshadowing or flashbacks? Is the story suspenseful? If so, what expectations on the part of the reader create this suspense? Does the story have a surprise ending?
7. *Characterization:* Who is the main character, or protagonist? Who are the other major and minor characters? What is revealed in the story about each character's appearance, personality, background, motivations, and relationships? What conflicts do these characters face? Which of these characters changes in the course of the story and in what ways? What roles do the minor characters play in advancing the action of the story?
8. *Devices of sound and figures of speech:* Does the story make use of special devices of sound such as onomatopoeia or parallelism? of figures of speech such as metaphor or hyperbole?
9. *Theme:* What is the theme, or message, of the story? How is this theme revealed?

When you write about a short story, you will probably want to select one of the elements from the above list as the focus of your composition. Then you can discuss how the other elements relate to it. For example, you might decide to focus on the theme of a particular short story. In your introductory paragraph, you would tell the title and author of the story and introduce its theme. In the first body paragraph, you might give a brief summary of the story's plot. In the second body paragraph, you might describe the main character and the conflict that he or she faces in the story. You would devote other body paragraphs to other important elements in the story that related to the theme. Finally, you would write a concluding paragraph that explained why the theme was significant.

Motivation for Writing Write this statement on the board: "The whole is *more* than the sum of its parts." Ask students to tell what the statement means, as it relates to a work of literature. (Accept various answers. Suggested response: In a work of literature we may be able to define the plot and characters, theme, and so on by themselves, but when we consider all these parts together as they relate to each other, we may come up with a better understanding of the work as a whole.)

Tell the class that in this lesson, and in Section 3 in general, they will learn more about interpreting a work of literature as a whole.

CASE STUDY: WRITING ABOUT A SHORT STORY

Chuck's English class had studied all the different elements of short stories. His teacher asked the class to write a composition of three to five paragraphs that analyzed an entire short story. Chuck decided to write about Edward Everett Hale's "The Man Without a Country," on page 185.

Prewriting

Chuck read the story once. He felt that the theme was an especially important one, so he decided that this theme would be the focus of his composition. Chuck did some freewriting to gather ideas about the theme:

> This story is so emotional! I never thought that a story about patriotism could be so moving. I really felt compassion for Nolan, even if he did swear that he didn't ever want to hear about the U.S. again—the story really made me think about what it means to be an American.

Next, to make sure that he had a clear idea of exactly what the theme was, he tried to state it in a sentence in his own words:

> Americans should realize how lucky they are to be citizens of the United States.

Chuck reread the story. He then made a chart in his notes lisitng other elements of the story and telling how they related to the theme. Here is a section from Chuck's prewriting notes:

- Author: Edward Everett Hale
- Title: "The Man Without a Country." The title suggests both the subject and the theme of the story.
- Point of view: First-person limited. This point of view allows the author to tell the story from the perspective of someone who had met Nolan and could appreciate his suffering.
- Central conflict: Nolan vs. his punishment. Nolan struggles to keep his feelings of longing for home under control. The conflict is internal, but the reader can see how painful it is for Nolan. This adds to the power of the theme.

Plot:

- Introduction: The young Nolan blindly joins Aaron Burr in his rebel activities.
- Inciting incident: When standing trial for his crime, Nolan says that he would like never to hear of the United States again.
- Development: The court grants Nolan his wish. He is transferred from ship to ship for the rest of his life, never being allowed to discuss his country with anyone. On one of these ships, he meets the narrator and tells him that he should realize how much the United States means to him.
- Resolution: On his deathbed, Nolan begs the captain of the ship to tell him what has happened in the United States in the last fifty years. The captain does, and Nolan dies in peace.
- Denouement: The captain discovers a note left by Nolan asking that a gravestone be erected in the U.S. with his name and some patriotic words on it.
- Characterization: Nolan, the protagonist, is characterized as lonely and withdrawn after losing his country. This shows how important the United States really is—it's tragic that Nolan has to lose it before he appreciates it.

Chuck made an outline for his composition. The outline showed that his composition would have four paragraphs, as follows:

- Introductory paragraph:
  - Author
  - Title
  - Theme

- First body paragraph:
  Summarize plot.
  Tell how plot reveals theme.
- Second body paragraph:
  Describe characterization of Nolan.
  Tell how this relates to theme.
- Concluding paragraph:
  Restate theme.
  Tell how theme is significant for all Americans.

Drafting and Revising

Chuck used his outline and his prewriting notes to write a draft of his composition. Then he revised his draft.

Proofreading and Publishing

Chuck proofread his composition and then made a clean copy of it. He shared his final copy with his classmates and his teacher.

ACTIVITIES AND ASSIGNMENTS

A. Read "The Man Without a Country," on page 185. Then use Chuck's notes and outline from the case study to write a four-paragraph composition on the short story. Revise and proofread the composition. Share your final copy with your classmates and your teacher.

B. Select one of the following short stories for a three- to five-paragraph composition: "Christmas Day in the Morning," on page 21; "The Day the Sun Came Out," on page 107; "The Tell-Tale Heart," on page 145; "The Six Rows of Pompons," on page 163; "The Gift-Giving," on page 175; or "Flowers for Algernon," on page 201. Follow the same steps that Chuck followed in the case study. Share the final copy of your composition with a small group of your classmates and with your English teacher.

Motivation for Writing Write this statement on the board: "I couldn't see the forest for the trees." Ask students what the statement might mean as it relates to a work of literature, say a poem.

(Accept various answers. Suggested response: The statement might mean the reader could only focus on the individual parts or aspects of the poem but could not see the poem as a whole.)

Tell the class that in this lesson they will learn more about how to interpret a poem as a whole.

Lesson 13: Writing About a Poem

In this handbook you have learned about some elements found in poetry—images, special devices of sound, figures of speech, theme, and so on. When you write about a poem, you must consider all of these elements and how they contribute to the poem as a whole.

It is important to understand a poem fully before you begin writing about it. Therefore, you should read the poem several times, both silently and aloud, to familiarize yourself with the way the poem achieves its effect. Make sure that you understand the meanings of all the words in the poem—if any are unfamiliar, look them up in a dictionary. Listen to the way the poem sounds, noticing the effect of the particular words the author has chosen. If the poem is a concrete poem, look carefully at the arrangement of the words on the page and think about how the shape relates to the poem's meaning. To make sure that you understand each line of the poem, try to paraphrase it, or put it into your own words.

The following list of questions will be helpful when you gather information for writing about a poem:

1. *Author:* Who is the poem's author?
2. *Title:* What is the title of the poem? Does the title suggest the poem's subject or theme?
3. *Genre:* What is the poem's genre, or type? Is it a lyric poem—a highly musical work that expresses emotion? Is it a narrative poem—one that tells a story? Is it a concrete poem—one with a shape that suggests its meaning?
4. *Stanza form:* Is the poem divided into stanzas? If so, how many lines does each stanza have? Is the poem written in some standard stanza form such as couplet, quatrain, sonnet, haiku, or limerick? Does each stanza function as a separate unit of meaning, like a paragraph in a composition?
5. *Devices of sound:* Is the poem in free verse or in some regular meter? If the poem has some regular meter, how many feet are there in an average line? What kind of foot is most common in the poem?

   Does the poem have a regular rhyme scheme? If so, what is this rhyme scheme?

   Does the poem make use of onomatopoeia? alliteration? consonance? assonance? internal rhyme? euphony? cacophony? parallelism? repetition? Does it have a refrain? What examples can you find of these devices?
6. *Imagery:* What images of sight are used in the poem? of sound? of taste? of touch? of smell? What effects do these images have?
7. *Figures of speech:* Does the poem contain examples of metaphor? of simile? of personification? of hyperbole? of understatement? Does the poet make use of symbols? puns? allusions? paradoxes? irony?
8. *Other literary devices:* What is the poem's general mood? Does this mood change in the course of the poem?

   What is the poem's setting? How is the setting related to the poem's mood? to the action of the poem?

   What seems to be the poem's central message, or theme? What do you think the writer's purpose was?

   Is the poem written in complete sentences?

   Does the poem use punctuation, capitalization, or spacing in special ways?

   Does the poem invite the reader to contrast two or more things?

CASE STUDY: WRITING ABOUT A POEM

Cory's English teacher asked the class to

write a composition analyzing a favorite poem. Cory decided to write about Naoshi Koriyama's "Jetliner," on page 536.

Prewriting

First Cory read the poem silently. He took note of the words *pondering* and *chandelier,* which were defined in the footnotes. Then he read the poem aloud, listening to the sounds of the words as he read them. He read the poem a third time and looked for examples of images and figures of speech. Cory then read the list of questions on page 784 and answered the questions in his notes. Here is a section from Cory's prewriting notes:

- Author: Naoshi Koriyama
- Title: "Jetliner"
- Stanza form: The poem has four stanzas of unequal length. Each stanza describes a distinct part of the process of an airplane's taking off.
- Devices of sound: The poem is written in free verse. There is no rhyme scheme.

  Onomatopoeia:
  "burning heart beating like thunders" (line 8);
  "howling, shouting, screaming, and roaring" (line 16)

  Alliteration:
  "*sh*arp eyes *sh*ining" (line 4);
  "*b*urning heart *b*eating" (line 8);
  "*s*oftly lifting . . . *s*oaring higher" (lines 19–20)

  Euphony:
  "soaring higher and higher and higher still/piercing the sea of clouds/up into the chandelier of stars" (lines 20–22)

  Cacophony:
  "kicking the dark earth hard" (line 12);
  "violent kick" (line 17)

  Repetition:
  "deep, deep breath" (line 5);
  "kicking the dark earth hard/. . . . / kicking the dark earth harder" (lines 12–14);
  "then he dashes, dashes like mad, like mad" (line 15);
  "soaring higher and higher and higher still" (line 20)

Cory finished answering the questions and then made a rough outline for his composition. He decided that the main point of his paper would be how the poem uses devices of sound and figures of speech to create a vivid picture of an airplane taking off.

Drafting and Revising

Cory wrote a draft of his composition from his outline and his prewriting notes. Then he revised his composition to make it clearer and more focused.

Proofreading and Publishing

Cory proofread his paper carefully. He made a clean final copy of his composition and shared it with his class discussion group.

ACTIVITIES AND ASSIGNMENTS

A. Finish Cory's prewriting and then write a composition about the poem "Jetliner." Follow these steps:

1. Read the poem several times, both silently and aloud. Then answer the questions in the list on page 784 under the headings *Imagery, Figures of Speech,* and *Other Literary Devices*. Organize your information into an outline for your composition.
2. Write a draft of the composition according to your outline. Then revise your draft, making sure that your main points are clear.
3. Proofread the composition for errors in spelling and mechanics. Then make a clean copy

of your paper and share it with a small group of your classmates.

B. Select one of the following poems for a two- or three-paragraph analysis: "Barbara Frietchie," on page 525; "Lyric 17," on page 532; "Reflections Dental," on page 542; "Ring Out, Wild Bells," on page 544; "Taught Me Purple," on page 551; "Four Little Foxes," on page 556; "Blow, Blow, Thou Winter Wind," on page 566; "January," on page 576; "Southbound on the Freeway," on page 588; "Identity," on page 598; or "The Choice," on page 604. Follow these steps when planning and writing your paper:

1. Read the poem silently. Look up any unfamiliar words in a dictionary. Read the poem aloud, paying attention to the way the poem sounds. Then read the poem silently again and look for examples of imagery and figurative language. In your prewriting notes, answer the questions from the list on page 784.
2. Decide what you think is the purpose of the poem. Write a topic sentence for your composition that tells this purpose. Then organize your notes to show how the writer accomplishes the purpose through specific techniques used in the poem. Make a rough outline that shows what information you will present in each paragraph of your paper.
3. Write a draft of your composition. Revise your draft, making sure that it has an introduction with a clear topic sentence, a body with supporting evidence for the topic sentence, and a solid conclusion.
4. Proofread your composition using the Checklist for Proofreading on page 772.
5. Make a clean final copy of your paper and share it with your classmates and with your teacher.

Lesson 14: Writing About Drama

DRAMA AS LITERATURE

One way to experience a drama is to read it as you would any other form of literature. Drama shares many common elements with short stories, novels, and narrative poetry. Dramas have plots, conflicts, settings, and characters. Like other types of writing, dramas have themes and use imagery, devices of sound, and figurative language.

DRAMA AS PERFORMANCE

There is one aspect of drama that sets it apart from all other types of literature. Drama is written specifically to be performed by actors in front of an audience. To experience the full effect of a drama, you must see it as a stage production. When you read a drama, you should constantly be thinking about what the work would be like in a performance.

The printed form of a drama is called its *script,* and it is composed of dialogue and stage directions. *Dialogue* simply means the words spoken by the characters. There are no quotation marks around the dialogue in a drama; each line follows the name of the character who speaks it. *Stage directions* are instructions for how the performance should appear and sound to the audience. When reading a drama, you will see the stage directions in brackets or parentheses; they will be italicized or underlined. They give such information as how the stage should look; how the characters should move and speak; what special effects of sound and lighting should be used; and what properties, or movable objects, should appear on stage.

Since a drama may be experienced in two very different ways—as literature or as performance—there are many possible approaches to writing about a drama. You could simply analyze one aspect of the drama, such as characterization, plot, conflict, or setting. A paper focusing on one of these topics would be very similar to the compositions you have written in the other parts of this handbook. Another approach to writing about a drama is to write about some aspect of its performance. You might describe how you would go about constructing the set for a particular scene in the drama or what costumes a certain character would wear. If you were able to attend an actual performance of the drama, you could write a critique of that performance, telling what you thought was good about it and what you thought should have been done differently.

CASE STUDY: WRITING ABOUT DRAMA

Pauline's English class studied how drama was similar to and different from other types of literature. Then her teacher asked the class to write an analysis of a drama. Pauline decided to write about *The Ugly Duckling,* the play by A. A. Milne, on page 245.

Prewriting

Pauline read the drama very carefully. Since she had not seen a performance of the play, she decided to write about it as a work of literature. She made the following list of plot elements:

- Introduction: In the conversation between the King and the Chancellor, we learn that Prince Simon is on his way to meet Princess Camilla. The Princess is not beautiful, and the King and Queen are worried that the Prince will refuse to marry her.
- Inciting incident: This takes place before the opening of the play. The King and

Motivation for Writing Ask students if they have ever heard the term "script doctor." Explain, if necessary, that a script doctor is someone who rewrites weak dramas, especially movie scripts, to make them better.

Ask students to imagine they are script doctors. Ask them to state the characteristics of a drama that they would look for in seeking to write a stronger script. (Accept various answers. Suggested response: A script doctor would look for interesting characters, a plot that hangs together well, a clear point of view, and so on.)

Note that the class will learn more about writing about drama in this lesson.

Queen have decided to let Dulcibella stand in for the Princess at her first meeting with the Prince.

- Development: Their Majesties' plan goes into action. Prince Simon and Princess Camilla meet accidentally and fall in love.
- Climax and resolution: Prince Simon's attendant must solve a riddle, but he is too stupid to figure it out. The Prince steps in and makes an excuse for him, and the wedding can go on as planned.
- Denouement: Princess Camilla tells her parents that she adores the Prince and leaves to prepare for the wedding. The King remarks that she doesn't look quite so plain any longer.
- Special techniques: The focus of the plot is the irony of situation that arises from the chance meeting of the Prince and Princess.

Pauline made one further note about *The Ugly Duckling*:

> This play is especially enjoyable in its written form because many of the stage directions contain many witty remarks that an audience would not experience.

Pauline decided that the main point of her paper would be to explain why *The Ugly Duckling* is a pleasure to read as well as to see performed. She made an outline for her composition showing how she would organize the information in her prewriting notes into three paragraphs.

Drafting and Revising

Pauline wrote a draft of her composition. She read her draft and realized that it did not really accomplish her purpose, which was to show why the drama was enjoyable to read. When she revised her composition, she added more specific details about the plot of the drama to make her writing more convincing.

Proofreading and Publishing

Pauline made a fresh copy of her revised draft and proofread it for errors in spelling and mechanics. Then she shared the final copy of her composition with her parents and her English teacher.

ACTIVITIES AND ASSIGNMENTS

A. Use Pauline's notes to write a three-paragraph composition about *The Ugly Duckling*. Follow these steps:

1. Read the drama carefully. Add to Pauline's notes any important details that you find are missing. Then make an outline for your composition. Your outline should have one section for each paragraph of your composition. In the introductory paragraph, tell what drama you're writing about and introduce the main point of your paper. In the body paragraph, give evidence to support your main point. In the concluding paragraph, summarize the main idea of your composition and perhaps comment on the theme of the play.
2. Use your outline to write a draft of your composition.
3. Revise your paper using the Checklist for Revision on page 769.
4. Proofread your composition and make a clean copy of it. Then share your final copy with your classmates and your teacher.

B. Select one of the following dramas for an original composition: *Back There,* on page 263; *Let Me Hear You Whisper,* on page 277; or *The Diary of Anne Frank,* on page 303. Follow these steps:

1. Read the drama carefully. Decide what approach you will take in writing about it—you can analyze it strictly as literature, or you can write about some aspect of its performance.
2. Decide on a single element of the drama—a particular character, the plot, the setting, and so on—that will serve as the focus of your

composition. Write a topic sentence that explains the main idea of your paper.

3. Make an outline for your composition. Be sure that you plan for a clear introduction, body, and conclusion.
4. Write a draft of your paragraph. Then revise it, making sure that all of your ideas are expressed clearly and are supported with evidence from the drama.
5. Proofread your composition using the Checklist for Proofreading on page 772. Then make a clean final copy of your paper for sharing with a small group of your classmates and with your teacher.

789

Motivation for Writing Ask students to imagine that they are TV producers who are considering which scripts to use in a certain drama series for next season. Ask students to consider what they would look for in a superior script.

(Accept various answers. Suggested response: Like the script doctor, the TV producer looks for interesting characters, a strong plot with a dramatic conflict, an original idea, and a clear development of that idea.)

Note that in this lesson, students will learn more about how to evaluate a literary work, whether it be a drama, poem, or short story.

SECTION 4: JUDGING A LITERARY WORK: EVALUATION

Lesson 15: Evaluating a Literary Work

WHAT IS AN EVALUATION?

An *evaluation* of a literary work is a judgment about its quality or value. Consider the following poem, which also appears on page 578:

WINTER MOON

Langston Hughes

How thin and sharp is the moon tonight!
How thin and sharp and ghostly white
Is the slim curved crook of the moon tonight!

Here is a statement that evaluates the poem:

> Langston Hughes's poem, "Winter Moon," is effective because it uses sense images so well. The poem gives readers a vivid, intense experience of the painful emotions surrounding a winter moon.

The evaluation expresses an opinion about the poem, not a fact. However, the opinion must be supported by facts. Consider the following evaluation of the same poem:

> Langston Hughes's poem, "Winter Moon," is effective because it uses sense images so well. The poem gives readers a vivid, intense experience of how comforting and cheerful a winter moon can be.

This statement also expresses an opinion, but it is not a valid opinion. That is, the opinion cannot be backed up by facts about the poem. The moon's "thin and sharp" edges suggest a painful image of touch, and the "ghostly white" color of the moon evokes a frightening, eerie feeling. Therefore, the evidence from the poem does not support the claim that it gives the reader a "comforting and cheerful" experience.

CRITERIA FOR EVALUATION

When you evaluate something, you need a set of *criteria,* or standards, for your judgment. The following list includes some of the most common criteria used for evaluating literature:

1. *Originality:* A work that deals with a subject never dealt with before or that approaches a topic in a new and different way is said to show originality. Writers who avoid trite or clichéd material and who show their readers fresh ways of looking at the world generally receive favorable evaluations of their work.
2. *Consistency or completeness of effect:* A writer usually tries to create a certain effect in a literary work. If the effect is spoiled through the author's carelessness, the overall quality of the work is lowered. For example, consider the following haiku:

   Loose creaking floorboards—
   I tiptoe through dark shadows.
   Boy, am I hungry!

   The first two lines create a serious, suspenseful mood, but the third line does not complete this effect. Therefore, the poem probably would not be evaluated favorably.
3. *Importance:* Some works are considered to be of higher value than others because they deal with topics of greater importance. A nonsense poem about how many jellybeans a boy can eat would not be valuable in terms of its message. A poem whose theme was world hunger, on the other hand, might be evaluated favorably because of the importance of its message.
4. *Moral or ethical message:* In many works, the

theme contains a message about how people should live their lives. A reader who agrees with the message will consider the work to be of greater value than a reader who does not agree with the message. For example, a person who believed the statement "It is important to stand up for one's own rights" would probably place a high value on the short story, "The Ninny," on page 159.

5. *Clarity:* Good literature should present the writer's ideas clearly. This does not mean that works that are difficult to understand at first are inferior to simple ones. Some of the best literary works require careful study before the reader can understand and appreciate what the writer has intended. However, if a work is difficult to make sense of because it is simply written in a careless or confusing manner, then the work might be judged to be of poor quality.

CASE STUDY: EVALUATING A LITERARY WORK

Cara's English teacher asked the class to write an evaluation of a poem. Cara decided to write about Walter de la Mare's "Silver," on page 564.

Prewriting

Cara read the poem several times, silently and aloud. Then she did some freewriting about the effect that the poem created:

> The title says it all—everything in this poem turns silver when the moon's beams hit it. Even things you wouldn't think of like a dog's paws and a mouse's claws. The poem makes me think of moonlight as especially beautiful—I hadn't ever really thought about how things looked in it before. Every line in the poem shows how the moonlight turns something silver.

Next Cara applied the criteria for evaluation in this lesson to the poem. Here is a section from Cara's prewriting notes:

- Originality: The topic—moonlight—isn't particularly original. However, the way the poet describes it is—for example, he says that even a mouse's claws look silver in the moonlight.
- Completeness of effect: The poem never strays from its purpose of describing the moonlight. The theme of silver is carried throughout the poem.
  The mood—one of quiet, peaceful beauty—is consistent throughout the poem.
- Clarity: The poem is not confusing or unclear. It is fairly simple, but very effective.

Cara decided that what made the poem especially valuable was the completeness of the effect that it created through images of sight. She made this the main point of her evaluation, and she wrote a topic sentence that introduced this idea. Then she made an outline for her paper that showed how she would organize the information she had gathered in her prewriting.

Drafting and Revising

Cara wrote a draft of her evaluation. When she read what she had written, she realized that some of her ideas would be unclear to her readers. She revised her draft, adding more specific details to make her main points clearer.

Proofreading and Publishing

Cara proofread her draft, correcting errors in grammar and usage, spelling, punctuation, and capitalization. Then she made a final copy of her evaluation for sharing with her classmates and with her teacher.

ACTIVITIES AND ASSIGNMENTS

A. Use Cara's prewriting notes to write an evaluation of "Silver." Follow these steps:

1. Read the poem several times. Review Cara's notes and add any important details that you find are missing from them.

2. Decide what criterion will be the focus of your evaluation. Write a topic sentence that tells the author and title of the poem and the main criterion that you will be using to evaluate it. Make a rough outline for your paper.
3. Write a draft of your paper. Make sure that it has a clear introduction, body, and conclusion. In the conclusion, make a general statement about the quality of the work as a whole.
4. Revise and proofread your composition. Make a final copy to share with your classmates in a small discussion group. Then turn your evaluation in to your teacher.

B. Select one of the following works for a one- to three-paragraph evaluation: "Charles," on page 79; "Gentleman of Río en Medio," on page 93; "The Day I Got Lost," on page 113; "The Tell-Tale Heart," on page 145; "Thank You, M'am," on page 169; *Let Me Hear You Whisper,* on page 277; "*Harriet Tubman: Guide to Freedom,*" on page 383; "The Trouble with Television," on page 463; "Dial Versus Digital," on page 477; "Paul Revere's Ride," on page 509; "The Secret Heart," on page 548; "Blue-Butterfly Day," on page 559; "Forgotten Language," on page 565; "The City Is So Big," on page 586; or "Identity," on page 598. Follow these steps:

1. Read the work carefully—if it is a poem, read it several times. Then freewrite about why you liked or did not like the work.
2. Apply the criteria listed in this lesson to the work. In your notes, write down how the work meets or does not meet each criterion.
3. Decide which criterion is the most appropriate for evaluating the work. Write a topic sentence that introduces the work and the central criterion that you will use to judge it. Then make an outline for the rest of your composition.
4. Draft, revise, and proofread your evaluation. Share your final copy with your classmates and with your teacher.

Lesson 16: Writing a Comparative Evaluation

WHAT IS A COMPARATIVE EVALUATION?

You learned in the last lesson that an evaluation is a judgment about the quality of a literary work. A *comparative evaluation* is one in which two or more works are evaluated side by side, exploring what makes one better or worse than the other(s).

One way to write a comparative evaluation is simply to apply the criteria listed in the preceding lesson to each of the works. For example, you might explain why one short story was more original than another short story.

Another approach to writing a comparative evaluation is to select a literary element that the works have in common—such as a subject, a theme, or a special technique—and to write about why one work is a better example of that element. For example, if you were comparing two poems that were both about a basball game, you might tell why one was more vivid and interesting than the other.

STEPS IN WRITING A COMPARATIVE EVALUATION

Begin by selecting the works that you will compare. The works must have something in common. You might choose to compare two short stories, three poems, or a drama and a short story with similar themes. When you have decided what specific works you will compare, list in your notes their authors and titles and the feature they have in common as follows:

- Works to be compared: John Greenleaf Whittier's poem, "Barbara Frietchie," and Henry Wadsworth Longfellow's poem, "Paul Revere's Ride"
- Feature to be compared: originality in presenting a historical event

The next step is to study each of the works carefully and to decide which author has done the better job of handling the feature. Gather evidence from the works to support your opinion.

When you write your comparative evaluation, begin with an introductory paragraph that tells what works you will be comparing and what feature you will be discussing. Then write body paragraphs about each work. In each body paragraph, give details from the work to show how the author has dealt with the feature you are comparing. Make sure that the details you give support your opinion about which work is superior. Finally, write a concluding paragraph that sums up your opinion about the comparative values of the works.

CASE STUDY: WRITING A COMPARATIVE EVALUATION

Joanna's English teacher asked the class to write a comparative evaluation of two poems.

Prewriting

Joanna decided to compare two poems with similar subjects. She selected Robert Frost's "Blue-Butterfly Day," on page 559, and John Updike's "January," on page 576, because each described a particular season. She wrote the following information in her prewriting notes:

- Works to be compared: "Blue-Butterfly Day," by Robert Frost, and "January," by John Updike
- Feature to be compared: imagery used to portray a season

Joanna studied the poems very carefully and decided that she liked the Updike poem better because it had more images of scenery. She then gathered evidence from the poems to

Motivation for Writing Ask students to suppose they are editors of the school literary magazine. How would they decide which was the better of two poems submitted for the publication?

(Accept various answers. Suggested response: Using the checklist developed in Lesson 13, page 784, editors might look for items the two poems have in common from the following list, and then decide which poem does a better job developing each item: stanza form, sound devices, imagery, figures of speech, mood, and theme.)

Tell students that they will learn more about how to compare and evaluate two works of literature in this lesson.

support her evaluation. Joanna made a rough outline for her paper showing how she would organize her information into four paragraphs.

Drafting and Revising

Joanna wrote a draft of her evaluation from her notes and her outline. Here are the first two paragraphs of her paper:

> Robert Frost's poem, "Blue-Butterfly Day," and John Updike's poem January both describe a certain season. Both are excellent, but maybe Updike's might be called "better" due to there are more images of scenery. The Frost one describes mainly only the butterflies.
>
> The images in "Blue-Butterfly Day" include "sky-flakes" in line 2, "unmixed color on the wing" in line 3, and "flowers that fly" in line 5. Their nice images. There are also images of touch as well. Like in the Last two lines: "They lie closed over in the wind and cling/Where wheels have freshly sliced the April mire." These images are farely specific—they describe the butterflies but not much info about the scenery around.

Joanna finished her draft. She then revised it, adding more details from the poems and making her sentences clearer. Then she made a fresh copy of her revised draft for proofreading.

Proofreading and Publishing

Joanna proofread her composition carefully. Then she shared the final copy of her comparative evaluation with her parents, her classmates, and her teacher.

ACTIVITIES AND ASSIGNMENTS

A. Finish writing Joanna's draft from the case study. Follow these steps:

1. Read the poems very carefully. Decide whether or not you agree with Joanna's evaluation. If you agree, gather information to support it; if you do not agree, gather information to support your own evaluation.
2. Rewrite the first two paragraphs of Joanna's evaluation if you disagree with her comparison of the poems. Finish the composition, writing another body paragraph discussing the Updike poem and a concluding paragraph.
3. Revise the draft. Make sure that your ideas will be understood by your readers. Then proofread the paper for errors in spelling and mechanics. Share the final copy of your evaluation with a small group of your classmates and with your teacher.

B. Write a comparative evaluation of one of the following pairs of literary works (suggestions for features to compare are in parentheses): "Barbara Frietchie," on page 525, and "Paul Revere's Ride," on page 509 (effective presentation of historical events); "Jetliner," on page 536, and "Song of the Sky Loom," on page 579 (effective use of figures of speech); "Four Little Foxes," on page 556, and "Ring Out, Wild Bells," on page 544 (effective use of devices of sound); or "Identity," on page 598, and "The Choice," on page 604 (effective examination of the subject of choices). Follow these steps:

1. Read both works carefully. Freewrite about why you liked one better than the other. Then select one literary element or criterion of evaluation that shows how the two works differ in quality. Write a topic sentence that explains why you think this criterion shows one work to be better than the other.
2. Gather information from both works that supports your topic sentence. Then organize your notes and make an outline for a four-paragraph composition. The first paragraph should introduce the two works and include your topic sentence. The second and third paragraphs—the body paragraphs—should each discuss one of the works and give examples that support your topic sentence. The concluding paragraph should summarize the main point of your evaluation.
3. Revise and proofread your draft. Then make a final copy of your comparative evaluation and

share it with a small group of your classmates who also wrote about the two works that you selected. Finally, share your paper with your teacher.

Motivation for Writing Remind students that they have learned about the elements of a short story—plot, character, setting, point of view, and theme—at various points in the year. Now it is time to put all this knowledge together by writing a short story.

Have the class break up into small groups to brainstorm for ideas for a short story which each member of the group can then develop individually.

Note that students can learn more about writing a short story in this lesson.

SECTION 5: WRITING CREATIVELY

Lesson 17: Writing a Short Story

In the preceding lessons of this handbook, you have learned how to analyze literature written by other writers. Now you will have the chance to write your own literary works. In this lesson you will learn about the process of writing a short story.

FINDING A STORY IDEA

The first step in planning a short story is to think of a subject to write about. It is sometimes helpful to brainstorm about the elements of short stories that you have studied in this handbook—setting, conflict, character, and theme, for example. The following are some suggestions for finding an idea for your short story:

1. Think of a particular time and place that interest you. The setting of a short story often gives rise to the action. For example, if you decided to set your story in the distant future, you might write about a conflict between characters over whether or not to place an earth colony on the planet Venus.
2. Imagine an interesting conflict that might involve the main character of your short story. The conflict might be internal—within the mind of the character—or external—between the character and another character, a group, or a nonhuman force such as a tornado.
3. Think of an interesting person whom you know in real life and create a character that has some of the qualities of this person.
4. Take an idea that you believe in strongly and think of a situation that would illustrate this idea. For example, if you think that honesty is an important value, create a story that will show why it is important.

DEVELOPING YOUR IDEA

When you have found an idea for one part of your story, start planning the other parts and thinking about how they will all fit together. The following list of questions will help you to develop the various parts of your story:

1. *Setting:* When and where does the story take place? What images of sight, sound, touch, taste, and smell can I use to describe the setting?
2. *Character:* Who is the main character? What is he or she like? How will I show what the character is like in the story? What other major characters will appear in the story? What will they be like? How will these characters relate to the main character? What minor characters will appear in the story? What roles will they play?
3. *Conflict:* What conflict will the main character be involved in? Will the conflict be internal—within the character's mind—or external—between the character and some outside force?
4. *Plot:* What events will take place in the story, and in what order?

   Introduction: What background information will I need to supply about the setting? about the characters?

   Inciting incident: What event will cause the central conflict of the story?

   Development: What events will occur as a result of the inciting incident?

   Climax: What will be the high point of interest or suspense in the story?

   Resolution: How will the conflict in the story end?

   Denouement: What events, if any, will occur after the resolution?

5. *Theme:* What will be the main idea of my story? How will I reveal this idea?
6. *Point of view:* Will the story be told from the first-person point of view—by a narrator who is a character in the story? Or will the story be told from the third-person point of view—by a narrator who is outside the action of the story? Will the narrator be limited or omniscient?

CASE STUDY: WRITING A SHORT STORY

Peter's English teacher asked the class to write an original short story for a literary contest in the school. Peter was excited about entering the contest, so he began thinking about the assignment right away.

Prewriting

First Peter needed an interesting idea for his story. He read the suggestions for finding a story idea in this lesson and brainstormed about setting, conflict, character, and theme. Here is a section from Peter's prewriting notes:

- Setting: the school cafeteria; a hut in the jungle; a deserted island; my dad's office building; on board a submarine
- Conflict: a fight with my best friend; a tiger is about to attack; there's no food or water; stuck in an elevator; deciding whether to attack an aircraft carrier
- Character: myself; my sister; my English teacher; an exchange student from India; the man who owns the candy store near the school
- Theme: friendship is really important; going to school isn't as bad as it seems sometimes; being in a position of authority means you have to make difficult decisions

Peter looked over his prewriting and decided that he would write a story about how he and his best friend got stuck in an elevator one day. He then made a list of the events that would take place in his story:

- Introduction: David and I skip school and go to my dad's office building. Dad was a kid once, so we hope he'll think it's funny. He works on the fourteenth floor, so we get into the elevator.
- Inciting incident: The elevator gets stuck somewhere near the ninth floor.
- Development: At first we think it's neat to be stuck, but then we start to get scared. We talk about what would happen if we never got out of the elevator. We wonder what our English teacher, Mrs. Mehl, would say tomorrow in class if we had died while skipping school.
- Climax: The elevator starts to shake. We're certain that we're going to fall to the bottom of the elevator shaft and die.
- Resolution: The elevator door opens. We take the stairs down to the ground floor.
- Denouement: We decide to go back to school, and we return just in time for English class. After class, we talk about how we've never enjoyed a class so much!

Peter planned to tell the story from the perspective of a character who takes part in the action, so the point of view would be first-person limited. Now that he had gathered all of his information, he was ready to begin writing his short story.

Drafting and Revising

Peter wrote a draft of his story, telling each of the events in order. Then he revised his draft, adding details that would create suspense for the reader.

Proofreading and Publishing

Peter proofread the revised draft of his story

797

for errors in spelling and mechanics. Then he made three final copies of his short story—one for his friend David, one for his English teacher, and one for the literary contest.

ACTIVITIES AND ASSIGNMENTS

A. Use Peter's notes from the case study to write a short story. Revise and proofread the story. Then share it with your classmates and with your teacher.

B. Write an original short story about any subject that interests you. Follow these steps when planning and writing your story:

1. To think of an idea for your story, brainstorm about setting, conflict, character, and theme as Peter did in the case study. Pick one or two of the best ideas. Then develop the other parts of your story.
2. Make a list in your notes of the events that will take place in your story under the following headings: Introduction, Inciting incident, Development, Climax, Resolution, and Denouement. If you wish to do so, you may also include any of the following elements: Suspense, Foreshadowing, Flashbacks, and Surprise ending.
3. Write a draft of your short story. Revise the draft, making sure that your writing is vivid and keeps the reader interested in the story.
4. Proofread your story for errors in grammar and usage, spelling, punctuation, capitalization, and manuscript form. Then make a final copy of your short story and share it with your classmates and with your teacher.

Lesson 18: Writing a Poem

The type of poem a writer chooses to write depends upon his or her subject and purpose. For example, if a poet wanted to describe a brief scene in a striking, vivid manner, a haiku would be an appropriate choice. A haiku consists of three short lines. The first and third lines have five syllables, and the second line has seven syllables. Haiku often use images of sight, sound, touch, taste, and smell. The following is an example of a haiku:

The spring lingers on
In the scent of a damp log
Rotting in the sun

—Richard Wright

Sometimes the subject of a poem is one that can be represented by a simple shape. In this case, a writer may decide to write a concrete poem. The letters, words, and punctuation in a concrete poem are arranged in a shape on the page that suggests its subject or meaning. For example, the following traditional Native American poem is a concrete poem:

A POEM ABOUT A WOLF MAYBE TWO WOLVES

he comes running
across the field where
he comes running

he comes running
along the hill where
he comes running

Free Verse

Many modern poets write a type of poetry known as *free verse.* Free verse has no formal restrictions—that is, it does not have a specific meter, rhyme scheme, or stanza form. It is usually written in unrhymed lines of varying lengths, and it may or may not be broken up into stanzas. Punctuation is sometimes used in unusual ways to create certain effects. Naoshi Koriyama's poem, "Jetliner," on page 536, is written in free verse. Here is the third stanza from that poem:

then . . . after a few . . . tense moments . . . /
of pondering
he roars at his utmost
and slowly begins to jog
kicking the dark earth hard
and now he begins to run
kicking the dark earth harder
then he dashes, dashes like mad, like/
mad
howling, shouting, screaming, and/
roaring

Notice that Koriyama has used ellipses in the first line of the stanza to emphasize the "tense moments . . . of pondering." The poem is not divided into sentences, nor is the first word in each line capitalized.

Poets who write in free verse attempt to create poetic effects from something other than the regular meter and rhyme scheme of formal structure. Poems written in free verse, however, require as much thought as poems written with formal structure. After you read the following case study, you will have the chance to write your own poem in free verse.

CASE STUDY: WRITING A POEM

Aimee's English class learned about several different types of poems. Then her teacher asked the class to write an original poem in free verse.

Prewriting

Aimee needed to think of a subject for her poem. She brainstormed to gather a number of possible ideas. Then she selected the idea she liked best—she decided to write about her favorite hobby, horseback riding.

Motivation for Writing Have students think of a poem from the poetry unit (pages 501-621) that they particularly liked, or another poem.

Have students plan how they could write a similar poem, using a similar topic and form.

Have students make notes on not only the topic and form, but the various literary devices that the poet uses, and how these might inspire their own creations.

Note that they will find out more about writing a poem in this lesson.

To gather ideas about her topic that she could use in her poem, Aimee freewrote for three minutes. She wrote down everything that came into her mind when she thought about horseback riding without worrying about punctuation or spelling.

Here is Aimee's freewriting:

> I love the exhilarating feeling of the wind in my face as I ride along—it's so refreshing and exciting and the horse—my favorite horse is named Comet—is so powerful but he's under my control—I can move along so effortlessly but I feel like I'm part of the horse at the same time and it's *my* legs that are galloping not just his. We're like one unit moving as a single person-horse.

Next Aimee wrote down the ideas she wanted to include in her poem in complete sentences, as if she were writing a paragraph about the topic. Here is what she wrote:

> I stand looking at my favorite horse, Comet. He is a graceful yet powerful animal. Then I get into the saddle, and when I give the signal, we start to move. We are no longer a person and a horse—we are a single person-horse. Comet moves into a gallop at my command—I'm in complete control—and we glide along effortlessly. I feel the wind in my face and I feel exhilaration and excitement at the same time. Somehow I'm more "me" when I'm riding Comet.

Aimee then made a list of the images of sight, sound, and touch that she would use in her poem.

Drafting and Revising

Aimee wrote a draft of he poem in free verse form. Here is her unrevised draft:

I face him—
A massive, powerful Other
With muscles rippling under
A shimering coat of hair.
He looks at me calmly,
As if giving consent,
And I climb aboard his great back.
A tiny signal that only he and I
Know about
And we are moving—
No longer a person
                    and
                        a horse
But now a single person-horse.
We glide along the ground—
His legs that are my legs
Beat out a regular rhythm
On the hard ground.
The wind slaps onto my face
To remind me that now I'm really
Alive—
Perhaps more alive then when
I was just me
Stumbling around
On two legs.

Aimee gave her poem a title: "Comet." Then she revised her draft, changing some words to make the poem flow more smoothly. When she was sure that her poem achieved the effect she intended it to, she made a clean copy of her revised draft for proofreading.

Proofreading and Publishing

Aimee proofread her poem for errors in spelling and punctuation. Then she made two final copies of her poem, one for her teacher and one for the school literary magazine.

ACTIVITIES AND ASSIGNMENTS

A. Revise the first draft of Aimee's poem in the case study. Change any words that you feel spoil the effect of the poem, and add a few more images of sight, sound, or touch where appropriate. Then proofread the poem and make a clean final copy of it. Share this copy with a small group of your classmates and with your teacher.

B. Write an original poem in free verse. Follow these steps:

1. To gather possible ideas for your poem, brainstorm for three to five minutes. Then select the best idea to be the subject of your poem.
2. Freewrite about your subject. Write down everything that comes to mind, especially any

personal experiences you've had with the subject.

3. Using your freewriting as a guide, write down in paragraph form what you want to say in your poem. Organize your paragraph in the order in which you plan to present your ideas in your poem.
4. Make a list of images of sight, sound, touch, taste, and smell that could be used to describe the subject. Also write down any figures of speech—hyperbole, personification, metaphor, or simile—that you might use in your poem.
5. Write a draft of your poem in free verse. Feel free to use punctuation and capitalization in innovative ways to express your ideas. Remember—you do not have to write in complete sentences if you do not wish to do so.
6. Revise your poem. Make sure that there are no lines or words that spoil the effect you are trying to create. If your poem is not very vivid, add more images or figures of speech.
7. Proofread your poem carefully. Then make a final copy of it for sharing. Read your poem aloud to a small group of your classmates before turning it in to your English teacher.

Motivation for Writing Ask who in the class is especially interested in planning a dramatic sketch or skit for presentation to the whole class. Have these individuals, and/or others you designate, lead small groups to plan a group of sketches.

Note that the sketches can be original or based on a literary work in the anthology or that they have read outside of class.

Tell students they can learn more about writing a dramatic sketch in this lesson.

Lesson 19: Writing a Short Dramatic Sketch

A *dramatic sketch* is a short scene, serious or comic, that makes a single point. Like a full-length drama, a dramatic sketch can be read in its written form or performed by actors before an audience.

ELEMENTS OF A DRAMATIC SKETCH

The title of a dramatic sketch is followed by a list of characters. The sketch itself is made up of dialogue and stage directions. The *dialogue,* or the words spoken by each character, follows the name of the character that speaks it. The characters' names are capitalized, as in these lines of dialogue from page 267 of *Back There:*

> MRS. LANDERS. Now what's the trouble?
> CORRIGAN. What did you say?
> MRS. LANDERS. What did I say to whom? When?
> CORRIGAN. To the lieutenant. To the officer. What did you just say to him?

The *stage directions* in a dramatic sketch tell how the sketch is to be performed on stage. They give information about how the setting should appear to the audience; how the characters should move and speak; what *properties,* or movable objects, should be used in the performance; and what special effects of lighting and sound should be used. Stage directions are italicized or underlined, and they appear in brackets or parentheses. Here are stage directions from Act I, Scene 2 of *The Diary of Anne Frank,* on page 303:

> [MR. FRANK *stops abruptly as he hears the sound of marching feet from the street below. Everyone is motionless, paralyzed with fear.* MR. FRANK *goes quietly into the room on the right to look down out of the window.* ANNE *runs after him, peering out with him. The tramping feet pass without stopping. The tension is relieved.* MR. FRANK, *followed by* ANNE, *returns to the main room and resumes his instructions to the group.*]

PLANNING A DRAMATIC SKETCH

When you plan to write a dramatic sketch, you must give careful consideration to all the elements that will make up the sketch. You must decide what the setting of the sketch will be and how that setting will be reproduced on stage. You must think about what you want each of the characters to look like and what costumes they will wear. You must decide how each character will move and speak. As in planning any narrative work, you must decide what events will take place in the sketch and in what order.

WRITING A DRAMATIC SKETCH

As you draft the sketch, you should bear in mind that it is meant to be performed for an audience. Stop from time to time and read the dialogue aloud to make sure that it sounds natural. Be sure that the setting is one that can be represented fairly easily on a stage. Where necessary, include stage directions to instruct the actors how to move and speak and the stage crew how to use special effects of lighting and sound.

CASE STUDY: WRITING A SHORT DRAMATIC SKETCH

Shirley's English teacher asked the class to write a short dramatic sketch based on a folktale or a narrative poem. Shirley decided to use John Greenleaf Whittier's poem, "Barbara Frietchie," on page 525.

Prewriting

Shirley read the narrative poem several

times. She thought about the setting and made the following notes about it:

- Time: cool September morning; 1860's
- Place: Frederick, Maryland
- Description of setting: cobblestone street with homes on both sides; lots of church spires in the distance
- Lighting: morning sun
- Properties: United States flag of the 1860's

Next Shirley thought about the characters and how she would portray each of them in a stage production. She made the following chart describing the characters in her prewriting notes:

Barbara Frietchie

- Appearance: old; bent over; gray hair; wearing a long skirt with an apron and a blouse
- Personality: proud; stubborn; brave
- Speech: loud, spirited, high-pitched voice
- Movement: slow, but deliberate and unafraid

Stonewall Jackson

- Appearance: tall and strong; wearing a slouched hat and a Confederate uniform; riding on horseback
- Personality: noble; a tough leader, but sensitive
- Speech: loud, strong voice, but a man of few words
- Movement: self-confident; gestures are bold and definite

Confederate soldiers

- Appearance: wearing Confederate uniforms
- Movement: obedient

Shirley listed, in order, the events that would take place in her dramatic sketch. Here are her notes:

- Barbara Frietchie appears on the empty street and picks up an American flag that is lying on the ground.
- She disappears into her house with the flag.
- The flag appears on a staff emerging from Barbara Frietchie's attic window.
- Stonewall Jackson leads rebel troops into the town; he looks around.
- Jackson sees the flag and orders his men to shoot it down.
- The Confederate soldiers aim their rifles at the house and shoot down the flag.
- When the firing has stopped, Barbara Frietchie appears at her window and says to Jackson and his men that they should shoot her instead of the flag.
- Jackson is moved by the old woman's courage and orders his men not to fire. The troop moves on through the town.
- The flag, now in shreds, flies from Barbara Frietchie's attic window all day while rebel troops march through the streets.

Drafting and Revising

Shirley wrote a draft of her dramatic sketch. First she wrote its title and the list of characters. Then she wrote the dialogue and stage directions that described the action of the sketch. When she had finished writing, she revised her draft, making sure that the dialogue sounded natural. She also added more stage directions to make the action clear.

Proofreading and Publishing

Shirley proofread her sketch for errors in spelling and mechanics. She and some of her friends performed the sketch for the rest of the class.

ACTIVITIES AND ASSIGNMENTS

A. Use Shirley's prewriting notes from the case study to write a short dramatic sketch based on "Barbara Frietchie." Start by creating a title and list of characters. Then write the dialogue and the stage directions. Revise and proofread the sketch, and share it with your classmates and your teacher.

B. Write an original dramatic sketch based on one of the following works: "The Adventure of the Speckled Band," on page 27; "*Harriet Tubman: Guide to Freedom,*" on page 383; "Paul Revere's Ride," on page 509; "William Stafford," on page 517; "Hammerman," on page 655; "The Foggy Stew," on page 669; "Tussle with a Bear," on page 681; or *The Pearl,* on page 695. Follow these steps:

1. Select a single scene from the narrative to portray in your sketch. Make a list of the characters in the scene and describe how each will look, act, and speak.
2. Think about how the setting of the scene could be reproduced on a stage. Write down your ideas for making the set in your notes.
3. List, in order, the events that will take place in your sketch.
4. Think of a title for your sketch and write it at the top of your paper. Then list the characters and give a brief description of each.
5. Write the dialogue and the stage directions for your sketch. Stop writing from time to time to read the dialogue aloud. Make sure that you include enough stage directions to make the action clear.
6. Revise and proofread your sketch. Suggest to your teacher that the sketch be performed or read aloud in front of the class.

Lesson 20: Writing a Personal Essay

A *personal essay* is a form of nonfiction writing that allows a writer to share his or her thoughts, feelings, and experiences with others. When you write a personal essay, you speak in your own voice about something important to you.

A personal essay is similar in some ways to the compositions about literature that you have learned about in preceding lessons. When you write, you must be sure that your essay has a clear introduction, body, and conclusion. You need a topic sentence that is supported by evidence. However, the evidence that you will use in a personal essay will not be from a literary work—it will be from your own thoughts and experiences.

The topic of a personal essay should be something especially important to you. Once you have decided on a topic, try freewriting to gather information for your essay. Write everything that you know and feel about the topic. Next you must decide what the purpose of your writing will be. Ask yourself whether you want to tell a story, to explain or describe something, or to persuade your readers to do or to believe something. Once you have a definite purpose in mind, you should write a sentence that tells what this purpose is. This sentence will be your thesis statement.

Include your thesis statement in the introduction of your essay. Then, in the body of your essay, give evidence to support the thesis statement. For example, if your thesis statement were something like "Yellowstone National Park is a great place to go for a family vacation," you might list in the body all the interesting things you and your family did when you went there. In the last section of your essay, the conclusion, summarize your main point.

When you revise your essay, make sure that you have made all of your ideas very clear. Also check to see that each statement in your writing is supported by evidence. Finally, proofread your essay and make a final copy for sharing.

CASE STUDY: WRITING A PERSONAL ESSAY

Howard's English class learned how personal essays are a way to share one's thoughts and feelings with others. Then his teacher asked the class to write an essay on any topic that was important to them.

Prewriting

Howard needed to come up with a topic for his essay. He tried brainstorming for five minutes, writing down all the possible topics he could think of. Here are some of the ideas that Howard considered:

- The time my paintings were displayed in the lobby of the school and everyone liked them
- Why math is my favorite subject in school
- How to draw birds
- Why it's important to treat people fairly
- The time I tried out for the basketball team and didn't make it

Howard decided to write about his experience of trying out for the basketball team. He wasn't sure that he could state in a sentence exactly why the event was significant to him, so he tried freewriting to gather ideas. Here is Howard's freewriting:

> When I didn't make the basketball team I was a mess. I vowed I'd never play basketball ever again. I was sure I was going to make the team. It was all I could do not to cry. I thought I'd never play hoop again but my friends were really nice about it though. When my mom and

Motivation for Writing Have students brainstorm for a list of ten ideas that are important to them at this point in their lives. Topics might include developing more personal freedom, or winning more recognition for some achievement.

Then tell students to decide which of these topics they would like to develop into a full-length personal essay.

Note that students may learn more about writing a personal essay in this lesson.

dad came home from work it was awfull—they marched in with big grins—thinking I had made the team. After about a week though I realized being so down in the dumps wasn't worth it. And I missed playing basketball just for fun—so I just lived with my disappointment and life went on as usual. Now I think back and realize that what I thought was so terrible really wasn't. Its OK to be disappointed sometimes. I got over it. I still play basketball and it's still fun and I still do my best. I'm even going to try out again for the team next year.

Howard read his freewriting and thought about the significance of his experience. He drafted the following thesis statement for his essay:

> I was really counting on making the basketball team, but when I didn't, it wasn't the end of the world.

He realized that the sentence was a bit too narrow, so he rewrote his thesis statement as follows:

> When you count on something and it doesn't come through, it's not the end of the world.

This sentence would inform his readers that his story had significance for everyone, not just for himself.

Howard made a rough outline for his essay. The outline showed how he would organize the introduction, body, and conclusion of his writing.

Drafting and Revising

Howard wrote a draft of his essay and then revised it, as shown in the box, with Howard's changes marked with standard editorial symbols.

Proofreading and Publishing

Howard proofread his draft. Then he made a final copy of it and shared it with his classmates and with his teacher.

¶Last year I tried out for the ~~hoop~~ basketball team. Sure I'd make it. I didn't. Although it took me a while to get over it, I realized that when you count on something and it doesn't come ~~threw~~ through, it's not the end of the world.

I got to school early the day the team list was posted outside the gym, eager to see my name. My name wasn't there, and I was really upset. I felt like walking out of school, ~~and~~ going home, and hiding in my room.

My friends saw that I was ~~a mess over~~ upset about something. When I told them I hadn't made the team, they ~~said all kinds of things. They~~ said, "Well, at least you tried your best," or they said, "Gee, I'm sorry to hear it." They seemed to understand how much it meant to me, ~~That~~ which helped. Soon I even wanted to play~~ed~~ basketball again.

I could have stopped doing things where I might not succeed, but then I wouldn't do very much. I'm still dis~~s~~appointed when things don't turn out the way I want, but I know I can handle it. In fact I still practice my jump shot and plan to try out for next year's team.

ACTIVITIES AND ASSIGNMENTS

A. Answer the following questions about the case study:

1. What run-on sentence did Howard correct when he revised his draft? what sentence fragments?
2. Where did Howard change language that was too informal?
3. Where did Howard combine sentences to make his writing smoother?
4. What corrections would Howard still have to make during proofreading?

B. Write your own personal essay. Follow these steps:

1. Think of a topic that is very important to you. If you need to do so, try brainstorming to gather ideas for possible topics.
2. When you have decided on a topic, try prewriting techniques such as freewriting, clustering, analyzing, questioning, or making charts and lists to gather information for your essay.
3. Decide what the purpose of your writing will be—to tell a story, to explain or describe something, or to persuade. Write a thesis statement that tells this purpose.
4. Make an outline that shows what information you will include in the introduction, body, and conclusion of your essay.
5. Use your outline to write a draft of your essay. Write as many drafts as you need to write. Then revise the draft that you are most pleased with. Make sure that your writing accomplishes its purpose.
6. Proofread your essay using the Checklist for Proofreading on page 772. Then make a clean final copy of your essay and share it with your classmates and with your teacher.

HANDBOOK OF LITERARY TERMS AND TECHNIQUES

ACT See *Drama.*

ALLITERATION *Alliteration* is the repetition of initial consonant sounds. Advertisers use alliteration to catch the ear of the reader or viewer, as in "*B*ooks for a *B*uck." In poetry alliteration is used to create a musical or rhythmic effect, to emphasize key words, or to imitate sounds. Consider the alliteration in Kenyan poet John Roberts's "The Searchers":

> I remember a dog ran out from an alley,
> *S*niffed my trousers, *s*cented rags
> And as I stooped to pat him ran back,
> *Cl*aws *cl*icking on the asphalt.

In these lines alliteration of the *s* sounds links two images of smell, while the consecutive *cl* sounds in the last line mimic the "clicking" of the dog's claws.
See *Onomatopoeia* and *Repetition.*

ALLUSION An *allusion* is a reference to a well-known person, place, event, literary work, or work of art. The title of A. A. Milne's play *The Ugly Duckling,* on page 245, alludes to a fairy tale by Hans Christian Andersen. The allusion invites the reader to compare the character Princess Camilla to the swan in Andersen's fairy tale. The Bible and classical mythology provide two of the most common sources of literary allusions. May Swenson's poem "By Morning" alludes to a famous Biblical story of the miraculous feeding of the Israelites:

> By morning we'll be children
>   feeding on manna
>
> a new loaf on every doorsill

Writers usually do not explain their allusions. They expect that their readers will be familiar with the things to which they refer. An active reader will think about the meaning of every allusion that he or she encounters.

ANAPEST See *Meter.*

ANECDOTE An *anecdote* is a brief story about an interesting, amusing, or strange event. Writers and speakers use anecdotes to entertain and to make specific points. In the entries from *Davy Crockett's Almanacs,* on page 679, legendary American folk hero Davy Crockett tells anecdotes about his outrageous frontier adventures. In "Tussle with a Bear," Crockett describes how he heroically killed a bear. "Davy Crockett's Dream" features the bizarre events in Crockett's dream.

ANTAGONIST An *antagonist* is a character or force in conflict with the main character, or protagonist. A character who acts as an antagonist usually desires some goal that is at odds with the goals of the protagonist. The struggle between the two, or central conflict, is the foundation of the story's plot. In Ursula K. Le Guin's "The Rule of Names," on page 69, the protagonist, Mr. Underhill, wants to guard and keep his treasure. Blackbeard, the antagonist, wants to take the treasure away from the wizard.

ATMOSPHERE See *Mood.*

AUTOBIOGRAPHY *Autobiography* is a form of nonfiction in which a person tells his or her own life story. An autobiographer may tell his or her entire life story or may concentrate on only part of it. Maya Angelou writes about her childhood in *I Know Why the Caged Bird Sings.* Eudora Welty's *One Writer's Beginnings* describes how she became a writer. Autobiographies often include most of the elements of good fiction: interesting stories and events, well-developed characters, and vivid descriptions of settings.

BALLAD A *ballad* is a songlike poem that tells a story, often one dealing with adventure and romance. Ballads have four- to six-line stanzas, with regular rhythms and rhyme schemes. Many ballads have a *refrain,* a line or group of lines repeated at the end of each stanza.

The earliest ballads, such as "Lord Randall" and "Barbara Allan," were not written down but rather were composed orally and then sung. Then they were passed by word of mouth from singer to singer and from generation to generation. Thus the ballads often changed dramatically over the course of time. By the time modern scholars began to collect folk ballads, most ballads existed in many different versions. Many writers of the modern era have created *literary ballads,* imitating the simplicity, structure, and diction of the ancient ballads. For example, Henry Wadsworth Longfellow's "Paul Revere's Ride," on page 509, borrows many elements from the folk ballad tradition.

BIOGRAPHY *Biography* is a form of nonfiction in which a writer tells the life story of another person. People often write biographies of people who are famous for their achievements. Ann Petry's *Harriet Tubman: Guide to Freedom* is an example of biography. Biographies are considered nonfiction because they deal with real people and events. Still, a good biography shares many of the qualities of all good narrative writing.
See *Autobiography.*

BLANK VERSE *Blank verse* is poetry written in unrhymed iambic pentameter lines. This form should not be confused with *free verse,* which is poetry that has no regular meter. A great deal of English poetry is written in blank verse because its meter is natural to the English language and because serious subjects are often best dealt with in unrhymed lines. William Wordsworth's "There Was a Boy" is in blank verse:

> There was a boy; ye knew him well, ye cliffs
> And islands of Winander! Many a time,
> At evening, when the earliest stars began
> To move along the edges of the hills,
> Rising or setting, would he stand alone.

CENTRAL CONFLICT See *Conflict.*

CHARACTER A *character* is a person or animal who takes part in the action of a literary work. The *main character,* or protagonist, is the most important character in the story, the focus of the reader's attention. Often the protagonist changes in some important way during the course of the story. A *minor character* takes part in the story's events but is not the main focus of attention. Minor characters sometimes help the reader learn about the main character.

Fictional characters are sometimes described as either round or flat. A *round character* is fully developed. The writer reveals the character's background and his or her personality traits, both good and bad. A *flat character,* on the other hand, seems to possess only one or two personality traits and little, if any, personal history. Characters can also be described as dynamic or static. A *dynamic character* changes in the course of a story. A *static character* does not change. Philip Nolan, in Edward Everett Hale's "The Man Without a Country," on page 185, is a round, dynamic character. In contrast, Paul Revere, in Longfellow's poem, on page 509, is flat and static.
See *Characterization, Hero/Heroine,* and *Motivation.*

CHARACTERIZATION *Characterization* is the act of creating and developing a character. Writers use two methods to create and develop characters—direct and indirect. When using *direct characterization,* the writer actually states a character's traits, or characteristics. Dorothy M.

Johnson used direct characterization in the following passage from "The Day the Sun Came Out," on page 107:

> Two weeks we had been moving when we picked up Mary, who had run away from somewhere that she wouldn't tell. Pa didn't want her along, but she stood up to him with no fear in her voice.

When using *indirect characterization,* the writer allows the reader to draw his or her own conclusions based on information presented by the author. In "The Adventures of the Speckled Band," on page 35, Arthur Conan Doyle provides indirect characterization of Dr. Roylott by means of his appearance, words, and actions:

> He stepped swiftly forward, seized the poker, and bent it into a curve with his huge brown hands.
>
> "See that you keep yourself out of my grip," he snarled, and hurling the twisted poker into the fireplace he strode out of the room.

CINQUAIN See *Stanza.*

CLIMAX See *Plot.*

CONCRETE POEM A *concrete poem* is one with a shape that suggests its subject. The poet arranges the letters, punctuation, and lines to create a visual image on the page. Guillaume Apollinaire's "Crown" is a concrete poem. Its letters and words are arranged in the shape of a jeweled crown.

CONFLICT A *conflict* is a struggle between opposing forces. Conflict is one of the most important elements of stories, novels, and dramas because it causes the actions that form the plot. In an *external conflict* a character struggles against some outside person or force, such as a storm, a jealous enemy, or a social convention. The conflict between Mr. Underhill and Blackbeard in "The Rule of Names," on page 69, is an external conflict.

In an *internal conflict* the struggle takes place within the protagonist's mind. The character struggles to reach some new understanding or to make an important decision. Philip Nolan, in "The Man Without a Country," on page 185, experiences an inner conflict as he comes to realize the importance of home and country. Literary works can have at the same time several conflicts, both internal and external. The most important conflict in a work is called the *central conflict.*
See *Plot.*

COUPLET See *Stanza.*

DACTYL See *Meter.*

DENOUEMENT See *Plot.*

DESCRIPTION A *description* is a portrait, in words, of a person, place, or object. Descriptive writing uses images that appeal to the five senses—sight, hearing, taste, smell, and touch.

In her poem "Desert Noon," Elizabeth Coatsworth uses images of sight to create a description of a desert scene in southwestern California:

> When the desert lies
> Pulsating with heat
> And even the rattlesnakes
> Coil among the roots of the mesquite
> And the coyotes pant at the waterholes—
> Far above,
> Against the sky,
> Shines the summit of San Jacinto,
> Blue-white and cool as a hyacinth
> With snow.

See *Image.*

DEVELOPMENT See *Plot.*

DIALECT A *dialect* is a form of a language spoken by people in a particular region or group. English, for example, has numerous dialects.

The English spoken in London differs from the English spoken in Liverpool. Likewise, the English spoken in Boston differs from the English spoken in Texas. Dialects differ in pronunciation, grammar, and word choice. Often they reflect the economic, geographic, and cultural differences among speakers of the same language.

Writers use dialects to make their characters seem true to life. For example, in "The House Guest," on page 85, the character named Bridgie speaks in the dialect of Northern Ireland:

> "Ya won't peach on me? Ya won't tell? Sometimes I just like swingin' around the neighborhood. I won't get lost and shame ya."

Mark Twain, Rudyard Kipling, and Zora Neale Hurston are three well-known writers who make effective use of dialect in their works.

DIALOGUE *Dialogue* is conversation between characters. Dialogue helps make stories more interesting and more realistic. In poems, novels, and short stories, dialogue is usually set off by quotation marks, as in this example from "The Day the Sun Came Out," by Dorothy M. Johnson:

> "Mushrooms ain't good eating," I said. "They can kill you."
>
> "Maybe," Mary answered. "Maybe they can. I don't set up to know all about everything, like some people do."

In a play, dialogue simply follows the name of the character who is speaking, as in these lines from *Let Me Hear You Whisper,* by Paul Zindel:

> HELEN: I don't have a TV.
> MISS MORAY: I'm sorry.
> HELEN: I'm not.

See *Dialect* and *Drama.*

DIMETER See *Meter.*

DRAMA A *drama* is a story written to be performed by actors. Although a drama is meant to be performed, one can also read the written version, or script, which contains the dialogue and stage directions. *Dialogue* is the words spoken by the actors. *Stage directions,* usually printed in brackets or parentheses and in italics, tell how the actors should look, move, and speak. They also describe the setting and desired effects of sound and lighting. Dramas are often divided into major sections called *acts.* These acts are then further divided into smallar sections called *scenes.*

In contemporary usage the term *drama* is often used to refer to serious or tragic plays, as opposed to lighter, comic plays.
See *Character, Dialogue,* and *Plot.*

DRAMATIC IRONY See *Irony.*

DYNAMIC CHARACTER See *Character.*

ESSAY An *essay* is a short, nonfiction work about a particular subject. An *expository essay* presents information, discusses ideas, or explains a process. "The Indian All Around Us," on page 457, is an example of an expository essay. A *narrative essay* tells a true story. "Forest Fire," on page 453, tells the story of Anaïs Nin's actual experiences during a forest fire near her Sierra Madre home. A *persuasive essay* tries to convince the reader to do something or to accept a particular conclusion. Robert MacNeil's "The Trouble with Television," on page 463, tries to convince the reader that television is a harmful influence. Finally, a *decriptive essay* presents a portrait, in words, of a person, place, or object. Travel writing provides many examples of descriptive essays. Few essays, however, are purely descriptive. It is important to remember, too, that an essay may combine elements of all four types of writing.
See *Description, Exposition, Narration,* and *Persuasion.*

EXPOSITION *Exposition* is writing or speech that explains or informs. Exposition may occur in both fiction and nonfiction writing. This Handbook of Literary Terms is an example of expository nonfiction because it explains the meanings of important literary terms and ideas.

The term *exposition* is also used to refer to the part of a story that introduces the basic elements of the plot: the characters, the setting, and the initial situation leading to the conflict. The exposition of *The Ugly Duckling,* on page 245, occurs in the opening conversation between the King and the Chancellor. Here the reader learns the identity of both characters and learns, too, that Prince Simon is arriving that day to ask Princess Camilla to marry him.
See *Plot.*

EXTENDED METAPHOR In an *extended metaphor,* as in a regular metaphor, a subject is spoken or written of as though it were something else. However, an extended metaphor differs from a regular metaphor in that several points of comparisons are suggested by the writer or speaker. Naoshi Koriyama uses extended metaphor in his poem "Jetliner," on page 536, to compare a jet plane to a runner.
See *Metaphor.*

FABLE A *fable* is a brief story, usually with animal characters, that teaches a lesson, or moral. The moral is usually stated at the end of the fable. The Greek slave Aesop wrote many fables in the sixth century B.C. that are still widely read today. Many familiar expressions, such as "cry wolf" and "sour grapes," come from Aesop's fables. Modern writers such as James Thurber and Mark Twain have also written fables.
See *Irony* and *Moral.*

FANTASY *Fantasy* is highly imaginative writing that contains elements not found in real life. Fantasy involves invented characters, invented situations, and sometimes invented worlds and creatures. Many science-fiction stories, such as Isaac Asimov's "Rain, Rain, Go Away," on page 13, contain elements of fantasy.
See *Science Fiction.*

FICTION *Fiction* is prose writing that tells about imaginary characters and events. Short stories and novels are works of fiction. Some writers base their fictional tales on actual experiences and real people, to which they add invented characters, dialogue, and settings. Other writers of fiction work entirely from their own imaginations.
See *Narration, Nonfiction,* and *Prose.*

FIGURATIVE LANGUAGE *Figurative language* is writing or speech that is not meant to be taken literally. The many types of figurative language are called *figures of speech.* These types include hyperbole, simile, metaphor, and personification. Writers use figurative language to express their meanings in fresh, vivid, surprising ways.
See *Hyperbole, Metaphor, Personification, Simile,* and *Symbol.*

FIGURE OF SPEECH See *Figurative Language.*

FLASHBACK A *flashback* is a section of a literary work that interrupts the sequence of events to relate an event from an earlier time. All the action in *The Diary of Anne Frank,* on page 303, except for the first and last scenes, is a flashback to events that occurred more than three years before the opening scene. Pearl Buck's "Christmas Day in the Morning," on page 21, is largely flashback. The story begins and ends with Rob as an elderly man, but the story's main action is a flashback to the Christmas of Rob's fifteenth year.

FLAT CHARACTER See *Character.*

FOLK BALLAD See *Ballad.*

FOLKTALE A *folktale* is a story that was composed orally and then passed from person to person by word of mouth. Types of folktales include fables, legends, myths, and tall tales. Most folktales are *anonymous:* No one knows who first composed them. In fact, folktales originated among people who could neither read nor write. These people entertained themselves by telling stories aloud, often ones dealing with heroes, adventure, romance, and magic.

In the modern era, scholars like the brothers Wilhelm and Jakob Grimm began collecting folktales and writing them down. Their collection, published as *Grimm's Fairy Tales,* includes such famous tales as "Cinderella," "Rapunzel," and "The Bremen Town Musicians."

American scholars have also collected folktales, often ones dealing with fanciful heroes such as Pecos Bill, Paul Bunyan, and Davy Crockett. See Carl Sandburg's retelling, "Paul Bunyan of the North Woods," on page 643.
See *Fable, Legend, Myth,* and *Oral Tradition.*

FOOT See *Meter.*

FORESHADOWING *Foreshadowing* is the use, in a literary work, of clues that suggest events that have yet to occur. Foreshadowing creates *suspense* by making the reader wonder what will happen next. In the short story, "A Retrieved Reformation," on page 61, O. Henry foreshadows later events in the story by means of certain details earlier in the tale. That Jimmy is no ordinary criminal but is rather an expert safecracker will become an important detail. The fact that he falls in love with a banker's daughter is a clue that his former trade might play a role in his new life. The fact that the prison warden told Jimmy, "You're not a bad fellow at heart," is another clue. Thus foreshadowing is a means of linking seemingly minor or unconnected details with important developments later in a work.

FREE VERSE *Free verse* is poetry not written in a regular rhythmical pattern, or meter. The following lines, from the South African poet Mongameli Mabona's "The Sea," are in free verse:

Ocean,
Green or blue or iron-gray,
As the light
Strikes you.
Primordial flood,
Relentless and remorseless
Like a woman in a rage.

In a free verse poem the poet is free to write lines of any length or with any number of rhythmic stresses, or beats. Thus free verse is less constraining than *metrical verse,* which requires set patterns of stresses.
See *Meter.*

GENRE A *genre* is a division or type of literature. Literature is generally divided into three major genres: poetry, prose, and drama. Each, in turn, is further divided into such standard literary categories as the following:

1. *Poetry:* lyric, epic, narrative, and dramatic poetry
2. *Prose:* fiction (novels, short stories) and nonfiction (essays, letters, biographies, autobiographies, and reports)
3. *Drama:* serious drama and tragedy, comic drama, farce, and melodrama

See *Drama, Poetry,* and *Prose.*

HAIKU *Haiku* is a three-line Japanese verse form. The first and third lines of a haiku have five syllables; the second line has seven syllables. A haiku usually presents a single, vivid image drawn from nature. See the two examples by Bashō and Moritake, on page 573.

HEPTAMETER See *Meter.*

HEPTASTITCH See *Stanza.*

HERO/HEROINE A *hero* or *heroine* is a character whose actions are inspiring or noble. In very old myths and stories, heroes and heroines often have superhuman powers. Hercules and Achilles are two examples of this type of hero. In modern literature, heroes and heroines tend to be ordinary people. All heroes and heroines struggle to overcome some great obstacle or problem. For example, in "The Day the Sun Came Out," on page 107, Mary is a heroine because she risks her life by eating wild mushrooms to determine if they are safe for the children to eat. In Beryl Markham's "The Captain and His Horse," on page 47, the hero is the Baron, the horse. The Baron helps save the lives of two of its riders in the story. By the end of the story, we learn that the Baron was decorated for bravery.

The word *hero* was originally used for male characters and *heroine* for females. However, it is now acceptable to use the term *hero* to refer both to males and to female characters.

HEXAMETER See *Meter.*

HUBRIS *Hubris* is the fault of excessive pride. In tragic works the hubris of the main character is usually the cause of the protagonist's downfall. In the famous Greek play *Oedipus Rex,* the hero's downfall is partly caused by his hubris. Likewise, in the contemporary novel *Things Fall Apart,* by the Nigerian writer Chinua Achebe, the hubris of the main character, Okonkwo, leads to his exile and eventual death.

HYPERBOLE *Hyperbole* is an exaggeration for effect. Because it makes a statement that is not meant to be taken literally, hyperbole is considered a figure of speech. Everyday speech is full of examples of hyperbole, such as "I'm so hungry I could eat a horse." Writers use hyperboles to create humor, to emphasize particular points, and to create dramatic effects. For example, a famous novel by Ralph Ellison begins with this powerful example of hyperbole, which gives his book its name:

> I am an invisible man.

See *Figurative Language.*

IAMB See *Meter.*

IMAGE An *image* is a word or a phrase that appeals to one or more of the five senses. Writers use images to create specific descriptions—to show how their subjects look, sound, smell, taste, and feel. The following lines from "Nightsong City," by the South African poet Dennis Brutus, contain several images of sound:

> The sound begins again:
> The siren in the night
> The thunder at the door
> The shriek of nerves in pain.
> Then the keen crescendo
> Of faces split by pain
> The wordless, endless wail
> Only the unfree know.

IMAGERY See *Image.*

INCITING INCIDENT See *Plot.*

IRONY *Irony* is the general name given to literary techniques that involve surprising, interesting, or amusing contradictions. In *verbal irony,* words are used to suggest the opposite of their usual meaning, as when a weak person is called "a born leader." In *dramatic irony,* there is a contradiction between what a character thinks and what the audience or reader knows to be true. An example can be found in "The Tell-Tale Heart," on page 145, in which the reader knows that the beating heart exists only in the main character's imagination. In *irony of situation,* an event occurs that directly contradicts the expectations of the characters or the reader. *The Ugly Duckling,* on page 245, provides an example of irony of situation. Princess Camilla and Prince Simon send good-looking substitutes to stand in for them at their arranged first meeting. When the Prince and Princess accidentally meet, they fall in love despite their appearances and despite the fact that they do not know each other's true identity. Note that this is also an example of dramatic irony, for the reader or audience does know these characters' true identities.

IRONY OF SITUATION See *Irony.*

LEGEND A *legend* is a widely told story about the past, one that may or may not have a foundation in fact. The stories of King Arthur of Britain and his knights of the Round Table are legends. Likewise, the stories that have survived about American folk heroes such as Pecos Bill and Paul Bunyan are legends. Legends usually contain fantastic details, such as incredible feats of strength or supernatural beings. "The Girl Who Hunted Rabbits," on page 635, is a Zuñi Indian legend about a brave young maiden who risks her life to find food for her family. In this legend the maiden is menaced by a cannibal demon, but she is saved by two war gods.
See *Folktale, Myth,* and *Oral Tradition.*

LIMERICK A *limerick* is a humorous, rhyming, five-line poem with a specific meter and rhyme scheme. Most limericks have three strong stresses in lines one, two, and five, and two strong stresses in lines three and four. Most follow the rhyme scheme *aabba.* See the two limericks on page 569.

LYRIC POEM A *lyric poem* is a highly musical verse that expresses the observations and feelings of a single speaker. They are called lyrics because they were, in ancient times, sung to the accompaniment of a lyre, a stringed instrument. Langston Hughes's "Harlem Night Song," on page 558, and Shakespeare's "Blow, Blow, Thou Winter Wind," on page 566 are examples of lyric poetry.

MAIN CHARACTER See *Character.*

METAMORPHOSIS A *metamorphosis* is a change in shape or form. In many ancient Greek and Roman myths, human beings are transformed by the gods into animals, trees, or flowers, as in the story of Daphne and Apollo. Daphne, a beautiful huntress who was being chased one day by the god Apollo, was transformed into a laurel tree by her father, the river god Peneus. The Roman poet Ovid incorporated many of these myths into his great Latin poem, *The Metamorphoses.* This poem is an important source of literary allusions to classical mythology.

Metamorphosis remains an important theme in contemporary literature as well. For example, the Australian writer B. Wongar begins his short story "Babaru, the Family" with this metamorphosis:

> Our mother has left us. She has not died or run away but has changed into a crocodile. Maybe it is better that way—not that we will see much of her, but it helps to know that she is not far off; should anything like that happen to any of us, we will be around in the bush together again.

See *Allusion* and *Myth.*

METAPHOR A *metaphor* is a figure of speech in which something is described as though it were something else. A metaphor, like a simile, works by pointing out a similarity between two things. For example, in Robert Frost's "The Road Not Taken," on page 600, the diverging roads are a metaphor for the major choices that people must make in their lives.

An *extended metaphor* is one that makes more than one point of comparison. Walt Whitman uses extended metaphor in his poem "O Captain! My Captain!" on page 534. He compares the United States to a ship, President Lincoln (who is not actually named in the poem) to the ship's captain, and national events to a ship's voyage.

See *Extended Metaphor* and *Figurative Language.*

METER The *meter* of a poem is its rhythmical pattern. This pattern is determined by the number and types of stresses, or beats, in each line. To describe the meter of a poem, you must *scan* its lines. Scanning involves marking the stressed and unstressed syllables of a poem. A slash mark (´) is used to signify a strong stress, while a weak stress is marked with a horseshoe symbol (˘). Here is an example of *scansion* using Elizabeth Barrett Browning's "The Cry of the Children":

Do ye hear the children weeping, O my
 brothers,
Ere the sorrow comes with years?
They are leaning their young heads against
 their mothers,
And that cannot stop their tears.

Each group of stresses within a line is called a *foot.* The following types of feet are common in English poetry:

1. *Iamb:* a foot with one weak stress followed by one strong stress, as in the word "reform"
2. *Trochee:* a foot with one strong stress followed by one weak stress, as in the word "flower"
3. *Anapest:* a foot with two weak stresses followed by one strong stress, as in the phrase "to the store"
4. *Dactyl:* a foot with one strong stress followed by two weak stresses, as in the word "formula"
5. *Spondee:* a foot with two strong stresses, as in the word "eighteen"
6. *Pyrrhic:* a foot with two weak stresses, as in the last foot of the word "fortu|nately"
7. *Amphibrach:* a foot with a weak syllable, one strong syllable, and another weak syllable, as in "the wandering minstrel"
8. *Amphimacer:* a foot with one strong syllable, one weak syllable, and another strong syllable, as in "black and white"

Depending on the type of foot that is most common in them, lines of poetry are described as being *iambic, trochaic, anapestic,* or *dactylic.*

Lines of poetry are also described in terms of the number of feet they contain:

1. *Monometer:* verse written in one-foot lines

One crow
melting snow

—Elizabeth Coatsworth, "March"

2. *Dimeter:* verse written in two-foot lines

The pitch | pines fade
into a | whiteness
that has blot|ted the marsh.

—Marge Piercy, "The Quiet Fog"

3. *Trimeter:* verse written in three-foot lines

A sat|urat|ed meadow,
 Sun-shaped | and jew|el small
A cir|cle scarce|ly wider
 Than the trees | around | were tall

—Robert Frost, "Rose Pogonias"

4. *Tetrameter:* verse written in four-foot lines

I have wrapped | my dreams in | silken | cloth,
And laid | them away | in a box | of gold;
Where long | will cling | the lips | of the moth,
I have wrapped | my dreams | in silken | cloth.

—Countee Cullen, "For a Poet"

5. *Pentameter:* verse written in five-foot lines

All things | within | this fad|ing world | hath
 end,

816

Adver|sity | doth still | our joys | attend;
No ties | so strong, | no friends | so dear |
and sweet,
But with | death's part|ing blow | is sure | to
meet.

—Anne Bradstreet, "Before the Birth of One of Her Children"

A six-foot line is called a *hexameter.* A line with seven feet is called a *heptameter.* A complete description of the meter of a poem tells both how many feet each line contains and what kind of foot occurs most often in the lines. Thus the lines from Anne Bradstreet's poem would be described as *iambic pentameter.* Poetry that does not have a regular meter is called *free verse.*
See *Blank Verse* and *Free Verse.*

MINOR CHARACTER See *Character.*

MOOD *Mood,* or *atmosphere,* is the feeling created in the reader by a literary work or passage. Writers use many methods to create mood, including images, dialogue, descriptions, characterization, and plot events. Often a writer creates a particular mood at the beginning of a work and then sustains this mood throughout. For example, the mood of Edgar Allan Poe's "The Tell-Tale Heart," on page 145, is one of nervous dread and terror. Sometimes, however, the mood of a work will change with each new twist of the plot.

For example, the mood of "Flowers for Algernon," on page 201, changes according to the fortunes of the main character. Notice how the mood of the following poem by Mari Evans changes in the last three lines:

if you have had your midnights
and they have drenched your barren guts with
tears
I sing you sunrise and love and someone to
touch

MONOMETER See *Meter.*

MORAL A *moral* is a lesson taught by a literary work. A fable usually ends with a moral that is directly stated. For example, the moral of Aesop's famous fable of the hare and the tortoise is this: "Sure and steady wins the race."

Novels, short stories, and poems often suggest certain lessons or morals, but these are rarely stated directly. Such morals must be inferred by readers from details contained in the works.
See *Fable.*

MOTIVATION A *motivation* is a reason that explains or partially explains a character's thoughts, feelings, actions, or speech. Writers try to make their characters' motivations, or motives, as clear as possible so that the characters will seem believable and lifelike. If a character's motives are not clear, then the character will seem flat and unconvincing.

Characters are often motivated by such common human feelings as love, greed, hunger, revenge, and friendship. For example, in "The Adventure of the Speckled Band," on page 27, fear motivates Miss Stoner to ask for Holmes's help. Holmes, in turn, is motivated by his intellectual interest in the case and by his sympathy for Miss Stoner.
See *Character.*

MYTH A *myth* is a fictional tale that explains the actions of gods or heroes or the origins of elements of nature. Myths were generally handed down by word of mouth for generations. "The Origins of Fire," on page 627, is a native American myth that explains how human beings came to use fire. The ancient Greek myth of Prometheus also seeks to explain the origins of fire.

Every ancient culture has its own *mythology,* or collection of myths. Those of the Greeks and

the Romans are called *classical mythology.* Myths often reflect the values of the cultures that give birth to them.
See *Oral Tradition.*

NARRATION *Narration* is writing that tells a story. Novels, short stories, biographies, histories, and autobiographies are common types of *prose narration,* or narrative. Epics and ballads are standard types of *verse narrative.* Whether in verse or prose, a good narrative usually contains interesting events, settings, and characters.
See *Narrative Poem* and *Narrator.*

NARRATIVE See *Narration.*

NARRATIVE POEM A *narrative poem* is a story told in verse. It often possesses the elements of fiction, such as characters, conflict, and plot. The events are usually told in *chronological order,* the order in which they happen. Narrative poems may be serious, like Longfellow's "Paul Revere's Ride," on page 509, or humorous, like "William Stafford," on page 517.

NARRATOR A *narrator* is a speaker or character who tells a story. There are several types of narrator, and the type that a writer chooses determines the story's *point of view.* If the narrator is a character who takes part in the story and who refers to herself or himself as *I,* this is *first-person narration.* For example, the narrator of Paul Darcy Boles's "The House Guest," on page 85, is the older brother in the household. He is a first-person narrator. If the narrator stands outside the action of the story, then this speaker is a *third-person narrator.* Loula Grace Erdman's "Grass Fire," on page 129, uses a third-person narrator.
See *Point of View.*

NONFICTION *Nonfiction* is prose writing that presents and explains ideas or that tells about real people, places, objects, or events. Histories, biographies, autobiographies, essays, and newspaper articles are all types of nonfiction.
See *Fiction.*

NOVEL A *novel* is a long work of fiction. Novels, like short stories, contain plot, character, conflict, and setting, but they are much longer than short stories. Thus they usually contain more characters, a greater variety of settings, and more complicated plots than do most short stories. A novel often contains, in addition to its major plot, one or more lesser stories, or subplots. Some famous novels include *Moby-Dick, David Copperfield,* and *the Red Badge of Courage.* John Steinbeck's novel *The Pearl* is included in this book.
See *Fiction.*

OCTAVE See *Stanza.*

ONOMATOPOEIA *Onomatopoeia* is the use of words that imitate sounds. *Hiss, crash, buzz, neigh, ring* and *jingle* are examples of onomatopoeia. In William Shakespeare's "Full Fathom Five," onomatopoeia is used to imitate the sound of a bell:

> Sea nymphs hourly ring the knell:
>   Ding-Dong.
> Hark! Now I hear them.
>   Ding-dong, bell.

ORAL TRADITION The *oral tradition* is the passing of songs, stories, and poems from generation to generation by word of mouth. Folk songs, ballads, fables, and myths are often the products of oral tradition. No one knows who created them. That is, they are *anonymous.* The ballad "John Henry," on page 663, is a product of the oral tradition. No one knows who first wrote this ballad. It has been passed from singer to singer for many years and, like most products of the oral tradition, exists in many different versions.
See *Folktale, Legend,* and *Myth.*

PARALLELISM See *Repetition.*

PENTAMETER See *Meter.*

PERSONIFICATION *Personification* is a type of figurative language in which a nonhuman subject is given human characteristics. The expressions "Father Time" and "Mother Earth" are examples of personification. The poem by Sylvia Plath on page 503 personifies mushrooms as meek, yet slightly sinister creatures:

Nudgers and shovers
In spite of ourselves.
Our kind multiplies:
We shall by morning
Inherit the earth.
Our foot's in the door.

See *Figurative Language.*

PERSUASION *Persuasion* is writing or speech that attempts to convince the reader to adopt an opinion or course of action. Advertisements are the most common forms of persuasion; they try to persuade people to buy certain products or services. Newspaper editorials, political speeches, and essays are other common forms of persuasive writing. In his essay "Dial Versus Digital," on page 477, Isaac Asimov tries to persuade his readers that something important has been lost in the change from dial to digital clocks and watches.

PLOT *Plot* is the sequence of events in a literary work. In most novels, short stories, dramas, and narrative poems, the plot involves two basic elements—characters and conflict. The plot usually begins with the *exposition,* which establishes the setting, identifies the characters, and introduces the basic situation. This is usually followed by the *inciting incident,* which introduces the *central conflict.* The *development* of the central conflict shows how the characters are affected by it. Eventually, the development reaches a high point of interest or suspense, the *climax.* The *falling action* of the conflict then follows. Any events that occur during the falling action make up the *resolution,* or *denouement.*

Some plots do not contain all of these parts. Short stories, for example, often do not include an exposition and a denouement. Sometimes, too, the inciting incident in a short story or novel has occurred before the opening of the story.

All the events that occur before the climax of a story make up its *rising action.* All the events that occur after the climax make up the *falling action.*
See *Conflict.*

POETRY *Poetry* is one of the three major types of literature, the others being prose and drama. Poetry is not easy to define, but we might say that poetry is language used in special ways. Most poems make use of concise, rhythmic, and emotionally charged language. The language of poetry usually emphasizes the re-creation of experiences over analysis of these experiences. Traditionally, poetry has differed from prose in making use of formal structural devices such as rhyme, meter, and stanzas. Some poems, however, are written out just like prose.

Major types of poetry include lyric poems, narrative poems, dramatic poems, and epics. Walter de la Mare's "Silver," on page 564, and Lew Sarett's "Four Little Foxes," on page 556, are lyric poems. Joaquin Miller's "Columbus," on page 521, and John Greenleaf Whittier's "Barbara Frietchie," on page 525, are narrative poems. In dramatic poetry, characters speak the poem in their own voices. An epic poem, such as Homer's *Iliad,* is a long, involved narrative poem about the exploits of gods and heroes.

POINT OF VIEW *Point of view* is the perspective, or vantage point, from which a story is told. The three most common points of view in narrative literature are first person, omniscient third-person, and limited third-person.

In a story from the *first-person point of view,*

the narrator is a character in the story. We see the story through his or her eyes. Most of the Sherlock Holmes stories, such as "The Adventure of the Speckled Band," on page 27, are told from a first-person point of view—that of Dr. Watson.

In a story written from the *omniscient,* or "all knowing," *third-person point of view,* the narrator is not a character in the story but views the events of the story through the eyes of more than one of the characters. Saki's "The Story-Teller," on page 3, uses the third-person omniscient point of view.

In a *third-person limited point of view,* the narrator is not a character, but he or she presents the story from the perspective of one of the characters. That character's thoughts, feelings, and experiences are the focus of attention. Pearl S. Buck's "Christmas Day in the Morning," on page 21, is an example of limited third-person narration.
See *Narrator.*

PROSE *Prose* is the ordinary form of written language. Most writing that is not poetry, drama, or song is considered prose. Prose fiction includes novels and short stories. Nonfiction prose includes essays, biography, autobiography, journalism, scientific reports, and historical writing.
See *Fiction, Genre,* and *Nonfiction.*

PROTAGONIST The *protagonist* is the main character in a literary work. Normally, the reader sympathizes with or at least learns to understand the protagonist. For example, in "The Man Without a Country," on page 185, the reader sympathizes with the protagonist, Philip Nolan, who has been exiled for life to a ship. In *The Diary of Anne Frank,* on page 303, the reader sympathizes with the protagonist, Anne Frank, who must deal with many hardships.

PYRRHIC See *Meter.*

QUATRAIN See *Stanza.*

REFRAIN A *refrain* is a regularly repeated line or group of lines in a poem or song. In Joaquin Miller's "Columbus," on page 521, the refrain is "Sail on! sail on! sail on!"

REPETITION *Repetition* is the use, more than once, of any element of language—a sound, a word, a phrase, a sentence, a grammatical pattern, or a rhythmical pattern. Repetition is used both in prose and in poetry. In prose fiction, a plot may be repeated, with variations, in a subplot, or a minor character may be similar to a major character in important ways. In poetry, repetition often involves the recurring use of certain words, images, structures, and devices. Rhyme and alliteration, for example, repeat sounds. A repeating rhyme pattern is called a *rhyme scheme.* A *refrain* is a repeated line or group of lines.

Another form of repetition, used in both prose and poetry, is *parallelism,* in which a grammatical pattern is repeated, though with some changes over time. José Garcia Villa's poem "Lyric 17," which appears on page 532, contains parallel repetition of the phrase "It must":

It must be slender as a bell,
And it must hold fire as a well.
It must have the wisdom of bows
And it must kneel like a rose.

RESOLUTION See *Plot.*

RHYME *Rhyme* is the repetition of sounds at the end of words. Poets use rhyme to create musical effects, and to emphasize and to link certain words and ideas. The most traditional type of rhyme is *end rhyme,* or rhyming words at the end of the lines. Alfred, Lord Tennyson, uses end rhyme in "Ring Out, Wild Bells" on page 544:

Ring out, wild bells, to the wild *sky,*
  The flying cloud, the frosty *light*:

The year is dying in the *night*;
Ring out, wild bells, and let him *die*.

Internal rhyme occurs when rhymes occur within lines. Notice, for example, the internal rhymes in this poem by Oliver Wendell Holmes:

In the street I heard a *thumping*; and I knew it
was the *stumping*
Of the Corporal, our old *neighbor,* on that leg
he *wore,*
With a knot of women *round him,*—it was lucky
I had *found him,*
So I followed with the others, and the Corporal
marched *before*.

RHYME SCHEME A *rhyme scheme* is a regular pattern of rhyming words in a poem. To indicate the rhyme scheme of a poem, one uses lower-case letters. For example, the following stanza, from Robert Frost's "Blue-Butterfly Day," on page 559, has an *abab* rhyme scheme:

It is blue-butterfly day here in *spring* *a*
And with these sky-flakes down in flurry
on *flurry* *b*
There is more unmixed color on the *wing* *a*
Than flowers will show for days unless
they *hurry*. *b*

RHYTHM *Rhythm* is the pattern of stresses, or beats, in spoken or written language.
See *Meter.*

ROUND CHARACTER See *Character.*

SCAN/SCANNING See *Meter.*

SCENE See *Drama.*

SCIENCE FICTION *Science fiction* is writing that tells about imaginary events that involve science or technology. Much science fiction is set in the future, often on planets other than Earth. Arthur C. Clarke's "Crime on Mars," on page 137, is a science-fiction story about a crime that takes place in a large Earth colony on Mars.
See *Fiction.*

SENSORY LANGUAGE *Sensory language* is writing or speech that appeals to one or more of the five senses. Writers use sensory language to make the ideas and events they describe more vivid and clear.
See *Image.*

SESTET See *Stanza.*

SETTING The *setting* of a literary work is the time and place of the action. The time includes not only the historical period—past, present, or future—but also the year, the season, the time of day, and even the weather. The place may be a specific country, state, region, community, neighborhood, building, institution, or home. Details such as dialects, clothing, customs, and modes of transportation are often used to establish setting. In most stories, the setting serves as a backdrop against which the characters act out the actions of the narrative. The setting of Ray Bradbury's "The Drummer Boy of Shiloh," on page 151, is an April night in 1862, during the Civil War, at a place named "Shiloh" near the Tennessee River, close to a church.

The setting of a story often helps to create a particular mood, or feeling. The mood of Ray Bradbury's story is one of nervous expectation—of fear mingled with resolve.
See *Conflict, Plot,* and *Theme.*

SHORT STORY A *short story* is a brief work of fiction. Like novels, most short stories contain a central conflict and one or more characters, the most important of which is the protagonist. Like lyric poems, short stories usually create a single effect, or dominant impression. The main idea, message, or subject of a short story is its *theme.*
See *Fiction.*

SIMILE A *simile* is a figure of speech that makes a direct comparison between two unlike subjects using *like* or *as.* Everday speech contains many similes, as in "quiet as a mouse," "like a duck out of water," "good as gold," and "old as the hills."

Writers use similes to create vivid, telling descriptions. Poetry, especially, relies on similes to point out new and interesting ways of looking at the world. For example, Richard García's poem "The City Is So Big," on page 586, contains this striking simile:

> And trains pass with windows shining
> Like a smile full of teeth.

SPEAKER The *speaker* is the imaginary voice assumed by the writer of a poem. In other words, the speaker is the character who tells the poem. Sometimes this speaker will identify himself or herself by name. At other times the speaker is more vague. Interpreting a poem often depends on inferring what the speaker is like based on the details that he or she provides.

SPONDEE See *Meter.*

STAGE DIRECTIONS *Stage directions* are notes included in a drama to describe how the work is to be performed or staged. Stage directions are usually printed in italics and enclosed within parentheses or brackets. They may indicate how the actors should speak their lines, how they should move, how the characters should be dressed, what the stage should look like, or what special effects of lighting or sound should be used. Here is an excerpt from Rod Serling's play *Back There,* on page 263, which includes stage directions:

> WILLIAM. [*Opening the door*] Well, April *is* spring, sir.
> CORRIGAN. It's getting there. What is the date, William?
> WILLIAM. April 14th [*Then he turns and grins at the attendant.*] 1965—right?

See *Drama.*

STANZA A *stanza* is a group of lines in a poem, considered as a unit. Many poems are divided into stanzas of equal length, with the stanzas separated by spaces. Stanzas are often like paragraphs in prose; each presents a single thought or idea.

Stanzas are usually named according to the number of lines they contain, as follows:

1. *Couplet:* a two-line stanza
2. *Tercet:* a three-line stanza
3. *Quatrain:* a four-line stanza
4. *Cinquain:* a five-line stanza
5. *Sestet:* a six-line stanza
6. *Heptastich:* a seven-line stanza
7. *Octave:* an eight-line stanza

In traditional poetry stanzas are often rhymed. However, not all rhyming poems use stanzas, nor do all poems that are divided into stanzas rhyme. Less traditional poetry contains stanzas of varying length, sometimes with, sometimes without, rhyme.

STATIC CHARACTER See *Character.*

SUBPLOT See *Novel.*

SURPRISE ENDING A *surprise ending* is a conclusion that violates the expectations of the reader. For example, the ending of Shirley Jackson's short story "Charles," on page 79, is a complete surprise to the reader. Laurie's parents are so convinced that Charles exists that the reader is as astonished as the narrator to discover that there is no Charles. The stories that Laurie has been telling to his parents are probably stories about himself. Often a writer will *foreshadow* the surprise ending by including seemingly minor details earlier in the story that make the later surprise appear a fair, if unexpected, ending.
See *Foreshadowing* and *Plot.*

SUSPENSE *Suspense* is a feeling of anxious uncertainty about the outcome of events in a literary work. Writers create suspense by raising questions in the minds of their readers. For

example, in Beryl Markham's "The Captain and His Horse," on page 47, suspense peaks when the buffaloes trap the narrator and the Baron. The reader worries and wonders whether they will escape and, if so, how. Suspense in a story can be especially intense if there are convincing, interesting characters about whom the reader cares strongly.
See *Plot.*

SYMBOL A *symbol* is anything that stands for or represents something else. Symbols are usually concrete objects or images that represent abstract ideas. For example, the eagle is often used as a symbol of freedom. Likewise, chains can symbolize slavery and oppression. In literature, concrete images are often used to represent, or symbolize, the themes of a literary work. For example, in Edgar Allan Poe's "The Tell-Tale Heart," on page 145, the beating heart of the old man could be a symbol of the old man's vengeance or of the main character's guilt. Symbols generally differ from metaphors or similes in that the reader or listener must infer what the symbol stands for. The writer or speaker does not explicitly make the comparison.
See *Figurative Language.*

TERCET See *Stanza.*

TETRAMETER See *Meter.*

THEME A *theme* is a central message, concern, or insight into life expressed in a literary work. A theme can usually be expressed by a one- or two-sentence statement about human beings or about life. For example, the theme of Edward Everett Hale's short story, "The Man Without a Country," on page 185, might be this: "Every man needs to feel allegiance to his native country, whether he always appreciates that country or not."

A theme may be stated directly or may be implied. In poems and in works of prose fiction the theme is rarely stated directly. More often, the other elements of the work—its language, imagery, plot, tone, and structure—suggest the theme. *Interpretation* involves uncovering the theme of a literary work by carefully considering the parts, or elements, of the work.

In nonfiction works, and especially in essays, the theme is often stated directly. The title of Robert MacNeil's "The Trouble with Television," on page 463, suggests in a general way what the theme of the essay is, and the essay itself states the theme explicitly: Television oversimplifies, distorts, and ultimately "decivilizes" human existence.

TONE *Tone* is the attitude toward the subject and audience conveyed by the language and rhythm of the speaker in a literary work. For example, the tone of Edgar Allan Poe's "The Tell-Tale Heart," on page 145, is frantic and sinister. The narrator of the story reveals, by his tone and by his actions, that he is dangerously insane. In contrast, the tone of John Updike's poem "January," on page 576, is light and humorous.
See *Mood.*

TRIMETER See *Meter.*

TROCHEE See *Meter.*

VERBAL IRONY See *Irony.*

HANDBOOK OF CRITICAL THINKING AND READING TERMS

ABSTRACT *adj.* Anything that is not concrete or definite is *abstract.* Writers make their abstract ideas clear by using specific examples and illustrations. Suppose, for instance, that a writer wants to convey the abstract idea that a character is happy. The writer might do this by showing the character smiling, whistling, walking briskly, and greeting others enthusiastically. Another way to express abstract ideas clearly is to use figures of speech, such as similes, metaphors, and personifications. For example, the simile "quiet as a mouse" uses a concrete image—a mouse—to convey the abstract idea of quietness.

ANALOGY *n.* An *analogy* is a comparison that explains one subject by pointing out its similarities to another subject. In "Concrete Mixers," on page 587, Patricia Hubbell compares concrete mixers to elephants:

> The drivers are washing the concrete mixers;
> Like elephant tenders they hose them down.
> Tough gray-skinned monsters standing
> ponderous,
> Elephant-bellied and elephant-nosed

To understand an analogy a reader must consider what qualities or characteristics the two subjects have in common.

An analogy may be expressed using a variety of literary techniques, which include simile, metaphor, and extended metaphor. See the explanations of these techniques in the Handbook of Literary Terms and Techniques.

ANALYSIS *n.* *Analysis* is the process of studying the parts of a whole. By studying the parts, you can often come to understand what the whole is all about. The process of analysis consists of the following steps:

1. Separate the whole into its parts.
2. Describe each part.
3. Look for connections between the parts and between each part and the whole.

For example, you might analyze Robert MacNeil's essay "The Trouble with Television," on page 463, by dividing it into these parts: the introduction, the body, the conclusion, and the main idea. Then you would think about these parts and how they are interrelated. See Sections 2 and 3 of the Handbook of Writing About Literature, on page 748, for more information about analyzing literary works.

ARGUMENT *n.* An *argument* is a set of statements consisting of a conclusion and one or more premises, or reasons for accepting the conclusion. In "Hokusai: The Old Man Mad About Drawing," on page 481, Stephen Longstreet presents the argument that Katsushika Hokusai is the Japanese artist whom westerners most like and understand. In the essay Longstreet supports his claim with specific reasons.

When you write about a literary work, you present arguments supporting conclusions that you have come to based on your reading. For example, you might argue that Robert Frost's "The Road Not Taken," on page 600, is about the choices that people make and the consequences of these choices. Of course, you would have to present evidence, or reasons, to support your conclusion. Never simply make claims about a work without supporting these claims with evidence.

Note that the term *argument* is also used to describe a brief summary, or synopsis, of a literary work. Thus a paragraph summarizing the plot of Paul Zindel's *Let Me Hear You Whisper,* on page 277, might be described as presenting the argument of the play.

See *Conclusion, Deduction, Evidence, Induction,* and *Inference.*

BANDWAGON See *Propaganda Techniques.*

BEGGING THE QUESTION See *Logical Fallacy.*

CATEGORIZATION *n.* *Categorization* is the process of placing objects or ideas into groups or categories. To categorize something, follow these steps:

1. Note the characteristics of the thing that you are studying.
2. Think of other things that share these characteristics.
3. Think of a name to refer to the whole group of things.

For example, to categorize Henry Wadsworth Longfellow's "Paul Revere's Ride," on page 509, you might begin by noting that the poem tells a story. Then you would think of other poems that share this characteristic. Finally, you would come up with a general term to describe all such poems, such as the term *narrative poem.*

CAUSE AND EFFECT *n. phrase* When an event precedes and brings about a second event, the first is said to be a *cause* and the second, an *effect.* The plot of a literary work often depends on cause-and-effect relationships. In a plot, one event causes another event, which causes another, and so on to the end of the work. For example, in O. Henry's "A Retrieved Reformation," on page 61, the main character, Jimmy, ceases to commit burglaries when he falls in love with Annabel. Falling in love is the cause, and Jimmy's reformation is the effect.

Cause-and-effect relationships also exist between the parts of a work and the responses of a reader. Writers choose their materials and techniques carefully to cause readers to feel certain effects. For example, in "The City Is So Big," on page 586, Richard García chooses his images carefully to cause the reader to feel how frightening a city can be.

CIRCULAR REASONING See *Logical Fallacy.*

COMPARISON *n.* *Comparison* is the process of observing and pointing out similarities. For example, a comparison of the American folk heroes Paul Bunyan and Davy Crockett might point out the following similarities: Each possessed great strength and courage. Each lived on the frontier. Each preferred a rugged life in the wilderness to life in a city or town. A comparison is often signaled by one of the following words or phrases: *similarly, likewise, also, in the same manner,* or *in the same way.*
See *Contrast.*

CONCLUSION *n.* A *conclusion* is an idea that follows reasonably from another idea or group of ideas. The conclusion of an argument should follow reasonably from the supporting statements, facts, and reasons. For example, in the essay "Dial Versus Digital," on page 477, Isaac Asimov presents several reasons to support his conclusion that something important has been lost in the change from dial clocks to digital clocks.

The word *conclusion* is also used, of course, to describe the ending of any written or spoken work. Whenever you write, you should make sure that your written product has a clear conclusion. That is, when a reader finishes your work, he or she should have a feeling of completeness. There are many ways to create this sense of an ending. The following are some common ways in which writers conclude their works:

1. By telling about the last of a series of events
2. By summarizing what has been said
3. By making a general statement about what has been said
4. By calling on readers to form some opinion or to take some action
5. By explaining the importance or value of what has been said
6. By connecting what has been said to something else of importance or value

CONTRAST *n.* *Contrast* is the process of observing and pointing out differences. When you contrast two things, you first note their individual characteristics. Then you note any differences in these characteristics. For example, you might note the following differences between people and computers:

1. People are conscious, but computers are not.
2. People have feelings, but computers do not.
3. People can act on their own, but computers cannot.

In writing, a contrast is often signaled by one of the following words or phrases: *in contrast, on the contrary, however, but,* or *on the other hand.*

DEDUCTION *n.* *Deduction* is a form of argument in which the conclusion has to be true if the premises are true. The following is an example of a deductive argument:

Premise 1: All lyric poems express the feelings of a speaker.
Premise 2: "The Secret Heart," by Robert P. Tristram Coffin, is a lyric poem.
Conclusion: "The Secret Heart," by Robert P. Tristram Coffin, expresses the feelings of a speaker.

As this example shows, if you accept the premises of a deductive argument, then you must accept the conclusion.

DEFINITION *n.* *Definition* is the process of explaining the meaning of a word or a phrase. Definition makes communication possible by establishing agreed-upon meanings for words.

The simplest type of definition, called *ostensive definition,* involves pointing to something and saying its name. If, for example, you point to an object and say, "bicycle" you are giving an ostensive definition of the word *bicycle.* Ostensive definition is often used to teach new words to small children.

Another common type of definition is *lexical definition*—the kind of definition found in dictionaries. A lexical definition uses words to explain the meanings of other words. Some types of lexical definition include definition by synonym, definition by antonym, definition by example, and genus and differentia definition.

In a *definition by synonym,* you use a word or a phrase that has the same meaning as the word or phrase that you are defining: A *film* is a "motion picture."

In a *definition by antonym,* you use a word or phrase that has an opposite meaning, along with a negative word such as *not: Tepid* water is water that is "neither very hot nor very cold."

In a *definition by example,* you list things to which the term being defined applies: *Scandinavia* includes Denmark, Sweden, Norway, and Finland.

In a *genus and differentia definition,* you first place the thing to be defined into a general category, or *genus.* Then you tell how the thing differs from other things in the same category:

To be defined: daisy
Genus, or group: flowers
Differentia: many white petals
round yellow center
petals extend out from middle
Definition: A daisy is "a flower with many white petals extending from a round, yellow middle."

The purpose of a definition is to make a reader or listener understand what is being said. Whenever you write, make sure that you define any terms that your audience might not otherwise understand. Use the methods of lexical definition explained here.

EITHER/OR FALLACY See *Logical Fallacy.*

EVALUATION *n.* *Evaluation* is the process of making judgments about the quality or value of something. The statement " 'Flowers for Algernon' is an excellent short story" is an evaluation. To evaluate a literary work, you must first analyze it. Once you identify the parts of a work and understand how these components contribute to the whole, you can then evaluate the work.

Tastes vary from person to person, and intelligent readers can disagree on the merits of a particular work. Still, some judgments about literary works are more reasonable than others

because they are based on sensible standards, or criteria. Most readers agree that literary works should contain believable plots, imaginative language, and interesting, convincing characters. Criteria such as these make evaluations of literary works possible. An effective, persuasive evaluation uses elements in the work—such as plot details, characters, and descriptions—as evidence to support the evaluation. Judgments such as "I hated it" or "It's the best" are unacceptable because they are too vague.
See *Opinion* and *Judgment.*

EVIDENCE *n.* *Evidence* is factual information presented to support an argument. In criminal trials, lawyers present known or new facts as evidence to prove or disprove the innocence of the defendant. In literary analysis or evaluation, the parts of a work—such as language, plot, characters, and tone—are the evidence that must be used to support an interpretation or judgment. For example, consider the statement, "The main character in Poe's 'The Tell-Tale Heart' is mad." You might support this interpretation by pointing out that he thinks the old man in the tale possesses an "evil eye" and that he thinks he hears his dead victim's heart beating.
See *Fact, Reason,* and *Support.*

FALSE ANALOGY See *Logical Fallacy.*

FACT *n.* A *fact* is a statement that can be proved true or false by evidence. For example, the following facts are true by definition:

$9/3 = 3$
A novel is a long, fictional prose narrative.

The following facts are true by observation:

William O. Douglas was a justice on the United States Supreme Court.
Tunisia is in Africa.

Facts are extremely important in literary works. An author uses them to develop characters, settings, and plots. A reader uses them as the evidence with which to make predictions, inferences, and evaluations.
See *Opinion.*

GENERALIZATION *n.* A *generalization* is a statement that applies to more than one thing. The following are generalizations:

John Greenleaf Whittier's poems usually rhyme.
Newspapers are reliable sources of information.

The first statement applies to more than one of Whittier's poems, and the second to more than one newspaper. *Deductive arguments* often begin with generalizations. Consider the following deductive argument:

Premise: (generalization) Shirley Jackson did not write any stories set in Sri Lanka.
Premise: Shirley Jackson wrote the story "Charles."
Conclusion: The story "Charles" is not set in Sri Lanka.

Inductive arguments, on the other hand, often end with generalizations. Consider the following argument:

Premise: Last month Mary read a book about Roberto Clemente.
Premise: Last week Mary read a book about Babe Ruth.
Premise: Now Mary is reading a history of the World Series.
Conclusion: (generalization) Mary likes to read about baseball.

Generalizations are useful for summarizing observations. True generalizations usually assert only that something is frequently or usually the case, not that it is always so. Be careful not to overgeneralize. For example, the statement "All of Ray Bradbury's stories are set on Mars" is an overgeneralization because many exceptions can be found. One way to avoid overgeneralizing is to limit your general statements by using qualifiers, such as *usually, often, generally, a few,* and *many.*
See *Conclusion* and *Stereotype.*

INDUCTION *n.* *Induction* is a form of argument in which the conclusion is probably but not necessarily true. For example, if you read several poems by Shel Silverstein and find that each is humorous, then you might conclude, "All of Shel Silverstein's poems are humorous." This conclusion may be true, but it is not necessarily true because you have not read all of Silverstein's poems. You would have to limit your conclusion by using a qualifier: "Many of Shel Silverstein's poems are humorous."
See *Generalization* and *Inference.*

INFERENCE *n.* An *inference* is any logical or reasonable conclusion based on known facts or accepted premises. Detectives such as Sherlock Holmes continually make inferences on the basis of the facts known to them. The conclusions of inductive and deductive arguments—Sherlock Holmes uses both kinds of reasoning—are inferences. In thinking about a literary work, the reader must constantly draw inferences from the details presented by the author. The author wants and expects the reader to do so. For example, Walt Whitman expected the readers of his "O Captain! My Captain!" on page 534 to infer that the real subject and inspiration of his poem was Abraham Lincoln. The emotional, heartrending nature of the poem and its repeated references to a beloved, nameless leader, coupled with the reader's knowledge of its background, or *context,* make this inference reasonable.

INTERPRETATION *n.* *Interpretation* is the process of determining the meaning or significance of speech, writing, art, music, or actions. The interpretation of a literary work involves many different processes. These include the following:

1. Reading carefully and actively and responding to each new detail, character, and plot incident
2. Breaking down the work into its parts, describing each, and looking for patterns, connections, and similarities among the parts
3. Examining your own responses to the work and identifying the details that help to create these responses
4. Unifying your observations by making generalizations, based on them, about the meaning or purpose of the work as a whole

Interpretation is usually aimed at identifying the theme of a literary work. For example, your reading of Pearl S. Buck's "Christmas Day in the Morning," on page 21, might lead you to this statement of theme: "Buck affirms the mysterious yet very practical ability of love to bring people together." Reasonable interpretations will take into account, directly or indirectly, all important parts of a work.
See *Analysis.*

JUDGMENT *n.* A *judgment* is a statement about the quality or value of something. Like arguments, judgments must be supported by facts and reasons. A sound judgment of a literary work, therefore, must be based on evidence from the text.
See *Evaluation* and *Opinion.*

LOGICAL FALLACY *n. phrase* A *logical fallacy* is an error in reasoning. People often commit such errors when they are attempting to persuade others to adopt some opinion or to take some action. The following logical fallacies are quite common:

1. *Begging the question:* This fallacy occurs when someone assumes the truth of the statement to be proved without providing any supporting evidence. For example: "All students who receive A's in algebra will go on to become great mathematicians." (No evidence is given to support the claim.)
2. *Circular reasoning:* This fallacy occurs when the evidence given to support a claim is simply a restatement of the claim in other words. For example: "I think the cafeteria food is delicious because it tastes good." (The second part of the sentence simply restates the original claim in different words.)

3. *Either/or fallacy:* This fallacy occurs when someone claims that there are only two alternatives when there are actually more. For example: "A high-school graduate can either get a job or join the armed forces." (This statement ignores other possibilities such as going to college.)
4. *False analogy:* This fallacy occurs when someone falsely assumes that two subjects are similar in some respect just because they are similar in some other respect. For example: "Paul lives in Iowa, and he is a farmer. Janet also lives in Iowa. Therefore, Janet must be a farmer." (The false assumption is made that because Paul and Janet live in the same state, they must also have the same occupation.)
5. *Post hoc, ergo propter hoc:* (a Latin phrase meaning "After this, therefore because of this") This fallacy occurs when someone falsely assumes that an event is caused by another event simply because of the order of the events in time. For example: "After Rose entered the room, Claire left. Claire must have left because she doesn't like Rose." (The two events might be completely unrelated. One cannot assume a cause-and-effect relationship on such flimsy evidence.)
6. *Overgeneralization:* This fallacy occurs when someone makes a statement that is too broad or too inclusive. For example: "All baseball players chew bubble gum." (While this statement might be true of some baseball players, it is certainly not true of all of them.)

When you do persuasive writing or speaking, try to avoid these logical fallacies. Also be on guard against these fallacies in the speech and writing of others.

MAIN IDEA *n. phrase* The *main idea* is the central point that a speaker or writer wants to communicate. For example, the main idea of Robert Frost's "The Road Not Taken," on page 600, is that making a difficult or unpopular choice can make a great difference in one's life. As in most works of poetry and fiction, however, this main idea is implied rather than stated directly. In essays that seek to persuade the reader, the thesis is usually directly stated early in the essay. This is especially true of essays that analyze or interpret a work of literature.
See *Purpose.*

OBJECTIVE *adj.* Something is *objective* if it has to do with a reality that exists independently of any particular person's mind or personal, internal experiences. Statements of fact are objective because anyone can, at least in theory, determine whether they are true. For example, the statement "John Steinbeck wrote *The Pearl*" is objective because it deals with an impersonal, extenal reality. On the other hand, the statement "*The Pearl* is a powerful book" is subjective because it reports one individual's personal, internal experience of the novel.

To be objective is to be fair. Judges and jurors in legal trials are expected to evaluate cases fairly and objectively by taking all the facts into account. Similarly, in writing about literature a critic will seem fair if he or she takes into account the important facts and details contained in the work.
See *Subjective.*

OPINION *n.* An *opinion* is a statement that can be supported by facts but that is not itself a fact. Opinions usually fall into one of three categories: judgments, predictions, or statements of obligation.

A *judgment* offers an evaluation of something:

Mr. García is an excellent teacher.

A *prediction* is a statement about the future:

New baseball teams will be added to the major leagues.

A *statement of obligation* tells how one should act:

Do unto others as you would have them do unto you.

A good citizen should keep up with current events.

Whenever you express an opinion, you should be prepared to support it with facts and with reasoned arguments. An opinion that you cannot back up is merely a prejudice.
See *Fact, Judgment,* and *Prediction.*

OVERGENERALIZATION See *Logical Fallacy.*

PARAPHRASE *n.* A *paraphrase* is a restatement in other words. Writing a paraphrase is an excellent way to test your understanding of a literary work. A paraphrase can also be used to support an interpretive argument when the exact words of the original are not essential to the argument. When you paraphrase a passage, be careful not to alter the meaning of the original. Simply put into your own words what the writer has said.

POST HOC, ERGO PROPTER HOC See *Logical Fallacy.*

PREDICTION *n.* *Prediction* is the act of making statements about the future. An active reader of a literary work continually makes predictions about what is going to happen next. These predictions are based on details provided in the work and on the reader's general knowledge about how people act and how the world operates.

In literary works prediction is possible because of the use of foreshadowing. *Foreshadowing* is the technique of providing clues about what is going to happen later in a work. See the definition of foreshadowing in the Handbook of Literary Terms and Techniques.
See *Opinion.*

PROBLEM SOLVING *n. phrase* *Problem solving* is the process by which a person comes up with a solution to some difficulty. Interpreting a literary work is a type of problem solving. So is planning a piece of writing. The following are some general guidelines for solving problems:

1. State the problem as clearly as you can.
2. Identify the goal that you want to reach. That is, determine what situation will exist when the problem is solved.
3. Examine the differences between the goal state (the situation that will exist when the problem is solved) and the initial state (the situation at the time when you begin working on the problem).
4. Take steps to reduce the differences between the initial state and the goal state.

The following are some rules of thumb, or *heuristics,* that are useful in solving problems:

1. Break the problem down into parts and solve the parts separately.
2. Think of a time when you solved a simpler problem of the same type. See if you can use the same solution.
3. Restate the problem in various ways. Doing so may give you some additional insight into the problem.
4. Ask someone to help you with parts of the problem that are especially difficult.
5. Ask "What if" questions to come up with possible solutions. Test each of these solutions.
6. Define the key terms or concepts involved in the problem.
7. Use general thinking strategies such as diagraming, freewriting, clustering, and brainstorming to come up with possible solutions.
8. Use means/ends analysis. That is, at each step in the solution, compare where you are with where you want to be. Take steps to reduce the differences between where you are and the desired goal.

PROPAGANDA TECHNIQUE *n. phrase* A *propaganda technique* is an improper appeal to emotion used for the purpose of swaying the opinions of an audience. The following propaganda techniques are quite common:

1. *Bandwagon:* This technique involves encouraging people to think or act in some way simply because other people are doing so.

For example: "All your neighbors are rushing down to Mistri Motors to take advantage of the year-end sale. You come, too!"

2. *Loaded words:* This technique involves using words with strong positive or negative connotations, or associations. Name-calling is an example of the use of loaded words. So is any use of words that are charged with emotion. For example: "No really *intelligent* voter would support his candidacy."
3. *Snob appeal:* This technique involves making a claim that one should act or think in a certain way because of the high social status associated with the action or thought. For example: "Felson's Furs—the feeling of luxury, for those who can afford the very best."
4. *Transfer:* This technique involves making an illogical association between one thing and something else that is generally viewed as positive or negative. For example: "The American pioneers worked hard because they cared about the future. If you care about the future of your family, then see your agent at Pioneer Insurance."
5. *Unreliable testimonial:* This technique involves having an unqualified person endorse a product, action, or opinion. For example: "Hi! I'm Bart Bearson. As a pro-football quarterback, I have to be concerned about my health. That's why I take Pro-Ball Vitamin Supplements."
6. *Vague, undefined terms:* This technique involves promoting or challenging an opinion by using words that are so vague or so poorly defined as to be almost meaningless. For example: "Try our *new* and *improved, all-natural* product!"

Avoid using propaganda techniques in your own speech and writing, and be on the alert for these techniques in the speech and writing of others.

PURPOSE *n.* The *purpose* is the goal or aim of a literary work. A writer's purpose may be to tell a story, to describe something, to explain or inform, to persuade, or simply to entertain. Often a work will combine several of these purposes. In her essay "The Sounds of Richard Rodgers," on page 473, Ellen Goodman has two major purposes: First, Goodman wants to explain Richard Rodgers's work. Second, she wants to persuade readers that it is possible for people to blend their work lives with their personal lives, as Richard Rodgers did.

In an essay the writer's purpose is often stated directly. The sentence or sentences that tell the purpose, or main idea, of the essay are called the thesis statement.
See *Main Idea.*

REALISTIC DETAILS/FANTASTIC DETAILS *n. phrases* A *realistic detail* is one that is drawn from actual or possible experience. A *fantastic detail* is one that is not based on actual experience and that is highly improbable or imaginary. Realistic details make plots, characters, descriptions, and statements seem true to life. Writers often use fantastic details to capture the reader's interest or imagination. Folktales, such as those about Paul Bunyan and Pecos Bill, often contain fantastic details about the hero's strength or courage. Fantastic details are also found in science-fiction stories, such as Arthur C. Clarke's "Crime on Mars," on page 137.

Few works consist entirely of fantastic details. More often fantastic and realistic details are combined. In "Crime on Mars," for example, Clarke sets the realistic details of a human crime against the fantastic background of a colony on another planet.

REASON *n.* A *reason* is a statement made in support of some conclusion. The term *reason* is also used to signify the human ability to think logically and rationally.
See *Argument* and *Conclusion.*

SOURCE *n.* A *source* is anything from which ideas and information are taken. Books, magazines, speeches, television programs, conversations, and personal experience may all serve as sources. Some books, such as dictionaries, encyclopedias, almanacs, and atlases, are specifically designed to be used as sources. A good source is one that is thorough, objective, and up-to-date.

There are two types of sources, primary and secondary. *Primary sources* are first-hand accounts. Conversations, speeches, documents, and letters are examples of primary sources. *Secondary sources* are accounts written by others, after the fact. For example, *One Writer's Beginnings* is a primary source of information about Eudora Welty's life because Welty wrote this book herself. On the other hand, a biography of Eudora Welty, written by another writer, is a secondary source of information about Welty. It merely summarizes or repeats information gained from other sources, such as *One Writer's Beginnings.*

Whenever you borrow facts and ideas from other sources, be sure to credit your sources by means of footnotes or end notes. If you do not credit them, you are committing the dishonest act called plagiarism.

STEREOTYPE *n.* A *stereotype* is a fixed or conventional notion or characterization. It is a type of overgeneralization or oversimplification. Some examples include the mad scientist, the absent-minded professor, and the beautiful princess. Although writers occasionally use stereotypes when they do not have sufficient space to develop a character fully, good writers generally avoid stereotyping. They know that carefully drawn characters and situations are more interesting to read about than tired, simplistic stereotypes.
See *Generalization.*

SUBJECTIVE *adj.* Something is *subjective* if it is based on personal reactions or emotions rather than on some objective reality. A reader's reaction to a work of literature is subjective because another reader may have a different reaction. Opinions are subjective statements, but not all opinions are equally valid. Sensible subjective statements about a literary work are based on evidence from the text. For example, if you find Goodrich and Hackett's play *The Diary of Anne Frank* powerful and moving, you should be able to identify some of the details in the play that make you feel this way.

When authors invent thoughts, dialogue, and actions for their characters, they are depicting the characters' subjective experiences. *The Diary of Anne Frank,* for example, recreates the subjective feelings and experiences of a young girl who, along with her family, is hiding from the Nazis during World War II.
See *Objective.*

SUMMARIZE *v.* To *summarize* something is to restate it briefly in different words. A brief summary of Pearl S. Buck's story, "Christmas Day in the Morning," might be as follows:

> The main character, an older man named Rob, recalls the Christmas when he was fifteen and gave his father a special gift: He got up early and milked the family's cows all by himself, a chore he had always helped his father with and had always hated. His father was delighted by this "present." Thinking back on this incident gives Rob the idea of doing something similar for his wife. So, Rob gets up early on Christmas morning to trim the Christmas tree and to write a love letter to his wife. Rob learned when he was fifteen how to give the gift of love, and he has remembered that lesson all of his life.

SUPPORT *v.* To *support* a statement is to provide evidence for it.
See *Argument* and *Evidence.*

TIME ORDER *n. phrase* *Time order* is organization by order of occurrence, that is, by chronological order. Many fiction and nonfiction works use time order to organize and present the events they describe.

TRANSFER See *Propaganda Technique.*

UNRELIABLE TESTIMONIAL See *Propaganda Technique.*

GLOSSARY

READING THE GLOSSARY ENTRIES

The words in this glossary are from selections appearing in your textbook. Each entry in the glossary contains the following parts:

1. The Entry Word. This word appears at the beginning of the entry, in boldface type.

2. The Pronunciation. The symbols in parentheses tell how the entry word is pronounced. If a word has more than one possible pronunciation, the most common of these pronunciations is given first.

3. The Part of Speech. Appearing after the pronunciation, in italics, is an abbreviation that tells the part of speech of the entry word. The following abbreviations have been used:

n. noun **p.** pronoun **v.** verb

adj. adjective **adv.** adverb **conj.** conjunction

4. The Definition. This part of the entry follows the part-of-speech abbreviation and gives the meaning of the entry word as used in the selection in which it appears.

KEY TO PRONUNCIATION SYMBOLS USED IN THE GLOSSARY

The following symbols are used in the pronunciations that follow the entry words:

Symbol	*Key Words*	*Symbol*	*Key Words*
a	asp, fat, parrot	b	bed, fable, dub
ā	ape, date, play	d	dip, beadle, had
ä	ah, car, father	f	fall, after, off
		g	get, haggle, dog
e	elf, ten, berry	h	he, ahead, hotel
ē	even, meet, money	j	joy, agile, badge
		k	kill, tackle, bake
i	is, hit, mirror	l	let, yellow, ball
ī	ice, bite, high	m	met, camel, trim
		n	not, flannel, ton
ō	open, tone, go	p	put, apple, tap
ô	all, horn, law	r	red, port, dear
o͞o	ooze, tool, crew	s	sell, castle, pass
o͝o	look, pull, moor	t	top, cattle, hat
yo͞o	use, cute, few	v	vat, hovel, have
yo͝o	united, cure, globule	w	will, always, swear
oi	oil, point, toy	y	yet, onion, yard
ou	out, crowd, plow	z	zebra, dazzle, haze
u	up, cut, color	ch	chin, catcher, arch
ur	urn, fur, deter	sh	she, cushion, dash
		th	thin, nothing, truth
ə	a in ago	t͟h	then, father, lathe
	e in agent	zh	azure, leisure
	i in sanity	ŋ	ring, anger, drink
	o in comply	'	[indicates that a following l or n is a syllabic consonant, as in *able* (ā' b'l)]
	u in focus		
ər	perhaps, murder		

A

abalone (ab' ə lō' nē) shell *n.* An oval shell with a pearly lining

abandonment (ə ban' dən mənt) *n.* Unrestrained freedom of actions or emotions

abduction (ab duk' shən) *n.* Kidnapping

aboriginal (ab' ə rij' ə n'l) *adj.* First; native

abyss (ə bis') *n.* Great depth

acquaintance (ə kwānt' 'ns) *n.* A person one has met

acquiescent (ak' wē es' ənt) *adj.* Agreeing without protest

acrid (ak' rid) *adj.* Sharp; bitter

acute (ə kyo͞ot') *adj.* Sensitive

ad-lib (ad' lib') *v.* To say or do things not in a script

adversary (ad' vər ser' ē) *n.* Enemy

affectation (af' ek tā' shən) *n.* Behavior not natural to a person intended to impress others

aghast (ə gast') *adj.* Horrified

airy (er' ə) *adj.* Lightness

alkaloid (al' kə loid') *adj.* Referring to certain bitter substances found chiefly in plants

allure (ə lo͝or') *v.* To tempt; attract

ally (al' ī) *v.* To join or to unite, connection between country, person, or group for a common purpose

alms (ämz) *n.* Money given to poor people

alterative (ôl' tə rāt' iv) *adj.* Causing a change

amble (am' b'l) *v.* To move at a smooth, easy pace

ambuscade (am' bəs kād') *n.* Place of surprise attack

amenity (ə men' ə tē) *n.* Pleasant quality

anachronism (ə nak' rə niz'm) *n.* Anything that seems to be out of its proper place in history

anemometer (an' ə mäm' ə tər) *n.* An instrument that determines wind speed

antagonist (an tag' ə nist) *n.* Opponent

anxious (aŋk' shəs) *adj.* Eagerly wishing

apathetic (ap' ə thet' ik) *adv.* Indifferent

apex (ā' peks) *n.* Highest point; peak

appall (ə pôl') *v.* To overwhelm with horror or shock

apparition (ap' ə rish' ən) *n.* A strange figure appearing suddenly or in an extraordinary way

applaud (ə plôd') *v.* To show approval or enjoyment by clapping the hands

appraisal (ə prā' z'l) *n.* Evaluation; judgment

apprehension (ap' rə hen' shən) *n.* A fearful feeling about the future; dread

apprentice (ə pren' tis) *v.* To contract to learn a trade under a skilled worker

arbitrary (är' bə trer' ē) *adj.* Based on one's preference or whim

archaeologist (är' kē äl' ə jist) *n.* Scientist who studies the life and culture of ancient people

archer (är′ chər) *n.* A person who shoots with bow and arrow
archipelago (ar′ kə pel′ ə gō′) *n.* A chain of many islands
ardent (är′ d′nt) *adj.* Passionate
aristocrat (ə ris′ tə krat′) *n.* A person belonging to the upper class
armory (är′ mər ē) *n.* A storehouse for weapons
articulated (är tik′ yə lāt′ əd) *adj.* Connected by joints
artifact (är′ tə fakt′) *n.* Any object made by human work, left behind by a civilization
askew (ə skyōō′) *adv.* Crookedly
assiduous (ə sij′ yoo wəs) *adj.* Careful and busy
atone (ə tōn′) *v.* Make amends for wrongdoing
august (ô gust′) *adj.* Honored
aura (ôr′ ə) *n.* An atmosphere or quality
avail (ə vāl′) *v.* To be of use
avarice (av′ ə ris) *n.* Greediness
aver (ə vʉr′) *v.* To declare
awed (ôd) *adj.* Having a mixed feeling of reverence, fear, and wonder
axioms (ak′ sē əmz) *n.* Truths or principles that are widely accepted

B

babel (ba′ b′l) *n.* A confusion of sounds
backfire (bak′ fīr′) *n.* A fire started to stop an advancing fire
bane (bān) *n.* Ruin
bank (baŋk) *v.* To tilt an airplane to the side when turning
banner (ban′ ər) *n.* Flag
barter (bär′ tər) *v.* To exchange goods
becalm (bi käm′) *v.* Not to move
bedraggle (bi drag′ ′l) *v.* To wet and soil
beguile (bi gīl′′) *v.* To charm
belfry (bel′ frē) *n.* The part of a tower that holds the bells
bellow (bel′ ō) *v.* Roar powerfully
benediction (ben′ ə dik′ shən) *n.* A blessing
benevolent (bə nev′ ə lənt) *adj.* Kindly
benign (bi nīn′) *adj.* Kindly
billow (bil′ ō) *n.* Large; spread out
bleating (blēt′ iŋ) *n.* The sound made by sheep
blunder (blun′ dər) *n.* A foolish or stupid mistake
bode (bōd) *v.* To foretell a future event
borne (bôrn) *v.* Carried
brace (brās) *n.* A pair of like things
bravado (brə vä′ dō) *n.* Bold, bragging behavior
bridle (brīd′ ′l) *n.* A head harness for guiding a horse
brimstone (brim′ stōn′) *n.* Another name for sulfur, a foul-smelling mineral
brine (brīn) *n.* Water full of salt and used for pickling
broach (brōch) *n.* Start a discussion about a topic
bullpen (bool′ pen′) *n.* A barred room in a jail, where prisoners are kept temporarily
bulwark (bool′ wərk) *n.* Protection; defense
buoyant (boi′ ənt) *adj.* Lighthearted

C

cadence (kād′ ′ns) *n.* Rhythmic flow of sound
cajole (kə jōl′) *v.* To coax gently
callous (kal′ əs) *adj.* Unfeeling
callowness (kal′ ō nəs) *n.* Youth and inexperience; immaturity
caper (kā′ pər) *n.* Slang term for criminal act
capitulation (kə pich′ ə lā′ shən) *n.* Surrender
carcass (kär′ kəs) *n.* The dead body of an animal
carillon (kar′ ə län′) *n.* A set of stationary bells, each producing one note of the scale
catapult (kat′ ə pult′) *v.* To launch
cataract (kat′ ə rakt′) *n.* Large waterfall
celestial (səl es′ chəl) *adj.* Of the sky
centrifugal (sen trif′ yə gəl) *adj.* Describing something that tends to move away from the center
cessation (se sā′ shən) *n.* A stopping
chancellor (chan′ sə lər) *n.* An official secretary
civic (siv′ ik) *adj.* Of a city
clairvoyant (kler voi′ ənt) *adj.* Having the ability to see what cannot be seen; keenly perceptive
coherence (kō hir′ əns) *n.* The quality of being connected in an intelligible way
commission (kə mish′ ən) *n.* Authority given to make something
commotion (kə mō′ shən) *n.* Noisy movement
communal (käm yoon′ ′l) *adj.* Shared by members of a group
compassionate (kəm pash′ ə nit) *adj.* Sympathizing deeply
compensation (käm′ pən sā′ shən) *n.* Equal reaction
compliance (kəm plī′ əns) *n.* Agreeing to a request
compound (käm pound′) *adj.* Mix
compulsory (kəm pul′ sər ē) *adj.* Required
conciliate (kən sil′ ē āt′) *v.* To make friends with
condemn (kən dem′) *v.* To disapprove of
confederate (kən fed′ ər it) *adj.* Accomplice; partner in crime
conjecture (kən jek′ chər) *v.* To guess from very little evidence
conjuration (kän′ jə rā′ shən) *n.* The making of a magic spell
conspicuous (kən spik′ yoo əs) *adj.* Noticeable
conspiratorial (kən spir′ ə tôr′ ē əl) *adj.* Secretive
constellation (kän stə lā′ shən) *n.* Brilliant cluster
convent (kän′ vənt) *n.* A girls′ boarding school run by nuns
conviction (kən vik′ shən) *n.* Strong belief
convolutions (kän′ və lū shənz) *n.* Uneven ridges on the brain′s surface
convulse (kən vuls′) *v.* To suffer a violent, involuntary spasm
cosseted (käs′ it əd) *adj.* Pampered; indulged
couch (kouch) *v.* To put into words
countenance (koun′ tə nəns) *n.* The face

834

covert (kuv′ ərt) *adj.* Concealed; hidden
cower (kou′ ər) *v.* To crouch or huddle from fear
cowling (kou′ liŋ) *n.* A removable metal covering for an engine
cowpuncher (kou′ pun cher) *n.* Cowboy
crane (krān) *n.* A large, slender bird with very long legs and neck
cranny (kran′ ē) *n.* Small, narrow opening
credo (krē′ dō) *n.* Set of personal beliefs
crevasse (kri vas′) *n.* A deep, narrow opening, as in a cliff
crevice (krev′ is) *n.* A narrow opening
crockery (kräk′ ər ē) *n.* Earthenware dishes, pots, and so on
crooner (kro͞on′ ər) *n.* Singer
crooning (kro͞on′ iŋ) *v.* Singing or humming in a low, gentle way
crosstie (krôs′ tī) *n.* Beam laid crosswise under railroad tracks to support them
crustaceans (krus tā′ shənz) *n.* Shellfish, such as lobsters, crabs, or shrimp
crypt (kript) *n.* An underground vault, used as a burial place
cryptic (krip′ tik) *adj.* Having hidden meaning
crystal (kris′ t'l) *n.* The transparent covering over the face of a watch
cunning (kun′ iŋ) *adj.* Skillful
cynical (sin′ ik l) *adj.* Disbelief as to the sincerity of people's intentions or actions

D

damask (dam′ əsk) *n.* A fine fabric of silk or linen with a woven design
daunt (dônt′) *v.* To intimidate or discourage
deference (def′ ər əns) *n.* Courteous respect
defray (di frā′) *v.* To pay the money for the cost of
delineate (di lin′ ē āt) *v.* To describe in detail
demise (di mīz′) *n.* Death
derision (di rizh′ ən) *n.* Contempt; ridicule
destine (des′ tin) *v.* To determine by fate
devour (di vour′) *v.* To eat up greedily
digital (dij′ it əl) *adj.* Giving a reading in digits, which are the numerals from 0 to 9
discreet (dis krēt′) *adj.* Careful about what one says or does
discreet surveillance (dis krēt′ sər vā′ ləns) *n.* Careful unobserved watch kept over a person
disheveled (di shev′ 'ld) *adj.* Untidy; messy
disposition (dis pə zish′ ən) *n.* One's nature or temperament
dissemble (di sem′ b'l) *v.* To conceal under a false appearance
dissentient (di sen′ shənt) *adj.* Differing from the majority
dissimulation (di sim′ yə lā′ shən) *n.* The hiding of one's feelings or purposes
dissolute (dis′ ə lo͞ot′) *adj.* Unrestrained
dissolution (dis′ ə lo͞o′ shən) *n.* The act of breaking down and crumbling
distend (dis tend′) *v.* To stretch out; to become swollen
diverge (də vurj′) *v.* To branch off
divert (də vurt′) *v.* To distract
divest (də vest′) *v.* To strip; to get rid of
doggedness (dôg′ id nis) *n.* Stubborness
dogie (dō′ gē) **calves** *n.* Motherless calves
drill (dril) *n.* Pointed tool used for making holes in hard substances
drive (drīv) *v.* To force by hitting
drowse (drouz) *n.* Sluggishness; doze
drove (drōv) *n.* Large number; crowd
dugout (dug′ out′) *n.* A shelter built into a hillside

E

edifice (ed′ i fis) *n.* Imposing structure
elaborate (i lab′ ər it) *adj.* Careful; painstaking
elder (el′ dər) *n.* Shrub or small tree
elixir (i lik′ sər) *n.* Magic potion
elusive (i lo͞o′ siv) *adj.* Hard to grasp mentally
emancipate (i man′ sə pāt) *v.* To free from the control or power of another
eminent (em′ ə nənt) *adj.* Well-known
encumber (in kum′ bər) *v.* To weigh down
engulf (in gulf′) *v.* To flow over; to swallow up
enigma (ə nig′ mə) *n.* An unexplainable event
enthusiasm (in tho͞o′ zē az′m) *n.* Intense or eager interest
enunciate (i nun′ sē āt′) *v.* To speak clearly and carefully
escarpment (e skärp′ mənt) *n.* A long cliff
esophagus (i säf′ ə gəs) *n.* The tube through which food passes to the stomach
eternal (i tur′ n'l) *adj.* Everlasting
euphemism (yo͞o′ fə miz′ əm) *n.* A less direct term that substitutes for a distasteful or offensive word or phrase
evacuee (i vak′ yo͞o wē′) *n.* One who leaves a place because of danger
evasion (i vā′ zhən) *n.* Avoidance
exception (ik sep′ shən) *n.* Exclusion
excrescence (iks kres′ 'ns) *n.* A natural outgrowth
exodus (ek′ sə dəs) *n.* Departure
expend (ik spend′) *v.* To use up
expound (ik spound′) *v.* To explain in careful detail
extravagence (ik strav′ ə gəns) *n.* Waste
extremity (ik strem′ ə tē) *n.* Dying stage
exult (ig zult′) *v.* To rejoice

F

fastidious (fas tid′ ē əs) *adj.* Not easy to please
fatalist (fā′ tə list) *n.* One who believes that all events are determined by fate
fatuous (fach′ oo wəs) *adj.* Foolish; blandly inane
feign (fān′) *v.* To make a false show of

feint (fānt) *v.* Make a pretense of attack
fell (fel) *n.* Rocky or barren hill
fertile (fur' t'l) *adj.* Rich; productive
fiscal (fis' kəl) *adj.* Having to do with finances
fissure (fish' ər) *n.* Narrow opening
fitting (fit' iŋ) *adj.* Proper
flag (flag) *v.* To signal to a train to stop
flamboyant (flam boi' ənt) *adj.* Too showy; extravagant
fleece (flēs) *n.* Soft, warm covering made of sheep's wool
fluctuate (fluk' choo wāt') *v.* To be constantly changing
flue (floo) *n.* The pipe in a chimney
flush (flush) *n.* A blush or glow
forbear (fôr ber') *v.* To refrain from
foresight (fôr' sīt) *n.* The act of seeing beforehand
forestall (fôr stôl') *v.* To prevent
forsaken (fər sā' kən) *adj.* Abandoned
fragrant (frā' grənt) *adj.* Covered with the odor of something
fretted (fret' əd) *adj.* Decoratively arranged
friction (frik' shən) *n.* The rubbing of the surface of one body against another
furtive (fur' tiv) *adj.* Sly or done in secret
futile (fyoot' 'l) *adj.* Useless; hopeless

G

galley (gal' ē) *n.* Cooking area on a ship
garnet (gär' nit) *n.* Deep red gem
garrison (gar' ə s'n) *n.* Military post or station
gentian (jen' shən) *n.* Herb with blue flowers
gesticulation (jes tik' yə lā' shən) *n.* Energetic hand or arm gesture
glean (glēn) *v.* To find out gradually bit by bit
gleeful (glē' fəl) *adj.* Merry
glisten (glis' 'n) *v.* To shine
glockenspiel (gläk' ən spēl') *n.* Musical instrument like xylophone
gnarled (närld) *adj.* Knotty and twisted
goad (gōd) *v.* To urge to action
gout (gout) *n.* Inflammation of the joints
gracious (grā' shəs) *adj.* Kind and generous
granite (gran' it) *adj.* Made of a type of very hard rock
gratification (grat' ə fi kā' shən) *n.* The act of pleasing
gross (grōs) *n.* Twelve dozen
guffaw (gə fô') *v.* To laugh in a loud, coarse way
guile (gīl) *n.* Craftiness
gumption (gump' shən) *n.* Courage, boldness
guttural (gut' ər əl) *adj.* Made in back of the throat; *n.* Sound produced in the throat
gyration (jī rā' shən) *n.* Circling or spiral movement

H

haggard (hag' ərd) *adj.* Having a tired look
harness (här' nis) *v.* To tie
hasp (hasp) *n.* Hinged metal fastening of a window
heft (heft) *v.* To lift; test the weight of
hie (hī) *v.* To hurry
hoarse (hôrs) *adj.* Sounding harsh
hobnailed (häb' nāld) *adj.* Having short nails put on the soles to provide greater traction
homage (häm' ij) *n.* Public expression of honor
homesteader (hōm' sted' ər) *n.* Settler in America in the 1800's
hook-and-eye (hook' and ī') *n.* A fastening device
horde (hôrd) *n.* Large moving group
horizon (hu rī' zən) *n.* The line that forms the apparent boundary between the earth and the sky
host (hōst) *n.* An army; a multitude
hover (huv' ər) *v.* To stay suspended in the air
hummock (hum' ək) *n.* Mound or small hill
hurtle (hurt' 'l) *v.* To move quickly
hybrid (hī' brid) *adj.* Grown from different varieties

I

ignominious (ig' nə min' ē əs) *adj.* Humiliating; degrading
impenetrable (im pen' i trə b'l) *adj.* Not able to be passed through
imperious (im pir' ē əs) *adj.* Overbearing, arrogant
imperturbable (im' pər tur' bə bl) *adj.* Unexcited; calm
impetuous (im pech' oo wəs) *adj.* Impulsive
inarticulate (in' är tik' yə lit) *adj.* Speechless or unable to express oneself
incantation (in' kan tā' shən) *n.* Magic words used to cast a spell
incarcerate (in kär' sər āt') *v.* Jail; imprison
incentive (in sen' tiv) *n.* Something that stirs up people or urges them on
incessant (in ses' 'nt) *adj.* Without interruption
incisors (in sī' zərz) *n.* The front teeth
incredulous (in krej' oo ləs) *adj.* Doubt or disbelief
indigent (in' di jənt) *adj.* Needy; poor
indignant (in dig' nənt) *adj.* Filled with anger over some injustice
indiscretion (in dis kresh' ən) *n.* Lack of good judgment
indiscriminate (in' dis krim' ə nit) *adj.* Random
indomitable (in däm' it ə b'l) *adj.* Not easily discouraged
indulgent (in dul' jənt) *adj.* Very tolerant
ineffectual (in' i fek' choo əl) *adj.* Without any effect
inevitable (in ev' ə tə b'l) *adj.* Unavoidable
inexorable (in ek' sər ə b'l) *adj.* Unwilling to give in
inexplicable (in eks' pli kə b'l) *adj.* Without explanation
inferiority complex (in fir' ē or' ə tē käm' pleks) *n.* Constant sense of worthlessness
inflammation (in' flə mā' shən) *n.* A state of redness, pain and swelling
infuse (in fyooz') *v.* To put into

ingot (iŋ′ gət) *n.* A mold in which metal is cast
inherent (in hir′ ənt) *adj.* Natural
initiation (i nish′ ē ā′ shən) *n.* The events during which a person becomes admitted as a member of a club
innumerable (i nōō′ mər ə b′l) *adj.* Too many to be counted
inquest (in′ kwest) *n.* Investigation
inquisitive (in kwiz′ ə tiv) *adj.* Curious
insidious (in sid′ ē əs) *adj.* Sly; crafty
insolent (in′ sə lənt) *n.* One who is boldly disrespectful
insolent (in′ sə lənt) *adj.* In a bold disrespectful way
insubordination (in′ sə bor′ d′n ā′ shən) *n.* Disobedience
insufferable (in suf′ ər ə b′l) *adj.* Unbearable
insular (in′ sə lər) *adj.* Isolated; detached
intercession (in′ tər sesh′ ən) *n.* A prayer said on behalf of another person
intercourse (int′ ər kôrs) *n.* Communication between people
intern (in′ tərn) *n.* A doctor serving a training period
intimation (in′ tə mā′ shən) *n.* Hint or suggestion
introspective (in′ trə spek′ tiv) *adj.* Looking into one's own thoughts and feelings
intuition (in′ too wish′ ən) *n.* Ability to know immediately without reasoning
invariable (in ver′ ē ə b′l) *adj.* Not changing
invincible (in vin′ sə b′l) *adj.* Unbeatable

J

jaded (jā′ did) *adj.* Worn-out
jocund (jäk′ ənd) *adj.* Cheerful; merry

K

kaleidoscopic (kə lī′ də skäp′ ik) *adj.* Constantly changing
keel (kēl) *n.* The chief structural beam extending along the entire length of the bottom of a boat or ship supporting the frame
keen (kēn) *adj.* Having a sharp cutting edge
keystone (kē′ stōn) *n.* A wedge-shaped piece at the top of an arch that locks other pieces into place
kindle (kin′ d′l) *v.* To ignite
kitchenette-furnished (kich ə net′ fur′ nisht) *adj.* Having a small, compact kitchen
knell (nel) *n.* The sound of a bell slowly ringing
knothole (nät′ hōl) *n.* A hole in a board where a knot has fallen out

L

lag (lag) *v.* To fall behind
lair (ler) *n.* Den of a wild animal
languorous (laŋ′ gər əs) *adj.* Slow and lazy
lateral (lat′ ər əl) *adj.* Toward the side
lee (lē) *n.* Sheltered place; the side away from the wind
leer (lir′) *v.* To look with malicious triumph
legacy (leg′ ə sē) *n.* Anything handed down, as from an ancestor
leprosy (lep′ rə sē) *n.* An infectious, disfiguring disease
lethargy (leth′ ər jē) *n.* Laziness or indifference
lichen (lī′ kən) *n.* Small plants of fungus and algae growing on rocks, wood, or soil
lilting (lilt′ iŋ) *adj.* With a light, graceful rhythm
limned (lim ′d) *adj.* Outlined
loam (lōm) *n.* Rich, dark soil
lobulated (läb′ yōō lāt′ əd) *adj.* Subdivided
lockjaw (läk′ jô′) *n.* A disease that causes jaw and neck muscles to become rigid
low (lō) *v.* To make the typical sound that a cow makes
lugubrious (loo gōō′ brē əs) *adj.* Sad
lumberjack (lum′ bər jak′) *n.* A person employed to cut down timber
luminance (loo′ mə nəns) *n.* Brightness
luminous (loo′ mə nəs) *adj.* Glowing in the dark

M

macabre (mə käb′ rə) *adj.* Gruesome
malignant (mə lig′ nənt) *adj.* Harmful; likely to cause death
malingerer (mə lin′ gər ər) *n.* One who pretends to be ill in order to escape work
mammoth (mam′ əth) *adj.* Huge
maneuver (mə nōō′ vər) *v.* To move in a planned way
mania (mā′ nē ə) *n.* Uncontrollable enthusiasm
manifold (man′ ə fōld′) *adj.* Many and varied
mantle (man′ t′l) *n.* Sleeveless cloak or cape
meditate (med′ ə tāt′) *v.* To think deeply
medium (mē′ dē əm) *n.* Means of communication
meets (mētz) *n.* A series of races or competitions
mercurial (mər kyoor′ ē əl) *adj.* Quick or changeable in behavior
Mercury (mur′ kyoo rē) *n.* In Roman mythology, the messenger of the gods
metamorphose (met′ ə môr′ fōs) *v.* To change or transform
meticulous (mə tik′ yoo ləs) *adj.* Extremely careful about details
mire (mīr) *n.* Deep mud
miscreants (mis′ krē ənts) *n.* Criminals
moccasin (mäk′ ə s′n) *n.* Heelless slipper of soft flexible leather
mode (mōd) *n.* Way; form
molding (mōl′ diŋ) *n.* Ornamental woodwork
monolithic (män′ ə lith′ ik) *adj.* Formed from a single block
morose (mə rōs′) *adj.* Gloomy
mote (mōt) *n.* A speck of dust or other tiny particle
mucilage (myōō′ s′l ij) *n.* Any watery solution of gum, glue, etc. used as an adhesive
muse (myōōz′) *v.* To think deeply
muslin (muz′ lin) *n.* Plain-woven, cotton fabric

musty (mus′ tē) *adj.* Having a stale, damp smell
muted (myo͞ot′ əd) *adj.* Muffled; subdued
mutineers (myo͞ot′ ′n irz′) *n.* People on a ship who revolt against their officers
mutinous (myo͞ot′ ′n əs) *adj.* Rebellious
mutual (myo͞o′ cho͞o wəl) *adj.* Having the same relationship toward each other

N

narcotic (när kät′ ik) *n.* Something that has a soothing effect
nebulous (neb′ yə ləs) *adj.* Vague; unclear and indefinite
negotiation (ni gō′ shē ā′ shən) *n.* Bargaining, or discussing to reach an agreement
nester (nest′ ər) *n.* A homesteader on the prairies in the mid-1800′s
neurosurgeon (no͝or′ ō sʉr′ jən) *n.* A doctor who operates on the nervous system
ninny (nin′ ē) *n.* Fool
nitwit (nit′ wit′) *n.* Stupid or silly person
nonchalant (nän′ shə länt′) *adj.* Casual
notions (nō′ shənz) *n.* Small, useful household items
nurture (nʉr′ chər) *v.* To nourish
nuzzle (nuz′ l) *v.* To rub with the nose

O

obdurate (äb′ do͝or ət) *adj.* Stubborn; unyielding
obliterate (ə blit′ ə rāt) *v.* To wipe out; leaving no traces
obscure (äb skyo͝or′) *adj.* Hidden; *v.* Hide
omen (ō′ mən) *n.* A thing or happening supposed to foretell a future event
ominous (äm′ ə nəs) *adj.* Threatening
oratorical (ôr′ ə tôr′ i k′l) *adj.* Of or characteristic of an orator, lofty, high-sounding
ornate (ôr nāt′) *adj.* Having fancy decorations
orthodontist (ôr′ thə dän′ tist) *n.* A dentist who straightens teeth
ostentatious (äs′ ten tā′ shəs) *adj.* Showy

P

paleontologist (pā′ lē än täl′ ə jist) *n.* Scientist who investigates prehistoric forms of life
palmated (pal′ māt əd) *adj.* Shaped like a hand with the fingers spread
palpate (pal′ pāt) *v.* To examine by touch
palpitant (pal′ pə tənt) *adj.* Quivering
pandemonium (pan′ də mō′ nē əm) *n.* A scene of wild disorder
panoply (pan′ ə plē) *n.* Magnificent covering or array
paradox (par′ ə däks′) *n.* A situation that seems to have contradictory qualities
paraphernalia (par′ ə fər nāl′ yə) *n.* Equipment
paroxysm (par′ ək siz′m) *n.* Outburst or convulsion
parson (pär′ sən) *n.* A clergyman
pelt (pelt) *n.* The skin and fur of an animal
perambulating (per am′ byo͞o lāt′ iŋ) *adj.* Walking
perch (pʉrch) *v.* To rest upon
peremptory (pər emp′ tə rē) *adj.* Absolute, without question
periscope (per′ ə skōp′) *n.* An instrument containing mirrors and lenses to see objects not in a direct line from the viewer; often used in submarines
perspiration (pʉr′ spə rā′ shən) *n.* Sweat
pertinacity (pʉr′ tə nas′ ə tē) *n.* Stubbornness
pervade (pər vād′) *v.* To spread throughout
petulant (pech′ o͝o lənt) *adj.* Impatient
phantasmagorical (fan taz′ mə gôr′ ik′l) *adj.* A rapid change, as in a dream
phantom (fan′ təm) *n.* Ghost-like figure
phoenix (fē′ niks) *n.* In Egyptian mythology, a beautiful bird
pinafore (pin′ ə fôr′) *n.* A sleeveless garment worn by little girls over a dress
pittance (pit′ ′ns) *n.* A small or barely sufficient allowance of money
placid (plas′ id) *adj.* Calm; quiet
plaintive (plān′ tiv) *adj.* Sorrowful; mournful
platform (plat′ fôrm) *n.* Statement of intention
plebeian (plē bē′ ən) *n.* A common, ordinary person or animal
plethoric (plə thôr′ ik) *adj.* Too full
plum (plum) *adj.* Here, first-class
poach (pōch) *v.* To cook gently in near-boiling water
pollen (päl′ ən) *n.* The yellow, powderlike cells formed in the stamen of a flower
ponder (pän′ dər) *v.* To think deeply
ponderous (pän′ dər əs) *adj.* Heavy; massive
portentous (pôr ten′ təs) *adj.* Pompous
portly (pôrt′ lē) *adj.* Large, heavy, and dignified
posterity (päs ter′ ə tē) *n.* Future generations
posthaste (pōst′ hāst′) *adv.* With great quickness
precarious (pri ker′ ē əs) *adj.* Insecure and dangerous
precipitate (pri sip′ ə tāt) *v.* To cause to happen
predecessor (pred′ ə ses′ ər) *n.* Someone who comes before another in a position
pre-eminent (prē em′ ən ənt) *adj.* Dominant
premonition (prē mə nish′ ən) *n.* An omen
prerequisite (pri rek′ wə zit) *n.* An initial requirement
presentable (pri zen′ tə b′l) *adj.* Suitable to be seen by others
pretext (prē tekst) *n.* A false reason or motive given to hide a real intention
primordial (prī môr′ dē əl) *adj.* Primitive
privation (prī vā′ shən) *n.* Lack of common comfort
procure (prō kyo͝or′) *v.* To obtain by some effort
prodigy (präd′ ə jē) *n.* A child of extraordinary genius
proffer (präf′ ər) *v.* To offer
profound (prə found′) *adj.* Deep
progeny (präj′ ə nē) *n.* Children
promote (prə mōt′) *v.* To give a higher position
propound (prə pound′) *v.* To propose; put forward for consideration

prospect (präs′ pekt) *n.* A likely candidate
protestation (prät′ is tā′ shən) *n.* Formal declaration or assertion
prow (prou) *n.* The frontmost part of a ship
prowess (prou′ is) *n.* Superior ability
pungent (pun′ jənt) *adj.* Sharp and stinging to the smell
purchase (pur′ chəs) *n.* A tight hold to keep from slipping
purgatory (pur′ gə tôr′ ē) *n.* A state or place of temporary punishment

R

rafter (raf′ tər) *n.* One of the beams that slopes from the ridge of a roof to the eaves and supports the roof
ram (ram) *v.* Heavy beams used to break down gates
rampage (ram′ pāj) *n.* An outbreak of violent behavior
rampant (ram′ pənt) *adj.* Unrestrained
raucous (rô′ kəs) *adj.* Boisterous; disorderly
ravaging (rav′ ij iŋ) *adj.* Severely damaging or destroying
recede (ri sēd′) *v.* To move farther away
reconnoiter (rē′ kə noit′ ər) *v.* To make an exploratory examination to get information about a place
recrudescence (rē′ kro͞o des′ əns) *n.* A fresh outbreak of something that has been inactive
redress (rē′ dres) *n.* The righting of wrongs
refute (ri fyo͞ot′) *v.* To disprove
regimen (rej′ ə mən) *n.* A regulated system of diet and exercise
remote (ri mōt′) *adj.* Distant
renounce (ri nouns′) *v.* To give up
replica (rep′ li kə) *n.* A copy of a work of art
repugnance (ri pug′ nəns) *n.* Extreme dislike
resolute (rez′ ə lo͞ot′) *adj.* Showing a firm purpose; determined
retribution (ret′ rə byo͞o′ shən) *n.* A punishment deserved for a wrong done
retrogression (ret′ rə gresh′ ən) *n.* A moving backward to a more primitive state
reverie (rev′ ər ē) *n.* Daydream
revue (ri vyo͞o′) *n.* A musical show with loosely connected skits, songs and dances
riveted (riv′ it əd) *adj.* Fastened or made firm
rollicking (räl′ ik iŋ) *adj.* Lively
ruction (ruk′ shən) *n.* Quarrel or noisy disturbance
ruddy (rud′ ē) *adj.* Having a healthy color
runt (runt) *n.* The smallest animal in a litter
ruse (ro͞oz) *n.* A trick or plan for fooling someone

S

sagacity (sə gas′ ə tē) *n.* High intelligence and sound judgment
sage (sāj) *n.* A plant used to flavor food
salient (sāl′ yənt) *adj.* Noticeable; prominent
sap (sap) *v.* To drain; to exhaust
sarcastic (sär kas′ tik) *adj.* Having a sharp, mocking tone intended to hurt another
sash (sash) *n.* The frame holding the glass panes of the window
sassafras (sas′ ə fras′) *n.* Dried root bark of the sassafras tree
sated (sāt′ əd) *adj.* Fully satisfied
savor (sā vər) *v.* To enjoy; appreciate
scores (skôrz) *n.* The music for a stage production or film, apart from the lyrics and dialogue
scorpion (skôr′ pē ən) *n.* Any of a group of poisonous arachnids found in warm regions
screech (skrēch) *n.* A shrill, high-pitched shriek or sound
scuttle (skut′ ′l) *v.* To run or move quickly
sect (sekt) *n.* Small group of people with the same leader and belief
semblance (sem′ bləns) *n.* Likeness; image
sensory (sen′ sər ē) *adj.* Of receiving sense impressions
sentinel (sen′ ti nəl) *n.* Guard
shanty (shan′ tē) *n.* Hut or shack
sheen (shēn) *n.* Shininess
shingle (shiŋ′ g′l) *v.* To cover the roof with shingles
shinny (shin′ ē) *v.* To climb by gripping with both hands and legs
shoal (shōl) *n.* Sand bar
shoon (sho͞on) *n.* Old-fashioned word for shoes
shun (shun) *v.* To avoid
simultaneous (si′ məl tā′ nē əs) *adj.* Taking place at the same time
sinew (sin′ yo͞o) *n.* A band of fibrous tissue that connects muscles to bones or to other parts and can also be used as thread for sewing
singular (sin′ gyə lər) *adj.* Exceptional; peculiar
sinister (sin′ is tər) *adj.* Threatening harm, evil, or misfortune
sire (sīr) *n.* Father
skeptic (skep′ tik) *n.* Person who doubts
slander (slan′ dər) *n.* Lies
slash (slash) *v.* To cut with a sweeping stroke
smoldering (smōl′ dər iŋ) *adj.* Fiery
snicker (snik′ ər) *v.* To laugh in a mean way
snide (snīd) *adj.* Intentionally mean
soliloquize (sə lil′ ə kwīz) *v.* To talk to oneself
somber (säm′ bər) *adj.* Dark; gloomy
specious (spē′ shəs) *adj.* Seeming to be true without really being so
specter (spek′ tər) *n.* A disturbing thought
spectral (spek′ trəl) *adj.* Ghostly
spike (spīk) *n.* A long thick metal nail used for splitting rock
spume (spyo͞om) *n.* Foam; froth
spurn (spurn) *v.* To reject scornfully
squall (skwôl′) *v.* To cry out or scream
stalk (stôk′) *v.* To secretly approach
starboard (stär′ bərd) *adj.* The right side of a ship, as one faces forward

839

starling (stär' liŋ) *n.* Dark-colored bird

static (stat' ik) *adj.* Not changing or progressing

stealthy (stel' thē) *adj.* Secret; quiet

steep (stēp) *adj.* A slope or incline having a sharp rise

stench (stench) *n.* An offensive smell

stifled (stī' f'ld) *adj.* Muffled; suppressed

stilted (stil' təd) *adj.* Unnatural; very formal

stimulus (stim' yə ləs) *n.* Something that rouses to action

stolid (stäl' id) *adj.* Showing little or no emotion

stratagem (stra' tə jəm) *n.* Plan for defeating an opponent

strife (strīf) *n.* Conflict

suavity (swä' və tē) *n.* Graceful politeness

subjunctive (səb juŋk' tiv) *n.* A particular form of a verb

successor (sək ses' ər) *n.* A person that follows or comes after another

suckle (suk' 'l) *v.* To nurse at the breast

suitor (so͞ot' ər) *n.* A man courting a woman

sultry (sul' trē) *adj.* Hot and humid

superfluous (soo pʉr' floo wəs) *adj.* More than is necessary

surcharged (sʉr' charjd) *adj.* Overcharged

surveillance (sər vā' ləns) *n.* Watch, inspection

swagger (swag' ər) *n.* Arrogance or boastfulness; *v.* To strut; walk with a bold step

swamp (swämp) *v.* To sink by filling with water

swarthy (swôr' thē) *adj.* Having a dark complexion

swoon (swo͞on) *v.* Faint

T

taciturn (tas' ə tʉrn') *adj.* Not likely to talk

tangible (tan' jə bəl) *adj.* Observable; understandable

taunt (tônt) *v.* To jeer at; to mock

taut (tôt) *adj.* Tightly stretched

teamster (tēm' stər) *n.* One who drives a team of horses to haul a load

teem (tēm) *v.* to swarm

tenacious (tə nā' shəs) *adj.* Holding on firmly

tendril (ten' drəl) *n.* Thin shoot from a plant

tenement (ten' ə mənt) *n.* A run-down apartment building

tenure (ten' yər) *n.* Time of residence

tepee (tē' pē) *n.* A cone-shaped tent of animal skins

thesis (thē' sis) *n.* Statement of position or proposition

tick (tik) *v.* To operate smoothly

tint (tint') *v.* To color

tipis (tē' pēz) *n.* Cone-shaped tents made of animal skins

tolerate (täl' ə rāt') *v.* To allow; permit

tortuous (tôr' cho͞o wəs) *adj.* Winding with repeated twists and turns

tousled-looking (tou' z'ld loo' kiŋ) *adj.* Rumpled or mussed

transient (tran' shənt) *adj.* Not permanent

tread (tred) *n.* Step

tremor (trem' ər) *n.* Shaking or vibration

trivial (triv' ē əl) *adj.* Of little importance

troubadour (tro͞o' bə dôr') *n.* Traveling singer, usually accompanying himself on a stringed instrument

trough (trôf) *n.* Long and narrow container for holding water or food for animals

U

unabashed (un ə bash' əd) *adj.* Unashamed

uncanny (un kan' ē) *adj.* Strange

undulate (un' dyo͞o lāt) *v.* To move in waves

unfurled (un fʉrld') *adj.* Unfolded

unobtrusive (un əb tro͞o' siv) *adj.* Not calling attention to oneself

unwonted (un wun' tid) *adj.* Not usual

uproariously (up rôr' ē əs lē) *adv.* Loudly and boisterously

usurp (yo͞o sʉrp') *v.* To take over

V

vacuous (vak' yoo wəs) *adj.* Empty; shallow

venture (ven' chər) *v.* To express oneself at the risk of criticism, objection, or denial

versatile (vʉr' sə t'l) *adj.* Having many uses

vicarage (vik' ər ij) *n.* A place where a member of the clergy lives

vicarious (vī kər' ē əs) *adj.* Experienced by one person or animal in place of another

vigorous (vig' ər əs) *adj.* Strong and energetic

viscera (vis' ər ə) *n.* Internal organs

vituperation (vī to͞o' pə rā' shən) *n.* Abusive language

voile (voil) *n.* A light cotton fabric

voracious (vô rā' shəs) *adj.* Eager to devour large quantities of food

W

waft (waf' t) *v.* To move lightly through the air

walleyed (wôl' īd') *adj.* Having eyes that turn outward

wan (wän) *adj.* Pale

waning (wān' iŋ) *adj.* A full moon shrinking to a new moon

wantonness (wän' tən nəs) *n.* Lack of discipline

whirl (hwʉrl) *v.* To drive with a rotating motion

willow-wild (wil' ō wild') *adj.* Slender and pliant, like a reed blowing in the wind

winch (winch) *n.* A machine used for lifting

wistful (wist' fəl) *adj.* Expressing vague yearnings

wizened (wiz' ənd) *adj.* Shrunken, and wrinkled wtih age

wormwood (wʉrm' wood) *n.* A plant that produces a bitter oil

wraith (rāth) *n.* Ghost

Y

yearling (yir' liŋ) *n.* An animal that is between one and two years old

yonder (yon' dər) *adj.* In the distance

yucca (yuk' ə) *n.* A desert plant with stiff leaves and white flowers

INDEX OF FINE ART

INDEX OF LITERATURE IN AMERICAN HISTORY

Reading literature is another way to learn history. Stories, poems, and plays show you how people lived and what they thought in different periods in time. The following chart presents selections from this book according to periods in American history.

THE NEW WORLD (Prehistory to 1750)

THE STRUGGLE FOR INDEPENDENCE (1750–1775)

A GROWING NATION (1776–1860)

THE NATION DIVIDED (1860–1865)

AMERICA IN A CHANGING TIME (1865–1900)

THE EARLY TWENTIETH CENTURY (1900–1950)

AMERICA TODAY (1950–Present)

INDEX OF SKILLS

ANALYZING LITERATURE

845

CRITICAL THINKING AND READING

SPEAKING AND LISTENING

STUDY AND RESEARCH

THINKING AND WRITING

UNDERSTANDING LANGUAGE

INDEX OF TITLES BY THEMES

SEARCH FOR JUSTICE AND DIGNITY

NEW AMERICANS AND THE IMMIGRATION EXPERIENCE

EXPERIENCES WITH WAR AND PEACE

INDIVIDUALS AND THE NEED FOR ACCEPTANCE

PASSAGES AND TRANSFORMATIONS

THE INDIVIDUAL AND SOCIETY

JOURNEY TO PERSONAL FULFILLMENT

A TIME FOR COURAGE

FANTASY AND THE UNEXPLAINED

THE ENVIRONMENT AND THE TOUCHED AND UNTOUCHED EARTH

A TIME FOR LAUGHTER

TECHNOLOGY: A TWO-EDGED SWORD

UNCONVENTIONAL CHARACTERS

OUR HERITAGE

INDEX OF AUTHORS AND TITLES

Page numbers in italics refer to biographical information.

ACKNOWLEDGMENTS (continued)

Dorothy Boles and Triangle Communications, Inc.
"The House Guest" by Paul Darcy Boles, copyright 1975 by Triangle Communications, Inc. All rights reserved. Originally appeared in *Seventeen* Magazine.

Borden Publishing Company
From "Hokusai: The Old Man Mad About Drawing" reproduced from *The Drawings of Hokusai* by Stephen Longstreet published by Borden Publishing Co., Alhambra, California.

Brandt & Brandt Literary Agents, Inc.
"Johnny Appleseed" from *A Book of Americans,* copyright 1933 by Rosemary and Stephen Vincent Benét; copyright renewed 1961 by Rosemary Carr Benét. "The Land and the Water" from *The Wind Shifting West* by Shirley Ann Grau, copyright © 1973 by Shirley Ann Grau. Reprinted by permission of Brandt & Brandt Literary Agents, Inc.

The Caxton Printers, Ltd.
"The Six Rows of Pompons" from *Yokohama, California* by Toshio Mori. The Caxton Printers, Ltd., Caldwell, Idaho.

Coward-McCann, Inc.
"Desert Noon" by Elizabeth Coatsworth, reprinted by permission of Coward-McCann, Inc., from *Compass Rose* by Elizabeth Coatsworth, copyright 1929 by Coward-McCann, Inc.; copyright renewed © 1957 by Elizabeth Coatsworth.

Curtis Brown Ltd., New York
"Journey to the Interior" from *A Short History of the Fur Trade* by Adrien Stoutenburg. Copyright © 1968 by Adrien Stoutenburg. Reprinted by permission of Curtis Brown, Ltd.

Curtis Brown Ltd., London
"The Ugly Duckling" by A. A. Milne. Copyright 1941 by A. A. Milne. Reprinted by permission of Curtis Brown Ltd., London.

Doubleday & Co., Inc.
"Rain, Rain, Go Away" by Isaac Asimov copyright © 1959 by King-Size Publishing, Inc. from *Buy Jupiter and Other Stories.* "A Retrieved Reformation" from *Roads of Destiny* by O. Henry. "My Wild Irish Mother" by Jean Kerr. Copyright © 1960 by McCall Corp. From *How I Got to be Perfect.* Reprinted by permission of Doubleday. Reprinted by permission of Doubleday & Co., Inc.

Mari Evans
"if you have had your midnights" from *Nightstar* by Mari Evans, published by CAAS, the University of California at Los Angeles, 1981. Reprinted by permission of the author.

Farrar, Straus and Giroux, Inc.
Adapted from "Charles" from *The Lottery* by Shirley Jackson. Copyright © 1948, 1949 by Shirley Jackson; copyright © renewed 1976, 1977 by Laurence Hyman, Barry Hyman, Mrs. Sarah Webster, and Mrs. Joanne Schnurer. Reprinted by special permission of Farrar, Straus and Giroux, Inc. "The Day I Got Lost" from *Stories for Children* by Isaac Bashevis Singer. Copyright © 1962, 1967, 1968, 1970, 1972, 1973, 1974, 1975, 1976, 1979, 1980, 1984 by Isaac Bashevis Singer. Reprinted by permission of Farrar, Straus and Giroux, Inc.

Richard García
"The City Is So Big" by Richard García, © 1973 by Richard García. Reprinted by permission of the author.

GRM Associates, Inc., Agents for the Estate of Ida M. Cullen
Lines from "For a Poet" from *On These I Stand: The Best-Loved Poems of Countee Cullen.* Copyright © 1925 by Harper & Brothers; copyright renewed 1953 by Ida M. Cullen. Reprinted by permission of GRM Associates, Inc., Agents for the Estate of Ida M. Cullen.

Harcourt Brace Jovanovich, Inc.
"Crime on Mars" copyright © 1960 by Davis Publications. Reprinted from *The Nine Billion Names of God* by Arthur C. Clarke. Excerpt from "Forest Fire" from *The Diary of Anais Nin 1947–1955* by Anais Nin, edited by Gunther Stuhlmann, copyright © 1974 by Anais Nin. "Paul Bunyan of the North Woods" and "They Have Yarns" from *The People, Yes* by Carl Sandburg, copyright 1936 by Harcourt Brace Jovanovich, Inc.; renewed 1964 by Carl Sandburg. From "For My Sister Molly Who In The Fifties" copyright © 1972 by Alice Walker, in her volume *Revolutionary Petunias & Other Poems.* Reprinted by permission of Harcourt Brace Jovanovich, Inc.

Harper & Row, Publishers, Inc.
Text of "Shooting Stars" from *This World Of Wonder* by Hal Borland (J. B. Lippincott), copyright © 1972, 1973 by Hal Borland. Slightly adapted from pp. 314–325 from *Of Men and Mountains* by William O. Douglas, copyright 1950 by Sidney Davis, Trustee of the William O. Douglas Trust. Renewed 1958 by Sidney Davis. Haiku, "The Falling Flower," by Moritake from *Poetry Handbook: A Dictionary of Terms,* 4th edition, by Babette Deutsch. Copyright © 1957, 1962, 1969, 1974 by Babette Deutsch. Reprinted by permission of Harper & Row, Publishers, Inc.

Harper & Row, Publishers, Inc., Joan Aiken, Jonathan Cape Ltd., and A. M. Heath & Company Ltd.
"The Gift Giving" from *Up the Chimney Down and Other Stories* by Joan Aiken, copyright © 1984 by Joan Aiken Enterprises Limited. Reprinted by permission.

Harvard University Press
"The Tell-Tale Heart" by Edgar Allan Poe from *Collected Works of Edgar Allan Poe* edited by Thomas Ollive Mabbott, copyright © 1978 by the President and Fellows of Harvard College. From *One Writer's Beginnings* by Eudora Welty, copyright © 1983, 1984 by Eudora Welty. Reprinted by permission of Harvard University Press.

John Hawkins & Associates, Inc.
Hokku poem ("The spring lingers on") by Richard Wright. Copyright by Richard Wright. Reprinted by permission of John Hawkins & Associates, Inc., New York.

Hill and Wang, a division of Farrar, Straus and Giroux, Inc.
"The Story-Teller" from *Collected and New Poems 1924–1963* by Mark Van Doren, copyright © 1963 by Mark Van Doren. Reprinted by permission of Hill and Wang, a division of Farrar, Straus and Giroux, Inc.

Henry Holt and Company, Inc.
"Blue-Butterfly Day" and "The Road Not Taken" copyright 1916, 1923 by Holt, Rinehart and Winston, Inc. and renewed 1944, 1951 by Robert Frost. Reprinted from *The Poetry of Robert Frost* edited by Edward Connery Lathem. Lines from "Rose Pogonias" copyright © 1969 by Holt, Rinehart and Winston, Inc. Reprinted from *The Poetry of Robert Frost* edited by Edward Connery Lathem, by permission of Henry Holt and Company, Inc.

Evelyn Tooley Hunt and Negro Digest
"Taught Me Purple" by Evelyn Tooley Hunt from *Negro Digest,* February 1964 © 1964 by Johnson Publishing Company, Inc. Reprinted by permission of Evelyn Tooley Hunt and NEGRO DIGEST.

Daniel Keyes
"Flowers For Algernon" (short story version) by Daniel Keyes. Copyright © 1959 and 1987 by Daniel Keyes. Reprinted by permission of the author. Edited for this edition.

Alfred A. Knopf, Inc.
"The Ninny" from *The Image of Chekhov* by Anton Chekhov, translated by Robert Payne. Copyright © 1963 by Alfred A. Knopf, Inc. "The Cyclone" from *Pecos Bill: Texas Cowpuncher* by Harold W. Felton. Copyright 1949 by Alfred A. Knopf, Inc. "Harlem Night Song" and "Winter Moon" from *Selected Poems of Langston Hughes* by Langston Hughes. Copyright 1926 by Alfred A. Knopf, Inc. and renewed 1954 by Langston Hughes. Lines from "The Quiet Fog" copyright © 1975 by Marge Piercy, reprinted from *The Twelve Spoked Wheel Flashing* by Marge Piercy. "January" from *A Child's Calendar* by John Updike. Copyright © 1965 by John Updike and Nancy Burkert. "Winter Ocean" copyright © 1960 by John Updike from *Telephone Poles* by John Updike. Reprinted by permission of Alfred A. Knopf, Inc.

Alfred A. Knopf, Inc. and Pierre Berton
Two maps ("The Country of the Klondike Fever" and "The Trail of '98") from *The Klondike Fever* by Pierre Berton. Copyright © 1958 by Pierre Berton. Reprinted by permission.

Alfred A. Knopf, Inc. and Olwyn Hughes Literary Agency
"Mushrooms" copyright © 1960 by Sylvia Plath. Reprinted from *The Colossus and Other Poems* by Sylvia Plath, by permission.

Naoshi Koriyama
"Jetliner" by Naoshi Koriyama is reprinted from *Poetry Nippon* (Summer 1970) by permission of the author. Copyright © 1970 by The Poetry Society of Japan, Nagoya, Japan.

Ursula K. Le Guin and her agent, Virginia Kidd
"The Rule of Names" from *The Wind's Twelve Quarters* by Ursula K. Le Guin, copyright © 1964, 1975 by Ursula K. Le Guin. "Talking About Writing" from *The Language of the Night: Essays on Fantasy and Science Fiction* by Ursula K. Le Guin, copyright © 1979 by Ursula K. Le Guin. Reprinted by permission of the author and the author's agent, Virginia Kidd.

The Literary Trustees of Walter de la Mare and The Society of Authors as their representative
"Silver" from *Collected Poems 1901–1918* by Walter de la Mare. Reprinted by permission.

Little, Brown and Company
"Sancho" from *The Longhorns* by J. Frank Dobie. Copyright 1941 by J. Frank Dobie. Copyright © renewed 1969 by J. Frank Dobie. *The Man Without a Country* by Edward Everett Hale. By permission of Little, Brown and Company.

Sterling Lord Literistic, Inc.
"A Poem About a Wolf Maybe Two Wolves" from *Shaking the Pumpkin* edited by Jerome Rothenberg. Copyright © 1972 by Jerome Rothenberg. Reprinted by permission of Sterling Lord Literistic, Inc.

Macmillan Publishing Company
Lines from "March" from *Summer Green* by Elizabeth Coatsworth. Copyright 1948 by Macmillan Publishing Company, renewed 1976 by Elizabeth Coatsworth Beston. "The Secret Heart" from *Collected Poems* by Robert P. Tristram Coffin. Copyright 1935 by Macmillan Publishing Company, renewed 1963 by Margaret Coffin Halvosa. "Advice to a Girl" from *Collected Poems* by Sara Teasdale. Copyright 1933 by Macmillan Publishing Company, renewed 1961 by Guaranty Trust Co. of N.Y. Reprinted with permission of Macmillan Publishing Company.

McIntosh and Otis, Inc.
"The Day the Sun Came Out" by Dorothy M. Johnson. Copyright 1953 by Dorothy M. Johnson; copyright renewed. Originally published in *Cosmopolitan* as "Too Soon a Woman" and reprinted by permission of McIntosh and Otis, Inc.

N. Scott Momaday
"New World" from *The Gourd Dancer* by N. Scott Momaday, copyright © 1976 by N. Scott Momaday. Reprinted by permission of the author.

William Morris Agency, Inc. on behalf of the authors
"Roberto Clemente: A Bittersweet Memoir" from *Great Latin Sports Figures* by Jerry Izenberg. Copyright © 1976 by Jerry Izenberg. Reprinted by permission of William Morris Agency, Inc. on behalf of the author. *Let Me Hear You Whisper* by Paul Zindel. Copyright © 1973 by Zindel Productions Incorporated. CAUTION: Professionals and amateurs are hereby warned that *Let Me Hear You Whisper* is subject to a royalty. It is fully protected under the copyright laws of the United States of America, and of all countries covered by the International Copyright Union (including the Dominion of Canada and the rest of the British Commonwealth), and of all countries covered by the Universal Copyright Convention and the Pan-American Copyright Convention, and of all countries with which the United States has reciprocal copyright relations. All rights, including professional, amateur, motion picture, recitation, lecturing, public reading, radio broadcasting, television, and the rights of translation into foreign languages, are strictly reserved. Particular emphasis is laid on the question of readings, permission for which must be secured from the author's agent in writing. All inquiries (except for amateur rights) should be addressed to Gilbert Parker, William Morris Agency, Inc., 1350 Avenue of the

Americas, New York, NY 10019. The amateur acting rights of *Let Me Hear You Whisper* are controlled exclusively by Dramatists Play Service, Inc., 440 Park Avenue South, New York, NY 10016. No amateur performance of the play may be given without obtaining in advance the written permission of the Dramatists Play Service, Inc., and paying the requisite fee.

The New York Times
"A to Z in Foods as Metaphors: Or, a Stew Is a Stew Is a Stew" by Mimi Sheraton, September 3, 1983. Copyright © 1983 by The New York Times Company. Reprinted by permission.

The New Yorker Magazine, Inc.
"Hog-Calling Competition" by Morris Bishop from "Limericks Long After Lear" from *The New Yorker,* October 3, 1936. Reprinted by permission; © 1936, 1964 The New Yorker Magazine, Inc.

North Point Press
"The Captain and His Horse" by Beryl Markham from *The Splendid Outcast: Beryl Markham's African Stories,* compiled by Mary S. Lovell. Copyright © 1987 by the Beryl Markham Estate. Reprinted by permission of North Point Press.

Harold Ober Associates Inc.
"Christmas Day in the Morning" by Pearl S. Buck, published in *Collier's,* December 23, 1955. Copyright © 1955 by Pearl S. Buck. Copyright renewed 1983. "Thank You, M'am" from *The Langston Hughes Reader* by Langston Hughes. Copyright © 1958 by Langston Hughes. Copyright renewed 1986 by George Houston Bass. Reprinted by permission of Harold Ober Associates Inc.

Julio Noboa Polanco
"Identity" by Julio Noboa Polanco from *The Rican,* Journal of Contemporary Puerto Rican Thought, copyright 1973. Reprinted by permission of the author.

Prentice-Hall, Inc.
"The Foggy Stew" from the book *True Tall Tall Tales of Stormalong: Sailor of the Seven Seas* by Harold W. Felton, © 1968. Used by permission of the publisher, Prentice-Hall, Inc., Englewood Cliffs, New Jersey. "Blow, Blow, Thou Winter Wind" (from *As You Like It,* II,vii, 174) by William Shakespeare, published in *Renaissance Poetry* edited by Leonard Dean. Reprinted by permission.

Présence Africaine, Paris
Lines from "The Sea" by Mongameli Mabona from *Présence Africaine* published in No. 57 (1st Quarterly, 1966). Reprinted by permission.

The Putnam Publishing Group
"The Girl Who Hunted Rabbits" from *Zuñi Folk Tales,* translated by Frank H. Cushing with an introdution by J. W. Powell.

Random House, Inc.
From *I Know Why the Caged Bird Sings* by Maya Angelou. Copyright © 1969 by Maya Angelou. "Raymond's Run" copyright © 1971 by Toni Cade Bambára. Reprinted from *Gorilla, My Love* by Toni Cade Bambara. From *The Diary of Anne Frank* by Frances Goodrich and Albert Hackett. Copyright 1954, 1956 as an unpublished work. Reprinted by permission of Random House, Inc. CAUTION: *The Diary of Anne Frank* is the sole property of the dramatists and is fully protected by copyright. It may not be acted by professionals or amateurs without written permission and the payment of a royalty. All rights, including professional, amateur, stock, radio broadcasting, television, motion picture, recitation, lecturing, public reading, and the rights of translation into foreign languages are reserved.

Reader's Digest
"The Indian All Around Us" by Bernard DeVoto. Reprinted with permission from the April 1953 *Reader's Digest.* Copyright © 1953 by The Reader's Digest Association, Inc.

Reader's Digest and Robert MacNeil
"The Trouble with Television" by Robert MacNeil (condensed from a speech delivered November 13, 1984, at the President's Leadership Forum, State University of New York at Purchase). Reprinted with permission from the March 1985 *Readers' Digest.*

Marian Reiner for Eve Merriam
"A Lazy Thought" from *Jamboree: Rhymes for All Times* by Eve Merriam. Copyright © 1962, 1964, 1966, 1973, 1984 by Eve Merriam. All rights reserved. Reprinted by permission of Marian Reiner for the author.

Molly Lou Reko, Robert Wilson, Sallie Erdman, and Elizabeth Erdman
"Grass Fire" from *The Edge of Time* by Loula Grace Erdman. Copyright 1950 by Loula Grace Erdman. Copyright renewed 1978 by the Amarillo National Bank. Reprinted by permission.

Andrea Reynolds, attorney-in-fact for André Milos
"The Adventure of the Speckled Band" from *The Complete Sherlock Holmes* by Sir Arthur Conan Doyle.

Russell and Volkening, Inc. as agents for the author
"Harriet Tubman: Guide to Freedom" from *Harriet Tubman: Conductor on the Underground Railroad* by Ann Petry. Copyright © 1955, renewed 1983 by Ann Petry. Reprinted by permission of Russell and Volkening, Inc. as agents for the author.

St. Martin's Press, Inc., New York, and Harold Ober Associates Inc.
"Debbie" from *All Things Wise and Wonderful* by James Herriot. Copyright © 1976, 1977 by James Herriot. Reprinted by permission.

Argelia Sedillo
"Gentleman of Rio en Medio" by Juan A. A. Sedillo, published in *New Mexico Quarterly,* 1939. Reprinted by permission.

Rod Serling
Back There by Rod Serling. Reprinted by permission of The Rod Serling Trust. All rights reserved.

Simon & Schuster, Inc.
"The Drummer Boy of Shiloh" from *The Machineries of Joy* by Ray Bradbury. Copyright © 1949, 1952, 1953, 1957, 1960, 1962, 1963, 1964, 1981 by Ray Bradbury. Reprinted by permission of Simon & Schuster, Inc. Pronunciation key from *Webster's New World Dictionary*—Second College Edition. Copyright © 1984 by Simon & Schuster, Inc. Reprinted by permission of Simon & Schuster, Inc.

Virginia Driving Hawk Sneve
"The Medicine Bag" by Virginia Driving Hawk Sneve, published in *Boy's Life,* March 1975. Reprinted by permission of the author.

Lloyd Sarett Stockdale
"Four Little Foxes" from *Slow Smoke* by Lew Sarett, copyright 1953 by Lew Sarett; Henry Holt and Company. Reprinted by permission of Lloyd Sarett Stockdale.

Sterling Lord Literistic, Inc.
"A Poem About a Wolf Maybe Two Wolves" from *Shaking the Pumpkin* edited by Jerome Rothenberg. Copyright © 1972 by Jerome Rothenberg. Reprinted by permission of Sterling Lord Literistic, Inc.

Summit Books, a division of Simon & Schuster, Inc.
"The Sounds of Richard Rodgers" from *At Large* by Ellen Goodman. Copyright © 1981 by The Washington Post Company. Reprinted by permission of Summit Books, a division of Simon & Schuster, Inc.

Sunstone Press
"Song of the Sky Loom" from Herbert Spinden's *Songs of the Tewa,* published by Sunstone Press, Santa Fe, New Mexico. Reprinted by permission.

May Swenson
"By Morning" by May Swenson is reprinted by permission of the author, copyright © 1954, renewed © 1982 by May Swenson, and originally appeared in *The New Yorker* under the title, "Snow By Morning." "Southbound on the Freeway" by May Swenson is reprinted by permission of the author, copyright 1963 by May Swenson, and was originally printed in *The New Yorker.* Reprinted by permission of the author.

University of Oklahoma Press
"The Origin of Fire" from *Indian legends From the Northern Rockies* by Ella E. Clark. Copyright © 1966 by the University of Oklahoma Press. Reprinted by permission.

The University of Tennessee Press
"Tussle with a Bear" and "Davy Crockett's Dream" by Davy Crockett from *The Tall Tales of Davy Crockett: The Second Nashville Series of Crockett Almanacs, 1839–1841.* An enlarged facsimile edition, with an introduction by Michael A. Lobaro. Copyright © 1987 by the University of Tennessee Press. Reprinted by permission.

Viking Penguin Inc.
"400-Meter Free Style" from *Our Ground Time Here Will Be Brief* by Maxine Kumin. Copyright 1989 by Maxine Kumin. "Reflections Dental" from *Times Three* by Phyllis McGinley. Copyright 1953 by Phyllis McGinley; copyright renewed © 1978 by Julie Elizabeth Háyden and Phyllis Hayden Blake. Originally published in *The New Yorker.* "The Choice" from *Enough Rope* by Dorothy Parker. Copyright 1926 by Dorothy Parker; copyright renewed 1953 by Dorothy Parker. "Hammerman" from *American Tall Tales* by Adrien Stoutenburg. Copyright © 1966 by Adrien Stoutenburg. "Lyric 17" from *Have Come, Am Here* by José Garcia Villa. Copyright 1942 by José Garcia Villa; copyright renewed © 1969 by José Garcia Villa. Reprinted by permission of Viking Penguin Inc. *The Pearl* by John Steinbeck. Copyright 1945 by John Steinbeck; copyright renewed © 1973 by Elaine Steinbeck, Thom Steinbeck, and John Steinbeck IV. Reprinted by permission of Viking Penguin Inc.

Viking Penguin Inc. and The Bodley Head Ltd.
"The Story-Teller" from *The Complete Short Stories of Saki (H. H. Munro).* Copyright 1930, renewed © 1958 by The Viking Press, Inc. Reprinted by permission.

David Wagoner
"Staying Alive" from *Collected Poems 1956–1976* by David Wagoner. Copyright © 1976 by Indiana University Press; copyright 1987 by David Wagoner. Reprinted by permission of the author.

Note: Every effort has been made to locate the copyright owner of material reprinted in this book. Omissions brought to our attention will be corrected in subsequent editions.

ART CREDITS

Cover and Title Page: *The Inspiration of Christopher Columbus, 1856,* José María Obregón, oil on canvas, 147 × 106 cm., Museo Nacional de Arte, Mexico City (INBA); **p. 1:** Millard Sheets, *Children and Pigeons in the Park, Central Park,* Kennedy Galleries, Inc.; **p. 11:** *James Folly General Store and Post Office,* Winfield Scott Clime, Three Lions; **p. 20:** *Pearl S. Buck* (detail), Vita Solomon, National Portrait Gallery, Smithsonian Institution, Gift of the Pearl S. Buck Foundation; **p. 23:** Nasjonalgalleriet, Oslo, Andrew Wyeth, *Albert's Son,* 1959; **p. 26:** *Sir Arthur Conan Doyle,* 1927 (detail), H. L. Gates, National Portrait Gallery, London; **p.71:** Cover of *A Wizard of Earth-Sea,* Yvonne Gilbert; **p. 75:** *The Sea Serpent,* Arthur Rakham, *Arthur Rakham's Book of Pictures;* **p. 83:** *Woman with Parasol,* Claude Monet, Scala/Art Resource; **p. 87:** *The Cloth Doll,* Robert Duncan; **p. 89:** *Street Vista in Winter,* Charles Burchfield, Kalamazoo Institute for Arts; **p. 93:** *The Sacristan of Trampas* (detail) by Paul Burlin, Courtesy Museum of New Mexico, Neg. No. 26622; **p. 110:** *A Log Cabin in a Clearing on the American Frontier,* 1826, The Granger Collection; **p. 117:** Charles E. Burchfield, *Lavender and Old Lace,* from the collection of The New Britain Museum of American Art (Charles F. Smith Fund), Photo credit: E. Irving Blomstrann; **p. 120:** *Perkins Cove* by Jane Betts, Collection of Wendy Betts; **p. 123:** *Clouds and Water,* 1930, Arthur G. Dove, The Metropolitan Museum of Art, The Alfred Stieglitz Collection, 1949, © Copyright 1979 by The Metropolitan Museum of Art; **p. 124:** Caldwell, Vivian, *Softly,* Private Collection; **p. 130:** *Herd of Buffalo Fleeing from Prairie Fire,* M. Straus, 1888, oil on canvas, Amon Carter Museum, Fort Worth; **p. 152:** *Drummer Boy,* Julian Scott, N. S. Mayer; **p. 155:** *The Battle of Shiloh, Tennessee (6–7 April,*

1862), 1886, Kurz and Allison, The Granger Collection; **p. 157:** Edward Hopper, *Rooms by the Sea,* Yale University Art Gallery, Bequest of Stephen Carlton Clark; **p. 168:** *Langston Hughes* by Winold Reiss (detail), 1925, National Portrait Gallery, Smithsonian Institution, Gift of W. Tjark Reiss, in memory of his father, Winold Reiss; **p. 170:** *Mother Courage (1974),* Charles White, National Academy of Design; **p. 172:** *Sunny Side of the Street,* Philip Evergood; **p. 184:** *Edward Everett Hale* (detail), Philip L. Hale, National Portrait Gallery, Smithsonian Institution; **p. 186:** *Officer of the Watch on the Horseblock, Heck's Iconographic Encyclopedia,* 1851, The New York Public Library, Astor, Lenox and Tilden Foundations; **p. 192:** Thomas Birch, *USS. Constitution and HMS. Guerriere* (Aug. 19, 1812), U.S. Naval Academy Museum; **p. 195:** *Warrant Officers' Mess, Heck's Iconographic Encyclopedia, 1851,* The New York Public Library, Astor, Lenox and Tilden Foundations; **pp. 240–41:** Hopper, Edward, *First Row Orchestra,* 1951, Hirshhorn Museum and Sculpture Garden, Smithsonian Institution, Gift of Joseph H. Hirshhorn Foundation; **p. 273:** *Assassination of Abraham Lincoln by Booth at Ford's Theatre,* The Granger Collection; **pp. 374–75:** *Miracle of Nature,* Thomas Moran, Three Lions; **p. 381:** *Many Brave Hearts,* Charles Demuth, Hirshhorn Museum and Sculpture Garden, Smithsonian Institution, Joseph Martin/Scala-Art Resource; **p. 384:** *Harriet Tubman Series, #7,* Jacob Lawrence, Hampton University Museum; **p. 386:** *Harriet Tubman Series, #16,* Jacob Lawrence, Hampton University Museum; **p. 388:** *Harriet Tubman Series, #10,* Jacob Lawrence, Hampton University Museum; **p. 404–5:** *Symbols,* Benny Andrew, Museum of Art, Wichita State University; **p. 410:** Samuel Langhorne Clemens (detail) by Frank Edwin Larson, National Portrait Gallery, Smithsonian Institution; **p. 411:** *The Great Mississippi Steamboat Race,* 1870, Currier & Ives, The Granger Collection; **p. 414:** *Samuel Clemens as a Young Man,* M. T. Papers; **p. 417:** *The Champions of the Mississippi,* Currier & Ives, Art Resource; **p. 429:** *Girl Reading Outdoors,* Fairfield Porter, **p. 432:** *In a Stampede,* 1888, Illustration by Frederic Remington, The Granger Collection; **p. 435:** *The American Cowboy,* Charlie Dye, Collection of Harold McCracken; **p. 446:** Cecilia Beaux, American, 1855–1942, *After the Meeting,* 1914, oil on canvas, 40-15/16 × 28⅛″ (104 × 71.5 cm), The Toledo Museum of Art, Toledo, Ohio, gift of Florence Scott Libbey; **p. 449:** Henri Matisse, *Woman before an Aquarium,* 1921, oil on canvas, 81.3 × 100.3 cm, Helen Birch Bartlett Memorial Collection, 1926.200, © 1987 The Art Institute of Chicago. All rights reserved; **p. 457:** Painted Buffalo Hide Shield, Jemez, New Mexico, Museum of the American Indian; **p. 458:** Painted Bowl: Deer Figure, Mimbres, New Mexico, Museum of the American Indian; **p. 459:** Jar with Animal Head Handle, Socorro County, New Mexico, Museum of the American Indian; **p. 464:** Hendler, Maxwell (1938–), *Afternoon Television,* Copyright 1977 by the Metropolitan Museum of Art, the Metropolitan Museum of Art, George A. Hearn Fund, 1977; **p. 467:** John Singer Sargent, 1856–1925, *Paul Helleu Sketching with His Wife,* 1889, oil on canvas, 25⅝ × 31¾″, The Brooklyn Museum, 20.640, Museum Collection Fund; **p. 477:** Dali, Salvador, *The Persistence of Memory,* 1931, (detail), oil on canvas 9½ × 13″, Collection, The Museum of Modern Art, New York, given anonymously; **p. 482:** Hokusai, Katsushika (1760–1849), *The Great Wave off Kanagawa,* from the series The Thirty-Six Views of Fuji, The Metropolitan Museum of Art, Bequest of Mrs. H. O. Havemeyer, 1929, The H. O. Havemeyer Collection; **p. 492:** *Trading Cards,* courtesy of Kitchen Arts & Letters; **p. 500:** *Above Witebsk,* 1922, Marc Chagall, Three Lions; **p. 507:** *Holy Mountain III* (1945), Horace Pippin, Hirshhorn Museum and Sculpture Garden, Smithsonian Institution, Scala/Art Resource; **p. 508:** *Henry Wadsworth Longfellow* (detail), Thomas B. Read, National Portrait Gallery, Smithsonian Institution; **p. 521:** *The Landing of Columbus,* 1876, Currier & Ives, The Harry T. Peters Collection, Museum of the City of New York; **p. 524:** John Greenleaf Whittier (detail), 1881, William Notman, National Portrait Gallery, Smithsonian Institution; **p. 529:** Joseph Stella, *The Brooklyn Bridge: Variation on an Old Theme,* 1939, oil on canvas, 70 × 42″, Collection of Whitney Museum of American Art, Purchase, Acq #42.15; **p. 533:** Copyright 1980 by the Metropolitan Museum of Art, Rosen, Severin, *Still Life: Flowers,* 1855, The Metropolitan Museum of Art, Purchase, Charles Allen Munn Bequest, Fosburgh Fund, Inc., Gift; Mr. and Mrs. J. William Middendorf II Gift; and Henry G. Keasbey Bequest, 1967; **p. 535:** Abraham Lincoln, National Portrait Gallery, Smithsonian Institution; **p. 538:** *Baron Alfred Tennyson,* c. 1840 (detail), S. Laurence, National Portrait Gallery, London; **p. 551:** Charles Webster Hawthorne, American, 1872–1930, *Summer Millinery,* 1915, oil on board 58½ × 46¾″, 71.659, The Chrysler Museum, Norfolk, VA, Gift of Walter P. Chrysler, Jr.; **p. 553:** Copyright 1981 by the Metropolitan Museum of Art, Seurat, Georges Pierre (1859–1891), *Invitation to the Sideshow (La Parade),* The Metropolitan Museum of Art, Bequest of Stephen C. Clark, 1960; **p. 554:** (second from top) see credit for p. 168; **p. 562:** *William Shakespeare* (detail), artist unknown, National Portrait Gallery, London; **p. 567:** *Trés Riches Heures du Duc de Berry: February,* Chantilly—Musée Condé, Giraudon/Art Resource; **p. 569:** *Hog Heaven,* Mike Patrick; **p. 571:** Rockwell Kent, *Shadows of Evening,* 1921–23, oil on canvas, 38 × 44″, Collection of Whitney Museum of American Art, Acq. #31.257; **pp. 572, 572:** Japanese, Lacquers, Meiji Period, XIX Century, Box, Manuscript, with tray, inside top cover lacquer (detail), The Metropolitan Museum of Art, Bequest of Benjamin Altman, 1913; **p. 574:** (second from top) see credit for p. 168, (third from top) see credit for p. 571 (detail); **pp. 576–77:** *Winter Twilight near Albany, N.Y.,* 1858, George Henry Boughton, Courtesy of the New York Historical Society, New York City; **p. 583:** *Houses of Murnau at Obermarkt,* 1908, Wassily Kandinsky, Lugano-Thyssen-Bornemisza Collection, Art Resource; **pp. 586–87:** *City at the Sea,* Helmut Kies, Three Lions; **p. 595:** *On the Promenade,* August Macke, Three Lions; **pp. 598–99:** *Seashore at Palavas,* 1854, Gustave Courbet, Musée Fabre, Montpellier; **p. 615:** Marc Chagall, *Green Violinist,* Solomon R. Guggenheim Museum, New York, Photo, David Heald; **pp. 622–23:** *Woodcutter on a Rock,* 1891, Winslow Homer, Private Collection; **pp. 626** (detail), **628:** Lightning, 1973, from the Weather Series, color lithograph, 39 × 32″, © Gemini Gel/David Hockney, 1973; **p. 630:** *Carl Sandburg* (detail), Miriam Svet, National Portrait Gallery, Smithsonian Institution; **p. 632:** *Baseball Player and Circus Performers,* John Zielinski, Sal Barracca & Associates; **p. 637:** *Indian Girl (1917),* Robert Henri, Indianapolis Museum of Art; **p. 642:** New York Public Library; **p. 643:** *Paul Bunyan Carrying a Tree on His Shoulder and an Ax in His Hand,* The Bettmann Archive; **pp. 654** (detail), **p. 656:** Museum of African American Art, Palmer C. Hayden, Collection, Gift of Miriam A. Hayden, Photograph by Armando Solis; **p. 664:** *A Man Ain't Nothin' but a Man,*

Palmer C. Hayden, Palmer C. Hayden Collection, Gift of Miriam A. Hayden, Photograph by Armando Solis; **p. 670:** *The Little Navigator,* New Bedford Whaling Museum; *Cigar Store Figure, Jack Tar, Portugese Sailor, Robin, Ship's Eye,* Shelburne Museum, Shelburne, Vermont; **p. 672:** *Sable Island: The Sailor's Graveyard,* John Frost, Abby Aldrich Rockefeller Folk Art Center, Williamsburg, Virginia; **p. 674:** New York Public Library Picture Collection; **p. 682:** *Davy Crockett, with the Help of His Dog, Fighting a Bear,* cover of the Crockett Almanac, 1841, The Granger Collection; **pp. 690–91:** *Mesa and Cacti,* Diego Rivera, Detroit Institute of Arts; **p. 693:** *La Molendera, 1924,* Diego Rivera, Museo de Arte Moderno, Reproduction authorized by El Instituto Nacional de Bellas Artes y Literatura; **p. 696:** *Peasant with Sombrero (Peon), 1926,* Diego Rivera, Galeria Arvil, Mexico City; **p. 699:** *Delfina and Dimas,* Diego Rivera, Private Collection; **p. 706:** *Two Mexican Women and a Child,* Diego Rivera, The Fine Arts Museum of San Francisco, M. H. deYoung Memorial Museum; **p. 718** *Group,* Jesus Guerrero Galván, Collection IBM Corporation, Armonk, New York; **p. 725:** *Mexican Peasant with Sombrero and Serape,* Diego Rivera, Mr. and Mrs. Dudley Smith Collection, Harry Ransom Humanities Research Center, The University of Texas at Austin; **p. 734:** *Cactus on the Plains (Hands), 1931,* Diego Rivera, Edsel and Eleanor Ford House, Grosse Point Shores, Michigan, Photograph by R. H. Hensleigh; **p. 741:** *The Sob, 1939,* David Alfaro Siquieros, Collection, The Museum of Modern Art, New York, Given Anonymously.

PHOTOGRAPH CREDITS

p. 9: The Granger Collection; **p. 12:** Thomas Victor; **pp. 16–17:** Ann and Myron Sutton/Shostal; **p. 46:** Beryl Markham, UPI/Bettmann Newsphotos; **p. 60:** UPI/Bettmann Newsphotos; **p. 68:** Thomas Victor; **p. 84:** AP/Wide World Photos; **p. 96:** Nikky Finney; **p. 97:** Cliff Feulner/The Image Bank; **p. 98:** Co Tentmeester/The Image Bank; **p. 101:** Audrey Gottlieb/Monkmeyer; **p. 103:** Steven E. Sutton/Duomo CWG VIII; **p. 106:** Montana Historical Society, Helena; **p. 112:** Thomas Victor; **p. 113:** Ken Karp; **p. 118:** AP/Wide World; **p. 128:** Bradford Bachrach; **p. 136:** UPI/Bettmann Newsphotos; **p. 144:** UPI/Bettmann Newsphotos; **p. 150:** Thomas Victor; **p. 158:** The Bettmann Archive; **p. 162:** Steven Y. Mori; **p. 164:** Steve Solum/Bruce Coleman; **p. 200:** Harry Snaveley; **p. 203:** The Memory Shop; **pp. 208, 217:** Phototeque; **p. 221:** The Memory Shop; **p. 229:** Ken Karp; **p. 233:** Tom Bean/The Stock Market; **p. 262:** International Creative Management; **p. 276:** AP/Wide World; **pp. 300, 301, 302:** UPI/Bettmann Newsphotos; **p. 304:** The Bettmann Archive; **pp. 306, 308, 311, 316, 328:** © by Anne Frank-Fonds/COSMOPRESS, Genève; **p. 333:** UPI/Bettmann Newsphotos; **pp. 337, 345, 349, 352, 358:** © by Anne Frank-Fonds/COSMOPRESS, Genève; **p. 363:** The Granger Collection; **p. 378:** J.P. Nacivet/Leo de Wys, Inc.; **p. 379:** Thomas Victor; **p. 395:** Ken McVey/After Image; **p. 398:** Jerry Wachter/Focus on Sports; **p. 402:** Wake Forest University; **p. 420:** UPI/Bettmann Newsphotos; **p. 422:** Jonathan T. Wright/Bruce Coleman; **p. 425:** Gordon Wiltsie/Bruce Coleman; **p. 430:** The Bettmann Archive; **p. 438:** John Wyand; **p. 444:** The Granger Collection; **p. 452:** AP/Wide World Photos; **p. 456:** The Bettmann Archive; **p. 462:** The Bettmann Archive; **p. 468:** Les Line; **p. 469:** Dennis diCicco/Peter Arnold, Inc.; **p. 472:** UPI/Bettmann Newsphotos; **p. 476:** Thomas Victor; **p. 480:** AP/Wide World; **p. 484:** Thomas Victor; **p. 486:** Simon Warner/The Brontë Society; **p. 494:** AP/Wide World; **p. 504:** E. R. Degginger; **p. 505:** AP/Wide World; **p. 520:** The Granger Collection; **p. 526:** © Henri Cartier-Bresson/Magnum; **p. 530:** (top) NYT Pictures, (middle) UPI/Bettmann Newsphotos; **p. 537:** George Hall/Woodfin Camp; **p. 538:** (top) Thomas Victor; (middle) AP/Wide World; **pp. 540–41:** Charles West/The Stock Market; **p. 542:** (left and right) Joel Gordon; **p. 543:** (left) Roy Morsch/The Stock Market, (right) Richard Dunoff/The Stock Market; **p. 545:** G. Cigolini/The Image Bank; **p. 546:** (top) AP/Wide World, (middle) The Bettmann Archive; **p. 549:** Ken Karp; **p. 554:** (top) Courtesy of Helen Sarett Stockdale and Lloyd Sarett Stockdale, (third from top) Dmitri Kessel/*Life* magazine, © Time Inc.; (bottom) Thomas Victor; **p. 557:** Kenneth W. Fink/Bruce Coleman; **p. 559:** Jane Burton/Bruce Coleman; **p. 562:** (top) © Faber & Faber Ltd., (middle) AP/Wide World; **p. 564:** Aram Gesar/The Image Bank; **p. 574:** (top) Thomas Victor, (bottom) Thomas Victor; **p. 578:** A. & J. Verkaik/The Stock Market; **pp. 580–81:** David Fitzgerald/After Image; **p. 584:** (middle) Harold Hornstein, (bottom) Thomas Victor; **pp. 588–89:** Tardos Camesi/The Stock Market; **p. 590:** AP/Wide World; **p. 592:** Focus on Sports; **p. 596:** (bottom) Dmitri Kessel/*Life* Magazine © Time, Inc.; **pp. 600–601:** Julius Fekete/The Stock Market; **p. 602:** (top) The Granger Collection; **p. 608:** Robin Seyfried; **p. 611:** Michael Melford/Wheeler Pictures; **p. 616:** Thomas Victor; **p. 662:** The Granger Collection; **p. 675:** The Granger Collection; **p. 678:** The Granger Collection; **p. 694:** UPI/Bettmann Newsphoto.

ILLUSTRATION CREDITS

pp. 4, 7, 28–29, 34, 38–39: The Art Source; **pp. 48–49, 54–55, 57:** Joel Spector; **pp. 109, 128, 140–141, 146, 160, 176–177, 180–181, 245, 249, 250–251, 256, 260:** The Art Source; **p. 265:** Chet Jezerski/Jeff Cavaty; **pp. 285, 297, 509, 512–513, 517, 646, 647, 654, 656:** The Art Source; **pp. 684–85:** Oliver Williams.